CANADIAN 12TH EDITION

AUDITING

THE ART AND SCIENCE OF ASSURANCE ENGAGEMENTS

ALVIN A. ARENS
PricewaterhouseCoopers Emeritus Professor,
Michigan State University

RANDAL J. ELDER
Syracuse University

MARK S. BEASLEY
North Carolina State University,
Deloitte Professor of Enterprise Risk Management

INGRID B. SPLETTSTOESSER
York University

PEARSON

Toronto

Vice-President, Editorial Director: Gary Bennett
Editor-in-Chief: Nicole Lukach
Acquisitions Editor: Megan Farrell
Marketing Manager: Jenna Wulff
Developmental Editor: Paul Donnelly
Project Manager: Richard di Santo
Manufacturing Manager: Jane Schell
Production Editor: Sandhya Gola, Cenveo Publisher Services
Copy Editor: Susan Bindernagel
Proofreaders: Nancy Carroll, Trish Jones
Permissions Researcher: Christina Beamish
Compositor: Cenveo Publisher Services
Art Director: Julia Hall
Interior and Cover Designer: Miriam Blier
Cover Image: George Diebold/Getty Images

10 9 8 7 6 5 4 3 2 CKV

Library and Archives Canada Cataloguing in Publication

Auditing : the art and science of assurance engagements / Alvin A. Arens ... [et al.].—Canadian 12th ed.

Includes index.
ISBN 978-0-13-279156-4

1. Auditing—Textbooks. I. Arens, Alvin A.

HF5667.A82 2012   657'.45   C2012-906497-1

PEARSON

ISBN 978-0-13-279156-4

Brief Contents

Contents

[Part 3] The Auditor's Risk Response: Audit of Cycles and Accounts 359

Preface

Welcome to the Canadian Twelfth Edition of *Auditing: The Art and Science of Assurance Engagements*. Standards are continuing to evolve and upgrade the quality of the auditing profession, and we have responded by also upgrading the quality of our text. I say we, because Shaweta Roopra, a Manager with Deloitte & Touche, Toronto, in National Assurance Services, has joined the writing team as a contributing author. Shaweta has provided valuable advice about IFRS, ASPE, and current auditing standards and practices that are embedded into every chapter of this text.

We have gone through every word, exhibit, and table carefully, trimmed what we could, added more risk-focused material, and added and revised figures and tables to better portray concepts. Shaweta's experience as a contract faculty member at York University for several years has enabled her to consider the teaching and communication focus as well as current auditing and accounting standards.

What's New to This Edition?

- Greater emphasis on risk assessment and strategic auditing.
- Clarity around auditing standards—New icons and text boxes highlight the changes that are occurring as Canada has adopted new international standards, and references to prior *CICA Handbook* sections have been removed.
- CondoCleaners.com—This running case with discussion questions about a small company, CondoCleaners.com, focuses attention on the auditing needs of small businesses. It has been expanded to appear in all chapters.
- Inclusion of adapted practice problems from past CGA Canada auditing examinations in each chapter.
- Learning Objective references have been added to all of the end-of-chapter discussion and practice problems and cases.
- Chapters are organized in a new order to facilitate progressive learning; details are provided below.

Students want more practical information and practice to illustrate the assurance material that can, at times, be quite technical. This new edition of *Auditing* therefore contains more stories and practice questions that relate to small and large businesses at home or from the international business perspective.

Objectives

This book is intended for use in an introductory auditing course, for one-semester or two-semester instruction at the undergraduate or graduate level. Using a risk-based approach, this text focuses on the auditor's decision-making processes. It is important to keep the underlying objective in mind—to assess risks and tailor the audit approach as a response to those risks. The evidence collected must enable the auditor's statement of opinion with respect to financial statements (and other types of information, as discussed in the last chapter). Assessing and documenting the risks associated with the client's business and the various components of the financial statements allows the auditor to target the fieldwork to specific objectives called audit assertions. If a student in auditing understands the risks to be addressed in a given audit area, the circumstances of the engagement, and the decisions to be made, he or she should be able to determine the appropriate evidence to gather and how to evaluate the evidence obtained.

The title of this book reflects the reality that auditing goes beyond financial statement auditing to other assurance services. Auditing is an art, as it requires considerable use of professional judgment, but it is also a science, resting upon a solid frame of technical skills and knowledge of multiple disciplines, including accounting, tax, and information systems. In incorporating substantial new material on risk assessment and corporate governance, our primary purpose is to integrate the most important concepts of financial statement auditing and the general assurance engagement framework. Electronic commerce, non-profit businesses, and many topics that engage professional judgment are highlighted by Problems and by specialized boxes: Auditing in Action and Audit Challenge.

Organization

This text is divided into four parts.

Part 1, The Auditing Profession (Chapters 1–4)

We begin by explaining the importance of assurance services, including auditing, and differentiating accounting from auditing. Then we talk about the different types of accountants and what they do. Chapter 1 now has increased content on internal auditing and internal auditors. In Chapter 2, we move to the role of public accounting firms and other organizations, such as the Office of the Auditor General of Canada, in doing audits. We show how the Sarbanes–Oxley Act, Canadian and international quality control standards, and the Canadian Public Accountability Board have resulted in methods that produce high-quality audits. The final product, the Independent Auditor's Report, is shown. Chapter 3, Professional Relationships, reflects the fact that professional rules of conduct govern the behaviour of the public accountant in the context of relationships with corporations, other business entities, and the users of reports. Two approaches to dealing with ethical dilemmas are discussed, with a recent approach called "Giving Voice to Values" (GVV), providing students with a proactive method for responding in accordance with their values. Independence standards using a threat-based model are applied to public and non-public engagements. Threats to independence and the way these are mitigated with good quality-control practices are thoroughly examined. Part 1 concludes with Chapter 4, which presents an investigation of the auditor's legal liability and the profession's response.

Part 2, The Audit Process (Chapters 5–11)

This section has been adapted to international terminology, whereby the audit process phases are grouped into three sections: Risk Analysis, Risk Response, and Reporting. Chapter 5 allocates eight phases to those three sections, integrating international standards with Canadian practice and standards. It explains the auditor's and management's responsibilities and the key role of the audit committee in corporate governance. Fraud risk is discussed by audit phase. Transaction cycles are explained with the help of the annual report and financial statements of Hillsburg Hardware Limited, a fictitious public company located in eastern Canada. Chapter 6 focuses on the development of a client risk profile in the context of the business environment. The risk-based audit approach with its large investment in up-front planning and the concepts of materiality, performance materiality, and the audit risk model are covered in Chapter 7. Chapter 8 links evidence decisions to assessed risks and includes general concepts of evidence accumulation. Chapter 9, Internal Controls and Control Risk, uses the components of internal control that are consistent with international standards. Fraud risk assessment is integrated with control risk assessment. Chapter 10 provides an overall strategic risk-based audit plan, linking planning to assertion-based audit programs, with a new section on the impact of client conversions to IFRS. Chapter 11 discusses sampling concepts relevant to the audit process.

Part 3, The Auditor's Risk Response: Audit of Cycles and Accounts (Chapters 12–18)

These chapters apply the concepts from Part 2 to the audit of multiple functional cycles. Each cycle chapter (12, 14 through 18) has an early discussion of risks of fraud and error in the cycle. This enables the ensuing discussion of controls and risk responses (audit procedures) to be related to these risks of fraud and error.

In Chapter 12 we start with sales, cash receipts, and the related income statement and balance sheet accounts, using further details from Hillsburg Hardware Limited as examples. Risks of error and fraud in the cycle lead to audit procedures for sales and cash receipts for particular internal control and audit objectives for tests of controls. Chapter 13 continues to use audit objectives and the results of internal controls tests to formulate tests of details of balances. Students will learn to apply audit sampling to the audit of sales, cash receipts, and accounts receivable by incorporating sampling into the appropriate test, showing the design, conduct, and evaluation of the sample.

The remaining chapters in Part 3 deal with a specific transaction cycle or part of a transaction cycle in much the same manner as Chapters 12 and 13 deal with the sales and collection cycle. Each chapter is meant to demonstrate the relationship of risks to internal controls and tests of controls for each broad category of transactions to the related balance sheet and income statement accounts. Cash in bank is the first of these chapters studied, since the audit of cash balances is related to most other audit areas.

Part 4, Completing the Audit, Reporting, and Offering Other Services (Chapters 19–21)

Completion of the audit depends on evaluating whether sufficient audit evidence has been gathered, in the context of the client risk profile and the audit risk model, to enable provision of an opinion on the financial statements. This final phase is explained in Chapter 19. Chapter 20 describes audit reports and variations to such reports. The chapter has significant changes due to the adoption of international standards resulting in a longer and more specific audit report, with the predecessor report now removed. The impact of events discovered after the report date are considered. The final chapter, Chapter 21, focuses on review and compilation engagements, a common service for small- and medium-sized businesses, both profit-oriented and non-profit-oriented. It also describes other types of assurance engagements, such as a report of assurance with respect to internal control over financial reporting, required by public companies under Section 404 of the Sarbanes–Oxley Act of 2002 in the United States.

Chapter Outline

Each chapter contains the following:

- Learning Objectives, listing the concepts that you should be able to address after reading the chapter.
- An opening vignette discussing a real-world topic to highlight a theme and the importance of the chapter. Each vignette describes the importance of the topic to auditors and provides questions to think about the topic further.
- A list of *CICA Handbook* sections or CASs referenced in the chapter, targeting additional readings.
- Figures and tables to illustrate, summarize, or clarify topics covered.

- Auditing in Action, Audit Challenge, and New Standards boxes identifying relevant challenges to auditors, successes and research, key current topics, further cases and questions, or recent events in the area.
- An icon (CAS) highlights discussions of new standards in the text.
- Essential terms defined in the margin and presented in boldface in the running text for easy reference.
- Concept Check questions placed at the end of each major chapter section, testing and reinforcing the section material.
- A summary expanding upon the learning objectives.
- Review questions for students to assess comprehension of chapter material.
- Discussion questions and one or two professional judgment problems offering real-world topics to which chapter content can be applied.
- Discussion questions about a small company, CondoCleaners.com, to focus attention on the needs of small business.
- ACL Problems that show students how audit software is used to perform specific types of audit tests.

MyAccountingLab

The moment you know. Educators know it. Students know it. It's that inspired moment when something that was difficult to understand suddenly makes perfect sense. Our MyLab products have been designed and refined with a single purpose in mind—to help educators create that moment of understanding with their students.

MyAccountingLab delivers **proven results** in helping individual students succeed. It provides **engaging experiences** that personalize, stimulate, and measure learning for each student. And it comes from a **trusted partner** with educational expertise and an eye on the future.

The MyAccountingLab for the Canadian Twelfth Edition of *Auditing: The Art and Science of Assurance Engagements* includes many valuable assessments and study tools to help students practise and understand key concepts from the text. Students can practise select end-of-chapter questions. (These questions, marked in orange in the text, must be assigned by the instructor beforehand.) They can also review key terms with glossary flashcards, access student PowerPoint slides, and explore integrated case content.

MyAccountingLab can be used by itself or linked to any learning management system. To learn more about how MyAccountingLab combines proven learning applications with powerful assessment, visit www.myaccountinglab.com.

Student Resources

COURSESMART FOR STUDENTS CourseSmart goes beyond traditional expectations—providing instant, online access to the textbooks and course materials you need at an average savings of 60 percent. With instant access from any computer and the ability to search your text, you'll find the content you need quickly, no matter where you are. And with online tools like highlighting and note-taking, you can save time and study efficiently. See all the benefits at www.coursesmart.com/students.

Instructional Support Materials

INSTRUCTOR'S RESOURCE MANUAL The Instructor's Resource Manual assists the instructor in teaching the course more efficiently. The features include instructions for assignments, practical examples to help the students understand the material, and helpful suggestions on how to effectively teach each chapter. This manual also includes guidelines for downloading ACL audit software, solutions to ACL problems, and additional ACL exercises.

INSTRUCTOR'S SOLUTIONS MANUAL This comprehensive resource provides detailed solutions to all the end-of-chapter review questions, multiple-choice questions, problems, and cases.

PEARSON TESTGEN A comprehensive testbank of questions has been prepared to accompany the new edition. The questions are rated by difficulty level and are correlated to learning objectives. The testbank is presented in a special computerized format known as Pearson TestGen. It enables instructors to view and edit the existing questions, add questions, generate tests, and print the tests in a variety of formats. Powerful search and sort functions make it easy to locate questions and arrange them in any order desired. TestGen also enables instructors to administer tests on a local area network, grade the tests electronically, and prepare the results in electronic or printed reports. Pearson TestGen is compatible with PC and Macintosh systems.

POWERPOINT SLIDES Electronic colour slides are available in Microsoft PowerPoint. The slides illuminate and build on key concepts in the text.

IMAGE LIBRARY The Image Library is an impressive resource that helps instructors create vibrant lecture presentations. Almost all figures and tables in the text are included and organized by chapter for convenience. These images can easily be imported into Microsoft PowerPoint to create new presentations or to add to existing ones.

COURSESMART FOR INSTRUCTORS CourseSmart goes beyond traditional expectations—providing instant, online access to the textbooks and course materials you need at a lower cost for students. And even as students save money, you can save time and hassle with a digital eTextbook that allows you to search for the most relevant content at the very moment you need it. Whether it's evaluating textbooks or creating lecture notes to help students with difficult concepts, CourseSmart can make life a little easier. See how when you visit www.coursesmart.com/instructors.

PEARSON eTEXT Pearson eText gives students access to the text whenever and wherever they have access to the internet. eText pages look exactly like the printed text, offering powerful new functionality for students and instructors. Users can create notes, highlight text in different colours, create bookmarks, zoom, click hyperlinked words and phrases to view definitions, and view in single-page or two-page view. Pearson eText allows for quick navigation to key parts of the eText using a table of contents and provides full-text search.

TECHNOLOGY SPECIALISTS Pearson's Technology Specialists work with faculty and campus course designers to ensure that Pearson technology products, assessment tools, and online course materials are tailored to meet your specific needs. This highly qualified team is dedicated to helping schools take full advantage of a wide range of educational resources, by assisting in the integration of a variety of instructional materials and media formats. Your local Pearson Education sales representative can provide you with more details on this service program.

Acknowledgments for the Canadian Twelfth Edition

Our world is changing. This text reflects some of those changes in the rapid pace of standards shifts in the external auditing profession. The feedback and assistance from individuals both inside and outside the profession, with different perspectives, have spurred on our creativity and reinforced the knowledge that we are all different and bring a broad spectrum of skills to the work we do.

I would like to thank the following individuals who contributed their time and energy in sharing their opinions and best practices, helping make this book representative not only of sound theory but of the actual work done in the field of audit and assurance:

Sophie Audousset-Coulier, Concordia University
Stacie Chappell, Western New England University
Phil Cowperthwaite, Cowperthwaite Mehta
Susan Fisher, Algonquin College
Kenneth Fox, University of Alberta
David Hiscock, University of Guelph–Humber
Joanne Jones, York University
Kelsie McKay, Georgian College
Bruce MacLean, Dalhousie University
N. Dawn McGeachy, Colby McGeachy
James Palanacki, Deloitte & Touche LLP
Wendy Popowich, NAIT
Linda A. Robinson, University of Waterloo
Peter Rumyee
William Sanjian Zhang, McGill University
Joseph Toste, Centennial College
Larry Yarmolinsky, Internal Audit Division, Government of Ontario
Douglas Yee, Sauder School of Business, BCIT

My biggest thanks goes to Shaweta Roopra, without whom I would not have had the time to complete this book. In addition to providing content, her invaluable guidance about which standards to review for a particular chapter helped me to focus my time.

In addition, I thank all the editorial and production staff at Pearson Canada for putting together a high-quality product, including Gary Bennett, Vice-President, Editorial Director; Megan Farrell, Acquisitions Editor; Nicole Lukach, Editor-in-Chief; Paul Donnelly, Developmental Editor; and Richard di Santo, Project Manager.

This book is dedicated to my family—Jake, Pat, and Mike—who did the extra chores around the house and cooked dinner while I worked late. Thank you; without your love and support this book would not have been possible.

Ingrid B. Splettstoesser

Thank-you, Ingrid Splettstoesser, for giving me an opportunity to be a contributing author to this book and for introducing me to the academic world. I would like to thank Deloitte & Touche LLP for the tremendous support and encouragement I received to enable me to contribute to this book. Finally, I would like to thank my family for their love and support through the authoring process.

Shaweta Roopra, Contributing Author

The auditing profession

Who are auditors and why are they important? These first four chapters provide background for performing strategic financial statement audits, which is our primary focus. This background will help you understand why auditors perform audits the way they do.

Our book begins with a who's who of assurance services, including auditing, and the role of accountants, public accounting firms, and other organizations in doing audits. The chapters in Part 1 emphasize the regulation and control of public accounting through auditing and ethical standards and discuss the legal responsibilities of auditors. We also talk about audit reports, which are the final products of audits.

1

The demand for an auditing and assurance profession

Don't all accountants do the same thing? No, not really. There are well-trained accountants who do only accounting, accountants who do auditing (public accountants or internal auditors), and accountants who have many other specializations, such as financial planning or forensics. This chapter will talk about many different types of accountants. You can use this information to help you consider the focus that your accounting career will take.

LEARNING OBJECTIVES

1 Identify the components of an audit and explain why there is a demand for audits. Explain the strategic differences between accounting and auditing, contrasting professional risks and rewards.

2 Link the nature of assurance services to examples of actual services provided. Distinguish audit engagements from other assurance and non-assurance services. Consider why financial statement auditors rely upon internal auditors.

3 Explore the different types of accountants and what they do.

Why Do Auditing?

It has been a busy day for Rong, Celia, Matt, and Ruyan. Their auditing professor gave them the assignment of finding the firm that they wanted to work for as their dream job, and they have spent a few hours each poring through a variety of websites. They each discovered unusual things that auditors do, and are excited about the potential opportunity. Let us hear what each of them has decided.

Rong wants to move to Ottawa and join the federal Office of the Auditor General's (OAG) team. "They do so many different types of audits! They audit the biggest financial statement in Canada, the government of Canada itself, with a team headed by several Directors. The *June 2011 Status Report of the Auditor General of Canada* describes several special examinations that were conducted, with diverse organizations and purposes. One of these was an insurance company, the Canada Deposit Insurance Corporation (CDIC), which helps protect savings of individuals in the event that a bank fails. The OAG found that the CDIC was doing its job well, they assessed whether 'assets are safeguarded and controlled.' Two other organizations did not do as well in that report. There were 'deficiencies' at the Freshwater Fish Marketing Corporation and the National Arts Centre Corporation. I think it would be really interesting auditing these large organizations that have an impact upon our lives."

Celia is interested in working with information systems and new technology companies. She wants to specialize in computer consulting or computer auditing. She chose one of Canada's largest CA (Chartered Accountant) public accounting firms, KPMG. This is how she explains her choice. "Information technology is an international language. If you specialize in tax, it changes from country to country, but computing technologies are international. So, by specializing in technology, I can work with any of the industries that KPMG specializes in. They do say on their website that they have an industry focus on several industries including information, communications, and entertainment. I like to travel, so if I worked for an international company, I could transfer to Hong Kong, Japan, Bermuda, or other parts of the world once I qualify as a CA and public accountant."

Matt is an entrepreneur at heart, and thinks that by working with the small business sector, he will be working with the fastest-growing sector of the economy. "Porter Hetu International is a CGA (Certified General Accountants) public accounting firm. They work with small and medium-sized organizations and individuals. It's great that the firm was started by two individuals, one a

Sources: 1. KPMG home page, **www.kpmg.com/ca/en**. 2. KPMG "Information, Communications and Entertainment (ICE)," **www.kpmg.com/Ca/en/WhatWeDo/Industries/ICE/Pages/default.aspx**. 3. Ministry of Finance April 1, 2010 Organizational Structure, **www.fin.gov.on.ca/en/about/rbplanning/rbp2010-11_orgchart.pdf**. 4. 2011 Status Report of the Auditor General of Canada, Chapter 7 – Special Examinations of Crown Corporations – 2010, **www.oag-bvg.gc.ca/internet/English/parl_oag_201106_07_e_35375.html**. 5. Office of the Auditor General of Canada, web page titled About Us, **www.oag-bvg.gc.ca/internet/English/au_fs_e_43.html**. 6. Porter Hetu International home page, **www.porterhetu.com/**. All accessed: June 27, 2011.

continued >

continued

French-Canadian and the other English-speaking. The firm is relatively young (founded in 1988), so I expect them to be rapidly responsive to businesses. I would like to specialize in tax once I obtain my CGA and public accounting designation. I know that many public accounting firms offer tax services, but working with an organization that focuses on small business is the way to go for me."

Ruyan wants to get to know a single organization very well so that she can help improve the way the organization functions and provide regular advice to management. "I think I want to be part of an internal audit team. Internal audit teams can be small, from one or two people, to large groups that are as big as an accounting firm, consisting of hundreds of people! I found the organization chart for the Ontario Ministry of Finance, which includes the Ontario Internal Audit Division for the province of Ontario. The Internal Audit Division has 11 different teams, including health, education, justice, and finance and revenue. I think if I worked on one of those teams that I could help the province run better."

WHAT DO YOU THINK?

1. What kind of audit specialization are you interested in?
2. Once you have your university degree, what kind of accounting designations would you pursue?
3. Who can you talk to so that you can learn more about your choices and decide on your future career path in public accounting or auditing?

PROFESSIONAL accountants assess risks of errors or fraud, provide examinations of controls, audit financial statements, and help businesses be more successful. As businesses become more complex and need more reliable information, auditors play a vital role, both in providing assurance on information other than financial statements and in providing business advisory and tax services. For example, businesses and consumers who use information technology and electronic communication networks such as the internet to conduct business and make decisions are concerned about the risks of unauthorized access to systems. Auditors are valued because of their technical knowledge and independence in providing assurances about such access, as well as their competence and experience in assisting companies to improve operations. Auditors often make and help implement recommendations that improve profitability by enhancing revenue or reducing costs, by reducing risks of errors and fraud, and by improving operational controls.

① Nature and Relevance of Auditing

To audit effectively, you need to learn the rules and procedures—the science—of auditing, after you have studied accounting, tax, finance, and management information systems. In addition, you need to practise this knowledge in a variety of situations and gain experience in the real world. The defined practice of **auditing**, below, includes several key words and phrases.

> **AUDITING** is the accumulation and evaluation of evidence about information to determine and report on the degree of correspondence between the information and established criteria. Auditing should be done by a competent, independent person.

Auditing—the accumulation and evaluation of evidence about information to determine and report on the degree of correspondence between the information and established criteria.

We will now look at each of these key phrases in turn.

INFORMATION AND ESTABLISHED CRITERIA To do an audit, there must be information in a verifiable form and some standards (criteria) by which the auditor can evaluate the information. Information can and does take many forms. Auditors routinely perform audits of quantifiable information, including companies' financial statements and individuals' federal income tax returns. Auditors also perform audits of more subjective information, such as the effectiveness of computer systems and the efficiency of manufacturing operations.

The criteria against which information is evaluated vary depending on the information being audited. For example, in the audit of historical financial statements by public accounting firms, the criteria are an accounting framework such as International Financial Reporting Standards (IFRS) or Accounting Standards for Private Enterprises (ASPE). To illustrate, this means that in the audit of RONA Inc.'s (**www.rona.ca**) financial statements, Raymond Chabot Grant Thornton LLP, the public accounting firm (**www.rcgt.com**), determines whether RONA Inc.'s financial statements have been prepared in accordance with the IFRS accounting standards. **Canada Revenue Agency auditors** use the provisions of the Income Tax Act to audit tax returns. In the audit of RONA's corporate tax return by the Canada Revenue Agency, the Income Tax Act, rather than an applicable reporting framework, would provide the criteria for assessment.

Canada Revenue Agency auditor—an auditor who works for the Canada Revenue Agency and conducts examinations of taxpayers' returns.

For more subjective information, such as auditing the effectiveness of computer operations, it is more difficult to establish criteria. Typically, auditors and the entities being audited agree on the criteria well before the audit starts. For a computer application, the criteria might, for example, include the absence of input or output errors.

ACCUMULATING AND EVALUATING EVIDENCE **Evidence** is defined as any information used by the auditor to assess whether the information being audited is stated in accordance with the established criteria. The quality and amount of evidence collected depends upon the risks of misstatement. The auditor devises an **audit strategy** to effectively plan the evidence-gathering process. Evidence takes many different forms, including oral representation of the auditee (client), written communication with outsiders, and observations by the auditor. Certain evidence (from a third party) is considered more reliable than other evidence (from the client). It is important to obtain a sufficient quality and volume of evidence to mitigate the risks of the audit. The process of determining the amount of evidence necessary and evaluating whether the information corresponds to the established criteria in the context of identified

Evidence—any information used by the auditor to assess whether the information being audited is stated in accordance with established criteria.

Audit strategy—a planned approach to the conduct of audit testing, taking into account assessed risks.

risks is a critical part of every audit. This means that the strategic audit approach is the primary subject of this text.

COMPETENT, INDEPENDENT PERSON The auditor must be qualified to understand the engagement risks and the criteria used. This includes competence in selecting the types and amount of evidence to accumulate and effectively evaluating evidence to reach the proper conclusion. The auditor also must be independent in mind and appearance. Independence is discussed further in Chapter 3. The competence of the individual performing the audit is of little value if he or she is biased in the accumulation and evaluation of evidence. Requirements in Canada vary, since public accounting is a provincial jurisdiction. In those provinces (such as Ontario, Quebec, Newfoundland, and Nova Scotia at time of writing) where a licence is required, the public accountant would be termed an LPA (licensed public accountant).

Independent auditor—a public accountant or accounting firm that performs audits of commercial and non-commercial entities.

Auditors reporting on company financial statements are often called **independent auditors**. Even though an auditor of published financial statements is paid a fee by a company, he or she is normally sufficiently independent to conduct audits that can be relied on by users. Absolute independence is impossible, but auditors strive to maintain a high level of independence to keep the confidence of users relying on their reports. Although **internal auditors** work for the company, they usually report directly to the audit committee to help maintain independence from the operating units being audited.

Internal auditor—an auditor employed by a company to audit for the company's board of directors and management.

Independent auditor's report—the communication of audit findings to users.

REPORTING The final stage in the audit process is the **independent auditor's report**—the communication of the audit findings to users. Reports differ in nature, but in all cases they must inform readers of the degree of correspondence between information and established criteria. Reports also differ in form and can vary from the auditor's standard opinion usually associated with financial statements to a customized report in the case of an audit of effectiveness.

Figure 1-1 summarizes the important ideas in the definition of auditing by illustrating an audit of an individual's tax return by a Canada Revenue Agency auditor.

The objective is to determine whether the tax return was prepared in a manner consistent with the requirements of the Income Tax Act. The auditor first considers the potential risk of incorrect or fraudulent tax reporting by comparing the statistics of the tax return with other tax returns and by considering factors such as the taxpayer's industry and past income. The auditor next examines supporting records provided by the taxpayer and from other sources, such as the taxpayer's employer or bank. After completing the audit, the Canada Revenue Agency (**www.cra-arc.gc.ca**) auditor will issue a report to the taxpayer assessing additional taxes, advising that a refund is due or stating that there is no change in the status of his or her return.

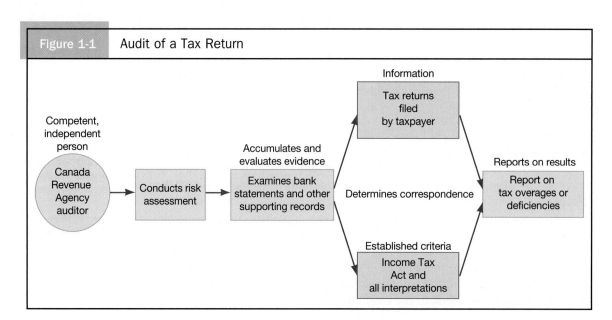

Figure 1-1 Audit of a Tax Return

Fraud Fighters: Demand for Forensic Accountants Remains Strong through Economic Downturn

When Ron Forster conducts interviews, he watches his subjects as much as he listens to them. Even a seemingly innocuous gesture—an interviewee moving his hand away from his face before answering a sensitive question—could be a sign the subject is lying. Mr. Forster is a forensic accountant, a growing subset of the accounting field focused on uncovering financial fraud.

And while forensic accountants do their share of number crunching and computer analysis, they also do work that resembles television crime show investigations. "Forensic accountants are really financial detectives," says Alex Brown of the United Kingdom Institute of Chartered Accountants' forensic group. Brown has worked on cases involving Caribbean money laundering, Eastern European smuggling, and major commercial disputes. Forensic accountants use rigorous accounting skills and a flair for investigation to sniff out fraud, uncover money laundering, and trace missing assets.

The day-to-day work of a forensic accountant involves interviewing key people, studying accounts and, increasingly, examining electronic documents. The ever-growing volume of such documentation means that there is now a new branch of forensic accounting. Specialist computing forensic experts often have a background in information technology and receive accounting training on the job.

Forensic accounting is booming and continues to expand through the recent global recession. Over a five-year period, the number of fraud examiners certified by the Association of Certified Fraud Examiners increased from just over 15,000 to nearly 25,000 with over 55,000 members as of June 2011. "During a declining economy, fraud activity often comes to light," says Marc Brdar, a forensic accountant in Pittsburgh. "Prosperity can hide a multitude of sins."

"I was attracted to forensic accountancy because, like science, you need to have investigative skills," says forensic trainee Amy Hawkins. "I really like the sleuthing side of the job, where you're finding out whodunit and where the money went." Forensic accountant Simon Bevan adds, "When you find that killer document, it 's a real reward for all your hard work."

Sources: Adapted from Association of Certified Fraud Examiners home page, **www.acfe.com**, accessed June 28, 2011. 2. Anya Sostek, "Fraud Fighters: Forensic Accountants on Front Line in Fight Against Fraud," *Pittsburgh Post Gazette*, March 29, 2009. 3. Amy McClellan, "Forensic Accountancy: Hot on the Trail of the Fraudsters," *The Independent*, April 26, 2006.

Distinction between Auditing and Accounting

Many financial statement users and members of the general public confuse auditing and accounting. The confusion occurs because most auditing is concerned with accounting information, and many auditors have considerable expertise in accounting matters. The confusion is increased by giving the title "public accountant" to individuals of any accounting designation who are qualified to perform the external audit function.

Accounting is the recording, classifying, and summarizing of economic events in a logical manner for the purpose of providing financial information for decision making. The function of accounting is to provide certain types of quantitative information that management and others can use to make decisions. Accountants must have a thorough understanding of the principles and rules that provide the basis for preparing the accounting information. Accountants also help to develop the systems used to record an entity's economic events in a timely way and at a reasonable cost.

When auditing accounting data, the concern is with evaluating whether recorded information reasonably reflects the economic events that occurred during the accounting period within specified dollar ranges (called materiality). The auditor must look at the organization's planning methods and risks, including its strategies and economic niches, as discussed further in Chapter 6. Since accounting standards are the criteria

Accounting—the recording, classifying, and summarizing of economic events in a logical manner for the purpose of providing financial information for decision making.

for evaluating whether the accounting information is properly recorded, any auditor involved with these data must also thoroughly understand the rules, such as accounting principles used in particular accounting frameworks for the audit of financial statements. These principles are constantly evolving as business practices and standards change—there are different accounting standards for public companies, private enterprises, not-for-profit organizations, and public sector entities. Throughout this text, the assumption is made that the reader has already studied accounting principles and standards for the appropriate type of entity under discussion.

Economic Demand for Auditing

Businesses, governments, and not-for-profit organizations use auditing services extensively. Publicly accountable organizations, such as businesses listed on securities exchanges or large not-for-profit organizations, are legally required to have an annual financial statement audit.

A look at the economic reasons for auditing highlights why auditing is valuable. Consider a bank manager's decision to make a loan to a business. The decision will be based on such factors as previous financial relations with the business and the financial condition of the business as reflected by its financial statements. Assuming the bank makes the loan, it will charge a rate of interest determined primarily by three factors:

1. *Risk-free interest rate.* This is approximately the rate the bank could earn by investing in Canada Treasury Bills for the same length of time as the business loan.
2. *Business risk for the customer.* This risk reflects the possibility that the business will not be able to repay its loan because of economic or business conditions such as a recession, poor management decisions, or unexpected competition in the industry.
3. **Information risk.** This risk reflects the possibility that the information upon which the business decision was made was inaccurate. A likely cause of the information risk is inaccurate financial statements.

Information risk—the risk that information upon which a business decision is made is inaccurate.

Auditing has no effect on either the risk-free interest rate or business risk. It can have a significant effect on information risk. If the bank manager is satisfied that there is low information risk, the risk is lowered and the overall interest rate to the borrower can be reduced. For example, assume a large company has total interest-bearing debt of approximately $1 billion. If the interest rate on that debt is reduced by only 1 percent, the annual savings in interest is $10 million. Many lenders such as banks require annual audits for companies with large bank loans outstanding.

As society becomes more complex, there is an increased likelihood that unreliable information will be provided to decision makers. There are several reasons for this: remoteness of information, bias and motives of provider, voluminous data, and the existence of complex exchange transactions.

Managers of businesses and the users of their financial statements may conclude that the best way to deal with information risk is simply to have the risk remain reasonably high. A small company may find it less expensive to pay higher interest costs than to increase the costs of reducing information risk (e.g., by having an audit).

For larger businesses, it is usually practical to incur such costs to reduce information risk. There are three main ways to do so:

1. The user may go to the business premises to examine records and obtain information about the reliability of the statements.
2. Management is responsible for providing reliable information to users. Users may evaluate the likelihood of sharing their information risk loss with management.
3. An independent audit is performed. This is the most common way for users to obtain more reliable information.

In addition to understanding accounting, the auditor must also possess expertise in risk assessment processes and the accumulation and interpretation of audit evidence. It is this expertise that distinguishes auditors from accountants. Determining the proper audit procedures that mitigate risks, deciding the number and types of items to test, and evaluating the results are tasks that are unique to the auditor.

② Assurance and Non-Assurance Services

Figure 1-2 shows the relationship between assurance and non-assurance services. Audits, reviews, reports on the effectiveness of internal control over financial reporting, and attestation services on information technology are all examples of attestation services, which are a subset of assurance services. Management consulting services, depending upon their purpose, could be assurance or non-assurance, while tax and bookkeeping services are non-assurance services.

Assurance Services

Assurance engagements, or "assurance services," are independent professional services that improve the quality of information for decision makers. The assurance engagement is an assurance service where the auditor issues a report about the reliability of an assertion (such as financial statements) prepared by another party (such as management). Assurance services are valued because the assurance engagement provider is independent and is perceived as unbiased with respect to the information examined.

Assurance services can be performed by auditors or by a variety of other professionals. For example, companies that perform television ratings are performing an assurance engagement. BBM Canada (**www.bbm.ca**), a not-for-profit television rating organization, and Nielsen Media Research Canada (**www.ca.nielsen.com**) conduct television rating studies. These organizations provide assurance that a specified number of viewers are watching the identified television shows. As shown in Table 1-1, for a television viewing attestation engagement, the information provided (the assertion) would be the number of viewers, while the reliability of the assertion is assessed using surveys or other technical tools.

Another example of a company that provides assurance services is the Canadian Council of Better Business Bureaus (CCBBB, **www.bbb.org/canada**). The CCBBB collects information about Canadian businesses. Some of the information is not

concept check

C1-1 List and explain the five key elements of the definition of auditing.

C1-2 Explain the difference between accounting and auditing.

C1-3 Describe the economic reasons for conducting an audit.

Assurance engagement—a service where a written communication is provided expressing an opinion about the reliability of an assertion made by another party; also called "assurance service."

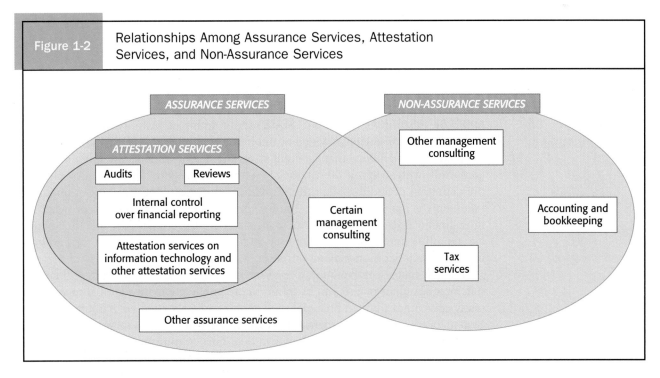

| Figure 1-2 | Relationships Among Assurance Services, Attestation Services, and Non-Assurance Services |

Table 1-1	Examples of Assurance Engagements That Are Also Attestation Engagements	

Component of Engagement	Television Viewing Attestation Engagement	Financial Statement Attestation Engagement
Name of engagement	Attestation engagement, television rating study	Attestation engagement, financial statement audit
Name of third party (the client)	Television network, such as CTV Television Network	Management of the client, e.g., management of RONA, on behalf of the shareholders
Information provided by the client (what is being tested)	Circulation figures used to promote advertising	Annual and quarterly financial statements
Party providing assurance	BBM Canada	Financial statement auditor
Type of report issued	Reach report or demographic reach report	Independent Auditor's Report

verified (and so would be considered equivalent to a compilation engagement, discussed below), while other information, such as details about current business scams, are verified, providing assurance regarding the specifics of those illegal activities.

The need for assurance is ongoing. Auditors have provided assurance services for years, particularly for historical financial statement information. Accounting firms have also performed assurance services related to lotteries and contests to provide assurance that winners were determined in an unbiased fashion in accordance with contest rules. More recently, auditors have been expanding the types of assurance services they perform, such as assurance engagements about company financial forecasts, website controls, and the security of information. The demand for assurance services is expected to grow as the demand for forward-looking information increases and as more real-time information becomes available through the internet.

A large category of assurance services provided by accounting firms is attestation services. The **attestation service** or engagement is a particular form of assurance service in which the auditor evaluates the information provided by one party, using suitable criteria, and issues a report about the reliability of this information to another party. Here, we use five categories to discuss attestation services:

1. Audit of historical financial statements.
2. Review of historical financial statements.
3. Attestation on internal control over financial reporting.
4. Attestation services on information technology.
5. Other attestation services that may be applied to a broad range of subject matter.

Attestation service—a special form of assurance engagement, such as a financial statement audit, in which the auditor evaluates the information provided by one party, using suitable criteria, and issues a report about the reliability of this information to another party.

AUDIT OF HISTORICAL FINANCIAL STATEMENTS Audits of historical financial statements are a major service provided by public accounting firms. In an audit of historical financial statements, management states that the statements are fairly stated in conformity with an applicable financial reporting framework. Table 1-1 shows (using the definition of auditing) that the responsible third party for the audit of financial statements is management. The auditor's report expresses an opinion on whether those financial statements conform, in all material respects, with the specified financial reporting framework. External users of financial statements rely on the auditor's report for their decision-making purposes.

Publicly traded companies in Canada are required to have audits of their financial statements. Auditor reports can be found in the public company's annual report, and many companies' audited financial statements can be accessed via the internet from System for Electronic Document Analysis and Retrieval (SEDAR) at **www.sedar.com**. This website, developed by the Canadian Securities Administrators (CSA) and CDS Inc., a subsidiary of the Canadian Depository for Securities Limited, has been available since 1997. It contains public filings, such as annual reports, management discussion and analysis, and press releases from public companies. Most public companies also have a website where copies of financial statements are posted. The auditor's report on financial statements is carefully worded to provide information to users (as discussed further in Chapter 20). The report lists the financial statements being audited and the responsibility of the auditors and management, and briefly describes how an audit is conducted before providing the auditor's opinion.

Many privately held companies also have annual financial statement audits to obtain financing from banks and other institutions. Government and not-for-profit organizations often have audits to meet the requirements of lenders or funding sources.

External users, such as shareholders and lenders, who rely on those financial statements to make business decisions, look to the independent auditor's report as an indication of the statements' reliability. They value the auditor's assurance because of the auditor's independence from the client, expertise, and knowledge of financial statement reporting matters. Figure 1-3 illustrates the relationships among the auditor, client, and financial statement users.

| Figure 1-3 | Relationships Among Financial Statement Auditor, Client, and External Users |

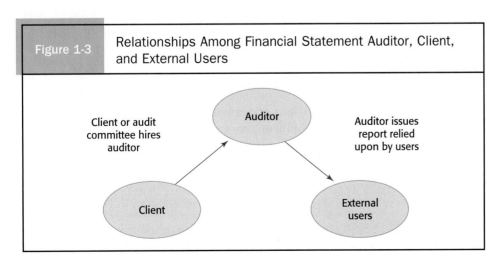

Client or audit committee hires auditor

Auditor

Auditor issues report relied upon by users

Client

External users

REVIEW OF HISTORICAL FINANCIAL STATEMENTS Many smaller, non-public companies want to issue financial statements to various users at a lower cost than an audit. They use a review, which provides a much lower degree of assurance than an audit. For a review, management also states that the financial statements are fairly stated in conformity with an applicable financial reporting framework, the same as for audits. A review provides moderate assurance, with the result that the public accountant (PA) provides a conclusion on the financial statements produced, rather than an opinion. Accordingly, the PA is required to do considerably less work than in an audit so the resulting cost is less. Reviews are discussed in more detail in Chapter 21.

ATTESTATION ON INTERNAL CONTROL OVER FINANCIAL REPORTING For an attestation on internal control over financial reporting, management states that internal controls have been developed and implemented following well-established criteria. Section 404 of the Sarbanes-Oxley Act in the United States requires publicly listed companies to report management's assessment of the effectiveness of internal control. The Act also requires auditors to evaluate management's assessment, which is an attestation of the effectiveness of internal control over financial reporting. This evaluation, which is integrated with the audit of the financial statements, increases user confidence about future financial reporting because effective internal controls reduce the likelihood of future misstatements in the financial statements. Canadian subsidiaries of U.S. companies and Canadian companies selling publicly listed shares in the United States would be subject to these requirements. This type of report is discussed further in Chapter 21.

ATTESTATION SERVICES ON INFORMATION TECHNOLOGY One of the major factors affecting the demand for other assurance services is the growth of the internet and electronic commerce. Concern over privacy and security of information on the internet continues as the volume of electronic commerce increases. The volume of real-time information available on the internet is shifting the need for assurance from historical information at a point in time, such as financial statements, to assurances about the privacy and reliability of processes generating information in a real-time format. For example, many business functions, such as ordering and making payments, are conducted over the internet and directly between computers using electronic data interchange (EDI). As transactions and information are shared online and in real time, there is an even greater demand for assurances about computer system controls surrounding information transacted electronically and the security of the information related to the transactions. Auditors can help provide assurance about these functions.

To respond to the growing need for assurance related to business transacted over the internet, the American Institute of Certified Public Accountants (AICPA) and the Canadian Institute of Chartered Accountants (CICA) developed two products (see also **www.webtrust.org**).

1. The *WebTrust* service is an electronic seal affixed to a website to assure the user that established criteria related to business practices, transaction integrity, and information processes have been met. The seal is a symbolic representation of the Public Accountant's report on management assertions about its disclosure of electronic commerce practices.
2. *SysTrust* provides assurance on information system reliability in areas such as security and data integrity. The accountant evaluates a company's computer systems using Trust Services principles and criteria, and determines whether controls over the system exist. The accountant then performs tests to evaluate the controls and prepares a report covering the specific period of the tests.

For an example of a WebTrust seal and report go to **www.confirmation.com**, an organization that provides audit confirmations electronically. You will see that confirmation.com has other types of assurance seals in addition to WebTrust.

OTHER ATTESTATION SERVICES Accountants may also prepare special reports for clients where the auditor provides an opinion on financial information other than financial statements or on compliance with an agreement or regulations. For example, an auditor might provide an opinion on the sales at a Shoppers Drug Mart in a Saskatoon shopping mall because the store's rent is based on sales and the owner of the mall requires an audit opinion.

OTHER ASSURANCE SERVICES There are almost no limits to the types of services that auditors can provide. A survey of large Certified Public Accountant (CPA) firms, performed by the AICPA Special Committee on Assurance Services, identified more than 200 assurance services currently provided. See also Chapter 21.

NON-ASSURANCE SERVICES Accounting firms perform numerous other services that generally fall outside the scope of assurance services. Some of these are related to financial statements, while others would be considered financial planning or management advisory services.

COMPILATIONS A compilation involves the accountant preparing financial statements from a client's records or from other information provided. Compilations are also called "Notices to Readers" or NTRs, after the name of the report issued with such engagements. A compilation is much less extensive than a review, and the cost is much less. No assurance is provided by a compilation, and readers are cautioned that the financial statements may not be appropriate for their purposes.

TAX SERVICES Accounting firms prepare corporate and individual tax returns for both audit and non-audit clients. In addition, sales tax remittance, tax planning, and other aspects of tax services are provided by most firms.

MANAGEMENT ADVISORY SERVICES Management advising includes services such as retirement planning and personal financial planning. Most accounting firms also provide services that enable businesses to operate more effectively, including simple suggestions for improving accounting systems, help with marketing strategies, computer installations, and pension benefit consulting. The firm offering these types of services needs to be aware of independence rules that prohibit the provision of some of these services to assurance clients, as discussed in Chapter 3.

ACCOUNTING AND BOOKKEEPING SERVICES Some small clients lack the personnel or expertise to prepare their own subsidiary records. Many small accounting firms work with accounting software packages to help clients record their transactions. Often such clients proceed with a compilation engagement.

When a PA conducts a review or an audit after doing bookkeeping work, he or she must take care to ensure that independence rules are properly followed. In particular, the PA must ensure that all transactions and journal entries are approved by management during the bookkeeping engagement. Additional prohibitions apply if the client is a public company.

Types of Audits and External Audit Reliance upon Internal Audit

Auditors perform three primary types of audits, as described and illustrated in Table 1-2.

1. **Financial statement audits**
2. **Compliance audits**
3. **Operational audits**

Financial statement audits are conducted by qualified public accountants. While compliance audits and operational audits are conducted by primarily government and internal auditors (discussed in the next section), public accountants may also do these types of engagements.

As part of the financial statement audit, external auditors evaluate whether their client's internal controls are designed and operate effectively and whether the financial statements are fairly presented. Because internal auditors spend all of their time with one company, their knowledge about the organization's operations and internal controls is much greater than the external auditors' knowledge.

Guidelines for conducting compliance or operational audits (the latter often termed "internal audits") for companies are not as well defined as for external audits. This occurs because of the wide variety of internal audits. Based on user requirements, the audit purpose, audit methods, and audit reports must be customized. Management of different companies may have widely varying expectations of the type and

Financial statement audit—an audit conducted to determine whether the financial statements of an entity are presented fairly, in all material respects, in conformity with an applicable financial reporting framework.

Compliance audit—(1) a review of an organization's financial records performed to determine whether the organization is following specific procedures, rules, or regulations set down by some higher authority; (2) an audit performed to determine whether an entity that receives financial assistance from a federal or provincial government has complied with specific laws and regulations.

Operational audit—a review of any part of an organization's operating procedures and methods for the purpose of evaluating economy, efficiency, and effectiveness.

Table 1-2	Examples of Three Types of Audits			
Type of Audit and Description	Example	Available Evidence	Information	Established Criteria
Financial Statement Audit: an audit conducted to determine whether the overall financial statements of an entity are stated in conformity with an applicable reporting framework	Perform annual audit of Trans-Canada Corporation's financial statements	Documents, records, and outside sources of evidence	TransCanada Corporation's financial statements	Reporting framework such as IFRS or ASPE
Compliance Audit: (1) a review of an organization's financial records performed to determine whether the organization is following specific procedures, rules, or regulations set down by some higher authority; (2) an audit performed to determine whether an entity that receives financial assistance from a federal or provincial government has complied with specific laws and regulations.	Determine if bank covenants for loan continuation have been met	Financial statements and calculations by the auditor	Company records	Loan agreement provisions
Operational Audit: a review of any part of an organization's operating procedures and methods for the purpose of evaluating economy, efficiency, and effectiveness.	Evaluate whether the computerized payroll processing for subsidiary H is operating economically, efficiently, and effectively	Error reports, payroll records, and payroll processing costs	Number of payroll records processed in a month, costs of the department, and error rate	Company standards for economy, efficiency, and effectiveness in payroll department

extent of auditing to be done by internal auditors. For example, management of one company may decide that internal auditors should be extensively involved in systems development, whereas others may decide that their work should focus primarily on financial controls and fraud audits.

RELATIONSHIP OF INTERNAL AND EXTERNAL AUDITORS There are both differences and similarities between the responsibilities and conduct of audits by internal and external auditors. The primary difference is to whom each party is responsible. The external auditor is responsible to financial statement users who rely on the auditor to add credibility to the statements. The internal auditors are responsible to management, although, to improve independence, they should report to the audit committee. Even with this important difference, there are many similarities between the two groups. Both must be competent as auditors and remain objective in performing their work and reporting their results. They both follow a similar methodology in performing their audits, including risk assessment, planning, and performing tests of controls and substantive tests. For financial statement audit work, they both use the audit risk model and materiality in deciding the extent of their tests of financial systems and evaluating results. Their decisions about materiality and risks may differ, however, because external users may have different needs than management.

External auditors justify reliance on internal auditors through the use of an audit risk model, explained in Chapter 7, and by following specified standards (discussed further in Chapter 19). The fee reduction of the external auditor is typically substantial when there is a highly regarded internal audit function and the external auditor can rely upon their work.

concept check

C1-4 Explain the difference between assurance and non-assurance engagements, providing an example of each.

C1-5 List and describe three types of audits, giving an example for each. Why is each type of audit important?

C1-6 Why is it important for external auditors to be able to rely upon internal auditors?

③ Professional Accountants and Their Work

Professional Accounting/Auditing Organizations

Auditors are trained professionals, frequently coming from the accounting profession. Various organizations perform auditing functions—external and internal—in Canada. Selected organizations and the designations awarded by the organizations are described below. These organizations require that individuals have a university degree and obtain relevant work experience. Each organization conducts research and develops, monitors, and comments upon standards relevant to its members. Because of the dynamic nature of business environments, each organization requires regular continuing professional development and offers continuing education programs. Professional organizations may offer specific programs of study leading to further specialist designations. Accounting organizations in Canada and around the world cooperate in conducting this research.

The *Canadian Institute of Chartered Accountants* (CICA, see **www.cica.ca**), publishes audit and assurance standards developed by the AASB (Auditing and Assurance Standards Board). The AASB, in consultation with an advisory board and others, sets the private- and public-sector auditing and assurance standards followed by public accountants in Canada. Current Canadian auditing standards are based upon international auditing standards. The CICA is one of the three major accounting organizations in Canada providing a professional designation relating to accounting and auditing, and it is the umbrella organization of the provincial institutes and *ordre* that regulate the CA profession in Canada. Members of the CICA are *chartered accountants* (CAs). The educational requirements for becoming a CA vary among provinces, with a common experience requirement of 30 months. All provinces require that an individual, to qualify as a CA, pass a national uniform examination administered by the CICA.

The *Certified General Accountants Association of Canada* (CGAAC, see **www.cga-online.org**) also provides a professional designation relating to accounting and assurance. CGAAC is the umbrella organization of the provincial associations and *ordre* that regulate the CGA profession in Canada. The use of the title "certified general accountant" (CGA) is awarded by CGAAC. Experience requirements are set at a minimum of two years in a combination of intermediate and senior positions in accounting or finance. Individuals, depending upon educational background, must pass a variety of subject-based national examinations, with an integrated capstone national examination.

The *Society of Management Accountants of Canada* (SMAC, see **www.cma-canada.org**), provides a professional designation relating to accounting and assurance and regulates the CMA profession in Canada. The SMAC administers the *Certified Management Accountant* (CMA) program, leading to the CMA designation. Students must pass examinations in required subject areas, pass a uniform national examination, and meet experience requirements.

At time of writing, the national CA, CGA and CMA (and many provincial/regional associations) were engaged in unification talks to create a single accounting organization that would offer a CPA (Chartered Professional Accountant) designation.

For an accountant to work as a public accountant, that is, do the work to assess financial statements and provide an opinion upon them, the person must complete the requirements of both an accounting designation (CGA, CMA, or CA) and in certain regions must hold a licence for public accountant (LPA). Requirements for registration as a public accountant vary by province.

Internal auditors and operational or compliance auditors may be accountants or come from any area of specialization, such as information systems, actuarial science, or psychology, before moving into the audit field.

Internal auditors look to *The Institute of Internal Auditors* (IIA, **www.theiia.org**) for professional guidance. The IIA is an organization that functions for internal auditors much as the CICA does for CAs, the CGAAC for CGAs, and the SMAC for CMAs; it establishes ethical standards and standards for the practice of internal auditing, provides education, and encourages professionalism of its approximately 103,000 members. The IIA has played a major role in the increasing influence of internal auditing. For example, the IIA has a highly regarded certification program resulting in the designation of Certified Internal Auditor (CIA) for those who meet the testing and experience requirements.

The Information Systems Audit and Control Association (ISACA, see **www.isaca.org**) awards the Certified Information Systems Auditor (CISA) designation to individuals passing an international examination and meeting experience requirements.

Both the IIA and ISACA have several classes of members, including associate and educational members, who can join the association to have access to publications and educational material but who would not be permitted to use the CIA or CISA designation until they have completed the necessary examination and experience requirements.

Types of Auditors

What type of auditing would you like to specialize in? Financial statement audits are conducted by public accountants skilled in accounting and auditing. Compliance audits also require skill in legislation, regulations, or policies that are being audited, as well as knowledge of controls-related processes. Operational audits may require a multidisciplined specialist team that understands clearly the organizational and operational facets under audit. Operational and compliance audits are often conducted by governmental and internal auditors. Depending upon their work experience and training, professional accountants have the skills to conduct all of these audits.

Here, we briefly discuss four types of auditors. They are public accountants, government auditors, Canada Revenue Agency auditors, and internal auditors. Throughout the text, we will frequently talk about the roles of specialist auditors, such as that of the tax expert when reviewing a financial statement audit, the information systems specialist when assessing information systems functions, and the forensic auditor when assessing fraud risks and conducting fraud audits.

PUBLIC ACCOUNTANTS Public accounting firms conduct financial statement audits or reviews. If the audit is due to a size requirement, or required by law, the audit is a statutory audit. Because of the widespread use of audited financial statements in the Canadian economy, as well as businesses' and other users' familiarity with these statements, it is common to use the terms "external auditor," "independent auditor," "public accountant," and "licensed public accountant" synonymously. PAs also complete many of the other types of engagements discussed in this chapter.

GOVERNMENT AUDITORS The Government of Canada and the various provincial governments each have an Auditor General who is responsible for auditing the ministries, departments, and agencies which report to that government. These government auditors may be appointed by a bipartisan legislative committee or by the government in that jurisdiction. They report to their respective legislatures and are responsible to the body appointing them. The primary responsibility of the government audit staff is to perform the audit function for government. The extent and scope of the audits performed are determined by legislation in the various jurisdictions. For example, in 1977, the federal parliament revised existing legislation by passing the Auditor General Act to require the Auditor General to report to the House of Commons on the efficiency and economy of expenditures or whether value for money had been received.

In 1984, the House of Commons passed Bill C-24, which amended the Financial Administration Act with respect to Crown corporations.[1] The implications are significant for auditors in public practice and in the government. Included among its requirements are the following:

1. Internal audits that look at financial matters or compliance with regulations and audits that look at whether or not the operations are conducted in an efficient, effective, and economic manner.
2. External audits of the financial statements.
3. Special examinations of efficiency, effectiveness, and economy (every five years).

The audit responsibilities of these government auditors are much like those of a public accounting firm. Most of the financial information prepared by various government agencies and, in some cases, by Crown corporations is audited by these government auditors before the information is submitted to the various legislatures. Since the authority for expenditures and receipts of government agencies is defined by law, there is considerable emphasis on compliance in these audits. In many provinces, experience as a government auditor fulfills the experience requirement for a professional designation. Auditor General reports are available online. (Refer to Table 1-3.)

An example of audit work in the public sector is the evaluation of the computer system controls of a particular purpose within a governmental unit. For a financial application, this could include access controls (quality of management supervision, segregation of duties) and controls executed both by human beings and by computer systems.

CANADA REVENUE AGENCY AUDITORS The Canada Revenue Agency has as its responsibility the enforcement of the federal tax laws as they have been defined by Parliament and interpreted by the courts. A major responsibility of this agency is to audit the returns of taxpayers to determine whether they have complied with the tax laws. The auditors who perform these examinations are referred to as Canada Revenue Agency auditors. These audits are solely compliance audits.

---

[1] The interested reader is referred to A Director's Introduction to the Audit and Special Examination Provisions of the Financial Administration Act (as amended by Bill C-24), published by the Canadian Comprehensive Auditing Foundation, from which this material is taken.

Table 1-3	Website Locations for Federal and Provincial Auditor General Offices
Canada:	**www.oag-bvg.gc.ca** (also the Auditor General for Northwest, Nunavut, and Yukon Territories)
Alberta:	**www.oag.ab.ca**
British Columbia:	**www.bcauditor.com**
Manitoba:	**www.oag.mb.ca**
New Brunswick:	**www.gnb.ca/oag-bvg/index-e.asp**
Newfoundland and Labrador:	**www.ag.gov.nl.ca/ag/**
Nova Scotia:	**www.gov.ns.ca/audg/**
Ontario:	**www.auditor.on.ca**
Prince Edward Island:	**www.assembly.pe.ca/auditorgeneral/index.php**
Quebec:	**www.vgq.gouv.qc.ca/default-EN.aspx**
Saskatchewan:	**www.auditor.sk.ca**

It might seem that the audit of returns for compliance with the federal tax laws would be a simple and straightforward problem. However, tax laws are highly complicated, and there are hundreds of volumes of court interpretations. Taxation problems could involve individual taxpayers, sales tax, goods and services tax, corporate taxes, or trusts. An auditor involved in any of these areas must have expertise in the applicable taxes to conduct the audit. The tax returns being audited vary from the simple returns of individuals who work for only one employer and take the standard tax deductions to the highly complex returns of multinational corporations.

INTERNAL AUDITORS Internal auditors, many of whom are members of the IIA, are employed by individual companies to audit for management. The internal audit group typically reports directly to the audit committee of the board of directors or a senior executive. Internal auditors' responsibilities vary considerably, depending upon the employer. Internal audit staff size can range from one or two to hundreds of employees, each of whom has diverse responsibilities, including many outside the accounting area. In recent years, many internal auditors have become involved in operational auditing or have developed expertise in evaluating computer systems. They also provide assistance in evaluating new systems prior to implementation and in assessing risks within the organization.

Modern internal auditing takes a proactive business advisory approach in contrast to traditional operational- and compliance-based audits. The need to emphasize consulting is evident from the definition of internal audit provided by the Institute of Internal Auditors: "an independent, objective assurance and consulting activity designed to add value and improve an organization's operations. It helps an organization accomplish its objectives by bringing a systematic, disciplined approach to evaluate and improve the effectiveness of risk management, control, and governance processes."

concept check

C1-7 List and describe three professional accounting organizations in Canada.

C1-8 Which professionals could conduct the audit of a company that manufactures automobiles? Provide examples of the types of assurance or non-assurance engagements they could conduct for this company.

To operate effectively, an internal auditor must be independent of the line functions in an organization but will not be independent of the entity as long as an employer–employee relationship exists. Internal auditors provide management with valuable information for making decisions concerning the efficient and effective operation of its business. Users from outside the entity, however, are unlikely to want to rely on information verified by internal auditors because of their lack of independence (explained further in Chapter 3). This lack of independence is the major difference between internal auditors and public accounting firms.

Summary

1. *What are the components of an audit?* An audit is an engagement where risk assessment, evidence collection, and evaluation are used to assess client information, such as a financial statements, using specific criteria, such as conformity with an applicable financial reporting framework. The results are reported by independent professionals.

   Why is there continued demand for audits? Audits provide added value to information since they provide independent assurance where the user of the report is remote from the provider, where the provider may be biased, or where data audited are voluminous or complex.

   What are the strategic differences between accounting and auditing? Accounting involves the actual preparation of underlying records, whereas auditing helps determine whether that recorded information reflects actual economic events. The auditor must plan the audit strategically, i.e., select evidence in response to identified risks of error or fraud.

2. *What are examples of the different types of engagements completed by auditors?* A financial statement audit is an attest engagement, a subset of assurance engagements.

   For an attest engagement, the client prepares the materials (such as the financial statements), and the auditor provides a written opinion on them, whereas for a specified auditing procedure engagement, the auditor may actually prepare the report (such as comments on lottery processes).

   Why do the financial statement auditors rely upon internal auditors? Having the PA rely upon internal audit saves the client money. Also, since the internal auditors work for the client full time, they are more familiar with the procedures at the client and are an important resource for the external auditors.

3. *What type of work do accountants complete?* Audits and assurance engagements are conducted by qualified accountants and other professionals. Public accountants (PAs), who audit financial statements as well as conducting these other engagements, can be CGAs, CMAs, or CAs in Canada. Although some CMAs provide assurance services, most CMAs are financial and management accounting professionals. CIAs and internal auditors often do operational audits and help management assess risks. There are also many specialist designations, such as the CISA.

MyAccountingLab

Make the grade with MyAccountingLab: The questions, exercises, and problems marked in orange can be found on MyAccountingLab. You can practise them as often as you want, and most feature step-by-step guided instructions to help you find the right answer.

Review Questions

1-1 ❶ Your local veterinarian is complaining about all of the "accountants" he has had to work with—the government has been in to look at his income taxes, the bookkeeper has been sick so he has had to hire someone else, and now you are coming in to do an audit. Using the definition of an audit, explain to the veterinarian what you will be doing with the financial statements.

1-2 ❶ Explain what is meant by determining the degree of correspondence between information and established criteria. What are the information and established criteria for the audit of Glickle Ltd.'s tax return by a Canada Revenue Agency auditor? What are they for the audit of Glickle Ltd.'s financial statements by a public accounting firm?

1-3 ❶ Explain why the auditor needs to know how to conduct a risk assessment.

1-4 ❶ What is the relationship between the risk assessment process and the collection of audit evidence?

1-5 ❷ Describe the different types of assurance engagements that could be provided for a hospital.

1-6 ❷ What are the differences and similarities among audits of financial statements, compliance audits, and operational audits?

1-7 ❷ List five examples of specific operational audits that could be conducted by an internal auditor in a manufacturing company.

1-8 ❷ Using a law firm as an example, describe the different audit, attestation, and assurance services that could be provided to the firm, with examples.

1-9 ❷ Explain why auditors need to be knowledgeable about e-commerce technologies.

1-10 ❸ Briefly describe the accounting organizations that exist in Canada and identify the professional designations they award. What roles do these organizations play for their members?

1-11 ❸ What are the major differences in the scope of the audit responsibilities for public accountants, auditors from the Auditor General's Offices, Canada Revenue Agency auditors, and internal auditors?

Discussion Problems

1-13 ❶ Daniel Charon is the loan officer of the Georgian Bay Bank. Georgian Bay Bank has a loan of $540,000 outstanding from Regional Delivery Service Ltd., a company specializing in the delivery of products of all types on behalf of smaller companies. Georgian Bay's collateral on the loan consists of 20 small delivery trucks with an average original cost of $45,000.

Charon is concerned about the collectibility of the outstanding loan and whether the trucks still exist. He therefore engages Susan Virms, public accountant, to count the trucks, using registration information held by Charon. She is engaged because she spends most of her time auditing used automobile and truck dealerships and has extensive specialized knowledge about used trucks. Charon requests that Virms issue a report stating:

1. Which of the 20 trucks is parked in Regional's parking lot on the night of June 30?

2. The condition of each truck, using the categories poor, good, and excellent.
3. The fair market value of each truck using the current "blue book" for trucks, which states the approximate wholesale prices of all used truck models based on the poor, good, and excellent categories.

REQUIRED
a. Identify which aspects of this narrative fit each of the following parts of the definition of auditing:
   (1) Information.
   (2) Established criteria.
   (3) Accumulates and evaluates evidence.
   (4) Competent, independent person.
   (5) Report of results.
b. Identify the greatest difficulties Virms is likely to face doing this assurance engagement.

1-14 ❶ ❷ Vial-tek has an existing loan in the amount of $1.5 million with an annual interest rate of 9.5 percent. The company provides an internal company-prepared financial statement to the bank under the loan agreement. Two competing banks have offered to replace Vial-tek's existing loan agreement with a new one. First National Bank has offered to loan Vial-tek $1.5 million at a rate of 8.5 percent but requires Vial-tek to provide financial statements that have been reviewed by a public accounting firm. Second National Bank has offered to loan Vial-tek $1.5 million at a rate of 7.5 percent but requires Vial-tek to provide financial statements that have been audited. The controller of Vial-tek approached a public accounting firm and was given an estimated cost of $12,000 to perform a review and $20,000 to perform an audit.

REQUIRED
a. Explain why the interest rate for the loan that requires a review report is lower than that for the loan that does not require a review. Explain why the interest rate for the

loan that requires an audit report is lower than the interest rate for the other two loans.
b. Calculate Vial-tek's annual costs under each loan agreement, including interest and costs for the public accounting firm's services. Indicate whether Vial-tek should keep its existing loan, accept the offer from First National Bank, or accept the offer from Second National Bank.
c. Assume that First National Bank has offered the loan at a rate of 8 percent with a review, and the cost of the audit has increased to $25,000 due to new auditing standards requirements. Indicate whether Vial-tek should keep its existing loan, accept the offer from First National Bank, or accept the offer from Second National Bank.
d. Explain why Vial-tek may desire to have an audit, ignoring the potential reduction in interest costs.
e. Explain how knowledge of e-commerce technologies and a strategic understanding of the client's business may increase the value of the audit service.

1-15 ❶ ❸ Projections indicated that there would be record numbers of homeless over the next few years, so the city decided that it was important to make shelters available. Accordingly, contracts were signed with two hotels in the downtown area over a three-year period. The hotels committed to have rooms available in the two coldest months of the year, and the city agreed to pay for the rooms at the rate of $40 per night. The hotel rooms were intended for homeless families.

At the same time, local churches got together and arranged to have volunteers staff the churches and provide hot meals so that the churches could be used as shelters by single individuals. The result was that the hotel rooms were

not used, and over a period of three years, the city paid almost $850,000 for empty rooms. This was publicized when the Auditor General for the city published his annual report.

REQUIRED
a. What objectives and criteria would the city Auditor General have used when conducting his audit of expenditures for the homeless?
b. Draft a section of the value-for-money report that would explain how the audit was conducted as well as the findings.
c. What recommendations for improvement might be included in the audit report?

1-16 ❶ ❷ ❸ Dave Czarnecki is the managing partner of Czarnecki and Hogan, a medium-sized local PA firm located outside of Kamloops. Over lunch, he is surprised when his friend James Foley asks him, "Doesn't it bother you that your clients don't look forward to seeing their auditors each year?" Dave responded, "Actually, many of my clients look forward to discussing their business with me. Auditing is only one of several services we provide. Most of our work for clients does not involve financial statement audits, and our audit clients seem to like interacting with us."

REQUIRED
a. Identify ways in which a financial statement audit adds value for clients.
b. List services other than audits that Czarnecki and Hogan likely provide.
c. Assume Czarnecki and Hogan has hired you as a consultant to identify ways in which they can expand their practice. Identify at least one additional service that you believe the firm should provide and explain why you believe this represents a growth opportunity for PA firms.

1-17 ❶ ❷ ❸ Joy Wu, a PA, is planning her first audit of a closely held small business. In prior years, Wu compiled the financial statements of the company. She also helped to set up its accounting system and supervised the work of the company's bookkeeper, who has limited knowledge of accounting. This year, management wants Wu to perform an audit because a local bank has requested audited financial statements as a condition for granting the company a large loan needed to expand operations. During her discussions with management, Wu agreed to conduct the audit and to continue to supervise the company's day-to-day accounting. This will facilitate the audit work by giving her a good knowledge of the company's business transactions. The company would like Wu to continue to closely advise and support management with the bank loan negotiations to secure the best possible loan terms.

REQUIRED
a. Describe the different types of work that Wu is considering, and the stakeholders involved in or affected by this work.
b. Assess the appearance of independence here. Is it possible for Wu to do all of this work and still be independent? Why or why not?

(Extract from AU2 CGA-Canada Examinations developed by the Certified General Accountants Association of Canada © 2010 CGA-Canada. Reproduced with permission. All rights reserved.)

Professional Judgment Problems

1-18 ❶ ❷ A small, but expanding, specialty home-products retailer recently implemented an internet portal that allows customers to order merchandise online. In the first few months of operation, their internet site attracted a large number of visitors; however, very few placed orders online. The retailer conducted several focus-group sessions with potential shoppers to identify reasons why shoppers were visiting the website without placing orders. Shoppers in the focus group made these comments:

1. "I am nervous about doing business with this retailer because it is relatively unknown in the marketplace. How do I know the product descriptions on the website are accurate and that the stated return policies are followed?"
2. "I am reluctant to provide my credit card information online. How do I know the transmission of my personal credit card information to the retailer's website is protected?"
3. "Retailers are notorious for selling information about customers to others. The last thing I want to do is enter personal information online, such as my name, address, telephone number, and e-mail address. I am afraid this retailer will sell that information to third parties and then I'll be bombarded with a bunch of junk e-mail messages!"
4. "Websites go down all the time due to system failures. How do I know the retailer's website will be operating when I need it?"

REQUIRED
Discuss whether this situation provides an opportunity for PAs to address these customer concerns. How could a PA provide assistance?

1-19 ❶ ❷ ❸ A large conglomerate is considering acquiring a medium-sized manufacturing company in a closely related industry. A major consideration by the management of the conglomerate in deciding whether to pursue the merger is the operational efficiency of the company. Management has decided to obtain a detailed report based on the intensive investigation of the operational efficiency of the sales department, production department, and research and development department.

REQUIRED
a. What professionals could the conglomerate hire to conduct the operational audit? What skills should be present in the audit team?
b. What major problems are the auditors likely to encounter in conducting the investigation and writing the report?

Case

1-20 ❶❷❸ Mont Louis Hospital, which is affiliated with a leading university, has an extremely reputable research department that employs several renowned scientists. The research department operates on a project basis. The department consists of a pool of scientists and technicians who can be called upon to participate in a given project. Assignments are made for the duration of the project, and a project manager is given responsibility for the work.

All major projects undertaken by the research department must be approved by the hospital's administrative board. Approval is obtained by submitting a proposal to the board outlining the project, the expected amount of time required to complete the work, and the anticipated benefits. The board also must be informed of major projects that are terminated because of potential failure or technological changes that have occurred since the time of project approval. An overall review of the status of open projects is submitted to the board annually.

In many respects, profit-making techniques utilized by business firms are applied to the management of the research department. For example, the department conducts preliminary research work on potential major projects that it has selected prior to requesting the board to approve the project and commit large amounts of time and money. The department also assesses the potential for grants for and for future revenues of the project. Financial reports for the department and each project are prepared periodically and reviewed with the administrative board.

Over 75 percent of the cost of operating the department is for labour. The remaining costs are for materials utilized during research. Materials used for experimentation are purchased by the hospital's central purchasing department. Once these materials are delivered, the research department is held accountable for their storage, their utilization, and the assignment of their costs to the projects.

In order to protect the hospital's right to discoveries made by the research department, staff members are required to sign waiver agreements at the time of hire and at certain intervals thereafter. The agreements relinquish the employees' rights to patent and royalty fees relating to hospital work.

The excellent reputation of Mont Louis is due, in part, to the success of the research department. The research department has produced quality research in the health-care field and has always been able to generate revenues in excess of its costs. The administrative board believes that the hospital's continued reputation for quality depends on a strong research department, and therefore the board has requested that the university's internal auditors perform an operational audit of the department. As part of its request for the operational audit, the board has presented a set of objectives that the internal audit is to achieve.

The operational audit to be conducted by the university's internal audit department should provide assurances as follows:

- The research department has assessed the revenues and cost aspects of each project to confirm that the revenue potential is equal to or greater than estimated costs.
- Appropriate controls exist to provide a means to measure how projects are progressing and to determine if corrective actions are required.
- Financial reports prepared by the research department for presentation to the administrative board properly reflect all revenues (both endowment and royalty sources and appropriated funding) and all costs.

REQUIRED

a. Evaluate the objectives presented by the administrative board to the university's internal audit department in terms of their appropriateness as objectives for an operational audit. Fully discuss the following:
   (1) The strengths of the objectives.
   (2) The modifications and/or additions needed to improve the set of objectives.

b. Outline, in general terms, the basic procedures that would be suitable for performing the audit of the research department.

c. Identify three documents that members of the university's internal auditing staff would be expected to review during the audit, and describe the purpose that the review of each document serves in carrying out the audit.

d. Discuss whether and how the work of the internal auditors could be used by the external auditors to reduce the cost of the financial statement audit.

(Adapted from CMA)

Ongoing Small Business Case: Thinking about CondoCleaners.com

1-21 ❶❸ Jim and Cecilia were having lunch at the public accounting firm cafeteria downtown and discussing the future. They had both been recently promoted to managers, with incomes approaching six figures. Cecilia and her husband had recently purchased a house, while Jim had accumulated a sizable nest egg, living with his parents. They were talking about the "departed ones"—their peers who had left the firm and were working as internal auditors or executives or had started their own business. Others had stayed with the firm but were now working as specialists in areas other than financial statement auditing. Jim had an idea that had been in the back of his head for two or three years—what about an online cleaning business? There were so many large condominium towers near the office—people could book their cleaning appointment online and then have the cleaning done within two or three days. Cecilia smiled, "I don't think I would take that kind of risk, having just committed to a mortgage, but I regret not using my skills in starting a new business."

REQUIRED

Using the definition of auditing, identify the types of skills that Jim and Cecilia have acquired at the public accounting firm. How would these skills translate into being able to run your own business? What types of skills might Jim need to run this new business?

2   The public accounting profession

As we saw in Chapter 1, public accountants (PAs) add value to information by providing assurance. What are the processes that help ensure that PAs do a good job? What is the difference in organizational structure between the large public accounting firms that earn over a billion dollars per year in Canada and the sole practitioner who works with small businesses? Future management accountants will use the information in this chapter to work with professional accounting firms. Future auditors (external, internal, government, or specialists) can use the chapter to see how quality assurance is maintained.

LEARNING OBJECTIVES

1 Describe the various organizational structures of public accounting firms.

2 Link the market forces that help ensure that audit and assurance engagements are completed to high standards of quality. Describe the organizations involved in the development and maintenance of Canadian GAAS (generally accepted auditing standards) for public accountants. Explain how these standards are enforced.

3 Examine the characteristics of quality control for financial statement audits. Explain how quality control is monitored,

including the role of the CPAB (Canadian Public Accountability Board).

STANDARDS REFERENCED IN THIS CHAPTER

CICA Standards

Section 5021 – Authority of auditing and assurance standards and other guidance for engagements other than audits of financial statements and other historical financial information

Section 5030 – Quality control procedures for assurance engagements other than audits of financial statements and other historical financial information

CSQC-1 – Quality control for firms that perform audits and reviews of financial statements and other assurance engagements

CAS 200 – Overall objectives of the independent auditor, and the conduct of an audit in accordance with Canadian Auditing Standards

CAS 220 – Quality control for an audit of financial statements

Leveraging the Power of Professional Judgment

What do the smallest of audits, completed in less than two days, have in common with the largest of audits that take thousands of people hours? Well, as explained at the beginning of this chapter, one similarity is the use of professional judgment, where the PA uses judgment to evaluate the risks associated with the engagement and match audit work to those risks. There are others, such as compliance with auditing standards and applicability of quality control procedures.

As you will find from studying auditing, there are hundreds of pages of auditing standards. Auditors who use bulky checklists and the full chain of command (such as having junior auditors' work supervised by a manager and then reviewed by a partner) will find that they cannot do a small audit in fewer than 12 hours. However, Phil Cowperthwaite, of Cowperthwaite Mehta in Toronto, has written a discussion document titled the "Anatomy of a 12-Hour Audit of Micro-Entities." Phil explained in his document and provided his audit training working papers to illustrate that yes, an audit can be done in such a brief time. It requires that field work be done by the partner with, perhaps, an onsite assistant, so that queries of staff can be cleared immediately. It requires a keen sense of judgment so that you know what to ask the client and which audit procedures relate to which risks and which audit tasks. Knowledge of audit standards must be current and embedded into concise checklists that are tailored to the industry, using predetermined and current industry knowledge. Finally, the audit must be automated using current tools.

Comparing this to the largest audits, which also must be done efficiently due to a highly competitive financial statement audit market, we will find that such audits are also highly automated (but using a broader variety of software tools), and that multiple levels of staff are used for those parts of the financial statement audit that suit them. Audit management conduct risk assessments, liaise with client executives and audit committees, and form the risk assessments that are key to the audit process. Junior staff conduct detailed audit procedures such as document inspection and examination of physical inventory. Specialized staff work with information technology, fraud assessments, tax, and conduct additional quality control work for high risk engagements.

IMPORTANCE TO AUDITORS

Both Phil's small firm and the largest firms engage in continuing research. Phil's firm is constantly refining the industry-specific checklists it uses in its smallest audits. Two areas of industry expertise, for example, include day care centres and associations. Phil was the CICA nominee voting member of the International Auditing and Assurance Standards Board (IAASB, see **http://ifac.org/IAASB/**) from 2006 to 2011 and as of writing (February 2012) is the CICA nominee voting member on the International Federation of Accountants Small and Medium Practices Committee (**www.ifac.org/about-ifac/small-and-medium-practices-committee**).

continued >

continued

The largest firms add to their industry expertise by creating databases of industry information for internal use and also by refining their database of audit procedures that they use for their engagements. Smaller firms may subscribe to software programs such as CCH Profit Driver or Sageworks ProfitCents to gain access to such information.

WHAT DO YOU THINK?

1. What are some examples of industry specializations for a small firm with fewer than ten people? Provide additional examples for a large firm. (Tip: Look at some accounting firm websites.)

2. How can public accountants ensure that they stay current in auditing standards and auditing techniques?

3. From this case and your knowledge of businesses, what would you need to do to stay current with knowledge of particular industry sectors, such as day cares or banks?

AS you can see from our opening vignette, research is important for all sizes and types of financial statement auditors. It is conducted by all accounting organizations in Canada and by national and international accounting organizations around the world. Good research is conducted by experienced auditors and research professionals. It is important in helping to ensure high quality, effective audits are conducted by public accounting firms.

Sources: 1. Cowperthwaite, Phil, Anatomy of a 12-Hour Audit of Micro-Entities, 2011, **www.cica.ca/cas/ site-utilities/item49214.pdf**, Accessed: August 21, 2011. 2. Cowperthwaite Mehta sample working paper file, undated, Received August 12, 2011. 3. Interview with Phil Cowperthwaite, August 12, 2011.

 ## Organization of Public Accounting Firms

Public Accounting Firms

There are currently more than 5,000 public accounting firms in Canada. These firms range in size from a sole practitioner to the more than 6,500 professional staff employed by Canada's largest public accounting firm, Deloitte & Touche LLP (see **www.deloitte.com**). Four size categories can be used to describe public accounting firms: "Big Four" international firms, other international or national firms, large local and regional firms, and small local firms.

INTERNATIONAL FIRMS How many "big" firms are there? In terms of revenue, the top three firms each earned Canadian revenues over $1 billion. These firms, plus three others, make up the Canadian firms with more than 1,500 employees each. Eight Canadian firms had more than 100 partners, and many regional firms have national and international affiliations.[1]

---

[1] Jeffrey, Gundi, "Firms end 2011 on upswing," *The Bottom Line*, 28(4), 2012, p. 13.

The six largest accounting firms in the world are Deloitte & Touche LLP (**www.deloitte.com**), PricewaterhouseCoopers LLP (**www.pwcglobal.com**), KPMG LLP (**www.kpmg.com**), Ernst & Young LLP (**www.ey.com**), Grant Thornton Canada (**www.grantthornton.com**), and BDO Dunwoody (**www.bdo.ca**).[2] They audit most of the 1,000 largest companies in Canada. Their gross revenues ranged from $426 million to over $1.5 billion for 2011.[3] These firms have offices that range in size from several hundred professionals in Toronto to smaller offices with fewer than 20 people. Due to large differences in size (the fourth-ranked firm, Ernst & Young LLP, was listed as having $870 million in annual revenue, with the fifth, Grant Thornton LLP, at less than $515 million), the four largest firms are commonly referred to as the "Big Four."

These international firms are so large because they need to be able to serve all major international cities as the globalization of businesses increases. For example, if a Canadian company has branches in the United States, Brazil, and Spain, the public accounting firm providing the audit in each of those countries must have auditors who are familiar with that country's laws, accounting practices, and auditing standards. Each of the largest firms now has the capability to serve all major international markets.

NATIONAL FIRMS Several other firms in Canada, such as Meyers Norris Penny LLP (**www.mnp.ca**) Collins Barrow National Cooperative (**www.collinsbarrow.com**), PKF Canadian Firms (**www.pkfnan.org**), and DFK Canada Inc. (**www.dfk.ca**), are referred to as national firms because they have offices in most major cities. Their revenue ranges are over $100 million.[4]

Audit Challenge 2-1 explains that some national or regional firms or associations of firms are operated by PAs with a CGA background. National or regional firms or associations of firms perform the same services as international firms and compete directly with them for clients. In addition, each is affiliated with firms in other countries and therefore has an international capability.

---

[2] *The Bottom Line*, April 2012, p. 13.
[3] Ibid., p. 13.
[4] Ibid., p. 16.

National and Regional CGA Firms

The largest-growing sector of business is the small business sector, since new businesses are always being formed. CGAAC has conducted research with respect to small business entrepreneurship by contacting its members who work with small businesses. This type of research is important to CGAs and other accountants who become PAs, since it gives them an opportunity to find out more about their primary client base.

Many CGAs in public practice work in a small office, often on their own or with only a few other partners. Regional or national public accounting firms grow by obtaining new clients or by buying or merging with such small public accounting firms. Examples of three such larger CGA firms are Porter Hetu International (**www.porterhetu.com**), EPR Canada Group Inc. (**www.epr.ca**) and Reid Hurst Nagy (**www.rhncga.com**). Porter Hetu International's Canadian website shows that the firm has offices in every province except Saskatchewan; EPR's online map shows offices in every province, while Reid Hurst Nagy is focused on western Canada, with offices in Richmond and Kelowna, B.C.

CRITICAL THINKING QUESTIONS

1. What qualities would each of these firms be looking for in potential new member offices? (Tip: Read the two CGA magazine articles listed as sources.)
2. How would these organizations ensure that consistent, high-quality work is provided by each member office?
3. What type of audit firm would you prefer to work for—one that provides service to only small businesses, or one that has a greater breadth of clientele, from small to medium-sized and public companies?

Sources: 1. Buckstein, Jeff, "The Client Shift," *CGA Magazine*, May–June 2002. 2. Cramp, Beverly, "Building National and Regional CGA Firms," *CGA Magazine*, January-February 2011, Retrieved from: **www.cga-canada.org/en-ca/AboutCGACanada/CGAMagazine/Pages/_ca_magazine_about.aspx**; Accessed: August 21, 2011.

LARGE LOCAL AND REGIONAL FIRMS There are fewer than 50 public accounting firms with professional staffs of more than 50 people. Some have only one office and serve clients primarily within commuting distance. Others have several offices in a province or region and serve clients within a larger radius. These firms compete with other public accounting firms, including the Big Four, for clients. Many of them become affiliated with associations of public accounting firms to share resources for such matters as technical information and continuing education.

SMALL LOCAL FIRMS Most of these public accounting firms have fewer than 25 professionals in their single office. They perform audits and related services primarily for smaller businesses and not-for-profit organizations, although some do have one or two clients with public ownership. Many small firms are resigning from these public company audits due to the need to register with the **Canadian Public Accountability Board** (CPAB, see **www.cpab-ccrc.ca**).

Canadian Public Accountability Board (CPAB)—an oversight organization for the audit of publicly listed companies that includes practice inspections.

Structure of Public Accounting Firms

The organization and structure of public accounting firms can vary depending on the nature and range of services offered by the firm. Three main factors influence the organizational structure of all firms:

1. *The need for independence from clients.* Independence permits auditors to remain unbiased in drawing conclusions about their clients' financial statements.
2. *The importance of a structure to encourage competence.* The ability of the structure to encourage competence permits auditors to conduct audits and perform other services efficiently and effectively.
3. *The increased litigation risk faced by auditors.* Firms continue to experience increases in litigation-related costs. Some organizational structures afford a degree of protection from lawsuits to individual firm members.

The organizational form used by many public accounting firms is that of a sole proprietorship or a partnership, although most provinces allow special-purpose limited liability partnerships or professional corporations. In a typical firm, several professionals join together to practise as partners, offering auditing and other services to interested parties. The partners normally hire professional staff to assist them in their work. Competence is developed by having a large number of professionals with related interests associated in one firm, which facilitates a professional attitude and continuing professional education.

The organizational hierarchy in a typical public accounting firm includes partners, managers, supervisors, seniors or in-charge auditors, and assistants, with a new employee usually starting as an assistant and spending two or three years in each classification before achieving partner status. The titles of the positions vary from firm to firm, but the basic structure is the same in all of them. When we refer in this text to the auditor, we mean the particular person performing some aspect of a financial statement audit. It is common to have one or more auditors from each level on larger engagements.

E-Commerce and Public Accounting Firm Operations

Like all industries, public accounting firms are using the internet to market their services. Firms of all sizes use the internet to highlight such things as office locations, affiliations, service lines, and industry specializations, and to provide reference tools and materials to existing and potential clients. Firm websites feature news and insights about business issues, such as updates on changes in tax laws and interactive forms to determine which type of retirement account to choose.

Public accounting firms use the internet to connect their global professional staff and to take advantage of online resources and databases. These resources are useful to PAs for staying current on emerging business and standards-setting issues. Databases such as Standard and Poor's Net Advantage Database and the Goldman Sachs Research Database provide extensive industry-specific information and coverage of companies. PAs use these on a subscription basis to stay current on industry developments and to obtain industry data useful for auditing and consulting.

❷ Responding to the Public Call for High-Quality Audits

High-profile failures, such as Enron and WorldCom, and frequently restated financial statements, such as those by Nortel, help explain why there is an increasing focus on standards and upon high-quality audits.

Professional Accounting Organizations

High-quality audits adhering to professional standards are promoted by professional organizations that serve as umbrella organizations for their members. The organizations coordinate the examination processes, provide for continuing education activities, fund research projects, produce relevant publications, and engage in standard setting and practice inspection processes.

RESEARCH AND PUBLICATIONS Each association has some form of monthly (or bimonthly) newsletter or national magazine. For example, in its role as representative of the CAs in Canada, the CICA publishes a wide range of materials. These include the monthly *CAmagazine* (**www.camagazine.com**), accounting and auditing research studies, and the biannual *Financial Reporting in Canada*. The CICA coordinates the Uniform Evaluation exam and publishes the Board of Evaluators' Report on each year's exam. It also coordinates the common activities of the provincial institutes and *ordre*.

The Certified General Accountants Association of Canada (CGAAC) plays a similar role in the professional lives of CGAs, as do the Society of Management Accountants of Canada for CMAs and the Institute of Internal Auditors for CIAs. For example, CGAAC publishes *CGA Magazine* (**www.cga-canada.org**), SMAC publishes *CMA*

Magazine (**www.managementmag.com**), and ISACA publishes *ISACA Journal* (**www.isaca.org/journal**). In addition, each association administers exams and provides professional guidance and continuing professional education. They also conduct research and publish materials of interest to their members and students.

CONTINUING EDUCATION Since all of these organizations require regular professional development, they are active in continuing professional education, sponsoring seminars, and developing and providing material for use by their membership. The CICA has six specializations for Chartered Accountants, in cooperation with other professional organizations. The ISACA also has specialized designations in information systems security and governance.

ESTABLISHING STANDARDS AND RULES The CICA has been given the authority by the Canada Business Corporations Act and the various provincial incorporating acts to set accounting and auditing and assurance standards that must be followed by public accountants doing audits of companies chartered under one of those Acts. This is done by stating that the financial statements should be prepared in accordance with the standards as set out in the *CICA Handbook*. In this role, the CICA supports research by its own research staff and, through grants, by others. Standards are codified in the *CICA Handbook*, and guidelines and rules for members and other public accountants to follow are also proposed. The *CICA Handbook* is produced in multiple parts: there is one part on assurance, and four parts on accounting.

Regulatory Influences on the Financial Statement Audit Process

Figure 2-1 uses the definition of auditing to illustrate components of the financial statement audit process. The figure shows key management actions, standards, and auditor actions. This figure helps us see regulatory influences on the component parts of the audit.

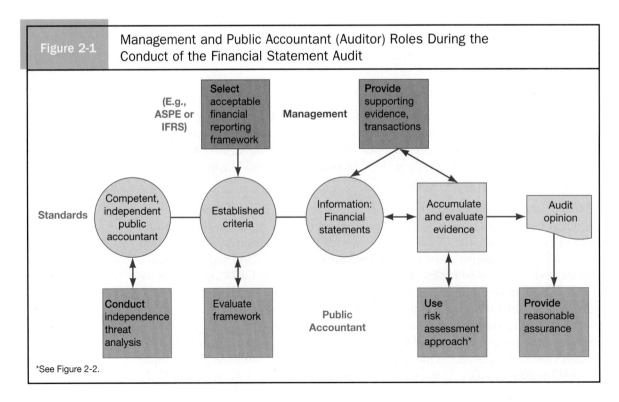

Figure 2-1 Management and Public Accountant (Auditor) Roles During the Conduct of the Financial Statement Audit

*See Figure 2-2.

Canada Has Embraced CASs

Canadian accounting and auditing standards have been modified to be in conformity with international standards because of an increasingly global business environment and a desire for efficiency in the standard-setting process. ISAs (International Standards on Auditing) have been adopted as Canadian Auditing Standards, CASs.

The CICA website (**www.cica.ca**) has a menu item titled "Canadian Standards in Transition" devoted to the transition to international standards. It includes reasons for the change and frequently asked questions (FAQs) about ISAs and CASs. The Canadian Auditing Standards Support Tool (at **www.cica.ca/cas/cas-comparative-mapping-tool/index.aspx**) is a helpful interactive tool that helps accountants identify which standards are relevant to which phases of the audit engagement. Similar standards information is available from the CGAAC website's assurance section, **www.cga-pdnet.org/en-CA/Pages/default.aspx**.

The ISAs already adopted focus on standards for the audit of financial statements. Some current Canadian standards combine guidance for the audit of financial statements and other types of assurance engagements. This means that the existing Canadian auditing and assurance standards will likely be rewritten to provide separate guidance for financial statement audits and other assurance engagements. In the meanwhile, we will be using both *CICA Handbook* section numbers and CAS numbers. The section numbers are called "Other Canadian Standards."

The CICA uses the terms *CICA Handbook—Assurance* or "Assurance Handbook" to refer to assurance standards. The *CICA Handbook—Assurance* has the following sections and subsections, many of which we will refer to in this text:

- Preface (facilitates an understanding of the scope and authority of the standards)
- Canadian Standards on Quality Control (containing quality control standards)
- Canadian Auditing Standards (the CASs)
- Other Canadian Standards (containing Handbook Sections about General Assurance and Auditing, Specialized Areas, Review Engagements, Related Services, and the Public Sector)
- Assurance and Related Services Guidelines

Canadian auditing and assurance standards are issued by the Auditing and Assurance Standards Board (AASB), which is composed of volunteers appointed by the Auditing and Assurance Standards Oversight Board (AASOB) and from the business community. Canadian auditing and assurance standards are based upon standards originally developed and released by IFAC's IAASB.

The conversion to CASs brings with it changes in terminology and a reorganization of Canadian standards, expected to be completed in the coming years. Each CAS is organized into the following sections: Introduction, Objective, Definitions, Requirements, Application, and Other Explanatory Material.

The process of establishing Canadian regulations has been influenced by the introduction of the Sarbanes-Oxley Act in the United States.[5] Some of these influences, such as the creation of the CPAB, are shown in Table 2-1.

It is important to consider these external influences as we talk about the nature of auditing, for it is in the eyes of external users and regulators that independence is assessed. Walking through the definition using Figure 2-1, we see that an independence threat analysis using the rules of professional conduct (explained further in Chapter 3) helps identify when a public accountant (or auditor) is independent. Prior to developing the financial statements, management will select an applicable financial reporting framework. As explained in Chapter 1, this framework is usually one of IFRS (International Financial Reporting Standards), ASPE (Accounting Standard for Private

---

[5] See **www.gpo.gov/fdsys/pkg/PLAW-107publ204/content-detail.html.**

Table 2-1	Influence of Sarbanes-Oxley Act on Canadian Regulations
Sarbanes-Oxley Requirement	**Effect on Canada**
Creation of the PCAOB (Public Company Accounting Oversight Board) to oversee listed company auditors and develop audit standards	Implementation of the CPAB to oversee Canadian audit professionals
Listed company management to certify the accuracy and completeness of financial statements	Same requirements implemented in Canada
Listed company management to certify existence of adequate internal controls and describe material changes to internal controls	Similar requirements implemented in Canada
Auditors required to provide an opinion on management's certification of internal controls	Not implemented in Canada
Increased independence requirements for auditors	Revisions of national and provincial rules of professional conduct for CAs and CGAs

Enterprises) or ASNPO (Accounting Standards for Not-for-Profit Organizations). The auditor is required to assess whether the framework selected by management is suitable. For U.S. reporting, the auditor will also need to be familiar with accounting frameworks acceptable in the United States.

When preparing the financial statements, management ensures that appropriate evidence exists to support the numbers and other disclosures contained within the financial statements. Sarbanes-Oxley in the United States and regulatory reporting requirements in Canada provide the clout to make management directly responsible for the financial statements. CASs state that the auditor can conduct the audit only if management agrees to provide this supporting evidence and both acknowledges and understands its responsibilities.

Canadian Auditing Standards require that the audit be conducted using a risk assessment approach. Part 2 of this text explains the risk assessment audit approach in detail, but an overview is provided in this chapter (see Figure 2-2). First, the auditor must identify and assess the potential risks of material misstatement in the financial

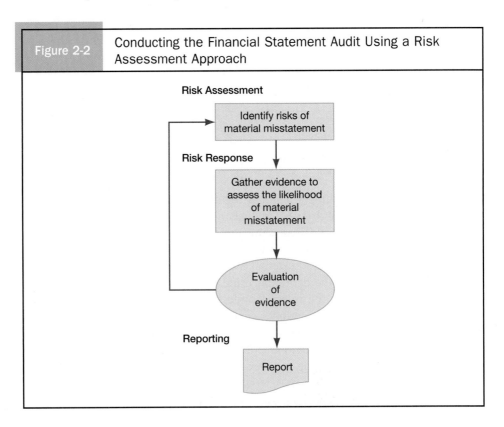

Figure 2-2	Conducting the Financial Statement Audit Using a Risk Assessment Approach

statements. Based upon these risks, the auditor will provide a risk response, which includes the design and execution of the evidence-gathering process to assess the likelihood of these material misstatements actually occurring. Canadian standards describe quality-control procedures and actions that the auditor should undertake during this process. The auditor continually evaluates evidence to enable preparation of the audit report. The audit report (discussed further in Chapter 20) is an opinion, not a guarantee, that provides reasonable assurance that the financial statements are free of material misstatement.

CAS   We will be examining CICA **Assurance Standards** throughout this text. Assurance Standards are issued by the **Auditing and Assurance Standards Board (AASB)**, as explained in the Preface to the CASs and *CICA Handbook* Section 5021 in the CICA Handbook—Assurance. These standards are the requirements underlying the audits, assurance engagements, and related services activities carried out by public accountants. These are considered to be authoritative requirements.

We will also use **Assurance and Related Services Guidelines** issued by the AASB. These Guidelines do not have the authority of Assurance Recommendations and are either interpretations of existing Recommendations or the views of the AASB on a particular matter of concern.

Ways Public Accountants Are Encouraged to Perform Effectively

Professional accounting organizations and other outside organizational influences have developed several mechanisms to increase the likelihood of appropriate audit quality and professional conduct. These are summarized in Figure 2-3 and discussed in the remainder of this and subsequent chapters. The codes of professional conduct of the various accounting bodies have a significant influence on members and are meant to provide a standard of conduct for all members, including those who are in public practice. The codes and related issues of professional conduct are examined in Chapter 3. Legal liability is studied in Chapter 4. Shaded circles indicate items discussed in this chapter.

Generally Accepted Auditing Standards

Auditing or assurance standards are general requirements designed to aid auditors in fulfilling their professional responsibilities in the audit of historical financial statements. They include quality control standards, consideration of management integrity about

Assurance Standards—a framework for the auditor to use to assist him or her in the conduct of an audit engagement; the authority underlying the audits and related services activities carried on by public accountants; the Requirements sections of CASs and the italicized portions of Other Canadian Standards in the *CICA Handbook*. They are issued by the Auditing and Assurance Standards Board.

Auditing and Assurance Standards Board (AASB)—an independent Board of the CICA that has the responsibility for issuing auditing and assurance standards for financial statement audits and other types of assurance and related services engagements

Assurance and Related Services Guidelines—interpretations of Assurance Standards or views of the Auditing and Assurance Standards Board on particular matters of concern; less authoritative than Assurance Recommendations.

Figure 2-3   Ways the Profession and Society Encourage Public Accountants to Conduct Themselves at a High Level

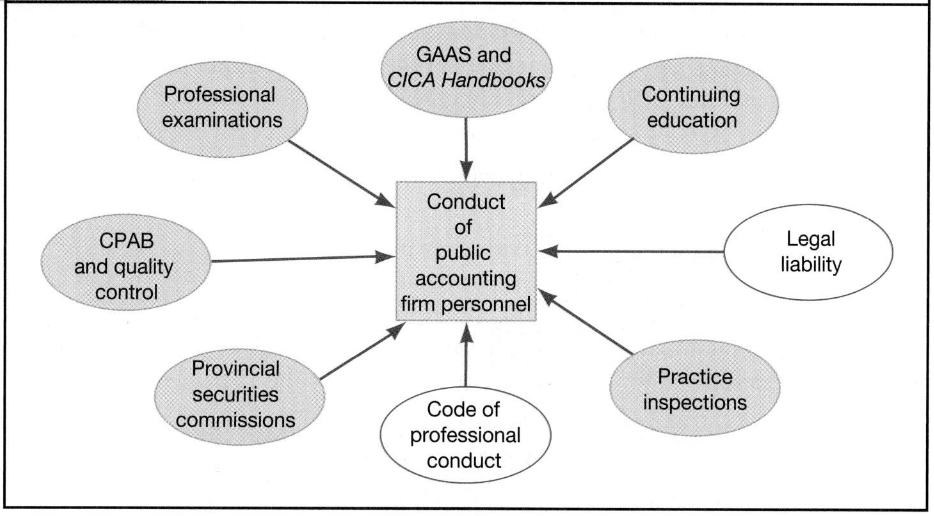

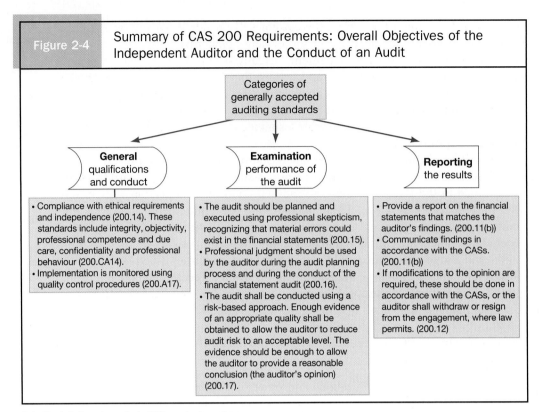

Figure 2-4 Summary of CAS 200 Requirements: Overall Objectives of the Independent Auditor and the Conduct of an Audit

Categories of generally accepted auditing standards

General qualifications and conduct

- Compliance with ethical requirements and independence (200.14). These standards include integrity, objectivity, professional competence and due care, confidentiality and professional behaviour (200.CA14).
- Implementation is monitored using quality control procedures (200.A17).

Examination performance of the audit

- The audit should be planned and executed using professional skepticism, recognizing that material errors could exist in the financial statements (200.15).
- Professional judgment should be used by the auditor during the audit planning process and during the conduct of the financial statement audit (200.16).
- The audit shall be conducted using a risk-based approach. Enough evidence of an appropriate quality shall be obtained to allow the auditor to reduce audit risk to an acceptable level. The evidence should be enough to allow the auditor to provide a reasonable conclusion (the auditor's opinion) (200.17).

Reporting the results

- Provide a report on the financial statements that matches the auditor's findings. (200.11(b))
- Communicate findings in accordance with the CASs. (200.11(b))
- If modifications to the opinion are required, these should be done in accordance with the CASs, or the auditor shall withdraw or resign from the engagement, where law permits. (200.12)

Note: Bracketed numbers refer to CAS paragraph numbers.

providing relevant evidence; professional qualities such as competence and independence requirements; evidence assessment and gathering requirements; and reporting requirements. Together, the material in the *CICA Handbook—Assurance*, research and other audit publications, plus best practices of public accounting firms comprise Canadian generally accepted auditing standards (GAAS).

Auditing standards in the United States are issued by the American Institute of Certified Public Accountants (**www.aicpa.org**) and the Public Company Accounting Oversight Board (PCAOB, see **www.pcaobus.org**), as described in New Standards 2-2. The AICPA is the umbrella organization for the CPA designation and the state CPA associations. Generally accepted auditing standards (GAAS) (also known as "Canadian generally accepted auditing standards") refers to the contents of the *CICA Handbook—Assurance*, published research and materials about auditing, plus Canadian generally accepted auditing practices.

CAS The broadest auditing standards available are overall objectives (also called general standards) discussed in CAS 200, summarized in Figure 2-4. These broad standards are not specific enough to provide any meaningful guide to practitioners, but they do represent a framework for further discussion of detailed standards.

CAS 200 explains the overall objectives of the public accountant when conducting an audit of financial statements. These objectives relate to the definition of auditing (200.11):

- Providing reasonable assurance that the financial statements are not materially misstated;
- Consideration of both potential fraud or error;
- Communicating whether the financial statements comply with an applicable financial reporting framework using the expression of an opinion;
- Reporting on the financial statements; and
- Communicating auditor findings in accordance with the CASs.

GENERAL: QUALIFICATIONS AND CONDUCT This standard stresses the important qualities the auditor should possess. In addition to technical competence obtained by a formal education in auditing and accounting, practical experience and continuing professional education are aspects of competence. The auditor must be technically qualified and experienced in those industries in which the auditor has clients.

The requirement involves due care in the performance of all aspects of auditing (discussed further in Chapter 4). This means that the auditor is a professional, responsible for fulfilling his or her duties diligently and carefully. As an illustration, due care includes consideration of the completeness of the working papers, the sufficiency of the audit evidence, and the appropriateness of the auditor's report. As a professional, the auditor must act in good faith, but he or she is not expected to make perfect judgments in every instance. Quality control procedures, discussed in the next section, help provide audit quality.

To conduct the audit effectively, the auditor must be free of bias. The importance of an objective state of mind and independence was stressed earlier in the definition of auditing. The Rules of Professional Conduct of the various provincial institutes of CAs and the *ordre* as well as CAS 200 stress the need for independence and the adherence to ethical standards. The rules of conduct of CGAAC also stress the need for independence of CGAs engaged in public accounting. The Canada Business Corporations Act (CBCA), which is similar to several of the provincial incorporating Acts, also requires the auditor to be independent. Public accounting firms are required to follow several practices to increase the likelihood of independence of all personnel. For example, there are established procedures for larger audits that utilize an audit committee whenever there is a dispute between management and the auditors that facilitate the auditors' independence from management, in addition to the requirements of confidentiality and professional behaviour. For example, the internal and external auditors usually report to the audit committee. An audit committee is a subcommittee of the board of directors of a company. So that the audit committee can provide effective oversight, the audit committee members must be independent, that is, be composed of directors not belonging to management, also strengthening audit independence. These topics are discussed further in Chapter 3.

EXAMINATION: PERFORMANCE OF THE ENGAGEMENT These standards require that the auditor conduct the audit using a risk-based approach, being skeptical about the potential for material misstatement (which includes errors or fraud) in the financial statements. Part 2 of this text discusses the components of the audit risk model as well as audit responsibilities and objectives, relating these to the auditor's objective of obtaining reasonable assurance that the financial statements are free of material misstatement.

A strategic and risk-based approach means that the client must be assessed in the context of the business environment, the corporate governance process, and the quality of internal controls. The decision as to how much and what quality of evidence to accumulate for a given set of circumstances requires professional judgment. A major portion of this book is concerned with the study of evidence accumulation and the circumstances affecting the amount needed. To provide an opinion requires planning, understanding the client's business, and gathering sufficient evidence.

To assist the auditor, the CBCA specifies the auditor's qualifications in Section 161 but also provides the auditor with statutory rights and responsibilities. These give the auditor the right to attend shareholder meetings and the right to have access to the necessary records, information, and explanations necessary to conduct the audit. These rights provide the auditor the access necessary for completion of the audit.

REPORTING: THE RESULTS Figure 2-5 shows that specific wording is required in the auditor's report. The report describes the auditor's responsibilities, management's responsibilities, the financial statements that were audited, the scope of the engagement, and the auditor's opinion. If the standard opinion cannot be provided, standards explain when and how the report should be modified. The audit report and the purpose of the individual sections are discussed in Chapter 20.

When the *CICA Handbook* is silent on an issue, the auditor may turn to other authoritative sources. These include the Statements on Auditing Standards (SASs) issued by the AICPA, the ISAs issued by the International Federation of Accountants,

Figure 2-5   Components of The Standard Auditor's Report

	Report section title
INDEPENDENT AUDITOR'S REPORT	**Report Title**
To the Shareholders of Hillsburg Hardware Limited	**Addressee**
We have audited the accompanying financial statements of Hillsburg Hardware Limited, which comprise the statements of financial position as at December 31, 2011 and December 31, 2010, and the statement of comprehensive income, statement of changes in equity and statement of cash flows for the years then ended, and a summary of significant accounting policies and other explanatory information.	**Introductory statement**
Management's Responsibility for the Financial Statements	**Management responsibility**
Management is responsible for the preparation and fair presentation of these financial statements in accordance with International Financial Reporting Standards, and for such internal control as management determines is necessary to enable the preparation of financial statements that are free from material misstatement, whether due to fraud or error.	
Auditor's Responsibility	**Auditor responsibility**
Our responsibility is to express an opinion on these financial statements based on our audits.	
We conducted our audits in accordance with Canadian generally accepted auditing standards. Those standards require that we comply with ethical requirements and plan and perform the audit to obtain reasonable assurance about whether the financial statements are free from material misstatement. An audit involves performing procedures to obtain audit evidence about the amounts and disclosures in the financial statements. The procedures selected depend on the auditor's judgment, including the assessment of the risks of material misstatement of the financial statements, whether due to fraud or error. In making those risk assessments, the auditor considers internal control relevant to the entity's preparation and fair presentation of the financial statements in order to design audit procedures that are appropriate in the circumstances, but not for the purpose of expressing an opinion on the effectiveness of the entity's internal control. An audit also includes evaluating the appropriateness of accounting policies used and the reasonableness of accounting estimates made by management, as well as evaluating the overall presentation of the financial statements.	
We believe that the audit evidence we have obtained is sufficient and appropriate to provide a basis for our audit opinion.	
Opinion	**Opinion paragraph**
In our opinion, the financial statements present fairly, in all material respects, the financial position of Hillsburg Hardware Limited as at December 31, 2011 and December 31, 2010, its financial performance and its cash flows for the years then ended in accordance with International Financial Reporting Standards.	
[signature of] Boritz, Kao, Kadous & Co., LLP	**Auditor's signature**
March 1, 2012	**Date of the auditor's report**
444 Transom Street Halifax, Nova Scotia B3M 3JP	**Auditor's address**

textbooks, journals, and technical publications. Materials published by the CICA, mentioned earlier in the chapter, such as audit technique studies, are particularly useful in furnishing assistance on specific questions.

International Auditing Standards

The CICA, the CGAAC, and the SMAC are members of the International Federation of Accountants (IFAC, see **www.ifac.org**), a body that seeks to harmonize auditing standards on a worldwide basis. IFAC, through the International Auditing and

Standards from the PCAOB in the United States

The Sarbanes-Oxley Act of 2002, signed into law on July 30, 2002, is considered by many observers to be the most important legislation affecting the American auditing profession since the 1933 and 1934 Securities Acts. The Sarbanes-Oxley Act was triggered by the bankruptcies and alleged audit failures involving Enron and WorldCom. The provisions of the Act apply to publicly held companies and their audit firms.

This Act established the Public Company Accounting Oversight Board (PCAOB), appointed and overseen by the Securities and Exchange Commission (SEC). The PCAOB provides oversight for auditors of public companies, including establishing auditing, ethics, independence, and quality control standards for public company audits and performing inspections of the quality controls at audit firms performing those audits. These activities were formerly the responsibility of the AICPA. The U.S. Auditing Standards Board (ASB) is still responsible for issuing pronouncements on auditing matters for all entities other than public companies. Although the PCAOB is responsible for setting standards, existing auditing standards remain in effect for public companies until the PCAOB develops specific guidance.

The PCAOB regularly issues new standards that have an impact on SEC registrants, including Canadian companies that file on the SEC. The most recent standards (effective with year-ends after December 15, 2010) concern the quality and extent of audit evidence.

Assurance Standards Board (IAASB), issues International Standards on Auditing (ISAs) and International Auditing Practice Notes (IAPNs) for the guidance of accountants in member countries. ISAs are standards and are authoritative, while IAPNs provide guidance and are not authoritative. Now that Canada has adopted the ISAs as CASs, our standard-setters are looking at the IAPNs for potential adoption. Prior to adopting international standards in Canada, the AASB issues exposure drafts explaining how the standards will be changed (if at all) and solicits feedback. Feedback is used to further revise exposure drafts and determine whether the proposed standard is acceptable.

In addition, the provincial securities commissions are members of the International Organization of Securities Commissions (IOSCO, see **www.iosco.org**). IOSCO members are concerned with securities that are issued by a company in one country and sold in a second country. For example, shares of Vale Inco Limited (**www.inco.com**), a Canadian corporation owned by a Brazilian company, are traded on the Toronto Stock Exchange under the jurisdiction of the Ontario Securities Commission (OSC, see **www.osc.gov.on.ca**) and on the New York Stock Exchange under the jurisdiction of the U.S. Securities and Exchange Commission (SEC, see **www.sec.gov**); Vale Inco's shares are said to be "cross-listed." Both the OSC and the SEC are members of IOSCO. IOSCO members are concerned about International Auditing and Assurance Standards as they have to decide on the quality, sufficiency, and appropriateness of evidence collected and the report issued for audits of financial statements submitted to them for cross-listing.

A Canadian auditor must conduct an audit of a Canadian or foreign company in accordance with Canadian GAAS (i.e., follow the *CICA Handbook*) and may, in addition, conduct the audit in accordance with international GAAS (i.e., the ISAs or the GAAS of another country such as the United States). Canada's adoption of international auditing standards facilitates the efficient completion of such international engagements. The auditor may report that the audit was conducted using Canadian and foreign GAAS. It is important to note that Canadian GAAS would be the floor in this case, and differences in the two standards may need to be identified.

Where there are reporting differences between Canadian GAAS and the ISAs or foreign GAAS, the auditor should follow Canadian reporting standards. The *CICA*

Handbook takes precedence over the ISAs when there is a conflict. A Canadian auditor who is engaged to conduct an examination in accordance with International Standards on Auditing would consult the most recent version of the ISAs.

③ Quality Control

For a public accounting firm, **quality control** comprises the methods used to make sure that the firm meets its professional responsibilities to clients. These methods include the organizational structure of the public accounting firm and the procedures the firm sets up. For example, a public accounting firm might have an organizational structure that assures the technical review of every engagement by a partner who has expertise in the client's industry.

A public accounting firm must make sure that generally accepted auditing standards are followed on every audit. Quality controls represent the mechanisms used by the firm that help it meet those standards consistently on every engagement. Quality controls are therefore established for the entire public accounting firm and all the activities in which the firm is involved; GAAS require that these standards are applied to each engagement on an individual basis.

CSQC-1 (Canadian standard on quality control) and CAS 220 (quality control for an audit of financial statements), the Canadian versions of the equivalent international standards, apply to assurance engagements for financial statements. Section 5030 (quality control procedures for assurance engagements other than audits of financial statements and other historical financial information) applies to other assurance engagements.

Elements of Quality Control

CAS

CICA Handbook Section CSQC-1 describes general standards of quality control that are applied to firms performing audit and review engagements with a focus on financial statements and financial data. Section 5030 provides similar standards for other types of assurance engagements. These are summarized in Table 2-2, where the general components of quality control are listed under a series of headings called elements of quality control.

These standards clarify the minimum policies and procedures that firms should have in place. PAs need to ensure that they adequately apply quality control to each audit engagement. For example, there are specific procedures to help ensure that differences of opinion on an engagement are brought forward and cleared before finalizing the engagement. We will be looking at these quality control procedures in more detail when we talk about the various phases of the audit engagement throughout this text.

Quality control standards complement the independence rules that are in place for PAs in response to increased demands for public accountability. After the Sarbanes-Oxley Act of 2002 was passed in the United States creating the PCAOB, a similar body was implemented in Canada called the Canadian Public Accountability Board (**www.cpab-ccrc.ca**). Rather than being legislated, the CPAB was created by the provincial securities commissions, the Office of the Superintendent of Financial Institutions, and the CICA. The CPAB's purpose is to help improve the public's confidence in independent auditing. This is accomplished by promoting high-quality audits. The CPAB has developed an oversight program that involves regular inspections of those public accounting firms that audit Canadian public companies. One of the items absent from the CPAB's mission statement is the development of auditing standards. This is a key difference between the Canadian and American approaches. Although the CPAB will provide feedback to the standard-setting process, it is up to the AASB and coordination with international standard-setting bodies.

Public accounting firms are required to register with the CPAB and are subject to a quality control inspection by the CPAB if they audit companies called "reporting

Table 2-2	Elements of Quality Control at the Firm Level

Element	Summary of Requirements
1. Leadership and responsibilities within the firm:	An organizational culture that provides quality should be present for audit and review engagements. Quality control procedures should be developed, documented, implemented, and communicated. Management within a firm should ensure that qualified personnel monitor and address non-compliance with quality control procedures. A firm should establish a formal code of conduct that includes procedures for individuals to disclose differences of opinion and any inappropriate conduct.
2. General ethical requirements:	The general ethical principles of integrity, objectivity, professional competence and due care, confidentiality, and professionalism should be addressed at the policy level, promoted by firm personnel, and monitored.
3. Independence:	Policies and procedures should be developed, communicated, and monitored to ensure that the firm complies with the independence requirements. Areas to be addressed are the extent of non-assurance services provided to audit and review clients, documentation of independence evaluations, partner rotation (where required), fee policies, partner compensation, and effects of litigation.
4. Client acceptance or continuance:	Policies and procedures for the client risk assessment processes should be present, including an evaluation of a potential client's management integrity and auditor competence and independence.
5. General human resource policies:	Adequate hiring policies (and documentation of their implementation) that ensure competence and integrity of personnel should be in place. Ongoing professional development of personnel should exist, with assignment to work that matches employee competence, and performance evaluation related to audit quality.
6. Extent of professional development:	Employees should be adequately trained in the skills needed to conduct audits and reviews. Both instructors and attendees are to be evaluated, with documentation of that evaluation.
7. Engagement performance:	Adequate processes and procedures should be in place to ensure that the audit or review is conducted in accordance with GAAS, that quality control procedures are followed for each engagement, and that the audit is appropriately documented. These include the use of software tools, supervision, review of work, use of internal or specialist consultation, and processes for handling differences of opinion.
8. Engagement quality control review:	Procedures for quality control review should exist to take place during the engagement and monitoring should occur after engagement completion. Policies in place should include use of second or independent partner review, technical review, documentation, and compliance with quality control processes. Processes should exist for following up internal and external complaints.
9. Documentation:	Policies should address extent of documentation, whether retained in hard copy or electronic format, file retention, storage, security and back-up for audit documentation, correspondence, policies, and procedures.

issuers." (The inspection process is discussed further in the next section.) The term "reporting issuers" is used to describe entities, such as profit-oriented businesses and mutual funds that have raised capital from the public, are listed on a Canadian stock exchange, and are required to file annual audited financial statements with their listing exchange. At the time of writing, there were 309[6] registered firms on the CPAB website. These include both CGA firms and CA firms.

Public accounting firms that do not audit reporting issuers are not subject to quality control inspection by the CPAB but are still required to have quality control standards in place. Quality control needs to be considered during all phases of the engagement, including client acceptance, continuance, planning, execution, and file review of the engagement.

---

[6]Canadian Public Accountability Board, **www.cpab-ccrc.ca**, Accessed: September 8, 2011.

Practice Inspection Comes Calling

For a CA or CGA functioning as a sole practitioner or working for a small public accounting office, the provincial practice inspectors will likely come to review audit files every three years, depending upon the province where the practice office is located. If the office does not conduct audits, the PA may not see them at all—the practice inspection team will ask to have the review engagement files sent to them. Inspections are conducted by qualified PAs, either CAs or CGAs, licensed by the same provincial association as the practitioner.

If the office is licensed to have articling students (an approved training office), the inspectors will review the ability of the office to provide sufficient, appropriate hours to the students, as well as the quality control procedures. Then, they will review the quality control manual, a sample of client files, and ask questions. The report will be discussed with the PA before being finalized.

If the inspectors find any files or quality control procedures unsatisfactory, the PA may be required to revise processes, attend training courses, or have more frequent practice inspections (that the PA would have to pay for). Provincial and national professional accounting organizations regularly provide articles that assist their members in maintaining a high quality of work, such as the online Outlook magazine published by the B.C. CGA Association.

Sources: 1. The Institute of Chartered Accountants of Ontario, Practice Inspection Overview, **www.icao.on.ca/CAfirms/PracticeInspection/1012page1417 aspx**, Accessed: September 8, 2011. 2. McDonald, M. "Ethics in focus," by Outlook, December 2010, p. 10-11, **www.cga-bc.org**, Accessed: September 8, 2011.

The quality control procedures that a public accounting firm employs will depend on the size of the firm, the number of practice offices, and the nature of the practice. The quality control procedures of a 150-office international firm with many complex multinational clients would vary considerably from those of a five-person firm specializing in small audits in one or two industries.

PRACTICE INSPECTION One of the ways in which the PA profession in Canada has dealt with quality control is through the establishment of practice inspections. The purpose of all practice inspections is to ensure the existence of, and adherence to, quality control standards. These inspections may be administered by professional associations, provincial institutes, *ordre*, or the CPAB.

Practice inspections may be conducted by accounting bodies independently of the CPAB. Practice inspection for CAs, for example, is administered by the provincial institute or *ordre* and is usually mandatory for CAs in public practice. A practice inspection of each practice unit (usually an office but possibly each partner in the office) is normally completed every three years but could be yearly if the practice unit is found not to maintain the level of practice standards set forth by the provincial practice inspection committee.

CPAB practice inspections may be conducted by a provincial accounting body, with the CPAB providing direction and reviewing the results. CPAB inspections are conducted annually for audit firms that have 50 or more reporting issuers. Audit firms having fewer reporting issuers may be inspected once every three years.

The CPAB publishes an annual report summarizing its findings, organized by size of firm. For example, the April 2011 report, available from the CPAB website, reveals that for the period ended December 2010, there were inspections of the four largest public accounting firms in Canada, 11 annual inspections, 25 recurring inspections, and 29 follow-up inspections. CPAB concerns cover a number of areas, such as lack of adequate engagement supervision and review, poor design of substantive analytical procedures, not enough or inappropriate audit evidence, not enough communication with the audit committee, and lack of consultation by smaller firms on complex, non-routine transactions. CPAB also noted in its major findings that excellent work was also present in the files that it selected for review.[7] CPAB noted in its report that 71 provincial practice inspections were conducted during 2010.

A Provincial Practice Inspection Committee can impose sanctions. These include reinspection the following year and referral to the Professional Conduct Committee, whose powers include requiring the member to take courses, removing the practice unit's right to train students, and expelling the member from their professional body and forfeiting the member's right to use the appellation Chartered Accountant or Certified General Accountant.

The CPAB could impose additional sanctions or restrictions such as engaging an independent monitor or limiting the right to audit reporting issuers. It could also make the inspection reports public but would do so only if the member firms were not addressing the recommendations for improvement.

Practice inspection can be beneficial to the profession and individual firms. The profession gains if reviews result in practitioners doing higher-quality audits. A firm can also gain if the practice inspection improves the firm's practices and thereby enhances its reputation and effectiveness and reduces the likelihood of lawsuits. Of course, practice inspection is costly. There is always a trade-off between costs and benefits.

Provincial Securities Commissions

Securities regulation in Canada is a provincial matter; therefore, companies that issue securities in Canada must abide by rules promulgated by the provincial securities commissions. The national umbrella organization, the Canadian Securities Administrators (**www.csa-acvm.ca**), sets policies to which the member commissions agree to adhere. The **provincial securities commissions** are responsible for administering the purchase and sale of securities within their jurisdictions.

Provincial securities commissions—provincial organizations with quasi-legal status that administer securities regulations within their jurisdictions.

Copies of the actual policy statements, which may include questions and answers and multimedia presentations about them, are available at the websites of the following provincial securities commissions' sites: British Columbia Securities Commission (**www.bcsc.bc.ca**), Alberta Securities Commission (**www.albertasecurities.com**), Ontario Securities Commission (**www.osc.gov.on.ca**), and l'Autorité des marches financiers (**www.lautorite.qc.ca/index.en.html**).

More specifics on some of these rules will be discussed in subsequent chapters. The CSA was responsible for the rule that required listed companies' auditors to participate in the oversight program of the CPAB. It also implemented the requirement that the listing company's Chief Financial Officer and Chief Executive Officer provide certification of annual and interim financial statements (as well as the accompanying management discussion and analysis and information forms filed with the exchanges). Another requirement is that every listed company must have an audit committee, with specifics about the composition and responsibilities of those audit committees.

Securities and Exchange Commission

Since many Canadian companies sell their stocks and borrow money in the United States, they must meet the requirements of the **Securities and Exchange Commission** (SEC). It is therefore appropriate to review the functions and operations of that body.

The overall purpose of the SEC, an agency of the U.S. federal government, is to assist in providing investors with reliable information upon which to make investment decisions. To this end, the Securities Act of 1933 requires most companies planning to issue new securities to the public to submit a registration statement to the SEC for approval. The Securities Exchange Act of 1934 provides additional protection by

Securities and Exchange Commission (SEC)—a U.S. federal agency that oversees the orderly conduct of the securities markets; the SEC assists in providing investors in public corporations with reliable information upon which to make investment decisions.

---

[7]Canadian Public Accountability Board, **www.cpab-ccrc.ca**, Accessed: September 10, 2011.

requiring the same companies and others to file detailed annual reports with the commission. The commission examines these statements for completeness and adequacy before permitting a company to sell its securities through the securities exchanges.

Although the SEC requires considerable information that is not of direct interest to CPAs, the securities acts of 1933 and 1934 require financial statements, accompanied by the opinion of an independent certified public accountant, as part of a registration statement. Specific reports, for example, interim financial information, changes in officers or directors, and certain related-party transactions also need to be filed.

Since large CPA firms usually have clients that must file one or more of these reports, and since the rules and regulations affecting filings with the SEC are extremely complex, most CPA firms have specialists who spend a large portion of their time making sure their clients satisfy all SEC requirements.

concept check

C2-6 What are the different ways that quality control is established and enforced for public accounting firms in Canada?

C2-7 Why is it important that PAs have high-quality financial statement audits?

The SEC has considerable influence in setting generally accepted accounting principles and disclosure requirements for financial statements as a result of its authority for specifying reporting requirements considered necessary for fair disclosure to investors. The SEC has power to establish rules for any CPA associated with audited financial statements submitted to the commission. Even though the commission has taken the position that accounting principles and auditing standards should be set by the PCAOB or the profession, the SEC's attitude is generally considered in any major change proposed by the Auditing Standards Board or equivalent U.S. standard-setting bodies.

The SEC requirements of greatest interest to CPAs are set forth in the commission's Regulation S-X and Accounting Series Releases, and Accounting and Auditing Enforcement Releases. These publications constitute important regulations, as well as decisions and opinions on accounting and auditing issues affecting any CPA dealing with publicly held companies.

Summary

1. *How are public accounting firms organized?* Small accounting firms are set up as sole proprietorships or partnerships, with most larger firms set up as limited liability partnerships.

   What are some of the largest public accounting firms? The four largest firms are Deloitte & Touche LLP, PricewaterhouseCoopers LLP, KPMG LLP, and Ernst & Young LLP.

2. *What market forces ensure that audit and assurance engagements are completed to high standards of quality?* The biggest threat is that a public accounting firm will be forced out of business due to legal liability. Provincial securities commissions and the CPAB are now involved to ensure that the quality of audits is high. Completion of audits to high ethical standards helps maintain the positive image of auditors. As have so many other businesses, auditing has adopted the use of information technology to help ensure the effective and efficient completion of audits.

   Which organizations develop and maintain the standards that public accountants use? In Canada, public accounting audit and assurance standards are the responsibility of the AASB. The AASB develops standards in consultation with many organizations and groups: other accounting organizations in Canada, CPAB, securities and exchange commissions, international and other national standard-setting organizations, individual PAs, and the business community.

   How does GAAS relate to risk mitigation? GAAS defines the standards to be used during the audit engagement, including quality control procedures and proper supervision. The auditor balances the cost of lawsuits against the cost of quality control in managing the auditor's risk of being sued.

   How are quality control standards enforced? Quality control inspections called practice inspections are conducted by the professional associations, the provincial institutes/*ordre*, and the CPAB.

3. *What is quality control, and how is it monitored?* Quality controls are policies and procedures used by a public accounting firm to ensure that it meets its professional responsibilities. Table 2-2 describes some of the characteristics of quality control. Public accounting firms are required to have a quality control manual and to monitor and enforce their quality control procedures. Feedback from practice inspections, such as those of the CPAB, help monitor quality controls so that public accounting firms can engage in continuing improvement.

Review Questions

2-1 ❶ What are the advantages and disadvantages of practising as a large public accounting firm rather than a small one?

2-2 ❶ What major characteristics of the organization and conduct of public accounting firms permit them to fulfill their social functions competently and independently?

2-3 ❶ Research the rules in your province with respect to accounting firm structure. Are LLPs permitted? What is the primary difference between a public accounting firm organized as a partnership and an LLP? Why would a public accounting firm choose to organize as an LLP?

2-4 ❶ How can a PA use the internet to assist the PA practice?

2-5 ❷ Although the *CICA Handbook* standards provide general guidance, the application of these standards is dependent upon particular circumstances. In practice, a professional accountant may encounter situations where *CICA Handbook* standards do not exist or may not apply. Since there is no substitute for the exercise of professional judgment in the determination of what constitutes fair presentation and good practice, it has been suggested that too much effort is being directed toward the development of standards. Discuss the issues raised in the above statements.
(Adapted from the CICA)

2-6 ❷ What benefits do organizations such as the CICA, CGAAC, and SMAC provide to their members?

2-7 ❷ What role does the *CICA Handbook* have in the professional activities of public accountants in Canada?

2-8 ❷ Distinguish between generally accepted auditing standards and generally accepted accounting principles, and give two examples of each.

2-9 ❷ Explain how an objective state of mind and due care contribute to a PA's qualifications to conduct a financial statement audit.

2-10 ❸ How did business failures by Enron and WorldCom affect quality control procedures for public accounting firms in Canada and the United States?

2-11 ❸ How has Sarbanes-Oxley affected the Canadian regulatory environment for PAs?

2-12 ❸ What is the role of the CPAB?

2-13 ❸ Describe the role of International Standards on Auditing. Discuss whether a PA who conducts an audit in accordance with generally accepted auditing standards simultaneously complies with international standards on auditing.

2-14 ❸ What is meant by the term "quality control" as it relates to a public accounting firm?

2-15 ❸ State what is meant by the term "practice inspection." What are the implications of the term for the public accounting profession?

Discussion Problems

2-16 ❶ A local PA, who has been in practice for several years, recently met with representatives of an internet service provider that is interested in developing a website for the PA's practice. The PA has been reluctant to develop an internet site but is willing to learn more about the types of information and resources that PAs often provide on their internet sites before making a final decision.

REQUIRED
a. Describe the types of resources and weblinks that PAs often provide on their websites.
b. State reasons why public accounting firms invest resources in creating sophisticated internet sites.
c. Discuss how the internet site can be a useful tool for a public accounting firm's accounting and auditing practice.

2-17 ❸ For each of the following procedures that are taken from the quality control manual of a public accounting firm, identify the applicable element of quality control from Table 2-2 on page 39 and explain why the procedure is important for the audit engagement.

a. Appropriate accounting and auditing research requires adequate technical reference materials. Each firm professional has online password access through the firm's

website to electronic reference materials on accounting, auditing, tax, and other technical information including industry data.

b. Each audit engagement of the firm is directed by a partner and, in most instances, a manager of the firm. On every engagement, an attempt is made to maintain continuity of at least a portion of the personnel.

c. Audit engagement team members enter their electronic signatures in the firm's engagement management software to indicate the completion of specific audit program steps. At the end of the audit engagement, the engagement management software will not allow archiving of the engagement file until all audit program steps have been electronically signed.

d. At all stages of any engagement, an effort is made to involve professional staff at appropriate levels in the accounting and auditing decisions. Various approvals of the manager or senior accountant are obtained throughout the audit.

e. No employee will have any direct or indirect financial interest, association, or relationship (for example, a close relative serving a client in a decision-making capacity) not otherwise disclosed that might be adverse to the firm's best interest.

f. Each office of the firm shall be visited at least annually by review persons selected by the director of accounting and auditing. Procedures to be undertaken by the reviewers are illustrated by the office review program.

g. Existing clients of the firm are reviewed on a continuing basis by the engagement partner. Termination may result if circumstances indicate that there is reason to question the integrity of management or its independence, or if accounting and auditing differences of opinion cannot be reconciled. Doubts concerning whether the client-auditor relationship should be continued must be promptly discussed with the director of accounting and auditing.

h. Individual partners submit the nominations of those persons whom they wish to be considered for partner. To become a partner, an individual must have exhibited a high degree of technical competence; must possess integrity, motivation, and good judgment; and must have a desire to help the firm progress through the efficient dispatch of the job responsibilities to which he or she is assigned.

i. Through the continuing employee evaluation and counselling program and through the quality control review procedures as established by the firm, educational needs are reviewed and formal staff training programs modified to accommodate changing needs. At the conclusion of practice office reviews, apparent accounting and auditing deficiencies are summarized and reported to the firm's director of personnel.

2-18 ③ The following comments summarize the beliefs of some practitioners about quality control and practice inspection:

Quality control and practice inspection are quasi-governmental methods of regulating the profession. There are two effects of such regulation. First, it gives a competitive advantage to national public accounting firms because they already need formal structures to administer their complex organizations. Quality control requirements do not significantly affect their structure. Smaller firms now need a more costly organizational structure, which has proven unnecessary because of existing partner involvement on engagements. The major advantage smaller public accounting firms have traditionally had is a simple and efficient organizational structure. Now that advantage has been eliminated because of quality control requirements. Second, quality control and practice inspection are not needed to regulate the profession. Elements of quality control have always existed, at least informally, for quality firms. Three things already provide sufficient assurance that informal quality control elements are followed without practice inspection. They are competitive pressures to do quality work, legal liability for inadequate performance, and a code of professional ethics requiring that PAs follow generally accepted auditing standards.

REQUIRED

a. State the pros and cons of these comments.

b. Evaluate whether control requirements and practice inspection are worth their cost.

Professional Judgment Problem

2-19 ② ③ The Mobile Home Manufacturing Company is audited by the public accounting firm Rossi and Montgomery. Mobile Home has decided to issue stock to the public and wants Rossi and Montgomery to perform all the audit work necessary to satisfy the requirements for filing with the OSC. The public accounting firm has never had a client go public before.

REQUIRED

a. What are the implications of Rossi and Montgomery accepting the engagement?

b. List the additional issues confronting the auditors when they file with the OSC as compared with dealing with a regular audit client.

Case

2-20 ② ③ Cheng, a recently qualified PA, has been assigned by his firm, Liu & Liu LLP, to serve as the senior auditor in charge of the fieldwork on a new audit engagement. The client is a medium-sized credit union that is heavily involved as a mortgage lender in the local real estate market. This is the first credit union that Liu & Liu is auditing. Cheng has not previously been involved in audits of financial institutions. The credit union's predecessor auditors resigned unexpectedly during the current fiscal year, and they have not responded to Liu & Liu's request for information for over one month. Liu & Liu has agreed to perform the engagement since the financial statement audit needs to be completed.

The client has provided Liu & Liu with the predecessor audit firm's unqualified opinion on last year's financial statements. The engagement partner tells Cheng to concentrate her efforts on understanding the client's business and internal control environment, including the credit union's internal control systems, but not to rely upon internal controls. Then, Cheng is to perform extensive tests on the key balance sheet asset and liability accounts, such as mortgage loans receivable. Cheng performs the audit as instructed, finds no material misstatements, and Liu & Liu issues an unqualified opinion on the financial statements.

REQUIRED

State whether or not the PA has violated generally accepted auditing standards. Justify your response.

(Extract from AU2 CGA- Canada Examinations developed by the Certified General Accountants Association of Canada © 2010 CGA-Canada. Reproduced with permission. All rights reserved.)

Ongoing Small Business Case: Planning for CondoCleaners.com

2-21 ❶ ❷ ❸ As a professional in the practice of giving advice, Jim knew when he had to ask questions, too. He called a lawyer friend of the family who owned a cleaning business at the other end of the country and was suitably cautioned, "It's very competitive, and you don't make much money. You'll have to succeed on volume. You're an accountant—crunch some numbers on what you expect!" Jim also talked to his family and peers at work, finding out that people who used cleaning services were primarily working couples or the elderly. Finally, he used the services of a local university marketing class to do some market research for him. This was totally new for Jim—as an experienced auditor, how could his skills help him in running a cleaning business?

REQUIRED

How is running a public accounting business similar to running a cleaning business?

3 Professional relationships: The role of ethics and independence

The public accountant (PA) is a professional who works with the audit committee, board of directors, management, and other professionals such as lawyers. In addition to providing a high quality of work, the PA is expected to be free from bias and to behave in an ethical manner. In this chapter, we will look at some of the issues and rules affecting the professional accountant's behaviours in relationship with others.

Rules of professional conduct are regularly updated by all accounting professions, and qualified accountants are expected to abide by these rules whether they work in public accounting, in industry, in education, or in the not-for-profit sector. As a potential PA, it is important that you understand how these rules govern your relationships with your fellow members and potential clients. If you will be working as a management accountant, specialist, or internal or government auditor, you will still be bound by the rules of the professional accounting organizations you are a member of. Some of those rules are discussed in this chapter.

LEARNING OBJECTIVES

1. Describe ethics and their relevance. Acquire tools to promote ethical conflict resolution (also known as working through an ethical dilemma).

2. Explain how PAs are different from other professionals. Examine the role of a code of professional conduct in encouraging PA ethical behaviour. Apply rules of professional conduct to case facts and identify violations.

3. Examine the threats to independence and explain how the threats can be mitigated. Discuss how the auditor's relationship with the audit committee affects independence. Identify some of the key rules of professional conduct and how are they enforced.

STANDARDS REFERENCED IN THIS CHAPTER
CICA Standards
CAS 220 – Quality control for an audit of financial statements

Section 5030 – Quality control procedures for assurance engagements other than audits of financial statements and other historical financial information

Section 7600 – Reports on the application of accounting principles

CSQC-1 – Quality control for firms that perform audits and reviews of financial statements and other assurance engagements

The Value of the Audit Depends on Auditor Independence

Bruce Smith is a senior auditor who works on the audit of the Canadian subsidiary of Ultimate Networks, an audit client in his firm's Hong Kong office. Bruce has watched the shares of Ultimate Networks soar for the last six months. Ultimate Networks is gaining market share, and he knows that their sales will continue to soar with the new technology that they have in the pipeline. Finally, he can't resist any longer. He calls his investment broker, John Rizzo, and places an order for 200 shares of Ultimate Network's shares. "Are you sure this is okay?" asked Rizzo. "I thought Ultimate Networks was one of the jobs that you enjoyed working at." Rizzo knows about professional responsibilities because he worked with Bruce at a PA firm prior to becoming an investment broker, and they remained friends. "Why don't you check it out and get back to me?" Rizzo added.

IMPORTANCE TO AUDITORS

The next morning, Bruce is glad that he has John Rizzo for an investment broker. The recent CPAB reports talked about the importance of independence and that it had uncovered some independence violations at member firms. Firms even had to recall audit reports. The result could have included partners and audit staff being terminated for making share investments similar to the investment that Bruce contemplated the day before. Bruce remembers that he is required to annually sign a statement that he does not own shares in a long list of client firms. In the past he had treated them as a formality and not really read through the list before signing it. It would have been a grave mistake for him to purchase those shares.

As he thinks about the requirement that he not own shares in an audit client, he concludes, "There are plenty of other good investments out there."

WHAT DO YOU THINK?

1. Independence is one of the most important characteristics of the external auditor. Why would someone like Bruce consider ignoring it?
2. How can firms help people like Bruce understand the importance of independence?
3. Should employees who violate independence rules be terminated from their employment immediately?

❶ Ethical Behaviour is a Cornerstone of Trust

What Are Ethics?

Ethics can be defined broadly as a set of moral principles or values. Each of us has such a set of values, although we may or may not have considered them explicitly. Philosophers, religious organizations, and other groups have defined, in various ways, ideal sets of moral principles or values. Examples of prescribed sets of moral principles or values at the implementation level include laws and regulations, church doctrines, codes of business ethics for professional groups such as CAs, CGAs, and CMAs, and codes of conduct within individual organizations such as accounting firms, corporations, and universities.

An example of ethical principles is included in Table 3-1 below. These principles were developed by combining principles from the Josephson Institute of Ethics (a non-profit organization focused on ethical quality) with ethical standards published by both an international coaching organization and a technical journal.

A search of the internet will reveal thousands of sites with published ethical standards, for example, the Canadian Standards Association (**www.csa.ca**).

It is common for people to differ in their moral principles or values and the relative importance they attach to these principles. These differences reflect life experiences, successes and failures, and the influences of parents, teachers, religious organizations, and friends.

NEED FOR ETHICS Ethical behaviour is necessary for a society to function in an orderly manner. It can be argued that ethics is the glue that holds a society together. Imagine, for example, what would happen if we could not depend on the people we deal with to be honest. If parents, teachers, employers, siblings, co-workers, and friends all consistently lied, it would be almost impossible for effective communication to occur.

The need for ethics in society is so important that many commonly held ethical values are incorporated into laws. However, many of the ethical values found in Table 3-1 cannot be incorporated into laws because of the judgmental nature of certain values.

Table 3-1	Illustrative Ethical Principles
The following list of ethical principles incorporates characteristics and values that many people and organizations associate with ethical behaviour.	
Trustworthiness	Be honest and reliable. Honour your agreements or promises, and do not intentionally mislead others. Be reliable—do your best to fulfill your commitments. Declare conflicts of interest. Act promptly to disclose hazards.
Respect	Be civil, courteous, and accepting of others, understanding the many differences that exist among people. Be unbiased in your decision making.
Responsibility	Be accountable for your own actions and aware of the actions of those you are supervising. Keep confidential information confidential. Use resources wisely and economically. Do not use the work of others without declaring the source. Identify your own competence levels and act within that competence.
Fairness	Judge actions and individuals on their merits, considering the equality of individuals and having regard for due process and transparency.
Caring	Act out of a positive intention to do no harm or to minimize harm. Be concerned for others, showing benevolence when it is within your ability to do so.
Citizenship	Obey laws, and assist others in obeying laws, including the reporting of offenders. Help your society function by participating in voting, volunteer work, and the conservation of resources.

Sources: 1. ASME Technical Journals, **www.asme.org**, Accessed: November 29, 2011. 2. International Coach Federation, **www.coachfederation.org**, Accessed: November 29, 2011. 3. The Josephson Institute, **www.josephsoninstitute.org**, Accessed: November 29, 2011.

WHY PEOPLE ACT UNETHICALLY Most people define unethical behaviour as conduct that differs from what they believe would have been appropriate given the circumstances. Each of us decides what constitutes ethical behaviour. It is important to understand what causes people to act in a manner that we decide is unethical.

There are two primary reasons why people act unethically: the person's ethical standards are different from those of society as a whole, or the person chooses to act selfishly. Both reasons may exist.

The person's ethical standards differ from general society's Extreme examples of people whose behaviour violates almost everyone's ethical standards are drug dealers, bank robbers, and larcenists.

Many far less extreme examples exist where others violate our ethical values. When people cheat on their tax returns, treat other people with hostility, lie on employment applications, or perform below their competence levels as employees, most of us regard that as unethical behaviour. If the other person has decided that this behaviour is ethical and acceptable, there is a conflict of ethical values.

The person chooses to act selfishly The difference between ethical standards that differ from general society's and acting selfishly is illustrated in the following example: Aaron finds a briefcase in an airport containing important papers and $1,000. He tosses the briefcase and keeps the money. He brags to his family and friends about his good fortune. Aaron's values probably differ from most of society's. Brenda faces the same situation but responds differently. She keeps the money but leaves the briefcase in a conspicuous place. She tells nobody and spends the money on a new wardrobe. It is likely that Brenda has violated her own ethical standards, but she has decided that the money was too important to pass up. She has chosen to act selfishly. What would you do? Shouldn't the briefcase and its entire contents be returned? Consider Carl who returns the entire briefcase and gets a reward of $500.

This example shows that unethical behaviour often results from selfish motives. Political scandals result from the desire for political power. Cheating on tax returns and expense reports is motivated by financial greed. Performing below one's competence and cheating on tests are due to laziness or perceived lack of time. In each case, the person knows that the behaviour is inappropriate but chooses to do it anyway because of the apparent personal sacrifice needed to act ethically.

An **ethical dilemma** is a situation a person faces in which a decision must be made about appropriate behaviour. A simple example of an ethical dilemma was finding a briefcase, which involves deciding whether to try to find the owner or to keep it. Far more difficult ethical dilemmas can arise in the auditing profession. Consider Qin Zhang. Qin is the senior auditor in-charge of the September 30, 2011, financial statement audit of Paquette Forest Products Inc., a forest products company that produces lumber and paper products in northern Manitoba. The company employs 375 people and is the main employer in the remote town of Duck Lake, Manitoba; the other businesses in Duck Lake provide goods and services to Paquette Forest Products and its employees. In the course of the audit, Qin discovers that the company has had a number of failures of the equipment that removes the sulphuric acid from the paper production process and, as a result, thousands of litres of untreated water have been dumped into the Loon River and Duck Lake. Qin learns that the cost of replacing the equipment so that no further spills are likely would strain cash reserves. If ordered to replace the equipment by the environment ministry, the company would be forced to raise additional capital or cease operations. What should Qin do?

Auditors, accountants, and other business people face many ethical dilemmas in their business careers. Dealing with a client who threatens to seek a new auditor unless an unqualified opinion is issued presents a serious ethical dilemma if an unqualified opinion is inappropriate. Deciding whether to confront a supervisor who has materially overstated departmental revenues as a means of receiving a larger bonus is tough to do. Continuing to be a part of the management of a company that harasses and mistreats employees or treats customers dishonestly is an ethical dilemma, especially if the manager has a family

Ethical dilemma—a situation in which a decision must be made about the appropriate behaviour.

to support and the job market is tight. Deciding whether or not to report the negligence of a supervisor to a partner is a problem you may face as a staff accountant.

RATIONALIZING UNETHICAL BEHAVIOUR There are alternative ways to resolve ethical dilemmas, but care must be taken to avoid methods that are rationalizations of unethical behaviour. The following are commonly employed rationalization methods that can easily result in unethical conduct:

1. *Everybody does it.* The argument that it is acceptable to falsify tax returns, cheat on exams, or sell defective products ("just obeying orders") is commonly based on the rationalization that everyone else is doing it and therefore it is acceptable.
2. *If it's legal, it's ethical.* Using the argument that all legal behaviour is ethical relies heavily on the perfection of laws. Under this philosophy, one would have no obligation to return a lost object to its owner unless the other person could prove that it was his or hers.
3. *Likelihood of discovery and consequences.* This approach relies on evaluating the likelihood that someone else will discover the behaviour. Typically, the person also assesses the severity of the penalty (consequences) if there is a discovery. An example is deciding whether to correct an unintentional overbilling to a customer when the customer has already paid the full billing. If the seller believes the customer will detect the error and respond by not buying in the future, the seller will inform the customer now; otherwise the seller will wait to see if the customer complains.

RESOLVING ETHICAL DILEMMAS In recent years, formal frameworks have been developed to help people resolve ethical dilemmas. The purpose of such frameworks is to help a person identify the ethical issues and decide on an appropriate course of action based on the person's own values. This six-step approach is intended to be a relatively simple approach to resolving ethical dilemmas:

1. Obtain the relevant facts.
2. Identify the ethical issues from the facts.
3. Determine who is affected by the outcome of the dilemma and how each person or group is affected.
4. Identify the alternatives available to the person who must resolve the dilemma.
5. Identify the likely consequence of each alternative.
6. Decide on the appropriate action.

A more recent approach, titled *Giving Voice to Values*[1] (GVV), provides a framework for dealing with ethical issues in a proactive way, with the assumption that the organization is willing to work to resolve ethical dilemmas and the person at the centre of the dilemma is willing to take action. The steps in the GVV Process[2] are:

1. *Identification:* Identifying the ethical issue, the values underpinning the different positions in this value conflict and the possibilities for action.
2. *Purpose and choice:* Considering your personal and professional purpose and choices.
3. *Stakeholder analysis:* Who is affected, what is at stake for them, and how do you connect with them?
4. *Powerful response:* Craft a useful, powerful response that you could use, taking into account multiple options, the need for additional information, working with allies, and who your audience would be.
5. *Scripting and coaching:* Further develop and practise your response (scripting) and get help (coaching).

We now use the GVV approach to consider an unfortunately common ethical dilemma that you might encounter in your future career.

---

[1] Gentile, M. C. & Hittner, J. 2010. *Giving Voice to Values: How to Speak Your Mind When You Know What's Right.* Yale University Press, New Haven.

[2] Chappell, S., M. Edwards and D. Webb. (2011) *Giving Voice to Values: A means of shifting the teaching and practices of business ethics,* 18th Annual International Vincentian Conference Promoting Business Ethics, St, John's University, New York, October 26–28, 2011.

Shifting Values Using the GVV Five-Step Approach

ETHICAL DILEMMA Bryan Longview has been working for six months as a staff assistant for De Souza & Shah, public accountants. Currently he is assigned to the audit of Reyon Manufacturing Corp. under the supervision of Karen Van Staveren, an experienced audit senior. There are three auditors assigned to the audit, including Karen, Bryan, and a more experienced assistant, Martha Mills. During lunch on the first day, Karen says, "It will be necessary for us to work a few extra hours on our own time to make sure we come in on budget. This audit isn't very profitable anyway, and we don't want to hurt our firm by going over budget. We can accomplish this easily by coming in a half hour early, taking a short lunch break, and working an hour or so after normal quitting time. We just won't write that time down on our time report." Bryan recalls reading in the firm's policy manual that working extra hours and not charging for them on the time report is a violation of De Souza & Shah's employment policy. He also knows that seniors are paid bonuses instead of overtime, whereas staff are paid for overtime but get no bonuses. Later, when Bryan discusses the issue with Martha, she says, "Karen does this on all of her jobs. She is likely to be our firm's next audit manager. The partners think she's great because her jobs always come in under budget. She rewards us by giving us good engagement evaluations, especially under the cooperative attitude category. Several of the other audit seniors follow the same practice."

1. *Identification:* Bryan recognizes that Karen's request violates firm policies and is underpinned by a desire to meet the expected budget and the value she places on career advancement. Bryan also knows that these practices affect the firm's quality control, since budgeting and time management will not be accurate. By violating one firm policy, he and his other team members could be on the slippery slope to violating other practices, such as signing off incomplete work.

2. *Purpose and choice:* Bryan takes the time to reconnect with his broader purpose of being an accountant: to contribute to the accurate reporting and financial survival of the organizations he serves. As such, he recognizes that it is partly his responsibility to change this practice of not recording overtime. He would like to be in compliance with his firm's practices and record his time honestly. Prior to acting, he needs to gather more information and think about the best way to move forward.

3. *Stakeholder analysis:* Bryan documents who the affected stakeholders are, as well as how they are affected both if he does give voice and does not give voice. Some of his analysis is shown in Table 3-2. To help him with crafting his response, he

Table 3-2	Extract from Bryan's Stakeholder Analysis	
Stakeholder	What's at stake if I DO give voice?	What's at stake if I DO NOT give voice?
Karen and other supervisors doing the same	• They have the option of changing their practices. • They could be demoted or otherwise affected. • They could receive a lower performance bonus.	• They are encouraged to employ these practices with other clients. • They receive a larger performance bonus. • They could be pressured into poor quality work that enables client management to receive higher performance bonuses.
Me and my other team members	• We are able to record our hours honestly. • We receive a higher wage (overtime). • We are motivated to produce high-quality work since the time and effort spent is recognized and rewarded.	• We will be under pressure to do the same at other clients. • We receive a lower wage. • We will be encouraged to follow the same practice when we become supervisors. • We are motivated to leave the firm and go to an employer where this practice does not exist.
De Souza and Shah firm	• Quality control standards are followed. • Jobs are properly billed and budgeted. • Employee training can focus on encouraging good job practices and discouraging poor recording.	• May result in underbilling clients in current and future engagements. • May be unable to realistically budget other engagements. • May affect the firm's ability to motivate and retain employees. • Firm could be sued for not following labour laws with respect to payment of overtime.

	Extract of Bryan's Inhibiting Arguments, Enabling Arguments	
Table 3-3	**and Levers Relevant to Accurate Recording of Hours Worked**	

Inhibiting Arguments	Enabling Arguments	Levers
Obedience to supervisor: It's not my responsibility; I'll get in trouble.	As an employee, it is everyone's job to ensure quality control.	Supervisors who change their practices to follow firm standards may be rewarded.
Standard practice: Everyone is doing this so it's standard practice.	Some supervisors are not doing this, and they are getting rewarded for good quality work.	A different supervisor on this engagement next year could detect the problem and cause problems for Karen.
Lack of materiality: It's just a few hours. It won't make any difference.	These hours add up over many engagements, and this affects our employer's profitability.	If the underbilling is detected, it could cause peer review problems with our employer.
Us versus them: I'll be targeted as a trouble maker by all of the supervisors.	Supervisors who record their work honestly will support me, as will the standards partner of our firm.	Karen and other supervisors will be supported by the standards partner for recording time accurately.

thinks about and develops a list of inhibiting arguments, enabling arguments, and levers he can use to support his case. He lists the top four arguments in Table 3-3.

4. *Powerful response*: Having identified the stakeholders involved and the arguments he may encounter, Bryan thinks about the logistics of how to move forward. Who should he speak with first? What data will he need to bring to each conversation? Bryan decides the first step is to talk to his university classmates. He finds out that one other person has been subjected to this same pressure at one of his clients, but that all of his other classmates have received peer mentor counselling at their firms. Apparently the firms know that this practice exists and want to stamp it out because it reduces the ability of junior employees to express themselves during engagements. He puts together a list of the firms with such programs and a summary of the benefits for such programs and the costs of not addressing these practices.

Bryan also talks confidentially to his provincial institute's peer support program and gains some valuable information and a sense of support for his intended strategy to raise this issue with Karen first.

5. *Scripting and coaching*: Armed with this information, Bryan writes out an opening statement that clearly frames the conversation as an opportunity for learning and moving towards best practice. He also assumes Karen will respond with each and every inhibiting argument and writes out his intended response. He practises in front of the mirror the things he would say to Karen. In his practice, he considers both a positive response and a negative response. He then makes an appointment with Karen, so that he can talk to her before the weekly time sheets are due.

The results? Only Bryan can tell us, but he is more likely to have a successful conversation with Karen that is businesslike and constructive.

② Professional Ethics and Principles of Conduct

Special Need for Ethical Conduct in Professions

Our society has attached a special meaning to the term "professional." A professional is expected to conduct himself or herself at a higher level than many other members of society. For example, when the press reports that a physician, clergyperson, member of Parliament, CA, CGA, or CMA has been indicted for a crime, most people feel more disappointment than when the same thing happens with people who are not labelled as professionals.

Some Ethical Violations Are More Severe Than Others

Bryan Longview's ethical dilemma involves a situation in which he is asked to work without regarding the time, which is sometimes called kitchen-tabling or eating time. One of the concerns with eating time is that it can lead to a more severe problem known as premature signoff, in which a staff person signs off as having completed work without performing the necessary procedures.

Tom Holton has far too busy a social life to work overtime. To make certain that work does not interfere with his other plans, he tests only part of the assigned sample. For example, if he is asked to test 25 cash disbursement transactions, he tests the first 15 but indicates that he has tested all 25. A supervisor, curious about Tom's amazing ability to beat the time budget, decides to carefully reperform Tom's work. When the firm discovers that Tom is signing off procedures without completing them, he is dismissed that day—no counselling out, no two weeks' notice.

The term "professional" carries a responsibility for conduct that extends beyond satisfying the person's responsibilities to himself or herself and beyond the requirements of our society's laws and regulations. This responsibility is to the public, to the client, and to fellow practitioners and includes honourable behaviour even if that means personal sacrifice. A CA, CGA, or CMA in public practice is a professional who carries that responsibility.

The underlying reason for a high level of professional conduct by any profession is the need for public confidence in the quality of service by the profession, regardless of the individual providing it. For the professional PA, it is essential that the client and external financial statement users have confidence in the quality of audits and other services. If users of services do not have confidence in physicians, judges, or PAs, the ability of those professionals to serve clients and the public effectively is diminished.

It is not practical for users to evaluate the performance of professional services because of their complexity. A patient cannot be expected to evaluate whether an operation was properly performed. A financial statement user cannot be expected to evaluate audit performance. Most users have neither the competence nor the time for such an evaluation. Public confidence in the quality of professional services is enhanced when the profession encourages high standards of performance and conduct on the part of all practitioners.

Increased competition sometimes makes public accounting firms concerned about keeping clients and maintaining a reasonable profit. Because of the increased competition, many public accounting firms have implemented philosophies and practices that are frequently referred to as "improved business practices." These include such things as improved recruiting and personnel practices, better audit quality control practices, effective office management, and tailored advertising and other promotional methods. Public accounting firms are also attempting to become more efficient in doing audits in a variety of ways, for example, through the use of computers, effective audit planning, and careful assignment of staff.

Standards for obtaining, renewing, and retaining PA licences or rights in many provinces (such as a minimum number of annual hours in provision of assurance services) mean that detailed engagement record keeping is crucial. For those accounting students who do not want to work in public practice, other types of work experience in industry are now possible.

DIFFERENCE BETWEEN PUBLIC ACCOUNTING FIRMS AND OTHER PROFESSIONALS Public accounting firms have a different relationship with users of financial statements than most other professionals have with the users of their services. Lawyers, for example, are

concept check

C3-1 What are the six ethical principles that many people and organizations associate with ethical behaviour?

C3-2 Describe an ethical dilemma. What are two approaches for resolving an ethical dilemma?

typically engaged and paid by a client and have the primary responsibility to be an advocate for that client. Public accounting firms are engaged by management for private companies and by the audit committee for public companies. The firms are paid by the company issuing the financial statements, but the primary beneficiaries of the audit are financial statement users. Often, the auditor does not know or have contact with those users but has frequent meetings and ongoing relationships with client personnel.

It is essential that users regard such public accounting firms as competent and unbiased. If users were to believe that such public accounting firms do not perform the valuable service of reducing information risk, the value of and demand for those firms' audit and other attestation reports would be reduced. This provides incentives for public accounting firms to conduct themselves at a high professional level.

Ways Professional Accountants in Public Practice Are Encouraged to Conduct Themselves Professionally

There are several ways in which society and the public accounting professions encourage those in public practice to conduct themselves appropriately and to do high-quality audits and related services. Figure 3-1 shows the most important ways. Several of these were discussed in Chapter 2, including GAAS requirements, the Recommendations of the *CICA Handbook*, professional examinations, quality control, the CPAB and provincial securities commissions, practice inspection, and continuing education. The ability of individuals to sue public accounting firms also exerts considerable influence on the way practitioners conduct themselves and audits. Legal liability is studied in Chapter 4.

The code of professional conduct of the PA's respective accounting body also has a significant influence on the practitioner. It is meant to provide a standard of conduct for members of that body. When professionals do not adhere to the standards of their profession, they are subject to a variety of potential sanctions. Table 3-4 explains that many of these are related to public release of information about the actions of the accountant, which is why the table is called "For Whom the Bell Tolls."

Code of Professional Conduct

A code of conduct can consist of general statements of ideal conduct or specific rules that define unacceptable behaviour. The advantage of general statements is

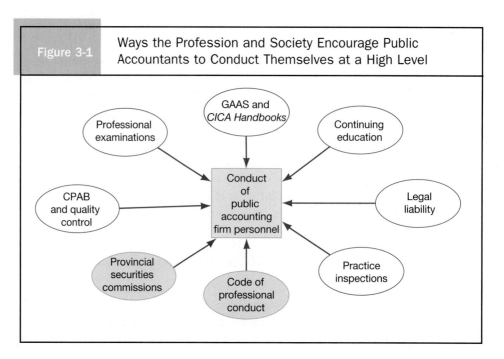

Figure 3-1 Ways the Profession and Society Encourage Public Accountants to Conduct Themselves at a High Level

Table 3-4	For Whom the Bell Tolls

Examples of Sanctions That Can Be Imposed Against PAs or Firms When Standards Are Violated
Publication of the name(s) of the violator(s) and the nature of the convicted offence
Sanctions from regulatory bodies such as the CPAB, OSC, or the SEC (e.g., refusal to accept new publicly listed clients for a period of time)
Refusal to renew PA licences for individuals or firms (with the CPAB)
Increased frequency of peer review
Appointment of an external monitor
Fines and/or payment of costs such as legal fees
Requirements to change quality control procedures
Mandatory education
Suspension of designation (e.g., CA, CGA, or CMA) or expulsion from the professional association

the emphasis on positive activities that encourage a high level of performance. The disadvantage is the difficulty of enforcing general ideals because there are no minimum standards of behaviour. The advantage of carefully defined specific rules is the enforceability of minimum behaviour and performance standards. The disadvantage is the tendency of some practitioners to define the rules as maximum rather than minimum standards. A second disadvantage is that some practitioners may view the code as the law and conclude that if some action is not prohibited, it must be ethical. A practitioner must consider the intent of the code in addressing whether a particular action is acceptable or not.

A professional code of conduct serves both the members of the body promulgating the code and the public. It serves members by setting standards the members must meet and providing a benchmark against which the members will be measured by their peers. The public is served because the code provides a list of standards that the members of the body should follow and helps determine expectations of members' behaviours. Yet such a code will be followed only in an organization with the appropriate organizational culture, as explained in Auditing in Action 3-2.

At present, most PAs in Canada are either CAs or CGAs. The provincial institutes and Quebec *ordre* of chartered accountants determine the rules of professional conduct for members and students of that provincial institute or *ordre*. The provincial institutes and *ordre* have harmonized their rules of professional conduct so that, generally, the same set of rules applies to all PAs in Canada. Certain rules (e.g., confidentiality, which is discussed below) apply to students as well as to members. All of the rules apply to members in public practice, while a smaller number also apply to members who are not engaged in the practice of public accounting.

We will restrict the remainder of our discussion to rules of conduct of British Columbia CGAs and Ontario CAs (as examples of provincial rules of conduct).

Generally the codes of conduct have attempted to accomplish both the objectives of general statements of ideal conduct and of specific rules. For example, the Rules of Professional Conduct of the Institute of Chartered Accountants of Ontario (ICAO) have principles that are stated in broad terms, the rules themselves, and additional guidance on the rules, called "interpretations." The ICAO, the Certified General Accountants Association of British Columbia (CGA-BC), and other organizations such as the Institute of Internal Auditors (IIA), provide discussions of current issues and examples of how to deal with particular ethical issues through regular newsletters sent to members. Figure 3-2 is illustrative of this. The structure is listed in order of increasing specificity: The principles provide ideal standards of conduct, whereas rules of conduct are more specific, and the interpretations or examples are very specific.

Research on Commitment Helps Explain Violations

Can you do the audit of an organization that you are marketing with? As explained in the next section, this could be a self-interest threat, because your own financial results are linked with those of the organization. One of the top international accounting firms was barred from accepting new SEC clients for six months as it both audited PeopleSoft Inc. as well as marketed and installed the software. The firm maintained that it was not violating the rules, yet this clearly violated the appearance of objectivity of the firm.

Tyler, Dienhart, and Thomas talked about the "command and control" versus the "values and integrity" approach to ethical compliance. In a values and integrity model, employees are encouraged to comply with ethical processes because they understand the goals of the processes, and they believe that they are fair. This encourages employees to come forward with what they believe are ethical violations. In the command and control model, as advocated by strict rules, employees are less likely to comply with rules and may not come forward with potential violations.

The most important finding discussed in Tyler et al.'s article was the fact that organizational culture is the most important variable in ethical compliance—more important than the type of ethical compliance program. This means that organizations that are focused on profits to the exclusion of anything else send the message to employees that ethics do not matter. Perhaps something like this happened at the accounting firm involved—the profits from software sales and installation were considered more important than independence.

Sources: 1. Morris, Floyd, "Big auditing firm gets 6-month ban on new business," *The New York Times*, April 17, 2004, **www.nytimes.com/2004/04/17/business/17ERNS.html**, Accessed: September 14, 2008. 2. Tyler, Tom, John Dienhart, and Terry Thomas, "The ethical commitment to compliance: Building value-based cultures," *California Management Review*, 50(2), Winter 2008, p. 21-51.

PRINCIPLES OF PROFESSIONAL CONDUCT The principles generally are characteristics that the professional body deems desirable in its members. An organization is judged by the behaviour of its members; therefore, one principle would be that members behave in a way that enhances the reputation of all the members. Members should act ethically and in a way that will serve the public interest. For example, CGA-BC at **www.cga-bc.org** talks about "safeguarding and advancing the interests of society," while the ICAO at **www.icao.on.ca** talks about "conduct[ing engagements] . . . in a manner which . . . serve[s] the public interest." Both CGAs and CAs are also told that they should not use confidential information for their own benefit and to avoid (and where unavoidable to disclose) conflicts of interest. When the courts discipline or

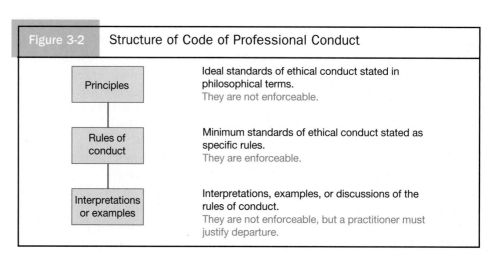

Figure 3-2	Structure of Code of Professional Conduct

Principles	Ideal standards of ethical conduct stated in philosophical terms. They are not enforceable.
Rules of conduct	Minimum standards of ethical conduct stated as specific rules. They are enforceable.
Interpretations or examples	Interpretations, examples, or discussions of the rules of conduct. They are not enforceable, but a practitioner must justify departure.

convict a member of a profession, the profession's reputation suffers along with that of the member. It is a mistake to think that only the member loses his or her reputation in such a situation.

Other common principles are that members act with integrity and due care in the performance of their professional activities; that they maintain (i.e., keep current) their professional competence; that they do not undertake work for which they lack the necessary competence; and that they behave in a professional way toward colleagues. The accountant must maintain confidentiality with respect to the affairs and business of the client. There is one principle that relates more specifically to PAs: The accountant should ensure that he or she maintains an independent or objective state of mind when providing assurance services (e.g., audits or reviews) for clients.

A careful examination of these ethical principles will indicate that most are applicable to any professional, not just professional accountants. For example, physicians should behave in a way that is not discreditable to their profession; they should act ethically and in a way that serves the public interest; and they should exercise integrity and due care. Physicians should maintain their professional competence and behave in a professional way toward their colleagues. They should not breach their clients' confidentiality. These principles will be explored more fully in the remainder of this chapter.

EXAMPLES OF RULES OF CONDUCT   The discussion that follows will consider some of the more important rules of conduct followed by PAs in Canada. A student interested in obtaining a particular professional designation (e.g., CA, CGA, or CMA) should refer to and become familiar with the specific rules of conduct of the provincial and national body to which he or she seeks admission.

While all the rules discussed below apply to members of the professional accounting bodies in public practice, some of the rules discussed do not apply to members who are not engaged in the practice of public accounting.

Figure 3-2 indicated that while principles may not be enforceable, the rules of conduct are. For that reason, the rules of conduct of the accounting bodies are stated in more precise language than the principles can be. Because of their enforceability, the rules are often called Rules or Code of Professional Conduct.

APPLICABILITY OF THE RULES OF CONDUCT   The rules of conduct for CAs and CGAs specifically state that while the rules are for all CAs and CGAs, respectively, certain rules, because of their nature, may apply only to members who are in public practice.

It would be a violation of the rules if someone did something on behalf of a member that would have been a violation if the member had done it. An example is a banker who states in a newsletter that Johnson and Able, public accountants, have the best tax department in the province and consistently get large refunds for their tax clients. This is likely to create false or unjustified expectations and is a violation of both the CA and CGA rules of conduct.

A member is also responsible for compliance with the rules by employees and partners.

DEFINITIONS   A few definitions must be understood to minimize misinterpretation of the rules to be discussed shortly.

- Client—the person(s) or entity that retains a member or his or her firm, engaged in the practice of public accounting, for the performance of professional services.
- Firm—a proprietorship or partnership engaged in the practice of public accounting, including individual partners thereof.
- Member—a member of the Canadian Institute of Chartered Accountants (and a provincial institute or *ordre*) or of the Certified General Accountants Association of Canada (and a provincial association) or of the Society of Management Accountants of Canada (and a provincial association).
- Practice of public accounting—representing oneself as a PA and at the same time performing for a client one or more types of services rendered by PAs.

concept check

C3-3 Explain the need for a code of professional ethics for PAs. In which ways should the PAs' code of ethics be similar to and different from those of other professional groups such as lawyers or dentists?

C3-4 List the three parts that may be part of the structure of a code of professional conduct, and state the purpose of each.

C3-5 What is meant by the statement, "The rules of professional conduct of a professional accounting organization should be regarded as a minimum standard?"

Professional Rules of Conduct for the Public Accountant

Independence

Generally, the rules of conduct promulgated by the accounting bodies require their members who are engaged in the practice of public accounting to be independent when they perform certain functions. For example, the rules require that auditors of historical financial statements be independent. **Independence** (impartiality in performing professional services) is also required for other types of attestation engagements such as review engagements.

Independence in auditing means taking an unbiased viewpoint in the performance of audit tests, the evaluation of the results, and the issuance of the auditor's report. If the auditor is an advocate for the client, a particular banker, or anyone else, he or she cannot be considered independent. Independence must be regarded as the auditor's most critical characteristic. The reason that many diverse users are willing to rely upon the professional PA's reports as to the fairness of financial statements is their expectation of an unbiased viewpoint.

PAs must maintain an independent attitude in fulfilling their responsibilities, and it is also important that the users of financial statements have confidence in that independence. These two objectives are frequently identified as "independence in fact" and "independence in appearance." **Independence in fact** exists when the auditor is actually able to maintain an unbiased attitude throughout the audit, whereas **independence in appearance** is the result of others' interpretation of this independence. If auditors are independent in fact but users believe them to be advocates for the client, most of the benefit of the audit function will be lost.

The Threats to Independence

In response to financial statement and management frauds, the professional accountant codes of conduct have adopted very specific rules of conduct with respect to independence. These rules are considered a foundation for providing public trust, since objectivity in an engagement relies upon auditor independence.

When deciding to accept a client or to continue an existing engagement, the PA is required to examine five threats to independence: self-interest threat, self-review threat, advocacy threat, familiarity threat, and intimidation threat. The PA is to assess threats when they exist and document the safeguards that were used to reduce the threats to an acceptable level. Table 3-5 lists and defines these threats to independence with examples. Table 3-6 describes safeguards that the firm can implement to either eliminate the threats or reduce them to an acceptable level.

Some of the threats affect overall independence. If you own shares in your client's business (**self-interest threat**) or are trying to help them obtain financing (**advocacy threat**), you stand to gain from the result of the financial statement audit.

The **self-review threat** means that you are auditing your own work. Imagine that you have assisted the client in designing an information system that calculates the costs for an inventory system. The new system seems to be working well, and there are excellent reports that track inventory movement and out-of-stock situations. However, during the design phase, you neglected to put in controls to highlight when the system creates a negative inventory situation, either due to either clerical or programming error.

What would you do during the audit? Perhaps you would be less likely to point out this error to the client in a management letter because it would imply that you did not properly perform your work during the system design. Alternatively, you might not detect the system inadequacy during your analysis of internal controls; you believe that it is such an excellent system that you do not need to complete a detailed analysis of internal controls. This example shows how a self-review threat can be very dangerous to the completion of a quality audit engagement.

Table 3-5   Threats to Independence

Threat to Independence (defined)	Examples
Self-interest threat—when the member could receive a benefit because of a financial interest in the client or in the financial results of the client or due to a conflict of interest.	The firm or member owns shares in or has made a loan to the client. The client fees are significant in relation to the total fee base of the PA or of the firm.
Self-review threat—when the PA is placed in the position of having to audit his or her own work or systems during the audit.	The reasons for this could be that the PA prepared original data or records for the client as part of a bookkeeping engagement or was an employee or officer of the organization. The PA could also have designed and implemented an accounting information system used to process client records.
Advocacy threat—when the firm or member is perceived to promote (or actually does promote) the client's position; that is, the client's judgment is perceived to direct the actions of the PA.	The PA is acting as an advocate in resolving a dispute with a major creditor of the client. The firm or PA is promoting the sale of shares or other securities for the client or is receiving a commission for such sales.
Familiarity threat—occurs when it is difficult to behave with professional skepticism during the engagement due to a belief that one knows the client well.	There is a long association between senior staff and the client (e.g., being on the engagement for 10 years). A former partner of the firm is now the chief financial officer of the client.
Intimidation threat—the client personnel intimidate the firm or its staff with respect to the content of the financial statements or with respect to the conduct of the audit, preventing objective completion of field work.	The client threatens to replace the audit firm over a disclosure disagreement. The client places a maximum upon the audit fee that is unrealistic with respect to the amount of work that needs to be completed.

With a **familiarity threat**, it may be that you were the audit junior on a job, worked as an assistant, then were promoted to supervisor and manager, and are now a partner. You have worked with the client for 15 years, and it seems that you know the strengths and weaknesses of all of the employees, juniors and executives alike. You may take it for granted that they are doing their jobs just as well this year as they did last year. However, you do not know that the controller is going through a messy divorce and the vice-president of finance has started gambling. They are both short of money, which gives them an incentive to manipulate the records and steal money from the company. The actual financial manipulation could lead to **intimidation threat**— where the senior accounting personnel expect you to overlook their manipulation or you may lose the audit. You have known these individuals for 15 years and think of them as friends, so what is a little financial statement manipulation among friends?

The independence rule situations listed in Table 3-7 help prevent independence threats from occurring. Some rules apply to all assurance engagements (e.g., financial

Familiarity threat—a threat to independence that occurs when it is difficult to behave with professional skepticism during the engagement.

Intimidation threat—a threat to independence that occurs when the client intimidates the public accounting firm or its staff with respect to the content of the financial statements or with respect to the conduct of the audit.

Table 3-6   Safeguards to Independence

Safeguard Category	Examples
Created by the profession or provided in legislation or securities exchange regulation	Education and training provided by the professional accounting body. Practice review provided by the professional accounting body or by the CPAB.
Provided by the client	A qualified, independent audit committee. A corporate code of ethics that provides for disclosure and resolution of conflicts. Competent client personnel.
Available within the firm's systems and procedures	Firm policies and procedures that promote awareness and ensure compliance for independence. Rotation of senior personnel on client engagements.

	Table 3-7	Applicability of Independence Rule			

	Prohibited Engagements if Situation Applies During Term of Engagement			
Independence Rule Situation	Audit of Listed Entity	Audit of Non-listed Entity	Other Assurance Engagement (e.g., review)	Non-assurance Service
Has direct or indirect financial interest	X	X	X	X
Exerts control over the entity	X	X	X	
Has a loan from or has a loan guaranteed by the entity (except in normal course of business; e.g., a bank)	X	X	X	
Has close business relationship	X	X	X	
Engagement staff accepted financial-related position at client within the last year	X			
Member of firm is officer or director	X	X	X	
Management decisions were made	X	X	X	
Prepared or changed originating source data or journal entry without management approval	X	X	X	
Accounting or bookkeeping services provided	X			
Valuation services provided	X			
Actuarial services provided	X			
Internal audit services provided	X			
Financial information systems design or implementation provided	X			
Expert opinion or service provided	X			
Legal services provided	X	X	X	
Human resources for senior positions provided	X			
Corporate finance services provided	X	X	X	

Note: Not all situations are listed. Please consult the rules of conduct for your provincial professional accounting association for more details.

statement audit and review for businesses of all sizes), while others apply only to an entity listed on a stock exchange with total market capitalization greater than $10 million, called a **listed entity**.

In addition to the specifics described in Table 3-7, where the member or firm is not allowed to complete the engagement, there are situations where only the person affected is to be excluded from the engagement team. These are situations where the student or member:

- Has made a loan to or guarantees a loan to the client.
- Has an immediate family member as a director, officer, or employee who can exert control over the engagement or who is in an accounting role.
- Was an employee with the client in a financial oversight position during the duration of the audit.

At the engagement level, independence rules for listed clients include the mandatory rotation of senior personnel (with reinstatement provisions after two years) as follows: the engagement partner and quality control partner after five years (seven years in some provinces); other partners who provide more than 10 hours of service after seven years. All services to a listed client must be approved by the audit committee.

Listed entity—an entity whose debts or shares are listed on a stock exchange and that has market capitalization and total assets greater than $10 million.

IESBA Code of Ethics for Professional Conduct

The International Ethics Standard Board for Accountants (IESBA) *Code of Ethics for Professional Accountants* is also a principles-based framework consisting of three parts. Part A establishes five fundamental principles related to integrity, objectivity, professional competence and due care, confidentiality, and professional behaviour. Part A also provides a conceptual framework that accountants can apply to identify threats to compliance with the fundamental principles, evaluate the significance of identified threats, and apply safeguards, when necessary, to eliminate the threat or reduce the threat to an acceptable level. Parts B and C of the IESBA Code describe how the conceptual framework applies in certain situations, including examples of safeguards and descriptions of situations where safeguards are not available to address threats. Part B applies to professional accountants in public practice while Part C applies to professional accountants in industry.

Source: International Ethics Standards Board for Accountants, Code of Ethics for Professional Accountants, **www.ifac.org**, Accessed: November 29, 2011.

A practical way for a PA to document the independence rules for each engagement is to fill in a checklist. A checklist actively states that the rules have been followed for the engagement and clearly identifies action taken where threats exist, with a conclusion stated for each engagement. This helps ensure that the assessment of independence is part of the quality assurance process for each engagement.

It seems from Table 3-7 that it would be difficult for a PA to provide comprehensive services to a client! What if you work for a small practice where the bulk of the work is accounting, bookkeeping, and review engagements? How is your work affected? Assuming that you and the other members of the firm have adequately addressed the five threats to independence, the primary practical concerns would be familiarity and self-review. There should be periodic change of staff at a client, where possible, and all transactions and journal entries should be discussed with and approved by the client before being processed.

Independence is far broader than simply preventing a financial interest, such as owning shares in a client. For the PA to be truly independent, all five threats must be considered and addressed for each engagement.

INDEPENDENCE THREAT ANALYSIS Public accounting firms are required to actively assess their ability to conduct an engagement prior to accepting (or renewing) the engagement. This means having policies and procedures in place to identify any new threats to independence, training employees, and monitoring the policies and procedures. If the current processes are not working (for example, employees may be investing in an organization unaware that it is a client of the firm), then new practices may be needed, such as having employees annually sign a form which lists every client, stating that they do not have any investments in those organizations. These new practices are an example of remedial action. Then, prior to accepting each engagement, audit management (such as the partner and the manager) is required to evaluate, in writing, the independence of the firm and the staff assigned to the engagement. This formal **independence threat analysis** forms part of the documentation for the engagement.

AUDIT COMMITTEE An **audit committee** is a selected number of members of a company's board of directors who provide a forum that is independent of management for both external and internal auditors. Most audit committees are made up of three to five or sometimes as many as seven directors. Incorporating Acts generally require that the audit committee must be independent outside directors (i.e., not part of company

Independence threat analysis—assessment of independence threats for a particular engagement.

Audit committee—selected members of a client's board of directors, who liase with and provide a forum for the auditors to remain independent of management.

management). Access to an active audit committee by internal and external auditors is one of the indicators of a healthy corporate governance structure. Most organizations that have debt or securities listed on a Canadian or American stock exchange (regardless of size) are required to have an audit committee consisting of at least three independent members who are also directors of the organization. Members of the audit committee are also required to be financially literate. The external auditor has the right to attend meetings of the audit committee and to call meetings if he or she feels they are necessary. Directors who become aware of any misstatements in issued financial statements must notify the auditor and the audit committee of the misstatements. A typical audit committee decides such things as which public accounting firm to retain and the scope of services the public accounting firm is to perform. The audit committee also meets with the public accounting firm to discuss the progress and findings of the audit and helps resolve conflicts between the public accounting firm and management. For the type of questions that directors would ask auditors, look at the 20 Questions Series, at **www.rogb.ca/director-series/20-question-series/index.aspx**.

At least annually, the auditor should inform the audit committee in writing of the following items: the level of the auditor's independence; all relationships between the auditor and his or her related business or practice and the entity and its related entities; and the total fees charged (separating out audit and non-audit services). The audit committee should also work directly with the internal auditors, approving their strategic plan and discussing their findings with them. The internal auditors should also be required to clarify the level of their independence.

AIDS TO MAINTAINING INDEPENDENCE The accounting profession and society, especially in the past decade, have been concerned about ensuring that (1) auditors maintain an unbiased attitude in performing their work (independence in fact) and (2) users perceive auditors as being independent (independence in appearance). Many of the elements shown in Figure 3-1 and other requirements or inducements encourage PAs to maintain independence in fact and appearance.

Legal liability The penalty involved when a court concludes that a practitioner is not independent can be severe, including criminal prosecution. The courts have certainly provided major incentives for auditors to remain independent. Legal liability is discussed in Chapter 4.

Rules of professional conduct The existing rules of conduct restrict PAs in their financial and business relationships with clients.

Generally accepted auditing standards Standards require the auditor to maintain an objective state of mind in all matters related to the assurance engagement.

Public accounting firm quality control processes Most public accounting firms establish policies and procedures to provide reasonable assurance that all engagement personnel are independent. Effective training, monitoring, and remedial action with respect to these processes help ensure compliance.

Audit committee An audit committee, as was discussed above, can help auditors remain independent of management.

Shopping for accounting principles Management may consult with other accountants on the application of accounting principles, often called "opinion shopping." Although consultation with other accountants is an appropriate practice, it can lead to a loss of independence in certain circumstances as a potential intimidation threat or self-interest threat. The existing auditor may feel intimidated if the new accounting treatment is not accepted. If a public accounting firm replaces the existing auditors on the strength of accounting advice offered but later finds facts and circumstances that require the public accounting firm change its position due to a self-interest threat, it may lose the client. The Auditing and Assurance Standards Board issued Section 7600, "Reports on the Application of Accounting Principles," setting out requirements that must be met when a public accounting firm is requested to provide a written opinion on the application of accounting principles or auditing standards by a party other than the client (also discussed in Chapter 20). Such an opinion would be issued for specific circumstances or transactions relating to an audit, review, or compilation client of another public accounting firm. It applies if the PA is asked to provide a generic or hypothetical opinion on the application of accounting principles, to make sure that both the incumbent auditor and the auditor providing the opinion have full information.

Approval of auditor by shareholders The Canada Business Corporations Act and other incorporating Acts require shareholders to approve the selection of a new auditor or the continuation of the existing one. Shareholders are usually a more objective group than is management.

Confidentiality

The rules of conduct for PAs state that members shall not disclose any confidential client information or employer information without the specific consent of the client or employer. The rules also prohibit using **confidential or inside information** to earn profits or benefits.

> **Confidential or inside information**—client information that may not be disclosed without the specific consent of the client except under authoritative professional or legal investigation.

The rule against disclosure does not apply if the member is called upon to disclose the information by the courts. Communication between auditor and client is not privileged as it is between lawyer and client; a court can require a PA to produce all files and documents held, including confidential advice provided. For this reason, the auditor must take care with information put into the file, recognizing that the file could appear as a court document. The rule against disclosure also does not apply if the member's professional body requires the confidentiality rule to be waived in connection with the body's exercise of its duties (e.g., when an auditor is called upon to produce working papers in connection with the disciplinary process or when an auditor is required to produce files as part of practice inspection).

While the rules of professional conduct with respect to confidentiality are quite clear, as you will discover in Chapter 4, the auditor may be confronted with a situation where he or she must choose between confidentiality and other rules of conduct or another course of action.

NEED FOR CONFIDENTIALITY During an audit or other type of engagement, practitioners obtain a considerable amount of information of a confidential nature, including officers' salaries, product pricing and advertising plans, and product cost data. If auditors divulged this information to outsiders or to client employees who have been denied access to the information, their relationship with management would become strained and, in extreme cases, would cause the client harm. The confidentiality requirement applies to all services provided by public accounting firms, including tax and management services.

Ordinarily, the public accounting firm's working papers can be provided to someone else only with the express permission of the client. This is the case even if a PA sells his or her practice to another public accounting firm or is willing to permit a successor auditor to examine the working papers prepared for a former client. Permission is not required from the client, however, if the working papers are subpoenaed by a court or are used as part of practice inspection. If the working papers are subpoenaed, the client should be informed immediately. The client and the client's lawyer may wish to challenge the subpoena.

Maintenance of the Reputation of the Profession

The rules of accounting bodies in Canada require their members to behave in the best interests of their profession and the public. This means accountants should not take advantage of the trust placed in them. An accountant should not be publicly critical of a colleague (i.e., by making a complaint about the colleague's behaviour to their professional body or by being critical, as a successor auditor, to the new client) without giving the colleague a chance to explain his or her actions first.

Actions by a member of a professional body—in law, medicine, or any other profession—reflect not only on the member but also on the body. For example, a lawyer who steals trust monies sullies not only his or her own reputation but also that of the law profession; the theft brings all lawyers into disrepute. Reputation is affected by anti-social behaviour such as harassment and discrimination, since such behaviour is considered abhorrent, resulting in professional disciplinary actions. Therefore, it is essential that an accountant behave in an exemplary manner as a member of the professional body.

Integrity and Due Care

The rules of conduct for professional accountants require members to act with integrity and due care. Integrity is one of the hallmarks of the profession. One of a professional accountant's most important assets is his or her reputation for honesty and fair dealing; if users of financial statements audited by or prepared by an accountant do not believe in the practitioner's honesty or fairness, the value of the financial statements or the audit is diminished. The professional accountant's behaviour with clients, colleagues, employers, and employees must be above reproach.

Due care in the performance of duties is also a hallmark of a professional. The PA has a legal duty of care to certain users of financial statements, as will be seen in Chapter 4. Due care means the application by a professional of a level of care and skill in accordance with what would reasonably be expected of a person of his or her rank and training.

Competence

Professional accountants, including PAs, have a responsibility to maintain their professional competence. The rules of conduct require practitioners to maintain competence; similarly, GAAS state the necessity of "adequate technical training and proficiency in auditing." The public expects that all professionals will strive to keep abreast of the latest techniques and methodologies. An auditor should not undertake an audit of a client unless that auditor has both knowledge of that client's business and industry and of the technical aspects of the audit. For example, the audit of an insurance company requires knowledge of auditing the policy reserves that form a significant part of the insurance company's liabilities. Many larger accounting firms form industry specialization groups within the firm that are responsible for all audits within their specialty.

auditing in action 3-4
Practice Firm Argues about Lawsuit Disclosure

ABCD LLP, a medium-sized regional CA firm, was contacted by Amy, the corporate controller of a public company, about conducting the audit of Model Manufacturing Limited (MML). Amy had attended several external training events with members of the firm and was known to the partners of ABCD LLP. ABCD conducted a due diligence investigation and was informed by MML about the existence of a defective products lawsuit that was being vigorously defended. The lawsuit was disclosed in MML financial statements but had not been accrued. ABCD accepted the audit engagement and, upon corresponding with MML lawyers, found that a judgment had actually been issued against MML for $400,000, which should have been accrued in the previous quarterly financial statements. ABCD argued about the disclosure with MML, which finally agreed to accrue the amount when the lawyers supported ABCD's request. ABCD was so disenchanted with MML management's attitude about disclosure that it resigned after having completed the current year's audit engagement.

An audit firm should decline a new audit if the firm either lacks or does not have access to the technical knowledge required to complete the audit. Similarly, an auditor within a firm should ensure that he or she has access to the technical knowledge required to complete the audit.

Members are encouraged to keep current in a variety of ways. The various institutes and the *ordre* of chartered accountants have practice inspections (discussed in Chapter 1) over a three-year period of all public practice units. Professional accountants are required to attend a certain number of continuing professional education courses a year.

Adherence to Accounting Standards and GAAS

Professional accounting bodies require their members in practice as PAs and working in industry not to associate with false or misleading information or to fail to reveal material omissions from financial statements. PAs can lose faith in management when information is withheld, as described in Auditing in Action 3-4, and it then becomes difficult to complete the audit engagement. Users of financial statements prepared by or audited by professional accountants are entitled to believe that the financial statements are complete and fairly present the financial position of the company, to believe that the financial statements are not false and misleading, and to rely on the integrity of the accountants involved.

Given that public trust of professional accountants does exist, if an accountant betrayed this trust and provided a clean opinion on financial statements known to be misleading, users would accept the statements as correct and would suffer a loss. Discovery that the PA was associated with false and misleading financial information or failed to reveal a material fact would destroy the accountant's reputation for integrity.

PAs are required to comply with professional standards when preparing and auditing financial statements. These standards would include the standards of the professional body but, more importantly, accounting standards and GAAS as set out in the *CICA Handbook*. As you learned in Chapter 1, the Canada Business Corporations Act and the incorporating Acts of many of the provinces require financial statements to be prepared according to accounting standards in conformity with an applicable accounting framework as specified by the *CICA Handbook* and also require the auditor's report to be in accordance with the standards of the *CICA Handbook*. The Canadian Securities Administrators, who set policy for the securities commissions and stock exchanges in Canada, also specify the *CICA Handbook* as the source of accounting standards.

Advertising and Solicitation

A profession's reputation is not enhanced if the members openly solicit one another's clients or engage in advertising that is overly aggressive, self-laudatory, or critical of other members of the profession or that makes claims that cannot be substantiated. As a consequence, the professional accounting bodies in Canada either explicitly or implicitly prohibit solicitation of another PA's client and advertising that is not in keeping with the profession's high standards.

Responding to a request for information from a client of another public accounting firm is not solicitation, nor is responding to an invitation to tender from another firm's client. Rather, solicitation is approaching the client of another public accounting firm to convince him or her to switch to one's own firm; it is a targeted act of seeking a specific professional engagement.

Advertising that is in good taste is acceptable. It may include complimentary material about the accounting firm but should not claim any superior skills or make promises that cannot be kept (e.g., a promise that certain favourable results will be achieved). Advertising is a general process of informing potential users of the availability of services.

Other Rules

Breaches of the rules The rules of conduct of the professional accounting bodies require members who are aware of a breach of the rules by another member to report that member to the profession's discipline committee after first advising the member of the intent to make a report. The bodies are self-regulating. It is important that the member be notified of the intent to report the breach in case there are mitigating circumstances of which the reporting member is not aware.

Contingent fees The charging of a fee based on the outcome of an audit, such as the granting of a loan by a bank, could easily impair the auditor's independence. Contingent fees are prohibited for audits, reviews, and any other engagements that require the auditor to be objective.

Communication with predecessor auditor The rules of conduct of the PAs and incorporating Acts such as the Canada Business Corporations Act require a (potential) successor auditor, prior to accepting an appointment as auditor, to communicate with the incumbent auditor to inquire if there are any circumstances of which the incumbent is aware that might preclude the successor from accepting the appointment. The successor would ask the potential client to authorize the incumbent to provide the information requested. If the client refuses to do so, the successor should be reluctant to accept the appointment because it is likely that the client is hiding something.

The rules also require that the incumbent respond to the successor's request and be candid in responding. The communication between the incumbent and the successor is important because it prevents a successor from unknowingly accepting an appointment that might, if all the facts were known, be rejected. For example, if the incumbent resigned after finding that management of the client was dishonest and was engaged in fraud, it is unlikely any public accounting firm would accept the client if the incumbent passed on that knowledge. In short, the required communication protects prospective successors, and thus the profession, from getting involved with undesirable clients. Review of the previous auditor's working papers is an important part of the audit process, as discussed further in audit planning.

Professional liability insurance Members practising public accounting are required to carry professional liability insurance. Two issues arise that can cause confusion: defining public accounting and the extent of work being done without remuneration.

For example, during tax season, individuals may prepare tax returns for family and friends at no charge. Since basic advice such as maximization of RRSP contributions is often included, this process is considered to be practising public accounting. However, if only a limited number of returns are being prepared for no remuneration, a public practice is not being carried on. If more than a handful of returns are being prepared and fees are being charged, either on a full- or part-time basis, then professional liability insurance is required.

Other rules The rules of conduct of the professional accounting bodies include many more rules than have been described here; an aspiring professional accountant should be aware of the rules of conduct of the professional body of which membership is sought.

Enforcement

concept check

C3-6 What are the five threats to independence? Describe each and provide an example.

C3-7 List three categories of safeguards to independence. Provide an example of each.

C3-8 Why are contingent fees prohibited for financial statement audits?

The rules of conduct for CAs are established and administered provincially. The rules of conduct for CGAs are promulgated by CGAAC. The provincial CGA associations have the power to add rules and have the responsibility for enforcing the rules.

As described in Table 3-4, the various professional bodies have the power to impose penalties ranging from public censure in the body's newsletter or requiring courses to be taken to upgrade skills to levying fines or expulsion. CPAB has the power to restrict a firm's ability to audit a listed entity. Since the professional accounting bodies are self-regulating, there is a danger that the public will perceive the disciplinary process as not being as stringent as it should be and that there is a reluctance to punish members who break the rules. This issue is being dealt with by including laypersons on the disciplinary committees and by the inspections supervised by CPAB. Information is also available to the public about findings of the discipline committees and actions taken by them.

International Quality Control Requires Inspector Cooperation

We have talked about the PCAOB and the CPAB, organizations that are responsible for oversight of public company audits in the United States and in Canada. There are similar oversight bodies around the world, such as the *Professional Oversight Board* in the United Kingdom.

As we will discuss later in this book, auditors of an organization may rely upon specialists (for example an inventory specialist in a jewelry store, or a pension specialist to evaluate pension liabilities). Auditors could also rely upon auditors in other offices around the world, auditors from their own firm or from other firms, to conduct the audit of international organizations. International audits require international quality control, both from the organization doing the audit, and from oversight bodies.

If an organization has a head office in London, England, it may be that the U.K oversight board would be the responsible quality control reviewer, while an organization in Canada would have the CPAB responsible. If the CPAB is responsible, it might choose to rely upon the working papers of quality control inspections completed by another organization, such as the PCAOB. This means that the CPAB would want to be certain about the quality of the inspection completed in the other country, and potentially have access to the working papers. Laws and procedures have, in fact, been developed so that these organizations can rely upon each other's work.

Source: G. Jeffrey, (March 2011) "Countries agree to share audit data," *The Bottom Line*, p. 5; Professional Oversight Board, **www.frc.org.uk/pob/**.

Summary

1. *What are ethics and why are they important?* Ethics are broad moral principles or values that help guide our behaviour and establish trustworthy, responsible, and fair relationships.

   How can I work through an ethical conflict (known as an ethical dilemma)? Two approaches are discussed in this chapter. A six-step framework that walks through information collection, analysis, and a decision is provided, as well as a five-step proactive approach that encourages resolution of the dilemma (identification, purpose and choice, stakeholder analysis, powerful response, and scripting and coaching).

2. *How are PAs different from other professionals?* The clients of PAs are individuals as well as management of corporations. In addition, PAs have a responsibility to users of financial statements such as shareholders and creditors. This is a more expanded responsibility than that of other professionals.

   What is the role of a code of professional conduct in encouraging accountant ethical behaviour? Such a code of conduct can have general statements of ideal conduct and specific rules that define unacceptable behaviour.

3. *What are the threats to independence?* There are five areas where independence must be considered: self-interest, self-review, advocacy, familiarity, and intimidation.

   How does the auditor's relationship with the audit committee affect independence? The audit committee can help the auditor remain independent of management by making the auditor retention decision, approving the services provided by the PA, discussing the audit progress and findings, and by helping to resolve conflicts between the public accounting firm and management.

   What are some of the key rules of professional conduct and how they are enforced? There are rules of professional conduct covering independence, confidentiality, maintenance of the reputation of the profession, integrity and due care, competence, adherence to professional standards, and advertising and solicitation. Rules of conduct are enforced by the professional accounting associations and by CPAB.

MyAccountingLab

Make the grade with MyAccountingLab: The questions, exercises, and problems marked in orange can be found on MyAccountingLab. You can practise them as often as you want, and most feature step-by-step guided instructions to help you find the right answer.

Review Questions

3-1 ❶ Using Table 3-1, explain how a professional accountant would embody each of the illustrated ethical principles.

3-2 ❶ When analyzing an ethical dilemma, why is a structured approach helpful?

3-3 ❷ Identify and explain factors that should keep the quality of audits high, even though advertising and tendering are allowed.

3-4 ❸ Distinguish between independence in fact and independence in appearance. State three activities that may not affect independence in fact but are likely to affect independence in appearance.

3-5 ❸ Why is an auditor's independence so essential?

3-6 ❸ What organization is responsible for developing ethics standards for accountants at the international level? What are the fundamental principles of the international ethics standards?

3-7 ❸ What consulting or nonaudit services are prohibited for auditors of public companies? What other restrictions and requirements apply to auditors when providing nonaudit services to public companies?

3-8 ❸ What is an independence threat analysis? When and why should it be completed?

3-9 ❸ Many people believe that a PA cannot be truly independent when payment of fees is dependent on the management of the client. Explain a way of reducing this appearance of lack of independence.

3-10 ❸ The auditor's working papers usually can be provided to someone else only with the permission of the client. What is the rationale for such a rule? What are the exceptions to this rule?

3-11 ❸ The rules of conduct of professional accountants require them to report a breach of the rules of conduct by a member to their profession's disciplinary body. What should they do before making such a report?

3-12 ❸ After accepting an engagement, a PA discovers that the client's industry is more technical than at first realized and that he or she (i.e., the accountant) is not competent in certain areas of the operation. What should the PA do in this situation?

3-13 ❸ For what types of engagements are contingent fees acceptable as charged by professional accountants?

3-14 ❸ Why is it so important that a successor auditor communicate with the incumbent before accepting an appointment as auditor? What should the successor do if the incumbent does not reply?

Discussion Questions and Problems

3-15 ❶ ❷ Diane Harris, a PA, is the auditor of Fine Deal Furniture, Inc. In the course of her audit for the year ended December 31, 2011, she discovered that Fine Deal had serious going-concern problems. Henri Fine, the owner of Fine Deal, asked Diane to delay completing her audit.

Diane is also the auditor of Master Furniture Builders Ltd., whose year end is January 31. The largest receivable on Master Furniture's list of receivables is Fine Deal Furniture; the amount owing represents about 45 percent of Master Furniture's total receivables, which, in turn, are 60 percent of Master Furniture's net assets. The management of Master Furniture is not aware of Fine Deal's problems and is certain the amount will be collected in full.

Master Furniture is in a hurry to get the January 31, 2011, audit finished because the company has made an application for a sizable loan from its bank to expand its operations. The bank has informally agreed to advance the funds based on draft financial statements submitted by Master Furniture just after the year end.

REQUIRED
What action should Diane take and why?

3-16 ❸ The following situations involve the provision of non-audit services. Indicate whether providing the service is a violation of the rules of professional conduct for PAs. Explain your answer.

a. Providing bookkeeping services to a listed entity. The services were preapproved by the audit committee of the company.
b. Providing internal audit services to a listed entity that is not an audit client.

c. Designing and implementing a financial information system for a private company.
d. Recommending a tax shelter to a client that is a publicly held listed entity. The services were preapproved by the audit committee.

e. Providing internal audit services to a listed entity audit client with the preapproval of the audit committee.
f. Providing bookkeeping services to an audit client that is a private company.

3-17 ❸ Each of the following scenarios involves a possible violation of the rules of conduct. Indicate whether each is a violation and explain why you think it is or is not.

a. John Brown is an PA, but not a partner, with three years of professional experience with Lyle and Lyle, Public Accountants, a one-office public accounting firm. He owns 25 shares of stock in an audit client of the firm, but he does not take part in the audit of the client and the amount of stock is not material in relation to his total wealth.

b. In preparing the corporate tax returns for a client, Phyllis Allen, a PA, observed that the deductions for contributions and interest were unusually large. When she asked the client for backup information to support the deductions, she was told, "Ask me no questions, and I will tell you no lies." Phyllis completed the return on the basis of the information acquired from the client.

c. A private entity audit client requested assistance of Kim Tanabe, a PA, in the installation of a computer system for maintaining production records. Kim had no experience in this type of work and no knowledge of the client's production records, so she obtained assistance from a computer consultant. The consultant is not in the practice of public accounting, but Kim is confident of her professional skills. Because of the highly technical nature of the work, Kim is not able to review the consultant's work.

d. Five small Moncton public accounting firms have become involved with an information project by taking part in an interfirm working paper review program. Under the program, each firm designates two partners to review the working papers, including the tax returns and the

financial statements, of another public accounting firm taking part in the program. At the end of each review, the auditors who prepared the working papers and the reviewers have a conference to discuss the strengths and weaknesses of the audit. They do not obtain the authorization from the audit client before the review takes place.

e. Roberta Hernandez, PA, serves as controller of a Canadian company that has a significant portion of its operations in several South American countries. Certain government provisions in selected countries require the company to file financial statements based on international standards. Roberta oversees the issuance of the company's financial statements and asserts that the statements are based on international financial accounting standards; however the standards she uses are not those issued by the International Accounting Standards Board.

f. Bill Wendal, a PA, set up a casualty and fire insurance agency to complement his auditing and tax services. He does not use his own name on anything pertaining to the insurance agency and has a highly competent manager, Renate Jones, who runs it. Bill frequently requests Renate to review with the management of an audit client the adequacy of the client's insurance if it seems underinsured. He feels that he provides a valuable service to clients by informing them when they are underinsured.

g. Michelle Rankin, a PA, provides tax services, management advisory services, and bookkeeping services and conducts audits for the same private company client. She requires management to approve, in writing, transactions and journal entries. Since her firm is small, the same person frequently provides all the services.

3-18 ❸ Each of the following situations involves possible violations of the rules of conduct that apply to professional accountants. For each situation, state whether it is a violation. Where there is a violation, explain the nature of the violation and the rationale for the existing rule.

a. Martha Painter, a PA, was appointed as the trustee of the So family trust. The So family trust owned the shares of the So Manufacturing Company, which is audited by another partner in Martha's office. Martha owns 15 percent of the shares of the So Manufacturing Company and is also a director of the company, in the position of Treasurer.

b. Marie Godette, LLB, has a law practice. Marie has recommended one of her clients to Sean O'Doyle, a PA. Sean has agreed to pay Marie 10 percent of the fee Sean receives from Marie's client.

c. Theresa Barnes, a PA, has an audit client, Choi, Inc., which uses another public accounting firm for management services work. Unsolicited, Theresa sends her firm's literature covering its management services capabilities to Choi on a monthly basis.

d. Alan Goldenberg leased several vehicles from his friend Norm. Norm said that he would give Alan a $200 commission for each referral. Alan referred to Norm several clients who were interested in leasing vehicles. After a few months, Alan was pleased to receive a cheque for $3,000 in the mail. Several of his clients had decided to change automobile leasing companies.

e. Edward Golikowski completed for his client financial projections that covered a period of three years. Edward was in a hurry and inadvertently stated that they covered five years; so he redid the client's calculations, rather than checking assumptions and doing field work, even though he attached an assurance report.

f. Marcel Poust, a PA, has sold his public accounting practice, which includes bookkeeping, tax services, and auditing to Sheila Lyons, a PA. Marcel obtained permission from all audit clients for audit-related working papers before making them available to Sheila. He did not get permission before releasing tax- and management services-related working papers.

3-19 ❸ Ann Archer serves on the audit committee of JKB Communications Inc., a telecommunications start-up company. The company is currently a private company. One of the audit committee's responsibilities is to evaluate the external auditor's independence in performing the audit of the company's financial statements. In conducting this year's evaluation, Ann learned that JKB Communications' external auditor also performed the following IT and e-commerce services for the company:

1. Installed JKB Communications' information system hardware and software selected by JKB management.
2. Supervised JKB Communications' personnel in the daily operation of the newly installed information system.
3. Customized a prepackaged payroll software application, based on options and specifications selected by management.
4. Trained JKB Communications' employees on the use of the newly installed system.
5. Determined which of JKB Communications' products would be offered for sale on the company's internet website.
6. Operated JKB Communications' local area network for several months while the company searched for a replacement after the previous network manager left the company.

REQUIRED

Consider each of the preceding services separately. Evaluate whether the performance of each service is a violation of the rules of professional conduct.

3-20 ❸ The following are situations that may violate the general rules of conduct of professional accountants. Assume in each case that the PA is a partner.

1. Simone Able, a PA, owns a substantial limited partnership interest in an apartment building. Juan Rodriquez is a 100-percent owner in Rodriquez Marine Ltd. Juan also owns a substantial interest in the same limited partnership as Simone. Simone does the audit of Rodriquez Marine Ltd.
2. Horst Baker, a PA, approaches a new audit client and tells the president that he has an idea that could result in a substantial tax refund in the prior year's tax return by application of a technical provision in a tax law that the client had overlooked. Horst adds that the fee will be 50 percent of the tax refund after it has been resolved by Canada Revenue Agency. The client agrees to the proposal.
3. Chantal Contel, a PA, advertises in the local paper that her firm does the audit of 14 of the 36 largest drugstores in the city. The advertisement also states that the average audit fee, as a percentage of total assets for the drugstores she audits, is lower than that of any other public accounting firm in the city.
4. Olaf Gustafson, a PA, sets up a small loan company specializing in loans to business executives and small companies. Olaf does not spend much time in the business because he works full time in his public accounting practice. No employees of Olaf's public accounting firm are involved in the small loan company.
5. Louise Elbert, a PA, owns a material amount of stock in a mutual fund investment company, which, in turn, owns stock in Louise's largest audit client. Reading the investment company's most recent financial report, Louise is surprised to learn that the company's ownership in her client has increased dramatically.

REQUIRED

Discuss whether the facts in any of the situations indicate violations of the rules of conduct for professional accountants. If so, identify the nature of the violation(s).

Professional Judgment Problems

3-21 ❸ Donna, a PA, is approached by the owner of one of her clients, for whom she normally compiles monthly and annual financial statements, to perform an audit of the company's inventories. The client, Fantastic Fashions Ltd., is a chain of retail clothing stores that operates in several local shopping malls. The owner explains that he is seeking new bank financing that will be secured by the inventories as collateral for the loan, and that the bank has requested an audit of the recorded inventories as a condition of granting the loan. The bank insists that it will lend no more than 75 percent of the amount of inventories as shown on an audited schedule of inventories that the owner has been asked to submit. Because the owner is in urgent need of cash, he offers to pay Donna an audit fee equal to 10 percent of the loan amount, and Donna agrees to these terms. She then performs an audit of the inventories in accordance with generally accepted auditing standards, and issues a standard unqualified audit opinion, except that the opinion paragraph reads as follows: "In my opinion, this schedule presents fairly, in all material respects, the inventories of Fantastic Fashions Ltd. as at March 31, 2012, in accordance with generally accepted accounting standards for private enterprises."

REQUIRED
Discuss whether Donna has violated the rules of conduct for professional accountants. If so, identify the nature of the violation(s).

3-22 ③ Joseph Smith was the chairman and chief operating officer of Maximum Software Limited, providing software solutions to companies in Manitoba. Joseph owned 40 percent of the company and had several silent partners who sat on the board of directors but did not participate in the company's operations. The chief financial officer of Maximum was Barbara Black, who had been with the company since its inception ten years ago.

Joseph was short of money, so he created a fictitious company and requested that Barbara send monthly cheques of $10,000 to this company, called Network Best, for consulting fees. Barbara agreed since Joseph approves the invoices. The controller, Samuel Chu, was a single parent with three children. Samuel did a normal credit check on Network Best and told Barbara that the company did not exist and the invoices should not be paid. Barbara berated Samuel and told him to keep quiet or he would lose his job. Joseph billed amounts through Network Best for three years.

REQUIRED
Assuming that all of the individuals described are qualified accountants, what rules of professional conduct were violated? What should Barbara or Samuel have done?

Case

3-23 ① ② ③ Barbara Whitley had great expectations about her future as she sat at her graduation ceremony in May 2011. She was about to receive her Master of Accountancy degree, and the following week she would begin her career on the audit staff of Green, Thresher & Co., a public accounting firm. Things looked a little different to Barbara in February 2012. She was working on the audit of Delancey Fabrics Ltd., a textile manufacturer with a calendar year end. The pressure was enormous. Everyone on the audit team was putting in 70-hour weeks, and it still looked as if the audit would not be done on time. Barbara was doing work in the property area, vouching additions for the year. The audit program indicated that a sample of all items over $10,000 should be selected, plus a non-statistical sample of smaller items. When Barbara went to take the sample, Jack Bean, the senior, had left the client's office and could not answer her questions about the appropriate size of the judgmental sample. Barbara forged ahead and selected 50 smaller items on her own judgment. Her basis for doing this was that there were about 250 such items, so 50 was a reasonably good proportion of such additions. Barbara audited the additions with the following results: The items over $10,000 contained no errors; however, the 50 small items contained a large number of errors. In fact, when Barbara projected them to all such additions, the amount seemed quite significant.

A couple of days later, Jack Bean returned to the client's office. Barbara brought her work to Jack in order to inform him of the problems she found, and got the following response: "My God, Barbara, why did you do this? You were supposed to look only at the items over $10,000, plus 5 or 10 little ones. You've wasted a whole day on that work, and we can't afford to spend any more time on it. I want you to throw away the schedules where you tested the last 40 small items and forget you ever did them."

When Barbara asked about the possible audit adjustment regarding the small items, none of which arose from the first 10 items, Jack responded, "Don't worry, it's not material anyway. You just forget it; it's my concern, not yours."

REQUIRED
a. In what way is this an ethical dilemma for Barbara?
b. Use the five-step Giving Voice to Values approach discussed in the chapter to resolve the ethical dilemma.

Ongoing Small Business Case: Quitting the Firm to Start CondoCleaners.com

3-24 ③ Jim has been thinking about CondoCleaners.com for the last three months now. He has been a bit distracted at work and has had some difficulty concentrating, as he has started organizing a request for proposal for his new website and for a market study to help him plan his approach. After discussions with the firm's personnel partner, he decided to give the firm four months' notice, rather than leaving in the middle of a busy season. The firm is sorry to see him go and has said that there will always be a job there for him. Jim is wondering if he should ask the current client he is working on, a marketing company, to complete a market survey for him.

REQUIRED
Explain why or why not Jim should use the services of his firm's audit client for the CondoCleaners.com market study. What other potential quality control or independence issues are caused by Jim's proposed new business?

4   Legal liability

Why can the auditor be sued when a business goes bankrupt? Isn't it management's responsibility to run the business? In this chapter, we will explore terminology associated with legal liability and look at how lawsuits and legislation have framed the public accounting legal environment. Future management accountants will learn how some of these same liability issues affect management, while potential public accountants will identify actions that they can take to mitigate the likelihood of lawsuits. Internal or government auditors and specialists are often involved in the development of assurance reports, so mitigation actions are relevant to them as well.

LEARNING OBJECTIVES

1 Explain how sources of legal liability are related to a distinction between business failure and audit failure. Describe the financial statement auditor's fiduciary responsibility and the money-laundering reporting requirements of the public accountant.

2 Explain why the accountant does not have the right of privileged communication. Define selected concepts and terms associated with the auditor's legal liability. Describe actions the public accountant should take if a client sues him or her.

3 Describe the groups of individuals or organizations, in addition to the client, who can sue the auditor. Explain how the auditor would defend against such suits, matching the type of defence to the nature of the suit. Consider whether the auditor can go to jail because of criminal liability.

4 List the actions that individual accountants and the profession can undertake to mitigate the risks of legal liability.

5 Identify the actions that accountants should take to determine which legislation has an impact on their work. Link those actions to standards of continuing education, quality control, and engagement completion.

STANDARDS REFERENCED IN THIS CHAPTER

CICA Standards

Section 5020 – Association

Section 9200 – Compilation engagements

It Takes the Net Profit from Many Audits to Offset the Cost of One Lawsuit

Orange and Rankle, LLP, a public accounting firm located in Nepean, Ontario, audited a small high-tech client that developed software for the gaming industry. A significant portion of the client's capital was provided by a syndicate of 40 limited partners. The owners of these interests, including several lawyers, were knowledgeable business and professional people.

Orange and Rankle audited the company for four consecutive years, from its inception, for an average annual fee of approximately $26,000. The audits were well done by competent auditors. In the middle of the fifth year of the company's existence, it became apparent that the marketing plan it had developed was overly optimistic and the company was going to require additional capital or a significant strategy change. The limited partners were polled and refused to provide the capital, as did the bank. The company folded and filed for bankruptcy. The limited partners lost their investment in the company. They subsequently filed a lawsuit against all parties involved in the enterprise, including the auditors.

IMPORTANCE TO AUDITORS

It was clear to the firm and to others who subsequently reviewed the audits that they complied with auditing standards in every way. Yet, over the next several years, the auditors proceeded through the process of preparing to defend themselves in the lawsuit. They went through complete discovery, hired an expert witness on auditing-related issues, filed motions, and so forth. They attempted a settlement at various times, but the plaintiffs would not agree to a reasonable amount. Finally, during the second day of trial, the plaintiffs settled for a nominal amount.

The total out-of-pocket cost to the audit firm was $250,000, not to mention personnel time, possible damage to their reputation, and general stress and strain. Thus, the cost of this suit, in which the auditors were completely innocent, was almost ten times the average annual audit fee earned from this client. However, by defending against this type of suit, firms discourage others from initiating similar lawsuits, since the plaintiffs also must spend their time and money to engage in the lawsuit.

WHAT DO YOU THINK?

1. Why should all firms defend themselves against lawsuits that do not have merit?
2. Should audits become more expensive to pay for these types of frivolous lawsuits? Why or why not?
3. How would you tell others that the quality of your work was good if you were conducting an audit?

continued >

continued

LICENSED public accountants (PAs) provide assurance in a variety of reports about financial information. Users of these reports could sue the PA if they believed there was a material representation that caused them a loss. As the auditors at Orange and Rankle learned the hard way, legal liability and its consequences are significant. It is the reason accountants carry liability insurance—to enable them to conduct their work in a professional manner and deal with lawsuits from clients and others. Sound quality control practices and adherence to independence rules and other professional standards and rules of conduct assist firms in preventing lawsuits.

This chapter discusses the nature of legal liability of public accountants. **Legal liability** arises due to the professional's obligation under the law to provide a reasonable level of care while performing work for those he or she serves. First, the reasons for increased litigation against public accountants are discussed. Then, specific legal responsibilities related to fiduciary duty and money laundering are described. This is followed by a detailed examination of the nature of the lawsuits and the sources of potential liability. Significant lawsuits involving public accountants that relate to the various issues are presented in summary form. You will note that the cases discussed come from the United States, the United Kingdom, and Canada; the legal systems in all three countries (except in Quebec, whose private law is based on French civil law[1]) are based on English common law; as a consequence, when judges in all three countries hand down decisions, while they have no obligation to follow decisions in the other countries, they will often refer to those decisions in the course of giving their own judgments. The options available to the profession and individual practitioners to minimize liability while meeting society's needs are presented. We close by looking at the importance of awareness of current legislation for accountants in management and public accounting.

[1]Smyth, J. E., D. A. Soberman, and A. J. Easson, *The Law and Business Administration in Canada*, Seventh Edition, (Toronto: Prentice Hall Canada Inc., 1995), p. 46–47.

① Appreciating the Legal Environment

Changed Legal Environment

Professionals have always had a duty to provide a reasonable level of care while performing work for those they serve. Audit professionals have a responsibility under common law to fulfill implied or expressed contracts with clients. They are liable to their clients for negligence and/or breach of contract should they fail to provide the services or should they fail to exercise due care in their performance. Auditors may also be held liable under the tort of negligence or provincial securities Acts to parties other than their clients in certain circumstances. The precise legal definition of the auditor's third-party liability continues to evolve. (Third parties are people who do not

Legal liability—the professional's obligation under the law to provide a reasonable level of care while performing work for those he or she serves.

Table 4-1	Conditions That Must Be Present for a Fiduciary Duty to Arise
• The fiduciary has the ability to exercise discretion or power	
• Discretion or power can be unilaterally exercised, and	
• The beneficiary is peculiarly vulnerable	

Sources: 1. The Supreme Court of Canada case of *Robert L. Hodgkinson v. David L. Sims and Jerry S. Waldman (File No. 23033, 1997)*. 2. Paskell-Mede, Mindy, "Fiduciary duty," *CAmagazine*, April 2004, p. 43–44, 49.

have a contract with the auditor.) The position of the Supreme Court of Canada at the time of writing remains that the auditor owes a duty of care to third parties who are part of a limited group of persons whom the auditor knows will use and rely on the audit, and that the auditor's knowledge extends to the purpose or transaction for which the financial statements would be used.

Note the use of the term "evolve" here; in Canada, as in other countries, lower courts are presenting other definitions. You will see further discussion of this shortly. Finally, in rare cases, auditors have also been held liable for criminal acts. A criminal conviction against an auditor can result only when it is demonstrated that the auditor acted with criminal intent.

As described in Chapter 1, professional accountants perform a variety of services in addition to financial statement audits. As independent advisors, they may prepare financial statements or financial projections. As accountants, they may record transactions, prepare payroll, make tax or remittance payments, or handle other parts of the accounting functions. These may trigger a fiduciary duty to the client and additional government reporting requirements with respect to money laundering.

Fiduciary duty suits are a growing body of Canadian law that has affected accountants and may also affect auditors. **Fiduciary duty**, as listed in Table 4-1, results when a party (such as an accountant) has an obligation to act for the benefit of another, and that obligation includes discretionary power. It has also been called a "duty of loyalty."

An LPAA PA conducting a financial statement audit would not have any fiduciary duty, as the PA is not acting on behalf of the organization or its stakeholders but is providing an opinion on the financial statements. The situations where an accountant is making payments on the client's behalf to a tax authority or is appointed as a trustee for an estate are examples where fiduciary duty could arise. A professional accountant acting as an officer or director of an organization would have a fiduciary duty to shareholders.

Canadian PAs are required to have controls in place to identify and track suspicious transactions and comply with the reporting requirements of the Proceeds of Crime (Money Laundering) and Terrorist Financing Act (PCMLTFA), which came into effect in 2001 and has had several revisions. This reporting needs to take place if the PA is doing specific work on behalf of the client (called triggering activities) that triggers the requirements of the Act. These activities are (1) receipt or payment of funds (e.g., tax payments or employee remittance payments), (2) purchase or sale of assets (e.g., marketable securities or real estate), or (3) transferring cash or securities (e.g., using electronic funds transfer to make employee remittances). If you engage or your firm engages in these activities, then cash transactions of $10,000 or more must be reported to FINTRAC (the Financial Transactions and Reports Analysis Centre of Canada). You would also be expected to have systems in place to help identify clients who might be terrorists and to identify suspicious transactions over $3,000. More information is available on the FINTRAC website (**www.fintrac-canafe.gc.ca**) and professional accounting websites. Penalties for PAs (and others) for failing to follow the requirements of the PCMLTFA include up to five years in jail and/or a fine of up to $2 million.

Fiduciary duty—a party (such as an accountant) has an obligation to act for the benefit of another, and that obligation includes discretionary power.

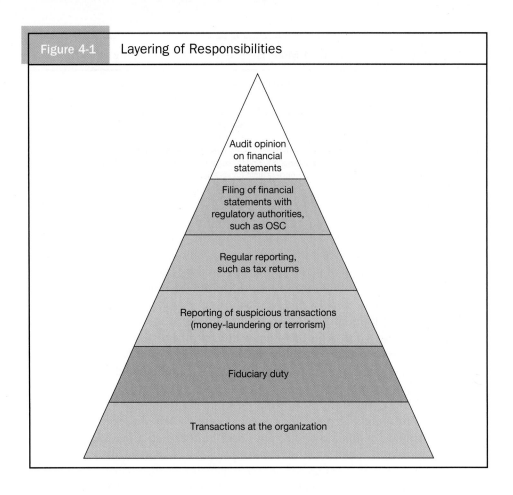

| Figure 4-1 | Layering of Responsibilities |

Audit opinion on financial statements

Filing of financial statements with regulatory authorities, such as OSC

Regular reporting, such as tax returns

Reporting of suspicious transactions (money-laundering or terrorism)

Fiduciary duty

Transactions at the organization

In addition to reporting requirements, there are also criminal offences associated with money laundering. Part XII.2 of the Criminal Code, Bill C-61, is known informally as the "proceeds of crime" legislation. In *R. v. Loewen* (1996), an accountant was convicted of laundering $125,000. The accountant stated to an undercover officer that he had a "few companies" through which he could move money. He then transferred the money through various accounts, retaining a commission. If this accountant were a professionally designated accountant, actions by the accountant's professional organization would have followed, likely expelling the accountant from the organization.

This case clearly demonstrates the accountant committing a criminal act. However, the legislation also applies to individuals who accept property (including fees), should they know or be willfully blind to the fact that the property was obtained illegally. Such individuals could be charged with possession or laundering. This is an additional incentive for accountants to be cautious when they have any doubts regarding management integrity.

Figure 4-1 shows how responsibilities are layered upon the basic transaction processing of an organization. If something goes wrong with any of the layers, problems occur. Decision makers are counted on to effectively process and organize transactions (a duty of loyalty). They are also expected to report suspicious transactions. Management accountants help ensure that accurate information is present in the underlying transactions in order to effectively prepare reports such as tax returns and financial statements. The latter are provided to regulators and are also audited by PAs. This figure helps show how auditors and regulators rely upon management in the conduct of their responsibilities.

Auditors' legal liability in assurance engagements is the main focus of this chapter. Sources, with examples, are shown in Table 4-2, along with the other potential claims or charges we have discussed.

Table 4-2   Major Sources of Auditors' Legal Liability

Source of Liability	Example of Potential Claim or Charge
Assurance Engagements	
Client—liability to client under common law	Client sues auditor for not discovering a defalcation during the audit.
Third party—liability to third parties under common law	Bank sues auditor for not discovering materially misstated financial statements.
Liability under provincial securities acts	A purchaser of stock issued by a company sues the auditor for not discovering materially misstated financial statements in a prospectus.
Criminal liability	Court prosecutes auditor under the Criminal Code of Canada for knowingly issuing an incorrect auditor's report.
Other Requirements	
Fiduciary duty—one party has an obligation to act for the benefit of another, and that obligation includes discretionary power	An accountant acting as trustee for a client invests in inappropriate investment vehicles and otherwise squanders the assets of the trust.
Proceeds of Crime (Money Laundering) and Terrorist Financing Act—obligation to report cash transactions and suspicious transactions and maintain control systems to track same	Five years in jail and/or a fine of up to $2 million for non-reporting of cash transactions over $10,000 or suspicious cash transfers
Criminal offence of possession or laundering	Transfer to legitimate organizations of money that was known to be proceeds of illegal activities, resulting in criminal charges.

DISTINCTION AMONG BUSINESS FAILURE, AUDIT FAILURE, AND AUDIT RISK

Many accounting and legal professionals believe that a major cause of lawsuits against public accounting firms is the lack of understanding by financial statement users of the difference between a business failure and an audit failure and between an audit failure and audit risk. These terms are first defined, followed by a discussion of how misunderstanding in the differences between the terms often results in lawsuits against auditors.

Business failure A **business failure** occurs when a business is unable to repay its lenders or meet the expectations of its investors due to economic or business conditions such as a recession, poor management decisions, or unexpected competition in the industry. The extreme case of business failure is filing for bankruptcy. As stated in Chapter 1, there is always some risk that a business will fail.

Audit failure An **audit failure** occurs when the auditor issues an inappropriate audit opinion as the result of an underlying failure to comply with the requirements of generally accepted auditing standards (GAAS). For example, the auditor may have assigned unqualified assistants to perform audit tasks, and because of their lack of competence and inappropriate supervision, they fail to find material misstatements that qualified auditors would have discovered.

Audit risk **Audit risk** is the risk that the auditor will conclude that the financial statements are fairly stated and an unqualified opinion can therefore be issued when, in fact, they are materially misstated. As will be shown in subsequent chapters, auditing cannot be expected to uncover all material financial statement misstatements. Auditing is limited by sampling, and certain misstatements and well-concealed frauds are extremely difficult to detect. This means that there is always some risk that the audit

Business failure—the situation when a business is unable to repay its lenders or meet the expectations of its investors because of economic or business conditions.

Audit failure—a situation in which the auditor issues an erroneous audit opinion as the result of an underlying failure to comply with the requirements of generally accepted auditing standards.

Audit risk—the risk that the auditor will conclude that the financial statements are fairly stated and an unqualified opinion can therefore be issued when, in fact, they are materially misstated.

will not uncover a material financial statement misstatement, even when the auditor has complied with GAAS.

Most accounting professionals agree that in most cases when an audit has failed to uncover material misstatements and the wrong type of audit opinion is issued, a legitimate question may be raised as to whether the auditor exercised due care. A PA who exercises **due care** is completing the audit with care, diligence, and skill. If the auditor failed to use due care in the conduct of the audit, then there is an audit failure. Then, the law often allows parties who suffered losses as a result of the auditor's breach of duty of care to recover some or all of the losses linked to the audit failure.

The difficulty arises when there has been a business failure but not an audit failure. For example, when a company goes bankrupt or cannot pay its debts, it is common for financial statement users to claim there was an audit failure, particularly when the most recently issued auditor's opinion indicates the financial statements were fairly stated. This conflict between users and auditors often arises because of what is referred to as the expectation gap between users and auditors. An **expectation gap** is the conflict between what some users expect from an auditor's report and what the auditor's report is designed to deliver; some users believe that an auditor's report is a guarantee for the accuracy of the financial statements, although the report is an opinion based on an audit conducted according to GAAS. Most auditors believe that conducting an audit in accordance with GAAS is all that can be expected of auditors. Many users believe auditors guarantee the accuracy of financial statements, and some users even believe the auditor guarantees the financial viability of the business. Fortunately for the profession, the courts continue to support the auditor's view.

Due care (during an audit)— completing the audit with care, diligence, and skill.

Expectation gap—the conflict between what some users expect from an auditor's report and what the auditor's report is designed to deliver; some users believe that an auditor's report is a guarantee for the accuracy of the financial statements, although the report is, in fact, an opinion based on an audit conducted according to GAAS.

auditing in action 4 - 1
Benefits from Research in Predicting Organizational Failures

Remember that one of the accounting standards relates to "going concern"—that an organization is able to continue operations in the future for at least one year. Auditors use ratios and financial modelling to help them assess the likelihood of business failure. Some of these financial models were first derived by researchers and tested against publicly available information about organizational failure and success. According to Statistics Canada, there were over 6,000 bankruptcies in 2007 alone, so analytical tools that help predict business failure are a welcome adjunct to the auditor's toolbox.

Dionne, Laajimi, Mejri, and Petrescu compared the results of three sets of calculations in their ability to predict bankruptcy defaults among Canadian public corporations. The authors used a model that examined stock market data (which predicted 61 percent of the defaults correctly), one that used financial statement data only (86 percent accuracy for defaults), and a combined or hybrid model that used both financial statement and stock market data (97 percent accuracy for defaults). What was most interesting was that splitting the time period studied in half resulted in a 100 percent accuracy prediction rate for defaults for the period 1996–2004. PAs can certainly use this kind of help when assessing the going-concern assumption!

Sources: 1. Dionne, Georges, Sadok Laajimi, Sofiane Mejri, and Madalina Petrescu, "Estimation of the default risk of publicly traded companies: Evidence from Canadian data," *Canadian Journal of Administrative Studies*, 25, 2008, p. 134–152. 2. Statistics Canada, "Bankruptcies, by industry, by province and territory," 2008, **www40.statcan.gc.ca/l01/cst01/econ11a-eng.htm**, Accessed: December 14, 2011.

IT is a difficult scenario—management fraud occurs and the financial statements are misstated. The business fails, and the bank or creditors lose money because asset accounts had been inflated. You think that is the worst—then management (who committed the fraud) turns around and sues the auditor. Luckily, the courts will not allow someone who benefited from a criminal action (e.g., fraud) to sue an auditor and recover money as part of the consequences of his or her fraud. Misleading the auditor includes deliberately withholding documentation. Even though the financial statements are misstated, the auditor relied upon management to prepare those financial statements.

A similar concept applies to directors. If directors rely upon the advice of management in making their decisions, they will not always be held liable for losses related to their decisions based upon that reliance.

CRITICAL THINKING QUESTIONS

1. How does management benefit from withholding information from auditors?
2. What effect does the absence of evidence have on the auditors?
3. How can lack of relevant disclosure affect the shareholders of a company?

Sources: 1. Paskell-Mede, Mindy, "Judging ill-gotten gains," *CAmagazine*, November 2002, p. 33-34. 2. Paskell-Mede, Mindy, "Obligated to reveal," *CAmagazine*, September 2007, 55, 57. 3. Rose, Jan, "Directors make mistakes," *CAmagazine*, November 2003, p. 36-38.

② Legal Terms Affecting PAs and Their Clients

Legal Concepts Affecting Liability

The licensed public accountant is responsible for every aspect of his or her public accounting work, including auditing, taxes, management advisory services, and accounting and bookkeeping services. Section 5020 of the *CICA Handbook*, "Association," helps explain the public accountant's involvement with an enterprise and with information issued by that enterprise. (There is no equivalent CAS proposed for Section 5020.) For example, if a public accountant negligently failed to properly prepare and file a client's tax return, the public accountant could be held liable for any penalties and interest the client was required to pay plus the tax preparation fee charged.

Most of the major lawsuits against public accounting firms have dealt with audited or unaudited financial statements. The discussion in this chapter deals primarily with these two aspects of public accounting. There, the areas of liability in auditing can be classified as (1) liability to clients, (2) liability to third parties under common law and statute law, and (3) criminal liability. First, we need to consider several legal concepts that apply to these types of lawsuits: the prudent person concept, liability for the acts of others, and the lack of privileged communication.

PRUDENT PERSON CONCEPT There is agreement within the profession and the courts that the auditor is not a guarantor or insurer of financial statements. The auditor is expected only to conduct the audit with due care. Even then, the auditor cannot be expected to be perfect.

The standard of due care to which the auditor is expected to be held is often referred to as the **prudent person concept**. This is the legal concept that a person has a duty to exercise reasonable care and diligence in the performance of his or her obligations to another.

LIABILITY FOR ACTS OF OTHERS The partners of a public accounting firm may have joint and several liability if a suit for tort or negligence is brought against the partnership. In other words, each partner may be held liable in a civil action for the tort or negligent actions of each of the other partners and employees in the partnership. Ontario provincial legislation has given accounting firms the ability to reduce their liability by forming **limited liability partnerships (LLPs)**. This is an organizational structure whereby only the person who does the work, those who supervise that person, and the firm itself are liable, but not other individual partners within the firm. In the absence of fraud or actual knowledge, only the person who did the work and those who supervised that

concept check

C4-1 List the sources of legal liability of a PA.

C4-2 Explain when a PA has a fiduciary duty to a client.

C4-3 How does Canadian money-laundering legislation affect a PA?

Prudent person concept—the legal concept that a person has a duty to exercise reasonable care and diligence in the performance of his or her obligations to another.

Limited liability partnership (LLP)—an organizational structure whereby only the person who does the work, those who supervise that person, and the firm itself are liable, but not other individual partners within the firm.

person, as well as the firm itself, would be liable. The auditor can also be held responsible for damages of others using the concept of joint and several liability. If an auditor is partially responsible but none of the other defendants has assets or insurance, then there will be an attempt to collect all damages from the auditor.

The partners may also be liable for the work of others on whom they rely. The groups an auditor is most likely to rely on are other public accounting firms engaged to do part of the work, internal auditors, and specialists called upon to provide technical information. Where a primary–secondary auditor relationship exists, the primary auditor would be entitled to rely upon the work of the secondary auditor, assuming that the primary auditor had conducted sufficient quality control work with respect to that secondary auditor. If the auditor proved that there was appropriate reliance on the work of a specialist, there would be an extremely strong defence that the auditor was not negligent and would not be liable to the plaintiff, assuming that GAAS were followed.

LACK OF PRIVILEGED COMMUNICATION Public accountants do not have the right under common law to withhold information from the courts on the grounds that the information is privileged. A court can subpoena information in an auditor's working papers. Confidential discussions between the client and auditor cannot be withheld from the courts. In the very specific situation where an accountant prepares documentation as a result of a lawyer's request to be used in existing or potential litigation, that documentation could be considered privileged (e.g., *Cineplex Odeon v. MNR [Ministry of National Revenue]*, 1994), as could confidential legal information provided by a client.

Definitions of Legal Terms

The material in the rest of the chapter can be studied more effectively if the most common legal terms affecting public accountants' liability are understood. Take a moment to review the terms in Table 4-3. Be sure to note the distinction between joint and several liability and separate and proportionate liability. In Canada, unless the charges are brought under provincial civil liability legislation (see New Standards 4-1), joint and several liability applies.

new standards 4-1
First Lawsuit Shows Effects of Changed Rules for Civil Liability

Effective December 31, 2005, the Ontario government enacted legislation as part of its Investor Confidence Initiative (comprising Bill 198, 2002; Bill 145, 2004; and Part XXIII.1 Ontario Securities Act) that both increases legal liability and reduces the amounts that auditors could be liable for. The legislation provides that both initial and secondary investors could sue (with court permission) where they relied upon information that was misrepresented (such as incorrect financial statements). Changes that would affect public accountants are proportional liability (they could be sued for only the portion for which they are judged to be at fault) and a cap on liability based upon a formula that is the greater of $1 million or the earnings from the client (and its affiliates) for the 12 months preceding the misrepresentation. These changes mean that more parties could sue the auditor but that the amount for which he or she would be liable would be less. The cap on liability does not apply if the defendant knew about the misrepresentation or failed to make known the misrepresentation on a timely basis.

An important aspect of this legislation is that the plaintiff does not need to prove that he or she relied upon the false information but only that there was a loss. However, the plaintiff must prove to a court that the action has merit before it can proceed. It may be that this process is slowing down the litigation process—there is one case dating from the Imax 2005 financial statements that was permitted to proceed according to lower courts, was appealed, and only in February 2011 was given the go ahead to proceed by the Ontario Superior Court of Justice.

Sources: 1. DiLieto, Rossana, Jean-Paul Bureaud, William J. Braithwaite, Peter Jervis, and G. Wesley Voorheis, "Preparing for Secondary Market Civil Liability," **www.apgo. net/newsletters/2005-12/ dwo_20051117_market-disclosure.pdf**, Accessed: November 11, 2009. 2. Morgan, Brian, "New liabilities," *CAmagazine*, June/July 2003, p. 34–36. 3. Paskell-Mede, Mindy, "The first of many issues," *CAmagazine*, August 2011, p. 44–45.

Table 4-3	Legal Terms Affecting PA Liability

Legal Term	Description
Terms Related to Negligence and Fraud	
Negligence	Failure to exercise reasonable care in the performance of one's obligations to another. For auditors, it is in terms of what other competent auditors would have done in the same situation.
Tort action for negligence	A legal action taken by an injured party against the party whose negligence resulted in the injury. A typical negligence action against a PA is a bank's claim that an auditor had a duty to uncover material errors in financial statements that had been relied on in making a loan.
Gross negligence	Lack of even slight care that can be expected of a person, tantamount to reckless behaviour.
Contributory negligence	When a person injured by a PA's negligence has also been negligent, and this negligence has also caused or contributed to the person's loss or injuries. A common example of such negligence is failure to give a PA information requested during the preparation of a tax return. The client later sues the accountant for improper preparation of the return. The court may hold that there was contributory negligence on the part of the client, and any damages that the client is awarded would be reduced in proportion to the amount that the client's own negligence was responsible for the loss. This defence is also used to reduce the effects of joint and several liability.
Fraud	A false assertion that has been made knowingly, without belief in its truth, or recklessly without caring whether or not it is true. An example is an auditor giving a standard (unqualified) opinion on financial statements that will be used to obtain a loan when the auditor knows the financial statements contain a material misstatement.
Constructive fraud	Existence of such recklessness that, even though there was no actual intent to defraud, a court will impute or construe fraud to the action. For example, if a PA failed to follow most of the generally accepted auditing standards, he or she may be found to have committed constructive fraud even though no intent to deceive financial statement users has been proven. (This concept has been used in foreign court cases but has not been used in Canadian cases. It is therefore not discussed further in this chapter. We will focus instead on negligence and fraud.)
Terms Related to Contract Law	
Breach of contract	Failure of one or both parties in a contract to fulfill the requirements of the contract. An example is the failure of a public accounting firm to deliver a tax return on the agreed-upon date. Parties who have a relationship that is established by a contract are said to have privity of contract. There can be privity of contract without a written agreement, but an engagement letter defines the contract more clearly.
Third-party beneficiary	A third party who does not have privity of contract but is known to the contracting parties and is intended to have certain rights and benefits under the contract. A common example is a bank that has a large loan outstanding at the balance sheet date and requires an audit as a part of its loan agreement.
Other Terms	
Common law	Laws developed through court decisions rather than through government statutes; also called "judge-made law" or "case law." An example is an auditor's liability to a bank related to the auditor's failure to discover material misstatements in financial statements that were relied upon in issuing a loan. Common law is always evolving as new precedents are set by the courts.
Statutory law	Laws and regulations that have been passed by a Canadian government body, either federal or provincial. The Canada Business Corporations Act is an important statutory law affecting auditors of companies incorporated under its jurisdiction.
Civil action	An action between individuals such as those that may be brought for breach of contract or tort.
Criminal action	An action brought under a provision of criminal statute law, for example, the Criminal Code of Canada.
Joint and several liability	The assessment against a defendant of the full loss suffered by a plaintiff, regardless of the extent to which other parties shared in the wrongdoing. For example, if management intentionally misstates financial statements, an auditor can be assessed the entire loss to shareholders if the company is bankrupt and management is unable to pay.
Separate and proportional liability	The assessment against a defendant of that portion of the damage caused by the defendant's negligence. For example, if the courts determine that an auditor's negligence in conducting an audit was the cause of 30 percent of the loss to a defendant, only 30 percent of the aggregate damage will be assessed to the public accounting firm.

Liability to Clients

The term "client" refers to the entity being audited and not to its owners or shareholders. Although the shareholders vote to appoint the auditors, the contract is between the enterprise and the auditors. In effect, shareholders are third parties and are discussed further, together with liability to other third parties, on page 85.

Lawsuits against public accountants from clients vary widely, including such claims as failure to complete an audit engagement on the agreed-upon date, inappropriate withdrawal from an audit, failure to discover a **defalcation** (theft of assets), and breach of the confidentiality requirements of public accountants. These lawsuits are relatively rare, and they do not receive the publicity often given to third-party suits. For example, in *Cameron v. Piers, Conrod & Allen*, an auditor was sued for issuing incorrect financial statements based upon incorrect information provided by a manager. The suit was not upheld because it was found that the auditor exercised reasonable care and skill.[2]

A typical lawsuit involves a claim that the auditor did not discover an employee defalcation as a result of negligence in the conduct of the audit. The lawsuit can be for breach of contract, a tort action for negligence, or both. Tort actions can be based on ordinary negligence or fraud. Note that, while it might sound odd for plaintiffs to claim under both breach of contract and negligence, the way each is proven and the amount of damages available under each might be different. By claiming under both, the plaintiff is covering all bases. The plaintiff cannot, however, be awarded damages twice for one event or loss.

The principal issue in cases involving alleged negligence is usually the level of care required. Although it is generally agreed that nobody is perfect, not even a professional, any significant misstatement will create a doubt regarding competence. In the auditing environment, failure to meet GAAS is often strong evidence of negligence. An example of an audit case raising the question of negligent performance by a public accounting firm is the case of *Haig v. Bamford et al.* (see Table 4-5 on page 85). Remember from the study of GAAS in Chapter 2 that determining due care and the amount and type of evidence to be obtained on an audit are subjective decisions. In a suit where negligence by an auditor was alleged, the court would hear evidence from one or more expert (auditing) witnesses. From this evidence, a judge or jury would decide what the typical public accountant would do, and what the accountant being sued should have done.

The question of level of care becomes more difficult in the environment of unaudited financial statements (i.e., a review or compilation) in which there are few accepted standards by which to evaluate performance. An example of a lawsuit dealing with the failure to uncover fraud in unaudited financial statements is *466715 Ontario Limited operating as Multi Graphics Print & Litho v. Helen Proulx and Doane Raymond* (1998).[3] There, the auditors were found to have competently completed their review engagement (which does not include controls assessment), and not liable for detecting fraud by the sole bookkeeper. The opposite finding occurred in *Italian Gifts v. Dixon*, 2000, where the court found that the auditor should have detected under-remitted sales taxes using analytical review as a test of plausibility in a review engagement (discussed further in Chapter 21). Since this was a consequence of the client's own errors, the auditor was only found to be 50 percent liable.[4]

---

[2] Rowan, Hugh, Q.C., "Stymied by management: A case of negligence?" *CAmagazine, April* 1986, p. 80–87.

[3] Kulig, P., "Doane Raymond absolved of wrongdoing," *The Bottom Line*, November 1, 1998, p. 14; and Trial judgment, Ontario Court (General Division), 95-CU-87608, August 20, 1998.

[4] Paskell-Mede, Mindy, "A limitation of liability," *CAmagazine*, November 2000, p. 47–48. Note that there is no equivalent CAS proposed for Section 9200.

Table 4-4	Six Auditor Defences
Defence	**Description**
Lack of duty to perform (also known as duty of care)	Liability is limited to foreseeable known users or users with a contract.*
Absence of misstatement	Also known as "no error"—the financial statements as relied upon are accurate in all material respects.
No damages	Even though the financial statements were materially misstated and the audit was negligently performed, the plaintiff did not suffer any damages.
Absence of negligence	The auditor conducted the audit in accordance with GAAS.
Absence of causal connection	a) It is irrelevant that the financial statements are materially misstated, as the user did not rely upon them, or b) the auditor is liable only for losses due to fraud after a time when they could or should have detected the fraud.
Contributory negligence	The party suing is also negligent.

*This defence is subject to legislation. For example, in Ontario, auditors have liability to investors, which is presently not the case under common law.

AUDITORS' DEFENCES AGAINST CLIENT SUITS FOR NEGLIGENCE The public accounting firm normally uses one or more of six defences (see Table 4-4) when there are legal claims of negligence by clients: lack of duty to perform the service, absence of (material) misstatement, no damages, absence of negligence, absence of causal connection, and contributory negligence.

Lack of duty The **lack of duty to perform** the service is a legal defence under which the professional claims that no contract existed with the plaintiff; therefore, no duty existed to perform the disputed service. For example, the public accounting firm might claim that errors were not uncovered because the firm did a review engagement, not an audit. A common way for a public accounting firm to demonstrate a lack of duty to perform is by use of an engagement letter.[5] Many litigation experts believe well-written engagement letters are one of the most important ways public accounting firms can reduce the likelihood of adverse legal actions. In *Kuziw et al. v. Abbott et al.* (1984) the court found a lack of duty to perform on the part of the accountant, because a compilation engagement was conducted, and the plaintiff had completed considerable research about the company before investing his funds.

Absence of misstatement Prior to addressing negligence, the defendant accountants could provide evidence that the financial statements were in accordance with accounting standards, that is, that there were no material errors. This means that even if the auditors had been negligent, the appropriate financial statements would not have differed materially from those on which the plaintiff relied. Then no grounds exist for suing the auditors, since the financial statements appropriately portray the financial situation of the organization and there was an **absence of misstatement**.

No damages (or reduced damages) It is possible that the financial statements were materially misstated and that the audit was negligently performed but that the plaintiff did not suffer any damages. This was one of the issues addressed by the Supreme

Lack of duty to perform—a legal defence under which the professional claims that no contract existed with the plaintiff; therefore, no duty existed to perform the disputed service; also applies to the concept of limiting liability to foreseeable known users.

Absence of misstatement—the financial statements appropriately portray the financial situation of the organization.

---

[5] Two types of letters that are commonly used by auditors to reduce potential liability to clients are an engagement letter and a management representation letter. An engagement letter is a signed agreement between the public accounting firm and the client identifying such items as whether an audit is to be done, other services to be provided, the date by which the work is to be completed, and the fees. The representation letter documents oral communication between auditors and management and states management's responsibilities for fair presentation in the financial statements.

Court of Canada in the case of *Hercules Management Ltd. v. Ernst & Young* (see Table 4-5 on page 85). A third party, the shareholders, claimed damages, but the Supreme Court stated that the damages were suffered by the corporate entity itself rather than by the shareholders. Thus, those plaintiffs (the shareholders) had no standing in law to claim the damages.

Absence of negligence This is a legal defence under which the professional claims that the disputed service was properly performed; an auditor would claim that the audit was performed according to GAAS. Even if there were undiscovered unintentional material misstatements (errors), intentional misstatements, or misrepresentations (fraud and other irregularities), the auditors would argue that they were not responsible if the audit was properly conducted. This occurs because there was an **absence of negligence**. The public accounting firm is not expected to be infallible.

It is likely that the courts will accept the *CICA Handbook* as evidence of appropriate standards of behaviour for the auditor, but it is possible that the courts could decide that an auditor who complied with the *Handbook* had been negligent. Such circumstances would be rare, but they could occur if the court thought the auditor had complied with the letter and not the spirit of the rules, or if accounting standards were not sufficiently informative.

Requiring auditors to discover all material misstatements would make them insurers or guarantors of the accuracy of the financial statements. In *Cameron v. Piers, Conrod & Allen* (previously discussed) the court ruled that the auditor had satisfied the prudent person concept by doing their best with the information available.

Absence of causal connection To succeed in an action against the auditor, the client must be able to show that there is a close causal connection between the auditor's breach of the standard of due care and the damages suffered by the client. For example, assume an auditor failed to complete an audit on the agreed-upon date. The client alleges that this caused a bank not to renew an outstanding loan, which caused damages. A potential auditor defence is that the bank refused to renew the loan for other reasons, such as the weakening financial condition of the client. The case of *Kuziw et al. v. Abbott et al.* (previously discussed) illustrates **absence of causal connection**—the legal defence under which the professional contends that the damages claimed by the client were not brought about by any act of the professional; the court ruled that the purchaser, Kuziw, did not rely on an incorrect auditor's report but rather had decided to purchase Graf-Tech based on other information.

Contributory negligence A defence of contributory negligence means that the public accounting firm claims that part or all of the loss arose because of the claimant's own negligence. For example, suppose the client is the claimant and argues that the public accounting firm was negligent in not uncovering an employee theft of cash. A likely contributory negligence defence is the auditor's claim that the public accounting firm informed management of a weakness in the internal controls that enhanced the likelihood of the fraud, but management did not correct it. Management often does not correct internal control weaknesses because of cost considerations, attitudes about employee honesty, or procrastination. The auditor is unlikely to lose this suit, assuming a strong contributory negligence defence, if the client was informed in writing of internal control weaknesses.

Contributory negligence is also a way to "share the blame" if the auditor could have detected the problem, but it was also due to the plaintiff's own actions. *Italian Gifts v. Dixon* (previously discussed) is an example of this type of contributory negligence, since the client made errors in remitting sales taxes that could have been detected by the auditors if they had conducted their review engagement correctly.

Absence of negligence —a legal defence under which the professional claims that the disputed service was properly performed; an auditor would claim that the audit was performed according to GAAS.

Absence of causal connection—a legal defence under which the professional contends that the damages claimed by the client were not brought about by any act of the professional.

concept check

C4-4 How could the legal environment in Canada increase or decrease auditor liability? (Cite court cases in your discussion.)

C4-5 Explain the difference between joint and several liability and proportional liability.

C4-6 Can the auditor withhold information from the courts? Why or why not?

③ Liability to Non-Clients

Liability to Third Parties under Common Law

A public accounting firm may be liable to third parties if a loss was incurred by the claimant due to reliance on misleading financial statements. Third parties are those with whom the auditor did not enter into a contract and include actual and potential shareholders, vendors, bankers and other creditors or investors, employees, and customers. A typical suit might occur when a bank is unable to collect a major loan from an insolvent customer. The bank will claim that misleading audited financial statements were relied upon in making the loan and that the public accounting firm should be held responsible because it failed to perform the audit with due care. Understanding when the auditor will be held liable calls for an understanding of the continuing evolution of this area of the law.

EVOLUTION OF LIABILITY The leading precedent-setting auditing case in third-party liability was a 1931 U.S. case, *Ultramares Corporation v. Touche* (see Table 4-5). It established the traditional common law approach known as the Ultramares doctrine. The case has been cited many times in England and Canada.

The key aspect of the Ultramares doctrine is that ordinary negligence is insufficient for liability to third parties because of the lack of privity of contract between the third party and the auditor. The judge commented that it would be inappropriate to hold the auditors liable to third parties in the circumstances, since this would open the doors to indeterminate liability of an indeterminate amount to an indeterminate number of people. The case was followed by other jurisdictions on the basis of the policy considerations underlying this judgment. In addition, Ultramares also held that if there had been fraud or **constructive fraud**, the auditor could be held liable to more general third parties.

The Supreme Court of Canada decided another important case on this issue in 1976. The case was *Gordon T. Haig v. Ralph L. Bamford et al.* (see Table 4-5). This case confirms the finding that lack of privity is not necessarily a valid defence. However, the Supreme Court decided it should not consider the foreseeability test (i.e., test #1), as it was not relevant to the particular circumstances. Instead, the narrower test of actual knowledge of the limited class was deemed to be appropriate. This means that in Canada, persons making negligent misstatements (in this case, auditors) are potentially

Constructive fraud—conduct that the law construes as fraud even though there was no actual intent to deceive; considered to be so reckless that the courts decide it is tantamount to fraud.

Table 4-5	Classic Lawsuits Defining Third-Party Liability Where the Auditors Had Been Found to Be Negligent	
Lawsuit	Nature of Claim	Effect on Defining Third-Party Liability
Ultramares Corporation v. Touche (1931)	Creditors sued due to losses where financial statements had been fraudulently misstated (inflated accounts receivable and accounts payable).	Only those who are party to a contract with the accountants can sue them when there is negligence.
Haig v. Bamford et al. (1976)	Investor sued due to investment losses where financial statements had a deposit included as revenue.	Three tests identified to define to whom the auditor owed a duty of care: 1. Foreseeability of the use of audited financial statements by the plaintiff. 2. Actual knowledge of the limited class who will rely on the audited statements. 3. Actual knowledge of the person who will rely on the audited statements.
Hercules Management Ltd. v. Ernst & Young (1997)	Investors of two failed companies sued due to the loss of value of their shares.	There is no general auditor liability to shareholders, since the loss of equity is really a loss suffered by the company.

liable to all those third parties who were members of a limited group of whom the auditors had knowledge at the time the audit was performed and to whom the audited financial statements were issued. For example, the test of actual knowledge would apply if an auditor were asked to give an opinion on financial statements to be shown to several local banks for purposes of obtaining a loan. The narrowest of the three tests, that the auditor must know the actual individual, was rejected as being too narrow.

Table 4-5 also refers to *Hercules Management v. Ernst & Young*, (1997), where the court ruled that the auditors had no special knowledge that the shareholders planned to use the financial statements for investment decisions and that there was no privity of contract. The auditors claimed in their defence that they owed no duty of care to the shareholders and the courts agreed.

AUDITOR DEFENCES AGAINST THIRD-PARTY SUITS The defences available to auditors in suits by clients are also available in third-party lawsuits (see Table 4-4).

The previous section outlined the lack of duty of care defence. The more recent cases in both the United Kingdom and Canada suggest that we now know that the limited class of users is to be defined in relation to the known purpose of the financial statements and that, therefore, each case should be decided on its own factual context. The class that the auditor is liable to is also subject to legislation. As explained in the previous section, secondary investors (those who purchase shares after an initial offering) can now also sue auditors under provincial legislation without needing to prove reliance on the information.

The second defence in third-party suits, absence of misstatement, is also known as "no error" in the financial statements. Thus, a plaintiff's damages would be inappropriately calculated because the financial statements on which they relied would have been accurate.

In no damages, the third party did not suffer a loss due to reliance—the loss may have occurred for other reasons, such as poor management or a worsening economic environment.

Next is non-negligent performance. If the auditor conducted the audit in accordance with GAAS, there is a strong inference of no negligence. Recognize, however, that non-negligent performance is difficult to demonstrate to a court. Proving lack of negligence normally involves a debate between experts hired by both sides. The judge, who is a layperson with respect to accounting and auditing, then assesses the credibility of the experts from both sides in order to make an independent decision based upon legal, accounting, and auditing concepts.

Absence of causal connection in third-party suits has two variations. The first occurs when there is a material misstatement in the financial statements, the second when there is a defalcation at the client or plaintiff's place of business. When there is a misstatement in the financial statements, the defence usually means non-reliance on the financial statements by the user. For example, assume the auditor can demonstrate that a lender relied upon an ongoing banking relationship with a customer, rather than the financial statements, in making a loan. The fact that the auditor was negligent in the conduct of the audit would not be relevant in that situation. In the case of a defalcation, the auditors would not be liable for the entire loss caused by the culprit (e.g., if there had been a certain amount of defalcation that had already taken place before the auditors could have been expected to detect it). Normally, the auditor is held liable only for additional fraud committed after the first date on which the whistle could have been blown. Another good example of "no causal connection" arises in tax cases where the client is required to pay additional taxes. The accountant would not be liable to reimburse the client for taxes paid but only for the interest and penalties, since nothing could have been done legitimately to avoid payment of the taxes.

Finally, it is possible to find contributory negligence if it could be said the claimants were themselves negligent, say, by ignoring other relevant information. It would be more common, however, for the auditor to defend on one of the other bases outlined above.

Criminal Liability

Fraud by anyone can be a criminal act, and the perpetrator can be subject to criminal prosecution. The criminal action would be brought by the Attorney General; conviction of a professional accountant for criminal liability would likely result in a charge of criminal misconduct by the professional accountant's institute (or *ordre*). **Criminal liability for auditors** is the possibility of being found guilty under criminal law for defrauding a person through knowing involvement with false financial statements.

For example, if the auditor of a company gave an unqualified auditor's report on the company's financial statements knowing that inventory was grossly overvalued, it is possible the auditor would be found guilty of criminal fraud and could be sued in a civil action.

Suppose in this case that inventory was to be valued at the lower of cost or market but the auditor deliberately did not include drastic decreases in market value that occurred in the second month following the balance sheet date. Failure to reflect all the information in the auditor's possession in the financial statements would make them misleading despite their being in accordance with the applicable financial reporting standards. This occurs when there are multiple alternatives under particular accounting frameworks or where the standards in the accounting framework require limited disclosure. The auditor could be judged guilty of fraud.

While there are almost no Canadian cases involving fraud, there have been several U.S. cases. Fraud, however, is interpreted more liberally in the United States. There the term "fraud" is used in civil cases, when errors in financial statement legal disclosures that benefit management or others occur. The leading case of criminal action against CPAs is *United States v. Simon*, which occurred in 1969. In this case, three auditors were prosecuted for filing false financial statements of a client with the government and held to be criminally liable. The consequences for these three men were significant. They lost their CPA certificates under the U.S. Rule 501 of the Code of Professional Conduct (acts discreditable) and were forced to leave the profession. *United States v. Simon* has been followed by three additional major criminal cases. In *United States v. Natelli* (1975), two auditors were convicted of criminal liability for certifying the financial statements of National Student Marketing Corporation that contained inadequate disclosures pertaining to accounts receivable.

In *United States v. Weiner* (1975), three auditors were convicted of securities fraud in connection with their audit of Equity Funding Corporation of America. Equity Funding was a financial conglomerate, the financial statements of which had been overstated through a massive fraud by management. The fraud was so extensive and the audit work so poor that the court concluded the auditors must have been aware of the fraud and were therefore guilty of complicity. In Canada, these auditors would likely have been found guilty of negligence.

In *ESM Government Securities v. Alexander Grant & Co.* (1986), a U.S. case, it was revealed by management to the partner in charge of the audit of ESM that the previous year's audited financial statements contained a material misstatement. Rather than complying with professional and firm standards in such circumstances, the partner agreed to say nothing in the hope that management would work its way out of the problem during the current year. Instead, the situation worsened, eventually to the point where losses exceeded $300 million. The partner was subsequently convicted of criminal charges for his role in sustaining the fraud and was handed a 12-year prison term. In this case, the partner personally benefited from the fraud and would likely also have been found guilty of fraud in Canada.

In the United States, the Sarbanes-Oxley Act of 2002 made it a felony to destroy or create documents to impede or obstruct a federal investigation. Under the Act, a person may face fines as well as imprisonment of up to 20 years for altering or destroying documents. These provisions were adopted following the *United States v. Andersen* (2002) case described in Figure 4-2, in which the government charged Andersen with

Criminal liability for auditors
—the possibility of being found guilty under criminal law; defrauding a person through knowing involvement with false financial statements.

In this case, the government charged Andersen with destruction of documents related to the firm's audit of Enron. During the period between October 19, 2001, when Enron alerted Andersen that the SEC had begun an inquiry into Enron's accounting for certain special-purpose entities, and November 8, 2001, when the SEC served Andersen with a subpoena in connection with its work for Enron, Andersen personnel shredded extensive amounts of physical documentation and deleted computer files related to Enron.

The firm was ultimately convicted of one count of obstruction of justice. The conviction was not based on the document shredding but on the alteration of a memo related to Enron's characterization of charges as non-recurring in its third-quarter 2001 earnings release, in which the company announced a loss of $618 million.

As a result of the conviction, Andersen was no longer able to audit publicly traded U.S. companies. The conviction was overturned in May 2005 by the U.S. Supreme Court because the instructions provided to the jury were too broad. The victory was largely symbolic since the firm effectively ceased operations after the original conviction.

obstruction of justice for the destruction and alteration of documents related to its audit of Enron. This case is another example of criminal liability in the United States.

Several practical lessons can be learned from these cases:

- An investigation of the integrity of management is an important part of deciding on the acceptability of clients and the extent of work to be performed.
- Independence in appearance and fact by all individuals on the engagement is essential, especially in a defence involving criminal actions.
- Transactions with related parties require special scrutiny because of the potential for misstatement.
- Accounting standards cannot be relied upon exclusively in deciding whether financial statements are fairly presented.
- Good documentation may be just as important in the auditor's defence of criminal charges as in a civil suit.
- The potential consequences of the auditor knowingly committing a wrongful act are so severe that it is unlikely that the potential benefits could ever justify the actions.

④ Auditor Liability Prevention

The Profession's Response to Legal Liability

There are a number of things the professional accounting associations and the public accounting profession as a whole can do to reduce the practitioner's exposure to lawsuits. The instituting of practice inspection by the provincial institute, CPAB, and *ordre* of members in public practice (discussed in Chapter 2) is one positive step in recognizing the additional responsibility that the public demands of professionals. Some of the others are discussed further below.

1. *Conduct research in auditing.* Continued research is important in finding better ways to do such things as uncovering unintentional material misstatements and management and employee fraud, communicating audit results to financial statement users, and making sure that auditors are independent. Significant research already takes place through the professional accounting associations, public accounting firms, and universities. For example, the University of Waterloo Centre for Information Integrity and Information Systems Assurance (see **http://accounting.uwaterloo.ca/uwcisa/**) has a variety of research and educational activities, including information systems assurance research.

2. *Set standards and rules.* The CICA must constantly set standards and revise them to meet the changing needs of auditing. New Canadian Auditing Standards, revisions of the rules of conduct of the various professional accounting bodies, and other pronouncements must be issued as society's needs change and as new technology arises from experience and research.

3. *Set requirements to protect auditors.* Professional accounting associations can help protect public accountants by setting requirements (such as independence rules) that better practitioners already follow.

4. *Establish practice inspection requirements.* The periodic examination of a firm's practices and procedures is a way to educate practitioners and identify firms not meeting the standards of the profession.

5. *Defend unjustified lawsuits.* It is important that public accounting firms continue to oppose unwarranted lawsuits even if in the short run the costs of winning exceed the costs of settling.

6. *Educate users.* It is important to educate investors and others who read financial statements as to the meaning of the auditor's opinion and the extent and nature of the auditor's work. Auditors do not test 100 percent of all records and do not guarantee the accuracy of the financial records or the future prosperity of the company. This means that there still could be errors or other misstatements in the financial statements.

7. *Sanction members for improper conduct and performance.* One characteristic of a profession is its responsibility for policing its own membership. The professional accounting bodies have disciplinary procedures that are designed to deal with the problems of inadequate performance by members.

8. *Lobby for changes in laws.* If the risk exposure of auditors to legal liability becomes too high, insurance will either be prohibitively expensive or unobtainable, and self-insurance is not an option. If the risk exposure does start to approach an unacceptable level, governments could be lobbied at least to ensure viable insurance coverage exists. Lobbying can produce results such as the June 1998 law permitting limited liability partnerships (LLPs) in Ontario and the more recent provincial legislative changes providing for secondary investor suits with liability ceilings.

The Individual Professional Accountant's Response to Legal Liability

Practising auditors may also take specific action to minimize their liability. Most of this book deals with that subject. A summary of several of these practices is included here.

1. *Deal only with clients possessing integrity.* The auditor needs to be alert to risk factors that may result in lawsuits. There is an increased likelihood of having legal problems when a client lacks integrity in dealing with customers, employees, units of government, and others. A public accounting firm needs procedures to evaluate the integrity of clients and should dissociate itself from clients found lacking.

2. *Hire qualified personnel and train and supervise them properly.* A considerable portion of most audits is done by young professionals with limited experience. Given the high degree of risk public accounting firms have in doing audits, it is important that these young professionals be qualified and well trained. Supervision of their work by more experienced, qualified professionals is also essential.

3. *Follow the standards of the profession.* A firm must implement procedures to make sure that all firm members understand and follow the Recommendations of the *CICA Handbook* and other authoritative sources of accounting standards and GAAS, their profession's rules of conduct, and other professional guidelines.

4. *Maintain independence.* Independence is more than merely financial. Independence in fact requires an attitude of responsibility separate from the client's interest. Much litigation has arisen from a too-willing acceptance by an auditor of a

client's representation or of a client's pressures. The auditor must maintain an attitude of healthy professional skepticism.

5. *Understand the client's business.* The lack of knowledge of industry practices and client operations has been a major factor in auditors failing to uncover errors in several cases. It is important that the audit team be educated in these areas.

6. *Perform quality audits.* Quality audits require that appropriate evidence be obtained and appropriate judgments be made about the evidence. It is essential, for example, that the auditor evaluate a client's internal controls and modify the quantity and quality of evidence obtained to reflect the findings. Well-documented and monitored quality control procedures help provide quality audits.

7. *Document the work properly.* The preparation of good working papers helps in organizing and performing quality audits. Quality working papers help an auditor defend an audit in court.

8. *Obtain an engagement letter and a management representation letter.* These two letters are essential in defining the respective obligations of client and auditor. They are helpful especially in lawsuits between the client and auditor and also in third-party lawsuits.

9. *Maintain confidential relations.* Auditors are under an ethical and sometimes legal obligation not to disclose client matters to outsiders.

10. *Carry adequate insurance.* A public accounting firm needs to have adequate insurance protection in the event of a lawsuit. Although insurance rates have risen considerably in the past few years as a result of increasing litigation, professional liability insurance is still available to all public accountants.

11. *Seek legal counsel.* Whenever serious problems occur during an audit, a public accountant would be wise to consult experienced counsel. In the event of a potential or actual lawsuit, the auditor should immediately seek an experienced lawyer.

concept check

C4-10 Who should respond to the audit profession's legal liability? Why?

C4-11 Why is international cooperation important in the limitation of legal liability?

⑤ Legislation and the Assurance Engagement

In the preceding sections of this chapter we discussed professional legal liability after the completion of an engagement. There are many other times when legislation has an impact on the PA. In this section we will talk about tax legislation, the Personal Information Protection and Electronic Documents Act (PIPEDA), and the importance of knowing the legislation that affects your client when conducting a financial statement audit.

Impact of Tax Legislation

There is an old saying that the only certainties are "death and taxes," yet the impact of taxes can be far from certain. We have municipal property taxes, sales and excise taxes, estate taxes, and income taxes for both the province and the country. PAs often decide to specialize in one or more forms of these taxes, performing quality control for the financial statement audit or doing special investigations and calculations for clients. Errors in tax calculations or assumptions can be large, resulting in refunds, enormous debts, or misstatements in the financial statements. This explains why most firms require a quality control tax person's sign-off of the client's tax returns before the financial statements are released for printing. Large errors can result in the loss of the client, liability for unpaid interest or penalty, or lawsuits. PAs need to be aware of recent tax rulings that might affect their clients, since a clarification of tax law could result in the ability to refile or change a tax return.

Many of the functions in an organization are impacted by the proper treatment of taxation. Organizations need to collect and remit payroll taxes and withholdings, collect and remit provincial sales taxes and the goods and services or harmonized sales tax, and correctly record their transactions so that they can calculate income tax. As an PA, you will be asked to identify potential risks of error at your client before examining client systems to identify key controls that mitigate those risks. Knowing your client's profit objectives, for example, can help determine whether there is a risk of over- or understatement of income taxes, which will affect the types of audit tests that you design.

Impact of Privacy Legislation

Besides Canada's federal privacy legislation, PIPEDA, there are also provincial privacy Acts and privacy protection provisions in provincial health-care Acts. International organizations would also be subject to the privacy legislation of their trading partners (suppliers and customers). Some countries have stricter legislation than Canada, while others have less comprehensive legislation. Most legislation embodies basic principles of data collection, data accuracy, and data confidentiality. For example, only authorized individuals should have access to data for legitimate business purposes, and data should be retained only as long as they have a business purpose. We will talk about some examples in Chapter 9, when we discuss corporate governance and the control environment. As an example here, consider that employees should be trained about privacy, be asked to annually sign a privacy policy document, and that privacy adherence should be monitored with violations resulting in remedial action.

As a licensed public accountant, you would include in your engagement letter a statement that you would keep client data confidential, securing your working paper files so that data stored in the files stay private. This means that your office should have appropriate security, as should your filing cabinets and your computer systems, so that only authorized individuals have access to client data files. It would be a public relations and legal liability disaster should client data files that you used for audit testing be leaked to the internet, resulting in investigations by Canada's Privacy Commissioner! As part of your client risk assessment, you will consider your client's data management policies and practices, which include privacy policies.

Some PAs specialize in privacy assurance engagements, helping clients assess their privacy practices and implement policies and procedures for effective privacy management in their organizations. Privacy is part of a well-run organization and needs to be considered together with effective security over information systems, appropriate authentication of users, and carefully designed individual access rights. All of these systems need to be working to help ensure privacy.[6]

Other Legislation and Audits

Think about other legislation that affects clients of financial statement audits. These include labour laws, municipal bylaws, expropriation laws, environmental laws, consumer safety laws, and numerous others. As an interested observer, you might become aware of these laws only when your client violates them and is on the front page of the newspaper. However, as an PA, assessing financial statement risks includes assessing fraud risks and the procedures in place at your client for assessing its own risks. This means that the client should be aware of the legislation that impacts it and communicate this information to you, its auditor. If the client does not have an effective risk assessment or quality control mechanism (for example, to prevent toxins from entering the food production system), then the auditor would need to carefully assess the going concern ability of the client if it were fined and sued for violations of health and safety regulations.

As part of their training, PAs will learn about effective risk management processes so that they can assess these at their client. Audit quality-control procedures include updating checklists used with clients to include questions about relevant new legislation that affects all clients and asking clients about their own processes in adhering to the laws in their jurisdictions, whether they be local, national, or international.

---

[6] If you are interested in learning more about privacy and privacy assurance engagements, there is a frequently-asked-questions page on the CICA website that provides links to further resources at **www.cica.ca/resources-and-member-benefits/privacy-resources-for-firms-and-organizations/faqs/item10442.aspx**.

concept check

C4-12 How can federal income tax legislation affect the financial statement audit?

C4-13 Why does the auditor need to consider environmental legislation during a financial statement audit?

Engagement completion will include communication with the client's lawyers to determine the status of lawsuits so that disclosure can be included in financial statements, or the financial records adjusted where judgment has occurred either for or against the client.

In this text, we will also learn about risk management from the perspective of the financial statement audit. Risk assessment helps identify risks of misstatement. A variety of audit procedures form the audit responses that can be taken to deal with the identified risks. Evaluation of the audit responses is a continuing process throughout the audit as well as at the end of the engagement, as team members communicate with each other and document the results of their field work.

Appendix 4A
Securities Legislation

In Chapter 2, it was pointed out that a number of Canadian companies were listed on American stock exchanges or sold securities in the United States or both and that these companies were therefore subject to the requirements of the U.S. Securities Act of 1933 and the Securities Exchange Act of 1934. The following discussion pertains to the civil liability of accountants under a typical Canadian securities act—the Ontario Securities Act—and relevant U.S. acts.

Ontario Securities Act Part XXIII, Civil Liability, deals with liability for misrepresentation in a prospectus. It applies not only to auditors but also to issuers, those selling securities, underwriters, and directors. Auditors are not referred to directly but are described in Section 130(1) as those "whose consent has been filed pursuant to a requirement of the regulations but only with respect to reports, opinions, or statements that have been made by them." The section states that the purchaser who purchases the security based on the prospectus is deemed to be relying on representations with respect to that prospectus. Thus, the issue of privity would be automatically dealt with in the event that the purchaser sued the auditor or others.

Section 130(8) goes on to state that all persons or companies specified in the first section are jointly and severally liable, but the amount recoverable (specified in the next paragraph of the Act) would not exceed the price at which the securities were offered to the public.

Section 131 specifies the same deemed reliance, liability, and amount recoverable in the context of a take-over bid circular.

U.S. Laws

Securities Act of 1933 This Act deals with the information in registration statements and prospectuses. It concerns only the reporting requirements for companies issuing new securities. The only parties that can recover from auditors under the 1933 Act are original purchasers of securities. The amount of the potential recovery is the original purchase price less the value of the securities at the time of the suit. If the securities have been sold, users can recover the amount of the loss incurred.

The Securities Act of 1933 imposes an unusual burden on the auditor. Section 11 defines the rights of third parties and auditors. These are summarized as follows:

- Any third party who purchased securities described in the registration statement may sue the auditor for material misrepresentations or omissions in audited financial statements included in the registration statement.
- The third-party user does not have the burden of proof that he or she relied on the financial statements or that the auditor was negligent or fraudulent in doing the

audit. The user must prove only that the audited financial statements contained a material misrepresentation or omission.

- The auditor has the burden of demonstrating as a defence that (1) an adequate audit was conducted in the circumstances or (2) all or a portion of the plaintiff's loss was caused by factors other than the misleading financial statements. The 1933 Act is the only U.S. common or statutory law where the burden of proof is on the defendant.
- The auditor has responsibility for making sure the financial statements were fairly stated beyond the date of issuance, up to the date the registration statement became effective, which could be several months later. For example, assume the audit report date for December 31, 2011, financial statements is February 10, 2012, but the registration statement is dated November 1, 2012. In a typical audit, the auditor must review transactions through the audit report date, February 10, 2012. In statements filed under the 1933 Act, the auditor is responsible to review transactions through the registration statement date, November 1, 2012.

Although the burden on auditors may appear harsh, there have been few cases tried under the 1933 Act.

SECURITIES EXCHANGE ACT OF 1934 The liability of auditors under the Securities Exchange Act of 1934 frequently centres on the audited financial statements issued to the public in annual reports or submitted to the SEC as a part of annual 10-K reports.

Every company with securities traded on national and over-the-counter exchanges is required to submit audited statements annually. There are obviously a much larger number of statements falling under the 1934 Act than under the 1933 Act.

In addition to annual audited financial statements, there is potential legal exposure to auditors for quarterly (10-Q), monthly (8-K), and other reporting information. The auditor is frequently involved in reviewing the information in these other reports; therefore, there may be legal responsibility. However, few cases have involved auditors for reports other than auditor's reports.

SEC SANCTIONS Closely related to auditors' liability is the SEC's authority to sanction. The SEC has the power in certain circumstances to sanction or suspend practitioners from doing audits for SEC companies. Rule 2(e) of the SEC's Rules of Practice says:

> The commission may deny, temporarily or permanently, the privilege of appearing or practising before it in any way to any person who is found by the commission: (1) not to possess the requisite qualifications to represent others, or (2) to be lacking in character or integrity or to have engaged in unethical or improper professional conduct.

In recent years, the SEC has temporarily suspended a number of individual CPAs from doing any audits of SEC clients. It has similarly prohibited a number of CPA firms from accepting any new SEC clients for a period, such as six months. At times, the SEC has required an extensive review of a major CPA firm's practices by another CPA firm. In some cases, individual CPAs and their firms have been required to participate in continuing education programs and to make changes in their practice. Sanctions such as these are published by the SEC and are often reported in the business press, making them a significant embarrassment to those involved.

FOREIGN CORRUPT PRACTICES ACT OF 1977 Another significant congressional action affecting both CPA firms and their clients was the passing of the Foreign Corrupt Practices Act of 1977. The Act makes it illegal to offer a bribe to an official of a foreign country for the purpose of exerting influence and obtaining or retaining business. The prohibition against payments to foreign officials is applicable to all U.S. domestic firms, regardless of whether they are publicly held or privately held, and to foreign companies filing with the SEC.

Apart from the bribery provisions that affect all companies, the law also requires SEC registrants under the Securities Exchange Act of 1934 to meet additional requirements. These include the maintenance of reasonably complete and accurate records and an adequate system of internal control. The law significantly affects all SEC companies and may affect auditors through their responsibility to review and evaluate systems of internal control as a part of doing the audit.

SARBANES-OXLEY ACT OF 2002 The Sarbanes-Oxley Act greatly increases the responsibilities of public companies and their auditors in the United States. The Act requires the CEO and CFO to certify the annual and quarterly financial statements filed with the SEC. In addition, as discussed in Chapter 9, management must report its assessment of the effectiveness of internal control over financial reporting, and for large companies, the auditor must provide an opinion on the effectiveness of internal control over financial reporting. As a result, auditors may be exposed to legal liability related to their opinions on internal control. The PCAOB also has the authority to sanction registered CPA firms for any violations of the Act.

Summary

1. *What are a public accountant's sources of legal liability?* Public accountants could be liable to clients and third parties such as shareholders and debt holders.

   How is this liability related to a distinction between business failure and audit failure? Financial statement users might confuse business failures, for example, due to bankruptcy, with an audit failure, where an audit was not conducted in accordance with GAAS, resulting in more frequent lawsuits.

   Does the financial statement auditor have a fiduciary duty? No. As explained on page 75, the PA would need to have discretionary power over funds to have a fiduciary duty.

   Does the PA have reporting obligations with respect to potential money-laundering? In some cases, yes. Page 75 describes triggering activities (basically receipt and disbursements of funds under certain conditions) that would require a PA to report financial transactions to FINTRAC.

2. *Do accountants have the right of privileged communication?* No. Accountants must disclose their working papers to the courts when subpoenaed.

   What other concepts or terms are associated with auditor's legal liability? The prudent person concept (pages 79–80) is an important concept, as are distinctions between negligence and fraud (page 81) and distinctions between contract and common law (pages 81–86).

   What should auditors do if a client sues them? With the assistance of legal counsel, assuming the conduct of an audit in accordance with GAAS, the auditor would likely pursue one of the defences listed in the chapter commencing on page 83.

3. *Who else can sue the auditor, besides the client?* Nonclients such as actual and potential shareholders, vendors, bankers, creditors, investors, employees, and customers can sue an auditor.

   How would the auditor defend against such suits? The auditor would use a series of defences used with clients, summarized in Table 4-4 (page 83).

   Can the auditor go to jail because of criminal liability? Yes, though this would likely occur only where the auditor was deliberately involved with materially incorrect financial statements and intended to mislead.

4. *What are individual accountants and the profession doing to respond to legal liability?* Individual accountants can undertake many actions (listed on pages 88–90) to help prevent lawsuits. The profession has made changes in the recent past, including participation with the CPAB, and numerous activities such as research (see pages 88–89).

5. *What should auditors do to determine the impact of legislation on the financial statement audit?* Auditors need to discuss with management the organization's risk assessment process, including identification and requirements of legislation for their business.

   How does the need to understand relevant legislation affect the audit process? Auditors need to have sufficient training to understand the legislation, identify sources of relevant legislation, and have checklists in their documentation to remind them to consider relevant legislation. Once relevant legislation is identified, the auditor incorporates consideration of the legislation into the planning and conduct of the audit.

   Link those actions to standards of continuing education, quality control, and engagement completion. Quality control, supervision, and clear documentation help auditors incorporate the results of their findings into their audit process.

MyAccountingLab

Make the grade with MyAccountingLab: The questions, exercises, and problems marked in orange can be found on MyAccountingLab. You can practise them as often as you want, and most feature step-by-step guided instructions to help you find the right answer.

Review Questions

4-1 ❶ State several factors that have affected the incidence of lawsuits against public accountants.

4-2 ❶ Distinguish between business risk and audit risk. Why is business risk a concern to auditors?

4-3 ❷ How does the prudent person concept affect the liability of the auditor?

4-4 ❷ A partner in a public accounting firm may be held liable for errors in the work of others. Identify at least two groups of such others and explain why the partner might be liable.

4-5 ❷ Differentiate between criminal action and civil action.

4-6 ❷ A common type of lawsuit against public accountants is for the failure to detect a defalcation. State the auditor's responsibility for such discovery. Give authoritative support for your answer.

4-7 ❷ What is meant by "contributory negligence"? Under what conditions will this likely be a successful defence?

4-8 ❸ Is the auditor's liability affected if the third party was unknown rather than known? Explain.

4-9 ❷❸ Distinguish among the auditor's potential liability to the client, liability to third parties under common law, and criminal liability. Describe one situation for each type of liability in which the auditor could be held legally responsible.

4-10 ❹ In what ways can the profession positively respond and reduce liability in auditing?

4-11 ❹ In what ways can an individual public accountant positively respond and reduce liability in auditing?

4-12 ❺ Describe two types of legislation that could affect the financial statement audit; explain why there is an impact.

Discussion Questions and Problems

4-13 ❸ Helmut & Co., a public accounting firm, was the new auditor of Mountain Ltd., a private company in the farm equipment and supply business.

In early February 2012, Helmut & Co. began the audit for the year ended December 31, 2011. The audit was to be run by Frost, a senior who had just joined Helmut from another firm. Frost was to be assisted by two juniors.

Sara Mountain, the president of Mountain Ltd., approached Frost and said that the Bank of Trail was prepared to increase its loan to Mountain upon receipt of the 2011 financial statements.

The juniors were assigned the accounts receivable and inventory sections, both of which were significant in relation to total assets, while Frost concentrated on the income statement and the remaining balance sheet accounts. The audit was finished quickly, and after a cursory review of the file and statements by Martin Helmut, senior partner of Helmut & Co., the signed auditor's report was appended to the financial statements, which were delivered to Mountain, which, in turn, sent them to the bank.

The bank increased the loan significantly, principally on the basis of the very successful year the company had enjoyed despite the fact that the farm supply business was depressed. Several months later, Mountain Ltd. made an assignment in bankruptcy. The trustee found that many accounts receivable were still outstanding from the balance sheet date and that inventory on hand included substantial quantities of obsolete and damaged goods that had been included in the year-end inventory at cost. In addition, the year-end inventory amount included inventory that had been sold prior to the year end. Bank of Trail sued Helmut & Co. for negligence.

REQUIRED

Discuss Helmut & Co.'s defence. Is lack of privity a defence in this case? Was Helmut & Co. negligent? Explain your answer fully.

4-14 ❷❸ Watts and Williams, a firm of PAs, audited the accounts of Sampson Skins, Inc., a corporation that imports and deals in fine furs. Upon completion of the audit, the auditors supplied Sampson Skins with 20 copies of the audited financial statements. The firm knew in a general way that Sampson Skins wanted that number of copies of the auditor's report in order to furnish them to banks and other potential lenders.

The balance sheet in question was misstated by approximately $800,000. Instead of having a $600,000 net worth, the corporation was insolvent. The management of Sampson Skins had doctored the books to avoid bankruptcy. The assets had been overstated by $500,000 of fictitious and non-existent accounts receivable and $300,000 of nonexistent skins listed as inventory when, in fact, Sampson Skins had only empty boxes. The audit failed to detect these fraudulent entries. Martinson, relying on the audited financial statements, loaned Sampson Skins $200,000. He is now seeking to recover his loss from Watts and Williams.

REQUIRED

State whether each of the following is true or false, and give your reasons:

a. If Martinson alleges and proves negligence on the part of Watts and Williams, he will be able to recover his loss.

b. If Martinson alleges and proves constructive fraud (i.e., gross negligence on the part of Watts and Williams), he will be able to recover his loss.

c. Martinson does not have a contract with Watts and Williams.

d. Unless actual fraud on the part of Watts and Williams can be shown, Martinson cannot recover his loan.

e. Martinson is a third-party beneficiary of the contract Watts and Williams made with Sampson Skins.

4-15 ❷ ❸ The public accounting firm of André, Mathieu & Paquette (AMP) was expanding very rapidly. Consequently, it hired several junior accountants, including Jim Small. The partners of the firm eventually became dissatisfied with Jim's production and warned him that they would be forced to terminate him unless his output increased significantly.

At that time, Jim was engaged in audits of several clients. He decided that to avoid being fired, he would reduce or omit entirely some of the standard auditing procedures listed in audit programs prepared by the partners. One of the public accounting firm's clients, Newell Corporation, was in serious financial difficulty and had adjusted several of the accounts being examined by Jim to appear financially sound. Jim prepared fictitious working papers in his home at night to support the supposed completion of auditing procedures assigned to him, although he, in fact, did not examine the adjusting entries. The public accounting firm rendered an unqualified opinion on Newell's financial statements, which were grossly misstated. Several creditors, relying on the audited financial statements, subsequently extended large sums of money to Newell Corporation.

REQUIRED

Would the public accounting firm be liable to the creditors who extended the money because of their reliance on the erroneous financial statements if Newell Corporation should fail to pay them? Explain.

(Adapted from AICPA)

4-16 ❷ Jan Sharpe recently joined the public accounting firm of Spark, Watts, and Wilcox. On her third audit for the firm, Jan examined the underlying documentation of 200 disbursements as a test of purchasing, receiving, vouchers payable, and cash disbursement procedures. In the process, she found 12 disbursements for the purchase of materials with no receiving reports in the documentation. She noted the exceptions in her working papers and called them to the attention of the audit supervisor. Relying on prior experience with the client, the audit supervisor disregarded Sharpe's comments, and nothing further was done about the exceptions.

Subsequently, it was learned that one of the client's purchasing agents and a member of its accounting department were engaged in a fraudulent scheme whereby they diverted the receipt of materials to a public warehouse while sending the invoices to the client. When the client discovered the fraud, the conspirators had obtained approximately $70,000, of which $50,000 was recovered after the completion of the audit.

REQUIRED

Discuss the legal implications and liabilities of Spark, Watts, and Wilcox as a result of the facts just described.

4-17 ❷ ❸ In confirming accounts receivable on December 31, 2009, the auditor found 15 discrepancies between the customer's records and the recorded amounts in the subsidiary ledger. A copy of all confirmations that had exceptions was turned over to the company controller to investigate the reason for the difference. He, in turn, had the bookkeeper perform the analysis. The bookkeeper analyzed each exception, determined its cause, and prepared an elaborate working paper explaining each difference. Most of the differences in the bookkeeper's report indicated that the errors were caused by timing differences in the client's and customer's records. The auditor reviewed the working paper and concluded that there were no material exceptions in accounts receivable.

Two years subsequent to the audit, it was determined that the bookkeeper had stolen thousands of dollars in the previous three years by taking cash and overstating accounts receivable. In a lawsuit by the client against the public accountant, an examination of the auditor's December 31, 2009, accounts receivable working papers, which were subpoenaed by the court, indicated that one of the explanations in the bookkeeper's analysis of the exceptions was fictitious. The analysis stated the error was caused by a sales allowance granted to the customer for defective merchandise the day before the end of the year. The difference was actually caused by the bookkeeper's theft.

REQUIRED

a. What are the legal issues involved in this situation? What should the auditor use as a defence if sued?

b. What was the public accountant's deficiency in conducting the audit of accounts receivable?

4-18 ③ Marino Rossi, a public accountant, audited the financial statements of Newfoundland Rugs Ltd. Cooke, the president of Newfoundland Rugs, told Marino that the company was planning a private placement of company bonds to raise $500,000 of needed capital. The audit proceeded smoothly, and the audited financial statements were issued.

Unknown to Marino, several significant receivables represented consignment accounts and not receivables, but Cooke had persuaded the companies involved to sign the receivable confirmations Marino had sent out, indicating they agreed that they owed the balances reported at the balance sheet date. In addition, a large number of rolls of low-quality interior carpeting had been classed as first quality. The effect of these two fraudulent acts resulted in a profit of $150,000 (instead of a loss of $480,000) and a positive net worth (instead of a negative net worth).

Newfoundland Rugs borrowed the money on the private placement and then went bankrupt several months later.

REQUIRED
a. Could the private-placement lenders succeed in a suit against Marino? If so, what must they prove?
b. What defence would Marino use?

Professional Judgment Problem

4-19 ③ Jackson is a sophisticated investor. As such, he was initially a member of a small group that was going to participate in a private placement of $1 million of common stock at Clarion Corporation. Numerous meetings were held between management and the investor group. Detailed financial and other information was supplied to the participants. Upon the eve of the completion of the placement, it was aborted when one major investor withdrew. Clarion then decided to offer $2.5 million of Clarion common stock to the public, registered with the OSC. Jackson subscribed to $300,000 of the Clarion public stock offering. Nine months later, Clarion's earnings dropped significantly, and as a result, the stock dropped 20 percent beneath the offering price.

Jackson sold his shares at a loss of $60,000 to Chang. Jackson seeks to hold liable all parties who participated in the public offering, including Clarion's accounting firm of Allen, Dunn, and Rose. Although the audit was performed in conformity with auditing standards, there were some relatively minor misstatements subsequently discovered in the financial statements that accompanied the share registration documents. It is believed by Clarion and Allen, Dunn, and Rose that the claim is without merit.

REQUIRED
a. What will be the likely basis of Jackson's suit?
b. What are the probable defences that might be asserted by Allen, Dunn, and Rose? Will the defences succeed?
c. If, subsequent to Chang's purchase of the shares at $240,000, a material misstatement was discovered in the financial statements, would your answers to questions (a) and (b) change? If Chang then lost $80,000 upon disposal of his shares, what suit would be available to Chang?

Case

4-20 ② ③ Aqua Inc. was a privately owned company that operated a marina business from two lakefront properties in northern Ontario. The company was started by two brothers. The company provided boat docking, sold gasoline and boating supplies, and was very successful.

Aqua's accountant, John Purd, is a PA who operated an accounting proprietorship in a nearby town. John offered only accounting, bookkeeping, and some investment counselling services. John's business has been successful, and he approached Aqua with a desire to purchase part of the Aqua business. John suggested that he would buy a one-third interest in the business by buying shares from the two brothers. The company could then issue a new class of non-voting shares, and they would all become very wealthy, almost immediately, just from the sale of the shares. John explained that this plan would make the existing shareholders wealthy without giving up control of the business.

John explained that Aqua would have to have audited financial statements to encourage potential investors and that he could save the company money by conducting the audit himself. John had to thoroughly analyze Aqua's books anyway as part of his due diligence in buying the shares for himself, so he would charge Aqua only a small fee for his audit services.

The brothers agreed with John's suggestion, and John bought a third of the company. John conducted the audit by himself over the next two months. As John had promised, he gave an unqualified audit opinion on the financial statements. As soon as the audit was completed, John found one of his own clients, New Investments Ltd., to buy the shares. After expenses, John and each of the two brothers received approximately $800,000. Unfortunately, Aqua's business failed in the following year, when it was discovered that Aqua did not own the lakefront properties, but had only leased them. When the leases expired, the landlord refused to enter a new lease and Aqua filed for bankruptcy. As the auditor, John was sued by Aqua's bank and by New Investments, both of whom claimed they had relied on the audited financial statements in their dealings with Aqua. John claimed that the two brothers had lied to him that the business owned the lakefront properties, so he was not responsible.

REQUIRED
a. As the auditor, identify to which parties John owed a duty of care. Explain your answer by statying why John would owe a duty of care to each party you mention.
b. Identify ethical violations by John.

Ongoing Small Business Case: CondoCleaners.com and the Law

4-21 ⑤ Jim is in the process of organizing the business details for his business, getting a website established, and preparing marketing documentation. To save money, he has decided to do the initial cleaning himself until he has enough business to hire staff. He did some of his training at home, substituting himself for the cleaning service that his parents used. Then, he asked friends of his family if he could clean their places. He investigated cleaning products and how they could be used and determined how quickly he could work.

REQUIRED

What legislation will Jim need to be concerned with when setting up his business? How will the legislation affect his website development process and the way that he runs his business?

The audit process

Part 2 presents the strategic audit process. An eight-phase audit process model starts with risk assessment (introduced in Chapter 3). To conduct risk assessment, you need to understand audit responsibilities and objectives (Chapter 5), a framework for audit planning and documentation (Chapter 6), the concepts of materiality and risk (Chapter 7), and the nature of audit evidence (Chapter 8). Key risks that the auditor assesses include those with respect to a control framework that includes fraud risks (Chapter 9).

It is essential to understand the material in these chapters because the information will be used extensively throughout the rest of the book. Chapter 10 summarizes and integrates audit planning and audit evidence mix. You will use these planning concepts and audit sampling (Chapter 11) throughout the rest of the book.

Many of the concepts throughout the remainder of the book are illustrated with examples based on Hillsburg Hardware Limited. The financial statements and other information from the company's annual report are included in the insert on pages 138–153.

5   Audit responsibilities and objectives

Now that you have an understanding of the environment within which an auditor functions, we can begin to look at the specifics of the financial statement audit. Management accountants will often be involved in preparing documents for the public accountant (PA) prior to the conduct of the financial statement audit, while internal or operational auditors may assist in working-paper preparation or actual audit testing. Specialists may assist in the audit in a variety of roles—so all types of accountants can benefit from knowing their responsibilities with respect to the audit.

LEARNING OBJECTIVES

1 Describe the objective of conducting an audit of financial statements. Explain the difference between management and auditor responsibilities with respect to the financial statements. Discuss how the financial statement auditor uses professional skepticism for the discovery and examination of potential material misstatements or illegal acts.

2 Examine the preplanning steps that the auditor completes before accepting the financial statement audit engagement. Document the importance of an engagement letter.

3 Describe the eight phases of a financial statement audit and provide an overview of the audit process.

4 Show how transactions underlying financial statements are divided into cycles. Describe the relationship between the cycle

approach and the financial statement audit. Explain relationships among the cycles and between the cycle approach and the control environment.

5 Describe management assertions about financial information. Relate management assertions to transaction-related audit objectives, balance-related audit objectives, and presentation and disclosure-related audit objectives.

STANDARDS REFERENCED IN THIS CHAPTER

CICA Standards

CAS 200 – Overall objectives of the independent auditor, and the conduct of an audit in accordance with Canadian auditing standards

CAS 210 – Agreeing the terms of audit engagements

CAS 240 – The auditor's responsibilities relating to fraud in an audit of financial statements

CAS 250 – Considerations of laws and regulations in an audit of financial statements

CAS 315 – Identifying and assessing the risks of material misstatement through understanding the entity and its environment

When is it "Worth Bothering"?

After the official interview about corporate governance and management policies, the external audit manager, Diane, invited Joe, the corporate controller, out to lunch. Joe started talking about some of his job frustrations.

"It's tough working in a unionized environment. We lose so much due to sick days! This makes it difficult to enforce the rules that we have for segregation of duties, particularly for refund policies. With over 60 different locations where payments or credit card payments are handled, there is a high risk of theft," said Joe.

Diane responded that this was also assessed as high risk by the organization's internal audit department, which had conducted audits of many of the locations in the past year.

"Yes, I know," responded Joe. "But when the internal auditor comes to me with these little thefts of $2,000 while I'm faced with losses in the hundreds of thousands of dollars due to absenteeism, I don't really feel like prosecuting these little thefts. My heart isn't in it, and I really feel like telling the internal audit to drop the whole thing." Diane, at a loss for words, kept eating and then asked, "When would it be worth bothering?"

IMPORTANCE TO AUDITORS

Diane's professional skepticism should now be kicked into high gear. Joe does not feel like prosecuting fraud, and it is likely that others in his accounting department know Joe's attitudes. What other areas does Joe "not care about"? Is there a problem with management apathy or employee apathy so that controls are no longer effective? After lunch, it would likely be a good idea for this client's audit team to have a meeting to update their risk assessments for this client, perhaps consulting with one of the firm's forensic audit specialists.

WHAT DO YOU THINK?

1. Do you think that this organization should prosecute all thefts or frauds? Why or why not?

2. What might Joe's attitude say about other problems or inefficiencies in the organization?

3. What questions might Diane ask of other financial managers or executives at the organization after her lunch with Joe?

FORENSIC auditors are accountants who have had training in fraud detection and gathering of documentation, often obtaining a professional designation such as Certified Fraud Examiner (CFE). Does this sound exciting to you? Although the possibility of tension and secrecy is present, sifting through information to support potential fraud requires meticulous attention to detail and skills in information technology. Think about what might make an audit engagement

Source: Based upon an interview with an accountant conducted by I. Splettstoesser-Hogeterp in June 2008.

continued >

continued

risky, and keep your ideas in mind as we go through the next few chapters. Risk assessment is a process that continues throughout the entire financial statement audit.

Before beginning the study of how to conduct an audit, it is necessary first to understand the objectives of an audit and what the auditor should do prior to accepting an audit engagement. Then, we look at the eight phases of the financial statement audit before considering how the financial statements are divided into cycles to facilitate the audit process, looking also at the relationships among the cycles. Management makes assertions (both implied and explicit) when preparing financial statements. The auditor uses these assertions to derive audit objectives. Knowledge of assertions and audit objectives help the auditor decide which audit tests to conduct (both to evaluate risks and as a risk response process), as discussed in the next chapter.

① The Objective of the Audit—Management and Auditor Responsibilities

Objective of Conducting an Audit of Financial Statements

CAS CAS 200 of the *CICA Handbook* explains that the purpose of the financial statement audit is to express an opinion on the financial statements. This opinion is an assessment of whether the financial statements are presented fairly, in the context of materiality (discussed in Chapter 7), in conformity with an applicable financial reporting framework as the criteria for the assessment.

Auditors accumulate evidence to enable them to reach conclusions about whether financial statements are fairly stated in all material respects and to issue an appropriate auditor's report.

When, on the basis of adequate evidence, the auditor concludes that the financial statements are unlikely to mislead a prudent user, the auditor gives an audit opinion on their fair presentation and associates his or her name with the statements. Although not an insurer or a guarantor of the fairness of the presentations in the statements, the auditor has considerable responsibility for notifying users as to whether or not the statements are properly stated. If the auditor believes the statements are not fairly presented or is unable to reach a conclusion because of insufficient evidence or prevailing conditions, the auditor has the responsibility to notify the users through the auditor's report.

Management's Responsibilities

The responsibility for adopting sound and appropriate financial reporting framework and corresponding accounting policies, maintaining adequate internal control, and making fair representations in the financial statements rests with management rather than with the auditor. The primary responsibility for internal control and the financial statements also rests with management, given that the entity's transactions and related assets, liabilities, and equity are within the direct knowledge and control of

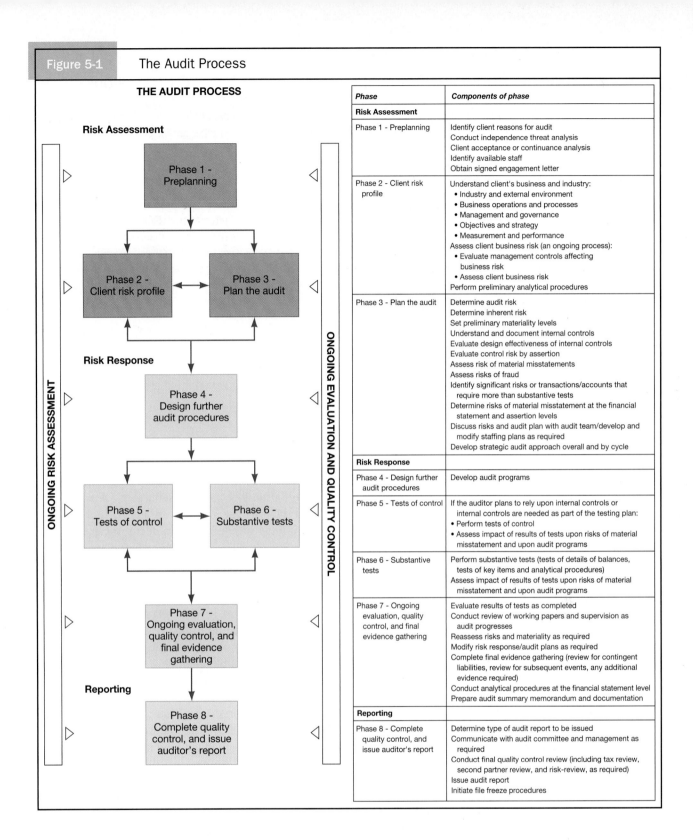

Figure 5-1 The Audit Process

THE AUDIT PROCESS

Phase	Components of phase
Risk Assessment	
Phase 1 - Preplanning	Identify client reasons for audit Conduct independence threat analysis Client acceptance or continuance analysis Identify available staff Obtain signed engagement letter
Phase 2 - Client risk profile	Understand client's business and industry: • Industry and external environment • Business operations and processes • Management and governance • Objectives and strategy • Measurement and performance Assess client business risk (an ongoing process): • Evaluate management controls affecting business risk • Assess client business risk Perform preliminary analytical procedures
Phase 3 - Plan the audit	Determine audit risk Determine inherent risk Set preliminary materiality levels Understand and document internal controls Evaluate design effectiveness of internal controls Evaluate control risk by assertion Assess risk of material misstatements Assess risks of fraud Identify significant risks or transactions/accounts that require more than substantive tests Determine risks of material misstatement at the financial statement and assertion levels Discuss risks and audit plan with audit team/develop and modify staffing plans as required Develop strategic audit approach overall and by cycle
Risk Response	
Phase 4 - Design further audit procedures	Develop audit programs
Phase 5 - Tests of control	If the auditor plans to rely upon internal controls or internal controls are needed as part of the testing plan: • Perform tests of control • Assess impact of results of tests upon risks of material misstatement and upon audit programs
Phase 6 - Substantive tests	Perform substantive tests (tests of details of balances, tests of key items and analytical procedures) Assess impact of results of tests upon risks of material misstatement and upon audit programs
Phase 7 - Ongoing evaluation, quality control, and final evidence gathering	Evaluate results of tests as completed Conduct review of working papers and supervision as audit progresses Reassess risks and materiality as required Modify risk response/audit plans as required Complete final evidence gathering (review for contingent liabilities, review for subsequent events, any additional evidence required) Conduct analytical procedures at the financial statement level Prepare audit summary memorandum and documentation
Reporting	
Phase 8 - Complete quality control, and issue auditor's report	Determine type of audit report to be issued Communicate with audit committee and management as required Conduct final quality control review (including tax review, second partner review, and risk-review, as required) Issue audit report Initiate file freeze procedures

management. In contrast, the auditor's knowledge of these matters and internal control is limited to that acquired during the audit.

The annual reports of public companies usually include a statement about management's responsibilities and relationship with the public accounting firm. The insert on page 146 presents a report of management's responsibility by the management of a large (fictionalized) retail hardware distributor, Hillsburg Hardware Limited. The first paragraph states management's responsibilities for the fair presentation of the financial statements, and the second paragraph discusses management's responsibilities with respect to internal control. The third paragraph comments on the audit committee, the board of directors, and their role with respect to the financial statements.

CAS

Management's responsibility for the fairness of the representations (assertions) in the financial statements carries with it the privilege of determining which disclosures it considers necessary. These responsibilities are described in detail in *CICA Handbook* CAS 210, Agreeing the terms of audit engagements. Although management has the responsibility for the preparation of the financial statements and the accompanying footnotes, it is acceptable for an auditor to draft this material for the client or to offer suggestions for clarification as long as management understands and approves to mitigate self-review threats as discussed in Chapter 3. In the event that management insists on financial statement disclosure that the auditor finds unacceptable, the auditor can either issue an adverse or qualified opinion or, as a last resort, withdraw from the engagement. Reporting is discussed further in Chapter 20.

The Canadian Securities Administrators (CSA), Canada's securities regulators, have filed rules that impose requirements similar to those of the U.S. Sarbanes-Oxley Act of 2002 for most companies listed on Canadian stock exchanges. The chief executive officer (CEO) and chief financial officer (CFO) of such companies must certify annual and interim financial statements as well as management discussion and analysis (MD&A) and certain information forms that are filed with the stock exchanges. Management is required to certify that it has reviewed the documents, that they do not contain any misrepresentations or material omissions and present fairly the financial condition of the company, and that disclosure controls and procedures or internal control over financial reporting have been designed, evaluated, and disclosed. If companies do not adhere to these rules, they will not be allowed to sell their shares or debt via Canadian stock exchanges.

Auditor's Responsibilities

CAS 200 (par. 15) explains the key role of professional skepticism in the audit of financial statements. We can break this paragraph into three chunks that need to be considered during each of the eight phases of the audit process used in this text:

- Be aware that there could be material misstatements in the financial statements (a state of mind)
- Use professional skepticism (be impartial and objective) when
- You are planning and conducting the audit (throughout the whole audit engagement).

The requirement for an attitude of skepticism does not mean that the auditor should plan and conduct the audit with an attitude of disbelief or of distrust in management. As shown in Table 5-1, management has many important responsibilities that, in most cases, management performs well and conscientiously. Rather, **professional skepticism** means that the auditor should not be blind to evidence that suggests that documents, books, or records have been altered or are incorrect. The auditor should not assume that management is dishonest, but the possibility of dishonesty must be considered. The concept of reasonable assurance indicates that the auditor is not an insurer or guarantor of the correctness of the financial statements.

There are several reasons the auditor is responsible for reasonable but not absolute assurance. First, most audit evidence results from testing a sample of a population, such as accounts receivable or inventory. Sampling includes some risk of not uncovering a material misstatement. The areas to be tested, the type, extent, and timing of those tests, and the evaluation of test results require significant judgment on the part of the auditor. Even with good faith and integrity, auditors can make mistakes and errors in judgment. Second, accounting representations from management contain complex estimates which involve uncertainty and can be affected by future events. Third, fraudulently prepared financial statements are often extremely difficult, if not impossible, for the auditor to detect, especially when there is collusion among management.

The *CICA Handbook*, in CAS 240, The auditor's responsibilities in relation to fraud in an audit of financial statements, details how the auditor should use professional skepticism when considering the risk of the financial statements containing material error or fraud and other irregularities. CAS 240 distinguishes between two types of misstatements: errors, and fraud and other irregularities. An **error** is an unintentional misstatement of the financial statements, whereas **fraud and other irregularities** are intentional. Two examples of errors are a mistake in extending price times quantity on a sales invoice and overlooking older raw materials in determining lower of cost or market for inventory.

For fraud and other irregularities, a distinction can be drawn between theft of assets, often called **defalcation** or **employee fraud**, and fraudulent financial reporting, often called **management fraud**. Employee fraud also includes corruption, such as managers or others taking bribes or having the corporation pay for personal expenses. One way of characterizing the difference is that employee fraud is perpetrated against the company, whereas management fraud is perpetrated for the apparent benefit of the company. An example of theft of assets is a clerk taking cash at the time a sale is made and not entering the sale in the cash register. An example of fraudulent financial reporting is the intentional overstatement of sales near the balance sheet date to increase reported earnings. In the case of the former, the company loses the money stolen; in the case of the latter, the company appears more profitable and, presumably, its stock rises in price.

It is usually more difficult for auditors to uncover fraud and other irregularities than errors. This is because of the intended deception associated with fraud and other irregularities. Table 5-2 shows how the auditor considers fraud risks throughout the audit. Not only the auditors but also professional accountants employed by management should be alert to errors, fraud, and other irregularities. We discuss fraud risk factors and the auditor's response further in subsequent chapters.

MANAGEMENT FRAUD Management fraud is inherently difficult to uncover because (1) it is possible for one or more members of management to override internal controls, and (2) there is typically an effort to conceal the misstatement. Management

Professional skepticism —the auditor should not be blind to evidence that suggests that documents, books, or records have been altered or are incorrect. The auditor should not assume that management is dishonest, but the possibility of dishonesty must be considered.

Error—an unintentional misstatement of the financial statements.

Fraud or other irregularity—an intentional misstatement of the financial statements.

Defalcation or employee fraud— theft of assets.

Management fraud—a fraud or other irregularity resulting in fraudulent financial reporting.

Table 5-1	Management and Auditor Responsibilities

Management's Responsibilities	Auditor's Responsibilities
• Adopt appropriate accounting framework.	• Use professional skepticism.
• Adopt sound accounting policies.	• Conduct the audit using a risk-based approach.
• Maintain adequate internal control.	• Conduct the audit to provide reasonable assurance about material misstatements.
• Make fair representations in the financial statements.	• Consider fraud and error.
• Acknowledge its responsibilities to the auditors.	• Issue a management letter if weaknesses are encountered that could result in a material error.
• Provide documentation and information for the audit process.	• Issue an appropriate report.

Table 5-2	Fraud Risk Assessment or Fraud Risk Response by Audit Phase

Audit Phase	Auditor Actions
Risk Assessment	
Phase 1: Preplanning	• Consider potential for management bias during client acceptance or continuance analysis. • Include management responsibility for fraud management in the engagement letter.
Phase 2: Client risk profile	• Note pressures and business practices that could be conducive to fraud. • When assessing corporate governance, evaluate effectiveness of risk management practices. • During preliminary analytical review, include analyses that could highlight unusual transactions or trends that could be indicative of fraud.
Phase 3: Audit plan	• Document internal controls that could prevent or detect fraud. • Evaluate design effectiveness of controls in mitigating fraud risks. • Assess risks of fraud overall and for each assertion where there is potential risk of material misstatement. • Discuss risks of fraud and effects on audit plan with audit team members.
Risk Response	
Phase 4: Design further audit procedures	• Include in audit programs audit techniques that address risks of fraud.
Phase 5: Tests of controls	• If reliance is intended upon controls that mitigate risks of fraud, perform tests of control, and assess the results of tests upon risks of fraud and upon audit programs.
Phase 6: Substantive tests	• Include in audit programs substantive tests that address significant risks of fraud.
Phase 7: Ongoing evaluation, quality control, and final evidence gathering	• Assess evidence from multiple sources for inconsistencies or unusual results that could be indicators of fraud. • Modify audit programs as required to investigate inconsistencies or unusual results.
Reporting	
Phase 8: Complete quality control, and issue auditor's report	• Communicate with audit committee and management results of audit and impact upon fraud risk management processes.

fraud may include omission of transactions or disclosures, fraudulent amounts, or misstatements of recorded amounts. Careful examination of journal entries and other adjustments made by management may help to identify risks of management fraud.

Audits cannot be expected to provide the same degree of assurance for the detection of material management fraud as is provided for an equally material error. Concealment by management makes fraud more difficult for auditors to find. The cost of providing equally high assurance for management fraud and for errors is economically impractical for both auditors and society.

Factors indicating potential management fraud The auditor is required to evaluate factors that may indicate an increased likelihood of management fraud. These are discussed further in Chapters 6 and 9.

EMPLOYEE FRAUD The profession has also been emphatic that the auditor has less responsibility for the discovery of employee fraud than for errors. If auditors were responsible for the discovery of all employee fraud, auditing tests would have to be greatly expanded because many types of employee fraud are extremely difficult, if not impossible, to detect. For example, if there is fraud involving the collusion of several employees that includes the falsification of documents or computer records, it is unlikely that such a fraud would be uncovered in a normal audit.

As the auditor assesses the likelihood of material management fraud, he or she should also evaluate the likelihood of material employee fraud. This is normally done initially as a part of understanding the entity's internal control and assessing control risk and fraud risk. Audit evidence should be expanded when the auditor finds an absence of adequate controls or failure to follow prescribed procedures, if he or she believes material employee fraud could exist.

COMPUTER FRAUD Computer fraud consists of fraud conducted with the assistance of computer software or hardware. This could include deliberately programming functions into a computer program so that it incorrectly calculates interest, placing unauthorized employees ("horses") on a computerized payroll system, falsifying an electronic mail message, obtaining "free" long-distance telephone services, or creating fraudulent electronic cash transactions.

As with other forms of error or fraud, the auditor cannot be expected to always detect immaterial fraud but should investigate unusual relationships or patterns. Good internal controls spanning the development, acquisition, and use of automated systems help to prevent computer fraud.

ILLEGAL ACTS CAS 250, Consideration of laws and regulations in an audit of financial statements, refers to non-compliance with legislation (par. 11) as occurring when the organization does not comply with laws and regulations that pertain to it. This can happen in error or deliberately and would result in an **illegal act**. Two examples of illegal acts are a violation of income tax laws and a violation of an environmental protection law. It is an auditor's responsibility to comply with generally accepted auditing standards (GAAS) and, as a result, the auditor may not detect non-compliance or become aware that an illegal act has occurred if management has not disclosed it to the auditor.

Illegal act—violation of or non-compliance with laws or government regulations.

The performance of an illegal act by management or an employee of a company may affect the company (and the financial statements) in a variety of ways. For example, the payment of a bribe by a subsidiary in a foreign country could lead to expulsion of the company and/or expropriation of the company's assets; both the balance sheet and income statement could be affected. Failing to properly dispose of untreated waste products could make the company liable for fines and penalties; the income statement could be affected. Even if the magnitude of the illegal act itself is not material, the consequences could be. The auditor must be interested in illegal acts so that their potential impact may be properly evaluated.

Direct-effect illegal act—illegal act whose result affects general ledger accounts and financial statement amounts

Indirect-effect illegal act—illegal act whose result does not affect general ledger accounts but may require disclosure in the notes to the financial statements

Preplanning the audit—actions taken prior to commencing detailed client risk analysis, which involve the following steps: identify client reasons for audit, conduct independence threat analysis, client acceptance or continuance analysis, identify available staff, and obtain signed engagement letter.

Risk Assessment

Phase 1 - Preplanning

Phase 2 - Client risk profile

Phase 3 - Plan the audit

Risk Response

Phase 4 - Design further audit procedures

Phase 5 - Tests of control

Phase 6 - Substantive tests

Phase 7 - Ongoing evaluation, quality control, and final evidence gathering

Reporting

Phase 8 - Complete quality control, and issue auditor's report

When an illegal act is discovered, the auditor must consider whether such an act is a reflection of the company's corporate culture. Are such acts condoned or encouraged by management? If management does not promote ethical behaviour, the auditor should question management's good faith and consider whether continued association with the client is desirable.

CAS 250 (par. 16) requires that the auditor requests written representation from management (or those charged with governance of the organization) with respect to non-compliance with laws or regulations or possible acts of non-compliance that would affect the financial statements or their notes. The section goes on to say that, other than inquiry of management, the auditor should not search for such illegal acts unless there is reason to believe they may exist.

Direct-effect illegal acts Certain violations of laws and regulations have a direct financial effect on specific account balances in the financial statements. For example, a violation of income tax laws directly affects income tax expense and income taxes payable. The auditor's responsibilities under CAS 250 for these **direct-effect illegal acts** are the same as for errors or fraud and other irregularities. As an example, on each audit, the auditor will evaluate whether there is evidence available to indicate material violations of federal or provincial tax laws. This might be done by discussions with client personnel and examination of reports issued by the Canada Revenue Agency after it has completed an examination of the client's tax return.

Indirect-effect illegal acts Most illegal acts affect the financial statements only indirectly. For example, if a company violates environmental protection laws, there is an effect on the financial statements only if there is a fine or sanction. Potential material fines and sanctions indirectly affect financial statements by creating the need to disclose a contingent liability for the potential amount that might ultimately be paid. This is called an **indirect-effect illegal act**. Other examples of illegal acts that are likely to have only an indirect effect are violations of insider securities trading regulations, employment equity laws, and employee safety requirements.

Auditing standards clearly state that the auditor provides no assurance that indirect-effect illegal acts will be detected. Auditors lack legal expertise, and the frequently indirect relationship between illegal acts and the financial statements makes it impractical for auditors to assume responsibility for discovering those illegal acts. One of the first things that an auditor would do upon discovering an illegal act would be to consult a lawyer.

Table 5-3 shows that there are three levels of responsibility that the auditor has for finding and reporting illegal acts. Depending upon the severity of the illegal act, the auditor must work with management and outside expertise to determine the audit response, which may include resignation from the engagement if the auditor can no longer trust executive management.

Before Accepting an Engagement, Preplanning Takes Place

Preplan the Audit

Preplanning the audit, which takes place prior to acceptance and early in the engagement, involves the following steps: identify the client's reasons for the audit, conduct an independence threat analysis, decide whether to accept or continue doing the audit for the client, select staff for the engagement, and obtain a signed engagement letter.

IDENTIFY CLIENT REASONS FOR AUDIT Two major factors affecting the appropriate evidence to accumulate are the likely financial statement users and their intended uses of the financial statements. It will be shown in Chapter 7 that the auditor is likely to

Audit situation (level of responsibility)	Example	Auditor action
No reason to believe *illegal acts exist*	Auditor has exercised professional skepticism and conducted the audit to search for errors or fraud. None were found. Legal letters indicate no lawsuits in progress, and there are indicators of management attitudes that promote honesty and disclosure throughout the organization.	• Continue to exercise professional skepticism throughout the completion of the engagement.
There is reason to believe *illegal acts may exist*	Minutes of Board of Directors meetings indicate an investigation by the Environmental Protection Agency. The auditor has observed, during the audit of payments, that there are unusually large payments going to foreign consultants that are poorly documented. Management is evasive when questioned about these payments.	• Consult legal advice or another specialist who is knowledgeable about the potential illegal act. • Inquire of management and the audit committee about these events at a level above those likely to be involved in the potential illegal act. • Consider accumulating additional evidence to determine if there actually is an illegal act. • Modify audit procedures throughout the audit to consider increased risk of fraud or illegal acts in other areas of the organization.
*It is **known** that there is an illegal act*	The auditor discovered a large payment made to the purchasing agent of a large customer of the client.	• Consult legal advice or another specialist who is knowledgeable about the potential illegal act. • Consider the effects on the financial statements, including disclosures. • Inform the audit committee and an appropriate level of management. • Modify audit procedures throughout the audit to consider increased risk of fraud or illegal acts in other areas of the organization. • Modify the independent auditor's report if financial statement treatment is inadequate. • Consider resigning from the engagement if senior management integrity is in question.

Table 5-3   Auditor Levels of Responsibility for Finding and Reporting Illegal Acts

accumulate more evidence when the financial statements are to be used extensively. This is the case for publicly held companies (such as Hillsburg), those with extensive indebtedness, and companies that are to be sold in the near future.

The most likely uses of the financial statements can be determined from previous experience in the engagement and discussion with management. Throughout the engagement, the auditor may obtain additional information as to why the client is having an audit and the likely uses of the financial statements.

CONDUCT INDEPENDENCE THREAT ANALYSIS The rules of conduct state that an auditor may conduct an audit only if independent. The five threats to independence (i.e., self-interest, self-review, advocacy, familiarity, and intimidation, see Chapter 3) must be explicitly assessed, and any potential threats described. The auditor then determines whether it is possible to implement safeguards to mitigate the threat (e.g., changing the partner in charge of an engagement to deal with the familiarity threat). If such safeguards can be put into place, or there are no threats, the engagement can be accepted. The auditor would communicate to the audit committee any such threats and how they had been dealt with.

If there are threats without compensating safeguards available, or the safeguards do not adequately mitigate the threat, the engagement must be declined.

CLIENT ACCEPTANCE OR CONTINUANCE A public accounting firm must use care in deciding which clients are acceptable. The firm's legal and professional responsibilities are such that clients who lack integrity or argue constantly about the proper conduct of the audit and fees can cause more problems than they are worth. Some public accounting firms may refuse clients in what they perceive to be high-risk industries, such as high technology, health, and casualty insurance, and may even discontinue auditing existing clients in such industries.

New client investigation Before accepting a new client, most public accounting firms investigate the company to determine its acceptability. To the extent possible, the prospective client's standing in the business community, financial stability, and relations with its previous public accounting firm should be evaluated. For example, many public accounting firms use considerable caution in accepting new clients from newly formed, rapidly growing businesses. Many of these businesses fail financially and expose the public accounting firm to significant potential liability.

For prospective clients that have previously been audited by another public accounting firm, the new (successor) PA (Public Accountant) is required to communicate with the predecessor auditor. The purpose of the requirement is to help the successor auditor evaluate whether to accept the engagement. The communication may, for example, inform the successor auditor that the client lacks integrity or that there have been disputes over accounting principles, audit procedures, or fees.

The burden of initiating the communication rests with the successor auditor. Permission must be obtained from the client before the communication can be made because of the confidentiality requirement in the rules of conduct of the professional accounting bodies. The predecessor auditor is required to respond to the request for information. In the event there are legal problems or disputes between the client and the predecessor, the latter's response can be limited to stating that no information will be provided. The successor should seriously consider the desirability of accepting a prospective engagement, without considerable investigation, if a client will not permit the communication or the predecessor will not provide a comprehensive response.

Even when a prospective client has been audited by another public accounting firm, other investigations are needed. Sources of information include local lawyers, other public accountants, banks, and other businesses.

Many practitioners take advantage of the internet as a search tool to learn more about the potential new client and its key operations by studying available client websites and by using search engines for other sites that discuss the potential client. In addition, they use database search tools or customized search engines to examine financial data or recent publications about the client. This information is useful in the client acceptance decision and throughout the audit if the client is accepted.

Continuing clients Considering whether or not to continue doing the audit of an existing client is as important a decision as deciding whether or not to accept a new client. For that reason, public accounting firms evaluate existing clients annually to determine whether there are reasons for not continuing to do the audit. Previous conflicts over such things as the appropriate scope of the audit, the type of opinion to issue, or fees may cause the auditor to discontinue association. The auditor may also determine that the client lacks basic integrity and therefore should no longer be a client. If there is a lawsuit against a public accounting firm by a client or a suit against the client by the public accounting firm, the firm should not do the audit because its independence could be questioned.

Even if none of the previously discussed conditions exist, the public accounting firm may decide not to continue doing audits for a client because of excessive risk. For example, a public accounting firm might decide that there is considerable risk of a regulatory conflict between a governmental agency and a client, which could result in financial failure of the client and, ultimately, lawsuits against the public accounting firm. Even if the engagement is profitable, the risk may exceed the immediate benefits of doing the audit.

As an example, consider Hillsburg Hardware Limited, audited by Berger, Kao, Kadous & Co., LLP (BKK), a firm in Halifax, Nova Scotia. BKK is part of a national association of firms, so it has access to specialists and national standards personnel. Hillsburg has been a client of BKK since the company was formed in 1980. Hillsburg management has generally been easy to work with, although at times there have been minor disagreements. Management turnover is low, and profits have been consistent, although recent earnings have declined in the wake of the current recession. BKK conducted a search on the internet and found that Hillsburg received positive press, primarily for local charitable work. Discussions with management indicated that the only major issue coming up that would affect the audit would be continuing enhancements to information systems.

Investigation of new clients and re-evaluation of existing ones are essential parts of deciding risk to the auditor. Assume that a potential client is in a reasonably risky industry and has management that has a reputation of integrity but is also known to take aggressive financial risks. The public accounting firm may choose not to accept the engagement. If the public accounting firm concludes that the client is still acceptable, the fee proposed to the client is likely to be affected. Audits with higher risks will normally result in higher audit costs, which should be reflected in higher audit fees.

IDENTIFY STAFF AVAILABLE FOR THE ENGAGEMENT Assigning the appropriate staff to the engagement is important to meet quality control standards in GAAS and to promote audit efficiency. If the auditor does not have the expertise or available staff to audit the client, then the engagement should be declined.

Staff must be assigned with competence and quality in mind. On larger engagements, there are likely to be one or more partners and staff at several experience levels doing the audit. Specialists in such technical areas as statistical sampling, provision of industry expertise, or information systems auditing may also be assigned. On smaller audits, there may be only one or two staff members.

A major consideration affecting staffing is the need for continuity from year to year. An inexperienced staff assistant is likely to become the most experienced non-partner on the engagement within a few years. Continuity helps the public accounting firm maintain familiarity with technical requirements and close interpersonal relations with the client's personnel. The extent of assistance provided by the client, including work done by the internal audit department, also affects staffing. Throughout the planning and conduct of the audit, the entire team meets to share information and to ensure awareness of risks.

OBTAIN A SIGNED ENGAGEMENT LETTER A clear understanding of the terms of the engagement should exist between the client and the public accounting firm. The terms should be in writing (ISA 210) to minimize misunderstandings. Management's responsibilities are clarified and clearly agreed upon prior to the auditor being able to accept the engagement. This is done using a signed engagement letter.

Signed engagement letter–a written agreement between the public accounting firm and the client as to the terms of the engagement for the conduct of the audit and related services.

The **engagement letter** is a written agreement between the public accounting firm and the client for the conduct of the audit and related services. It should specify whether the auditor will perform an audit, a review, or a compilation, plus any other services such as tax returns or management services. It should also state any restrictions to be imposed on the auditor's work, deadlines for completing the audit, assistance to be provided by the client's personnel in obtaining records and documents, and schedules to be prepared for the auditor. If the client has an internal audit department, it will also specify the role of that department during the audit. It often includes an agreement on fees. The engagement letter is also a means of informing the client that the auditor is not responsible for the discovery of all or any acts of fraud.

The engagement letter does not affect the public accounting firm's responsibility to external users of audited financial statements, but it can affect legal responsibilities to the client. For example, if the client sued the public accounting firm for failing to find a material misstatement, one defence a public accounting firm could use would be a signed engagement letter stating that a review, rather than an audit, was agreed upon.

Engagement letter information is important in planning the audit principally because it affects the timing of the tests and the total amount of time the audit and other services will take. If the deadline for submitting the audit report is soon after the balance sheet date, a significant portion of the audit must be done before the end of the year. When the auditor is preparing tax returns and a management letter, or if client assistance is not available, arrangements must be made to extend the amount of time for the engagement. Client-imposed restrictions on the audit could affect the procedures performed, auditor independence, and possibly even the type of audit opinion issued. An example of an engagement letter for the audit of Hillsburg Hardware Limited is given in Figure 5-2. The financial statements for Hillsburg Hardware Limited are included on pages 138–153.

concept check

C5-4 Why does the auditor assess clients for acceptability prior to conducting the audit engagement?

C5-5 What are some of the typical reasons that a client wants a financial statement audit?

C5-6 Describe the sections in an engagement letter and explain the relevance of each section.

③ Audit Phases

The financial statement audit is a strategic process—this means that forward planning is conducted with regular ongoing evaluation of work to date so that adjustments can be made to the process as needed in response to risks and findings to date. The goal is to gather sufficient, high-quality evidence to provide an audit opinion. As we discuss the eight phases (shown and described in Figure 5-1 on page 103), keep in mind that these are part of one audit and that in practice the auditor will go back and forth between phases as risks and findings are documented and evaluated.

Think about a recent decision that you made that involved multiple steps, such as deciding which major to select in school. You would have looked at your own preferences, talked to people, gathered information from the internet, and considered the impact on your future job. Some data are easy to gather, some are quantitative (e.g., which courses you would have to take), and some are qualitative (which courses do you like or dislike, and how strongly). Perhaps when you found out that you would have a low income in one discipline, you changed your strategy and looked at another discipline. Perhaps this even caused you to switch gears totally and start looking at another university.

Figure 5-2   Engagement Letter

June 14, 2010

Boritz, Kao, Kadous & Co., LLP
Halifax, Nova Scotia
B3M 3JP

Mr. Rick Chulick, President
Hillsburg Hardware Limited
2146 Willow Street
Halifax, Nova Scotia
B3H 3F9

Dear Mr. Chulick:

The purpose of this letter is to outline the terms of our engagement to audit the financial statements of Hillsburg Hardware Limited for the year ending December 31, 2010.

Objective, scope, and limitations

Our statutory function as auditor of Hillsburg Hardware Limited is to report to the shareholders by expressing an opinion on Hillsburg Hardware Limited's financial statements. We will conduct our audit in accordance with Canadian generally accepted auditing standards and will issue an audit report.

It is important to recognize that there are limitations inherent in the auditing process. Since audits are based on the concept of selective testing of the data underlying the financial statements, they are subject to the limitation that material misstatements, if they exist, may not be detected. Because of the nature of fraud, including attempts at concealment through collusion and forgery, an audit designed and executed in accordance with Canadian generally accepted auditing standards may not detect a material fraud. Further, while effective internal control reduces the likelihood that misstatements will occur and remain undetected, it does not eliminate the possibility. For these reasons, we cannot guarantee that misstatements or other illegal acts, if present, will be detected.

Our responsibilities

We will be responsible for performing the audit in accordance with Canadian generally accepted auditing standards. These standards require that we plan and perform the audit to obtain reasonable assurance about whether the financial statements present fairly, in all material respects, the financial position results of operations, and cash flows in accordance with International Financial Reporting Standards. Accordingly, we will design our audit to provide reasonable, but not absolute, assurance of detecting fraud, errors, and other irregularities that have a material effect on the financial statements taken as a whole, including illegal acts the consequences of which have a material effect on the financial statements.

One of the underlying principles of the profession is a duty of confidentiality with respect to client affairs. Accordingly, except for information that is in or enters the public domain, we will not provide any third party with information related to Hillsburg Hardware Limited without Hillsburg Hardware Limited's permission, unless required to do so by legal authority, by the rules of professional conduct/code of ethics, or to satisfy the requirements of the Canadian Public Accountability Board.

We will communicate in writing to the Audit Committee the relationships between us and Hillsburg Hardware Limited that, in our professional judgment, may reasonably be thought to bear on our independence. Further, we will confirm our independence with respect to Hillsburg Hardware Limited.

The objective of our audit is to obtain reasonable assurance that the financial statements are free of material misstatement. However, if we identify any of the following matters, they will be communicated to the appropriate level of management, including the Audit Committee:

(a) misstatements, other than trivial errors;
(b) fraud;
(c) misstatements that may cause future financial statements to be materially misstated;
(d) illegal or possibly illegal acts, other than those considered inconsequential;
(e) significant weakness in internal control; and
(f) certain related-party transactions.

The matters communicated will be those that we identify during the course of our audit. Audits do not usually identify all matters that may be of interest to management in discharging its responsibilities. The type and significance of the matter to be communicated will determine the level of management to which the communication is directed.

We will consider Hillsburg Hardware Limited's internal control over financial reporting solely for the purpose of determining the nature, timing, and extent of auditing procedures necessary for expressing our opinion on the financial statements. This consideration will not be sufficient for us to render an opinion on the effectiveness of internal control over financial reporting.

continued >

| Figure 5-2 | Engagement Letter *(Continued)* |

Management's responsibilities

Management is responsible for:

(a) The fair presentation of Hillsburg Hardware Limited's financial statements in accordance with generally accepted accounting standards;

Completeness of information:

(b) providing us with and making available complete financial records and related data and copies of all minutes of meetings of shareholders, directors, and committees of directors;

(c) providing us with information relating to any known or probable instances of non-compliance with legislative or regulatory requirements, including financial reporting requirements;

(d) providing us with information relating to any illegal or possibly illegal acts, and all facts related thereto;

(e) providing us with information regarding all related parties and related-party transactions;

Fraud and error:

(f) the design and implementation of internal controls to prevent and detect fraud and error;

(g) an assessment of the risk that the financial statements may be materially misstated as a result of fraud;

(h) providing us with information relating to fraud or suspected fraud affecting the entity involving
  (i) management, (ii) employees who have significant roles in internal control, or (iii) others, where the fraud could have a material effect on the financial statements;

(i) providing us with information relating to any allegations of fraud or suspected fraud affecting the entity's financial statements communicated by employees, former employees, analysts, regulators, or others;

(j) communicating its belief that the effects of any uncorrected financial statement misstatements aggregated during the audit are immaterial, both individually and in the aggregate, to the financial statements taken as a whole;

Recognition, measurement, and disclosure:

(k) providing us with an assessment of the reasonableness of significant assumptions underlying fair value measurements and disclosures in the financial statements;

(l) providing us with any plans or intentions that may affect the carrying value or classification of assets or liabilities;

(m) providing us with the measurement and disclosure of transactions with related parties;

(n) providing us with an assessment of significant estimates and all known areas of measurement uncertainty;

(o) providing us with claims and possible claims, whether or not they have been discussed with Hillsburg Hardware Limited legal counsel;

(p) providing us with information relating to other liabilities and gain or loss contingencies, including those associated with guarantees, whether written or oral, under which Hillsburg Hardware Limited is contingently liable;

(q) providing us with information on whether or not Hillsburg Hardware Limited has satisfactory title to assets, liens or encumbrances on assets, and assets pledged as collateral;

(r) providing us with information relating to compliance with aspects of contractual agreements that may affect the financial statements;

(s) providing us with information concerning subsequent events; and

(t) providing us with written confirmation of significant representations provided to us during the engagement on matters that are
  (i) directly related to items that are material, either individually or in the aggregate, to the financial statements;
  (ii) not directly related to items that are material to the financial statements but are significant, either individually or in the aggregate, to the engagement; and
  (iii) relevant to your judgments or estimates that are material, either individually or in the aggregate, to the financial statements.

Coordination of the Audit

Assistance is to be supplied by your personnel, including preparation of schedules and analysis of accounts, as described in a separate attachment.

Fees

Our fees are based on the amount of time required at various levels of responsibility, plus out-of-pocket expenses (i.e., travel, printing, telephone, and communications) payable upon presentation of billing. We will notify you immediately of any circumstances we encounter that could significantly affect our estimate of total fees.

continued >

We appreciate the opportunity to be of service to Hillsburg Hardware Limited. The above terms of our engagement shall remain operative until amended, terminated, or superseded in writing.

If you have any questions about the contents of this letter, please raise them. If the services as outlined are in accordance with your requirements and if the above terms are acceptable, please sign the copy of this letter in the space provided and return it to us.

Yours very truly,

J.E. Boritz
Boritz, Kao, Kadous & Co., LLP
Accepted by:
Title: President
Date: June 14, 2010

A strategic audit process is similar. You will see that, as we describe decisions to be made during the audit (for example, whether to rely upon internal controls), the answer can have a major impact upon the actions taken during the audit.

The eight phases of the audit are broken down into three sections: Risk Assessment, Risk Response, and Reporting. In practice, information moves back and forth among these sections and phases, as you will see when we discuss examples. In the **risk assessment** section, the auditor identifies what could go wrong with the financial statements and the approaches for dealing with the risks. Substantial information must be collected and analyzed about the industry, business environment, and client to identify and assess these risks. Then, the auditor moves to **risk response**, where specific audit programs and processes are designed and tests conducted to obtain reasonable assurance with respect to the financial statements in the context of assessed risks. Finally, in the **reporting** section, the auditor decides upon the report to be issued, issues the report, and communicates with management and the audit committee.

For any given audit, there are many ways an auditor can accumulate evidence to meet the overall audit objectives. Two overriding considerations affect the approach the auditor selects: (1) sufficient, high-quality audit evidence must be accumulated to meet the auditor's professional responsibility, and (2) the cost of accumulating the evidence should be balanced against the quality of the evidence.

Risk assessment—the auditor identifies what could go wrong with the financial statements and the approaches for dealing with the risks.

Risk response—specific audit programs and processes are designed and tests conducted to obtain reasonable assurance with respect to the financial statements in the context of assessed risks.

Reporting—the auditor decides upon the type of independent auditor's report to be issued, issues the report, and communicates with management and the audit committee.

Risk Assessment

In these phases the auditor finds out about the client and the client's industry and business environment. A phrase that describes risks is "what could go wrong"? For example, you would likely not replace your car unless it were old and needed repairs, and you were going on a long trip and wanted to avoid breakdowns. Similarly, in the audit engagement, the auditor needs to know "what could go wrong" in the financial statements, the client industry, or business, before tailoring the risk response to those assessed risks. The three phases of risk assessment are preplanning (to decide whether the audit should proceed), client risk assessment (to identify and document preliminary client business risks), and audit planning (to organize documentation and risks into an audit framework and develop a tailored strategic audit approach). Chapters 6 through 10 cover risk assessment and the audit planning process.

PHASE 1—PREPLANNING As explained in the previous section, the auditor first decides whether to accept the new client or continue with the existing client. This is a mutual decision, often following a lengthy proposal and discussion phase for new clients. Only if the decision is to proceed with the engagement does the auditor provide an engagement letter and continue on to the remaining phases of the audit.

PHASE 2—CLIENT RISK PROFILE Unique aspects of different businesses are reflected in the financial statements. An audit of a life insurance company could not be performed with due care without an understanding of the unique characteristics of that industry. Imagine attempting to audit a client in the bridge construction industry without understanding the construction business and the percentage-of-completion method of accounting. Neither audit could be effectively conducted without an awareness of the business environments and regulatory environments within which these businesses function. Industries operate within the broader context of the local, national, and international economy and are subject to changes in accounting standards, foreign-exchange rates, interest rates, overall demand, or raw material prices. Once the auditor understands the industry, then the auditor can more effectively understand and assess the client's for the purposes of developing a client risk profile, which is discussed further in Chapter 6. The knowledge of industry and business helps the auditor develop expectations of client results in the context of the overall business environment to properly conduct preliminary **analytical procedures** that help assess the ability of the client to continue as a going concern and to focus further audit work. Although we have set client risk profile as a separate phase, note that there is an ongoing risk assessment process (left sidebar of Figure 5-1) that includes continual re-evaluation of client business risk as well as of the risks described in Phase 3.

> **Analytical procedures**—use of comparisons and relationships to determine whether account balances or other data appear reasonable.

PHASE 3—PLAN THE AUDIT Developing the client risk profile (Phase 2) and planning the audit are two sets of activities that are closely linked and completed in parallel. As information about the client is gathered, it is structured and analyzed as part of an audit planning model, such as the audit risk model (explained further in Chapter 7).

Based upon the purpose of the audit, the projected users, and the business risk of the client (the risk that the client will fail to achieve its objectives, discussed further in Chapters 6 and 7), the auditor will determine audit risk, representing the willingness to accept potential material error in the financial statements. The knowledge of the business, industry, and environment will enable the auditor to assess the likelihood of material misstatement in the financial statements as a whole or by assertion before the consideration of internal controls (known as inherent risk). Using the financial results of the client, the auditor will set preliminary materiality levels.

After the auditor gains an understanding of internal control, he is in a position to evaluate how effective controls should be in preventing and detecting errors or fraud and other irregularities (measured as control risk). Control risk includes specifically considering the risks of fraud. This evaluation involves identifying specific controls that reduce the likelihood that errors or fraud and other irregularities will occur and not be detected and corrected on a timely basis. Supervisory, managing, or monitoring controls are specifically identified as having important effects. This process is referred to as evaluating control risk, and it is completed by assertion, for each material account or class of transactions.

Using the assessed inherent risks and assessed control risks, the auditor will then determine the risks of material misstatement at the financial statement and assertion levels, which helps identify the depth of audit work required for the individual accounts and transaction streams. On an ongoing basis, these risks and the audit plan are discussed with the audit team, and audit plans are modified as required. The nature of these risks and their relationships within the audit risk model are explained further in Chapter 7.

The outcome of the planning process is a strategic audit approach for the audit overall and for the components of the audit (accounts with potential for material error, or material transaction streams). This strategic process must be approved by audit team management before it is implemented. The ongoing process of evaluation and quality control (right sidebar of Figure 5-1) ensures that a high quality audit is conducted for all phases.

Risk Response

The concept of risk response refers to the fact that the audit is designed to respond to identified risks with audit programs and tests addressing those risks. The four risk response phases are the design of further audit procedures (describing audit tests to be conducted); tests of control (in response to control risk and accounts that require more than substantive tests); substantive tests; and ongoing evaluation, quality control, and final evidence gathering. Chapters 10 through 19 address the risk response process.

PHASE 4—DESIGN FURTHER AUDIT PROCEDURES The audit procedures (or audit tests) are prepared to respond to the risks of material misstatement identified in the risk assessment phases of the audit. The auditor considers the balance of different types of tests, the type of sampling to be used to actually conduct the tests, and adding unpredictability (or randomness) to the testing process. The tests are conducted in relationship to the materiality levels determined, dealing with specific risks such as the potential for management bias or override, fraud risks, or complex transactions identified.

PHASE 5—TESTS OF CONTROL Where the auditor has decided to rely upon internal controls, the auditor must test the effectiveness of the controls or rely upon tests of controls conducted in one of the prior two years if the control has characteristics that permit extended reliance. (This concept is discussed further in Chapter 9—controls do not have to be tested every year.) For example, assume that the client's order entry software requires that all amounts over $10,000 must be entered twice. This control is directly related to the accuracy of sales. One possible test of the effectiveness of this control is for the auditor to enter a transaction over $10,000 and observe whether the system requests a second entry. **Tests of controls** are audit procedures that test the effectiveness of control policies and procedures in support of a reduced assessed control risk.

> **Tests of controls**—audit procedures to test the effectiveness of control policies and procedures in support of a reduced assessed control risk.

As the tests are completed, the results are evaluated to determine if there should be any changes in assessed risks or in the design of the audit procedures.

PHASE 6—SUBSTANTIVE TESTS There are three general categories of substantive procedures: analytical procedures, tests of details of balances, and tests of key items. Analytical procedures are those that assess the overall reasonableness of transactions and balances using comparisons and relationships. An example of an analytical procedure that would provide some assurance for the accuracy of both sales transactions and accounts receivable is to have the auditor run an exception report (using audit software) of sales transactions for unusually large amounts and compare total monthly sales to prior years. If a company is consistently using incorrect sales prices, significant differences are likely.

Tests of details of balances are specific procedures intended to test for monetary misstatements in the balances in the financial statements. An example related to the accuracy of accounts receivable is direct written communication with the client's customers. Tests of ending balances are essential to the conduct of the audit because most of the evidence is obtained from a source independent of the client and therefore considered to be of high quality.

> **Tests of details of balances**—an auditor's tests for monetary errors or fraud and other irregularities in the details of balance sheet and income statement accounts.

Tests of key items focus on specific transactions that could be at risk of matrial error. For example, the purchase of shares in a subsidiary company may be at risk of incorrect valuation. Similarly, the auditor may choose to examine the activity between the company and a related party to ensure that the amounts have been recorded correctly.

> **Tests of key items**—audit tests that focus on specific transactions that could be at risk of material error.

There is a close relationship among the general review of the client's circumstances, results of understanding internal control and assessing control risk, analytical procedures, and the substantive tests of the financial statement account balances. If the auditor has obtained a reasonable level of assurance for any given audit objective by performing tests of controls and analytical procedures, the tests of details for that objective can be significantly reduced. In most instances, however, some tests of details of significant financial statement account balances are necessary.

PHASE 7—ONGOING EVALUATION, QUALITY CONTROL, AND FINAL EVIDENCE GATHERING
This phase links to all of the other phases of the audit engagement. As the results of the tests and other information gathered throughout the audit are compiled, audit management (the supervisor, manager, and partner) works with the audit team to assess the impact upon assessed risks and procedures designed as a response. This means that supervision and quality control are ongoing, as working papers are regularly reviewed and unusual items followed up. It may also result in a revision to materiality (if there are large unrecorded errors) or the audit programs (if risk revision occurs as a result of audit testing).

After the auditor has completed all the procedures for each audit objective and for each financial statement account, it is necessary to combine the information obtained into an audit summary memorandum to reach an overall conclusion as to whether the financial statements are fairly presented. This is a highly subjective process that relies heavily on the auditor's professional judgment. In practice, the auditor continuously combines the information obtained as he or she proceeds through the audit.

Reporting

PHASE 8—REPORTING When the audit is completed, the PA must issue an auditor's report to accompany the client's published financial statements. The report must meet well-defined technical requirements that are affected by the scope of the audit and the nature of the findings. These reports are studied in Chapter 20. Prior to releasing the report, the auditor will conduct final quality control reviews (such as tax, second partner, or risk reviews). The auditor will also issue a management letter and report to management and the audit committee about the outcome of the audit.

Entity-level controls—controls that affect the entire organization.

④ **Entity-Level Controls and Financial Statement Cycles**

Corporate Governance and Entity-Level Systems

Prior to looking at specific cycles, the auditor will inquire about and document corporate governance systems such as the policies and procedures employed by the board of directors, the audit committee, and senior management. As you will discover in later chapters, actions at the corporate governance level have a significant impact upon the level of risk assigned to the audit of the organization.

There are also many **entity-level controls**, such as supervision policies and information technology general controls that affect multiple or all transaction cycles. For example, controls over program changes affect all systems that have automated information systems, as do security and access controls. Prior to working with individual transaction cycles, the auditor would document, evaluate, and test (where reliance is warranted) these entity-level controls (Chapter 9).

Financial Statement Cycles

Individual accounts and cycles within the audit are assessed using audit assertions. Figure 5-3 explains how these assertions are developed in the context of the objectives of the audit. Dividing the financial statements into smaller segments or components makes the audit more manageable and aids in the assignment of tasks to different members of the audit team. For example, most auditors treat capital assets and notes payable as different segments. Each segment is audited separately but not independently (e.g., the audit of capital assets may reveal an unrecorded note payable). After the audit of each segment is completed, including interrelationships with other segments, the audit results are combined and re-evaluated. A conclusion can then be reached about the financial statements taken as a whole.

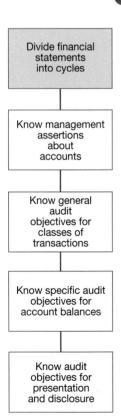

Figure 5-3   Five Steps to Develop Audit Assertions

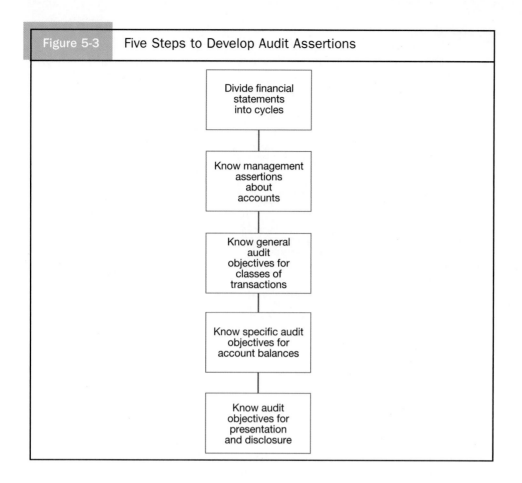

THE CYCLE APPROACH TO SEGMENTING AN AUDIT A common way to divide an audit is to keep closely related types (or classes) of transactions and account balances in the same segment. This is called the **cycle approach**. For example, sales, sales returns, cash receipts, and charge-offs of uncollectable accounts are four classes of transactions that cause accounts receivable to increase and decrease, all part of the sales and collection cycle. Similarly, payroll transactions and accrued payroll are a part of the human resources and payroll cycle.

Cycle approach—a method of dividing an audit by keeping closely related types of transactions and account balances in the same segment.

The logic of using the cycle approach can be seen by thinking about the way transactions are reported in journals and summarized in the general ledger, trial balance and financial statements. Figure 5-4 shows that transaction details (normally from computer files) are organized into journals, the totals posted to the general ledger and other records (such as master files or databases). The general ledger is reported as a trial balance and summarized as financial statements.

To the extent that it is practical, the cycle approach combines transactions recorded in different subsystems with the general ledger balances that result from those transactions.

The following is a list of cycles explained in detail in this text:

- Sales and collection cycle.
- Human resources and payroll cycle.
- Acquisition and payment cycle.
- Inventory and distribution cycle.
- Capital acquisition and repayment cycle.

Each of these cycles is so important that it is part of the title of one chapter in this book.

To illustrate the application of cycles to audits, Figure 5-5 presents the December 31, 2010, general trial balance of Hillsburg Hardware Limited. The financial statements prepared from this trial balance are included in the insert on pages 146–150.

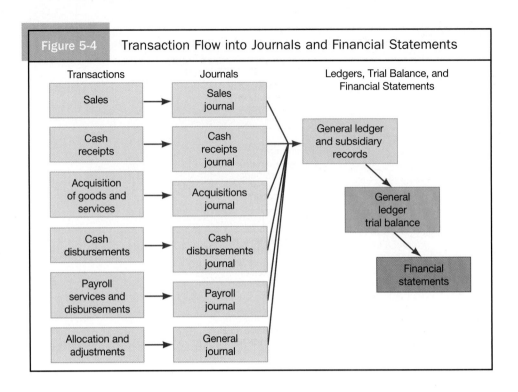

| Figure 5-4 | Transaction Flow into Journals and Financial Statements |

Prior-year figures usually included for comparative purposes are excluded from Figure 5-5 in order to focus on transaction cycles. A trial balance is used to prepare financial statements and is a primary focus of every audit. The letter representing a cycle is shown for each account in the left column beside the account name. Each account has at least one cycle associated with it, and only cash and inventories are part of two or more cycles.

The cycles used in this text are shown again in Table 5-4. The accounts for Hillsburg Hardware Limited are summarized by cycle and include the transaction types that typically appear in each cycle.

The following observations expand the information contained in Table 5-4.

All general ledger accounts and transaction types for Hillsburg Hardware Limited are included at least once. For a different company, the number and types of transactions and general ledger accounts would differ, but all would be included.

Some transaction types and general ledger accounts are included in more than one cycle. When that occurs, it means the transaction type is used to record transactions from more than one cycle and indicates a tie-in between the cycles. The most important general ledger account included in and affecting several cycles is the general cash account (cash in bank). General cash connects most cycles.

The capital acquisition and repayment cycle is closely related to the acquisition and payment cycle. The acquisition of goods and services includes the purchase of inventory, supplies, and general services in performing the main business operations. Transactions in the capital acquisitions cycle are related to financing the business, such as issuing stock or debt, paying dividends, and repaying debt. The same transaction type is used to record transactions for both cycles, and the transactions are similar. There are two reasons for treating capital acquisition and repayment separately from the acquisition of goods and services. First, the transactions are related to financing a company rather than to its operations. Second, most capital acquisition and repayment cycle accounts involve few transactions, but each is often highly material and therefore should be audited extensively. For both reasons, it is more convenient to separate the two cycles.

The inventory and distribution cycle is closely related to all other cycles, especially for a manufacturing company. The cost of inventory includes raw materials (acquisition and payment cycle), direct labour (human resources and payroll cycle), and manufacturing overhead (acquisition and payment and human resources and payroll

Figure 5-5   Hillsburg Hardware Limited Adjusted Trial Balance

HILLSBURG HARDWARE LIMITED
TRIAL BALANCE
December 31, 2010

		Debit	Credit
S,A,P,C	Cash in bank	$ 827,568	
S	Trade accounts receivable	20,196,800	
S	Allowance for uncollectible accounts		$ 1,240,000
S	Other accounts receivable	945,020	
A,I	Inventories	29,864,621	
A	Prepaid expenses	431,558	
A	Land	3,456,420	
A	Buildings	32,500,000	
A	Computer and delivery equipment	3,758,347	
A	Furniture and fixtures	2,546,421	
A	Accumulated amortization		31,920,126
A	Trade accounts payable (1)		4,483,995
C	Notes payable		4,179,620
P	Accrued payroll		1,349,800
P	Accrued payroll expenses		119,663
C	Accrued interest		149,560
C	Dividends payable		1,900,000
A	Goods and services tax payable (net) (1)		235,994
A	Accrued income tax		795,442
C	Long-term notes payable		24,120,000
A	Deferred tax		738,240
A	Other accrued payables		829,989
C	Capital stock		8,500,000
C	Retained earnings		11,929,075
S	Sales		144,327,789
S	Sales returns and allowances	1,241,663	
I	Cost of goods sold	103,240,768	
P	Salaries and commissions	7,738,900	
P	Sales payroll benefits	1,422,100	
A	Travel and entertainment—selling	1,110,347	
A	Advertising	2,611,263	
A	Sales and promotional literature	321,620	
A	Sales meetings and training	924,480	
A	Miscellaneous sales expense	681,041	
P	Executive and office salaries	5,523,960	
P	Administrative payroll benefits	682,315	
A	Travel and entertainment—administrative	561,680	
A	Computer maintenance and supplies	860,260	
A	Stationery and supplies	762,568	
A	Postage	244,420	
A	Telephone and fax	722,315	
A	Rent	312,140	
A	Legal fees and retainers	383,060	
A	Auditing and related services	302,840	
A	Amortization	1,452,080	
S	Bad debt expense	3,323,084	
A	Insurance	722,684	
A	Office repairs and maintenance	843,926	
A	Miscellaneous office expense	643,680	
A	Miscellaneous general expense	323,842	
A	Gain on sale of assets		719,740
A	Income taxes	1,746,600	
C	Interest expense	2,408,642	
C	Dividends	1,900,000	
	(1) These accounts were grouped together on the financial statements	$237,539,033	$237,539,033

Note: Letters in the left-hand column refer to the following transaction cycles: S = Sales and collection, A = Acquisition and payment, P = Human resources and payroll , I = Inventory and distribution, C = Capital acquisition and repayment.

cycles). The sale of finished goods involves the sales and collection cycle. Because inventory is material for most manufacturing or distribution companies, it is common to borrow money using inventory as security. In those cases, the capital acquisition and repayment cycle is also related to inventory and distribution.

	Table 5-4	Cycles Applied to Hillsburg Hardware Limited	

		General Ledger Account Included in the Cycle	
Cycle	Transaction Types Included in the Cycle (See Figure 5-4)	Balance Sheet	Income Statement
Sales and collection	Sales Cash receipts Journal entries	Cash in bank Trade accounts receivable Allowance for uncollectable accounts Other accounts receivable	Sales Sales returns and allowances Bad-debt expense
Acquisition and payment	Acquisitions Cash disbursements Journal entries	Cash in bank Inventories Prepaid expenses Land Buildings Computer and delivery equipment Furniture and fixtures Accumulated amortization Trade accounts payable Goods and services tax payable Accrued income tax Deferred tax Other accrued payables	Advertising^S Amortization Auditing^A and related services Computer maintenance and supplies Gain on sale of assets Income taxes Insurance^A Legal fees and retainers^A Miscellaneous general expense^A Miscellaneous office expense^A Miscellaneous sales expense^S Office repairs and maintenance Postage^A Rent^A Sales and promotional literature^S Sales meetings and training^S Stationery and supplies^A Taxes^A Telephone and fax^A Travel and entertainment—selling^S Travel and entertainment—administrative^A
Human resources and payroll	Payroll Journal entries	Cash in bank Accrued payroll Accrued payroll benefits	Salaries and commissions^S Sales payroll benefits^S Executive and office salaries^A Administrative payroll benefits^A
Inventory and distribution	Acquisitions Sale Journal entries	Inventories	Cost of goods sold
Capital acquisition and repayment	Acquisitions Cash disbursements Journal entries	Cash in bank Notes payable Accrued interest Long-term notes payable Accrued interest Capital stock Retained earnings Dividends Dividends payable	Interest expense

S = Selling expense
A = General and administrative expense

RELATIONSHIPS AMONG CYCLES Figure 5-6 illustrates the relationship of the cycles to one another. In addition to the five cycles, general cash is also shown. Each cycle is studied in detail in later chapters.

Figure 5-6 shows that cycles have no beginning or end except at the origin and final disposition of a company. A company begins by obtaining capital, usually in the form of cash. In a manufacturing company, cash is used to acquire raw materials, capital assets, and related goods and services to produce inventory (acquisition and payment cycle). Cash is also used to acquire labour for the same reason (human

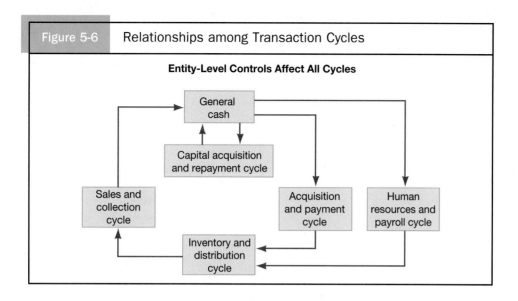

Figure 5-6 Relationships among Transaction Cycles

Entity-Level Controls Affect All Cycles

resources and payroll cycle). Acquisition and payment and human resources and payroll are similar in nature, but the functions are different enough to justify separate cycles. The combined result of these two cycles is inventory (inventory and distribution cycle). At a subsequent point, the inventory is sold and billings and collections result (sales and collection cycle). The cash generated is used to pay dividends and interest and to start the cycles again. The cycles interrelate in much the same way in a service company, where there will be no inventory, but there may be unbilled receivables and work-in-progress of unbilled services.

RELATIONSHIPS AMONG TRANSACTION CYCLES Transaction cycles are of major importance in the conduct of the audit. For the most part, auditors treat each cycle separately during the audit. Although auditors take care to interrelate different cycles at different times and be aware of the interrelationships among the cycles, they must treat the cycles somewhat independently in order to manage complex audits effectively.

auditing in action 5-2

Sinks in Cycles

How do sinks relate to audit cycles? An audit senior was working at a client that manufactured a variety of sinks and bathtubs. During her observation of inventory, she found certain colours and brands tucked back in a corner, gathering dust and dirt.

She asked management to transfer inventory data into a spreadsheet so that she could further analyze the impact on the financial statements. It turned out that certain sinks were overvalued in the financial statements. Management made an adjustment and wrote down the value by several thousand dollars.

This meant that in future sales, less cash would be received (as the sinks were worth less). Less revenue and accounts receivable will be recorded in the sales and collection cycle.

The inventory value was written down, reducing the cost of inventory. Coordination with the purchasing department would mean that the company would no longer purchase the colours in question (deep greens and purples) and would purchase other colours instead.

This example shows that a single audit observation (and the resulting journal entry) is linked to several financial statement cycles.

Source: Discussion between an audit supervisor, summer 2008, and I. Splettstoesser-Hogeterp.

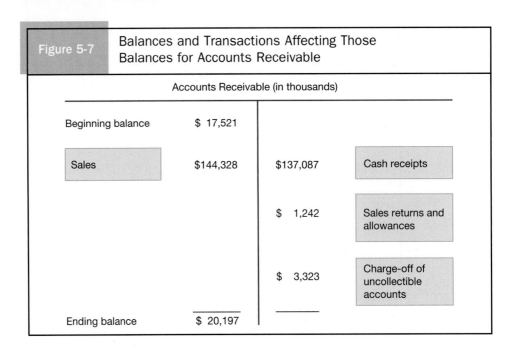

Figure 5-7 Balances and Transactions Affecting Those Balances for Accounts Receivable

Accounts Receivable (in thousands)

Beginning balance	$ 17,521		
Sales	$144,328	$137,087	Cash receipts
		$ 1,242	Sales returns and allowances
		$ 3,323	Charge-off of uncollectible accounts
Ending balance	$ 20,197		

Setting Audit Objectives

Auditors conduct audits consistent with the cycle approach by performing audit tests of the transactions making up ending balances and also by performing audit tests of the account balances themselves. Figure 5-7 illustrates this important concept by showing the four classes of transactions that determine the ending balance in accounts receivable. Assume that the beginning balance of $17,521 was audited in the prior year and is therefore considered reliable. If the auditor could be completely sure that each of the four classes of transactions was correctly stated, the auditor could also be sure that the ending balance of $20,197 was correctly stated. However, it may be impractical for the auditor to obtain complete assurance about the correctness of each class of transactions, resulting in less than complete assurance about the ending balance in accounts receivable. Then, overall assurance can be increased by auditing the ending balance of accounts receivable. Auditors have found that, generally, the most efficient way to conduct audits is to obtain some combination of assurance for each class of transactions and for the ending balance in the related account.

As shown in Table 5-6, for any given class of transactions, there are several audit objectives that must be met before the auditor can conclude that the transactions are properly recorded. They are called transaction-related audit objectives (or assertions) in the remainder of this book. For example, there are **transaction-related audit objectives** specific to sales and sales returns and allowances.

Similarly, there are several audit objectives that must be met for each account balance. They are called balance-related audit objectives. For example, there are balance-related audit objectives specific to accounts receivable and balance-related audit objectives specific to accounts payable. It will be shown later that the transaction-related and balance-related audit objectives (also called assertions), are somewhat different but closely related. Throughout the remainder of this text, the term audit objectives refers to both transaction-related and balance-related audit objectives.

There is a third group, called presentation and disclosure audit objectives that are specific to the presentation and disclosure of financial statements, also shown in Table 5-6.

Before examining audit objectives in more detail, it is necessary to understand management assertions. These are studied next.

Audit objectives specific to a transaction, balance, or presentation and disclosure—transaction-related, balance- related, or presentation and disclosure audit objectives used to tailor the audit process to transactions, events, balances, or disclosures.

concept check

C5-9 How do entity-level controls affect cycles?

C5-10 Why does the audit process use cycle?

C5-11 List two typical cycles.

⑤ Management Assertions and Audit Objectives

Management Assertions

Management assertions are implied or expressed representations by management about (i) classes of transactions or events, (ii) related account balances in the financial statements, and (iii) the classification, presentation, or disclosure of information in the financial statements. As an illustration, the management of Hillsburg Hardware Limited asserts that cash of $827,568 (see Figure 5-5) was present in the company's bank accounts or on the premises as of the balance sheet date. Unless otherwise disclosed in the financial statements, management also asserts that the cash was unrestricted and available for normal use. Similar assertions exist for each asset, liability, equity, revenue, and expense item in the financial statements. These assertions apply to classes of transactions, account balances, and all of the material in the financial statements, including the notes.

Management assertions are directly related to accounting standards in alignment with their selected accounting framework. These assertions are part of the criteria that management uses to record and disclose accounting information in financial statements. Return to the definition of auditing in Chapter 1, on page 5. It states, in part, that auditing is a comparison of information (financial statements) to established criteria (conformity with an applicable financial reporting framework). Auditors must therefore understand the assertions to do adequate audits.

CAS International and Canadian auditing standards (CAS 315.A111) classify assertions into three categories:

1. Assertions about classes of transactions and events for the period under audit.
2. Assertions about account balances at period end.
3. Assertions about financial statement presentation and disclosure.

The specific assertions included in each category are listed in Table 5-5. The assertions are grouped so that assertions related across categories of assertions are included on the same table row. We will use these groupings to first discuss the management assertions, then discuss the audit objectives.

ASSERTIONS ABOUT CLASSES OF TRANSACTIONS AND EVENTS Management makes several assertions about transactions. These assertions also apply to other events that are reflected in the accounting records, such as recording depreciation and recognizing pension obligations.

Occurrence The occurrence assertion concerns whether recorded transactions included in the financial statements actually occurred during the accounting period.

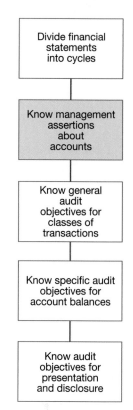

Management assertions—implied or expressed representations by management about classes of transactions; related account balances; and classification, presentation, or disclosures in the financial statements.

Table 5-5	Management Assertions for Each Category of Assertions	
Assertions about classes of transactions and events	**Assertions about account balances**	**Assertions about presentation and disclosure**
Occurrence	Existence	Occurrence and
	Rights and obligations	Rights and obligations
Completeness	Completeness	Completeness
Accuracy		Accuracy and
	Valuation and	Valuation
	Allocation	
Cutoff		
Classification		Classification and
		Understandability

For example, management asserts that recorded sales transactions represent exchanges of goods or services that actually took place.

Completeness This assertion addresses whether all transactions that should be included in the financial statements are in fact included. For example, management asserts that all sales of goods and services are recorded and included in the financial statements.

The completeness assertion addresses matters opposite from the occurrence assertion. The completeness assertion is concerned with the possibility of omitting transactions that should have been recorded, whereas the occurrence assertion is concerned with inclusion of transactions that should not have been recorded. Thus, violations of the occurrence assertion relate to account overstatements, whereas violations of the completeness assertion relate to account understatements. The recording of a sale that did not take place is a violation of the occurrence assertion, whereas the failure to record a sale that did occur is a violation of the completeness assertion.

Accuracy The accuracy assertion addresses whether transactions have been recorded at correct amounts. Using the wrong price to record a sales transaction and an error in calculating the extensions of price times quantity are examples of violations of the accuracy assertion.

Cutoff The cutoff assertion addresses whether transactions are recorded in the proper accounting period. Recording a sales transaction in December when the goods were not shipped until January violates the cutoff assertion.

Classification The classification assertion addresses whether transactions are recorded in the appropriate accounts. Recording administrative salaries in cost of sales is one example of a violation of the classification assertion.

ASSERTIONS ABOUT ACCOUNT BALANCES Assertions about account balances at year-end are about amounts shown in the balance sheet (called the *Statement of Financial Position* under IFRS).

Existence The existence assertion deals with whether assets, liabilities, and equity interests included in the balance sheet actually existed on the balance sheet date. For example, management asserts that merchandise inventory included in the balance sheet exists and is available for sale at the balance sheet date.

Rights and obligations This assertion addresses whether assets are the rights of the entity and whether liabilities are the obligations of the entity at a given date. For example, management asserts that assets are owned by the company or that amounts capitalized for leases in the balance sheet represent the cost of the entity's rights to leased property and that the corresponding lease liability represents an obligation of the entity.

Completeness This assertion addresses whether all accounts and amounts that should be presented in the financial statements are in fact included. For example, management asserts that notes payable in the balance sheet include all such obligations of the entity.

The completeness assertion addresses matters opposite from the existence assertion. The completeness assertion is concerned with the possibility of omitting items from the financial statements that should have been included, whereas the existence assertion is concerned with inclusion of amounts that should not have been included. Violations of the existence assertion relate to account overstatements, while violations of the completeness assertion relate to account understatements. Inclusion of a receivable for a customer that does not exist violates the existence assertion, whereas the failure to include a receivable from a customer violates the completeness assertion.

Valuation and allocation The valuation and allocation assertion deals with whether assets, liabilities, and equity interests have been included in the financial statements at appropriate amounts, including any valuation adjustments to reflect asset amounts at net realizable value. For example, management asserts that property is recorded at historical cost and that such cost is systematically allocated to appropriate accounting periods through depreciation. Similarly, management asserts that trade accounts receivable included in the balance sheet are stated at net realizable value.

ASSERTIONS ABOUT PRESENTATION AND DISCLOSURE With increases in the complexity of transactions and the need for expanded disclosures about these transactions, assertions about presentation and disclosure have increased in importance.

Occurrence and rights and obligations This assertion addresses whether disclosed events have occurred and are the rights and obligations of the entity. For example, if the client discloses that it has acquired another company, it asserts that the transaction has been finalized.

Completeness This assertion deals with whether all required disclosures have been included in the financial statements. As an example, management asserts that all material transactions with related parties have been disclosed in the financial statements.

Accuracy and valuation The accuracy and valuation assertion deals with whether financial information is disclosed fairly and at appropriate amounts. Management's disclosure of the amount of unfunded pension obligations and the assumptions underlying these amounts is an example of this assertion.

Classification and understandability This assertion relates to whether amounts are appropriately classified in the financial statements and footnotes, and whether the balance descriptions and related disclosures are understandable. For example, management asserts that the classification of inventories as finished goods, work-in-process, and raw materials is appropriate, and the disclosures of the methods used to value inventories are understandable.

Auditors may use different terms to express the management assertions as long as all the aspects included in Table 5-5 (page 125) are addressed. The auditor should consider the relevance of each assertion for each significant class of transactions, account balance, and presentation and disclosure. Relevant assertions have a meaningful bearing on whether the account is fairly stated and are used to assess the risk of material misstatement and the design and performance of audit procedures. For example, valuation is likely to be a relevant assertion for accounts receivable, but not for cash.

After the relevant assertions have been identified, the auditor can then develop audit objectives for each category of assertions. The auditor's audit objectives follow and are closely related to management assertions. That is not surprising because the auditor's primary responsibility is to determine whether management assertions about financial statements are justified. The reason for using audit objectives, rather than the assertions, is to provide a framework to help the auditor accumulate sufficient appropriate evidence and decide the proper evidence to accumulate given the circumstances of the engagement. The objectives remain the same from audit to audit, but the evidence varies, depending on the circumstances.

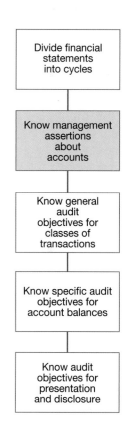

Transaction-Related Audit Objectives

The auditor's **transaction-related audit objectives** follow and are closely related to management assertions about classes of transactions. There is a difference between general transaction-related audit objectives and specific transaction-related audit objectives for each class of transactions. The five general transaction-related audit objectives discussed here are applicable to every class of transactions and are stated in broad terms. Specific transaction-related audit objectives are also applied to each class of transactions but are stated in terms tailored to a specific class of transactions, such

Transaction-related audit objectives—five audit objectives that must be met before the auditor can conclude that the total for any given class of transactions is fairly stated. The general transaction-related audit objectives are occurrence, completeness, accuracy, cutoff, and classification.

as sales transactions. Once the auditor establishes general transaction-related audit objectives, they can be used to develop specific transaction-related audit objectives for each class of transactions being audited, as shown in Table 5-6.

GENERAL TRANSACTION-RELATED AUDIT OBJECTIVES

Occurrence—recorded transactions occurred Inclusion of a sale in the sales files or journal when no sale occurred violates the occurrence objective, as the sale is then fictitious or does not belong to the organization. This objective is the auditor's counterpart to the management assertion of occurrence.

Completeness—all transactions are recorded This objective deals with whether all transactions that should be included in the files or journals have actually been included. Failure to record a sale when a sale occurred violates the completeness objective. The objective is the counterpart to the management assertion of completeness.

The occurrence and completeness objectives emphasize opposite audit concerns: occurrence deals with potential overstatement and completeness with unrecorded transactions (understatement).

Accuracy—recorded transactions are recorded appropriately Depending upon the way that records or information systems are organized, accuracy can have up to three components: (i) initial data entry, (ii) summarization, and (iii) posting.

Accuracy of data entry for sales transactions would be violated if the quantity of goods shipped were different from the quantity billed, the wrong selling price were used for billing, or there were extension or adding errors (perhaps due to program errors) during billing. These three parts of accuracy match the management assertion of accuracy.

Summarization is the process of grouping or totalling some transactions for the purpose of posting. For example, the sales account may have only a daily total of the

Table 5-6 Examples of Management Assertions, General Audit Objectives, and Specific Audit Objectives

	Audit Objectives about **transactions** or events	Audit Objectives about **transactions** or events	Audit Objectives about **account balances** at the end of the period	Audit Objectives about **account balances** at the end of the period	Audit Objectives about **presentation and disclosure**	Audit Objectives about **presentation and disclosure**
Management Assertion	*General Audit Objective*	*Specific Audit Objective: Sales*	*General Audit Objective*	*Specific Audit Objective: Inventory*	*General Audit Objective*	*Specific Audit Objective: Inventory*
Existence or Occurrence	Occurrence	Recorded sales are for shipments made to nonfictitious customers	Existence	All recorded inventories exist at the balance sheet date (i.e., are real)	Occurrence	Inventory balances are based on transactions that actually occurred that pertain to the entity, resulting in actual inventory amounts on hand
Rights and Obligations			Rights and obligations (ownership)	Inventories belong to the company (i.e., are not being held on consignment)	Rights and obligations (ownership)	Inventory belongs to the company
Completeness	Completeness	All existing sales transactions are recorded	Completeness	All existing inventory has been counted and included in inventory	Completeness	Disclosures about inventory are fully included (e.g., consignment terms described)
Accuracy	Accuracy	Recorded sales are for the amount of goods shipped and are correctly billed and recorded			Accuracy	The inventory balance shown on the financial statements is materially correct.
Valuation			Valuation	Inventories have been written down where net realizable value is less than book value.	Valuation	The inventory balance shown on the financial statements is shown at an appropriate amount.
Allocation			Allocation	Inventory amounts and adjustments are allocated to the correct period in the correct accounts at the correct amount.		
Cutoff	Cutoff	Sales are recorded on the correct dates.				
Classification	Classification	Sales transactions are recorded in the correct account.			Classification	Inventory information is presented in the correct accounts, e.g., as raw materials, work-in-progress, or finished goods.
Understandability					Understandability	Inventory information is clearly shown.

transactions from the sales sub-system. A summarization error occurs in sales if the daily total is added incorrectly or the total of internet sales is not added correctly.

Posting is the process of recording transactions to the general ledger account. Many systems post every single transaction to the general ledger, while others record only a daily, weekly, or monthly total. A posting error occurs if the wrong sales amount was updated to the customer master file or the wrong total for internet sales was transferred to the general ledger. Since the posting of transactions to subsidiary records, the general ledger, and other related master files is typically accomplished automatically by computerized accounting systems, the risk of random human error in posting is minimal. Once the auditor has established that the automated information systems are functioning properly, there is a reduced concern about both summarization and posting errors.

Cutoff—transactions are recorded on the correct dates A timing error (the management assertion of cutoff) occurs if transactions are not recorded on the dates the transactions took place. A sales transaction, for example, should be recorded on the date of shipment or when risks of ownership are transferred.

Classification—transactions included in the client's records are properly classified Examples of misclassifications of sales are including cash sales as credit sales, recording a sale of operating capital assets as revenue, and misclassifying commercial sales as residential sales.

SPECIFIC TRANSACTION-RELATED AUDIT OBJECTIVES The general transaction-related audit objectives must be applied to each material type (or class) of transaction in the audit. Such transactions typically include sales, cash receipts, acquisitions of goods and services, payroll, and others. Table 5-6 on page 129 lists the five transaction-related audit objectives. It includes the general form of the objectives, the application of the objectives to sales transactions, and the management assertions.

Balance-Related Audit Objectives

Balance-related audit objectives are five audit objectives (see Table 5-6) that must be met before the auditor can conclude that any given account balance is fairly stated.

Balance-related audit objectives are similar to the transaction-related audit objectives just discussed. They also follow from management assertions, and they provide a framework to help the auditor accumulate sufficient appropriate evidence. General balance-related audit objectives are applied to specific account balances, resulting in specific balance-related audit objectives.

Because of the way audits are done, balance-related audit objectives are almost always applied to the ending balance in balance sheet accounts, such as accounts receivable, inventory, and notes payable. Balance-related objectives are also applied to certain income statement accounts. These usually involve non-routine transactions and unpredictable expenses, such as legal expense or repairs and maintenance. Other income statement accounts are closely related to balance sheet accounts and are tested simultaneously (e.g., amortization expense with accumulated amortization, interest expense with notes payable).

When using the balance-related audit objectives as a framework for auditing balance sheet account balances, the auditor accumulates evidence to verify detail that supports the account balance, rather than verifying the account balance itself. For example, in auditing accounts receivable, the auditor obtains a listing of the aged accounts receivable balances from the client that agrees with the general ledger balance (see page 451 for an illustration). The accounts receivable balance-related audit objectives are applied to the customer accounts in that listing.

GENERAL BALANCE-RELATED AUDIT OBJECTIVES

Existence—amounts included exist Inclusion of an account receivable from a customer in the accounts receivable trial balance when there is no receivable from that customer violates the existence objective. Similarly, if the same inventory is accidentally

Balance-related audit objectives—five audit objectives that must be met before the auditor can conclude that any given account balance is fairly stated. The general balance-related audit objectives are existence, rights and obligations, completeness, valuation, and allocation.

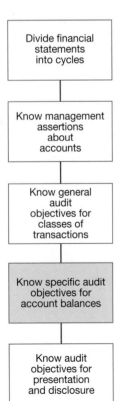

Divide financial statements into cycles

↓

Know management assertions about accounts

↓

Know general audit objectives for classes of transactions

↓

Know specific audit objectives for account balances

↓

Know audit objectives for presentation and disclosure

counted twice and thus inventory is inflated, the existence objective has been violated. This objective is the auditor's counterpart to the management assertion of existence or occurrence.

Rights and obligations In addition to existing, most assets must be owned before they can be included in the financial statements. Similarly, liabilities must belong to the entity. Rights are always associated with assets and obligations with liabilities.

Completeness—all amounts are recorded Failure to include an account receivable from a customer when the receivable exists violates the completeness objective. Forgetting to count and include certain types of inventory does the same. This includes the concept that all transactions have been summarized and posted (also called *detail tie-in*) to the account.

The existence and completeness objectives emphasize opposite audit concerns: existence deals with potential overstatement and completeness deals with unrecorded amounts (understatement).

Valuation (realizable value)—assets are included at the amounts estimated to be realized This objective concerns whether an account balance has been reduced for declines from historical cost to net realizable value or properly valued if fair value accounting is being used (such as for marketable securities). Examples of when this objective applies are considering the adequacy of the allowance for uncollectable accounts receivable, writedowns of inventory for obsolescence, or revaluation of fixed assets. The objective applies only to asset accounts and is part of the management valuation assertion.

Allocation—amounts included are appropriate Allocation includes several concepts: (i) accuracy of adjustment or recorded amount, (ii) timing of the adjustment and (ii) adjustment to the correct accounts.

Accuracy of adjustment requires that the correct adjustment or allocation be calculated. For example, the write-down of inventory must be correctly determined, and the amortization of fixed assets should be for an appropriate amount that reflects the useful life (and fair value if fair value accounting is used. *Timing of adjustment* refers to the allocation of the adjustment to the correct financial periods. For example, a write-down of inventory should pertain to the current fiscal period, while amortization of fixed assets needs to be allocated to the periods while the asset was in productive use.

Adjustment to correct accounts requires that the adjustment be posted to the correct general ledger accounts. Changes in inventory values would be posted to cost of goods sold for the current period, while changes to the fair value of assets could be posted to equity accounts. If the useful life an asset has changed, this could result in postings to both the current year's amortization costs and to equity accounts. This is closely related to the transaction-related audit objective of classification, since the adjustment transactions should be posted to the correct general ledger accounts.

If the transactions are posted correctly, then the balances will also be recorded in the correct accounts. For example, on the accounts receivable listing, receivables must be separated into short-term and long-term, and amounts due from affiliates, officers, and directors must be classified separately from amounts due from customers. Inventory should be correctly classified by type. An adequate chart of accounts that differentiates among the different types of assets and liabilities is an important enabler of correct transaction classification and of general ledger account allocation.

SPECIFIC BALANCE-RELATED AUDIT OBJECTIVES After the general balance-related audit objectives are understood, specific balance-related audit objectives for each account balance on the financial statements can be developed. There should be at least one specific balance-related audit objective for each general balance-related audit objective unless the auditor believes that the general balance-related audit objective is not relevant or is unimportant in the circumstances. There may be more than one specific balance-related audit objective for a general balance-related audit objective. For example, specific balance-related audit objectives for rights and obligations of the inventory of Hillsburg Hardware Limited could include that (1) the company has title to all inventory items listed, and (2) inventories are not pledged as collateral unless it is disclosed.

Presentation and Disclosure-Related Audit Objectives

Presentation and disclosure audit objectives There are seven general audit objectives used to examine the financial statements. These are occurrence, rights and obligations (ownership), completeness, accuracy, valuation, classification, and understandability.

Financial statements are summary documents used to communicate information directly to users. For example, an organization may have several cash accounts that show up only as one line on the financial statements. Financial statement audit objectives are associated with the quality of the information provided in the financial statements. If a complex investment is described in a confusing manner, the reader cannot understand what the business is doing. The underlying purpose of these audit objectives is to assess whether financial information portrays (through the transactions, accounts, and notes) the actions of the organization in a way that reflects the underlying economic reality of what actually occurred. For example, in the notes in the Hillsburg Hardware Limited financial statements on pages 146–150, there is a clear description of accounting policies used by the business. Table 5-6 (on page 129) relates general and specific audit objectives to management assertions. The same concepts that apply to transaction-related and balance-related audit objectives apply equally to the presentation and disclosure audit objectives.

The key difference is the general presentation and disclosure-related audit objective of understandability.

Understandability—account balances and related disclosure requirements are clearly presented in the financial statements The auditor will need to assess the financial statements and notes from the perspective of a reasonably informed business user to determine whether the information is presented in a clear way, portraying the events and actions of the organization. For example, industry-specific methods would be shown, as described in the Hillsburg Hardware Limited financial statements (note 2), where vendor allowances and rebates are included in other receivables (see page 150). These types of explanations help the reader to understand the nature of the business transactions included in the accounts.

SPECIFIC PRESENTATION AND DISCLOSURE-RELATED AUDIT OBJECTIVES By looking at each amount or note in the financial statements, the auditor can develop specific presentation and disclosure-related audit objectives. These would be linked to the type of account and the nature of the communication issue. For example, assets might have valuation, classification, and understandability as specific audit objectives. Table 5-6 on page 129 provides examples for inventory.

How Audit Objectives Are Met

The auditor must obtain sufficient appropriate audit evidence to support all management assertions in the financial statements. As stated earlier, this is done by accumulating evidence in support of some appropriate combination of transaction-related, balance-related, presentation and disclosure audit objectives. Table 5-6 (page 129) shows examples of these audit objectives.

The auditor plans the appropriate combination of audit objectives and the evidence that must be accumulated to meet them by following the structured eight-phase audit process shown in Figure 5-1. The risk assessment phases help the auditor identify those assertions where there is the greatest likelihood of misstatement. Then, the risk response phases are used to design further audit procedures which are completed to assess evidence using the assertions. The use of assertions to help organize evidence enables the completion of a high-quality audit with the appropriate audit report.

Divide financial statements into cycles

Know management assertions about accounts

Know general audit objectives for classes of transactions

Know specific audit objectives for account balances

Know audit objectives for presentation and disclosure

---

concept check

C5-12 What are management assertions about financial information?

C5-13 How does the auditor use management assertions during the financial statement audit?

C5-14 What are the three different types of audit objectives? Provide an example of each for the completeness audit objective.

Summary

1. *What is the objective of conducting an audit of financial statements?* The auditor expresses an opinion about the fairness of presentation of the financial statements.

   Explain the difference between management and auditor responsibilities with respect to the financial statements and the discovery and correction of material misstatements or illegal acts. Management is responsible for designing internal controls to prevent and detect errors, fraud, and illegal acts. These controls should be concerned with errors of all sizes, not just material errors. Auditors are concerned with material misstatements as they consider the financial statements in the context of users. Auditors express an opinion on the financial statements that have been prepared by management.

2. *Describe the preplanning steps that the auditor completes prior to accepting the financial statement audit.* The auditor goes through a client acceptance or continuance decision process, identifies the client's reasons for an audit, and conducts an independence threat analysis.

   Why is an engagement letter important? The engagement letter clarifies the responsibilities of both the auditor and the client and is used to minimize misunderstandings.

3. *List the eight phases of a financial statement audit, and provide an overview of the audit process.* The eight phases are divided into three groups. First there are three risk assessment phases: pre-planning (phase 1); client risk profile (2); and planning the audit (3). This is followed by four risk response phases: designing further audit procedures (4); tests of control (5); substantive tests (6); and ongoing evaluation, quality control, and final evidence gathering (7). The final phase is complete quality control

and issue of the auditor's report (8). These phases allow the auditor to collect sufficient appropriate audit evidence to state an opinion on the financial statements.

4. *Show how financial statements are divided into cycles.* The smaller segments or components are cash; capital acquisition and repayment; acquisition and payment; human resources and payroll; inventory and distribution; and sales and collection.

   How is this cycle approach related to the financial statement audit? One aspect of evidence gathering is the auditor testing classes of transactions that are part of the transaction cycles.

   What is the relationship among the cycles? The cycles show that transactions are related to each other, since the cycles interrelate. For example, cash has a role in each of the cycles—payment of sales, purchase of materials, and acquisition of debt.

   What is the relationship between the cycle approach and entity-level controls? Entity-level controls affect all cycles, as the corporate governance structure includes policies and procedures for all transactions.

5. *Describe management assertions about financial information.* Management assertions are implied or expressed representations about classes of transactions and accounts in the financial statements.

   Relate management assertions to general transaction-related audit objectives and general balance-related audit objectives. Transaction-related and balance-related audit objectives follow from and are closely related to management assertions and provide a framework to help the auditor collect audit evidence.

MyAccountingLab Make the grade with MyAccountingLab: The questions, exercises, and problems marked in orange can be found on MyAccountingLab. You can practise them as often as you want, and most feature step-by-step guided instructions to help you find the right answer.

Review Questions

5-1 ❶ State the objective of the audit of financial statements. In general terms, how do auditors meet that objective?

5-2 ❶ Distinguish between management's and the auditor's responsibilities for the financial statements being audited.

5-3 ❶ Explain two important characteristics of professional skepticism.

5-4 ❶ Distinguish between the terms "errors" and "fraud and other irregularities." What is the auditor's responsibility for finding each?

5-5 ❶ Distinguish between management fraud and employee fraud. Discuss the likely difference between these two types of fraud on the fair presentation of financial statements.

5-6 ❶ Define the term "illegal act." What is the auditor's responsibility with respect to illegal acts by clients?

5-7 ❷ What factors should an auditor consider prior to accepting an engagement?

5-8 ❷ What is the purpose of an engagement letter? Explain how it is important to both the auditor and management.

5-9 ❸ Identify the eight phases of the audit. Provide an example of an activity completed in each phase.

5-10 ❹ Describe what is meant by the cycle approach to auditing. What are the advantages of dividing the audit into different cycles?

5-11 ❹ Why are sales, sales returns and allowances, bad debts, cash discounts, accounts receivable, and allowance for uncollectable accounts all included in the same cycle?

5-12 (4) How are entity-level controls related to cycles?

5-13 (5) Distinguish between general audit objectives and management assertions. Why are the general audit objectives more useful to auditors?

5-14 (5) Explain the differences among transaction-related, balance-related, and presentation and disclosure-related audit objectives.

5-15 (5) An acquisition of equipment repairs by a construction company is recorded in the incorrect accounting period. Which transaction-related audit objective has been violated? Which transaction-related objective has been violated if the acquisition has been capitalized as a capital asset rather than expensed?

5-16 (5) A banker found a set of financial statements difficult to read, and the disclosures seemed to be incomplete. Which presentation and disclosure-related objectives have been violated? Why?

5-17 (5) Distinguish between the existence and completeness balance-related audit objectives. State the effect on the financial statements (overstatement or understatement) of a violation of each in the audit of accounts payable.

5-18 (5) Identify the management assertion and general balance-related audit objective for this specific balance-related audit objective: All recorded fixed assets exist at the balance sheet date.

Discussion Questions and Problems

5-19 (1) Frequently, questions have been raised regarding the responsibility of the independent auditor for the discovery of fraud (including defalcations and other similar irregularities) and concerning the proper course of conduct of the independent auditor when his or her examination discloses specific circumstances that arouse suspicion about the existence of fraud.

REQUIRED
a. What are (1) the function and (2) the responsibilities of the independent auditor in the examination of financial statements? Discuss fully, but do not include fraud in this discussion.
b. What are the responsibilities of the independent auditor for the detection of fraud and other irregularities? Discuss fully.
c. What is the independent auditor's proper course of conduct when his or her examination discloses specific circumstances that arouse his or her suspicion as to the existence of fraud and other irregularities?
(Adapted from AICPA)

5-20 (1) It is well accepted that, throughout the conduct of the ordinary audit, it is essential to obtain large amounts of information from management and to rely heavily on management's judgments. After all, the financial statements are management's representations, and the primary responsibility for their fair presentation rests with management, not the auditor. For example, it is extremely difficult, if not impossible, for the auditor to evaluate the obsolescence of inventory as well as management can in a highly complex business. Similarly, the collectibility of accounts receivable and the continued usefulness of machinery and equipment are heavily dependent on management's willingness to provide truthful responses to questions.

REQUIRED
Reconcile the auditor's responsibility for discovering material misrepresentations by management with these comments.

5-21 (1) Recently there have been a significant number of highly publicized cases of management fraud involving the misstatement of financial statements. Although most client managements possess unquestioned integrity, a very small number, given sufficient incentive and opportunity, may be predisposed to fraudulently misstate reported financial conditions and operating results.

REQUIRED
a. What distinguishes management fraud from other types of fraud?
b. What are an auditor's responsibilities, under generally accepted auditing standards, to detect management fraud?

c. What are the characteristics of management fraud that an auditor should consider in order to fulfill the auditor's responsibilities for detecting management fraud under generally accepted auditing standards?
d. Three factors that heighten an auditor's concern about the existence of management fraud include (1) an intended public placement of securities in the near future, (2) management compensation dependent on operating results, and (3) a weak internal control environment evidenced by lack of concern for basic controls and disregard of the auditor's recommendations. What other factors should heighten an auditor's concern about the existence of management fraud?
(Adapted from AICPA)

5-22 ❷ Guilin & Partners is a PA firm that has audited ZFL for the past five years. During the past year, ZFL has grown to include exports to Asia. The president and the controller both retired last year. The new management met with Guilin this year to discuss this year's audit and hope to reduce the audit fees. ZFL's new management suggested that since the company had received an unqualified audit opinion every year from Guilin, less audit work would be needed this year. They also suggested that there was no need for an engagement letter this year since Guilin's staff was very familiar with the company. The managing partner at Guilin, Tim, explained to the controller that there were new accounting principles being applied this year because differential reporting rules no longer applied to the company. Tim also explained the audit process in more detail to the controller and president, who then agreed that the audit fees requested by Guilin were reasonable.

REQUIRED

Explain why you would or would not require an engagement letter this year. Support your answer.

(Extract from AU1 CGA -Canada Examinations developed by the Certified General Accountants Association of Canada © 2011 CGA-Canada. Reproduced with permission. All rights reserved.)

5-23 ❸ Following are seven audit activities.

a. Examine invoices supporting recorded fixed asset additions.

b. Review industry databases to assess the risk of material misstatement in the financial statements.

c. Summarize misstatements identified during testing to assess whether the overall financial statements are fairly stated.

d. Test computerized controls over credit approval for sales transactions.

e. Send letters to customers confirming outstanding accounts receivable balances.

f. Perform analytical procedures comparing the client with similar companies in the industry to gain an understanding of the client's business and strategies.

g. Compare information on purchases invoices recorded in the acquisitions journal with information on receiving reports.

REQUIRED

For each activity listed above, use Figure 5-1 to indicate in which phase of the audit the procedure was likely performed.

5-24 ❼ The following general ledger accounts are included in the trial balance for an audit client, Jones Wholesale Stationery Store.

Income tax expense
Income tax payable
Accounts receivable
Advertising expense
Travel expense
Bonds payable
Common stock
Unexpired insurance
Furniture and equipment
Cash
Notes receivable
Purchases
Sales salaries expense

Allowance for doubtful accounts
Inventory
Property tax expense
Interest expense
Amortization expense— furniture and equipment
Retained earnings
Sales
Salaries, office and general
Telephone and fax expense

Accumulated amortization of furniture and equipment
Notes payable
Property tax payable

Bad-debt expense
Interest receivable
Insurance expense
Interest income
Accrued sales salaries
Rent expense
Prepaid interest expense

REQUIRED

a. Identify the accounts in the trial balance that are likely to be included in each transaction cycle. Some accounts will be included in more than one cycle. Use the format that follows.

b. How would the general ledger accounts in the trial balance most likely differ if the company were a retail store rather than a wholesale company? How would they differ for a hospital or a government unit?

Cycle	Balance Sheet Accounts	Income Statement Accounts
Sales and collection		
Acquisition and payment		
Human resources and payroll		
Inventory and distribution		
Capital acquisition and repayment		

5-25 ❺ The following are two specific balance-related audit objectives in the audit of accounts payable.

1. All accounts payable included on the list represent amounts due to valid vendors.

2. There are no unrecorded accounts payable.

The list referred to in the objectives is the aged accounts payable trial balance produced using the supplier master file. The total of the list equals the accounts payable balance on the general ledger.

a. Explain the difference between these two specific balance-related audit objectives.

b. For the audit of accounts payable, which of these two specific balance-related audit objectives would usually be more important? Explain.

5-26 ⑤ The following (1 through 17) are the balance-related, transaction-related, and presentation- and disclosure-related audit objectives.

Assertions about classes of transactions and events	Assertions about account balances	Assertions about presentation and disclosure
1. Occurrence	6. Existence	11. Occurrence and
	7. Rights and obligations	12. Rights and obligations
2. Completeness	8. Completeness	13. Completeness
3. Accuracy		14. Accuracy and
	9. Valuation and	15.Valuation
	10. Allocation	
4. Cutoff		
5. Classification		16. Classification and
		17. Understandability

REQUIRED

Identify the specific audit objective (1-17) that each of the following specific audit procedures (a. through l.) satisfies in the audit of sales, accounts receivable, and cash receipts for the current fiscal year.

a. Examine a sample of duplicate sales invoices to determine whether each one has a shipping document attached.

b. Add all customer balances in the accounts receivable trial balance and agree the amount to the general ledger.

c. For a sample of sales transactions selected from the sales journal, verify that the amount of the transaction has been recorded in the correct customer account in the accounts receivable total field of the customer master file.

d. Inquire of the client whether any accounts receivable balances have been pledged as collateral on long-term debt and determine whether all required information is included in the footnote description for long-term debt.

e. For a sample of shipping documents selected from shipping records, trace each shipping document to a transaction recorded in the sales journal.

f. Discuss with credit department personnel the likelihood of collection of all accounts with a balance greater than $100,000 and greater than 90 days old as of the year end.

g. Examine sales invoices for the last five sales transactions recorded in the sales journal in the current year and examine shipping documents to determine that they are recorded in the correct period.

h. For a sample of customer accounts receivable balances at the year end, examine subsequent cash receipts in the following month to determine whether the customer paid the balance due.

i. Determine whether all risks related to accounts receivable are adequately disclosed.

j. Foot the sales journal for the month of July (half way through the fiscal year) and trace postings to the general ledger.

k. Send letters to a sample of accounts receivable customers to verify whether they have an outstanding balance at the fiscal year end.

l. Determine whether long-term receivables and related party receivables are reported separately in the financial statements.

Professional Judgment Problem

5-27 ① ③ Jane was the audit supervisor in charge of the audit of an advertising agency. Unfortunately, two other audit supervisors in the office resigned and moved on to other positions. Rather than hiring or promoting another supervisor, the firm reallocated clients. Jane was asked to take on some of the other audit clients and spend less time reviewing files and supervising staff. The audit managers and partners were expected to do a more thorough audit review to help compensate for the fewer than usual number of supervisors.

Jane felt harried, and her audit staff at the advertising agency were upset that she had not been present there for several days. The tax provision looked complex, and Jane decided to leave the tax section for the tax area to review.

To Jane's horror, she discovered six months later that the tax provision had been incorrect by over $100,000. The client was upset that the financial statements were materially in error and decided to seek other auditors.

Using your knowledge of audit standards and the audit process, explain which audit phases were poorly executed in the audit of the advertising agency. Provide suggestions for improvement to help prevent this type of error in the future.

Case

5-28 ❶ Rene Ritter opened a small grocery and related products convenience store in 1990 with the money she had saved working as a Loblaws store manager. She named it Ritter Dairy and Fruits. Because of the excellent location and her fine management skills, Ritter Dairy and Fruits grew to three locations by 1995. By that time, she needed additional capital. She obtained financing through a local bank at 2 percent above prime, under the condition that she submit quarterly financial statements reviewed by a public accounting firm approved by the bank. After interviewing several firms, she decided to use the firm of Gonzalez & Fineberg, PAs, after obtaining approval from the bank.

By 1999, the company had grown to six stores, and Rene developed a business plan to add another 10 stores in the next several years. Ritter's capital needs had also grown, so Rene decided to add two business partners who both had considerable capital and some expertise in convenience stores. After further discussions with the bank and continued conversations with the future business partners, she decided to have an annual audit and quarterly reviews done by Gonzalez & Fineberg, even though the additional cost was almost $15,000 annually. The bank agreed to reduce the interest rate on the $4,000,000 loan to 1 percent above prime.

By 2004, things were going smoothly, with the two business partners heavily involved in the day-to-day operations and the company adding two new stores per year. The company was growing steadily and was more profitable than they had expected. By the end of 2005, one of the business partners, Fred Warnest, had taken over responsibility for accounting and finance operations, as well as some marketing. Annually, Gonzalez & Fineberg did an in-depth review of the accounting system, including internal controls, and reported their conclusions and recommendations to the board of directors. Specialists in the firm provided tax and other advice. The other business partner in the dairy, Ben Gold, managed most of the stores and was primarily responsible for building new stores. Rene was president and managed four stores.

In 2009, the three business partners (now the executive management of the company) decided to go public to enable them to add more stores and modernize the existing ones. The public offering was a major success, resulting in $25 million in new capital and nearly 1,000 shareholders. Ritter Dairy and Fruits added stores rapidly, and the company remained highly profitable under the leadership of Ritter, Warnest, and Gold.

Rene retired in 2012 after a highly successful career. During the retirement celebration, she thanked her business partners, employees, and customers. She also added a special thanks to the bank management for their outstanding service and to Gonzalez & Fineberg for being partners in the best and most professional sense of the word. She mentioned their integrity, commitment, high-quality service in performing their audits and reviews, and considerable tax and business advice for more than two decades.

REQUIRED

a. Explain why the bank imposed a requirement of a quarterly review of the financial statements as a condition of obtaining the loan at 2 percent above prime. Also, explain why the bank did not require an audit and why the bank demanded the right to approve which public accounting firm was engaged.

b. Explain why Ritter Dairy and Fruits agreed to have an audit performed rather than a review, considering the additional cost of $15,000.

c. What did Rene mean when she referred to Gonzalez & Fineberg as "partners"? Does the PA firm have an independence problem?

d. What benefit does Gonzalez & Fineberg provide to shareholders, creditors, and management in performing the audit and related services?

e. What are the responsibilities of the PA firm to shareholders, creditors, management, and others?

Ongoing Small Business Case: Transaction Flows at CondoCleaners.com

5-29 ❹ ❺ Jim is doing preliminary planning to organize transaction flows at CondoCleaners.com. His secure website will use a credit card service to process customer payments, which will be deposited directly into the business bank account. He will pay for expenses using his own credit card or personal cheque, then submit expenses to the company monthly. Once he decides to hire employees, he will initially do the payroll calculations himself and issue cheques manually.

REQUIRED

a. List the financial statement cycles that will be present at CondoCleaners.com. For each financial statement cycle, list three general ledger accounts that will likely be present at the company.

b. Using Figure 5-4 as a guide, draw a flow diagram showing how sales will be processed at CondoCleaners.com.

c. Describe three specific transaction-related audit objectives that you would use to audit the sales revenue at CondoCleaners.com.

2011 Annual Report

HILLSBURG HARDWARE LIMITED 2011 ANNUAL REPORT

CONTENTS

Rick Chulick, President and Chief Operating Officer

DEAR SHAREHOLDERS: March 29, 2012

We are proud to announce another year of noticeable improvement.

In last year's letter we stated, "We are committed to increasing the efficiency and effectiveness of operations through cost savings and productivity improvements. In addition, we intend to maintain and further develop our customer base through recently implemented post-sale service programs." The operating results in this report demonstrate that our objectives have been achieved, resulting in a net income increase of $740,000 from 2010 to 2011. This amounts to 15 cents per share, a 23.2% increase from last year. Our goal in the current year is to further improve the results of operations and create value for shareholders. In doing so, we will focus primarily on the following three strategic components of our business plan:

1. Post-sale service arrangements designed to further develop and maintain our customer base.

2. Aggressive advertising campaigns that allow us to penetrate markets dominated by national wholesale hardware store chains.

3. Implementation of new warehouse technology designed to increase productivity and reduce stocking and distribution costs.

We will report our progress throughout the year.

Christopher J. Kurran
Chief Executive Officer

Rick Chulick
President and Chief Operating Officer

2

HISTORY

Hillsburg Stores Ltd. began operations in 1980 in Halifax, Nova Scotia, as a retail hardware store chain. On September 25, 1986, Hillsburg merged with Handy Hardware and Lumber Company, which established the concept of selling high-quality hardware through wholesale distribution outlets in 1981, to form Handy-Hillsburg, Inc., a provincial corporation. On June 5, 1990, after spinning off all of its lumber-related assets to Handy Corporation, the company changed its name to Hillsburg Hardware, Ltd. On October 22, 1992, the company reincorporated as a federal company and changed its name to Hillsburg Hardware Limited (heareafter referred to as "the Company"), which trades on the TSX under the symbol "HLSB."

OVERVIEW

Hillsburg Hardware Limited is a wholesale distributor of hardware equipment to a variety of independent, high-quality hardware stores in the eastern part of Canada. The primary products are power and hand tools, landscaping equipment, electrical equipment, residential and commercial construction equipment, and a wide selection of paint products.

More than 90% of the Company's products are purchased from manufacturers and shipped either directly to customers or to the main warehouse in Halifax, Nova Scotia, where shipments are combined to minimize the costs of freight and handling.

Hardware retailers, now more than ever, find it advantageous to purchase from us rather than directly from manufacturers. We make it possible for smaller, independent retailers to purchase on an as-needed basis, rather than in bulk. Moreover, we offer our customers a range of high-quality products that cannot be found at most national chains.

We also offer far more post-sale services to customers than are offered by manufacturers and other national distributors. We simplify the purchasing process by assigning each customer a permanent salesperson. Each salesperson becomes involved in the sales process and also acts as a liaison between the customer and post-sale service areas. For example, when customers experience technical problems with recently purchased hardware, their salesperson has the responsibility to coordinate both exchanges and warranty repairs with the manufacturer. This process adds value for customers and makes post-sales service more efficient and less problematic. Low turnover and extensive training of our salespeople enhance this service.

To further encourage customer loyalty, each customer is given access to our internal database system—ONHAND (Online Niche-Hardware Availability Notification Database). The ONHAND system lets customers check the availability of hard-to-find products instantly over the Internet. Moreover, the system includes data such as expected restock dates for items that are currently sold out and expected availability dates for items that will soon be introduced to the market.

Because of the two aforementioned processes, we have managed to maintain a repeat-customer base. Nearly 75% of all first-time customers make at least one additional purchase within one year of their first purchase.

Recently, there have been major consolidations in the wholesale hardware industry. We believe this consolidation trend is advantageous to our operations as a distributor of hard-to-find, high-quality hardware equipment. The recent consolidation of Builder's Plus Hardware, Inc., one of the top ten largest national hardware store chains, is a case in point. One month after the consolidation, Builder's Plus decided not to carry high-end construction and landscaping equipment in order to focus on what it called the "typical hardware customer."

PRODUCTS

To more effectively manage inventory, we carefully monitor the composition of net sales by category of items sold. The following chart indicates the percentage of net sales by class of merchandise sold during the years 2011, 2010, and 2009:

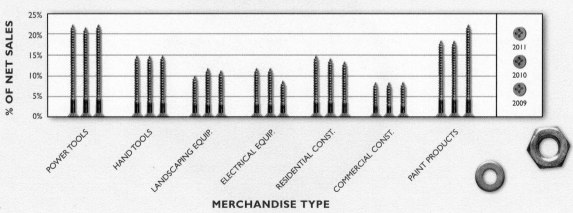

MARKETING PROGRAM

This year, the Company made a significant investment in a new advertising campaign. Various radio, newspaper, magazine, and television advertisements were purchased at the local and regional levels using the Company's new catchphrase, "Hardware for Hard Workers." The new jingle has been partially responsible for the fiscal 2011 increase in sales of 9%.

CUSTOMERS

The majority of our customers are located in Nova Scotia, Prince Edward Island, New Brunswick, and Newfoundland and Labrador. Our current customer base consists of more than 400 independently owned hardware stores. Approximately 25% of our customers make up more than 80% of total sales revenue. To promote long-standing relationships with customers, we offer an array of incentive and customer appreciation programs. Since these programs were implemented in 2001, customer satisfaction ratings have improved steadily in each subsequent year.

SUPPLIERS

We purchase hardware and other products from more than 300 manufacturers. No single vendor accounted for more than 5% of our purchases during fiscal 2011, but our 25 largest vendors accounted for nearly 35%. We currently have long-term supply agreements with two vendors: Mechanical Tools and Painter's Paradise. These agreements are in effect until the end of fiscal year 2012. The combined dollar amount of each contract is not expected to exceed 5% of total purchases for the year.

COMPETITORS

There are other regional wholesale hardware distributors that compete with the Company, but national wholesale hardware store chains dominate the industry. Most of our competitors are not only larger, but have greater financial resources than our company. Eight national chains exist in the geographic area in which Hillsburg Hardware Limited operates. Of the eight national chains, Hardware Bros., Tools & Paint, and Construction City account for a significant portion of the wholesale hardware market share and also carry the hard-to-find and high-quality items we provide. The success of our business depends on our ability to keep distribution costs to a minimum and our customers satisfied through superior customer service.

The chart that follows is a breakdown of market share in the wholesale hardware market by competitor category, including the 2% market share held by the Company. The chart illustrates that we have considerable opportunity for sales growth.

EMPLOYEES

Hillsburg Hardware currently employs 319 individuals. The majority of our employees are involved in day-to-day sales. Because of our marketing and customer relations strategy, we make significant investments in ongoing training and professional development activities. Each year employees are required to attend 75 hours of professional training. Each employee receives a performance evaluation at least four times per year, usually once each quarter. Our turnover is among the lowest in the industry because of our compensation, training, and evaluation programs. We regard our employees as our most valuable asset.

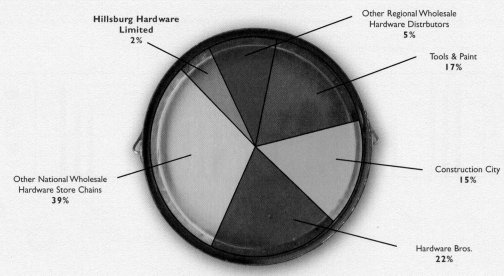

- Hillsburg Hardware Limited 2%
- Other Regional Wholesale Hardware Distrbutors 5%
- Tools & Paint 17%
- Construction City 15%
- Hardware Bros. 22%
- Other National Wholesale Hardware Store Chains 39%

PROPERTIES

The Company owns and operates its main warehouse and an administrative office. The main warehouse and administrative office are in the same 475,000 square-foot building. We also rent a second warehouse for $312,000 annually. The building, located in Sydney, Nova Scotia, serves as an off-site storage facility.

LEGAL PROCEEDINGS

On September 3, 2010, a suit was filed in the Municipal Court in Yarmouth, Nova Scotia against the Company. The product liability suit, "*Don Richards* v. *Hillsburg Hardware Limited*" is related to injuries that resulted from an alleged defective design of a tractor manufactured by Silo-Tractor, a Canadian corporation. The suit is currently in pretrial proceedings. In the opinion of our legal counsel, the suit is without merit. We intend to vigorously defend our position.

The Company does not believe any other legal issues materially affect its finances.

EXECUTIVE OFFICERS

The following list provides names and present positions of the Company's officers:

NAME	POSITION
John P. Higgins	Chairman of the Board
Rick Chulick	President and Chief Operating Officer (a)
Christopher J. Kurran	Chief Executive Officer (b)
Avis A. Zomer	Chief Financial Officer
Brandon S. Mack	Vice-President, Sales and Marketing
Mary R. Moses	Vice-President, Merchandising
Vanessa M. Namie	Vice-President, Operations (c)
Joseph A. Akuroi	Vice-President, Quality Assurance (d)

(a) Mr. Chulick has been President and Chief Operating Officer of the Company since November 2001. Mr. Chulick was Chairman of the Board from 2004 to 2006.
(b) Mr. Kurran has been Chief Executive Officer of the Company since September 2001. Prior to his role as CEO, Mr. Kurran was employed from 1992 to 2000 by Trini Enterprises, an industrial distributor.
(c) Ms. Namie has been employed by the Company since its inception in 1992. She has held her current position since 2000 and served as an operations manager from 1992 to 2000.
(d) Mr. Akuroi was Chief Operating Officer and President of Hardware Bros., one of the ten largest wholesale hardware chains in the country, from 1998 to 2003.

CONTROLS AND PROCEDURES

Pursuant to securities commission rules, we have carefully evaluated the effectiveness of the design and operation of our disclosure controls and procedures. After careful review of all controls and procedures, our Chief Executive Officer and Chief Financial Officer implemented a new control over the internal verification and timely recording of sales transactions. In compliance with requirements, the CEO and CFO have certified to the OSC that internal controls are operating effectively in all material respects. The Company will continue to monitor the effectiveness of all disclosure controls and procedures and make modifications whenever necessary.

INFORMATION REGARDING COMMON EQUITY

Hillsburg Hardware Limited's common stock currently trades on the TSX under the symbol "HLSB." The following chart shows the high and low prices of the Company's common stock by quarter for the years 2011 and 2010:

	2011		2010	
	High	Low	High	Low
Quarter 1	12.50	9.05	13.30	10.00
Quarter 2	12.55	10.10	12.75	10.25
Quarter 3	12.30	10.99	14.10	9.75
Quarter 4	12.40	8.95	11.50	8.20

On March 23, 2011, there were 1,250 shareholders of our common stock.

DIVIDEND POLICY

Dividend payments on common stock are authorized annually by the Board of Directors. For 2011, dividend payments totaled $1.9 million, which is $0.38 per share.

HLSB +12.40

To the Shareholders of Hillsburg Hardware Limited

We have audited the accompanying financial statements of Hilllsburg Hardware Limited, which comprise the statements of financial position as at December 31, 2011and December 31, 2010, and the statement of comprehensive income, statement of changes in equity and statement of cash flows for the years ended December 31, 2011 and December 31, 2010, and a summary of significant accounting policies and other explanatory information.

Management s Responsibility for the Financial Statements

Management is responsible for the preparation and fair presentation of these financial statements in accordance with International Financial Reporting Standards, and for such internal control as management determines is necessary to enable the preparation of financial statements that are free from material misstatement, whether due to fraud or error.

Auditor s Responsibility

Our responsibility is to express an opinion on these financial statements based on our audits. We conducted our audits in accordance with Canadian generally accepted auditing standards. Those standards require that we comply with ethical requirements and plan and perform the audit to obtain reasonable assurance about whether the financial statements are free from material misstatement.

An audit involves performing procedures to obtain audit evidence about the amounts and disclosures in the financial statements. The procedures selected depend on the auditor's judgment, including the assessment of the risks of material misstatement of the financial statements, whether due to fraud or error. In making those risk assessments, the auditor considers internal control relevant to the entity's preparation and fair presentation of the financial statements in order to design audit procedures that are appropriate in the circumstances, but not for the purpose of expressing an opinion on the effectiveness of the entity's internal control. An audit also includes evaluating the appropriateness of accounting policies used and the reasonableness of accounting estimates made by management, as well as evaluating the overall presentation of the financial statements.

We believe that the audit evidence we have obtained in our audits is sufficient and appropriate to provide a basis for our audit opinion.

Opinion

In our opinion, the financial statements present fairly, in all material respects, the financial position of Hillsburg Hardware Limited as at December 31, 2011 and December 31, 2010, its financial performance and its cash flows for the years ended December 31, 2011 and December 31, 2010 in accordance with International Financial Reporting Standards..

Berger, Kao, Kadous & Co., LLP

Berger, Kao, Kadous & Co., LLP
March 21, 2012
Halifax, Nova Scotia

7

FINANCIAL STATEMENTS

Management s Accountability

To Our Shareholders:

The management of Hillsburg Hardware Limited is responsible for the accompanying Financial Statements and all other information in the annual report. The financial statements have been prepared by management in accordance with International Financial Reporting Standards, which recognize the necessity of relying on some best estimates and informed judgments. All financial information in the annual report is consistent with the Financial Statements.

To discharge its responsibilities for financial reporting and safeguarding of assets, management depends on the Company's systems of internal accounting control. These systems are designed to provide reasonable assurance that the financial records are reliable and form a proper basis for the timely and accurate preparation of financial statements. Management meets the objectives of internal accounting control on a cost-effective basis through the prudent selection and training of personnel, adoption and communication of appropriate policies, and employment of an internal audit program.

The Board of Directors oversees management's responsibilities for financial statements primarily through the activities of its Audit Committee, which is composed solely of Directors who are neither officers nor employees of the Company. This Committee meets with management and the Company's independent auditors, Berger, Kao, Kadous & Co., LLP, to review the financial statements and recommend approval by the Board of Directors. The Audit Committee is also responsible for making recommendations with respect to the appointment and remuneration of the Company's auditors. The Audit Committee also meets with the auditors, without the presence of management, to discuss the results of their audit, their opinion on internal accounting controls, and the quality of financial reporting.

The financial statements have been audited by Berger, Kao, Kadous & Co., LLP, whose appointment was ratified by shareholder vote at the annual shareholders' meeting.

John P. Higgins	Christopher J. Kurran	Avis A. Zomer
Chairman of the Board	Chief Executive Officer	Chief Financial Officer

8

HILLSBURG HARDWARE LIMITED

Statement of financial position at 31 December 2011(in thousands)

ASSETS	2011	2010
Non-current assets		
Land	3,456	3,456
Buildings	32,500	32,500
Equipment, furniture, and fixtures	6,304	8,660
Less: Accumulated Amortisation	(31,920)	(33,220)
Total Property, plant and equipment	$10,340	$10,896
Total non-current assets	**10,340**	**10,896**
Current assets		
Inventories	29,865	31,600
Trade receivables (net of allowances of $1,240 and $1,311)	18,957	16,210
Other receivables	945	915
Prepaid Expenses	432	427
Cash and bank balances	828	743
Total current assets	51,027	49,895
Total assets	**$61,367**	**$60,791**
EQUITY AND LIABILITIES		
Capital		
Issued Capital	$8,500	$8,500
Retained earnings	13,963	11,929
Total Equity	22,463	20,429
Non-current liabilities		
Notes payable	24,120	26,520
Deferred Income tax liability	738	722
Other long-term payables	830	770
Total non-current liabilities	25,688	28,012
Current liabilities		
Trade accounts payable	4,720	4,432
Notes payable	4,180	4,589
Accrued payroll	1,350	715
Accured payroll taxes	120	116
Accrued interest and dividends payable	2,050	1,975
Accrued income tax	796	523
Total current liabilities	**13,216**	**12,350**
Total Liabilties	**38,904**	**40,362**
Total equity and liabilities	**$61,367**	**$60,791**

"We offer our customers a range of high-quality products that cannot be found at most national chains."

9

HILLSBURG HARDWARE LIMITED STATEMENT OF COMPREHENSIVE INCOME FOR THE YEAR ENDED 31 DECEMBER 2011 (in thousands)		
	2011	2010
Revenue	$1,43,086	$1,31,226
Cost of sales	1,03,241	94,876
Gross profit	39,845	36,350
Selling, general, and administrative expenses	(32,475)	(29,656)
Interest Expense	(2,409)	(2,035)
Gain on sale of assets	720	—
Profit before tax	5,681	4,659
Income tax expense	(1,747)	(1,465)
Total comprehensive income for the year	$3,934	$3,194
Earnings per share	$0.79	$0.64

CHANGES IN EQUITY

HILLSBURG HARDWARE LIMITED STATEMENT OF CHANGES IN EQUITY				
	Common Stock		Contributed	Retained	Total
	Shares	Par value	Surplus	Earnings	Shareholders Equity
Balance as at December 31, 2009	5000	$5,000	$3,500	$10,635	$19,135
Net Income				3,194	3,194
Dividends paid				(1,900)	(1,900)
Balance as at December 31, 2010	5000	$5,000	3,500	11,929	20,429
Net Income				3,934	3,934
Dividends paid				(1,900)	(1,900)
Balance as at December 31, 2011	5000	$5,000	$3,500	$13,963	$22,463

10

CASH FLOWS

	2011	2010
HILLSBURG HARDWARE LIMITED		
STATEMENTS OF CASH FLOWS (in thousands)		
Year Ended December 31, 2011		
	2011	**2010**
Cash Flows from Operating Activities		
Cash flows provided by (used in) operating activities		
Net Income	$ 3,934	$ 3,194
Amortisation	1,452	1,443
Loss on sale of assets	(720)	–
Deferred income taxe liability increase (decrease)	16	(8)
Changes in non-cash working capital		
Trade and other receivables	(2,777)	(393)
Inventories	1,735	(295)
Prepaid expenses	(5)	(27)
Accounts payable	288	132
Accrued liabilities	714	77
Income taxes payable	273	23
Net Cash provided by operating activities	4,910	4,146
Cash Flows from investing activities		
Capital expenditures	(10,500)	(1,800)
Sale of equipment	10,324	–
Net cash used in investing activities	(176)	(1,800)
Cash flows from financing activities		
Dividend payment	(1,900)	(1,900)
Proceeds (repayments) from borrowings (net)	(2,749)	(423)
Net cash used in financial activities	(4,649)	(2,323)
Net increase in cash	85	23
Cash at the beginning of year	743	720
Cash at the end of year	$ 828	$ 743

II

1. DESCRIPTION OF SIGNIFICANT ACCOUNTING POLICIES AND BUSINESS

We are a wholesale distributor of high-quality power tools, hand tools, electrical equipment, landscaping equipment, residential and commercial construction equipment, and paint products. The majority of our customers are smaller, independent hardware stores located in Nova Scotia, Prince Edward Island, New Brunswick, and Newfoundland and Labrador.

Allowance for Doubtful Accounts: Our allowance for doubtful accounts is maintained to account for expected credit losses. Estimates of bad debts are based on individual customer risks and historical collection trends. Allowances are evaluated and updated when conditions occur that give rise to collection issues.

Inventory: Inventories are stated at the lower of cost and net realizable value. Costs of inventories are determined on a first-in-first-out basis. Net Realizable value represents the estimated selling price for inventories less all estimated costs of completion and costs necessary to make the sale. To present accurately the estimated net realizable value of the accounts, we adjust inventory balances when current and expected future market conditions, as well as recent and historical turnover trends, indicate adjustments are necessary.

Property and Equipment: Land, buildings, computers and other equipment, and furniture and fixtures are stated at historical cost. Depreciation is calculated on a straight-line basis over estimated useful lives of the assets. Estimated useful lives are 20 to 35 years for buildings and 2 to 10 years for equipment and furniture and fixtures.

Revenue Recognition: Revenue is measured at the fair value of the consideration received or receivable. Revenue is reduced for estimated customer returns, rebates and other similar allowances. Revenue from sale of goods is recognized when the goods are delivered and titles have passed at which time all the following conditions are satisfied: (i) the company has transferred to the buyer the significant risks and rewards of the ownership of goods, (ii) the company retains neither continuing managerial involvement to the degree usually associated with ownership nor effective control over the goods sold, (iii) the amount of revenue can be measured reliably, (iv) it is probable that the economic benefits associated with the transaction will flow to the company, and (v) the costs incurred or to be incurred in respect of the transaction can be measured reliably.

Income Taxes: The deferred income tax liability account includes temporary differences between financial accounting income and taxable income. The account consists largely of temporary differences related to (1) the valuation of inventory, (2) depreciation, and (3) other accruals.

2. OTHER RECEIVABLES

The other receivables balance consists largely of vendor allowances and vendor rebates. When vendor allowances and vendor rebates are recognized (all activities required by the supplier are completed, the amount is determinable, and collectibility is reasonably certain), they are recorded as reductions of costs of goods sold.

3. NOTES PAYABLE

Notes payable for the year ended December 31, 2011 consists of three notes payable to the bank. Each note carries a fixed interest rate of 8.5%. One note for $4,180,000 matures in June 2012 and the other two mature on December 31, 2013. During 2011, there was an additional note outstanding in the amount of $4,400,000, which was paid off during October 2011.

4. COMMITMENTS

The Company is currently committed to an operating lease that expires in 2014. Rental payments for the remainder of the lease are set at $312,000 per annum.

5. SEGMENT REPORTING

The Company operates in one segment. The breakdown of revenues (in thousands) from different products is listed in the chart below:

SEGMENT REPORTING		
	2011	2010
Power Tools	$ 31,479	$ 27,557
Hand Tools	21,463	19,684
Landscaping Equipment	14,309	15,645
Electrical Equipment	17,170	15,849
Residential Construction Merchandise	18,372	15,949
Commercial Construction Merchandise	10,498	9,815
Paint Products	25,755	23,621
	$1,43,086	**$1,31,226**

6. EARNINGS PER SHARE

Earnings per share calculations for 2011 and 2010 were computed as follows:

Numerators
(net income in thousands): $3,934, and $3,194

Denominators
(shares of common stock): 5,000,000
(unchanged for all years)

Diluted earnings per share were the same as basic earnings per share for all years.

12

**Management's Discussion and Analysis
of Financial Condition and Results of Operations**

The following discussion and analysis of the results of our operations and our financial condition are based on the financial statements and related notes included in this report. When preparing the financial statements, we are frequently required to use our best estimates and judgments. These estimates and judgments affect certain asset, liability, revenue, and expense account balances. Therefore, estimates are evaluated constantly based on our analyses of historical trends and our understanding of the general business environment in which we operate. There are times, however, when different circumstances and assumptions cause actual results to differ from those expected when judgments were originally made. The accounting policies referred to in Note 1 to the financial statements, in our opinion, influence the judgments and estimates we use to prepare our financial statements.

RESULTS OF OPERATIONS

For the year ended December 31, 2011, gross profit increased by 9.6% or $3,495,000 from 2010. This increase in gross profit more than offsets the increase in operating expenses from 2010 to 2011 of $2,819,000 or 9.5%. The increase in gross margin largely explains the operating income increase of $676,000.

For the year ended December 31, 2010, gross profit increased by $2,389,000 or 7% from 2009. Total operating expenses increased by $1,219,000 or approximately 4.3% from 2009. The increase in gross profit offset the total operating expense increase, and the net result was a $1,170,000 increase in operating income.

Net Sales: From 2010 to 2011 net sales increased by $11,860,000 or 9%. The increase in net sales can be explained largely by an aggressive advertising campaign that the Company organized during the second half of 2011. Net sales for 2010 increased by $8,541,000 or 7% from 2009, which is consistent with industry-wide average revenue growth of 7% from 2009 to 2010.

Gross Profit: Gross profit as a percentage of net sales stayed relatively stable at 27.68% and 27.70% in 2009 and 2010, respectively, but increased to 27.85% in 2011. The 2011 increase is mostly due to improved vendor incentive programs, our focus on cost containment, and increases in the resale values of certain commodities such as PVC piping material and certain types of metal wiring. While gross profit percentages in the industry have declined somewhat, our position as a niche provider in the overall hardware market allows us to charge premium prices without losing customers.

Selling, General and Administrative Expenses: Selling expenses increased by $1,911,000 or 14.8% from 2010 to 2011 and by $805,000 or 6.7% from 2009 to 2010. As a percentage of net sales, selling expenses increased by 0.52% since 2010 and decreased by 0.03% from 2009 to 2010. The increase in selling expenses as a percentage of net sales from 2010 to 2011 is due to our new advertising campaign and increased expenditures on sales meetings and training.

General and administrative expenses increased by $908,000 or 5.4% from 2010 to 2011 and by $414,000 or 2.5% from 2009 to 2010. As a percentage of net sales, general and administrative expenses decreased by 0.42% since 2010 and decreased by 0.55% from 2009 to 2010. The overall increase from 2010 to 2011 was caused mostly by unexpected repairs needed to reattach and replace damaged shelving units in our main warehouse building.

Interest Expense: In 2011 interest expense increased by $374,000, or approximately 18.4%, compared to 2010. The increase was due to an overall interest rate increase and the restructuring of debt covenants that are less restrictive but demand higher interest rates. In 2010 interest expense decreased by $138,000 or 6.4% compared to 2009. The 2010 decrease was mainly due to the Company's decision to decrease the level of long-term debt. The average interest rates on short- and long-term debt during 2011 were approximately 10.5% and 8.5% respectively.

LIQUIDITY

During 2011, our working capital requirements were primarily financed through our line of credit, under which we are permitted to borrow up to the lesser of $7,000,000 or 75% of accounts receivable outstanding less than 30 days. The average interest rate on these short-term borrowings in 2011 was approximately 10.5%.

Cash provided by operating activities for 2011 and 2011 was $4,910,000 and $4,146,000 respectively. The change from 2010 to 2011 is primarily due to the increase in net income. Increases in receivables were largely offset by decreases in inventories and increases in payables and other current liabilities. The increase in cash provided from operating activities of $1,491,000 from 2009 to 2010 is largely the result of the increase in net income and smaller increases in receivables and merchandise inventory in 2010 compared to 2009. We believe that cash flow from operations and the available short-term line of credit will continue to allow us to finance operations throughout the current year.

STATEMENT OF CONDITION

Merchandise inventory and trade accounts receivable together accounted for over 95% of current assets in both 2011 and 2010. Merchandise inventory turned over approximately 3.4 times in 2011 and 3.0 times in 2009. Average days to sell inventory were 108.6 and 120.9 in 2011 and 2010 respectively. Net trade receivables turned over approximately 7.6 times in 2011 and in 2010. Days to collect accounts receivable computations were 48.1 and 48.0 in 2011 and 2010 respectively. Both inventory and accounts receivable turnover are lower than industry averages. We plan for this difference to satisfy the market in which we operate. Our market consists of smaller, independent hardware stores that need more favourable receivable collection terms and immediate delivery of inventory. Because we hold large amounts of inventory, we are able to fill orders quicker than most of our competitors even during the busiest times of the year.

OUTLOOK

During 2011 we experienced another year of noticeable improvement. The Company's financial performance can largely be attributed to (1) a continued focus on cost containment, (2) productivity improvements, (3) aggressive advertising, and (4) the implementation of programs designed to enhance customer satisfaction.

During 2012, we will continue to apply the same strategic efforts that improved 2011 performance. We are also implementing a new warehouse information system designed to increase productivity and reduce stocking and distribution costs. Management believes that earnings growth will be primarily driven by (1) continued focus on customer satisfaction, (2) penetration into markets currently dominated by national wholesale hardware store chains, and (3) the use of technology to attract additional customers and promote more efficient operations.

INFORMATION CONCERNING FORWARD-LOOKING STATEMENTS

This report contains certain forward-looking statements (referenced by such terms as "expects" or "believes") that are subject to the effects of various factors including (1) changes in wholesale hardware prices, (2) changes in the general business environment, (3) the intensity of the competitive arena, (4) new national wholesale hardware chain openings, and (5) certain other matters influencing the Company's ability to react to changing market conditions. Therefore, management wishes to make readers aware that the aforementioned factors could cause the actual results of our operations to differ considerably from those indicated by any forward-looking statements included in this report.

HILLSBURG HARDWARE LIMITED
FIVE-YEAR FINANCIAL SUMMARY (in thousands, except for per share amounts)

STATEMENT OF FINANCIAL POSITION DATA:

	2011	2010	2009	2008	2007
Current assets	$ 51,027	$ 49,895	$ 49,157	$ 47,689	$ 46,504
Total assets	61,367	60,791	59,696	57,441	51,580
Long-term notes payable	24,120	26,520	26,938	25,432	25,223
Current liabilities	13,216	12,350	12,173	12,166	9,628
Total shareholders equity	22,463	20,429	19,135	18,756	15,764

STATEMENT OF COMPREHENSIVE INCOME DATA:

	2011	2010	2009	2008	2007
Revenue	$ 143,086	$ 131,226	$ 122,685	$ 120,221	$ 117,115
Cost of sales	103,241	94,876	88,724	88,112	85,663
Gross profit	39,845	36,350	33,961	32,109	31,452
Profit before income taxes	5,681	4,659	3,351	3,124	1,450
Net income	3,934	3,194	2,279	2,142	994
Cash provided by operating activities	4,910	4,146	2,655	1,811	1,232
Per common share data:					
Net income	$ 0.79	$ 0.64	$ 0.46	$ 0.43	$ 0.22
Cash dividends per share	$ 0.38	$ 0.38	$ 0.38	$	$
Common shares outstanding	5,000	5,000	5,000	5,000	4,500

KEY OPERATING RESULTS AND FINANCIAL POSITION RATIOS:

	2011	2010	2009	2008	2007
Gross profit (%)	27.85%	27.70%	27.68%	26.71%	26.86%
Return on assets (%)	9.30%	7.73%	5.72%	5.73%	2.86%
Return on common equity (%)	26.49%	23.55%	17.69%	18.10%	9.50%

14

6   Client risk profile and documentation

How does an auditor decide whether a client is risky or not? This chapter identifies and talks about the many parts involved in developing and updating a client risk profile. The auditor needs to examine not only the industry and the business environment but also many details about the client and its governance process before deciding upon client business risk, overall risks of material misstatement, and risks of fraud. After these risks have been assessed, the auditor can move on to the audit plan. Management accountants can use this information to develop actions to mitigate risks, while public accountants (PAs), internal auditors, and specialists may be involved in the risk assessment process.

business risk. State why it is important to document related parties and transactions with them. Explain how preliminary analytical review is used during planning.

3 Determine what working papers the auditor retains to document the financial statement audit. Explain the purposes of working papers. Describe the common characteristics of high-quality working papers.

STANDARDS REFERENCED IN THIS CHAPTER

CICA Standards

CAS 230 – Audit documentation

CAS 300 – Planning an audit of financial statements

CAS 315 – Identifying and assessing the risks of material misstatement through understanding the entity and its environment

CAS 550 – Related parties

LEARNING OBJECTIVES

1 Explain the importance of an adequate audit planning process. Link the audit planning process to the development of a client risk profile. Explain the components of understanding the client's business and industry and assessing client business risk.

2 Describe the type of evidence that the auditor collects when developing the client risk profile and assessing client

Pssst—Would You Like to Buy a Town?

The aerial photographs of the town showed lush greenery and an ocean frontage. Other photos pictured a deserted shopping mall and deserted suburban streets, complete with mowed lawns. The American-owned mining town of Kitsault, B.C., had an asking price of $7 million according to the *Toronto Star* October 2, 2004. The town was abandoned two years after completion, in 1983, when the prices for molybdenum (used to strengthen steel) dropped, making the mine in Kitsault unprofitable.

In 2008, Avanti Mining was planning on reopening the mine, as it had resource estimates completed on the molybdenum content of the mine, believing that over 235 million pounds could be sold. It based its decision to purchase the mine in October 2008 on prices of US$20 per pound for molybdenum. Its website indicates that in the entire time that the Kitsault mine had previously been in operation (1967–1972 and 1981–1982), only about 30 million pounds of the metal had been mined. It has taken the last four years for the company to find business partners, complete an environmental assessment and work on obtaining permits for re-opening the mine.

Will Avanti succeed at Kitsault when other producers around the world have failed? Freeport-McMoRan Copper & Gold Inc. owns the Henderson molybdenum mine near Denver, Colorado. In November 2008, it announced that it would be reducing the labour force at that mine from 700 to 600 (a 100-employee lay-off) because of a drop in molybdenum prices down to US$12 per pound—a 60-percent price drop.

IMPORTANCE TO AUDITORS

The stories of these two mining companies illustrate how many businesses are vulnerable to raw material market prices and the importance of understanding the marketplace within which a business operates. Mines are sellers of basic metals, so they are particularly vulnerable to price changes. The unfolding credit crunch in 2008 was reflected in price drops for metals. Molybdenum prices from March 2006 to September 2008 had climbed gradually from the mid-US$20 range to upward of US$30 before dropping to about US$12 in November 2008, wiping out the gains of the past few years. A two-year chart of molybdenum prices shows fluctuations between about $13 and $18 per pound (per **www.infomine.com**).

Some companies can increase their prices for finished goods when prices for raw materials increase; others cannot. As market prices drop, companies may be forced to shed assets or change the way they run their operations to stay profitable.

WHAT DO YOU THINK?

1. Look at the appliances in your kitchen—refrigerators, stoves, microwaves, and toasters. Many raw materials were used to make these products—aluminum, plastic, and steel. If

continued >

continued

the cost of raw materials rose, what would happen to the companies that produced these appliances?

2. Why could or couldn't they increase their prices? How does raw material price volatility affect companies that produce appliances?

3. How would raw material price volatility affect the risk profile of your client, a major refrigerator producer?

The stories about molybdenum mines underline the importance of knowing both our client's operations and the external business environment. They also link to valuation issues in the financial statements, for if the metal goes down in price, then so will the inventory of the finished goods of that metal. Knowledge of the external environment helps detect such potential risks of misstatement in the financial statements. In this chapter, we will discuss two audit phases that comprise part of the audit risk assessment process (Phase 1, preplanning, was discussed in Chapter 5). Here, we will cover Phase 2, the Client Risk Profile, in considerable detail. We will also overview Phase 3, Plan the Audit, which is discussed in the next few chapters, completed in Chapter 10.

Sources: 1. Associated Press, "Henderson molybdenum production cut; Climax on hold," *Rocky Mountain News*, November 10. 2008, **www.rockymountainnews.com**, Accessed: November 30, 2008. 2. "Avanti Mining Finalizes Purchase of the Past Producing Kitsault Molybdenum Mine, British Columbia," October 20, 2008, News Release, **www.aventi.com**, Accessed: November 30, 2008. 3. Girard, Daniel, "Modern-day ghost town on the block," *Toronto Star*, October 2, 2004, p. H1, H3. 4. "Investment Mine," **www.infomine.com**, Accessed: November 30, 2008.5. Avanti Mining Inc., Kitsault Mine web site: **www.avantimining.com/s/Home.asp** and **www.avantimining.com/s/Kitsault.asp**; Accessed: January 10, 2012.

① The Importance of Audit Planning

Generally accepted auditing standards require adequate planning. This planning is done in response to risk assessment. The auditor should plan and perform the audit to reduce audit risk to an acceptably low level that is consistent with the objective of the audit. This means that the auditor conducts enough work to detect material misstatements to the targeted level of assurance, the complement of risk. (If audit risk is 3 percent, the auditor works to achieve 97 percent assurance of detecting material misstatements in the financial statements.) The purpose of planning is to provide for effective conduct of the audit (CAS 300, par. 04). If assistants are employed, they should be properly supervised, so the audit plan should include supervision methods for the audit team (CAS 300, par. 11).

CAS

CAS 300 (par. 9) states that the auditor must develop an audit plan that includes the following components:

- The nature, timing, and extent of audit procedures for the purpose of risk assessment.
- The nature, timing, and extent of additional audit procedures, linked to the individual audit assertions.

- Any other audit procedures that are needed for the audit to be conducted in accordance with GAAS (the exact wording is to state that the audit is conducted in compliance with the CASs).

This means that the audit plan includes a description of what the auditor will do during all phases of the audit, including preplanning and completion of the client risk profile. The audit plan is finalized when risk assessments are complete, which is why we describe Phase 3 of the audit as Plan the Audit. This is where the auditor determines the strategic approach for the audit.

There are three main reasons why the auditor should plan engagements properly: to enable the auditor to obtain sufficient appropriate audit evidence for the circumstances, to help keep audit costs reasonable, and to avoid misunderstandings with the client. Obtaining sufficient appropriate audit evidence is essential if the public accounting firm is to minimize legal liability and maintain a good reputation in the professional community. Keeping costs reasonable helps the firm remain competitive and thereby retain its clients, assuming the firm has a reputation for doing quality work. Avoiding misunderstandings with the client is important for good client relations and for facilitating quality work at reasonable costs. For example, suppose he or she informs the client that the audit will be completed before June 30 but is unable to finish it until August because of inadequate staff. The client is likely to be upset with the public accounting firm and may even sue for breach of contract.

Before the auditor can develop a detailed plan of action, he or she must have a clear understanding of the risks of material misstatement in the financial statements—the "what could go wrong" picture. Part of this risk assessment occurs before the client is accepted or before the decision to continue with the client takes place (during Phase 1, Preplanning, explained in Chapter 5). At that time, the auditor assesses the financial viability of the client as part of acceptance or continuance, identifies the client's reasons for an audit, conducts an independence threat analysis, obtains an engagement letter, and considers staffing for the engagement.

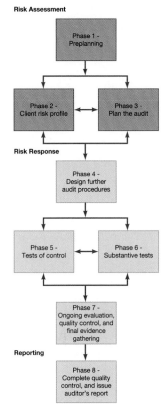

Develop Client Risk Profile

THE RELEVANCE OF A CLIENT RISK PROFILE In Phase 2, Client Risk Assessment, the auditor develops a thorough understanding of the client's business and industry to assess client business risk and to assess the risk of material misstatements or fraud for the financial statements overall. In Phase 3, the Audit Plan, the auditor moves to working with the audit risk model (discussed in Chapter 7). It is a knowledge of the relationships of those risks that drives the collection of data about the client. Our figure of the audit process shows the relationships between Phases 2 and 3 as cyclical—the auditor will keep working on the Client Risk Profile until sufficient information has been collected to determine Phase 3 audit risk, assess overall inherent risk, and decide upon materiality levels. However, the client risk profile will be updated if needed, as the audit progresses through later stages.

Figure 6-1 illustrates the auditor's strategic approach to understanding the client's business and industry, which is used to assess client business risk.

UNDERSTAND CLIENT'S BUSINESS AND INDUSTRY A thorough understanding of the client's business and industry and knowledge about the company's operations are essential for doing an adequate audit. The nature of the client's business and industry affects client business risk and the risk of material misstatements in the financial statements. (Recall that client business risk is the risk that the client will fail to meet its objectives.) In recent years, several factors have increased the importance of understanding the client's business and industry:

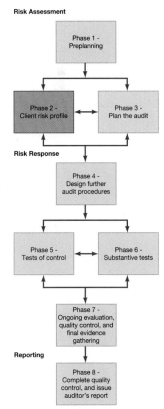

- Information technology connects client companies with major customers and suppliers. As a result, auditors need greater knowledge about major customers and suppliers and related risks.

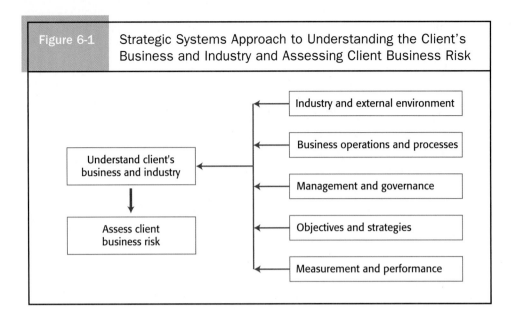

Figure 6-1 Strategic Systems Approach to Understanding the Client's Business and Industry and Assessing Client Business Risk

- Understand client's business and industry
  - Industry and external environment
  - Business operations and processes
  - Management and governance
  - Objectives and strategies
  - Measurement and performance
- Assess client business risk

- Clients have expanded operations globally, often through joint ventures or strategic alliances.
- Information technology affects internal client processes, improving the quality and timeliness of accounting information.
- The increased importance of human capital and other intangible assets has increased accounting complexity and the importance of management judgments and estimates.
- Auditors need a better understanding of the client's business and industry to provide additional value-added services to clients. For example, audit firms often offer assurance and consulting services related to information technology and risk management services to non-public audit clients, which requires an extensive knowledge of these clients' industries.

auditing in action 6-1
Teaming Up by Industry

A high level of knowledge of a client's industry and business is so critical to conducting quality audits and providing tax and consulting services that many accounting firms provide specialized expertise by industry. Here is a sample of Canadian firms:

www.kpmg.com/Ca/en/WhatWeDo/ Industries lists the following sectors: building, construction and real estate; consumer markets; energy; financial services; high growth markets; industrial markets; information, communications, and entertainment; mining; private equity; public sector; and special interests.

www.grantthornton.ca/sectors has privately held business; public companies; manu-

facturing and distribution; professional services; financial services; real estate; construction; and hospitality as its industry segments.

Rita Zelikman, Chartered Accountant, (**www. ritazelikman.com**), lists financial statement preparation; review engagements; taxation and tax planning; computerized bookkeeping, business consulting, and help with incorporating.

Organizing along industry or expertise lines helps public accounting firms focus their resources to better understand their client's business and provide value-added services.

Sources: 1. Grant Thornton, **www.grantthornton.ca/sectors**. 2. KPMG, **www.kpmg.com/Ca/en/WhatWeDo/Industries**. 3. Rita Zelikman, CA, **www.ritazelikman.com**. All accessed: January 10, 2011.

CAS 315, Identifying and assessing the risks of material misstatement through understanding the entity and its environment, requires the auditor to obtain knowledge of the entity's business and environment in order to assess risks and conduct the audit. The section lists factors to be understood in the external business environment, internal structures, internal controls, and risk assessment processes. This chapter and the next several chapters cover information to be documented and assessed, including internal controls, corporate governance, and fraud risks.

INDUSTRY AND EXTERNAL ENVIRONMENT There are three primary reasons for obtaining a good understanding of the client's industry:

1. Risks associated with specific industries may affect the auditor's assessment of client business risk and acceptable audit risk—and may even influence auditors against accepting engagements in riskier industries, such as high technology, biochemical, or small financial service organizations.

2. Certain inherent risks are typically common to all clients in certain industries. Familiarity with those risks aids the auditor in assessing their relevance to the client. Examples include potential inventory obsolescence in the fashion clothing industry, potential accounts receivable collection risks in the consumer loan industry, and risks of inadequate reserves for losses in the casualty insurance industry.

3. Many industries have unique accounting requirements that the auditor must understand to evaluate whether the client's financial statements are in accordance with the applicable financial reporting framework. For example, if the auditor is doing an audit of a city government, the auditor must understand governmental accounting and auditing requirements. Unique accounting requirements exist for construction companies, railways, not-for-profit organizations, financial institutions, and many other organizations.

Many auditor litigation cases (like those described in Chapter 4) could be the result of the auditor's failure to fully understand the nature of transactions in the client's industry. For example, several major accounting firms in the United States paid the federal government large settlements related to audits of failed savings and loans. In some of these audits, the auditors failed to understand the nature of significant real estate transactions. Currently, some firms internationally are facing lawsuits due to the declines in the values of asset-backed paper.

The auditor must also understand the client's external environment, including such things as economic conditions, extent of competition, and regulatory requirements. For example, auditors of utility companies need more than an understanding of the industry's unique regulatory accounting requirements. They must also know how recent deregulation in this industry has increased competition and how fluctuations in energy prices impact firm operations. To develop effective audit plans, auditors of all companies must have the expertise to assess external environment risks.

Knowledge of the client's industry can be obtained in different ways. These include discussions with the auditor in the firm who was responsible for the engagement in previous years and with other auditors in the firm currently on similar engagements, as well as conferences with the client's personnel, including internal auditors. Many of the larger public accounting firms have industry specialists who can be consulted for their expertise. Smaller firms that do not have the expertise can consult the practice advisory service of their professional body. There are often industry audit guides, textbooks, and technical magazines available for the auditor to study in most major industries. Some auditors subscribe to specialized journals for those industries to which they devote a large amount of time. Considerable knowledge can also be obtained by participating actively in industry associations and training programs.

BUSINESS OPERATIONS AND PROCESSES Knowledge about the client's business that differentiates it from other companies in its industry is also needed. This knowledge will help the auditor more effectively assess audit risk and inherent risk and will also

Table 6-1	Examples of Analytical Procedures Performed During Planning
Purpose	Analytical Procedure Performed During the Planning Phase
Understand the client's industry and business	Calculate key ratios for the client's business and compare them with industry averages.
Assess going concern	Calculate the debt-to-equity ratio and compare it with those of previous years and successful companies in the industry.
Indicate possible misstatements	Compare the gross margin with those of prior years, looking for large fluctuations.
Reduce detailed tests	Compare prepaid expenses and related expense accounts with those of prior years.

be useful in designing analytical procedures. Table 6-1 provides examples of analytical procedures that the auditor could use.

The auditor should understand factors such as major sources of revenue, key customers and suppliers, sources of financing, and information about related parties that may indicate areas of increased client business risk. For example, many technology firms are dependent on one or a few products that may become obsolete due to new technologies or stronger competitors. Dependence on a few major customers may result in material losses from bad debts or obsolete inventory. Here we will expand on four areas: operational and reporting structure, technology infrastructure, touring the plant and offices, and identifying related parties.

Operational and reporting structure Companies filing their financial statements with a securities commission, companies whose securities are traded in a public market, and all life insurance enterprises are required to disclose segment information by industry and by geographic area and the amount of export sales. Auditors must have sufficient knowledge of a company's business to enable them to evaluate whether segment information should be disclosed and, if so, to determine whether the appropriate segment information has been disclosed by the client.

The auditor's working paper files include the history of the company, a list of the major lines of business, and a record of the most important accounting policies in previous years. Study of this information and discussions with the client's personnel aid in understanding the business.

Where multiple corporate structures are involved, the relationship and ownership of the organizations should be documented, as should reporting lines of key management personnel. The auditor will also determine whether the organization operates in a centralized or decentralized fashion by looking at the flow of information in an overview manner, that is, whether financial statements are managed and prepared divisionally, departmentally, or at head office, and who is responsible for development and coordination of the business. The auditor would also note the size and responsibilities of the management team.

Technology infrastructure An overview description of the type of information systems in use would cover hardware, software, maintenance processes, and level of integration. For example, does the organization use mainframe computing, local area networks, electronic data interchange (EDI), or have a corporate website that is capable of processing transactions? Is packaged or customized software used to process transactions and provide reporting? An organization is likely to have advanced automated systems when its systems have one or more of the following characteristics:

- Custom-designed operational or strategic information systems.
- Use of database management systems or ERP (enterprise resource planning) systems.
- Use of data communications (including the internet).

- Use of paperless systems such as electronic data interchange or electronic funds transfer.
- A complex hardware or software processing configuration.

The existence of each of these characteristics affects the nature of information systems processing at the organization and so also affects the audit process, as discussed further in Chapter 9.

Touring the plant and offices A tour of the client's facilities is helpful in obtaining a better understanding of the client's business and operations because it provides an opportunity to observe operations first-hand and to meet key personnel. The actual viewing of the physical facilities aids in understanding physical safeguards over assets and in interpreting accounting data by providing a frame of reference in which to visualize such assets as inventory in process, data processing equipment, and factory equipment. The knowledge of the physical layout also facilitates getting answers to questions later in the audit.

With such first-hand knowledge, the auditor is better able to identify problem areas such as unused equipment or potentially unsaleable inventory. Discussions with non-accounting employees during the tour and throughout the audit also help the auditor learn more about the client's business to aid in assessing inherent risk.

Identifying related parties Transactions with related parties are important to auditors because they must be properly recorded and disclosed in the financial statements if they are material or information about them could affect decision making. Generally accepted accounting standards for IFRS, ASPE, and ASNPO require disclosure of the nature of the related-party relationship; a description of transactions, including dollar amounts; and amounts due from and to related parties. Transactions with related parties are not arms-length transactions. There is a risk that they were not valued at the same amount as they would have been if the transactions had been with an independent party. Most auditors assess inherent risk as high for related parties and related-party transactions, both because of the accounting disclosure requirements and the lack of independence between the parties involved in the transactions.

The auditor should identify all related parties and related-party transactions, as both quantitative and qualitative considerations are used to decide whether related-party transactions should be disclosed. A party is considered to be a related party if it has the ability to influence decisions, either directly or indirectly. A **related-party transaction** is any transaction between the client and a related party. Common examples include sales or purchase transactions between a parent company and its subsidiary, exchanges of equipment between two companies owned by the same person, and loans to officers. A less common example, called economic dependence, is the potential for exercise of significant influence on an audit client by, for example, its most important supplier or customer, lender, or borrower.

Related-party transaction—any transaction between the client and a related party.

Because material related-party transactions must be properly recorded in accordance with accounting standards and disclosed, all related parties need to be identified and included in audit documentation early in the engagement. Having all related parties included in the audit files, as well as making sure all auditors on the team know who the related parties are, helps auditors identify undisclosed related-party transactions as they do the audit. Common ways of identifying related parties include inquiry of management, review of shareholder and board minutes, review of OSC or SEC filings, and examining shareholder listings to identify principal shareholders.

For publicly listed entities that have shares traded on the SEC, the auditor needs to be aware of regulatory restrictions. The Sarbanes–Oxley Act prohibits related-party transactions that involve personal loans to any director or executive officer of a public company. Banks and other financial institutions in the United States, as in Canada, however, are permitted to make normal loans, such as residential mortgages, to their directors and officers using market rates.

As part of gathering knowledge of business, the auditor will do a search of newspapers and news sites about the company. The following three events illustrate problems at companies.

Niko Resources Ltd. (Calgary, Alberta), an oil and gas company, was fined $9.499 million and placed under a three year probation in June 2011. The cause? Providing access to a vehicle and travel expenses (estimated at close to $200,000) to a government official of Bangladesh. The apparent purpose of these bribes was to suppress government action after explosions occurred at Niko natural gas fields. Niko was prosecuted under Canada's Corruption and Foreign Public Officials Act.

In early January 2012, Valle Foam Industries (Brampton, Ontario) and its affiliate Domfoam International Inc. (Montreal, P.Q.) were fined $12.5 million by the Competition Bureau. The two companies admitted that they worked with their competitors to fix the prices of their foam products for over 11 years after a two-year investigation.

The above two cases provide graphic examples of lack of management integrity that resulted in huge fines. The auditors of these companies would now need to be alert for potential additional control violations or illegal acts.

The third example is a theft of 2,700 units of the then most recent line of BlackBerry smart telephones, stolen from a Mississauga warehouse, valued at over $1 million. The auditor would use this information to dig further about the level of insurance held by the owners of the smartphones and assess whether the quality of physical security at the company warranted increasing the risk of future losses.

Sources: 1. Areliano, Nestor E., "Million-dollar BlackBerry heist remains unsolved," August 29, 2011, **www.itbusiness.ca**, Accessed: August 31, 2011. 2. Jackson, Emily, "Brampton firm fined $12.5 million," *Toronto Star*, January 7, 2012, p. B2. 3. Lauren Krugel, "Niko fined $9.5M for Bangladeshi bribe," *Toronto Star*, June 25, 2011, p. B3.

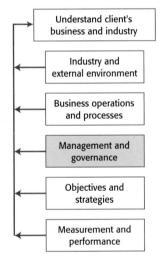

MANAGEMENT AND GOVERNANCE Since management establishes a company's strategies and business processes, an auditor should assess management's philosophy and operating style and its ability to identify and respond to risk, as these significantly influence the risk of material misstatements in the financial statements.

A firm's governance includes its organizational structure, as well as the activities of the board of directors and the audit committee. Corporate governance will be discussed further in Chapter 9. An effective board of directors helps ensure that the company takes only appropriate risks, while the audit committee, through oversight of financial reporting, can reduce the likelihood of overly aggressive accounting.

Three closely related types of legal documents and records should be examined early in the engagement: articles of incorporation and bylaws, minutes of board of directors' and shareholders' meetings, and contracts. Some information, such as effects of contracts, must be disclosed in the financial statements. Other information, such as authorizations in the board of directors' minutes, is useful in other parts of the audit. Early knowledge of these legal documents and records enables auditors to interpret related evidence throughout the engagement and to make sure there is proper disclosure in the financial statements.

Articles of incorporation and bylaws The **articles of incorporation**, granted by the federal government or by the province in which the company is incorporated, is the legal document necessary for recognizing a corporation as a separate entity. It includes the exact name of the corporation, the date of incorporation, the kinds and amounts of capital stock the corporation is authorized to issue, and the types of business activities the corporation is authorized to conduct. In specifying the kinds of capital stock, it also includes such information as the voting rights of each class of stock, preferences and conditions necessary for dividends, and prior rights in liquidation.

Articles of incorporation—a legal document granted by the federal or provincial jurisdiction in which a company is incorporated that recognizes a corporation as a separate entity. It includes the name of the corporation, the date of incorporation, capital stock the corporation is authorized to issue, and the types of business activities the corporation is authorized to conduct.

The **bylaws** include the rules and procedures adopted by the shareholders of the corporation. They specify such things as the fiscal year of the corporation, the frequency of shareholder meetings, the method of voting for directors, and the duties and powers of the corporate officers.

The auditor must understand the requirements of the articles of incorporation and the bylaws in order to determine whether the financial statements are properly presented. The correct disclosure of the shareholders' equity, including the proper payment of dividends, depends heavily on these requirements.

Code of ethics Companies frequently communicate the entity's values and ethical standards through policy statements and codes of conduct. For U.S. SEC filers, in response to requirements in the Sarbanes–Oxley Act, the SEC requires each public company to disclose whether it has adopted a code of ethics that applies to senior management, including the CEO, CFO, and principal accounting officer or controller. A company that has not adopted such a code must disclose this fact and explain why it has not done so. The SEC also requires companies to promptly disclose amendments and waivers to the code of ethics for any of those officers. For any organization, a code of ethics and the processes to ensure adherence are a powerful signal of corporate conduct. Auditors should become knowledgeable about the company's code of ethics and examine any changes and waivers of the code of conduct that have implications for the governance system and related integrity and ethical values of senior management.

Minutes of meetings and contracts The **corporate minutes** are the official record of the meetings of the board of directors and shareholders. They include summaries of the most important topics discussed at these meetings and the decisions made by the directors and shareholders. The auditor should read the minutes to obtain information that is relevant to performing the audit. There are two categories of relevant information in minutes: authorizations, and discussions by the board of directors affecting inherent risk.

Common authorizations in the minutes include compensation of officers, new contracts and agreements, acquisitions of property, loans, and dividend payments. While reading the minutes, the auditor should identify relevant authorizations and include the information in the working papers by making an abstract of the minutes or by obtaining a copy and underlining significant portions. Some time before the audit is completed, there must be a follow-up of this information to ensure that management has complied with decisions made by the shareholders and the board of directors. As an illustration, the authorized compensation of officers should be traced to each individual officer's payroll record as a test of whether the correct total compensation was paid. Similarly, the auditor should compare the authorizations of loans with notes payable to make certain that these liabilities are recorded.

Information included in the minutes affecting the auditor's assessment of inherent risk is likely to involve more general discussions. To illustrate, assume that the minutes state that the board of directors discussed two topics: changes in the company's industry that affect the usefulness of existing machinery and equipment, and a possible lawsuit by Environment Canada for chemical seepage at a plant in Ontario. The first discussion is likely to affect the inherent risk of obsolete equipment and the second one the inherent risk of an illegal act; both could affect the financial statements (the valuation of fixed assets and the disclosure of a contingent liability).

Clients become involved in different types of contracts that are of interest to the auditor. These can include such diverse items as long-term notes and bonds payable, stock options, pension plans, contracts with vendors for future delivery of supplies, software usage and maintenance contracts, government contracts for completion and delivery of manufactured products, royalty agreements, union contracts, and leases.

Most contracts are of primary interest in individual parts of the audit and, in practice, receive special attention during the different phases of the detailed tests. For

Bylaws—the rules and procedures adopted by a corporation's shareholders, including the corporation's fiscal year and the duties and powers of its officers.

Corporate minutes—the official record of the meetings of a corporation's board of directors and shareholders in which corporate issues such as the declaration of dividends and the approval of contracts are documented.

example, the provisions of a pension plan would receive substantial emphasis as a part of the audit of the unfunded liability for pensions. The auditor should review and abstract the documents early in the engagement to gain a better perspective of the organization and to become familiar with potential problem areas.

The existence of contracts often affects the auditor's assessed inherent risk. For example, assume that the auditor finds early in the audit that the client has signed several sales contracts with severe non-performance clauses committing the company to deliver specified quantities of its product at agreed-upon prices during the current and next five years. The inherent risk for total sales, liabilities for penalties, and sales commitment disclosures are likely to be assessed as high in this situation.

Corporate governance The auditor will also consider the quality of management and governance in place at the client. Chapter 9 explains that internal controls are logically grouped into several levels or categories. The first level discussed is the control environment, the level of controls established by senior management. Since senior management, the board of directors, and the Audit Committee have a pervasive effect on the company, it is important that their policies, procedures, and key decisions be considered when developing a client risk profile. Previous material collected, such as minutes of directors' meetings and information about related parties, helps build a profile of the control environment. Discussions with the audit committee and with senior management about their decision-making processes and the ways that policies are implemented help complete the picture. The auditor will also consider risk assessment practices, including fraud risk management, also discussed further in Chapter 9.

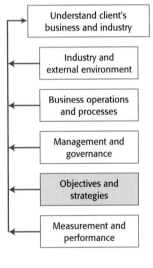

CLIENT OBJECTIVES AND STRATEGIES Strategies are approaches followed by the entity to achieve organizational objectives. Auditors should understand client objectives related to:

1. Reliability of financial reporting.
2. Effectiveness and efficiency of operations.
3. Compliance with laws and regulations.

Budgeting processes, financial targets, and press releases are sources of financial objectives. If there is undue management pressure to meet targets, these can bias management's intentions with respect to the methods used for recording transactions, increasing pressures for financial statement fraud. The quality of transaction processing systems and information systems will affect the timeliness and accuracy of information that is recorded and summarized into the financial statements. By understanding management objectives and biases, as well as the type of accounting systems in use, the auditor knows of potential pressures on the financial statements.

Auditors need knowledge about operations to assess client business risk, inherent risk, and control risk in the financial statements. For example, product quality can have a significant impact on the financial statements through lost sales and through warranty and product liability claims. In Canada, in 2008 and later, there were recalls of lead-painted toys, potentially listeria-infected meat, and cars and other vehicles with potential defects. Such recalls cost millions of dollars, having a major effect on the financial statements.

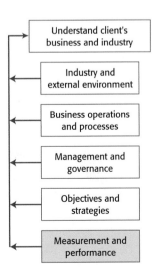

As part of understanding the client's objectives related to compliance with laws and regulations, the auditor should become familiar with the terms of its contracts and other legal obligations, explained in the previous section.

A clear code of ethics that indicates the organization's intentions to abide by laws and regulations, together with monitoring on the part of management to support compliance, help reduce the inherent risks associated with violations of laws and regulations.

MEASUREMENT AND PERFORMANCE A client's performance measurement system includes key performance indicators that management uses to measure progress toward its objectives. These indicators go beyond financial statement figures, such as sales and net income, to include measures tailored to the client and its objectives. Such key performance indicators may include market share, sales per employee, unit sales growth, unique visitors to a website, same-store sales, and sales per square foot for a retailer.

Inherent risk of financial statement misstatements may be increased if the client has set unreasonable objectives or if the performance measurement system encourages aggressive accounting. For example, a company's objective may be to have the leading market share of industry sales. If management and salespeople are compensated on the basis of achieving this goal, there is increased incentive to record sales before they have been earned or record sales for non-existent transactions. In such a situation, the auditor is likely to increase assessed inherent risk and the extent of testing for the occurrence and cutoff transaction-related audit objectives for sales.

Performance measurement includes ratio analysis and benchmarking against key competitors. As part of understanding the client's business, the auditor should perform ratio analysis or review the client's calculations of key performance ratios.

ASSESS CLIENT BUSINESS RISK The auditor uses knowledge gained from the strategic understanding of the client's business and industry to assess client business risk, the risk that the client will fail to achieve its objectives. Client business risk can arise from any of the factors affecting the client and its environment. For example, new technology can render a client's products obsolete.

The auditor's primary concern is the risk of material misstatements in the financial statements due to client business risk. For example, companies often make strategic acquisitions or mergers that depend on successfully combining the operations of two or more companies. If the planned synergies do not develop, the fixed assets and goodwill recorded in the acquisition may be impaired, affecting fair presentation in the financial statements.

The auditor's assessment of client business risk considers the client's industry and other external factors as well as the client's business strategies, processes, and other internal factors. The auditor also considers management controls that may mitigate business risk, such as effective risk assessment practices and corporate governance. After evaluating client business risk, the auditor can assess the risk of material

audit challenge 6 - 1
Understanding Airship Solutions

AS an auditor conducting a financial statement audit, it is important for you to understand your client and the business environment that it operates in.

But what if the business is a new niche that does not really fit as part of an existing industry grouping? Take a look at the Toronto distributor of Airship Solutions, founded in 2006. (There are also six other locations around the world, at the time of writing.) Airship Solutions is the worldwide manufacturer of the Airship blimps, manufactured to be filled with non-exploding helium.

Apparently, outside blimps are an environmentally friendly way to take high-quality aerial photographs. They also provide a highly visible form of advertising. So, we might look at aerial photography or aerial advertising. A search on the internet reveals that there are also many balloon companies that sell indoor blimps of various sizes, starting at US$400. The product that Airship provides is much more than a balloon, starting at $3,600 Canadian.

Airship is a high technology company, using CAD (computer-aided design) techniques to design its products. Its website states that the blimps are designed to earn Australian Civil Aviation Safety Authority certification; this certification allows the blimps to be flown where there are large groups of people.

CRITICAL THINKING QUESTIONS

1. How would you decide what would be a reasonable gross margin for Airship Solutions? What sources of information would you use?

2. How vulnerable would Airship be to downturns in the economy? Why?

3. What sources of information would you use to provide yourself with a thorough knowledge of this business?

Sources: 1. "Airship Solutions," **www.airship.com.au**, Accessed: January 10, 2012. 2. Langton, Jerry, "Blimp maker has high hopes," *Toronto Star*, October 20, 2008, p. B1, B4. 3. "Southern Balloon Works," **www.southernballoonworks.com**, Accessed: December 1, 2008.

concept check

C6-1 List each of the five components of understanding the client's business and industry, and provide an example of an audit step for the component.

C6-2 How does assessing client business risk fit into the client risk profile?

misstatement in the financial statements and then apply the audit risk model to determine the appropriate extent of audit evidence. (Use of the audit risk model will be discussed in Chapter 7.)

Management is a primary source for identifying client business risks. In public companies, management should conduct thorough evaluations of relevant client business risks that affect financial reporting to be able to certify quarterly and annual financial statements and to evaluate the effectiveness of disclosure controls and procedures. The Sarbanes–Oxley Act requires management to certify that it has informed the auditor and audit committee of any significant deficiencies in internal control, including material weaknesses. Such information enables auditors to better evaluate how internal controls may affect the likelihood of material misstatements in financial statements.

② Client Risk Profile Evidence Gathering and Preliminary Analytical Review

Development of the client risk profile is the second risk assessment phase in the audit process. The first phase (pre-planning), described in Chapter 5, uses similar evidence gathering techniques. These techniques are also used in further risk assessment techniques (such as inherent risk assessment and control risk assessment) discussed in later chapters.

Client Risk Profile Evidence Gathering

In Chapter 8 we describe the types of evidence that the auditor can collect. During the risk assessment process, the auditor uses primarily four of types of evidence:

1. *Inquiries of management and others:* Thorough discussion with management will enable the auditor to target risk assessment and evidence gathering. In addition to what has already been discussed, inquiry helps the auditor determine the role and nature of organizational culture in promoting a positive ethical climate at the business, as well as determining management's style and roles. Sales, marketing, and production personnel are a valuable source of information from which to obtain an overview of business functioning.
2. *Observation:* The plant tour is an important example of observation. It can also corroborate statements that were made during inquiries.
3. *Inspection:* Examining key organizational contracts, reports, and minutes are valuable examples of inspection.
4. *Analytical procedures:* Analysis is used during many phases of the audit but is particularly relevant during risk assessment to highlight areas where inquiries of management need to be made and to target additional audit work.

In developing the client risk profile (and updating it throughout the course of the audit), the auditor will consider the evidence gathered in pre-planning, as well as what was present in the prior year's audit file. One of the first techniques used is analytical review, as it can provide a quick snapshot of financial results.

Preliminary Analytical Review

Auditors perform preliminary analytical procedures to better understand the client's business and to help assess client business risk. One such procedure compares client ratios with industry or competitor benchmarks to provide an indication of the company's performance. Such preliminary tests can reveal unusual changes in ratios compared with those of prior years, or to industry averages, and help the auditor identify areas with increased risk of misstatements that require further attention during the audit.

The Hillsburg Hardware Ltd. example is used to illustrate the use of preliminary analytical procedures as part of audit planning. Table 6-2 presents key financial ratios for Hillsburg Hardware Ltd., along with comparative industry information that auditors might consider during audit planning.

| Table 6-2 | Examples of Planning Analytical Procedures for Hillsburg Hardware Ltd. |

Selected Ratios	Hillsburg 12/31/11	Industry 12/31/11	Hillsburg 12/31/10	Industry 12/31/10
Short-Term Debt-Paying Ability				
Cash ratio	0.06	0.22	0.06	0.20
Quick ratio	1.50	3.10	1.45	3.00
Current ratio	3.86	5.20	4.04	5.10
Liquidity Activity Ratios				
Accounts receivable turnover	7.59	12.15	7.61	12.25
Days to collect accounts receivable	48.11	30.04	47.96	29.80
Inventory turnover	3.36	5.20	3.02	4.90
Days to sell inventory	108.65	70.19	120.86	74.49
Ability to Meet Long-Term Obligations				
Debt to equity	1.73	2.51	1.98	2.53
Times interest earned	3.06	5.50	3.29	5.60
Profitability Ratios				
Gross profit percent	27.85	31.00	27.70	32.00
Profit margin ratio	0.05	0.07	0.05	0.08
Return on assets	0.13	0.09	0.12	0.09
Return on common equity	0.25	0.37	0.24	0.35

These ratios are based on the Hillsburg Hardware Ltd. financial statements. (See the insert in Chapter 5 on pages 147–150). Hillsburg's Annual Report to Shareholders described the company as a wholesale distributor of hardware equipment to independent, high-quality hardware stores in eastern Canada. The company is a niche provider in the overall hardware industry, which is dominated by national chains like Home Depot and Rona. Hillsburg's auditors identified potential increased competition from national chains as a specific client business risk. Hillsburg's market consists of smaller, independent hardware stores. Increased competition could affect the sales and profitability of these customers, likely affecting Hillsburg's sales and the value of assets such as accounts receivable and inventory. An auditor might use ratio information to identify areas where Hillsburg faces increased risk of material misstatements.

The profitability measures indicate that Hillsburg is performing fairly well despite the increased competition from larger national chains. Although lower than the industry averages, the liquidity measures indicate that the company is in good financial condition, and the leverage ratios indicate additional borrowing capacity. Because Hillsburg's market consists of smaller, independent hardware stores, the company holds more inventory and takes longer to collect receivables than the industry average.

In identifying areas of specific risk, the auditor is likely to focus on the liquidity activity ratios. Inventory turnover has improved but is still lower than the industry average. Accounts receivable turnover has declined slightly and is lower than the industry average. The collectability of accounts receivable and inventory obsolescence are likely to be assessed as high inherent risks and will therefore likely warrant additional attention in the current year's audit. These areas likely received additional attention during the prior year's audit as well.

Analytical procedures are further described in Chapter 8, which also shows the calculations for the 2011 Hillsburg figures on page 245 in Figure 8A-5. Figure 8-3 also shows common-size financial statements for Hillsburg, another form of analytical review.

concept check

C6-3 What are the four types of evidence gathering used by the auditor for risk assessment?

C6-4 Provide an example of two types of analytical review that are used during the development of the client risk profile.

Refer to Figure 6-1 (see page 158). After obtaining an understanding of the client in the context of its business environment and assessing client business risk, the auditor is ready to move on to planning using the audit risk model. As explained in Chapter 7, this involves determining audit risk, inherent risk, materiality levels, risks of material misstatement, and control risk. These are discussed further in subsequent chapters.

③ The Nature of Audit Working Papers

Working Papers

CAS

Working papers (audit documentation)—the written or electronic audit documentation kept by the auditor to support audit conclusions; these include risk assessments, procedures or tests performed, information obtained, and conclusions reached.

As explained in CAS 230, Audit documentation, **working papers** are the written or electronic **audit documentation** kept by the auditor to support audit conclusions; these include risk assessments, procedures or tests performed, information obtained, and conclusions reached. Working papers should include all the information the auditor considers necessary to conduct the examination adequately and to provide support for the auditor's report.

PURPOSES OF WORKING PAPERS The overall objective of working papers is to aid the auditor in providing reasonable assurance that an adequate audit was conducted in accordance with GAAS. More specifically, the working papers, as they pertain to the current year's audit, provide a basis for planning and documenting all phases of the audit, a record of the evidence accumulated, the results of the tests, support for determining the proper type of auditor's report, and a basis for review by supervisors and partners. Proper controls need to be in place to ensure that the working papers are completed on time (within 60 days of the audit report date according to CAS 230 par. A21) and that the file is archived at that time. Increasingly, working papers are maintained as computerized files using specialized software, the only paper component being documentation provided by the client or external parties.

CAS

BASIS FOR PLANNING THE AUDIT If the auditor is to plan the current year's audit adequately, the necessary reference information must be available in the working papers. The papers include such diverse planning information as conclusions on client risk analysis, descriptive information about internal control, a time budget for individual audit areas, the audit program, and the results of the preceding year's audit.

Record of the evidence accumulated and the results of the tests The working papers are the primary means of documenting that an adequate audit was conducted in accordance with Canadian GAAS. If the need arises, the auditor must be able to demonstrate to regulatory agencies, such as the British Columbia Securities Commission, and to the courts that the audit was well planned and adequately supervised; the evidence accumulated was appropriate, sufficient, and timely; and the auditor's report was proper considering the results of the examination.

Support for determining the proper type of auditor's report The working papers provide an important source of information to assist the auditor in deciding the appropriate auditor's report to issue in a given set of circumstances. The data in the papers are useful for evaluating the adequacy of audit scope and the fairness of the financial statements.

Basis for review The working papers are the primary frame of reference used by supervisory personnel to evaluate whether sufficient appropriate evidence was accumulated to justify the auditor's report.

In addition to the purposes directly related to the auditor's report, the working papers can also serve as the basis for preparing tax returns, filings with the provincial securities commissions, and other reports. They are a source of information for issuing communications to the audit committee and management concerning various matters such as internal control weaknesses or operations recommendations.

Working papers also provide a frame of reference for training personnel and aid in planning and coordinating subsequent audits.

File archive CAS 230 explains that the final version of the audit file should be assembled within 60 days after the date of the audit report. At that time, firms initiate a "file freeze," also called a file archive. This means that if any additional information is added after that date, it needs to be separately identified and added at the front of the file, rather than throughout the working papers. Such additional information would need to be carefully assessed to ensure that it does not affect any of the audit conclusions. This method of archiving the file helps maintain the integrity of the audit conclusions.

CONTENTS AND ORGANIZATION Each public accounting firm establishes its own approach to preparing and organizing working papers, and the beginning auditor must adopt his or her firm's approach. The emphasis in this text is on the general concepts common to all working papers.

Figure 6-2 illustrates the organization of a typical set of working papers. They contain virtually everything involved in the financial statement audit. There is a definite logic to the type of working papers prepared for an audit and the way they are arranged in the files, even though different firms may follow somewhat different approaches. Firms organize their working papers using electronic folders that correspond to the phases of the audit. Table 6-3 lists common categories of working papers, the typical contents of those working papers, and examples. Many firms have most of the documents in electronic form, including scanned documents from the client. The current electronic working paper file includes all documents pertaining to the current audit, including the client working trial balance and financial statements. The current file is built from a roll-forward of the prior year file, use of firm databases and standards, and addition of current field work such as tests of controls included as supporting

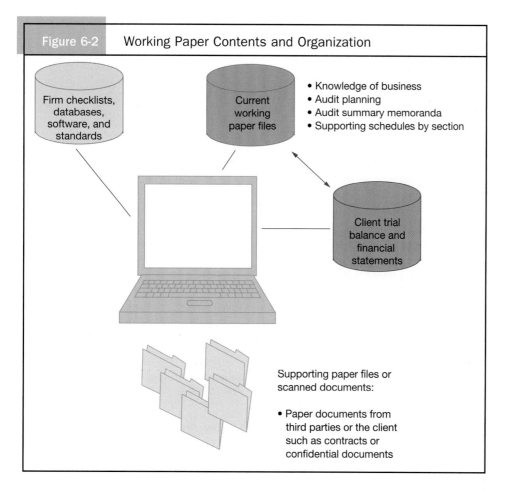

| Figure 6-2 | Working Paper Contents and Organization |

Firm checklists, databases, software, and standards

Current working paper files
- Knowledge of business
- Audit planning
- Audit summary memoranda
- Supporting schedules by section

Client trial balance and financial statements

Supporting paper files or scanned documents:

- Paper documents from third parties or the client such as contracts or confidential documents

Table 6-3	Typical Electronic Working Papers and Their Purpose

Category of working paper and typical content	Examples of working papers included
Knowledge of business: historical and continuing information about the business	Articles of incorporation, bylaws, bond indentures, significant contracts such as executive remuneration and long-term debt agreements, documentation of corporate governance processes
Audit planning: risk analysis documents, calculation of materiality, staff scheduling, completed planning checklists, audit programs, flowcharts and documentation supporting internal controls (which could also be filed in the supporting schedule section)	Analytical procedures from the prior and current audit, analysis and conclusions for control risk overall
Audit summary memoranda:	
Supporting schedules by section: Analytical procedures, completed checklists by section, audit programs by section, copies of scanned documents, multi-year working papers, contracts that are specific to a particular account, documentation of controls that pertain to particular accounts or transaction flows (which could also be filed in the supporting schedule section)	*Current year:* analysis of control risk by assertion by cycle and account, audit programs for tests of control and tests of detail by account, copies of insurance policies or large fixed asset addition invoices that were examined *Multi-year:* long-term debt, shareholders' equity accounts, fixed asset and depreciation, notes payable (which include prior year and current year analyses)

schedules. Use of electronic documents permits flexibility in organization. For example, the internal control documentation for the sales cycle could be included in the audit planning section or in the supporting schedule section for sales, with cross-referencing so that it can be rapidly located.

Working papers are password protected so that only the audit team members can access the client file, and once a staff member has completed a document, they

auditing in action 6 - 3
Research on Importance of Information Technology

How many businesses do you know that do their work without information systems? Only the very smallest organizations process their transactions or do their work with paper and pencil nowadays. This applies to auditing firms as well.

Most working papers are prepared using software. There could be firm software for risk analysis and materiality decisions, databases containing industry-based audit programs, and templates for calculating information such as interest expense and prepaids. For every type of working paper that you can think of, it is likely that software or a spreadsheet template is available. Such automation can help the audit firm cope with frequent changes in audit standards.

In addition, software is used for audit time budgets, time recording, and the management of the audit firm, such as software for billing, payroll, general ledger, and financial statements. Information systems specialists use a variety of software to conduct computer-assisted audit tests geared to the risks and needs of the audit team.

Research into the perceived importance of technology use showed that use of technology was more frequent for analytical procedures, audit report preparation, sampling, searching the internet, and automated working papers. More complex risk analysis systems (such as those used to detect the potential for fraud) were less frequently used.

Sources: 1. Janvrin, Diane, James Bierstaker, and D. Jordan Lowe, "An examination of audit information technology use and perceived importance," *Accounting Horizons*, 22(1), 2008, p. 1–21. 2. Stroude, Linda, "No rest for the auditor," *CAmagazine*, August 2008, p. 33–34.

can make no further changes. The documents are archived and logged to track which changes were made by staff, supervisors, managers or partners.

Since the basis for preparing the financial statements is the general ledger, the amounts included in the general ledger are the focal point of the examination. As early as possible after the balance sheet date, the auditor obtains the client financial statements and a copy of the general ledger accounts and their year-end balances (usually in electronic form, called the trial balance). Working papers are typically organized by groups of accounts that correspond to a line or segment of financial statement accounts. For example, one supporting schedule section would be cash, while another would be accounts receivable.

PREPARATION OF WORKING PAPERS The proper preparation of supporting schedules to document the audit evidence accumulated, the results found, and the conclusions reached are an important part of the audit. The auditor must recognize the circumstances requiring the need for a schedule and the appropriate design of schedules to be included in the files. Although the design depends on the objectives involved, working papers should possess certain characteristics:

- Each working paper should be properly identified with such information as the client's name, the period covered, a description of the contents, the name of the preparer, the date of preparation, and an index code. Where automated working-paper software is used, defaults can be set up in the software, simplifying this process.
- Working papers should be indexed and cross-referenced to aid in organizing and filing. One type of indexing uses alphabetic characters. The primary or "lead" schedule for cash would be indexed as A-1, the individual supporting working papers for details about general ledger accounts making up the total cash on the financial statements indexed as A-2 through A-4, and so on, as additional working papers are required.
- Completed working papers must clearly indicate the audit work performed. This is accomplished in three ways: by a written statement in the form of a memorandum, by initials or name beside the audit procedures in the audit program, and by notations directly on the working paper schedules. Notations on working papers are accomplished by the use of tick marks or symbols written adjacent to the detail on the body of the schedule. These notations must be clearly explained at the bottom of the working paper.
- Each working paper should include enough information to fulfill the objectives for which it was designed. If the auditor is to prepare working papers properly, the auditor must be aware of his or her goals. For example, if a working paper is designed to list the detail and show the verification of support of a balance sheet account, such as prepaid insurance, it is essential that the detail on the working paper reconcile with the trial balance general ledger insurance account.
- The conclusions that were reached about the segment of the audit under consideration should be plainly stated.

The common characteristics of well-designed working papers are indicated in Figure 6-3.

OWNERSHIP OF WORKING PAPERS The working papers prepared during the engagement, including those prepared by the client for the auditor, are the property of the auditor. The only time anyone else, including the client, has a legal right to examine the working papers is when they are subpoenaed by a court as legal evidence or when they are required by the PA's professional organization in connection with disciplinary proceedings or practice inspection. At the completion of the engagement, working papers are retained on the public accounting firm's premises for future reference or sent offsite for secure archiving.

CONFIDENTIALITY OF WORKING PAPERS The need to maintain a confidential relationship with the client was discussed in Chapter 3. It was noted that the rules of conduct

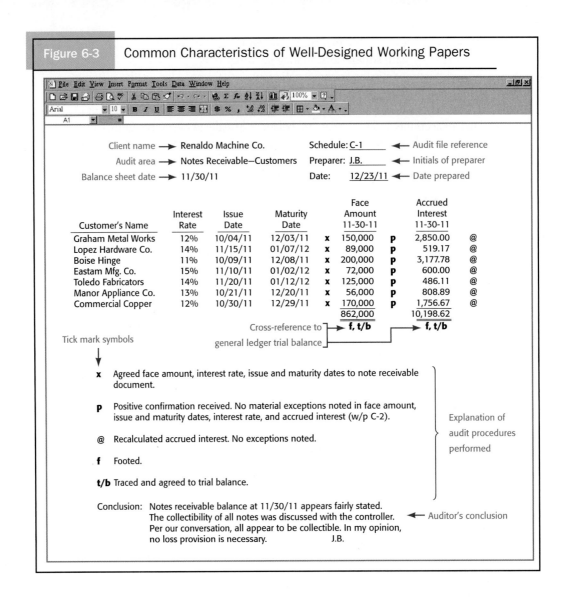

Figure 6-3 Common Characteristics of Well-Designed Working Papers

Client name → Renaldo Machine Co.　　Schedule: C-1 ← Audit file reference
Audit area → Notes Receivable—Customers　Preparer: J.B. ← Initials of preparer
Balance sheet date → 11/30/11　　　Date:　12/23/11 ← Date prepared

Customer's Name	Interest Rate	Issue Date	Maturity Date		Face Amount 11-30-11		Accrued Interest 11-30-11	
Graham Metal Works	12%	10/04/11	12/03/11	x	150,000	p	2,850.00	@
Lopez Hardware Co.	14%	11/15/11	01/07/12	x	89,000	p	519.17	@
Boise Hinge	11%	10/09/11	12/08/11	x	200,000	p	3,177.78	@
Eastam Mfg. Co.	15%	11/10/11	01/02/12	x	72,000	p	600.00	@
Toledo Fabricators	14%	11/20/11	01/12/12	x	125,000	p	486.11	@
Manor Appliance Co.	13%	10/21/11	12/20/11	x	56,000	p	808.89	@
Commercial Copper	12%	10/30/11	12/29/11	x	170,000	p	1,756.67	@
					862,000		10,198.62	

Cross-reference to → **f, t/b** → **f, t/b**
general ledger trial balance

Tick mark symbols ↓

x　Agreed face amount, interest rate, issue and maturity dates to note receivable document.

p　Positive confirmation received. No material exceptions noted in face amount, issue and maturity dates, interest rate, and accrued interest (w/p C-2).

@　Recalculated accrued interest. No exceptions noted.

f　Footed.

t/b　Traced and agreed to trial balance.

⎫
⎬ Explanation of audit procedures performed
⎭

Conclusion:　Notes receivable balance at 11/30/11 appears fairly stated. The collectibility of all notes was discussed with the controller. ← Auditor's conclusion
Per our conversation, all appear to be collectible. In my opinion, no loss provision is necessary.　　　J.B.

---

of the professional accounting bodies require their members not to disclose any confidential information obtained in the course of a professional engagement except with the consent of the client or, as was noted above, when required by the courts or by the professional accounting associations.

During the course of the examination, auditors obtain a considerable amount of information of a confidential nature, including officer salaries, product pricing and advertising plans, and product cost data. If auditors divulged this information to outsiders or to client employees who have been denied access, their relationship with management would be seriously strained. Furthermore, having access to the working papers would give employees an opportunity to alter information on them. For these reasons, care must be taken to protect the working papers at all times.

Ordinarily, the working papers can be provided to someone else only with the express written permission of the client; the client owns the data on the working papers. This is the case even if a PA sells his or her practice to another public accounting firm. Permission is not required from the client, however, if the working papers are subpoenaed by a court or are used in connection with disciplinary hearings or practice inspection conducted by the auditor's professional body. The auditor would normally consult with a lawyer and inform the client in these cases.

concept check

C6-5 Provide an example of a form of security that should be maintained over each of physical and electronic working papers.

C6-6 Give two examples of types of working papers that would be included in a current working paper file.

Summary

1. *Why is adequate planning essential to the audit planning process?* Planning helps ensure that the auditor gathers enough evidence of suitable quality, assists in keeping audit costs reasonable, helps avoid misunderstandings with the client, and it is required by GAAS.

   How is the audit planning process linked to the development of a client risk profile? Risk assessment is a key portion of the audit plan. By assessing risks associated with the client's operations and management processes and stating a conclusion on client business risk, the auditor helps target the audit evidence gathering process.

   How is a client risk profile developed? The client risk profile has two main parts: developing an understanding of the client's business and industry, and assessing client business risk. Understanding of the client's business and industry includes the industry and external environment, business operations and processes, management and governance, objectives and strategies, and measurement and performance processes. Assessing client business risk involves looking at the results of the understanding of the client's business and industry to assess the likelihood that the organization will meet its objectives. The auditor will also consider management's risk assessment and control procedures and results of preliminary analytical review.

2. *What type of evidence does the auditor collect when compiling the client risk profile?* The auditor uses inquiries of management and others, observation, inspection, and analytical procedures.

   Why is it important to document related parties and transactions with them? Clear identification of related parties helps the auditor ensure that this information is clearly and properly disclosed in the financial statements. The monetary amount of related-party transactions (if material) also needs to be disclosed.

   How does analytical review aid the client risk assessment process? Analytical review can help assess the going-concern assumption and whether the company is achieving its business goals. It also provides a quick way for looking for reasonableness of financial data and for targeting further audit field work in response to assessed risks.

3. *What working papers does the auditor retain to document the planning and risk profile process?* The auditor will document observations of the client's business, relevant industry and environment characteristics, as well as information gathered about the client's business (e.g., related parties, extracts from articles of incorporation, bylaws, minutes), and conduct preliminary analytical review. Supported conclusions for each of the risk factors will be included.

   What are the purposes of working papers? They are a written record (in either paper or electronic form) providing information collected during the audit, supporting the conclusions reached in the audit opinion, and demonstrating that the audit was conducted in accordance with Canadian GAAS.

   What are the common characteristics of high-quality working papers? The design will reflect clarity of purpose, allowing others to clearly see the work that the auditor has completed so that it can be reperformed if necessary. They will also demonstrate that adequate supervision and review were completed during the audit.

MyAccountingLab

Make the grade with MyAccountingLab: The questions, exercises, and problems marked in orange can be found on MyAccountingLab. You can practise them as often as you want, and most feature step-by-step guided instructions to help you find the right answer.

Review Questions

6-1 ❶ What benefits does the auditor derive from planning audits?

6-2 ❶ Identify the major steps in developing the client risk profile. Provide an example of audit evidence for each step.

6-3 ❶ List the types of information the auditor should obtain or review as a part of understanding the industry and external environment. Provide one specific example of how the information will be useful in conducting an audit.

6-4 ❶ When a PA has accepted an engagement from a new client that is a manufacturer, it is customary for the PA to tour the client's plant facilities. Discuss the ways in which the PA's observations made during the course of the plant tour will be of help as he or she plans and conducts the audit.

6-5 ❶ An auditor acquires background knowledge of the client's industry as an aid to his or her audit work. How does the acquisition of this knowledge aid the auditor in distinguishing between obsolete and current inventory?

6-6 ❶ Jennifer Bailey has many clients in the manufacturing business. She has worked in this sector for many years and believes that she knows the industry well. Explain why it is important for Jennifer to develop a client risk profile every year. For each step of the client risk profile, list the benefits to the inclusion of this task as part of the client risk analysis process.

6-7 ❶ Identify the three categories of client objectives that the auditor should understand. Indicate how each objective may affect the auditor's assessment of inherent risk and evidence accumulation.

6-8 ① What is the purpose of the client's performance measurement system? Give examples of key performance indicators for the following businesses: (1) a chain of retail clothing stores, (2) an internet portal, (3) a hotel chain.

6-9 ① Define client business risk, and describe several sources of client business risk. What is the auditor's primary concern when evaluating client business risk?

6-10 ① Describe top management controls and their relationship to client business risk. Give two examples of effective management and governance controls.

6-11 ① ② Your firm has performed the audit of Danko Inc. for several years, and you have been assigned the responsibility for the current audit. How would your review of the articles of incorporation and bylaws for this audit differ from that of the audit of a client that was audited by a different public accounting firm in the preceding year?

6-12 ① ② Identify four types of information in the client's minutes of the board of directors' meetings that are likely to be relevant to the auditor. Explain why it is important to read the minutes early in the engagement.

6-13 ① ② For the audit of Radline Manufacturing Company, the audit partner asks you to carefully read the new mortgage documents from Green Bank and extract all pertinent information. List the information in a mortgage that is likely to be relevant to the auditor.

6-14 ② Define what is meant by a "related party." What are the auditor's responsibilities for related parties and related-party transactions?

6-15 ② Charles Ngu is assessing the management and governance structure of Major Appliance Manufacturing Co. Describe four types of evidence that Charles would gather, and state the relevance of the evidence to the assessment of the management and governance structure of the company.

6-16 ③ Explain why it is important for working papers to include each of the following: identification of the name of the client, period covered, description of the contents, initials of the preparer, date of the preparation, and an index code.

6-17 ③ Why is it essential that the auditor not leave questions or exceptions in the working papers without an adequate explanation?

6-18 ③ What type of working papers can be prepared by the client and used by the auditor as a part of the working-paper file? When client assistance is obtained in preparing working papers, describe the proper precautions the auditor should take.

6-19 ③ Who owns the working papers? Under what circumstances can they be used by other people?

Discussion Questions and Problems

6-20 ① ② The minutes of the board of directors of Marygold Catalogue Company Ltd. for the year ended December 31, 2011, were provided to you.

Meeting of February 16, 2011

Ruth Ho, chair of the board, called the meeting to order at 4:00 p.m. The following directors were in attendance:

Margaret Aronsond	Claude La Rose
Fred Brick	Lucille Renolds
Henri Chapdelaine	J. T. Schmidt
Ruth Ho	Marie Titard
Homer Jackson	Roald Asko

The minutes of the meeting of October 11, 2010, were read and approved.

Marie Titard, president, discussed the new marketing plan for wider distribution of catalogues in the western market. She made a motion for approval of increased expenditures of approximately $50,000 for distribution costs, which was seconded by Roald Asko and unanimously passed.

The unresolved dispute with the Canada Revenue Agency over the tax treatment of leased office buildings was discussed with Harold Moss, the tax partner from Marygold's public accounting firm, Moss & Lawson. In Mr. Moss's opinion, the matter would not be resolved for several months and could result in an unfavourable settlement.

J. T. Schmidt moved that the computer equipment that was no longer being used in the Kingston office, since new equipment had been acquired in 2010, be donated to the Kingston Vocational School for use in their repair and training program. Margaret Aronson seconded the motion and it was unanimously passed.

Annual cash dividends were unanimously approved as being payable April 30, 2011, for shareholders of record April 15, 2011, as follows:

Class A common — $10 per share

Class B common — $5 per share

Officers' bonuses for the year ended December 31, 2010, were approved for payment March 1, 2011, as follows:

Marie Titard — President $26,000
Lucille Renolds — Vice-President $12,000
Roald Asko — Controller $12,000
Fred Brick — Secretary-Treasurer $9,000

Meeting adjourned 6:30 p.m.

Fred Brick, Secretary

Meeting of September 15, 2011

Ruth Ho, chair of the board, called the meeting to order at 4:00 p.m. The following directors were in attendance:

Margaret Aronson	Claude La Rose
Fred Brick	Lucille Renolds
Henri Chapdelaine	J. T. Schmidt
Ruth Ho	Marie Titard
Homer Jackson	Roald Asko

The minutes of the meeting of February 16, 2011, were read and approved. Marie Titard, president, discussed the improved sales and financial condition for 2011. She was pleased with the results of the catalogue distribution and cost control for the company. No action was taken.

The nominations for officers were made as follows:

President—Marie Titard

Vice-President—Lucille Renolds

Controller—Roald Asko

Secretary-Treasurer—Fred Brick

Salary	2011	2012
Marie Titard, President	$90,000	$95,400
Lucille Renolds, Vice-President	$60,000	$63,600
Roald Asko, Controller	$60,000	$63,600
Fred Brick, Secretary-Treasurer	$40,000	$42,400

The nominees were elected by unanimous voice vote.

Salary increases of 6 percent, exclusive of bonuses, were recommended for all officers for 2012. Marie Titard moved that such salary increases be approved; the proposal was seconded by J. T. Schmidt and unanimously approved.

Roald Asko moved that the company consider adopting a pension/profit-sharing plan for all employees as a way to provide greater incentive for employees to stay with the company. Considerable discussion ensued. It was agreed without adoption that Asko should discuss the legal and tax implications with lawyer Cecil Makay and a public accounting firm reputed to be knowledgeable about pension and profit-sharing plans, Able and Bark.

Roald Asko discussed the expenditure of $58,000 for acquisition of an information system for the Kingston office to replace equipment that was purchased in 2010 and has proven ineffective. Asko moved that the transaction be approved; the move was seconded by Jackson and unanimously adopted. Fred Brick moved that a loan of $36,000 from Kingston Bank be approved. The interest is floating at 2 percent above prime. The collateral is to be the new hardware and software being installed in the Kingston office. A chequing account, with a minimum balance of $2,000 at all times until the loan is repaid, must be opened and maintained if the loan is granted. The proposal was seconded by La Rose and unanimously approved.

Lucille Renolds, chair of the audit committee, moved that the public accounting firm of Moss & Lawson be selected again for the company's annual audit and related tax work for the year ended December 31, 2012. This was seconded by Aronson and unanimously approved.

Meeting adjourned 6:40 p.m.

Fred Brick, Secretary

REQUIRED

a. How do you, as the auditor, know that all minutes have been made available to you?

b. Read the minutes of the meetings of February 16 and September 15. Use the format on the next page to list and explain information that is relevant to the 2011 audit.

c. Read the minutes of the meeting of February 16, 2011. Did any of that information pertain to the December 31, 2010, audit? Explain what the auditor should have done during the December 31, 2010, audit with respect to the 2011 minutes.

Information Relevant to 2011 Audit	Audit Action Required
1.	
2.	

6-21 ❶ ❷ During the audit of Xtra Technology Inc. (XTI), Andrea found the following journal entry occurring at the end of each month:

Inventory	DR $20,000.00
Cost Variance	CR $20,000.00

The accounting manager told Andrea that this was a regular entry made every month to account for the deviation from actual cost to standard costing for inventory. Andrea was skeptical of this explanation as it was the same every month, and there were other journal entries that appeared to deal with the cost variances adequately, so she asked for the supporting documents for the entries. The accounting manager told her that there were no supporting documents as this was an automatic entry made every month, authorized by the controller. He had never considered checking it before. When Andrea asked the controller about the entries, she discovered that the company purchased inventory from a company controlled by the same company that owned a controlling interest in XTI. The $20,000 was actually a purchase, but they preferred to record it as a cost variance. The controller told Andrea not to be concerned about it and that the parent company's auditors would take case of all transactions between the two companies in its consolidated accounting.

REQUIRED

Assume that you are a manager with the audit firm and Andrea reports to you. Explain your concerns, if any, over the information that Andrea has learned.

(Extract from AU1 CGA- Canada Examinations developed by the Certified General Accountants Association of Canada © 2011 CGA-Canada. Reproduced with permission. All rights reserved.)

6-22 ❷ In your audit of Canyon Outdoor Provision Company's financial statements, the following transactions came to your attention:

1. Canyon Outdoor's operating lease for its main store is with York Properties, which is a real estate investment firm owned by Travis Smedes. Mr. Smedes is a member of Canyon Outdoor's board of directors.

2. One of Canyon Outdoor's main suppliers for kayaks is Hessel Boating Company. Canyon Outdoor has purchased kayaks and canoes from Hessel for

the last 25 years, under a long-term contract arrangement.

3. Short-term financing lines of credit are provided by Cameron Bank and Trust. Suzanne Strayhorn is the lending officer assigned to the Canyon Outdoor account. Suzanne is the wife of the largest investor of Canyon Outdoor.

4. Hillsborough Travel partners with Canyon Outdoor to provide hiking and rafting adventure vacations. The owner of Hillsborough Travel lives in the same neighborhood as the CEO of Canyon Outdoor. They are acquaintances, but not close friends.

5. The board of directors consists of several individuals who own stock in Canyon Outdoor. At a recent board meeting, the board approved its annual dividend payable to shareholders effective June 1.

REQUIRED

a. Define what constitutes a "related party."

b. Which of the preceding transactions would most likely be considered to be a related party transaction?

c. What financial statement implications, if any, would each of the above transactions have for Canyon Outdoor?

d. What procedures might auditors consider to help them identify potential related party transactions for clients like Canyon Outdoor?

ABC Company Inc.
Notes Receivable
31/12/11

Schedule _____ Date
Prepared by _JD_ 21/1/12
Approved by _PP_ 5/2/12

Acct 110			Maker			
	Apex Co.	Ajax, Inc.	J. J. Co.	P. Smith	Martin-Peterson	Tent Co.
Date						
Made	15/6/10	21/11/10	1/11/10	26/7/11	12/5/10	3/9/11
Due	15/6/12	Demand	$200/mo	$1000/mo	Demand	$400/mo
Face amount	5000<	3591<	13180<	25000<	2100<	12000<
Value of Security	none	none	24000	50000	none	10000
Notes:						
Beg. bal.	4000^{PWP}	3591^{PWP}	12780^{PWP}	–	2100^{PWP}	–
Additions				25000		12000
Payments	>(1000)	>(3591)	>(2400)	>(5000)	>(2100)	>(1600)
End bal.						
① Current	3000 ✓	–	2400 ✓	12000	–	4800
② Long-term	–	–	7980	8000	–	5600
③ Total	3000 C	-0-	10380 C	20000 C	-0-	10400 C
Interest						
Rate	5%	5%	5%	5%	5%	6%
Pd. to date	none	paid	31/12/11	30/9/11	paid	30/11/11
Beg. bal.	104^{PWP}	-0-^{PWP}	24^{PWP}	-0-	-0-^{PWP}	-0-
④ Earned	175 ✓	102 ✓	577 ✓	468 ✓	105 ✓	162 ✓
Received	-0-	>(102)	>(601)	>(200)	>(105)	>(108)
⑤ Accrued 31/12/11	279	-0-	-0-	268	-0-	54

✓ - Tested

PWP-Agrees with prior year's working papers.

① Total of $22,200 agrees with working trial balance.

② Total of $21,580 agrees with working trial balance.

③ Total of $43,780 agrees with working trial balance.

④ Total of $1,589 agrees with miscellaneous income analysis in operations W/P.

⑤ Total of $601 agrees with A/R lead schedule.

6-23 ❶ ❷ ❸ You have been assigned the audit of your city's largest car dealership. The car dealership has been one of your firm's audit clients for many years. It is modern and is located in a building owned by the dealership corporation. The company has recently spent almost $100,000 modernizing its vehicle repair bays, with new wiring and lift jacks.

REQUIRED

For each of the five components of understanding the client's business and industry, provide specific examples of the work that you would do to develop your understanding, and how you would document your understanding in the working paper files.

6-24 ❸ Do the following with regard to the working paper for ABC Company Inc. shown on the previous page:
a. List the deficiencies in the working paper.
b. For each deficiency, state how the working paper could be improved.
c. Prepare an improved working paper using electronic spreadsheet software. Include an indication of the audit work done as well as the analysis of the client data.

Professional Judgment Problems

6-25 ❶ ❷ The internet has dramatically increased global e-commerce activities. Both traditional "brick and mortar" businesses and new dot-com businesses use the internet to meet business objectives. For example, eBay successfully offers online auctions as well as goods for sale in a fixed-price format.
a. Identify three specific business strategies that explain eBay's decision to offer goods for sale at fixed prices.
b. Describe three business risks related to eBay's operations. How do these risks affect your assessment of eBay's client business risk?
c. Acquisitions by eBay include PayPal, an online payment service, and Skype, an internet communications company. Discuss possible reasons why eBay made these strategic acquisitions.
d. Identify possible risks that could lead to material misstatements in the eBay financial statements if business risks related to its operations, including recent acquisitions, are not effectively managed.

6-26 ❶ ❷ You are engaged in the annual audit of the financial statements of Maulack Corp., a medium-sized wholesale company that manufactures light fixtures. The company has 25 shareholders. During your review of the minutes, you observe that the president's salary has been increased substantially over the preceding year by the action of the board of directors. His present salary is much greater than salaries paid to presidents of companies of comparable size and is clearly excessive. You determine that the method of computing the president's salary was changed for the year under audit. In previous years, the president's salary was consistently based on sales. In the latest year, however, his salary was based on net income before income taxes. Maulack Corp. is in a cyclical industry and would have had an extremely profitable year, except that the increase in the president's salary siphoned off much of the income that would have accrued to the shareholders. The president is a minority shareholder of the company.

REQUIRED

a. What is the implication of this condition for the fair presentation of the financial statements?
b. Discuss your responsibility for disclosing this situation.
c. Discuss the effect, if any, that the situation has on:
   1. The fairness of the presentation of the financial statements.
   2. The consistency of the application of accounting principles.

(Adapted from AICPA)

Case

6-27 ❶ ❷ ❸ Winston Black was an audit partner at Henson, Davis, LLP. He was in the process of reviewing the audit files for the audit of a new client, McMullan Resourcing. McMullan was in the business of heavy construction. Winston was conducting his first review after the field work had been substantially completed. Normally, he would have done an initial review during the earlier planning phases as required by his firm's policies; however, he had been overwhelmed by an emergency with his largest and most important client. He rationalized not reviewing the details of the client risk analysis or other audit planning information because (1) the audit was being overseen by Sara Beale, a manager in whom he had confidence, and (2) there were a few days of field work left, where any additional audit work could be completed.

Winston then found that he was confronted with several problems. First, he found that his firm may have accepted McMullan without complying with its new client acceptance procedures. McMullan came to Henson, Davis on a recommendation from a friend of Winston's. Winston got "credit" for the new business, which was important to him because it would affect his compensation from the firm. Because Winston was busy, he told Sara to conduct a new client acceptance review and let him know if there were any problems. He never heard from Sara and assumed everything was in order. In reviewing Sara's preplanning documentation, he saw a check mark in the box "contact prior auditors" but found no details indicating if it was done. When he asked Sara about this, she responded:

"I called Gardner Smith (the responsible partner with McMullan's prior audit firm) and left a voicemail message for him. He never returned my call. I talked to Ted McMullan about the change of auditors, and he told me that he informed Gardner about the change and that Gardner said, 'Fine, I'll help in any way I can.' Ted said Gardner sent over copies of analyses of fixed assets and equity accounts, which Ted gave to me. I asked Ted why they replaced Gardner's firm, and he told me it was over the tax contingency issue and the size of their fee. Other than that, Ted said the relationship was fine."

The tax contingency issue that Sara referred to was a situation in which McMullan had entered into litigation with a bank from which it had received a loan. The result of the litigation was that the bank forgave McMullan several hundred thousand dollars in debt. This was a windfall to McMullan, and they recorded it as a capital gain, taking the position that it was not regular income. The prior auditors disputed this position and insisted that a contingent tax liability be recorded. This upset McMullan, but the company agreed in order to receive an unqualified opinion. Before hiring Henson, Davis as their new auditors, McMullan requested that Henson, Davis review the situation. Henson, Davis believed the contingency was remote and agreed to the elimination of the contingent liability.

The second problem involved a long-term contract with a customer in Montreal. Under IFRS, McMullan was required to recognize income on this contract using the percentage-of-completion method. The contract was partially completed as of the year end and was material to the financial statements. When Winston went to review the copy of the contract in the audit files, he found three things. First, there was a contract summary prepared by the sales manager that set out its major features. Second, there was a copy of the contract written in French. Third, there was a signed confirmation (in English) confirming the terms and status of the contract. The space on the confirmation requesting information about any contract disputes was left blank, indicating no such problems.

Winston's concern about the contract was that to recognize income in accordance with IFRS, the contract had to be enforceable. Often, contracts contain a cancellation clause that might mitigate enforceability. Because he was not able to read French, Winston could not tell whether the contract contained such a clause. When he asked Sara about this, she responded that she had asked the company's vice-president of sales about the contract and he told her that it was their standard contract. The company's standard contract did have a cancellation clause in it, but it required mutual agreement and could not be cancelled unilaterally by the buyer.

REQUIRED

a. Evaluate whether Henson, Davis, LLP, complied with generally accepted auditing standards in their acceptance of McMullan Resources as a new client. What can they do at this point in the engagement to resolve any deficiencies if they exist?

b. Consider whether sufficient audit work has been done with regard to McMullan's Montreal contract. If not, what more should be done?

c. Evaluate and discuss whether Winston and Sara conducted themselves in accordance with generally accepted auditing standards.

Ongoing Small Business Case: Management-Prepared Working Papers at CondoCleaners.com

6-28 ② ③ Since the owner, Jim, is a qualified accountant, he would like to reduce professional fees by assisting with the preparation of working papers. Jim has purchased a basic accounting software package, which he uses to record transactions. He still does all the accounting for his business.

REQUIRED

List five working papers that Jim could prepare for the audit of his business by your firm. What concerns would you have about the working papers prepared by Jim? What additional audit work would your firm need to do to be able to rely upon these working papers?

7 Materiality and risk

We have not "talked any numbers" yet. How does the auditor assess the financial statements to decide what should be tested? What is the model used to organize and assess risks during the audit process? In this chapter, we will explain the audit risk model and how it is used for planning. We will also examine the key concept of materiality. Together with the information of the previous chapter, where we discussed the client risk profile and audit planning, the concepts of materiality and risk will allow us to move on to Chapter 8, where we will talk about evidence. All types of auditors and accountants can benefit from an awareness of materiality to help them assess when to investigate unusual items; risk assessment concepts help identify where the focus of audit procedures or control processes should be.

LEARNING OBJECTIVES

1 State the components of the audit risk model and describe the process used to assess audit risk. Explain why the auditor needs to consider client business risk during the financial statement audit. Describe engagement risk in auditing.

2 Describe the factors the auditor considers when assessing inherent risk.

3 Examine how materiality is used to assess the amount of work conducted during an audit engagement. List quantitative and qualitative factors that an auditor considers when setting materiality, allocating materiality to segments, and setting performance materiality.

4 Relate the components of the audit risk model to the amount of evidence that should be collected during an audit. Link materiality to the use of the audit risk model. Describe drawbacks associated with the use of the audit risk model during field work assessment.

STANDARDS REFERENCED IN THIS CHAPTER

CICA Standards

CAS 200 – Overall objectives of the independent auditor, and the conduct of an audit in accordance with Canadian auditing standards

CAS 315 – Identifying and assessing the risks of material misstatement through understanding the entity and its environment

CAS 320 – Materiality in planning and performing an audit

CAS 450 – Evaluation of misstatements identified during the audit

Explain to Me One More Time How You Did a Good Job, but the Company Went Broke

Maxwell Spencer is a senior partner in his firm, and one of his regular duties is to attend the firm's annual training session for newly hired auditors. He loves doing this because it gives him a chance to share his many years of experience with inexperienced people who have bright and receptive minds. He covers several topics formally during the day and then sits around and "shoots the breeze" with participants during the evening hours. Here we listen to what he is saying.

"Suppose you are a retired 72-year-old man. You and your wife, Minnie, live on your retirement fund, which you elected to manage yourself rather than receive income from an annuity. You concluded that your years in business gave you the ability to earn a better return than what the annuity would provide.

"So when you retired and got your bundle, you called your broker and discussed with him what you should do with it. He told you that the most important thing was to protect your principal and recommended that you buy bonds. You settled on three issues that your broker and his firm believed were good ones, with solid balance sheets: (1) an entertainment company that was building a series of amusement parks across Canada, (2) a fast-growing alternative energy company, and (3) a major life insurance company. All you have to do is sit back and clip your coupons.

Ah, 'the best-laid plans of mice and men' . . . First, the entertainment company went broke, and you can look forward to recovering only a few cents on the dollar over several years. Then the alternative energy company failed, and you might get something back—eventually. Finally, the life insurance company was closed by the government and has to default on all of its outstanding bonds. A recovery plan has been initiated, but don't hold your breath. Your best strategy is to re-apply for your old job or do temp work somewhere."

IMPORTANCE TO AUDITORS

"Now, what could the auditors of these three entities ever say to you about how they planned and conducted their audits and decided to issue an unqualified opinion that would justify that opinion in your mind? You don't care about business failure versus audit failure, or risk assessment and reliability of audit evidence, or any of that technical mumbo jumbo. The auditors were supposed to be there for you when you needed them, and they weren't. And materiality? Anything that would have indicated a problem is material for you.

"The message is, folks, that it's a lot easier to sweat over doing a tough audit right than it is to justify your judgments and decisions after it's too late. And there's nothing that can help you if you think that a harmed investor will ever see things from your point of view."

continued >

WHAT DO YOU THINK?

1. What does Maxwell's story tell you about the relevance of potential business failure to the auditor?

2. Think about the responsibilities of the auditor versus the responsibility of management in strategic planning and environmental assessment. How do the requirements to consider knowledge of the external business environment deal with the issues raised by Maxwell?

AUDITORS would like to do a thorough, high-quality audit that provides value to both the users of the financial statements and their clients. At the same time, auditors need to balance the costs of conducting the audit against the risk of being sued. This chapter explains important tools for conducting a high-quality audit—assessment of risks, use of an audit risk model, and the use of materiality during the audit.

Users are indirectly informed of the importance of risks and materiality by means of the auditor's report (discussed further in Chapter 20). The scope paragraph in an auditor's report includes two important phrases that are directly related to materiality and risk. These phrases are emphasized in the following two sentences of a standard scope paragraph.

> I conducted my audit in accordance with Canadian generally accepted auditing standards. Those standards require that I comply with ethical requirements and plan and perform an audit to **obtain reasonable assurance** whether the financial statements are **free of material misstatement**.

The phrase *obtain reasonable assurance* is intended to inform users that auditors do not guarantee or ensure the fair presentation of the financial statements. The phrase communicates that there is some risk that the financial statements are not fairly stated even when the opinion is unqualified. The phrase *free of material misstatements* is intended to inform users that the auditor's responsibility is limited to material financial information. Materiality is important because it is impractical for auditors to provide assurances on immaterial amounts.

We start this chapter by looking at specific types of risks considered during the audit process, then work through the audit risk model, a framework for assessing and documenting risks during the financial statement audit process. After a detailed look at inherent risk, one of the components of the audit risk model, we work with materiality before bringing these concepts together.

Risk in Auditing and the Audit Risk Model

Risk

Risk in auditing means that the auditor accepts some level of uncertainty in performing the audit function. The auditor recognizes, for example, that there is uncertainty about the appropriateness of evidence, about the effectiveness of a client's internal control, and whether the financial statements are fairly stated when the audit is completed.

An effective auditor recognizes that risks exist and deals with those risks in an appropriate manner. Most risks that auditors encounter are difficult to measure and require careful thought for an appropriate response. For example, assume the auditor determines that the client's industry is undergoing significant technological changes, which affect both the client and the client's customers. This change may affect the obsolescence of the client's inventory, collectability of accounts receivable, and perhaps even the ability of the client's business to continue. Responding to these risks properly is essential to achieving a quality audit.

ILLUSTRATION CONCERNING RISKS AND EVIDENCE Before discussing the audit risk model, an illustration for a hypothetical company is provided in Table 7-1 as a frame of reference for the discussion. The illustration shows that the auditor has decided on a "medium" willingness to accept the risk that material misstatements exist after the audit is complete for all five cycles (consideration A). It is common for auditors to want an equal likelihood of misstatements for each cycle after the audit is finished to permit the issuance of an unqualified opinion. Next, the table shows that there are differences among cycles in the frequency and size of expected misstatements (B). For example, there are almost no misstatements expected in the human resources and payroll cycle but many in inventory and distribution. The reason may be that the payroll transactions are highly routine, whereas there may be considerable complexities in recording inventory. Similarly, internal control is believed to differ in effectiveness among the five cycles (C). For example, internal controls in human resources and payroll are considered highly effective, whereas those in inventory and distribution are considered ineffective.

The previous considerations (A, B, C) affect the auditor's decision about the appropriate extent of evidence to accumulate (D). For example, because the auditor expects few misstatements in human resources and payroll (B) and internal control is

Table 7-1	Illustration of Differing Evidence among Cycles				
	Sales and Collection Cycle	Acquisition and Payment Cycle	Human Resources and Payroll Cycle	Inventory and Distribution Cycle	Capital Acquisition and Repayment Cycle
A Auditor's willingness to permit material misstatements to exist after completing the audit (audit risk)	Low willingness (medium)	Low willingness (medium)	Low willingness (medium)	Low willingness (medium)	Low willingness (medium)
B Auditor's assessment of expectation of material misstatement before considering internal control (inherent risk)	Expect some misstatements (medium)	Expect many misstatements (high)	Expect few misstatements (low)	Expect many misstatements (high)	Expect few misstatements (low)
C Auditor's assessment of effectiveness of internal control to prevent or detect material misstatements (control risk)	Medium effectiveness (medium)	High effectiveness (low)	High effectiveness (low)	Low effectiveness (high)	Medium effectiveness (medium)
D Extent of evidence the auditor plans to accumulate (detection risk)	Medium level (medium)	Medium level (medium)	Low level (high)	High level (low)	Medium level (medium)

effective (C), the auditor plans for less evidence collection in the human resources and payroll cycle (D) than for inventory and warehousing. Recall that the auditor has the same (medium) level of willingness to accept material misstatements after the audit is completed for all five cycles (A), but a different extent of evidence is needed for various cycles. The difference is caused by differences in the auditor's expectations of misstatements before considering internal control and differing assessments of internal control by cycle.

AUDIT APPROACH The overall audit approach designed by most firms is strategic — overview tactical plans are developed that take into account the client's objectives and strategies considering the broader business environment within which the client operates. Chapter 5 described the many steps involved in the audit process. Risk assessment helps the auditor gather the information needed to formulate conclusions for the audit risk model, which we discuss next. As part of the planning process, the auditor decides upon a strategic approach for each cycle to plan the evidence mix. Throughout this process, the audit staff meet on an as-needed basis, with full team meetings held at key decision points throughout the engagement.

Figure 7-1 shows the relationship among the components of the audit risk model (audit risk, inherent risk, control risk, and detection risk). Think of the small circles falling down the page as potential material errors. Let us use the inventory and distribution cycle as an example. Many types of material errors could occur, such as recording incorrect quantities, incorrect prices, theft of inventory, and double shipments to clients. These potential errors are errors that could occur if we do not have controls, so they are errors due to the inherent nature of the system—perhaps a complex system with costly inventory that is easy to steal, resulting in many potential errors (circles).

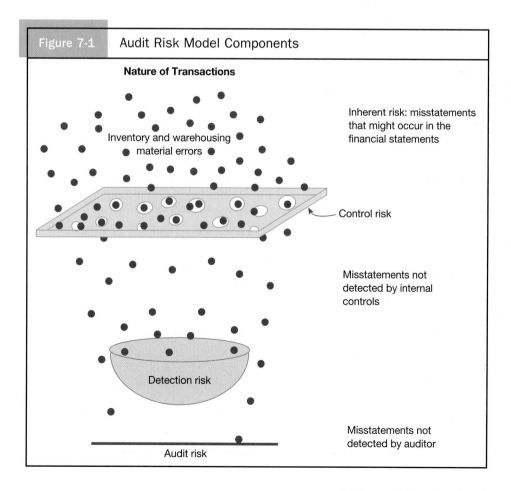

Figure 7-1	Audit Risk Model Components

Nature of Transactions

Inventory and warehousing material errors

Inherent risk: misstatements that might occur in the financial statements

Control risk

Misstatements not detected by internal controls

Detection risk

Misstatements not detected by auditor

Audit risk

In reality, there may not be any material errors or there may be many. Since inherent risk for the inventory and distribution cycle has been assessed as high, there are many potential material errors falling into the internal controls tray.

The purpose of internal controls is to prevent, detect, and correct errors in the financial statements. If controls are good, then there are no holes (or very small ones) in the internal controls tray, and internal controls will prevent or detect these potential errors so that they can be corrected. This is called low internal control risk. If internal controls are poor (such as in the figure), then the client will not prevent or detect the errors, and the circles (potential material errors) continue to fall (and are present in the financial statements when the auditor conducts audit testing). This means that the auditor would not rely upon internal controls, and would assess control risk as high.

An accurate control risk assessment for Figure 7-1 would result in the auditor deciding that in the inventory and distribution cycle, there is low effectiveness in internal controls, so that there will be no reliance upon internal controls. This means that the auditor will need to conduct substantive testing to detect and quantify the errors. The detection of these errors is represented as a bowl—the auditor "catches" the errors using substantive audit procedures.

The bowl has to be large enough and the substantive procedures effective enough to detect most of the material errors. This high level of audit testing brings the auditor's detection risk (the risk of not catching an error) down to a low level. For example, if the auditor decided that medium audit risk was required, then the auditor would be prepared to accept up to 5 percent likelihood of missing a material error. If the auditor had decided upon a low audit risk, then the bowl would have to be even larger, so that perhaps only 1 percent of the errors would go undetected.

It is important that the auditor assess both inherent risk and control risk to know how much testing should be completed to achieve the desired audit risk.

Audit Risk Model for Planning

This way of dealing with risk in planning audit evidence is called the application of the **audit risk model**, a formal model reflecting the relationships among audit risk (AR), inherent risk (IR), control risk (CR), and planned detection risk (PDR). The audit risk model is discussed in the *CICA Handbook* in CAS 200, Overall objective of the independent auditor, and the conduct of an audit in accordance with Canadian auditing standards. A thorough understanding of the audit risk model is essential to effective auditing and to the study of the remaining chapters of this book.

The audit risk model is used primarily for planning purposes in deciding how much evidence to accumulate in each cycle. It is usually stated as follows: $AR = IR \times CR \times PDR$, where AR = audit risk, IR = inherent risk, CR = control risk, and PDR = planned detection risk (CAS 200 refers to this as detection risk).

AUDIT RISK **Audit risk** is a measure of how willing the auditor is to accept that the financial statements may be materially misstated after the audit is completed and an unqualified opinion has been reached. When the auditor decides on a lower audit risk, it means the auditor wants a higher level of assurance. Auditors sometimes refer to the terms "audit assurance," "overall assurance," or "level of assurance" instead of "audit risk." **Audit assurance** or any of the equivalent terms is the complement of audit risk, that is, one minus audit risk. For example, audit risk of 2 percent is the same as audit assurance of 98 percent. In other words, audit risk of 2 percent means the auditor is willing to accept a 2-percent risk that there are material errors in the financial statements. At the same time, a 98-percent level of assurance has been obtained that the financial statements are free of material errors. Zero risk would be certainty, and a 100-percent risk would be complete uncertainty. Complete assurance (zero risk) of the accuracy of financial statements is not economically practical. It has already been established in Chapter 5 that the auditor cannot guarantee the complete absence of material misstatements.

Using the audit risk model, there is a direct relationship between audit risk and planned detection risk, and an inverse relationship between audit risk and planned evidence. Refer to Figure 7-1 to help understand this relationship. For example, as the level of audit risk decreases (i.e., the auditor wants more assurance), more evidence needs to be gathered (a bigger audit bowl), planned detection risk is reduced, and more assurance is needed from audit evidence. As we will discuss in the next chapter, auditors also often assign more experienced staff or have an additional independent review of the working papers for a client with lower audit risk.

INHERENT RISK Inherent risk is a measure of the auditor's assessment of the likelihood that a material misstatement might occur in the first place, that is, before considering the effectiveness of internal accounting controls. Inherent risk is the susceptibility of the financial statements to material misstatement, assuming no internal controls exist. If the auditor concludes that there is a high likelihood of misstatements, ignoring internal controls, the auditor would conclude that inherent risk is high. Internal controls are ignored in setting inherent risk because they are considered separately in the audit risk model as control risk. In Table 7-1, inherent risk (B) has been assessed high for inventory and lower for human resources and payroll and capital acquisitions and repayments. The assessment was likely based on discussions with management, knowledge of the company, and results of prior-year audits. For example, there may be thousands of inventory transactions of many different types, with prior-year files showing many errors. Payroll, personnel, and capital acquisition transactions could occur less frequently and be more frequently checked by outside parties (e.g., banks may process payroll, and contracts may be reviewed externally for capital acquisitions). Factors to be examined when assessing inherent risk are discussed in the next section of this chapter. Inherent risk is normally assessed at the account balance assertion (audit objective) level.

> **Inherent risk**—a measure of the auditor's assessment of the likelihood that there are material misstatements in a segment before considering the effectiveness of internal controls.

CONTROL RISK Control risk is a measure of the auditor's assessment of the likelihood that misstatements exceeding a tolerable amount in a segment will not be prevented or detected by the client's internal control. Control risk represents (1) an assessment of whether a client's internal control is effective for preventing or detecting misstatements and (2) the auditor's intention to rely on internal controls and assign a value to control risk as part of the audit plan. For example, assume the auditor concludes that internal control is completely ineffective to prevent or detect misstatements. This is the likely conclusion for inventory and warehousing in Table 7-1 (C). The auditor would therefore assign 100 percent control risk factor (the numerical maximum) to control risk, which means "no reliance."

> **Control risk**—a measure of the auditor's assessment of the likelihood that misstatements exceeding materiality in a segment will not be prevented or detected by the client's internal controls

Before auditors can use a control risk of less than 100 percent, they must do three things: obtain an understanding of the design of the client's internal control, evaluate the design effectiveness of those controls based on the understanding, and test internal control for operational effectiveness. Understanding internal controls is required for all audits. Assessing design effectiveness and tests of controls are required when the auditor chooses to set control risk below 100 percent and to place reliance on the controls. Internal controls and control risk are discussed further in Chapter 9.

PLANNED DETECTION RISK Planned detection risk is a measure of the risk that audit evidence for a segment will fail to detect material misstatements, should such misstatements exist. There are two key points about planned detection risk. First, it is dependent on the other three factors in the model. Planned detection risk will change only if the auditor changes one of the other factors. Second, it determines the amount of evidence the auditor plans to accumulate (which grows inversely with the size of planned detection risk). Using the complement of detection risk, at 5 percent detection risk, the auditor needs to provide 95 percent assurance (a bowl in Figure 7-1 that would catch 95 percent of the potential errors) so that the evidence collected will detect material errors. If planned detection risk is reduced to 2 percent, the auditor needs to accumulate more evidence (to obtain 98 percent assurance that evidence

> **Planned detection risk**—a measure of the risk that audit evidence for a segment will fail to detect misstatements exceeding materiality, should such misstatements exist; PDR = AR / (IR × CR).

collected will detect material errors). For example, in Table 7-1 (D), planned detection risk is low for inventory and distribution, which causes planned evidence to be high. The opposite is true for human resources and payroll, which has high planned detection risk, requiring less evidence gathering.

A numerical example is provided to solve for detection risk, even though it is not practical to measure as precisely as these numbers imply. The numbers used below are for the inventory and distribution cycle in Table 7-1.

$$AR = 3.5\% \quad \text{(medium risk to be accepted)}$$
$$IR = 100\% \quad \text{(high risk of errors expected)}$$
$$CR = 100\% \quad \text{(low effectiveness of internal controls)}$$
$$AR = IR \times CR \times PDR \text{ or}$$
$$PDR = \frac{AR}{(IR \times CR)}$$
$$PDR = 0.035 / 1 \times 1 = 0.035 \text{ or } 3.5\%$$

(Auditor plans 3.5 percent risk of not detecting errors and seeks 96.5 percent assurance from substantive tests.)

RELATIONSHIPS AMONG AUDIT RISK MODEL COMPONENTS The audit risk desired affects the amount of evidence to be gathered. As audit risk decreases, assurance required increases and more evidence must be gathered, making the audit more costly.

Inherent risk and planned detection risk have an inverse relationship. Using Figure 7-1, we can see that when more material errors are likely to exist (inherent risk assessed as higher), if control risk stays the same, the detection risk bowl must be larger (more evidence to be gathered and lower detection risk).

Similarly, if inherent risk stays constant but control risk is higher (there are more holes in the control risk tray, letting more material errors through), then we again have to increase the size of our detection risk bowl (more evidence gathering needed and smaller detection risk). There is also an inverse relationship between the two types of risk.

CLIENT BUSINESS RISK AND ENGAGEMENT RISK **Client business risk**, as explained in the previous chapter, is the risk that the client will fail to achieve its objectives, leading to business failure. Client business risk is related to the accounting concept of going concern, which addresses whether the client will be in operation for another year or longer. When the auditor assesses that client business risk will be high, then the auditor may decide to not retain or accept the client, or gather additional evidence to support potential accounts that may need to be adjusted (such as fixed assets or marketable securities).

Engagement risk, or **auditor business risk**, is the risk that the auditor or audit firm will suffer harm after the audit is finished. Engagement risk is closely related to client business risk. For example, if a client declares bankruptcy after an audit is completed, the likelihood of a lawsuit against the public accounting firm increases, even if the quality of the audit was good.

CAS **CHANGING AUDIT RISK FOR BUSINESS RISK** Current standards use the term **business risk** to apply to clients (CAS 315, par. 4b). However, as described above, we will specifically use "client business risk" when we discuss clients. If a client decides to enter into a new product line that does poorly and does not recognize that the line needs to be disposed of, the decision could affect the entity's ability to continue as a going concern. The auditor assesses the entity's strategies as part of the development of a client risk profile. Client business risk is also considered when setting audit risk and materiality.

With respect to the audit firm, if the audit firm acquires clients that do not pay their bills, are dishonest, and result in significant litigation against the firm, then the PA firm itself will perhaps have a poor reputation and have going concern problems

Client business risk—the risk that the client will fail to achieve its objectives.

Engagement risk or auditor business risk—the risk that the auditor or audit firm will suffer harm after the audit is finished.

Business risk—includes auditor business risk and client business risk due to poor strategic decisions. The way firms handle auditor business risk or engagement risk is through client continuance or acceptance reviews and with techniques such as quality assurance during the audit.

Research has indicated that several factors affect client business risk. Only three of those are discussed here: the degree to which external users rely on the financial statements, the likelihood that a client will have financial difficulties after the auditor's report is issued, and the integrity of management (including the potential for fraud). These factors also affect audit risk.

The degree to which external users rely on the statements When external users place heavy reliance on the financial statements, it is appropriate that audit risk be decreased. When the statements are heavily relied on, a great social harm could result if a material misstatement were to remain undetected in the financial statements. The cost of additional evidence can be more easily justified when the loss to users from material misstatements is substantial.

Several factors are good indicators of the degree to which financial statements are relied on by external users:

- *Client's size.* Generally speaking, the larger a client's operations, the more widely used the statements will be. The client's size, measured by total assets or total revenues, will have an effect on audit risk.
- *Distribution of ownership.* The statements of publicly held corporations are normally relied on by many more users than those of private or closely held corporations. For these companies, the interested parties include the provincial securities administrators such as the British Columbia Securities Commission, perhaps the SEC, financial analysts, creditors, suppliers, the government, and the general public. The availability of financial statements on the internet allows for easy downloading of financial statement information for publicly traded companies.
- *Nature and amount of liabilities.* When statements include a large number of liabilities, they are more likely to be used extensively by actual and potential creditors than when there are few liabilities.

The likelihood that a client will have financial difficulties after the auditor's report is issued If a client is forced to file for bankruptcy or suffers a significant loss after completion of the audit, there is a greater chance of the auditor's being required to defend the quality of the audit than if the client were under no financial strain. The loss could be due to fraud, the loss of a major customer, or a computer disaster that cripples the company for a period of time. There is a natural tendency for those who lose money in a bankruptcy or because of a stock price reversal to file suit against the auditor. This can result from the honest belief that the auditor failed to conduct an adequate audit or from the users' desire to recover part of their loss regardless of the adequacy of the audit work.

If the auditor believes the chance of financial failure or loss is high, and there is increased business risk for the auditor, audit risk should be reduced. If a lawsuit does occur, the auditor will then be in a better position to defend the audit successfully. The total audit evidence and costs will increase, but this is justifiable because of the additional risk of lawsuits the auditor faces.

It is difficult to predict financial failure, but certain factors are good indicators of its increased probability:

- *Liquidity position.* If a client is constantly short of cash and working capital, it indicates a future problem in paying bills. The auditor must assess the likelihood and significance of a weak liquidity position getting worse.
- *Profits (losses) in previous years.* When a company has rapidly declining profits or increasing losses for several years, the auditor should recognize the future solvency problems the client is likely to encounter. It is also important to consider the changing profits relative to the balance remaining in retained earnings.

- *Method of financing growth.* The more a client relies on debt as a means of financing, the greater the risk of financial difficulty if the client's operations become less successful. It is also important to evaluate whether permanent assets are being financed with short-term or long-term loans. Large amounts of required cash outflows during a short period of time can force a company into bankruptcy.
- *Nature of the client's operations.* Certain types of businesses are inherently riskier than others. For example, other things being equal, there is a much greater likelihood of bankruptcy of a start-up technology company dependent on one product than of a diversified food manufacturer.
- *Extent of reliance upon technology and quality of support strategies.* The more a client relies upon technology, the more important it is that the client has an adequate backup and disaster recovery plan in the event of hardware or software failure. Support strategies, such as maintenance in the event of minor hardware or software problems, need to be high quality so that relatively minor problems, such as failure in a communications processor, do not cause operational shut downs. Appendix 7A, starting on page 205, describes the phases of a typical disaster recovery plan.
- *Competence of management.* Competent management is constantly alert for potential financing difficulties and modifies its operating methods to minimize the effects of short-run problems. The ability of management must be assessed as a part of the evaluation of the likelihood of bankruptcy.

audit challenge 7-1

Would Your Client Recover This Quickly from a Major Fire?

A major insurance company located in downtown Toronto on Bay Street occupied several floors of a high-rise building. On the tenth floor, there was a data centre housing mainframe computers, disk drives, printers, and telecommunications equipment for communicating with hundreds of insurance brokers and insurance offices. The data centre was physically separated from the offices, with an automated fire extinguishing system. On the ninth floor, immediately below the data centre, was an open area with personal computers used by the actuaries (individuals who analyze mortality rates and thus determine how much the company should charge for life insurance). On the sixth floor was a tape vault housing backup data and programs from the data centre.

On a Friday prior to a long weekend, the ninth floor open area caught fire. It was a massive fire, blackening the entire area and blowing out windows. Smoke filtered up to the tenth floor, where it seeped through holes in the data centre's walls (caused by previous movement of office partitions that had been attached to the data centre's walls). The operators (who had not been adequately trained) panicked and did not push the 15-cm-wide red button beside the exit door that would have automatically shut off the power to all systems. Instead, they rapidly left the room. Although the fire extinguishing system was activated, smoke continued to seep in, and half of the disk drives crashed.

As firefighters doused the fire on the ninth floor, large volumes of water poured onto the ninth floor and below, hitting the top of the tape vault and cracking it. (The tape vault was located in the building's "water well," where the water was supposed to flow so that it did not filter through the floors and ceilings of multiple floors.) Luckily, only about 5 cm of water settled in the bottom of the tape vault.

On Saturday morning, a human chain of 300 people transferred backup media to Bay Street, where transport trucks loaded with mainframe computing equipment and peripherals waited, hooked up to the telephone cables at the front of the building. On Tuesday morning, the mainframe systems were up and running, as if nothing had happened to the tenth floor. The ninth floor actuaries were not so lucky. All of their backup media, which were kept in their desks on the ninth floor, had been destroyed.

However, one of the actuaries had gone on holiday one week prior to the fire. Thinking that he would do some work at home, he had taken a copy of the system with him when he left. Needless to say, he was a hero when he returned a week after the fire.

CRITICAL THINKING QUESTIONS

1. What would have been the likely consequences if the company had been unable to restore operations to the main data centre until one week later? What about three weeks later?
2. This scenario indicates the importance of disaster recovery planning for central systems as well as decentralized systems. What other systems need to be backed up and why?
3. How does the quality of an organization's disaster recovery planning affect client business risk?

Table 7-2	Methods Practitioners Use to Assess Audit Risk and Client Business Risk

Factors	Methods Used by Practitioners to Assess Audit Risk and Client Business Risk
External users' reliance on financial statements	• Examine the financial statements, including footnotes. • Read minutes of board of directors' meetings to determine future plans. • Examine filings with the provincial securities commission for a publicly held company. • Discuss financing plans with management.
Likelihood of financial difficulties	• Analyze the financial statements for financial difficulties using ratios and other analytical procedures. • Examine historical and projected cash flow statements for the nature of cash inflows and outflows. • Assess adequacy of disaster recovery plans.
Management integrity (including potential fraud)	• Follow the procedures discussed in Chapter 5 for client acceptance and continuance.

Management's integrity (including potential fraud) As discussed in Chapter 5, as a part of new client investigation and continuing client evaluation, if a client has questionable integrity, the auditor is likely to assess audit risk lower, not accept the audit, or even resign from the audit. Companies with low integrity often conduct their business affairs in a manner that results in conflicts with their shareholders, regulators, and customers. These conflicts, in turn, often reflect on the users' perceived quality of the audit and can result in lawsuits and other disagreements. An obvious example of a situation in which management's integrity is questionable is prior criminal conviction of a key member of management. Other examples of questionable integrity might include frequent disagreements with previous auditors, the Canada Revenue Agency, the provincial securities commission, or the stock exchange where the company is listed. Frequent turnover of key financial and internal audit personnel and ongoing conflicts with labour unions and employees may also indicate integrity problems.

To assess audit risk, the auditor must first assess each of the factors affecting audit risk. Table 7-2 illustrates the methods used by auditors to assess each of the three factors already discussed. You can see after examining Table 7-2 that the assessment of each of the factors is highly subjective, which means that the overall assessment is also

concept check

C7-1 Using the audit risk model, holding all factors equal, what happens to detection risk if control risk goes down? Why?

C7-2 Why should the auditor consider client business risk when determining audit risk?

auditing in action 7-1
Assessing Audit Risk in Practice

Henry Rinsk, of Links, Rinsk & Rodman, Public Accountants, is the partner responsible for the audit of Hungry Food Restaurants Ltd., a chain of nine Manitoba family restaurants. The firm has audited Hungry Food for 10 years and has always found management competent, cooperative, and easy to deal with. Hungry Food is family owned with a business succession plan in place, profitable, liquid, and with little debt. Management has a reputation in the commu-

nity of high integrity and good relationships with employees, customers, and suppliers.

After meeting with the other partners as part of the firm's annual client continuation meeting, Henry recommends that audit risk for Hungry Food be assessed as high. For Links, Rinsk & Rodman, this means no expansion of evidence, a "standard" review of working papers, and a "standard" assignment of personnel to the engagement.

highly subjective. A typical evaluation of audit risk is high, medium, or low, where a low audit risk assessment means a "risky" or large client requiring more extensive evidence, assignment of more experienced personnel, and/or a more extensive review of working papers.

② Inherent Risk Assessment

Inherent Risk

The inclusion of inherent risk in the audit risk model is one of the most important concepts in auditing. It implies that auditors should attempt to predict where misstatements are most or least likely in the financial statement segments. This information affects the total amount of evidence the auditor is required to accumulate and influences how the auditor's efforts to gather the evidence are allocated among the segments of the audit. Inherent risk for the client as a whole is considered in the development of the client risk profile (discussed in the previous chapter), while the audit risk model is used to consider inherent risk for each audit objective for material account balances, classes of transactions, and disclosures.

The audit risk model shows the common impact that inherent and control risks have on detection risk. For example, an inherent risk of 40 percent and a control risk of 60 percent affect detection risk and planned evidence the same as an inherent risk of 60 percent and a control risk of 40 percent. In both cases, the overall risk of material misstatement is the same. In both cases, multiplying IR by CR results in a denominator in the audit risk model of 24 percent. The combination of inherent risk and control risk can be thought of as the expectation of misstatements after considering the effect of internal controls on inherent risk, termed the **risk of material misstatements**. Inherent risk is the expectation of misstatements before considering the effect of internal controls.

Risk of material misstatements— the expectation of misstatements after considering the effect of internal controls on inherent risk.

Table 7-3 describes major factors at the client that the auditor considers when assessing inherent risk. In addition, the auditor also considers the results of previous audit, and whether this is a repeat or new audit engagement.

audit challenge 7-2
Inherent Risks, Estimating Risks of Disaster

ONLINE-ONLY companies rely upon the internet and upon effective security practices to keep their businesses going. Zappos.com, an international website that sells clothing, shoes, and bags, displayed the following message today (January 16, 2012) when a search was placed: "We are so sorry—we are not accepting international traffic. If you have any questions please email us at **help@zappos.com**." The company shut down international traffic after it announced a data breach that affected over 24 million customers. Customers were advised to change their passwords. Clearly a website that is down cannot sell any of its products.

What about larger disasters, such as plant explosions? In Toronto, on August 10, 2008, the Sunrise Propane Industrial Gases distribution plant experienced an explosion that resulted in the death of a firefighter and an employee as well as the evacuation of five streets within a one-block radius of the plant. The corporate buildings were almost completely destroyed. Edmonton's AT Plastics had an explosion on October 24, 2008, that injured nine workers. The Edmonton business was renamed Celanese

EVA Performance Polymers Inc. in August 2009. A substantial investment was required to enable resumption of operations.

CRITICAL THINKING QUESTIONS

1. How would you assess the inherent risk of an online business versus a manufacturer of dangerous chemicals? What factors did you consider in your assessment?
2. Which financial statement accounts are most susceptible to risk for an online retailer suxh as Zappos? For an organization that produces dangerous chemicals? Why?

Sources: 1. Freeman, Sunnay and Bill Taylor, "Residents return after blast," August 11, 2008, **www.thestar.com**, Accessed: November 26, 2008. 2. Macdonald, Jim, 'It sounded like a bomb,' says resident after blast in Edmonton plastics plant," *Toronto Star*, October 25, 2008, p. A25. 3. Ochre Media, "Celanese Unveils EVA Performance Polymers Business Unit," June 26, 2009, **www.plastics-technology.com/news/news_archives.asp?NewsID=256**, Accessed: August 24, 2009. 4. Zappos.com home page: **www.zappos.com**, Accessed: January 16, 2012. 5. Lucian Constantin, "International Zappos customer access blocked after data breach," January 16, 2012. **itbusiness.ca**, Accessed: January 16, 2012.

Table 7-3	Major Client Factors the Auditor Considers When Assessing Inherent Risk

Factor and areas most likely affected	Examples of how it can affect inherent risk
Nature of client's business: accounts such as inventory, accounts and loans receivable and other fixed assets most likely affected (see also Chapter 5)	• Frequently changing technology increases risk of inventory obsolescence. • Stable industry (such as banking) decreases inherent risks overall.
Nature of data processing systems: type of programming affects quality of programs; complexity affects error rates	• Customized programs increase inherent risks or programming errors while packaged software decreases it. • Complex configurations are harder to understand and manage, increasing the likelihood of out-of-date programming or data loss.
Extent of use of data communications: increased data communications increases risks of data breach or of unauthorized access	• Use of the internet increases inherent risks associated with data compromise or data loss. • Use of electronic funds transfers (such as EDI, online banking) increases inherent risks associated with cash.
Integrity of management: low integrity increases risks of unauthorized transactions or of financial statement fraud	• Management that is dominated by one or a few individuals who lack integrity, risks of financial statement fraud increase, increasing inherent risks. • Indicators of honest management lowers inherent risks.
Client motivation: biases to lower taxes or increase management bonuses	• Small business with a bias to lower taxes increases inherent risks associated with revenue completeness and expenses occurrence. • Senior management motivation to increase profits or revenue due to contingent bonuses increase inherent risks of revenue cutoff and existence.
Results of previous audits: recurrence of the same type of errors	• Errors in cutoff in prior years are likely to recur, increasing inherent risks of cutoff errors. • Absence of errors in prior years reduces inherent risks.
Presence of related parties: transactions with these parties could be misstated or not adequately disclosed	• The transactions between a parent and subsidiary company are not at arms-length, increasing inherent risks of valuation and accuracy. • Inherent risk of completeness and understandability of disclosures increases.
Presence of non-routine or complex transactions: lack of knowledge increases potential for error	• Inherent risks of accuracy and allocation increase for non-routine purchases of fixed assets or other items. • Financial instruments could be recorded incorrectly (higher inherent risks of accuracy) or not disclosed in an understandable way.
Presence of accounts or transactions requiring judgment: management biases may result in increased risk of misstatement	• If management is biased towards higher profits due to a management bonus, then judgments in accounts such as bad debt allowance or liability for warranty payments could result in higher inherent risks of valuation.
Susceptibility of assets to misappropriation: liquid assets are more prone to theft	• Organizations that handle cash or liquid inventory (such as jewellery) would have higher inherent risks of completeness or existence.

RESULTS OF PREVIOUS AUDITS Errors found in the previous year's audit have a high likelihood of occurring again in the current year's audit. This happens because many types of errors are systemic in nature, and organizations are often slow in making changes to eliminate them. Therefore, an auditor would be negligent if the results of the preceding year's examination were ignored during the development of the current year's audit program. For example, if the auditor found a significant number of errors in pricing inventory, inherent risk would likely be high, and extensive testing would have to be done in the current audit as a means of determining whether the deficiency in the client's system had been corrected. If, however, the auditor has found no errors for the past several years in conducting tests of an audit area, the auditor is justified in reducing inherent risk, provided that changes in relevant circumstances have not occurred.

INITIAL VERSUS REPEAT ENGAGEMENT Auditors gain experience and knowledge about the likelihood of misstatements after auditing a client for several years. The lack of previous years' audit results would cause most auditors to use a larger inherent risk for initial audits than for repeat engagements in which no material misstatements had been found. Most auditors set a high inherent risk in the first year of an audit and reduce it in subsequent years as they gain experience.

The auditor will also consider the quality and nature of the data at the client (called the population).

ASSESSMENTS OF MAKEUP OF THE POPULATION The individual items making up the total population also frequently affect the auditor's expectation of material misstatement. For example, most auditors would use a higher inherent risk for accounts receivable when most accounts are significantly overdue than when most accounts are current. Similarly, the potential for misstatements in inventory purchased several years ago would normally be greater than for inventory purchased in the past few months. Transactions with affiliated companies, amounts due from officers, cash disbursements made payable to cash, and accounts receivable outstanding for several months are examples of situations requiring a larger inherent risk assessment and therefore greater investigation because there is usually a higher likelihood of misstatement than in more typical transactions.

ASSESSING INHERENT RISK The auditor must evaluate the preceding factors and decide on an appropriate inherent risk level for each cycle, account, type of disclosure, and audit objective. Some factors, such as the integrity of management, will affect many or perhaps all cycles, whereas others, such as nonroutine transactions, will affect only specific accounts or audit objectives.

The Importance of Materiality

CAS

Neither CAS 320, Materiality in planning and performing an audit, nor CAS 450, Evaluation of misstatements identified during the audit, defines **materiality**; instead, it is spoken of in terms of three key concepts in the context of an audit (CAS 320 par. 2). The first is that a misstatement is material if it affects the decision of a knowledgeable financial statement user, and second, that materiality is relative to circumstances surrounding the decision and the nature of the information. A third point raised by the CAS is that the auditor considers users of financial statements as a group, rather than considering each user individually (such as a bank, bondholder, or shareholder).

The auditor's responsibility is to determine whether financial statements are materially misstated. If the auditor determines that there is a material misstatement, he or she will bring it to the client's attention so that a correction can be made. If the client refuses to correct the statements, a modified opinion must be issued (Chapter 20 explains types of opinions, such as qualified or an adverse opinion). The type of opinion issued will depend on how material and pervasive the misstatement is. Auditors must, therefore, have a thorough knowledge of the application of materiality.

A careful reading of the characteristics of materiality reveals the difficulty auditors have in applying materiality in practice. It emphasizes the decisions of users who have a reasonable knowledge of business and economic activities and who rely on the statements to make decisions. Auditors, therefore, must have knowledge of the likely users of their clients' financial statements and the decisions that are being made. For example, if an auditor knows financial statements will be relied on in a buy–sell agreement for the entire business, the amount that the auditor considers material may be smaller than for an otherwise similar audit. In practice, auditors often do not know who the users are or what decisions will be made. This is why the auditor obtains knowledge of the business environment, of the client, of the purpose of the audit, and of risks before developing materiality.

There are six closely related steps in applying materiality during the planning and conduct of the audit. They are shown in Figure 7-2 and discussed in this section. The auditor starts by setting a preliminary judgment about materiality ((Step 1, called simply "materiality"), then adjusts that number based upon expected errors and past experience to establish performance materiality (Step 2). **Performance materiality** is an amount lower than the calculated materiality, to provide an allowance for undetected material errors during the conduct of the audit. Performance materiality is allocated to the segments of the audit (Step 3), as shown in the first bracket of the figure. These three steps, which are part of planning, are our primary focus for the discussion of materiality in this chapter. Step 4 occurs throughout the engagement, where auditors estimate the amount of misstatements in each segment as they evaluate audit evidence. The final two steps are done near the end of the audit during the engagement completion phase and are part of evaluating the results of audit tests.

CAS 450 suggests that an auditor be concerned with several levels of misstatement in assessing whether or not there is a material misstatement:

1. **Identified misstatements**—the actual misstatements discovered in the sample tested; they have not been corrected by management.
2. **Likely or projected misstatements**—the projection of the actual misstatements in the sample to the population; the misstatements have not been corrected by management or could be disagreements of opinion with management.
3. **Likely aggregate misstatement**—the sum of the identified misstatements and likely misstatements in the financial statements.
4. **Further possible misstatements**—the misstatements over and above the likely aggregate misstatement that result from the imprecision in the sampling process.
5. **Maximum possible misstatement**—the sum of likely aggregate misstatement plus further possible misstatements.

The auditor is sure of an identified misstatement because it was determined to be the misstatement in the sample. The projection of that error to the population plus other actual identified misstatements—the likely misstatement—is based on the assumption that the sample is representative of the population. The auditor is fairly certain about the likely aggregate misstatement when he or she is talking to the client about making an adjustment; if the likely aggregate misstatement exceeds materiality, the auditor will require an adjustment.

Further possible misstatement is based on the imprecision in the sampling process. There are two risks: (1) the sample may not be representative, and (2) the auditor may misinterpret evidence.[1] The auditor recognizes that further possible misstatements are possible but not probable. It would not be appropriate to ask the client to make an adjustment for further possible misstatements by virtue of their very definition.

Step 1. Set Materiality

Ideally, an auditor decides early in the audit the combined amount of misstatements in the financial statements that would be considered material. CAS 320 par. 6 explains that the auditor uses materiality during the audit and when conducting the audit to

Performance materiality—an amount less than materiality that the auditor uses to plan and conduct the financial statement audit engagement, to reduce the likelihood that uncorrected errors exceed materiality.

Identified misstatements—the actual misstatements discovered in the sample tested; the misstatements have not been corrected by management.

Likely or projected misstatements—the projection of the actual misstatements in the sample to the population; the misstatements have not been corrected by management or there is a disagreement with management; see also "Direct projection method of estimating misstatement."

Likely aggregate misstatement—the sum of the identified misstatements and likely misstatements in the financial statements.

Further possible misstatements—the misstatements over and above the likely aggregate misstatement that result from the imprecision in the sampling process.

Maximum possible misstatement—the sum of likely aggregate misstatement plus further possible misstatements.

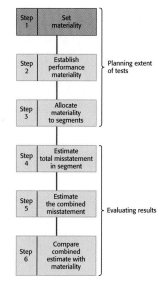

---

[1] These two risks are called "sampling risk" and "nonsampling risk" respectively. They are discussed in detail in Chapter 11.

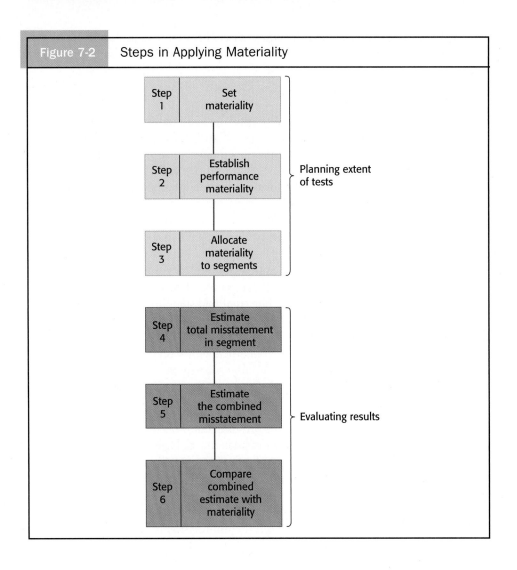

Figure 7-2 Steps in Applying Materiality

Step 1 — Set materiality

Step 2 — Establish performance materiality

Step 3 — Allocate materiality to segments

⎫ Planning extent of tests

Step 4 — Estimate total misstatement in segment

Step 5 — Estimate the combined misstatement

Step 6 — Compare combined estimate with materiality

⎬ Evaluating results

determine the nature, timing, and extent of the auditing procedures. This judgment is one of the most important decisions the auditor makes. It requires considerable professional judgment.

The reason for setting materiality is to help the auditor plan the appropriate evidence to accumulate. If the auditor sets a low dollar amount, more evidence is required than for a high amount. Examine again the financial statements of Hillsburg Hardware Limited, in Chapter 5 on pages 147–150. What do you think is the combined amount of misstatements that would affect decisions of reasonable users? Do you believe a $100 misstatement would affect users' decisions? If so, the amount of evidence required for the audit is likely to be beyond that for which the management of Hillsburg Hardware can pay. Do you believe a $1 million misstatement would be material? Most experienced auditors would say that amount is far too large as a combined materiality amount for Hillsburg.

FACTORS AFFECTING JUDGMENT ABOUT MATERIALITY Several factors affect setting materiality for a given set of financial statements. The most important of these are discussed below.

Materiality is a relative rather than an absolute concept A misstatement of a given magnitude might be material for a small company, whereas the same dollar error could be immaterial for a large one. For example, a total error of $1 million would be extremely material for Hillsburg Hardware Limited because net income before tax is about $5.7 million. It would be immaterial for a company such as IBM, which has total assets and net income of several billion dollars. Hence, it is not possible to establish any dollar-value guidelines for materiality applicable to all audit clients.

Bases with a percentage applied are needed for evaluating materiality Since materiality is relative, it is necessary to have bases to which a percentage is applied. Common bases include the following:

1. 5 to 10 percent of net income before taxes. This number can be fairly volatile so most auditors use normalized net income (i.e., net income adjusted for unusual and non-recurring items such as a large inventory writedown) or average net income.
2. 1/2 percent to 5 percent of gross profit.
3. 1/2 percent to 1 percent of total assets.
4. 1/2 percent to 5 percent of shareholders' equity.
5. 1/2 percent to 2 percent of revenue.
6. The weighted average of methods 1 to 5.
7. A reducing percentage of the greater of revenue and assets.
8. 1/2 percent to 2 percent of expenses or revenue as suggested by the guideline for non-profit entities.

Current practice also includes exponential models, in which materiality starts low for small bases, rises exponentially, and then levels off. Also, scaled amounts are used that are larger than the percentages shown above. Those methods that use a range of percentages generally suggest that the largest percentage be used for smaller entities and the smallest percentage be used for larger entities. For example, under method 1, 10 percent would be used if the entity were small and 5 percent if it were very large; some percentage between 5 percent and 10 percent would be used for entities between the two extremes. The auditor uses professional judgment and past experience to determine the appropriate method.

Impact of qualitative factors Certain types of misstatements are likely to be more important to users than others, even if the dollar amounts are the same. The auditors cannot plan to detect smaller amounts but must react if they are discovered. For example, small amounts involving fraud and other irregularities are usually considered more important than unintentional errors of equal dollar amounts because fraud reflects on the honesty and reliability of the management or other personnel involved. To illustrate, most users would consider an intentional misstatement of inventory as being more important than clerical errors in inventory of the same dollar amount. In addition, while the amount of a fraud may be less than materiality, the impact of fraud on the entity may be in excess of materiality. For example, assume materiality for an entity with worldwide operations was $200 million. An illegal payment in another country of $25,000 would be less than materiality but could lead, if the illegal payment were to be discovered by the authorities in the other country, to fines or seizure in that country of the entity's assets. The fines or seizures could be many times the amount of the illegal payment, resulting in loss of income or other damages that exceeded materiality.

ILLUSTRATIVE GUIDELINES The CICA currently does not provide specific materiality guidelines to practitioners. The concern is that such guidelines might be applied without considering all the complexities that should affect the auditor's final decision.

To show the application of materiality, illustrative guidelines are provided. They are intended only to help you better understand the concept of applying materiality in practice. The guidelines are stated in Figure 7-3 in the form of a policy guideline for a public accounting firm.

APPLICATION TO HILLSBURG HARDWARE LIMITED Using the illustrative guidelines for McCutcheon & Wilkinson in Figure 7-3, it is now possible to decide on a preliminary judgment about materiality for Hillsburg Hardware Limited (see Table 7-4).

Figure 7-3   Illustrative Materiality Guidelines

MCCUTCHEON & WILKINSON, CHARTERED ACCOUNTANTS
Edmonton, Alberta T6G 1N4
(780) 432-6900

POLICY STATEMENT   Sally J. Wilkinson
No. 32 IC   Karen McCutcheon
Title: Materiality Guidelines

Professional judgment is to be used at all times in setting and applying materiality guidelines. In general, the following policies are to be applied:

1. The combined total of misstatements in the financial statements exceeding 10 percent is normally considered material. A combined total of less than 5 percent is presumed to be immaterial in the absence of qualitative factors. Combined misstatements between 5 percent and 10 percent require the greatest amount of professional judgment to determine their materiality.
2. The 5 to 10 percent must be measured in relation to the appropriate base. Many times there is more than one base to which errors should be compared. The following guides are recommended in selecting the appropriate base:
   a. *Income statement.* Combined misstatements in the income statement should ordinarily be measured at 5 to 10 percent of operating income before taxes. A guideline of 5 to 10 percent may be inappropriate in a year in which income is unusually large or small. When operating income in a given year is not considered representative, it is desirable to substitute as a base a more representative income measure, such as normalized net income before taxes or average operating income for a three-year period.
      In the case of clients who operate in industries where operating income before taxes is not considered to be a useful base, ½ percent to 2 percent of revenue will be used as a guideline.
   b. *Balance sheet.* Combined misstatements in the balance sheet should originally be evaluated for total assets. For total assets, the guideline should be between ½ and 1 percent, applied in the same way as for the income statement. An alternative is to use ½ percent to 5 percent of shareholders' equity.
3. Qualitative factors should be carefully evaluated on all audits. In many instances they are more important than the guidelines applied to the income statement and balance sheet. The intended uses of the financial statements and the nature of the information on the statements, including footnotes, must be carefully evaluated.
4. If the guideline for the income statement is less than those selected for the balance sheet, the lesser amount should be used as a guideline for all misstatements that affect operating income before taxes. Misstatements such as misclassification errors would be evaluated using the greater amount.

Assuming the auditor for Hillsburg Hardware decided that the general guidelines are reasonable, the first step would be to evaluate whether any qualitative factors significantly affect the materiality judgment. If not, considering the income statement base first, the auditor must decide that if combined misstatements on the income statement were less than $248,000, the statements would be considered fairly stated. If the combined misstatements exceeded $496,000, the statements would not be considered fairly stated. If the misstatements were between $248,000 and $496,000, a more careful consideration of all facts would be required. The auditor then applies the same process to the other three bases. Given the suggested guidelines calculated above and

Table 7-4   Preliminary Judgment about Materiality

	Maximum		Minimum	
	Percentage	Dollar Amount (in thousands)	Percentage	Dollar Amount (in thousands)
Profit before taxes	5	248	10	496
Gross profit	1/2	199	5	1,992
Total assets	1/2	307	1	614
Total equity	1/2	112	5	1,123
Revenue (net sales)	1/2	715	2	2,862

the fact that Hillsburg Hardware is a public company with a limited number of share-holders, the auditor would probably decide to use the larger of the net income bases, $496,000, as materiality. Gross profit is also a base that fluctuates less from year to year than net income since companies may have fluctuating income levels.

Step 2. Establish Performance Materiality

Materiality adjusted for the effect of net anticipated misstatements to determine materiality available for unanticipated misstatements is called performance materiality. Our continued application to Hillsburg Hardware is shown in Figure 7-4. The auditor is simply reducing the materiality of $496,000 for net anticipated misstatements of $55,000 to determine that $441,000 will be available for unanticipated misstatements. A useful analogy would be that of an individual going out for the evening who has $60 for dinner and a movie but needs $10 for cab fare home. The amount available for spending for the evening is $50, not $60. Similarly, the amount available for unanticipated misstatements is really $441,000, not $496,000.

The auditor may change the materiality during the audit if, for example, a new user of the financial statements is identified or if many errors were encountered during the audit and the auditor wants to widen the scope of testing. The use of performance materiality provides leeway for such a change. This revised figure and the reasons would need to be carefully documented, and field work completed to date reassessed in the context of the new materiality level.

Step 3. Allocate Planning Materiality to Segments

Some auditors allocate materiality to segments once they have determined materiality available for unanticipated misstatements. They use the amounts allocated to

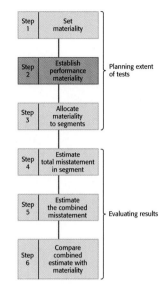

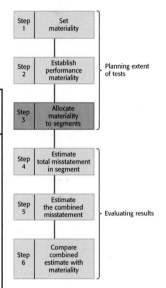

Figure 7-4	Tolerable Misstatement Allocated to Hillsburg Hardware Limited Accounts	

	Balance Dec. 31, 2010 (in Thousands)	Tolerable Misstatement (in Thousands)
Property, plant, and equipment	10,340	48 (a)
Other current assets	1,377	60 (b)
Inventories	29,865	265 (c)
Trade accounts receivable (net)	18,957	265 (c)
Cash	$ 828	$ 6 (d)
Total assets	$61,367	
Trade accounts payable	$ 4,720	106 (e)
Notes payable—total	28,300	0 (a)
Accrued payroll and payroll tax	1,470	60 (c)
Accrued interest and dividends payable	2,050	0 (a)
Other liabilities	2,364	72 (c)
Capital stock and capital in excess of par	8,500	0 (a)
Retained earnings	13,963	NA (f)
Total liabilities and equity	$61,367	$882 (2 × $441)

NA = Not applicable
(a) Small tolerable misstatement as a percent of account balance because most of the balance is in land and buildings, which is unchanged from the prior year and need not be audited.
(b) Large tolerable misstatement as a percent of account because account can be verified at extremely low cost, probably with analytical procedures, if tolerable misstatement is large.
(c) Large tolerable misstatement because account is large and requires extensive sampling to audit the account.
(d) Zero or small tolerable misstatement because account can be completely audited at low cost and no misstatements are expected.
(e) Moderately large tolerable misstatement because a relatively large number of misstatements are expected.
(f) Not applicable—retained earnings is a residual account that is affected by the net amount of the misstatements in the other accounts.

Table 7-5	Calculation of Performance Materiality		
Materiality, based on net income before extraordinary items			$496,000
Less			
Anticipated misstatements from specific tests		$50,000	
Carry forward misstatements from the previous year		80,000	
Anticipated client corrections		(75,000)	55,000
Performance materiality available for unanticipated misstatements			$441,000

determine sample sizes and the amount of testing required. However, many auditors use total performance materiality in audit planning on the grounds that the auditor is concerned about the aggregate misstatement in the financial statements as a whole, which needs to be applied consistently to all of the accounts and disclosures. Auditing in Action 7-2 provides an example where allocating materiality to segments is appropriate.

The allocation of planning materiality to segments (Step 3 in Figure 7-2) is done because auditors accumulate evidence by cycles or accounts rather than for the financial statements as a whole. If auditors have a preliminary judgment about materiality for each segment, it helps them to decide the appropriate audit evidence to accumulate. Materiality is modified by segment in response to differences in anticipated errors and risks by segment. It may also be modified because of a particular reliance on those accounts. For example, if the client is using accounts receivable and inventory as collateral on a loan, the auditor might want to collect more evidence on those accounts. For an accounts receivable balance of $1,000,000, for example, the auditor should accumulate more evidence if a misstatement of $50,000 is considered material than if $300,000 were considered material.

When allocation of materiality is used, it is allocated primarily to balance sheet rather than income statement accounts because most income statement misstatements have an equal effect on the balance sheet due to the effects of the double-entry bookkeeping system. For example, a $20,000 overstatement of accounts receivable is also a $20,000 overstatement of sales. Materiality would be allocated to either income statement or balance sheet accounts, not both, because doing so would result in double counting.

ALLOCATION ILLUSTRATED When auditors allocate materiality to account balances, the materiality allocated to any given account balance is referred to as the "tolerable misstatement" for that account (see also Chapter 11). For example, if an auditor decides to allocate $100,000 of a total preliminary judgment about materiality of $200,000 to accounts receivable, tolerable misstatement for accounts receivable is $100,000. This means that the auditor is willing to consider accounts receivable fairly stated if it is misstated by $100,000 or less.

Auditors face three major difficulties in allocating materiality to balance sheet accounts:

1. Auditors expect certain accounts to have more misstatements than others.
2. Both overstatements and understatements must be considered.
3. Audit costs affect the allocation of tolerable misstatements.

Figure 7-4 on the previous page illustrates the approach followed by the auditors of Hillsburg Hardware Limited. It summarizes the balance sheet, combining certain accounts, and shows the allocation of total materiality of $441,000 (10 percent of earnings, less the effect of anticipated misstatements). Professional judgment and auditor risk assessments are used to allocate these amounts. Some of the rationale for allocation is shown at the bottom of Figure 7-4. For example, it was decided that there would be no allocation of tolerable misstatement to notes payable, even though it is as large as inventories. This happens because even if tolerable misstatement had been allocated to notes payable, confirmations would still have been necessary. It was therefore more efficient to allocate amounts to inventories. A smaller amount, $60,000, was allocated to other current assets (other accounts receivable and prepaid expenses) and to accrued payroll and payroll taxes. These amounts can easily be verified within $60,000 using analytical procedures, which are low cost. If tolerable misstatement were lower, more costly audit procedures such as inspection of documents and confirmation would need to be used.

In practice, it is often difficult to predict in advance which accounts are most likely to be misstated and whether misstatements are likely to be overstatements or understatements. This is why past experience at the same client is used to help allocate materiality. Similarly, the relative costs of auditing different account balances may be hard to estimate, which is why auditors track their time by audit segment for effective audit budgeting. It is a difficult professional judgment decision to allocate the planning materiality to accounts. Those firms that do so have developed rigorous guidelines and use statistical methods.

Steps 4, 5, and 6. Estimate Misstatement and Compare

The first three steps in applying materiality involve planning, while the last three steps in Figure 7-2 result from performing audit tests. These steps are introduced here and discussed in greater detail in later chapters.

When the auditor performs audit procedures for each segment of the audit, a summary schedule is kept of all misstatements found. For example, assume the auditor finds six client errors in a sample of 200 in testing inventory costs (identified misstatement). These misstatements are used to estimate the total misstatements in inventory (step 4). The total is referred to as an "estimate" or often a "projection" because only a sample, rather than the entire population, was audited. The projected misstatement amounts (likely misstatements) for each account are combined on the summary schedule (step 5), and then the combined misstatements for all accounts (likely aggregate misstatement) is compared with materiality (step 6) or with performance materiality.

Table 7-6 is used to illustrate the last three steps in applying materiality. For simplicity, only three accounts are included and the calculation of likely misstatements for accounts receivable and for inventory are shown. The materiality is $50,000 (performance materiality is not shown). The likely misstatements are calculated based on actual audit tests. Assume, for example, that in auditing inventory, the auditor found $3,500 of net overstatement errors in a sample of $50,000 of the total population of $450,000. One way to calculate the estimate of the misstatements is to make a direct projection from the sample to the population and add an estimate for sampling error (further possible misstatements). The **direct projection method of estimating misstatement** (likely misstatement) is done by dividing the net misstatements in the sample by the total sampled, then multiplying the result by the total recorded population value:

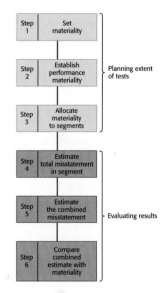

Direct projection method of estimating misstatement—net misstatements in the sample, divided by the total sampled, multiplied by the total recorded population value; see also "Likely misstatements."

$$\frac{\text{Net misstatements in the sample (\$3,500)}}{\text{Total sampled (\$50,000)}} \times \begin{array}{c}\text{Total recorded}\\\text{population value}\\(\$450,000)\end{array} = \begin{array}{c}\text{Direct projection}\\\text{estimate (\$31,500)}\end{array}$$

The estimate for **sampling error** results because the auditor has sampled only a portion of the population. (This is discussed in detail in Chapters 11, 12, and 13.) It is the amount by which a projected likely misstatement amount could be different from an actual (and unknown) total as a result of the sample not being representative. In this simplified example, the estimate for sampling error is assumed to be 50 percent of the direct projection of the misstatement amounts for the accounts where sampling was used (accounts receivable and inventory).

Sampling error—error that results because the auditor has sampled only a portion of the population.

In combining the misstatements in Table 7-6 on the next page, note that the likely misstatements for the three accounts add to $43,500. The total sampling error (further possible misstatements) quite often is different from the sum of the sampling errors

| | Table 7-6 | Illustration of Comparison of Maximum Possible Misstatement to Materiality |

	Maximum Possible Misstatement		
Account	Likely Misstatement	Sampling Error	Total
Cash	$ 0	N/A	$ 0
Accounts receivable	$12,000	$ 6,000[1]	$18,000
Inventory	$31,500	$15,750[2]	$47,250
Total estimated misstatement amount	$43,500	$21,750	$65,250
Materiality			$50,000

N/A = Not applicable; cash audited 100%. (1) 12,000 × 50% (assumed) (2) 31,500 × 50% (assumed)

since varying levels of certainty must be incorporated and the total is usually calculated as a numeric range. Sampling error represents the maximum error in account details not audited.

It is unlikely that this maximum error amount would exist in all accounts subjected to sampling. Sampling methodology (see Chapters 11, 12, and 13) provides for determining a combined sampling error that takes this into consideration.

Table 7-6 shows that the maximum possible misstatement for the three accounts of $65,250 exceeds materiality of $50,000. Furthermore, the major area of difficulty is inventory, where the maximum possible misstatement is $47,250. Because the estimated maximum possible misstatement exceeds materiality, the financial statements are not acceptable. The auditor can either determine whether the estimated aggregate misstatement actually exceeds $50,000 by performing additional audit procedures or ask the client to make an adjustment for likely misstatements. Assuming additional audit procedures are performed, they would be concentrated in the inventory area.

If the estimated maximum possible misstatement for inventory had been $24,000 ($16,000 plus $8,000 sampling error), the auditor would not need to expand audit tests, since the total maximum possible misstatement would be less ($18,000 + $24,000 = $42,000) than the $50,000 materiality. It is likely that the auditor would have accepted the balances in the three accounts.

concept check

C7-5 What is the difference between materiality and performance materiality? How does the use of performance materiality affect the audit process?

C7-6 What are the advantages and disadvantages of allocating materiality to segments?

auditing in action 7-2
Reasonable Materiality Is Hard Work

What to do? OilCo has acquired a subsidiary, which has resulted in assets increasing by over $100 million to $195 million. Of the growth, $68 million is in inventory and $80 million in goodwill. Firm standards result in a calculation of materiality of only about $50,000 based on gross margin, while revenue results in only a slightly higher number of $100,000.

This means that sample sizes for inventory would approach 300 for completeness, existence, and accuracy, to obtain a reasonable level of assurance.

Can an average be taken? Since it is for only a partial year, can the whole year's materiality be used?

The firm's standards department gave the following advice: An average does not make sense when operations have changed. Using an artificially high materiality increases engagement risk for the auditor. Rather than trying to increase materiality with reasons that do not make sense, focus on the parts of the audit that are risky, that is, inventory and goodwill, spending less time on other parts of the engagement.

Source: Correspondence about materiality from an audit firm to I. Splettstoesser-Hogeterp, Fall 2008.

④ Relating Risk and Materiality to Audit Performance

Summary of Audit Risk Model Risks

Figure 7-5 summarizes the factors that affect audit risk, inherent risk, and control risk. Based on the determined audit risk, the conclusion reached with respect to inherent risk, and both the conclusion and extent of reliance determined for control risk, the auditor determines the planned detection risk and, combined with materiality, the planned audit evidence to be accumulated.

Other Materiality and Risk Considerations

AUDIT RISK FOR SEGMENTS Both control risk and inherent risk are typically estimated for each cycle, each account, and each audit objective and are likely to vary from cycle to cycle, account to account, and objective to objective on the same audit. Internal controls may be more effective for inventory-related accounts than for those related to capital assets. Control risk would therefore also be different for different accounts depending on the effectiveness of the controls. Factors affecting inherent risk, such as susceptibility to defalcation and routineness of the transactions, are also likely to differ from account to account. For that reason, it is normal to have inherent risk vary for different accounts in the same audit unless there is some strong overriding factor of concern such as management integrity.

Audit risk is ordinarily set by the auditor for the entire audit and held constant for each major cycle and account. Auditors normally use the same audit risk for each segment because the factors affecting audit risk are related to the entire audit, not to individual accounts. For example, the extent to which financial statements are relied on for users' decisions is usually related to the overall financial statements, not just

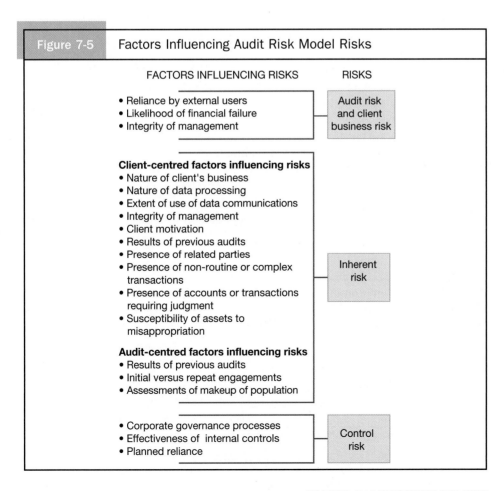

Figure 7-5   Factors Influencing Audit Risk Model Risks

FACTORS INFLUENCING RISKS — RISKS

- Reliance by external users
- Likelihood of financial failure
- Integrity of management

→ Audit risk and client business risk

Client-centred factors influencing risks
- Nature of client's business
- Nature of data processing
- Extent of use of data communications
- Integrity of management
- Client motivation
- Results of previous audits
- Presence of related parties
- Presence of non-routine or complex transactions
- Presence of accounts or transactions requiring judgment
- Susceptibility of assets to misappropriation

Audit-centred factors influencing risks
- Results of previous audits
- Initial versus repeat engagements
- Assessments of makeup of population

→ Inherent risk

- Corporate governance processes
- Effectiveness of internal controls
- Planned reliance

→ Control risk

one or two accounts. In the illustrations that follow in this and subsequent chapters, a common audit risk is used for segments and for the financial statements as a whole.

Because control risk and inherent risk may vary from cycle to cycle, account to account, or objective to objective, planned detection risk and required audit evidence will also vary. For example, inventory might require extensive testing on an engagement due to weak internal controls and concern about obsolescence due to technological changes in the industry. On the same engagement, accounts receivable may require little testing because of effective internal controls, fast collection of receivables, excellent relationships between the client and customers, and good audit results in previous years. Similarly, for a given audit of inventory, an auditor may assess that there is a higher inherent risk of a valuation misstatement because of the higher potential for obsolescence but a low inherent risk of a classification misstatement because there is only purchased inventory.

RELATING RISKS TO BALANCE-RELATED OR DISCLOSURE-RELATED AUDIT OBJECTIVES It is common in practice to assess inherent and control risks for each audit objective.

MEASUREMENT LIMITATIONS One major limitation in the application of the audit risk model is the difficulty of measuring quantitatively the components of the model, which are highly subjective.

Instead of numeric values, many auditors use terms such as "low," "medium," and "high" to document their risk assessment. Audit firms have developed automated systems that help the auditor to ensure that the appropriate questions have been answered and assist in the documentation and tabulation of conclusions reached. Table 7-7 shows how auditors can use such subjective assessments to decide on the appropriate amount of evidence to accumulate for a particular transaction cycle. For example, in situation 1, the auditor has decided to accept a high audit risk. The auditor has concluded that there is a low risk of misstatement in the cycle (inherent risk) and that internal controls are effective. Therefore, a high detection risk is appropriate. As a result, a low level of evidence is needed. Situation 3 is at the opposite extreme. If both inherent and control risks are high but the auditor wants a low audit risk, considerable evidence is required. The other three situations fall between the two extremes.

It is equally difficult to quantitatively measure the amount of evidence implied by a given planned detection risk. A typical audit program that is intended to reduce detection risk to the planned level is a combination of several audit procedures, each using a different type of evidence that is applied to different audit objectives. Where statistical methods are not employed, auditors subjectively evaluate whether sufficient evidence has been planned to satisfy a planned detection risk of low, medium, or high. Considerable professional judgment is needed to decide on the type and quality of evidence, discussed further in Chapter 8 and subsequent chapters. Continuing research in audit firms is used to help auditors to determine the mix of evidence required and to devise more effective means of gathering evidence as the nature of business transactions change.

Table 7-7	Relationships of Risk to Evidence				
Situation	Audit Risk	Inherent Risk	Control Risk	Planned Detection Risk	Amount of Evidence Required
1	High	Low	Low	High	Low
2	Low	Low	Low	Medium	Medium
3	Low	High	High	Low	High
4	Medium	Medium	Medium	Medium	Medium
5	High	Low	Medium	Medium	Medium

Research on Risk Monitoring and Control

Many organizations operate in specialized industries that have unique economic, regulatory, and accounting issues. In an effort to provide auditor or management guidance, the CICA issues practice alerts and director alerts. For example, the CICA website (**www.cica.ca**) has a section titled "What's New" in Canadian Auditing Standards at **www.cica.ca/focus-on-practice-areas/small-and-medium-practices-(smp)/implementing-the-assurance-standards-tax/index.aspx**, where you will find a series of Practice Alerts. "Enhancing Professional Skepticism" (February 2012) provides tips for auditors to improve their audit of related parties and accounting estimates (among other topics), and you can find a Not-for-Profit Director Alert dated December 2011 that describes changes to legislation for federally incorporated charities. CGAAC provides similar alerts to its members in its PPM (Public Practice Manual) materials.

In applying the audit risk model, auditors are concerned about both over- and under-auditing, but most auditors are more concerned about the latter. Under-auditing exposes the public accounting firm to legal liability and loss of professional reputation.

Practising auditors develop various types of spreadsheets, templates, or computerized links to aid in relating the considerations affecting audit evidence to the appropriate evidence to accumulate. One such spreadsheet in printed form is included in Figure 7-6 for the audit of accounts receivable for Hillsburg Hardware Limited. The five balance-related audit objectives introduced in Chapter 5 are included in the columns at the top of the spreadsheet. Rows one and two are audit risk and inherent risk, which were studied in this chapter. Materiality is included at the bottom of the worksheet. The following decisions were made in the audit of Hillsburg Hardware Limited:

- Materiality. The preliminary judgment about materiality was set at $496,000 (10 percent of earnings before income taxes and extraordinary items of $4,961,000).
- Audit risk. Audit risk was assessed as high because of the good financial condition of the company, high management integrity, and the relatively few public shareholders, about 1,000.
- Inherent risk. Inherent risk was determined to be low for all balance-related audit objectives except valuation. In past years, there have been audit adjustments to the allowance for uncollectable accounts because it was found to be understated.

Planned detection risk would be approximately the same for each balance-related audit objective in the audit of accounts receivable for Hillsburg Hardware Limited if the only three factors the auditor needed to consider were audit risk, inherent risk, and materiality. The evidence planning spreadsheet shows that other factors must be considered before making the final evidence decisions. Control risk for the different transaction types is examined separately, as is the impact of analytical procedures. These are studied in subsequent chapters and will be integrated into the evidence planning spreadsheet at that time.

RELATIONSHIP OF MATERIALITY AND RISK AND AUDIT EVIDENCE The concepts of materiality and risk in auditing are closely related and inseparable. Materiality is a measure of magnitude or size while risk is a measure of uncertainty. Taken together they measure the uncertainty of amounts of a given magnitude. For example, the statement that the auditor plans to accumulate evidence such that there is only a five-percent risk (audit risk) of failing to uncover misstatements exceeding materiality of $25,000 (materiality) is a precise and meaningful statement.

Figure 7-6

Evidence Planning Spreadsheet to Decide Tests of Details of Balances for Hillsburg Hardware Limited—Accounts Receivable

	Existence	Rights and Obligations	Completeness	Valuation	Allocation
Audit risk	high	high	high	high	high
Inherent risk	low	low	low	low	low
Control risk – Sales					
Control risk – Cash receipts					
Control risk – Additional controls					
Analytical procedures					
Planned detection risk for tests of details of balances					
Planned audit evidence for tests of details of balances					

Materiality $496,000

As a general rule, there is a fixed relationship among materiality, risk, and audit evidence. If one of those components is changed, then one or both of the remaining components must also change to achieve the same audit risk. For example, if evidence is held constant and materiality is decreased, then the risk that a material but undiscovered misstatement could exist must increase. Similarly, if materiality were held constant and risk reduced, the required evidence would increase.

Evaluating Achieved Audit Risk

After the auditor plans the engagement and accumulates audit evidence, results of the audit can also be stated in terms of the audit risk model. However, research has shown that using the planning model to evaluate total audit results may result in an understatement of **achieved audit risk**.[2] Achieved audit risk is the numeric value of audit risk using the assessed inherent risk; the value of control risk after documenting, evaluating, and testing internal controls (or the set value based on nonreliance); and the achieved detection risk.

During evaluation, the relationships can be used, but professional judgment, rather than simple reliance on the formula, is required to ensure that sufficient evidence has been collected.

Achieved audit risk—the numeric value of audit risk using the assessed inherent risk; the value of control risk after documenting, evaluating, and testing internal controls (or the set value based on nonreliance); and the achieved detection risk.

---

[2] Research on U.S. Statement of Auditing Standards 47, which provides an evaluation form of the audit planning model, indicates that the formula can result in an understatement of achieved audit risk if the formula is used to evaluate total evidence collected.

The relationships show us that when insufficient evidence has been collected to achieve a specified audit risk, the following theoretical ways could be used to reduce achieved audit risk to the targeted level:

- *Reduce assessed inherent risk.* Because inherent risk is assessed by the auditor based on the client's circumstances, this assessment is done during planning and is typically not changed unless new facts are uncovered as the audit progresses. Changing inherent risk is outside of the control of the auditor.
- *Reduce assessed control risk.* Assessed control risk is affected by the client's internal controls and the auditor's tests of those controls. Auditors can reduce control risk by more extensive tests of controls if the client has effective controls.
- *Reduce achieved detection risk by increasing substantive audit tests.* Auditors reduce achieved detection risk by accumulating evidence using analytical procedures and tests of details of balances. Additional audit procedures, assuming that they are effective, and larger sample sizes both reduce achieved detection risk. This option is the only option of the three that is considered reasonable under current auditing standards unless the auditor concludes that there was an error in the original assessments of inherent or control risk.

No difficulties occur when the auditor accumulates planned evidence and concludes that the assessment of each of the risks was reasonable or better than originally thought. The auditor will conclude that sufficient appropriate audit evidence has been collected for that account or cycle.

concept check

C7-7 How does materiality affect planned evidence?

C7-8 What risks are considered before conducting tests of details?

Appendix 7A
Disaster Recovery Planning

Disaster recovery planning for potential information technology disruptions is a subset of business continuity planning, which relates to the disruptions or threats to the organization as a whole The purpose of a disaster recovery plan (DRP) is to enable a business to continue operations in the event of failure of part or all of its information systems. Something as simple as a hard drive crash (in which the reading head of the hard drive fails, destroying the head, the disk, and the data on it) can cause enormous problems if a company has not given careful thought to contingency procedures. Think of your own personal computer. What would you do if this terrible event occurred? Audit Challenge 7-1 on page 188 describes how an insurance company fared when it had a fire that destroyed some personal computers and disk drives and also caused other equipment failures.

Gary Baker's concise article in *CAmagazine*[3] several years ago breaks down the disaster recovery process into five phases. The phases are as follows:

1. **MANAGEMENT COMMITMENT TO THE CONCEPT OF DISASTER RECOVERY PLANNING** Preparation of a disaster recovery plan (DRP) is time-consuming and requires the provision of funds and human resources. If management is not fully committed to this process, the resources will not be provided, and the activity will falter.

2. **RANKING OF BUSINESS PROCESSES** The entity needs to ask, "What will happen if process X is not available?" Can the payroll be paid? Can goods be shipped out of the door? For organizations using paperless systems and electronic data interchange or electronic commerce, operations will likely cease if those systems are unavailable. Users need to identify what would happen if particular application processes were

---

[3] Baker, G., "Quick recoveries," *CAmagazine*, August 1995, p. 49–50, 53.

unavailable and the likely impact that this would have on the business. Baker suggests using one-day, three-day, and seven-day time frames when conducting this ranking.

3. IDENTIFYING MINIMUM RESOURCES REQUIRED From step 2, the entity will have identified applications that were critical to ongoing operations. Resources required to restore these operations (and perhaps some noncritical systems as well) now need to be identified and costed. Where multiple alternatives exist, they should be similarly identified and costed.

4. PREPARE A DATA CENTRE PLAN AND A USER PLAN The data centre plan addresses technical issues and procedures, such as obtaining hardware and software backup, and ensuring appropriate telecommunications access. The user plan identifies activities required to resume operations and can include manual alternative activities that would be completed if computing resources were unavailable.

5. TEST THE PLAN This trial run will help both data processing personnel and users identify any shortcomings in the DRP and provide a subsequent schedule for remedying those shortcomings.

There are a variety of technical publications and articles that can be used by organizations to prepare a disaster recovery plan or to obtain more detailed guidance on the components of planning.[4] In addition to those issues mentioned by Baker, it is important that an entity have current offsite backup of its systems, carry adequate appropriate insurance coverage, and continue to maintain its disaster recovery plans once the DRP has initially been developed.

Audit Impact The existence of an effective disaster recovery plan is linked to the auditor's assessment of the viability of the entity as a going concern. If an entity using integrated Electronic Data Interchange (EDI), Electronic Funds Transfers (EFTs), and automated shipping systems were to lose these systems and not have an effective DRP, the entity would likely fail if it could not recover its systems within a short period of time. Thus, the auditor might consider either lowering the numeric value of audit risk or asking the client to disclose the lack of appropriate disaster recovery plans in a note to the financial statement.

---

[4] See, for example, Doughty, K., "Business continuity: A business survival strategy," *Information Systems Control Journal*, 1, 2002, p. 28–36.

Summary

1. *What are the components of the audit risk model?* Table 7-1 describes and illustrates audit risk, inherent risk, control risk, and (planned) detection risk.

   Why does the auditor need to consider business risk, both for the client (called client business risk) and for the auditor (termed engagement risk)? Business risk is about not achieving business objectives, resulting in business failure or bankruptcy. If the client fails, then the auditor could be sued. If the auditor fails in doing the audit work correctly, the audit report could be incorrect, also resulting in the auditor being sued (and potentially going out of business).

2. *When assessing inherent risk, what does the auditor consider?* The text lists major factors (page 191) that are related to the nature of the client business, the integrity of its management, the types of transactions or processes, and the susceptibility of transactions to error or manipulation, as well as auditor-centred factors, such as whether it is an initial or repeat engagement.

3. *How is materiality used to assess the amount of work conducted during an audit engagement?* Materiality is used to assess the impact that potential errors might have on users of the financial statements. The auditor needs to conduct the audit such that the statements are free of material errors to a specified assurance level. Since materiality affects sample size, as materiality decreases, so does the need for increased audit testing.

What quantitative and qualitative factors does an auditor consider when setting materiality? The auditor uses professional judgment to choose a base against which to calculate materiality. The numerical value decided upon is based upon factors such as the client risk profile, the extent of fluctuation of bases, and the amount of assurance required.

4. How do the components of the audit risk model relate to the amount of evidence that should be collected during an audit? Assessments are completed to the individual cycle, account, and audit objective level. These assessments are used, together with professional judgment, to decide upon the nature, quality, and quantity of evidence collected, resulting in a detailed audit program.

How does materiality fit in with the audit risk model? The auditor decides upon materiality using professional judgment, with full awareness of the same information that is used to estimate the components of the audit risk model (Figure 7-1 on page 183). Then, materiality is used to help decide upon the amount of evidence that is collected on an assertion-by-assertion basis. Materiality and the components of the audit risk model do not directly affect each other, but both affect the amount of evidence collected.

What problems arise with the use of the audit risk model if risks change once the audit fieldwork has commenced? In the end, the auditor must have sufficient evidence to state an audit opinion. If risk changes indicate that more evidence is required, the auditor needs to collect additional evidence.

If the opposite occurs, then the auditor has collected too much evidence—however, auditors would tend to err in this direction rather than collecting too little evidence.

MyAccountingLab

Make the grade with MyAccountingLab: The questions, exercises, and problems marked in orange can be found on MyAccountingLab. You can practise them as often as you want, and most feature step-by-step guided instructions to help you find the right answer.

Review Questions

7-1 ❶ Define the "audit risk model" and explain each term in the model.

7-2 ❶ Explain the causes of an increased or decreased planned detection risk.

7-3 ❶ When does the auditor assess client business risk? Why?

7-4 ❶ How does engagement risk (auditor business risk) affect the audit process?

7-5 ❶ Explain why inherent risk is estimated for segments rather than for the overall audit. What is the effect on the amount of evidence the auditor must accumulate when inherent risk is increased from medium to high for a segment?

7-6 ❶ Explain the relationship between audit risk and the legal liability of auditors.

7-7 ❶ State the categories of circumstances that affect audit risk, and list the factors that the auditor can use to indicate the degree to which each category exists.

7-8 ❷ Explain the effect of extensive misstatements found in the prior year's audit on inherent risk, planned detection risk, and planned audit evidence.

7-9 ❸ Define the term "materiality" as it is used in accounting and auditing. What is the relationship between materiality and the phrase "obtain reasonable assurance" used in the auditor's report?

7-10 ❸ Explain why materiality is important but difficult to apply in practice.

7-11 ❸ What is meant by "planning materiality"? Identify the most important factors affecting the development of this figure.

7-12 ❸ Assume Rosanne Madden, a PA, is using 5 percent of net income before taxes as her major guideline for evaluating materiality. What qualitative factors should she also consider in deciding whether misstatements may be material?

7-13 ❸ Differentiate between identified misstatements, likely or potential misstatements, and further possible misstatements. Explain why all three are important.

7-14 ❸ How would the conduct of an audit of a medium-sized company be affected by the company's being a small part of a large conglomerate as compared with its being a separate entity?

7-15 ❹ Auditors have not been successful in measuring the components of the audit risk model. How is it possible to use the model in a meaningful way without a precise way of measuring the risk?

Discussion Questions and Problems

7-16 ❶ You are the proprietor of an PA firm with a growing audit practice. You have accepted the audit of T-Division, one of six separate Canadian divisions of a large, private multinational corporation. Each division operates as a separate entity. The manager of each division receives a salary, plus a bonus based on the net profit of the division. In each division, the manager has the authority over all other employees for buying materials, production issues, accounting, and personnel matters.

James has reached the level of manager of the T-Division by working very hard and demanding high production levels of his staff. James has advised you that he wants to see all questions you have about accounting issues and he assures you that he will personally make sure that they are taken care of, without any more effort on your behalf. James explained that he has managed three other divisions in the past for this company, and each one received a "clean audit report," which helped his career. He wants to ensure that T-Division also gets a "clean" audit report and to keep the auditor's work at a minimum.

REQUIRED

a. Determine whether you would set the overall audit risk as high, medium, or low for your audit of T-Division. Justify your response.

b. Identify and briefly explain two other items of information about T-Division, besides what you already know, that would be important for you to consider in determining the proper level of audit risk.

(Extract from AU1 CGA- Canada Examinations developed by the Certified General Accountants Association of Canada © 2009 CGA-Canada. Reproduced with permission. All rights reserved.)

7-17 ❶ ❷ You are the auditor in charge of the audit of the municipality of Sackville, New Brunswick. The municipality has a budget of about $65 million and has had a balanced budget for the last three years. There are about 10 people in the accounting office and the rest of the employees are operational, dealing with supervision of roadwork, garbage collection, and similar matters. Many services are outsourced, minimizing the need for employees. The municipality has a chief executive officer and a controller and reports to the council of elected representatives.

REQUIRED

For each of the following situations, state a preliminary conclusion for audit risk, inherent risk, control risk, and detection risk. Justify your conclusions. State any assumptions that are necessary for you to reach your conclusions.

1. This is the first year that you have been auditing Sackville. There has been extensive turnover after the recent election. Costs are out of control, and it looks like it

may be necessary to raise realty taxes by as much as 15 percent.

2. For four years now, you have been auditing Sackville. The employees are experienced, and any control recommendations that you have suggested have been discussed and, where feasible, implemented. There is a tiny budget surplus this year, and it looks as if a balanced budget is in sight again for next year.

3. Sackville is being hit by bad press. It seems that one of the purchasing agents set up a fictitious company and was billing the municipality for goods that had not been received. To make it worse, the purchasing agent's wife was the assistant accountant. The office of the provincial Auditor General has sent a letter to the controller of Sackville stating that the municipality has been selected for audit by the provincial Auditor General's Office based on a random sample and that the provincial auditors will be arriving within two weeks of the completion of your audit.

7-18 ❶ ❸ Some accountants have suggested that the auditor's report should include a statement of materiality level and audit risk that the auditor used in conducting the audit.

REQUIRED

a. The proponents of such disclosure believe that the information would be useful to users of the financial statements being reported on. Explain fully why you think they have this view.

b. Some accountants oppose such disclosure. Explain why you think they are not in favour of it.

c. What is your position on the issue?

7-19 ❸ Statements of earnings and financial position for Prairie Stores Corporation are shown on the next page.

REQUIRED

a. Use professional judgment in determining materiality based on revenue, net income before taxes, total assets, and shareholders' equity. Your conclusions should be stated in terms of percentages and dollars.

b. Assume you complete the audit and conclude that financial statement misstatements exceed materiality. What should you do?

c. As discussed in part (b), likely net earnings from continuing operations before income taxes were used as a base for materiality when completing the audit. Discuss why most auditors use before-tax net earnings instead of after-tax net earnings when calculating materiality based on the income statement.

Statement of Earnings
Prairie Stores Corporation

	For the 52 Weeks Ended		
	March 30, 2012	April 1, 2011	April 1, 2010
Revenue			
Net sales	$8,351,149	$6,601,255	$5,959,587
Other income	59,675	43,186	52,418
	8,410,824	6,644,441	6,012,005
Costs and expenses			
Cost of sales	5,197,375	4,005,548	3,675,369
Marketing, general, and administrative expenses	2,590,080	2,119,590	1,828,169
Provision for loss on restructured operations	64,100	–	–
Interest expense	141,662	46,737	38,546
	7,993,217	6,171,875	5,542,084
Earnings from continuing operations before income taxes	417,607	472,566	469,921
Income taxes	196,700	217,200	214,100
Earnings from continuing operations	220,907	255,366	255,821
Provision for loss on discontinued operations, net of income taxes	20,700	–	–
Net earnings	$200,207	$255,366	$255,821

Statement of Financial Position
Prairie Stores Corporation

Assets	March 30, 2012		April 1, 2011	
Current assets				
Cash		$39,683		$37,566
Temporary investments (at cost, which approximates market)		123,421		271,639
Receivables, less allowances of $16,808 in 2012 and $17,616 in 2011		899,752		759,001
Inventories				
Finished product	680,974		550,407	
Raw materials and supplies	443,175		353,795	
		1,124,149		904,202
Deferred income tax benefits		9,633		10,468
Prepaid expenses		57,468		35,911
Total current assets		2,254,106		2,018,787
Land, buildings, equipment at cost, less accumulated amortization		1,393,902		1,004,455
Investments in affiliated companies and sundry assets		112,938		83,455
Goodwill and other intangible assets		99,791		23,145
Total assets		$3,860,737		$3,129,842
Liabilities and Shareholders' Equity				
Current liabilities				
Notes payable		$280,238		$113,411
Current portion of long-term debt		64,594		12,336
Accounts and drafts payable		359,511		380,395
Accrued salaries, wages, and vacations		112,200		63,557
Accrued income taxes		76,479		89,151
Other accrued liabilities including goods and services tax		321,871		269,672
Current liabilities		1,214,893		928,522
Long-term debt		730,987		390,687
Other noncurrent liabilities		146,687		80,586
Accrued income tax liability		142,344		119,715
Total liabilities		2,234,911		1,519,510
Shareholders' equity				
Common stock issued, 51,017 shares in 2012 and 50,992 in 2011		200,195		199,576
Retained earnings		1,425,631		1,410,756
Total shareholders' equity		1,625,826		1,610,332
Total liabilities and shareholders' equity		$3,860,737		$3,129,842

7-20 ③ ④ You are evaluating audit results for current assets in the audit of Quicky Plumbing Co. You set the materiality for current assets at $12,500 for overstatements and at $20,000 for understatements. The estimated and actual misstatement ranges are shown below.

REQUIRED

a. Justify a lower materiality for overstatements than understatements in this situation.

b. Explain why the totals of the tolerable misstatements exceed materiality for both understatements and overstatements.

c. Explain how it is possible that three of the estimates of total misstatement have both an overstatement and an understatement.

d. Assume that you are not concerned whether the estimate of misstatement exceeds tolerable misstatement for individual accounts if the total estimate is less than materiality.

1. Given the audit results, should you be more concerned about the existence of material overstatements or understatements at this point in the audit of Quicky Plumbing Co.?

2. Which account or accounts will you be most concerned about in (1)? Explain.

e. Assume that the estimate of total overstatement amount for each account is less than tolerable misstatement, but that the total overstatement estimate exceeds materiality.

1. Explain why this would occur.

2. Explain what the auditor should do.

Account	Tolerable Misstatement		Estimate of Total Misstatement	
	Over-statements	Under-statements	Over-statements	Under-statements
Cash	$ 2,000	$ 3,000	$ 2,000	$ 0
Accounts receivable	12,000	18,000	4,000	19,000
Inventory	8,000	14,000	3,000	10,000
Prepaid expenses	3,000	5,000	2,000	1,000
Total	$25,000	$40,000	$11,000	$30,000

7-21 ① ② ④ Following are six situations that involve the audit risk model as it is used for planning audit evidence requirements in the audit of inventory.

REQUIRED

a. Explain what low, medium, and high mean for each of the four risks and planned evidence.

b. Fill in the blanks for planned detection risk and planned evidence using the terms low, medium, or high.

c. Using your knowledge of the relationships among the foregoing factors, state the effect on planned evidence (increase or decrease) of changing each of the following five factors, while the other three remain constant:

1. An increase in audit risk.
2. An increase in control risk.
3. An increase in planned detection risk.
4. An increase in inherent risk.
5. An increase in inherent risk and a decrease in control risk of the same amount.

Risk	Situation					
	1	2	3	4	5	6
Acceptable audit risk	High	High	Low	Low	High	Medium
Inherent risk	Low	High	High	Low	Medium	Medium
Control risk	Low	Low	High	High	Medium	Medium
Planned detection risk	–	–	–	–	–	–
Planned evidence	–	–	–	–	–	–

7-22 ① ② ③ ④ The following are concepts discussed in this chapter:

1. Materiality
2. Control risk
3. Risk of fraud
4. Estimated total misstatement in a segment
5. Planned detection risk
6. Estimate of total (combined) misstatement
7. Acceptable audit risk
8. Tolerable misstatement
9. Inherent risk
10. Risk of material misstatement
11. Known misstatement

REQUIRED

a. Identify which items are *audit planning decisions* requiring professional judgment.

b. Identify which items are *audit conclusions* resulting from application of audit procedures and requiring professional judgment.

c. Under which circumstances is it acceptable to change those items in part a after the audit is started? Which items can be changed after the audit is 95 percent complete?

Professional Judgment Problem

7-23 **①②** Joe Whitehead is planning the audit of a newly obtained client, Henderson Energy Corporation, for the year ended December 31, 2011. Henderson Energy is regulated by the provincial utility commission and, because it is a publicly traded company, the audited financial statements must be filed with the OSC (Ontario Securities Commission).

Henderson Energy is considerably more profitable than many of its competitors, largely due to its extensive investment in information technologies used in its energy distribution and other key business processes. Recent growth into rural markets, however, has placed some strain on 2011 operations. Additionally, Henderson Energy expanded its investments into speculative markets and is also making greater use of derivative and hedging transactions to mitigate some of its investment risks. Because of the complexities of the underlying accounting associated with these activities, Henderson Energy added several highly experienced accountants to its financial reporting team. Internal audit, which has direct reporting responsibility to the audit committee, is also actively involved in reviewing key accounting assumptions and estimates on a quarterly basis.

Whitehead's discussions with the predecessor auditor revealed that the client has experienced some difficulty in correctly tracking existing property, plant, and equipment items. This largely involves equipment located at its multiple energy production facilities. During the recent year, Henderson acquired a regional electric company, which expanded the number of energy production facilities.

Whitehead plans to staff the audit engagement with several members of the firm who have experience in auditing energy and public companies. The extent of partner review of key accounts will be extensive.

REQUIRED

Based on the above information, identify factors that affect the risk of material misstatement in the December 31, 2011, financial statements of Henderson Energy. Indicate whether the factor increases or decreases the risk of material misstatement. Also, identify which audit risk model component is affected by the factor. Use the format below:

Factor	Effect on the Risk of Material Misstatement	Audit Risk Model Component
Henderson is a new client	Increases	Inherent risk

Case

7-24 **①②** In the audit of Whirland Chemical Company, a large publicly traded company, you have been assigned the responsibility for obtaining background information for the audit. Your firm is auditing the client for the first time in the current year as a result of a dispute between Whirland and the previous auditor over the proper valuation of work-in-process inventory and the inclusion in sales of inventory that has not been delivered but has, for practical purposes, been completed and sold.

Whirland Chemical has been highly successful in its field in the past two decades, primarily because of many successful mergers negotiated by Bert Randolph, the president and chairman of the board. Even though the industry as a whole has suffered dramatic setbacks in recent years, Whirland continues to prosper, as evidenced by its constantly increasing earnings and growth. Only in the last two years have the company's profits turned downward. Randolph has a reputation for having been able to hire an aggressive group of young executives by using relatively low salaries combined with an unusually generous profit-sharing plan.

A major difficulty you face in the new audit is that Whirland lacks the highly sophisticated accounting records expected of a company of its size. Randolph believes that profits come primarily from intelligent and aggressive action based on forecasts, not by relying on historical data that come after the fact. Most of the forecast data are generated by the sales and production department rather than by the accounting department. The personnel in the accounting department do seem competent but somewhat overworked and underpaid relative to other employees. One of the recent changes that will potentially improve the record-keeping is the installation of sophisticated information systems. Not all of the accounting records are fully integrated yet, but such major areas as inventory and sales are included in the new system.

The first six months' financial statements for the current year include a profit of approximately only 10 percent less than that of the first six months of the preceding year, which is somewhat surprising, considering the reduced volume and the disposal of a segment of the business, Mercury Supply Co. The disposal of this segment was considered necessary because it had become increasingly unprofitable over the past four years. At the time of its acquisition from Roger Randolph, a brother of Bert Randolph, the company was highly profitable and was considered a highly desirable purchase. The major customer of Mercury Supply Co. was the Mercury Corporation, which is owned by Roger Randolph. Gradually, the market for its products declined as Mercury Corporation began diversifying and phasing out its primary products in favour of more profitable business. Even though Mercury Corporation is no longer buying from Mercury Supply Co., it compensates by buying a large volume of other products from Whirland Chemical.

The only major difficulty Whirland faces right now, according to financial analysts, is underfinancing. There is a high amount of current debt and long-term debt because of the depressed capital markets. Management is reluctant to obtain equity capital at this point because the increased number of shares would decrease the earnings per share even more than 10 percent. At the present time, Randolph is negotiating with several cash-rich companies in the hope of being able to merge with them as a means of overcoming the capital problems.

REQUIRED

a. List the major concerns you would have when assessing inherent risk and audit risk for the audit of Whirland Chemical Company. Explain why they are potential problems. Provide a conclusion (high, medium, or low) for inherent risk and audit risk.

b. State the appropriate approach to investigating the significance of each item you listed in (a).

Ongoing Small Business Case: Materiality for CondoCleaners.com

7-25 ❸ CondoCleaners.com has been in business now for three years. The current year's annual sales is $320,000, with cost of goods sold at $275,000. There is no debt, and the company has fixed assets of $4,250 (a personal computer and vacuum cleaners). The company currently provides cleaning services for 12 clusters of downtown condominium units.

REQUIRED

Calculate preliminary materiality for CondoCleaners.com for the current year of operations.

8   Audit evidence

What does an auditor examine to provide assurance about the quality of the financial statements? When has enough information been collected? These are difficult questions, and this chapter examines the nature of evidence that is collected. All types of auditors will make decisions about the types of audit tests they will conduct in response to assessed risks. This chapter provides a toolkit of the different types of evidence and the factors that need to be considered to select high-quality evidence.

LEARNING OBJECTIVES

1 Describe five evidence decisions made during the audit process. Relate audit evidence decisions to qualities affecting persuasiveness of evidence.

2 List and explain the seven general methods of evidence collection. Explain the importance of automated audit techniques in supporting the conduct of recalculation and reperformance.

3 Discuss methods used to choose the types of evidence to collect. Use criteria to assess the reliability of evidence. Link audit standards to mandated evidence collection processes.

4 Define analytical procedures and state when they are used during the audit process. Describe the advantages and disadvantages of the five major types of analytical procedures as part of the evidence collection process.

STANDARDS REFERENCED IN THIS CHAPTER

CICA Standards

CAS 315 – Identifying and assessing the risks of material misstatement through understanding the entity and its environment

CAS 330 – The auditor's responses to assessed risks

CAS 500 – Audit evidence

CAS 520 – Analytical procedures

CAS 505 – External confirmations

Sometimes the Most Important Evidence Is Not Found in the Accounting Records

Crenshaw Properties was a real estate developer that specialized in self-storage facilities that it sold to limited partner investors. Crenshaw's role was to identify projects, serve as the general partner with a small investment, and raise capital from mortgage funds or other lenders such as banks and credit unions. Crenshaw had an extensive network of people who marketed these investments on a commission basis. As general partner, Crenshaw earned significant fees for related activities, including promotional fees, investment management fees, and real estate commissions.

The investments were successful, and business prospered. The value of self-storage facilities increased in line with the real estate market, and values were booming. But sales started to slow down in 2011 and continued to slow into 2012.

George Crenshaw received a shock when he went to the bank in mid-2012 to secure mortgages for his next construction project. The bank requested detailed valuations of all of the properties in the Crenshaw Properties portfolio. It also wanted quarterly cash flow reporting, to be reviewed by the company's auditors, and a personal guarantee from George Crenshaw before considering provision of more mortgage funds.

Upon analysis of the valuations and a cash flow statement, the bank declined the mortgage to Crenshaw Properties, saying that the company's margins needed to increase and costs needed to be cut before it would consider lending additional funds. Crenshaw Properties wants to sell off some assets to continue operations, but the depressed real estate market may make this difficult.

IMPORTANCE TO AUDITORS

Crenshaw Properties ran into difficulties in financing because of the international credit crunch triggered by falling real estate values, turmoil in the asset-backed paper market, lower bank liquidity, and the subsequent tightening credit market. Lack of financing and decreased real estate values could mean that Crenshaw will no longer be a going concern if it cannot reorganize and cut costs.

As part of their audits in 2011 and 2012, the auditors should have considered the values of the assets held by Crenshaw, with the resultant impact on borrowing capacity and the ability of the company to continue operations.

WHAT DO YOU THINK?

1. What other factors could affect the ability of Crenshaw Properties to continue operations? How would the auditors find out about these factors?

continued >

2. How does general knowledge of the economy help the auditor when conducting the financial statement audit? What about specific industry knowledge?

WHAT other types of companies or business activities could be affected by a credit crunch? Virtually every organization uses banking facilities and has debt. The inability to renew debt or borrow money can cripple an organization. As an auditor, you need to think about both the big-picture risks involved in a company's operations, as well as the small-picture risks associated with individual transactions and potential errors. Evidence helps the auditor assess risks and decide upon the likelihood of potential misstatement in the financial statements.

Audit Evidence and Associated Decisions

Nature of Evidence

Audit evidence was defined in Chapter 1 as any information used by the auditor to determine whether the financial statement being audited is stated in accordance with the established criteria. The information is a decision tool—it varies widely in the extent to which it persuades the auditor whether financial statements are stated in conformity with an acceptable financial reporting framework. Evidence includes persuasive information, such as the auditor's count of marketable securities, and less persuasive information, such as responses to questions by the client's employees.

Evidence is gathered in all phases of the audit process—in the risk assessment process, to help the auditor decide where there could be a risk of material misstatement in the financial statements; as a response to risks at the assertion level; and to document quality control, supervision, and overall conclusions about the type of audit report.

AUDIT EVIDENCE CONTRASTED WITH LEGAL AND SCIENTIFIC EVIDENCE The use of evidence is not unique to auditors. Evidence is also used extensively by scientists, lawyers, historians, and many others to support their decisions.

Through television, most people are familiar with the use of evidence in legal cases dealing with the guilt or innocence of a party charged with a crime such as robbery. In legal cases, there are well-defined rules of evidence enforced by a judge for the protection of the innocent. It is common, for example, for legal evidence to be judged inadmissible on the grounds that it is irrelevant, prejudicial, or based on hearsay.

Similarly, in scientific experiments, the scientist obtains evidence to draw conclusions about a theory. Assume, for example, a medical scientist is evaluating a new medicine that may provide relief to asthma sufferers. The scientist will gather evidence from a large number of controlled experiments over an extended period of time to determine the effectiveness of the medicine.

Table 8-1	Characteristics of Evidence for a Scientific Experiment, a Legal Case, and an Audit of Financial Statements		
Basis of Comparison	Scientific Experiment Involving Testing a Medicine	Legal Case Involving an Accused Thief	Audit of Financial Statements
Use of the evidence	Determine effects of using the medicine	Decide guilt or innocence of accused	Determine if statements are fairly presented
Nature of evidence	Results of repeated experiments	Direct evidence and testimony by witnesses and party involved	Various types of audit evidence generated by the auditor, third parties, and the client
Party or parties evaluating evidence	Scientist	Jury and judge	Auditor
Certainty of conclusions from evidence	Vary from uncertain to near certainty	Requires establishing guilt beyond a reasonable doubt	High level of assurance
Nature of conclusions	Recommend or not recommend use of medicine	Innocence or guilt of party	Issue one of several alternative types of auditor's reports
Typical consequences of incorrect conclusions from evidence	Society uses ineffective or harmful medicine	Guilty party is not penalized, or innocent party is found guilty	Statement users make incorrect decisions, and auditor may be sued

The auditor also gathers evidence to draw conclusions. Different evidence is used by auditors than by scientists or lawyers, and it is used in different ways, but in all three cases, evidence is used to reach conclusions. Table 8-1 illustrates key characteristics of evidence from the perspective of a scientist doing an experiment, a legal case involving an accused thief, and an auditor of financial statements. There are six bases of comparison. Note the similarities and differences among the three professions.

Audit Evidence Decisions

CAS 330, The auditor's responses to assessed risks, explains that the auditor needs to link completed audit work to the assessed risks at the assertion level (transactions, balances, or financial statement disclosures), as well as documenting the conclusions and results of the audit procedures (par. 28). Identifying risks helps the auditor determine the appropriate types and amount of evidence to accumulate to be satisfied that the components of the client's financial statements and the overall statements are fairly stated. This judgment is important because of the prohibitive cost of examining and evaluating all available evidence. For example, in an audit of financial statements of most organizations, it is impossible for the public accountant (PA) to examine the contents of all computer files or available evidence such as cancelled cheques, vendors' invoices, customer orders, payroll time records, and the many other types of documents and records.

The auditor's decisions on evidence accumulation can be broken into the following five subdecisions:

1. Which risks could result in a risk of material misstatement (RMM) at the assertion level.

2. Which audit procedures to use (their "nature").

3. What sample size to select for a given procedure (the "extent" of a test).

4. Which particular items to select from the population.

5. When to perform the procedures (the "timing").

IDENTIFYING RISKS BY ASSERTION For each major class of transactions and material general ledger account, the auditor looks at the potential for RMM. Knowledge of the industry, business, and operating procedures at the client will help the auditor complete this assessment. For example, at Hillsburg Hardware, the auditor may decide that risk of obsolescence of inventory (the valuation assertion) is high due to frequent new product announcements and the potential for economic recession, while the risk of accuracy (recording the quantity, cost, and mechanical calculations) is low due to the high quality of information systems and monitoring controls at the company.

AUDIT PROCEDURES An **audit procedure** is the detailed instruction for the collection of a particular type of audit evidence that is to be obtained at some time during the audit. For example, evidence such as physical inventory counts, comparisons of cancelled cheques with cash disbursements, journal entries, and shipping document details is collected using audit procedures.

Audit procedure—detailed instruction for the collection of a type of audit evidence.

Audit procedures need to be detailed and specific—what is being done, how it is being done, and when. The auditor will consider manual and automated procedures, depending upon their cost. For example, the following is an audit procedure for the verification of cash disbursements:

- During the interim audit (when), obtain the cash disbursements report (how), and for the outstanding cheques, compare the payee name, amount, and date on the cancelled cheque with the cash disbursement report (what).

SAMPLE SIZE Once an audit procedure is determined, it is possible to vary the sample size from one to all the items in the population being tested. In the audit procedure above, suppose there are 6,600 outstanding cheques to be traced to the cash disbursements report. The auditor might select a sample size of 40 cheques for comparison. The decision as to how many items to test must be made by the auditor for each audit procedure. The sample size for any given procedure is likely to vary from audit to audit. Sampling is discussed further in Chapter 11.

ITEMS TO SELECT After the sample size has been determined for a particular audit procedure, it is still necessary to decide which items to test. If the auditor decides, for example, to select 40 cancelled cheques from a population of 6,600 for comparison with the cash disbursements journal, several different methods can be used to select the specific cheques to be examined. The auditor could (1) select a week and examine the first 40 cheques, (2) select the 40 cheques with the largest amounts (also known as "key items"), (3) select the cheques randomly, or (4) select those cheques the auditor thinks are most likely to be in error. A combination of these methods could also be used. The sampling method and size is related to assessed risks and would need to be approved by the audit manager or partner.

TIMING An audit of financial statements usually covers a period such as a year, and an audit is often not completed until several weeks or months after the end of the fiscal period. The timing of audit procedures can vary from early in the accounting period to long after it has ended. Normally the financial statement audit is completed one to three months after year end.

Audit procedures often incorporate sample size, items to select, and timing. The following is a more complete version of the audit procedure previously used to include all five audit evidence decisions. (Italics identify the assertion, timing, number of items to select, and sample size decisions.)

- *Occurrence*: During the interim audit, obtain the *October* bank reconciliation and cash disbursements report, and compare the payee name, amount, and date on the cancelled cheque with the cash disbursements report for a *randomly selected sample of 40* outstanding cheque numbers.

AUDIT PROGRAM The detailed instructions for the entire collection of evidence for an audit area is called an **audit program**. Normally, there is an audit program for each component of the audit (e.g., accounts receivable and sales). An example of an audit program that includes audit procedures (the how), sample size, items to select (the what), and timing (the when) is given on page 327 in Table 10-6. The right side of the audit program also includes the audit objectives for each procedure, as studied in Chapter 5.

Persuasiveness of Evidence

Generally accepted auditing standards (GAAS) require the auditor to obtain sufficient appropriate audit evidence to be able to draw reasonable conclusions on which to base the audit opinion. Because of the nature of audit evidence and the cost considerations of doing an audit, it is unlikely that the auditor will be completely convinced that the opinion is correct. However, the auditor must be persuaded that his or her opinion is correct with a high level of assurance. By combining all evidence from the entire audit, the auditor is able to decide when he or she is sufficiently persuaded to issue an auditor's report.

Persuasiveness of evidence is the degree to which the auditor is convinced that the evidence supports the audit opinion; the three determinants of persuasiveness are sufficiency (enough evidence), appropriateness (quality and relevance), and timeliness (covering the appropriate period).

SUFFICIENCY The quantity of evidence obtained determines its **sufficiency** (CAS 500, par. 5[e]). Quantity is measured primarily by the sample size the auditor selects. For a given audit procedure, the evidence obtained from a sample of 50 would ordinarily be more sufficient than that from a sample of 25.

There are several factors that determine the appropriate sample size in audits. The two most important are the auditor's expectation of errors and the effectiveness of the client's internal controls. To illustrate, assume that, during the audit of Lau Computer Parts Inc., the auditor concludes that there is a high likelihood of obsolete inventory due to the nature of the client's industry. The auditor would sample more inventory items for obsolescence in an audit such as this than in one where the likelihood of obsolescence was low. Similarly, if the auditor concludes that a client has effective rather than ineffective internal controls over recording capital assets, a smaller sample size in the audit of purchases of capital assets is required. The particular items tested also affect the sufficiency of evidence. Samples containing population items with large dollar values, items with a high likelihood of error, and items that are representative of the population are usually considered sufficient. This means that sufficiency requires enough items, enough representative items, and enough dollar value to be tested.

APPROPRIATENESS **Appropriateness** refers to the quality of evidence, that is, the degree to which the evidence can be considered relevant and reliable. If evidence is considered to be highly appropriate, it is a great help in persuading the auditor that the financial statements are fairly stated. For example, if an auditor counted inventory, that evidence would be more appropriate than if management gave the auditor its own figures. Generally, the more appropriate the evidence, the less evidence is needed. Evidence is appropriate when it is both relevant and reliable.

Appropriateness of evidence depends on the audit procedures selected. Appropriateness cannot be improved by selecting a larger sample size or different population items. It can be improved only by selecting audit procedures that improve either the relevance or the reliability of the evidence.

RELEVANCE **Relevant evidence** pertains to the audit objective the auditor is testing. For example, assume the auditor is concerned that a client is failing to bill

Will It Stand Up in Court?

Rhonda McMillan had been the in-charge auditor on the audit of Blaine Construction Company in 2006. Now she is sitting here, in 2012, in a room full of attorneys who are asking her questions about the 2006 audit. Blaine was sold to another company in 2007 at a purchase price that was based primarily on the 2006 audited financial statements. Several of the large construction contracts showed a profit in 2006 using the percentage of completion method, but they ultimately resulted in large losses for the buyer. Because Rhonda's firm audited the 2006 financial statements, the buyer is trying to make the case that Rhonda's firm failed in their audit of contract costs and revenues.

The buyer's attorney is taking Rhonda's deposition and is asking her about the audit work she did on contracts. Referring to the audit files, his examination goes something like this:

Attorney   Do you recognize this exhibit, and if you do, would you please identify it for us?

Rhonda   Yes, this is the summary of contracts in progress at the end of 2006.

Attorney   Did you prepare this schedule?

Rhonda   I believe the client prepared it, but I audited it. My initials are right here in the upper right-hand corner.

Attorney   When did you do this audit work?

Rhonda   I'm not sure, I forgot to date this one. But it must have been about the second week in March, because that's when we did the field work.

Attorney   Now I'd like to turn your attention to this tick mark next to the Baldwin contract. You see where it shows Baldwin, and then the red sort of cross-like mark?

Rhonda   Yes.

Attorney   In the explanation for that tick mark it says: "Discussed status of job with Elton Burgess. Job is going according to schedule and he believes that the expected profit will be earned." Now my question is, Ms. McMillan, what exactly was the nature and content of your discussion with Mr. Burgess?

Rhonda   Other than what is in the explanation to this tick mark, I have no idea. I mean, this all took place over five years ago. I only worked on the engagement that one year, and I can hardly even remember that.

Rhonda's work was not adequately documented, and what was there indicated that her testing relied almost exclusively on management inquiry without any required corroboration. The evidence collected was not sufficient and not relevant. Her audit firm was required to pay a significant settlement for damages to the buyer.

---

customers for shipments (completeness transaction-related audit objective). If the auditor selected a sample of duplicate sales invoices and traced each to related shipping documents, the evidence would not be relevant for the completeness objective because it tests for occurrence instead. A relevant procedure would be to compare a sample of shipping documents with related duplicate sales invoices to determine if each shipment had been billed. The reason the second audit procedure is relevant and the first is not is that the shipment of goods is the normal criterion used for determining whether a sale has occurred and should have been billed. By tracing from shipping documents to duplicate sales invoices, the auditor can determine if shipments have been billed to customers. When the auditor traces from duplicate sales invoices to shipping documents, it is impossible to find unbilled shipments.

Relevance can be considered only in terms of specific audit objectives.

RELIABILITY   **Reliability of evidence** increases when it is obtained from (1) the auditor's direct knowledge, (2) an independent provider, (3) a client with effective internal

> **Reliability of evidence**—evidence is reliable when it is obtained from (1) the auditor's direct knowledge, (2) an independent provider, (3) a client with effective internal controls, (4) qualified providers such as law firms and banks, (5) objective sources, or (6) consistent and multiple sources.

controls, (4) qualified providers such as law firms and banks, (5) objective sources, or (6) consistent or multiple sources.

(1) Auditor's direct knowledge Evidence obtained directly by the auditor through observation, reperformance, and inspection is more appropriate than information obtained indirectly. For example, if the auditor observes recent fixed asset additions, notes serial numbers, and traces the historical cost from original invoices, the evidence would be more reliable than if the auditor relied on documents and calculations provided by the controller.

(2) Independence of provider Evidence obtained from a source outside the entity is more reliable than that obtained from within, assuming that the external party is arm's length from the organization. For example, external evidence such as communications from banks, lawyers, or customers is generally regarded as more reliable than answers obtained from inquiries of the client. Similarly, documents that originate from outside the client's organization are considered more reliable than those that originate within the company and have never left the client's organization. An example of external evidence is an insurance policy, whereas a purchase requisition is internal evidence.

(3) Effectiveness of client's internal controls When a client's internal controls are effective, evidence obtained from the client is more reliable than when controls are weak, as discussed further in Chapter 9. For example, if internal controls over sales and billing are effective, the auditor can obtain more accurate and complete evidence from sales invoices and shipping documents than if the controls are inadequate. When considering internal controls, the auditor also considers the likelihood of management override and the pervasive impact of management integrity.

(4) Qualifications of individuals providing the information Even when the source of information is independent, the evidence will not be reliable unless the individual providing it is qualified to do so. For this reason, communications from law firms and bank confirmations are typically more highly regarded than accounts receivable confirmations from persons not familiar with the business world. Also, evidence obtained directly by the auditor may not be reliable if he or she lacks the qualifications to evaluate the evidence. For example, examination of an inventory of diamonds by an auditor who is not trained to distinguish between diamonds and glass would not provide reliable evidence of the existence of diamonds. The auditor needs to consider the qualifications of providers with respect to each source of evidence, whether it be from management, internal auditors, or external specialists.

(5) Degree of objectivity Objective evidence is more reliable than evidence that requires considerable judgment to determine whether it is correct. Examples of objective evidence include confirmation of accounts receivable and bank balances, the physical count of securities and cash, and the adding (footing) of a list of accounts payable to determine if it is the same as the balance in the general ledger. Examples of subjective evidence include communication from a client's lawyers as to the likely outcome of outstanding lawsuits against the client, observation of obsolescence of inventory during physical examination, and inquiries of the credit manager about the collectability of non-current accounts receivable. In evaluating the reliability of subjective evidence, the qualifications of the person providing the evidence are important.

(6) Consistency from multiple sources With respect to a particular assertion, the auditor could use multiple sources of evidence. Consider, for example, obsolescence of inventory at Hillsburg Hardware. The auditor could calculate inventory turnover, review recent purchasing invoices, talk to shipping personnel, and observe physical inventory in the warehouse. If shipping personnel stated that no old stock existed, but the auditor observed old inventory (perhaps dusty or dirty boxes of products), then the auditor would need to investigate further to clarify the inconsistency. Evidence with all sources consistent is more reliable than inconsistent evidence.

TIMELINESS The **timeliness** of audit evidence can refer either to when it was accumulated or to the period covered by the audit. Evidence is usually more persuasive for balance sheet accounts when it is obtained as close to the balance sheet date as possible. For example, the auditor's count of marketable securities on the balance sheet date would be more persuasive than a count two months earlier. For income statement accounts, evidence is more persuasive if there is a sample from the entire period under audit rather than from only a part of the period. For example, a random sample of sales transactions for the entire year would be more persuasive than a sample from only the first six months.

Timeliness—the timing of audit evidence in relation to the period covered by the audit.

COMBINED EFFECT The persuasiveness of evidence can be evaluated only after considering the combination of sufficiency, appropriateness, and timeliness in the context of the RMM for that audit objective. A large sample of evidence is not persuasive unless it is relevant to the audit objective being tested. A large sample of evidence that is neither appropriate nor timely is also not persuasive. Similarly, a small sample of only one or two pieces of appropriate and timely evidence also lacks persuasiveness. The auditor must evaluate the degree to which all three qualities have been met in deciding persuasiveness.

To illustrate the characteristics shown in Table 8-2, assume an auditor is verifying inventory that is a major item in the financial statements. Generally accepted auditing standards require that the auditor be reasonably persuaded that inventory is not materially misstated. First, the auditor identifies the RMM for the audit objectives about inventory. For example, there could be a high risk for incompleteness due to many small items that can be easily stolen. The auditor must obtain a sufficient amount of appropriate and timely evidence about inventory. This means deciding which procedures to use for auditing inventory (such as an inventory count conducted by the auditor) to satisfy the appropriateness requirement, as well as determining the proper sample size (based upon risk and statistical tables) and items to select from the population (likely those most easily stolen or of high value) to satisfy the sufficiency requirement. Finally, the auditor must determine the timing of these procedures (such as at the same time as the client conducts an inventory count). The combination of these

Table 8-2	Audit Evidence Decisions and Qualities Affecting Persuasiveness of Evidence
Audit Evidence Decisions	**Qualities Affecting Persuasiveness of Evidence**
Likelihood of risk of material misstatement	Level of assessed risks, by assertion

Audit procedures	Appropriateness
	   Relevance
	   Reliability
	      Auditor's direct knowledge
	      Independence of provider
	      Effectiveness of internal controls
	      Qualifications of provider
	      Objectivity of evidence
	      Consistency of evidence

Sample size	Sufficiency and adequate sample size
Items to select	Based upon sampling methods chosen

Timing	Timeliness
	   When procedures are performed
	   Portion of period audited

last four evidence decisions must result in sufficiently persuasive evidence to satisfy the auditor that inventory is materially correct. The audit program for inventory will reflect these decisions.

concept check

C8-1 How is audit evidence similar to legal evidence?

C8-2 List the five evidence decisions that the auditor makes. Explain their relevance to the audit process.

PERSUASIVENESS AND COST In making decisions about evidence for a given audit, both persuasiveness and cost must be considered. It is rare when only one type of evidence is available for verifying information. The persuasiveness and cost of all alternatives should be considered before selecting the best type or types. The auditor's goal is to obtain a sufficient amount of timely, reliable evidence that is relevant to the information being verified and to do so at reasonable cost. Automated audit procedures can often allow for high volumes of testing at a lower cost than manual testing, as discussed further in Chapter 11.

 ## Methods of Evidence Collection

Types of Audit Evidence

The *CICA Handbook* specifies that audit evidence may be obtained through the methods of inspection, observation, external confirmation, recalculation, reperformance, and analytical procedures and inquiry. These terms are defined and explained in CAS 500, par. A10 to A25.

The order in which these methods are listed and discussed should not be interpreted as implying the relative strengths of the types or categories of evidence. In other words, the fact that "inspection" appears at the top of the list does not mean that any evidence belonging to that category is automatically stronger than evidence belonging to another category. The quality of each type of evidence, regardless of type, must be evaluated carefully.

Before beginning the study of types of evidence, it is useful to show the relationships among auditing standards, which were studied in Chapter 1, types of evidence, and the five evidence decisions discussed earlier in this chapter. These relationships are shown in Figure 8-1. Note that the standards are general, whereas audit procedures are specific. Types of evidence are used in many procedures.

audit challenge 8-1
Computer Glitches Affect Thousands

HOW would you feel if you received a tax assessment that was based on incorrect information? Now imagine you were required to pay additional taxes. CIBC's Amicus unit, administering 3,061 customers of President's Choice Financial, sent incorrect tax information to Canada Revenue Agency (CRA), while sending different (correct) information to the customers. The incorrect information sent to CRA stated that the customers had cashed in some of their 2003 RRSPs, resulting in tax reassessments.

How is it possible that computer systems could send different information to two different parties? The *Toronto Star* reported that the cause was the switch from a manual to a computer-based system. This would mean that there was either a large-scale programming error or data entry error.

In November 2007, Air Canada's reservation systems encountered communications problems with airports so that tickets and tags could not be printed, stranding travellers for over five hours, again affecting "thousands" of customers. The problem was identified as a computer error of some kind, with no further information provided.

CRITICAL THINKING QUESTIONS

1. If a client has problems in delivering services, what is the likelihood that there are also information systems processing errors in the accounting systems?
2. What kinds of checks and balances should be in place when an organization implements program changes?
3. How does the quality of information systems affect your perception of the quality of internal control?

Sources: 1. Laidlaw, Stuart, "Tax error blamed on systems update," *Toronto Star*, January 27, 2005, p. D3. 2. Olive, David, "CIBC is really, really sorry," *Toronto Star*, January 27, 2005, p. D3. 3. Teotino, Isabel, "Airline glitch strands travellers," *Toronto Star*, November 17, 2007, p. A10.

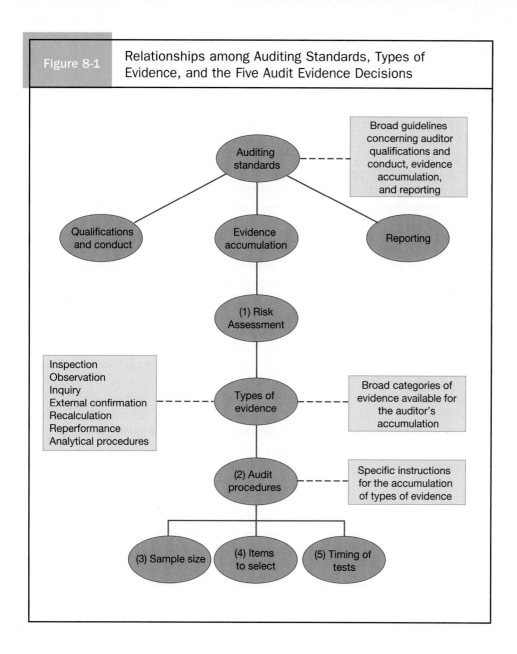

Figure 8-1 Relationships among Auditing Standards, Types of Evidence, and the Five Audit Evidence Decisions

INSPECTION Inspection (also called "physical examination or physical inspection") is the auditor's inspection or count of a tangible asset or document. This type of evidence is most often associated with inventory and cash but is also applicable to the verification of securities, notes receivable, and tangible capital assets. The distinction between the inspection of assets, such as marketable securities and cash, and the inspection of documents, such as cancelled cheques and sales documents, is important for auditing purposes. If the object being examined, such as a sales invoice, has no inherent value, the source is called documentation. For example, before a cheque is signed, it is a document; after it is signed, it becomes an asset; and when it is cancelled, it becomes a document again.

Inspection, which is a direct means of verifying that an asset actually exists (existence objective), is regarded as one of the most reliable and useful types of audit evidence. Generally, inspection is an objective means of determining both the quantity and the description of the asset. In some cases, it is also a useful method for evaluating an asset's condition or quality. However, inspection is not sufficient evidence to verify that existing assets are owned by the client (rights and obligations objective) since assets could be on consignment, and the auditor may not be qualified to judge such qualitative factors as obsolescence or authenticity (net realizable value for the valuation

Inspection—the auditor's physical examination or count of a tangible asset, or inspection of a document.

objective). Proper valuation for financial statement purposes usually cannot be determined by inspection.

OBSERVATION **Observation** is the use of the senses to assess selected activities. Throughout the audit, there are many opportunities to exercise sight, hearing, touch, and smell to evaluate a wide range of things. For example, the auditor may tour a plant to obtain a general impression of a client's facilities, observe whether equipment is rusty to evaluate obsolescence, and watch individuals perform accounting tasks to determine whether the persons assigned responsibilities are performing them. Observation is rarely enough by itself because there is the risk that the client's personnel involved in accounting activities are aware of the auditor's presence. They may do their work to a higher standard when the audit is present. Other kinds of corroborative evidence will also be used.

EXTERNAL CONFIRMATION **External confirmation** describes the receipt of a written or oral response from an independent third party verifying the accuracy of information that was requested by the auditor. The request is made to the client, and the client asks the independent third party to respond directly to the auditor in writing. Since confirmations come from sources that are independent of the client, they are a highly regarded and often-used type of evidence. External confirmations are relatively costly to obtain and may cause some inconvenience to those asked to supply them. If oral confirmations are used, they must be followed up with a written summary to provide adequate documentation for the audit file.

Whether or not confirmations should be used depends on the reliability needs of the situation as well as the alternative evidence available. Traditionally, confirmations are not used to verify individual transactions between organizations, such as sales transactions, because the auditor can use inspection of documents for that purpose. Similarly, confirmations are seldom used in the audit of capital-asset additions because these can be verified adequately by inspection of documentation and physical examination of the asset. While external confirmations are generally a very reliable form of evidence, the auditor must be aware that the third party providing the confirmation may be careless or not competent, may not have the correct information, or may be a related party.

CAS 505, External confirmations, states that external evidence is considered more reliable than evidence obtained from within the organization. It also says that the use of confirmations needs to be tailored to the risk assessments concluded by the auditor. Practically, this means that confirmations be used unless the auditor has alternative

---

auditing in action 8-2

Not in Canada Yet—Secure Electronic Audit Bank Confirmations

Bank confirmations have traditionally been mailed in paper form, using a prescribed format. Several factors have promoted the use of electronic confirmations of bank balances and other information in the United States. U.S. auditing standard AU 330 clarified that confirmation requests may be transmitted and received electronically. In 2010, Bank of America announced that it would only respond to bank confirmation requests submiiteed electronically through a designated third-party service provider. The third party provides a secure environment for transmitting the confirmation to authenticated confirmation respondents, reducing the risk of interception and response time. A search of the internet reveals a site called **www.confirmation. com** which provides audit confirmations that can even be accessed by your smart phone. It handles accounts receivable and accounts payable confirmations as well as bank confirmations.

Sources: 1. Interpretation No. 1 of AU 330, "Use of Electronic Confirmations," **www.aicpa.org**. 2. Guidance for Dealing with Electronic Confirmations, November 13, 2008 **www.journalofaccountancy.com**. 3. Capital Confirmation Inc. home page, **www.confirmation.com**, Accessed: January 19, 2012.

Table 8-3	Information Frequently Confirmed

Information	Source
Assets	
Cash in bank	Bank
Accounts receivable	Customer
Notes receivable	Maker
Owned inventory out on consignment	Consignee
Inventory held in public warehouses	Public warehouse
Cash surrender value of life insurance	Insurance company
Liabilities	
Accounts payable	Creditor
Notes payable	Lender
Advances from customers	Customer
Mortgages payable	Mortgagor
Bonds payable	Bondholder
Owners' Equity	
Shares outstanding	Registrar and transfer agent
Other Information	
Insurance coverage	Insurance company
Contingent liabilities	Company law firm(s), bank, and others
Bond indenture agreements	Bondholder
Collateral held by creditors	Creditor

high-quality evidence or believes for some reason that the confirmations received would be unreliable. The major types of information that are frequently confirmed, along with the source of the confirmation, are indicated in Table 8-3.

To be considered reliable evidence, confirmations must be controlled by the auditor from the time they are prepared until they are returned. If the client controls the preparation of the confirmation, performs the mailing, or receives the responses, the auditor has lost control and with it independence; thus the reliability of the evidence is reduced.

RECALCULATION **Recalculation** involves rechecking the computations and mathematical work completed by the client during the period under audit. Rechecking of computations consists of testing the client's arithmetical accuracy. It includes such procedures as extending sales invoices and inventory, adding data files, reports and subsidiary ledgers, and checking the calculation of amortization expense and prepaid expenses.

> Recalculation—repeating or checking the mathematical accuracy of calculations completed by the client.

When done manually, recalculation involves selecting a sample of transactions. However, many auditors use computer-assisted audit techniques so that recalculation can occur for a whole class of transactions. For example, in the inventory file, quantity on hand times unit price can be extended, added, and agreed to the general ledger control total.

REPERFORMANCE The redoing of other procedures such as internal controls (i.e., non-mathematical procedures) is called **reperformance**, or **parallel simulation**. This could include rechecking of transfers of information, which consists of tracing amounts to verify that when the same information is included in more than one place, it is recorded at the same amount each time. For example, the auditor normally completes limited tests to verify that the information in the sales history files has been included for the proper customer and at the correct amount in the subsidiary accounts receivable files and is accurately summarized in the general ledger.

> Reperformance or parallel simulation—the redoing of procedures and internal controls (other than mathematical calculations) of the client by the auditor.

Reperformance, particularly the process of checking posting and summarization, relies heavily upon the use of computer-assisted audit tests. The general term computer-assisted audit tests (CAATs) is used to describe tests that the auditor conducts using computer software or using the data or systems of the client. The two most common forms of CAATs are the use of test data and generalized audit software.

Test data **Test data** involves the use of fictitious transactions to determine whether client programs are functioning as described. For Hillsburg Hardware, test data are used to determine whether the system rejects transactions that it should reject, such as invalid customer numbers, unapproved prices, unapproved credit terms, or invalid dates. This is the most common use of test data for reperformance, since the client data files need not be disrupted and the testing can be performed quickly and efficiently.

Should the auditor choose to verify that programs are calculating invoice extensions correctly (a test of recalculation), test data that show the expected result would need to be prepared and then entered into the client system. Such a test would result in an invoice being calculated and posted against a client account. A credit transaction would need to be created to reverse this invoice test from the client records (i.e., customer master file, transaction files, general ledger, and inventory files). Some of the inconvenience could be avoided by also establishing a fictitious client, but then the auditor has inserted deliberate fictitious transactions in the client's systems. This is the major drawback of test data. It is also a point-in-time test and verifies that the programs being tested are functioning as tested at the time of the test. The auditor needs to conduct additional tests to determine that these same programs were used during the period under audit.

An **integrated test facility** overcomes the problems with test data by allowing the auditor to use test data in a test environment where it does not affect client accounting records. However, it can be used only with clients who have established such a capability during the initial set-up of their accounting systems.

Generalized audit software **Generalized audit software** consists of a software package that is used by the auditor to run routines against client data. Two common packages in Canada are Audit Command Language for Personal Computers (ACL-PC) and Interactive Data Extraction and Analysis (IDEA). The auditor obtains a copy of the client data files and runs one or more of the following types of activities against the data file. The examples shown are typical tests that would be run against the customer master file together with open item accounts.

- *Mathematical calculations*: addition of debit and credit amounts, extensions.
- *Aging functions*: aging of the accounts to recreate figures in the aged accounts receivable trial balance.
- *Comparisons*: between the outstanding balance and the credit limit.
- *Sampling*: using random, dollar-unit, interval, or stratification.

Reperformance is also referred to as parallel simulation. For example, if the auditor recreates the aged accounts receivable trial balance using client data, this is parallel simulation. This is a dual-purpose test since it ensures the mechanical accuracy of the aging process (a substantive test) while also verifying that the client's aging program is functioning correctly (a controls test).

ANALYTICAL PROCEDURES Analysis is used to identify the components of a financial statement item so that its characteristics can be considered during planning. **Analytical procedures** use comparisons and relationships between financial and non-financial information to determine whether account balances appear reasonable. An example is comparing the gross margin percent in the current year with that of the preceding year. For certain audit objectives or small account balances, analytical procedures may be the only evidence needed. For other accounts, other types of evidence may be reduced when analytical procedures indicate that an account balance appears reasonable. In some cases, analytical procedures are also used to isolate accounts or transactions that should be investigated more extensively to help in deciding whether additional verification is needed. An example

---

Computer-assisted audit tests (CAATs)—tests that the auditor conducts using computer software or using the data or systems of the client.

Test data—the use of fictitious transactions to determine whether client programs are functioning as described.

Integrated test facility—the use of test data in a test environment where it does not affect the client accounting records.

Generalized audit software—a software package that is used by the auditor to run routines against client data.

Analytical procedures—use of comparisons and relationships to determine whether account balances or other data appear reasonable.

is comparison of the current period's total repair expense with previous years' and investigation of the difference, if it is significant, to determine the cause of the increase or decrease.

CAS 520 of the *CICA Handbook* states that analytical procedures should be used on all audits to conduct risk assessments and at or near the end of the audit when assessing the financial statements as a whole. For certain audit objectives or small account balances, analytical procedures alone may be sufficient evidence. In most cases, however, additional evidence beyond analytical procedures is also needed to satisfy the requirement for sufficient competent evidence.

Because analytical procedures are an important part of planning audits, performing tests of each cycle, and completing audits, their use is studied more extensively at the end of this chapter, and in most of the remaining chapters of this book. Normally, specialized software or spreadsheet templates are used to perform analytical procedures.

INQUIRY **Inquiry of the client** is the obtaining of written or oral information from the client in response to questions from the auditor. Inquiry cannot be regarded as conclusive because it is not from an independent source and may be biased in the client's favour. As an illustration, when the auditor wants to obtain information about the client's method of recording and controlling accounting transactions, he or she usually begins by asking the client how internal controls operate. Later, the auditor performs a walk-through and tests of controls to determine if the controls function as described.

> **Inquiry of the client**—the obtaining of written or oral information from the client in response to questions during the audit.

Internal versus External Documentation

The documents examined by the auditor are the records used by the client to provide information for conducting its business in an organized manner. Since each transaction in the client's organization is normally supported by at least one document or computer file, there is a large volume of this type of evidence available. For example, the client often retains a customer order, a shipping document, and a duplicate sales invoice for each sales transaction. These same documents, whether in paper or electronic form, are useful evidence for verification by the auditor of the accuracy of the client's records for sales transactions. Documentation is a form of evidence widely used in every audit because it is usually readily available to the auditor at a relatively low cost. Sometimes it is the only reasonable type of evidence available.

Documents can be conveniently classified as internal or external. An **internal document** is one that has been prepared and used within the client's organization and is retained without ever going to an outside party such as a customer or a vendor. Examples of internal documents include duplicate sales invoices, employees' time reports, exception reports, and inventory receiving reports. An **external document** is one that has been in the hands of someone outside the client's organization who is a party to the transaction being documented but that is either currently in the hands of the client or readily accessible. In some cases, external documents originate outside the client's organization and end up in the hands of the client. Examples of this type of external document are vendors' invoices, cancelled notes payable, and insurance policies. Other documents, such as cancelled cheques, originate with the client, go to an outsider, and are finally returned to the client.

> **Internal document**—a document, such as an employee time report, that is prepared and used within the client's organization.

> **External document**—a document, such as a vendor's invoice, that has been used by an outside party to the transaction being documented and that the client now has or can easily obtain.

Whether an auditor will accept a document as reliable evidence depends on whether it is internal or external, and when internal, whether it was created and processed under conditions of good internal control. Internal documents created and processed under conditions of weak internal control may not be reliable evidence, because there could be errors or deliberate changes.

Since external documents have been in the hands of both the client and another party to the transaction, there is some indication that both members are in agreement about the information and the conditions stated on the document. This explains why external documents are regarded as more reliable evidence than internal ones. Some external documents have exceptional reliability because they are prepared with considerable care and have been reviewed by lawyers or other qualified experts. Examples include title papers to property such as land, insurance policies, indenture agreements, and contracts.

When auditors use documentation to support recorded transactions or amounts, it is often referred to as **vouching**. To vouch recorded acquisition transactions, the auditor might, for example, trace from the acquisitions report to supporting vendors' invoices and receiving reports and thereby satisfy the occurrence objective. If the auditor traces from receiving reports to the acquisitions report to satisfy the completeness objective, it would not be appropriate to call it vouching, since this would be reperformance. The term "vouching" is broad, and the audit program and audit workpapers always need to clearly explain what type of tracing or comparison was done, rather than simply using the term "vouching."

Many documents are available only in electronic form. For example, many companies use EDI (Electronic Data Interchange—the electronic exchange of standardized business transactions). Purchase, shipping, billing, cash receipt, and cash disbursement transactions may be available only in electronic form. Financial statement assertions most affected by EDI are completeness and accuracy. The auditor would also need to assess authorization of transactions, resulting in a need to test automated controls for these objectives.

Other forms of automation, such as image processing systems, whereby documents are scanned and converted into electronic images rather than being stored in paper format, also require changes in audit techniques. Auditors need to assess the strength of such electronic evidence based upon controls in place over changes to such documents, just as they would assess the strength of internal paper documentation.

Choosing the Right Type of Evidence

Evidence During Risk Assessment, Risk Response and Reporting

Table 8-4 provides examples of the *What, Why, and How* for each section of the financial statement audit process: risk assessment, risk response, and reporting. The *What* of an audit procedure needs to specifically state what the auditor is doing, i.e., what type of evidence is being collected, frequently using the evidence types that we have stated. The *Why* uses assessed risks or audit assertions to link the audit work to its purpose. Finally, the *How* provides detailed audit steps that will enable the work to be completed. When selecting evidence, the auditor needs to consider reliability and cost while providing sufficiency, relevance, and timeliness.

Risk assessment is used as the basis of targeting field work and other procedures. CAS 315 requires the auditor to use inquiry (e.g., to ask management about its risk assessment process), analytical procedures (e.g., to consider relationships in the financial statements), as well as observation and inspection. CAS 315 goes on to describe the work that the auditor should complete to obtain an understanding of the entity, its business environment, and systems of internal control. In this phase, the auditor will conduct fewer tests than in the other phases.

Risk response involves designing the audit procedures, conducting tests of controls, and conducting substantive tests (and dual purpose tests) to respond to the risks of material misstatement identified at the assertion level. The most common types of evidence collection methods for tests of control are inspection, inquiry, reperformance, and dual purpose tests, as we will see in later chapters. For substantive tests, all types of evidence are used.

Reporting provides to the client the final audit report, after quality control procedures have been completed (including second partner, standards, and tax). It also includes statutory reporting (of issues such as material weaknesses found) to the audit committee, and management letters that promote more effective controls based upon findings during the audit engagement.

CAS

	Examples of the "What, Why, and How" of Audit Procedures for Risk Assessment, Risk Response, and Reporting

Table 8-4

What are you doing?	Why are you conducting this work?	How will you perform the procedure?
Risk Assessment		
Inspect prior-year working papers.	Identify errors or risks that need to be considered this year.	Read audit summary memoranda, carry forward errors from the unadjusted error sheets, and read notes to the client financial statements.
Inspect publicly available information about the entity.	Update risk assessments, and identify potential new risks.	Conduct internet searches using the name of the company, its officers, management, and key suppliers or customers.
Perform high-level analytical review.	Identify areas of the financial statements that look unusual or are significant to tailor subsequent field work.	Prepare common-size income statements, obtain client current trial balance, and run through firm software to calculate ratios and trends.
Risk Response		
Observe the competence of employees (test of control)	Determine the likelihood that employees will competently do their work and perform internal controls as documented.	When at the client, note employee attitudes, diligence towards completing their work, frequency of errors, and effectiveness of supervision.
Recalculate totals of all subledgers and trace to general ledger accounts (dual purpose test).	Satisfy completeness and accuracy assertions to ensure that underlying electronic data files match totals in the general ledger and financial statements.	Obtain client transactions in electronic form as data files. Using the assistance of information systems audit staff, transfer the data to audit software so that it can be added. Trace the totals from the reports obtained to the general ledger.
Send positive confirmations to customers (substantive test).	Verify the existence, accuracy, and valuation of accounts receivable.	Send confirmations to all customers with current balances exceeding $125,000, amounts over $25,000 over 90 days, and a statistical sample of the remainder.
Reporting		
Second partner review of working paper files (quality control).	Determine that evidence collected was adequate to support the audit report to be issued.	Read audit summary memorandum and review supporting documentation as required.
Finalize management letter and other communications to the audit committee.	Communicate to audit committee and management material errors or other required material; help improve effectiveness of operations.	Use material from working papers and communicated from audit manager to finalize these documents.
Prepare audit report.	Communicate the results of the audit.	Use standard wording or suggested wording from firm's database.

Reliability of Types of Evidence

The first five criteria for determining the reliability of evidence (independence of provider, effectiveness of controls, auditor's direct knowledge, qualifications of provider, and objectivity of evidence), discussed in the first section of this chapter, are related to the seven types of evidence in Table 8-5. Several observations are apparent from a study of this table.

First, the effectiveness of the client's internal controls (discussed further in the next chapter) has a significant effect on the reliability of most types of evidence. For example,

Table 8-5

Table 8-5   Reliability of Types of Evidence Collection Methods

Type of Evidence	Criteria to Determine Reliability				
	Independence of Provider	Effectiveness of Client's Internal Control	Auditor's Direct Knowledge	Qualifications of Provider	Objectivity of Evidence
Inspection	High (auditor does)	Varies	High	Normally high (auditor does)	High
Observation	High (auditor does)	Varies	High	Normally high (auditor does)	Medium
Inquiries of the client	Low (client provides)	Not applicable	Low	Varies	Varies—low to high
External Confirmation	High	Not applicable	Low	Varies—usually high	High
Recalculation	High (auditor does)	Varies	High	High (auditor does)	High
Reperformance	High (auditor does)	Varies	High	High (auditor does)	High
Analytical procedures	High/low (auditor does/client responds)	Varies	High	Not applicable	Low

automated calculations and procedures from a company with effective internal controls are more reliable than manual calculations because the calculations are more likely to be consistent. Similarly, analytical procedures will not be appropriate evidence if the internal controls that produced the data provide inaccurate information.

Second, both inspection and reperformance are likely to be highly reliable if internal controls are effective. These two types of evidence effectively illustrate that equally reliable evidence may be completely different. Inspection involves examining an asset (such as inventory, or a fixed asset such as equipment) at a point in time, while reperformance can be used to redo work that has occurred throughout the year, such as posting of transactions or comparison of documents.

Third, some types of evidence are rarely sufficient to provide competent evidence to satisfy any objective. From examining Table 8-5 we see that observation, inquiries of the client, and analytical procedures are examples of this.

Cost of Types of Evidence

The two most expensive types of evidence are inspection and external confirmation. Inspection is costly because it normally requires the auditor's presence when the client is counting the asset, often on the balance sheet date. For example, inspection of inventory can result in several auditors travelling to widely separated geographical locations. External confirmation is costly because the auditor must follow careful procedures in the confirmation preparation, mailing, receipt, and follow-up of nonresponses and exceptions.

Reperformance and analytical procedures are moderately costly. The cost is lowered if client personnel locate documents for the auditor and organize them for convenient use. Analytical procedures require the auditor to decide which analytical procedures to use, enter or transfer data to make the calculations, and evaluate the results. Doing so may take considerable time.

The three least expensive types of evidence are observation, inquiries of the client, and recalculation. Observation is normally done together with other audit procedures. An auditor can easily observe whether client personnel are following appropriate inventory counting procedures at the same time he or she counts a sample of inventory (physical examination). Inquiries of clients are done extensively on every audit and normally have a low cost. Certain inquiries may be costly, such as obtaining written statements from the client documenting discussions throughout the audit.

Recalculation can vary in cost. It can be low when it involves simple calculations and tracing that can be done at the auditor's convenience. Costs per transaction are reduced when the auditor's computer software is used to perform these tests after obtaining a copy of the client data files.

Application of Types of Evidence to Evidence Decisions

An application of three types of evidence to the last four evidence decisions for one audit objective is shown in Table 8-6. First, review the examples in columns 4 and 5 of Table 5-6 on page 129. These are the specific balance-related objectives that would apply to the audit of inventory for Hillsburg Hardware Limited. The overall objective is to obtain persuasive evidence (sufficient, appropriate, and timely), at reasonable cost, that inventory is materially correct. The auditor must therefore decide which audit procedures to use to satisfy each objective, what the sample size should be for each procedure, which items from the population to include in the sample, and when to perform each procedure.

The completeness objective from Table 5-6 (see page 129) is selected for further study: inventory quantities agree with items physically on hand. Several types of evidence collection methods are available to satisfy this objective. Table 8-6 lists three types of evidence and gives examples of the last four evidence decisions for each type.

Mandated Evidence Collection

CAS 330, The auditor's responses to assessed risks, provides three opportunities when specific types of tests should be conducted as part of the evidence mix: when substantive tests may not be sufficient, for the financial statement closing process, and for significant risks.

TESTS OF CONTROLS WHERE SUBSTANTIVE PROCEDURES ARE INSUFFICIENT With highly automated systems, such as electronic data interchange and electronic banking, primary reliance upon accuracy and completeness of transactions could rest with the computer programs functioning correctly. This is an example where substantive

Table 8-6	Types of Evidence and Decisions for a Specific Audit Objective*			
		Evidence Decisions		
Type of Evidence	Audit Procedure	Sample Size	Items to Select	Timing
Observation	Observe client's personnel counting inventory to determine whether they are properly following instructions.	All count teams	Not applicable	Balance sheet date
Inspection	Count a sample of inventory and compare quantity and description to client's counts.	120 items	40 items with large dollar value, plus 80 randomly selected	Balance sheet date
Reperformance	Compare quantity on client's perpetual records to quantity on client's counts.	70 items	30 items with large dollar value, plus 40 randomly selected	Balance sheet date

*Completeness Balance-related audit objective: Inventory quantities on the client's perpetual records agree with items physically on hand.

procedures alone (for example, recalculation of interest charges) could not provide sufficient evidence with respect to an assertion. CAS 330 par. 8(b) requires that, in such cases, the auditor should also design and perform tests of controls.

FINANCIAL STATEMENT CLOSING PROCESS Unfortunately, financial statements are subject to manipulation. If management, or others, choose to misstate financial statements, they could process journal entries that do not have adequate support or authorization. This could result in the financial statements disagreeing with the underlying financial records. Because of these risks, the auditor is required to

a. compare the underlying accounting records (such as subsidiary ledgers or computer files) to the general ledger accounts with reconciliation to the financial statements and
b. review those material adjustments or journal entries and their supporting documentation that are part of the financial statement preparation process (CAS 330, par. 20).

SUBSTANTIVE PROCEDURES REQUIRED FOR SIGNIFICANT MATERIAL RISKS As part of the risk assessment process, the auditor identifies those audit objectives, transactions, and accounts that are prone to a high risk of material misstatement. CAS 330 par. 21 mandates that tests of details (substantive procedures) should be completed for such accounts. For example, if the auditor believes that there is a potential for material misstatement in the bad-debt allowance for accounts receivable (valuation audit objective) and has already conducted detailed analytical review, further specific tests of detail, such as looking at individual accounts for their collectability (e.g., the extent of payments received subsequent to the year end) would be required.

concept check

C8-6 How does the quality of internal controls affect evidence?

C8-7 Describe two audit techniques that the auditor should use to reduce the risk of financial statement misstatement during the financial statement closing process.

Special Terms

Audit procedures are the detailed steps, usually written in the form of instructions, for the accumulation of the seven types of audit evidence. They should be sufficiently clear to explain to members of the audit team what is to be done, why and how.

Several different terms are commonly used to describe audit procedures. These are presented and defined in Table 8-7 on the next page. To help you understand the terms, an illustrative audit procedure and the type of evidence are shown in the table.

④ Analytical Procedures and Their Role

Analytical Procedures

Analytical procedures use financial and non-financial data in meaningful comparisons and relationships to determine whether account balances or other data appear reasonable. The results of the analytical procedures help in designing the nature, timing, and extent of other audit procedures so that sufficient appropriate audit evidence may be obtained and the appropriate opinion given in the auditor's report.

For example, the auditor might compare current year recorded commissions expense to total recorded sales multiplied by the average commission rate as a test of the overall reasonableness of recorded commissions. For this analytical procedure to be relevant, the auditor has likely concluded that recorded sales are correctly stated, all sales earn a commission, and there is an average actual commission rate that is readily determined.

CAS

CAS 520 provides standards for the use of analytical review. It is recommended that the auditor use analysis in planning the audit, as a substantive procedure, and in the overall evaluation of the financial statements. The auditor would evaluate the reliability of the information that is used for the analytical procedures, as well as follow up and corroborate any explanations that management gives when discussing the results.

Table 8-7	Terms, Audit Procedures, and Types of Evidence	
Term and Definition	**Illustrative Audit Procedure**	**Types of Evidence**
Examine—A reasonably detailed study of a document or record to determine specific facts about it.	Examine a sample of vendors' invoices or data to determine whether the goods or services received are reasonable and of the type normally used by the client's business.	Inspection
Scan—A less detailed examination of a document or record to determine if there is something unusual warranting further investigation.	Scan the sales report, looking for large and unusual transactions. For large sales history files, use audit software to run an exception report for large amounts.	Analytical procedures
Read—An examination of written information to determine facts pertinent to the audit and the recording of those facts in a working paper.	Read the minutes of a board of directors' meeting, and summarize all information that is pertinent to the financial statements in a working paper.	Inspection
Compute—A calculation done by the auditor independent of the client.	Compute the inventory turnover ratios, and compare to previous years as a test of inventory.	Analytical procedures
Recompute—A calculation done to determine whether a client's calculation is correct.	Recompute the unit sales price times the number of units for a sample of duplicate sales invoices, and compare the totals to the client's calculations.	Recalculation
Foot—An addition of a column of numbers to determine if the total is the same as the client's.	Foot the sales history files using audit software, and compare all totals to the general ledger.	Recalculation
Trace—An instruction normally associated with documentation or reperformance. The instruction should state what the auditor is tracing and where it is being traced from and to. Frequently, an audit procedure that includes the term "trace" will also include a second instruction, such as "compare" or "recompute."	Trace a sample of sales transactions from the sales reports to sales invoices, and compare customer name, date, and the total dollar value of the sale. Trace postings from the sales reports to the general ledger accounts.	Recalculation Reperformance
Compare—A comparison of information in two different locations. The instruction should state which information is being compared in as much detail as practical.	Select a sample of sales invoices and compare the unit selling price as stated on the invoice to the master files of unit selling prices authorized by management.	Reperformance
Count—A determination of assets on hand at a given time. This term should only be associated with the type of evidence defined as physical examination.	Count petty cash on hand at the balance sheet date.	Inspection
Observe—The act of observation should be associated with the type of evidence defined as observation.	Observe whether the two inventory count teams independently count and record inventory quantities.	Observation
Inquire—The act of inquiry should be associated with the type of evidence defined as inquiry.	Inquire of management whether there is any obsolete inventory on hand at the balance sheet date.	Inquiries of client

Purposes and Timing of Analytical Procedures

The most important reasons for utilizing analytical procedures are discussed in this section. As a part of that discussion, the appropriate timing is also examined.

UNDERSTANDING THE CLIENT'S BUSINESS In Chapter 6, there is a discussion of the need to obtain knowledge about the client's industry and business. Analytical procedures are one of the techniques commonly used in obtaining that knowledge.

By conducting analytical procedures where the current year's unaudited information is compared with prior years' audited information, changes are highlighted. These changes can represent important trends or specific events, all of which will influence audit planning. For example, a decline in gross margin percentages over time may indicate increasing competition in the company's market area and the need to consider inventory pricing more carefully during the audit. Similarly, an increase in the balance in capital assets may indicate a significant acquisition that must be reviewed.

ASSESSMENT OF THE ENTITY'S ABILITY TO CONTINUE AS A GOING CONCERN The likelihood of financial failure must be considered by the auditor in the assessment of audit-related risks as well as in connection with management's use of the going-concern assumption in preparing the financial statements. For example, if a higher-than-normal ratio of long-term debt to net worth is combined with a lower-than-average ratio of profits to total assets, a relatively high risk of financial failure may be indicated. Not only would such conditions affect the audit plan, they may indicate that substantial doubt exists about the entity's ability to continue as a going concern, which would require disclosure in the notes to the financial statements.

INDICATION OF THE PRESENCE OF POSSIBLE MISSTATEMENTS IN THE FINANCIAL STATEMENTS **Unusual fluctuations** occur when significant differences are not expected but do exist or when significant differences are expected but do not exist. In either case, one of the possible reasons for an unusual fluctuation is the presence of an accounting error, fraud, or other irregularities. If the unusual fluctuation is large, the auditor must determine the reason for it and whether the cause is a valid economic event, not an error or fraud. For example, in comparing the ratio of the allowance for uncollectable accounts receivable to gross accounts receivable with that of the previous year, the auditor may discover that the ratio had decreased while, at the same time, accounts receivable turnover also decreased. The combination of these two pieces of information would indicate a possible understatement of the allowance. Such *attention directing* results in the performance of more detailed procedures by the auditor in the specific audit areas where errors or fraud and other irregularities might be found.

REDUCTION OF DETAILED AUDIT TESTS When analytical procedures support account balances, it is possible to perform fewer detailed tests in connection with those accounts. For example, if analytical procedure results of a small account balance such as prepaid insurance are favourable, no detailed tests may be necessary. In other cases, certain audit procedures can be eliminated, sample sizes can be reduced, or the timing of the procedures can be moved farther away from the balance sheet date.

CAS **TIMING** There are three CASs that state a requirement to use analytical procedures: CAS 315 during risk assessment, CAS 330 for use as a general risk response technique, and CAS 520 as substantive procedures and at the completion phase of the engagement. CAS 315 par. 6 requires risk assessment that includes analysis, used in the planning phase to determine the nature, extent, and timing of other auditing procedures to be performed. Use of analytical procedures during planning helps the auditor identify significant matters requiring special consideration later in the engagement. Refer to the figure inside the cover of the text. Preliminary analytical review conducted in Phase 2—client risk profile is used in Phase 3—Plan the audit. For example, the calculation of inventory turnover before inventory price tests are done may indicate the need for special care during those tests.

Analytical procedures are often done during the testing phase of the examination in conjunction with other audit procedures in Phase 6 as substantive tests. For example, the prepaid portion of each insurance policy might be compared with the same policy for the previous year as a part of doing tests of prepaid insurance.

CAS 520 par. 6 states that analytical procedures should be used near the end of the audit. Included in Phase 7, and used in Phases 7 and 8, such tests are useful as a final review for material misstatements or financial problems and help the auditor take a final "objective look" at the financial statements that have been audited. It is common for a partner to do a detailed review of the analytical procedures during the final review of working papers and financial statements. Typically, a partner has a good understanding of the client and its business because of ongoing relationships.

Unusual fluctuations—significant unexpected differences, indicated by analytical procedures, between the current year's unaudited financial data and other data used in comparisons.

Figure 8-2   Timing and Purposes of Analytical Procedures

Purpose	(Required) Risk Assessment Planning: Phases 2, 3	Substantive Tests Phase 6	(Required) End of Audit Phases 7, 8
Understand client's industry and business and assess risks	X		
Assess going concern	X		
Indicate possible misstatements (attention directing)	X		X
Reduce detailed tests		X	

Knowledge of the client's business combined with effective analytical procedures is a way to identify possible oversights in an audit.

The purposes of analytical procedures for each of the three different times they are performed are shown in Figure 8-2. The shaded boxes in the matrix indicate that certain purposes are applicable to a certain phase. Note that purposes vary for different phases of the audit. Analytical procedures are performed during the planning phase for all four purposes, whereas the other two phases are used primarily to determine appropriate audit evidence and to reach conclusions about the fair presentation of financial statements.

Five Types of Analytical Procedures

An important part of using analytical procedures is selecting the most appropriate procedures. There are five major types of analytical procedures. In each case, auditors compare client data with the following:

1. Industry data.
2. Similar prior-period data.
3. Client-determined expected results.
4. Auditor-determined expected results.
5. Expected results using non-financial data.

COMPARE CLIENT AND INDUSTRY DATA Suppose you are doing an audit and obtain information about the client and the averages in the client's industry (Table 8-8).

Table 8-8   Example of Comparison of Client and Industry Data

	Client		Industry	
	2012	2011	2012	2011
Inventory turnover	3.4%	3.5%	3.9%	3.4%
Gross margin percent	26.3%	26.4%	27.3%	26.2%

If we look only at client information for the two ratios shown, the company appears to be stable with no apparent indication of difficulties. However, compared with the industry, the client's position has worsened. In 2011, the client did slightly better than the industry in both ratios. In 2012, it was a half percent worse. Although these two ratios by themselves may not indicate significant problems, the example illustrates how comparison of client data with industry data may provide useful information about the client's performance. For example, the company may have lost market share, its pricing may not be competitive, it may have incurred abnormal costs, or it may have obsolete items in inventory.

The Financial Post Company (**www.financialpost.com**) and Dun & Bradstreet Canada Limited (**www.dnb.ca**) accumulate financial information for thousands of larger companies and compile the data for different lines of business; local credit bureaus compile data for companies in their community. Many public accounting firms purchase these publications for use as a basis for industry comparisons in their audits.

The most important benefits of industry comparisons are that they are an aid to understanding the client's business and are an indication of the likelihood of financial failure. The ratios in Dun & Bradstreet Canada, for example, are primarily of a type that bankers and other credit executives use in evaluating whether a company will be able to repay a loan. The same information is useful to auditors in assessing the relative strength of the client's capital structure, its borrowing capacity, and its likelihood of financial failure.

A major weakness of using industry ratios for auditing is the difference between the nature of the client's financial information and that of the firms making up the industry totals. Since the industry data are broad averages, the comparisons may not be meaningful unless the auditor takes into account the unique characteristics of the client.

COMPARE CLIENT DATA WITH SIMILAR PRIOR-PERIOD DATA Suppose the gross margin for a company has been between 26 and 27 percent for each of the past four years but is 23 percent in the current year. This decline in gross margin should be a concern to the auditor. The cause of the decline could be a change in economic conditions. However, it could also be caused by misstatements in the financial statements, such as sales or purchase cut-off errors, unrecorded sales, overstated accounts payable, or inventory costing errors. The auditor should determine the cause of the decline in gross margin and consider the effect, if any, on evidence accumulation.

The following are common examples of analytical procedures using client data:

Compare the current year's balance with that for the preceding year One of the easiest ways to make this test is to include the preceding year's adjusted trial balance results in a separate column of the current year's trial balance spreadsheet. The auditor can easily compare the current year's and previous year's balance to decide early in the audit whether a particular account should receive more than the normal amount of attention because of a significant change in the balance. For example, if the auditor observes a substantial increase in supplies expense, the auditor should determine whether the cause was an increased use of supplies, a misstatement in the account due to a misclassification, or a misstatement in supplies inventory, or a combination of both.

Compare the detail of a total balance with similar detail for the preceding year If there have been no significant changes in the client's operations in the current year, much of the detail making up the totals in the financial statements should also remain unchanged. By comparing the detail of the current period with a similar detail of the preceding period, it is often possible to isolate information that needs further examination. Comparison of details may take the form of details over time or details at a point in time. A common example of the former is comparing the monthly totals for the current and preceding years for sales, repairs, and other accounts. An example of the latter is comparing the details of loans payable at the end of the current year with those at the end of the preceding year.

Table 8-9   Internal Comparisons and Relationships

Ratio or Comparison	Possible Misstatement
Raw material turnover for a manufacturing company.	Misstatement of inventory or cost of goods sold or obsolescence of raw material inventory.
Sales commissions divided by net sales.	Misstatement of sales commissions.
Sales returns and allowances divided by gross sales.	Misclassified sales returns and allowances or unrecorded returns or allowances subsequent to year end.
Sales taxes payable (current year) divided by sales taxes payable (preceding year).	Failure to properly accrue sales taxes owing at year end.
Each of the individual manufacturing expenses as a percentage of total manufacturing expense.	Significant misstatement of individual expenses within a total.

Compute ratios and percentage relationships for comparison with previous years
The comparison of totals or details with previous years as described in the two preceding paragraphs has two shortcomings. First, it fails to consider growth or decline in business activity. Second, relationships of data to other data, such as sales to cost of goods sold, are ignored. Ratio and percentage relationships overcome both shortcomings. The earlier example about the decline in gross margin is a common percentage relationship used by auditors.

Table 8-9 describes five ratios and the possible misstatements they could detect to show the usefulness of ratio analysis. In all cases, the comparisons should be with calculations made in previous years for the same client. There are many potential ratios and comparisons available for use by an auditor. Appendix 8A and subsequent chapters dealing with specific audit areas describe other examples. Normally, the auditor will arrange to have trial balance information entered annually into audit software that calculates a range of ratios and comparisons automatically.

Many of the ratios and percentages used for comparison with previous years are the same ones used for comparison with industry data. For example, it is useful to compare current year gross margin with industry averages and those of previous years. The same can be said for most of the ratios described in Appendix 8A beginning on page 241.

There are also numerous potential comparisons of current and prior-period data beyond those normally available from industry data. For example, the ratio of each expense category to total sales can be compared with those of previous years. Similarly, in a multi-unit operation (e.g., a retail chain), internal comparisons for each unit can be made with previous periods (e.g., the revenue and expenses of individual retail outlets in a chain of stores can be compared).

Auditors often prepare vertical common-size financial statements for one or more years that display all items as a percentage of a common base, such as sales. Vertical common-size financial statements allow for comparison between companies or for the same company over different periods, revealing trends and providing insight into how different companies compare. Vertical common-size income statement data for the past three years for Hillsburg Hardware are included in Figure 8-3 on the next page. The auditor should calculate income statement account balances as a percent of sales when the level of sales has changed from the prior year—a likely occurrence in many businesses. Hillsburg's sales have increased significantly over the prior year. Note that accounts such as cost of goods sold, sales salaries, and commissions have also increased significantly but are fairly consistent as a percent of sales, which we expect for these accounts.

The auditor is likely to require further explanation and corroborating evidence for the changes in advertising, bad-debt expense, and office repairs and maintenance.

Figure 8-3   Hillsburg Hardware Vertical Common-Size Income Statement

HILLSBURG HARDWARE LIMITED
VERTICAL COMMON-SIZE INCOME STATEMENT
Three Years Ending December 31, 2011

	2011 (000) Preliminary	2011 % of Net Sales	2010 (000) Audited	2010 % of Net Sales	2009 (000) Audited	2009 % of Net Sales
Sales	$144,328	100.87	$132,421	100.91	$123,737	100.86
Less: Returns and allowances	1,242	0.87	1,195	0.91	1,052	0.86
Net sales	143,086	100.00	131,226	100.00	122,685	100.00
Cost of sales	103,241	72.15	94,876	72.30	88,724	72.32
Gross profit	39,845	27.85	36,350	27.70	33,961	27.68
Selling expense						
Salaries and commissions	7,739	5.41	7,044	5.37	6,598	5.38
Sales payroll benefits	1,422	0.99	1,298	0.99	1,198	0.98
Travel and entertainment	1,110	0.78	925	0.70	797	0.65
Advertising	2,611	1.82	1,920	1.46	1,790	1.46
Sales and promotional literature	322	0.22	425	0.32	488	0.40
Sales meetings and training	925	0.65	781	0.60	767	0.62
Miscellaneous sales expense	681	0.48	506	0.39	456	0.37
Total selling expense	14,810	10.35	12,899	9.83	12,094	9.86
Administration expense						
Executive and office salaries	5,524	3.86	5,221	3.98	5,103	4.16
Administrative payroll benefits	682	0.48	655	0.50	633	0.52
Travel and entertainment	562	0.39	595	0.45	542	0.44
Computer maintenance and supplies	860	0.60	832	0.63	799	0.65
Stationery and supplies	763	0.53	658	0.50	695	0.57
Postage	244	0.17	251	0.19	236	0.19
Telephone and fax	722	0.51	626	0.48	637	0.52
Rent	312	0.22	312	0.24	312	0.25
Legal fees and retainers	383	0.27	321	0.25	283	0.23
Auditing and related services	303	0.21	288	0.22	265	0.22
Amortization	1,452	1.01	1,443	1.10	1,505	1.23
Bad debt expense	3,323	2.32	3,394	2.59	3,162	2.58
Insurance	723	0.51	760	0.58	785	0.64
Office repairs and maintenance	844	0.59	538	0.41	458	0.37
Miscellaneous office expense	644	0.45	621	0.47	653	0.53
Miscellaneous general expense	324	0.23	242	0.18	275	0.22
Total administrative expenses	17,665	12.35	16,757	12.77	16,343	13.32
Total selling and administrative expenses	32,475	22.70	29,656	22.60	28,437	23.18
Operating income	7,370	5.15	6,694	5.10	5,524	4.50
Other income and expense						
Interest expense	2,409	1.68	2,035	1.55	2,173	1.77
Gain on sale of assets	(720)	(0.50)	0	0.00	0	0.00
Earnings before income taxes	5,681	3.97	4,659	3.55	3,351	2.73
Provision for income taxes	1,747	1.22	1,465	1.12	1,072	0.87
Net income	$ 3,934	2.75	$ 3,194	2.43	$ 2,279	1.86

- Note that advertising expense has increased as a percent of sales. One possible explanation is the development of a new advertising campaign.
- The dollar amount of bad-debt expense has not changed significantly but has decreased as a percent of sales. The auditor needs to gather additional evidence to determine whether bad-debt expense and the allowance for doubtful accounts are understated.

- Repairs and maintenance expense has also increased. Fluctuations in this account are not unusual if the client has incurred unexpected repairs. The auditor should investigate major expenditures in this account to determine whether they include any amounts that should be capitalized as a fixed asset.

COMPARE CLIENT DATA WITH CLIENT-DETERMINED EXPECTED RESULTS Since **budgets** represent the client's expectations for the period, an investigation of the most significant areas in which differences exist between budgeted and actual results may indicate potential misstatements. The absence of differences may also indicate that misstatements are unlikely. It is common, for example, in the audit of local, provincial, and federal governmental units, to use this type of analytical procedure.

Budgets—written records of the client's expectations for the period; a comparison of budgets with actual results may indicate whether or not misstatements are likely.

Whenever client data are compared with budgets, there are two special concerns. First, the auditor must evaluate whether the budgets were realistic plans. In some organizations, budgets are prepared with little thought or care and therefore are not realistic expectations. Such information has little value as audit evidence. The second concern is the possibility that current financial information in the budget was changed by client personnel to conform to the actual results. If that has occurred, the auditor will find no differences in comparing actual data with the budget, even if there are misstatements in the financial statements. Discussing budget procedures with client personnel is done to satisfy the first concern. Assessment of control risk and detailed audit tests of actual data are usually done to minimize the likelihood of the latter concern.

COMPARE CLIENT DATA WITH AUDITOR-DETERMINED EXPECTED RESULTS A second common type of comparison of client data with expected results occurs when the auditor calculates *the expected balance for comparison with the actual balance*. In this type of analytical procedure, the auditor makes an estimate of what an account balance should be by (1) relating it to some other balance sheet or income statement account or accounts, or (2) by making a projection based on some historical trend.

An example of *calculating an expected value based on relationships of accounts* is the independent calculation of interest expense on long-term notes payable by multiplying the ending monthly balance in notes payable by the average monthly interest rate (see Figure 8-4 on the next page). This independent estimate based upon the relationship between interest expense and notes payable is used to test the reasonableness of recorded interest expense.

An example of *using a historical trend* would be where the moving average of the allowance for uncollectable accounts receivable as a percentage of gross accounts receivable is applied to the balance of gross accounts receivable at the end of the audit year to determine an expected value for the current allowance.

COMPARE CLIENT DATA WITH EXPECTED RESULTS USING NON-FINANCIAL DATA Suppose that, in auditing a hotel, you can determine the number of rooms, room rate for each room, and occupancy rate. Using those data, it is relatively easy to estimate total revenue (rooms × occupancy rate × room rate) from rooms to compare with recorded revenue. The same approach can sometimes be used to estimate such accounts as tuition revenue at universities (average tuition × enrollment), factory payroll (total hours worked × wage rate), and cost of materials sold (units × materials cost per unit).

The major concern in using non-financial data is the accuracy of the data. In the previous illustration, it is appropriate to use an estimated calculation of hotel revenue as audit evidence only if the auditor is satisfied with the accuracy of the count of the number of rooms, room rate, and occupancy rate. It would be more difficult for the auditor to evaluate the accuracy of the occupancy rate than the other two items.

Using Statistical Techniques and Computer Software

STATISTICAL TECHNIQUES Several statistical techniques that aid in interpreting results can be applied to analytical procedures. The advantages of using statistical techniques are the ability to do more sophisticated calculations and provide objectivity.

Figure 8-4

Hillsburg Hardware Overall Tests of Interest Expense
December 31, 2011

Hillsburg Hardware Limited
Overall Test of Interest Expense
12/31/11

Schedule __N-3__ Date
Prepared by __TM__ __3/06/12__
Approved by __JW__ __3/12/12__

Interest expense per general ledger   2,408,642 [1]

Computation of estimate:

  Short-term loans:

    Balance outstanding at month-end: [2]

Jan.	2,950,000
Feb.	3,184,000
Mar.	3,412,000
Apr.	3,768,000
May	2,604,000
June	1,874,000
July	1,400,000
Aug.	1,245,000
Sept.	1,046,000
Oct.	854,000
Nov.	2,526,000
Dec.	4,180,000
Total	29,043,000

Average ($\div$12) 2,420,250 @ 10.5% [3]   254,126

  Long-term loans:

Beginning balance   26,520,000 [2]
Ending balance   24,120,000 [2]
             50,640,000

Average ($\div$2) 25,320,000 @ 8.5% [4]   2,152,200

Estimated total interest expense   2,406,326

Difference   2,316 [5]

Legend and Comments
[1] Agrees with general ledger and working trial balance.
[2] Obtained from general ledger.
[3] Estimated based on examination of several notes throughout the year with rates ranging from 10% to 11%.
[4] Agrees with permanent file schedule of long-term debt.
[5] Difference not significant. Indicates that interest expense per books is reasonable.

The most common statistical technique for analytical procedures is regression analysis. Regression analysis is used to evaluate the reasonableness of a recorded balance by relating (regressing) the total to other relevant information. For example, the auditor might conclude that total selling expenses should be related to total sales, the previous year's selling expenses, and the number of salespeople. The auditor would then use regression analysis to statistically determine an estimated value of selling expenses for comparison with recorded values or to assess the profitability of different product lines.

Audit software—software used to automate preparation of audit working papers or the analysis of client data files.

AUDITOR'S COMPUTER SOFTWARE Computer-based **audit software** can be used to prepare audit working papers and perform extensive analytical procedures as a by-product of other audit testing. In the past several years, most public accounting firms have implemented a variety of computer software as tools for doing more efficient and effective audits. One feature common to all such software is the ability to input or import the client's general ledger into the auditor's computer system. These are linked

Working Paper Document Management

How many documents do you have on your personal computer? You may have several hundred, pertaining to correspondence, courses that you have worked on, or other types of projects. My system has over 200,000 files from different versions of courses and books that I have written over the years.

Audit firms regularly update their forms to reflect current standards and best business practices. It can be difficult to ensure that employees are using the current version, though, if the practice is to download versions onto their personal computer systems.

Best practices require audit firms to have current forms and documents accessible on a central server to audit staff. Employees are required to use only the forms from the central server every time they add a document to the audit file.

This helps to ensure that only authorized employees access current forms (by means of password access) and that only up-to-date forms are used, since they are always obtained from the central server.

Source: Interviews with accounting firms held in summer 2008 and winter 2012 by I. Splettstoesser-Hogeterp.

to working papers and cross-referenced, saving many hours of tedious working-paper referencing. Some systems also link directly to client data.

The general ledger information for the client is saved and carried forward in the auditor's automated working paper files year after year. The existence of current and previous years' general ledger information on the auditor's computer files permits extensive and inexpensive computerized analytical calculations. The analytical information can also be shown in different forms such as graphs and charts to help interpret the data.

A major benefit of computerized analytical procedures is the ease of updating the calculations when adjusting entries to the client's statements are made. If there are several adjusting entries to the client's records, the analytical procedures calculations can be quickly revised. For example, a change in inventory and cost of goods sold affects a large number of ratios. All affected ratios can be recalculated immediately.

concept check

C8-8 Why are analytical procedures an important part of the planning process?

C8-9 How can audit software assist the analytical review process?

Appendix 8A
Common Financial Ratios

Auditors' analytical procedures often include the use of general financial ratios during planning and final review of the audited financial statements. These are useful for understanding the most recent events and financial status of the business and for viewing the statements from the perspective of a user. The general financial analysis may be effective in identifying possible problem areas for additional analysis and audit testing as well as business problem areas for which the auditor can provide other assistance. This appendix presents a number of widely used general financial ratios.

Short-Term Debt-Paying Ability

Many companies follow an operating cycle whereby production inputs are obtained and converted into finished goods and then sold and converted into cash. This requires an investment in working capital; that is, funds are needed to finance inventories and accounts receivable. A majority of these funds come from trade creditors and the balance comes from initial capitalization, bank borrowings, and positive net cash flow from operations.

$$\text{Current ratio} = \frac{\text{current assets}}{\text{current liabilities}}$$

$$\text{Quick ratio} = \frac{\text{cash + marketable securities + net accounts receivable}}{\text{current liabilities}}$$

$$\text{Cash ratio} = \frac{\text{cash + marketable securities}}{\text{current liabilities}}$$

The net working capital position of a company is the excess of current assets over current liabilities and is also measured by the current ratio. Presumably, if net working capital is positive (i.e., the current ratio is greater than 1.0), the company has sufficient available assets to pay its immediate debts; and the greater the excess (the larger the ratio), the better off the company is in this regard. Companies with a comfortable net working capital position are considered preferred customers by their bankers and trade creditors and are given favourable treatment. Companies with inadequate net working capital are in danger of not being able to obtain credit.

However, this is a somewhat simplistic view. The current assets of companies will differ in terms of both valuation and liquidity, and these aspects will affect a company's ability to meet its current obligations. One way to examine this problem is to restrict the analysis to the most available and objective current assets. The quick ratio eliminates inventories from the computation, and the cash ratio further eliminates accounts receivable. Usually, if the cash ratio is greater than 1.0, the company has good short-term debt-paying ability. In some cases, it is appropriate to state marketable securities at market value rather than cost in computing these ratios (see Figure 8A-1).

Short-Term Liquidity

If a company does not have sufficient cash and cash-like items to meet its obligations, the key to its debt-paying ability will be the length of time it takes the company to convert less liquid current assets into cash. This is measured by the short-term liquidity ratios (see Figure 8A-2).

The two turnover ratios—accounts receivable and inventory—are very useful to auditors. Trends in the accounts receivable turnover ratio are frequently used in assessing the reasonableness of the allowance for uncollectable accounts. Trends in the inventory turnover ratio are used in identifying a potential inventory obsolescence problem.

Figure 8A-2   Short-Term Liquidity Ratios

$$\text{Average accounts receivable turnover} = \frac{\text{gross credit sales net of returns}}{\text{average gross receivables}}$$

$$\text{Average days to collect (or number of days' sales in accounts receivable)} = \frac{\text{average gross receivables} \times 365}{\text{gross credit sales net of returns}}$$

$$\text{Average inventory turnover} = \frac{\text{cost of goods sold}}{\text{average inventory}}$$

$$\text{Average days to sell (or average days' sales in inventory)} = \frac{\text{average inventory} \times 365}{\text{cost of goods sold}}$$

$$\text{Average days to convert inventory to cash} = \text{average days to sell} + \text{average days to collect}$$

When the short-term liquidity ratios (and the current ratio) are used to examine a company's performance over time or to compare performance among companies, differences in inventory accounting methods, fiscal year ends, and cash-credit sales mix can have a significant effect. With regard to inventories, a few companies have adopted the LIFO (last in, first out) method. This can cause inventory values to differ significantly from FIFO (first in, first out) values. When companies with different valuation methods are being compared, the company's LIFO value inventory can be adjusted to FIFO to obtain a better comparison.

When two companies have different fiscal year ends, such that one is on a natural business year that corresponds to the business cycle and the other is not, the simple average gross receivables and inventory figures for the former will be lower. This will tend to cause the company with a natural business year to appear more liquid than it really is. An averaging computation with quarterly data can be used for further comparison.

Finally, the use of net sales per the financial statements in the receivables liquidity ratios can cause distortion when a significant portion of sales is for cash. This will be somewhat mitigated when the proportions are fairly constant among periods or companies for which comparisons are being made.

Ability to Meet Long-Term Debt Obligations and Preferred Dividends

A company's long-run solvency depends on the success of its operations and on its ability to raise capital for expansion or even survival over periods of temporary difficulty. Common shareholders will benefit from the leverage obtained from borrowed capital that earns a positive net return.

A key measure in evaluating this long-term structure and capacity is the debt-to-equity ratio (see Figure 8A-3). If this ratio is too high, it may indicate the company has used up its borrowing capacity and has no cushion for future events. If it is too low, it may mean available leverage is not being used to the owners' benefit. If the ratio is trending up, it may mean earnings are too low to support the needs of the enterprise. And, if it is trending down, it may mean the company is doing well and setting the stage for future expansion.

The tangible net assets-to-equity ratio indicates the current quality of the company's equity by excluding those assets whose realization is wholly dependent on future operations, such as goodwill. This ratio can be used to better interpret the debt-to-equity ratio.

The ability to make interest payments is more a function of the company's ability to generate positive cash flows from operations in the short run, as well as over time. Times interest earned shows how easily the company can make interest (and preferred dividend) payments, assuming earnings trends are stable.

Operating and Performance Measurement

All creditors and investors, therefore, are interested in the results of operations of a business enterprise, with the result that a number of operating and performance ratios are

Figure 8A-3	Long-Term Debt and Preferred Dividends Ratios

$$\text{Debt-to-equity ratio} = \frac{\text{total liabilities}}{\text{total equity}}$$

$$\text{Tangible net assets-to-equity ratio} = \frac{\text{total equity} - \text{intangible assets}}{\text{total equity}}$$

$$\text{Times interest earned} = \frac{\text{operating income}}{\text{interest expense}}$$

$$\text{Times interest and preferred dividends earned} = \frac{\text{operating income}}{\text{interest expense} + [\text{preferred dividends}/(1 - \text{tax rate})]}$$

Figure 8A-4	Operating and Performance Ratios

$$\text{Earnings per share} = \frac{\text{earnings} - \text{preferred dividends}}{\text{number of common shares}}$$

$$\text{Efficiency ratio} = \frac{\text{gross sales net of returns}}{\text{tangible operating assets}}$$

$$\text{Profit margin ratio} = \frac{\text{operating income}}{\text{gross sales net of returns}}$$

$$\text{Profitability ratio} = \frac{\text{operating income}}{\text{tangible operating assets}}$$

$$\text{Return on total assets ratio} = \frac{\text{income before interest} + \text{taxes}}{\text{total assets}}$$

$$\text{Return on common equity ratio} = \frac{\text{income before taxes} - [\text{preferred dividends}/(1 - \text{tax rate})]}{\text{common equity}}$$

Leverage ratios (computed separately for each source of capital other than common equity, for example, short-term debt, long-term debt, deferred taxes) =

$$\frac{(\text{return on total assets} \times \text{amount of source}) - \text{cost attributable to source}}{\text{common equity}}$$

$$\text{Book value per common share} = \frac{\text{common equity}}{\text{number of common shares}}$$

in use (see Figure 8A-4). The most widely used operating and performance ratio is earnings per share, which is an integral part of the basic financial statements for most companies. Several additional ratios can be calculated and will give further insights into operations.

The first of these is the efficiency ratio. This shows the relative volume of business generated from the company's operating asset base. It shows whether sufficient revenues are being generated to justify the assets employed. When the efficiency ratio is low, there is an indication that additional volume should be sought before more assets are acquired. When the ratio is high, it may be an indication that assets are being fully utilized (i.e., there is little excess capacity) and an investment in additional assets will soon be necessary.

The second ratio is the profit margin ratio. This shows the portion of sales that exceeds cost (both variable and fixed). When there is weakness in this ratio, it is generally an indication that either (1) gross margins (revenues in excess of variable costs) are too low, or (2) volume is too low in relationship to fixed costs.

Two ratios that indicate the adequacy of earnings relative to the asset base are the profitability ratio and the return on total assets ratio. These ratios show the efficiency and profit margin ratios combined.

An important perspective on the earnings of the company is what kind of return is provided to the owners. This is reflected in the return (before taxes) on common equity. If this ratio is below prevailing long-term interest rates or returns on alternative investments, owners will perceive that they should convert the company's assets to some other use, or perhaps liquidate, unless return can be improved.

An interesting supplemental analysis is provided through leverage analysis. Here, the proportionate share of assets for each source of capital is multiplied by the company's return on total assets. This determines the return on each source of capital. The result is compared with the cost of each source of capital (e.g., interest expense), and a net contribution by capital source is derived. If this amount is positive for a capital source, it may be an indication that additional capital should be sought. If the leverage is negative from a capital source, recapitalization alternatives and/or earnings improvements should be investigated. It is also helpful to use this leverage analysis when considering the debt-to-equity ratio.

Figure 8A-5 Ratio Illustration Using Hillsburg Hardware Limited

Earnings per share $= \dfrac{3,934 - 0}{5,000} = \$0.79$

Current ratio $= \dfrac{51,027}{13,216} = 3.86$

Quick ratio $= \dfrac{828 + 0 + 18,957}{13,216} = 1.50$

Cash ratio $= \dfrac{828}{13,216} = 0.06$

Accounts receivable turnover $= \dfrac{143,086}{(20,197 + 17,521)/2} = 7.59$ times

Days to collect $= \dfrac{18,859 \times 365}{143,086} = 48.11$ days

Inventory turnover $= \dfrac{103,241}{(29,865 + 31,600)/2} = 3.36$ times

Days to sell $= \dfrac{30,733 \times 365}{103,241} = 108.65$ days

Days to convert to cash $= 108.65 + 48.11 = 156.76$ days

Debt to equity $= \dfrac{38,904}{22,463} = 1.73$

Tangible net assets to equity $= \dfrac{22,463}{22,463} = 1.00$

Times interest earned $= \dfrac{7,370}{2,409} = 3.06$ times

Times interest and preferred dividends earned $= \dfrac{7,370}{2,409 + 0/(1 - 0.31)} = 3.06$ times

Efficiency ratio $= \dfrac{143,086}{29,865 + 10,340} = 3.56$

Profit margin ratio $= \dfrac{7,370}{143,086} = 0.05$

Profitability ratio $= \dfrac{7,370}{29,865 + 10,340} = 0.18$

Return on total assets $= \dfrac{5,681 + 2,409}{61,367} = 0.13$

Return on common equity $= \dfrac{5,681 - 0/(1 - 0.31)}{22,463} = 0.25$

Leverage ratios:

Current liabilities $= \dfrac{(0.13 \times 13,216) - 0}{22,463} = 0.08$

Notes payable $= \dfrac{(0.13 \times 28,300) - 2,409}{22,463} = 0.06$

Book value per common share $= \dfrac{22,463}{5,000} = \$4.49$

The final operating and performance ratio is book value per common share. This shows the combined effect of equity transactions over time.

The usefulness of these ratios in making comparisons over time or among companies is reduced by inconsistent classification of operating versus non-operating items, inventory methods, amortization methods, research and development costs, and off-balance-sheet financing.

Illustration

Computation of the various ratios is illustrated in Figure 8A-5 using the financial statements of Hillsburg Hardware Limited introduced in Chapter 5.

Summary

1. *What are the five evidence decisions that need to be made?* After identifying the risk associated with audit objectives (1), the auditor needs to select audit procedures (2), choose sample size (3), decide on items to select (4), and determine the timing of the actual conduct of the procedures (5).

    What does the auditor mean by the phrase "sufficient appropriate audit evidence"? The auditor needs to have enough evidence that is relevant to the financial statement accounts to state an opinion on the financial statements.

2. *List and explain the seven general methods of evidence collection.* These are inspection (physical examination of a tangible asset or document); observation (using senses, such as watching); external confirmation (written or oral response from an independent third party); recalculation (computing mathematical items such as sales invoices and comparing to client results); reperformance (redoing internal control procedures); analytical procedures (use of comparisons and relationships); and inquiries of the client (obtaining written or oral details);.

    Why are automated audit procedures particularly helpful with recalculation and reperformance? Comparisons and calculations are often repeated for thousands of transactions. Having computer-assisted audit procedures redo this work for all transactions rather than a sample helps to increase the effectiveness of audit procedures.

3. *How does the auditor choose the type of evidence to collect?* The auditor uses criteria such as the independence of the provider, the effectiveness of internal controls, the qualifications of the provider (including the auditor), and the objectivity of the evidence in the context of the specific financial statement assertions that are being examined, as well as the overall risk of the engagement and the materiality of the account or balance. The auditor considers multiple sources so that consistency can be assessed among them.

    Describe the times when particular types of evidence collection are mandated. The auditor needs to evaluate and test internal controls when substantive procedures are not sufficient, conduct tests of the financial statement closing process, and perform tests of detail when the risk of material misstatement for an account or transaction stream is high.

4. *What are analytical procedures?* They are the use of financial and non-financial data in meaningful comparisons and relationships to assess the reasonableness of account balances or other data.

    What is their role in the evidence collection process? They are used in all phases of the audit, and are required during the planning and completion phases.

    Describe five major types of analytical procedures. Client data can be compared with industry data, prior-period data, client-determined expected results, auditor-determined expected results, or non-financial data. Advantages and disadvantages are discussed starting on page 232.

MyAccountingLab

Make the grade with MyAccountingLab: The questions, exercises, and problems marked in orange can be found on MyAccountingLab. You can practise them as often as you want, and most feature step-by-step guided instructions to help you find the right answer.

Review Questions

8-1 **1** Discuss the similarities and differences between evidence in a medical test and evidence in the audit of financial statements.

8-2 **1** List the five major evidence decisions that must be made on every audit.

8-3 **1** Describe what is meant by an audit procedure. Why is it important for audit procedures to be carefully worded?

8-4 **1** Describe what is meant by an audit program for accounts receivable. What four things should be included in an audit program?

8-5 **1** Explain why the auditor can only be persuaded with a reasonable level of assurance, rather than convinced, that the financial statements are correct.

8-6 **1** Identify the three factors that determine the persuasiveness of evidence. How are these three factors related to audit procedures, sample size, items to select, and timing?

8-7 **1 3** Identify the characteristics that determine the appropriateness of evidence. For each characteristic, provide one example of a type of evidence that is likely to be appropriate.

8-8 **2** List the seven types of audit evidence included in this chapter, and give two examples of each.

8-9 **2** What are the four characteristics of the definition of a confirmation? Distinguish between a confirmation and external documentation.

8-10 **2** Distinguish between internal documentation and external documentation as audit evidence, and give three examples of each.

8-11 **4** Explain the importance of analytical procedures as evidence in determining the fair presentation of the financial statements.

8-12 **4** Your client, Harper Ltd., has a contractual commitment as a part of a bond indenture to maintain a current ratio of 2.0. If the ratio falls below that level on the balance sheet date, the entire bond becomes payable immediately. In the current year, the client's financial statements show that the ratio has dropped from 2.6:1 (or 2.6) to 2.05:1 (or 2.05) over the past year. How would this situation affect your audit plan?

8-13 ④ Distinguish between attention-directing analytical procedures and those intended to reduce detailed substantive procedures.

8-14 ④ Gail Gordon, PA, has found ratio and trend analysis relatively useless as a tool in conducting audits. For several engagements, she computed the industry ratios included in publications by The Financial Post Company and compared them with client ratios. For most engagements, the client's business was significantly different from the industry data in the publication, and the client would automatically explain away any discrepancies by attributing them to the unique nature of its operations. In cases in which the client had more than one branch in different industries, Gail found the ratio analysis no help at all. How could Gail improve the quality of her analytical procedures?

8-15 ④ It is imperative that the auditor follow up on all material differences discovered through analytical procedures. What factors affect such investigations?

8-16 ④ Explain the purpose of common-size financial statements.

Discussion Questions and Problems

8-17 ① ② ③ The following are eight situations, each containing two means of accumulating evidence:

1. Confirm accounts receivable with business organizations versus confirming receivables with consumers.
2. Physically examine 8-cm steel plates versus examining electronic parts.
3. Examine duplicate sales invoices when several competent people are checking one another's work versus examining documents prepared by a competent person in a one-person staff.
4. Physically examine inventory of parts for the number of units on hand versus examining them for the likelihood of inventory being obsolete.
5. Confirm a bank balance versus confirming the oil and gas reserves with a geologist specializing in oil and gas.
6. Confirm a bank balance versus examining the client's bank statements.
7. Physically count the client's inventory held by an independent party versus confirming the count with an independent party.
8. Physically count the client's inventory versus obtaining a count from the company president.

REQUIRED

a. For each of the eight situations, state whether the first or second type of evidence is more reliable.
b. For each situation, state which of the factors discussed in the chapter affect the appropriateness of the evidence.

8-18 ① ② ③ ④ In the audit of Worldwide Wholesale Inc., you performed extensive ratio and trend analyses. No material exceptions were discovered except for the following:

1. Commission expense as a percentage of sales had stayed constant for several years but has increased significantly in the current year. Commission rates have not changed.
2. The rate of inventory turnover has steadily decreased for four years.
3. Inventory as a percentage of current assets had steadily increased for four years.
4. The number of days' sales in accounts receivable has steadily increased for three years.
5. Allowance for uncollectable accounts as a percentage of accounts receivable has steadily decreased for three years.
6. The absolute amounts of amortization expense and amortization expense as a percentage of gross fixed assets are significantly smaller than in the preceding year.

REQUIRED

a. Evaluate the potential significance of each of the exceptions above for the fair presentation of financial statements.
b. State the follow-up procedures you would use to determine the possibility of material misstatements.
c. What do these changes indicate about the overall financial position of Worldwide Wholesale Inc.?

8-19 ❶ ❷ ❸ ❹ As part of the analytical procedures of Mahogany Products, Inc., you perform calculations of the following ratios:

Ratio	Industry Averages 2012	Industry Averages 2011	Mahogany Products, Inc. 2012	Mahogany Products, Inc. 2011
1. Current ratio	3.30	3.80	2.20	2.60
2. Days to collect receivables	87.00	93.00	67.00	60.00
3. Days to sell inventory	126.00	121.00	93.00	89.00
4. Purchases divided by accounts payable	11.70	11.60	8.50	8.60
5. Inventory divided by current assets	0.56	0.51	0.49	0.48
6. Operating earnings divided by tangible assets	0.08	0.06	0.14	0.12
7. Operating earnings divided by net sales	0.06	0.06	0.04	0.04
8. Gross margin percentage	0.21	0.27	0.21	0.19
9. Earnings per share	$14.27	$13.91	$2.09	$1.93

REQUIRED

For each of the preceding ratios:

a. State whether there is a need to investigate the results further and, if so, the reason for further investigation.

b. State the approach you would use in the investigation.

c. Explain how the operations of Mahogany Products, Inc. appear to differ from those of the industry.

8-20 ❷ ❸ Parts, Inc. sells electrical components to large department stores and also has a few cash sales to electricians. Sales invoices are prepared for all sales. Cash sales are recorded to the cash receipts journal and cash is deposited to the bank each day. All sales to large stores are credit sales and are handled by sales clerks by telephone or facsimile. The sales clerk takes the customer's request, checks the authorized customer list for credit limits (if it is a credit sale), prepares the sales invoice, and sends one copy to the inventory control department, who sends the ordered goods to the shipping department. For cash sales, the inventory control clerk brings the items sold to the sales counter and the goods are given to the purchaser at the time of sale. For credit sales, the shipping clerk signs the inventory control copy of the sales invoice and then prepares a shipping invoice. A third copy of the sales invoice is forwarded to the accounting department so that a clerk can enter the sale into the sales journal. The shipping invoices are maintained in the shipping department in case a shipment needs to be checked. All goods are shipped FOB shipping point.

REQUIRED

a. Design two audit procedures that will provide evidence of the existence of sales. Identify the nature of the procedure, the documents you are using, and explain why these procedures will show whether recorded sales are valid.

b. Design two audit procedures that will provide evidence of the completeness of sales. Identify the nature of the procedure, the documents you are using, and explain why these procedures will show whether recorded sales are complete.

(Extract from AU1 CGA -Canada Examinations developed by the Certified General Accountants Association of Canada © 2011 CGA-Canada. Reproduced with permission. All rights reserved.)

8-21 ❷ ❸ List two examples of audit evidence that the auditor can use in support of each of the following:

a. Recorded amount of entries in the purchase journal.
b. Physical existence of inventory.
c. Accuracy of accounts receivable.

d. Ownership of capital assets.
e. Liability for accounts payable.
f. Obsolescence of inventory.
g. Existence of petty cash.

8-22 ❷ ❸ Seven different types of evidence were discussed. The following questions concern the reliability of that evidence:

a. Explain why confirmations are normally more reliable evidence than inquiries of the client.

b. Describe a situation in which confirmation will be considered highly reliable and another in which it will not be reliable.

c. Under what circumstances is the physical observation of inventory considered relatively unreliable evidence?

d. Explain why recalculation tests are highly reliable but of relatively limited use.

e. Give three examples of relatively reliable documentation and three examples of less reliable documentation. What characteristics distinguish the two?

f. Give several examples in which the qualifications of the respondent or the qualifications of the auditor affect the reliability of the evidence.

g. Explain why analytical procedures are important evidence even though they are relatively unreliable by themselves.

8-23 ❷ ❸ The following audit procedures were performed in the audit of inventory to satisfy specific balance-related audit objectives as discussed in Chapter 5. The audit procedures assume the auditor has obtained the inventory count records that list the client's inventory. The general balance-related audit objectives from Chapter 5 are also included.

AUDIT PROCEDURES

1. Using audit software, extend unit prices times quantity, foot the extensions, and compare the total with the general ledger.
2. Trace selected quantities from the inventory listing to the physical inventory to make sure the items exist and the quantities are the same.
3. Question operating personnel about the possibility of obsolete or slow-moving inventory.
4. Select a sample of quantities of inventory in the factory warehouse, and trace each item to the inventory count sheets to determine if it has been included and if the quantity and description are correct.
5. Using both this year's and last year's inventory data files, compare quantities on hand and unit prices, printing any with greater than a 30 percent or $15,000 variation from one year to the next.
6. Examine sales invoices and contracts with customers to determine if any goods are out on consignment with customers. Similarly, examine vendors' invoices and contracts with vendors to determine if any goods on the inventory listing are owned by vendors.
7. Send letters directly to third parties who hold the client's inventory and request that they respond directly to us.

GENERAL BALANCE-RELATED AUDIT OBJECTIVES

Existence

Rights and obligations

Completeness

Valuation

Allocation

REQUIRED

a. Identify the type of audit evidence used for each audit procedure.

b. Identify the general balance-related audit objective or objectives satisfied by each audit procedure.

8-24 ❸ ❹ In auditing the financial statements of a manufacturing company, the PA has found that the traditional audit trail has been replaced by an electronic one. As a result, the PA may place increased emphasis on automated internal controls and on analytical procedures of the data under audit. These tests, which are also applied in auditing visibly posted accounting records, include the computation of ratios that are compared with prior-year ratios or with industry-wide norms. Examples of analytical procedures are the computation of the rate of inventory turnover and the computation of the number of days' sales in receivables.

REQUIRED

a. Discuss the advantages to the public accountant of the use of analytical procedures in an audit.

b. In addition to the computations given in part (c), list five ratios that an auditor may compute during an audit on balance sheet accounts and related income accounts. For each ratio listed, name the two (or more) accounts used in its computation.

c. When an auditor discovers that there has been a significant change in a ratio when compared with the preceding year's, he or she considers the possible reasons for the change. Give the possible reasons for the following significant changes in ratios:

1. The rate of inventory turnover (ratio of cost of sales to average inventory) has decreased from the preceding year's rate.
2. The number of days' sales in receivables (ratio of average daily accounts receivable to sales) has increased over the prior year.

(Adapted from AICPA)

Professional Judgment Problem

8-25 ❶ ❷ ❸ ❹ Your province administers to students in public schools and high schools standardized tests of reading, writing, and mathematics. Reports are produced both by school and for the province overall describing how students fared in these tests. Recently, the Annual Report of the Office of the provincial Auditor General evaluated this testing process. The report was thorough, describing the process and how it was audited and providing some observations and recommendations. One observation related to the methods of monitoring and comparing student progress. Issues raised were as follows:

- Not enough information is collected in student information systems about student practices such as homework assignment, homework completion, and whether remedial assistance was provided or available.
- There were questions about the accuracy of information recorded about students.
- Concerns were raised about the comparability of data for students from school to school.
- Information systems may not be capable of retaining sufficient student data.

a. Using the seven different types of evidence listed in Table 8-5 on page 230, identify the evidence that the provincial auditor's office might have collected to reach the conclusions described above. For each type of evidence, explain who would have provided the evidence, and note the level of objectivity of such evidence. Justify your answer.

b. What would be the relevant transaction-related audit objectives considered during this audit? List at least one audit procedure that could have been conducted for each of the transaction-related audit objectives from Chapter 5 that you consider to be relevant.

Case

8-26 ❶ ❷ ❸ Grande Stores is a large department store chain with catalogue operations. The company has recently expanded from 6 to 43 stores by borrowing from several large financial institutions and from a public offering of common stock. A recent investigation has disclosed that Grande materially overstated net income. This was accomplished by understating accounts payable and recording fictitious supplier credits that further reduced accounts payable. An OSC investigation was critical of the evidence gathered by Grande's audit firm, Montgomery & Ross, in testing accounts payable and the supplier credits.

The following is a description of some of the fictitious supplier credits and unrecorded amounts in accounts payable, as well as the audit procedures.

1. McClure Advertising Credits—Grande had arrangements with some vendors to share the cost of advertising the vendor's product. The arrangements were usually agreed to in advance by the vendor and supported by evidence of the placing of the ad. Grande created a 114-page list of approximately 1,100 vendors, supporting advertising credits of $300,000. Grande's auditors selected a sample of 4 of the 1,100 items for direct confirmation. One item was confirmed by telephone, one traced to cash receipts, one to a vendor credit memo for part of the amount and cash receipts for the rest, and one to a vendor credit memo. Two of the amounts confirmed differed from the amount on the list, but the auditors did not seek an explanation for the differences because the amounts were not material.

    The rest of the credits were tested by selecting 20 items (one or two from each page of the list). Twelve of the items were supported by examining the ads placed, and eight were supported by Grande debit memos charging the vendors for the promotional allowances.

2. Springbrook Credits—Grande created 28 fictitious credit memos totalling $257,000 from Springbrook Distributors, the main supplier of health and beauty aids to Grande. Grande's controller initially told the auditor that the credits were for returned goods, then said they were a volume discount, and finally stated they were a payment so that Grande would continue to use Springbrook as a supplier. One of the Montgomery & Ross staff auditors concluded

that a $257,000 payment to retain Grande's business was too large to make financial sense.

The credit memos indicated that the credits were for damaged merchandise, volume rebates, and advertising allowances. The audit firm requested a confirmation of the credits. In response, Jon Steiner, the president of Grande Stores, placed a call to Mort Seagal, the president of Springbrook, and handed the phone to the staff auditor. In fact, the call had been placed to an officer of Grande. The Grande officer, posing as Seagal, orally confirmed the credits. Grande refused to allow Montgomery & Ross to obtain written confirmations supporting the credits. Although the staff auditor doubted the validity of the credits, the audit partner, Mark Franklin, accepted the credits based on the credit memoranda, telephone confirmation of the credits, and oral representations of Grande officers.

3. Ridolfi Credits—$130,000 in credits based on 35 credit memoranda from Ridolfi, Inc., were purportedly for the return of overstocked goods from several Grande stores. A Montgomery & Ross staff auditor noted the size of the credit and that the credit memos were dated subsequent to year end. He further noticed that a sentence on the credit memos from Ridolfi had been obliterated by a felt-tip marker. When held to the light, the accountant could read that the marked-out sentence read, "Do not post until merchandise received." The staff auditor thereafter called Harold Ridolfi, treasurer of Ridolfi, Inc. and was informed that the $130,000 in goods had not been returned and the money was not owed to Grande by Ridolfi. Steiner advised Franklin, the audit partner, that he had talked to Harold Ridolfi, who claimed he had been misunderstood by the staff auditor. Steiner told Franklin not to have anyone call Ridolfi to verify the amount because of pending litigation between Grande and Ridolfi, Inc.

4. Accounts Payable Accrual—Montgomery & Ross assigned a senior with experience in the retail area to audit accounts payable. Although Grande had poor internal control, Montgomery & Ross selected a sample of 50 for confirmation of the several thousand vendors who did business with Grande. Twenty-seven responses were received, and 21 were reconciled to Grande's records. These tests indicated an unrecorded liability of approximately $290,000

when projected to the population of accounts payable. However, the investigation disclosed that Grande's president made telephone calls to some suppliers who had received confirmation requests from Montgomery & Ross and told them how to respond to the request.

Montgomery & Ross also performed a purchases cutoff test by vouching accounts payable invoices received for nine weeks after year end. The purpose of this test was to identify invoices received after year end that should have been recorded in accounts payable. Thirty percent of the sample ($160,000) was found to relate to the prior year, indicating a potential unrecorded liability of approximately $500,000. The audit firm and Grande eventually agreed on an adjustment to increase accounts payable by $260,000.

REQUIRED
Identify deficiencies in the sufficiency and appropriateness of the evidence gathered in the audit of accounts payable of Grande Stores.

Ongoing Small Business Case: Banking at CondoCleaners.com

8-27 ❶ ❷ ❸ Jim has two bank accounts, one for payroll and one for processing other transactions at CondoCleaners.com. He will have sales transactions (credit card deposits from the credit card service provider), payroll transactions for his employees, and expense cheques from himself, costs for suppliers and equipment, salary and bonus cheques to himself, and bank charges.

REQUIRED
a. Describe the internal and external documentation that will likely be available for the audit of CondoCleaners.com.
b. For each of the seven methods of evidence collection, provide an example of an audit step that you could use for the audit of the cash transactions or balances at CondoCleaners.com.

9   Internal controls and control risk

"Why bother testing internal controls? We can just look at the numbers and the supporting documents, can't we?" Well, no! First of all, audit standards require that the auditor understand internal controls. Second, in a large organization with millions of transactions, ignoring internal controls would lead to a very expensive audit. For an organization of any size, the ability to rely on the procedures performed by computer software (such as calculations) reduces the amount of audit work required. Management accountants will find this information helpful as they choose to design internal controls for their organization. Internal, external, and specialist auditors frequently are called upon to assess internal controls.

LEARNING OBJECTIVES

1 State the three primary objectives of effective internal control. Describe the differing perspectives of the client and the auditor with respect to internal controls. State the purpose of understanding controls when substantive tests are not enough for auditing a particular assertion. Identify the three basic concepts that enable an auditor's study of internal controls. Describe the conditions where fraud is most likely to exist.

2 Explain the five components of the COSO (Committee of Sponsoring Organizations of the Treadway Commission) internal control framework and relate these to the audit process. Describe those control features that the auditor could look for that could reduce fraud risks.

3 Define information technology governance. Describe the attributes of good IT governance. State the impact of general IT controls on the audit planning process. State the effects of information systems on the eight-phase audit process.

4 Describe what the auditor does to obtain an understanding of internal controls. State how control risk is assessed, documented, and tested. Identify key controls, and link control risk by assertion to audit strategy and further audit procedures. Explain how different types of internal control reports affect tests of controls.

5 Identify important risks and controls in small businesses.

STANDARDS REFERENCED IN THIS CHAPTER

CICA Standards

CAS 240 – The auditor's responsibilities relating to fraud in an audit of financial statements

CAS 265 – Communicating deficiencies in internal control to those charged with governance and management

CAS 315 – Identifying and assessing the risks of material misstatement through understanding the entity and its environment

CAS 330 – The auditor's responses to assessed risks

CAS 610 – Using the work of internal auditors

CSAE 3416 – Reporting on controls at a service organization

Section 5025 – Standards for assurance engagements other than audits of financial statements and other historical financial information

Section 5925 – An audit of internal control over financial reporting that is integrated with an audit of financial statements

Section 9110 – Agreed-upon procedures regarding internal control over financial reporting

Rogue Trader Circumvents Controls Causing $7 Billion in Losses

The size of the trading losses at French bank Société Générale were staggering. Jérôme Kerviel, a junior trader with a modest base salary of around $70,000, had gambled more than the bank's entire net worth in high-risk bets involving unauthorized trades related to European stock index funds.

Kerviel's role was to make trades that bet whether European stock markets would rise or fall. Each bet was supposed to be offset by a trade in the opposite direction to keep risk at a minimum, with the bank making profit or loss based on the difference between the parallel bets. However, within months of joining the trading desk, he began placing his bets all in one direction, rather than hedging the trades as he was expected to do. One bet paid off handsomely after an attack on the London transport system sent European markets into a dive. "Bingo, 500,000 euros," Kerviel said in an interview with investigators. This success led him to make even bolder bets.

Société Générale played up their use of computer systems to ward off risk. The bank's equity-derivatives unit had not experienced a major incident in 15 years. "We didn't think it was possible," said one Société Générale executive discussing the losses. Unfortunately, Kerviel knew how to mask his trades to avoid detection. He masked his positions with fake trades, creating the illusion that his positions were hedged.

Keeping his trades hidden required constant vigilance. Kerviel needed to continue to delete and re-enter fake trades to avoid detection. As a result, he regularly skipped holidays and rarely took vacation. "It is one of the rules of controls: a trader who doesn't take holidays is a trader who doesn't want his books to be seen by others," Kerviel stated to investigators.

Finally, a fictitious trade made in the name of a German brokerage house triggered an alarm in Société Générale's systems. Under repeated questioning, Kerviel revealed that his bets had over 50 billion euros at risk for the bank. By the time the French bank unwound the bets, it had lost 4.9 billion euros ($7.4 billion), nearly destroying the 145-year-old bank.

IMPORTANCE TO AUDITORS

At Kerviel's June 2010 trial, one of the bank's former executives admitted that the bank failed by creating an environment where there was "too much trust." And, his former boss commented, "If you're not looking for anything, you don't find anything." Was it really "too much trust," or simply inadequate control systems that did not identify violations of bank procedures? External auditors must test internal controls to be able to rely upon them—management must do the same.

continued >

continued

WHAT DO YOU THINK?

1. What management attitudes permitted these huge exposures to occur?
2. What actions on the part of the bank could have prevented or detected the losses?
3. What would the role of the external auditor be in the detection of these losses?

THE opening story involving Société Générale demonstrates how deficiencies in internal control can cause significant losses resulting in material misstatements in financial statements. Financial reporting problems of companies such as Enron and Nortel also exposed serious deficiencies in internal control. To address these concerns, Section 404 of the Sarbanes-Oxley Act in the United States requires auditors of public companies to assess and report on the effectiveness of internal control over financial reporting, in addition to their report on the audit of financial statements. In Canada, although public company management must attest to the quality of the company's internal controls, assessment by the auditors is not required.

Chapter 9 is the fourth chapter dealing with financial statement audit risk assessment. The study of internal control, assessment of control risk, and related evidence gathering is a major component in the audit risk model studied in Chapter 7. Control risk is "CR" in the audit risk model. It was explained in Chapter 7 that planned audit evidence can be reduced when there are effective internal controls. This chapter shows why and how this can be done.

To understand how internal control is used in the audit risk model, knowledge of key internal control concepts is needed. Accordingly, this chapter focuses on the meaning and objectives of internal control from both the client's and the auditor's point of view, the components of internal control, and the auditor's methodology for assessing and testing control risks, which include risks of fraud.

Sources: Adapted from 1.Clark, Nicola and Katrin Behnhold, "A Société Générale Trader Remains a Mystery as His Criminal Trial Ends," *The New York Times*, June 25, 2010. 2. Gauthier-Villars, David and Carrick Mollenkamp, "Portrait Emerges of Rogue Trader at French Bank," *The Wall Street Journal*, February 2–3, 2008, p. A1.

 ## Differing Perspectives of Internal Control

Internal control—the policies and procedures instituted and maintained by the management of an entity in order to provide reasonable assurance that management's objectives are met.

A system of **internal control** consists of policies and procedures designed to provide management with reasonable assurance that the company achieves its objectives and goals. These policies and procedures are often called controls, and collectively, they make up the entity's internal control. There are three broad objectives in designing an effective internal control system:

1. *Reliability of financial reporting.* As we discussed in Chapter 5, management is responsible for preparing statements for investors, creditors, and other users. Management has both a legal and professional responsibility to be sure that the

information is fairly presented in accordance with reporting requirements under an acceptable accounting framework such as ASPE or IFRS.

2. *Efficiency and effectiveness of operations.* Controls within a company encourage efficient and effective use of its resources to optimize the company's goals. An important objective of these controls is accurate financial and nonfinancial information about the company's operations for decision making.

3. *Compliance with laws and regulations.* In the United States, public companies are required to issue a report about the operating effectiveness of internal control over financial reporting. In Canada, management is required to report on the effectiveness of internal controls. Public, nonpublic, and not-for-profit organizations are required to follow many laws and regulations. Some relate to accounting only indirectly, such as environmental protection and human rights laws. Others are closely related to accounting, such as income tax regulations and fraud.

Client Perspectives on Internal Control

Management designs systems of internal control to accomplish all three objectives. As we shall see in the next section, this contrasts with the auditor's focus in both the audit of financial statements and the audit of internal controls that is on relevant controls: those that have an impact on the reliability of financial reporting, plus those controls over operations and compliance with laws and regulations that could materially affect financial reporting.

The internal control system consists of governance processes as well as many specific policies and procedures designed to provide management with reasonable assurance that the goals and objectives that it believes to be important to the entity will be met.

Control systems must be cost beneficial. The controls adopted are selected by comparing the costs to the organization to the benefits expected. One benefit to management, but certainly not the most important, is the reduced cost of an audit when the auditor evaluates internal control as good or excellent and assesses control risk as much below maximum (i.e., as low).

Management typically has the following objectives in designing effective internal control.

Maintaining reliable control systems Management must have reliable control systems so that it will have accurate information for conducting its operations and producing financial statements. For example, the price to charge for products is based in part on information about the cost of making the products. Information must be reliable and timely if it is to be useful to management for decision making.

Safeguarding assets The physical assets of a company can be stolen, misused, or accidentally destroyed unless they are protected by adequate controls. The same is true of non-physical assets such as important records (e.g., confidential business proposals or research and development data) and accounting records (e.g., accounts receivable balances, financial details). Safeguarding certain assets and records has become increasingly important since the advent of computer systems and the implementation of consumer privacy protection laws. Large amounts of information stored on computer media can be destroyed or stolen if care is not taken to protect them. Management safeguards assets by controlling access and by comparisons of assets with records of those assets.

Optimizing the use of resources The controls within an organization are meant to optimize use of resources by preventing unnecessary duplication of effort and waste in all aspects of the business and by discouraging other inefficient use of resources.

Preventing and detecting error and fraud The internal controls of a company play an important role in the prevention and detection of error or fraud and other irregularities. The cost of preventing a particular misstatement should be balanced against the likelihood of the misstatement occurring and the amount of the misstatement that could occur.

AUDITOR PERSPECTIVES Evaluation of internal control and the associated control risk is part of the audit planning process. The auditor considers control risk together with inherent risk to evaluate whether there is a risk of financial statement misstatement at the level of the financial statements as a whole or for individual transactions, accounts, or disclosures at the assertion level (see the CAS 315 section, Risk assessment procedures and related activities). The quality of the internal controls affects the extent of tests of details conducted by the auditor.

Management's internal control objectives go beyond financial statement objectives. In other words, there are aspects of internal control that are of interest to management but not to the auditor; consequently, the auditor does not concern himself or herself with those aspects of internal control in planning the audit. An example would be internal controls that have been set up by management to ensure that accurate information about the company's market share is collected and provided to the company's marketing department.

CAS

Relevant controls—controls that are relevant to the financial statement audit (by preventing or detecting errors or helping to ensure the reliability of financial reporting)

CAS 315 paragraph 12 explains that the auditor considers internal control that is relevant to the financial statement audit. **Relevant controls** normally pertain to cycles of events (transactions) that lead to information recorded in the financial statements. However, other systems, such as manufacturing quality control, could be relevant if the client has had quality control problems that have resulted in numerous product returns and the auditor is attempting to assess the value of inventory. The auditor examines whether internal controls prevent, detect, or correct errors or other misstatements. The auditor can consider inherent risks together with control risks by assertion or can consider inherent and control risks separately. This text generally considers them separately, although practice varies. When risks of error are high, the auditor will expand tests of details, potentially abandoning tests of controls altogether.

CONTROLS RELATED TO THE RELIABILITY OF FINANCIAL REPORTING The auditor is interested primarily in controls that relate to the first of management's internal control objectives: maintaining reliable control systems. This is the area that directly impacts the reliability of the financial statements and their related assertions and therefore impacts the auditor's objective of determining that the financial statements are fairly stated.

As stated in Chapter 5, auditors have significant responsibility for the discovery of management and employee fraud and, to a lesser degree, certain types of illegal acts. Auditors are therefore also concerned with a client's controls over the safeguarding of assets and compliance with applicable laws and regulations if they affect the fairness of the financial statements. Internal controls, if properly designed and implemented, can be effective in preventing and detecting fraud.

Controls affecting internal management information, such as budgets and internal performance reports, should also be examined. These types of information are often important sources for the auditor because they can be used to develop expectations for analytical procedures. If the controls over these internal reports are considered inadequate, the value of the reports as evidence diminishes.

Emphasis on controls over classes of transactions The emphasis by auditors is on controls over classes of transactions rather than on account balances or disclosures. The reason is that the accuracy of the results of the accounting system (account balances and financial statement balances) is heavily dependent upon the accuracy of the inputs and processing (transactions). For example, if products sold, units shipped, or unit selling prices are incorrectly billed to customers for sales, both sales and accounts receivable will be misstated. If controls are adequate to ensure billings, cash receipts, sales returns and allowances, and charge-offs are correct, the ending balance in accounts receivable is likely to be correct. Disclosures rely upon management identification, which are audited separately, for example by review of minutes of Board meetings.

In the study of internal control and assessment of control risk, therefore, auditors are primarily concerned with the **transaction-related audit objectives**, discussed in Chapter 5. These objectives were discussed in detail on page 124. Table 9-1 illustrates the development of transaction-related audit objectives for sales transactions.

During the study of internal control and assessment of control risk, the auditor does consider internal controls over account balances where relevant. For example, transaction-related audit objectives typically have no effect on two balance-related audit objectives: valuation, and rights and obligations. The auditor is likely to make a separate evaluation as to whether management has implemented internal controls for each of these two balance-related audit objectives where there is a potential for material misstatement.

When substantive procedures are insufficient The auditor may identify some risks that cannot be effectively tested by substantive tests alone. For example, there may be a risk of incomplete recording of electronic commerce transactions or the risk of inaccurate calculation of invoices due to transfer of information from other subsystems. When such risks are present, the auditor is required to obtain an understanding of the

> **Transaction-related audit objectives**—five audit objectives that must be met before the auditor can conclude that the total for any given class of transactions is fairly stated. The general transaction-related audit objectives are occurrence, completeness, accuracy, cutoff, and classification.

Table 9-1	Sales Transaction-Related Audit Objectives
Transaction-Related Audit Objectives—General Form	**Specific Sales Transaction-Related Audit Objectives**
Occurrence	Recorded sales are for shipments made to nonfictitious customers of the entity.
Completeness	Existing sales transactions are recorded.
Accuracy	Recorded sales are for the amount of goods shipped and are appropriately billed and recorded.
Cutoff	Sales are recorded on the correct dates.
Classification	Sales transactions are recorded in the correct accounts.

controls (perhaps in information systems) that address those risks (CAS 315 par. 30) and then test those controls if reliance is intended.

Consider the whole picture The auditor's frame of reference is the potential risk of material misstatements at the financial statement level. So, after considering the potential for misstatements at the detailed assertion level for transactions and account balances, it is important to step back and look at the financial statements as a whole. For example, does it appear that there is a frequent risk of understatement for more than one asset account, or a frequent risk of completeness errors for multiple types of transactions? If so, consider the impact on the financial statements as a whole.

Studying Internal Control

KEY CONCEPTS There are three basic concepts underlying the study of internal control and assessment of control risk: management's responsibility, reasonable assurance, and inherent limitations.

Management's responsibility Management, not the auditor, must establish and maintain the entity's controls. This concept is consistent with the requirement that management, not the auditor, is responsible for the preparation of financial statements in accordance with an acceptable accounting framework.

Reasonable assurance A company should develop internal controls that provide reasonable, but not absolute, assurance that the financial statements are fairly stated. Internal controls are developed by management after considering both the costs and benefits of the controls. Management is often unwilling to implement an ideal system because the costs may be too high. For example, it is unreasonable for auditors to expect the management of a small company to hire several additional accounting personnel to bring about a small improvement in the reliability of accounting data. It is often less expensive to have auditors do more extensive auditing than to incur higher internal control costs.

Inherent limitations Internal controls cannot be regarded as completely effective, regardless of the care followed in their design and implementation. Even if systems personnel could develop, design, and program an ideal system, the effectiveness of the system would also depend on the competency and dependability of the people using it. For example, assume that a procedure for counting inventory is carefully developed and requires two employees to count independently. If neither of the employees understands the instructions or if both are careless in doing the counts, the count of inventory is likely to be incorrect. Even if the count is right, management might override the procedure and instruct an employee to increase the count of quantities in order to improve reported earnings. Similarly, the employees might decide to overstate the counts intentionally to cover up a theft of inventory by one or both of them. This collaborative effort among employees to defraud is called **collusion**.

Because of these inherent limitations of controls and because auditors cannot have more than reasonable assurance of the controls' effectiveness, there is almost always some level of control risk greater than zero. Therefore, even with the most effectively designed internal controls, the auditor must obtain audit evidence beyond testing the controls for every material financial statement account.

As part of studying internal control, the auditor also studies the risks of fraud.

Conditions for Fraud

Three conditions for fraud arising from fraudulent financial reporting and misappropriations of assets are described in paragraph A1 of the *CICA Handbook* CAS 240. As shown in Figure 9-1, these three conditions are referred to as the **fraud triangle**.

1. *Incentives/Pressures.* Management or other employees have incentives or pressures to commit fraud.

Collusion—a cooperative effort among employees to defraud a business of cash, inventory, or other assets.

Fraud triangle—represents the three conditions of fraud: incentives/pressures, opportunities, and attitudes/rationalization.

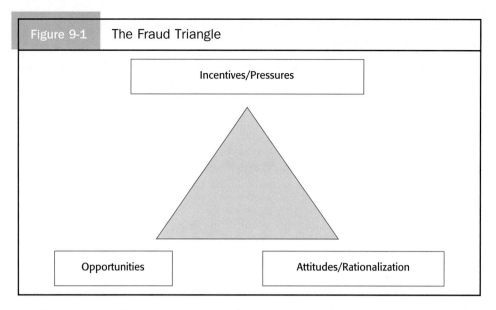

Figure 9-1   The Fraud Triangle

Incentives/Pressures

Opportunities

Attitudes/Rationalization

2. *Opportunities.* Circumstances provide opportunities for management or employees to commit fraud.

3. *Attitudes/Rationalization.* An attitude, character, or set of ethical values exists that allows management or employees to intentionally commit a dishonest act, or they are in an environment that imposes pressure sufficient to cause them to rationalize committing a dishonest act.

RISK FACTORS FOR FRAUDULENT FINANCIAL REPORTING An essential consideration by the auditor in uncovering fraud is identifying factors that increase the risk of fraud. These are referred to as **fraud risk factors** or red flags of fraud. Table 9-2 below

Fraud risk factors—entity factors that increase the risk of fraud.

Table 9-2   Examples of Risk Factors for Fraudulent Financial Reporting

Three Conditions of Fraud		
Incentives/Pressures	Opportunities	Attitudes/Rationalization
Management or other employees have incentives or pressures to materially misstate financial statements.	Circumstances provide an opportunity for management or employees to misstate financial statements.	An attitude, character, or set of ethical values exists that allows management or employees to intentionally commit a dishonest act, or they are in an environment that imposes pressure sufficient to cause them to rationalize committing a dishonest act.
Examples of Risk Factors	Examples of Risk Factors	Examples of Risk Factors
Financial stability or profitability is threatened by economic, industry, or entity operating conditions. Examples include significant declines in customer demand and increasing business failures in either the industry or overall economy.	Significant accounting estimates involve subjective judgments or uncertainties that are difficult to verify.	Inappropriate or ineffective communication and support of the entity's values.
Excessive pressure for management to meet the requirements or expectations of third parties, such as the terms of debt covenant requirements.	Ineffective board of directors or audit committee oversight over financial reporting.	Known history of violations of securities laws or other laws and regulations.
Management or the board of directors' personal net worth is materially threatened by the entity's financial performance.	High turnover or ineffective accounting, internal audit, or information technology staff.	Management's practice of making overly aggressive or unrealistic forecasts to analysts, creditors, and other third parties.

provides examples of fraud risk factors for each of the three conditions of fraud for fraudulent financial reporting.

Incentives/Pressures A common incentive for companies to manipulate financial statements is a decline in the company's financial prospects. A decline in earnings may threaten the company's ability to obtain financing and continue as a going concern. Companies may also manipulate earnings to meet analysts' forecasts of anticipated earnings for the quarter, to meet debt covenant restrictions, or to artificially maintain or inflate stock prices. In some cases, management may manipulate earnings just to preserve their reputation. Management with significant wealth tied up in stock options may have an incentive to inflate stock prices to increase the profits they earn personally when the options are exercised.

Opportunities Financial statements of all companies are potentially subject to manipulation. However, the risk of fraudulent financial reporting is greater for companies in industries where significant judgments and estimates are involved. For example, valuation of inventories is subject to greater risk of misstatement for companies with diverse inventories in many locations or where the inventory could be obsolete.

Opportunities for misstatement are greater if there is turnover in accounting personnel or other weaknesses in accounting and information processes. In many cases of fraudulent financial reporting, the company had an ineffective audit committee and board of director oversight of financial reporting.

Attitudes/Rationalization The attitude of top management toward financial reporting is a critical risk factor in assessing the likelihood of fraudulent financial statements. This attitude is commonly referred to as the "tone at the top," and it is relevant to fraud risks because a poor tone at the top increases the risk of fraud and results in a poor internal control environment. If the CEO or other top managers display a disregard for the financial reporting process, for example, by consistently issuing overly optimistic forecasts or by being overly concerned about meeting analysts' earnings forecasts, fraudulent financial reporting is more likely. Also, management's character or set of ethical values may make it easier for it to rationalize a fraudulent act.

RISK FACTORS FOR MISAPPROPRIATION OF ASSETS The same three fraud triangle conditions apply to misappropriation of assets. However, in assessing risk factors, greater emphasis is placed on individual incentives and opportunities for theft. Table 9-3 provides examples of fraud risk factors for each of the three conditions of fraud for misappropriation of assets.

Incentives/Pressures Financial pressures are a common incentive for employees who misappropriate assets. Employees with excessive financial obligations or with drug abuse or gambling problems may steal to meet their personal financial or other needs. Managers should be alert for signs of these problems in employees with access to assets or accounting records. While a background check should be performed for all potential employees, a credit check may be included for those who will have access to assets. Dissatisfied employees may steal because of a sense of entitlement or as a form of attack against their employers. Companies can reduce fraud risk by dealing fairly with employees and monitoring employee morale.

Opportunities Opportunities for theft exist in all companies. However, opportunities are greater in companies with accessible cash or with inventory or other valuable assets, especially if the assets are small or readily transportable. For example, thefts of laptop computers are fairly common and much more frequent than thefts of desktop systems. Retailers and other organizations that receive revenue in the form of cash are also susceptible to theft. Surveillance methods and inventory coding and tracking systems can reduce the potential for theft. For example, casinos

Table 9-3	Examples of Risk Factors for Misappropriation of Assets	

Three Conditions of Fraud		
Incentives/Pressures	Opportunities	Attitudes/Rationalization
Management or other employees have incentives or pressures to misappropriate material assets.	Circumstances provide an opportunity for management or employees to misappropriate assets.	An attitude, character, or set of ethical values exists that allows management or employees to intentionally commit a dishonest act, or they are in an environment that imposes pressure sufficient to cause them to rationalize a dishonest act.
Examples of Risk Factors	Examples of Risk Factors	Examples of Risk Factors
Personal financial obligations create pressure for those with access to cash or other assets susceptible to theft to misappropriate those assets.	Presence of large amounts of cash on hand or inventory items that are small, of high value, or are in high demand.	Disregard for the need to monitor or reduce risk of misappropriating assets.
Adverse relationships between management and employees with access to assets susceptible to theft motivate employees to misappropriate those assets. Examples include the following: • Known or expected employee layoffs. • Promotions, compensation, or other rewards inconsistent with expectations.	Inadequate internal control over assets due to lack of the following: • Appropriate segregation of duties or independent checks. • Appropriate job applicant screening for employees performing key control functions. • Mandatory vacations for employees with access to assets.	Disregard for internal controls by overriding existing controls or failing to correct known internal control deficiencies.

handle extensive amounts of cash with minimal formal records of cash received. As a result, casinos make extensive use of video and human surveillance. On a more basic scale, one Canadian fast food chain has a small sign attached to its cash registers advising patrons that if they do not receive a receipt, their meal is free. This simple control ensures that the sales are recorded in the cash register. Such a control costs the company nothing to implement, and every patron becomes a watchdog.

Weak internal controls create opportunities for theft. Inadequate separation of duties is practically a licence for employees to steal. Whenever employees have custody or even temporary access to assets and maintain the accounting records for those assets, the potential for theft exists. As an example, if inventory storeroom employees also maintain inventory records, it is relatively easy for them to take inventory items and cover the theft by adjusting the accounting records.

Fraud is more prevalent in smaller businesses and not-for-profit organizations because it is more difficult for these entities to maintain adequate separation of duties. However, even large organizations may fail to maintain adequate separation in critical areas. Our opening story illustrates how this can lead to large losses.

Attitudes/Rationalization

Management's attitude toward controls and ethical conduct may allow employees and managers to rationalize the theft of assets. If management cheats customers through overcharging for goods or engaging in high-pressure sales tactics, employees may feel that it is acceptable for them to behave in the same fashion by cheating on expense or time reports.

concept check

C9-1 Why does management implement internal controls?

C9-2 Does the auditor document all internal controls? Why or why not?

C9-3 Can account balances be tested with control testing only? Why or why not?

C9-4 What is the difference between earnings management and income smoothing?

C9-5 Define misappropriation of assets and give two examples.

② COSO Components of Internal Control

COSO (the Committee of Sponsoring Organizations of the Treadway Commission, **www.coso.org**) has representatives from the American Accounting Association, the American Institute of Certified Public Accountants, Financial Executives International, the Institute of Management Accountants, and the Institute of Internal Auditors. A review of the website will show that the first report issued by COSO was in 1997 with respect to fraud, while their now commonly used integrated internal control framework was released in 1992. COSO continues to issue new material, as the box on strengthening enterprise risk oversight shows.

COSO's Internal Control—Integrated Framework describes five components of internal control that management designs and implements to provide reasonable assurance that its control objectives will be met. Each component contains many controls, but auditors concentrate on those designed to prevent or detect material misstatements in the financial statements. The COSO internal control components comprise the following:

1. Control environment.
2. Risk assessment.
3. Control activities.
4. Information and communication.
5. Monitoring.

Figure 9-2 shows that the control environment is the umbrella for the other four components. Without an effective control environment, the other four components are unlikely to result in effective internal control, regardless of their quality.

The Control Environment

The essence of an effectively controlled organization lies in the attitude of its management. If top management believes control is important, others in the organization will sense that and respond by conscientiously observing the policies and procedures established. On the other hand, if it is clear to members of the organization that control is not an important concern to top management and is given "lip service" rather than meaningful support, it is almost certain that control objectives will not be effectively achieved. Individuals responsible for overseeing the strategic direction of the entity and the accountability of the entity, including financial reporting and disclosure, are called **those charged with governance**. Corporate governance strategies have a major impact on the control environment and the other components of internal control. These strategies result in the use of **entity-level controls,** those controls that are implemented for multiple transaction cycles or for the entire organization.

The **control environment** consists of the actions, policies, and procedures that reflect the overall attitudes of top management, the directors, and the owners of an entity about control and its importance to the entity. It is the implementation of the attitudes and strategies of those charged with governance. For the purpose of

Those charged with governance— individuals responsible for overseeing the strategic direction of the entity and the accountability of the entity, including financial reporting and disclosure.

Entity-level controls—those controls that are implemented for multiple transaction cycles or for the entire organization.

Control environment—the actions, policies, and procedures that reflect the overall attitudes of top management, directors, and owners of an entity about control and its importance to the entity.

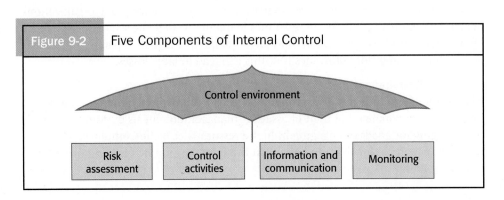

Figure 9-2	Five Components of Internal Control

Strengthening Enterprise Risk Oversight

The recent financial crisis is leading to a renewed focus on how senior executives approach risk management, including the board's role in risk oversight. Companies exist to provide value for stakeholders, but face uncertainty in their attempts to grow stakeholder value. A challenge for management is to determine how much uncertainty to accept, and how to effectively deal with uncertainty and associated risks. Senior executives are working to strengthen risk oversight so that both management and the board are better informed about emerging risk exposures, particularly those impacting strategy.

A recent COSO thought paper, Strengthening Enterprise Risk Oversight for Strategic Advantage, highlights four specific areas where senior management can work with its board to enhance the board's risk oversight capabilities:

1. Discuss risk management philosophy and appetite: Unless the board and management fully understand the level of risk that the organization is willing and able to take, it will be difficult for the board and management to effectively oversee critical risk exposures.

2. Understand risk management practices: For many organizations, the approach to risk management is ad hoc, informal, and implicit, leaving executives and boards with an incomplete view of key risks.

3. Review the portfolio of risks in relation to risk appetite: Ultimately, the goal is to evaluate whether existing risk exposures are in line with stakeholder appetite for risks.

4. Be informed of the most significant risks and related responses: Because risks constantly evolve, management needs a process that provides timely and robust information about risks arising across the organization.

These four areas build on COSO's Enterprise Risk Management—Integrated Framework, which provides core principles for effective identification, assessment, and management of enterprise risks.

Sources: Adapted from 1. Strengthening Enterprise Risk Management for Strategic Advantage, COSO, 2009; 2. Enterprise Risk Management—Integrated Framework, COSO, 2004 **www.coso.org**.

---

understanding and assessing the control environment, the auditor should consider the most important control subcomponents.

ACTIVE INTEGRITY AND PROMOTION OF ETHICAL VALUES The methods of communicating and reinforcing a culture of honesty and high ethical values are the product of the entity's ethical and behavioural standards. They include management's actions to remove or reduce incentives and temptations that might prompt personnel to engage in dishonest, illegal, or unethical acts. They also include the communication of entity values and behavioural standards to personnel through policy statements, codes of conduct, and by example.

COMMITMENT TO COMPETENCE Competence is the knowledge and skills necessary to accomplish tasks that define an individual's job. Commitment to competence includes management's consideration of the competence levels for specific jobs and how these skills translate into required skills and knowledge.

THE BOARD OF DIRECTORS OR AUDIT COMMITTEE PARTICIPATION AND OVERSIGHT The board of directors is essential for effective corporate governance because it has ultimate responsibility to make sure management implements proper internal control and financial reporting processes. An effective board of directors is independent of management, and its members stay involved in and scrutinize management's activities. Although the board delegates responsibility for internal control to management, it must regularly assess these controls. The audit committee considers the potential for management override of internal controls and oversees management's fraud risk assessment process, as well as antifraud programs and controls.

To assist the board in its oversight, the board creates an audit committee that is charged with oversight responsibility for financial reporting. The audit committee is also responsible for maintaining ongoing communication with both external and internal auditors, including the approval of audit and non-audit services done by auditors for public companies. This allows the auditors and directors to discuss matters that might relate to such things as the integrity or actions of management.

The audit committee's independence from management and knowledge of financial reporting issues are important determinants of its ability to effectively evaluate internal controls and financial statements prepared by management. The major exchanges (TSX, NYSE, AMEX, and NASDAQ) require that listed companies have an audit committee composed entirely of independent directors who are financially literate. One method of assessing the quality of corporate governance is the evaluation of the effectiveness of the audit committee's oversight of the company's external financial reporting and internal control over financial reporting.

MANAGEMENT PHILOSOPHY AND OPERATING STYLE Management, through its activities, provides clear signals to employees about the importance of control. For example, does management take significant risks or is it risk-averse? Do policies exist to protect information and ensure privacy and confidentiality? Are profit plans and budget data set as "best possible" plans or "most likely" targets? Can management be described as "fat and bureaucratic," "lean and mean," "dominated by one or a few individuals," or "just right"? Does management use aggressive accounting to ensure budgets and goals are met? Understanding these and similar aspects of management's philosophy and operating style gives the auditor a sense of its attitude about control.

ORGANIZATIONAL STRUCTURE The entity's organizational structure defines the lines of responsibilities and authority that exist. By understanding the client's organizational structure, the auditor can learn the management and functional elements of the business and perceive how control-related policies and procedures can be carried out.

HUMAN RESOURCE POLICIES AND PRACTICES The most important aspect of any system of controls is personnel. If employees are competent and trustworthy, other controls can be absent, and reliable financial statements will still result. Honest, efficient people are able to perform at a high level even when there are few other controls to support them. Even if there are numerous other controls, incompetent or dishonest people can reduce the system to a shambles.

Because of the importance of competent, trustworthy personnel in providing effective control, the method by which persons are hired, evaluated, and compensated is an important part of internal control.

METHODS OF ASSIGNING AUTHORITY AND RESPONSIBILITY The methods of communicating assignment of authority and responsibility must take into account the reporting relationships and responsibilities existing within the entity and the entity's culture. Care must be taken that such issues as the entity's policy on ethical and social issues and organizational goals and objectives are considered. The communications might include such methods as memoranda from top management about the importance of control and control-related matters, formal organizational and operating plans, employee job descriptions and related policies, and policy documents covering employee behaviour such as conflicts of interest and formal codes of conduct, including policies forbidding software copyright violation. Management also has the responsibility to manage risks of fraud and should allocate resources to these tasks. This includes identifying and measuring fraud risks, taking steps to mitigate identified risks, and monitoring controls that prevent and detect fraud.

MANAGEMENT CONTROL METHODS These are the methods that management uses to supervise the entity's activities. Do there exist policies indicating the status of electronic communications? Have logical access and monitoring methods (e.g., passwords and logging) been implemented to reinforce rights of usage as defined? Management methods that monitor the activities of others enhance the effectiveness of internal control in two ways. First, the implementation of such methods sends a clear message about the importance of control. Second, the methods serve to detect misstatements that may have occurred.

An example that illustrates management control methods is an effective budgeting system including subsequent periodic reports of the results of operations compared with budgets. An organization that has effective planning identifies material differences between actual results and the plan, and takes appropriate corrective action at the proper management level.

SYSTEMS DEVELOPMENT METHODOLOGY Management has the responsibility for the development and implementation of the entity's systems and procedures. The auditor should know whether management has a methodology for developing and modifying automated and manual systems and procedures or whether change occurs on an ad hoc basis.

MANAGEMENT REACTION TO EXTERNAL INFLUENCES While external influences are beyond management's control, management should be aware of these influences and be prepared to react appropriately. For example, management (and its tax advisors) should be knowledgeable about the tax laws in filing corporate tax returns so that an audit by the Canada Revenue Agency would not uncover any surprises.

Management should be aware of changes in the economy and technology in the entity's industry. For example, a retailing company should be aware of a potential downturn in the economy that could lead to reduced sales. The company should probably reduce its level of inventory in such a situation.

INTERNAL AUDIT An effective, competent, independent, and well-trained internal audit department, which reports to the audit committee of the board of directors, can greatly enhance the operations of an entity. Internal auditors are becoming more involved in planning and assessment activities, such as systems development audits, as well as monitoring the effectiveness of other control-related policies and procedures and performing operational audits.

In addition to its role in the entity's control environment, an adequate internal audit staff can contribute to reduced external audit costs by providing direct assistance to the external auditor. CAS 610 defines the way internal auditors affect the external auditor's evidence accumulation. If the external auditor obtains evidence that supports the competence, integrity, and objectivity of internal auditors, then the external auditor can rely on the internal auditors' work in a number of ways.

After obtaining information about each of the subcomponents of the control environment, the auditor uses this understanding as a basis for assessing management's and the directors' attitudes and awareness about the importance of control. For example, the auditor might determine the nature of a client's budgeting system as a part of understanding the design of the control environment. The operation of the budgeting system might then be evaluated in part by inquiry of budgeting personnel to determine budgeting procedures and follow up on differences between budget and actual.

Risk Assessment

Risk assessment for financial reporting is management's identification and analysis of risks relevant to the preparation of financial statements in conformity with an applicable financial reporting framework. For example, if a company frequently sells products at a price below inventory cost because of rapid technology changes, it is essential for the company to incorporate adequate controls to overcome the risk of overstating inventory.

The auditor obtains knowledge about management's risk assessment process by determining how management identifies risk relevant to financial reporting, evaluates its

Risk assessment—management's identification and analysis of risks relevant to the preparation of financial statements in conformity with an applicable financial reporting framework.

significance and likelihood of occurrence, and decides the actions needed to address the risks. Questionnaires and discussions with management are the most common ways to obtain this understanding.

Risk assessment is part of a cycle that can be used to address organizational risks. For example, the following five basic principles should be part of an effective fraud risk management process:

1. As part of the corporate governance process, the board of directors and senior management should clarify their expectations regarding fraud risk in a written policy.
2. Fraud risk exposures should be assessed.
3. Controls and actions to prevent or mitigate fraud risks should be established, based upon cost-benefit, management, and board assessments. Table 9-4 provides a list of control features that could reduce fraud risks, with an explanation of benefits for each control feature.
4. In the event that prevention or mitigation fails, controls and actions should be present to help detect fraud.
5. Communication, reporting, and monitoring should be used to update the fraud management process organization-wide and on a timely basis. The process should include practices and actions that will be undertaken in the event that a potential fraud is detected.

After Step 5, the organization would return to Step 1, perhaps annually. All entities, regardless of size, structure, nature, or industry, face a variety of risks from external and internal sources that must be managed. Because economic, industry, regulatory, and operating conditions constantly change, management is challenged with developing mechanisms to identify and deal with risks associated with change. Identifying and analyzing risk is an ongoing process and a critical component of effective internal control. Management must focus on risks at all levels of the organization and take actions necessary to manage them. An important first step is for management to identify factors that may increase risk. Failure to meet prior objectives, quality of personnel, geographic dispersion of company operations, significance and complexity of

Table 9-4	Control Features that Could Reduce Fraud Risks
Control feature	**How it could reduce fraud risks**
Management and board promotion of a culture of honesty and high ethics.	Implementation of programs and controls that are based on core values create an environment that reinforces acceptable behaviour and expectations of each employee.
Audit committee oversight of management and internal auditors.	Assists in creating an effective "tone at the top" by reinforcing zero tolerance for fraud; serves as a deterrent for management fraud by having a direct reporting relationship with internal and external auditors.
Specific management responsibilities for managing risks of fraud.	Reduces perceived opportunities to commit and conceal fraud. Results in improved internal controls by actively considering risks and implementing controls to mitigate the risks.
Articulated and effective fraud risk management process	Results in clear matching of controls to risks, and keeping risk assessments, controls, and monitoring processes current.
Effective general and application control activities that address specific risks of fraud, such as segregation of duties, passwords and user access rights that limit functions to those needed to complete their jobs, and monitoring of exceptions such as unusual traffic on networks	Prevents unauthorized access to assets, helps to detect potential unauthorized access to assets

core business processes, introduction of new information technologies, and entrance of new competitors all represent examples of factors that may lead to increased risk. Once a risk is identified, management estimates the significance of that risk, assesses the likelihood of the risk occurring, and develops specific actions that need to be taken to reduce the risk to an acceptable level. Management's risk assessment differs from, but is closely related to, the auditor's risk assessment discussed in Chapter 7. Management assesses risks as a part of designing and operating internal controls to minimize errors and fraud. Auditors assess risks to decide the evidence needed in the audit. If management effectively assesses and responds to risks, the auditor will typically need to accumulate less evidence than when management fails to identify or respond to significant risks.

Control Activities

COSO describes **control activities** (also known as **application controls**) as the policies and procedures, in addition to those included in the other four components, that help ensure that necessary actions are taken to address risks in the achievement of the entity's objectives. There are potentially many such control activities in any entity, including both manual and automated controls. The control activities in individual transaction cycles generally fall into the following five groups, which are discussed further in this section.

1. Adequate segregation of duties.
2. Proper authorization of transactions and activities.
3. Adequate documents and records.
4. Physical and logical control over assets and records.
5. Independent checks of performance and recorded data.

Before we consider the above groups, let us look at some terminology that helps us navigate the different types of controls that are present in automated information systems.

GENERAL (COMPUTER) CONTROLS When an organization uses automated information systems, general information systems controls (normally called **general controls**) are used to describe internal control activities that could affect multiple classes of transactions or multiple groups of accounts. Table 9-5 lists general control categories and illustrates how they pertain to automated accounting systems (also called "application systems").

> **Control activities (also known as application controls)—** policies and procedures that help ensure that necessary actions are taken to address risks in the achievement of the entity's objectives.
>
> **Application controls (also known as control activities)—**the set of manual, computer-assisted, or fully automated controls that comprise the controls for a particular transaction stream.
>
> **General controls—**internal controls for automated information systems pertaining to more than one transaction cycle or group of accounts.

Table 9-5	General Controls* and Their Relationship to Accounting Systems*	
Manual Information System	**Automated Systems**	
	General Control* Categories	
	• Organization and management controls	
	• Systems acquisitions, development, and maintenance controls	
	• Operations and information systems support	
Accounting System*	Application System*	
Accounting System* Control Activities	Application System* Control Activities	
• Manual controls	• Manual controls	
	• Computer-assisted controls	
	• Fully automated controls	

*"Accounting systems" and "application systems" are used as synonymous terms. "General controls" are also known as "general IT controls."

- *Organization and management controls.* Policies and procedures related to controls should be established, and segregation of incompatible functions should exist.
- *Systems acquisition, development, and maintenance controls.* Application systems could be purchased, developed, or otherwise acquired. Once acquired, changes may need to be made. Established methodologies and control systems should be in place to provide reasonable assurance that the systems (or changes) are authorized and efficient and function in a manner consistent with organizational objectives.
- *Operations and information systems support.* Systems should be available when needed and used for authorized purposes. This section covers employee operational training, adequate documentation of day-to-day procedures, business continuity planning and information systems recovery, and physical and logical security.

Table 9-6 provides examples of sample objectives and the general control activities used to implement the objectives for each general control category. For the purposes of brevity, the examples are illustrative only and do not include all of the procedures that an organization would require to achieve the specific objective.

ACCOUNTING (OR APPLICATION) CONTROL ACTIVITIES As shown in Table 9-5, an individual **accounting system** (also called an "application system") can have different types of control activities (policies and procedures). An example of an application system would be a sales system, which processes sales transactions initiated either by telephone order or by a purchase order form received in the mail. Such a sales system is part of a transaction cycle (sales, receivables, receipts). The transaction cycle could include a separate information systems process for sales, accounts receivable, and cash receipts. So, multiple application systems could be part of a transaction cycle.

Continuing the sales system example, the sales system could have manual control activities (such as approving large sales by the sales manager), computer-assisted control activities (such as the credit manager reviewing a credit exception report prior to releasing orders for processing), or fully automated control activities (such as having the information system calculate sales taxes due on the sale). For simplicity, we will use the terms "controls" and "control activities" as synonyms.

ADEQUATE SEGREGATION OF DUTIES Six general categories of activities should be separated from one another. These are custody of assets, recording or data entry of

Accounting system—the set of manual and/or computerized procedures that collect, record, and process data and report the resulting information; also known as "application system" or "functional system."

Table 9-6	Examples of General Controls	
General Control Category	Sample General Control Objective	Relevant General Control Policy or Procedure
Organization and management controls	Individuals using the organization's systems should have access to only those systems required to do their job effectively. (Segregation of duties)*	1. Managers are to describe necessary access rights by job description. 2. Unique user identification codes and passwords are to be assigned to each employee.
Systems acquisition, development, and maintenance controls	Current authorized versions of payroll programs are in use at all times. (Authorization of transactions and activities)*	1. Management is to monitor government budgets to understand the timing of payroll table changes. 2. The software supplier is to be contacted to ensure that updated payroll software is received on a timely basis.
Operations and information systems support	Online systems should be fully operational between 8:00 a.m. and 6:00 p.m., Monday through Saturday. (Safeguards over use of assets)*	Duplicate hardware resources are to be kept functional for hardware systems.

*The phrase in parentheses shows the specific type of control activity required.

transactions, systems development or acquisition and maintenance, computer operations, reconciliation, and authorization of transactions and activities.

Naturally, the extent of **separation of duties** depends heavily on the size of the organization. In many small companies, it is not practical to segregate the duties to the extent suggested. In these cases, the auditor will likely choose to not rely upon internal controls.

Separation of duties—segregation of the following activities in an organization: custody of assets, recording/data entry, systems development/acquisition and maintenance, computer operations, reconciliation, and authorization.

Separation of custody of assets from accounting The reason for not permitting the person who has temporary or permanent custody of an asset to account for that asset is to protect the firm against theft. Indirect access, such as access to cheque signature images, also must be separate. When one person performs both custody and accounting functions, there is an excessive risk of that person's disposing of or using the asset for personal gain and adjusting the records to hide the theft or use. If the cashier, for example, receives cash and is responsible for data entry of cash receipts and sales, it is possible for the cashier to take the cash received from a customer and adjust the customer's account by failing to record a sale or by recording a fictitious credit to the account.

Separation of operational responsibility from recording or data entry of transactions If each department or division in an organization were responsible for preparing its own records and reports, there would be a tendency to bias the results to improve its reported performance. In order to ensure unbiased information, record-keeping is typically included in a separate accounting department under the controller.

Separation of systems development or acquisition and maintenance from accounting Systems development or acquisition comprises activities that create (or purchase) new methods of processing transactions, thus changing the way information is entered, displayed, reported, and posted against files or databases. Maintenance activities involve changes to these processes. These functions should be monitored to ensure that only authorized programs and systems consistent with management objectives are put into place. A programmer who could enter data could enter transactions (e.g., a wage rate increase) and then suppress the logs or other reports showing the transaction. Here are two job functions in this grouping:

- *Systems analyst.* The systems analyst is responsible for the general design of the system. The analyst sets the objectives of the overall system and the specific design of particular applications.
- *Programmer.* Based on the individual objectives specified by the systems analyst, the programmer develops documentation such as flowcharts for the application, prepares computer instructions, may test the program, and documents the results.

If there is inadequate control over software systems or over individual programs, then the auditor would be unable to rely on activities handled by those systems. For example, imagine being unable to rely on interest calculations made by a bank or on the aging in the accounts receivable aged trial balance. These types of situations occur when the auditor is unable to rely on system or program changes. When the entity has systems development or maintenance functions, a quality assurance group may test the functioning of the new systems or changes, helping ensure that inadvertent errors and unauthorized functions have not been introduced.

Separation of computer operations from programming and accounting These job functions include basic procedures such as handling output reports and taking backup copies of information, and more complex functions such as set-up of functional access rights in password systems and development of information systems recovery procedures. Help-desk or computer support personnel may also be included in this area. Personnel who have physical access to media or the capability to set access rights could steal confidential information or give themselves the right to do anything on the system (called a "super-user"). Separation from authorization, from entry of transactions data, and from the ability to change programs makes it harder for personnel to suppress a trail of their activities.

Separation of reconciliation from data entry Reconciliation involves comparing information from two or more sources, or independently verifying the work that has been completed by others. For example, preparation of a bank reconciliation by the accounting manager independent of the accounts receivable or accounts payable personnel would detect unauthorized use or disbursements of cash.

For batch-based computer systems, a data control group handles the flow of transactions from users, passing the transactions to data entry after logging the number of them, then matching output to logged details to help ensure that all transactions have been recorded, before passing the transactions and reports back to users. An independent check by someone other than the data entry person of key information entered, such as payroll rates or customer credit limits, also serves as a form of data control function.

Proper authorization of transactions and activities If possible, it is desirable to prevent persons who authorize transactions from having control over the related assets. For example, the same person should not authorize the payment of a vendor's invoice and also sign the cheque in payment of the bill. The authorization of a transaction and the handling of the related asset by the same person increase the possibility of defalcation within the organization. A person who authorizes transactions and handles computer operations could suppress printouts documenting the transactions. Similarly, a programmer who could authorize transactions could set up a fictitious supplier, authorize payments to that supplier, then alter the accounts payable programs so that the transactions did not print on reports.

Authorization also includes authorization of new programs and changes to programs since this affects the way that transactions are processed.

Every transaction must be properly authorized if controls are to be satisfactory. Authorization can be either general or specific. **General authorization** means that management establishes policies for the organization to follow. Subordinates are instructed to implement these general authorizations by approving all transactions within the limits set by the policy. Examples of general authorization are the use of fixed prices for the sale of products, credit limits for customers, and fixed reorder points for making purchases. General authorization can be implemented manually or embedded within computer programs—for example, where computer systems check for and reject orders if they cause a customer's accounts receivable balance to exceed the established credit limit.

Specific authorization (or approval) has to do with individual transactions. Management is often unwilling to establish a general policy of authorization for some transactions. Instead, it prefers to make authorizations on a case-by-case basis. One example is the authorization of a sales transaction by the sales manager for a used-car company. Another example is that grocery clerks are authorized to reverse only small transactions; for larger transactions, a supervisor must insert a key or type a password before the transaction can be completed.

ADEQUATE DOCUMENTS AND RECORDS Documents and records are the physical objects (paper or electronic files) on which transactions are entered and summarized. They include such diverse items as sales invoices, purchase orders, subsidiary records, sales journals, and employee time cards. Both documents of original entry and records on which transactions are entered are important, but the inadequacy of documents normally causes greater control problems.

Documents and computer files perform the function of transmitting information throughout the client's organization and among different organizations. These records must be adequate to provide reasonable assurance that all assets are properly controlled and all transactions correctly recorded. For example, if the receiving department fills out a receiving report when material arrives, the accounts payable department can verify the quantity and description on the vendor's invoice by comparing it with the information on the receiving report. In addition to data entries, programming errors that result in inaccurate processing can also result in inaccurate records.

General authorization
—company-wide policies for the approval of all transactions within stated limits.

Specific authorization
—case-by-case approval of transactions not covered by company-wide policies.

The following principles dictate the proper design and use of documents, electronic transactions, and input screens. Documents should be:

- Prenumbered or automatically numbered consecutively to facilitate control over missing records, and to aid in locating records when they are needed at a later date (significantly affects the transaction-related audit objective of completeness).
- Prepared at the time a transaction takes place, or as soon thereafter as possible. When there is a longer time interval, records are less credible and the chance for misstatement is increased (affects the transaction-related audit objective of cutoff).
- Sufficiently simple and described to ensure that they are clearly understood.
- Designed for multiple use whenever possible to minimize the number of different forms. For example, a properly designed and used shipping document can be the basis for releasing goods from storage to the shipping department, informing billing of the quantity of goods to bill the customer and the appropriate billing date, and updating the perpetual inventory records.
- Constructed in a manner that encourages correct preparation. This can be done by providing a degree of internal check within the form or record. For example, a document might include instructions for proper routing, blank spaces for authorizations and approvals, and designated column spaces for numerical data. Input screens would label fields that are to be entered, provide input entry edits (e.g., checking on valid date), and prevent users from proceeding until all relevant information has been completed.

Chart of accounts A control closely related to documents and records is the **chart of accounts**, which lists and classifies transactions into individual balance sheet and income statement accounts. The chart of accounts is an important control because it provides the framework for determining the information presented to management and other financial statement users. The chart of accounts is helpful in preventing classification errors if it accurately and precisely describes which type of transactions should be in each account.

Chart of accounts—a listing of all the entity's accounts, which classifies transactions into individual balance sheet and income statement accounts.

Systems documentation The procedures for proper record-keeping should be spelled out in systems documentation (in a manual or company intranet) to encourage consistent application. The documentation should provide enough information to facilitate adequate record-keeping and the maintenance of proper control over assets, and could include procedural manuals, software user manuals, program documentation, and computer operations procedures.

PHYSICAL AND LOGICAL CONTROL OVER ASSETS AND RECORDS If assets are left unprotected, they can be stolen. If records are not adequately protected, they can be duplicated, stolen, damaged, or lost. When a company is highly computerized, it is especially important to protect its computer equipment, programs, and data files. The equipment and programs are expensive and essential to operations. The data files are the records of the company and, if damaged, could be costly or even impossible to reconstruct.

An important type of protective measure for safeguarding physical assets and records is the use of physical precautions. An example is the use of storerooms for inventory to guard against pilferage. Fireproof safes and safety deposit vaults for the protection of assets such as currency and securities are other important physical safeguards.

We use three categories of controls related to safeguarding data-processing equipment, programs, and data files. As with other types of assets, *physical controls* are used to protect the computer facilities. Examples are locks on doors to the computer room and terminals, adequate storage space for software and data files to protect them from loss, and proper fire-extinguishing systems. Next, *logical access controls* deal with having software that ensures that only authorized people can use the equipment and have access to software and data files. An example is an online access password system. Finally, *backup and recovery procedures* are actions an organization can take in the event of a loss of equipment, programs, or data. For example, having a backup copy of programs and critical data files stored in a safe remote location together with information systems recovery procedures is important for maintaining business continuity.

INDEPENDENT CHECKS OF PERFORMANCE AND RECORDED DATA The last category of control activity is the careful and continuous review of the other controls, often referred to as **independent checks** on performance or internal verification. The need for independent checks arises because internal control tends to change over time unless there is a mechanism for frequent review. Personnel are likely to forget or intentionally fail to follow procedures or become careless unless someone observes and evaluates their performance.

An essential characteristic of the persons performing internal verification procedures is independence from the individuals originally responsible for preparing the data. The least expensive means of internal verification is the separation of duties in the manner previously discussed. For example, when the bank reconciliation is performed by a person independent of the accounting records and handling of cash, there is an opportunity for verification without incurring significant additional costs.

Computerized accounting systems can be designed so that many internal verification procedures can be automated as part of the system, such as separate addition of subsidiary files for agreement to general ledger totals.

Information and Communication

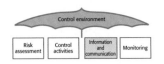

The purpose of an entity's **accounting information and communication systems** is to initiate, record, process, and report the entity's transactions and to maintain accountability for the related assets. An accounting information and communication system has several subcomponents, typically made up of classes of transactions such as sales, sales returns, cash receipts, acquisitions, and so on. For each class of transactions, the accounting system must satisfy all of the six transaction-related audit objectives identified earlier in Table 9-1. For example, the sales accounting system should be designed to ensure that all shipments of goods by a company are correctly recorded as sales (completeness and accuracy objectives) and are reflected in the financial statements in the proper period (cutoff objective). The system must also avoid duplicate recording of sales and recording a sale if a shipment did not occur (occurrence objective).

To understand the design of the accounting information system, the auditor determines (1) the major classes of transactions of the entity; (2) how those transactions are initiated and recorded; (3) what accounting records exist and their nature; (4) how the system captures other events that are significant to the financial statements, such as declines in asset values; and (5) the nature and details of the financial reporting process followed, including procedures to enter transactions and adjustments in the general ledger.

Monitoring

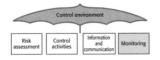

Monitoring activities deal with ongoing or periodic assessment of the quality of internal control performance by management to determine that controls are operating as intended and that they are modified as appropriate for changes in conditions. Information for assessment and modification comes from a variety of sources including studies of existing internal controls, internal auditor reports, exception reporting on control activities, reports by regulators such as the Office of the Superintendent of Financial Institutions, feedback from operating personnel, and complaints from customers about billing charges.

INTERNAL AUDIT FUNCTION For many companies, especially larger ones, a competent internal audit department is essential to effective monitoring of internal controls. For an internal audit function to be effective, it is important that the internal audit staff be independent of both the operating and accounting departments and that it report directly to a high level of authority within the organization, usually the audit committee of the board of directors.

In addition to its role in monitoring an entity's internal controls, an adequate internal audit staff can contribute to reduced external audit costs by providing direct assistance to the external auditor.

SIZE OF BUSINESS AND INTERNAL CONTROL The size of a company does have a significant effect on the nature of internal control activities and the specific monitoring controls. It is more difficult to establish adequate separation of duties in a small company. It would also be unreasonable to expect a small firm to have internal auditors. However, even though it may not be common to formalize policies in manuals, it is certainly possible for a small company to have competent, trustworthy personnel with clear lines of authority; proper procedures for authorization, execution, and recording of transactions; adequate documents, records, and reports; physical controls over assets and records; and, to a limited degree, checks on performance.

A major control available in a small company is the knowledge and concern of the top operating person, who is frequently an owner-manager. Knowledge about and having a personal interest in the organization and a close relationship with the personnel (often called "executive controls") make possible careful evaluation of the competence of the employees and the effectiveness of the overall systems. For example, internal control can be significantly strengthened if the owner conscientiously performs such duties as signing all cheques after carefully reviewing supporting documents, reviewing bank reconciliations, examining accounts-receivable statements sent to customers, approving credit, examining all correspondence from customers and vendors, and approving the write off of bad debts.

SUMMARY OF INTERNAL CONTROL A description of the COSO components of internal control discussed in the preceding sections (control environment, risk assessment, control activities, information and communication, monitoring) is included in Table 9-7 with examples.

concept check

C9-6 Can a small business implement all five COSO internal control levels? Why or why not?

C9-7 Which of the five categories of COSO internal controls is most important? Justify your response.

Table 9-7	COSO Components of Internal Control	

Internal Control		
Component	**Description of Component**	**Examples**
Control environment	Actions, policies, and procedures that reflect the overall attitude of top management, directors, and owners of an entity about internal control and its importance	• Commitment to competence • Board of director and audit committee participation • Management's philosophy and operating style • Organizational structure • Human resource policies and practices
Risk assessment	Management's identification and analysis of risks relevant to the preparation of financial statements in conformity with an applicable financial reporting framework	Risk assessment processes: • Identify factors affecting risks • Assess significance of risks and likelihood of occurrence • Determine actions necessary to manage risks Categories of management assertions that must be satisfied: • Assertions about classes of transactions and other events • Assertions about account balances • Assertions about presentation and disclosure
Control activities	Policies and procedures that management has established to meet its objectives for financial reporting	Types of specific control activities: • Adequate separation of duties • Proper authorization of transactions and activities • Adequate documents and records • Physical control over assets and records • Independent checks on performance
Information and communication	Methods used to initiate, record, process, and report an entity's transactions and to maintain accountability for related assets	Transaction-related audit objectives that must be satisfied: • Occurrence • Completeness • Accuracy • Cutoff • Classification
Monitoring	Management's ongoing and periodic assessment of the quality of internal control performance to determine whether controls are operating as intended and are modified when needed	• Review department exception reports • Conduct annual employee evaluations

③ IT (Information Technology) Governance and the Audit of General Information Systems Controls

As shown in Figure 9-3, IT governance needs to be considered in terms of the organization's overall mission, vision, and business strategy. After discussing IT governance, we will look at the relationship between general information systems controls and the financial statement audit planning process. IT governance would be assessed by the auditor in Phase 2 of the audit process, as part of understanding the client's business (management and governance).

IT Governance

IT governance is the overall process that enables an organization to provide information systems resources that meet business needs. It starts with the control environment and moves down to control activities that manage acquisition of resources and monitoring such as keeping the disaster recovery plan current. Accomplishing IT governance means that responsible management needs to have the authority and methodologies to accomplish the organization's IT goals.

In addition to adding value, the goal of IT governance is to help prevent disastrous failures, such as information systems implementations that make transaction processing cumbersome or too costly. IT governance rests within a coherent information systems strategy that is developed and aligned with the organizational strategy and culture and updated as necessary.

IT governance is a crucial subset of corporate governance. Similar to the assessment of overall corporate governance, evaluation of IT governance starts with the cultural and operating environment of the management information systems (MIS) functional areas. MIS should be viewed as a partner within the business rather than an adversary or servant. **IT dependence** should be avoided. Such dependence occurs when there is a disconnection between the business strategy and the MIS operations, exhibited when senior management, such as other executives and the board, abdicate

IT governance—the policies, practices, and procedures that help IT resources add value while considering costs and benefits.

IT dependence—a disconnection between the business strategy and the MIS operations.

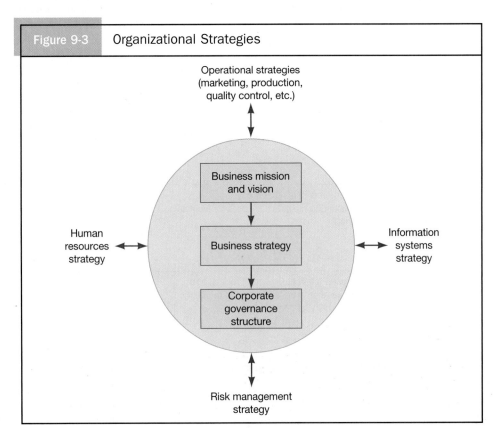

| Figure 9-3 | Organizational Strategies |

Auditing Security Policies

It seems that wherever you look, there are security breaches or attempted attacks on private data involving hundreds of thousands or even millions of individuals. In early 2011, Sony experienced several breaches—exposing data of more than 75 million customers. In December 2011, Mark Zuckerberg, the founder of Facebook, had his Facebook account hacked. Even a website that specializes in security, DigiNotar in Holland, which issues security certificates, was hacked—with the result that phony digital certificates were issued. Organizations must be increasingly vigilant and keep current with their security policies.

When considering an organization's security policy, the auditor will look at several characteristics:

1. *Is the policy comprehensive?* For example, does it consider regulatory requirements (such as privacy laws), security threats that are linked to the enterprise's risk assessments, and all of the different types of information systems in use at the organization?

2. *Is the policy current?* In addition to new technologies and software, the organization needs to update the policy for changes in laws and regulations, consider new threats (such as new viruses), and update its software (perhaps due to updates in data encryption practices).

3. *Has the policy been communicated?* Using the COSO framework, information and communication means that employees have been trained, the policy has been implemented, and this communication is part of controls and monitoring.

4. *Is it compulsory?* Practices that are optional likely will not be in use. Controls and business practices should help make the policy a routine part of organizational life.

5. *Is it realistic?* The security policy should have a broad set of principles that can readily be converted into controls and actions that can be implemented by the systems and people of the organization.

The internal or external auditor charged with evaluation of the security policy will look at each of the above characteristics and design tests that will help examine them.

Sources: 1. Associated Press. "Hackers hit security in Dutch cyber-raid," *Toronto Star*, September 6, 2011, p. B4. 2. Chandra, Ishwar, "The five C's of IT policy," *Internal Auditor*, December 2008, p. 23-23. 3. Kopun, Francine, "Into the Breach," *Toronto Star*, December 8, 2011,, p. B1;4.Zeffer, Kim, "FBI Arrests U.S. Suspect in LulzSec Sony Hack: Anonymous Also Targeted," September 22, 2011, **www.wired.com**, Accessed: January 26, 2012.

---

supervision of IT. This tends to result in the reliance upon a small group of individuals within the organization for MIS needs, requirements, or operations. Instead, the CIO (chief information officer) should be a participant in executive meetings, with feedback, decision making, and information flowing among members of the executive team and other parts of the organization. There should be an absence of political games with respect to IT and other resources within the organization. For example, a history of failed, over-budget, or problematic information systems implementations could be an indication of inadequate management of issues such as data ownership and succession planning associated with IT.

The use of an information systems steering committee with executive membership helps guide and oversee MIS processes. Control and audit are considered throughout the development, operations, and maintenance of systems. For example, for e-commerce systems or business functions that make extensive use of other online systems, reconciliation, audit, and testing capabilities should be built into systems, rather than added on after development is complete.

A value realization and delivery framework helps the MIS department to accomplish both the demand and supply side of operations. As each system is considered and evaluated, there should be continuous assessment for alignment with the business needs and strategies. Purchasing or implementing systems simply because they are the "newest toy on the block" results in fragmented, inefficient processing. However, environmental scanning with respect to new technologies adopted or available can help the organization identify obsolescence or other factors that could require IT changes.

Examination and assessment of MIS throughout the systems life cycle can be facilitated by internal audit or by rotational testing by the external auditors. Operational objectives such as effectiveness, efficiency, and economy are used. The organization could develop or purchase metrics to monitor and control the value assessment process.

Impact of General Information Systems Controls on the Planning Phases of the Audit

Let us look at audit issues in each of the three general control categories described in Table 9-6.

ORGANIZATION AND MANAGEMENT CONTROLS The method of organizing and managing the organization will vary based upon factors such as overall size, the functions that are outsourced, and whether the organization has packaged off-the-shelf programs or customized software. Packaged software will have fewer programming errors, and normally cannot be altered by the client, increasing the potential reliance on accuracy of programming. The nature and organization of the hardware technology supporting the organization are also a factor: for example, mainframe versus local area networks, methods of data communications, and presence of web-based purchasing or sales networks will affect the type of security controls that should be in place.

When documenting their understanding of internal controls, auditors will consider segregation of duties (discussed in Chapter 5), and the quality of documented policies and procedures affecting topics such as data ownership, data management, software ownership, privacy, and code of conduct with respect to technology. The auditor will also consider the level of technical expertise present at the organization and the access rights of specialized jobs such as database management, operating systems software support, operations job control specialists, security officers, privacy officers, business continuity coordinators, web masters, and specialized expertise in a variety of programs or programming languages.

A key question to ask is, "which personnel are super-users?" Super-users are individuals who, because of their expertise and function, have access to supervisory software or the ability to circumvent normal controls due to their expertise. For example, an operating systems software specialist works with operating systems and technical utilities, changing security features, utility software, and the programming languages processed by the system. Such a person can circumvent security software. Another typical super-user is the person or team that manages security, passwords, and user access. Such individuals could set up a new user account under an assumed name that gives them access to all systems, with the potential to change their own wage rate or set up fictitious customers or suppliers. Super-users are also common in small businesses with limited segregation of duties.

Management needs to be aware of the risks associated with super-users so that effective compensating controls can be established (such as careful independent review of payroll wage rates and customer credit limits). The auditor aware of such risks will increase the control risks associated with affected assertions and look for such compensating controls. Read Audit Challenge 9-2 on the next page, which overviews Hillsburg Hardware's general controls. Were there any super-users for either the old or current configurations?

SYSTEMS, ACQUISITION, DEVELOPMENT, AND MAINTENANCE CONTROLS Organizations employ a wide variety of software serving a broad range of purposes, such as providing the user interface, providing security, managing hardware and software, communicating information, and recording and processing transactions. Here, we focus on the process used to obtain software that serves the organization's needs.

Hillsburg Hardware Limited in Transition

BACK in 1995, when Hillsburg Hardware Limited had only 50 customers, the industry standard of a local area network with a single central server was more than adequate. All software consisted of standard packaged software. There were no onsite data processing personnel, and operating functions were shared among accounting and general staff. The receptionist was responsible for initiating backup before she left in the evening and the general manager kept a copy offsite at his home. The controller was responsible for maintaining password security profiles that controlled access rights. General controls were as follows:

- *Organization and management controls* Management had a policy of establishing segregation of duties as much as possible with the existing personnel. Functions considered incompatible with respect to financial systems were separated.
- *Systems acquisition, development, and maintenance controls* All software used was packaged software. The software was used in its original form (not modified). Software was obtained only in object code (machine language), so it could not be modified by Hillsburg Hardware personnel.
- *Operations and information systems support* Company offices were open from 8:00 a.m. to 5:00 p.m. The network was left up and running 24 hours per day. A maintenance contract was kept with a major support organization to provide onsite support in the event of equipment failure. Staff were initially trained in the software packages used and had software manuals to refer to in the event of queries. The controller prepared a set of instructions (about three pages) to be used in the event that a major disaster destroyed the building and the local area network. These instructions were intended to allow Hillsburg Hardware Limited personnel to resume operations at a local area network owned by their support organization for a fee of $500 per hour.

Two years ago, Hillsburg finally updated its aging collection of systems to an integrated database management system running on a mid-range minicomputer as the main server. Smaller servers were introduced to host email and office management products (such as word processing and spreadsheets). More sophisticated packaged accounting software was acquired, with support provided by the software supplier. Data in the databases can be exported into spreadsheet files so that staff can prepare their own reports if needed.

The company now has over 200 workstations (a combination of microcomputers and specialized cash registers) updating information and accessing the storage systems attached to the minicomputer, and three full-time information systems personnel. The information systems manager works on and supervises a range of functions, such as technical support for staff and clients and updating the website. The website was custom developed, but maintenance is handled internally. Passwords are maintained by the controller's executive assistant.

To maintain security, data from the ONHAND (Online Niche-Hardware Availability Notification Database) customer database is ported across to a group of stand-alone high-end microcomputers every night so that customers can inquire about the availability of products and the status of their orders via the internet. Internet access by customers is handled via an ISP (Internet Service Provider). Hillsburg decided that there would be no direct data communications access from the minicomputer and from staff computers—a small group of machines is available for staff to check email. This machine configuration is also used for electronic data interchange transactions between Hillsburg and 10 key suppliers. Transactions are copied to and from the minicomputer systems three times per day.

- *Current organization and management controls* There has been no change in policy. Duties are segregated as much as practical. Information systems support personnel do not have access to accounting data.
- *Current systems acquisition, development, and maintenance controls* Accounting software is still packaged software, maintained externally. Information systems personnel cannot change the accounting software. The website and the electronic data interchange software are maintained internally. Changes to these two pieces of software must be approved jointly by the chief financial officer and the vice-president, operations.
- *Current operations and information systems support* All systems have current anti-virus software, and firewalls are in place for the group of internet-accessible machines. Company offices are now open from 7:00 a.m. to 6:00 p.m. All systems are left up and running 24 hours a day. There is a more comprehensive backup and disaster recovery plan. Selected staff walk through this plan as a test every six months to ensure that systems changes have been accounted for. There are maintenance plans for all purchased hardware and software.

CRITICAL THINKING QUESTIONS

1. Describe IT governance controls that should be in place at Hillsburg Hardware Limited. State the purpose of each control that you describe.
2. List general controls present for the current systems at Hillsburg Hardware Limited for each general control category. For each control, state the risk that the control mitigates and how the auditor would test the control.
3. Identify apparent or potential control weaknesses for the current systems at Hillsburg Hardware Limited. What risks are associated with these weaknesses? What compensating controls would you look for?

Information Technology Control Guidelines[1] breaks down the software acquisition process into three general categories:

- In-house development (employees within the entity determine user requirements and build the software using one of many alternative development approaches).
- Systems acquisition (software is acquired from an outside vendor and implemented as is, or modified and implemented).
- Turnkey software development (custom software development is contracted to an outside party).

When understanding the client's business and controls, the auditor will document the processes used to acquire information technology and look for controls to ensure that systems acquired or maintained produce reliable financial data. Where custom program development is routinely undertaken, formal methodologies with appropriate checkpoints should exist, as should a method of evaluating systems once they have been implemented. Policies to monitor ongoing program changes should also exist. When software systems are purchased, management should ensure that the software is consistent with organizational objectives.

Table 9-8	Impact of Information Systems on Financial Statement Audit Phases
Audit Phase	**Example of Impact of Automation on Audit Process**
Risk Assessment	
1. Preplanning	• Identify availability of specialist expertise in the audit staff.
2. Client risk profile	• Understand information systems hardware and software infrastructure. • Document and assess IT governance processes.
3. Plan the audit	• Document and assess IT control environment including IT general controls and disaster recovery plans. • Test general controls where reliance is intended. • Document and assess key automated and combined application controls; consider each application separately to ensure adequate controls, such as segregation of duties, are in place, using passwords or other techniques.
Risk Response	
4. Design further audit procedures	• Design audit programs, considering the use of computer-assisted audit techniques and the ability to access data in client files.
5. Tests of control	• Test automated and combined application controls where reliance is intended. • Consider use of computer-assisted audit techniques for tests of controls (such as the use of test data and integrated test facilities).
6. Substantive tests	• Conduct substantive or dual-purpose tests by means of direct access to client data files (consider the use of spreadsheet software, generalized audit software, or specialized report writers).
7. Ongoing evaluation, quality control, and final evidence gathering	• Ongoing evaluation should incorporate team meetings and recommendations from IT specialists assigned to the engagement.
Reporting	
8. Complete quality control and issue auditor's report	• Consider independent information systems specialist review for high-risk engagements.

[1] *Information Technology Control Guidelines*, 3rd Edition, 1998, published by the Canadian Institute of Chartered Accountants.

Impact of information systems on the eight-phase audit process Every audit that you encounter will likely have heavily automated systems, with some advanced issues, such as data communications, web-based sales or purchasing, in-house custom development, or enterprise-wide processing (also called enterprise resource processing).

Table 9-8 on the previous page lists the audit phases, with examples of the impact of automation on the audit process. The main points from Table 9-8 are the reliance on and integration of findings from information systems audit specialists for quality of IT governance, general controls, and use of advanced methods of testing automated or combined information systems controls. Specialists could be used to develop or run computer-assisted audit techniques.

concept check

C9-8 Provide two examples of effective IT governance practices.

C9-9 List the three categories of general controls. For each category, provide an example of an audit step that could be conducted.

C9-10 List two tasks that information systems audit specialists could complete during the financial statement audit.

④ Internal Controls and the Audit Process

Overview of Internal Controls and the Audit Process

Figure 9-4 describes the steps involved in auditing internal controls. First, we need to understand and document the relevant internal controls (those that have an impact on the financial statements) before evaluating the design effectiveness, which helps us decide which controls could be tested or where there could be gaps (weaknesses) in control systems. This information allows the auditor to assess control risk and consider control risk together with inherent risk to identify potential risks of material misstatement. If the auditor relies on internal controls, tests of controls are designed and executed, then evaluated. The results of the evaluation could result in re-assessment of risks or reporting to management, which could also result in redesign of audit tests.

1. OBTAIN AN UNDERSTANDING OF RELEVANT CONTROLS

Reasons for understanding internal control sufficient to plan the examination The auditor must obtain understanding of the client's internal control sufficient to plan the examination for every audit and to assess risks. This includes documenting internal controls that could prevent or detect fraud. Refer to the inside front cover of this text: understanding internal control occurs during Phases 1 through 3. The extent of that understanding must, at a minimum, be sufficient to adequately plan the examination in terms of four specific planning matters.

Auditability The auditor must obtain information about the integrity of management and the nature and extent of the accounting records to be satisfied that sufficient appropriate audit evidence is available to support the financial statement balances and the auditor's report. This decision will be made during Phase 1, prior to client acceptance or continuance, and reassessed as the audit continues.

Potential material misstatements The understanding should allow the auditor to identify the types of potential errors or fraud and other irregularities that might affect the financial statements and to assess the risk that such misstatements might occur in amounts that are material to the financial statements.

Planned detection risk Control risk in the planning form of the audit risk model directly affects detection risk for each audit objective [PDR = AR / (IR × CR)]. Information about internal control is used to assess control risk for each control objective, which, in turn, affects planned detection risk and planned audit evidence.

Design of tests The information obtained should allow the auditor to design effective tests of the financial statement balances (or transactions or disclosures) for each audit assertion. Such tests include tests for monetary correctness of transactions and balances, as well as analytical procedures. These are discussed in more detail in the next chapter.

Understanding the components of internal controls Relevant controls from each of the components of internal control must be studied, understood, and documented.

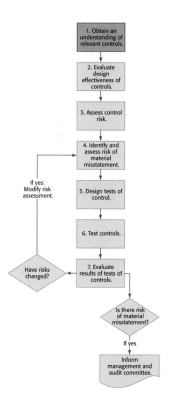

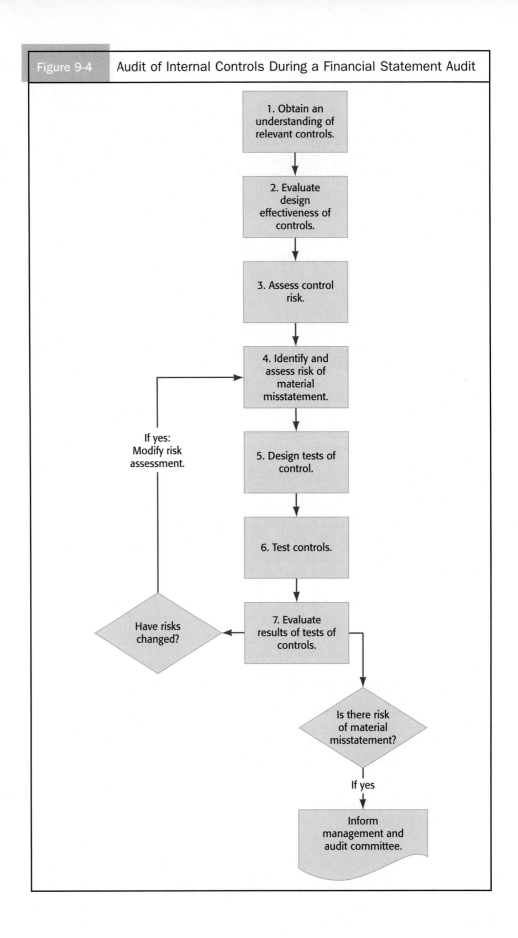

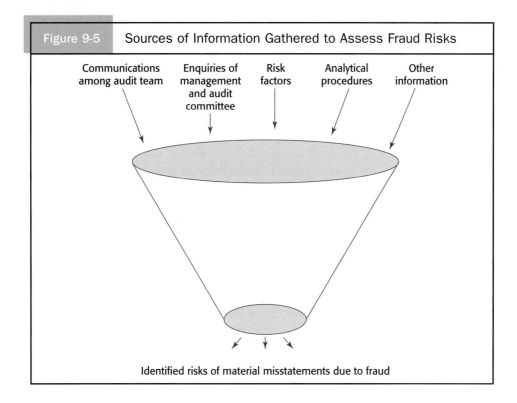

Figure 9-5   Sources of Information Gathered to Assess Fraud Risks

As part of this process, the auditor assesses whether controls actually appear to be in place as described, for example by asking for an example of the control or by selecting a small sample and testing the control.

During this process, the auditor will also look for potential fraud risks. Figure 9-5 illustrates how information gathered throughout this understanding phase is used to assess fraud risks. This information is considered in the context of the three conditions for fraud: incentives/pressures, opportunities, and attitudes/rationalization. Auditors should consider the following:

- Information obtained from communications among audit team members about their knowledge of the company and its industry, including how and where the company might be susceptible to material misstatements due to fraud.
- Responses to auditor inquiries of management about its risk management process, including views of the risks of fraud and about existing programs and controls to address specific identified fraud risks.
- Specific risk factors for fraudulent financial reporting, revenue recognition, and misappropriation of assets.
- Analytical procedures results obtained during planning that indicate possible, implausible, or unexpected analytical relationships.
- Knowledge obtained through other procedures, such as client acceptance and retention decisions, interim review of financial statements, and consideration of inherent or control risks.

Understanding the control environment   Information is obtained about the control environment for each of the subcomponents discussed. The auditor then uses the understanding as a basis for assessing management's and the directors' attitudes and awareness about the importance of control. For example, the auditor might determine the nature of a client's budgeting system for the company as a whole (which applies to multiple departments) as a part of understanding the design of the control environment. The description of the budgeting system might be obtained in part by (1) inquiry of budgeting personnel to determine budgeting procedures and (2) follow-up of differences between budget and actual amounts. The auditor might also examine client schedules comparing actual results to budgets and ask about the monitoring of variances that is done.

Understanding general controls The nature and level of complexity of automation in the information systems used at the organization will affect the amount of effort required by the auditor to understand general controls. The auditor obtains information about the organizational structure of the information systems processing department, and the hardware and software configuration of computing systems, and a general description of the types of automated systems in use. This information is used to plan the extent of work required to understand general controls. For example, if the organization has programmers on staff and many of its financial systems use customized software, then the auditor will need to spend time documenting the processes used to authorize, design, test, implement, and change such software.

Understanding the accounting system To understand the design of the accounting system, the auditor determines (1) the major classes of transactions of the entity; (2) how those transactions are initiated; (3) what accounting records and data files exist and their nature; (4) how transactions are processed from initiation to completion, including a description of processing handled by computer programs; and (5) the nature and details of the financial reporting process followed. Typically, this is accomplished and documented by a narrative description of the system or by flowcharting. The operation of the accounting system is often determined by tracing one or a few transactions through the accounting system (called a **transaction walk-through**).

Transaction walk-through—the tracing of selected transactions through the accounting system.

Understanding the control activities Auditors obtain an understanding of the control environment, general computer controls, and accounting system in a similar manner for most audits, but obtaining an understanding of control activities varies. For smaller clients, it is common to identify few or even no control activities because controls are often ineffective due to limited personnel. In that case, a high assessed level of control risk is used; that is, control risk is assessed at the maximum of 100 percent. For clients with extensive controls where the auditor believes controls are likely to be excellent, it is often appropriate to identify many relevant controls during the controls understanding phase before deciding on the key controls to be tested. The extent to which controls are identified is a matter of audit judgment. The key part of this process is obtaining enough understanding so that controls can be understood for each audit assertion, allowing for design of audit tests.

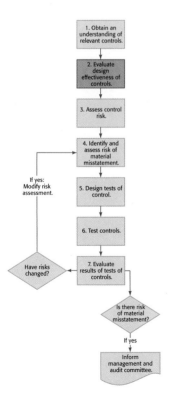

2. EVALUATE DESIGN EFFECTIVENESS OF CONTROLS FOR RISK ASSESSMENT Once an understanding of internal control that is sufficient for audit planning is obtained, two major assessments must be made.

Assess whether the financial statements are auditable The first assessment is whether the entity is auditable. The factors that determine auditability are the control environment, with reference to corporate governance structures and an emphasis on the integrity of management, and the adequacy of accounting methods. Many audit procedures rely to some extent on the representations of management. For example, it is difficult for the auditor to evaluate whether inventory is obsolete or identify all related parties without honest and complete information from management. If management lacks integrity, management may provide false representations causing the auditor to rely on unreliable evidence.

The accounting records serve as a direct source of audit evidence for most audit objectives. If the accounting records are deficient, necessary audit evidence may not be available. For example, if the client has not kept duplicate sales invoices and vendors' invoices or data files have become corrupted, it would normally not be possible to do an audit. Unless the auditor can identify an alternative source of reliable evidence, or unless appropriate records can be constructed for the auditor's use, the only recourse may be to consider the entity unauditable.

When it is concluded that the entity is not auditable, the auditor discusses the circumstances with the client (usually at the highest level) and either withdraws from the engagement or issues a disclaimer form of auditor's report (discussed further in Chapter 20).

Consider design effectiveness of controls Documentation of internal controls includes assessing controls by applying audit assertions to transaction streams. Where the auditor has identified accounts that cannot be tested only by substantive tests, the auditor will also have documented internal controls for those accounts.

During examination of design effectiveness, the auditor:

1. Considers whether relevant controls are present for all relevant assertions and to prevent or detect fraud.
2. Evaluates which controls are more important for the relevant assertions (these are key controls).
3. Examines potential weaknesses in internal control to determine whether there are compensating controls (alternative controls).

3. ASSESS CONTROL RISK The auditor assesses control risk at the assertion level and also at the financial statement level overall. The following discussion looks at the reasoning involved in assessing control risk.

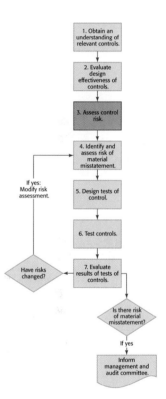

Determine the level of control risk supported by the understanding obtained After obtaining an understanding of internal control, the auditor makes an initial assessment of control risk. Control risk is a measure of the auditor's expectation that internal controls will neither prevent material misstatements from occurring nor detect and correct them if they have occurred.

The initial assessment is made for each transaction-related audit objective for each major type of transaction. For example, the auditor makes an assessment of the occurrence objective for sales and a separate assessment for the completeness objective. There are different ways to express this expectation. Some auditors use a subjective expression such as high, moderate, or low. Others use numerical probabilities such as 1.0, 0.6, or 0.2.

The initial assessment usually starts with consideration of the control environment and then of general computer controls. If the attitude of management is that control is unimportant, it is doubtful that general controls or detailed control activities will be reliable. If general controls are inadequate, then the individual automated systems affecting the transaction cycles will not be reliable. The best course of action in that case is to assume that control risk for all transaction-related audit objectives is at maximum (such as high or 1.0). On the other hand, if management's attitude is positive, the auditor then considers the specific policies and procedures within the control environment, the accounting system, and control activities. Those policies and procedures are used as a basis for an assessment below maximum.

There are two important considerations about the assessment. First, the flow of reasoning needs to be documented with adequate support. In many audits, particularly of smaller companies, the auditor assumes that the control risk is at maximum whether or not it actually is. The auditor's reason for taking this approach is that he or she has concluded that it is more economical to audit the financial statement balances more extensively rather than to conduct tests of controls. This conclusion is reached after a clear understanding of the internal controls is obtained, which is a requirement under GAAS. Second, when the auditor believes control risk is lower, the level of control risk assessed must match the evidence obtained. For example, suppose the auditor believes that control risk for unrecorded sales is low but has gathered little evidence in support of control activities for the completeness objective. The auditor's assessment of control risk for unrecorded sales must then be either moderate or high. It could be low only if additional evidence were obtained in support of the pertinent controls.

Decide on the appropriate assessed control risk The auditor can choose to set control risk based upon the quality of the controls (for example, at low or medium), or could set control risk higher (i.e., not rely upon the controls) and do substantive testing instead. This recognizes the trade-off between the costs of testing relevant controls and the costs of substantive tests that would be avoided by reducing assessed control risk. Assume, for example, that for the occurrence and accuracy transaction-related audit objectives for sales, the auditor believes that the cost of confirming accounts receivable could be reduced by $5,000 by incurring $2,000 to support a lower assessed control risk. Then, it is worth testing controls since the overall cost of the audit will be lower.

Where the client uses paperless systems or advanced automated processes such as electronic data interchange, the auditor may be required to rely upon internal controls. Then, the cost-benefit decision is applied among alternative tests of controls rather than choosing between tests of controls and tests of details.

4. IDENTIFY AND ASSESS RISK OF MATERIAL MISSTATEMENT

Financial statement level During the understanding of internal control, the auditor should keep an eye out for potential pervasive factors that could result in a risk of material misstatement at the financial statement level. For example, if there is a new information system being installed and there are insufficient general controls over the conversion of information from the old system to the new system, the auditor may need to conduct additional tests of details to test whether material errors occurred during the implementation of the new system. The auditor is required to consider revenue recognition as a significant risk, which would be highlighted if management has a bias to overstate income to meet publicized earnings targets.

Assertion level The auditor will consider those assertions where there is the greatest likelihood of material misstatement if the controls are not functioning. For example, if there are many sales at each month end, then the auditor might consider that cutoff and completeness need to be carefully considered at the year end.

The auditor may have identified individual audit assertions for an account or risks at the financial statement level where controls do not exist or were found to be implemented in a manner that still results in the potential for misstatements. The auditor will also consider inherent risks in making this assessment. These risks will be discussed with management as well as considered during the design of both tests of controls and tests of details.

5. AND 6. DESIGN AND CONDUCT TESTS OF CONTROLS
Assessing control risk requires the auditor to consider the design of controls to evaluate whether they would be effective in meeting specific transaction-related audit objectives. In order to use specific relevant controls as a basis for assessing control risk below maximum, specific evidence must be obtained about their effectiveness throughout all (or most) of the period under audit. The procedures to gather evidence about design and use in operation during the understanding phase are called **procedures to obtain an understanding**. The procedures to test effectiveness of controls in support of assessing control risk below maximum are called **tests of controls**.

7. EVALUATE RESULTS; INTEGRATE WITH PLANNED DETECTION RISK AND SUBSTANTIVE TESTS
The result of the preceding steps is the determination of the assessed level of control risk by audit objective for each of the entity's major transaction types. Where the assessed level of control risk is below maximum, it will be supported by specific tests of controls. These assessments are then related to the balance-related audit objectives and disclosure-related audit objectives for the accounts and disclosures affected by the major transaction types. The appropriate level of detection risk for each balance-related and disclosure-related audit objective is then determined using the audit risk model.

Where the results of tests of controls support the design of controls as expected, the auditor uses the same assessed control risk. If, however, the tests of controls indicate the controls did not operate effectively, the assessed level of control risk (and the potential

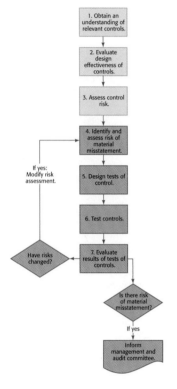

Procedures to obtain an understanding—procedures used by the auditor to gather evidence about the design and implementation of specific controls.

Tests of controls—audit procedures to test the effectiveness of controls in support of control risk assessed below maximum.

effect on the risks of material misstatements) must be reconsidered. For example, the tests may indicate that frequent program changes occurred during the year or that the person applying the control made frequent errors. Then a higher assessed level of control risk would be used unless additional controls relating to the same transaction-related audit objectives could be identified and found to be effective.

The reconsideration could result in different tests of controls or changes to the planned tests of details. Any internal control weakness that could result in a material misstatement must be documented and communicated to management and those charged with governance (such as the audit committee).

AUDIT PROCEDURES AND THEIR DOCUMENTATION Now that we have reviewed the process of auditing internal controls during a financial statement audit, we will look more closely at internal control audit procedures and methods of documenting internal controls. There is an enormous amount of information that is collected and organized to obtain a useful picture of how an organization handles its information and processes. There are many different ways of collecting and displaying the controls found to enable useful assessment.

Procedures to Obtain the Necessary Understanding

In practice, the study of a client's internal control and assessment of control risk varies from client to client. For smaller clients, many auditors obtain a level of understanding sufficient only to assess whether the statements are auditable, evaluate the control environment for management's attitude, and determine the adequacy of the client's accounting system. Often, for efficiency, control activities are not tested, control risk is assumed to be maximum, and detection risk is therefore low. This approach is called a substantive audit approach.

For many larger clients, especially for repeat engagements, the auditor plans on a low assessed level of control risk for most parts of the audit before the audit starts. This approach is called a combined audit approach. The auditor has identified the risks of material misstatement and determined that internal controls can be relied on. The auditor next obtains an understanding of the control environment and the accounting system at a fairly detailed level. Then the auditor identifies relevant controls that will reduce control risk, makes an assessment of control risk, and finally tests the controls for effectiveness. The auditor can conclude that control risk is low only after all three steps are completed.

PROCEDURES RELATING TO UNDERSTANDING, DESIGN EFFECTIVENESS, AND IMPLEMENTATION The auditor's procedures to obtain an understanding of internal control attempt to find out about the elements of internal control, see that they have been implemented, and document the information obtained in a useful manner. The following are procedures relating to understanding, design effectiveness, and implementation.

Update and evaluate auditor's previous experience with the entity Most audits of a company are done annually by the same public accounting firm. Except for initial engagements, the auditor begins the audit with a great deal of information about the client's internal controls developed in prior years. Because systems and controls change infrequently, this information can be updated and carried forward to the current year's audit.

Make inquiries of client personnel A logical starting place for updating information carried forward from the previous audit or for obtaining information initially is with appropriate client personnel. Inquiries of client personnel at the management, supervisory, and staff level will usually be conducted as part of obtaining an understanding of the design of internal control. Care must be taken to document the information collected.

Read client's policy and systems manuals To design, implement, and maintain its internal controls, an entity must have extensive documentation of its own. This includes policy manuals and documents (e.g., a corporate code of conduct) and systems manuals and documents (e.g., an accounting manual and an organization chart). This information is studied by the auditor and discussed with company personnel to ensure that it is properly interpreted and understood.

Examine documents and records The control environment, the details of the accounting system, and the application of control activities will involve the creation of many documents and records. By inspecting actual completed documents and records, the auditor can bring the contents of the manuals to life and better understand them. Inspection also provides evidence that the control policies and procedures have been placed in operation.

For businesses with large volumes (such as hundreds of thousands or millions of transactions) or paperless systems, the auditor is likely to use computer-assisted tests and online viewing of transactions as an alternative to viewing paper documents.

Observe the entity's activities and operations In addition to inspecting completed documents and records, the auditor can observe client personnel in the process of preparing them and carrying out their normal accounting and control activities. When the client uses paperless systems, this may require the running of test transactions through the system to verify the understanding, or specialist computer audit assistance. This further enhances understanding and verifies that control policies and procedures have been implemented.

Observation, inspection of documents and records, and inquiry can be conveniently and effectively combined in the form of the transaction walk-through mentioned earlier. With that procedure, the auditor selects a few documents for the initiation of a transaction type and traces them through the entire accounting process. At each stage of processing, the auditor makes inquiries and observes current activities, in addition to inspecting completed documentation for the transactions selected.

DOCUMENTATION OF THE UNDERSTANDING Three commonly used methods of documenting the understanding of internal control are narratives, flowcharts, and internal control questionnaires. These may be used separately or in combination, as discussed below. The auditor will use those that are most efficient in the client circumstances; that is, for a simple system a narrative will be enough, whereas for a more complex system flowcharts are more effective. The internal control questionnaire is used to document auditor conclusions and provide cross-references to supporting documentation.

Narrative A **narrative** is a written description of a client's internal controls. A proper narrative of an accounting system and related controls includes four characteristics:

- *The origin of every document and record in the system.* For example, the description should state where customer orders come from and how sales invoices are prepared.
- *All processing that takes place.* For example, if sales amounts are determined by a computer program that multiplies quantities shipped by stored standard prices, that should be described.
- *The disposition of every document and record in the system.* The updating of computer files, method of storing of documents, and transferral to customers or discarding of documents should be described.
- An *indication of controls relevant to the assessment of control risk.* These typically include separation of duties (e.g., separating recording cash from handling cash), authorization and approvals (e.g., credit approvals), and the nature of internal verification (e.g., comparison of unit selling price to sales contracts).

Flowchart An internal control **flowchart** is a symbolic, diagrammatic representation of the client's documents and their sequential flow in the organization. An adequate flowchart includes the same four characteristics identified above for narratives.

Flowcharting is useful primarily because it can provide a concise overview of the client's system as an analytical tool in evaluation. A well-prepared flowchart aids in

Narrative—a written description of a client's internal controls, including the origin, processing, and disposition of documents and records, and the relevant control activities.

Flow chart—a diagrammatic representation of the client's documents and records, and the sequence in which they are processed.

identifying inadequacies by facilitating a clear understanding of how the system operates. For most uses, it is superior to narrative descriptions as a method of communicating the characteristics of a system, especially to show adequate separation of duties. It is easier to follow a diagram than to read a description. It is also usually easier to update a flowchart, particularly one that is stored electronically, than a narrative. Most auditor flowcharting is now completed using automated working-paper software. The auditor may also use the automated program or automated systems flowcharts that have been prepared by client software systems.

It would be unusual to use both a narrative and a flowchart to describe the same system, since both are intended to describe the flow of documents and records in an accounting system. Sometimes the combination of a flowchart with a supporting narrative is used. The decision to use one or the other or a combination of the two is dependent on two factors: relative ease of understanding by current- and subsequent-year auditors and relative cost of preparation.

Internal control questionnaire An **internal control questionnaire** asks a series of questions about the controls in each audit area, including the control environment, as a means of indicating to the auditor aspects of internal control that may be inadequate. In most instances, it is designed to require a "yes" or "no" response, with "no" responses indicating potential internal control deficiencies. Where automated working-paper software is used, the responses can be automatically linked and cross-referenced to supporting documentation and to weakness investigation working papers.

> **Internal control questionnaire**—a series of questions about the controls in each audit area used as a means of gaining an understanding of internal control.

The primary advantage of the questionnaire is the ability to cover each audit area thoroughly and reasonably quickly at the beginning of the audit. The primary disadvantage is that individual parts of the client's systems are examined without providing an overall view, although recently developed internal control documentation software overcomes this weakness. In addition, a standard questionnaire is often inapplicable to some audit clients, especially smaller ones.

Figure 9-6 on the next page illustrates part of an internal control questionnaire for the sales and collection cycle of Hillsburg Hardware Limited. The questionnaire is also designed for use with the five transaction-related audit objectives. Note that each objective (A through F) is part of a transaction-related objective as it applies to sales transactions (see shaded portions). The use of both questionnaires and flowcharts is highly desirable for understanding the client's system. Flowcharts provide an overview of the system, and questionnaires are useful checklists to remind the auditor of many different types of controls that should exist. When properly used, a combination of these two approaches should provide the auditor with an excellent description of the system.

It is often desirable to use the client's narratives or flowcharts and have the client fill out the internal control questionnaire, as long as any subsequent reliance on controls is adequately substantiated with testing. When understandable and reliable narratives, flowcharts, and questionnaires are not available from a client, which is frequently the case, the auditor must prepare them. Many auditors rely on electronic auditing tools, including industry-specific checklists and industry-specific flowcharting templates that can be completed and viewed electronically.

Assessing Control Risk

Once the auditor has obtained descriptive information and evidence in support of the design and operation of internal control, an **assessment of control risk** by transaction-related audit objective can be made. This is normally done separately for each major type of transaction in each transaction cycle. For example, in the sales and collection cycle, the types of transactions usually are sales, sales returns and allowances, cash receipts, and the provision for and write-off of uncollectable accounts.

> **Assessment of control risk**—a measure of the auditor's expectation that internal controls will neither prevent material misstatements from occurring nor detect and correct them if they have occurred; control risk is assessed for each transaction-related audit objective in a cycle or class of transactions.

IDENTIFY TRANSACTION-RELATED AUDIT OBJECTIVES The first step in the assessment is to identify the transaction-related audit objectives to which the assessment applies.

Figure 9-6 Partial Internal Control Questionnaire for Sales

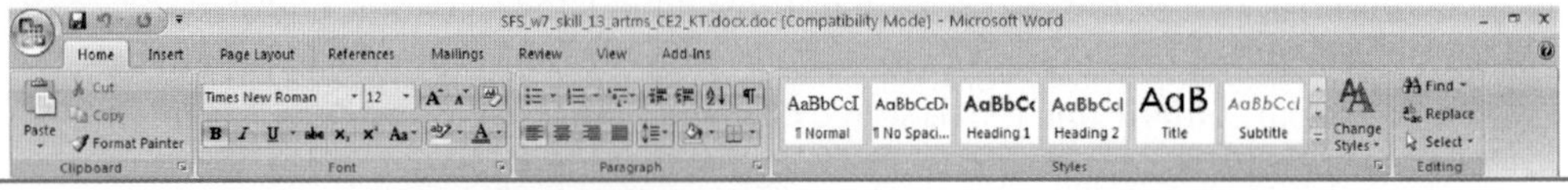

Client _Hillsburg Hardware Limited_ — Audit Date _12/31/11_

Auditor _MSW_   Date Completed _9/30/11_   Reviewed by _AR_   Date Completed _10/1/11_

Objective (shaded) and Question	Yes	No	N/A	Remarks
Sales				
A. Recorded sales are for shipments actually made to existing customers.				
1. Is customers' credit approved by a responsible official, and is access to change credit limit master files restricted?	✓			_Approved By Chief Financial Officer_
2. Is the recording of sales supported by authorized shipping documents and approved customer orders?	✓			_Pam Dilley examines underlying documentation._
3. Is there adequate separation of duties between billing, recording sales, and handling cash receipts?	✓			
4. Are sales invoices prenumbered and accounted for?		✓		_Prenumbered but not accounted for. Additional substantive testing required._
B. Existing sales transactions are recorded.				
1. Is a record of shipments maintained?	✓			
2. Are shipping documents controlled from the office in a manner that helps ensure that all shipments are billed?	✓			_By Pam Dilley_
3. Are shipping documents prenumbered and accounted for?	✓			
C. Recorded sales are for the amount of goods shipped and are correctly billed and recorded.				
1. Is there independent comparison of the quantity on the shipping documents to the sales invoices?	✓			
2. Is an authorized price list used, and is access to change the price master file restricted?	✓			
3. Are monthly statements sent to customers?	✓			
D. Sales transactions are properly included in the master files and are correctly summarized.				
1. Does the computer automatically post transactions to the accounts receivable master file and general ledger?	✓			
2. Is the accounts receivable master file reconciled with the general ledger on a monthly basis?	✓			_By Erma, the chief accountant_
E. Recorded sales transactions are properly classified.				
1. Is there independent comparison of recorded sales to the chart of accounts?			✓	_All sales are on account and there is only one sales account._
F. Sales are recorded on the correct dates.				
1. Is there independent comparison of dates on shipping documents to dates recorded?		✓		_Unmatched and unrecorded shippers are reviewed weekly._

This is done by applying the transaction-related audit objectives introduced earlier, which are stated in general form, to each major type of transaction for the entity.

IDENTIFY SPECIFIC RELEVANT CONTROLS The next step is to identify the specific relevant controls that contribute to accomplishing each transaction-related audit objective. The auditor identifies pertinent controls by proceeding through the descriptive information about the client's system. Those policies and procedures that, in his or her judgment, provide control over the transaction involved are identified. In doing this, it is often helpful to refer back to the types of controls that might exist and ask if they do exist. For example: Is there adequate segregation of duties, and how is it achieved? Are the documents used well designed? Are there controls over inputting to the computer system?

The auditor should identify and include those controls that are expected to have the greatest impact on meeting the transaction-related audit objectives. These are often termed **key controls**. The reason for including mainly key controls is that they will be sufficient to achieve the transaction-related audit objectives and should provide audit efficiency.

IDENTIFY AND EVALUATE WEAKNESSES **Internal control weaknesses** are defined as the absence of adequate controls, which increases the risk of misstatements existing in the financial statements. If, in the judgment of the auditor, there are inadequate controls to satisfy one of the transaction-related audit objectives, expectation increases of a misstatement occurring. For example, if no internal verification of the accuracy of payroll transactions is taking place, the auditor may conclude there is a weakness in internal control.

A four-step approach can be used for identifying significant internal control weaknesses.

Identify existing controls Because weaknesses are the absence of adequate controls, the auditor must first know which controls exist. The methods for identifying existing controls have already been discussed.

Identify the absence of key controls Internal control questionnaires, narratives, and flowcharts are useful to identify areas in which key controls are lacking and the likelihood of misstatements is increased. When control risk is assessed as moderate or high, there is usually an absence of controls.

Determine potential material misstatements that could result This step is intended to identify specific errors or fraud and other irregularities that are likely to result from the absence of controls. The importance of a weakness is proportionate to the magnitude of the errors or fraud and other irregularities that are likely to result from it.

Consider the possibility of compensating (or mitigating) controls A **compensating (or mitigating) control** is a control elsewhere in the system that offsets a weakness. Note that any control can be a compensating control. A common example in a smaller company is active involvement of the owner to compensate for lack of segregation of duties. When a compensating control exists, the weakness is no longer a concern because the potential for misstatement has been sufficiently reduced.

Figure 9-7 on the next page shows the documentation of weaknesses for the sales and collection cycle of Hillsburg Hardware Limited. The "Effect on Audit Evidence" column shows the effect of the weakness on the auditor's planned audit programs.

The Control Risk Matrix

Many auditors use a control matrix to assist in the control-risk assessment process. Most controls affect more than one transaction-related audit objective, and often several different controls affect a given transaction-related audit objective. These complexities make a **control risk matrix** a useful way to summarize and assess control risk.

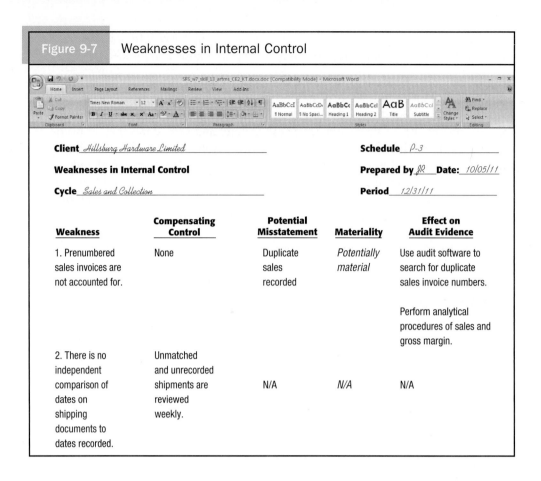

Figure 9-7   Weaknesses in Internal Control

Client _Hillsburg Hardware Limited_   Schedule _P-3_

Weaknesses in Internal Control   Prepared by _JR_ Date: _10/05/11_

Cycle _Sales and Collection_   Period _12/31/11_

Weakness	Compensating Control	Potential Misstatement	Materiality	Effect on Audit Evidence
1. Prenumbered sales invoices are not accounted for.	None	Duplicate sales recorded	_Potentially material_	Use audit software to search for duplicate sales invoice numbers. Perform analytical procedures of sales and gross margin.
2. There is no independent comparison of dates on shipping documents to dates recorded.	Unmatched and unrecorded shipments are reviewed weekly.	N/A	_N/A_	N/A

The control risk matrix matches key internal controls and internal control weaknesses with transaction-related audit objectives as a tool for assessing control risk.

Figure 9-8 illustrates the use of a control risk matrix for sales transactions of Hillsburg Hardware Limited. In constructing the matrix, the transaction-related audit objectives for sales were listed as column headings, and pertinent controls that were identified were listed as headings for the rows. In addition, where significant weaknesses were identified, they were also entered as row headings below the listing of key controls. The body of the matrix was then used to show how the controls contribute to the accomplishment of the transaction-related audit objectives and how weaknesses impact the objectives. In this illustration, a "C" was entered in each cell where a control partially or fully satisfied an objective, and a "W" was entered to show the impact of the weaknesses.

Assess Control Risk Once controls and weaknesses have been identified and matched to transaction-related audit objectives, there can be an assessment of control risk. Referring to Figure 9-8, the auditor assessed control risk for Hillsburg's sales by reviewing each column for pertinent controls and weaknesses, and asking, "What is the likelihood that a material misstatement of the type to be controlled would not be prevented or detected and corrected by these controls, and what is the impact of the weaknesses?" If the likelihood is high, then the control risk is high.

Link to risk of material misstatement and substantive testing Once control risk has been assessed, the auditor documents the effect on the risk of material misstatement by assertion and the effect on substantive testing. This is usually done by having a question either at the top or bottom of the checklist and the control risk assessment. For example, the internal control questionnaire would ask about the extent of intended reliance upon internal controls and which audit assertions had a potential for material misstatement; the control matrix would ask about the impact upon substantive testing or whether there were specific assertions that needed to be tested

Internal Control	Recorded sales are for shipments actually made to nonfictitious customers (occurrence).	Existing sales transactions are recorded (completeness).	Recorded sales are for the amount of goods shipped and are correctly billed and recorded (accuracy).	Sales transactions are properly included in the accounts receivable master file and are correctly summarized (accuracy).	Sales are recorded on the correct dates (cutoff).	Sales transactions are properly classified (classification).
Credit is approved automatically by computer by comparison to authorized credit limits (C1).	C					
Recorded sales are supported by authorized shipping documents and approved customer orders (C2).	C		C			
Separation of duties for billing, recording of sales, and handling of cash receipts (C3).	C	C		C		
Shipping documents are forwarded to billing daily and are billed on the subsequent day (C4).	C				C	
Shipping documents are prenumbered and accounted for weekly (C5).		C			C	
Batch totals of quantities shipped are compared with quantities billed (C6).	C	C	C			
Unit selling prices are obtained from the price list master file of approved prices (C7).			C			
Sales transactions are internally verified (C8).						C
Statements are mailed to customers each month (C9).	C		C	C		
Computer automatically posts transactions to the accounts receivable subsidiary records and to the general ledger (C10).				C		
Accounts receivable master file is reconciled to the general ledger on a monthly basis (C11).				C		
There is a lack of internal verification for the possibility of sales invoices being recorded more than once (W1).	W					
There is a lack of control to test for timely recording (W2).					W	
Assessed control risk	Medium	Low	Low	Low	High	Low*

*Because there are no cash sales, classification is not a problem.
C = Control; W = Weakness.
Note: This matrix was developed using an internal control questionnaire, part of which is included in Figure 9-3 (page 262), as well as flowcharts and other documentation of the auditor's understanding of internal control. Weaknesses are carried to an investigation sheet, shown in Figure 9-4 (page 280), for assessment.

because substantive testing was not sufficient for that audit assertion. See Figures 9-6 and 9-7 for examples.

Figure 9-7 (page 290) shows that the auditor has considered the two weaknesses in the control matrix. The first risk could lead to a potential material misstatement, so the auditor will conduct additional audit tests to quantify the potential effect. The second apparent weakness has a compensating control, so it is then no longer a weakness—the

Figure 9-9	Internal Control Letter

CHESLEY & BEDARD
Chartered Accountants
2016 Village Boulevard
Ottawa, Ontario K1S 5B6

February 12, 2012

Audit Committee
Airtight Machine Inc.
1729 Athens Street
Ottawa, Ontario K1N 6N5

In planning and performing our audit of the financial statements of Airtight Machine Inc. for the year ended December 31, 2011, we considered its internal control in order to determine our auditing procedures for the purpose of expressing our opinion on the financial statements and not to provide assurance on internal control. However, we noted certain matters involving internal control and its operation that we consider to be of such significance that we believe they should be reported to you. The matters being reported involve circumstances coming to our attention relating to significant deficiencies in the design or operation of internal control that, in our judgment, could adversely affect the organization's ability to record, process, summarize, and report financial data consistent with the assertions of management in the financial statements.

The matter noted is that there is a lack of independent verification of the data entry of the customer's name, product number, and quantity shipped on sales invoices and credit memos. As a consequence, errors in these activities could occur and remain uncorrected, adversely affecting both recorded net sales and accounts receivable. This deficiency is particularly significant because of the large size of the average sale of Airtight Machine Inc.

This report is intended solely for the information and use of the audit committee, board of directors, management, and others in Airtight Machine Inc.

Very truly yours,

Chesley & Bedard

Chesley & Bedard

control matrix would be updated, and the "W" changed to a "C" with the compensating internal control that "unmatched and unrecorded shipments are reviewed weekly."

Internal control letter and related matters During the course of obtaining an understanding of the client's internal control and assessing control risk, auditors obtain information that is of interest to the audit committee in fulfilling its responsibilities. Generally, such information concerns significant deficiencies in the design or operation of internal control (weaknesses).

CAS

AUDIT COMMITTEE COMMUNICATIONS According to CAS 265, the auditor is required to communicate material internal control weaknesses in writing to "the audit committee or equivalent." If the client does not have an audit committee, then the communication should go to the person (or persons) in the organization who has (have) overall responsibility for internal control, such as the board of directors or the owner-manager. An illustrative **internal control letter** communicates these significant internal control weaknesses and is shown in Figure 9-9.

MANAGEMENT LETTERS In addition to significant weaknesses in internal control, auditors often observe less significant internal control-related matters as well as opportunities for the client to make operational improvements. These types of matters should also be communicated to the client. The form of communication is often a separate letter for that purpose, called a **management letter**, which communicates less significant weaknesses or potential operational improvements to management. This letter

Internal control letter—a letter from the auditor to the audit committee or senior management detailing significant weaknesses in internal control.

Management letter—the auditor's written communication to management to point out less significant weaknesses in internal control and possibilities for operational improvements.

needs to be clearly identified as a derivative report to indicate that the purpose of the engagement was not to determine weaknesses in internal control but that they were identified as a by-product of the audit. The letter would also indicate that the auditors may not have found all weaknesses.

Impact of General Controls on Application Control Reliance

As described earlier and shown in Table 9-5 (page 281), general (computer) controls are controls over automated information systems with respect to organization and management; systems acquisition, development, and maintenance; and operations and information systems support. Table 9-6 (page 288) provided examples of general (computer) controls.

Since general controls affect multiple transaction cycles, the quality of general controls should be assessed prior to the decision as to whether reliance will be placed on controls or procedures in automated accounting systems. The effect of general controls is discussed separately below for the three types of application controls that can occur in automated accounting systems (see Table 9-5).

Manual controls **Manual controls** are performed by individuals without reliance on reports or screens prepared by automated information systems. For example, goods received from a supplier are counted and recorded on a receiving report, then compared to the bill of lading that came with the shipment on the truck. General controls would have limited impact on these controls.

Manual controls—are performed by individuals without reliance on reports or screens prepared by automated information systems.

Computer-assisted controls **Computer-assisted controls** are performed by individuals with the assistance of a computer report or computer information. For example, inventory counts are recorded in the computer system. A report is printed identifying differences between the perpetual records and the inventory count so that a different count team can verify the discrepancy. Should general controls be inadequate, the computer information used as a basis for completing this control could be unreliable.

Computer-assisted controls—controls that have a manual component and a computerized component, such as an individual using a computerized exception report to complete a task.

Fully automated controls **Fully automated controls** are performed using only automated information systems, with no manual or human intervention. For example, every morning, prior to commencing sales order processing, the accounts receivable subsystem automatically adds the accounts receivable open item file and transfers the total to a reconciliation file, where another program compares the total with the accounts receivable balance in the general ledger. If there is a difference, a warning message is sent to the accounts receivable data entry clerk. Normally, fully automated controls can best be tested with control tests. Computer-assisted audit tests that would be suitable would include test data, integrated test facilities, or reperformance (using generalized audit software). Such controls are vulnerable to general control failures, such as poor program testing.

Fully automated controls—controls that are undertaken without human intervention, such as a credit check where transactions are automatically rejected.

When identifying key controls in a system, the auditor may have identified a combination of manual, computer-assisted, and fully automated controls. For example, when considering credit approval prior to shipment, a manual control would require that each shipment be manually approved and initialled. A computer-assisted control would have the computer system print a report for the credit manager of questionable orders. The credit manager would review the report and determine which orders should be shipped. A fully automated control would have the computer system automatically reject all orders that caused customers to exceed their credit limit.

For an auditor to consider placing reliance upon either a computer-assisted or fully automated control, the auditor must have reasonable assurance that general controls over the computerized portion of the controls are effective. In particular, program change controls and access controls must be effective.

- *Program change controls.* There should be sufficient controls in place to ensure that programs throughout the year were adequately controlled. This provides reasonable assurance that there were no unauthorized program changes and that programs functioned consistently throughout the year.
- *Access controls.* Physical and logical access controls should exist to prevent unauthorized access to programs and data and to document access so that accountability can be established. If unauthorized access to programs or data can be obtained, then the auditor would not be able to place reliance on the results of those programs or data throughout the year.

Should the auditor conclude that general controls are adequate, then the auditor has the choice of relying on any of the different types of controls in the accounting system that are identified as key controls (i.e., manual, computer-assisted, or fully automated). Should general controls be poor, then the auditor may be able to rely on only manual controls. Alternatively, the auditor may decide to assess control risk at maximum and not rely on any internal controls.

Tests of Controls

The controls that the auditor has identified as reducing control risk (the key controls) must be supported by tests of controls to make sure they have been operating effectively throughout all, or most of, the audit period. For example, in Figure 9-8 (page 291), each key control must be supported by sufficient tests of controls if the auditor will be relying upon the control.

PROCEDURES FOR TESTS OF CONTROLS Four types of audit procedures are used to support the operation of key internal controls. They are as follows:

Make inquiries of appropriate entity personnel Although inquiry is not generally a strong source of evidence about the effective operation of controls, it is an appropriate form of evidence. For example, the auditor may determine that unauthorized personnel are not allowed access to computer files by making inquiries of the person who controls set up of user identification codes and functional access rights.

Inspection of documents, records, and reports Many controls leave a clear trail of documentary evidence. Suppose, for example, that when a customer order is received, it is used to update a customer accounts receivable record, which is approved for credit using the computer system. Orders that cause the customer to exceed the credit limit are printed and reviewed by the sales manager. The sales manager initials the listing for those orders that are to be accepted. (See the first and second key controls in Figure 9-8.) The auditor examines the credit exception report and ensures that required signatures or initials are present. Since this is a computer-assisted control (reliance on an automated exception report), the auditor reviews the general controls file to ensure that general controls are adequate prior to the conduct of this test. The auditor may examine a personal guarantee in a bank loan file if there is a need to increase credit, and this provides supporting evidence of the credit-granting process.

Observe control-related activities Other types of control-related activities do not leave an evidential trail. For example, separation of duties relies on specific persons performing specific tasks, and there is typically no documentation of the separate performance. (See the third key control listed in Figure 9-8.) For controls that leave no documentary evidence, the auditor generally observes them being applied. For computer-based controls, the auditor may consider the use of test data to determine whether the control is functioning. **Test data** are fictitious transactions entered in controlled circumstances and processed through the client systems. The auditor compares anticipated results with results that actually occurred from processing the transactions.

Reperform client procedures There are also control-related activities for which there are related documents and records but whose content is insufficient for the auditor's

Test data—fictitious transactions entered in controlled circumstances and processed through the client systems.

purpose of assessing whether controls are operating effectively. For example, assume prices on sales invoices are automatically retrieved from the computer master file by client personnel and not overridden. (See the seventh key control in Figure 9-8.) There is no documentation of this control, since it relies upon an automated process. In these cases, it is common for the auditor to actually reperform the control activity to see whether the proper results were obtained. For this example, the auditor can reperform the procedure by tracing the sales prices to the authorized price in the master file in effect at the date of the transaction. Reperformance can also be automated. For example, if the company uses a complex algorithm to calculate its allowance for bad debts based on sales throughout the year, the algorithm could be duplicated and recalculated using **generalized audit software** (general purpose software capable of reading and testing client data using special-purpose modules such as extraction, sampling, and graphing). If no misstatements are found, the auditor can conclude that the procedure is operating as intended.

Generalized audit software— general purpose software capable of reading and testing client data using special-purpose modules such as extraction, sampling, and plotting.

EXTENT OF PROCEDURES The extent to which tests of controls are applied depends on the intended assessed level of control risk. The lower the assessed level of control risk, the more extensive the tests of controls must be both in terms of the number of controls tested and the number of items tested. For example, if the auditor wants to use a low assessed level of control risk, a larger sample size for documentation, observation, and reperformance procedures should be applied.

Reliance on evidence from prior year's audit If evidence was obtained in the prior year's audit that indicates a key control was operating effectively and the auditor determines that it is still in place, the extent of the tests of that control may be reduced substantially in the current year and tested as a minimum every third year. If auditors determine that a key control has been changed since it was last tested, they should test it in the current year. When there are a number of controls tested in prior audits that have not been changed, auditors should test some of those controls each year to ensure that there is a rotation of controls testing throughout the three-year period.

Testing of controls related to significant risks Significant risks are those risks that the auditor believes require special audit consideration. When the auditor's risk assessment procedures identify significant risks, the auditor is required to test the operating effectiveness of controls that mitigate these risks in the current year audit if the auditor plans to rely on those controls to support a control risk assessment below 100 percent. The greater the risk, the more audit evidence the auditor should obtain that controls are operating effectively.

Testing less than the entire audit period Ideally, tests of controls should be applied to transactions and controls for the entire period under audit. However, it is not always possible to do so. Where less than the entire period is tested, the auditor should determine whether changes in controls occurred in the period not tested and obtain evidential matter about the nature and extent of any changes. Controls dealing with financial statement preparation occur monthly, quarterly, or at year end and should therefore be tested at those times.

RELATIONSHIP OF TESTS OF CONTROLS TO PROCEDURES TO OBTAIN AN UNDERSTANDING You will notice that there is a significant overlap between tests of controls and procedures to obtain an understanding. Both include inquiry, inspection, and observation. There are two primary differences in the application of these common procedures between phases. The auditor needs to understand internal control only as it applies to the financial statements as a whole and to relevant assertions relating to significant account balances or classes of transactions. In other words, the procedures to gain an understanding are applied only to certain control policies and procedures that have been instituted by the client. The auditor will obtain knowledge about the design of the relevant policies and procedures and determine whether or

Table 9-9	Relationship of Planned Assessed Level of Control Risk and Extent of Procedures

Planned Assessed Level of Control Risk

Type of Procedure Used	High Level: Obtaining an Understanding Only	Lower Level: Tests of Controls
Inquiry	Yes—extensive	Yes—some
Inspection	Yes—with transaction walk-through	Yes—using sampling
Observation	Yes—with transaction walk-through	Yes—at multiple times
Reperformance	No	Yes—using sampling

not they have been implemented. Tests of controls, on the other hand, are applied only when control risk has been assessed below maximum, and then only to relevant key controls.

The second difference is that procedures to obtain an understanding are performed only on one or a few transactions or, in the case of observations, at a single point in time. Tests of controls are performed on larger samples of transactions (perhaps 20 to 100), and often observations are made at more than one point in time.

For key controls, tests of controls other than reperformance are essentially an extension of related procedures to obtain an understanding. For that reason, when auditors plan at the outset to obtain a low assessed level of control risk, they may combine both types of procedures and perform them simultaneously.

Table 9-9 illustrates this concept in more detail, showing how audit procedures are used differently. Where only the required minimum study of internal control is planned, the auditor will conduct a transaction walk-through. The auditor determines that the audit documentation is complete and accurate, and observes that the control-related activities described are in operation.

When the control risk is assessed below maximum, a transaction walk-through is performed and a larger and more varied sample of documents is inspected for indications of the effectiveness of the operation of controls. Similarly, when observations are made, they will be more extensive and often at several points in time. Also, reperformance is an important test of some controls.

Two Audit Approaches

As we have explained, there are two approaches an auditor may take for a specific financial statement assertion: the substantive approach, where the auditor does not rely on internal controls; and the combined approach, where the auditor assesses control risk below maximum and does rely on internal controls.

A substantive approach is used when the auditor cannot rely on the internal controls with respect to a particular assertion or when it is not cost-effective to rely on the controls for that assertion. Control risk is set at high for that assertion; planned detection risk will therefore be low and the extent of evidence will be high. The auditor will obtain a sufficient understanding of the control environment and the accounting system to plan the audit and document the understanding and the control risk assessment; there would be no tests of controls.

A combined approach is used when the auditor can rely on the internal controls with respect to a particular assertion and control risk can be assessed at low. Even though a combined approach could be used if control risk is set at medium, it is normally not done in practice. Because control risk is set at low for that assertion, planned detection risk will be high and the extent of evidence will be low. The auditor will obtain an understanding of the control environment, the accounting system, and the control activities sufficient to plan the audit and document the understanding and the control risk assessment; controls would be tested to support the assessment of low with the extent of testing varying inversely with the assessment.

Expansion of Internal Control Testing

For some companies, the auditor reports upon management's assessment of internal control. Such a report is required by Section 404(b) of the Sarbanes-Oxley Act of 2002, affecting Canadian companies that are subsidiaries of American companies or that register securities for sale in the United States. A sample report is shown in Chapter 21. In Canada, public companies report on the quality of their internal controls but these reports do not need to be audited. However, it is likely that these companies will still want some form of assurance from their auditors about the quality of their internal controls. Section 9110, Agreed-upon procedures regarding internal control over financial reporting, discussed in Chapter 21, talks further about this type of reporting.

Since management's assessment of internal control covers internal control over financial reporting, the scope of the Section 404(b) internal control assessment is different from the scope of the financial statement audit. The auditor will need to assess whether additional testing is required (i.e., more testing than is needed for satisfaction of the audit assertions). Figure 9-10 describes potential differences in scope between the nature of internal control testing for an audit of internal control and an audit of financial statements. The figure shows that management is concerned about additional controls that the auditor would not rely upon in the audit of the financial statements, requiring the auditor to do additional testing to be able to provide assurance upon management's assessment of internal control.

Section 5925 of the *CICA Handbook*, An audit of internal control over financial reporting performed that is integrated with an audit of financial statements, is substantially equivalent to the U.S. standard. The application and explanatory material at the end of the standard walks through the entire engagement, discussing roles, risk assessment, criteria, planning, fieldwork, and reporting in detail. As with other engagements, management accepts responsibility for the internal controls, and the same auditor who conducts the financial statement audit performs the audit of management's internal control assessment.

As part of the fieldwork, the auditor should test entity-level controls (such as the control environment and general computer controls) as well as more specific preventative and detective controls. To assist in the risk assessment process, the auditor is required to segregate transactions into one of three categories: routine, non-routine, or estimation. Only those controls that achieve a control objective are tested, and testing varies from year to year. The testing extends past the end of the fiscal year to those periods that help ensure that the financial statements are properly completed, for example, until February 15 for a December year end if that is the time when the

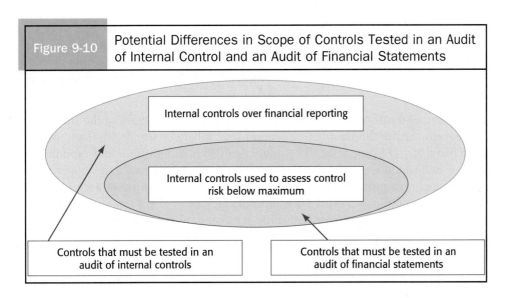

| Figure 9-10 | Potential Differences in Scope of Controls Tested in an Audit of Internal Control and an Audit of Financial Statements |

Internal controls over financial reporting

Internal controls used to assess control risk below maximum

Controls that must be tested in an audit of internal controls

Controls that must be tested in an audit of financial statements

concept check

C9-11 How is management's risk assessment relevant to the audit?

C9-12 What is the role of monitoring to support internal controls?

C9-13 Describe the audit strategy that the auditor uses when there is reliance upon key internal controls.

final accrual journal entries are made for the fiscal year. Procedures are also described for the reporting and handling of weaknesses in internal control.

⑤ Small Business Controls

Our discussions of internal control have indicated that small businesses frequently rely on owner/manager supervision. This is true whether a business uses manual or automated information systems. In this section, we examine the likely characteristics of a small business using the control framework of Figure 9-2 (page 259), Five Components of Internal Control.

Control Environment

The quality of the control environment depends on the attitudes of the owner/ manager. If the owner/manager adequately supervises employees, hires only competent employees, and encourages practices such as the use of confidential passwords, then the organization will have a more positive control environment and lower fraud risks than a situation in which the owner is an absentee and encourages the use of illegal copies of software.

Risk Assessment

Most small business owners are very clearly aware of their risks but do not have a formal method of documenting and assessing such risks. For example, they may be aware of the volatility of raw material prices or that there is an increased risk of uncollectability of accounts receivable. The auditor might recommend to small business owners that they consider periodically meeting with outside advisors, such as an advisory committee, to help them more formally assess risks within the businesses. Small business owners frequently underestimate fraud risks because they are prone to trusting their employees. A periodic credit check on employees or spot checking employee activity on a random basis can help assure the owner that employees are executing their activities conscientiously.

Control Activities

GENERAL CONTROLS

Organization and management controls There are often fewer people in the accounting department, perhaps even only one person; thus, segregation of duties may not be possible. Controls are often informal, lacking written authorization procedures. The owner/manager can readily override controls by personally performing clerical or operating functions.

Systems acquisition, development, and maintenance controls Use of packaged software is common in the accounting systems. A variety of software packages are available; they range in quality. Where programming is undertaken, controls over changes may be poor since an informal process will likely be used rather than a structured approach.

Operations and information systems support Primarily because of the small size of the organization, the information systems are likely to be simpler systems, using a centralized form of processing. The entity is unlikely to have in-house expertise in systems and would normally place reliance on software and hardware suppliers for system support and maintenance. Passwords may be in use but are in a simple form (e.g., the accounting personnel may have a single password that allows access to all systems and all functions. Note that this is a major control weakness and individual user access codes and passwords should be recommended.)

APPLICATION CONTROL ACTIVITIES When a software package is used and the entity is not capable of making changes to the software (since most software packages are provided only in machine code), certain controls in the software become important. For example, calculations in invoicing and inventory costing (recalculation), posting of transactions to subsidiary systems and to the general ledger (accuracy of summarization and posting), and aging of accounts receivable (valuation) are all functions normally present in software packages; these assist the business and the auditor can rely on them.

PRACTICAL CONTROLS TO BE EXERCISED BY THE OWNER/MANAGER For controls to be practical in a small business, they need to be activities that can be performed in a short period of time; otherwise it is unlikely that an owner/manager will implement them.

Systems acquisition, development, and maintenance controls It is important that the owner/manager understand the nature of software used by the business and how business needs might change. This includes software maintenance needs. For example, if the company uses a payroll package, then the company should expect to receive an upgrade whenever tax rates change. The owner should ensure that authorized programs are implemented (i.e., only valid, copyrighted materials should be implemented). If program changes are implemented, an employee should be assigned to test and keep a record of changes. Most small businesses have a lack of expertise in the selection, design, and operation of their automated information systems and frequently call on their accountant as a business advisor to help in these areas.

Operations and information systems support Backups should be made daily, with at least two copies of recent data and systems kept offsite. Although a formal disaster recovery plan may not be contemplated, the entity should have a current contact for hardware and software support in the event of system problems. At a minimum, documentation to provide for ongoing operations, such as a list of the procedures that are normally completed on a daily, weekly, and monthly basis, should be present.

APPLICATION CONTROL PROCEDURES These procedures include controls to prevent fraud. The most important control concept here is the separation of authorization from the recording of transactions and owner/manager controls. As in other sizes of business, the owner/manager needs to remain vigilant to prevent computer fraud and other types of fraud. Chapters 12 through 18 indicate that the owner should perform certain key activities, such as signing payroll cheques with a supporting payroll journal, signing accounts payable cheques with supporting documentation, and reviewing master file information.

concept check

C9-14 What is the key internal control risk at a small business, and how can a small business owner deal with it?

C9-15 How does a software package support a good control environment for a small business?

Summary

1. *What are the three primary objectives of internal control?* Organizations establish internal control to (i) help ensure reliable financial reporting, (ii) enable efficient and effective operations, and (iii) comply with laws and regulations.

   What are the different perspectives of the client and the auditor? The client is concerned about meeting organizational goals, which include having accurate information, safeguarding assets, optimizing the use of resources, and preventing and detecting error and fraud. The auditor needs to assess the overall risk of the engagement by considering the components of internal control, including the control environment and the controls over classes of transactions within the context of reasonable assurance.

   What does it mean that "substantive tests are not enough"? In some situations, it may be difficult to test a particular assertion using substantive tests alone. For

example, in a highly automated operation, information systems may perform controls such as matching of documentation, calculations, and posting. In such cases, the auditor would find that testing of details would not provide sufficient assurance and would need to conduct control testing of the automated controls.

   What are the three basic concepts that enable an auditor's study of internal controls? (1) Management is responsible for the establishment and maintenance of the entity's controls, (2) controls help provide reasonable assurance of the fairness of the financial statements, and (3) internal controls cannot be completely effective (inherent limitations).

   What are the conditions where fraud is most likely to exist? The three conditions are incentives, opportunity, and rationalization.

2. *What are the five components of internal control using the COSO framework?* They are control environment, risk assessment, control activities, information and communication, and monitoring.

Which controls does the auditor look for as indicators of lower fraud risks? The auditor will look for management and board promotion of a culture of high ethics, effective audit committee oversight of management and internal auditors, specific assignment management responsibilities for managing risks of fraud, an effective fraud risk management process, and adequate general and application controls to prevent and detect fraud.

3. *What is IT governance?* IT governance is the set of policies, procedures, and practices that help IT resources add value while considering costs and benefits.

How do IT general controls affect the audit planning process? Auditors need to understand general IT controls prior to determine the effectiveness of application controls. If general controls are sound, then the auditor may be able to place reliance upon automated or combined application controls.

How do information systems affect the audit process? The extent of client automation (Table 9-8) affects every phase of the audit process. Auditors may need to use IT audit specialists at clients who use advanced automated systems as part of the audit team.

4. *What does the auditor do to obtain an understanding of internal controls?* After assessing the integrity of management, the auditor uses inquiry, inspection, and observation to understand the control environment and uses inquiry, inspection, observation, and reperformance to understand general controls, accounting systems, and control and monitoring procedures.

How is control risk assessed, documented, and tested? After obtaining an understanding of internal control, the auditor evaluates the design effectiveness of internal controls to consider whether the financial statements are auditable. Then, general controls are assessed for their impact upon control risk for the individual transaction cycles and audit objectives in the transaction cycles. Finally, each audit objective is examined for each transaction type to determine the potential risk of material misstatement based on potential reliance on internal controls for that audit objective. Normally, software is used in the documentation of this process. The auditor will then design tests of controls for those key controls where reliance will be placed, test the controls, and evaluate the results of the tests of controls. If testing corroborates the operational effectiveness of the controls, then control risk is assessed at the targeted level.

What are relevant key controls? Relevant key controls are those that the auditor could rely upon and test that pertain to the financial statement audit.

Why is it important to link control risk to audit strategy and procedures? The auditor is better able to design substantive procedures that compensate for risks during the audit engagement and thus conduct a better quality audit.

What other types of internal control reports can an auditor issue? The auditor can issue an opinion on management's assessment of internal control and also issue special reports on internal control.

How do such internal control reports affect audit tests? An opinion on management's assessment of internal control is conducted at the same time as the financial statement audit and may include tests of additional controls, thus expanding the amount of work that would be completed during the financial statement audit engagement.

5. *What are important risks and controls for small businesses?* Small business owners face many of the risks of other businesses, but a unique risk for them is fraud or error due to lack of segregation of duties. This is mitigated by the strong level of commitment and hands-on activities conducted by most owners (such as signing cheques) and the use of well-designed software packages.

MyAccountingLab

Make the grade with MyAccountingLab: The questions, exercises, and problems marked in orange can be found on MyAccountingLab. You can practise them as often as you want, and most feature step-by-step guided instructions to help you find the right answer.

Review Questions

9-1 ❶ Describe the three broad objectives management has when designing effective internal control.

9-2 ❶ Describe which of the three categories of broad objectives for internal controls are considered by the auditor in an audit of both the financial statements and internal control over financial reporting. Why are these categories considered?

9-3 ❶ Compare management's concerns about internal control with those of the auditor.

9-4 ❶ Frequently, management is more concerned about internal controls that promote operational efficiency than about those that result in reliable financial data. How can the independent auditor persuade management to devote more attention to controls affecting the reliability of accounting information when management has this attitude?

9-5 ❶ What are the three conditions of fraud often referred to as "the fraud triangle"?

9-6 ❶ Give examples of risk factors for fraudulent financial reporting for each of the three fraud conditions: incentives/pressures, opportunities, and attitudes/rationalization.

9-7 **2** What are the five components of internal control in the COSO internal control framework? Provide an example of a control for each component.

9-8 **2** What is the relationship among the five components of internal control?

9-9 **2** What is meant by the "control environment"? What are the factors the auditor must evaluate to understand it?

9-10 **2** What is the relationship between the control environment and control systems?

9-11 **2** The separation of operational responsibility from record keeping is meant to prevent different types of misstatements than the separation of the custody of assets from accounting. Explain the difference in the purposes of these two types of separation of duties.

9-12 **2** Distinguish between general and specific authorization of transactions, and give one example of each type.

9-13 **2** Explain what is meant by "independent checks on performance," and give five specific examples.

9-14 **2** Discuss the importance of the control environment, or "setting the tone at the top," in establishing a culture of honesty and integrity in a company.

9-15 **2** Describe the five principles that should be addressed in an effective fraud risk management process.

9-16 **3** What is the purpose of an information systems steering committee? How does such a committee support effective corporate governance?

9-17 **3** What is the relationship between IT governance and corporate governance?

9-18 **3** What is IT dependence and how can it be prevented?

9-19 **3** List three categories of general controls. For each category, provide an example of an effective control.

9-20 **3** You are auditing a manufacturing company with three different locations. For each phase of the finan-cial statement audit, provide an example of the impact of automation on the audit process.

9-21 **3** Why does the auditor need to assess controls over information systems acquisition, development, and maintenance?

9-22 **4** Distinguish between obtaining an understanding of internal control and assessing control risk. Also, explain the methodology the auditor uses for each.

9-23 **4** Define what is meant by a "control" and a "weakness in internal control." Give two examples of each in the sales and collection cycle.

9-24 **4** Describe the seven steps in assessing control risk during a financial statement audit.

9-25 **4** Distinguish between the objectives of an internal control questionnaire and the objectives of a flowchart for documenting information about a client's internal control. State the advantages and disadvantages of each of these two methods.

9-26 **4** Describe what is meant by "key control" and "control deficiency."

9-27 **4** Explain what is meant by "significant deficiencies" as they relate to internal control. What should the auditor do when he or she has discovered significant deficiencies in internal control?

9-28 **4** Explain what is meant by "tests of controls." Write one inspection of documents test of control and one reperformance test of control for the following internal control: hours of time cards are re-added by an independent payroll clerk and initialled to indicate performance.

9-29 **4** Distinguish between a substantive approach and a combined approach in auditing a financial statement assertion.

9-30 **5** What control processes should a small business have for IT operations and support?

Discussion Questions and Problems

9-31 **1** During audit planning, an auditor obtained the following information:

1. Management has a strong interest in employing inappropriate means to minimize reported earnings for tax-motivated reasons.
2. Assets and revenues are based on significant estimates that involve subjective judgments and uncertainties that are hard to corroborate.
3. The company is marginally able to meet exchange listing and debt covenant requirements.
4. Significant operations are located and conducted across international borders in jurisdictions where differing business environments and cultures exist.

5. There are recurring attempts by management to justify marginal or inappropriate accounting on the basis of materiality.
6. The company's financial performance is threatened by a high degree of competition and market saturation.

REQUIRED
Classify each of the six factors into one of these fraud conditions: incentives/pressures, opportunities, or attitudes/rationalization.

9-32 **2** The following are errors or fraud and other irregularities that have occurred in Fresh Foods Grocery Store Ltd., a wholesale and retail grocery company.

1. The incorrect price was used on sales invoices for billing shipments to customers because the incorrect price was entered into a computer file.

2. A vendor's invoice was paid twice for the same shipment. The second payment arose because the vendor sent a duplicate copy of the original two weeks after the payment was due.
3. Employees in the receiving department stole some sides of beef. When a shipment of meat was received, the receiving department filled out a receiving report and forwarded it to the accounting department for the amount of goods actually received. At that time, two sides of beef were put in an employee's pickup truck rather than in the storage freezer.
4. During the physical count of inventory of the retail grocery, one counter wrote down the wrong description of several products and miscounted the quantity.
5. A salesperson sold several hundred kilos of lamb at a price below cost because she did not know that the cost of lamb had increased in the past week.

6. On the last day of the year, a truckload of beef was set aside for shipment but was not shipped. Because it was still on hand, it was counted as inventory. The shipping document was dated the last day of the year, so it was also included as a current-year sale.

REQUIRED
a. For each error or fraud and other irregularity, identify one or more types of controls that were absent.
b. For each error or fraud and other irregularity, identify the objectives that have not been met.
c. For each error or fraud and other irregularity, suggest a control to correct the deficiency.

9-33 ❶❷❹ Froggledore Realty Limited is a brokerage firm that employs 35 real estate agents. The agents are given an office and basic telephone service (estimated at a $250 value per month) and are paid on a commission basis. The building has wireless computing so that agents can bring in their own computers. Each office has its own lock, and agents are responsible for the contents of their offices. Calls that come into the office are allocated to agents based upon their region in the city, with each agent having a clearly defined region for sales.

Potential purchasers who call in are assigned to the on-call listed agent. The office manager is responsible for accounting and for supplying the office with software and other supplies. She purchased a copy of real estate sales management software (for $750) for the office and has been burning copies, which she sells to new real estate agents for $100; she figures it pays for her time (she usually burns them on her home computer).

The owner of the business, Jim Froggledore, has told her and the accounting staff to bring in any invoices that they have for home computing so that he can use them for the business. Depending upon how well the company does, Jim gives employees a 10- to 20-percent bonus at the end of the year for the invoices.

Jenny, the receptionist, is a freelance writer and has been writing advertising copy for the business in her spare time. She charges for this as an editing contract from her small business and takes supplies from the office, which she and her husband (not employed by Jim) use for their business.

Jim recently had the offices renovated, with new carpeting and wallpaper, by his sister's business. She also painted the recently renovated basement at Jim's home and installed indoor/outdoor carpeting on his patio; all of this was included in the bill to the business. Jim prorated the invoice and charged the real estate agents for the renovations to the office.

REQUIRED
a. Assess the quality of corporate governance at Froggledore Realty Limited.
b. Is the company auditable? Why or why not?
c. If you did decide to audit the company, what audit approach would you use?
d. Are there any additional audit procedures that would be required? Why or why not? List any additional audit procedures that you would recommend, stating the fraud risk that they address and the associated audit objective.

9-34 ❷❹ Recently, you had lunch with some friends at a new restaurant in your neighbourhood. After ordering, the server entered his password into a computer and punched in your order. The server continued taking orders and you noticed the cook removing a small printout and placing it on the wall in front of him (presumably your order). When the food was ready, it was placed directly below your order. The server looked at the printout, put it in his pocket, and then brought your order to the table.

When you finished eating, the server again entered his password and printed two copies of your bill. One copy was attached to the order slip, and the second was brought to you. You decided to pay by credit card, so two copies of the credit card authorization were brought to the table for signature. You kept one and the signed copy was returned to the server.

REQUIRED
a. What internal controls (manual, computer-assisted, and automated) are present at the restaurant?
b. How could the manager of the restaurant evaluate the effectiveness of the controls?
c. What are the costs and benefits of the restaurant's controls?

9-35 ② ④ Hans & Co. LLP, is auditing CCC Inc.'s 2011 financial statements. The firm previously audited the company's 2009 and 2010 financial statements. The 2009 audit resulted in a qualified opinion because the auditors were unable to verify the opening inventory for that year, but the 2010 audit resulted in an unqualified opinion. Julia worked on the previous two audits and is familiar with most of the staff at CCC, including the accounting manager, Marcus. Julia was scheduled to meet with Marcus on Monday morning to meet any new staff and have a tour of the office. The accounting manager was unable to meet with Julia on Monday, and instead sent her the following email:

Julia,

I have to take next week off for personal reasons. Therefore, I prepared this email for you. As you are probably aware, CCC Inc. has suffered some loss of sales due to the general economic slowdown experienced by many companies. The office procedures and internal controls are the same as last year. You will have many new staff to meet this year as employee turnover has been high. CCC had to reduce wages for most staff by 20% to stay profitable, so several employees complain that they are underpaid, and about 30% of the staff actually left for new jobs. As for my own position,

accounting manager, my wages were only reduced by 10%, because managers are expected to work harder than other staff. The staff generally do not believe that we work harder, but, for example, the controller has refused to take any vacation for the past year and does not want to take her vacation for the next two years. One of the controller's many responsibilities is to approve all payments and purchases from CCC's subsidiary company, CCC-2 Ltd. (As you know from last year's audit, CCC owns 60% of the voting shares of CCC-2 and senior executives of both companies own the remaining shares—40%). Being able to purchase goods and materials from CCC-2 at below market prices is a second reason that CCC has remained profitable, even in the poor economy, so it's very helpful that the controller is never away on vacation. I will be back on the office next week, so we can meet next Monday instead.

Regards, Marcus

REQUIRED

Assess control risk at CCC. Justify your response.

(Extract from AU1 CGA- Canada Examinations developed by the Certified General Accountants Association of Canada © 2011 CGA-Canada. Reproduced with permission. All rights reserved.)

9-36 ② ③ ⑤ Metro Plastics Limited is a medium-sized manufacturer of rigid plastics. It produces casings for printers, telephones, computer screens, and other types of equipment. It also produces stand-alone plastics, such as baskets and jars. Recently, Metro Plastics was purchased by a large food manufacturing conglomerate. The previous owner of Metro Plastics has agreed to stay on for three years to help provide management transition. He has also been asked to provide a presentation to the board of the conglomerate about the corporate governance and risk management practices of his company. The owner of Metro Plastics has come to you to

provide some guidance about the type of information that he should provide to the board.

REQUIRED

a. What type of information should he provide to the board about corporate governance? List three corporate governance controls that might have been present at the owner-managed company.

b. What type of information should he provide about risk management practices at Metro Plastics? List three risk management practices that might have been present at the owner-managed company.

Professional Judgment Problem

9-37 ⑤ Gaboria Frank is the owner of Frankincents Machining Limited, a custom machining centre with 10 full-time employees and a part-time bookkeeper, Norma, who comes in two days a week. Norma convinced Gaboria to purchase a small business suite of accounting packages and a desktop computer with a laser printer. Norma has set up the records on the computer, and all accounting work is now handled using the accounting packages (i.e., order entry, accounts receivable, cash disbursements, general ledger, and payroll). It took Norma about three months, and she initially had some difficulty balancing the subsystems, but everything

seems to be functioning properly now. Frank did not consult with you, his accountant, prior to implementing the systems.

REQUIRED

a. Identify the risks associated with the current method of handling accounting records at Frankincents Machining Limited.

b. Identify those activities that Frank should handle in sales, accounts receivable, cash disbursements, and payroll. Explain why.

Case

9-38 **②** **③** Friggle Corp. is a leasing and property management company located in Alberta. It provides financing to organizations wishing to purchase equipment or property and manages apartments and condominium properties. The company decided that it was time to upgrade its local area network. It decided also to purchase new accounting software but wanted to retain its old unit maintenance software, which, although 10 years old, had an easy-to-use interface that allowed maintenance personnel to track the maintenance work that they did in each unit. The controller, Joe, decided that the company should purchase the software from Midland Computers, which was owned by his brother-in-law, Tom. The prices were comparable with those of other computer networks that he priced, and Midland happened to be close by. Using materials from industry magazines, Joe decided that the best property management software to buy would be from Quebec; the software had received rave reviews about being easy to use.

The implementation was scheduled for the weekend after the June month-end close so that systems could be up and running by the following Monday. To Joe's horror, when he arrived at work on Monday, computers were still being unpacked and installed. Tom had difficulty following the installation instructions for the accounting software, which was not up and running until the end of the week. General ledger details had to be manually entered, since the software could not handle the structure of the old accounts. At the end of two weeks, Joe had the old system put back up so that Friggle could catch up on transactions and get some work out the door. It took three months of 12-hour days for all accounting staff to get the new system operational. Unfortunately, the old maintenance systems would not work with the new operating system, and a new maintenance system had to be evaluated and purchased.

REQUIRED

Assess IT governance at Friggle Corp. For weaknesses that you identify, provide recommendations for improvement.

ACL Problem

9-39 This problem requires the use of ACL software, use "Metaphor_APTrans_2002 file in ACL_Demo." The suggested command or other source of information needed to solve the problem requirement is included at the end of each question.

REQUIRED

a. For each of the computer-assisted audit procedures listed in part (c), identify the audit objective(s) associated with the test. Justify your response.

b. For each of the procedures listed in part (c), state the fraud risk that is addressed by the audit procedure. Justify your response.

c. Run the following ACL tests:

1. Total the Invoice Amount column for comparison with the general ledger balance of $276,841.33 (Total Field).

2. Recalculate unit cost times quantity and identify any extension misstatements (Filter).

3. Products that Metaphor purchases should not exceed $100 per unit. Print any purchase for subsequent follow-up where unit cost exceeded that amount (Filter).

4. Identify the three vendors from which the largest total-dollar accounts payable transactions occurred during 2002 (Summarize and Quick Sort).

5. For each of the three vendors in question 4, list any transactions that exceeded $15,000 for subsequent follow-up. Include the vendor number, invoice number, and invoice amount (Filter. Note that the Vendor Number is actually a character rather than a number, so you need to enclose it in quotes when using it in an expression.).

6. Vendor numbers 10134 and 13440 are parties related to Metaphor. Print any accounts payable transactions with these two vendors (Filter). Also, determine the total amount of transactions with each vendor (Summarize).

d. Identify audit procedures that are required to follow up any unusual results from each ACL audit test. Explain the purpose of each audit procedure.

Ongoing Small Business Case: COSO Controls at CondoCleaners.com

9-40 Jim's business is booming, and within six months, he has gone from his first cluster of four condominiums to 30 condominium towers within the downtown core that are serviced by his cleaning staff. Jim hired his first supervisor, Vagney, this month and has spent the past week training her and thinking about changes he can now make to internal controls. Vagney has a schedule of cleaning and drops in unannounced while cleaning is being done to do quality control checks. She has been assigned the responsibility of purchasing cleaning supplies from local department stores when they are on sale as well as scanning for specials to help reduce cleaning supply costs.

Jim still does the accounting, including payroll for his six full-time employees, who are paid a base pay of 20 hours per week. Jim does the scheduling to make sure that each employee receives at least 20 hours of work per week, then schedules the remaining cleaning around those 20 hours, trying to minimize the number of trips that employees need to make.

However, with a thriving business doing, at minimum, 150 hours of cleaning per week in personal condominium units ranging in size from bachelor units to luxury three-bedroom units, Jim is feeling burned out. During the Christmas lull, he decides to take some time off and reassess the direction that he is going. He also wants to make sure that he has key risks at his business addressed.

REQUIRED

a. Using the framework of COSO, describe each internal control category, and provide an example of controls that are present or could be present at CondoCleaners.com.

b. Identify three risks that could affect CondoCleaners.com. For each risk, provide a control that could be used to mitigate the risk.

10 Audit strategy and audit program

There are so many different types of businesses—how can there be a common approach to the financial statement audit? Just like the architect of a multi-storey office tower, the financial statement auditor carefully plans his or her strategy, identifying the risks involved with the client and developing an audit approach to complete the engagement. Internal auditors and specialists may participate in the financial statement audit and need to be aware of their role in the overall plan. Management accountants will be answering auditor questions and providing evidence to the auditors.

LEARNING OBJECTIVES

1 Explain what an audit strategy is. Determine the role of audit planning in the financial statement audit. Describe the purpose of an audit program. State the purpose of the five types of audit tests. Describe the role of dual-purpose tests.

2 Explain why determining evidence mix is a dynamic process. Explain how the auditor chooses the types of audit tests to be completed.

3 Describe the methodology for designing tests of controls and tests of details in the audit program. Link this methodology to the selection of audit tests by assertion.

4 Describe the impact on the audit process of a client conversion to IFRS (International Financial Reporting Standards). Relate the risks specific to IFRS conversion to how the audit process responds to those risks.

STANDARDS REFERENCED IN THIS CHAPTER

CICA Standards

CAS 240 – The auditor's responsibilities relating to fraud in an audit of financial statements

CAS 315 – Identifying and assessing the risks of material misstatement through understanding the entity and its environment

CAS 330 – The auditor's responses to assessed risks

CAS 520 – Analytical procedures

Clients Have Changed and So Have Audits

Jared and Gabrielle were comparing notes on two of their clients. Jared's client was implementing new enterprise-wide resource software—an integrated suite of programs that have a database core. Unfortunately, the implementation did not go well. There was a programming error in the new implementation that resulted in work-in-progress work orders being set to zero at the time of the conversion. Although new orders were handled properly, about 3,000 jobs were affected. These were noticed about two weeks after the conversion as billing cycles were concluded and inventory-to-job-cost reconciliations went out of whack.

Gabrielle was enthusiastic about her client's mass customization, with skirts and pants produced to individual orders as well as smaller production runs for retail store clients. The client had purchased software and hardware that enabled the linking of orders to the production system. The software and hardware were also able to reduce inventory of work in progress and finished goods by streamlining the link between ordering, production, and shipping. The client found that customer loyalty for customized work was very high.

IMPORTANCE TO AUDITORS

Investigation of data errors and review of account reconciliations after the software conversion at Jared's client meant that the client's year-end financial statement results were delayed by almost two months. Jared and his staff spent numerous hours reviewing data conversion plans with the client and helped compare information that was transferred from the old computer systems to the new data. The client was late filing its reports with the stock exchange, suspended trading of its shares for a month, and was threatened with delisting of its stock.

Jared was thankful that he had taken some extra information systems courses at university. He was also planning to take the Certified Information Systems Auditor Examination and move into the information systems audit group at his firm.

Gabrielle enthused about her client's new systems. "My client is finally starting to make some money on its line of custom-made skirts and pants. Lower inventory overall meant that we had to use only two staff members on the inventory count and were able to reduce the fieldwork on inventory by over 30 percent." Inventory was individually tracked, and the new information systems were found to be reliable and robust.

These two examples illustrate how the quality of the information systems and their conversion had an impact on the audit strategy and the resultant detailed testing of two different clients.

continued >

continued

WHAT DO YOU THINK?

1. With the discovery of a major program error at Jared's client, what is the likelihood that there would be other program errors? How would this affect the time spent on gathering information about control systems?

2. Are the two systems described above strategic information systems? Why or why not? How does the nature of the system affect client business risk?

THINK about the two businesses that Jared and Gabrielle discussed. How do information systems affect the way a business is run? What impact would this have on the audit planning processes? Most businesses, even small ones, use technology in the execution of their transactions. It is important to understand how such technology is related to business processes in order to adequately plan and execute the financial statement audit.

This chapter examines the role of an audit strategy in the financial statement audit. It also looks at two phases of the financial statement audit in detail: Phase 3—Plan the Audit, which is the last risk assessment phase, and Phase 4—Design Further Audit Procedures, the first risk response phase. This critical fourth phase specifies the entire audit program, including audit procedures, sample sizes, items to select, and timing of the testing.

Sources: 1. Schlosser, Julie, "A handful of companies are finally perfecting made-to-order for the masses. Here's how," *Fortune*, December 13, 2004. 2. Rainer, R. K., Jr., C. G. Cegielski, I. Splettstoesser-Hogeterp, C. Sanchez-Rodriguez, *Introduction to Information Systems*, Mississauga: John Wiley & Sons Canada, Ltd., 2011). 3. Songini, Marc L., "Bungled ERP installation whacks Asyst," *Computerworld*, 39(2), 2005.

 ## Audit Strategy and Audit Tests

In this section, we will use the example of Hillsburg Hardware Limited to describe the top-down process used to develop an audit strategy in the financial statement audit. We will also look at the "tools of the trade"—the types of audit tests that can be used.

Audit Strategy and Hillsburg Hardware Limited

Audit strategy—a planned approach (either "combined" or "substantive") to the conduct of audit testing, taking into account assessed risks.

An **audit strategy** consists of a planned approach to the conduct of audit testing, taking into account assessed risks. This means that the strategy can be developed only after the client risk profile has been developed and risks assessed. The audit strategy is the last step of Phase 3—Plan the Audit.

The preplanning phase (Phase 1) has been completed. As explained in our chapters so far, Hillsburg Hardware Limited (Hillsburg) is a continuing client that has been responsive to recommendations for improvement from the auditors. There are no independence issues for the audit firm Berger, Kao, Kadous & Co., LLP (BKK), which has obtained an engagement letter and has confirmed with the client that there are no independence issues. BKK would likely assign an information systems audit specialist to the audit team to assist with the documentation and evaluation of general and application controls.

Chapter 6 explained how the client risk profile would be developed (Phase 2 of the audit process), starting with an understanding of the client's business and industry. As a hardware wholesaler, Hillsburg would compete with other wholesalers and also with hardware retailers that offer discounts to commercial purchasers (such as Home Depot and Rona). This industry is suffering as consumers and businesses cut back on discretionary purchases. The Company Description (page 3 of the Hillsburg 2011 annual report) provides an overview of the business. The auditor would develop a picture of the overall business context by considering Hillsburg's local and regional competitors. A description of the business includes the quality of management and governance: Hillsburg has an active audit committee and a board that meet regularly. Although Hillsburg has not implemented an enterprise-wide risk management framework, each functional area conducts a risk assessment (including fraud risk assessment), which is evaluated by the executive management team at a semi-annual day-long retreat. Board members are invited to the retreat, and normally the chair of the board and a second board member who is also on the audit committee attend the retreat. The result of this retreat is incorporated into a risk assessment evaluation and plan that is discussed with the whole board at its quarterly meeting. Each functional area is expected to contribute to the annual strategic plan, which is similarly discussed with the board. The information systems department participates in the strategic planning exercises to ensure that computing plans address business needs and that technology capabilities are considered during the planning process. This contributes to a lower client business risk and a high quality control environment (understanding and document internal controls, part of Phase 3 of the audit process).

Figure 10-1 shows the process that the audit team has followed to complete Phase 2 of the Hillsburg Audit, development of the client risk profile. The audit team members assigned to the engagement are as follows:

Partner: Joe Anthony
Manager: Leslie Ngan
Senior: Fran Moore
Assistants: Mitch Bray and one person to be assigned later

Figure 10-1 shows that work has been completed to understand the client's business and industry, assess client business risk, and complete preliminary analytical review. As part of the understanding of business, Figure 10-2 shows a partial organization chart that includes selected accounting and operating personnel. As a result of this field work and audit team consultation, client business risk (included in the risk summary in Table 10-1 on page 310) has been assessed as low. Table 10-2 shows the role of the audit team planning meeting that occurred after the client risk profile had been developed.

In Phase 3, Plan the Audit, the auditor uses the audit risk model (discussed in Chapter 7), to assist with planning. Refer to the inside cover plate of this text for the list of tasks that are completed in this phase. They are numerous and encompass large tasks such as understanding and evaluating internal controls, covered in Chapter 9. To organize completion of the phase, an audit team planning meeting (described in Table 10-2) is used to determine risks and set materiality.

Selected conclusions reached for Hillsburg are summarized in Table 10-1. Further conclusions are discussed in subsequent chapters where we examine individual transaction cycles and accounts. The audit risk for Hillsburg has been assessed at low, as it is a public company registered with the OSC, with current and long-term bank debt. This means that a high level of evidence will need to be collected.

Inherent risk for the financial statements as a whole has been assessed as low, primarily due to the good quality of corporate governance and monitoring processes in place at the company. This decreases the likelihood of material misstatements.

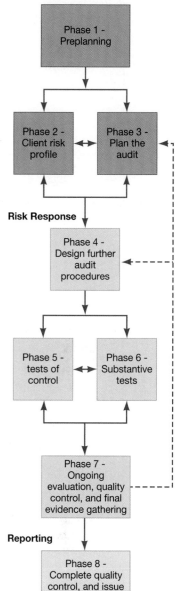

Risk Assessment

Phase 1 - Preplanning

Phase 2 - Client risk profile

Phase 3 - Plan the audit

Risk Response

Phase 4 - Design further audit procedures

Phase 5 - tests of control

Phase 6 - Substantive tests

Phase 7 - Ongoing evaluation, quality control, and final evidence gathering

Reporting

Phase 8 - Complete quality control, and issue auditor's report

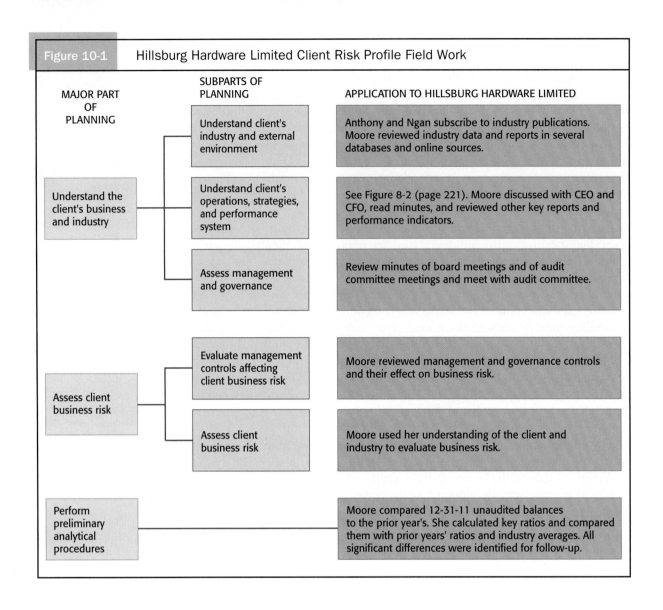

Figure 10-1 Hillsburg Hardware Limited Client Risk Profile Field Work

MAJOR PART OF PLANNING	SUBPARTS OF PLANNING	APPLICATION TO HILLSBURG HARDWARE LIMITED
Understand the client's business and industry	Understand client's industry and external environment	Anthony and Ngan subscribe to industry publications. Moore reviewed industry data and reports in several databases and online sources.
	Understand client's operations, strategies, and performance system	See Figure 8-2 (page 221). Moore discussed with CEO and CFO, read minutes, and reviewed other key reports and performance indicators.
	Assess management and governance	Review minutes of board meetings and of audit committee meetings and meet with audit committee.
Assess client business risk	Evaluate management controls affecting client business risk	Moore reviewed management and governance controls and their effect on business risk.
	Assess client business risk	Moore used her understanding of the client and industry to evaluate business risk.
Perform preliminary analytical procedures		Moore compared 12-31-11 unaudited balances to the prior year's. She calculated key ratios and compared them with prior years' ratios and industry averages. All significant differences were identified for follow-up.

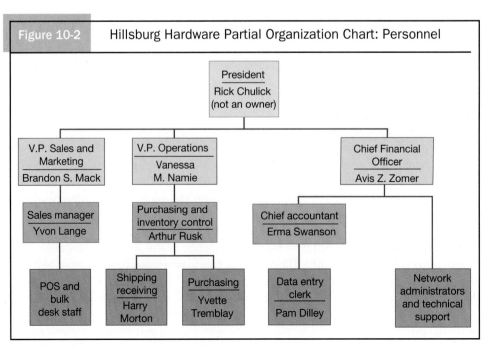

Figure 10-2 Hillsburg Hardware Partial Organization Chart: Personnel

Table 10-1	Hillsburg Hardware Limited Overall Risk Summary	

Type of Risk	Conclusion	Comments
Client business risk	Low	Although financial position is deteriorating, the company has plans of actions and strategies to deal with potentially plummeting revenue.
Audit risk	Low	Primary reasons include public company with long-term and current debt holder (bank).
Inherent risk	Low	Corporate governance and management integrity have been assessed as good. Results of previous audits indicate limited disagreements with the auditors and no related-party transactions. Primary judgment areas are valuation of accounts receivable and inventory, where many years of history and current data are available to assess.
Preliminary materiality	$496,000	$441,000 available for the current year after considering anticipated misstatements ($50,000), carry-forward misstatements ($80,000), and anticipated client corrections ($75,000).
Control risk	Low to medium	Varies by cycle and assertion. Areas where substantive testing will be insufficient: order entry assertions, assertions for electronic data interchange (EDI) transactions, assertions for automated payments.
Fraud risk	Low to moderate	Low for all transaction areas except for customer refunds (where it is moderate). Required significant areas of revenue recognition and journal entries to be tested.
Risk of material misstatements	Low to moderate	Revenue recognition is mandated to be a significant risk. Overall low risk, except for accounts receivable and inventory valuation, which are moderate.

As calculated in Chapter 7 in Table 7-5, preliminary materiality is $496,000, but only $441,000 (performance materiality) is available for the current year. Materiality will be used to help decide the scope of testing, the sample size, and to evaluate the results of testing. Control risk varies by cycle and assertion but is generally of good quality. There are three areas—order entry, EDI transactions, and automated payments—where it is considered that substantive testing will not be enough, as there is significant reliance upon automated systems in these areas.

Design effectiveness of internal controls by cycle, control risk by assertion, and risks of fraud by assertion are considered in Chapters 12 through 18. Overall risk

Table 10-2	Audit Planning Meeting Agenda—Meeting Held after Completion of Phase 1 (Preplanning) and Phase 2 (Client Risk Profile)

Review status of industry and client position in it.
Review prior year audit files and determine changes at the client.
Consider changes in management.
Identify and update inherent risk factors, biases, motivations, and fraud risks by financial statement overall, accounts, and cycles.
Set audit risk.
Set materiality, performance materiality, and levels of tolerable misstatement.
Organize risk factors by effects: financial statement overall, accounts, and cycles.
Identify assertions where substantive testing is not enough and there is a risk of material misstatement: financial statement overall, accounts, and cycles.

of fraud is considered low, except for customer refunds, whose risk is considered moderate. Note that customer refunds are considered a high-risk fraud area in the retail industry and that good quality controls at Hillsburg lowered fraud risk to moderate for the company.

The audit team has concluded that the overall risk of material misstatement for the financial statements is low. One of the exceptions relates to the mandated standards in CAS 240 that require revenue recognition to be considered a significant risk. The auditors have also raised the risk levels for accounts receivable valuation and inventory valuation due to the recession, which could result in accounts receivable collection problems and inventory obsolescence if these accounts are not carefully managed. The related working papers, conclusions, and assessments have been discussed with the audit team.

The audit team has decided that its overall audit strategy will be a combined approach, that is, an approach that includes both tests of control and substantive tests. The reasons for this approach will be explained in the next section, Evidence Mix Decisions, where we look at the top-down transaction cycle audit process.

Before considering those decisions, we take a closer look at the purpose of the different types of audit tests and how those tests are used in risk assessment and in the second major component of the audit, Risk Response.

Purpose of Different Audit Tests

Types of tests—the five categories of audit tests auditors use to determine whether financial statements are fairly stated: risk assessment procedures, procedures to obtain an understanding of internal control, tests of controls, analytical procedures, and tests of details of balances.

Substantive procedures—audit procedures that are used to quantify the amount of potential error in an account or transaction stream.

TYPES OF TESTS Auditors use five **types of tests** to determine whether financial statements are fairly stated: (1) risk assessment procedures, (2) procedures to obtain an understanding of internal control, (3) tests of controls, (4) analytical procedures, and (5) tests of details of balances. Note that we use the term **substantive procedures** to describe audit procedures that are used to quantify the amount of potential error in an account or transaction stream. There are two types of substantive tests: analytical procedures and tests of detail. (This means that analytical procedures are a type of test that is used for multiple purposes.) CAS 330 requires substantive tests where the auditor has identified a significant risk at the assertion level. If the auditor is not using tests of control, then analytical procedures are not enough—tests of detail must be used.

Since we have indicated earlier that the auditor must assume that revenue recognition is a significant risk (unless there is evidence to the contrary), this means that revenue recognition substantive testing will normally be conducted. The auditor is also required to conduct substantive tests related to the financial statement closing process.

Tests of controls, substantive tests of transactions, detailed analytical procedures, and tests of details of balances are completed in response to the auditor's assessment of the risk of material misstatements. The combination of all five types of audit procedures provides the basis for the auditor's opinion.

We now discuss each of these five types of tests in turn.

Risk assessment procedures—used to assess the likelihood of material misstatement (inherent risk plus control risk) in the financial statements.

Risk assessment procedures **Risk assessment procedures** are used to assess the likelihood of material misstatement (inherent risk plus control risk) in the financial statements. Chapter 6 described how the auditor obtains an understanding of the client's business and industry to assess client business risk and develop a client risk profile. Chapter 7 described how auditors perform procedures to assess inherent risk, and Chapter 9 discussed control risk. Collectively, procedures performed to obtain an understanding of the entity and its environment, including obtaining an understanding of internal controls, represent the auditor's risk assessment procedures.

Procedures used to obtain an understanding—procedures used by the auditor to gather evidence about the design and implementation of specific controls.

Procedures to obtain an understanding of internal control A major subset of the auditor's risk assessment procedures are those used to obtain an understanding of internal control. **Procedures used to obtain an understanding**, audit procedures used to gather evidence about the design and effectiveness of implementation of internal control, were studied in Chapters 6 and 9. During the development of the client risk profile, the auditor used these techniques to understand the client's business and industry, which included controls over management and governance, strategic planning, risk assessment, and monitoring. In Phase 3, Plan the Audit, the auditor must focus attention on both the design and the operation of aspects of internal control to the extent necessary to plan the rest of the audit effectively. A critical point is that the understanding obtained must be supported with evidence. The purpose of these procedures is to provide both understanding and evidence to support that understanding. These examples of audit procedures that relate to the auditor's understanding of internal control were identified:

- Update and evaluate the auditor's previous experience with the entity.
- Make inquiries of client personnel.
- Read client's policy and systems manuals.
- Inspect documents and records.
- Walk through transactions to verify flow of transactions and controls.
- Observe entity activities and operations.

Tests of controls A major use of the auditor's understanding of internal control is to assess control risk for each transaction-related audit objective. Examples are assessing the accuracy objective for sales transactions as low and the occurrence objective as moderate. Where the auditor believes control policies and procedures are effectively designed, and where it is efficient to do so, he or she will choose to assess control risk at a level that reflects that evaluation. This risk assessment is affected by the extent of automation of controls. In paperless systems or systems that rely fully upon automated controls, such as automatic reordering or EDI for document exchange, the auditor may be required to conduct tests of controls. This occurs as it may not be possible to reduce the risk of material misstatement for a specific transaction-related audit objective to an acceptably low level using only substantive tests. Audit procedures that test the effectiveness of controls in support of a reduced control risk are called **tests of controls**.

Tests of controls are performed to determine the effectiveness of both the design and the operation of specific internal controls. These tests include the following types of procedures:

Tests of controls—audit procedures to test the effectiveness of controls in support of a reduced assessed control risk.

- Make inquiries of appropriate client personnel.
- Examine documents, records, and reports.
- Observe control-related activities.
- Reperform client procedures.

The first two procedures are the same as those used to obtain an understanding of internal control. Performing tests of controls can be thought of as a continuation of the audit procedures used to develop a client risk profile or to obtain an understanding of internal control. The main difference is that with tests of controls, the objective is more specific and the tests are more extensive and linked to the level of risk associated with the assertion being tested. For example, if the client's budgeting process is to be used as a basis for assessing a low level of risk that expenditures are misclassified, in addition to the procedures described in the example given for obtaining an understanding, the auditor might also select a recent budget report, trace its contents to source records, prove its mathematical accuracy, examine all variance reports and memos that flow from it, talk to responsible personnel about the follow-up actions they took, and examine documentation in support of those actions. The purpose of tests of controls is to determine that any of the five transaction-related audit objectives that have a risk of material misstatement have been tested for the affected classes of transactions. For example, the auditor will perform tests of controls to test whether recorded sales transactions occurred and actual transactions are recorded. The auditor also performs these tests to determine if recorded sales transactions are accurately recorded, recorded in the appropriate period, correctly classified, and accurately summarized and posted to the general ledger and data files. If the auditor is confident that transactions were correctly recorded in the journals and correctly posted, he or she can be confident that general ledger totals are correct.

To illustrate typical tests of controls, it is useful to return to the control risk matrix for Hillsburg Hardware Limited in Figure 9-8, page 291. For each of the 11 controls included in Figure 9-8, Table 10-3 (below) identifies a test of controls that might be performed to test its effectiveness. Note that no test of control is performed for the weaknesses in Figure 9-8. It would make no sense to determine if the absence of a control is being adequately performed.

Analytical procedures—use of comparisons and relationships to determine whether account balances or other data appear reasonable.

Analytical procedures As discussed in Chapter 8, **analytical procedures** involve comparisons of recorded amounts to expectations developed by the auditor to determine whether account balances or other data seem reasonable. They often involve the calculation of ratios by the auditor for comparison with previous years' ratios and other related data. For example, the auditor could compare sales, collections, and

Table 10-3	Illustration of Tests of Controls
Illustrative Key Controls	**Typical Tests of Controls**
Credit is approved automatically by the computer by comparison with authorized credit limits (C1).	Review exception report and ensure approval by credit manager (inspection).
Recorded sales are supported by authorized shipping documents and approved customer orders, which are attached to the duplicate sales invoice (C2).	Examine a sample of duplicate sales invoices to determine that each one is supported by an attached, authorized shipping document and approved customer order (inspection).
There is separation of duties between billing, recording sales, and handling cash receipts (C3).	Observe whether personnel responsible for handling cash have no accounting responsibilities, and inquire about their duties (observation and inquiry).
Shipping documents are forwarded to billing daily and billed the subsequent day (C4).	Observe whether shipping documents are forwarded daily to billing, and observe when they are billed (observation).
Shipping documents are issued in numerical order by the computer and are accounted for weekly (C5).	Account for a sequence of shipping documents, and trace each to the sales journal (inspection and reperformance).
Shipping documents are batched daily and compared with quantities billed (C6).	Examine a sample of daily batches, recalculate the shipping quantities, and trace totals to reconciliation with input reports (reperformance).
Unit selling prices are obtained from the price list master file of approved prices (C7).	Examine a sample of sales invoices, and match prices to master file prices list. Review changes to price file throughout the year for proper approval (reperformance and inspection).
Sales transactions are internally verified (C8).	Examine document package for internal verification (inspection).
Statements are mailed to all customers each month (C9).	Observe whether statements are mailed for one month, and inquire about who is responsible for mailing the statements (observation and inquiry).
Once the batch of sales transactions is entered, the computer automatically posts transactions to the accounts receivable subsidiary records and to the general ledger (C10).	Trace postings from the batch of sales transactions to the accounts receivable subsidiary records and general ledger (reperformance).
Accounts receivable master file is reconciled to the general ledger on a monthly basis (C11).	Examine evidence of reconciliation for test month, and test accuracy of reconciliation (inspection and reperformance).

audit challenge 10-1
Testing Data Accuracy

HAVE you heard the term "garbage-in, garbage-out?" The term applies to quality of information—if you enter poor quality data into information systems, then the resulting reports upon which decisions are made are as poor as the data (i.e., garbage).

Think about a document that would be entered at an organization like Hillsburg Hardware Limited, such as a supplier invoice. It will have supplier name, date, invoice amount, and purchase details, such as item number, item description, quantity purchased, extended value, subtotal, taxes, and total.

To prevent data entry errors, most automated systems have features such as input edits whose role is to prevent accidental keying errors. Let us look at the date, for example, which contains a day, month, and year. The month should be between 1 and 12 and should likely be the current month. The day must be between 1 and 31 and should have a logical relationship to the month (for example, February cannot have day 31). The year should likely be the current year.

In addition to data entry controls, there are comparison, or matching, controls. Vendor names can be matched to vendor numbers, item numbers to existing numbers on file, and invoice details to previously recorded purchase order details.

CRITICAL THINKING QUESTIONS

1. Identify five different automated controls that could be applied to the invoice number of a vendor invoice that are not included in our examples.
2. What are some of the things that could go wrong if an item price is entered incorrectly? (These are risks—use audit assertions to describe the risks.)
3. For each risk you listed in (2), state a control that could prevent the risk or detect the error if it should occur. State whether the control you identified is preventive or detective.

accounts receivable in the current year to amounts in previous years and calculate the gross margin percentage for comparison with those in previous years. Analytical procedures are used in multiple audit phases, particularly for risk assessment, to understand the organization, to reduce detailed tests, and to assist with final evaluation.

Analytical procedures (discussed in Chapter 6) are (1) substantive procedures, (2) planning procedures to be used in designing the nature, extent, and timing of other audit procedures and (3) assessment procedures (when used in the final evidence gathering phase). When used as substantive procedures, they would be performed at a detailed level. For example, the auditor could calculate the gross margin for each product to identify which products might be incorrectly priced or have an incorrect cost. The auditor would also need to assess the quality of the data that are being for the analytical procedure. For example, as discussed in Audit Challenge 10-1 above, if the auditor were to use analytical review about individual stores' gross margins, then the auditor would ensure that gross margin data were accurately recorded in the client's system.

Tests of details of balances Tests of details of balances focus on the ending general ledger balances for both balance sheet and income statement accounts, but the primary emphasis in most tests of details of balances is on the balance sheet. (Terms such as "detailed tests" and "direct tests of balances" may be used interchangeably with "tests of details of balances.") Tests of details are audit procedures testing for monetary errors or fraud and other irregularities. They are applied to balance-related audit objectives that are considered to have a risk or material misstatement. Examples include direct communication in writing with customers for accounts receivable, physical examination of inventory, and examination of vendors' statements for accounts payable. These tests of ending balances are essential to the conduct of the audit because, for the most part, the evidence is obtained from a source independent of the client and, thus, is considered to be highly reliable. Examples of tests of details of balances for the financial statement closing process include tracing to underlying records, such as tracing each financial statement figure to the general ledger accounts and tracing journal entries to supporting documents. The extent of these tests depends on the results of controls and analytical procedures.

Tests of details of balances— audit procedures testing for monetary errors or fraud and other irregularities to determine whether the five balance-related audit objectives have been satisfied for each significant account balance.

A substantive test is a procedure designed to test for dollar amounts of errors or fraud and other irregularities directly affecting the correctness of financial statement balances. Such errors or fraud and other irregularities are a clear indication of misstatements of the accounts. The two main types of substantive procedures, analytical procedures and detailed tests of balances, are directed to significant account balances or classes of transactions because of the potential for a misstatement occurring (inherent risk) and because of the potential for a misstatement not being prevented or detected (control risk).

DUAL-PURPOSE TESTS An auditor may perform auditing procedures that are both tests of controls and substantive procedures on the same sample of transactions or account balances for efficiency; such procedures are known as **dual-purpose tests**. Dual-purpose tests provide evidence of whether or not the controls being tested were operating effectively during the period and whether there are misstatements in the data produced by the accounting system. Reperformance always simultaneously provides evidence about both controls and monetary correctness.

Dual-purpose tests are often cost effective when performed with the assistance of software, for example, generalized audit software. The auditor obtains a copy of the transaction file—for example, the detailed sales transaction history file. Substantive tests the auditor would do on such a transaction file include the following:

- Adding up the transactions, providing subtotals by month, and agreeing the subtotals to the general ledger (accuracy of totals, posting, and summarization).
- Adding up the individual lines of the invoice and comparing with the total for each invoice, printing exceptions (accuracy of totals).

Both tests would also serve a control testing purpose. Differences between the monthly totals and general ledger postings would indicate problems with the software that performs these functions. Differences between the auditor invoice total and the system invoice total could indicate a programming error, where invoices were not being added up correctly. Testing the accuracy of a program would be considered a control test.

SUMMARY OF TYPES OF TESTS Figure 10-3 summarizes the types of tests. Procedures to obtain an understanding of internal control and tests of controls are concerned with preparing a client risk profile and evaluating whether controls are sufficiently effective to justify reducing control risk and thereby reducing substantive audit tests. Analytical procedures emphasize the overall reasonableness of transactions and the general ledger balances, and tests of details of balances emphasize the ending balances in the general ledger. Together, the four types of audit tests enable the auditor to gather sufficient appropriate audit evidence to express an opinion on the financial statements.

Observe in Figure 10-3 that all five types of tests are used to satisfy sufficient appropriate audit evidence requirements. Also, observe that procedures to obtain an understanding and tests of controls reduce control risk, whereas the two substantive tests are used to satisfy planned detection risk.

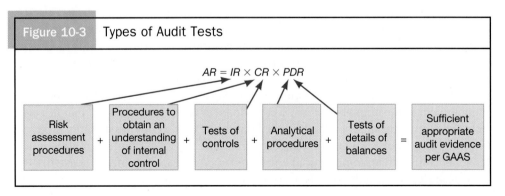

| Figure 10-3 | Types of Audit Tests |

$$AR = IR \times CR \times PDR$$

| Risk assessment procedures | + | Procedures to obtain an understanding of internal control | + | Tests of controls | + | Analytical procedures | + | Tests of details of balances | = | Sufficient appropriate audit evidence per GAAS |

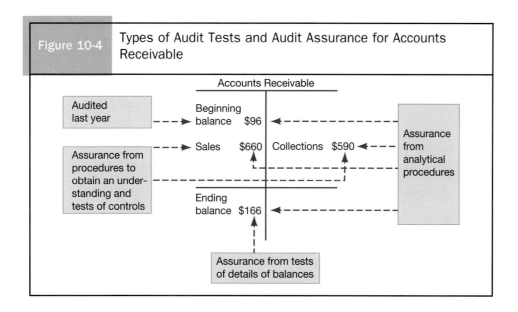

Figure 10-4	Types of Audit Tests and Audit Assurance for Accounts Receivable

Figure 10-4 shows how four types of tests are used to obtain a high level of assurance in the audit of one account, accounts receivable. The auditor can increase overall assurance by increasing the assurance obtained from any of the tests.

Evidence Mix Decisions

Evidence Mix Responds to Audit Strategy

Figure 10-5 shows that evidence mix is a response to risks. The strategic audit process is a methodical process: after preplanning (Phase 1) and after client risk profile (phase 2), the process continues. If controls are working as designed (and are cost-effective to test), then the auditor will conduct more tests of controls and fewer substantive tests. If controls are not functioning or are too expensive to test, then the auditor will conduct more tests of details.

This audit process is a dynamic process, since there is ongoing client business risk assessment with regular audit team interaction. If information arises that alters any of the risk assessments, then the audit plans are changed to reflect the changes in risks. At the same time there is ongoing field work evaluation and quality control to ensure that audit field work is affective and results in sufficient, appropriate audit evidence.

Relationship between Tests and Evidence

The control testing audit programs and the substantive testing audit programs will specify the type of evidence to be used in audit procedures (audit tests), the sample size, the items to select and the timing of the testing.

Only certain types of evidence are obtained through each of the four types of tests. Table 10-4 summarizes the relationship between types of tests and types of evidence. Several observations about the table follow:

- Procedures to obtain an understanding of internal control and tests of controls involve inspection, recalculation, observation, inquiry, and reperformance.
- External confirmation is the only test that is primarily a test of details of balances.
- Inquiries of clients are made with every type of test.
- Inspection, recalculation, and reperformance are used for every type of test except analytical procedures.

concept check

C10-1 How is the audit strategy linked to the audit risk assessment processes?

C10-2 List the five types of audit tests, and provide an example of each that would be relevant to Hillsburg Hardware Limited.

Figure 10-5

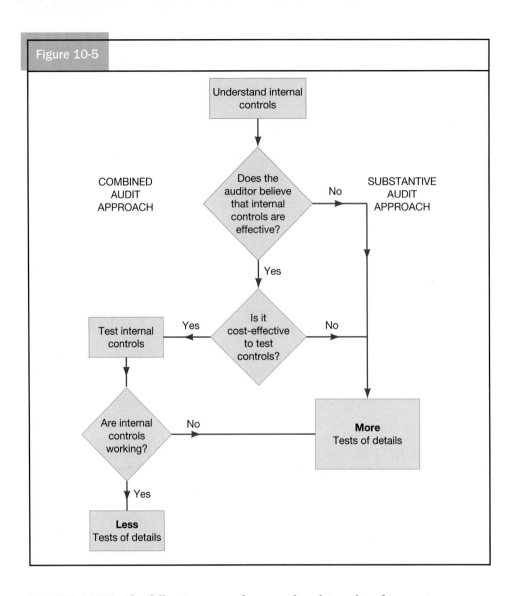

RELATIVE COSTS The following types of tests are listed in order of increasing cost:

- Analytical procedures.
- Procedures to obtain an understanding of internal control and tests of controls.
- Tests of details of balances.

| Table 10-4 | Relationship between Types of Tests and Evidence |

	Type of Evidence						
Type of Test	Inspection	Observation	Inquiries of the Client	External Confirmation	Recalculation	Reperfor-mance	Analytical Procedures
Procedures to obtain an understanding of internal control	✓	✓	✓		✓	✓	
Tests of controls	✓	✓	✓		✓	✓	
Analytical procedures			✓				✓
Tests of details of balances	✓		✓	✓	✓	✓	

The reason analytical procedures are least costly is the relative ease of making calculations and comparisons. Often, considerable information about potential misstatements can be obtained by simply comparing two or three numbers and looking for unusual relationships. Tests of controls are also low in cost because the auditor is making inquiries and observations, examining such things as initials on documents and outward indications of other control procedures, and conducting reperformance, recalculations, and tracings. Frequently, tests of controls can be done on a large number of items in a few minutes, especially if computer-based work, such as the use of test data, is included. Tests of details of balances are almost always considerably more costly than any of the other types of procedures. It is costly to send confirmations and to count assets. Because of the high cost of tests of details of balances, auditors usually try to plan the audit to minimize their use, focusing these tests upon high-risk and materially large areas.

Naturally, the cost of each type of evidence varies in different situations. For example, the cost of an auditor's test counting of inventory (a substantive test of the details of the inventory balance) frequently depends on the nature and dollar value of the inventory, its location, and the number of different items.

RELATIONSHIP BETWEEN TESTS OF CONTROLS AND SUBSTANTIVE TESTS An exception in a test of controls is an indication of the likelihood of errors or fraud and other irregularities affecting the dollar value of the financial statements. However, an exception in a substantive test is a financial statement misstatement. Exceptions in tests of controls are often referred to as "control test deviations." Control test deviations are significant only if they occur with sufficient frequency to cause the auditor to believe there may be material dollar misstatements in the statements. Additional substantive tests should then be performed to determine whether dollar misstatements have actually occurred (called a weakness investigation, as explained in Chapter 9). If controls are working well, then the number of substantive tests can be reduced.

As an illustration, assume that the client's controls require an independent clerk to verify the quantity, price, and extension of each supplier's invoice, after which the clerk must initial the original invoice to indicate performance. A test of control audit procedure would be to examine a sample of suppliers' invoices for the initials of the person who verified the quantitative data. If there is a significant number of documents without initials, the auditor should follow up with tests to determine if there are any monetary misstatements. This can be done by extending the tests of the suppliers' invoices to include verifying prices to purchase orders, reperforming extensions and footings, or by increasing the sample size for the confirmation of accounts payable (test of details of balances). Of course, even though the control is not operating effectively, the invoices may be correct. This will be the case if the persons originally preparing the supplier invoices did a conscientious and competent job. Similarly, even if there is an initial, there may be monetary misstatements due to the clerk initialling without performance or with careless performance of the internal control procedure.

TRADE-OFF BETWEEN TESTS OF CONTROLS AND SUBSTANTIVE TESTS As explained in Chapter 9, there is a trade-off between tests of controls and substantive tests. The auditor makes a decision while planning the control risk assessment. If control risk is assessed as high, the auditor would follow a substantive approach; if control risk is assessed lower, the auditor could follow a combined approach. Tests of controls must be performed to determine whether the lower assessed control risk is supported. If it is, planned detection risk in the audit risk model is increased and substantive procedures can therefore be reduced. If the control testing reveals that the controls are not functioning, or it is very costly to test internal controls, the auditor may still end up with a substantive approach. Figure 10-6 shows the relationship between substantive tests and control risk assessment (including tests of controls) at differing levels of internal control effectiveness.

The shaded area in Figure 10-6 is the maximum assurance obtainable from control risk assessment and tests of controls. For example, at any point to the left of

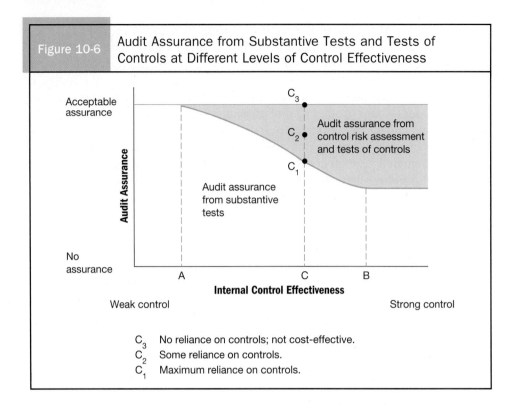

Figure 10-6 Audit Assurance from Substantive Tests and Tests of Controls at Different Levels of Control Effectiveness

C_3 — No reliance on controls; not cost-effective.
C_2 — Some reliance on controls.
C_1 — Maximum reliance on controls.

point A, assessed control risk is 1.0 because the auditor evaluates internal control as ineffective. Remember that auditing standards require that the auditor always understand internal controls as part of the audit planning process. At a large organization such as a bank or technology manufacturer, if controls are not reliable, you may not be able to conduct an effective audit. It will be almost impossible to do a substantive audit of an organization that processes hundreds of thousands of transactions (or more) daily.

Any point to the right of point B results in no further reduction of control risk because the public accounting firm has established the minimum assessed control risk that it will permit.

After the auditor determines the effectiveness of the client's internal controls, it is appropriate to select any point within the shaded area (that is between A and B) of Figure 10-6 consistent with the level of control risk that the auditor determines is appropriate. To illustrate, assume that the auditor contends that internal control effectiveness is at point C. Tests of controls at the C_1 level would provide the minimum control risk, given internal control. The auditor could choose to perform no tests of controls (point C_3), which would support a control risk of 1.0. Any point between the two, such as C_2, would also be appropriate. If C_2 is selected, the audit assurance from tests of controls is $C_3 - C_2$ and from substantive tests is $C - C_2$. The auditor will likely select C_1, C_2, or C_3 based upon the relative cost of tests of controls and substantive tests.

Evidence Mix and Audit Strategy

There are significant variations in the extent to which the four types of tests can be used in different audits for differing levels of inherent risk and internal control effectiveness. There can also be variations from cycle to cycle within a given audit, from account balance to account balance within a particular cycle, and even between assertions for a particular account balance. This combination of the four types of tests to obtain sufficient appropriate audit evidence for a cycle or account balance is known as **audit evidence mix**. Audit evidence mix is based upon the selected audit strategy.

Audit evidence mix—the combination of the four types of tests to obtain sufficient appropriate audit evidence for a cycle or account balance.

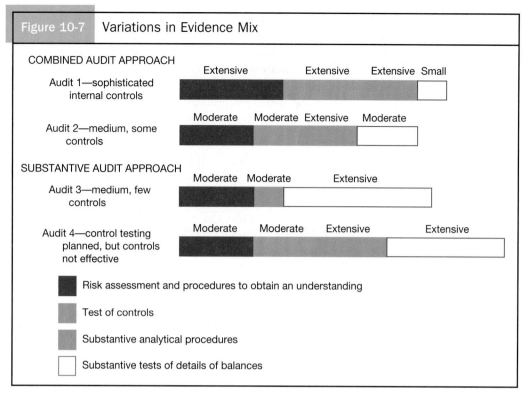

Figure 10-7 Variations in Evidence Mix

COMBINED AUDIT APPROACH

Audit 1—sophisticated internal controls

Extensive · Extensive · Extensive · Small

Audit 2—medium, some controls

Moderate · Moderate · Extensive · Moderate

SUBSTANTIVE AUDIT APPROACH

Audit 3—medium, few controls

Moderate · Moderate · Extensive

Audit 4—control testing planned, but controls not effective

Moderate · Moderate · Extensive · Extensive

■ Risk assessment and procedures to obtain an understanding

■ Test of controls

■ Substantive analytical procedures

□ Substantive tests of details of balances

Note: Auditors in all of the audits have completed client risk profiles, have knowledge of the business, and have completed planning analytical procedures.

Figure 10-7 above shows the audit evidence mix for four different audits. In each case, considerable time was spent accumulating knowledge of business and in risk assessment, as well as completing analytical review for planning purposes. Assume sufficient appropriate audit evidence was accumulated for all audits. Audit 1 is of a large company, while Audits 2 through 4 are of medium-sized companies. An analysis of each audit follows. Refer also to Figure 10-5 during this discussion.

auditing in action 10-1
Research and the Audit Process

How does understanding the external environment relate to risks of financial statement misstatement? A possible source of financial statement bias is the intention of the company to influence customers and suppliers. Raman and Shahrur (2008) found that earnings management was related to the amount of research and development investments by suppliers and customers in the next period.

This means that a company that is looking for customer or supplier financial support when developing a new product could be motivated to overstate its earnings. This research article illustrates the importance of discussing non-financial issues, such as potential new product development, with clients.

Nedard and Johnstone (2004) looked at how auditors adjusted their audit process in response to increased risks, specifically earnings manipulation risk and risk of poor corporate governance. Their results would indicate that in response to such issues as the risk of financial statement manipulation (perhaps due to new product development or high management bonuses), auditors charge more. This is reflected in both increased hours worked on the audit (that is, more testing was conducted), and the auditors actually charging a higher hourly rate, reflecting perhaps the worry associated with high-risk engagements.

Sources: 1. Bedard, Jean C. and Karla M. Johnstone, "Earnings manipulation risk, corporate governance risk, and auditors' planning and pricing decisions," *The Accounting Review*, 79(2), 2004. 2. Raman Kartik and Husayn Shahrur, "Relationship-specific investments and earnings management: Evidence on corporate suppliers and customers," *The Accounting Review*, 83(4), 2008, p. 1041–1081.

Analysis of Audit 1—sophisticated internal controls This client is a large company with sophisticated internal controls, justifying a combined audit approach. The auditor performs extensive tests of controls and relies heavily on the client's internal controls to reduce substantive tests. Extensive analytical procedures are also performed to reduce tests of details of balances, which are, therefore, minimized. Because of the emphasis on tests of controls and analytical procedures, this audit can be done less expensively than other types of audits.

Analysis of Audit 2—medium, some controls This company is medium-sized, with some controls and some inherent risks. Using a combined audit approach, the auditor has decided to do a medium amount of testing for all types of tests except analytical procedures, which will be done extensively.

Analysis of Audit 3—medium, few controls This company is medium-sized but has few effective controls and significant inherent risks. Management has decided that it is not cost-effective to implement better internal controls. This results in a substantive approach: no tests of controls are done because reliance on internal control is inappropriate when controls are insufficient. The emphasis is on tests of details of balances, but some analytical procedures are also done. The reason for limiting analytical procedures is the auditor's expectations of misstatements in the account balances. The cost of the audit is likely to be relatively high because of the amount of detailed substantive testing.

Analysis of Audit 4—medium, ineffective controls The original plan on this audit was to follow the approach used in Audit 2 (a combined audit approach). However, the auditor found extensive control test deviations and significant misstatements using dual-purpose tests and analytical procedures. The auditor, therefore, concluded that the internal controls were not effective and reverts to a wholly substantive approach. Extensive tests of details of balances are performed to offset the unacceptable results of the other tests. The costs of this audit are higher because tests of controls and dual-purpose tests were performed but could not be used to reduce tests of details of balances.

Figure 10-7 shows the relative mix of audit evidence types. It does not reflect total audit cost since the costs associated with the tests will vary, depending on the specific test selected and the extent of computerized support used for conducting the tests.

concept check

C10-3 Which audit test is the least costly to develop and conduct? Why?

C10-4 If an auditor conducts tests of controls but finds that controls are not functioning effectively, what is the effect upon substantive tests? Why?

③ Creating the Audit Programs

Design of the Audit Programs

An audit program identifies the audit steps that are the auditor's response to the identified risks. A combined audit approach is appropriate for most audits; such an approach includes both tests of controls and substantive procedures. The audit program for most audits is designed in three parts: tests of controls, analytical procedures, and tests of details of balances. There will likely be a separate set of audit programs for each transaction cycle. An example in the sales and collection cycle might be tests of controls audit programs for sales and cash receipts; an analytical procedures audit program for the entire cycle; and tests of details of balances audit programs for cash, accounts receivable, bad-debt expense, allowance for uncollectable accounts, and miscellaneous accounts receivable.

TESTS OF CONTROLS Refer to Figure 10-8. The tests of controls audit program normally includes a descriptive section documenting the understanding obtained about internal control, linking relevant key controls to risks that the auditor has identified in the planning meeting, by assertion. The audit file will also contain the procedures (those necessary to obtain an understanding of internal control and to determine the design effectiveness of those internal controls) performed in order to assess control

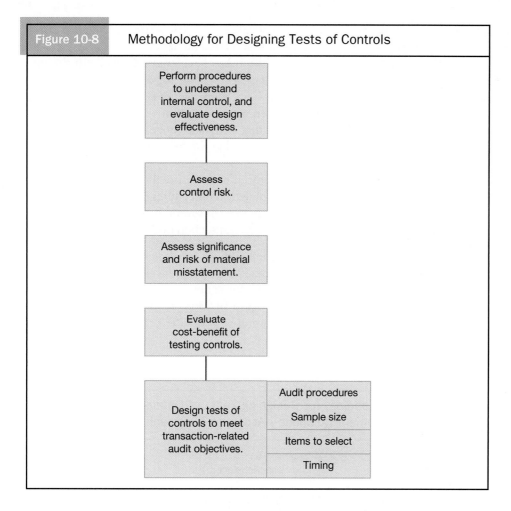

Figure 10-8 Methodology for Designing Tests of Controls

Perform procedures to understand internal control, and evaluate design effectiveness.

Assess control risk.

Assess significance and risk of material misstatement.

Evaluate cost-benefit of testing controls.

Design tests of controls to meet transaction-related audit objectives.
- Audit procedures
- Sample size
- Items to select
- Timing

risk. After assessing control risk, the auditor will assess the significance of the risks and determine the risk of material misstatements at the assertion level.

Then, the auditor will design tests of controls for those tests that are considered cost-effective to address risks at the assertion level. The first four steps in Figure 10-8 were described in more detail in Chapter 9 (refer to Figure 9-4). When controls are effective and planned control risk is low (i.e., the auditor chooses to rely on internal controls), a combined audit approach will be used and there will be tests of controls. Some dual-purpose tests may also be included. If control risk is assessed at maximum, the auditor will use a substantive audit approach (i.e., only substantive procedures will be used), as illustrated in Figure 10-5. The procedures already performed in obtaining an understanding of internal control may affect tests of controls.

For each transaction-related audit assertion where the auditor determines that reliance will be placed on controls, the auditor will select one or more audit procedures. The audit program will also describe sample size, the items to select, and timing. For example, an audit procedure to determine that recorded sales are for shipments actually made to non-fictitious customers (occurrence), the auditor would examine copies of sales invoices for supporting bills of lading and customer's purchase orders. The sample size of 44 would be determined based upon risks and estimated error rates (discussed further in the next two chapters). Items could be selected using the random number generator in your spreadsheet software, and tested at the interim audit, three months prior to the year end of the client.

ANALYTICAL PROCEDURES Many auditors perform extensive analytical procedures on all audits because they are relatively inexpensive. As stated in Chapter 8, analytical procedures are performed at three different stages of the audit: in the planning stage to help the auditor decide the other evidence needed to satisfy audit risk, during the audit in conjunction with tests of details of balances as part of substantive procedures, and near the end of the audit as a final test of reasonableness.

CAS CAS 315, Identifying and assessing the risks of material misstatement through understanding the entity and its environment, requires the use of analytical procedures during the planning phase of the audit. CAS 520 provides standards to ensure the effectiveness of analytical procedures when used as substantive procedures, although their use is optional. CAS 520 also states that analytical procedures are required as a final evaluation technique when assessing whether the financial statements are fairly stated and consistent with other evidence.

Choosing the appropriate analytical procedures requires the auditor to use professional judgment. The appropriate use of analytical procedures and illustrative ratios is discussed in Chapter 8. There are also examples in several subsequent chapters that provide typical analytical procedures for each transaction cycle.

TESTS OF DETAILS OF BALANCES The methodology for designing tests of details of balances is linked to the balance-related audit objectives developed in Chapter 5. In planning tests of details of balances to satisfy those objectives, many auditors follow a methodology such as the one shown in Figure 10-9 for accounts receivable. Designing such procedures is subjective and requires considerable professional judgment.

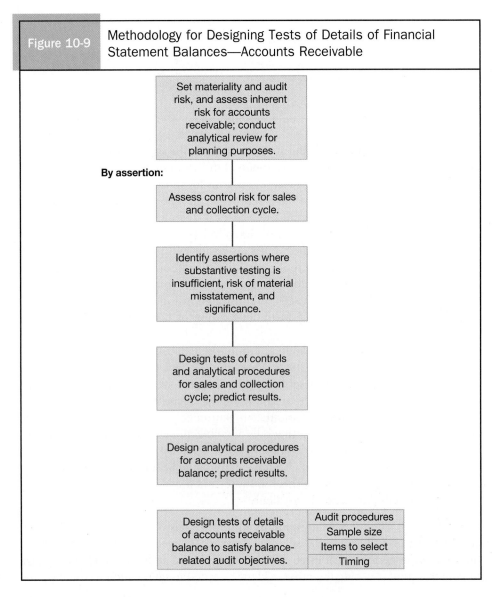

Figure 10-9 Methodology for Designing Tests of Details of Financial Statement Balances—Accounts Receivable

Set materiality audit risk and assess inherent risk for accounts receivable Setting the preliminary judgment about materiality for the audit as a whole is an auditor decision that was discussed in Chapter 6. The auditor could choose a different materiality for accounts receivable (which would be called tolerable misstatement for the account). A lower materiality would result in more testing of details. Analytical review for planning purposes, used together with a good knowledge of business and the industry, allows the auditor to identify obvious warning signals of error or fraud.

As discussed in Chapter 7, audit risk is normally decided for the audit as a whole, rather than by cycle. A rare exception might be when the auditor believes that a misstatement of a specific account, such as accounts receivable, would negatively affect users more than the same size misstatement of any other account. For example, if accounts receivable is pledged to a bank as security on a loan, audit risk may be set lower for sales and collections than for other cycles.

Inherent risk is assessed by identifying any aspect of the client's history, environment, or operations that indicates a high likelihood of misstatement in the current year's financial statements. This emphasizes the need for a broad-based knowledge of business that links risks to the external business environment. Once inherent risk has been assessed for the financial statements as a whole, it is assessed at the assertion level. Considerations affecting overall inherent risk applied to accounts receivable include makeup of accounts receivable, nature of the client's business, and sales trends. An account balance for which inherent risk has been assessed as high would result in more evidence accumulation than for an account with low inherent risk.

Inherent risk also can be extended to individual audit objectives. For example, because of adverse economic conditions in the client's industry, the auditor may conclude that there is a high risk of uncollectable accounts receivable (valuation objective). Inherent risk could still be low for all other objectives.

Assess control risk Control risk is discussed in detail in Chapter 9 and in earlier parts of this chapter. This methodology would be applied to both sales and collection in the audit of accounts receivable. As illustrated in Figure 10-5, effective controls reduce control risk and therefore the extent of evidence required for substantive procedures; inadequate controls increase the substantive evidence needed.

Identify high-risk assertions Assertions can be high risk for several reasons. The auditor may have identified the assertion as having a significant risk of fraud or material misstatement. For example, if there is an economic downturn and the client has customers with high credit limits, the auditor may want to spend additional time testing the valuation assertion, as the uncollectability of a single large account could have a significant effect. Also, there could be some assertions where substantive testing alone is not enough, due to extensive reliance on automated systems, for example with automated credit checks. In the latter case, the auditor may decide that testing of internal controls could be effective, especially where general controls over program changes and information systems access are of high quality.

Design tests of controls and analytical procedures and predict results The methodology for designing tests of controls and analytical procedures was discussed earlier in this section and will be illustrated in subsequent chapters. The tests are designed with the expectation that certain results will be obtained. These predicted results affect the design of tests of details of balances as discussed below.

Design tests of details of balances to satisfy balance-related audit objectives The planned tests of details of balances include audit procedures, sample size, items to select, and timing. Procedures must be selected and designed for each account and each balance-related audit objective within each account.

A difficulty the auditor faces in designing tests of details of balances is the need to predict the outcome of the tests of controls and analytical procedures before they are performed. This is necessary because the auditor should design tests of details of balances during the planning phase, but the appropriate design depends on the outcome

Table 10-5	Timing of Selected Audit Tests		
Risk Assessment	Plan and design audit approach, update understanding of internal control, update audit program, and perform preliminary analytical procedures.	31/8/11	
Risk Response	Perform tests of controls for first nine months of the year.	30/9/11	
	Confirm accounts receivable. Observe inventory.	31/10/11	
	Count cash, perform cut-off tests, and request various other confirmations.	31/12/11	Balance sheet date
	Do analytical procedures, complete tests of controls, and do most tests of details of balances.	07/1/12	Books closed
	Summarize results, review for contingent liabilities, review for subsequent events, accumulate final evidence including analytical procedures, and finalize audit.	08/3/12	Last date of field work
Reporting	Finalize and issue auditor's report after financial statements are approved.	15/3/12	

of the other tests. In planning tests of details of balances, the auditor usually predicts that there will be few or no exceptions in tests of controls and analytical procedures, unless there are reasons to believe otherwise. If the results of the tests of controls and analytical procedures are not consistent with the predictions, the tests of details of balances will need to be increased as the audit progresses. This occurred in our example of Audit 4 in Figure 10-7.

TIMING OF AUDIT TESTS Audit tests can be conducted throughout the year, or, for a small audit, may be conducted in a concentrated period of time. Table 10-5 shows typical timing for the different types of audit tests that we have conducted, for a client with a December year end. Because of their low cost, it is common to use analytical procedures whenever they are relevant.

The table shows that tests of details of balances are normally done last. On some audits, all are done after the balance sheet date. When clients want to issue statements soon after the balance sheet date, however, the more time-consuming tests of details of balances will be done at interim audit dates prior to year end with additional work being done to **roll forward** the audited interim-date balances to year end. (A roll forward involves substantive work on journal entries and other activities during this period.) Substantive tests of balances performed before year end provide less assurance and are not normally done unless internal controls are effective.

Roll forward—substantive work on journal entries and transactions from a date prior to the balance sheet date to the year end.

ILLUSTRATIVE AUDIT PROGRAM Table 10-6 shows the tests of details of balances segment of an audit program for accounts receivable. The format used relates the audit procedures to the balance-related audit objectives and presentation and disclosure audit objectives. Note that most procedures satisfy more than one objective. Also, more than one audit procedure is used for each objective. Audit procedures can be added or deleted as the auditor considers necessary. Sample size, items to select, and timing can also be changed for most procedures.

The audit program in Table 10-6 was developed after consideration of all the factors affecting tests of details of balances and is based on several assumptions about inherent risk, control risk, and the results of tests of controls and analytical procedures. If those assumptions change, the planned audit program will require revision. For example, analytical procedures could indicate potential errors for several balance-related audit objectives, tests of controls results could indicate weak internal controls, or new facts could cause the auditor to change inherent risk.

Sample Size	Items to Select	Timing*	Tests of Details of Balances Audit Procedures	Existence (B, PD)	Rights (B, PD)	Completeness (B, PD)	Accuracy (PD)	Valuation (B, PD)	Allocation (B)	Classification (PD)
Trace 20 items; foot 2 pages and all subtotals	Random	I	1. Obtain an aged list of receivables: trace open items to supporting invoice detail, foot schedule, and trace to general ledger.			x				
All	All	Y	2. Obtain an analysis of the allowance for doubtful accounts and bad debt expense: test accuracy, examine authorization for write-offs, and trace to general ledger.	x		x	x	x		
100	30 largest 70 random	I	3. Obtain direct confirmation of accounts receivable and perform alternative procedures for non-responses.	x	x	x	x		x	x
N/A	N/A	Y	4. Review accounts receivable control account for the period. Investigate the nature of, and review support for, any large or unusual entries or any entries not arising from normal journal sources. Also investigate any significant increases or decreases in sales toward year end.	x	x			x	x	x
All	All	Y	5. Review receivables for any that have been assigned or discounted.		x					
N/A	N/A	Y	6. Investigate collectibility of account balances.					x		
All	All	Y	7. Review lists of balances for amounts due from related parties or employees, credit balances, and unusual items, as well as notes receivable due after one year.	x						x
30 transactions for sales and cash receipts; 10 for credit memos	50% before and 50% after year end	Y	8. Determine that proper cutoff procedures were applied at the balance sheet date to ensure that sales, cash receipts, and credit memos have been recorded in the correct period.						x	

Balance–Related (B) and Presentation and Disclosure (BD)

Accounts Receivable Audit Objectives

*I – Interim; Y – Year end; N/A – Not applicable

Most large public accounting firms develop their own standard audit programs, organized by industry, often linked by audit objective to databases including lists of expected controls and likely audit tests. Smaller firms often purchase similar audit programs from outside organizations. Standard audit programs are normally computerized and can easily be modified to meet the circumstances of individual audit engagements. Examples of standard audit programs available for purchase are the CICA's *Professional Engagement Manual* (PEM) and CGA Canada's *Professional Practice Manual* (PPM). These manuals are available in paper form, online, or on CD-ROM and contain audit programs as well as general and industry-specific checklists that auditors can use and modify for individual engagements.

Standard audit programs, whether developed internally or purchased from an outside organization, can dramatically increase audit efficiency if they are used properly. They should not be used, however, as a substitute for an auditor's professional judgment. Because each audit is different, it is usually necessary to add, modify, or delete steps within a standard audit program in order to accumulate sufficient and appropriate audit evidence.

SELECTION OF AUDIT TESTS BY ASSERTION Refer to Table 5-5, Management assertions for each category of assertion, which we also use as our audit assertions. Table 5-5 shows that some of the assertions relate to all three areas: transactions, balances, and presentation and disclosure (for example, completeness). This is why the tests of detail in Table 10-6 address both the balance-related audit objectives and the presentation and disclosure audit objectives (except for understandability).

Tests of details of balances must be designed to satisfy balance-related audit objectives for each account. At the same time, these tests of detail provide assurance regarding the information that is presented in the financial statements, assuming that the auditor traces the general ledger balances to the financial statements.

The extent of substantive tests can be reduced when transaction-related audit objectives have been satisfied by tests of controls. It is, therefore, important to understand how each transaction-related audit objective relates to each balance-related audit objective.

This direct relationship can be illustrated by looking at sales transactions. If there are controls to ensure that all sales transactions that occur are recorded in the accounts receivable, then these controls can provide assurance with respect to the balance-related audit objective of completeness and the presentation and disclosure objective of completeness for revenue shown in the financial statements.

The relationship among the three types of audit objectives is discussed further in Chapter 12.

In addition to conducting tests to assess the fairness of the transactions and accounts shown in the financial statements, the auditor is required to examine and analyze the financial statements and the related notes with respect to the audit assertions. To do so, the auditor uses presentation and disclosure-related audit objectives, as explained in Chapter 5. The first four objectives are similar to the transaction-related and balance-related audit objectives. The final audit objective, understandability, requires the auditor to examine the statements and notes from the perspective of a knowledgeable business user to assess whether information has been clearly presented.

concept check

C10-5 List the type of information that would be included in an audit program.

C10-6 Describe the type of testing required when the auditor has identified an assertion to have a significant risk of material misstatement.

4 The Audit Process and Client Conversion to IFRS

In your accounting courses, you will have learned about several accounting frameworks, including IFRS and ASPE. In Canada, publicly accountable companies were required to adopt IFRS in 2011 as their financial reporting framework. Major efforts took place at large organizations to undertake this change. This is an ongoing issue, as small companies grow or are acquired by larger companies and may then be required to change their accounting framework from ASPE to IFRS. Table 10-7 describes how these changes present several additional risks which the auditor will need to consider.

The auditor will follow a risk-based approach when considering the impact of the IFRS conversion upon the audit plan. For example, when gathering knowledge of business, the auditor will consider the IFRS competencies of management, the Board of Directors, and the Audit Committee. When assessing control risk, the auditor will consider the quality of the processes that the client is using, such as:

- Knowledge and training of employees with financial reporting responsibilities,
- The source and quality of data for new and expanded financial statement disclosures under IFRS; and

Table 10-7

Risks of Error or Misstatement during IFRS Conversion

Potential bias in selection of accounting policies: At the time of conversion, the client has the opportunity to select accounting principles that are acceptable under IFRS. The client could select accounting policies that bias income or other presentations in the financial statements.

Incorrect implementation of accounting policies: The client's staff and management may lack familiarity with the new standards and guidance, and may not adequately document transactions to effectively implement the new accounting policies or to correctly calculate opening balances under IFRS.

Inconsistent internal controls: Since record-keeping practices may need to change, internal controls may change. Such controls may not be consistently applied due to lack of training or other reasons, resulting in an increase in the risks of material error.

Manipulation of transition adjustments: The client may attempt to record misstatements found in previously reported Canadian generally accepted accounting principles financial results as IFRS transition adjustments, a deliberate misstatement of the transition adjustments.

Errors in opening balance sheet: There may be omissions or other errors in the opening IFRS balance sheet adjustments.

Lack of consistency in group financial statements: Business units or subsidiaries may not be consistent with the parent company's IFRS accounting policies, and these differences may not be corrected upon consolidation.

Spreadsheet accounting: If reconciliations are maintained in spreadsheets, there is an increased risk of manual error in the entering information or when doing calculations.

- Segregation of duties and approvals during the IFRS conversion process, such as of initial review and approval of IFRS-related accounting policy decisions.

It is possible that materiality will change for subsequent audits if the basis of reporting income has changed. If the change to IFRS reduces income (and thus materiality) for a subsequent year, it may mean that additional field work may be required on the audit of the opening balances. This means, that, if auditors are aware that their client will be converting to IFRS, the auditors might choose to use a lower performance materiality when conducting their audit of the prior year.

If controls over the IFRS conversion process are poor, then the auditor may need to use a substantive audit approach for the conversion process, increasing the cost of the audit.

concept check

C10-7 Why does the auditor need to know how to audit an IFRS conversion?

C10-8 Explain why the auditor might not be able to use a combined audit approach of an IFRS conversion.

Summary

1. *What is an audit strategy?* An audit strategy comprises a planned approach to the conduct of audit testing, taking into account assessed risks. The audit strategy is either substantive or combined (substantive plus control testing).

   What is the role of audit planning? Audit planning describes a structured process to document risks according to the audit risk model, to document and evaluate internal controls, and to design an audit program in response to assessed risks.

   What is the purpose of an audit program? An audit program lists the audit procedures that the auditor con-ducts as the risk response phase of the audit. This includes tests of control and substantive tests.

   What are the five different types of audit tests? The five types of audit tests are (1) risk assessment procedures, (2) procedures to obtain an understanding of internal control, (3) tests of controls, (4) analytical procedures, and (5) tests of details of balances. Together, detailed analytical procedures and tests of details of balances are called substantive tests.

   Which type of test is a dual-purpose test? What is the purpose of such a test? A substantive test (remember that a substantive test comprises both analytical procedures and tests of details and is used to quantify errors) can be used both to quantify errors and as a test of controls.

2. *What is evidence mix?* Evidence mix is the phrase used to explain the proportion of the different types of tests used in the audit engagement.

Why is evidence mix selection a dynamic process? As the audit progresses and the auditor's risks assessments change, the auditor is required to modify the evidence collection process.

How does the auditor choose the types of audit tests to be completed? Audit tests are selected based upon the level of assessed risks. For example, tests of control are conducted only if control risk is set below maximum and there is a potential for reliance upon internal controls.

3. *What is the methodology for selecting audit tests for the audit program?* The audit program is designed to ensure that sufficient competent evidence is gathered for each class of transaction (or account or disclosure) for each relevant audit assertion. Audit tests are linked to the audit assertion in the context of assessed risks.

4. *How does a client's conversion to IFRS affect the audit process?* There are a number of additional risks to consider, such as inappropriate accounting policy selection and implementation. The auditor responds to these risks by auditing the client's IFRS implementation.

MyAccountingLab

Make the grade with MyAccountingLab: The questions, exercises, and problems marked in orange can be found on MyAccountingLab. You can practise them as often as you want, and most feature step-by-step guided instructions to help you find the right answer.

Review Questions

10-1 ❶ What are the five types of tests auditors use to determine whether financial statements are fairly stated? Identify which tests are performed to assess control risk and which tests are performed to achieve planned detection risk. Also, identify which tests will be used when auditing internal control over financial reporting.

10-2 ❶ Review the phases of the financial statement audit. List each phase that involves risk assessment. State which types of audit procedures would be used during each phase that you listed.

10-3 ❶ What is the purpose of risk assessment procedures, and how are they related to or different from the four other types of audit tests?

10-4 ❶ ❸ Distinguish between a test of controls and a substantive procedure. Give two examples of each.

10-5 ❶ Explain what is meant by "recalculation" and "reperformance." Give an example of each type of audit evidence. Why are recalculation and reperformance often dual-purpose tests?

10-6 ❶ ❷ ❸ An auditor may perform tests of controls and substantive procedures simultaneously as a matter of audit convenience. However, the substantive procedures and sample size are, in part, dependent upon the results of the tests of controls. How can the auditor resolve this apparent inconsistency?

10-7 ❸ Explain how the calculation of the gross margin percentage and the ratio of accounts receivable to sales, and their comparison to that of previous years, are related to the confirmation of accounts receivable and other tests of the accuracy of accounts receivable.

10-8 ❶ ❷ ❸ Distinguish between a combined audit approach and a substantive audit approach. Give one example of when each might be appropriate for the acquisition and payment cycle.

10-9 ❷ ❸ Assume that the client's internal controls over the recording and classifying of capital asset additions are considered weak because the individual responsible for recording new acquisitions has inadequate technical training and limited experience in accounting. How would this situation affect the evidence you should accumulate in auditing permanent assets as compared with another audit in which the controls are excellent? Be as specific as possible.

10-10 ❶ ❸ For each of the seven types of evidence discussed in Chapter 8, identify whether the evidence is applicable to procedures for risk assessment, obtaining an understanding of internal control, tests of controls, analytical procedures, or tests of details of balances.

10-11 ❶ ❷ ❸ The following are three decision factors related to the assessed level of control risk: effectiveness of internal controls, cost-effectiveness of a reduced assessed level of control risk, and results of tests of controls. Identify the combination of conditions for these three factors that is required before a reduction in substantive procedures is permitted.

10-12 ❸ Explain the relationship between the methodology for designing tests of controls in Figure 10-8 (page 323) to the methodology for designing tests of details of balances in Figure 10-9 (page 324).

10-13 ❶ ❷ ❸ Why is it desirable to design tests of details of balances before performing tests of controls? State the assumptions the auditor must make in doing this. What does the auditor do if the assumptions prove to be incorrect?

10-14 ❷ ❸ Why do auditors frequently consider it desirable to perform audit tests throughout the year rather than wait until year end? List several examples of evidence that can be accumulated prior to year end.

10-15 ❹ Alphatori Company's shares have been purchased by a food conglomerate, a public company. How will this change in ownership affect the accounting framework in use by Alphatori? How will the change in accounting framework affect the audit of Alphatori?

Discussion Questions and Problems

10-16 ❶ The following are 11 audit procedures taken from an audit program:

1. Add the supplier balances in the accounts payable master file, and compare the total with the general ledger.
2. Examine vendors' invoices to verify the ending balance in accounts payable.
3. Compare the balance in employee benefits expense with previous years'. The comparison takes the increase in employee benefits rates into account.
4. Discuss the duties of the cash disbursements bookkeeper with him or her, and observe whether he or she has responsibility for handling cash or preparing the bank reconciliation.
5. Confirm accounts payable balances directly with vendors.
6. Use generalized audit software to run a gap test on the cheques issued during the year. (Print a list of cheque numbers omitted from the normal cheque number sequencing.)
7. Examine the treasurer's initials on monthly bank reconciliations as an indication of whether they have been reviewed.
8. Examine vendors' invoices and other documentation in support of recorded transactions in the acquisitions journal.
9. Multiply the commission rate by total sales, and compare the result with commission expense.
10. Examine vendors' invoices and other supporting documents to determine whether large amounts in the repair and maintenance account should be capitalized.
11. Examine the initials of vendors' invoices that indicate internal verification of pricing, extending, and footing by a clerk.

REQUIRED

a. Indicate whether each procedure is a test of controls, an analytical procedure, or a test of details of balances.
b. Identify the type of evidence for each procedure.

10-17 ❶ ❷ ❸ Jennifer Schaefer, a public accountant, follows the philosophy of performing interim tests of controls on every December 31 audit as a means of keeping overtime to a minimum. Typically, the interim tests are performed some time between August and November.

REQUIRED

a. Evaluate her decision to perform interim tests of controls.

b. Under what circumstances is it acceptable for her to perform no additional tests of controls as part of the year-end audit tests?
c. If she decides to perform no additional testing, what is the effect on other tests she performs during the remainder of the engagement?

10-18 ❶ ❷ ❸ Kim Bryan, a new staff auditor, is confused by the inconsistency of the three audit partners to whom she has been assigned on her first three audit engagements. On the first engagement, she spent a considerable amount of time in the audit of cash disbursements by examining cancelled cheques and supporting documentation, but almost no time was spent on the verification of capital assets. On the second engagement, a different partner had her do less intensive tests in the cash disbursements area and take smaller sample sizes than in the first audit even though the company was much larger. On her most recent engagement under a third audit partner, there was a thorough test of cash disbursement transactions, far beyond that of the other two audits, and an extensive verification of capital assets. In fact, this partner insisted on a complete physical examination of all capital assets recorded on the books. The total audit time on the most recent audit was longer than that of either of the first two audits in spite of the smaller size of the company. Bryan's conclusion is that the amount of evidence to accumulate depends on the audit partner in charge of the engagement.

REQUIRED

a. State the differences in risk assessments that could affect the amount of evidence accumulated in each of the three audit engagements as well as the total time spent.
b. What could the audit partners have done to help Bryan understand the differences in the audit emphasis on the three audits?
c. Explain how these three audits are useful in developing Bryan's professional judgment. How could the quality of her judgment have been improved by the audits?

10-19 ❷ ❸ Assume that the client's internal controls over the recording and classifying of fixed asset additions are considered deficient because the individual responsible for recording new acquisitions has inadequate technical training and limited experience in accounting.

REQUIRED

a. What value would you assign to control risk? Why?
b. How will this situation affect the evidence you should accumulate in auditing fixed assets as compared with another audit in which the controls are excellent? Be as specific as possible.

10-20 ❷ ❸ Beds and Spreads, Inc. specializes in bed and bath furnishings. Its inventory system is linked through the company's website to key suppliers. The auditor identified the following internal controls in the inventory cycle:

1. The computer initiates an order only when perpetual inventory levels fall below prespecified inventory levels in the inventory master file.
2. The sales and purchasing department managers review inventory reorder points for reasonableness on a monthly basis. Approved changes to reorder points are entered into the master file by the purchasing department manager and an updated printout is generated for final review. Both managers verify that all changes were entered correctly and initial the final printout indicating final approval. These printouts are maintained in the purchasing department.
3. The computer will initiate a purchase order only for inventory product numbers maintained in the inventory master file.
4. The purchasing department manager reviews a computer-generated exception report that highlights weekly purchases that exceed $10,000 per vendor.

5. Salesclerks send damaged merchandise on the store shelves to the back storage room. The sales department manager examines the damaged merchandise each month and prepares a listing showing the estimated salvage value by product number. The accounting department uses the listing to prepare a monthly adjustment to recorded inventory values.

REQUIRED

Consider each of the preceding controls separately.
a. What type of risk or potential error could occur if the control were absent?
b. State whether the control is manual, computer-assisted, or fully automated.
c. Describe how the extent of testing of each control would be affected in subsequent years if general controls, particularly controls over program and master file changes, are effective.
d. For each control,
   • provide an example of an audit procedure to test the control; and
   • state the transaction-related audit objective associated with the audit procedure.

10-21 ❷ ❸ The following are audit procedures from different transaction cycles:

1. Use audit software to foot and cross-foot the cash disbursements journal, and trace the balance to the general ledger.
2. Select a sample of entries in the acquisitions journal, and trace each one to a related vendor's invoice to determine whether one exists.
3. Examine documentation for acquisition transactions before and after the balance sheet date to determine whether they are recorded in the proper period.
4. Inquire of the credit manager whether each account receivable on the aged trial balance is collectable.
5. Compute inventory turnover for each major product, and compare with that of previous years.
6. Confirm with lenders a sample of notes payable balances, interest rates, and collateral.
7. Use audit software to foot the accounts payable trial balance, and compare the balance with the general ledger.

REQUIRED

a. For each audit procedure, identify the transaction cycle being audited.
b. For each audit procedure, identify the type of evidence.
c. For each audit procedure, identify whether it is a test of control or a substantive test (indicating whether it is a test of details of balances or an analytical procedure).
d. For each audit procedure, identify the related audit objective(s).
e. Specifically assess the purpose of each audit procedure, as follows:
   • For tests of control, state the risk (potential error) that is being assessed.
   • For analytical procedures, state a possible result that you would expect.
   • For tests of detail, state the type of material error that you would be quantifying.

10-22 ❷ ❸ The following are three situations, all involving private companies, in which the auditor is required to develop an audit strategy:

1. The client has inventory at approximately 50 locations in a three-province region. The inventory is difficult to count and can be observed only by travelling by automobile. The internal controls over acquisitions, cash disbursements, and perpetual records are considered effective. This is the fifth year that you have done the audit, and audit results in past years have always been excellent. The client is in excellent financial condition.

2. This is the first year of an audit of a medium-sized company that is considering selling its business because of severe underfinancing. A review of the acquisition and payment cycle indicates that controls over cash disbursements are excellent but controls over acquisitions cannot be considered effective. The client lacks receiving reports and a policy as to the proper timing to record acquisitions. When you review the general ledger, you observe that there are many large adjusting entries to correct accounts payable.

3. You are doing the audit of a small loan company with extensive loans receivable from customers. Controls over

granting loans, collections, and loans outstanding are considered effective, and there is extensive follow-up of all outstanding loans weekly. You have recommended a new computer system for the past two years, but management believes the cost is too great, given their low profitability. Collections are an ongoing problem because many of the customers have severe financial problems. Because of adverse economic conditions, loans receivable have significantly increased and collections are less than normal. In previous years, you have had relatively few adjusting entries.

REQUIRED

a. For audit 1, recommend an evidence mix for the five types of tests for the audit of inventory and cost of goods sold. Justify your answer. Include in your recommendations both tests of controls and substantive tests.

b. For audit 2, recommend an evidence mix for the audit of the acquisition and payment cycle, including accounts payable. Justify your answer.

c. For audit 3, recommend an evidence mix for the audit of outstanding loans. Justify your answer.

Professional Judgment Problem

10-23 ❶ ❷ ❸ ❹ Sidhu, a PA, is planning his first audit of Microservices Ltd., a local retailer of computers and related products. Microservices is a new company, and this is the client's first fiscal year of operations. The owner has explained to Sidhu that she wants an audit from the beginning of the fiscal year and for the next several years so that she can build a credible financial track record. She then plans to make a public offering of shares, when market conditions are favourable. Sidhu recommended to the company (which the owner accepted) that the applicable accounting framework to be used should be ASPE.

Because the company is small and has few employees, Sidhu decides to ignore the company's internal controls and rely solely on substantive tests of transactions and details in this first audit engagement. Sidhu believes that this approach

will allow him to perform an audit at minimum cost, and hence charge a minimum audit fee. In later years, as the client's systems become better developed, Sidhu plans to modify his audit approach to incorporate some reliance on the client's internal controls and thereby reduce his level of substantive testing. Before beginning the audit, Sidhu discusses this audit plan with the owner, who fully agrees with Sidhu that this is the most efficient way to proceed, given the circumstances.

REQUIRED

Assess Sidhu's actions, using Canadian auditing standards.

(Extract from AU2 CGA -Canada Examinations developed by the Certified General Accountants Association of Canada © 2010 CGA-Canada. Reproduced with permission. All rights reserved.)

Case

10-24 ❶ ❷ ❸ Gale Brewer, a public accountant, had been the partner in charge of the audit of Merkle Manufacturing Company, a nonpublic company, for 13 years. Merkle had had remarkable growth and profits in the past decade, primarily as a result of the excellent leadership provided by Bill Merkle and other competent executives. Gale had always enjoyed a close relationship with the company and prided herself on having made over the years several constructive comments that had aided in the success of the firm. Several times in the past few years, Gale's firm had considered rotating a different audit team onto the engagement, but this had been strongly resisted by both Gale and Bill.

For the first few years of the audit, internal controls were inadequate and the accounting personnel had inadequate qualifications for their responsibilities. Extensive audit evidence was required during the audit, and numerous adjusting entries were necessary. However, because of Gale's constant prodding, internal controls improved gradually and competent personnel were hired. In recent years, there were normally no audit adjustments required, and the extent of the evidence accumulation was gradually reduced. During the past three years, Gale was able to devote less time to the audit because of the relative ease of conducting the audit and the cooperation obtained throughout the engagement.

In the current year's audit, Gale decided that the total time budget for the engagement should be kept approximately the same as in recent years. The senior in charge of the audit, Phil Warren, was new on the job and highly competent, and he had the reputation of being able to cut time off budgets. The fact that Bill had recently acquired a new division through merger would probably add to the time, but Phil's efficiency would probably compensate for it.

The interim tests of controls took somewhat longer than expected because of the use of several new assistants, a change in the accounting system to computerize the inventory and other accounting records, a change in accounting personnel, and the existence of a few more errors in the tests of the system. Neither Gale nor Phil was concerned about the budget deficit, however, because they could easily make up the difference at year end.

At year end, Phil assigned the responsibility for inventory to an assistant who also had not been on the audit before but was competent and extremely fast at his work. Even though the total value of inventory increased, Phil reduced the size of the sample from that of other years because there had been few errors in the preceding year. The assistant found several items in the sample that were overstated as a result of errors in pricing and obsolescence, but the combination of all of the errors in the sample was immaterial. Accordingly, Phil decided that adjustments to control risk were not warranted. The assistant completed the tests in 25 percent less time than the preceding year's tests. The entire audit was completed on schedule and in slightly less time than the preceding year's.

There were only a few adjusting entries for the year, and only two of them were material. Gale was extremely pleased with the results and wrote a special letter to Phil and the inventory assistant complimenting them on their efficiency during the audit.

Six months later, Gale received a telephone call from Bill and was informed that the company was in serious financial trouble. Subsequent investigation revealed that the inventory had been significantly overstated. The major cause of the misstatement was the inclusion of obsolete items in inventory (especially in the new division), errors in pricing as a result of a programming error in the new computer system, and the inclusion of nonexistent inventory in the final inventory listing, which had been printed two weeks after the inventory count had actually been conducted. The new controller had been directed to intentionally overstate the inventory to compensate for the reduction in sales volume from the preceding year.

REQUIRED

a. Following the sequence of the phases in the audit process, list the major deficiencies in the audit, and state why they took place.

b. What things should have been apparent to Gale or Phil in the conduct of the audit?

c. If Gale's firm is sued by creditors, what is the likely outcome?

Ongoing Small Business Case: Auditing Revenue Recognition at CondoCleaners.com

10-25 ❷ ❸ As explained in this chapter and in previous chapters, revenue recognition is likely to have the potential for material misstatement at most audits. Recall that orders for cleaning are placed two or more days ahead of time and paid for by credit card at the time of booking. Jim records sales in his accounting records, from the internet transactions.

REQUIRED

a. What sales audit assertions are subject to misstatement at CondoCleaners.com?

b. What data would you ask Jim, the owner of CondoCleaners.com, to include in his accounting records to ensure adequate tracking of sales information is possible?

c. List the audit procedures that you would conduct to audit revenue recognition at CondoCleaners.com. For each audit procedure, list the audit assertion that it addresses, and state the risk of misstatement that it addresses.

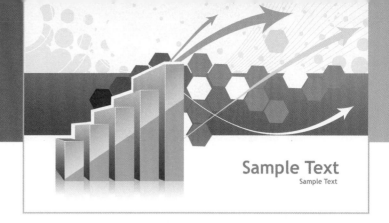

Sample Text
Sample Text

11   Audit sampling concepts

Since the auditor uses testing of transactions, there needs to be a way of choosing which items will be examined. Then, once the items have been chosen and audited, it is important to extrapolate the results to the population. In this chapter, you will look at the different types of sampling methods that an auditor is likely to use and the role of judgment during the sampling process. You will also see a real application of sampling for control testing at Hillsburg Hardware Limited. All types of auditors need to decide which items to select for sampling. Management accountants may use sampling to decide which items to monitor in their role as management.

LEARNING OBJECTIVES

1 Define sampling. Decide when an auditor would use statistical rather than nonstatistical sampling. Contrast the different types of nonprobabilistic (nonstatistical) sampling methods used by auditors. Provide examples of computer-assisted audit tests (CAATs) for nonstatistical sampling.

2 Explain the three different ways that an auditor can select a statistical sample. List three common statistical sampling methodologies used by auditors. Provide examples of CAATs for statistical sampling.

3 Describe the 14 steps in planning and selecting a sample, performing the tests, and evaluating the sample. Define an anomaly. Design field work that is required for an auditor to confirm that an error or misstatement is an anomaly.

STANDARDS REFERENCED IN THIS CHAPTER

CICA Standard

CAS 500 – Audit evidence

CAS 530 – Audit sampling

What Is an Error?

Brookes & Company, LLP, uses random samples when performing audit tests whenever possible. It believes that this gives it the best chance of getting representative samples of its clients' accounting information. In the audit of Sorofu Products, a company that sells and distributes jewellery, a random sample of 60 items was selected from a population of 18,250 items in doing a test of unit and total costs. Only one of the 60 items selected was in error, but it was large. In investigating the error, Harold Brakowski, the audit staff person doing the test, was told by Sorofu's controller that the error occurred while the regular inventory clerk was on vacation and was really only an "isolated error."

When Harold extrapolated the error, he obtained a significantly material overstatement of inventory. As an alternative to adjustment, he asked the human resources manager for vacation records, and determined that the inventory clerk was, indeed, on vacation for two weeks and that the error had occurred during that time. However, due to the size of the error, the audit team decided that additional substantive testing was required for that two-week period. Thirty more items were selected from that two-week period, and three additional errors were found. However, two were overstatements and one was an understatement, with the net result that the auditors could conclude that the errors in inventory at the year end were, overall, immaterial.

IMPORTANCE TO AUDITORS

Auditing standards require that errors be extrapolated to the entire population. However, Harold's investigation of the inventory costing error at Sorofu enabled him to split the costing transactions into two populations: a large population of transactions that were prepared while the inventory clerk was present and a smaller population that covered the clerk's two-week vacation. By obtaining an understanding of the costing process for these two populations, audit tests were designed to address them in accordance with the related risks. There was a much higher risk of error when the inventory clerk was absent, so more tests of detail were required to quantify the risk of material misstatement.

WHAT DO YOU THINK?

1. How would the firm's audit response have differed if it turned out that the inventory clerk had not been not on vacation when the error occurred?

2. Describe three risks (or potential errors) that could occur at Sorofu with respect to inventory costing. For each risk, describe an audit step that the auditor could use to investigate the risk.

continued >

THE situation at Sorofu shows us that sampling needs to be conducted in the context of the risks of error or misstatement. Samples are selected so that further testing can be conducted on the items selected. These could be tests of control or tests of detail. In this chapter, we will look at many different types of sampling. Some are more suited to control testing or to tests of detail, and certain methods are suitable for both types of testing.

1 The Nature of Sampling

CAS Due to the nature of the audit, the auditor does not examine all the available evidence but rather selects evidence from the available population. Sampling is not required, but CAS 530, Audit sampling, explains in the definition section that **audit sampling** occurs when (1) less than 100 percent of the items in the population under examination are being audited, and (2) each item (described as a sampling unit) in the population could be selected as part of the sample. As sampling is part of the audit process, it must be tied to the auditor's risk assessments.

Auditing using sampling means dealing with three aspects of audit sampling: (1) planning the sample and selecting the sample, (2) performing the tests, and (3) evaluating the results. We use the sales and collection cycle and its transactions as a frame of reference for discussing these concepts, but the concepts apply to every cycle. In Chapter 12 we provide an applied example of these concepts to tests of controls, and Chapter 13 applies audit sampling to tests of details of balances. Figure 11-1, which uses the same information as Figure 10-3, shows how audit sampling is related to the types of audit tests.

> **Audit sampling**—occurs when (1) less than 100 percent of the items in the population under examination are being audited, and (2) each item (described as a sampling unit) in the population could be selected as part of the sample.

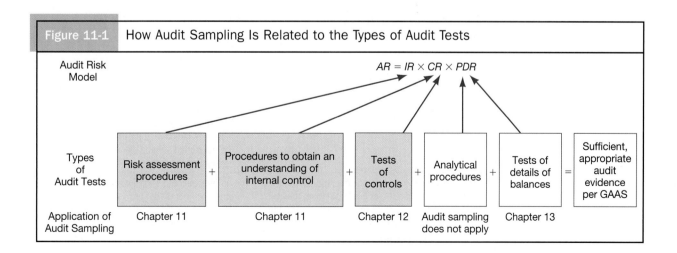

Figure 11-1 How Audit Sampling Is Related to the Types of Audit Tests

Representative Samples

Population—the body of data about which the auditor wishes to generalize.

Whenever an auditor selects a sample from a **population** (the data being tested), the objective is to obtain a sample that is representative. A **representative sample** has similar characteristics in the sample of audit interest as the population. For example, assume that a client's internal controls require a clerk to attach a shipping document to every duplicate sales invoice but that the procedure is not followed exactly 3 percent of the time. If the auditor selects a sample of 100 duplicate sales invoices and finds three shipping documents missing, the sample is highly representative. If two or four such exceptions are found in the sample, the sample is reasonably representative. If many missing items or no missing items are found, the sample is nonrepresentative.

Representative sample—a sample with the same characteristics as those of the population.

In practice, auditors do not know whether a sample is representative, even after all testing is completed. Auditors increase the likelihood of a sample being representative by using care in sample design, selection, and evaluation.

Nonsampling risk—occurs when audit tests do not uncover exceptions existing in the sample.

Nonsampling risk (or nonsampling error, see Table 11-1) occurs when audit tests do not uncover exceptions existing in the sample. In the previous example, three shipping documents were not attached to duplicate sales invoices, and if the auditor concluded that no exceptions existed (i.e. the population was acceptable), there was a nonsampling error.

The two causes of nonsampling error are the auditor's failure to recognize exceptions and inappropriate or ineffective audit procedures. An auditor might fail to recognize an exception because of exhaustion, boredom, or lack of understanding of what constitutes an exception. Take, for example, the control of attaching a shipping document to the duplicate sales invoice. An exception would be defined as a missing document or a shipping document that does not agree to the sales invoice. An ineffective audit procedure for these exceptions would be the selection of a sample of shipping documents to determine if each is attached to a set of duplicate sales invoices. The auditor in this case would be unable to determine whether there were numerous sales invoices unsupported by shipping documents, since such sales invoices could not be selected. (The auditor should have selected the sample from the invoices, not the shipping documents.) Careful design of audit procedures and proper supervision and instruction are ways to reduce nonsampling risk.

Sampling risk—results from testing less than the entire population.

Table 11-1 explains that **sampling risk** (sampling error) results from testing less than the entire population. Even with zero non-sampling error, there is always a chance that a sample is not representative. For example, if a population has a three-percent exception rate, the auditor could easily select a sample of 100 items containing no exceptions or many.

Table 11-1	Nonsampling Risk and Sampling Risk with Examples	
Type of risk and definition		**Example**
Nonsampling risk—the chance of exception when audit tests do not uncover exceptions existing in the sample; caused by failure to recognize exceptions and by inappropriate or ineffective audit procedures; synonymous with "nonsampling error."		The auditor reviews credit limit increases to the master file (master file change forms) for approval. Due to the poor handwriting, the auditor does not recognize when an unauthorized person signs four credit limit increases indicating approval. The auditor did not obtain sample signatures prior to conducting the test.
Sampling risk—the chance of exception inherent in tests of less than the entire population; may be reduced by using an increased sample size and using an appropriate method of selecting sample items from the population.		The auditor selected a random sample of shipping documents that provided an error of 1%, when the actual error rate was closer to 5% due to a new employee making numerous errors in one week (which was not sampled).

There are two ways to control sampling risk: making careful sample size decisions and by using an appropriate method of selecting sample items from the population. Increasing sample size will reduce sampling risk, and vice versa. At the extreme, testing all the items of a population will have a zero sampling risk (since this is no longer sampling). Statistical sampling method increases representativeness. This does not eliminate or even reduce sampling risk, but it does allow the auditor to measure the sample risk associated with a given sample size in a reliable manner.

Statistical versus NonStatistical Sampling and Probabilistic versus Nonprobabilistic Sample Selection

Before discussing the methods of sample selection to obtain representative samples, it is useful to make distinctions between statistical versus nonstatistical sampling, and probabilistic versus nonprobabilistic sample selection.

STATISTICAL VERSUS NONSTATISTICAL SAMPLING Audit sampling methods can be divided into two broad categories: statistical sampling and nonstatistical sampling. These categories are similar in that they both involve three phases:

1. Plan the sample.
2. Select the sample and perform the tests.
3. Evaluate the results.

The purpose of planning the sample is to make sure that the audit tests are performed in a manner that provides the desired sampling risk and minimizes the likelihood of nonsampling error. Selecting the sample involves deciding how to select sample items from the population. Performing the tests involves examining documents and performing other audit tests. Evaluating the results is the drawing of conclusions based on the audit tests.

Assume that an auditor selects a sample of 100 duplicate sales invoices from a population, tests each to determine if a shipping document is attached, and determines that there are three exceptions. Let's look at those actions step-by-step:

Action	Step
• Determine that a sample size of 100 is needed	1. Plan the sample.
• Decide which 100 items to select from the population.	2. Select the sample.
• Perform the audit procedure for each of the 100 items and determine that three exceptions exist.	Perform the tests.
• Reach conclusions about the likely exception rate in the total population when the sample exception rate equals three percent.	3. Evaluate the results.

Statistical sampling differs from nonstatistical sampling in that, through the application of mathematical rules, it allows the quantification (measurement) of sampling risk in planning the sample (step 1) and evaluating the results (step 3). (You may remember calculating a statistical result at a 95-percent **confidence level**, which is a statement of probability, in a statistics course. The 95-percent confidence level provides a five-percent sampling risk.)

In nonstatistical sampling, the auditor does not quantify sampling risk. Instead, the auditor selects those sample items that he or she believes will provide the most useful information in the circumstances, and conclusions are reached about populations on a judgmental basis. For that reason, the selection of non-statistical samples is often termed **judgmental sampling**.

PROBABILISTIC VERSUS NONPROBABILISTIC SAMPLE SELECTION AND THEIR APPLICATION Both probabilistic and nonprobabilistic sample selection fall under step 2. When using **probabilistic sample selection**, the auditor randomly selects items such that each population item has a known probability of being included in the sample. This process requires great care and uses one of several methods discussed shortly.

Statistical sampling—the use of mathematical measurement techniques to calculate formal statistical results and quantify sampling risk.

Confidence level—statement of probability.

Judgmental sampling—use of professional judgment rather than statistical methods to select sample items for audit tests.

Probabilistic sample selection—a method of sample selection in which it is possible to define the set of all possible samples, every possible sample item has a known probability of being selected, and the sample is selected by a random process.

In **nonprobabilistic sample selection**, the auditor selects sample items using professional judgment rather than probabilistic methods. Auditors can use one of several nonprobabilistic sample selection methods.

Auditing standards permit auditors to use either statistical or nonstatistical sampling methods. However, it is essential that each method be applied with due care. All steps of the process must be followed carefully. When statistical sampling is used, the sample *must be a probabilistic one*, and appropriate statistical evaluation methods must be used with the sample results to make the sampling risk computations. Auditors may make nonstatistical evaluations when using probabilistic selection, but it is never acceptable to evaluate a nonprobabilistic sample using statistical methods.

Three types of sample selection methods are commonly associated with nonstatistical audit sampling. All three methods are nonprobabilistic. Four types of sample selection methods are commonly associated with statistical audit sampling. All four methods are probabilistic.

The nonprobabilistic (judgmental) sample selection methods are:

- Directed sample selection.
- Block sample selection.
- Haphazard sample selection.

The probabilistic sample selection methods are:

- Simple random sample selection.
- Systematic sample selection.
- Probability proportionate-to-size sample selection.

Stratified sample selection (the use of data "layers") can be applied to both nonprobabilistic and probabilistic sample selection methods.

We will now discuss each of these sample selection methods, starting with nonprobabilistic methods.

Nonprobabilistic Sample Selection

Nonprobabilistic sample selection methods are those that do not meet the technical requirements for probabilistic sample selection. Since these methods are not based on strict mathematical probabilities, the representativeness of the sample may be difficult to determine. The information content of the sample, including its representativeness, will be based on the knowledge and skill of the auditor in applying his or her judgment in the circumstances.

DIRECTED SAMPLE SELECTION **Directed sample selection** is a nonprobabilistic method of sample selection in which each item in the sample is selected on the basis of some judgmental criteria established by the auditor. The auditor does not rely on equal chances of selection, but rather deliberately selects items according to the criteria. Some auditors consider certain directed samples to be a form of analytical review. The important issue is ensuring that the test is clearly defined and its audit role identified. The criteria may relate to representativeness, or they may not. Table 11-2 shows commonly used criteria.

Computer-assisted audit tests (CAATs) could be used to list the directed samples or to provide survey summaries that enable the auditor to identify at-risk transactions. These kinds of items can be efficiently investigated by the auditor, and the results can be applied to the population only on a judgmental basis. For example, the results of examining a selection of old accounts receivable (perhaps those over 90 days old) can be applied only to the total balance of old receivables, not to the entire accounts receivable population. The reasoning underlying the evaluation of such samples is that if none of the higher-risk items selected contain misstatements, then it is less likely that a material misstatement exists in the population.

Table 11-2	Commonly Used Directed Sample Selection Methods and Examples	

Commonly Used Direct Sample Selection Method	Examples
Items most likely to contain misstatements	• Receivables outstanding for a long time. • Purchases from and sales to officers or affiliates.
Items containing selected population characteristics	• Adjustments to sales in the last month of the year. • All transactions from the legal expense account.
Large dollar coverage	• All sales transactions that equal 75% of materiality or higher. • Repairs and maintenance expenses that are greater than $10,000 (or 10% of materiality).

BLOCK SAMPLE SELECTION In **block sample selection,** auditors select the first item in a block and the remainder of the block is chosen in sequence. One example of a block sample is the selection of a sequence of 100 sales transactions from the sales journal for the third week of March. A total sample of 100 could also be selected by taking 5 blocks of 20 items each, 10 blocks of 10, or 50 blocks of 2. In Audit Challenge 11-1, reviewing all supplier comments in date order is also a block sample.

> **Block sample**—a nonprobabilistic method of sample selection in which items are selected in measured sequences.

If few blocks are used, the probability of obtaining a nonrepresentative sample is too great, considering the possibility of such things as employee turnover, changes in the accounting system, and the seasonal nature of many businesses. CAATs can be used to increase audit coverage by running a gap test on all transactions. A gap test will go through all transactions in the sequence for the whole year (e.g., invoice numbers) and identify which numbers are missing.

A common use of block testing is testing cut-off. The auditor would select a block of invoices, receiving documents, and shipping documents spanning both sides of the year-end date to ensure that the transactions were recorded in the proper period. CAATs could be used to list the transactions that occurred during the period that the auditor is interested in. If the number of transactions is large (e.g., thousands of transactions per day), the auditor might choose a subsample of transactions from the block using one of the other sampling methods discussed in this chapter.

audit challenge 11-1
Playing with Numbers?

YOU found a gorgeous antique desk on eBay for an unbelievable price—only $250! The eBay statistics said that the seller had completed over 600 transactions with a 99-percent positive feedback rate, so you decided to use your credit card and buy it. You waited and waited, and four weeks later you still had not received the desk. Checking eBay again, you found that there were at least 75 negative feedback comments about customers not receiving their products, all posted within a period of three weeks. It turned out that someone had hacked into the seller's accounts and was taking the money. The positive feedback statistics were no longer valid.

Think about your auditing client, a financial organization that specializes in selling mutual funds and high-risk investments. For the last five years, the company's profits have

increased steadily, at the rate of about 20 percent per year. Now, due to the crash in worldwide stock markets and the decline in the values of funds, the company has laid off over 60 percent of its sales and administrative staff. Some sales are still occurring, but the company is having trouble meeting its payroll without dipping into its line of credit, which the bank has reduced.

CRITICAL THINKING QUESTIONS

1. What do these two examples tell us about the relationship between statistics and the environment?
2. What type of sample are the eBay data?
3. How could sampling have been used to predict potential difficulties with stock market and mutual fund values?

HAPHAZARD SAMPLE SELECTION When the auditor goes through a population and selects items for the sample without regard to their size, source, or other distinguishing characteristics, he or she is attempting to select without bias. This is called a **haphazard sample selection**. If the Audit Challenge 11-1 eBay samples were selected without regard to date order, then this would have been a haphazard sample.

The most serious shortcoming of haphazard sample selection is the difficulty of remaining completely unbiased in the selection. Because of the auditor's training and "cultural bias," certain population items are more likely than others to be included in the sample. For example, auditors may be inclined to select larger amounts or amounts from the middle of a period or to avoid round dollar amounts.

Although haphazard and block sample selection appear to be less logical than directed sample selection, they are often useful as audit tools and should not be ignored. In some situations, the cost of more complex sample selection methods outweighs the benefits obtained from using them. For example, assume that the auditor wants to trace credits from the accounts receivable transaction history files to the duplicate bank deposit slips and other authorized sources as a test for fictitious credits in the data files. A haphazard or block approach is simpler and much less costly than other selection methods in this situation and would be employed by many auditors.

concept check

C11-1 During the audit, a new staff member failed to record a client's 10-cent calculation error as an error. What type of error or risk does this mistake exemplify? Why?

C11-2 Provide two examples of directed sample selection that could be used for the audit of inventory.

❷ Probabilistic and Statistical Samples

Probabilistic Sample Selection

Statistical sampling requires a probabilistic sample to measure sampling risk. For probabilistic samples, the auditor uses no judgment about which sample items are selected, except in choosing which of the four selection methods to use. Most generalized audit software (GAS) is capable of running all of these sample selection methods. If sample sizes are high and data are accessible, it is likely more cost-effective for the auditor to use GAS rather than selecting the sample manually.

SIMPLE RANDOM SAMPLE SELECTION A simple **random sample** is one in which every possible combination of population items has an equal chance of constituting the sample. Simple random sampling is used to sample populations where each item is considered to have the same characteristics for audit purposes. For example, a simple random sample of 60 items contained in the cash disbursements journal throughout the year could be selected. Appropriate auditing procedures would be applied to the 60 items selected, and conclusions would be drawn and applied to all cash disbursement transactions recorded for the year.

Random number selection methods When a simple random sample is obtained, a method must be used that assures that all items in the population have an equal chance of selection. Suppose that in the above example there were a total of 12,000 cash disbursement transactions for the year. A simple random sample of one transaction would be such that each of the 12,000 transactions would have an equal chance of being selected. This would be done by obtaining a random number between 1 and 12,000. If the number was 3,895, the auditor would select and test the 3,895th cash disbursement transaction recorded in the cash disbursements journal.

Random numbers are a series of digits that have equal probabilities of occurring over long runs and that have no discernible pattern. Some accounting firms have specialized software that they use to select random numbers.

Replacement versus nonreplacement sampling Random numbers may be obtained with replacement or without replacement. In replacement sampling, an element in the population can be included in the sample more than once, whereas in nonreplacement sampling, an element can be included only once. If the random number corresponding to an item is selected more than once in nonreplacement sampling, it is not included in the sample a second time. Although both selection approaches are consistent with sound statistical theory, auditors normally use non-replacement sampling.

SYSTEMATIC SAMPLE SELECTION In **systematic selection** (also known as "systematic sampling"), the auditor calculates an interval and then methodically selects the items for the sample based on the size of the interval. The interval is determined by dividing the population size by the number of sample items desired. For example, if a population of sales invoices ranges from 652 to 3,151 and the desired sample size is 125, the interval is 20 [(3,151– 651) / 125]. The auditor must now select a random number between 0 and 19 to determine the starting point for the sample. If the randomly selected number is 9, the first item in the sample is invoice number 661 (652 + 9). The remaining 124 items are 681 (661 + 20), 701 (681 + 20), and so on through item 3,141.

The advantage of systematic sampling is its ease of use. For most populations, the systematic sample can be drawn quickly, the approach automatically puts the numbers in sequence, and the appropriate documentation is easy to develop.

A major problem with systematic selection is the possibility of bias. Because of the way systematic selection works, once the first item in the sample is selected, all other items are chosen automatically. This causes no problem if the characteristic of interest, such as a possible control deviation, is distributed randomly throughout the population; however, in some cases, characteristics of interest may not be randomly distributed. For example, if a control deviation occurred at a certain time of the month or with certain types of documents, a systematic sample could have a higher likelihood of failing to be representative than a simple random sample. It is important, therefore, when systematic selection is used, to consider possible patterns in the population data that could cause sample bias.

A variation of systematic sample selection by unit of interest is used by the **probability-proportionate-to-size (PPS)** sampling methods described in the next section. Here, the individual dollar is considered the unit of interest. The interval is determined based upon a statistical formula, and the transactions associated with that dollar interval are selected.

Systematic selection—a probabilistic method of sampling in which the auditor calculates an interval (the population size divided by the number of sample items desired) and selects the items for the sample based on the size of the interval and a randomly selected number between zero and the sample size.

Probability-proportionate-to-size sampling (PPS)—A modified form of physical attribute sampling method that focuses on the individual dollar (or unit of currency, such as Euro) as the unit of interest, rather than a physical unit. This is also called simply proportionate-to-size, monetary unit sampling, or dollar unit sampling.

auditing in action 11-1
Slicing Sales Data

Sales become accounts receivable. Customers who no longer buy could become delinquent debtors. Inventory that is not sold could become an inventory write-down. This means that looking at and analyzing sales data can not only help management improve their businesses but can help auditors value assets on the balance sheet.

Advanced tools, such as online analytical processing (known as OLAP), allow businesses to obtain current data as events happen rather than at month end.

For example, Grand & Toy in Canada uses a program called Defector Detector to identify customers who have not made purchases in the last four weeks (or other defined periods) and colour-codes information about customers based upon the length of time that purchases have not been made. Sales representatives then go to visit these customers to follow up.

Black Photo Corporation earns extra revenue by selling sales statistics to its vendors. Vendors can purchase information about their weekly sales at Black's stores. The vendor can then consult with Black's about sales mix and which products should be stocked on shelves. This helps the vendor increase sales and helps Black's have inventory that is more readily saleable.

Both Grand & Toy and Black's are using exception reporting, also known as directed sample selection. Auditors conduct directed sampling by identifying the items that they would like to examine and then selecting those transactions either manually or using computer-assisted audit tests. At both of the above organizations, it is likely that client software could be used to assist with the sampling process.

Sources: 1. Lysecki, Sarah, "Grand & Toy employs software to sniff out 'defectors'," 2005, **http://itbusiness.ca**, Accessed: January 15, 2009. 2. Schick, Shane, "Black's takes snapshot of store performance," **http://itbusiness.ca, Accessed: January 15, 2009.**

STRATIFIED SAMPLE SELECTION When a sample is stratified, it is split into multiple smaller sets or layers, of which each set has a similar characteristic. For example, stratification can occur by dollar amount (sales over $50,000; sales under that amount), by location (foreign versus domestic), or by another criteria, such as whether commissions will be paid (sales from head office versus sales made by travelling sales personnel). This can improve the efficiency of the audit by focusing work on transactions that may be more subject to material error. After data are stratified, the sample will be selected using one of the methods previously discussed (either probabilistic or non-probabilistic).

Statistical Sampling Methodologies

Once the decision has been made to conduct statistical sampling, the auditor may choose from three broad categories of statistical sampling: attribute, probability-proportionate-to-size (PPS), and variables. (Discovery sampling is also described, but this is a subset of attribute sampling.) These methods are based upon underlying **sampling distributions**, statistical frequency distributions such as binomial or normal distributions, which are covered in a statistics course. Review your statistics text to examine these distributions.

All three categories of sampling can be used for tests of controls or tests of details, although attribute sampling is normally used for controls testing, whereas PPS and variables sampling are normally used for tests of details.

ATTRIBUTE SAMPLING **Attribute sampling** is used to estimate the proportion of items in a population containing a characteristic or **attribute** of interest. This proportion is called the **occurrence rate** or **exception rate** and is the ratio of the items containing the specific attribute to the total number of population items. The occurrence rate is usually expressed as a percentage. For example, an auditor might conclude that the exception rate, the rate where control violations occurred for the internal verification of sales invoices, is approximately three percent, meaning that invoices are not properly verified three percent of the time. This methodology is designed to answer the question, "How many items contain errors?"

Auditors are interested in the occurrence of the following types of exceptions in populations of accounting data:

Table 11-3	Types of Statistical Sampling, Purpose, and Examples	
Type of Statistical Sample and Purpose	**Example**	**Textbook reference for detailed application**
Attribute sampling: estimate the frequency of a characteristic or of errors; used mainly for tests of controls	• Select a sample to determine frequency of times that credit limit is not authorized.	Chapter 12, Section 4
Discovery sampling: used to determine whether a type of event has occurred	• Select a sample to find out whether any potentially fraudulent transactions have been processed.	NA
Monetary unit sampling (MUS): used to find likely dollar range of error	• Select a sample of accounts receivable confirmations, circulate, and evaluate to determine the likely dollar range of error in accounts receivable.	Chapter 13, Section 4
Variance Estimation Sampling: used to determine a point estimate of the value of a population	• Select a sample of accounts receivable confirmations, circulate, and estimate the total dollar value of accounts receivable.	NA

1. Deviations from the client's established controls (i.e. controls not being followed).
2. Monetary errors or fraud and other irregularities in populations of transaction data.
3. Monetary errors or fraud and other irregularities in populations of account balance details.

Knowing the occurrence rate of exceptions is helpful for the first two types of exceptions, which relate to transactions. Therefore, auditors make extensive use of audit sampling that measures the occurrence or exception rate when performing tests of controls. With the third type of exception, the auditor usually needs to estimate the total dollar amount of the exceptions because a judgment must be made about whether the exceptions are material. When the auditor wants to know the total amount of a misstatement, he or she will use methods that measure dollars, such as PPS or variables methodologies.

Attribute sampling is used primarily for tests of controls, but auditors also use attribute sampling for substantive procedures when performing dual-purpose tests. Attribute sampling may be based on physical units (e.g., invoices) or monetary units (e.g., dollars). In the case of the former, the occurrence or exception rate would be a percentage; in the case of the latter, the exception would be a monetary amount. Whenever attribute sampling is used in this text, it refers to attribute statistical sampling for physical units (such as an invoice).

An example of attribute sampling applied to tests of controls is shown in Chapter 12, Section 4.

Discovery sampling **Discovery sampling**, a special type of attribute sampling, is used when the auditor is looking for very few or near zero deviations. For example, if the auditor suspects that fraud or other irregularities exist in the data, the sample size needs to be designed to provide the assurance of finding at least one example of the fraud or other irregularity.

If sales for the year were made up of 15,000 transactions with a dollar value of $30 million, the sampling unit for physical unit attribute sampling would be an invoice, while the sampling unit for monetary unit sampling, MUS (or DUS or PPS), would be each of the thirty million dollars. In the case of the former, each of the 15,000 invoices would have an equal chance of selection; in the case of the latter, each of the $30 million would have an equal chance of selection.

Monetary unit sampling allows the result of the testing to be stated in dollar terms. This allows the auditor to specify a dollar range of potential errors for a specified confidence level. It also increases the probability that larger transactions, totalling larger dollar amounts than smaller transactions, will be selected since, for example, an invoice including $150,000 will be 10,000 times more likely to be selected than one of $15. Monetary unit sampling is appropriate for tests of controls (as a dual purpose test) and for tests of details.

VARIABLES SAMPLING Variables sampling is used when the auditor desires a dollar or quantitative conclusion with respect to the test conducted. The general class of methods called variables sampling includes several techniques.

concept check

C11-3 List the three features of probabilistic sample selection.

C11-4 List one advantage and one disadvantage associated with systematic sample selection.

③ Steps in Conducting the Sampling Process

Planning, Selecting, and Evaluating a Sample

Audit sampling is applied to tests of controls and tests of details through a set of 14 well-defined steps shown in Figure 11-2. The steps are divided into four sections: plan the sample, select the sample, perform the audit procedures, and evaluate the results. Since the terminology varies depending upon whether attribute sampling or MUS are used, the type of sampling involved is noted in brackets in the figure. Table 11-4 summarizes the audit sampling steps in words separately for attribute sampling and for MUS sampling. It is important to follow these steps carefully as a means

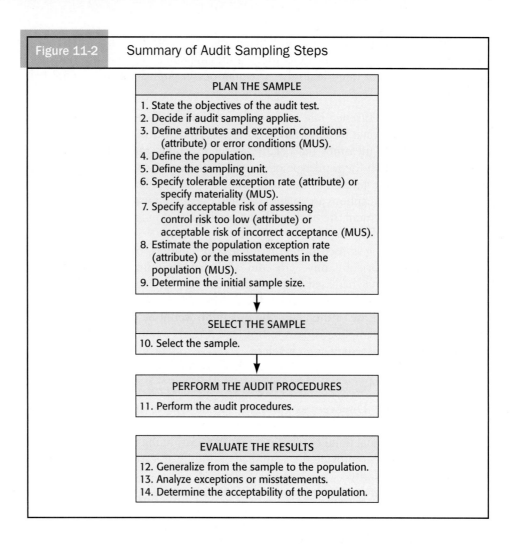

Figure 11-2   Summary of Audit Sampling Steps

PLAN THE SAMPLE

1. State the objectives of the audit test.
2. Decide if audit sampling applies.
3. Define attributes and exception conditions (attribute) or error conditions (MUS).
4. Define the population.
5. Define the sampling unit.
6. Specify tolerable exception rate (attribute) or specify materiality (MUS).
7. Specify acceptable risk of assessing control risk too low (attribute) or acceptable risk of incorrect acceptance (MUS).
8. Estimate the population exception rate (attribute) or the misstatements in the population (MUS).
9. Determine the initial sample size.

SELECT THE SAMPLE

10. Select the sample.

PERFORM THE AUDIT PROCEDURES

11. Perform the audit procedures.

EVALUATE THE RESULTS

12. Generalize from the sample to the population.
13. Analyze exceptions or misstatements.
14. Determine the acceptability of the population.

of ensuring that both the auditing and the sampling aspects of the process are properly applied. The steps provide an outline of the discussion that follows. Table 11-4 compares these steps for tests of controls (e.g., attribute sampling).

The general process of each step is described briefly in this chapter, and related definitions are provided for new terms. The steps will be described further in the application examples, with illustrations of the type of documentation that would be included in the audit working paper file. All phases of the process require the use of professional judgment, for example in deciding risk factors, interpreting errors, and deciding whether the population is acceptable. Chapter 12 provides an example of tests of controls using statistical and physical unit attribute sampling, and Chapter 15 does the same for tests of details using nonstatistical and MUS sampling.

The Planning phase of the sampling process is about:

- deciding *why* you are sampling (relating to the objectives of the audit test, and deciding if sampling is appropriate),
- then determining *what* you would be looking for (the attributes, exceptions, or dollar errors), then
- locating *where* you will find your sample (the population), and
- *how* you will locate your item in the population (the sampling unit).
- Next, *risks* need to be set (tolerable exception rate or materiality; acceptable risks of assessing control risk too low or acceptable risk of incorrect acceptance) based upon your overall audit plan and the risks in the cycle, and
- an *error estimation* takes place about the population so that you can
- decide *how many* items to select using statistical guidelines.

Table 11-4	Summary of Attribute and MUS Audit Sampling Steps

Steps—Attribute Sampling for Tests of Controls	Steps—MUS Sampling for Tests of Details
Plan the Sample	**Plan the Sample**
1. State the objectives of the audit test.	1. State the objectives of the audit test.
2. Decide if audit sampling applies.	2. Decide if audit sampling applies.
3. Define attributes and exception conditions.	3. Define misstatement conditions.
4. Define the population.	4. Define the population.
5. Define the sampling unit.	5. Define the sampling unit.
6. Specify tolerable exception rate.	6. Specify materiality.
7. Specify acceptable risk of assessing control risk too low.	7. Specify acceptable risk of incorrect acceptance.
8. Estimate the population exception rate.	8. Estimate misstatements in the population.
9. Determine the initial sample size.	9. Determine the initial sample size.
Select the Sample	**Select the Sample**
10. Select the sample.	10. Select the sample.
Perform the Audit Procedures	**Perform the Audit Procedures**
11. Perform the audit procedures.	11. Perform the audit procedures.
Evaluate the Results	**Evaluate the Results**
12. Generalize from the sample to the population.	12. Generalize from the sample to the population.
13. Analyze the exceptions.	13. Analyze the misstatements.
14. Determine the acceptability of the population.	14. Determine the acceptability of the population.

1. STATE THE OBJECTIVES OF THE AUDIT TEST The overall objectives of the test must be stated in terms of the risks addressed and the transaction cycle being tested. A typical control objective for the sales cycle would be to test the completeness assertion by verifying goods shipped have been invoiced, while a test of detail could be accuracy of accounts receivable.

2. DECIDE IF AUDIT SAMPLING APPLIES The term "population" represents the body of data about which the auditor wishes to generalize.

Audit sampling applies whenever the auditor plans to reach conclusions about a population based on a sample. Since sampling is very common, sampling is likely for most audit steps since the auditor will not look at all transactions.

The auditor should examine the audit program and decide those audit procedures where audit sampling applies. For example, in the following incomplete audit program (which is missing risks and assertions), sampling could be used for procedures 3 through 5.

1. Review sales transactions for large and unusual amounts (analytical procedure or directed sample).
2. Observe whether the duties of the accounts receivable clerk are separate from the handling of cash (test of control).
3. Examine a sample of duplicate sales invoices for the following:

    a. Credit approval by the credit manager (test of control).
    b. The existence of an attached shipping document (test of control).
    c. Inclusion of a chart of accounts number (test of control).

4. Select a sample of shipping documents, and trace each to related duplicate sales invoices for existence (test of control).
5. Compare the quantity on each duplicate sales invoice with the quantity on related shipping documents (test of control).

Audit sampling is inappropriate for the first two procedures in this audit program. The first is an analytical procedure. The second is an observation procedure for which no documentation exists to perform audit sampling.

For tests of details, while it is common to sample in many accounts, there are situations when sampling does not apply. The auditor may decide to audit only items over $5,000 and ignore all others because the total of the smaller ones is immaterial. In this case, the auditor has not sampled but has conducted a **census** of the strata over $5,000, which consists of auditing all of the transactions that satisfy a particular criteria. Similarly, if the auditor is verifying capital asset additions and there are many small additions and one extremely large purchase of a building, the auditor may decide to ignore the small items entirely. Again the auditor has not sampled but has focused on high-value items instead.

Census, conducting—consists of auditing all of the transactions that satisfy a particular criteria.

CAS **3. DEFINE ATTRIBUTES AND EXCEPTION OR ERROR CONDITIONS** Whenever audit sampling is used, the auditor must carefully define the characteristics (attributes) being tested and the exception conditions (see Table 11-5). CAS 500, Considering the relevance and reliability of audit evidence, requires that items that are audited relate to the audit test. The precise statement of what constitutes an attribute guides the staff person who performs the audit when identifying exceptions.

For example, based on the portion of the partial test-of-control audit program described in Step 2, the first attribute that can be tested by means of sampling is whether the duplicate sales invoice is approved for credit (Procedure 3a). The approval is the attribute, or item of interest. A control deviation in a manual system would be a lack of initials indicating credit approval. The absence of the defined attribute for any sample item will be an exception for that attribute.

Table 11-5	Terms Used in Planning Audit Sampling		
Sampling Step	Term Related to Planning	Test of control (e.g., for Attribute Sample)	Test of detail (e.g., for MUS Sample)
3	Define the item of interest.	Identify the characteristic or attribute of interest.	Individual dollars.
3	Define exceptions or errors.	Define the control deviation (an exception).	Normally any monetary difference (an error).
6	Specify tolerable exception rate (TER).	Specify the exception rate the auditor will permit in the population.	N/A
6	Specify performance materiality.	N/A	Use performance materiality available for the audit or allocated to the cycle or account.
7	Acceptable risk of assessing control risk too low (ARACR).	The risk that the auditor is willing to take of accepting a control as effective when the true population exception rate is greater.	N/A
7	Acceptable risk of incorrect acceptance (ARIA).	N/A	The risk that the auditor is willing to take of accepting a balance as correct when the true misstatement is greater than materiality.
8	Estimated population exception rate (EPER).	The advance estimate of the percentage of exceptions in the population.	N/A
8	Estimated misstatements in the population.	N/A	The advance estimate of total dollar error in the population.

Audit sampling for tests of details of balances measures monetary misstatements in the population. The audit test could be sending a confirmation and comparing the confirmed amount to the recorded amount for the sampled clients. Any dollar difference between the confirmed amount and the recorded amount would be an exception.

4. DEFINE THE POPULATION The auditor must sample from the entire population as it has been defined. The auditor may generalize only about that population that has been sampled. For example, in performing tests of controls of occurrence for sales, the auditor would define the population as all recorded sales for the year. If the auditor samples from only one month's transactions, it is invalid to draw conclusions about the invoices for the entire year.

It is important that the auditor carefully define the population in advance, being consistent with the objectives of the audit tests. For different tests in the audit program of the same cycle, it may be necessary to define more than one population for a given set of audit procedures. For example, if the auditor intends to trace from sales invoices to shipping documents and from shipping documents to duplicate sales invoices, there are two populations (i.e., one population of shipping documents and another of duplicate sales invoices).

The population for tests of details of accounts receivable using MUS or other dollar-based tests is defined as the recorded dollar population, the accounts receivable general ledger balance. The auditor then evaluates whether the recorded population is overstated or understated. It is also important to test the population for completeness before a sample is selected to ensure that all population items will be properly subjected to the sample selection process.

Population for stratified sampling The purpose of stratification is to permit the auditor to emphasize certain population items and de-emphasize others. In most audit sampling situations, auditors want to emphasize the larger recorded values; therefore, stratification is typically done on the basis of the size of recorded dollar values.

5. DEFINE THE SAMPLING UNIT The physical sampling unit when conducting tests of controls must be consistent with the objectives of the audit tests. The definition of the population and the planned audit procedures usually dictate the appropriate sampling unit. For example, if the auditor wants to determine how frequently the client fails to bill a customer's order (completeness), the sampling unit must be defined as the customer's order. If, however, the objective is to determine whether the proper quantity of the goods described on the customer's order is accurately shipped and billed, it is possible to define the sampling unit as the customer's order, the shipping document, or the duplicate sales invoice.

The sampling unit for nonstatistical audit sampling in tests of details of balances is almost always the item making up the account balance. For accounts receivable, it is the total balance for a specific customer account name or number, or an unpaid invoice, in the accounts receivable master file (or accounts receivable trial balance listing). For statistical sampling, such as MUS, the definition of the sampling unit is an individual dollar outstanding as part of the customer balance.

6. SPECIFY TOLERABLE EXCEPTION RATE OR SPECIFY MATERIALITY Establishing the **tolerable exception rate (TER)** (see Table 11-5) requires professional judgment on the part of the auditor. TER represents the exception rate that the auditor will permit in the population and still be willing to use the assessed control risk. Exceptions could be control deviations and/or the amount of monetary errors or fraud and other irregularities in the transactions established during planning. For example, assume that the auditor decides that TER for the attribute of sales invoice credit approval is 6 percent. This means that the auditor has decided that even if 6 percent of the sales invoices are not approved for credit, the credit approval control is still effective in terms of the assessed control risk included in the audit plan. The suitable TER relates to the risk associated with the audit assertion being tested, and to materiality. TER has a significant impact on sample size. A larger sample size is needed for a lower

> **Tolerable exception rate (TER)—** the exception rate that the auditor will permit in the population and still be willing to use the assessed control risk and/or the amount of monetary errors or fraud and other irregularities in the transactions established during planning.

TER than for a higher TER. For example, a larger sample is required for a TER of 4 percent than for a TER of 6 percent.

For sampling for tests of details, materiality is used during the sampling process.

7. SPECIFY ACCEPTABLE RISK OF ASSESSING CONTROL RISK TOO LOW OR ACCEPTABLE RISK OF INCORRECT ACCEPTANCE Whenever a sample is taken (statistical or nonstatistical), there is a risk that the quantitative conclusions about the population will be incorrect. This is always true unless 100 percent of the population is tested (called a census).

For audit sampling in tests of controls, that risk is called the **acceptable risk of assessing control risk too low (ARACR)** (Table 11-5). ARACR is the risk that the auditor is willing to take of accepting a control as effective (or a rate of monetary errors or fraud and other irregularities as tolerable) when the true population exception rate is greater than the tolerable exception rate (TER), a false positive. To illustrate, assume that TER is 6 percent, ARACR is 10 percent, and the true population exception rate is 8 percent. The control in this case is not acceptable because the true exception rate of 8 percent exceeds TER. The auditor, however, does not know the true population exception rate. The ARACR of 10 percent means that the auditor is willing to take a 10-percent risk of concluding that the control is effective after all testing is completed, even when it is ineffective. If the auditor finds the control effective in this illustration, he or she will have over-relied on the system of internal control (used a lower assessed control risk than justified). ARACR is the auditor's measure of sampling risk.

For tests of details, **acceptable risk of incorrect acceptance (ARIA)** is the risk that the auditor is willing to take of accepting a balance as correct when the true misstatement in the balance is greater than materiality. ARIA is the term equivalent to acceptable risk of assessing control risk too low (ARACR) for tests of controls. It is a false positive associated with sampling and tests of details.

There is an inverse relationship between ARIA and required sample size. If, for example, the auditor decides to reduce ARIA from 10 percent to 5 percent, the required sample size would increase because the auditor wants a larger safety margin in making sure that there is less likelihood of a false positive. By reducing ARIA, we are increasing the required sampling assurance that the balance is correct from 90 percent to 95 percent, thus resulting in a larger sample size (i.e., the gathering of more evidence).

Acceptable risk of assessing control risk too low (ARACR)—the risk that the auditor is willing to take of accepting a control as effective or a rate of monetary errors or fraud and other irregularities as tolerable, when the true population exception rate is greater than the tolerable exception rate.

Acceptable risk of incorrect acceptance (ARIA)—the risk that the auditor is willing to take of accepting a balance as correct when the true misstatement in the balance is greater than materiality.

audit challenge 11-2
The Danger of "False Positives"

SERVER farms that deal with highly sensitive information have multiple layers of security, for example the use of a physical magnetic stripe card with password to enter the building and a hand-scan with password to enter the server room. If a person who is authorized to enter the server room is rejected by the hand-scan machine (perhaps due to having a dirty hand or a cut on the hand), this is called a "false negative." This is dealt with by having the person contact support and a supervisor and having his or her identity verified and the system improved with an additional scan. Should an unauthorized person be able to enter with stolen identification and gain access with an unauthorized hand-scan, this would be a "false positive." From the perspective of the server farm organization, the false positive is far more dangerous, since an unauthorized person gains access to the building. (You may remember from your statistics course that a false negative is known as an incorrect rejection or alpha risk, while a false positive is known as an incorrect acceptance or beta risk.)

ARACR and ARIA represent the risk of "false positives." If the auditor sets ARACR or ARIA at 5 percent, then the auditor is deciding that a 5 percent risk can be taken of actually accepting the population when it is actually incorrect.

CRITICAL THINKING QUESTIONS

1. Explain, in your own words, the impact of a false acceptance (false positive) of material misstatements in the financial statements to the client and to a major user of the financial statements, such as a bank. What is the impact of a false rejection (false negative)?
2. Which is more hazardous to an auditor's financial health, false acceptance or false rejection of a material misstatement? Why?

The primary factor affecting the auditor's decision about ARIA is assessed control risk in the audit risk model. When internal controls are effective, control risk can be reduced, permitting the auditor to increase ARIA. This, in turn, reduces the sample size required for the test of details of the related account balance.

8. ESTIMATE THE POPULATION EXCEPTION RATE OR THE MISSTATEMENTS IN THE POPULATION Auditors should make an advance **estimate of the population exception rate (EPER)** to plan the appropriate sample size (Table 11-5). If the EPER is low, a relatively small sample size will satisfy the auditor's tolerable exception rate because a less precise estimate is required.

Auditors often use the preceding year's audit results to estimate EPER. If prior year results are not available, or if they are considered unreliable, the auditor can take a small preliminary sample of the current year's population to develop an estimate. It is not critical that the estimate be precise, because the current year's sample exception rate is ultimately used to estimate the population characteristics. If a preliminary sample is used, it can be included in the total sample, as long as appropriate sample selection procedures are followed.

For example, assume that an auditor takes a preliminary sample of 30 items to estimate the EPER that considers the entire population. Later, if the auditor decides that a total sample size of 100 is needed, only 70 additional items will need to be properly selected and tested.

Similarly, for tests of details sampling, the auditor makes this estimate based on prior experience with the client and by assessing inherent risk, considering the results of tests of controls and of analytical procedures already performed.

> **Estimated population exception rate (EPER)**—the exception rate the auditor expects to find in the population before testing begins.

9. DETERMINE THE INITIAL SAMPLE SIZE Four factors determine the initial sample size for audit sampling for tests of controls: population size, TER, ARACR, and EPER. Population size is not nearly as significant a factor as the others and typically can be ignored since once the population size is sufficiently large, the sample size required levels off.

Nonstatistical sampling uses professional judgment rather than a statistical formula (or tables) to determine sample size.

The **initial sample size**, determined by professional judgment, is preliminary because the exceptions or errors in the actual sample must be evaluated before it is possible to know whether the sample is large enough to achieve the objectives of the tests.

> **Initial sample size**—sample size determined by professional judgment (nonstatistical sampling) or by statistical tables (attribute sampling).

auditing in action 11-2
Sampling Standards and Resources

Do you like statistics? Perhaps you could make your living being a consultant in sampling. Samples are taken by tax auditors, Auditor General auditors, and internal auditors, as well as financial statement auditors and research organizations.

Ghement Statistical Consulting Company (**www.ghement. ca**) conducts training sessions and helps others design, conduct, and evaluate their sampling.

Many organizations provide standards with respect to sampling. For example, the Statistical Society of Canada (**www.ssc. ca**) promotes standards for high-quality education in statistics, while the federal Auditor General in Ottawa has standards that indicate when certain forms of sampling are most appropriate in value-for-money audits.

Examination of actual audit reports completed by auditor general offices in Canada as well as internal auditors of various government organizations provides insight into how sampling is important in evaluating the effectiveness of controls. For example, the internal audit report of year-end cash cut-off for the Canada Border Services Agency showed that internal auditors used the key-item approach. They selected 68 transactions of $100,000 or larger.

Their report described the errors in cut-off, with an overall conclusion that the $2 million in errors they found was immaterial to the total $1.3 billion population.

Sources: 1. Canada Border Services Agency, "Internal audit report of fiscal 2007–2008 year-end cash cut-off procedures," **http://cbsa-asfc.gc.ca/agency-agence/reports-rapports/ae-ve/2008/iaryccp_rvipde-eng.html**. 2. Ghement Statistical Consulting Company, **www.ghement.ca**. 3. Office of the Auditor General, "Conducting Surveys, Section 4: Sampling," **www.oag-bvg.gc.ca/internet/English/meth_gde_e_19725.html**. All accessed: February 17, 2012.

For attribute or MUS sampling, sample size is determined using a statistical formula embedded in software, or using tables.

When the auditor uses stratified sampling, the sample size must be allocated among the strata. For example, if you had three strata, the first being amounts over $350,000, the second for amounts between $500 and $349,999, and the third for all amounts under $500, you would select all of the items over $350,000 (a census), and an MUS sample with an interval of perhaps $400,000 from the remaining two layers. This would result in you obtaining many large dollar amounts and fewer small ones in your sample. Knowing the total dollar amounts in each stratum would help you determine that your sample would be the correct size. The Selection phase is about obtaining the items that will be tested.

10. SELECT THE SAMPLE After the auditor has computed the initial sample size for the audit sampling application, he or she must choose the items in the population to be included in the sample. The sample can be chosen by using any of the probabilistic or nonprobabilistic methods discussed earlier in the chapter. It is important for the auditor to use a method that will permit meaningful conclusions about the sample results.

For stratified monetary unit sampling, the auditor selects samples individual dollars associated with transactions independently from each stratum, as explained in Step 9. The auditor must determine the physical unit to perform the audit tests. For example, to perform the audit procedures, the auditor must identify the population item that corresponds to the 457,376th dollar, for example, the 125th invoice transaction.

In the Performance phase, audit procedures are performed.

11. PERFORM THE AUDIT PROCEDURES The auditor performs the test of control audit procedures by examining each item in the sample to determine whether it is consistent with the definition of the attribute and records in the working papers details of all the exceptions found. When audit procedures have been completed for a test of control sampling application, there will be a sample size and a number of exceptions for each attribute.

To perform the test of detail audit procedures, the auditor applies the appropriate audit procedures to each item in the sample to determine whether it is correct or contains a misstatement. For example, in the confirmation of accounts receivable, the auditor mails the sample of confirmations as described in Chapter 13 and determines the amount of misstatement in each account confirmed. For non-responses, alternative procedures are used to determine the misstatements. The auditor tracks the recorded value and the audited value so that the aggregate client misstatement can be determined.

CAS

The auditor will only obtain meaningful results from using audit sampling if the audit procedures are applied carefully. This includes testing a transaction for each sample item selected. CAS 530 requires that if the test cannot be conducted for the item selected, then the auditor must select another transaction. For example, the auditor might select an invoice to conduct a pricing test and find that the item selected was an adjustment invoice, so the pricing test cannot be conducted. In that case, the auditor must select an additional item. The audit program should explain in advance how such cases would be handled. For example, the audit program might say that the auditor should choose the next transaction.

Evaluation of the results involves extrapolating results from the sample to the population (called generalization), more carefully looking at the impact of the exceptions or errors found, and deciding whether the population is acceptable based upon the original objectives of the testing (i.e., using the assessed risks, tolerable levels of error or performance materiality).

Sample exception rate (SER)—
the number of exceptions in the
sample divided by the sample size.

12. GENERALIZE FROM THE SAMPLE TO THE POPULATION For tests of controls, the **sample exception rate (SER)** can be calculated easily from the actual sample results. SER equals the actual number of exceptions divided by the actual sample size. The population exception rate is different from the sample exception rate; the chance that they are exactly the same is too small.

Following is an approach used to estimate the error rate in the population when conducting a nonstatistical sample:

Subtract the sampling exception rate from the tolerable exception rate, which is called calculated sampling error (TER − SER = calculated sampling error), and evaluate whether calculated sampling error is sufficiently large to indicate that the true population exception rate is acceptable. For example, if an auditor takes a sample of 100 items for an attribute and finds no exceptions (SER = 0), and TER is 5 percent, calculated sampling error is 5 percent (TER of 5 percent − SER of 0 = 5 percent). On the other hand, if there had been four exceptions, calculated sampling error would have been 1 percent (TER of 5 percent − SER of 4 percent). It is much more likely that the true population exception rate is higher than 5 percent when the auditor has found a 4 percent error rate. Therefore, most auditors would probably find the population acceptable based on the first sample result of no errors in the sample and not acceptable based on the second.

In practice, auditors tend to test controls when they expect no exceptions. If no exceptions are found, then the control is considered to be reliable. However, when exceptions are found, it is more likely that the controls cannot be relied on, unless the situation(s) causing the control exception can be isolated (as discussed in the Step 13).

When generalizing tests of details, the auditor deals with dollar amounts rather than with exceptions. The auditor must generalize from the sample to the population by (1) projecting misstatements from the sample results to the population and (2) considering sampling error and sampling risk (ARIA).

For an example of these calculations, refer to Chapter 13, Section 4.

13. ANALYZE EXCEPTIONS OR MISSTATEMENTS In addition to determining the SER for each attribute control tested and evaluating whether the true but unknown exception rate is likely to exceed the tolerable exception rate, the auditor analyzes individual exceptions to determine the breakdown in the internal controls that caused them. Exceptions could be caused by carelessness of employees, misunderstood instructions, intentional failure to perform procedures, or many other factors. It is important that any such misstatements be discussed with management and potentially included in the management letter.

The nature of an exception and its cause have a significant effect on the evaluation of control risk by assertion. For example, if all the exceptions in the tests of internal verification of credit authorization for sales invoices occurred while the person normally responsible for performing the tests was on vacation, control risk would be set as high during this period. The auditor could choose to test the period substantively when the employee was on vacation and rely on internal controls for the remainder of the year. This type of exception is called an **anomaly**, because it is an exception or misstatement that is nonrepresentative of the population as a whole. CAS 530 requires that the auditor investigate such anomalies, conducting additional audit procedures, with the goal of verifying that the anomaly really is different and not representative of the population for the rest of the year.

Misstatements discovered during tests of details could also be caused by control exceptions, which explains why many tests of details are considered to be dual-purpose tests. For example, in confirming accounts receivable, suppose that all misstatements resulted from the client's failure to record returned goods. The auditor would determine why that type of misstatement occurred so often (perhaps due to lack of training in the receiving department), the implications of the misstatements on other audit areas (such as increased likelihood of cutoff errors requiring more substantive testing), and the potential impact on the financial statements (revenue allocated to the wrong period). An important part of misstatement analysis is deciding whether any modification of client business risk or the audit risk model is needed. If the auditor concluded that the failure to record the returns resulted from a breakdown of internal controls, it might be necessary

Anomaly—an exception or misstatement that is nonrepresentative of the population as a whole.

CAS

to reassess control risk for accuracy and cutoff. That would probably cause the auditor to reduce control testing and shift to substantive testing for the affected assertions.

14. DETERMINE THE ACCEPTABILITY OF THE POPULATION For tests of controls, it was shown under Step 12 that most auditors subtract SER from TER when they use non-statistical sampling. If the auditor concludes that the difference is sufficiently large, the control being tested can be used to support assessed control risk as planned, provided a careful analysis of the cause of exceptions does not indicate the possibility of other significant problems with internal controls.

When the auditor concludes that TER – SER is too small to conclude that the population is acceptable, the auditor must take specific action. Three courses of action can be followed.

Revise TER or ARACR This alternative should be followed only when the auditor has concluded that the original specifications were too conservative. Relaxing either TER or ARACR may be difficult to defend if the auditor is ever subjected to a review by a court or to a peer review.

Expand the sample size An increase in the sample size has the effect of decreasing the sampling error if the actual sample exception rate does not increase. Of course, SER may also increase or decrease if additional items are selected.

Revise assessed control risk If the results of the tests of controls do not support the planned assessed control risk, the auditor should revise assessed control risk upward. The effect of the revision is likely to increase tests of details of balances. For example, if tests of controls of credit approval indicate that approval procedures are not being followed, the auditor may not be able to rely on the control and will therefore conduct additional substantive tests at year end. This is most likely to be done through tests of the bad-debt allowance for accounts receivable and of bad-debt expense for the year.

For tests of details, an auditor using nonstatistical sampling cannot formally measure sampling error. Professional judgment is used to consider the possibility that the true population misstatement aggregated with other misstatements exceeds materiality. This is done by considering

1. the difference between the point estimate and materiality,
2. the extent to which items in the population have been audited 100 percent (such as large dollar items),
3. whether misstatements tend to be offsetting or in only one direction,
4. the amounts of individual misstatements, and
5. the sample size.

Suppose that materiality is $40,000. If the point estimate of misstatements is $6,589, it is likely that the population is acceptable.

Suppose that materiality is $12,000, only $5,411 greater than the point estimate. In that case, other factors would be considered. For example, if the larger items in the population were audited 100 percent, then any unidentified misstatements would be restricted to smaller items. If the misstatements tend to be offsetting and are relatively small in size, the auditor may conclude that the true population misstatement is likely to be less than materiality. Also, the larger the sample size, the more confident the auditor can be that the point estimate is close to the true population misstatement value. Therefore, the auditor would be more willing to accept that the true population misstatement is less than tolerable misstatement in this example, where the sample size is considered large, than where it is considered moderate or small. For statistical sampling of controls, the auditor uses a formula (or a table) to determine the likely range of error and the acceptability of the population. For MUS and variables statistical sampling, a formal decision rule that uses a likely range of misstatement is used for deciding the acceptability of the population. The decision rule will be illustrated in Chapter 13, along with the illustration of a specific sample selection.

concept check

C11-5 An auditor is counting a sample of inventory items. Provide two examples of potential errors or misstatement that could occur.

C11-6 The auditor has decided to circularize accounts payable confirmations. What is the likely population?

Summary

1. *What is sampling?* Sampling occurs when someone looks at less than 100 percent of the items in a population.

    Why would an auditor use statistical rather than nonstatistical sampling? With statistical sampling, the auditor can quantify sampling risk and also calculate a statistical result.

    What are the different types of nonprobabilistic (nonstatistical) sampling methods used by auditors? The three types are directed (items likely to contain misstatements, items containing selected population characteristics, or large dollar amounts), block, and haphazard.

    How can CAATs facilitate nonstatistical sampling? When populations are large and data are available, the auditor could select the samples using automated systems. For example, spreadsheets could be used to list high dollar value items, or GAS could be used for gap or block tests.

2. *What are the three different ways that an auditor can select a statistical sample?* The auditor could use a random number table, generate random numbers using computer software, or use systematic selection with a random start.

    List three common statistical sampling methodologies used by auditors. These are attribute sampling, probability-proportionate-to-size sampling (also known as monetary unit sampling or dollar unit sampling), and variables sampling.

    How can CAATs assist statistical sampling? Generalized audit software or other software could be used to select and evaluate the samples.

3. *Describe the 14 steps in planning and selecting a sample, performing the tests, and evaluating a sample.* These steps are listed in Figure 11-2 and Table 11-4.

    What are four additional issues the auditor should consider during the sampling process? The auditor needs to ensure that random sampling occurs, but it is also important to generalize mathematically to provide for statistical measurement. The planning, selection, execution, and evaluation of the sampling process need to be adequately documented. Any internal control exceptions or other errors found should be properly communicated to management and the audit committee. Both judgmental and statistical sampling require extensive use of professional judgment.

    What is an anomaly and how does it affect evaluation of audit results? An anomaly is an error or misstatement that does not generalize to the entire population being audited. If it were generalized, it would result in an inaccurate projection of error. However, the auditor needs to conduct and document audit steps that confirm that the error or misstatement is indeed an anomaly.

Review Questions

11-1 ❶ State what is meant by a "representative sample," and explain its importance in sampling audit populations.

11-2 ❶ Explain the major difference between statistical and nonstatistical sampling. What are the three main parts of statistical and nonstatistical methods?

11-3 ❶ Explain what is meant by "block sampling," and describe how an auditor could obtain five blocks of 20 sales invoices from a sales journal.

11-4 ❶ Distinguish between a sampling error and a non-sampling error. How can each be reduced?

11-5 ❶ Define what is meant by "sampling risk." Does sampling risk apply to nonstatistical sampling, MUS, attribute sampling, and variables sampling? Explain.

11-6 ❶ Define "stratified sampling," and explain its importance in auditing. How could an auditor obtain a stratified sample of 30 items from each of the three strata in the confirmation of accounts receivable?

11-7 ❶ Explain the difference between replacement sampling and nonreplacement sampling. Which method do auditors usually follow? Why?

11-8 ❶ What are the two types of simple random sample selection methods? Which of the two methods is used most often by auditors, and why?

11-9 ❶ Describe systematic sample selection, and explain how an auditor would select 35 numbers from a population of 1,750 items using this approach. What are the advantages and disadvantages of systematic sample selection?

11-10 ❶ What major difference between tests of controls and tests of details of balances makes attribute sampling inappropriate for tests of details of balances?

11-11 ❶ Outline a situation for which discovery sampling would be used.

11-12 ❶ Distinguish between random selection and statistical measurement. State the circumstances under which one can be used without the other.

11-13 ❶ Describe what is meant by a "sampling unit." Explain why the sampling unit for verifying the existence of recorded sales differs from the sampling unit for testing for the possibility of omitted sales.

11-14 ❶ Explain the difference between an attribute and an exception condition. State the exception condition for the following audit procedure: the duplicate sales invoice has been initialled, indicating the performance of internal verification.

11-15 ❶ Distinguish between the point estimate of the total misstatements (likely misstatement) and the true value of the misstatements in the population. How can each be determined?

11-16 ❶ Identify the factors an auditor uses to decide the appropriate TER. Compare the sample size for a TER of 6 percent with that of 3 percent, all other factors being equal.

11-17 ❶ Identify the factors an auditor uses to decide the appropriate ARACR. Compare the sample size for an ARACR of 10 percent with that of 5 percent, all other factors being equal.

11-18 ❶ State the relationship between each of the following:
a. ARACR and sample size.
b. Population size and sample size.
c. TER and sample size.
d. EPER and sample size.

11-19 ❶ Explain what is meant by "analysis of exceptions," and discuss its importance.

Discussion Questions and Problems

11-20 ❶❷❸ For the audit of Carbald Supply Company, Farda is conducting a test of sales for the first nine months of the fiscal year ended December 31, 2012. Incorrect revenue recognition has been assessed as a significant risk. Materiality is set at $750,000.

Included in the audit procedures are the following:
1. Foot and cross-foot the sales journal and trace the balance to the general ledger.
2. Review all sales transactions for reasonableness.
3. Select a sample of recorded sales from the sales journal and trace the customer name and amounts to duplicate sales invoices and the related shipping document.
4. Select a sample of shipping document numbers and perform the following tests:
   4.1 Trace the shipping document to the related duplicate sales invoice.
   4.2 Examine the duplicate sales invoice to determine whether copies of the shipping document, shipping order, and customer order are attached.
   4.3 Examine the shipping order for an authorized credit approval.
   4.4 Examine the duplicate sales invoice for an indication of internal verification of quantity, price, extensions, and footings; trace the balance to the accounts receivable master file.
   4.5 Compare the price on the duplicate sales invoice with the sales price in the product master file and the quantity with the shipping document.
   4.6 Trace the total on the duplicate sales invoice to the sales journal and the accounts receivable master file for customer, name, amount, and date.

REQUIRED
a. State the audit objective associated with each of the audit procedures.
b. Identify those audit procedures which are potential controls with respect to revenue recognition. Justify your response.
c. Identify those audit procedures where computer-assisted audit tests (CAATs) can be used for all or part of the audit procedure. State the process that the CAATs can complete.
d. What type of sampling would you use for these audit procedures? Justify your response.
e. State the appropriate sampling unit, define the attribute that you would test, and define exception conditions for each of the audit procedures.
f. Which of the audit procedures are dual-purpose tests? Justify your response.

11-21 ❷❸ Lam, a PA, is auditing the financial statements of his client, Harvesters Ltd., a company that sells and distributes agricultural equipment across Canada. Lam has performed a preliminary evaluation of the company's internal control over sales transactions, and has concluded that the quality of system design is very good. The system was developed for the client and installed by a well-respected consulting firm, and the system relies heavily on automated information systems. Lam decides that performing tests of control using computer-assisted audit techniques would likely be cost-effective. In addition, after completing his assessment of control risk over revenue transactions, Lam plans to use monetary-unit sampling to verify the client's recorded accounts receivable at year end.

In planning the engagement, Lam has assessed materiality to be $175,000.

REQUIRED
a. Explain the basic principles of sample selection for monetary unit (dollar unit) sampling.
b. Also discuss how computer-assisted audit techniques could be used to assist in sample selection, assuming that the population of year-end accounts receivable is available to Lam as a data file compatible with his software.
c. Assume that the client's recorded accounts receivable total $2,000,000 at year end and that Lam examines a valid random sample of 50 dollar units, and finds two errors as follows:

	Account number 26751	Account number 87523
Recorded amount	$20,000	$10,000
Amount confirmed by customer	10,000	NIL

Both errors were caused by the client's failure to record equipment returned by customers, where the equipment was deemed to be defective. The client agrees with the customer's position in both cases.

What further action is required on the part of the auditor with respect to these errors?

11-22 ❸ For the examination of the financial statements of Scotia Inc., Rosa Schellenberg, a public accountant, has decided to apply nonstatistical audit sampling in the tests of sales transactions. Based on her knowledge of Scotia's operations in the area of sales, she decides that the estimated population deviation rate is likely to be three percent and that she is willing to accept a 5-percent risk that the true population exception rate is not greater than 6 percent. Given this information, Rosa selects a random sample of 150 sales invoices from the 5,000 prepared during the year and examines them for exceptions. She notes the following exceptions in her working papers.

REQUIRED

a. Which of the invoices in the table should be defined as an exception?
b. Explain why it is inappropriate to set a single acceptable TER and EPER for the combined exceptions.
c. State the appropriate analysis of exceptions for each of the exceptions in the sample.

Invoice No.	Comment
5028	Sales invoice had incorrect price, but a subsequent credit note was sent out as a correction.
6791	Voided sales invoice examined by auditor.
6810	Shipping document for a sale of merchandise could not be located.
7364	Sales invoice for $2,875 has not been collected and is six months past due.
7625	Client unable to locate the printed duplicate copy of the sales invoice.
8431	Invoice was dated three days later than the date of the shipping document.
8528	Customer purchase order is not attached to the duplicate sales invoice.
8566	Billing is for $100 less than it should be due to a pricing error.
8780	Client is unable to locate the printed duplicate copy of the sales invoice.
9169	Credit is not authorized, but the sale was for only $7.65.

11-23 ❸ You have been asked to do planning for statistical testing in the control testing of the audit of cash receipts. Following is a partial audit program for the audit of cash receipts:

1. Review the cash receipts journal for large and unusual transactions.
2. Trace entries from the prelisting of cash receipts to the cash receipts journal to determine whether each is recorded.
3. Compare customer name, date, and amount on the prelisting with the cash receipts journal.
4. Examine the related remittance advice for entries selected from the prelisting to determine whether cash discounts were approved.
5. Trace entries from the prelisting to the deposit slip to determine whether each has been deposited.

REQUIRED

a. Identify which audit procedures can be tested using attributes sampling. Justify your response.
b. State the appropriate sampling unit for each of the tests in part (a).
c. Define the attributes that you would test for each of the tests in part (a). State the audit objective associated with each of the attributes.
d. Define exception conditions for each of the attributes that you described in part (c).
e. Which of the exceptions would be indicative of potential fraud? Justify your response.

Professional Judgment Problems

11-24 ❸ An audit partner is developing an office training program to familiarize her professional staff with statistical decision models applicable to the audit of dollar-value balances. She wants to demonstrate the relationship of sample sizes to population size and variability and the auditor's specifications as to tolerable misstatement and ARIA. The partner prepared the table on the next page to show comparative population characteristics and audit specifications of the two populations.

In items (1) through (5) below, indicate for the specific case from the table that follows the required sample size to be selected from Population 1 relative to the sample from Population 2.

1. In case 1 the required sample size from Population 1 is _____.
2. In case 2 the required sample size from Population 1 is _____.
3. In case 3 the required sample size from Population 1 is _____.
4. In case 4 the required sample size from Population 1 is _____.
5. In case 5 the required sample size from Population 1 is _____.

Your answer should be selected from the following responses:

a. Larger than the required sample size from Population 2.
b. Equal to the required sample size from Population 2.
c. Smaller than the required sample size from Population 2.
d. Indeterminate relative to the required sample size from Population 2.
(Adapted from AICPA)

	Characteristics of Population 1 Relative to Population 2		Audit Specifications as to a Sample from Population 1 Relative to a Sample from Population 2	
	Size	Estimated Population Exception Rate	Tolerable Misstatement	ARIA
Case 1	Equal	Equal	Equal	Lower
Case 2	Equal	Larger	Larger	Equal
Case 3	Larger	Equal	Smaller	Higher
Case 4	Smaller	Smaller	Equal	Higher
Case 5	Larger	Equal	Equal	Lower

Case

11-25 ❶❷❸ PA has just completed the accounts receivable confirmation process in the audit of Danforth Paper Company Ltd., a paper supplier to retail shops and commercial users. Following are the data related to this process:

Accounts receivable recorded balance	$2,760,000
Number of accounts	7,320

A nonstatistical sample was taken as follows:

All accounts over $10,000 (23 accounts)	$465,000
77 accounts under $10,000	$81,500
Materiality	$100,000

Inherent and control risk are both high.
No relevant analytical procedures were performed.

The table at right gives the results of the confirmation procedures.

REQUIRED

a. What type of non-statistical sampling method would PA have used? Justify your response.
b. Explain the advantages and disadvantages of using stratified sampling for the Danforth Paper Company Ltd. sample selection.
c. If statistical sampling were used, which method would be used? Justify your response.
d. Describe the process that would be used to evaluate the results of the nonstatistical sample. Consider both the direct implications of the misstatements found and the effect of using a sample.

	Recorded Value	Audited Value
Items over $10,000	$465,000	$432,000
Items under $10,000	81,500	77,150
Individual misstatements for items under $10,000:		
Item 12	5,120	4,820
Item 19	485	385
Item 33	1,250	250
Item 35	3,975	3,875
Item 51	1,850	1,825
Item 59	4,200	3,780
Item 74	2,405	0
	19,285	14,935

Ongoing Small Business Case: Sampling at CondoCleaners.com

11-26 ❶❷ There are about 350 payroll transactions and about 1,500 sales transactions in the current year under audit at CondoCleaners.com. The only material asset account is fixed assets.

REQUIRED

What type of sampling might be suitable at Condo-Cleaners.com? Justify your response.

3

The auditor's risk response: audit of cycles and accounts

To understand how auditing is done in practice, it is important to understand how auditing concepts are applied to specific auditing areas. The sales and collection cycle is the first area we look at for a detailed application of auditing concepts. This cycle is an important part of every audit and varies in complexity depending upon the nature of the client. These two chapters apply the concepts you have learned in previous chapters to the audit of sales, cash receipts, and the related income statement and balance sheet accounts in the cycle.

The objective of Chapter 12 is to help you learn the risk-based methodology for designing tests of controls for sales, cash receipts, and the other classes of transactions in the sales and collection cycle. Chapter 13 presents the continuation of the risk-based methodology for designing audit procedures for the audit of account balances in the sales and collection cycle.

Each of Chapters 14 to 17 deals with a specific transaction cycle or part of a transaction cycle in much the same manner as Chapters 12 and 13 cover the sales and collection cycle. These latter four chapters demonstrate the relationship of risks, internal controls, tests of controls, substantive tests of transactions, and analytical procedures to the related balance sheet and income statement accounts in the cycle and to tests of details of balances.

12 Audit of the sales and collection cycle: Tests of controls

Now that we have looked at the planning of the audit, including the risk assessment process, it is time to look at the execution phase—what are the risks associated with sales? How do we actually design and conduct the testing in response to these risks? Which tests are conducted and for what purpose? In this chapter, we look at the testing of internal controls for the sales and collection cycle. Management accountants will find this valuable when designing internal controls to mitigate risks, while auditors (financial, internal, and specialists) use their knowledge of internal controls to help assess risks and design audit tests.

LEARNING OBJECTIVES

1 Identify and describe typical records and transactions in the sales cycle. Describe the risks of fraud or error in the cycle. Explain how the functions and records in the cycle help to prevent or detect fraud or error.

2 State the relationship between overall audit planning risks and risks for sales and collections cycle assertions. Explain how the evaluation of general controls affects the audit of the sales and collection cycle. Describe the methodology for designing tests of controls for sales.

3 Describe the methodology for designing controls over sales returns and allowances, cash receipts transactions and uncollectable accounts. State the effect of the results of tests of controls on the audit.

4 Illustrate the risk assessment and audit of sales and cash receipts using Hillsburg Hardware Limited to describe the typical audit process through tests of controls. Relate audit tests and the sampling methodologies used to the purpose of the audit tests.

STANDARDS REFERENCED IN THIS CHAPTER

CICA Standards

CAS 240 – The Auditor's Responsibilities Relating to Fraud in an Audit of Financial Statements

Section 3400 – Revenue

IAS 18 – Revenue

The Choice Is Simple—Rely on Internal Control or Resign

Major Financial Inc. is one of the largest clients managed out of the Montreal office of a Big Four firm. It is a financial services conglomerate with almost 200 offices in Canada and the United States, as well as branch offices overseas. The company has over 200,000 major accounts receivable, with millions of smaller accounts. It processes hundreds of millions of sales and other transactions annually.

The company's national computer centre is in a large environmentally controlled room containing mainframe computers and a great deal of supporting equipment. There are two complete systems serving online systems, one serving as a backup for the other, as systems failure would stop operations in all of the company's branches.

The company has an excellent system of checks and balances whereby branch office transaction totals are reconciled to head office data processing control totals daily; these, in turn, are reconciled to outside bank account records monthly. Whenever this regular reconciliation process indicates a significant out-of-balance condition, procedures are initiated to resolve the problem as quickly as possible. There is an internal audit staff that oversees any special investigative efforts that are required.

Because Major Financial Inc. is a public company, it must file its annual report with the Quebec and Ontario securities commissions within 90 days of its fiscal year end. In addition, the company likes to announce annual earnings and issue its annual report as soon after year end as feasible. Under these circumstances, there is always a great deal of pressure on the public accounting firm to complete the audit quickly.

IMPORTANCE TO AUDITORS

Major Financial is a high-profile audit client with numerous risks. There are many users of the financial statements and a great deal of work that needs to be completed by the internal and external auditors in a short period of time.

A standard audit planning question is, how much shall we rely on internal control? In the case of the Major Financial audit, there is only one possible answer: as much as we can. Otherwise, how could the audit possibly be completed to meet the reporting deadlines, let alone keep audit cost to a reasonable level? Accordingly, the public accounting firm conducts the audit with significant reliance on general information systems controls, specific data processing controls, reconciliation processes, and internal audit procedures. It tests these controls extensively and performs many of its audit procedures prior to year end. In all honesty, if Major Financial Inc. did not have excellent internal controls, the public accounting firm would admit that an audit of the company just could not be done.

continued >

WHAT DO YOU THINK?

1. Which financial institution do you bank with? Think of at least three controls that are present when you conduct your banking. What are the risks that these controls mitigate?

2. Recall that there can be manual, automated, or combined internal controls. Classify the controls that you identified in (1) above using these categories. Which type of control do you think is more reliable for your financial institution? Why?

3. Client business risk may have been considered low for financial institutions in the past. How do recent asset valuation issues in the financial sector affect client business risk for financial institutions?

VERY large organizations process millions of transactions and may have thousands (or even millions) of customers. The role of sampling, whether for tests of controls or tests of details, becomes important, as does the methodology used to conduct such sampling. What types of samples would you use for such large clients? Judgmental or statistical or both? Think about the different ways that you could use sampling for clients such as Major Financial Inc. as you go through this chapter.

① The Typical Sales Cycle

The overall objective in the audit of the sales and collection cycle is to evaluate whether the account balances affected by the cycle are fairly presented in conformity with an applicable financial reporting framework.

Look at the adjusted trial balance for Hillsburg Hardware Limited in Figure 5-5. Accounts on the trial balance affected by the sales and collection cycle are identified by the letter S in the left margin. For other audits, the names and the nature of the accounts may vary, of course, depending on the industry and client involved. There are differences in account titles for a service company, a retail company, and an insurance company, but the basic concepts are the same. To provide a frame of reference for understanding the material in this chapter, a retail outlet with consumers and commercial customers, such as Hillsburg Hardware, is assumed.

Risks of Fraud or Error in the Sales and Collection Cycle

CAS Revenue and related accounts receivable and cash accounts are especially susceptible to manipulation and theft. For example, Table 12-1 shows a selection of major risks of error or fraud in the sales and collection cycle. This explains why CAS 240.26 requires the auditor to presume that there are risks of fraud with respect to revenue recognition (overstatement of revenue) for all clients. Surveys support the assumption that 5 percent of all organizations will experience some type of fraud (based on ACFE studies, see Figure 12-1), and more than 60 percent of financial statement fraud is revenue fraud (see COSO study,

	Risks of Misappropriation of Assets, Other Fraud or Illegal Acts	Risks of Inadequate Disclosure or Incorrect Presentation of Financial Information, Including Fraudulent Financial Reporting
Risks of Error		
Orders are shipped to a customer with a bad credit rating.		Consignment sales are recorded as revenue.
	Inventory is stolen and the sale is recorded as a fictitious sale (no shipping document).	
Incorrect recognition of revenue percentage for long-term contracts or complex revenue instruments.		Fictitious revenue transactions are recorded and reported.
	Revenue is recorded when goods have not been delivered.	
Sales are recorded twice (duplicated) or accidentally omitted.		Subsequent period revenue is deliberately recorded in the current period.
	"Channel stuffing:" inventory is shipped to customers with favourable terms, such as right of return, so that the client retains risks of ownership.	
Sales are recorded for the incorrect quantity or the incorrect price.		Financing transactions (borrowings) are recorded as revenue.
	Long-term service revenue (such as the provision of maintenance) is recorded as current revenue.	

Table 12-1 above: **Major Risks of Error or Fraud in the Sales and Collection Cycle**

www.coso.org/documents/COSOReleaseonFraudulentReporting2010PDF_001.pdf).
These high rates of fraud using revenue support the auditor's need to carefully assess risks and design audit tests for the audit of the sales and collection cycle.

Revenue is susceptible to manipulation for several reasons. Overstatement of revenues often increases net income by an equal amount because related costs of sales are often not recorded for fictitious or prematurely recognized revenues. Also, financial analysts and other market participants place increasing emphasis on revenue growth. There are three main types of revenue manipulations:

- Fictitious revenues (occurrence objective): Documents supporting fictitious sales could be created, or other transactions, such as financing arrangements, could be misclassified as revenue;
- Premature revenue recognition (cutoff assertion): Subsequent period sales are recorded as current period sales, "bill-and-holds" could take place (goods are invoiced but not shipped), side arrangements that change the terms of sale, such as consignment, or not meeting requirements for recording revenue; and
- Manipulation of adjustments: Returns and allowances could be hidden (not recorded, completeness assertion); or understatement of bad debts (valuation assertion for accounts receivable).

A look at the transaction flow and controls in the cycle will help us to see how the risks of error, misstatement, or fraud can be mitigated.

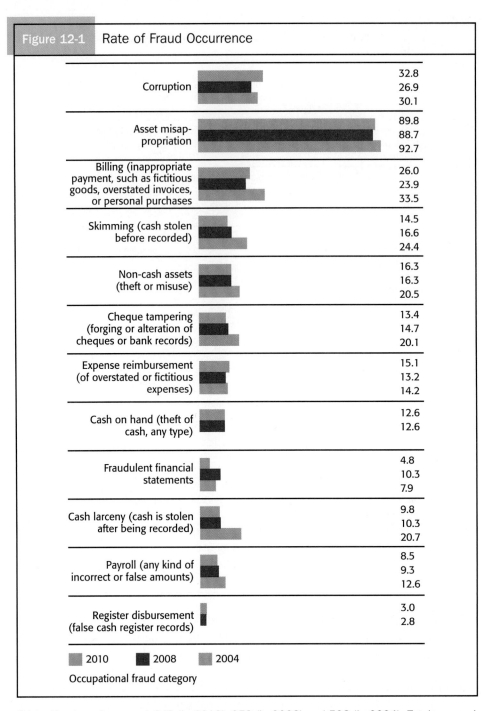

Figure 12-1 | Rate of Fraud Occurrence

Occupational fraud category	2010	2008	2004
Corruption	32.8	26.9	30.1
Asset misappropriation	89.8	88.7	92.7
Billing (inappropriate payment, such as fictitious goods, overstated invoices, or personal purchases	26.0	23.9	33.5
Skimming (cash stolen before recorded)	14.5	16.6	24.4
Non-cash assets (theft or misuse)	16.3	16.3	20.5
Cheque tampering (forging or alteration of cheques or bank records)	13.4	14.7	20.1
Expense reimbursement (of overstated or fictitious expenses)	15.1	13.2	14.2
Cash on hand (theft of cash, any type)	12.6	12.6	
Fraudulent financial statements	4.8	10.3	7.9
Cash larceny (cash is stolen after being recorded)	9.8	10.3	20.7
Payroll (any kind of incorrect or false amounts)	8.5	9.3	12.6
Register disbursement (false cash register records)	3.0	2.8	

"*Note:* Number of cases: 1,843 (in 2010), 959 (in 2008) and 508 (in 2004). Totals exceed 100 percent as some frauds involved multiple types. Methods of data collection changed in 2006, where comparatives and similar category totals were not provided.

Source: Association of Certified Fraud Examiners, "Report to the Nation on Occupational Fraud and Abuse," 2010, 2008, 2004, HYPERLINK www.acfe.com, Accessed: February 20, 2012

Classes of transactions in the sales and collection cycle—the categories of transactions for the sales and collection cycle in a typical company: sales, cash receipts, sales returns and allowances, charge-off of uncollectable accounts, and bad-debt expense.

A brief summary of the way accounting information flows through the various accounts in the sales and collection cycle is illustrated in Figure 12-2 by the use of T-accounts. This figure shows that there are generally six **classes of transactions** (the categories of transactions) included **in the sales and collection cycle**, flowing to the general ledger accounts noted below beside the class of transaction (CR = credit, DR = debit):

- Sales (cash and sales on account net of cash discounts taken): CR sales, DR accounts receivable and discounts taken.

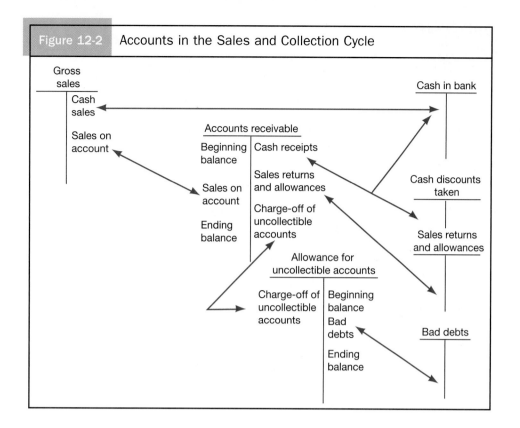

Figure 12-2   Accounts in the Sales and Collection Cycle

- Cash receipts: DR cash in bank, CR accounts receivable.
- Sales returns and allowances: DR sales returns and allowances, CR accounts receivable.
- Write-off of uncollectable accounts: CR accounts receivable, DR allowance for uncollectable accounts.
- Bad-debt expense: DR bad-debt expense, CR allowance for uncollectable accounts
- Master file changes: (no effect on general ledger accounts; effect is on master iles).

Nature of the Sales and Collection Cycle

The **sales and collection cycle** involves the decisions and processes necessary for the transfer of the ownership of goods and services to customers after they are made available for sale. It begins with a request by a customer (or a customer selecting and picking up a product) and ends with the conversion of material or service into an account receivable or cash.

There are two types of data stored: semi-permanent and transaction, as shown in Table 12-3. **Semi-permanent (or master file) data** in the sales and collection cycle are data that are established when a customer starts purchasing and is updated as customer information changes. For example, customer name, credit limit, and billing address are included, and the data are generally used for the processing of multiple transactions. **Transaction information** is based upon customer activity, with normally one or more transactions for each activity, such as a sale.

The nature of computer processing used within a transaction cycle determines potential controls available in the system. For example, transactions can be processed using groups of transactions (also called **batch processing**), or they can be processed one at a time with immediate update against the data files (called **online processing**). Many companies use both methods. Payroll or interest on overdue accounts may be processed weekly in batch mode, while sales orders received over the telephone may be recorded as received. Groups of transactions are controlled as a group, with records being counted and totals reconciled and posted, while online transactions are controlled individually, using data entry edits and numeric sequencing.

Sales and collection cycle— involves the decisions and processes necessary for the transfer of the ownership of goods and services to customers after they are made available for sale; begins with a request by a customer and ends with the conversion of material or service into an account receivable, and ultimately into cash.

Semi-permanent (or master file) data—in the sales and collection cycle, data that are established when a customer starts purchasing and is updated as customer information changes; generally used for the processing of multiple transactions.

Transaction information— information based on customer activity. There is normally one transaction for each activity. In the sales and collection cycle, examples include sale or cash payment transactions.

Batch processing—transaction processing using groups of transactions.

Online processing—the processing of transactions one at a time with an immediate update against the data files.

Table 12-2	Typical Information Included in Accounts Receivable or Sales Computer Data Files

Semi-permanent Information	Transaction Information
Semi-permanent information is often called master file data. It is established when a customer starts purchasing, and it is updated as customer information changes.	Transaction information is based on customer activity, and there is normally one transaction for each activity, such as a sale or cash payment.
Customer number or code	Customer number or code
Customer name	Customer name
Customer billing address	Transaction type (sale, credit, payment, adjustment)
Customer shipping address	
Customer phone number	Transaction date
Credit limit	Transaction amount
Payment terms (includes applicable discounts)	Transaction detail (item detail)
Year-to-date sales	Transaction tracking (the individual who entered the transaction)
Current balance outstanding	

AUTOMATIC TRANSACTIONS, CONTROLS, AND LOGS Documentation and assessment of systems should include automatic transactions or automatic controls. For example, sales could generate automatic reduction of inventory (in a point-of-sale system) or an automated system could prevent a sale if it causes a customer to exceed a credit limit. Many systems also do the posting to the general ledger automatically (such as having each transaction posted to the general ledger, or having daily totals posted).

Most systems have transaction logs that identify who has entered, modified or deleted transactions by associating user identification codes (user IDs) with the activity. As discussed in Chapter 9, individuals who enter transactions (such as sales) should not have access to assets. The auditor can use transaction logs to evaluate segregation of duties.

Business Functions in the Cycle and Related Documents and Records

Business functions in a sales and collection cycle—the key activities that an organization must complete to execute and record business transactions for sales, cash receipts, sales returns and allowances, charge-off of uncollectable accounts, and bad debts.

The business functions for a cycle are the key activities that an organization must complete to execute and record business transactions. Table 12-3 lists the common **business functions** in the sales and collection cycle, typical documents and records, and the purposes of those documents or records, which could be in paper or electronic form.

PROCESSING CUSTOMER SALES ORDERS The request for goods by a customer is the starting point for the entire cycle. It may be received by telephone, by letter, electronically, by a printed form that has been sent to prospective and existing customers, through salespeople, or in other ways. Legally, it is an offer to buy goods under specified terms. If the client does not provide a purchase order, many organizations create an internal sales order document to provide a record of the goods that are going to be shipped. To prevent data entry errors, input edits should be present (for example, reasonableness on quantity, matching of customer number to master file, and checking for valid postal codes). Internal sales orders should be sequentially numbered (and accounted for) to ensure that all sales orders processed are billed. In fact, the sales order number may follow through the entire process and be the same number used for the shipping document and invoice.

In a retail store environment, the customer order is absent, as the customer picks the product and takes it to a point-of-sale terminal.

GRANTING CREDIT For new customers, an external credit report from a credit rating agency should be obtained to help determine the credit limit which will be entered on an approved credit change form and recorded in the customer master file. Before goods are shipped, a properly authorized person or automated control system must

Table 12-3	Business Functions, Related Documents and Records and Their Purposes for the Sales and Collection Cycle	
Business Function	**Documents and Records**	**Purpose of Document or Record**
Processing customer sales orders	Customer (purchase) order	Specifies the products and quantities (and often prices) of the products purchased.
Granting credit	External credit report	Provides external information about the credit-worthiness of the customer.
	Credit change form or credit approval form*	Documents the approved credit limit (or changes to it) for entry into the customer master file.
	Accounts receivable trial balance	A report that lists the amount owed by each customer, either in total or by invoice, usually showing the age (e.g. 30 days, 60 days).The report is also used to assist the collection process.
Shipping goods	Shipping document	Records the quantity and type of goods shipped to the customer.
	Bill of lading	Records the packages, weights, and sizes shipped using an external trucking company.
	Change of address form*	Records authorized address change or shipping address change for the customer, for entry into the customer master file.
Billing customers and recording sales	Sales invoice	A document sent to the customer that describes the quantity of goods sold, the price, other charges such as shipping, taxes, as well as terms of payment.
	Sales journal/history report	A listing of sales transactions for a particular period (e.g. day, week), which may include sales returns.
	Summary sales report	Totals from the sales journal, including general ledger distribution.
	Monthly statements	The customer's accounts receivable activity. It starts with the opening balance, shows a listing of sales, cash, and adjustments transactions and totals for a particular customer.
Processing and recording cash receipts	Remittance advice	Document received with cheque payment or sent as a record of electronic payment that lists the date of payment, amounts, and invoices paid.
	Cash prelisting	A separate record of cash and cheques received, prepared immediately upon receipt of funds.
	Bank deposit slip	A listing of amounts, by customer, deposited in the bank and used at the bank to deposit cheques and cash.
	Bank deposit listing	A record of the bank deposit detail used by the accounting system.
	Cash receipts journal	A listing of all cash received and deposited in the bank that also lists the accounts receivable entries made, by customer.
Processing and recording sales returns and allowances	Returns receiving report	Receiving document that identifies the quantity, item, and state of repair of returned items.
	Credit memo	A transaction and document that reduces the amount due from a customer, usually in the same format as a sales invoice, but with a negative amount.
	Sales returns and allowances journal	Transaction listing of credit notes and other reductions to sales.
Writing off uncollectable accounts receivable	Uncollectable account authorization form	A document that describes which accounts are to be written off, and why.
Providing for bad debts	Journal entry authorization	Journal entry to provide for estimated bad debts.
Maintaining semi-permanent data	Master file change form*	Description of and authorization of addition, change, or deletion of sales prices or customer data.
	Master file change report	Report of master file changes processed.

Notes: * Some organizations may use a multi-purpose master file change form. "Journal" and "history report" are synonymous terms.

approve credit to the customer for sales on account. Sales are automatically authorized as long as the account receivable (the balance outstanding in the master file or listed on an accounts receivable trial balance) stays within the authorized credit limit. Once the balance approaches the credit limit, exception reports are printed for the credit manager to review and approve, or other methods are used to determine whether credit limits should be extended or individual sales should continue to be approved. Weak practices in credit approval or in changing the credit limit in the master file frequently result in excessive bad debts and accounts receivable that may be uncollectable. In a retail environment, consumers pay cash or by credit card, where the purchase must be within the limit available on the credit card.

SHIPPING GOODS Before shipment, the company needs to have a way to make sure that the product is in inventory. Then, products are picked and the shipping document is prepared as a record of goods that are shipped. Details will be different from the customer order if not all products are on hand (perhaps leading to a back-order for the customer). This critical function is the first point in the cycle where company assets are given up and is normally the time when revenue is recognized assuming that title to the goods has passed. If an external shipping company is used to ship goods, a bill of lading (or courier slip) will be used to track packages and quantities given to the trucking company. Accurate shipping addresses are important, so any changes to customer shipping addresses in the customer master file must be supported by an approved change of address form or similar written document. Companies that maintain perpetual inventory records also update them on the basis of shipping information. The retail point-of-sale terminal produces a sales slip that tracks both inventory (the items taken) and records the total sale, so there is no shipping function or separate shipping document for such sales.

BILLING CUSTOMERS AND RECORDING SALES To ensure that there are no unauthorized changes to shipping documents or invoices, only approved individuals should have access to these functions. Once shipping information has been entered and the shipping document printed, it is locked so that no further changes can be made, and the sales invoice is automatically prepared. If the sales invoice is not automatically prepared with the same reference number, there need to be controls in place to ensure that all shipments are billed (by tracking document numbers) and the numeric continuity of both documents must be accounted for. Automatic invoicing also prevents calculation errors (assuming systems are programmed correctly) and prevents the same shipment from being billed twice. Approved prices would be retrieved from the sales price master file and should match the customer order. The authorized price includes consideration of freight charges, insurance, and terms of payment.

In most systems, billing of the customer includes preparation of a multicopy sales invoice and updating of the sales transactions file, customer master file, and general ledger files for sales and accounts receivable. This information is used to generate the sales journal and, along with cash receipts and miscellaneous credits, allows preparation of the accounts receivable trial balance.

Point-of-sale systems, such as those seen at many retail counters, often combine data entry and update for shipment, inventory, sales systems, and cash receipts with the entry of a single transaction. The single data entry transaction results in multiple transactions in the information systems, that is, shipment records, inventory changes, sales records, and cash receipts information.

PROCESSING AND RECORDING CASH RECEIPTS Processing and recording cash receipts includes receiving, depositing, and recording cash. Cash includes both currency and cheques. A potential fraud risk is the possibility of theft. Theft can occur before receipts are entered in the records, as illustrated in the first example in Audit Challenge 12-1, or later. The risk of theft is reduced in the handling of cash receipts when cash handling is separated from deposit and recording in the accounts, and when all cash must be deposited in the bank and recorded on a timely basis.

Cereal Hamburgers and Stale Cars

CASH. More cash for me, please, to support my lifestyle. This seems to be what underlies the innovative ways that employees or owners of businesses steal or engage in fraud.

Consider the case of the staff at a club-based restaurant. Staff were conspiring to provide more saleable products by adding cereal to hamburgers and watering down liquor. This enabled them to take the cash from about every fifth sale without recording it. Staff conspired to ensure that reports and supporting documents all reconciled so that the thefts could not easily be detected. Internal auditors became suspicious of the club because there was never any problem with the accounting records—they were too perfect!

This example illustrates the importance of considering past practices when examining documentation and considering documentation in the context of human behaviours.

In our second example, a car dealership was experiencing cash flow problems due to lower sales. The owner told his employees to deceive the bank about trade-ins that were received on the purchase of new cars.

As trade-ins could be used as security for the bank loan (they were part of the inventory that secured the loan), the car dealership was able to inflate its inventory by adding increasingly more fictitious used-car inventory. It did this by resending old sales documents with slight alterations. The bank asked only for the front page of the documentation, which made this alteration easy. Subsequent to the detection of the fraud, the bank changed its procedures to require more rigorous documentation and periodic spot checks of client inventory.

CRITICAL THINKING QUESTIONS

1. What are the characteristics of good documentation that make it so important for record keeping?
2. Identify some common documentation errors that could easily occur. Were the internal auditors of the club right to believe that perfect documentation was a problem?

Sources: 1. Jacka, J. Mike, "Roundtable," *Internal Auditor Journal*, August 2004, p. 91-92. 2. Miles, William, "Selling cars already sold," *Fraud Magazine*, January/February 2009, 23(1), p. 14-15, 58.

Some companies engage a bank or others to assist in the processing of cash receipts from customers. This could involve a lockbox system, whereby customers mail payments to a post office box address. The external organization is responsible for opening all receipts, maintaining records of all payments by customers received at the lockbox address, and depositing receipts into the company's bank account on a timely basis. In other cases, receipts are submitted electronically from customers' bank accounts to a company bank account through the use of electronic funds transfer (EFT). For consumer purchases by credit card on websites, the issuer of the credit card uses EFT to transfer funds into the company's bank account (less commission) almost immediately after the sale. For both lockbox systems and EFT, the bank provides information to the company to prepare the cash receipt entries in the company's accounting records. The use of both lockboxes and EFT allows for faster deposit of cash receipts into company bank accounts and often reduces risks associated with company personnel handling cash receipts since it separates cash handling from accounting entry.

The remittance advice is an independent external document that provides the dollar amount and invoice number that is being paid and could be a "tear-off" portion of the original invoice, or a "tear-off" portion to the customer cheque. Some organizations have a separate person (such as the receptionist) prepare a list of the remittance advices or payments prior to preparing a bank statement, which is called a cash prelisting. Others simply take the cheques and remittance advice amounts and transfer them directly to a bank deposit slip. Amounts received should be compared to invoice amounts as a check on accuracy and completeness when the bank detail is recorded. Recording of amounts received will result in a bank deposit listing, a cash receipts journal, and postings to cash and accounts receivable (by customer). Detailed postings should be reconciled to the total bank deposit to ensure completeness and accuracy, and only performed by authorized persons to prevent unauthorized changes.

PROCESSING AND RECORDING SALES RETURNS AND ALLOWANCES When a customer is dissatisfied with the goods purchased, the seller frequently accepts the return of goods or grants a reduction in the charges. The company prepares a returns receiving document (which may be a regular receiving report marked "return") for the returned goods and returns them to inventory. Damaged goods returns must be independently approved from the shipping department so that potential theft cannot be hidden as "damaged goods." Returns and allowances must be correctly and promptly recorded by a person who does not have access to the physical asset or access to cash, so that someone cannot steal goods or steal cash and hide the theft as a return of goods in the customer accounts. Approved credit memos would be used for returns and allowances (reductions in price) and should either have their own numeric sequence or be part of the sales invoice sequence numbers.

WRITING OFF UNCOLLECTABLE ACCOUNTS RECEIVABLE Despite the diligence of credit departments, some customers may not pay their bills. When the company concludes that an amount is no longer collectable, it must be written off. Typically, this occurs after a customer files bankruptcy or the account is turned over to a collection agency. Proper accounting requires an authorized adjustment for these uncollectable amounts.

PROVIDING FOR BAD DEBTS The provision for bad debts is an accounting estimate that allows for current period sales that the company believes it will be unable to collect in the future. It should be approved by a person independent of the accounting for accounts receivable (so that theft cannot be hidden as a bad debt allowance) and should either be consistent with prior years or any differences justified.

MASTER FILE CHANGE The customer master file is a file for maintaining semi-permanent data used for processing sales, payments, and other transactions associated with customers. The master file information is provided by the customer and reviewed and approved by the client prior to set-up. Approval is necessary for the credit limit and payment terms in particular and for changes to these fields. It is also important that customers provide changes, such as those to shipping addresses, in writing, since an incorrect shipping address would result in goods being shipped to an incorrect (or unauthorized) location. This approval may be evidenced by a master file change form. The changes can then be authorized by an appropriate individual prior to entry. The sales price master file will be used to retrieve prices for sales invoices and credit notes, so any additions, changes, or deletions to this file should be independently authorized. Any master file changes should be printed or emailed to a person independent of the one who entered the data, to prevent unauthorized changes and to allow for checking of accuracy of data entry.

② Sales Cycle Audit Planning

Risk Assessment and the Sales Cycle

Our previous chapters have explained the audit planning process. Risk assessment comprises the first three phases of the audit: preplanning, client risk profile, and planning the audit. It is only then that the auditor can decide upon the risk response, which includes the design and conduct of further audit procedures, including control testing of the sales and collection cycle, discussed in this chapter. Table 12-4 on the next page lists each of the risk assessments (except control risk, discussed in the next section) that the auditor would have conducted during the risk assessment phase and how each affects the audit of this cycle.

Table 12-4 shows that, as risks increase, the auditor is required to conduct more audit testing. The tests conducted could be tests of control or substantive tests. Let us consider the risks associated with the car dealership discussed in Audit Challenge 12-1. Client business risk for an automobile dealership may be high: such a business is at risk of failure due to decreasing automobile sales as many people lose their jobs and delay major purchases, such as automobiles. If the dealership has loans secured

Table 12-4 Risk Assessment and the Sales and Collection Cycle

Risk Type	Impact Upon Sales and Collection Cycle
Client business risk	Increased client business risk could lead to greater risks of misstatement of sales.
Audit risk	As audit risk decreases, the level of assurance required increases and the extent of testing required increases.
Inherent risk—overall	As inherent risk increases, the extent of testing required increases; inherent risks associated with the handling of cash directly affect certain audit assertions in sales (e.g., completeness).
Risk of material misstatement—overall	Management biases due to bonus incentives or stated earnings forecasts could increase the risk of misstatement of sales.
Risk of fraud—overall	Poor fraud risk management could result in increased risks of fraud, with a need to increase the extent of testing.
Identify significant risks	Revenue recognition is considered a significant risk unless the auditor has evidence to the contrary that can be clearly documented (CAS 240.A28-A30); this means that controls over revenue recognition need to be assessed and increased testing is required of assertions that affect revenue recognition.

CAS

by inventory or accounts receivable with bank covenants, there could be an incentive to manipulate the timing of sales or even the actual amounts of sales (the occurrence objective) to secure or maintain bank funding.

The auditor will consider client business risk and the users of the financial statements in setting audit risk. Many car dealerships have as users the bank, the automobile manufacturer, owners, employees, and regulatory agencies such as Canada Revenue Agency. As economic uncertainty increases, users may scrutinize financial statements more closely, causing the auditor to lower audit risk. The extent of audit testing would need to be increased for all sales audit assertions where there was a risk of material misstatement (e.g., completeness, accuracy, existence, cutoff).

Inherent risks at the dealership, discussed in Chapter 7, would be based on the auditor's assessment of corporate governance, management integrity, client motivation, and the results of previous audits. It is likely that the auditor would somewhat increase inherent risk for a car dealership in light of current economic trends. Risk of material misstatement overall would be moderate, depending upon factors such as revenue from vehicle repairs and maintenance, mix of variable and fixed costs (for example, are premises leased or owned?), and specific issues identified by the auditor. The exception could be the collectability of sales (valuation of accounts receivable), which could have increased risks, depending upon how sales of vehicles are financed. To effectively assess these risks, the auditor must know auditing standards for revenue, and how to apply them, as discussed in Auditing in Action 12-1.

Risk of fraud increases as the quality of the enterprise risk management process (including fraud risk assessment by management) declines and as the quality of internal controls overall declines. The auditor would pay particular attention to monitoring and supervisory controls, depending upon the size of the car dealership. The above risk assessments, including the supporting documentation of internal controls, are integrated into the auditor's control risk assessment.

Prior to examining specific controls for the sales and collection cycle, the auditor identifies assertions that may be prone to a risk of material misstatement, such as occurrence and cutoff of sales. To identify these assertions, the auditor will look at the nature of corporate governance and its effects on sales. For example, if management is remunerated using bonuses or frequently issues ambitious revenue forecasts, it may be prone to overstating revenue in the current period. Also, prior to considering specific controls by cycle, the auditor will consider the results of the general controls assessment for the client.

Assessing Revenue Recognition Policies: ASPE versus IFRS

How would you record income for capital leases, such as those sold by Xerox Corporation? The leases include sale of an asset, financing costs, and service components over a period of several years. *ASPE Handbook* Section 3400.05 supports immediate recognition of the sale of the capital asset portion, since Xerox has likely transferred the "risks and rewards" of ownership. The amount allocated to the capital asset would likely be based upon the value of the asset if it were sold without financing. The service revenue would be allocated as time passes (i.e., the service

performance has been delivered, 3400.07), while the financing income would likely be allocated based upon market interest rates at the time of the sale. (References for similar standards under IFRS are IAS 18.14).

Since Xerox is a public company, it would not be using ASPE. The key difference between IFRS and ASPE for revenue recognition is IAS 18.14(b), which states that revenue can only be recognized when the organization no longer has control over the asset or goods sold or when there is no longer any ongoing management involvement of the goods or services sold.

Effect of General Controls

As described in Chapter 9, the auditor documents general controls that are pervasive and that affect multiple transaction cycles. For example, access and control policies and program change control procedures affect multiple cycles. If unauthorized individuals could access and establish or change credit limits, this would cause problems with collectability of accounts. Similarly, the existence of excellent program change controls that have been tested would allow the auditor to place reliance on programs within each of the transaction cycles, such as the calculation of invoices and aging of accounts receivable. Poor program change controls would suggest that the auditor could potentially rely on only manual controls in the transaction cycle. If unauthorized individuals could change how the accounts receivable aging is calculated or how invoices are calculated, the transactions would be unreliable. Prior to documenting controls and assessing control risk in an individual cycle, the auditor reviews the general controls working-paper file to determine the general controls in place and determines whether reliance can be placed on these controls. This assessment may be completed by a specialist within the auditor's firm and is based on the auditor's risk assessment process.

Methodology for Designing Tests of Controls for Sales

The methodology for obtaining an understanding of internal controls and designing tests of controls for sales is shown in Figure 12-3. This methodology was studied in general terms in Chapters 9 and 10. It is applied specifically to sales in this section. The bottom box in Figure 12-3 shows the four evidence decisions the auditor must make.

Note that the audit tests are in the context of risks of material misstatement. Risks at the individual cycle level are stated in terms of assertions. For example, there could be a material risk that sales are made to fictitious customers (occurrence), that sales are recorded in the incorrect period (cutoff), or that the client has not recorded revenue appropriately (accuracy). Revenue recognition would be addressed by the affected assertions; for example, sales might be classified incorrectly (classification) or deliberately overstated (occurrence).

As we walk through Figure 12-3 we will also use Table 12-5, which lists the specific transaction-related audit objectives for sales along with relevant key controls and common tests of controls for those controls.

Figure 12-3 Methodology for Designing Tests of Controls for Sales

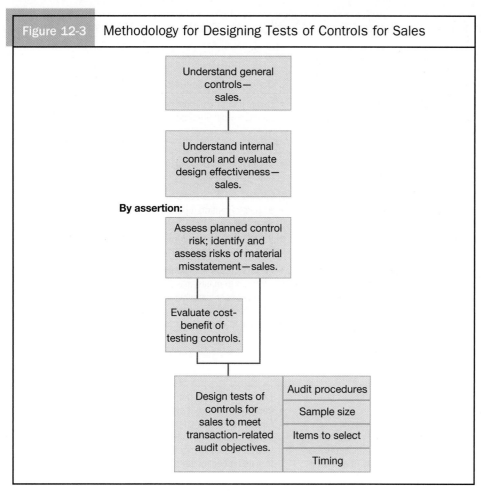

Note: For additional details, refer to Figure 9-6.

UNDERSTAND GENERAL CONTROLS—SALES The auditor needs to consider the type of information systems (e.g. packaged, customized) and its functions (batch, online, web-based) to assess whether programmed controls can be relied upon and whether controls need to be considered when data is transferred or summarized from one system to another. Some systems have access rights that allow entry into all functions of a cycle, while other systems have access rights that can be tailored to individual menu items. If a company has the latter type of system, it may be able to restrict master file changes and credit note generation. If these restrictions were not possible, then the auditor would look for other types of controls, such as the printing and review of reports that identify accurate, authorized master file changes have taken place.

The nature of programs in use affects the relevance of program change controls. When a company has purchased a software package and is unable to change the package, program change controls are normally excellent, since the programs cannot be changed. If the company has custom-developed software with appropriate standards, documentation, and testing, controls over program changes are also likely to be assessed as good. When a company has informal program change procedures, poor testing, or no formal authorization of program changes, for example, program change controls are considered poor. This suggests that the auditor cannot rely on programs during the audit.

Problems with program change procedures or with access controls can have a strong impact on the auditor's assessment of control risk. The auditor may choose not to rely on any programmed or interdependent internal controls for clients with such control weaknesses.

UNDERSTAND INTERNAL CONTROL AND EVALUATE DESIGN EFFECTIVENESS—SALES Chapter 9 discussed how auditors obtain an understanding of internal control. A typical

Transaction-Related Audit Objective	Key Internal Controls	Common Tests of Controls
Recorded sales are for shipments actually made to non-fictitious customers (occurrence).	• Shipping records and sales invoices cannot be produced if the customer number is invalid.	• Use test data and observe rejection of invalid customer numbers when entered by client staff into online system.
	• Recording of sales is supported by authorized shipping documents and approved customer purchase orders.	• Inspect copies of sales invoices for supporting bills of lading and customers' purchase orders.
	• Review exception reports that include unusual or large items extracted from sales transaction or customer master files.	• Inspect exception reports for evidence of review by authorized individual • Inspect the sales journal, general ledger, or trial balance for large or unusual items.*
	• Approval is required to commence selling goods to a new customer, to set up a new customer in the master files, or to change semi-permanent billing information. • A separate password is required to update customer master file information. • Master file changes are printed on numerically controlled reports and reviewed by management.	• Inspect master file change forms for authorization, and compare to master file change reports. • Review paper customer files for credit authorization forms and approval to accept customer. • Determine who has access to master file change password. • Inspect master file change report for evidence of review.
	• Credit is approved before shipment takes place using manual review, or • Orders causing balances to exceed credit limits are either not shipped (prevented by a programmed control), or require supervisor approval such as (i) the entry of a supervisor password prior to shipment or (ii) written approval of a credit limit exception report.	• Examine customer purchase order for credit approval. • Verify that password system has separate functionality for data entry and credit approval and that appropriate persons are assigned these functions. • Use test data to verify the programmed control that customers exceeding their credit limits will have their orders rejected. • Examine credit limit exception report for approval.
	• Sales invoices are sequentially prenumbered and properly accounted for (also satisfies completeness), or • Computer automatically generates sequential invoice numbers.	• Account for integrity of numerical sequence of sales invoices using block test. • Use generalized audit software to identify gaps in invoice numbers used.
	• Monthly statements are sent to customers; complaints receive independent follow-up (also satisfies accuracy).	• Observe whether statements are mailed, and inspect customer correspondence files.
All existing sales transactions are recorded (completeness).	• Shipping documents are sequentially prenumbered and accounted for. • Computer checks for gaps in shipping document numbers (i.e., orders shipped but not billed) and prints a report of missing numbers for independent follow-up.	• Account for integrity of numerical sequence of shipping documents using block test. • Trace shipping documents to associated sales invoices and entry into sales history file and accounts receivable customer master file. • Inspect report of missing shipping document numbers for evidence of independent follow-up.
Recorded sales are for the amount of goods shipped and are correctly billed and recorded (accuracy).	• Invoices are prepared using authorized prices, terms, freight, and discounts established in master files.	• Inspect approved computer printout of unit selling prices and compare to invoice details.
	• Shipping documents are matched to invoices, or • Shipping details are automatically used as the invoicing source. • Approved unit selling prices are entered into the master files and used for all sales. • Invoices are prepared using prices from an approved price list.	• Trace details on sales invoices to shipping documents, price lists, and customers' purchase orders. • Compare inventory selling prices in master files to approved master file change forms and invoice details.

Transaction-Related Audit Objective	Key Internal Controls	Common Tests of Controls
Recorded sales are for the amount of goods shipped and are correctly billed and recorded (accuracy). *(continued)*	• Batch totals of sales invoices are compared with computer summary reports of sales transactions. • Application software programs are used to calculate invoice extensions, calculate sales taxes, insert additional charges, and calculate invoice totals.	• Inspect file of batch totals for initials of data control clerk; compare totals to summary reports. • Recompute information on sales invoices.
	• Transactions are summarized on a timely basis for posting to the general ledger. • Customer master file is periodically printed for independent review. • Aged accounts receivable trial balances are reviewed for reasonableness.	• Trace sales journal entries to copies of sales orders, sales invoices, and shipping documents. • Foot journals, and trace postings to general ledger and accounts receivable master files.
	• Subsidiary accounts receivable records are periodically balanced to the general ledger. • Customer master file totals are compared with general ledger balance monthly, and differences are investigated. • Run-to-run totals are compared and reconciled (i.e., previous monthly accounts receivable total plus transactions reconciles to current month totals).	• Examine initials on general ledger account reconciliation indicating comparison. • Use generalized audit software to add up the outstanding accounts receivable transactions and the balances in the accounts receivable master file. Compare both independent totals with the accounts receivable general ledger balance.
Sales are recorded on the correct dates (cutoff).	• Invoices are prepared using a date equal to the shipping date (or specify the shipping date on the invoice). • System checks reasonableness of date entered. • Management reviews sales and cost of sales analytical reports for reasonableness.	• Compare dates of recorded sales transactions with dates on shipping records. • Inspect shipping records for unbilled shipments and for unrecorded sales. • Verify management walk-through of analytical reports using inquiry or inspect for evidence of follow-up.
Sales transactions are classified to the correct account (classification).	• Adequate chart of accounts is used. • Invoices can be posted only to valid customer accounts. • Posting is done automatically to sales account based upon batch totals or individual transactions. • Management reviews exception reports of unusual customer data.	• Inspect chart of accounts for adequacy. • Inspect customer master file to identify general ledger accounts used for posting. • Conduct manual walk-through of transactions from source to general ledger posting. • Inspect summary reports verifying posting process. • Inquire whether any out-of-balance conditions occurred during the year. • Inspect exception reports for evidence of review.

* This analytical procedure can also apply to other objectives, including completeness, accuracy, and timing.

approach for sales is to conduct interviews, review internal audit working papers, study the clients' flowcharts, prepare an internal control questionnaire, and perform walk-through tests of sales. Figure 10-2 provided an extract of the organization chart for Hillsburg Hardware Limited. Refer to Figure 10-2 and Figure 12-6, a flowchart for Hillsburg Hardware Limited sales and cash receipts. The auditor would develop such documentation to examine whether there are potential key controls that could be relied upon and to identify potential weaknesses in internal controls (called "evaluation of design effectiveness"), discussed further in the last section of this chapter.

ASSESS PLANNED CONTROL RISK; IDENTIFY AND ASSESS RISKS OF MATERIAL MISSTATEMENT—SALES The auditor uses the information obtained in understanding and evaluating design effectiveness of internal control to assess control risk. There are four essential steps to this assessment, all of which were discussed in Chapter 9.

- First, the auditor needs a framework for assessing control risk. The framework for all classes of transactions is the risks associated with the five transaction-related audit objectives. For sales, the audit objectives are shown for Hillsburg Hardware in

Figure 12-7. The auditor would include in the risk assessment process any significant risks identified earlier in the audit, or as required by auditing standards. For example, the auditor is required to consider revenue recognition as a significant risk and to document controls with respect to revenue recognition. The auditor will also consider risks over financial statement presentation and disclosure with respect to sales.

- Second, the auditor must identify the key internal controls and weaknesses for sales. These are also shown in Figure 12-7. The controls and weaknesses will be different for every audit.
- After identifying the controls and weaknesses, the auditor relates them to the objectives and cross-references them to supporting working papers. This is also shown in Figure 12-7 with Cs and Ws in appropriate columns.
- Finally, the auditor provides a conclusion for assessed control risk for each objective by evaluating the controls and weaknesses for each objective (see bottom row of Figure 12-7).

After assessing control risk, the auditor decides upon the risk of material misstatement for each audit assertion. Where there is a risk of material misstatement, the auditor is required to increase substantive tests in addition to conducting control tests (if control tests are conducted), affecting the design of the audit program.

The auditor will look for the following key control activities in this cycle:

- Separation of duties: separation of entry of sales data from entry of cash receipts (to prevent theft of cash and then hiding it in the records); separation of credit limit approval from sales (since sales employees may receive bonuses based upon sales and could be motivated to provide higher credit limits to unworthy customers); independent verification of key data, such as credit limits and other master file data, control totals, and journal entries such as bad debt write-offs.
- Proper authorization: authorization by management or independent individuals should be provided and documented for (i) credit prior to a sale, (ii) removal of goods for shipment, and (iii) sales prices, terms and charges, to ensure that only authorized goods are shipped at appropriate prices to customers with good credit risks;
- Adequate documents and records: accurate, complete transactions that cannot be altered should be retained in paper or electronic format that documents the sales-related business events (orders, shipments, sales, returns, credits, adjustments, and master file changes) and can be traced from origin to the general ledger accounts;
- Sequentially numbered documents: automatic sequential numbering that is accounted for and monitored should be present for all transaction types (invoices/credit notes, shipments, adjustments, and master file changes);
- Mailing of statements: these should be mailed by someone independent of the entry of sales or cash receipts (so that customers could report unusual entries in their statements);
- Independent verification processes: handled by people or software, verification can involve checking numerical continuity, matching of orders to shipments to invoices, and production of exception reports for independent follow up.

EVALUATE COST BENEFIT OF TESTING CONTROLS After the auditor has identified the key internal controls and weaknesses and assessed risks, he or she decides whether substantive tests will be reduced sufficiently to justify the cost of performing tests of controls. Auditors make this decision with the assistance of a matrix such as the one illustrated in Figure 12-7. At the same time, auditors will also identify assertions where substantive testing is not sufficient and tests of controls are required to reduce risks of material misstatements to a sufficient level.

Refer to Figure 12-3 and Table 12-5.

Transaction-related audit objectives (column 1 of Table 12-5) The **transaction-related audit objectives in the sales and collection cycle** included in Table 12-5 are derived from the framework developed in Chapters 5 and 9. Although certain internal controls satisfy more than one objective, it is desirable to consider each objective separately to facilitate a better assessment of control risk.

Key internal controls (column 2 of Table 12-5) Organizations establish internal controls for sales to achieve their business objectives. The auditor looks for key controls that are designed to achieve the five transaction-related audit objectives discussed in Chapters 5 and 9. If the controls necessary to satisfy any one of the objectives are inadequate, the likelihood of risk of material misstatements related to that objective is increased, regardless of the controls for the other objectives. The methodology for determining existing controls was studied in Chapter 9.

The source of the controls in this column is a list of potential key controls that would be included in a control risk matrix such as the one illustrated in Figure 12-7. A control satisfies more than one audit objective if there is more than one C for that control on the control risk matrix.

Common tests of controls (column 3 of Table 12-5) For each internal control on which the auditor chooses to rely, he or she designs a **test of control in the sales and collection cycle** to verify its effectiveness. Tests of controls include dual-purpose audit procedures that both test internal controls and test for monetary errors or fraud and other irregularities. Observe that the tests of controls in column 3 in Table 12-5 relate directly to the key internal controls.

Tests of controls in the sales and collection cycle—audit procedures performed to determine the effectiveness of both the design and operations of specific internal controls.

DESIGN TESTS OF CONTROLS FOR SALES For each relevant key control on which the auditor plans to rely to reduce assessed control risk, he or she must design one or more tests of controls to verify its effectiveness. For example, if the internal control is having the sales system identify orders that cause customers to go over their credit limit and having the orders printed for subsequent approval (occurrence), the test of control would include verifying that the application system is functioning as designed and inspecting the credit exception report for approval.

A common test of control for sales is accounting for a sequence of various types of documents. The test of continuity of sales invoices tests the completeness and occurrence assertions, while the test of continuity of shipping documents is a test of completeness. Called a "block test," while doing the test the auditor will watch for omitted and duplicate numbers or invoices outside the normal sequence as indicators of potential error. Should the auditor choose to use generalized audit software, then a gap test can be conducted by scanning the entire transaction history file and identifying any gaps in the numeric sequence (and also looking for duplicates).

Tests of controls for separation of duties are usually restricted to the auditor's observations of activities and discussions with personnel. For example, it is possible to observe whether the billing clerk has access to cash when opening incoming mail or depositing cash. It is usually also necessary to ask personnel what their responsibilities are and if there are any circumstances where their responsibilities are different from the normal policy. For example, the employee responsible for billing customers may state that he or she does not have access to cash. Future discussion may uncover that when the cashier is on vacation, that person takes over the cashier's duties. Allocation of password functionality should also be reviewed to ensure that individuals have not been assigned functions that are incompatible.

Several of the tests of controls in Table 12-5 can be performed using test data. For example, one of the key internal controls to prevent fraudulent or fictitious transactions is the inclusion of procedures to ensure that only approved information was entered into the customer master files. If a non-existent customer number is entered into the computer, it would be rejected. The auditor can test this control by asking client staff to enter non-existent customer numbers into the computer after making sure that the computer control is in operation and then observing the rejection of the entry.

DUAL-PURPOSE OR WEAKNESS INVESTIGATION TESTS BY ASSERTION Some tests of controls also quantify monetary errors, for example, tests of accuracy that reperform calculations and trace transaction totals to the general ledger. As discussed in previous chapters, these are dual-purpose tests. Such tests that can be used to quantify the extent of potential error have two purposes. They can be used as a dual-purpose test (for assessing control risk and for quantifying errors) or as a **weakness investigation test** since they can quantify the potential dollar effect of monetary errors or fraud and other irregularities due to control weaknesses. The following sections describe potential risks or misstatements that could occur by assertion. Then, specific audit tests to investigate or quantify the potential misstatement are discussed.

Weakness investigation tests—tests conducted to determine whether a material error or material misstatement could occur due to a control weakness.

Recorded sales occurred (occurrence) For this objective, the auditor is concerned with the possibility of three types of misstatements:

- sales being included in the journals for which no shipment was made,
- sales recorded more than once (duplicates), and
- shipments being made to non-existent customers and recorded as sales (fictitious sales).

There is an important difference between finding intentional and unintentional overstatements of sales. An unintentional overstatement normally also results in a clear overstatement of accounts receivable, which can often be found through confirmation procedures. In fraud, the perpetrator will attempt to conceal the overstatement, making it more difficult for auditors to find. Substantive tests of transactions may be necessary to discover overstated sales in these circumstances.

Recorded sale for which there was no shipment The auditor can trace from selected entries in the sales journal to make sure that related copies of the shipping and other supporting documents exist. If the auditor is concerned about the possibility of a fictitious duplicate copy of a shipping document, it may be necessary to trace the amounts to the perpetual inventory records as a test of whether inventory was reduced. Paperless systems would require the assistance of a specialist and the use of audit software to conduct such comparisons.

Sale recorded more than once Duplicate sales can be determined by reviewing a numerically sorted list of recorded sales transactions for duplicate invoice or shipping document numbers or by running generalized audit software tests to identify all duplicated numbers.

Shipment made to non-existent customers This type of fraud normally occurs only when the person recording sales is also in a position to authorize shipments or alter master file data. When internal controls are weak, it is difficult to detect fictitious shipments. Audit software could be used to look for post office box addresses, duplicated addresses, or addresses the same as those of employees.

All existing sales transactions are recorded (completeness) In many audits, the auditor is not as concerned about the completeness objective for sales on the grounds that overstatements of assets and income are a greater concern in the audit of sales transactions than their understatement. An exception would be where the auditor suspects that cash sales are being pocketed, which would affect gross margins.

An effective procedure to test for unbilled shipments is tracing selected shipping documents from a file in the shipping department to related duplicate sales invoices and the sales journal. To conduct a meaningful test using this procedure, the auditor must be confident that all shipping documents are included in the sample population. This can be done by accounting for a numerical sequence of the documents (block test).

Direction of tests It is important that you understand the difference between tracing from source shipping documents to the journals and tracing from the journals back to supporting documents. Figure 12-4 shows the direction of tests: going from the journals or sales invoice to the shipping document is a test for nonexistent sales transactions (occurrence objective), whereas going from the shipping document to the sales invoice or journals is a test for omitted transactions (completeness objective).

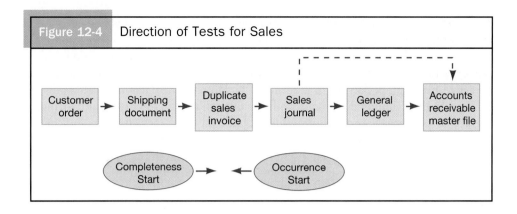

Figure 12-4 Direction of Tests for Sales

When testing for the other five transaction-related audit objectives, the direction of tests is usually not relevant. For example, the accuracy of sales transactions can be tested by tracing from a duplicate sales invoice to a shipping document, or vice versa.

Recorded sales are accurately recorded (accuracy) The accurate recording of sales transactions concerns shipping the correct amount of goods ordered, using the correct price when billing for the amount of goods shipped, and accurately recording the amount billed in the accounting records. The proper inclusion of all sales transactions in the customer master file is essential because the accuracy of these records affects the client's ability to collect outstanding receivables. Similarly, the sales transactions must be correctly totalled and posted to the general ledger if the financial statements are to be correct.

Reperformance to ensure the accuracy of each of these aspects is ordinarily conducted in every audit. A common approach is to start with entries in the sales journal and compare the total of selected transactions with customer master file totals and duplicate sales invoices. Prices on the duplicate sales invoices are normally compared with the customer purchase order and an approved price list, extensions and footings are recomputed, and the details listed on the invoices are compared with shipping records for description, quantity, and customer identification. Where reliance is placed on computer-based systems to perform mathematical calculations, the auditor may use test data to ensure that these calculations are properly performed or use generalized audit software and dual-purpose tests to reperform the calculations.

In every audit, it is necessary to perform some clerical accuracy tests of the summarization and posting process by footing the journals and tracing the totals and details to the general ledger and the master files to check whether there are intentional or unintentional misstatements in the processing of sales transactions. For most large systems, this is accomplished using generalized audit software, whereby the auditor obtains the client data files and does reperformance (such as footings or other calculations).

The extent of such tests is affected by the quality of the internal controls. Tracing individual transactions to a posting source is typically done as part of fulfilling other transaction-related audit objectives (such as completeness), but footing the sales journal and tracing the totals to the general ledger is done particularly for accuracy.

The comparison of tests of controls and substantive procedures for the accuracy objective is a good example of how audit time can be saved when effective internal controls exist. In manual systems, the test of controls for this objective takes minimal time because it involves examining only an initial or other evidence of internal verification. The test data approach can also be effective, since only a small number of transactions need be processed to verify that calculations are correct to determine that automated systems are functioning correctly. As the sample size for substantive procedures can be reduced if this control is effective, a significant saving will result from performing the test of controls of accuracy due to its lower cost.

Sales are recorded on the correct dates (cutoff) It is important that sales are billed and recorded as soon as possible after shipment takes place to prevent the unintentional omission of transactions from the records and to make sure sales are recorded in the proper period. At the same time that tests of controls with respect to the accuracy objective are being performed, it is common to compare the date on selected bills of lading or other shipping documents with the date on related duplicate sales invoices and the sales journal or sales history file. Significant differences in dates indicate a potential cutoff problem and the need to do additional substantive cutoff testing at the year-end date. Many computer systems require that the shipping date match the invoice date or that the invoice date be within a specified time of the current date, which will reduce the potential for cutoff errors.

Recorded sales are properly classified (classification) Charging the correct general ledger account is less of a problem in sales than in some other transaction cycles, but it is still important to check. When there are cash and credit sales, it is important not to debit accounts receivable for a cash sale or to credit sales for collection of a receivable. It is also important not to classify sales of operating assets, such as buildings, as sales. For those companies using more than one sales classification, such as companies issuing segmented earnings statements, proper classification is essential.

It is common to test sales for proper classification as part of testing for accuracy. The auditor examines supporting documents to determine the proper classification of a given transaction and compares this with the actual account in which it is recorded. Most computer-based systems, whether batch or online, are set to post to the appropriate sales general ledger account automatically. The auditor then must determine the controls in place to ensure that unusual transactions are recorded to the correct account.

Design format audit program— the audit procedures resulting from the auditor's decisions about the appropriate audit procedures for each audit objective; this is used to prepare a performance format audit program

Performance format audit program— the audit procedures for a class of transactions organized in the format that they will be performed; prepared from a design format audit program.

Revenue recognition and other significant risks The auditor will determine whether there are controls over revenue recognition, such as selection of appropriate recognition methods, and monitoring of controls over the other assertions that affect revenue recognition. Results of techniques described above, such as review of journal entries and tests of timing and accuracy, would be used to evaluate whether weaknesses exist here. The auditor would evaluate the results of the overall testing process for sales to determine whether further tests are needed.

DESIGN- AND PERFORMANCE-FORMAT AUDIT PROCEDURES The information presented in Table 12-5 is in a **design format** intended to help auditors design audit programs that satisfy the transaction-related audit objectives in a given set of circumstances. If certain objectives are important in a given audit or when the controls are different for different clients, the methodology helps the auditor design an effective and efficient audit program.

It is likely to be inefficient to do the audit procedures as they are stated in the design format of Table 12-5. In converting from a design to a **performance format**, procedures are combined and organized into the sequence in which they will be performed. This will allow the auditor to accomplish the following:

- Eliminate duplicate procedures.
- Make sure that when a given document is examined, all procedures to be performed on that document are done at that time.
- Do the procedures in the most effective order. For example, by footing the journal and reviewing the journal for unusual items first, the auditor gains a better perspective on doing the detailed tests.

The process of converting from a design to a performance format is illustrated for the Hillsburg Hardware Limited case application. The design format specific to Hillsburg Hardware is shown in Table 12-7. The performance format is in Figure 12-8.

concept check

C12-4 Explain the impact of client business risk on the sales and collection cycle. Include the impact on revenue recognition.

C12-5 How do general controls over access rights affect the sales cycle?

C12-6 What are the three types of misstatements that are associated with the occurrence objective for sales?

③ Methodology for Control Testing in the Remainder of the Cycle

Sales Returns and Allowances

The major risk for sales returns is that material sales returns could occur after the year end. The auditor would then need to test that these returns were matched to the correct period sales. Sales allowances (also called "volume rebates") are rebates or discounts that customers receive if they achieve a particular sales volume. The risk with such amounts is that material sales allowances could be matched to the incorrect period, resulting in an overstatement (or understatement) of sales.

The transaction-related audit objectives and the client's methods of controlling misstatements are essentially the same for processing credit memos for sales returns and allowances as those described for sales, with two important differences. The first relates to materiality. In many instances, sales returns and allowances are so immaterial that they can be ignored in the audit altogether. The second major difference relates to emphasis on objectives. For sales returns and allowances, the primary emphasis is normally on testing the existence of recorded transactions as a means of uncovering any theft of cash from the collection of accounts receivable that has been covered up by a fictitious sales return or allowance.

Although the emphasis for the audit of sales returns and allowances is often on testing the existence of recorded transactions, the completeness objective is the most important. Unrecorded sales returns and allowances can be material and can be used by a company's management to overstate net income, as illustrated in Auditing in Action 12-2. However, because the objectives and methodology for auditing sales

auditing in action 12-2
Sales Can Be Returned (and Come Back to Haunt You)

Significant sales returns can occur due to product defects or because the client shipped unwanted product (known as "channel stuffing"). Evaluating the completeness of sales returns is an important part of the financial statement audit process. Bausch & Lomb experienced significant returns due to both product defects and channel stuffing.

Late in 1993, Bausch & Lomb, Inc. informed its independent distributors that they would have to purchase up to two years' inventory of contact lenses. The lenses had to be purchased before December 24, when Bausch & Lomb closed its books. The distributors claimed that their oral agreements with Bausch & Lomb meant they would not have to pay for the lenses until they were sold. If these agreements existed, the shipments of lenses should not have been recognized as sales. Analytical review should detect sales manipulation of such a high order of magnitude.

Ten months after the December sales, most of the lenses had not been sold and Bausch & Lomb had collected less than 15 percent of the accounts receivable from the sales. In October 1994, Bausch & Lomb agreed to take back three-quarters of the inventory that had been shipped the previous December, resulting in an unexpected charge to quarterly earnings.

In 2006, Bausch & Lomb was forced to recall all of its ReNu with MoistureLoc contact lens solution because of a reported association with eye infections. Although the company's CEO estimated that costs associated with the recall would be in the $50 million to $70 million range, an analyst estimated that the potential liability from the recall could rise to the $500 million to $1 billion level. The auditors would need to make sure that such liabilities were adequately recorded or disclosed in the financial statements.

Source: Adapted from: 1. Maremont, Mark, "Numbers game at Bausch & Lomb?", *Business Week*, December 19, 1994, 108–110. 2. Lebowitz, Jack D. and Vadim A. Mzhen, "Worldwide recall of Bausch and Lomb contact lens MoistureLoc solution," May 19, 2006, **www.marylandaccidentlawblog.com/2006/05/worldwide_recall_of_bausch_and_1.html**, Accessed: July 26, 2009.

returns and allowances are essentially the same as for sales, we will not include a detailed study of the area.

Internal Controls and Tests of Controls for Cash Receipts

The most at-risk assertion for cash receipts is also completeness—has all cash been recorded in the accounts and not been stolen? The same methodology used for designing tests of controls over sales transactions is used for designing tests of controls over cash receipts. Cash receipts tests of controls audit procedures are developed around the same framework used for sales; that is, given the transaction-related audit objectives, key internal controls for each objective are determined so that control risk and the risks of material misstatement can be evaluated. Then, tests of controls are developed for each control to be tested to ensure the control is working and to determine monetary errors for each objective. As in all other audit areas, the tests of controls depend on the controls the auditor has identified to reduce the assessed level of control risk.

Key internal controls and common tests of controls to satisfy each of the internal control objectives for cash receipts are listed in Table 12-6. The third column, of tests of controls, is controls that are used to detect whether controls have been followed (termed "general tests of controls"). The second column of tests of controls, used for quantification of potential errors, could serve as dual-purpose tests.

An essential part of the auditor's responsibility in auditing cash receipts is identification of weaknesses in internal control that increase the likelihood of fraud. In expanding on Table 12-6, the emphasis will be on those audit procedures that are designed primarily for the discovery of fraud.

DETERMINE WHETHER CASH RECEIVED WAS RECORDED The most difficult type of cash defalcation for the auditor to detect is that which occurs before the cash is recorded in the cash receipts journal or other cash listing, especially if the sale and cash receipt are recorded simultaneously. For example, if a grocery store clerk takes cash and intentionally fails to register the receipt of cash on the cash register, it is extremely difficult to discover the theft. To prevent this type of fraud, internal controls such as those included in the second objective in Table 12-6 are implemented by many companies. The type of control will depend on the type of business. For example, the controls for a retail store in which the cash is received by the same person who sells the merchandise and rings up the cash receipts (termed "point-of-sale" or "POS" systems) should be different from the controls for a company in which all receipts are received through the mail several weeks after the sales have taken place. In a point-of-sale system, the sale must be recorded for the customer to receive a receipt. This may also remove the item from inventory, but, most important, it provides a control total that must be reconciled to the total cash (including credit card or debit card amounts) that is received during the day.

It is normal practice to trace from remittance advices, prelists of cash receipts (if available), or the duplicate bank deposit slip to the cash receipts journal and subsidiary accounts receivable records as a test of the recording of actual cash received.

Proof of cash receipts—an audit procedure to test whether all recorded cash receipts have been deposited in the bank account by reconciling the total cash receipts recorded in the cash receipts journal for a given period with the actual deposits made to the bank.

PREPARE PROOF OF CASH RECEIPTS A useful audit procedure to test whether all recorded cash receipts have been deposited in the bank account is a **proof of cash receipts**. In this test, the total cash receipts recorded in the cash receipts data files for a given period, such as a month, are reconciled with the actual deposits made to the bank during the same period. There may be a difference in the two due to deposits in transit and other items, but the amounts can be reconciled and compared. The procedure cannot detect cash receipts that have not been recorded in the journals or time lags in making deposits, but it can help uncover recorded cash receipts that have not been deposited, unrecorded deposits, unrecorded loans, bank loans deposited directly into the bank account, and similar errors or misstatements. A proof of cash receipts and cash disbursements is illustrated in Figure 14-6. This somewhat time-consuming

	Summary of Transaction-Related Audit Objectives, Key Controls, and Tests of Controls for Cash Receipts		
Table 12-6			
Transaction-Related Audit Objective	**Key Internal Control**	**General Tests of Controls**	**Quantitative/Dual-Purpose Tests of Controls**
Recorded cash receipts are for funds actually received by the company (occurrence).	Separation of duties between handling cash and record keeping or data entry.	Observe separation of duties.	Inspect the cash receipts journal, general ledger, and accounts receivable master file or trial balance for large and unusual amounts.*
	Independent reconciliation or review of bank accounts.	Observe independent reconciliation of bank account.	Trace from cash receipts listing to duplicate deposit slip and bank statements.
All cash received is recorded in the cash receipts journal (completeness).	Separation of duties between handling cash and record keeping.	Discussion with personnel and observation.	Trace from remittances or prelisting to duplicate bank deposit slip and cash receipts journal.
	Use of remittance advices or a prelisting of cash.	As above.	Inspect reconciliation reports of credit card or electronic funds transfer receipts.
	Immediate endorsement of incoming cheques.	Observe immediate endorsement of incoming cheques.	
	Internal verification of the recording of cash receipts.	Inspect indication of independent internal verification.	
	Regular monthly statements to customers.	Observe whether monthly statements are sent to customers.	
	Authorized use of POS to simultaneously record the sale, cash received, and reduce inventory.	Observe whether use of POS is controlled, such as by means of unique access codes and passwords.	
Cash receipts are deposited and properly recorded at the amount received (accuracy).	Approval of cash discounts.	Inspect remittance advices for proper approval.	Inspect remittance advices and sales invoices to determine whether discounts allowed are consistent with company policy.
	Regular reconciliation of bank accounts.	Inspect monthly bank reconciliations.	
	Comparison of batch totals with duplicate deposit slips and computer summary reports.	Inspect file of batch totals for initials of data control clerk; compare totals with summary reports.	
	Regular monthly statements to customers.	Observe whether statements are mailed.	Foot cash receipts journals, and trace postings to general ledger and accounts receivable master file.
	Comparison of customer master file or aged accounts receivable trial balance totals with general ledger balance.	Inspect documentation verifying that comparison was completed.	
Cash receipts are recorded on correct dates (cutoff).	Procedure requiring recording of cash receipts on a daily basis.	Observe unrecorded cash at any point in time.	Compare dates of deposits with dates in the cash receipts journal.
Cash receipts are properly classified (classification).	Use of adequate chart of accounts or automatic posting to specified accounts.	Review chart of accounts and computer-assigned posting accounts.	Examine documents supporting cash receipts for proper classification.

* This analytical procedure can also apply to other objectives, including completeness, accuracy, and cutoff.

procedure is ordinarily used only when controls are weak. In rare instances in which controls are extremely weak, the period covered by the proof of cash receipts may be the entire year.

TEST TO DISCOVER LAPPING OF ACCOUNTS RECEIVABLE **Lapping of accounts receivable**, which is a common type of defalcation, is the postponement of entries for the collection of receivables to conceal an existing cash shortage. The defalcation is perpetrated by a person who handles cash receipts and then enters them into the computer system. He or she takes the cash, defers recording the cash receipts from one customer, and covers the shortages with the receipts of another customer. These, in turn, are covered in the accounting records from the receipts of a third customer a few days later. The employee must continue to cover the shortage through repeated lapping, replace the stolen money, or find another way to conceal the shortage.

This defalcation can be prevented by separation of duties. It can be detected by comparing the name, amount, and dates shown on remittance advices with cash receipts journal entries and related duplicate deposit slips. Since the procedure is relatively time-consuming, it is ordinarily performed only when there is a specific concern with potential defalcation because of a weakness in internal control.

Audit Tests for Uncollectable Accounts

The major risk with uncollectable accounts is that write-offs are used to conceal the theft of cash. Occurrence of recorded write-offs is the most important transaction-related audit objective that the auditor should keep in mind in the verification of the write-off of individual uncollectable accounts. A major concern in testing accounts written off as uncollectable is the possibility of the client covering up a defalcation by charging off accounts receivable that have already been collected. The major control for preventing this type of misstatement is proper authorization of the write-off of uncollectable accounts by a designated level of management only after a thorough investigation of the reason the customer has not paid.

A typical control procedure is the examination of approvals by the appropriate person. For a sample of accounts charged off, it is also usually necessary for the auditor to examine correspondence in the client's files verifying the uncollectability of the accounts. The auditor can also examine credit reports such as those provided by Dun & Bradstreet Canada Limited (see **www.dnb.ca**) or Equifax (see **www.equifax.com/home/en_ca**).

Effect of Results of Tests of Controls

The results of the tests of controls have a significant effect on the remainder of the audit, especially on the tests of details of balances part of substantive procedures. The parts of the audit most affected by the tests of controls for the sales and collection cycle are the balances in accounts receivable, cash, bad-debt expense, and allowance for doubtful accounts. Furthermore, if the results of the control tests are unsatisfactory, it is necessary to do additional substantive testing for sales, sales returns and allowances, charge-off of uncollectable accounts, and processing of cash receipts.

At the completion of the tests of controls, it is essential to analyze each control test exception to determine its cause and the implication of the exception on assessed control risk, which may affect the supported detection risk and thereby the substantive procedures.

The most significant effect of the results of the tests of controls in the sales and collection cycle is on the confirmation of accounts receivable. The type of confirmation, the size of the sample, and the timing of the test are all affected. We consider these effects in the next chapter.

Figure 12-5 illustrates the major accounts in the sales and collection cycle and the types of audit tests typically used to audit these accounts. This figure also shows how the audit risk model discussed in Chapter 7 relates to the audit of the sales and collection cycle.

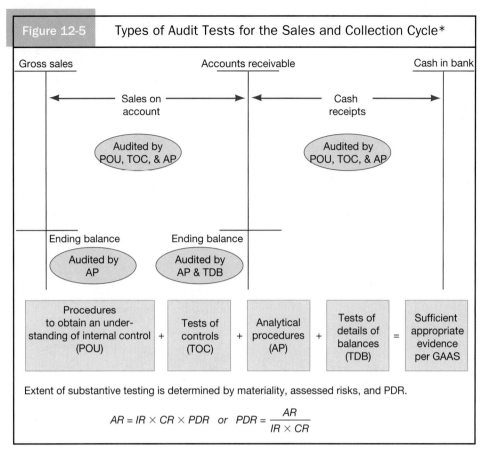

Figure 12-5 Types of Audit Tests for the Sales and Collection Cycle*

Gross sales   Accounts receivable   Cash in bank

Sales on account — Audited by POU, TOC, & AP

Cash receipts — Audited by POU, TOC, & AP

Ending balance — Audited by AP

Ending balance — Audited by AP & TDB

| Procedures to obtain an understanding of internal control (POU) | + | Tests of controls (TOC) | + | Analytical procedures (AP) | + | Tests of details of balances (TDB) | = | Sufficient appropriate evidence per GAAS |

Extent of substantive testing is determined by materiality, assessed risks, and PDR.

$$AR = IR \times CR \times PDR \quad or \quad PDR = \frac{AR}{IR \times CR}$$

*See Figure 12-2 for accounts.

Example of a Sales Audit

Case Illustration—Hillsburg Hardware Limited

The concepts for testing the sales and collection cycle presented in this chapter are now illustrated for Hillsburg Hardware Limited. The company's financial statements and the general ledger trial balance were shown in Chapter 5. Additional information was included in other chapters. A study of this case is intended to illustrate a methodology for designing audit procedures and integrating different parts of the audit.

Hillsburg Hardware Limited is a retail hardware company that focuses on selling high-quality power tools to individuals and the home improvement construction market. It is based in eastern Canada. A preliminary analytical review has shown continued maintenance of profit margins. This is a long-term continuing audit client, and there have never been any significant misstatements discovered in the tests. During the current year, a major change has occurred. The chief accountant left the company and has been replaced by Erma Swanson. There has also been some turnover of other accounting personnel.

The overall assessment by management is that the accounting personnel are reasonably competent and highly trustworthy. The president, Rick Chulick, has been the chief operating officer for approximately 10 years. He is regarded as a highly competent, honest individual who does a conscientious job. The following information is provided from the auditor's files:

- *The organization chart and flowchart of internal control prepared for the audit.* This information is included in Figures 10-2 and 12-6. Sales returns and allowances for this client are too immaterial to include in the flowchart or to verify in the audit.

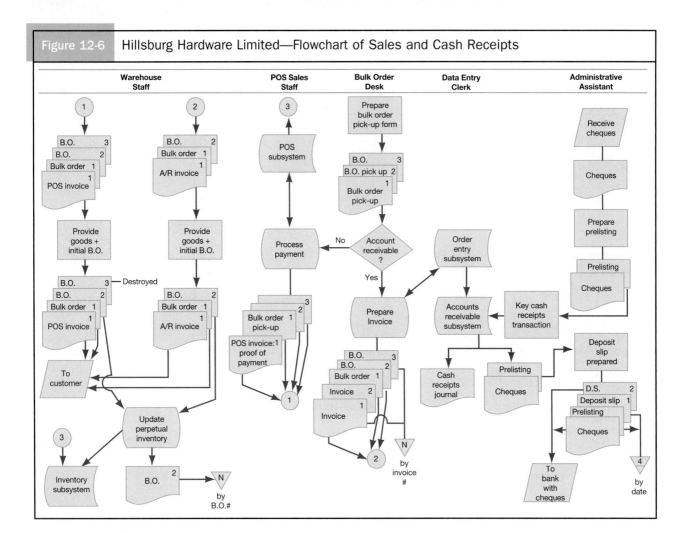

Notes

1. All correspondence is sent to the chief financial officer.
2. An exception report of missing bulk order numbers is printed weekly by the data entry clerk. The chief accountant discusses this with the warehouse staff supervisor to ensure that follow-up is undertaken.
3. All subsystems are posted to the general ledger on a daily basis after the close of business. The order-entry subsystem is also posted to the accounts receivable subsystem on a daily basis.
4. All prices in the point-of-sale (POS) system are based on prices in the master file. Should an override be necessary (e.g., due to damaged goods), the sales manager must enter his or her password to approve the price change. All such overrides will be printed on an exception report by the data entry clerk on a weekly basis. This report is reviewed by the chief accountant.
5. All prices used for accounts receivable are based on the same prices as in the POS system, with the customer discount applied. Customer discounts are negotiated at the time of customer approval, and range from 10 to 25 percent, based on the customer's projected and actual sales volume. Required on all accounts receivable invoices is an authorized customer signature that matches the signature on the in-house credit card.

6. Changes to the price master file and the customer master file for credit limits must be co-approved by the sales manager and the chief accountant on a master file change form. These changes are entered by the data entry clerk, and a sequentially numbered master file change report printed. This report is reviewed by the chief accountant for accuracy of data entry.
7. Payment at the POS desks can be made by cash, credit card, or debit card. Stand-alone credit card authorization and debit card entry machines are used to process non-cash payments. Daily totals (i.e., cash drawer, debit card totals, credit card totals) must equal the total sales recorded at each POS terminal.
8. There are two POS terminals for immediate payment and two bulk order desk terminals, where staff can inquire after inventory status and can prepare accounts receivable invoices using the order entry system for pre-authorized customers.
9. Warehouse staff compare bulk order quantities to amounts paid for or invoiced prior to providing goods, and initial the customer invoice. Customers sign copy 2 of the bulk order to indicate that goods have been taken.
10. An aged accounts receivable trial balance is printed weekly by the data entry clerk for follow-up by the chief accountant.

As part of the follow-up, the trial balance total is compared to the general ledger accounts receivable balance.

11. Statements are sent to customers monthly.

12. The administrative assistant stamps incoming cheques with a restrictive endorsement immediately upon receipt.

13. Deposits are made daily by the administrative assistant. Cash from the POS terminals is counted, recorded on the duplicate deposit slip, and added to the total of cheques received for the day.

14. Daily cash receipts postings from the POS system and the accounts receivable system are reconciled to the duplicate deposit slip by the data entry clerk.

15. The bank account is reconciled by the chief accountant on a monthly basis.

16. All bad-debt expenses and write-offs of bad debts are approved by the chief financial officer after being initiated by the chief accountant.

17. Financial statements are printed monthly by the data entry clerk and reviewed by the chief financial officer and the president.

18. All management (i.e., sales, purchasing and inventory control, accounting, and the president) meet on a weekly basis to review exception reports and discuss weekly internal financial results. These meetings are not minuted.

Procedures for other locations are similar and not shown in this flow chart to simplify the discussion.

- *Internal controls and weaknesses, and assessment of control risk for sales and cash receipts.* An appropriate approach to identifying and documenting internal controls and weaknesses and assessing control risk is included for sales in Figure 12-7 and for cash receipts in Figure 12-8. There are several things the auditor, Francine Martel, did to complete each matrix. First, she identified internal controls from flowcharts, internal control questionnaires, and discussions with client personnel. Only flowcharts are available in the Hillsburg case. Second, she identified weaknesses using the same sources. Third, she decided which transaction-related audit objectives are affected by the internal controls and weaknesses. Finally, she assessed control risk using the information obtained in the preceding three steps. The objective-by-objective matrices in Figures 12-7 and 12-8 were used primarily to help Francine effectively assess control risk.

- *The risk of material misstatement overall in sales and in revenue recognition.* These are considered low due to the stability of the organization and the preparation of reasonable financial statement projections that take into account the changing economic climate. Controls over the quality of financial statement disclosure are good, with both the chief financial officer and the president engaged in discussion to ensure clarity and completeness of disclosures. The auditors have been satisfied in the past with the quality and completeness of disclosures.

- *Tests of controls for each internal control.* The tests of controls for sales are included in the third and fifth columns of Table 12-7 and for cash receipts in the same columns in Table 12-8. The source of the internal controls is Figure 12-7 for sales and Figure 12-8 for cash receipts. Francine decided the appropriate tests for each control. These were approved by the audit manager prior to conducting the tests.

Note that certain objectives in Tables 12-7 and 12-8 have only programmed controls (e.g., sales classification and cutoff and cash receipts classification), or existing controls are such that there are weaknesses (e.g., occurrence in Table 12-7; completeness in Table 12-8). The tests of controls listed in the fifth columns of Tables 12-7 and 12-8 are dual-purpose tests designed to determine if the client's accounting transactions exist, are complete, are accurate, are properly classified, are recorded on the correct dates, and are summarized in the journals and correctly posted to the appropriate accounts. Tests such as these, described in Chapter 10, are both tests of controls and substantive procedures. The purpose of such tests is to assist the auditor in assessing control risk and also in quantifying the potential amount of error when conducted as substantive tests.

Francine decided on the tests of controls for each transaction-related audit objective listed in the third and fifth columns of Table 12-7 (sales) and Table 12-8 (cash receipts) for the different objectives after considering assessed control risk, the tests of controls listed in the third column, and weaknesses of internal control for that objective.

Internal Controls	Recorded sales are for shipments actually made to non-fictitious customers (occurrence).	Existing sales transactions are recorded (completeness).	Recorded sales are for the amount of goods shipped and are correctly billed and recorded (accuracy).	Sales transactions are updated correctly to the customer master file and the posting to the general ledger summed these transactions correctly (accuracy).	Sales are recorded on the correct dates (cutoff).	Sales transactions are properly classified (classification).
Scanned POS sales must be paid by cash, credit card, or debit card. (C1) **P**	C		C			
All external and internal credit card purchases require customer signature on the invoice. (C2)	C					
Bulk order pick-up form is matched to invoice and initialed. (C3)	C		C			
Credit is approved prior to customer account being established. (C4)	C					
Monthly statements are sent to accounts receivable customers. (C5)	C		C	C		
Bulk order forms are prenumbered, and the number is entered on the invoice. Computer system flags missing numbers on an exception report. (C6) **P**		C	C			
POS invoices and accounts receivable invoices are automatically numbered by the computer. (C7) **P**		C	C			
All invoices are prepared using prices in the inventory master file. (C8) **P**			C			
Accounts receivable terms are based on the customer master file. (C9) **P**			C			
Price overrides must be approved by sales manager password. (C10) **P**			C			
Sales manager overrides are printed on an exception report and reviewed by the chief accountant. (C11) **P**			C			
Sales control account is coded into computer system, and all POS and bulk sales are posted to that account. (C12) **P**						C
The invoice date is automatically the computer system date. (C13) **P**					C	
Posting to the data files is automatically handled by the computer system. (C14) **P**				C		
Aged accounts receivable trial balance is compared to general ledger balance monthly. (C15)				C		
Weakness — Evidence of follow-up on exception report of missing bulk order numbers is not documented. (W1)		W				
Assessed control risk	Low	Medium	Low	Low	Low	Low

Note: **P**—These controls are either programmed controls or interdependent controls (where part of the control is programmed and part of the control is handled by a person).

C = Control

W = Weakness

Figure 12-8

Figure 12-8   Assessment of Control Risk Matrix for Hillsburg Hardware Limited—Cash Receipts

	Recorded cash receipts are for funds actually received by the company (occurrence).	Cash received is recorded in the cash receipts journal (completeness).	Cash receipts are deposited at the amount received (accuracy).	Cash receipts are properly included in the customer master file and are correctly summarized (accuracy).	Cash receipts are recorded on the correct dates (cutoff).	Cash receipts transactions are properly classified (classification).
Cash Receipts Transaction–Related Audit Objectives						
Internal Controls						
Accountant reconciles bank account. (C1)	C		C			
Cheques are stamped with a restrictive endorsement. (C2)		C				
Statements are sent to customers monthly. (C3)		C	C			
Bank deposit slip reconciled to POS and accounts receivable postings. (C4)	C	C	C			
Cash is automatically posted to cash and accounts receivable accounts. (C5)						C
System date is used for data entry. (C6)					C	
Cash receipts are deposited daily. (C7)					C	
Entry of correct customer number results in automatic posting to that customer master file record. (C8)				C		
Accountant compares accounts receivable master file total with general ledger account. (C9)				C		
Weaknesses						
Prelisting of cash is not used to verify recorded cash receipts. (W1)		W				
Administrative assistant handles cheques after they are returned from cash receipts. (W2)		W				
Data entry clerk has access to cash receipts and maintains accounts receivable records. (W3)		W				
Assessed control risk	Low	High	Low	Low	Low	Low

C = Control
W = Weakness

These tables assume that there is a potential for material misstatement in each of the objectives and that substantive tests overall can be reduced by the conduct of these tests. For illustrative purposes, we have included thorough tests, although in practice auditors might decide to conduct tests of controls only where risks of misstatement are moderate to high.

Note that the objective-by-objective format in Tables 12-7 and 12-8 is used to help Francine more effectively determine the appropriate tests. She could have chosen tests of controls just as easily by selecting tests of controls for each internal control included in Figures 12-7 and 12-8. Most audit firms use automated working-paper software that allows them to simultaneously work on audit objective assessment and the preparation of audit testing plans without the preparation of multiple lists, as shown in this text. The multiple lists are shown here to assist in understanding of the audit process.

Table 12-7	Internal Controls and Tests of Controls for Hillsburg Hardware Limited—Sales* (Design Format)			

Transaction-Related Audit Objective	Existing Control†	Tests of Control, General	Weakness	Tests of Control, Dual-Purpose
Recorded sales are for shipments actually made to non-fictitious customers (occurrence).	Scanned POS sales must be paid by cash, credit card, or debit card. (C1) All external and internal credit card purchases require customer signature on the invoice. (C2) Bulk order pick-up form is matched to invoice and initialed. (C3) Credit is approved prior to customer account being established. (C4) Monthly statements are sent to accounts receivable customers. (C5)	Review POS procedures manual and discuss with POS staff. (6) Examine a sample of invoices for customer signature. (13.1) Examine a selection of invoices for matching bulk order form and initial. (13.3, 13.4) Examine a sample of master file change forms for evidence of approval. (14.1, 14.2) Observe whether monthly statements are mailed. (7)	Evidence of follow-up on exception report of missing bulk order numbers is not documented. (W1)	Use generalized audit software to print a list of customers exceeding their credit limit. (4.1)
All existing sales transactions are recorded (completeness).	Bulk order forms are prenumbered, and the number is entered on the invoice. Computer system flags missing numbers on an exception report. (C6) POS invoices and accounts receivable invoices are automatically numbered by the computer. (C7)	Review a sample of sales invoices for bulk order form number. (13.2) Observe system in use, and observe incremental assignment of invoice numbers. (1.2, 2.1)		Use generalized audit software to print a report of all gaps in the bulk order forms. (4.2) Use generalized audit software to print a report of all gaps in the invoice numbers. (4.3, 4.4)
Recorded sales are for the amount of goods shipped and are correctly billed and recorded (accuracy).	All invoices are prepared using prices in the inventory master file. (C8) Accounts receivable terms are based on the customer master file. (C9) Price overrides must be approved by sales manager password. (C10) Sales manager overrides are printed on an exception report and reviewed by the chief accountant. (C11) Posting to the data files is automatically handled by the computer system. (C14) Aged accounts receivable trial balance is compared with general ledger balance monthly. (C15)	Observe invoice preparation process. (1.3, 2.2) Request bulk order staff to enter a different term, and see if computer rejects it. (2.3) Request staff to override a price, and observe whether sales manager password is required. (1.4, 2.4) Discuss disposition of exception reports with chief accountant, and review report for evidence of review. (8) Conduct walk-through testing to verify that posting process is functioning correctly for daily posting. (5.1, 5.2, 5.3)		Use generalized audit software to print a report of unusual credit terms, and trace to customer master file approval form. (4.5, 4.7) Compare aged accounts receivable trial balance total with general ledger's. (4.6)
Sales are recorded on the correct dates (timing).	The invoice date is automatically the computer system date. (C13)	Observe invoice preparation process. (1.5, 2.5)		
Sales transactions are properly classified (classification)	Sales control account is coded into computer system, and all POS and bulk sales are posted to that account. (C12)	Examine a daily sales summary to verify account allocation. (5.1)		

---

*The procedures are summarized into a performance format in Figure 12-9. The number in parentheses after the procedure refers to Figure 12-9.

†Only the primary (key) control(s) for each objective is (are) shown. Most objectives are also affected by one or more additional controls.

TESTS OF CONTROLS AUDIT PROGRAM IN A PERFORMANCE FORMAT The tests of controls in Table 12-7 and Table 12-8 are combined into one audit program in Figure 12-9. The cross-referencing of the numbers in parentheses shows that no procedures have been added to or deleted from Figure 12-9. The reasons Francine

Table 12-8	Internal Controls and Tests of Controls for Hillsburg Hardware Limited—Cash Receipts* (Design Format)			
Transaction-Related Audit Objective	Existing Control†	Tests of Control, General	Weakness	Tests of Control, Dual-Purpose
Recorded cash receipts are for funds actually received by the company (occurrence).	Accountant reconciles bank account. (C1) Bank deposit slip reconciled to POS and accounts receivable postings. (C4)††	Observe whether Erma Swanson reconciles the bank account. (9)		Review the journals and transaction files for unusual transactions and amounts using GAS. (4.7) Summarize and prepare analysis of credits using GAS. (4.7, 4.8) Prepare a proof of cash receipts. (18) Examine a sample of daily reconciliations, verifying agreement to postings and to bank statement. (16)
All cash received is recorded in the cash receipts journal (completeness).	Cheques are stamped with a restrictive endorsement. (C2) Statements are sent to customers monthly. (C3)	Observe whether a restrictive endorsement is used on cash receipts. (10) Observe whether monthly statements are mailed. (7)	Prelisting of cash is not used to verify recorded cash receipts. (W1) Administrative assistant handles cheques after they are returned from data entry. (W2) Data entry clerk has access to cash receipts and maintains accounts receivable records. (W3)	Obtain the prelisting of cash receipts, and trace amounts to the cash receipts journal, testing for names, amounts, and dates. (19) Compare the prelisting of cash receipts with the duplicate deposit slip, testing for names, amounts, and dates. (16)
Recorded cash receipts are deposited at the amount received and properly recorded (accuracy).	Accountant reconciles bank account. (C1) Statements are sent to customers monthly. (C3) Accountant compares aged accounts receivable trial balance total with general ledger account. (C9) Entry of correct customer number results in automatic posting to that customer master file record. (C8)	Observe whether Erma reconciles the bank account. (9) Observe whether monthly statements are mailed. (7) Observe whether Erma compares total with general ledger account. (12) Observe data entry and conduct walk-through test. (3)		The procedures for the occurrence objective also fulfill this objective. Foot and cross-foot the cash receipts journal using GAS, and trace totals to the general ledger on a test basis. (4.8)
Cash receipts are recorded on correct dates (cutoff).	System date is used for data entry. (C6) Cash receipts deposited daily. (C7)	Observe whether bank deposits are made daily. (11)		Trace the total from the cash receipts journal to the bank statement, testing for a delay in deposit. (16)
Cash receipts are properly classified (classification).	Cash is automatically posted to cash and accounts receivable accounts. (C5)	Conduct walk-through. (5.4) Observe system use. (3.1)		Examine prelisting for proper account classification. (17)

GAS 5 generalized audit software.

* The procedures are summarized into a performance format in Figure 12-9. The number in parentheses after the procedure refers to Figure 12-9.

† Only the primary (key) control(s) for each objective is (are) shown. Most objectives are also affected by one or more additional controls.

†† This control also satisfies completeness and accuracy.

TESTS OF CONTROLS AUDIT PROCEDURES FOR SALES AND CASH RECEIPTS

(Sample Size and the Items in the Sample Are Not Included)

Tests of Programs

1. Observe use of POS system to verify that
   1.1 POS sales must be paid by cash, credit card, or debit card.
   1.2 POS invoices are automatically numbered by the computer.
   1.3 Invoices are prepared using prices automatically pulled from the inventory master file.
   1.4 Price overrides must be approved using the sales manager password. (Request an attempt to enter an override.)
   1.5 Invoice date is equal to computer system date.
2. Observe use of bulk order desk and accounts receivable sales data entry to verify that
   2.1 Accounts receivable invoices are automatically numbered by the computer.
   2.2 Invoices are prepared using prices automatically pulled from the inventory master file.
   2.3 Credit terms are pulled automatically from the customer master file. (Request an attempt to enter an incorrect credit term.)
   2.4 Price overrides must be approved using the sales manager password. (Request an attempt to enter an override.)
   2.5 Invoice date is equal to computer system date.
3. Observe cash receipts data entry process to verify that
   3.1 System date is used for data entry.

Tests of Data Using Generalized Audit Software—Included with Substantive Field Work of Accounts Receivable

4. Obtain transaction history file, open item accounts receivable file and customer master file, and conduct the following tests:
   4.1 List customers with balances exceeding their credit limit.
   4.2 List gaps in bulk order form numbers.
   4.3 List gaps in POS invoice numbers.
   4.4 List gaps in accounts receivable invoice numbers.
   4.5 List customers with discount terms exceeding 25 percent.
   4.6 Foot open item file and customer master file and agree to general ledger.
   4.7 Summarize debits and credits by customer. Prepare graphs displaying analysis of debit and credit patterns.
   4.8 Summarize cash receipts and prepare totals by day and month.

Walk-through Tests

5. Conduct walk-through tests of three transactions for each of the following activities to verify that programs are functioning as described:
   5.1 POS daily sales summary is posted to correct general ledger accounts.
   5.2 Accounts receivable daily sales are posted to correct general ledger accounts.
   5.3 Sales transactions are posted to correct customer master file accounts.
   5.4 Cash receipts are posted to correct general ledger accounts.

General Tests

6. Review system procedures and discuss with personnel to verify that procedures are being followed as described.
7. Observe whether monthly statements are mailed.
8. Discuss disposition of exception reports with appropriate member of management independently to verify consistency of treatment.
9. Observe whether the accountant reconciles the bank account.
10. Observe whether a restrictive endorsement is used on cash receipts.
11. Observe whether bank deposits are made daily.
12. Observe whether the accountant compares the accounts receivable trial balance total with the general ledger account.

Tests for Billing of Customers and Recording of Sales in the Accounts

13. Select a sample of customer invoices using a random selection process, and
    13.1 Ensure that the invoice copy has a customer signature.
         If the sale was for bulk goods:
    13.2 Verify that the bulk order form number was entered on the invoice.
    13.3 Verify that the bulk order form product description and quantity matches the invoice details.
    13.4 Locate the warehouse copy of the bulk order form and verify that the customer signature on the warehouse copy of the bulk order form matches the signature on the invoice copy.
14. Select a sample of customer master file change forms using a random selection process, and
    14.1 Verify that appropriate approvals are present.
    14.2 Trace to printout, confirming data entry of the change and verifying presence of chief accountant's initials.

Tests for Processing Cash Receipts and Recording the Amounts in the Records

15. Obtain the December prelistings of cash receipts, and trace amounts to the cash receipts journal, testing for names, amounts, and dates.
16. Compare the prelisting of cash receipts with the duplicate deposit slip, testing for names, amounts, and dates. Trace the total from the cash receipts journal to the duplicate bank deposit slip and the total per the duplicate bank deposit slip to the bank statement, testing for a delay in deposit. For those delayed deposits, also trace the totals to the POS system and accounts receivable sales system totals.
17. Examine prelisting for proper account classification.
18. Prepare a proof of cash receipts.
19. Trace selected entries from the cash receipts journal to entries in the customer master file, and test for dates and amounts.
20. Trace selected credits from the accounts receivable master file to the cash receipts journal, and test for dates and amounts.

prepared the performance format audit program were to eliminate audit procedures that were included more than once in Tables 12-7 and 12-8 and to include them in an order that permits audit assistants to complete the procedures as efficiently as possible. Note the large number of programmed controls, walk-through tests, and general tests. These illustrate that in automated systems, where programmed controls can be relied on due to good general controls, the time spent on control testing can be reduced, since the effort required to conduct these tests is considerably less than the effort required to conduct sampling and tests of attributes through sampling. The generalized audit software tests are conducted at the same time as the substantive tests for accounts receivable (discussed further in the next chapter).

Application of Attribute Sampling

To illustrate the sampling for the tests of controls concepts of Chapter 11, the sampling for some of the tests described in Figure 12-9 is now conducted. The parts of the tests of the sales and collection cycle included here are the tests of payment approval by the customer, shipment verification of bulk orders, and approval of customer master file changes. It should be kept in mind that the procedures for Hillsburg Hardware Limited were developed specifically for that client and would probably not be applicable to a different audit. The audit procedures for these tests are taken from step 13 and 14 of Figure 12-9 (Tests for Billing of Customers and Recording of Sales in the Accounts). Each working paper would also have information showing who completed the work, when it was completed, and who reviewed the working papers. Refer to Figure 11-2, Summary of Audit Sampling Steps. We have already completed Step 1, Stating the objectives of the test (these are the Audit Program steps listed in Figure 12-9 and their associated audit objectives in Table 12-7), and Step 2, as we have decided that attribute sampling applies.

STEP 3. DEFINE THE ATTRIBUTES OF INTEREST The attributes used in this application are taken directly from the audit program, as shown in Figure 12-10. Test 13.4 is looking for a customer signature, so the attribute is the signature itself. In Step 13.2 the auditor looks for the bulk order form entered on the invoice and in 13.3 that the bulk order form details (description and quantity) match the invoice. Note that audit step 13.4 actually has two attributes: first, that the warehouse copy of the bulk order form has the customer signature and second, that the customer signature on the invoice and bulk order form are the same.

The definition of the attribute is a critical part of attribute sampling and conducting a high-quality audit process, since it makes clear to the auditor what is being looked for during the audit process.

STEP 4. DEFINE THE POPULATION Table 12-7 shows that audit tests 13.1, 13.3, and 13.4 are for the occurrence objective, which means that our direction of test should start with the journals or sales transactions and then move towards the shipping documents, so our population is the sales invoices generated by both the POS system, shown in the third column of Figure 12-6 and the credit sales invoices that create accounts receivable (shown in the second column of Figure 12-6 as an "A/R invoice"). Test 13.2 is for completeness; however, the direction of the test also satisfies occurrence, since it is asking for us to review the bulk sales invoice for a supporting bulk order number. It is appropriate for us to also do this test starting from the sales invoices, since we have another test (Test 4.2) that uses generalized audit software (GAS) to provide a report of all gaps in the bulk order forms and will provide a dual-purpose test of errors in completeness.

The population consists of all of the POS invoices for the entire calendar year and the credit sales invoices. Figure 12-10 shows that there are 142,622 POS invoice transactions (ending number 283294 minus beginning number 140672) and 3,231 credit sales invoice numbers (ending number 6831 minus 3600 beginning number).

STEP 5. DEFINE THE SAMPLING UNIT If the population is correctly described, the sampling unit derives straight from the nature of the population. Our unit is the POS invoice.

Figure 12-10	Attribute Sampling Data Sheet

Client Hillsburg Hardware Limited   **Year end** 31/12/11

Audit Area Tests of Controls—Billing Function and   **Pop. size** 145,853
Recording of Sales

Define the objective(s) Examine duplicate sales invoices and related documents to determine if the system has functioned as intended and as described in the audit program.

Define the population precisely (including stratification, if any) POS invoices and credit sales invoices for the period 1/1/11 to 31/12/11. First POS number = 140672. Last POS number = 283294. First credit sales invoice number = 3600. Last credit sales invoice number = 6831

Define the sampling unit, organization of population items, and random selection procedures Sales invoice number, POS invoice numbers, and credit recorded in the sales files sequentially; random sampling.

Description of Attributes	Planned Audit				Actual Results			
	EPER	TER	ARACR	Initial sample size	Sample size	Number of exceptions	Sample exception rate	CUER
1. Invoice copy has customer signature. (13.1)	0	3	10	76				
For Bulk Sales: 2. Bulk order form number is entered on invoice details. (13.2)	2	8	10	48				
3. Bulk order form details match invoice details. (13.3)	0	4	10	57				
4. Warehouse copy of bulk order form has customer signature. (13.4)	1	4	10	96				
5. Customer signature on warehouse copy of bulk order form matches signature on invoice. (13.4)	0	3	10	76				

Intended use of sampling results:

1. Effect on Audit Plan:

2. Recommendations to Management:

STEP 6. ESTABLISH TER The tolerable exception rate (TER) for each attribute is decided on the basis of the auditor's judgment of what exception rate is material. The failure to have a customer signature on an invoice (or order) would be highly significant, since this could mean an inability to collect funds from a sale that is also an account receivable or from a credit card organization. Therefore, as indicated in Figure 12-10, the lowest TER (3 percent) is chosen for attributes 1 and 5 that pertain to signatures. The incorrect billing of the customer for bulk sales represents potentially significant misstatements, but no misstatement is likely to apply to the full amount of the invoice. As a result, a 4-percent TER is chosen for matching of the bulk order form details and customer signature on that form. The second attribute has a higher TER, since it is of less importance for the audit.

STEP 7. SPECIFY ARACR An acceptable risk of assessing control risk too low (ARACR) of 10 percent is chosen because there are numerous other controls, such as programmed controls and management review of exception reports.

STEP 8. ESTIMATE EPER The estimated population exception rate (EPER) is based on previous years' results, modified slightly upward due to the change in personnel.

STEP 9. DETERMINE INITIAL SAMPLE SIZE Initial sample size for each attribute is determined from Table 12-9 on the basis of the above considerations and is shown in the "initial sample size" column of the table in Figure 12-13. (For example, use the 10-Percent ARACRT portion of Table 12-9, read along the first row [0.00 EPER] to the second column [3.0 TER] where you will find 75, the initial sample size for the first attribute.) Note that the estimated population error rates are very low in Figures 12-10 and 12-13, ranging from 0 to 2 percent. In practice, many auditors will only conduct tests of controls if their estimated population exception rate is 0, since encountering errors could mean that the auditor cannot rely on the controls.

Sampling information is summarized for all attributes in Figure 12-13. For convenience in selection and evaluation, the auditor decided to select a sample of 75 for attribute 1, 50 for attributes 2 and 3, 100 for attribute 4, and 75 for attribute 5. On the basis of past experience, the decision was made to select 30 samples from the POS invoices and the remainder from credit sales invoices, since these have a greater proportion of bulk sales orders.

STEP 10. SELECT THE SAMPLE The random selection for the case is straightforward except for the need for different sample sizes for different attributes. This problem can be overcome by selecting a random sample of 50 for use on all five attributes followed by another sample of 25 for attributes 1 and 5, and an additional 25 for attribute 4. Spreadsheet software using the @RAND function was used to calculate random numbers. For example, the first ten random numbers selected were: 177611, 163763, 217029, 235986, 150176, 197303, 153469, 213150, 144408, and 269030. Once all random numbers had been selected, they were sorted in ascending sequence. Audit staff then went to client files and pulled the selected documents from the client files.

STEP 11. PERFORM THE PROCEDURES The audit procedures that are included in the audit program and summarized in the attribute sampling data sheet must be carefully performed for every item in the sample. As a means of documenting the tests and providing information for review, it is common to include a worksheet of the results. Some auditors prefer to include a worksheet containing a listing of all items in the sample; others prefer to limit the documentation to identifying the exceptions, which we have used. Figure 12-11 summarizes the exceptions found during the inspection process.

STEP 12- GENERALIZE TO THE POPULATION At the completion of the testing, the exceptions are tabulated to determine the number of exceptions in the sample for each attribute. This enables the auditor to compute the sample exception rate and determine the **computed upper exception rate (CUER,** a statistical measure of the maximum likely upper error rate) using Table 12-10. The exceptions for Attribute 1 were considered not to be true exceptions since signatures are not required on invoices for purchases made by cash on POS invoices, although they are required for all other types of purchases, so we use a zero sample exception rate (SER) for Attribute 1. Using Table 12-10, the lower half (10 Percent ARACR), locate the column that corresponds to the SER of O—this is the first column. Then, read along the row until you locate the sample size, which is 75. The table shows a sample size of 70 with a CUER of 3.2, and a sample size of 80 with a CUER of 2.8. This means that the CUER for a sample size of 75 is half way between these two numbers at 3.0, and there is a 10 percent probability that the real population error rate is higher than 3 percent. There is a 90 percent likelihood that the real population error rate is 3 percent or lower. The other CUER figures were determined in a similar manner.

For example, CUER of 3 percent with ARACR of 10 percent means that there is a 10 percent likelihood that the maximum population error rate (which is unknown) exceeds 3 percent.

Computed upper exception rate (CUER)– a statistical measure of the maximum likely upper error rate for a given ARACR.

Table 12-9 Determining Sample Size for Attribute Sampling

5-Percent ARACR

Estimated Population Exception Rate (in percentage)	Tolerable Exception Rate (in percentage)										
	2	3	4	5	6	7	8	9	10	15	20
0.00	149	99	74	59	49	42	36	32	29	19	14
0.25	236	157	117	93	78	66	58	51	46	30	22
0.50	*	157	117	93	78	66	58	51	46	30	22
0.75	*	208	117	93	78	66	58	51	46	30	22
1.00	*	*	156	93	78	66	58	51	46	30	22
1.25	*	*	156	124	78	66	58	51	46	30	22
1.50	*	*	192	124	103	66	58	51	46	30	22
1.75	*	*	227	153	103	88	77	51	46	30	22
2.00	*	*	*	181	127	88	77	68	46	30	22
2.25	*	*	*	208	127	88	77	68	61	30	22
2.50	*	*	*	*	150	109	77	68	61	30	22
2.75	*	*	*	*	173	109	95	68	61	30	22
3.00	*	*	*	*	195	129	95	84	61	30	22
3.25	*	*	*	*	*	148	112	84	61	30	22
3.50	*	*	*	*	*	167	112	84	76	40	22
3.75	*	*	*	*	*	185	129	100	76	40	22
4.00	*	*	*	*	*	*	146	100	89	40	22
5.00	*	*	*	*	*	*	*	158	116	40	30
6.00	*	*	*	*	*	*	*	*	179	50	30
7.00	*	*	*	*	*	*	*	*	*	68	37

10-Percent ARACR

Estimated Population Exception Rate (in percentage)	2	3	4	5	6	7	8	9	10	15	20
0.00	114	76	57	45	38	32	28	25	22	15	11
0.25	194	129	96	77	64	55	48	42	38	25	18
0.50	194	129	96	77	64	55	48	42	38	25	18
0.75	265	129	96	77	64	55	48	42	38	25	18
1.00	*	176	96	77	64	55	48	42	38	25	18
1.25	*	221	132	77	64	55	48	42	38	25	18
1.50	*	*	132	105	64	55	48	42	38	25	18
1.75	*	*	166	105	88	55	48	42	38	25	18
2.00	*	*	198	132	88	75	48	42	38	25	18
2.25	*	*	*	132	88	75	65	42	38	25	18
2.50	*	*	*	158	110	75	65	58	38	25	18
2.75	*	*	*	209	132	94	65	58	52	25	18
3.00	*	*	*	*	132	94	65	58	52	25	18
3.25	*	*	*	*	153	113	82	58	52	25	18
3.50	*	*	*	*	194	113	82	73	52	25	18
3.75	*	*	*	*	*	131	98	73	52	25	18
4.00	*	*	*	*	*	149	98	73	65	25	18
4.50	*	*	*	*	*	218	130	87	65	34	18
5.00	*	*	*	*	*	*	160	115	78	34	18
5.50	*	*	*	*	*	*	*	142	103	34	18
6.00	*	*	*	*	*	*	*	182	116	45	25
7.00	*	*	*	*	*	*	*	*	199	52	25
8.00	*	*	*	*	*	*	*	*	*	60	25

*Sample is too large to be cost-effective for most audit applications.

Notes: 1. This table assumes a large population. 2. Sample sizes are the same in certain columns even when expected population exception rates differ because of the method of constructing the tables. Sample sizes are calculated for attributes sampling using the expected number of exceptions in the population, but auditors can deal more conveniently with expected population exception rates. For example, in the 15-percent column for tolerable exception rate, at an ARACR of 5 percent, initial sample size for most EPERs is 30.

1. *Invoice copy has customer signature. (13.1)*

   Three exceptions found.

   POS invoices # 163763, 213150, and 237619 did not have customer signatures. These were all cash sales (i.e., not paid by credit card or debit card).

2. *Bulk order form number entered on invoice. (13.2)*

   Four exceptions found.

   POS invoice # 242681 missing bulk order number, although copy was attached.

   Credit sales invoice # 5802, 6137, and 8713 missing bulk order number, although copy was attached.

   No exceptions found for attributes 3, 4, and 5.

STEP 13. EXCEPTION ANALYSIS The final part of the application consists of analyzing the deviations to determine their cause and drawing conclusions about each attribute tested. Exception information is summarized in Figure 12-13 and Table 12-11. CUER exceeds TER for attribute 2; attribute 3 had no errors but the achieved CUER was slightly higher at 4.5. It is essential that some conclusion concerning follow-up action be drawn and documented for unacceptable CUER results. The exception analysis and conclusions reached are illustrated in Table 12-11, where the auditor concludes that there is no financial effect of errors in attribute 2, the bulk order form number missing (since copies of all bulk order forms were attached and there were no differences between the bulk order form and the invoice) The bottom of the data sheet Figure 12-13 explains that there is no effect on the audit.

STEP 14. DETERMINE THE ACCEPTABILITY OF THE POPULATION The controls tested for attributes 1 through 5 of the billing function and recording of sales can be relied on, even though the bulk order invoice number was not recorded on the sales invoice, since there were no deviations in any of the other controls. Thus, the sales population is acceptable.

Figure 12-12 shows how the auditor would test Audit Program Tests 14-1 and 14-2, which pertains to master file changes. Attribute 1 is the presence of appropriate approvals on the master file change form, while Attribute 2 is inspection of independent verification with supporting evidence (chief accountant's initials). The bottom half of Table 12-11 describes the exceptions that arose with respect to testing of master file changes, where the auditor concluded that additional testing of the bad debt allowance would be needed. Master file change forms and data entry verification reports were approved using existing policies, except where the designated individual

Figure 12-12	Testing of Master File Change Forms

Objectives: As listed in Figure 12-9 (14.1 and 14.2); authorization of master file change forms and proof of data entry verification.

Sampling: Applies to use of master file change forms throughout the year.

Population: Master file change forms used throughout the year. First form number used: 1201. Last form used: 2132.

TER: 5   **ARACR:** 10   **EPER:** 0   **Initial Sample Size:** 45

Results of Performing Procedures: Three exceptions found, on form # 1288, 1510, and 1599. In the first instance, signature of sales manager was missing. In the second and third, the signature of the chief accountant was missing. In all cases, the indicated person was on holiday. Also, for the latter two forms, the data entry report was initialed by the sales manager, since the chief accountant was absent.

	No. of Exceptions	Sample Exception Rate	CUER
Attribute 1	3	6.7	14.2
Attribute 2	2	4.4	11.4

Table 12-10 — Evaluating Sample Results Using Attribute Sampling: Tables for Determining Computed Upper or Lower Exception Rate

Sample Size	0	1	2	3	4	5	6	7	8	9	10
Actual Number of Deviations Found											

5-Percent ARACR

Sample Size	0	1	2	3	4	5	6	7	8	9	10
25	11.3	17.6	*	*	*	*	*	*	*	*	*
30	9.5	14.9	19.5	*	*	*	*	*	*	*	*
35	8.2	12-9	16.9	*	*	*	*	*	*	*	*
40	7.2	11.3	14.9	18.3	*	*	*	*	*	*	*
45	6.4	10.1	13.3	16.3	19.2	*	*	*	*	*	*
50	5.8	9.1	12-1	14.8	17.4	19.9	*	*	*	*	*
55	5.3	8.3	11.0	13.5	15.9	18.1	*	*	*	*	*
60	4.9	7.7	10.1	12-4	14.6	16.7	18.8	*	*	*	*
65	4.5	7.1	9.4	11.5	13.5	15.5	17.4	19.3	*	*	*
70	4.2	6.6	8.7	10.7	12-6	14.4	16.2	18.0	19.7	*	*
75	3.9	6.2	8.2	10.0	11.8	13.5	15.2	16.9	18.4	20.0	*
80	3.7	5.8	7.7	9.4	11.1	12-7	14.3	15.8	17.3	18.8	*
90	3.3	5.2	6.8	8.4	9.9	11.3	12-7	14.1	15.5	16.8	18.1
100	3.0	4.7	6.2	7.6	8.9	10.2	11.5	12-7	14.0	15.2	16.4
125	2.4	3.7	4.9	6.1	7.2	8.2	9.3	10.3	11.3	12-2	13.2
150	2.0	3.1	4.1	5.1	6.0	6.9	7.7	8.6	9.4	10.2	11.0
200	1.5	2.3	3.1	3.8	4.5	5.2	5.8	6.5	7.1	7.7	8.3

10-Percent ARACR

Sample Size	0	1	2	3	4	5	6	7	8	9	10
20	10.9	18.1	*	*	*	*	*	*	*	*	*
25	8.8	14.7	19.9	*	*	*	*	*	*	*	*
30	7.4	12-4	16.8	*	*	*	*	*	*	*	*
35	6.4	10.7	14.5	18.1	*	*	*	*	*	*	*
40	5.6	9.4	12-8	15.9	19.0	*	*	*	*	*	*
45	5.0	8.4	11.4	14.2	17.0	19.6	*	*	*	*	*
50	4.5	7.6	10.3	12-9	15.4	17.8	*	*	*	*	*
55	4.1	6.9	9.4	11.7	14.0	16.2	18.4	*	*	*	*
60	3.8	6.3	8.6	10.8	12-9	14.9	16.9	18.8	*	*	*
70	3.2	5.4	7.4	9.3	11.1	12-8	14.6	16.2	17.9	19.5	*
80	2.8	4.8	6.5	8.3	9.7	11.3	12-8	14.3	15.7	17.2	18.6
90	2.5	4.3	5.8	7.3	8.7	10.1	11.4	12-7	14.0	15.3	16.6
100	2.3	3.8	5.2	6.6	7.8	9.1	10.3	11.5	12-7	13.8	15.0
120	1.9	3.2	4.4	5.5	6.6	7.6	8.6	9.6	10.6	11.6	12-5
160	1.4	2.4	3.3	4.1	4.9	5.7	6.5	7.2	8.0	8.7	9.5
200	1.1	1.9	2.6	3.3	4.0	4.6	5.2	5.8	6.4	7.0	7.6

* Over 20 percent.

Note: This table presents computed upper deviation rates as percentages. Table assumes a large population.

was absent. However, this enables a single individual to approve credit and customer master file changes, which could lead to manipulation. The auditor should conduct additional weakness investigation testing by examining master file changes during the period when one of these two individuals was absent or on holiday. If, once additional testing was done, no unusual transactions are discovered, the auditor can then accept the population, although additional testing of the bad-debt allowance is still advisable.

Impact of Test of Controls Results on Audit Planning

After the tests of controls have been performed, it is essential to analyze each test of control exception to determine its cause and the implication of the exception on assessed control risk, which may affect the supported detection risk and the planned extent of substantive procedures.

Figure 12-13	Attribute Sampling Data Sheet, Completed

Client	Hillsburg Hardware Limited	**Year End** 31/12/11
Audit Area	Tests of Controls—Billing Function and Recording of Sales	**Pop. Size** 145,853

Define the objective(s) Examine duplicate sales invoices and related documents to determine if the system has functioned as intended and as described in the audit program.

Define the population precisely (including stratification, if any) POS invoices and credit sales invoices for the period 1/1/11 to 31/12/11. First POS number = 140672. Last POS number = 283294. First credit sales invoice number = 3600. Last credit sales invoice number = 6831.

Define the sampling unit, organization of population items, and random selection procedures Sales invoice number, POS invoice numbers, and credit recorded in the sales files sequentially; random sampling.

Description of Attributes	Planned Audit				Actual Results				
	EPER	TER	ARACR	Initial sample size	Sample size	Number of exceptions	Sample exception rate	CUER	
1. Invoice copy has customer signature. (13.1)	0	3	10	76	75	0	0	3	
For Bulk Sales: 2. Bulk order form number is entered on invoice details. (13.2)	2	8	10	48	50	4	8	15.4	
3. Bulk order form details match invoice details. (13.3)	0	4	10	57	50	0	0	4.5	
4. Warehouse copy of bulk order form has customer signature. (13.4)	1	4	10	96	100	0	0	2.3	
5. Customer signature on warehouse copy of bulk order form matches signature on invoice. (13.4)	0	3	10	76	75	0	0	3	

Intended use of sampling results:

1. **Effect on Audit Plan:** Controls tested using attributes #1, 3–5 can be relied upon. Policies and procedures to remedy #2 should be discussed with management. No additional audit procedures required, since no financial impact.

2. **Recommendations to Management:** See attached weakness investigation.

Table 12-11   Analysis of Exceptions

Attribute	Number of Exceptions	Nature of Exceptions	Effect on the Audit and Other Comments
1, sales	3	Three POS invoices paid by cash did not have customer signatures. Each invoice was for less than $50.	No effect on the audit. Hillsburg policy has been clarified that cash purchase invoices do not require customer signature.
2, sales	4	One POS invoice and three credit sales invoices did not have the bulk order number on the face of the invoice, although the invoice copy was attached.	These omissions would show on the bulk order form exception report showing missing bulk order numbers. Management indicated that, unfortunately, new employees often forget to record this number, resulting in an excessive number of items on the exception report. This usually eases off. Since this does not have a financial effect on the audit (there were no errors in goods shipped), no further audit work is required.
1, master file changes	3	Three master file change forms for new credit accounts were approved by only the sales manager or the chief accountant.	Additional work on the bad-debt allowance should be completed in the event that bad credit risks have been approved. Master file changes submitted during the period of these managers' absence should be reviewed for unusual items.
2, master file changes	2	Two data entry verification reports of master file changes were verified by the sales manager rather than by the chief accountant.	See above.

Figure 12-14   Evidence Planning Spreadsheet to Determine Tests of Details of Balances for Hillsburg Hardware Limited—Accounts Receivable

	Existence (or Occurrence)	Rights and Obligations	Completeness	Valuation	Allocation	Presentation and Disclosure
Audit risk	High	High	High	High	High	High
Inherent risk	Low	Low	Low	Medium	Low	Low
Control risk – Sales	Medium	Not applicable	Low	High	Low	Not applicable
Control risk – Cash receipts	High	Not applicable	Low	Not applicable	Low	Not applicable
Control risk – Additional controls	None	Low	None	None	None	Low
Analytical procedures						
Planned detection risk for tests of details of balances						
Planned audit evidence for tests of details of balances						

Materiality $496,000

For Hillsburg Hardware, assume that there were no other deviations for these tests beyond those described in Figure 12-11 and analyzed in Table 12-11. This means that the auditor can accept the planned control risk in all areas except the valuation assertion about account balances (due to the exceptions found with the master file changes). As noted on Table 12-11, the auditor will conduct additional tests of details on the bad debt allowance and the master file changes.

UPDATE THE EVIDENCE PLANNING SPREADSHEET After completing tests of controls, the auditor should complete rows 3 through 5 of the evidence planning spreadsheet. Recall from Chapter 9 that the control risk rows could have been completed before the tests of controls were done, and then modified if the test results were not satisfactory. An updated evidence planning spreadsheet is shown in Figure 12-14. The spreadsheet is used to determine the extent of substantive tests required for the cycle.

The most significant effect of the results of the tests of controls in the sales and collection cycle is on the confirmation of accounts receivable. The type of confirmation, the size of the sample, and the timing of the test are all affected by the results of tests of controls. The effect of the tests on accounts receivable, bad-debt expense, and allowance for uncollectable accounts is further considered in the next chapter.

COMMUNICATION WITH MANAGEMENT In addition to adjusting the audit procedures, the auditor should ensure that management is informed of all exceptions and that the impact of the exceptions is appropriately discussed. As the weaknesses are encountered, the auditor will conduct such a discussion verbally (as illustrated in Table 12-11), and also issue a management letter, in which the exception is described, the implications of the exception explained, and recommendations for improvement in procedures identified. For the sales and collection cycle, the auditor would communicate in writing the exceptions with respect to master file change form approval, and recommend that another individual provide a second signature on these forms in the event of the sales manager's or chief accountant's absence. The individual recommended to do this likely would be the president of the organization. The management letter should be copied to the audit committee.

concept check

C12-10 When deciding upon which controls to test, the auditor considers cost-effectiveness. Which types of controls are likely the least costly to test? Justify your response.

C12-11 The auditor is estimating the population exception rate (EPER) in the range of 10 to 15 percent. What type of testing would the auditor conduct? Why?

Summary

1. *What are typical records and transactions in the sales cycle?* There are typically six classes of transactions included in the sales and collection cycle: sales, cash receipts, sales returns and allowances, charge-off of uncollectable accounts, bad-debt expenses, and master file changes. Records include the customer master file and the transaction history file, with periodic listings such as sales journals and an aged accounts receivable trial balance.

   What are some important risks of fraud in the cycle and how can they be prevented or detected? Table 12-1 lists typical risks of fraud and error. The most significant one is the potential for overstatement of revenue, which can be prevented by effective and honest corporate governance (audit committee and management oversight), and adequate segregation of duties.

2. *How is risk assessment linked to the sales cycle?* The auditor considers risks to evaluate the likelihood of material misstatement in sales, accounts receivable, and allowance accounts. The auditor will also assess the likelihood of revenue recognition misstatements when designing audit tests in the cycle.

   How do general controls affect the audit of the sales and collection cycle? General controls affect multiple transaction cycles, so weaknesses in general controls, such as program change controls or access controls, would mean that the auditor might not be able to rely on programmed functions or segregation of duties. Strengths in general controls may allow the auditor to rely on those controls enforced by automated systems.

   Describe the methodology for designing tests of controls for sales. The auditor needs to understand and evaluate design effectiveness of general controls that apply to sales, as well as the application controls within the sales cycle. Then, the auditor assesses planned control risk for sales and identifies and assesses the risks of material misstatements in the sales cycle. The cost benefit of testing controls is examined by assertion prior to designing tests of controls for the cycle. Where desired, dual-purpose or weakness investigation tests are designed. An audit program in a performance format is used to conduct the tests.

3. *Describe the methodology for controls over sales returns and allowances, cash receipts transactions, and uncollect-*

able accounts. The general methodology is the same for every transaction type. It depends upon the risk for the transaction type and associated assertions as well as the materiality of the transactions.

What is the effect of the results of tests of controls on the audit? Where controls are functioning as described, the auditor may be able to reduce tests of details. As tests of controls tend to be less expensive to conduct than tests of details, this can result in an overall lower-cost high-quality audit.

4. *What is the typical audit process for tests of controls?* Hillsburg Hardware Limited is used to illustrate how the many possible controls are narrowed down to the relevant key controls in place at an organization for the audit assertions. Then, tests are designed and a sample selected. To conduct the testing, the audit steps are reorganized into a performance format that facilitates efficient completion of like audit procedures. When testing is completed, the results are evaluated and the effect on the audit identified.

MyAccountingLab

Make the grade with MyAccountingLab: The questions, exercises, and problems marked in orange can be found on MyAccountingLab. You can practise them as often as you want, and most feature step-by-step guided instructions to help you find the right answer.

Review Questions

12-1 ❶ Describe the nature of the following documents and records, and explain their use in the sales and collection cycle: bill of lading, sales invoice, customer master file, credit memo, remittance advice, and monthly statement to customers.

12-2 ❶ Describe the risks of error and fraud in the sales and collection cycle. Relate each risk of error or fraud to a relevant audit assertion.

12-3 ❶ Explain the importance of proper credit approval for sales. What effect do adequate controls in the credit function have on the auditor's evidence accumulation?

12-4 ❶ Distinguish between bad-debt expense and write-off of uncollectable accounts. Explain why they are audited in completely different ways.

12-5 ❶ List the transaction-related audit objectives for the verification of sales transactions. For each objective, state one internal control that the client can use to reduce the likelihood of misstatements.

12-6 ❶ List the most important duties that should be segregated in the sales and collection cycle. Explain why it is desirable that each duty be segregated.

12-7 ❶ Explain how prenumbered shipping documents and sales invoices can be useful controls for preventing misstatements in sales.

12-8 ❶ What three types of authorizations are commonly used as internal controls for sales? For each authorization, state a test of controls that the auditor could use to verify whether the control was effective in preventing misstatements.

12-9 ❶ Explain the purpose of footing and cross-footing the sales journal and tracing the totals to the general ledger.

12-10 ❶ What is the difference between the auditor's approach in verifying sales returns and allowances and that for sales? Explain the reasons for the difference.

12-11 ❶ Explain why auditors usually emphasize the detection of fraud in the audit of cash. Is this consistent or inconsistent with the auditor's responsibility in the audit? Explain.

12-12 ❶ List the transaction-related audit objectives for the verification of cash receipts. For each objective, state one internal control that the client can use to reduce the likelihood of misstatements.

12-13 ❶ List several audit procedures the auditor can use to determine whether all cash received was recorded.

12-14 ❶ Explain what is meant by "proof of cash receipts," and state its purpose.

12-15 ❶ Explain what is meant by "lapping," and discuss how the auditor can uncover it. Under what circumstances should the auditor make a special effort to uncover lapping?

12-16 ❶ What audit procedures are most likely to be used to verify accounts receivable charged off as uncollectable? State the purpose of each of these procedures.

12-17 ❶ Under what circumstances is it acceptable to perform tests of controls for sales and cash receipts at an interim date?

12-18 ❶ Deirdre Brandt, a public accountant, tested sales transactions for the month of March in an audit of the financial statements for the year ended December 31, 2012. Based on the excellent results of the tests of controls, she decided to significantly reduce her substantive tests of details of balances at year end. Evaluate this decision.

12-19 ❶ BestSellers.com sells fiction and non-fiction books to customers through the company's website. Customers place orders for books via the website by providing their name, address, and credit card number and expiration date. What internal controls could BestSellers.com implement to ensure that shipments of books occur only for customers who have the ability to pay for those books? At what point would BestSellers.com be able to record the sale as revenue?

12-20 ❶ ABC is a small manufacturing company that sells all of its products on credit; payment is normally due within 30 days. What are the risks associated with credit sales? What controls can ABC implement to mitigate these risks?

Discussion Questions and Problems

12-21 ❶❷ Items 1 through 8 are selected questions of the type generally found in internal control questionnaires used by auditors to obtain an understanding of internal control in the sales and collection cycle. In using the questionnaire for a particular client, a "yes" response to a question indicates a possible internal control, whereas a "no" indicates a potential weakness.

1. Are sales invoices independently compared with customers' orders for prices, quantities, extensions, and footings?
2. Are sales orders, invoices, and credit memoranda issued and filed in numerical sequence, and are the sequences accounted for periodically?
3. Are the selling function and cash register functions independent of the cash receipts, shipping, delivery, and billing functions?
4. Are all COD, scrap, equipment, and cash sales accounted for in the same manner as charge sales, and is the record keeping independent of the collection procedure?
5. Is the collection function independent of, and does it constitute a check on, billing and recording sales?
6. Are customer master files balanced regularly to general ledger control accounts by an employee independent of billing functions?
7. Are cash receipts entered in the accounts receivable system by persons independent of the mail-opening and receipts-listing functions?
8. Are receipts deposited intact on a timely basis?

REQUIRED

a. For each of the questions above, state the transaction-related audit objectives being fulfilled if the control is in effect.
b. For each control, list a test of control to test its effectiveness.
c. For each of the questions above, identify the nature of the potential financial misstatements.
d. For each of the potential misstatements in part (c), list an audit procedure to determine whether a material error exists.

12-22 ❶❷ YourTeam.com is an online retailer of college and professional sports team memorabilia, such as hats, shirts, pennants, and other sports logo products. Consumers select the university, college, or professional team from a pull-down menu on the company's website. For each listed team, the website provides a product description, picture, and price for all products sold online. Customers click on the product number of the items they wish to purchase. YourTeam.com has established the following internal controls for its online sales:

1. Only products shown on the website can be purchased online. Other company products not shown on the website are unavailable for online sale.
2. The online sales system is linked to the perpetual inventory system that verifies quantities on hand before processing the sale.
3. Before the sale is authorized, YourTeam.com obtains credit card authorization codes electronically from the credit card clearing house.
4. Online sales are rejected if the customer's shipping address does not match the credit card's billing address.
5. Before the sale is finalized, the online screen shows the product name, description, unit price, and total sales price for the online transaction. Customers must click on the Accept or Reject sales buttons to indicate approval or rejection of the online sale.
6. Once customers approve the online sale, the online sales system generates a Pending Sales file, which is an online data file that is used by warehouse personnel to process shipments. Online sales are not recorded in the sales journal until warehouse personnel enter the bill of lading number and date of shipment into the Pending Sales data file.

REQUIRED

a. For each control, identify the transaction-related audit objective(s) being fulfilled if each control is in effect.
b. For each control, describe potential financial misstatements that could occur if the control were not present.
c. For each control, identify an important general control that would affect the quality of the control.
d. For each control, list a test of control to test its effectiveness.

12-23 ❷ Jintian Clothing Ltd. manufactures sportswear and sells it to large department stores in Western Canada. The company records sales in a sales journal. When a customer orders merchandise, a sales clerk prepares a sales invoice. The credit manager must approve all sales to new customers, and a record is kept of all approved customers with their credit limit, as established by the credit manager. The

company manufactures several styles of sportswear, and each item is listed in a catalogue with the price updated quarterly.

Sales are recorded when goods are shipped. When the goods are shipped, the shipping clerk prepares a bill of lading in triplicate, with one part retained in the shipping department, one part accompanying the shipment, and one part forwarded to accounting. The accounting department matches the bill of lading to the sales invoice, records the sale, and adjusts the inventory records. All documents are sequentially pre-numbered.

REQUIRED

Prepare an audit plan to test the internal control objectives of occurrence, completeness, and accuracy at Jintian Clothing Ltd.

12-24 ❷ ❹ Lenter Supply Corp. is a medium-sized distributor of wholesale hardware supplies in southern Manitoba. It has been a client of yours for several years and has instituted excellent internal control over sales at your recommendation.

In providing control over shipments, the client has pre-numbered "warehouse removal slips" that are used for every sale. It is company policy never to remove goods from the warehouse without an authorized warehouse removal slip. After shipment, two copies of the warehouse removal slip are sent to billing for the computerized preparation of a sales invoice. One copy is stapled to the duplicate copy of a pre-numbered sales invoice, and the other copy is filed numerically. In some cases, more than one warehouse removal slip is used for billing one sales invoice. The lowest warehouse removal slip number for the year is 14682 and the highest is 37521. The lowest sales invoice number is 47821 and the highest is 68507.

In the audit of sales, one of the major concerns is the effectiveness of the controls in making sure that all shipments are billed. You have decided to use audit sampling in testing internal controls.

REQUIRED

a. State an effective audit procedure for testing whether shipments have been billed. What is the sampling unit for the audit procedure?

b. Assuming that you expect no deviations in the sample but are willing to accept a TER of 3 percent, at a 10-percent ARACR, what is the appropriate sample size for the audit test? You may complete this assignment using non-statistical sampling or attribute sampling.

c. Design a random selection plan for selecting the sample from the population using random numbers. Select the first 10 sample items using the random number generation function of your spreadsheet (@RAND for Excel). Organize the random numbers in ascending order.

d. Your supervisor suggests the possibility of performing other sales tests with the same sample as a means of efficiently using your audit time. List two other audit procedures that could conveniently be performed using the same sample, and state the purpose of each of the procedures.

e. Is it desirable to test the occurrence of sales with the random sample you have designed in part (c)? Why or why not?

12-25 ❸ You were asked in February 2013 by the board of management of your church to review its accounting procedures. As part of this review, you have prepared the following comments relating to the collections made at weekly services and record-keeping for members' pledges and contributions:

1. The finance committee is responsible for preparing an annual budget based on the anticipated needs of the various church committees and for the annual fall "pledge campaign" during which most members make a commitment to contribute a certain amount to the church over the following year.

2. The financial records are maintained by the treasurer who has authority to sign cheques drawn on the church bank account.

3. The ushers take up the collection during the services each Sunday and place it uncounted in a deposit bag in the church safe.

4. The treasurer, who is retired, comes in Monday morning, counts the collection, and deposits it into the church's bank account. Some members use predated numbered envelopes, but most do not. The treasurer enters members' contributions into a spreadsheet for the numbered envelopes only.

5. The treasurer issues receipts to each member every January based on the spreadsheet amounts. The contributions up to 2011 had always exceeded the amounts pledged so

that the value of receipts given out was less than total contributions; the excess was recorded as "loose" or "open" collection. In 2012, the total of the receipts given out by the treasurer exceeded the total funds received by the church.

6. The church is registered as a charity under the Income Tax Act and is required to file a return each year to comply with its rules. The chairperson of the finance committee is upset because the church has received a letter from the Canada Revenue Agency in connection with the return for 2012 because the return showed receipts given exceeded the funds actually received. The letter indicated that such differences could result in removal of the church's ability to issue income tax receipts.

REQUIRED

Identify the risks of error or fraud, identify control weaknesses, and recommend improvements in procedures at the church for the following:

a. Collections made at weekly services.

b. Record-keeping for members' pledges and contributions. Use the methodology for identifying weaknesses that was discussed in Chapter 9. Organize your answer as follows:

RISKS   WEAKNESS   RECOMMENDED IMPROVEMENT

(Adapted from AICPA)

12-26 ❸ ❹ The following is a partial audit program for the audit of cash receipts:

1. Review the cash receipts journal for large and unusual transactions.
2. Trace entries from the prelisting of cash receipts to the cash receipts journal to determine if each is recorded.
3. Compare customer name, date, and amount on the prelisting with the data on the cash receipts journal.
4. Examine the related remittance advice for entries selected from the prelisting to determine if cash discounts were approved.
5. Trace entries from the prelisting to the deposit slip to determine if each has been deposited.

REQUIRED
a. Identify which audit procedures could be tested using attribute sampling.
b. What is the appropriate sampling unit for the tests in part (a)?
c. List the attributes for testing in part (a).
d. Assume an ARACR of 5 percent and a TER of 8 percent for tests of controls. The estimated population deviation rate for tests of controls is 2 percent. What is the initial sample size for each attribute?

12-27 ❹ The following are auditor judgments and audit sampling results for six populations. Assume large population sizes.

	1	2	3	4	5	6
EPER (in percentage)	2	0	3	1	1	8
TER (in percentage)	6	3	8	5	20	15
ARACR (in percentage)	5	5	10	5	10	10
Actual sample size	100	100	60	100	20	60
Actual number of exceptions in the sample	2	0	1	4	1	8

REQUIRED
a. For each population, did the auditor select a smaller sample size than is indicated by using attribute sampling tables for determining sample size? Evaluate, selecting either a larger or smaller size than those determined in the tables.
b. Calculate the SER and CUER for each population.
c. For which of the six populations should the sample results be considered unacceptable? What options are available to the auditor?
d. Why is analysis of the exceptions necessary even when the populations are considered acceptable?
e. For the following terms, identify which is an audit decision, a non-statistical estimate made by the auditor, a sample result, or a statistical conclusion about the population:
  1. EPER.
  2. TER.
  3. ARACR.
  4. Actual sample size.
  5. Actual number of exceptions in the sample.
  6. SER.
  7. CUER.

Professional Judgment Problems

12-28 ❶ ❷ Parts for Wheels, Inc. has historically sold auto parts directly to consumers through its retail stores. Due to competitive pressure, Parts for Wheels installed an internet-based sales system that allows customers to place orders through the company's website. The company hired an outside website design consultant to create the sales system because the company's IT personnel lack the necessary experience.

Customers use the link to the inventory parts listing on the website to view product descriptions and prices. The inventory parts listing is updated weekly. To get the system online quickly, management decided not to link the order system to the sales and inventory accounting systems. Customers submit orders for products through the online system and provide credit card information for payment. Each day, accounting department clerks print submitted orders from the online system. After credit authorization is verified with the credit card agency, the accounting department enters the sale into the sales system. After that, the accounting department sends a copy of the order to warehouse personnel who process the shipment. The inventory system is updated on the basis of bills of lading information forwarded to accounting after shipment.

Customers may return parts for full refund if returned within 30 days of submitting the order online. The company agrees to refund shipping costs incurred by the customer for returned goods.

REQUIRED
a. Describe deficiencies in Parts for Wheels' online sales system that may lead to material misstatements in the financial statements. State which audit assertion is affected.
b. For each deficiency listed in part (a), identify changes in manual procedures that could be made to minimize risks, without having to reprogram the current online system.
c. Describe potential customer concerns about doing business online with Parts for Wheels. For each concern, provide one or more controls that could be implemented to address the concerns.

12-29 ❹ In performing tests of controls and substantive tests of transactions for the Oakland Hardware Company, Ben Frentz, a public accountant, is concerned with the internal verification of pricing, extensions, and footings of sales invoices, and the accuracy of the calculations. In testing sales using audit sampling, a separate attribute is used for the test of control (the presence of matching shipping documents) and the substantive test of transactions (the accuracy of calculation). Because internal controls are considered good, Frentz uses a 10-percent ARACR, a zero EPER, and a 5-percent TER for both attributes. Therefore, the initial sample size is 45 items, which Ben rounds up to 50.

In conducting the tests, the auditor finds three sample items for which there were no matching shipping documents, but in all cases the invoices are for services (such as product repairs or installation). No sales invoice tested in the sample has a financial misstatement. Complete the following requirements using either a non-statistical sampling or an attributes sampling approach.

REQUIRED

a. Estimate or determine the CUER for both attributes, assuming a population of 5,000 sales invoices.

b. Decide whether each control is acceptable.

c. Discuss the most desirable course of action that the auditor should follow in deciding the effect of the CUER exceeding the TER.

d. Explain how it is possible that the sample had three control deviations but no transactions involved monetary misstatements.

e. How would you analyze exceptions in this case?

Case

12-30 ❶ ❷ Meyer's Pharmaceutical Company, a drug manufacturer, has the following internal controls for billing and recording accounts receivable:

1. An incoming customer's purchase order is received in the order department by a clerk who enters the information into the sales management system. The system assigns an internal sequential number to the sales order. For existing customers, once the customer number has been entered, the information system automatically retrieves the customer's name and address and credit limit. The clerk visually compares this information to the purchase order, writes the customer number and internal sales order number on the customer purchase order form, then enters the item number and quantity ordered. The clerk then initials the purchase order as entered, and stamps the date entered on the purchase order. The sales management system multiplies the number of items by the unit price and adds the extended amounts to produce the total amount of the invoice. The clerk visually compares the total invoiced with the purchase order. If Meyer's prices are less than the customer prices, the order is processed. If Meyer's prices are higher, the clerk sets the order status as "Pending" and takes the purchase order to the sales department for follow-up. The clerk will release the order from the "Pending" status to credit check only when one of the sales supervisors has approved the order. For large differences (greater than $500), the customer is requested to initiate a revised purchase order.

2. The sales management system compares the sum of the new customer order plus existing accounts receivable for the customer with the credit limit for the customer. If the amount is less than the credit limit, then the order is accepted. If the amount exceeds the credit limit, a warning is displayed on the screen, and the order is not accepted but is given the status of "Pending." All pending orders are listed on a report and printed daily for review by the credit department. Approval is granted only if credit limits are increased and authorized by the credit manager on a credit limit change form, after appropriate investigation.

3. The sales management system compares ordered amounts with inventory, and if items are in stock, prints a three-part sales order shipping document and bill of lading, which is sent to the shipping department. After the order has been shipped, two copies of the shipping document are given to the accounting department. The third copy of the sales order and bill of lading are sent with the goods to the customer.

4. An accounts receivable clerk retrieves the sales order using the sales order number, enters the quantities shipped, and generates the invoice. One copy of the shipping document goes with the invoice to the customer, and another copy is stapled to the company copy of the invoice and filed numerically. The sales order number is listed on the invoice.

5. Sales are recorded online, that is, as each invoice is prepared, it is posted against the customer master file. Each day, a daily sales journal is printed. The sales and accounts receivable posting is recorded by automatic journal entry at the end of each day, after the daily sales journal is printed. The journal entry is printed at the bottom of the daily sales journal.

REQUIRED

a. Flowchart the billing function as a means of understanding the system.

b. Identify the potential risks of misstatement (error or fraud) that could occur at Meyer's.

c. For each risk identified in part (b), identify internal controls present at Meyer's that could prevent or detect the potential misstatement. State the audit objectives associated with each internal control.

d. Have all of the transaction-related audit objectives for sales been covered in part (c)? If not, list internal controls over sales for the remaining transaction-related audit objectives.

e. For each of the internal controls in parts (c) and (d), list a useful test of control to verify the effectiveness of the control.

f. For each transaction-related audit objective for sales, list appropriate substantive tests, considering internal controls.

ACL Problem   *ACL*

12-31 ❷ This problem requires the use of ACL software, use the Metaphor_AR_2002 file in ACL_Demo (in the Tables folder). The suggested command or other source of information needed to solve the problem requirement is included at the end of each question.

a. Determine the total number and amount of September 2002 transactions in the file (Filter, Count, and Total Field). What audit tests would you conduct with this information? What audit assertions are associated with the audit test?

b. Determine and print the total amount for each of the five types of 2002 transactions for comparison with the general ledger (Summarize). (AA = adjustment, CN = credit note, IN = invoice, PM = payments, TR = transfers) Which transaction type has the highest count?

How would you use this information during the audit process?

c. For sales invoices (IN), determine the number of transactions, total amount, largest amount, and average size (Filter and Statistics). Why would the auditor be interested in the size of the largest sale?

d. Determine the difference in the number of days between the invoice date (DATE1) and the due date (DUE) for sales invoices (IN), and evaluate the impact upon internal controls (Computed Field).

e. To better decide the sales invoices to select for testing, you decide to stratify 2002 sales invoices (IN) after excluding all invoices less than $300. Print the output (Filter and Stratify). On the basis of your results, assess whether $300 is a reasonable stratification level.

Ongoing Small Business Case: Commercial Accounts at CondoCleaners.com

12-32 ❶ ❷ Many of the condominium towers that comprise CondoCleaners.com's customer base have stores or businesses located in or near the towers. Jim has decided to further expand his business by offering cleaning services to businesses. Unlike residential customers, commercial accounts generate accounts receivable, as customers would be billed monthly for their cleaning services.

REQUIRED
What controls should Jim put in place to ensure the collectability of his commercial accounts? Why are these controls important?

13 Completing the tests in the sales and collection cycle: Accounts receivable

Substantive tests are considered the "finishing touch" for the audit of an account, yet they are also part of a continuous top-down audit process. Controls testing provides information about the quality of the client's systems so that the auditor has enough detail to design the tests of detail. In this chapter, we will look at one specific account—trade accounts receivable—and examine how the testing is designed, selected, executed, and evaluated. All types of auditors will conduct substantive tests such as those described here to quantify potential misstatements, while management accountants will find the results of such testing useful when deciding whether adjustments should be posted to accounts.

LEARNING OBJECTIVES

1 Identify and describe the risk-based process for designing tests of details of balances for accounts receivable. Explain the relationship between transaction-related, balance-related, and presentation and disclosure audit objectives for the sales and collection cycle.

2 Explain when and why analytical review procedures are completed as part of the audit of sales and accounts receivable. Demonstrate how analytical procedures can detect poten-

tial fraud and economic dependency issues. Link substantive testing to the audit risk model.

3 Describe the accounts receivable tests of detail audit tests that would be completed for each audit assertion. Discuss reasons supporting the importance of confirmation.

4 Illustrate the risk assessment and substantive tests of accounts receivable using Hillsburg Hardware Limited. Describe the execution and evaluation of monetary unit sampling (MUS).

STANDARDS REFERENCED IN THIS CHAPTER

CICA Standards

CAS 505 – External confirmations

Section 3840 – Related-party transactions

Section 3841 – Economic dependence

Section 4460 – Disclosure of related party transactions by not-for-profit organizations

IAS 24 – Related party transactions

When More Isn't Better

On Cindy Veinot's first audit assignment, she is asked to handle the confirmation of accounts receivable. The audit client is a retailer with a large number of customer accounts. In previous years, Cindy's firm had confirmed these accounts using negative confirmations. Last year, 200 negative confirmations were sent one month prior to year end. Those that were returned showed only timing differences; none represented a misstatement in the client's books.

Before the current year's planned confirmation date, Cindy performs a review of internal controls over sales and cash receipts transactions. She discovers that a new online system for sales transactions has been implemented, but the client is having considerable problems getting it to work properly. There were a significant number of misstatements in recording sales during the past few months. Cindy's tests of controls and substantive tests of sales transactions also identify similar misstatements.

When Cindy asks her supervisor what to do, the supervisor responds, "No problem, Cindy. Just send 300 confirmation requests instead of the usual 200." Cindy recalls from her auditing class that negative confirmation requests are not considered good evidence when there are weak controls. Because customers are asked to respond only when there are differences, the auditor cannot be confident of the correct value for each misstatement in the sample. Cindy concludes that expanding the sample size is the wrong solution. When Cindy discusses her concerns with her supervisor, who responds, "You are absolutely right. I spoke too quickly. We need to sit down and think about a better strategy to find out if accounts receivable is materially misstated."

IMPORTANCE TO AUDITORS

Cindy felt comfortable talking to her supervisor about her disagreement with the audit approach that had been used in the past. A good working relationship among members of the audit team enables junior staff to question the decisions of senior staff, either to improve the audit process or to help clarify the work that needs to be done. It is also important to have the knowledge to ask questions like Cindy did. It may be that changes in internal controls or changes in sampling methods or quantities tested require new procedures to be conducted.

WHAT DO YOU THINK?

1. What other questions could Cindy have asked that would have helped her assess the audit approach for accounts receivable?
2. How do system changes affect the substantive tests conducted at an audit?

continued >

continued

3. What information would Cindy require to select a sample for positive accounts receivable confirmations?

THE relationship between analytical procedures as a substantive test and tests of detail and planned detection risk are shown in Figure 13-1, using the audit risk model. We consider tests of controls for the sales and collection cycle, discussed in chapter 3, to be part of Phase 2 of the audit process. (Recall that Phase 1 is planning.) Tests of details of balances for the sales and collection cycle, studied in this chapter, are done in Phase 3. Audit programs including both tests of controls and substantive tests are written at the same time. However, prior to conducting substantive tests, the auditor would review the results of the control tests and update the audit planning process to decide whether changes are needed to assessed risks. This chapter walks you through the completion of the audit of the sales and collection cycle.

① Designing Tests of Details of Balances for Accounts Receivable

Methodology for Designing Tests of Details of Balances

Figure 13-2 shows the methodology that auditors follow in determining the appropriate tests of details of balances for accounts receivable. Substantive tests (comprising analytical review and tests of details) comprise Phase 6 in the risk response portion of the eight-phase audit process model introduced in Chapter 5. The methodology for designing tests of details was introduced in Chapter 10. This methodology integrates both the audit risk model and the types of audit tests that are shown in Figure 13-1.

Recall that prior to designing audit tests the auditor will conduct preplanning (Phase 1), build a client risk profile (Phase 2) that includes preliminary analytical

| Figure 13-1 | Relationship between Analytical Procedures as a Substantive Test and Tests of Details of Balances to Planned Detection Risk |

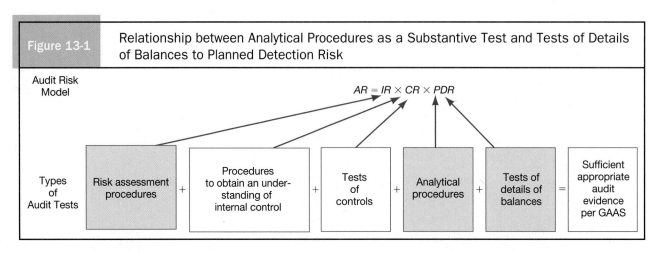

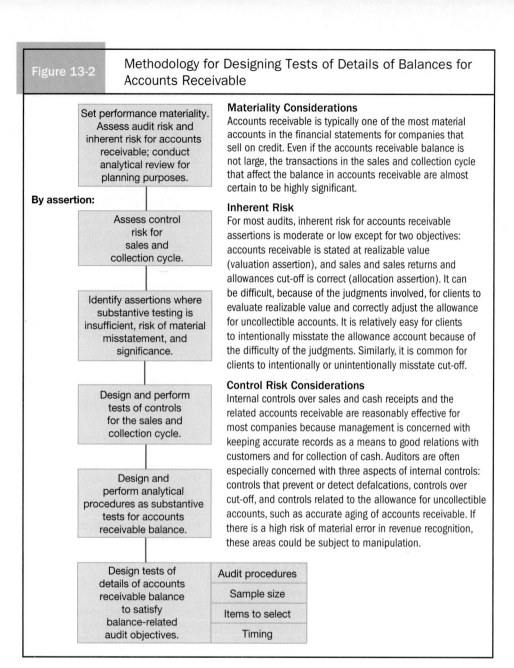

Figure 13-2 Methodology for Designing Tests of Details of Balances for Accounts Receivable

Set performance materiality. Assess audit risk and inherent risk for accounts receivable; conduct analytical review for planning purposes.

By assertion:

Assess control risk for sales and collection cycle.

Identify assertions where substantive testing is insufficient, risk of material misstatement, and significance.

Design and perform tests of controls for the sales and collection cycle.

Design and perform analytical procedures as substantive tests for accounts receivable balance.

Design tests of details of accounts receivable balance to satisfy balance-related audit objectives.

| Audit procedures |
| Sample size |
| Items to select |
| Timing |

Materiality Considerations

Accounts receivable is typically one of the most material accounts in the financial statements for companies that sell on credit. Even if the accounts receivable balance is not large, the transactions in the sales and collection cycle that affect the balance in accounts receivable are almost certain to be highly significant.

Inherent Risk

For most audits, inherent risk for accounts receivable assertions is moderate or low except for two objectives: accounts receivable is stated at realizable value (valuation assertion), and sales and sales returns and allowances cut-off is correct (allocation assertion). It can be difficult, because of the judgments involved, for clients to evaluate realizable value and correctly adjust the allowance for uncollectible accounts. It is relatively easy for clients to intentionally misstate the allowance account because of the difficulty of the judgments. Similarly, it is common for clients to intentionally or unintentionally misstate cut-off.

Control Risk Considerations

Internal controls over sales and cash receipts and the related accounts receivable are reasonably effective for most companies because management is concerned with keeping accurate records as a means to good relations with customers and for collection of cash. Auditors are often especially concerned with three aspects of internal controls: controls that prevent or detect defalcations, controls over cut-off, and controls related to the allowance for uncollectible accounts, such as accurate aging of accounts receivable. If there is a high risk of material error in revenue recognition, these areas could be subject to manipulation.

review, and conduct and document a variety of risk assessments that are used to develop a strategic audit approach by cycle (Phase 3). In Phase 4, the auditor will then develop the audit programs, tests of control, and substantive tests. The results of the tests of control (Phase 5), discussed in the previous chapter, are evaluated (which includes reassessing client business risks and fraud risks) before conducting the substantive tests (Phase 6), which are the focus of this chapter. Analytical procedures, described in the next section, will be completed first and reviewed before conducting the tests of detail.

Determining the appropriate tests of details of balances evidence is complicated because it must be decided on an objective-by-objective basis. There are several interactions that affect the evidence decision. For example, the auditor must consider inherent risk, which may differ by objective, and control risk, which also may vary by objective. The emphasis on a particular objective will vary depending upon the auditor's assessment of the likelihood of material misstatement.

Standards require that the auditor consider the risk of material misstatement for revenue recognition as high. The amount of work conducted in sales and accounts receivable will also be affected by the auditor's assessment of the quality of internal controls over revenue recognition. Where the auditor believes that biases or the potential of revenue manipulation exists, there will be increased tests of details

Balance-Related Audit Objective	Presentation and Disclosure-Related Audit Objective	Risk of Material Misstatement in Accounts Receivable	Example Tests of Detail of Balances to Respond to the Risk
Existence	Occurrence	Revenue is recorded when goods have not been delivered (or were delivered in the subsequent period), overstating both revenue and accounts receivable.[++]	Use generalized audit software (GAS) to compare details and dates of invoices to shipment and customer order details for the current year and the month subsequent to the year end.
Rights and obligations	Rights and obligations	Consignment sales are recorded as revenue, overstating both revenue and accounts receivable.[*]	Include confirmation of terms of sale with accounts receivable confirmations.
Completeness	Completeness	Shipments are made that are not billed (or were billed in the subsequent period), understating both revenue and accounts receivable.[++]	Same as occurrence. Conduct tests to ensure that the shipping detail and invoice detail data files are complete prior to conducting GAS testing.
Allocation (accuracy of recording)	Accuracy	Sales recorded at the incorrect quantity or the incorrect price result in revenue and accounts receivable that are over or under stated.	Use generalized audit software to (1) match sales invoice price details to authorized prices in the sales price master files and (2) same as occurrence.
Valuation	Valuation	Orders were shipped to a bad credit risk, resulting in uncollectable accounts that are not included in the bad debt allowance.[*]	(1) Using GAS, reperform aging of accounts receivable, (2) select confirmations and conduct appropriate confirmation procedures, (3) conduct audit of bad debt allowance.
Allocation (to correct period and correct account)	Classification	Long-term service revenue (such as the provision for maintenance) is recorded as current revenue or in the wrong period, overstating revenue and accounts receivable.	Read customer contracts and audit the criteria used to allocate revenue to components of the sales contract.
	Understandability	The nature of related parties is described too briefly to be of use; the description of related party sales transactions is unclear; users misunderstand the nature of the relationships and are misled.[+]	Read the notes to the financial statements and compare to audited information about related party transactions for understandability.

[*] This risk also pertains to occurrence.
[+] This risk is not listed on Table 12.1.
[++] This risk also pertains to allocation if the risk is due to shipment or billing in the next period.

of accounts receivable and increased use of dual-purpose tests for tests of control. Table 13-1 describes how some of the risks from Table 12-1 affect accounts receivable. It also provides example tests of detail of balances that would both respond to the risk and quantify the size of potential errors or misstatements. Note that some of the tests apply to multiple audit assertions.

To help manage the decision-making process for the appropriate tests of details of balances, auditors often use an **evidence planning spreadsheet**. This spreadsheet was first introduced in Chapter 7 (Figure 7-6) and further amplified in Chapter 12 (Figure 12-14). The completed evidence planning spreadsheet is included as Figure 13-8. This spreadsheet is directly related to the top-down methodology in Figure 13-2.

Evidence planning spreadsheet—a working paper used to help the auditor decide whether planned audit evidence for tests of details of balances should be low, medium, or high for each balance-related audit objective.

ACCOUNTS RECEIVABLE BALANCE-RELATED AUDIT OBJECTIVES The five general balance-related audit objectives used to help the auditor decide the appropriate audit evidence (shown in the first column of Table 13-1) are the same for every account balance and are applied to accounts receivable as accounts receivable balance-related audit objectives (Table 13-5).

The first five columns in the evidence planning spreadsheet in Figure 13-8 include the balance-related audit objectives. The auditor uses the factors in the rows to aid in assessing planned detection risk for accounts receivable, by objective. All of these factors are decided during audit planning. They were studied in Chapters 7 through 12.

ACCOUNTS RECEIVABLE PRESENTATION AND DISCLOSURE-RELATED AUDIT OBJECTIVES These seven objectives shown in the second column of Table 13-1 concern fair disclosure and representation of the accounts receivable balance in the financial statements.

Evidence planning for these objectives are included in Figure 13-8. Specific presentation and disclosure audit objectives for accounts receivable are shown Table 13-5.

We will now walk through the methodology in Figure 13-2, which represents the top-down strategic audit approach, as applied to the tests of details of balances for accounts receivable.

SET PERFORMANCE MATERIALITY, ASSESS AUDIT RISK AND INHERENT RISK FOR ACCOUNTS RECEIVABLE, AND CONDUCT PLANNING ANALYTICAL REVIEW Setting materiality starts with the auditor making the preliminary judgment about materiality for the entire financial statements, then adjusting that for anticipated misstatements to establish performance materiality (see Chapter 7). Figure 13-8 shows the performance materiality of $441,000 that was set for the Hillsburg Hardware audit by including the amount on the bottom of the evidence planning spreadsheet.

Audit risk is assessed for the financial statements as a whole and is not usually allocated to various accounts or objectives. Figure 13-8 shows an audit risk of high for every accounts receivable objective, which will permit a higher planned detection risk (and less planned evidence) for accounts receivable than if audit risk were low. Inherent risk is assessed for each objective and was assessed at low for all objectives except valuation for Hillsburg Hardware.

Planning analytical review is conducted to help target audit field work and look for unusual relationships. Appendix 8A illustrated the calculation of several ratios for Hillsburg Hardware. As an example, referring to the Hillsburg Hardware balance sheet at the end of Chapter 5, the accounts receivable balance for the current year is higher, yet the allowance for bad debts is lower. The auditor would conduct additional testing to justify the lower bad-debt allowance, particularly given current economic conditions.

ASSESS CONTROL RISK FOR THE SALES AND COLLECTION CYCLE The methodology for assessing control risk was studied in general in Chapter 9 and applied to sales and cash receipts transactions in Chapter 12. The framework used to identify control activities and internal control weaknesses was a control risk matrix. Examples are included in Figures 12-7 and 12-8.

The auditor must relate control risk for transaction-related audit objectives in the cycle to the balance-related and presentation and disclosure-related audit objectives in deciding planned detection risk and planned evidence for tests of details of balances. Figure 13-3 shows the relationship between transaction-related and balance-related objectives for the two primary classes of transactions in the sales and collection cycle (sales and cash receipts), and also between the transaction-related audit objectives and presentation and disclosure audit objectives for sales transactions. For example, assume that the auditor concluded that control risk for both sales and cash receipts transactions is low for the accuracy transaction-related audit objective. The auditor can, therefore, conclude that controls for some of the allocation balance-related audit objective for accounts receivable are effective. If sales returns and allowances and charge-off of uncollectable accounts receivable

Figure 13-3 Relationship between Transaction-Related, Balance-Related, and Presentation and Disclosure-Related Audit Objectives for the Sales and Collection Cycle

Class of Transactions	Transaction-Related Audit Objectives	Accounts Receivable Balance-Related Audit Objectives					Accounts Receivable Presentation and Disclosure Audit Objectives						
		Existence	Rights and Obligations	Completeness	Valuation	Allocation	Occurrence	Rights and Obligations	Completeness	Accuracy	Valuation	Classification	Understandability
Sales	Occurrence	X					X						
	Completeness			X					X				
	Accuracy					X				X			
	Cutoff					X							
	Classification					X						X	
Cash receipts	Occurrence			X									
	Completeness	X											
	Accuracy					X							
	Cutoff												
	Classification												

Legend:
- Assertions where there is no parallel
- Allocation is multi-faceted
- Existence & completeness complement each other when considering controls in sales & cash use

are significant, assessed control risk must also be considered for these two classes of transactions.

Several aspects of the relationships in Figure 13-3 deserve special mention:

- For sales, the occurrence transaction-related audit objective affects the existence balance-related audit objective, but for cash receipts, the occurrence transaction-related audit objective affects the completeness balance-related audit objective, since the recording of a valid cash receipt will help ensure that all accounts receivable are recorded.
- A similar relationship exists for the completeness transaction-related audit objective. The reason for this somewhat surprising conclusion is that an increase in sales increases accounts receivable, but an increase in cash receipts decreases accounts receivable. For example, recording a sale that did not occur violates the occurrence transaction-related audit objective and existence balance-related audit objective (both overstatements). Recording a cash receipt that did not occur violates the occurrence transaction-related audit objective, but it violates the completeness balance-related audit objective for accounts receivable because a receivable that is still outstanding is no longer included in the records if the duplicated or fictitious cash receipt is posted against a valid account receivable.

Two accounts receivable balance-related audit objectives are not affected by assessed control risk for the sales and cash receipts classes of transactions. These are valuation and rights and obligations. Similarly, the three presentation and disclosure audit objectives of rights and obligations, valuation, and understandability are not affected by the assessed control risk for the sales transactions. When the auditor wants to reduce assessed control risk below maximum for these objectives, separate controls are identified and tested (such as those that pertain to the adequacy of the bad debt provision). This was discussed in Chapter 9.

The auditor makes a separate assessment of control risk for objectives related to the accounts receivable balance, as shown in Figure 13-8.

IDENTIFY AT-RISK ASSERTIONS Figure 13-2 indicates three ways that the auditor assesses the assertions to identify high risks of material misstatement. The first is identifying those assertions where substantive testing may be insufficient. For example, if shipping documents and sales invoices are sent electronically (via electronic data interchange, EDI), and cash is received electronically, the auditor would be required to evaluate the controls over these processes. Substantive testing could be substantially reduced for the assertions of accuracy and completeness where general and automated application controls are found to be good.

Secondly, the auditor targets testing based upon risk of material misstatement. The most likely misstatements could occur with valuation (due to the judgments involved in setting the bad-debt allowance), cutoff (if sales are recorded in the wrong period), and occurrence (if there is a bias to overstating revenue). The auditor would then increase substantive tests for these assertions.

Finally, the auditor must increase testing where it is concluded that there are significant risks of misstatement, such as for revenue recognition. Other potential significant errors could arise with complex sales transactions or with foreign exchange exposure on accounts receivable. The auditor would increase testing for the assertions that pertain to these risks.

DESIGN AND PERFORM TESTS OF CONTROLS Chapter 12 dealt with deciding audit procedures and sample size for tests of controls and evaluating the results of those tests. The results of the tests of controls determine whether assessed control risk for sales and cash receipts needs to be revised. The evidence planning spreadsheet in Figure 13-8 shows three rows for control risk (sales, cash receipts, and additional controls) based on the completion and evaluation of those tests.

The next two sections focus separately on the two types of substantive tests, analytical procedures as a substantive test and tests of details.

Concept check

C13-1 Why is accounts receivable often an important account to audit?

C13-2 Which balance-related audit objectives are not affected by control risk for classes of transactions? Why?

C13-3 Why is valuation a highly at-risk assertion for accounts receivable?

The Importance of Analytical Procedures

As discussed in Chapter 8, analytical procedures are used throughout the audit: during planning, when performing detailed tests, and as a part of completing the audit. Those analytical procedures affecting accounts receivable or the sales cycle that are done during planning and when performing detailed tests are discussed in this chapter.

Table 13-2	Analytical Procedures for Planning for Sales and Collection Cycle
Analytical Procedure for Planning	**Possible Misstatement**
Compare bad-debt expense as a percentage of gross sales with previous years'.	Uncollectable accounts receivable that has not been provided for.
Compare number of days that accounts receivable is outstanding with previous years'.	Overstatement or understatement of allowance for uncollectable accounts and bad-debt expense.
Compare aging categories as a percentage of accounts receivable with previous years'.	Overstatement or understatement of allowance for uncollectable accounts and bad-debt expense.
Compare allowance for uncollectable accounts as a percentage of accounts receivable with previous years'.	Overstatement or understatement of allowance for uncollectable accounts.

audit challenge 13-1

Analyzing Great Western Lumber

LESLEY Stopps, a public accountant, is the auditor for Great Western Lumber Company Ltd., a wholesale wood milling company. Lesley calculates the gross margin for three product lines and obtains industry information from published data as listed at the end of this box.

In discussing the results, the controller states that Great Western has always had a higher gross margin on hardwood products than the industry because it focuses on the markets where it is able to sell at higher prices instead of emphasizing volume. The opposite is true of plywood where it has a reasonably small number of customers, each of which demands lower prices because of high volume. The controller states that competitive forces have caused reductions in plywood gross margin for both the industry and Great Western in 2010 and 2011. Great Western has traditionally had a somewhat lower gross margin for softwood than the industry until 2012, when the gross margin went up significantly due to aggressive selling.

Lesley observed that most of what the controller said was reasonable given the facts. Hardwood gross margin for the industry was stable and approximately 3.5 to 4 percent lower than Great Western's every year. Industry gross margin for plywood has declined annually but is about 10 percentage points higher than Great Western's. Industry gross margin for softwood has been stable for the three years, but Great Western's has increased by a fairly large amount.

CRITICAL THINKING QUESTIONS

1. The change in Great Western's softwood gross margin from 20.3 to 23.9 percent is a concern. What calculation helps to quantify the risk of material misstatement?
2. Identify the potential causes of the change in gross margin.
3. How would potential over- or understatements discussed in (2) affect the audit process?

	Great Western and Industry Gross Margins					
	2012 Gross Margin %		2011 Gross Margin %		2010 Gross Margin %	
	Great Western	Industry	Great Western	Industry	Great Western	Industry
Hardwood	36.3	32.4	36.4	32.5	36.0	32.3
Softwood	23.9	22.0	20.3	22.1	20.5	22.3
Plywood	40.3	50.1	44.2	54.3	45.4	55.6

Note: Industry figures are fictitious.

Design and Perform Analytical Procedures for Planning

Most year-end analytical procedures are done after the balance sheet date but before tests of details of balances. Where auditors also provide assurance on quarterly financial results, analytical review procedures are updated periodically throughout the year.

Table 13-2 presents examples of the major types of ratios and comparisons for the sales and collection cycle that could be used for planning purposes and potential misstatements that may be indicated by the analytical procedures. It is important to observe in the "Possible Misstatement" column that both balance sheet and income statement accounts are affected. For example, when the auditor performs analytical procedures for sales, evidence is being obtained about both sales and accounts receivable.

There are many potential warning signals or symptoms of revenue fraud. One of the most important ways of detecting these is by analytical procedures.

Analytical procedures for planning, especially gross margin percentage and accounts receivable turnover, often signal revenue frauds. Fictitious revenue overstates the gross margin percentage, and premature revenue recognition also overstates gross margin if the related cost of sales is not recognized. Fictitious revenues also lower accounts receivable turnover because the fictitious revenues are not collected. Table 13-3 includes comparative sales, cost of sales, and accounts receivable data for a company in which the financial statements included fictitious revenue. Note how the accounts receivable increased, as there were no cash receipts to pay for the

Table 13-3	Example of the Effect of Fictitious Receivables on Accounting Ratios		
	2012	2011	2010
Sales[a]	$265	$185	$105
Cost of sales	(155)	(115)	(67)
Gross profit	110	70	38
Gross profit percentage	42%	38%	36%
Year-end accounts receivable	70	38	20
Accounts receivable turnover[b]	3.8	4.9	5.3

[a]Dollar amounts in millions.
[b]Accounts receivable turnover calculated as Sales/Ending accounts receivable.

fictitious revenues. A higher gross profit percentage, which increased from 36 percent to 42 percent, and lower accounts receivable turnover ratio, which declined from 5.3 to 3.8, helped signal fictitious revenue and accounts receivable. When performing analytical procedures, the more years available to analyze, the more informative the trend analysis will be.

In some frauds, management generated fictitious revenues to make analytical procedures results, such as gross margin, similar to the prior years. In frauds like this, analytical procedures that compare client data with similar prior-period data are typically not useful to signal the fraud. Analytical procedures should also compare client data with industry performance data. Auditors should be aware of the risk of material misstatement related to revenue when the gross margin of the industry is declining, while the entity under audit has remained stable.

Design and Perform Analytical Procedures as Substantive Tests

Analytical procedures that are conducted as substantive tests are used to either quantify error, to provide assurance that numbers are reasonable, or to further target tests of detail. Table 13-4 provides examples of such tests. Analysis by product or product line provides assurance with respect to pricing. Analysis by customer helps to identify (among other things) whether growth (or decline) of sales or collections overall

Table 13-4	Analytical Procedures as Substantive Tests for Sales and Collection Cycle	
Analytical Procedure as a Substantive Test	**Possible Misstatement**
Compare gross margin percentage with previous years' (by product line).	Overstatement or understatement of sales and accounts receivable (errors in sales pricing).
Compare sales by month (by product line) over time.	Overstatement or understatement of sales and accounts receivable (cutoff errors).
Examine relationship between sales and cost of sales (for example, using regression analysis).	Understatement or overstatement of sales and accounts receivable (errors in sales or cost pricing).
Compare sales returns and allowances as a percentage of gross sales with previous years' (by product line).	Understatement or overstatement of sales returns and allowances and accounts receivable (timing errors).
Compare individual customer balances over a stated amount with previous years'.	Misstatements in accounts receivable and related income statement accounts (inadequate bad debt allowance or overstated sales).

have been consistent by customer, or whether there are any significantly high volume customers that need to be disclosed in the notes to the financial statements (such as required by Section 3841, Economic Dependence).

In addition to the analytical procedures in Tables 13-2 and 13-4, there should also be a review of accounts receivable for large and unusual amounts. Individual receivables that deserve special attention are large balances; accounts that have been outstanding for a long time; receivables from affiliated companies, officers, directors, and other related parties; and credit balances. The auditor should review the listing of accounts (aged trial balance) or run exception tests using GAS against the customer master file at the balance sheet date to determine which accounts should be investigated further.

The auditor's conclusion about analytical procedures for the sales and collection cycle is incorporated into the third row from the bottom on the evidence planning spreadsheet in Figure 13-8.

The Relationship Between Assertions and Tests of Detail

DESIGN TESTS OF DETAILS OF ACCOUNTS RECEIVABLE The appropriate tests of details of balances depend upon the factors incorporated into the evidence planning spreadsheet in Figure 13-8. The second row from the bottom of Figure 13-8 shows planned detection risk for each accounts receivable balance-related and presentation and disclosure-related audit objective (see Table 13-5). Planned detection risk for each objective in Figure 13-8 is an auditor decision, decided by subjectively combining the conclusions reached about each of the factors listed above that row.

Combining the factors that determine planned detection risk by assertion is complex because the measurement for each factor is imprecise and the appropriate weight to be given each factor is highly judgmental. On the other hand, the

Table 13-5 Specific Balance-Related and Presentation and Disclosure-Related Audit Objectives for Accounts Receivable

Specific Balance-Related Audit Objective	Specific Presentation and Disclosure Audit Objective
The accounts receivable on the aged accounts receivable trial balance exist. (existence)	The accounts receivable balance and related information disclosed in the financial statements occurred. (occurrence)
The accounts receivable are valid receivables that are due to the company. (rights and obligations)	The disclosed receivables and related information are valid receivables that are due to the company. (rights and obligations)
All existing accounts receivable have been included in the records and are fully summarized and posted. (completeness)	All disclosures that pertain to accounts receivable that should have been disclosed are included in the financial statements. (completeness)
Accounts receivable are stated at net realizable value, with any valuation adjustments appropriately recorded. (valuation)	The net realizable value information disclosed in the financial statements is fairly stated. (valuation)
Accounts receivable balances are appropriately recorded (accurately, in the correct period, in the correct account), including any related adjustments. (allocation)	Accounts receivable information is disclosed fairly and at the appropriate amounts. (accuracy)
	Accounts receivable accounts and information are appropriately presented and described. (classification)
	Accounts receivable accounts and information are clearly expressed. (understandability)

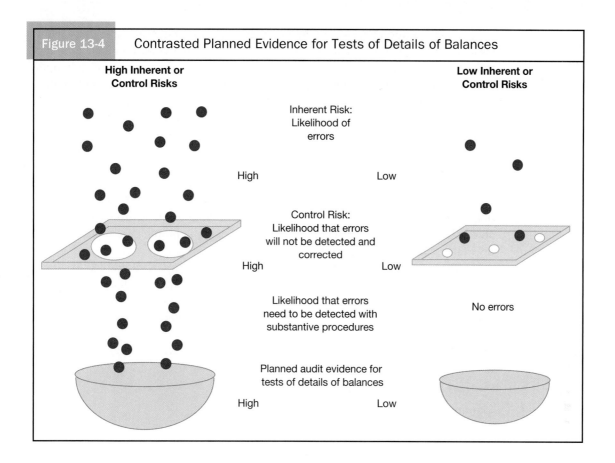

Figure 13-4   Contrasted Planned Evidence for Tests of Details of Balances

High Inherent or Control Risks		Low Inherent or Control Risks
	Inherent Risk: Likelihood of errors	
High		Low
	Control Risk: Likelihood that errors will not be detected and corrected	
High		Low
	Likelihood that errors need to be detected with substantive procedures	No errors
	Planned audit evidence for tests of details of balances	
High		Low

relationship between each factor and planned detection risk is well established. Figure 7-1 illustrated these relationships. Figure 13-4 contrasts how changes in inherent and control risks affect detection risk and thus the planned amount of audit evidence for tests of details of balances. For example, the left side of the diagram shows high inherent risk (many errors likely) and high control risk (the control risk tray has large holes in it). The right side shows low inherent risk (few errors likely) and low control risk (the control risk tray has only a few very small holes). The auditor knows that a high inherent risk or high control risk decreases planned detection risk and increases planned substantive tests. Good results from dual-purpose tests (that confirm that controls are functioning and there are no material errors, such as shown on the right) can lead to increased planned detection risk and decreased planned substantive tests.

The bottom row in Figure 13-8 shows the planned audit evidence for tests of details of balances for accounts receivable, by objective. Planned audit evidence is the complement of planned detection risk (i.e. if planned detection risk is low you need the opposite: high evidence collection).

Tests of Details of Balances for Balance-Related and Presentation and Disclosure-Related Audit Objectives

RELATIONSHIP OF TYPES OF TESTING TO AUDIT OBJECTIVES Table 13-5 shows that five of the balance-related audit objectives (B-RAOs) have parallels in presentation and disclosure-related audit objectives (P&D-RAOs). This means that if the auditor has adequately tested the accounts (for example, for existence), then if that same number shows on the financial statements, the general ledger account portion of the P&D-RAO for existence has been satisfied. The auditor would then also need to audit separately disclosures about the account in the financial statements (such as disclosure about accounts receivable from related parties) to adequately audit the P&D-RAO for existence.

The classification P&D-RAO does not have a parallel B-RAO (Table 13-5). However, recall that there is a classification transaction-related control objective. If controls are adequate to ensure accurate classification, then the auditor can rely upon those controls. Otherwise, the auditor will need to substantively test that classification is correct in the financial statements.

There is neither a B-RAO nor a transaction-related audit objective parallel to the understandability P&D-RAO. This means that the auditor will need to separately audit the information disclosed in the financial statements to assess whether it is understandable.

Tests of details of balances for all cycles emphasize balance sheet accounts, but income statement accounts are included because they are verified more as a byproduct of the balance sheet tests. For example, if the auditor confirms account receivable balances and finds overstatements due to mistakes in billing customers, there are overstatements of both accounts receivable and sales.

Confirmation of accounts receivable is the most important test of details of accounts receivable. The discussion of potential tests of details of balances for accounts receivable that follows assumes that the auditor has completed an evidence planning spreadsheet similar to the one in Figure 13-8 and has decided planned detection risk for tests of details for each B-RAO and each P&DB-RAO. The audit procedures selected and their sample size will depend heavily on whether planned evidence for a given objective is low, medium, or high.

Recorded accounts receivable exist (existence)
Confirmation of customers' balances is most important.

- For non-response or inability to confirm, auditors examine (1) supporting documents to verify the shipment of goods and (2) evidence of subsequent cash receipts to determine whether the accounts were collected.

The client has rights to accounts receivable (rights and obligations)

- Determine whether the receivables have been pledged as collateral, assigned to someone else, factored, or sold at discount by inquiring of management and reviewing minutes of Directors' Meetings.
- To verify details, send confirmations to banks, and examine correspondence files.

All valid accounts receivable are included (completeness)

- Compare the customer master file with the file of outstanding transactions and with the general ledger (to verify that all customer balances have been included).

Accounts receivable is valued correctly (valuation)

Valuation (of accounts receivable)—the amount of the outstanding balances in accounts receivable that will ultimately be collected.

- Inspect carefully the non-current accounts on the aged accounts receivable trial balance (see Figure 13-5 for example) to determine which have not been paid subsequent to the balance sheet date.
- Compare size and age of unpaid balances with similar information from previous years to evaluate whether the amount of non-current receivables is increasing or decreasing over time.
- Examine credit files, discuss with the credit manager, and review customer correspondence files as needed. Consider past history to determine the percentage of current accounts that need to be allowed for.
- Conduct substantive analytical review over time (trend analysis) of bad debts to evaluate quality of accounts receivable.
- Verify accuracy of bad debt expense as a residual, checking validity of charges to the bad debt expense if needed.

Accounts receivable balances and details are appropriately recorded and disclosed (allocation and accuracy)

Numerical accuracy of the account balance and details:

Figure 13-5 Aged Accounts Receivable Trial Balance Summary for Hillsburg Hardware Limited

Hillsburg Hardware Limited
Accounts Receivable
Aged Trial Balance
31/12/10

Schedule
Prepared by Client
Approved by

Date
5/1/11

Account Number	Customer	Balance 31/12/10	Aging, Based on Invoice Date				
			0–30 days	31–60 days	61–90 days	91–120 days	over 120 days
101011	Adams Supply Ltd.	73,290	57,966	15,324			
101044	Argonaut, Inc.	1,542	1,542				
101100	Atwater Brothers	85,518	85,518				
101191	Beekman Bearings Corp.	14,176	12,676		1,500		
101270	Brown and Phillips	13,952				13,952	
101301	Christopher Plumbing Ltd.	105,231	104,656	125	150	200	100
109733	Travellers Equipment Ltd.	29,765	29,765				
109742	Underhill Parts and Maintenance	8,963	8,963				
109810	UJW Co. Ltd.	15,832		9,832	6,000		
109907	Zephyr Plastics Corp.	74,300	60,085	14,215			
		20,196,800	10,334,169	5,598,762	2,598,746	1,589,654	75,469

- Same as for existence: Confirmation of accounts selected from the accounts receivable trial balance is the most common test of details of balances for the accuracy of accounts receivable.
- For non-response, or accounts that cannot be circulated, auditors examine supporting documents, in the same way as described for the existence objective.

Accuracy of the total and agreement between sub-ledger and general ledger, including allocation to correct accounts:

- Based on the **aged trial balance** (a listing of the balances in the accounts receivable customer master file at the balance sheet date, see Figure 13-8), whose total should agree with the general ledger account. Reperform addition of the aged accounts receivable trial balance for total column and the columns depicting the aging. If the quantity of accounts is large, it is best to use GAS (generalized audit software) to conduct as many of the tests as practical. By performing the additions, aging, and subtotalling for each customer, the auditor conducts the dual purpose tests of verifying that the programs performing these functions are working correctly as well as quantifying any error. At the same time, samples for confirmation can be selected and unusual transactions identified using the auditor's criteria. For example, balances that exceed their credit limits, or outstanding transactions over a certain size, or extremely old outstanding transactions could be listed. These would be used during tests of the relevant audit objectives.
- Compare the total on the trial balance with the general ledger accounts receivable account.

Trace a sample of individual balances to supporting documents, such as duplicate sales invoices, to verify the customer name, balance, and proper aging. For most large clients, this testing is most effectively completed using generalized audit software. The auditor obtains a copy of both the customer master file and the outstanding accounts receivable transactions.

- *Accuracy cut-off for accounts receivable.* (**Cut-off misstatements** can occur for sales, sales returns and allowances, and cash receipts.)

Aged accounts receivable trial balance—a listing of the balances in the accounts receivable master file at a particular date (such as the balance sheet date), broken down according to the amount of time elapsed between the date of sale and the effective date of the report.

Cut-off misstatements—misstatements that take place as a result of current period transactions being recorded in a subsequent period, or subsequent period transactions being recorded in the current period.

- Update planning for cutoff: first, decide on the appropriate criteria for cutoff; second, evaluate whether the client has established adequate procedures to ensure a reasonable cutoff; and third, test whether a reasonable cutoff was obtained.
- Sales cutoff. When the client's internal controls are adequate, the cutoff can usually be verified by obtaining the shipping document number for the last shipment made at the end of the period and comparing this number with current and subsequent period recorded sales, to verify that shipments were invoiced in the correct accounting period.
- Sales returns and allowances cutoff. For most companies, sales returns and allowances are recorded in the accounting period in which they occur, under the assumption of approximately equal, offsetting errors at the beginning and end of each accounting period. This is acceptable as long as the amounts are not significant. Examine supporting documentation for a sample of sales returns and allowances recorded during several weeks subsequent to the closing date to determine the date of the original sale. If the amounts recorded in the subsequent period are significantly different from unrecorded returns and allowances at the beginning of the period under audit, an adjustment must be considered. If internal controls for recording sales returns and allowances are evaluated as ineffective, a larger sample is needed to verify cutoff. The auditor tests for a cash receipts cutoff misstatement (frequently referred to as "holding the cash receipts open") by tracing recorded cash receipts to subsequent period bank deposits on the bank statement. If there is a delay of several days, this could indicate a cutoff misstatement.
- Evaluate accounts receivable confirmation responses for **timing differences** that could indicate cutoff errors.

Timing difference (in an accounts receivable confirmation)—a reported difference in a confirmation from a debtor that is determined to be a timing difference between the client's and debtor's records and therefore not a misstatement.

ACCOUNTS RECEIVABLE ARE PROPERLY CLASSIFIED

- Evaluate the classification of accounts receivable by reviewing the aged trial balance for material receivables from affiliates, officers, directors, or other related parties.
- If notes receivable or accounts that should not be classified as a current asset are included with the regular accounts, request that they be segregated.
- If the credit balances in accounts receivable are significant, request reclassification as accounts payable.

ACCOUNTS RECEIVABLE PRESENTATION AND DISCLOSURES ARE FAIRLY STATED AND UNDERSTANDABLE In addition to testing for the proper statement of the dollar amount in the general ledger, the auditor must also determine that information about the sales and collection cycle (such as revenue and accounts receivable) is fairly presented and disclosed in the financial statements. The auditor must decide whether the client has properly combined amounts and disclosed related-party information in the statements. Section 3840.51 for ASPE (Accounting Standards for Private Enterprises), Section 4460.07 for ASNPO (Accounting Standards for Not-for-Profit Organizations) and IAS 24.18-19 for IFRS (International Financial Reporting Standards) require the same types of information to be disclosed: describe the relationships to the related parties, the transactions (including those where no amounts were exchanged), the amount recognized in the financial statements and how it was measured, and any terms associated with loans, contractual obligations, commitments, or contingent liabilities. This information is to be separately disclosed and not commingled with other transactions. IAS 24.17 also requires disclosure of key management salaries and benefits. Even small amounts (below the threshold of materiality) are to be disclosed.

- Evaluate the adequacy of the footnotes: required footnote disclosure includes information about the pledging, discounting, factoring, assignment of accounts receivable, and amounts due from related parties.

- Determine that trade accounts receivable is segregated from related-party accounts receivable, and that different types of material transactions are clearly listed as separate line items to facilitate the classification and understandability objectives.
- Read management's discussion and analysis (MD&A) to determine whether there are any inconsistencies with the financial statements or other information that the auditor has collected in the course of the audit.

External Confirmation of Accounts Receivable

One of the most important audit procedures is the external confirmation of accounts receivable. As explained in Section 505.6 and in Chapter 8, external confirmations are a direct written response to the auditor, although the auditor could obtain it electronically. CAS 505 explains that an external confirmation uses "direct written response," which can be in multiple forms: paper or electronic. Auditing in Action 13-1 illustrates that electronic confirmations sent by electronic mail or other service providers are being used to provide faster response or improve response rates. Confirmation is used to satisfy the existence, accuracy, and allocation (cutoff aspect) audit objectives.

The use of external confirmations is not required. However, if the auditor did not confirm receivables, he or she would gain the required assurance by other means such as review of subsequent payments or examination of documentation supporting the receivable balance. The application and explanatory material of CAS 505 points out that confirmations may be more relevant to certain assertions (such as existence), and leaves the use of confirmations up to the auditor. Generally, the auditor will send confirmations unless the following are true:

auditing in action 13-1
Better and Faster Confirmations?

It is a tight deadline, and the audit is supposed to be completed within two weeks of the year end. The auditors planned their work well and did substantial control testing prior to the year end, as well as sending confirmations as of the end of November rather than the end of December. Yet some confirmations are best done at the end of the year, due to the risks involved.

Fortunately, the client's banks can now confirm electronically. Also, the client uses online banking, so audit staff were able to observe the client's bank balances as of December 31 by being present and asking the client to log in to all of its accounts and print off details.

Other techniques included having the client telephone customers ahead of time, letting them know that a confirmation request was coming and asking for their cooperation. Auditors obtained email addresses of major customers from the client, and emailed key confirmations as attachments ahead of time, giving the customers the option of printing off and faxing the signed confirmations. In all cases, supporting details of the outstanding invoices were provided, making it easier for the customers to respond to the confirmation request.

The client did not want one major customer confirmed, and the auditors did extensive alternative procedures for this client, as required by current standards, including running an online credit check on the customer to determine its existence and financial stability.

Key to all of these techniques is obtaining high-quality evidence that supports the information in the financial statements. Confirmation fraud does occur (where the client colludes with the customer or the confirmation is sent to a client-controlled address), so the auditor must be aware of potential management bias in overstating revenue (and accounts receivable) when using confirmation.

Sources: 1. Fox, Brian C., "Audit confirmation article falls short," *Journal of Accountancy*, June 2008, **www.journalofaccountancy.com/Issues/2008/Jun/AuditConfirmationArticleFallsShort**, Accessed: May 8, 2012. 2. McConnell, Donald. K. and Charles H. Schweiger, "Better Evidence Gathering," *Journal of Accountancy*, April 2008, **www.journalofaccountancy.com/Issues/2008/Apr/BetterEvidenceGathering**, Accessed: February 19, 2009.

- Accounts receivable are immaterial. This is common for certain companies such as retail stores with primarily cash or credit card sales.
- The auditor considers confirmations ineffective evidence because response rates will likely be inadequate or unreliable. In certain industries, such as hospitals, response rates to confirmations are very low.
- The combined level of inherent risk and control risk is low, and other substantive evidence can be accumulated to provide sufficient evidence. If a client has effective internal controls and low inherent risk for the sales and collection cycle, the auditor should be able to satisfy the evidence requirements by tests of controls, substantive tests of transactions, and analytical procedures.

Although the remaining sections in this chapter refer specifically to the confirmation of accounts receivable from customers, the concepts apply equally to other receivables such as notes receivable, amounts due from officers, and employee advances.

CAS **ASSUMPTIONS UNDERLYING CONFIRMATIONS** An auditor makes two assumptions when accepting an external confirmation from a third party as evidence. The first is that the person returning the confirmation is independent of the company and thus will provide an unbiased response. If this assumption is invalid, as would be the case if the confirmation of a fraudulent accounts receivable were sent to a company owned by an associate of the person committing the fraud, the value of the returned confirmation becomes zero. The second assumption is that the person returning the confirmation has knowledge of the account and the intent of the confirmation and has carefully checked the balance to his or her books and records to ensure that the confirmation is in agreement. However, this second assumption may also not always be valid. Research has shown that some people return confirmations without really checking the balance; such a confirmation would have no value. CAS 505 requires the auditor who has any doubts about the quality of the confirmation (due to the skills of the respondent or due to his or her lack of independence) to undertake additional audit procedures.

In performing confirmation procedures, the auditor must decide the type of confirmation to use, timing of the procedures, sample size, and individual items to select.

Confirmation Decisions

Type of confirmation Two common types of confirmations are used for confirming accounts receivable: positive and negative. A **positive confirmation** is a communication addressed to the debtor requesting him or her to confirm directly with the auditor whether the balance as stated on the confirmation request is correct or incorrect. Figure 13-6 illustrates a positive confirmation in the audit of Island Hardware Ltd. A variation of the first type of confirmation includes a listing of outstanding invoices making up the balance or a copy of the client customer statement attached by the auditor to the confirmation request. The listing of invoices is useful when the debtor uses a voucher system for accounts payable, and attaching the statement makes it easier for the debtor to respond. The auditor could also request confirmation of terms of sale to verify that title to the goods has passed to help identify potential consignment sales.

A second type of positive confirmation, often called a **blank confirmation form**, does not state the amount on the confirmation but requests the recipient to fill in the balance or furnish other information. Because blank forms require the recipient to determine the information requested before signing and returning the confirmation, they are considered more reliable than confirmations that include the information. Research shows, however, that response rates are usually lower for blank confirmation forms. These forms are preferred for accounts payable confirmations when the auditor is searching for understatement of accounts payable.

A **negative confirmation** is also addressed to the debtor but requests a response only when the debtor disagrees with the stated amount. Figure 13-7 illustrates a negative

Positive (accounts receivable) confirmation—a letter, addressed to the debtor, requesting that the recipient indicate directly on the letter whether the stated account balance is correct or incorrect and, if incorrect, by what amount.

Blank confirmation form—a letter, addressed to the debtor, requesting the recipient to fill in the amount of the accounts receivable balance; considered a positive confirmation.

Negative confirmation—a letter, addressed to the debtor, requesting a response only if the recipient disagrees with the amount of the stated account balance.

Figure 13-6   Example Positive Confirmation

Cockburn, Pedlar & Co.

Chartered Accountants
Cabot Bldg.
P.O. Box 123
3 King Street North
St. John's, Newfoundland
A1C 3R5

Garner Hardware
80 Main Street
Cornerbrook, Newfoundland
A2H 1C8

August 15, 2012

To Whom It May Concern:

Re: Island Hardware Ltd.
   In connection with our audit of the financial statements of the above company, we would appreciate receiving from you confirmation of your account. The company's records show an amount receivable from you of $175.00 on June 30, 2012.
   Do you agree with this amount? If you do, please sign this letter in the space below. However, if you do not, please note at the foot of this letter or on the reverse side the details of any differences.
   Please return this letter directly to us in the envelope enclosed for your convenience.

Sincerely,

Cockburn, Pedlar & Co.

Cockburn, Pedlar & Co.

Per:

Please provide Cockburn, Pedlar & Co. with this information.

J. Doe

_____

J. Doe, Accountant, Island Hardware Ltd.

The above amount, owed by me (us) at the date mentioned.

_____

confirmation in the audit of Island Hardware Ltd. It is a gummed label and would be attached to a customer's monthly statement. Often, the client can print the auditor's negative confirmation request directly onto the customer statements.

A positive confirmation is more reliable evidence because the auditor can perform follow-up procedures if a response is not received from the debtor. With a negative confirmation, failure to reply cannot be regarded as a correct response since the debtor may have ignored the confirmation request. This explains why CAS 505 states that negative confirmation should be used only when risks of material misstatement are low and when the following are true:

- The items to be confirmed are homogeneous (i.e., similar in nature) and comprise small account balances.
- No or few exceptions are likely.
- There is an expectation that the negative confirmations will be read and considered.

Offsetting the reliability disadvantage, negative confirmations are less expensive to send than positive confirmations, and thus more can be distributed for the same total cost. Negative confirmations cost less because there are no second requests and no follow-up of non-responses.

| Figure 13-7 | Example Negative Confirmation |

AUTIOR'S ACCOUNT CONFIRMATION

Please examine this statement carefully. If it does NOT agree with your records, please report any exceptions directly to our auditors

> Cockburn, Pedlar & Co.
> Cabot Bldg.
> P.O. Box 123
> 3 King Street North
> St. John's, Newfoundland
> A1C 3R5

who are making an examination of our financial statements. A stamped, addressed envelope is enclosed for your convenience in replying.

Do not send your remittance to our auditors.

Positive confirmations are more effective when the following exist:

- Individual balances of relatively large amounts.
- Few debtors or account balances.
- No suspicions or evidence of fraud or serious error.

Typically, when negative confirmations are used, the auditor puts considerable emphasis on the effectiveness of internal control as evidence of the fairness of accounts receivable and assumes the large majority of the recipients will provide a conscientious reading and response to the confirmation request. Negative confirmations are often used for audits of municipalities, retail stores, banks, and other industries in which the receivables are due from the general public. In these cases, more weight is placed on tests of controls than on confirmations.

The primary factors affecting the confirmation decision are the materiality of total accounts receivable, the number and size of individual accounts, control risk, inherent risk, the effectiveness of confirmations as audit evidence, and the availability of other audit evidence.

Timing The most reliable evidence from confirmations is obtained when they are sent as close to the balance sheet date as possible, as opposed to confirming the accounts several months before year end. This permits the auditor to test directly the accounts receivable balance on the financial statements without making any inferences about the transactions taking place between the confirmation date and the balance sheet date. However, as a means of completing the audit on a timely basis, it is frequently convenient to confirm the accounts at an interim date. This works well if internal controls are adequate and can provide reasonable assurance that sales, cash receipts, and other credits are properly recorded between the date of the confirmation and the end of the accounting period. Other factors the auditor considers in making the decision are the materiality of accounts receivable and the auditor's exposure to lawsuits because of the possibility of client bankruptcy and similar risks as measured by the auditor's evaluation of client business risk.

If the decision is made to confirm accounts receivable prior to year end, it will be necessary to test the transactions occurring between the confirmation date and the balance sheet date. The nature of testing depends upon the length of time between the confirmation date and the year end and the quality of internal controls. Testing could include examining such internal documents as duplicate sales invoices, shipping documents, and evidence of cash receipts, in addition to performing internal control testing, or analytical procedures of the intervening period.

Sample size The main considerations affecting the number of confirmations to send are as follows:

- Performance materiality.
- Inherent risk and risk of material misstatement (relative size of total accounts receivable, number of accounts, prior-year results, and expected misstatements).
- Assessed control risk.
- Achieved detection risk from other substantive tests (extent and results of analytical procedures as substantive tests and other tests of details).
- Type of confirmation (negatives normally require a larger sample size).

These factors are discussed further for Hillsburg Hardware in the next section.

Selection of the items for testing Some type of stratification is desirable with most confirmations. A typical approach to stratification is to consider both the size of the outstanding balance and the length of time an account has been outstanding as a basis for selecting the balances for confirmation. In most audits, the emphasis should be on confirming larger and older balances, since these are most likely to include a significant misstatement. However, it is also important to sample some items from every material stratum of the population. In many cases, the auditor selects all accounts above a certain dollar amount and selects a statistical sample from the remainder.

CAS **Refusal to permit confirmation** Management may refuse the auditor permission to send certain confirmations, perhaps because there is a dispute about the account. In such cases, CAS 505 requires the auditor to corroborate management's statements and to conduct alternative audit procedures (which would be similar to procedures conducted for non-responses, discussed below). For example, if an account is under dispute, the auditor would examine correspondence with the client and consider whether the account is still collectable. The auditor needs to consider whether management's reasons for not confirming the account are reasonable and how this fits in to other assessed risks.

MAINTAINING CONTROL After the items for confirmation have been selected, the auditor must maintain control of the confirmations until they are returned from the debtor. If the client's assistance is obtained in preparing the confirmations, enclosing them in envelopes, or putting stamps on the envelopes, close supervision by the auditor is required. The public accounting firm's return address must be included on all envelopes to make sure that undelivered mail is received by the public accounting firm. Similarly, self-addressed return envelopes accompanying the confirmations must be addressed for delivery to the public accounting firm's office. It is even important to mail the confirmations outside the client's office. All these steps are necessary to ensure independent communication between the auditor and the customer.

FOLLOW-UP ON NON-RESPONSES Non-responses to positive confirmations do not provide audit evidence. Similarly, for negative confirmations, the auditor cannot conclude that the recipient received the confirmation request and verified the information requested. Negative confirmations do, however, provide some evidence of the existence assertion. For example, if the address does not exist, the envelope will be returned to the auditor's offices.

It is common when the auditor does not receive a response to a positive confirmation request to send a second and even a third request for confirmation. Even with these efforts, some debtors will not return the confirmation. The auditor can then (1) perform alternative procedures or (2) treat the non-response as an error to be projected from the sample to the population in order to assess its materiality. The objective of the following **alternative procedures** is to determine by a means other than confirmation whether the non-confirmed account existed and was properly stated at the confirmation date.

Subsequent cash receipts Evidence of the receipt of cash subsequent to the confirmation date includes remittance advices, entries in the cash receipts records, or perhaps even subsequent credits in the supporting records. On the one hand, the examination of evidence of subsequent cash receipts is a highly useful alternative procedure because it is reasonable to assume that a customer would not make a payment unless it were for an existing receivable. On the other hand, the fact of payment does not establish whether there was an obligation on the date of the confirmation, since the payment could pertain to sales after the confirmation date. This is why care should be taken to specifically match each unpaid sales transaction with evidence of its payment as a test for disputes or disagreements over individual outstanding invoices as well as for matching to the correct period.

Duplicate sales invoices These are useful in verifying the actual issuance of a sales invoice and the actual date of the billing.

Shipping documents These are important in establishing whether the shipment was actually made and as a test of cutoff (allocation assertion).

Correspondence with the client Usually, the auditor does not need to review correspondence as a part of alternative procedures, but correspondence can be used to disclose disputed and questionable receivables not uncovered by other means.

The extent and nature of the alternative procedures depend primarily upon the materiality of the non-responses, the types of misstatements discovered in the confirmed responses, the subsequent cash receipts from the non-responses, and the auditor's conclusions about internal control. It is normally desirable to account for all unconfirmed balances with alternative procedures even if the amounts are small, as a means of properly generalizing from the sample to the population.

ANALYSIS OF DIFFERENCES When the confirmation requests are returned by the customer, it is necessary to determine the reason for any reported differences. In many cases, they are caused by timing differences between the client's and the customer's records. It is important to distinguish between these and the exceptions, which represent misstatements of the accounts receivable balance. The most commonly reported types of differences in confirmations follow.

Alternative procedure (for confirmations)—the follow-up of a positive confirmation not returned by the debtor with the use of documentation evidence to determine whether the recorded receivable exists and is collectable.

Payment has already been made Reported differences typically arise when the customer has made a payment prior to the confirmation date, but the client has not received the payment in time for recording before the confirmation date. Such instances should be carefully investigated to determine the possibility of a cash receipts cut-off misstatement, lapping, or a theft of cash.

Goods have not been received These differences may result because the client records the sale at the date of shipment and the customer records the purchase when the goods are received. The time the goods are in transit is frequently the cause of differences reported on confirmations. These should be investigated to determine the possibility of the customer not receiving the goods at all or the existence of a cut-off misstatement on the client's records.

The goods have been returned The client's failure to record a credit memo could result from timing differences or the improper recording of sales returns and allowances. Like other differences, these must be investigated.

Clerical errors and disputed amounts Reported differences in a client's records can occur when the customer states that there is an error in the price charged for the goods, the goods are damaged, the proper quantity of goods was not received, or other problems. These differences must be investigated to determine whether the client is in error and what the amount of the error is.

In most instances, the auditor asks the client to reconcile the difference and asks the client to communicate with the customer to resolve any audit disagreements. The auditor must carefully verify the client's conclusions on each significant difference.

DRAWING CONCLUSIONS When all differences have been resolved, including those discovered in performing alternative procedures, it is important to re-evaluate internal control. Each client misstatement must be analyzed to determine whether it was consistent or inconsistent with the original assessed level of control risk. If there is a significant number of misstatements that are inconsistent with the assessment of control risk, then it is necessary to revise the assessment and consider the effect of the revision on the audit.

It is also necessary to generalize from the sample to the entire population of accounts receivable. Even though the sum of the misstatements in the sample may not significantly affect the financial statements, the auditor must consider whether the population is likely to be materially misstated. This conclusion can be reached by using statistical sampling techniques or a non-statistical basis.

Auditing Hillsburg Hardware Accounts Receivable

Case Illustration—Hillsburg Hardware Limited

The Hillsburg Hardware Limited case illustration used in Chapter 12 continues here to include the determination of the tests of details of balances audit procedures in the sales and collection cycle. Recall that the risk of material misstatement in sales and revenue recognition were considered to be low.

Table 13-6 includes selected comparative trial balance information for the sales and collection cycle for Hillsburg Hardware Limited. Some of that information is used to illustrate several analytical procedures in Table 13-7. None of the analytical procedures indicated potential misstatements except the ratio of the allowance of uncollectable accounts to accounts receivable. The explanation at the bottom of Table 13-7 comments on the potential error.

Fran Moore prepared the evidence planning spreadsheet in Figure 13-8 as an aid to decide the extent of planned tests of details of balances. The source of each of the rows is as follows:

Table 13-6

Selected Comparative Information for Hillsburg Hardware Limited—Sales and Collection Cycle

	Dollar Amounts (in thousands)		
	31-12-11	31-12-10	31-12-09
Gross sales	$144,328	$132,161	$123,438
Sales returns and allowances	1,242	935	753
Gross profit	39,845	36,350	33,961
Accounts receivable	20,197	17,521	13,852
Allowance for uncollectable accounts	1,240	1,311	1,283
Accounts receivable (net)	18,957	16,210	12,569
Bad-debt expense	3,323	2,496	2,796
Total current assets	51,027	49,895	49,157
Net earnings before taxes and extraordinary items	6,401	4,659	3,351
Number of accounts receivable	415	385	372
Number of accounts receivable with balances over $150,000	19	17	16

- *Performance materiality.* The preliminary judgment about materiality was set at $496,000, with performance materiality for the audit and accounts receivable set at $441,000.
- *Assessed audit risk.* Fran assessed audit risk as high (0.05) because of the good financial condition of the company, its financial stability, and the relatively few users of the financial statements. The company has a large working capital line of credit.
- *Inherent risk.* Fran assessed inherent risk as low for all objectives except valuation. In past years, there have been audit adjustments to the allowance for uncollectable accounts because it was found to be understated. Given the decrease in credit availability overall in the financial system, there could be increased pressure on the collectability of accounts receivable this year.
- *Control risk.* Assessed control risk for sales and collections is taken from the assessment of control risk matrix for sales and cash receipts, modified by the results of the tests of controls. The control risk matrix is shown in Figures 13-7 and 13-8. The results of the tests of controls in Chapter 12 were consistent with the preliminary

Table 13-7

Analytical Procedures for Planning for Hillsburg Hardware Limited—Sales and Collection Cycle

	31-12-11	31-12-10	31-12-09
Gross profit	27.8%	27.7%	27.7%
Sales returns and allowances/gross sales	0.9%	0.7%	0.6%
Bad-debt expense/net sales	2.3%	1.9%	2.3%
Allowance for uncollectable accounts/accounts receivable	6.1%	7.5%	9.3%
Number of days receivables outstanding	48.1	43.6	39.6
Net accounts receivable/total current assets	37.2%	32.5%	25.6%

Note: Allowance as a percentage of accounts receivable has declined from 7.5 percent to 6.1 percent. Number of days receivable outstanding and economic conditions do not justify this change. Potential misstatement is approximately $282,758 ($20,197,000 × [0.075 × 0.061] = Total accounts receivable times the percentage decline).

Figure 13-8

Evidence Planning Spreadsheet to Determine Tests of Details of Balances for Hillsburg Hardware Limited—Accounts Receivable

	Existence (or Occurrence) (B, PD)	Rights and Obligations (B, PD)	Completeness (B, PD)	Valuation (B, PD)	Accuracy or Allocation (B, PD)	Classification (PD)	Understand-ability (PD)
Audit risk	High	High	High	High	High	High	High
Inherent risk	Low	Low	Low	Medium	Low	Low	Low
Control risk – Sales	Medium	Not applicable	Low	High	Low	Low	Not applicable
Control risk – Cash receipts	High	Not applicable	Low	Not applicable	Low	Low	Not applicable
Control risk – Additional controls	None	Low	None	None	None	None	Low
Analytical procedures as substantive tests	Good results	Not applicable	Good results	Unaccept-able results	Good results	Good results	Not applicable
Planned detection risk for tests of details of balances	Medium	High	High	Low	High	High	High
Planned audit evidence for tests of details of balances	Medium	Low	Low	High	Low	Low	Low

Performance Materiality $441,000

Note: B = Balance-related audit objectives, PD = Presentation and disclosure-related audit objectives.

assessments of control, except for the valuation objective. The initial assessment was low, but tests of controls results changed the assessment to high.

- *Analytical procedures.* Fran chose to use analytical procedures for planning to obtain medium levels of assurance from analytical procedures, as described in Table 13-7. This resulted in the detection of a potential material misstatement due to a lower bad debt allowance than expected, and the need to do a high level of tests of details for the valuation assertion.
- *Planned detection risk and planned audit evidence.* These two rows are decided for each objective based on the conclusions in the other rows.

Table 13-8 shows the tests of details audit program for accounts receivable and for the allowance for uncollectable accounts by audit objective (for both B-RAO and P&D-RAO combined, since it is typical to do these tests together). The audit program reflects the conclusions for planned audit evidence on the planning spreadsheet in Figure 13-8. Table 13-9 shows the audit program in a performance format. The audit procedures are identical to those in Table 13-8 except for procedure 2, which is an analytical procedure. The numbers in parentheses in Table 13-8 are a cross-reference between the two tables.

Using Monetary Unit Sampling to Select and Evaluate Confirmations

To illustrate the sampling for tests of details described in Chapter 11, monetary unit sampling is now conducted using accounts receivable data. Since Hillsburg Hardware has numerous accounts receivable, only portions of the population will be shown during this illustration.

Table 13-8

Balance-Related and Presentation and Disclosure-Related Audit Objectives and Audit Program for Hillsburg Hardware Limited—Sales and Collection Cycle (Design Format)

Balance-Related Audit Objective	Audit Procedure
The accounts receivable on the aged trial balance exist (existence and allocation).	Confirm accounts receivable using positive confirmations. Confirm all amounts over $150,000 and a statistical sample of the remainder. (7) Perform alternative procedures for all confirmations not returned on the first or second request. (8) Use generalized audit software (GAS) to provide reports of the following: • All customers with balances exceeding their credit limit. (1.3) • All customers with discount terms exceeding 25 percent. (1.4) • Debit and credit totals by customer. (1.5) • Customers with balances over $150,000. (1.6) • A dollar-unit sample of the remainder. (1.6) Foot open item file and customer master file and agree to general ledger. (1.1, 1.2)
The client has rights to the accounts receivable on the trial balance (rights and obligations and understandability).	Inspect the minutes of the board of directors' meetings for any indication of pledged or factored accounts receivable. (5) Inquire of management whether any receivables are pledged or factored. (5) Inspect financial statements including notes to determine that information about accounts receivable has been accurately and clearly disclosed. (13)
Existing accounts receivable are included in the aged trial balance (completeness).	Agree details of customers selected using GAS to the aged accounts receivable trial balance listing. (6)
Accounts receivable is stated at realizable value (valuation).	Use GAS to reperform aging for the aged accounts receivable trial balance. (1.7) Agree totals by aging category to the trial balance listing. (1.7, 1.8) Discuss with the credit manager the likelihood of collecting older accounts. (9) Inspect subsequent cash receipts and the credit file on all accounts over 90 days, and evaluate whether the receivables are collectable. (9) Evaluate whether the allowance is adequate after performing other audit procedures relating to collectability of receivables. (10)
Transactions in the sales and collection cycle are recorded in the proper period (allocation).	Select the last 40 sales transactions from the current year's sales journal and the first 40 from the subsequent year's, and trace each to the related shipping documents, checking for the date of actual shipment and the correct recording. (11) Inspect large sales returns and allowances after the balance sheet date to determine whether any should be included in the current period. (12)
Accounts receivable on the aged trial balance are properly classified (classification).	Inspect the receivables listed on the aged trial balance for notes and related-party receivables. (3) Inquire of management whether there are any related-party notes or long-term receivables included in the trial balance. (4)

Notes: The procedures are summarized in a performance format in Table 13-9. The number in parentheses after the procedure refers to Table 13-9 .

The steps followed are based on the 14 steps in planning, selecting, and evaluating a sample, as shown in Chapter 11.

Step 1. Objectives of the audit test When auditors sample for tests of details of balances, the objective is to determine whether the account balance being audited is fairly stated. The audit objective here is to determine the amount of monetary error associated with the existence, accuracy, and cut-off of accounts receivable. This will be accomplished by sending and evaluating confirmations of the accounts receivable balance as of December 31.

Step 2. Deciding if audit sampling applies Sampling can be used to select the smaller items to be confirmed, since the auditor has decided that all amounts greater than $150,000 will be confirmed (a census test for the strata of items greater than $150,000).

Table 13-9

Tests of Details of Balances Audit Program for Hillsburg Hardware Limited—Sales and Collection Cycle (Performance Format)

1. Obtain a copy of the customer master file and the accounts receivable open item transaction file as of December 31, and perform the following:

   1.1 Foot both the customer master file and the accounts receivable open item file.

   1.2 Agree the totals of the two files to each other and to the general ledger account balance.

   1.3 List all customers with balances exceeding their credit limit.

   1.4 List all customers with discount terms exceeding 25 percent.

   1.5 Provide a report that shows total debits and total credits of open items by customer.

   1.6 List customer and transaction details for all customers exceeding $150,000 and a dollar-unit sample of customers with balances below $150,000.

   1.7 Reperform the aging of the open items to derive the aged accounts receivable trial balance by customer.

   1.8 Agree the totals by aging category to the client-prepared aged accounts receivable trial balance.

2. Calculate analytical procedures indicated in carry-forward working papers (not included), and follow up any significant changes from prior years.

3. Inspect the receivables listed on the aged trial balance for notes and related-party receivables.

4. Inquire of management whether there are any related-party notes or long-term receivables included in the trial balance.

5. Inspect the minutes of the board of directors' meetings, and inquire of management to determine whether any receivables are pledged or factored.

6. Agree details of customers selected using GAS to the aged accounts receivable trial balance listing.

7. Confirm accounts receivable using positive confirmations. Confirm all amounts over $150,000 and those selected in step 1.6.

8. Perform alternative procedures for all confirmations not returned on the first or second request.

9. Discuss with the credit manager the likelihood of collecting older accounts. Inspect subsequent cash receipts and the credit file on all larger accounts over 90 days, and evaluate whether the receivables are collectable.

10. Evaluate whether the allowance is adequate after performing other audit procedures relating to collectability of receivables.

11. Select the last 40 sales transactions from the current year's sales journal and the first 40 from the subsequent year's, and trace each to the related shipping documents, checking for the date of actual shipment and the correct recording.

12. Inspect large sales returns and allowances after the balance sheet date to determine whether any should be included in the current period.

13. Inspect financial statements, including notes to determine that information about accounts receivable has been accurately and clearly disclosed.

Step 3. Define the error conditions Any monetary error between the amount recorded in the customer master file or the open item invoice amount and the confirmed amount is considered to be an error condition.

OBJECTIVES, DECIDING IF SAMPLING APPLIES, POPULATION, AND SAMPLING UNIT

Step 4. Define the population Hillsburg Hardware has total accounts receivable outstanding of $20,196,800. Since the sampling unit is defined as an individual dollar, the population size is equal to the total outstanding accounts receivable. However, the population is being divided into two strata. High dollar amounts over $150,000 are all being confirmed. A sample will thus be selected from the remainder.

The population for each stratum consists of the total of uncollected sales invoice amounts in that dollar range.

Step 5. Objectives, deciding if sampling applies, population, and sampling unit The sampling unit is defined as an individual dollar selected by the MUS program, with a random start. For each dollar selected, the total balance for that customer will be confirmed.

Step 6. Specify materiality For this example, tolerable misstatement for both overstatements and understatements is performance materiality of $441,000, the materiality figure for Hillsburg Hardware for total accounts receivable.

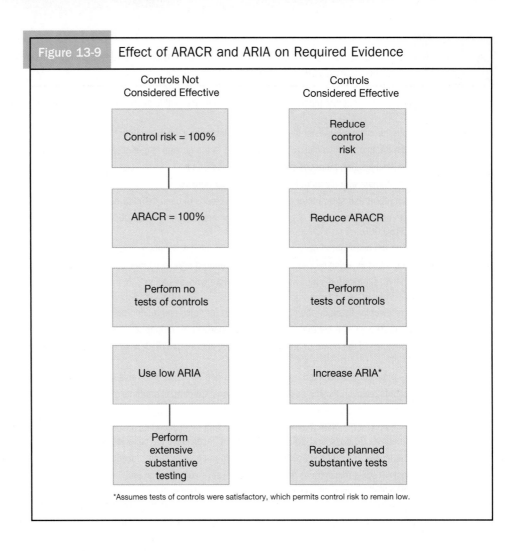

Figure 13-9 Effect of ARACR and ARIA on Required Evidence

Controls Not Considered Effective

Control risk = 100%

ARACR = 100%

Perform no tests of controls

Use low ARIA

Perform extensive substantive testing

Controls Considered Effective

Reduce control risk

Reduce ARACR

Perform tests of controls

Increase ARIA*

Reduce planned substantive tests

*Assumes tests of controls were satisfactory, which permits control risk to remain low.

Step 7. Set acceptable risk of incorrect acceptance Setting ARIA is a matter of professional judgment and is often reached with the aid of the audit risk model. It is set at 5 percent for this example. Figure 13-9 shows how setting ARIA (acceptable risk of incorrect acceptance, the risk of accepting a population when it is in fact unacceptable) is related to the quality of internal controls. The poorer the quality of internal controls (increased control risk), the lower the auditor will set ARIA so that more substantive testing is conducted. If controls are considered effective (the right side of Figure 13-9), then the auditor is relying upon internal controls and less substantive testing is required, so ARIA can be higher. ARIA is set at 5 percent since Figure 13-8 shows that there is high control risk for valuation, medium control risk for existence, and no control testing for additional controls (e.g. for bad debt allowance). Due to the potential misstatement described in the note at the bottom of Table 13-7 and the current economic conditions, the auditors of Hillsburg Hardware have decided that substantive testing levels will need to be high for the audit of accounts receivable.

Step 8. Estimate the misstatements in the population Normally the estimate of the population exception rate for MUS is zero percent, as it is most appropriate to use MUS when no misstatements or only a few are expected. Where misstatements are expected, the total dollar amount of expected population misstatements is estimated and then expressed as a percentage of the population recorded value. In this example, some overstatement is expected based upon the analytical procedures for planning shown in Table 13-7 and based on past experience, so a 0.5-percent expected exception rate is used.

To determine the sample size, the auditor also needs to make assumptions about how much error there will be in items that contain a misstatement. This is termed

Table 13-10	Listing of Assumptions and Facts for Accounts Receivable Sample	
Tolerable misstatement (same for upper and lower)		$441,000
Tolerable misstatement allocated to lower dollar stratum		$300,000
Average percent of misstatement assumption, overstatements		50%
Average percent of misstatement assumption, understatements		100%
ARIA		5%
Accounts receivable–recorded value		$20.2 million
Accounts receivable–amounts less than $150,000		$13-1 million
Estimated misstatement in accounts receivable		0.5%

tainting in *Dollar Unit Sampling: A Practical Guide for Auditors.*[1] Again, there may be a separate assumption for the upper and lower bounds. This is also a matter of professional judgment. Assumptions should be based on the auditor's knowledge of the client and past experience, and if less than 100 percent is used, the assumptions must be clearly defensible. For this example, 50 percent tainting is used for overstatements and 100 percent for understatements. (If a $200 customer balance has a $40 error, then the tainting is 20 percent.)

Assumptions up to Step 8 are listed in Table 13-10.

Step 9. Determine the initial sample size The sample size for the strata of amounts less than $150,000 is calculated as shown in Table 13-11.

Since only one sample is taken for both overstatements and understatements, the larger of the two computed sample sizes would be used, in this case 157 items.

Step 10. Select the sample The sample of items less than $150,000 is being selected using generalized audit software with monetary unit sampling. The software will use the ARACR, TER, and EPER to calculate a dollar interval, and then choose the accounts that correspond to that dollar interval. For example, if the dollar interval is $140,000 (the interval is normally less than performance materiality) and the random start is $6586, then the accounts would be summed until the cumulative total

> Tainting–the average percent of misstatement for population dollars that contain a misstatement (used with MUS sampling).

Table 13-11	Illustration of Sample Size Calculation	
	Upper Bound	Lower Bound
Tolerable misstatement	300,000	300,000
Average percent of error assumption (divide by):	0.50	1.00
equals	600,000	300,000
Recorded population value (divide by):	13,100,000	13,100,000
Allowable percent error bound (TER)	4.6%	2.3%
Estimated population exception rate (EPER)	0.5%	0.5%
Required sample size from the attributes table (Table 12.9) 5% ARACR, 5% and 3% TER, and 0.5% EPER	93	157

Note: The 5% TER comes from rounding the 4.6% up to 5%.

[1] Leslie, Donald A., Albert D. Teitlebaum, and Rodney J. Anderson, *Dollar Unit Sampling: A Practical Guide for Auditors* (Toronto: Copp Clark Pitman, 1979), p. 122–123, 390.

reaches $6,586; this identifies the first account to be selected. When the cumulative total reaches $146,586 ($140,000 + $6,586), the second account to be selected is identified. In this way, all 157 accounts will be selected.

The statistical methods used to evaluate monetary unit samples permit the inclusion of a physical unit in the sample more than once. For example, an item that was $700,000 or larger would be "selected" twice, since it is twice the size of the sample interval. This is handled at Hillsburg Hardware Limited by having the data divided into two strata—the larger amounts of greater than $150,000 are all being selected.

One problem using MUS (monetary unit sampling) selection is that population items with a zero recorded balance have no chance of being selected even though they could contain misstatements. Similarly, small balances that are significantly understated have little chance of being included in the sample. This problem can be overcome by doing specific audit tests for zero- and small-balance items, assuming that they are of concern.

Another problem is the inability to include negative balances, such as credit balances in accounts receivable, in the MUS sample. It is possible to ignore negative balances for MUS selection and test those amounts by some other means. An alternative is to treat them as positive balances (which is readily done with audit software by simply using absolute values) and add them to the total number of monetary units being tested; however, this complicates the evaluation process.

Fran determined from earlier generalized audit software tests that credit amounts were insignificant and decided that no separate audit work would be done on those amounts.

Step 11. Perform the audit procedures The auditor will obtain the customer accounts receivable details (the physical unit) for each selected number, prepare the confirmations, and send the confirmations.

Fran ensured that audit staff on the engagement properly handled the accounts receivable confirmation process. Confirmations were prepared and mailed, second requests were sent, discrepancies were reviewed, and alternative procedures were conducted for those items selected for which no replies were received.

Step 12. Generalize from the Sample to the Population (For the purposes of illustration, we will do the generalization process twice, once without errors, and then again with errors in the results.) First, we will generalize from the sample to the population when no misstatements are found using MUS. Assume that during the audit, no misstatements were uncovered in the sample (which is actually highly unlikely for confirmations). The auditor next wants to determine the maximum amount of overstatement and understatement amounts that could exist in the population and still provide a sample with no misstatements. These are the upper misstatement bound and the lower misstatement bound, respectively. Assuming an ARIA of 5 percent, and using Table 12-10, both the upper and lower bounds are determined by locating the intersection of the sample size (157) and the actual number of misstatements (0) in the same manner as for attribute sampling. The CUER of 2 percent on the table for 150 items represents both the upper and lower bound, expressed as a percentage. (For greater accuracy, we could extrapolate between the 150 and 200 sample size row, but the number is slightly less than 2.0, so by using 2.0 we are being conservative.)

Thus, based on the sample results and the misstatement bounds from the table, the auditor can conclude with a 5-percent sampling risk that no more than 2 percent of the dollar units in the population are misstated. To convert this percent into dollars, the auditor must make an assumption about the average percent of misstatement for population dollars that contain a misstatement. This assumption significantly affects the misstatement bounds. To illustrate the effects of tainting assumptions, we again use two different examples: first Fran's assumptions are shown, that is, a 50-percent misstatement assumption for overstatements and a

100-percent assumption for understatements, and a second assumption is shown with a 100-percent misstatement assumption for overstatements and a 200-percent assumption for understatements.

Assumption 1 with no errors (Fran's) Overstatement amounts equal 50 percent; understatement amounts equal 100 percent; misstatement bounds at a 5-percent ARIA are:

> Upper misstatement bound = population × computer upper (or lower) exception rate × tainting
> Upper misstatement bound = $13,100,000 × 2% × 50% = $131,000
> Lower misstatement bound = $13,100,000 × 2% × 100% = $262,000

The assumption is that, on the average, those population items that are overstated are misstated by half of the full dollar amount of the recorded value. Since the misstatement bound is 2 percent, the dollar value of the misstatement is not likely to exceed $131,000 (2 percent times 50 percent of the total recorded dollar units in the population). If all the amounts are overstated, there is an overstatement of $131,000. If they are all understated, there is an understatement of $262,000, since the assumption is that every understated amount is misstated by an amount equal to the misstatement (100 percent).

The assumption of 50 percent misstatements is very conservative, especially for overstatements. Assume that the actual population exception rate is 2 percent. The following two conditions both have to exist before the $131,000 properly reflects the true overstatement amount:

1. All amounts have to be overstatements. Offsetting amounts would have reduced the amount of the overstatement.
2. All population items misstated have to be 50 percent misstated. There could not, for example, be a misstatement such as a cheque written for $226 that was recorded as $262. This would be only a 13.7 percent misstatement (262 – 226 = 36 overstatement; 36/262 = 13.7 percent).

In the calculation of the misstatement bounds of $131,000 overstatement and $262,000 understatement, the auditor did not calculate a point estimate and precision amount (which is done for judgmental sampling). This is because statistical tables used include both a point estimate and a precision amount to derive the upper exception rate. Even though the point estimate and precision amount are not calculated for MUS, they are implicit in the determination of misstatement bounds and can be determined from the tables. For example, in this illustration, the point estimate of error is zero (the error rate times the population) and the statistical precision is $131,000 for overstatement and $262,000 for understatement.

Assumption 2 with no errors Overstatement amounts equal 100 percent; understatement amounts equal 200 percent; misstatement bounds at a 5-percent ARIA are:

> Upper misstatement bound = population × computer upper (or lower) exception rate × tainting
> Upper misstatement bound = $13,100,000 × 2% × 100% = $262,000
> Lower misstatement bound = $13,100,000 × 2% × 200% = $524,000

The justification for a larger percent for understatements is the potential for a larger misstatement in percentage terms. For example, an accounts receivable recorded at $20 that should have been recorded at $200 is understated by 900 percent [(200 – 20)/20], whereas one that is recorded at $200 that should have been recorded at $20 is overstated by 90 percent [(200 – 20)/200].

Generalizing when misstatements are found This section presents the evaluation method used when there are misstatements in the sample. The same illustration is continued; the only change is the assumption about the misstatements. The sample size remains at 157 and the recorded population value is still $13,100,000, but now five misstatements in the sample are assumed. The misstatements are shown in Table 13-12.

When there are errors in the sample, we need to do the following calculations:

- *Overstatement and understatement amounts are dealt with separately and then combined.* First, initial upper and lower misstatement bounds are calculated separately for overstatement and understatement amounts. Next, a point estimate of overstatements and understatements is calculated. The point estimate of understatements is used to reduce the initial upper misstatement bound, and the point estimate of overstatements is used to reduce the initial lower misstatement bound. The method and rationale for these calculations will be illustrated by using the four overstatements and one understatement amounts in Table 13-12 .

- A *different misstatement assumption and calculation is made for each misstatement using the error limit tables, including the zero misstatements.* When there were no misstatements in the sample, an assumption was required as to the average percent of misstatement for the population items misstated. The misstatement bounds were calculated showing several different assumptions. Now that misstatements have been found, sample information is available to use in determining the misstatement bounds. The misstatement assumption is still required, but it can be modified based on these actual misstatement data.

Where misstatements are found, a 100-percent assumption for all misstatements is not only exceptionally conservative, it is inconsistent with the sample results. A common assumption in practice, and the one followed in this book, is that the actual sample misstatements are representative of the population misstatements. This assumption requires the auditor to calculate the percent that each sample item is misstated as a layer (misstatement ÷ recorded balance) and apply that percent to the population. In that way each layer is added to obtain an estimate of the total misstatement.

The calculation of the percent for each misstatement is shown in the last column in Table 13-12. As will be explained shortly, a misstatement assumption is still needed for the zero misstatement portion of the computed results. For this example, a 50-percent misstatement assumption is used for the zero misstatement portion for overstatements and 100 percent for understatement misstatement bounds. The errors must be sorted in descending order (from largest to smallest) by both overstatements and understatements before doing the misstatement bounds calculation. The last column of Table 13-12 shows the order that the errors will be sorted into.

- *The auditor must deal with layers of the computed upper or lower exception rate from the attribute sampling table* (see Table 12-10) *for the ARIA assumption used.* The reason for doing so is that there is a different misstatement assumption for each misstatement. Layers are calculated by first determining the exception rate from the table for each misstatement and then calculating the projection for each layer. Table 13-13 shows the layers in the attribute sampling table for the example

Table 13-12	Misstatements Found				
Customer No.	Recorded Accounts Receivable Amount	Audited Accounts Receivable Amount	Misstatement	Misstatement ÷ Recorded Amount	Over- or Understate- ment Rank Order
102073	$ 6,200	$ 6,100	$ 100	0.016	3 (Over)
105111	12,910	12,000	910	0.070	2 (Over)
105206	4,322	4,450	(128)	(0.030)	1 (Under)
107642	23,000	22,995	5	0.0002	4 (Over)
109816	8,947	5,947	3,000	0.335	1 (Over)

Table 13-13 — Percent Misstatement Bounds

Number of Misstatements	Upper Precision Limit from Table	Increase in Precision Limit Resulting from Each Misstatement (Layers)
0	0.020	0.020
1	0.031	0.011
2	0.041	0.010
3	0.051	0.010
4	0.060	0.009

at hand. The layers were determined by reading across the table for a sample size of 150 from the 0 through 4 exception columns.

Upper misstatement bound = population × computer upper (or lower) exception rate × tainting

The way we interpret this table and the need for layers is in the context of the above formula. When there were no errors, we assumed that any not-found errors in the whole population had an error rate of 50 percent for overstatements and 100 percent for understatements. So we used 2 percent from the 150 sample. Our actual errors in Table 13-12 were less than 50 percent, so we can no longer assume a 50 percent error rate for all of the errors. We found four errors, so we allocate the 6 percent from the error rate table (sample size row 150 and column 4 errors at 5 percent ARACR) in layers, using the actual percentage error found. The second column of Table 13-14 shows how that 6 percent was allocated, with the note under the table explaining the calculation of the error percentage allocation.

Table 13-14 — Illustration of Calculating Initial Upper and Lower Misstatement Bounds

Number of Misstatements (1)	Upper Precision Limit Portion* (2)	Recorded Value (3)	Misstatement Unit Error Assumption (4)	Bound Portion (Columns 2 × 3 × 4) (5)
Overstatements				
0	0.020	$13,100,000	0.50	$131,000
1	0.011	$13,100,000	0.335	48,274
2	0.010	$13,100,000	0.070	9,170
3	0.010	$13,100,000	0.016	2,096
4	0.009	$13,100,000	0.0002	24
Upper precision limit	0.06			
Initial misstatement bound				$190,564
Understatements				
0	0.020	$13,100,000	1.00	$262,000
1	0.011	$13,100,000	0.03	4,323
Lower precision limit	0.031			
Initial misstatement bound				$266,323

* ARIA of 5 percent. Sample size of 150.
Note: Upper precision Limit portions are calculated as follows (in percentages): Layer 1: 3.1–2.0; Layer 2: 4.1–3.1; Layer 3: 5.1–4.1; Layer 4: 6.0–5.1.

Table 13-15 Illustration of Calculating Adjusted Misstatement Bounds

Number of Misstatements	Unit Misstatement Assumption	Sample Size	Recorded Population	Point Estimate	Bounds
Initial overstatement bound					$190,564
Understatement misstatement					
1	0.030	150	$13,100,000	$ 2,620	(2,620)
Adjusted overstatement bound					$187,944
Initial understatement bound					$266,323
Overstatement misstatements					
1	0.335				
2	0.070				
3	0.016				
4	0.0002				
Sum	0.4212	150	$13,100,000	$36,785	(36,785)
Adjusted understatement bound					$229,538

Notes: 150 is used as sample size for illustrative purposes; Point estimate = Unit misstatement assumption / sample size × recorded population.

- *Misstatement assumptions must be associated with each layer.* The most common method of associating misstatement assumptions with layers is to be conservative by associating the largest dollar misstatement percents with the largest layers. Table 13-14 shows the association. For example, the largest percent misstatement was 0.335 for customer 109816. This misstatement is associated with the layer factor of 0.011 (3.1%–2.0%), the largest layer where misstatements were found. The portion of the upper precision limit related to the zero misstatement layer has a misstatement assumption of 50 percent, which is still conservative. Table 13-14 shows the calculation of misstatement bounds before consideration of offsetting amounts.

  The upper misstatement bound was calculated as if there were no understatement amounts, and the lower misstatement bound was calculated as if there were no overstatement amounts, which is a conservative approach to estimating the upper and lower bounds.

Adjustment for offsetting amounts Most MUS users believe that the approach just discussed is overly conservative when there are offsetting amounts. If an understatement misstatement is found, it is logical and reasonable that the bound for overstatement amounts should be lower than it would be had no understatement amounts been found, and vice versa. The adjustment of bounds for offsetting amounts (Table 13-15) is made as follows: (1) a point estimate of misstatements is made for both understatement and overstatement amounts, and (2) each bound is reduced by the opposite point estimate.

The point estimate for overstatements is calculated by multiplying the average overstatement amount in the dollar units audited by the recorded value. The same approach is used for calculating the point estimate for understatements. In the example, there is one understatement amount of 3 percent or 3 cents per dollar unit in a sample of 150. (We use 150 as the sample size for illustrative purposes since that is the row that we used on the statistical sample tables. It results in a slightly larger point estimate of error than the actual sample size of 157.) The understatement point estimate is therefore $2,620 (0.03/150 × $13,100,000, the average percentage error per item times the population). Similarly, the overstatement point estimate is $36,785 [(0.335 + 0.07 + 0.016 + 0.0002)/150 × $13,100,000].

Table 13-15 on page 440 shows the adjustment of the bounds that follow from this procedure. The initial upper bound of $190,564 is reduced by the estimated most likely understatement error of $2,620 to an adjusted bound of $187,944. The initial lower bound of $266,323 is reduced by the estimated most likely overstatement amount of $36,785 to an adjusted bound of $229,538. Thus, given the methodology and assumptions followed, the auditor concludes that there is a 5-percent risk that accounts receivable is overstated by $187,944 or more, or understated by more than $229,538. It should be noted that if the misstatement assumptions were changed, the misstatement bounds would also change. The method used to adjust the bounds for offsetting amounts is one of several in current use. The method illustrated here is taken from Leslie, Teitlebaum, and Anderson.[2] All the methods in current use are reliable and somewhat conservative.

The seven steps in Table 13-16 summarize the calculation of the adjusted misstatement bounds for monetary unit sampling when there are offsetting amounts. The evaluation process for MUS is complex and is best handled using computer software.

Step 13 Analyze the Misstatements Fran and her staff analyzed the errors described in Table 13-12. The first two overstatement errors were due to accumulated discounts taken by customers that had not been properly removed from the accounts receivable. The understatement was due to a credit note that had accidentally been issued twice, and the large $3,000 difference was due to a change in discount rate. This customer had reached such a high volume of purchases that it was moved to a higher discount level, but Hillsburg staff did not implement the discount on a timely basis. In addition to calculating misstatement bounds, Fran will discuss with Hillsburg staff their management of discounts to ensure that these errors are corrected and to determine how future errors can be prevented. Fran could also have initiated additional substantive procedures to further quantify the extent of the dollar errors associated with discount differences.

Table 13-16	Calculation of Adjustment Misstatement Bounds for MUS with Offsetting Amounts
Steps to Calculate Adjusted Misstatement Bounds	**Calculation for Misstatements in Table 13-12**
1. Determine misstatement for each sample item, keeping overstatements and understatements separate.	Table 13-12 Four overstatements, one understatement
2. Calculate misstatement per dollar unit in each sample item (misstatement/recorded value).	Table 13-12 0.016, 0.07, 0.0002, 0.335
3. Layer misstatements per dollar unit from highest to lowest, including the percent misstatement assumption for sample items not misstated.	Table 13-14 0.5, 0.335, 0.07, 0.016, 0.0002
4. Determine upper precision limit using attribute sampling table, and determine the percent misstatement bound for each misstatement (layer).	Table 13-14 Total of 6 percent for four overstatements; calculate five layers. Total of 3.1 percent for one understatement; calculate two layers.
5. Calculate initial upper and lower misstatement bounds for each layer and total.	Table 13-14 Total of $190,564 and $266,323
6. Calculate point estimate for overstatements and understatements.	Table 13-15 $2,620 for overstatements $36,785 for understatements
7. Calculate adjusted upper and lower misstatement bounds.	$187,944 adjusted overstatement bound $229,538 adjusted understatement bound

[2] Leslie, Teitlebaum, and Anderson, op. cit.

Step 14 Determine the acceptability of the population Whenever a statistical method is used, a decision rule is needed to decide whether the population is acceptable. The decision rule for MUS is as follows:

If both the lower misstatement bound (LMB) and upper misstatement bound (UMB) fall between the understatement and overstatement tolerable misstatement amounts, accept the conclusion that the book value is not misstated by a material amount; otherwise, conclude that the book value may be misstated by a material amount.

Using Table 13-15, if there are no errors in the large amounts that were separately tested (those over $150,000), then the accounts receivable population is acceptable, since both the upper and lower bounds are less than the performance materiality of $441,000. The auditor will need to carry these upper and lower bounds to an unadjusted error summary sheet for overall evaluation together with the results of the audit tests for other cycles and accounts.

Action when a population is rejected When one or both of the error bounds lie outside the tolerable misstatement limits and the population is not considered acceptable, the auditor has several options. In this example, Fran could wait until tests of other audit areas were completed to see if materiality of $441,000 were exceeded for the aggregated misstatements. Alternatively, she could perform expanded tests in other areas, increase the sample size in the expectation that there were no errors in the expanded sample, ask that the account balance be adjusted, or request the client correct the population (which would then have to be reaudited). If the aggregated errors exceed materiality and the client will not adjust the accounts, the auditor will have to consider refusing to give an unqualified audit opinion.

Summary

1. *What is the process for designing tests of details of balances for accounts receivable?* Figure 13-2 provides a context: After setting materiality, assessing control risk, and designing and testing internal control, the auditor designs tests of details for each audit assertion based upon the risk of material misstatement for that assertion.

   What is the relationship between transaction-related, balance-related and presentation and disclosure-related audit objectives for the sales and collection cycle? Figure 13-3 illustrates these relationships.

2. *When and why are analytical review procedures completed as part of the audit of sales and accounts receivable?* Analytical procedures are completed during planning, as part of substantive testing and as part of completing the audit. For the detailed testing, account specific ratios are calculated. Ratios could also be calculated for customers or products to provide more assurance.

   How is the amount of substantive testing related to the audit risk model? The extent of detailed testing is related to the value of planned detection risk. As planned detection risk decreases, the amount of assurance required from tests of detail increases, resulting in the need for more substantive testing.

3. *Describe the accounts receivable audit tests that would be completed for each audit assertion.* Table 13-8 provides examples.

   Why is confirmation one of the most important audit procedures? It is a multipurpose technique that addresses several audit assertions: existence, accuracy, and the cut-off aspect of allocation.

4. *Provide examples of risk assessments and examples of tests of detail.* Section 4 provides a risk assessment for Hillsburg Hardware, and Tables 13-8 and 13-9 list many audit procedures that could be conducted as a result of that risk assessment. For example, generalized audit software is used for parallel simulation—recreation of the aged accounts receivable trial balance totals by customer.

   How is monetary unit sampling (MUS) executed and evaluated? The 14-step audit process described in Chapter 11 is used. Based upon materiality, ARACR, TER, and EPER, software is used to calculate a dollar interval. Then, that dollar interval is used together with a random start to select the sample. After audit tests are completed, software can be used to calculate upper and lower precision limits, or these can be calculated manually using statistical tables.

Review Questions

13-1 ❶ Distinguish between tests of details of balances and tests of controls for the sales and collection cycle. Explain how the tests of controls affect the tests of details.

13-2 ❶ Explain the relationship of each of the following to the sales and collection cycle: flowcharts, assessing control risk, tests of controls, and tests of details of balances.

13-3 ❶ Customers purchasing products through a company's website generally pay for those goods by providing their personal credit card information. Describe how a company's sale of products through its website affects the auditor's tests of accounts receivable in the financial statement audit.

13-4 ❷ List five analytical procedures for the sales and collection cycle. For each test, describe a misstatement that could be identified.

13-5 ❸ Identify the five accounts receivable balance-related audit objectives. For each objective, list one audit procedure.

13-6 ❸ Identify the seven accounts receivable presentation and disclosure-related audit objectives. For each objective, list one audit procedure.

13-7 ❸ Which of the five accounts receivable balance-related audit objectives can be partially satisfied by confirmations with customers?

13-8 ❸ Distinguish between accuracy tests of gross accounts receivable and tests of the realizable value of receivables.

13-9 ❸ Explain why you agree or disagree with the following statement: "In most audits, it is more important to test carefully the cutoff for sales than for cash receipts." Describe how you perform each type of test assuming the existence of prenumbered documents.

13-10 ❸ Evaluate the following statement: "In many audits in which accounts receivable is material, the desire to confirm customer balances is a waste of time and would not be performed by competent auditors if it were not required by auditing standards. When internal controls are excellent and there is a large number of small receiv-

ables from customers who do not recognize the function of confirmation, it is a meaningless procedure. Examples include well-run utilities and department stores. In these situations, tests of controls and substantive tests of transactions are far more effective than confirmations."

13-11 ❸ Distinguish between a positive and a negative confirmation, and state the circumstances in which each should be used. Why do public accounting firms often use a combination of positive and negative confirmations on the same audit?

13-12 ❸ In what circumstances is it acceptable to confirm accounts receivable prior to the balance sheet date?

13-13 ❸ State the most important factors affecting the sample size in confirmations of accounts receivable.

13-14 ❸ In Chapter 11, one of the points brought out was the need to obtain a representative sample of the population. How can this concept be reconciled with the statement in this chapter that the emphasis should be on confirming larger and older balances, since these are most likely to contain misstatements?

13-15 ❸ Define what is meant by "alternative procedures," and explain their purpose. Which alternative procedures are the most reliable? Why?

13-16 ❸ Explain why the analysis of differences is important in the confirmation of accounts receivable even if the misstatements in the sample are not material.

13-17 ❸ State three types of differences that might be observed in the confirmation of accounts receivable that do not constitute misstatements. For each, state an audit procedure that would verify the difference.

13-18 ❹ An auditor is determining the appropriate sample size for testing inventory valuation using MUS. The population has 2,620 items valued at $12,625,000. The tolerable misstatement for both understatements and overstatements is $500,000 at a 10-percent ARIA. No misstatements are expected in the population. Calculate the preliminary sample size using a 100-percent average misstatement assumption.

Discussion Questions and Problems

13-19 ❶❷❸ During his interim audit visit, Charles Ai determined that one of the subsidiary companies of Mega Big Limited had experienced some very serious problems with respect to the credit management and collection of trade accounts receivable. During the first six months of the year, the accounts receivable of this subsidiary had almost doubled, the number of days' sales in accounts receivable had increased from 39 days to 64 days, and bad-debt expense had risen sharply.

REQUIRED

Prepare an outline of the steps that should be taken to investigate the nature and causes of the credit and collection problems. (Do not consider the possibility of fraud.)

13-20 ❶❷❸ Charles is an articling public accounting student working on his first financial statement audit engagement. The client is BBB Appliances Inc. One of his duties was to prepare an aging of the company's accounts receivables.

His audit supervisor explained that the company's receivables have increased from $650,000 last year to $950,000 this year, which in both cases exceeds materiality. These amounts are given as security to the bank for the company's short-term bank loan. Total assets have increased from $4,000,000 to $4,300,000 and total sales have increased from $10,300,000 to $10,900,000 in the year. Charles knows that his firm will be relying on the procedure of positive confirmations to verify valuation, but is wondering why his supervisor has also arranged for a review of the corporate minutes of BBB's board of directors' meetings.

REQUIRED

a. Provide examples of evidence that Charles could obtain related to the accounts receivable and the bank loan from BBB's board of directors' meeting minutes.

b. Using *one* of your examples from part (a), explain how Charles could use that evidence in inspecting the adequacy of BBB's financial statement notes.

c. Using only the information above for BBB [ignore your answers to parts (a) and (b)], provide examples of analytical procedures for planning that Charles could use to conduct risk assessment procedures in the audit of BBB's financial statements. Show your calculations.

(Extract from AU1 CGA - Canada Examinations developed by the Certified General Accountants Association of Canada © 2010 CGA-Canada. Reproduced with permission. All rights reserved.)

13-21 ❶ ❷ ❸ The following are audit procedures in the sales and collection cycle:

1. Examine a sample of shipping documents to determine whether each has a sales invoice number included on it.
2. Examine a sample of non-cash credits in the accounts receivable master file to determine if the accounting supervisor has initialled supporting documents for each, indicating internal verification.
3. Discuss with the sales manager whether any sales allowances have been granted after the balance sheet date that may apply to the current period.
4. Add the columns on the aged trial balance, and compare the total with the general ledger.
5. Observe whether the controller makes an independent comparison of the total in the general ledger with the trial balance of accounts receivable.
6. Compare the date on a sample of shipping documents throughout the year with related duplicate sales invoices and the accounts receivable master file.
7. Examine a sample of customer orders and see if each has a credit authorization.

8. Compare the date on a sample of shipping documents a few days before and after the balance sheet date with related sales journal transactions.
9. Compute the ratio of allowance for uncollectable accounts divided by accounts receivable, and compare with those of previous years.

REQUIRED

a. For each procedure, identify the applicable type of audit evidence.
b. For each procedure, identify which of the following it is:
   (1) Test of control.
   (2) Analytical procedure (state whether it is for planning or as a substantive test).
   (3) Test of details of balances.
c. For those procedures you identified as a test of control, what transaction-related audit objective or objectives are being satisfied?
d. For those procedures you identified as a test of details of balances, what balance-related or presentation and disclosure-related audit objective or objectives are being satisfied?

13-22 ❶ ❸ The following misstatements are sometimes found in the sales and collection account balances:

1. Cash received from collections of accounts receivable in the subsequent period are recorded as current period receipts.
2. The allowance for uncollectable accounts is inadequate due to the client's failure to reflect depressed economic conditions in the allowance.
3. Several accounts receivable are in dispute due to claims of defective merchandise.
4. The pledging of accounts receivable to the bank for a loan is not disclosed in the financial statements.
5. Goods shipped and included in the current period sales were returned in the subsequent period.
6. Long-term interest-bearing notes receivable from affiliated companies are included in accounts receivable.

7. The aged accounts receivable trial balance total does not equal the amount in the general ledger.
8. Several accounts receivable balances in the accounts receivable master file are not included in the aged trial balance report.
9. One accounts receivable customer included in the accounts receivable master file is included in the aged trial balance twice.

REQUIRED

a. For each misstatement, identify the balance-related or presentation and disclosure audit objective to which it pertains.
b. For each misstatement, list an internal control that should prevent it.
c. For each misstatement, list one test of details of balances audit procedure that the auditor can use to detect it.

13-23 ❶ ❸ André Auto Parts Inc. sells new parts for foreign automobiles to auto dealers. Company policy requires that a prenumbered shipping document be issued for each sale. At the time of pickup or shipment, the shipping clerk writes the date on the shipping document. The last shipment made in the fiscal year ended August 31, 2012, was recorded on document 2167. Shipments are billed in the order that the billing clerk receives the shipping documents.

For late August and early September, shipping documents are billed on sales invoices as follows:

Shipping Document No.	Sales Invoice No.
2163	4332
2164	4326
2165	4327
2166	4330
2167	4331
2168	4328
2169	4329
2170	4333
2171	4335
2172	4334

The August and September sales journals include the following information:

Sales Journal—August 2012

Day of Month	Sales Invoice No.	Amount of Sale
30	4326	$ 726.11
30	4329	1,914.30
31	4327	419.83
31	4328	620.22
31	4330	47.74

Sales Journal—September 2012

Day of Month	Sales Invoice No.	Amount of Sale
1	4332	$2,641.31
1	4331	106.39
1	4333	852.06
2	4335	1,250.50
2	4334	646.58

REQUIRED

a. What are the accounting standards for a correct sales cutoff, i.e., recording sales in the correct period?

b. Which sales invoices, if any, are recorded in the wrong accounting period, assuming a periodic inventory? Prepare an adjusting entry to correct the accounts for the year ended August 31, 2012.

c. Assume that the shipping clerk accidentally wrote August 31 on shipping documents 2168 through 2172. Explain how that would affect the correctness of the financial statements. How would you, as an auditor, discover that error?

d. Describe, in general terms, the audit procedures you would follow in making sure the cutoff for sales is accurate at the balance sheet date.

e. Identify internal controls that would reduce the likelihood of cutoff errors. How would you test each control?

13-24 ❷ Johnson Clock Company sells specialty clocks, watches, and other timekeeping devices. Since its inception, the company has sold items through its home office store and at industry and collector trade shows around the country. To meet the demand from collectors around the world, the company began selling items through its website. Recent financial information about Johnson's sales is summarized in the tables on the next page.

REQUIRED

Using the information given, design and perform analytical procedures for the sales and collection cycle at Johnson Clock Company. On the basis of the results of your analytical procedures, describe how the results related to the internet-based sales differ from the home office and trade show sales.

	Year Ended 12/31/12	Year Ended 12/31/11	Year Ended 12/31/10
Sales:			
Home office	$1,279,480	$1,218,552	$1,163,851
Trade show	773,265	739,259	704,391
Internet-based	147,772	122,462	52,884
Sales Returns:			
Home office	$ 25,589	$ 23,152	$ 25,605
Trade show	13,946	13,676	12,679
Internet-based	13,254	11,022	4,760

	Year Ended 12/31/12	Year Ended 12/31/11	Year Ended 12/31/10
Cost of Goods Sold:	$831,662	$816,429	$768,142
Home office	491,023	480,518	454,332
Trade show	81,275	66,129	28,822
Internet-based			
Receivables related to sales from:	$126,195	$123,524	$127,545
Home office	74,149	68,862	67,544
Trade show	3,239	3,020	1,159
Internet-based			
Tolerable misstatement for sales and receivables is $12,000.			

13-25 ❸ You have been assigned to the confirmation of aged accounts receivable for the audit of the Blank Paper Company Ltd. You have tested the trial balance and selected the accounts for confirmation. Before the confirmation requests are mailed, the controller asks to look at the accounts you intend to confirm in order to determine whether she will permit you to send them.

She reviews the list and informs you that she does not want you to confirm six of the accounts on your list. Two of them have credit balances, one has a zero balance, two of the other three have a fairly small balance, and the remaining balance is highly material. The reason she gives is that she feels the confirmations will upset these customers because "they are kind of hard to get along with." She does not want the credit balances confirmed because it may encourage the customers to ask for a refund.

In addition, the controller asks you to send an additional 20 confirmations to customers she has listed for you. She does this as a means of credit collection for "those who won't know the difference between a public accountant and a credit collection agency."

REQUIRED
a. Is it acceptable for the controller to review the list of accounts you intend to confirm? Discuss.
b. Discuss the appropriateness of sending the 20 additional confirmations to the customers.
c. If the auditor complies with the controller's requests, what additional audit work is required?
d. Assuming the auditor complies with all of the controller's requests, what is the effect on the auditor's opinion?

13-26 ❸ You have been assigned to the first examination of the accounts of Duck Lake Inc. for the year ending March 31, 2012. Accounts receivable is confirmed on December 31, 2011, and at that date the receivables consisted of approximately 200 accounts with balances totalling $956,750. Seventy-five of these accounts with balances totalling $650,725 were selected for confirmation. All but 20 of the confirmation requests have been returned; 30 were signed without comments, 14 had minor differences which have been cleared satisfactorily, while 11 confirmations had the following comments:

1. We are sorry but we cannot answer your request for confirmation of our account, as Duck Lake Inc. uses an accounts payable voucher system.
2. The balance of $1,050 was paid on December 13, 2011.
3. The balance of $7,750 was paid on January 5, 2012.
4. The balance noted above has been paid.
5. We do not owe you anything as at December 31, 2011, as the goods, represented by your invoice dated December 30, 2011, number 25050, in the amount of $11,550, were received on January 5, 2012, on FOB destination terms.

6. An advance payment of $2,500 made by us in November 2011 should cover the two invoices totaling $1,350 shown on the statement attached.
7. We never received these goods.
8. We are contesting the propriety of this $12,525 charge. We think the charge is excessive.
9. Amount is okay. As the goods have been shipped to us on consignment, we will remit payment upon selling the goods.
10. The $10,000, representing a deposit under a lease, will be applied against the rent due to us during 2012, the last year of the lease.
11. Your credit memo dated December 5, 2011, in the amount of $440, cancels the balance above.

REQUIRED

What steps would you take to satisfactorily clear each of the above 11 comments?

(Adapted from AICPA)

13-27 ❼ The following are the entire outstanding accounts receivable for Stan's Bookbinding Company Ltd. The population is smaller than would ordinarily be the case for statistical sampling, but an entire population is useful to show how to select samples by monetary unit sampling.

REQUIRED
a. Select a sample using systematic MUS sampling. Materiality is $50,000 and an appropriate MUS interval is $35,000. Use a starting point of 1857. Identify the physical units selected.
b. Why would an auditor use MUS?

Population Item	Recorded Amount	Population Item	Recorded Amount
1	$ 1,410	11	$ 2,270
2	9,130	12	50
3	660	13	5,785
4	3,355	14	940
5	5,725	15	1,820
6	8,210	16	3,380
7	580	17	530
8	44,110	18	955
9	825	19	4,490
10	1,155	20	17,140

Population Item	Recorded Amount	Population Item	Recorded Amount
21	$ 4,865	31	$ 935
22	770	32	5,595
23	2,305	33	930
24	2,665	34	4,045
25	1,000	35	9,480
26	6,225	36	360
27	3,675	37	1,145
28	6,250	38	6,400
29	1,890	39	100
30	27,705	40	8,435
			$207,295

13-28 ④ You intend to use MUS as a part of the audit of several accounts for Roynpower Manufacturing Inc. You have done the audit for the past several years, and there has rarely been an adjusting entry of any kind. Your audit tests of all tests of controls for the transactions cycles were completed at an interim date, and control risk has been assessed as low. You therefore decide to use an ARIA of 10 percent for all tests of details of balances.

You intend to use MUS in the audit of the three most material asset balance sheet account balances: accounts receivable, inventory, and marketable securities. You feel justified in using the same ARIA for each audit area because of the low assessed control risk.

The recorded balances and related information for the three accounts are as follows:

	Recorded Value
Accounts receivable	$ 3,600,000
Inventory	4,800,000
Marketable securities	1,600,000
	$10,000,000

Net earnings before taxes for Roynpower are $2,000,000. You decide that materiality will be $100,000 for the client.

The audit approach will be to determine the total sample size needed for all three accounts. A sample will be selected from all $10 million, and the appropriate testing for a sample item will depend on whether the item is a receivable, inventory, or marketable security. The audit conclusions will pertain to the entire $10 million, and no conclusion will be made about the three individual accounts unless significant misstatements are found in the sample.

REQUIRED

a. Evaluate the audit approach of testing all three account balances in one sample.

b. Calculate the required sample size for each of the three accounts assuming you decide that the tolerable misstatement in each account is $100,000. (Recall that tolerable misstatement equals preliminary judgment about materiality for MUS.)

c. How would you identify which sample item in the population to audit for the number 4,627,871? What audit procedures would be performed?

d. Assume you select a sample of 100 sample items for testing and you find one misstatement in inventory. The recorded value is $987.12, and the audit value is $887.12. Calculate the misstatement bounds for the three combined accounts, and reach appropriate audit conclusions.

Professional Judgment Problem

13-29 ❶❷❸❹ For each of the following situations:

a. Discuss the key issues to address in determining whether or not revenue should be recognized.

b. Identify additional information required or audit procedures to be performed by the auditor to quantify or otherwise audit the issues identified in (a).

c. Use revenue recognition criteria for IFRS to explain how the client should recognize revenue.

1. A cell phone provider sells phone hardware and associated voice and data services. The typical contract includes a $200 upfront initial charge and $50 per month for the next two years for voice and data services. The company proposes to recognize 50 percent of revenue immediately, 25 percent at the end of the first year, and 25 percent at the end of second year.

2. Heavy Duty Construction Equipment Builders builds custom machinery for construction companies. Currently, it is producing machinery for a customer construction company for $25 million. The contracted date to complete the machinery was October, and the company met the contract date. It is now December, and the customer acknowledges the contract and confirms

the amount; however, the customer construction company has requested Heavy Duty Construction to hold the machinery as the construction site where the equipment will be used is not yet under development. Expected start has been delayed and will be sometime within the next 6 to 18 months.

3. Bakers Appliances have developed a new line of business where they will be selling bakeware appliances over the internet. The other lines of business have no return policy, hence no return allowance has ever been set by the company. However, since this is a new line of business, website sales grant each purchaser the right of return for a full refund within one year of date of purchase if the customer is unhappy with the product or finds the product defective.

4. Burer Technologies is a high-growth company that sells custom photographic software, which is a very rapidly changing industry. In order to achieve growth, management has empowered the sales staff to make special deals with clients (discounts and payment terms) to increase sales in the fourth quarter of the year. The sales deals include a price break and an increased salesperson commission.

Case

13-30 ❶❷❸ You are auditing the financial statements of the Reis Company, a small manufacturing firm that has been your client for several years. Because you were busy working on another engagement, you sent a staff accountant to begin the audit, with the suggestion that she start with accounts receivable.

Using the prior year's working papers as a guide, the auditor prepared a trial balance of the accounts, aged them, prepared and mailed positive confirmation requests, examined underlying support for charges and credits, and performed other work she considered necessary to obtain evidence about the validity and collectability of the receivables. At the conclusion of her work, you reviewed the working papers she prepared and found she had carefully followed the prior year's working papers.

Reis Company acquired the assets of another corporation during the year, so the nature and quality of its accounts receivable have changed. It has many more smaller accounts, as well as three larger international clients involving foreign exchange sales transactions. Sales have gone up substantially, and the accounts receivable balance has doubled. Two of the international accounts are over six months old and involve complex hedging transactions.

REQUIRED

a. What auditing standards have been violated by the personnel in the above case? Explain why you feel the standards you list have been violated.
b. How do the acquisition and the change in the nature of sales and accounts receivable affect control risk and inherent risk of accounts receivable?
c. Describe additional audit procedures that are required to effectively complete the audit of sales and accounts receivable.

ACL Problem ACL

13-31 ❶ ❷ ❹ This problem requires the use of ACL software. Use the Metaphor_Trans_All file in ACL Demo, which is a file of outstanding sales invoices (each row represents an invoice transaction). The suggested command or other source of information needed to solve the problem requirement is included at the end of each question.

a. Determine the total number of invoices (read the bottom of the Metaphor_Trans_All file screen) and total unpaid invoices outstanding (NEWBAL) for comparison with the general ledger (Total Field). What audit procedures would you perform using this information?
b. How many of the invoices included a finance charge (FINCHG), and what was the total amount of the finance charges (Filter, Count Records, and Total Field)? What is the impact of locating finance charges on your assessment of the bad-debt allowance?
c. Determine and print accounts receivable outstanding from each customer and total the amount for comparison with part (a); note: remove the filter from step (b) first (Summarize and Total Field). Which customer number has the largest balance due?

d. What is the largest and smallest account balance outstanding (Quick Sort)? How would you use the information from parts (c) and (d) to assist your decision making with respect to the circularization of accounts receivable? How would you use the information to satisfy presentation and disclosure audit objectives?
e. For the account with the largest balance, prepare and print an aging of the account from the transaction file using the statement date labeled "STMTTDT." Use the aging date as of 4/30/2003 and "NEWBAL" as the subtotal field (Filter and Age). What additional testing could you do with aging (using current and prior year's information) to assist with the assessment of the allowance for bad debts?
f. To better decide which customers to select for confirmation, you decide to stratify customer balances into two intervals after excluding all balances less than $5,000. How many balances are greater than $5,000? Print the output (Filter and Stratify). Assess the reasonableness of this stratification approach.

Ongoing Small Business Case: Bad Debts at CondoCleaners.com

13-32 ❶ ❸ Jim has obtained close to 50 commercial accounts for cleaning. Most customers pay well, although there are about five customers to whom he has to give reminder calls. If the account goes more than 30 days overdue, he cancels service, and no further services are provided to that customer. So far, he has done this for two accounts, which cost him about $500.

To Jim's surprise, when he walked into one of the condominium shopping malls, he found notices on three of the stores that they would be moving out. When he talked to the owners, he heard that, in the current round of lease negotiations, the condominium was increasing their rents by over 30 percent, in line with current commercial rates in the neighbourhood. Those who were moving out were leasing from the condominium corporation, rather than owning their units.

REQUIRED

How will this announcement affect Jim's business? How does this affect inherent risk of the 12 commercial accounts that Jim has in this building?

14 Audit of cash balances

"Cash" is available in many different ways—via cheque, credit card, and debit card or transferred electronically into your bank account. It is the way that we acquire assets and discharge our debts, so it has a pivotal role in the accounting process, being one side of many different types of transactions. Here, we will look at different types of cash accounts and how they are audited. Management accountants need to understand how to control cash, while many types of auditors may be asked to design or execute audit programs pertaining to cash.

LEARNING OBJECTIVES

1 Identify the different types of cash accounts. Explain the relationship between cash and the other transaction cycles. Describe the risks of fraud or error in the cycle.

2 Link the audit of cash to corporate governance and control processes. Relate the functions and records of the cash cycle to prevention or detection of fraud and error. Describe the steps in auditing the general cash account.

3 Identify the additional audit procedures conducted when there is suspicion of fraud. Define "kiting" and explain how it is audited.

4 Explain how an audit of the payroll cash account differs from the audit of the general cash account. Identify the special considerations that exist for EFT (electronic funds transfer) transactions. Explain how petty cash is audited.

STANDARDS REFERENCED IN THIS CHAPTER

ASPE

Section 1540 – Cash flow statement

IFRS

IAS 7 – Statement of cash flows

IAS 23 – Borrowing costs

Satyam Fraud of Over $1 Billion Could Have Been Detected

In January 2009, Ramalinga Raju, the founder of India's then fourth largest computer outsourcing company, Satyam Computer Services, confessed to having engaged in financial statement fraud for many years. Cash was overstated by more than US$1 billion, income was overstated substantially, and debt was overstated. Cash balances for September 2008 that were listed as about $1.04 billion in the financial statements were actually only about $66 million. Apparently, bank confirmations were not sent for many of Satyam's bank accounts, debt details were not confirmed, and differences between those bank confirmations actually sent and amounts reported by Satyam were not followed up by the company's auditors, PriceWaterhouse India.

The basic audit procedures of confirming cash and bank debt with the bank and maintaining control over the confirmations are normally used to verify cash and bank debt accounts. This type of fraud would normally be detected by such audit procedures.

Three years later, in March 2012, the U.S. Securities and Exchange Commission (SEC) fined Satyam US$10 million and PriceWaterhouse (PW) India US$7.5 million. Additional requirements accompanying the fine included a prohibition for PW India from accepting U.S.-based clients for six months, specific requirements to improve quality control processes, and the requirement to appoint an external independent monitor to make sure that the quality control measures were adopted.

IMPORTANCE TO AUDITORS

Auditors who do not perform required audit procedures can be sued and may not detect financial statement fraud, as occurred at Satyam. It is also important that auditors follow up differences between management reporting and what the external party (the bank) reports. Such differences are red flags for fraud if they cannot be explained and substantiated.

WHAT DO YOU THINK?

1. Remember the fraud triangle. What would have motivated Satyam's founder to misstate financial statements to the extent described?
2. What actions on the part of auditors would provide opportunity for Satyam's owner to commit fraud?
3. What journal entries would be recorded by Satyam to record the fictitious journal entries? How could such journal entries be detected by the auditors?

Sources: 1, "SEC slaps $17.5-million fine on Satyam, PriceWaterhouse," *The Hindu*, March 9, 2012, **www.thehindu.com/news/national/article1605665.ece.** 2. Murthy, Raja, January 10, 2009, "Satyam fraud check switches to PwC," online *Asian Times*, **www.atimes.com/atimes/South_Asia/KA101Df02.html** 3. Norris, Floyd, "Indian Accounting Firm is Fined $7.5 Million Over Fraud at Satyam," *The New York Times*, April 5, 2011, **www.nytimes.com**. All accessed: March 10, 2012

continued >

AS an auditing student, you can understand the importance of monitoring cash and making sure that the company has enough to pay its bills. Yet, we need to remember that not all internal controls are perfect and that harried employees may not carefully check all the documents pertaining to recording of cash, especially journal entries prepared by management.

Evidence accumulated for cash balances depends heavily on the results of the tests in the transaction cycles. Understanding the cash account is important because it links to all of those cycles. The auditor needs to consider the assessed risks from each cycle when auditing cash.

We start by looking at how cash is processed in an organization, before examining corporate governance and control issues. Then, we look at audit procedures conducted for different types of cash accounts.

Cash and the Transaction Cycles

Types of Cash Accounts

It is important to understand the different types of cash accounts because the auditing approach to each varies. Table 14-1 describes the major types of cash accounts or balances. Although cash management is not really a cycle (since its transactions come from other cycles), we refer to it here as a cycle for convenience.

Figure 14-1 shows the relationship of general cash to the other cash accounts. All cash either originates from or is deposited into general cash. This chapter focuses on three types of accounts: the general cash account, the imprest payroll bank account, and the imprest petty cash fund.

Risks of Fraud or Error in the Cash Cycle

Cash transactions arise because of activities in other cycles, such as receiving revenue (cash receipts), paying for expenses (miscellaneous payments), paying for inventory (payment of purchases), payment of employee wages (payroll expense), receipt or payment of debt (capital cycle). This means that the errors in processing cash or cash fraud could affect any cycle. Table 14-2 shows examples of the major types of error or fraud that could occur. Since cash impacts every cycle, there are many different types of error or fraud that impact this cycle. For further examples, refer to Chapter 12 and Chapters 15 to 18.

Cash in the Bank and Transaction Cycles

A brief discussion of the relationship between cash in the bank and the other transaction cycles serves a dual function: it highlights the importance of the tests of various transaction cycles to the audit of cash, and it aids in further understanding the integration of the different transaction cycles.

The general cash account is considered significant in almost all audits, even when the ending balance is immaterial. The amount of cash flowing into and out of the cash

Table 14-1	Major Types of Cash Accounts or Balances and Their Purposes
Type of Cash Account or Balance	**Purpose of Cash Account**
General cash account—the primary bank account for most organizations; virtually all cash receipts and disbursements flow through this account at some time.	• Used to make payments (for expenses and capital assets) and to record cash received from operations (such as cash sales and accounts receivable). • Small companies who have only one account have this type of account.
Imprest payroll account—a bank account to which the exact amount of payroll for the pay period is transferred from the general cash account. A fixed balance, such as $1,000, may also be kept in the account.	• Used to pay employees, and may also be used to pay employee remittances to Canada Revenue Agency. • Helps improve control over cash and reduce time to reconcile bank accounts.
Branch bank account—a separate bank account maintained at a local bank by a branch of a company. Can be either a general cash account or an imprest type account. Usage depends upon what is authorized by head office.	• Provides for more rapid deposits and/or payments at the local level. • Builds business relationships with local banks.
Imprest petty cash fund—a fund of cash maintained within the company for small cash payments; its fixed balance is comparatively small, and it is periodically reimbursed.	• Used for small cash purchases that can be paid more conveniently and quickly by cash than by cheque (e.g. office supplies)
Cash equivalents – short term, highly liquid investments (such as term deposits) that have a known value and an insignificant risk of change in value (Section 1540.06, IAS 7.6). Where bank overdrafts are in normal use (i.e. a fluctuating bank balance), the bank overdraft would also be considered a cash equivalent, even though it is a liability rather than an asset.	• Used to manage fluctuating cash balances so that cash is available for short-term operating needs.

account is frequently larger than for any other account in the financial statements. Furthermore, the susceptibility of cash to defalcation is greater than for other types of assets because most other assets must be converted to cash to make them usable.

In the audit of cash, an important distinction should be made between verifying the client's reconciliation of the balance on the bank statement to the balance in the general ledger and verifying whether recorded cash in the general ledger correctly

Figure 14-1	Relationship of General Cash to Other Cash Accounts

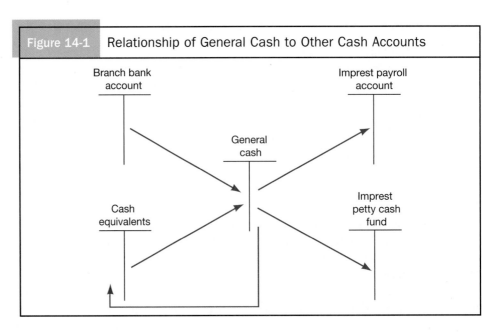

Table 14-2 — Examples of Major Risks of Error or Fraud in the Cash Cycle

Risk of Error	Risk of Misappropriation of Assets, Other Fraud or Illegal Acts	Risks of Inadequate Disclosure or Incorrect Presentation of Financial Information, including Fraudulent Financial Reporting
Cash received could be posted in the incorrect period.		Funds received as debt financing could be recorded as revenue.
	Payments in cash (rather than by cheque) could be stolen rather than recorded.	
Cash received could be recorded at the wrong amount.		Cash received from related parties could be recorded as cash received from general operations.
	Payments could be made to a fictitious supplier for goods not received.	
Suppliers could be paid twice for their invoices.		Failure to disclose payments to associated companies or companies controlled by the company.
	Management steals cash by authorizing personal payments (e.g. home renovations) as business expenses.	
Employees could be paid using the wrong wage rate.		Cash equivalents are incorrectly classified as marketable securities.
	Blank cheques are stolen and signatures forged to steal funds, or bank accounts are hacked into and cash stolen.	

reflects all cash transactions that took place during the year. It is relatively easy to verify the client's reconciliation of the balance in the bank account to the general ledger, which is the primary subject of this chapter, but a significant part of the total audit of a company involves verifying whether cash transactions are properly recorded by considering cash transactions in each cycle. For example, each of the following misstatements ultimately results in the improper payment of, or the failure to receive, cash, but none will normally be discovered as a part of the audit of the bank reconciliation:

Sales and accounts receivable transaction cycle

- Failure to bill a customer.
- Billing a customer at a lower price than called for by company policy.
- A defalcation of cash by interception of collections from customers before they are recorded. The account receivable is charged off as a bad debt.
- Fictitious refunds, whereby the employee takes the refund.

Acquisition and payment cycle

- Duplicate payment of a vendor's invoice.
- Improper payments of officers' personal expenditures.
- Payment for raw materials that were not received.

Human resources and payroll cycle

- Payment to an employee for more hours than he or she worked.
- Payment to fictitious employees.

Capital acquisition and repayment cycle

- Payment of interest to a related party for an amount in excess of the going rate.

If these misstatements are to be uncovered in the audit, their discovery must come about through tests of controls. The first four misstatements could be discovered as part of the audit of the sales and collection cycle, the next three in the audit of the acquisitions and payment cycle, the next two in the tests of the human resources and payroll cycle, and the final one in the audit of the capital acquisition and repayment cycle.

Entirely different types of misstatements are normally discovered as part of the tests of a bank reconciliation. For example:

- Failure to include on the outstanding cheque list a cheque that has not cleared the bank, even though it has been recorded in the cash disbursements journal.
- Cash received by the client subsequent to the balance sheet date but recorded as cash receipts in the current year.
- Deposits recorded as cash receipts near the end of the year, deposited in the bank, and included in the bank reconciliation as a deposit in transit.
- Payments on notes payable that were debited directly to the bank balance by the bank but were not entered in the client's records.

concept check

C14-1 Describe the difference between a general cash account and an imprest bank account.

C14-2 For each of the following transaction cycles, provide an example of an error in cash that would affect the cycle: sales and accounts receivable, acquisition and payment, human resources and payroll.

② Audit of the General Cash Account

Controls over cash are identified in every transaction cycle. For example, cash received at point-of-sale terminals is reconciled to sales, bank reconciliations are independently prepared, accounts receivable write-offs need to be independently authorized, and payments for products are made only with authorized purchase orders with supporting receiving documents. Thus, the auditor will consider the results of control risk for every transaction cycle when coming to a conclusion about controls over cash.

In addition, management attitudes toward cash and the nature of the treasury management function are important factors. In Chapter 4, we talked about money laundering. If a business has plenty of cash but there never seem to be any customers about (such as at a restaurant), then the business could be engaging in money laundering. If a company has invested in questionable marketable securities that are no longer liquid (such as occurred with the asset-backed-paper fiasco in 2008 and the $50 billion mutual-fund Madoff fraud in the United States), then the company will be in a cash squeeze, as it can no longer liquidate its investments.

Cycle-based indicators that could lead to cash liquidity problems could be gradually aging accounts receivable, obsolete inventory or poorly managed inventory, inability to take advantage of cash discounts in accounts payable, and difficulty meeting payroll or income tax obligations. By asking management about its policies with respect to cash management and cash investment, as well as gathering information from the different cycles, the auditor will obtain information about the likelihood of cash misstatements.

In testing the year-end balance in the general cash account, the auditor must accumulate sufficient evidence to evaluate whether cash, as stated on the balance sheet, is fairly stated and properly disclosed in accordance with the balance-related audit objectives (B-RAO). Rights to general cash, its classification on the balance sheet, and the valuation of cash are usually not a problem due to the inherent nature of cash.

The methodology for auditing year-end cash is essentially the same as for all other balance sheet accounts. This methodology is shown in Figure 14-2.

INTERNAL CONTROLS Internal controls over the year-end cash balances in the general account can be divided into two categories: (1) controls over the transaction cycles affecting the recording of cash receipts and disbursements and (2) independent bank reconciliations.

Controls affecting the recording of cash transactions are discussed in chapters pertaining to those cycles. For example, in the acquisition and payment cycle, major

Figure 14-2

Methodology for Designing Tests of Details of Balances for Cash in the Bank

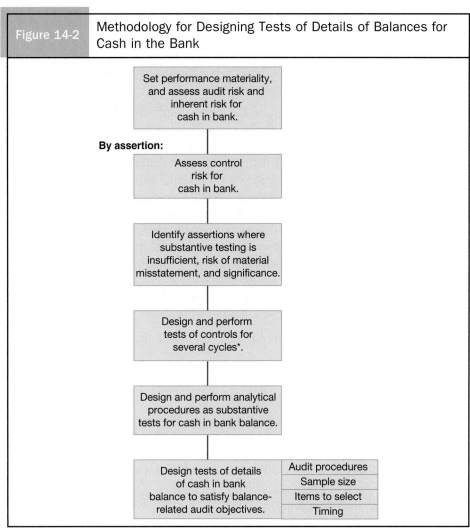

Set performance materiality, and assess audit risk and inherent risk for cash in bank.

By assertion:

Assess control risk for cash in bank.

Identify assertions where substantive testing is insufficient, risk of material misstatement, and significance.

Design and perform tests of controls for several cycles*.

Design and perform analytical procedures as substantive tests for cash in bank balance.

Design tests of details of cash in bank balance to satisfy balance-related audit objectives.

| Audit procedures |
| Sample size |
| Items to select |
| Timing |

*Cycles affected include sales and collection, acquisition and payment, human resources and payroll, and capital acquisition and repayment.

controls include the adequate segregation of duties between the cheque signing and the accounts payable functions, the signing of cheques by only a properly authorized person, the use of prenumbered cheques that are printed on special paper, adequate control of blank and voided cheques, careful review of supporting documentation by the cheque signer before cheques are signed, and adequate internal verification. If the controls affecting cash-related transactions are adequate, it is possible to reduce the audit tests of the year-end bank reconciliation.

Materiality considerations The cash balance is immaterial on most audits, but the cash transactions affecting the balance are almost always extremely material. There is, therefore, often potential for material misstatement of cash.

Inherent risk considerations Because cash (since it is highly liquid) is more susceptible to theft than other assets, there is high inherent risk for the existence objective. If there is a high volume of activity there is also a higher chance of manipulation. The existence objective is usually the focus in auditing cash balances. Typically, inherent risk is low for all other objectives.

Control risk considerations There are several considerations for control risk.

- Internal control effectiveness over cash balances varies significantly for different companies. The most important internal control is independent bank reconciliations.
- Internal controls over cash receipts and disbursements are important considerations in the audit and were discussed in earlier chapters.

- If there are debt covenants related to cash or liquidity position, then there could be a bias towards manipulation of cash balances.
- Individuals who are super users or have incompatible functions granted to them using computer systems (e.g., ability to steal cash and alter the accounting records) could result in control risk being assessed as high.

A monthly **bank reconciliation** of the differences between the cash balance recorded in the general ledger and in the general bank account on a timely basis by someone independent of the handling or recording of cash receipts and disbursements is an essential control over the cash balance. The reconciliation is important to ensure that the books reflect the same cash balance as the actual amount of cash in the bank after consideration of reconciling items, but even more important, the independent reconciliation provides a unique opportunity for an independent internal verification of cash receipts and disbursements transactions. If the bank statements are received unopened by the reconciler and physical control is maintained over the statements until the reconciliations are complete, the cancelled cheques, deposit information, and other documents included in the statement can be examined without concern for the possibility of alteration, deletions, or additions. A careful bank reconciliation by competent client personnel includes the following:

- Compare cancelled cheques with the cash disbursements journal for date, payee, and amount.
- Examine cancelled cheques for signature, endorsements, and cancellation.
- Compare deposits in the bank with recorded cash receipts for date, customer, and amount.
- Account for the numerical sequence of cheques, and investigate missing ones.
- Reconcile all items causing a difference between the book and the bank balance, and verify their propriety.
- Reconcile total debits on the bank statement with the totals in the cash disbursements journal.
- Reconcile total credits on the bank statement with the totals in the cash receipts journal.
- Review month-end interbank transfers for propriety and proper recording.
- Follow up on outstanding cheques and stop-payment notices.

Because of the importance of the monthly reconciliation of bank accounts, another common control for many companies is having a responsible employee review the monthly reconciliation as soon as possible after its completion.

ANALYTICAL PROCEDURES In many audits, the year-end bank reconciliation is verified on a 100-percent basis. Testing the reasonableness of the cash balance is therefore less important than for most other audit areas.

It is common for auditors to compare the ending balance on the bank reconciliation, deposits in transit, outstanding cheques, and other reconciling items with the prior-year reconciliation. Similarly, auditors normally compare the ending balance in cash with previous months' balances. These analytical procedures may uncover misstatements in cash.

AUDIT PROCEDURES FOR YEAR-END CASH A major consideration in the audit of the general cash balance is the possibility of fraud. The auditor must extend his or her procedures in the audit of year-end cash to determine the possibility of a material fraud when there are inadequate internal controls, especially the improper segregation of duties between the handling of cash and the recording of cash transactions in the accounting records.

The starting point for the verification of the balance in the general bank account is obtaining a bank reconciliation, such as the one shown in Figure 14-3, from the client for inclusion in the auditor's working papers. Note that the last number in the working paper is the adjusted balance in the general ledger. Although the bank reconciliation

Figure 14-3   Working Paper for a Bank Reconciliation

Microsoft Excel - Book2

File Edit View Insert Format Tools Data Window Help Acrobat

Arial   10   B I U $ % ,

A1   =

Clawson Industries
Bank Reconciliation
12/31/11

Schedule	A-2	Date	
Prepared by	Client / DED	1/10/12
Approved by	SW	1/18/12

Acct. 101 – General account, First Canadian Bank

Balance per Bank		109713	X A-2/1
Add:			
Deposits in transit			
12/30	10017 ✓		
12/31	11100 ✓	21117	
Deduct			
Outstanding cheques			
# 7993	12/16	3068 X	
8007	12/16	9763 X	
8012	12/23	11916 X	
8013	12/23	14717 X	
8029	12/28	A-7	37998 X	
8038	12/30	A-7	10000 X	<87462>
Other reconciling items: Bank error			
Deposit for another bank customer credited to general account by bank, in error		<15200>	A-3
Balance per bank, adjusted		28168	T/B
		W	
Balance per general ledger before adjustments		32584	A-1
Adjustments:			
Unrecorded bank service charge	216		A-3
Non-sufficient funds cheque returned by bank, not collectable from customer	4200	<4416>	C-3/1
Balance per general ledger, adjusted		28168	A-1
		W	

X Traced and agreed to bank confirmation.
✓ Traced deposit to the December 2011 cash receipts records and to the January 2012 bank cut-off statement, noting its proper classification as a deposit in transit at 12/31/11
X Traced cheque to December 2011 cash disbursements records and to the January 2012 bank cut-off statement, noting its proper classification as an outstanding cheque at 12/31/11
T/B Traced to 12/31/11 adjusted trial balance
W Footed

Testing for Greed, Using Generalized Audit Software (GAS) as an Analytical Tool

DOES something seem unusual at your client but you cannot quite put your finger on it? Perhaps there seems to be less cash than usual and purchases are slightly up, reducing costs of goods sold, but sales have not increased.

Consider asking the client for a copy of its entire transaction file for purchasing and payments and running a series of investigative analytical review procedures.

You could run totals of purchases by supplier and by month and look for round amounts, duplicate payments or suppliers with addresses that are the same as employee addresses. You could also ask for the payroll data file and match last names of employees with names of supplier contacts.

In any event, you will get more information about the nature of transactions and have more confidence about where to focus your audit work.

You could also identify actions that would help the company improve its purchases: for example, by testing purchases for raw materials, you could look for discrepancies in purchase cost from one supplier to the next and ask about the supplier selection process to ensure that all purchases are approved.

CRITICAL THINKING QUESTIONS

1. If you had a copy of the sales returns for a particular store, what types of data analysis would you do on the returns to look for potential fictitious returns (i.e., theft of cash)?
2. What types of transaction inquiries would you run on cash receipts in the accounts receivable file to test for lapping (i.e., theft of cash by crediting accounts receivable to the incorrect account)?

is normally prepared manually or using a spreadsheet, many accounting systems allow the client to use computerized systems to prepare the list of outstanding cheques.

The frame of reference for the audit tests is the bank reconciliation. The B-RAO and presentation and disclosure-related audit objectives (P&D-RAO) and common tests of details of balances are shown in Table 14-3. The actual audit procedures depend on the risks and controls in the transaction cycles for the client. Also, because of their close relationship in the audit of year-end cash, the existence of recorded cash in the bank, accuracy, and inclusion of existing cash (completeness) are combined. These three objectives are the most important ones for cash and therefore receive the greatest attention.

The following three procedures are discussed thoroughly because of their importance and complexity.

Receipt of a bank confirmation The direct receipt to the auditor's location of a confirmation from every bank or other financial institution with which the client does business is necessary for every audit, except when there are an unusually large number of inactive accounts. If the bank does not respond to a confirmation request, the auditor must send a second request or ask the client to telephone the bank. As a convenience to PAs as well as to bankers who are requested to fill out bank confirmations, the CICA has approved the use of a **standard bank confirmation form,** through which the bank responds to the auditor's request for information about the client's bank balances, loan information, and contingent liabilities. Figure 14-4 is an illustration of such a completed standard bank confirmation. This standard form has been agreed upon by the CICA and the Canadian Bankers Association. CGAAC and the Canadian Bankers Association have approved a similar bank confirmation form for use by CGAs.

The importance of bank confirmations in the audit extends beyond the verification of the actual cash balance. It is typical for the bank to confirm loan information and bank balances on the same form. The confirmation in Figure 14-4 includes three outstanding loans and a contingent liability (the guarantee). Information on liabilities to the bank for notes, mortgages, or other debt typically includes the amount of the loan, the date of the loan, its due date, interest rate, and the presence of collateral.

The auditor completes the sections labelled "client," "chartered accountant," "financial institution," and "confirmation date"; a signing officer from the client signs

> **Standard bank confirmation form**—a form approved by the CICA or CGAAC and Canadian Bankers Association through which the bank responds to the auditor's request for information about the client's bank balances, loan information, and contingent liabilities.

Table 14-3

Table 14-3 Balance-Related Audit Objectives and Presentation and Disclosure-Related Audit Objectives with Tests of Details of Balances for General Cash in the Bank

Balance-Related Audit Objective or Presentation and Disclosure-Related Audit Objective	Common Tests of Details of Balances Procedures	Comments
Cash in the bank as stated on the reconciliation exists (existence).	Obtain and test a bank confirmation.	(See extended discussion.)
Existing cash in the bank is included (completeness).	Obtain and test a cutoff bank statement.	(See extended discussion.)
Cash in the bank as stated on the reconciliation is accurate (accuracy).	Test the bank reconciliation, for example: Foot the outstanding cheque list, electronic payments list, and deposits in transit list. Prove the bank reconciliation as to additions and subtractions, including all reconciling items. Trace the book balance on the reconciliation to the general ledger. Perform extended tests of the bank reconciliation. Prepare proof of cash. Test for kiting.	(See extended discussion.) The first three procedures are the most important objectives for cash in the bank. The procedures are combined because of their close interdependence. The last three procedures should be done only when there are internal control weaknesses.
Cash presented in the financial statements is properly valued (valuation).	Determine exchange rates used by the client to present cash in foreign currencies and recalculate the amounts.	The auditor will need to determine that the appropriate exchange rate calculation method is used, that the method is disclosed in the financial statements, and that it is consistently applied.
Cash receipts and cash disbursements transactions are recorded in the proper period (allocation).	*Cash receipts:* Count the cash on hand on the first day of the year and subsequently trace to deposits in transit and the cash receipts journal. Trace deposits in transit to subsequent period bank statement (cutoff bank statement). *Cash disbursements:* Record the last cheque number used on the last day of the year, and subsequently trace to the outstanding cheques and the cash disbursements journal. Trace outstanding cheques to subsequent period bank statement.	When cash receipts received after year end are included in the journal, a better cash position than actually exists is shown. It is called the "holding open the cash receipts" journal. The "holding open the cash disbursements" journal reduces accounts payable and usually overstates the current ratio. The first procedures listed for each of receipts and disbursement allocation (cutoff) tests requires the auditor's presence on the client's premises at the end of the last day of the year.
Cash in the bank is presented in the correct accounts and properly described (classification).	Examine minutes, loan agreements, and obtain confirmation for restrictions on the use of cash and compensating balances. Review financial statements to make sure (a) material savings accounts and guaranteed investment certificates, if access is restricted, are disclosed separately from cash in the bank; (b) cash restricted to certain uses and compensating balances are adequately disclosed; and (c) bank overdrafts are included as current liabilities.	An example of a restriction on the use of cash is cash deposited with a trustee for the payment of mortgage interest and taxes on the proceeds of a construction mortgage. A compensating balance is the client's agreement with a bank to maintain a specified minimum in its chequing account.
Information about cash its uses, and restrictions are presented clearly (understandability).	Examine financial statements, particularly the cash flow statement, and the notes to the financial statements to determine that all relevant information is presented clearly.	The auditor would evaluate understandability from the perspective of a knowledgeable user.

in the "client" box authorizing the bank to provide the information; and the auditor sends the confirmation to the bank. While the bank should exercise due care in completing the confirmation, errors can occur. The auditor may wish to communicate with the bank if there is any information on the returned confirmation about which he or she is doubtful or if any information that was expected is not reported.

After the bank confirmation has been received by the auditor, the balance in the bank account confirmed by the bank should be traced to the amount stated on the bank reconciliation. All other information on the bank reconciliation should be

Figure 14-4

Standard Confirmation of Financial Institution Account Balance Information

BANK CONFIRMATION

(Areas to be completed by client are marked §, while those to be completed by the financial institutions are marked †)

FINANCIAL INSTITUTION	CLIENT (Legal Name) §
(Name, branch, and full mailing address) §	Koa Foods Inc.
Bank of Columbia	St. Jacobs, Ontario
Westmount & Old Post Road	NOL 1KO
Waterloo, Ontario	The financial institution is authorized to provide the details requested herein to the below-noted firm of accountants
N2L 5M1	§ *J Koa*
CONFIRMATION DATE § December 31, 2011	Client's authorized signature
(All information to be provided as of this date)	Please supply copy of the most recent credit facility agreement
(See Bank Confirmation Completion Instructions)	(initial if required) § _____

1. LOANS AND OTHER DIRECT AND CONTINGENT LIABILITIES (If balances are nil, please state.)

NATURE OF LIABILITY/ CONTINGENT LIABILITY †	INTEREST (Note rate per contract) RATE †	DATE PAID TO †	DUE DATE †	DATE OF CREDIT FACILITY AGREEMENT †	AMOUNT AND CURRENCY OUTSTANDING †
Loan	8%	31/12/11	Demand	5/5/06	$90,000
Loan	9%	30/11/11	30/5/13	1/4/05	$120,000
Loan	10%	31/12/11	Demand	1/6/07	$20,000
Guarantee	N/A		N/A	1/1/00	$8,000

ADDITIONAL CREDIT FACILITY AGREEMENT(S)

Note the date(s) of any credit facility agreement(s) not drawn upon and not referenced above †

2. DEPOSITS/OVERDRAFTS

TYPE OF ACCOUNT §	ACCOUNT NUMBER §	INTEREST RATE §	ISSUE DATE (if applicable) §	MATURITY DATE (if applicable) §	AMOUNT AND CURRENCY (Bracket if Overdraft) †
General	65422	—	—	—	$109,713
Payroll	65432	—	—	—	$4,000

EXCEPTIONS AND COMMENTS
(See Bank Confirmation Completion Instructions) †

STATEMENT OF PROCEDURES PERFORMED BY FINANCIAL INSTITUTION †
The above information was completed in accordance with the Bank Confirmation Completion Instructions.

Bill Brown

Authorized signature of financial institution

Branch Contact   W. Brown   (519) 884-1921

Name and telephone number

Please mail this form directly to our chartered accountant in the enclosed addressed envelope.

Name:	Kadous & Co.
Address:	P.O. Box 1939
	Waterloo, Ontario N2L 1G1
Telephone:	(519) 999-1234
Fax:	(519) 999-1235

Developed by the Canadian Bankers Association and the Canadian Institute of Chartered Accountants

traced to the relevant audit working papers. In any case, if the information is not in agreement with client records, an investigation must be made of the difference.

Receipt of a cut-off bank statement A **cut-off bank statement** includes a partial-period bank statement and the related cancelled cheques, duplicate deposit slips, and other documents included with bank statements, mailed by the bank directly to the public accounting firm's office. The purpose of the cutoff bank statement is to verify the reconciling items on the client's year-end bank reconciliation with evidence that is inaccessible to the client. To fulfill this purpose, the auditor requests that the client have the bank send directly to the auditor the bank statement for 7 to 10 days subsequent to the balance sheet date.

Cut-off bank statement—a partial-period bank statement and the related cancelled cheques, duplicate deposit slips, and other documents included in bank statements, mailed by the bank directly to the auditor. The auditor uses it to verify reconciling items in the client's year-end bank reconciliation.

Many auditors prove the subsequent-period bank statement if a cut-off statement is not received directly from the bank. The purpose of this proof is to test whether the client's employees have omitted, added, or altered any of the documents accompanying the bank statement. It is a test for intentional misstatements. The auditor performs the proof in the month subsequent to the balance sheet date by (1) footing all the cancelled cheques, electronic payments, debit memos, deposits, and credit memos; (2) checking to see that the bank statement balances when the footed totals are used; and (3) reviewing the items included in the footings to make sure they were cancelled by the bank in the proper period and do not include any alterations.

Tests of the bank reconciliation The reason for testing the bank reconciliation is to verify whether the client's recorded bank balance is the same amount as the actual cash in the bank except for deposits in transit, outstanding cheques, and other reconciling items. In testing the reconciliation, the cut-off bank statement provides the information for conducting the tests. Several major procedures are involved:

- Verify that the client's bank reconciliation is mathematically accurate.
- Trace the balance on the cut-off statement to the balance per bank on the bank reconciliation. A reconciliation is incomplete until these two are the same.
- Trace cheques included with the cut-off bank statement to the list of outstanding cheques on the bank reconciliation and to the cash disbursements journal. All cheques (or electronic payments) that cleared the bank after the balance sheet date and were included in the cash disbursements journal should also be included on the outstanding cheque (or outstanding payment) list. If a cheque (or electronic payment) was included in the cash disbursements journal, it should be included as an outstanding cheque (or payment) if it did not clear before the balance sheet date. Similarly, if a cheque (or payment) cleared the bank prior to the balance sheet date, it should not be on the bank reconciliation.
- Investigate all significant cheques or payments included on the outstanding cheque list that have not cleared the bank on the cut-off statement. The first step in the investigation should be tracing the amount of any items not clearing to the cash disbursements journal. The reason for the cheque not being cashed should be discussed with the client, and if the auditor is concerned about the possibility of fraud (such as deliberate holding of cheques), the vendor's accounts payable balance should be confirmed to determine whether the vendor has recognized the receipt of the cash in its records. In addition, the cancelled cheque should be examined prior to the last day of the audit if it becomes available.
- Trace deposits in transit to the subsequent bank statement. All cash receipts not deposited in the bank at the end of the year should be traced to the cut-off bank statement to ensure they were deposited shortly after the beginning of the next fiscal year.
- Account for other reconciling items on the bank statement and bank reconciliation. These include such items as bank service charges, bank errors and corrections, and unrecorded note transactions debited or credited directly to the bank account by the bank. These reconciling items should be carefully investigated to ensure they have been treated properly by the client.

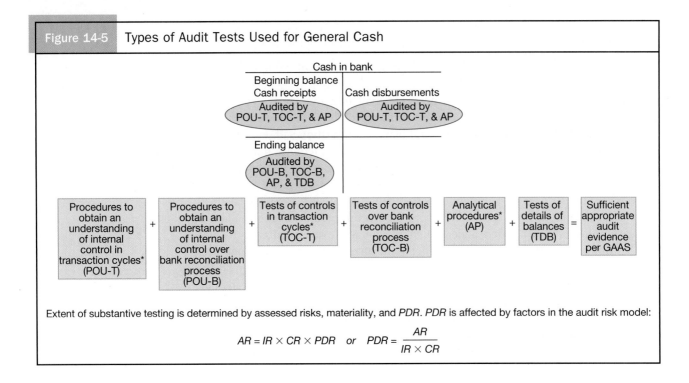

Figure 14-5 Types of Audit Tests Used for General Cash

Extent of substantive testing is determined by assessed risks, materiality, and *PDR*. *PDR* is affected by factors in the audit risk model:

$$AR = IR \times CR \times PDR \quad or \quad PDR = \frac{AR}{IR \times CR}$$

Figure 14-5 illustrates the types of audit tests (excluding risk assessment) used to audit the general cash account. This figure also shows how the audit risk model discussed in Chapter 7 relates to the audit of the general cash account.

③ Fraud-Oriented Procedures

concept check

C14-3 Why do the risks of every transaction cycle affect cash?

C14-4 What is the purpose of a bank reconciliation?

It is often necessary for auditors to extend their year-end audit procedures to test more extensively for the possibility of material fraud when there are material internal control weaknesses. Many fraudulent activities are difficult, if not impossible, to uncover; nevertheless, auditors are responsible for making a reasonable effort to detect fraud when they have reason to believe it may exist. Satyam, discussed in our opening vignette, had an annual growth rate of 24 percent, which was greater than the industry average, which should cause the auditor to increase fraud risks. The following procedures for uncovering fraud are discussed in this section: extended tests of the bank reconciliation, proofs of cash, and tests for kiting.

Extended tests of the bank reconciliation When the auditor believes that the year-end bank reconciliation may be intentionally misstated, it is appropriate to perform extended tests of the year-end bank reconciliation. The purpose of the extended procedures is to verify whether all transactions included in the journals for the last month of the year were correctly included in or excluded from the bank reconciliation and to verify whether all items in the bank reconciliation were correctly included. Let us assume that there are material internal control weaknesses and that the client's year end is December 31. A common approach is to start with the bank reconciliation for November and compare all reconciling items with cancelled cheques and other documents in the December bank statement. In addition, all remaining cancelled cheques and deposit slips in the December bank statement should be compared with the December cash disbursements and receipts journals. All uncleared items in the November bank reconciliation and the December cash disbursements and receipts journals should be included in the client's December 31 bank reconciliation. Similarly, all reconciling items in the December 31 bank reconciliation should be items from the November bank reconciliation and December's journals that have not yet cleared the bank.

The primary tests of the ending cash balance are tests of details of balances.

In addition to the tests just described, the auditor must also carry out procedures subsequent to the end of the year using the bank cut-off statement. These tests would be performed in the same manner as previously discussed.

Proof of cash Auditors sometimes prepare a proof of cash when the client has material internal control weaknesses in cash. A **proof of cash** is a four-column working paper used to reconcile the bank's records of the client's beginning balance, cash deposits, cleared cheques, and ending balance for the period with the client's records. It includes the following:

- A reconciliation of the balance on the bank statement with the general ledger balance at the beginning of the proof-of-cash period.
- A reconciliation of cash receipts deposited with the cash receipts journal for a given period.
- A reconciliation of cancelled cheques or electronic payments clearing the bank with the cash disbursements journal for a given period.
- A reconciliation of the balance on the bank statement with the general ledger balance at the end of the proof-of-cash period.

A proof of cash can be performed for one or more interim months, the entire year, or the last month of the year. Figure 14-6 on the next page shows a four-column proof of cash for an interim month.

The auditor uses a proof of cash to determine whether the following occurred:

- All recorded cash receipts were deposited.
- All deposits in the bank were recorded in the accounting records.
- All recorded cash disbursements were paid by the bank.
- All amounts that were paid by the bank were recorded.

The concern in an interim-month proof of cash is not with adjusting account balances, but rather with reconciling the amounts per accounting records and the bank.

When the auditor does a proof of cash, he or she is combining tests of controls and tests of details of balances. For example, the proof of the cash receipts is a test of recorded transactions, whereas the bank reconciliation is a test of the balance in cash

auditing in action 14-1
Positive Pay Reduces Cheque Fraud

Positive pay is an automated fraud detection tool offered by most banks. An organization using positive pay sends a file of issued cheques to the bank each day that cheques are written. The file sent to the bank includes the cheque number, account number, issue date, and dollar amount. The positive pay service matches the account number, cheque number, and dollar amount of each cheque presented for payment against the list of cheques provided by the organization. All three components of the cheque must match exactly for the cheque to be paid. When a cheque is presented that does not match, it is reported as an exception and an image of the cheque is sent to the organization so that it can make a pay/no pay decision and can either instruct the bank to pay or return the cheque.

These are good controls that assist the client in preventing cheque fraud. Auditors who have clients with this capability would need to consider controls over the issuing of the cheque details to the bank as well as controls over who has the ability to instruct the bank to either pay or return the cheque in addition to the positive-pay features provided by the bank.

Sources: 1. "CIBC Positive Pay," **www.cibc.com/ca/commercial/business-solutions/cash-management/positive-pay.html**. 2. "RBC Express Positive Pay," **www.rbcroyalbank.com/commercial/cashmanagement/1rx-positive.html**. All accessed: March 11, 2012.

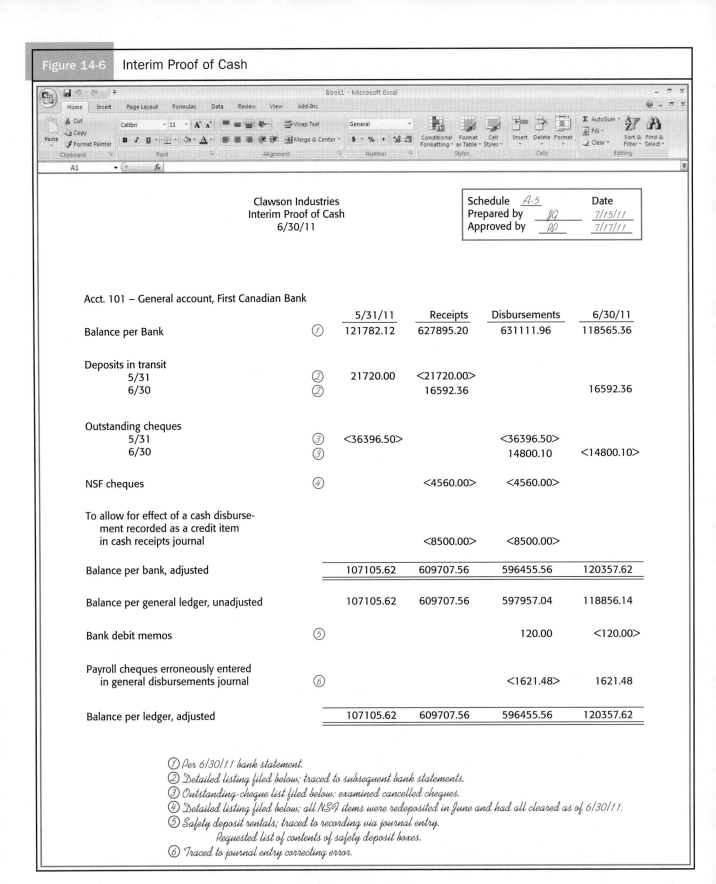

Figure 14-6 Interim Proof of Cash

Clawson Industries
Interim Proof of Cash
6/30/11

Schedule _A-5_   Date
Prepared by   JG   7/15/11
Approved by   RP   7/17/11

Acct. 101 – General account, First Canadian Bank

		5/31/11	Receipts	Disbursements	6/30/11
Balance per Bank	①	121782.12	627895.20	631111.96	118565.36
Deposits in transit					
5/31	②	21720.00	<21720.00>		
6/30	②		16592.36		16592.36
Outstanding cheques					
5/31	③	<36396.50>		<36396.50>	
6/30	③			14800.10	<14800.10>
NSF cheques	④		<4560.00>	<4560.00>	
To allow for effect of a cash disbursement recorded as a credit item in cash receipts journal			<8500.00>	<8500.00>	
Balance per bank, adjusted		107105.62	609707.56	596455.56	120357.62
Balance per general ledger, unadjusted		107105.62	609707.56	597957.04	118856.14
Bank debit memos	⑤			120.00	<120.00>
Payroll cheques erroneously entered in general disbursements journal	⑥			<1621.48>	1621.48
Balance per ledger, adjusted		107105.62	609707.56	596455.56	120357.62

① Per 6/30/11 bank statement.
② Detailed listing filed below; traced to subsequent bank statements.
③ Outstanding-cheque list filed below; examined cancelled cheques.
④ Detailed listing filed below; all NSF items were redeposited in June and had all cleared as of 6/30/11.
⑤ Safety deposit rentals; traced to recording via journal entry.
     Requested list of contents of safety deposit boxes.
⑥ Traced to journal entry correcting error.

at a particular time. The proof of cash is an excellent method of comparing recorded cash receipts and disbursements with the bank account and with the bank reconciliation. However, the auditor must recognize that the proof of cash disbursements is not for discovering cheques written for an improper amount, fraudulent cheques, or other misstatements in which the dollar amount appearing on the cash disbursements records is incorrect. Similarly, the proof of cash receipts is not useful for uncovering the theft of cash receipts or the recording and deposit of an improper amount of cash.

Tests for kiting Embezzlers occasionally cover a defalcation of cash by a practice known as **kiting**: transferring money from one bank to another and improperly recording the transaction, which overstates cash. The day before the balance sheet date, a cheque is drawn on one bank account and immediately deposited in a second account for credit before the end of the accounting period. In making this transfer, the embezzler is careful to make sure that the cheque is deposited at a late enough date that it does not clear the first bank until after the end of the period. Assuming that the bank transfer is not recorded until after the balance sheet date, the amount of the transfer is recorded as an asset in both banks. Although there are other ways of perpetrating this fraud, each involves the basic device of increasing the bank balance to cover a shortage by the use of bank transfers.

A useful approach to test for kiting, as well as for unintentional errors in recording bank transfers, is listing all bank transfers made a few days before and after the balance sheet date and tracing each to the accounting records for proper recording. An example of a bank transfer schedule is included in Figure 14-7. The working paper shows that there were four bank transfers shortly before and after the balance sheet date.

There are several things that should be audited on the bank transfer schedule:

- The accuracy of the information on the bank transfer schedule should be verified. The auditor should compare the disbursement and receipt information on the schedule with the cash disbursements and cash receipts journals to make sure that

> **Kiting**—the transfer of money from one bank account to another and improperly recording the transfer so that the amount is recorded as an asset in both accounts; used by embezzlers to cover a defalcation of cash.

Figure 14-7 Bank Transfer Working Paper

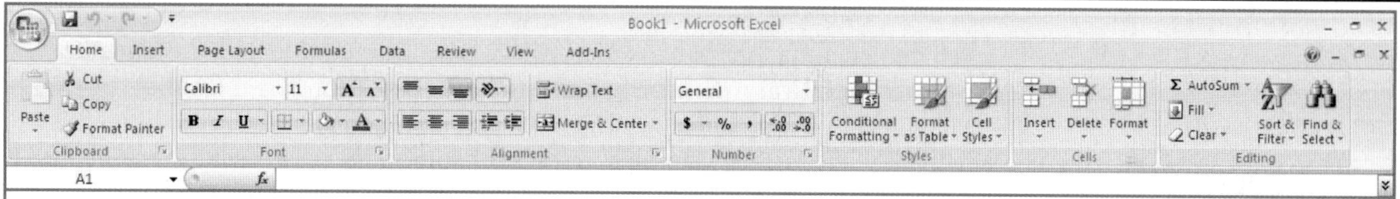

Clawson Industries
Schedule of Interbank Transfers
December 31, 2011

Schedule _A-7_
Prepared by _Client / DED 1/10/12_
Approved by _SW 1/18/12_

	Disbursements					Receipts	
Cheque No. (1)	Bank (2)	Amount (3)	Date Recorded in Books (4)	Date Paid by Bank (5)	Bank (6)	Date Recorded in Books (7)	Date Received by Bank (8)
#8018	First Canadian - general	$20,642✓	12-26-11⊗	12-28-11□	Federal Charter - payroll	12-28-11⊘	12-29-11□⊘
#8029	First Canadian - general	$37,998✓ A-2	12-28-11✗	01-02-12□	Federal Charter - savings	12-29-11⊘	12-29-11□⊘
#8038	First Canadian - general	$10,000✓ A-2	12-30-11✗	01-08-12□	Federal Charter - savings	12-30-11⊘	01-03-12□ⓦ
#8085	First Canadian - general	$21,014✓	01-02-12⊗	01-08-12□	Federal Charter - payroll	01-03-12⊘	01-08-12□⊘

✓ Traced to cash disbursements records.
⊘ Traced to cash receipts records.
✗ Cheque included as outstanding on bank reconciliation.
⊗ Cheque not included as outstanding on bank reconciliation.
ⓦ Receipt included as a deposit in transit.
□ Traced to bank statement.
⊘ Receipt not included as a deposit in transit.

Note: Examined cash disbursements and cash receipts records for cheques to and deposits from bank accounts. None included except those listed above.

it is accurate. Similarly, the dates on the schedule for transfers that were received and disbursed should be compared with the bank statement. Finally, cash disbursements and receipts journals should be examined to ensure that all transfers a few days before and after the balance sheet date have been included on the schedule. The symbol explanations on the working paper in Figure 14-7 indicate that these steps have been taken.

- The bank transfers must be recorded in both the receiving and disbursing banks. If, for example, there were a $10,000 transfer from Bank A to Bank B but only the disbursement was recorded, this could be evidence of an attempt to conceal a cash theft.

- The date of the recording of the disbursements and receipts for each transfer must be in the same fiscal year. In Figure 14-7, the dates in the two "date recorded in books" columns [columns (4) and (7)] are in the same period for each transfer; therefore, they are recorded correctly. If a cash disbursement was recorded in the current fiscal year and the receipt in the subsequent fiscal year, it might be an attempt to cover a cash shortage.

- Disbursements on the bank transfer schedule should be correctly included in or excluded from year-end bank reconciliations as outstanding cheques. In Figure 14-7, the 12-31-11 bank reconciliation should include outstanding cheques for the second and third transfers but not the other two. [Compare the dates in columns (4) and (5).] Understating outstanding cheques on the bank reconciliation indicates the possibility of kiting.

- Receipts on the bank transfer schedule should be correctly included in or excluded from year-end bank reconciliations as deposits in transit. In Figure 14-7, the 12-31-11 bank reconciliation should indicate a deposit in transit for the third transfer but not for the other three. (Compare the dates for each transfer in the last two columns.) Overstating deposits in transit on the bank reconciliation indicates the possibility of kiting.

concept check

C14-5 When could kiting occur and what does it do? How would it be accomplished?

C14-6 How can the auditor test for kiting?

Even though audit tests of bank transfers are usually fraud-oriented, they are often performed on audits in which there are numerous bank transfers, regardless of the internal controls. When there are numerous intercompany transfers, it is difficult to be sure that each is correctly handled unless a schedule of transfers near the end of the year is prepared and each transfer is traced to the accounting records and bank statements. In addition to the possibility of kiting, inaccurate handling of transfers could result in a misclassification between cash and accounts payable. Due to the materiality of transfers and the relative ease of performing the tests, many auditors believe that the tests should always be performed.

4 Additional Examples of Cash Auditing

AUDIT OF THE PAYROLL BANK ACCOUNT Tests of the payroll bank reconciliation should take only a few minutes if there is an imprest payroll account and an independent reconciliation of the bank account such as that described for the general account. Typically, the only reconciling items are outstanding cheques and, for most audits, the great majority clear shortly after the cheques are issued. In testing the payroll bank account balances, it is necessary to obtain a bank reconciliation, a bank confirmation, and a cut-off bank statement. The reconciliation procedures are performed in the same manner as those described for general cash. Naturally, extended procedures are necessary if the controls are inadequate or if the bank account does not reconcile with the general ledger imprest cash balance.

The discussion in the preceding paragraph should not be interpreted as implying that the audit of payroll is unimportant. Chapter 15 will show the reader that the most important audit procedures for verifying payroll are tests of controls. Most common payroll misstatements will be discovered by those procedures rather than by checking the imprest bank account balance.

AUDIT OF ELECTRONIC CASH TRANSACTIONS As described in Audit Challenge 14-2, many organizations receive cash or make cash payments electronically. For a typical small to medium-sized business, electronic cash receipts are used if the business sells to customers over the counter and accepts debit or credit card payments from those customers. Electronic cash payments include automatic payments for loans, insurance, and payroll to employees. More sophisticated or larger businesses could use **electronic data interchange** (EDI—the electronic transfer of business documents, such as invoices or purchase orders) with their **electronic funds transfers** (EFTs—the electronic transfer of funds, either as payment or receipt, e.g., using a debit card).

Electronic data interchange (EDI)—the electronic transfer of business documents, such as invoices and purchase orders.

Electronic funds transfer (EFT)—the electronic transfer of funds, either as payment or receipt (e.g., using a debit card).

CONTROL OVER DEBIT CARD CASH RECEIPTS When a business accepts debit card payments from its customers, the customer swipes his or her debit card and enters a personal identification number (PIN) to authorize the transfer of funds from the customer's bank account to the organization's bank account. Depending upon the type of system used by the client, there could be one copy of the printed receipt or two (since the client may simply store the receipt electronically). A printed receipt does go to the customer, either as a separate piece of paper or listed on the bottom of the sales invoice.

Although most debit card transactions are processed accurately, a very small percentage are not. The organization should therefore continue its cash reconciliation functions as part of the bank reconciliation for these electronic transactions. Most organizations keep track of payment methods automatically using their point-of-sale (POS) systems. Thus, the daily sales are broken down by cash, debit card, credit card, cheque, and accounts receivable. When performing the bank reconciliation, the debit card total should agree with the amounts automatically deposited into the bank. This reconciliation should be handled by a person independent of the POS function. These receipts should be tested as part of the sales and receivables transaction cycle.

Control over Electronic Payments

AUTOMATIC PRE-AUTHORIZED MONTHLY PAYMENTS Loan payments, interest payments, and insurance payments made on monthly or other regular intervals are based on a loan agreement or regular invoice. When the bank statement is sent to an organization, the only evidence of this payment will likely be a line on the bank statement showing the amount, a reference number, and possibly the name of the company that was paid.

audit challenge 14-2
Electronic Payments

MANY organizations use electronic funds transfers (EFTs) when they are transferring cash among banks, collecting from customers, paying employees, and paying vendors. Under these systems, cash is transferred instantly. For example, when Hillsburg Hardware Limited receives a debit card payment from ABC Hardware Ltd., the cash is transferred immediately from ABC's bank account to Hillsburg's bank account. No cheque is issued.

EFTs such as those via debit card and electronic data interchange (EDI) have the potential to improve internal controls, since there is no cash handling by employees. However, the risk of incorrect transfers or theft by unauthorized transfers still exists.

When assessing internal controls, the auditor needs to evaluate and document controls in all software involved (data communications, data transfer, specialized EDI programs,

and access). With electronic payments, year-end balances of accounts receivable, accounts payable, or inventory may be reduced since funds are received closer to the date of the transaction. Where funds are transferred electronically, there is an increased need for the enhanced security features of encryption, access control, and authentication (verifying the identity of the parties to a transaction).

CRITICAL THINKING QUESTIONS

1. When accounts receivable and inventory are small (i.e., immaterial), what type of audit testing is used for the sales and accounts receivable transactions? Why?
2. What is the role of password protection in the use of EDI and EFT? How does the auditor test such controls?

The organization under audit should have controls to ensure that only authorized amounts are set up for payment and that all automatic withdrawals are recorded in the accounts in the period made. These payments should be tested as part of the purchases and payments cycle.

PAYROLL PAYMENTS As with a payroll paid by cheque, payroll payments made electronically should be made using an imprest bank account.

Payment is usually initiated by the organization sending to the bank or other financial institution a set of forms or electronic data files specifying how much employees should be paid, what deductions should be made, the appropriate tax withholdings, and the bank accounts to which the funds should be transferred. The bank may (or may not) do the actual calculations, process payments, and send either a listing or a data file to the organization of payments made.

Again, there is a two-step authorization phase here. The first step covers master file information (e.g., wage rate, withholdings rate, bank account number), and the second covers the actual wages paid in a specific pay period. These controls should be documented, evaluated, and tested as part of the human resource and payroll cycle. As part of control over cash, a person independent of payroll should verify bank account numbers used for payments and should verify that payments from the imprest bank account match the payroll journal.

AUDIT OF ELECTRONIC RECEIPTS AND PAYMENTS The extent of audit work conducted on the bank reconciliation depends on the assessed quality of internal controls. There are usually fewer outstanding bank transactions for electronic transactions than for paper transactions sent via mail, since the timing difference between invoice and receipt is minimal.

When client personnel prepare the bank reconciliation, electronic payments should be agreed to an authorized schedule of such payments by date, payee account number, and amount. The auditor would review the authorized schedule of payments and controls over its preparation. Similarly, deposits would be traced to the client's POS system records.

For the imprest payroll account reconciliation, the auditor would review the documentation received from the bank and agree details to the reconciliation.

Audit of Petty Cash

Petty cash is a unique account because it is frequently immaterial in amount, and yet it is verified on most audits. The account is verified primarily because of the potential for defalcation and the client's expectation of an audit review even when the amount is immaterial.

INTERNAL CONTROLS OVER PETTY CASH The most important internal control for petty cash is the use of an imprest fund that is the responsibility of one individual. In addition, petty cash funds should not be mingled with other receipts, and the fund should be kept separate from all other activities. There should also be limits on the amount of any expenditure from petty cash, as well as on the total amount of the fund. The type of expenditure that can be made from petty cash transactions should be well defined by company policy.

Whenever a disbursement is made from petty cash, adequate internal controls require a responsible official's approval on a prenumbered petty cash form. The total of the actual cash and cheques in the fund plus the total unreimbursed petty cash forms that represent actual expenditures should equal the total amount of the petty cash fund stated in the general ledger. Periodically, surprise counts and a reconciliation of the petty cash fund should be made by the internal auditor or another responsible official.

When the petty cash balance runs low, a cheque payable to the petty cash custodian should be written on the general cash account for the replenishment of petty cash. The cheque should be for the exact amount of the prenumbered vouchers that are submitted as evidence of actual expenditures. These vouchers should be verified by the accounts payable clerk and cancelled to prevent their reuse.

AUDIT TESTS FOR PETTY CASH The emphasis in verifying petty cash should be on testing petty cash transactions rather than the ending balance in the account. Even if the amount of the petty cash fund is small, there is potential for numerous improper transactions if the fund is frequently reimbursed.

An important part of testing petty cash is first determining the client's procedures for handling the fund by discussing internal control with the custodian and examining the documentation of a few transactions. As a part of obtaining an understanding of internal control, it is necessary to identify internal controls and weaknesses. Even though most petty cash systems are not complex, it is often desirable to use a flowchart and an internal control questionnaire, primarily for documentation in subsequent audits. The tests of controls depend on the number and size of the petty cash reimbursements and the auditor's assessed level of control risk. When control risk is assessed at a low level and there are few reimbursement payments during the year, it is common for auditors not to test any further for reasons of immateriality. When the auditor decides to test petty cash, the two most common procedures are counting the petty cash balance and carrying out detailed tests of one or two reimbursement transactions. In such a case, the primary procedures should include footing (adding) the petty cash vouchers supporting the amount of the reimbursement, accounting for a sequence of petty cash vouchers, examining the petty cash vouchers for authorization and cancellation, and examining the attached documentation for reasonableness. Typical supporting documentation includes cash register tapes, invoices, and receipts.

Petty cash tests can ordinarily be performed at any time during the year, but as a matter of convenience, they are typically done on an interim date. If the balance in the petty cash fund is considered material, which is rarely the case, it should be counted at the end of the year. Unreimbursed expenditures should be examined as part of the count to determine whether the amount of unrecorded expenses is material.

concept check

C14-7 How do EDI and EFTs affect the audit trail at a business?

C14-8 How do EDI and EFTs affect the audit process?

Summary

1. *What are the different types of cash accounts?* They are the general cash account, the imprest payroll account, branch bank accounts, an imprest petty cash fund, and cash equivalents.

    Explain the relationship between cash and the other transaction cycles. Cash flows in and out of the cash account, with the other side of the accounting entry normally being in a different transaction cycle. For example, payroll payments, accounts payable payments, and receipts from sales all are recorded via the cash account.

    What are some of the risks of error or fraud in the cash cycle? Table 14-3 lists examples of major errors or fraud, which can be related to transactions from any cycle.

2. *How does the auditor consider corporate governance and internal controls when conducting the audit of cash?* The auditor evaluates and assesses controls in the other cycles and their impact upon cash. During the risk assessment process, the auditor will examine the control environment with respect to cash management and consider the impact upon all of the transaction cycles.

    Describe the steps in auditing the general cash account. Figure 14-2 described the risk-based audit approach as it applies to cash. After assessing control risk on an assertion basis, tests of controls are designed and performed, followed by the design and completion of tests of details. Year-end procedures include obtaining a bank confirmation and a bank cutoff statement, as well as tests of the bank reconciliation and the extent of testing will be based upon assessed control risk including risks of fraud.

3. *What additional procedures are conducted when there is suspicion of fraud?* Extended tests of the bank reconciliation or a proof of cash could be completed.

    What is "kiting" and how is it audited? If kiting (taking advantage of timing differences between banks to inflate cash) is suspected, then the auditor would prepare a bank transfer working paper.

4. *How is an audit of the payroll cash account different from the audit of the general cash account?* The payroll account may be an imprest account, containing only payroll cheques issued to employees. Having only a single transaction type means that it is easier to audit the account.

What special considerations exist for EFT transactions? Such transactions could involve complex software and access controls, requiring an increased reliance on automated computer controls.

How is petty cash audited? The auditor would likely examine controls over petty cash and conduct a petty cash count.

MyAccountingLab

Make the grade with MyAccountingLab: The questions, exercises, and problems marked in orange can be found on MyAccountingLab. You can practise them as often as you want, and most feature step-by-step guided instructions to help you find the right answer.

Review Questions

14-1 ❶ What is meant by an "imprest bank account" for a branch operation? Explain the purpose of using this type of bank account.

14-2 ❶ ❷ Explain the relationship among the initial assessed level of control risk, tests of controls for cash receipts, and tests of details of cash balances.

14-3 ❶ ❷ Explain the relationships among the initial assessed level of control risk, tests of controls for cash disbursements, and tests of details of cash balances. Give one example in which the conclusion reached about internal controls in cash disbursements would affect the tests of cash balances.

14-4 ❶ ❷ Assume that a client with excellent internal controls uses an imprest payroll bank account. Explain why the verification of the payroll bank reconciliation ordinarily takes less time than the tests of the general bank account, even if the number of cheques exceeds those written on the general account.

14-5 ❶ ❷ ❸ Why is there a greater emphasis on the detection of fraud in tests of details of cash balances than for other balance sheet accounts? Give two specific examples that demonstrate how this emphasis affects the auditor's evidence accumulation in auditing year-end cash.

14-6 ❷ Why is the monthly reconciliation of bank accounts by an independent person an important internal control over cash balances? Which individuals would generally not be considered independent for this responsibility?

14-7 ❷ Evaluate the effectiveness and state the shortcomings of the preparation of a bank reconciliation by the accountant in the manner described in the following statement: "When I reconcile the bank account, the first thing I do is to sort the cheques in numerical order and find which numbers are missing. Next I determine the amount of the uncleared cheques by referring to the cash disbursements journal. If the bank account reconciles at that point, I am all finished with the reconciliation. If it does not, I search for deposits in transit, cheques from the beginning of the outstanding cheque list that still have not cleared, other reconciling items, and bank errors until it reconciles. In most instances, I can do the reconciliation in 20 minutes."

14-8 ❷ How do bank confirmations differ from positive confirmations of accounts receivable? Distinguish between them in terms of the nature of the information confirmed, the sample size, and the appropriate action when the confirmation is not returned after the second request. Explain the rationale for the differences between these two types of confirmations.

14-9 ❷ Evaluate the necessity for following the practice described by an auditor: "In confirming bank accounts, I insist upon a response from every bank the client has done business with in the past two years, even though the account may be closed at the balance sheet date."

14-10 ❷ Describe what is meant by a cutoff bank statement and state its purpose.

14-11 ❷ Why are auditors usually less concerned about the client's cash receipts cutoff than the cutoff for sales? Explain the procedure involved in testing for the cutoff for cash receipts.

14-12 ❷ How would a company's bank reconciliation reflect an electronic deposit of cash received by the bank—from credit card agencies that make payments on behalf of customers purchasing products from the company's website—but not recorded in the company's records?

14-13 ❸ When the auditor fails to obtain a cutoff bank statement, it is common to "prove" the entire statement for the month subsequent to the balance sheet date. How is this done and what is its purpose?

14-14 ❸ Distinguish between "lapping" and "kiting." Describe audit procedures that can be used to uncover each.

14-15 ❸ Explain why, in verifying bank reconciliations, most auditors emphasize the possibility of a non-existent deposit in transit being included in the reconciliation and an outstanding cheque being omitted rather than the omission of a deposit in transit and the inclusion of a non-existent outstanding cheque.

14-16 ❹ Distinguish between the verification of petty cash reimbursements and the verification of the balance in the fund. Explain how each is done. Which is more important?

Discussion Questions and Problems

14-17 ❶ ❷ You are auditing general cash for Trail Supply Corp. for the fiscal year ended July 31. The client has not prepared the July 31 bank reconciliation. After a brief discussion with the owner, you agree to prepare the reconciliation with assistance from one of Trail Supply's clerks. You obtain the following information:

	General Ledger	Bank Statement
Beginning balance	$ 4,611	$ 5,753
Deposits		25,056
Cash receipts journal	25,456	
Cheques cleared		(23,615)
Cash disbursements journal	(21,811)	
July bank service charge		(87)
Note paid directly		(6,100)
NSF cheque		(311)
Ending balance	$ 8,256	$ 696

June 30 Bank Reconciliation

Information in General Ledger and Bank Statement	
Balance per bank	$5,753
Deposits in transit	600
Outstanding cheques	1,742
Balance per books	4,611

In addition, the following information is obtained:
1. The total of outstanding cheques on June 30 was $1,692.
2. The total for cheques that were recorded in the July disbursements journal was $20,467.
3. A cheque for $1,060 cleared the bank but had not been recorded in the cash disbursements journal. It was for an acquisition of inventory. Trail Supply uses the periodic inventory method.
4. A cheque for $396 was charged to Trail Supply but had been written on an associated company's bank account.
5. Deposits included $600 from June and $24,456 for July.
6. The bank withdrew from Trail Supply's account a non-sufficient funds (NSF) customer cheque totaling $311. The credit manager concluded that the customer intentionally closed its account and that the owner had left the city. The account was turned over to a collection agency.
7. The bank deducted $5,800 plus interest from Trail Supply's account for a loan made by the bank under an agreement signed four months ago. The note payable was recorded at $5,800 on Trail Supply's books.

REQUIRED
a. Prepare a bank reconciliation that shows both the unadjusted and adjusted balances per the general ledger.
b. Identify the nature of adjustments required.
c. What audit procedures would you use to verify each item in the bank reconciliation?

14-18 ❶ ❷ ❸ The following are fraud and other irregularities that might be found in the client's year-end cash balance. (Assume the balance sheet date is June 30.)
1. A cheque was omitted from the outstanding cheque list on the June 30 bank reconciliation. It cleared the bank July 7.
2. A cheque was omitted from the outstanding cheque list on the bank reconciliation. It cleared the bank September 6.
3. Cash receipts collected on accounts receivable from July 2 to July 5 were included as June 29 and 30 cash receipts.
4. A loan from the bank on June 26 was credited directly to the client's bank account. The loan was not entered in the books as of June 30.
5. A cheque that was dated June 26 and disbursed in June was not recorded in the cash disbursements journal, but it was included as an outstanding cheque on June 30.
6. A bank transfer recorded in the accounting records on July 2 was included as a deposit in transit on June 30.
7. The outstanding cheques on the June 30 bank reconciliation were underfooted by $2,000.

REQUIRED
a. Assuming that each of these misstatements was intentional, state the most likely motivation of the person responsible.
b. What control could be instituted for each intentional misstatement to reduce the likelihood of occurrence?
c. List an audit procedure that could be used to discover each misstatement.

14-19 ❸ Regional Transport Company is a large branch of a national company. Regional maintains its own bank account. Cash is periodically transferred to the central head office account in Montreal. On the branch account's records, bank transfers are recorded as a debit to the home office clearing account and a credit to the branch bank account. Similarly, the home office account is recorded as a debit to the central bank account and a credit to the branch office clearing account. Gordon Light is the accountant on staff for both the home office and the branch bank accounts. Because he also reconciles the bank account, the senior auditor, Cindy Marintette, is concerned about this internal control weakness.

As a part of the year-end audit of bank transfers, Cindy asks you to schedule the transfers for the last few days in 2012 and the first few days of 2013. You prepare the following list:

Amount of Transfer	Date Recorded in the Home Office Cash Receipts Journal	Date Recorded in the Branch Office Cash Disbursements Journal	Date Deposited in the Home Office Bank Account	Date Cleared the Branch Bank Account
$12,000	12-27-12	12-29-12	12-26-12	12-27-12
26,000	12-28-12	01-02-13	12-28-12	12-29-12
14,000	01-02-13	12-30-12	12-28-12	12-29-12
11,000	12-26-12	12-26-12	12-28-12	01-03-13
15,000	01-02-13	01-02-13	12-28-12	12-31-12
28,000	01-07-13	01-05-13	12-28-12	01-03-13
37,000	01-04-13	01-06-13	01-03-13	01-05-13

REQUIRED

a. State the appropriate audit procedures you should perform in verifying each bank transfer.
b. Prepare any adjusting entries required in the home office records.
c. Prepare any adjusting entries required in the branch bank records.

d. State how each bank transfer should be included in the December 31, 2012, bank reconciliation for the home office account after your adjustments in part (b).
e. State how each bank transfer should be included in the December 31, 2012, bank reconciliation of the branch bank account after your adjustments in part (c).

14-20 ❸ You are doing the first-year audit of Sherman School District and have been assigned responsibility for doing a four-column proof of cash for the month of October 2012. You obtain the following information:

1. Balance per books	September	30	$ 8,106
	October	31	3,850
2. Balance per bank	September	30	5,411
	October	31	6,730
3. Outstanding cheques	September	30	$ 916
	October 31		1,278
4. Cash receipts for October	per bank		26,536
	per books		19,711
5. Deposits in transit	September	30	3,611
	October 31		693

6. Interest on a bank loan for the month of October, charged by the bank but not recorded, was $596.
7. Proceeds on a note of the Jones Company were collected by the bank on October 29 but were not entered on the books:

Principal	$3,300
Interest	307
	$3,607

8. On October 26, a $407 cheque of the Billings Company was charged to Sherman School District's account by the bank in error.
9. Dishonoured cheques are not recorded on the books unless they permanently fail to clear the bank. The bank treats them as disbursements when they are dishonoured and as deposits when they are redeposited. Cheques totaling $609 were dishonoured in October; $300 was redeposited in October and $309 in November.

REQUIRED

a. Prepare a four-column proof of cash for the month ended October 31. It should show both adjusted and unadjusted cash.
b. Prepare all adjusting entries.

14-21 ❷❹ Santasgiftworld.com is an online retailer of children's toys. The chief executive officer has noticed that margins have been deteriorating over those of previous years due to an increase in cost of goods sold coupled with a much faster increase in freight out and bad-debt expenses. He has also heard through the grapevine that some customers have complained of unauthorized charges on their credit cards. Other customers have complained of placing orders and never having received them, necessitating replacement shipments. Still more complaints of unauthorized charges have been received from individuals claiming never to have ordered products at all. You have been contacted to help Santasgiftworld.com improve its operations

and to prevent possible litigation arising from continuing problems of this type.

Santasgiftworld.com employs 100 individuals. Its customer base consists mainly of individuals but also smaller toy stores, day-care centres, and schools, all of which order through the company website. The website has pages where customers can view all of the products and prices. There is a virtual shopping cart available for each customer once he or she has set up an account. A customer choosing to make a purchase simply clicks on the direct link to the shopping cart from the desired product and proceeds to checkout. There the customer is prompted to choose a major credit card payment method and enter the shipping address. Once this information has been entered, the customer chooses a shipping method: Canada Post, UPS, or Federal Express. The customer is then informed of the total price and the date to expect shipment.

Every two hours, the orders placed on the website are reviewed, then entered into the company's main database for fulfillment. Once an order is shipped, credit card information is extracted and transmitted for settlement in Santasgiftworld .com's favour.

Orders have been placed with the company, but the customers in question honestly deny ever submitting those orders. It turns out that many of those orders had been placed by the children of the customers, without the customers' knowledge. The children were able to gain access to their parents' accounts after the web ordering system recognized cookies on the hard drives. When the children went to the website, the page recognized them as the users of the account and gave them authorized access to make purchases.

REQUIRED

Identify control weaknesses at Santasgiftworld.com. For each control weakness,
a. State the exposure created.
b. Provide a recommendation to prevent or detect the exposure.
c. Provide an audit test of detail that could be used in assessing the impact on the financial statements.
d. Identify the audit objective(s) addressed by the audit tests.

Professional Judgment Problem

14-22 ❷ ❸ Yip-Chuk Inc. had weak internal control over its cash transactions. Facts about its cash position at November 30 were as follows:

The cash account showed a balance of $18,901.62, which included undeposited receipts. A credit of $100 on the bank's records did not appear on the records of the company. The balance per bank statement was $15,550. Outstanding cheques were no. 62 for $116.25, no. 183 for $150.00, no. 284 for $253.25, no. 8621 for $190.71, no. 8623 for $206.80, and no. 8632 for $145.28.

The cashier, Khalid Nasser, embezzled all undeposited receipts in excess of $3,794.41 and prepared the reconciliations shown in the table on the right.

REQUIRED
a. Prepare a supporting schedule showing how much Khalid embezzled.
b. How did he attempt to conceal his theft?

Balance, per general ledger, November 30		$18,901.62
Add: Outstanding cheques		
8621	$190.71	
8623	206.80	
8632	145.28	
		442.79
		19,344.41
Less: Undeposited receipts		3,794.41
Balance per bank, November 30		15,550.00
Deduct: Unrecorded credit		100.00
True cash balance, November 30		$15,450.00

c. Using only the information given, name two specific features of internal control that were apparently missing.
  (AICPA adapted)

Case

14-23 ❶ ❷ Three years ago, Peng started a business providing translation and document services to businesses that source goods from China for the Canadian retail market. At first, Peng did all of the work himself, marketing his services to potential customers, receiving orders, translating documents, suggesting improvements for wording, billing accounts, preparing the bank deposits, and maintaining the account information in a simple accounting system. The business has now grown to include preparing various advertising materials for foreign companies that sell goods in China.

Peng has hired you as the accounting manager and two other clerical staff, Xiaoli and Weihua, to handle the new accounting system and the accounting needs of the organization. Peng has suggested that the accounting duties include the following responsibilities:

Xiaoli	Weihua	Peng	Accounting Manager
• Receives enquiries from new customers and arranges for Peng to contact them (1) • Receives vendor invoices • Records the sales and receivables (2)	• Prepares the bank deposit • Keeps custody of payments received and takes the deposit to the bank (3) • Prepares the bank reconciliation (4)	• Provides service quotes for new customers • Determines what prices to charge for services • Authorizes the quoted price	• Authorizes a vendor invoice for payment (5) • Records vendor invoices in the accounts payable system (6)

a. Review the listed duties that are numbered (1) through (6). Indicate whether the duty should be reassigned, and why.

b. Prepare a revised table of duties that takes into consideration the reasons that you mentioned in Part a.
(CGA Adapted)

Ongoing Small Business Case: PayPal.com Problems at CondoCleaners.com

14-24 ❶ ❷ ❸ To increase his reach with customers in condominium towers, Jim has decided to accept payment from users of PayPal.com in addition to the credit card payments that he was accepting via his secure website. Jim had been using PayPal.com for about three months. One morning he received emails from several of his upset customers complaining that they had been billed several times for the same service. Yet when Jim looked at his PayPal records, he found that only one payment had been processed in his favour. Upon contacting the affected customers, Jim found that the customers had responded to a phishing email from someone pretending to belong to CondoCleaners.com customer support and had given their payment information to unauthorized individuals who had copied the transaction information and collected additional money. This means that someone had hacked into his company's website and accessed his customer email list.

REQUIRED

What are Jim's responsibilities in this case? What actions would you suggest that he take?

15　Audit of the human resources and payroll cycle

A payroll payment helps us buy groceries, pay rent or a mortgage, and pay for tuition. For many workers, it may be the crucial reason to show up for work every day. For a business, it can be the largest expense—if payroll is too high, gross margins are too low and the company could go into receivership. Good human resource policies help a business hire competent, honest employees who help provide for an effective and honest control environment. Management accountants implement controls over payroll and human resources, while various types of auditors examine payroll to evaluate those controls and to consider the risks of payroll fraud.

LEARNING OBJECTIVES

1 Explain the importance of the human resources and payroll cycle. Describe the risks of fraud or error in the cycle. Explain how the functions and records in this cycle help to prevent or detect fraud or error.

2 List typical audit tests of controls by assertion.

3 Consider the impact of outsourcing on the controls over, and the audit of, payroll. Apply these principles to other application cycles.

4 Highlight the misstatements that could be detected by an analytical review of payroll. Describe tests of details for the liability and expense accounts in the human resources and payroll cycle. Explain how analytical review and tests of details help the auditor achieve assurance for audit objectives about presentation and disclosure.

STANDARDS REFERENCED IN THIS CHAPTER

CICA Standards

CAS 402 – Auditor considerations relating to an entity using a service organization

CSAE 3416 – Reporting on controls at a service organization

IAS 24 – Related party disclosures

Viral Can Be a Good Word or a Nasty Surprise

Viral networking is an advertising or connection phrase of the present—it is the way that you communicate by word of mouth, electronically. The method is being used to promote organization-wide social networks intended to keep employees happy, connected, and well-informed. Such systems are being adopted by a broad range of organizations, including accounting firms.

One large example is IBM, which started with an internal directory of 450,000 employees in 2000. The directory was so heavily used that IBM created its social network called Beehive that is behind the company's firewall. IBM claims that the site fosters innovation, as employees talk electronically, rather than around the water cooler or coffee machine. The site is an important tool that is the subject of ongoing research at IBM.

Such social networking can encourage employees to make effective use of their existing tools for communication. In this way, the viral approach can be positive. However, an unhappy employee can also destroy a company by planting a virus.

A contract employee of Fannie Mae (in the United States) was charged with planting Trojan horse (delayed) computer malware at the company in January 2009. Employed there for three years, he had access to hardware (servers) and operating system-level software. The Trojan horse was set to delete company employees' access to all 4,000 servers and then destroy all of the corporate data by overwriting them with zeros. Thankfully, the malware was detected by a senior computer engineer. Had the malware been executed, the effects on the company could have been minor or disastrous, depending upon the quality of its disaster recovery and quality assurance processes. As discussed later in this chapter, Trojan horse software is also being used to steal money from many businesses.

IMPORTANCE TO AUDITORS

Auditors examine risks and controls in the human resources and payroll cycle for several reasons, including evaluating the quality of segregation of duties (which affects every financial cycle) and the quality of controls over payment of payroll. Internal auditors may be concerned about what is posted on a social networking site if confidential strategic planning information can be readily posted. Employee termination procedures should include disabling employee access to both transaction processing systems and internal social network sites. This is an

Sources: 1. Brandel, Mary, "The new employee connection: social networking behind the firewall," *Computerworld*, August 11, 2008, **www.computerworld.com**, Accessed: September 2, 2008. 2. Kloppott, Freeman, "Ex-Fannie Mae worker charged with planting computer virus," *The Examiner*, January 29, 2009, **www.dcexaminer.com**, Accessed: January 29, 2009. 3. Geyer, Werner, Joan DiMicco, Beth Brownholtz, Casey Dugan and David R. Millen. 2011. "IBM Watson Research Center, Project: Beehive," **http://domino.watson.ibm.com/cambridge/research.nsf/0/8b6d4cd6 8fc12b52852573d1005cc0fc?opendocument**, Accessed: November 15, 2011.

continued >

added administrative process that developers of social network sites may not have considered. Auditors can contribute by pointing out the need for such procedures.

All types of auditors would have nightmares about the potential for employees planting a virus if the organization's controls over preventing and detecting these were poor. Times of economic transition, when employees are concerned about their jobs, or when a corporation is engaged in contentious activities, could increase the risks of internal sabotage. Auditors can help to point out these risks and provide recommendations to improve controls.

WHAT DO YOU THINK?

1. What risks might be present in the payroll cycle with respect to the use of an organization's internal information systems, including social networking sites?

2. How does employee motivation affect the quality of internal controls?

3. During what phases of the audit does the auditor assess employee motivation? Provide examples of audit techniques that the auditor would use to assess employee motivation to correctly execute internal control procedures.

OUR opening vignette illustrates the importance of motivated employees in implementing effective internal controls. If the senior computer engineer at Fannie Mae had not been browsing through computer files, then the Trojan horse malware would not have been detected.

1 The Nature and Importance of the Human Resources and Payroll Cycle

The **human resources and payroll cycle** is the transaction cycle that begins with the hiring of personnel. It includes obtaining and accounting for services from the employees. It ends with payment to the employees for the services performed and to the government and other institutions for withheld and accrued employee benefits. It involves the employment and payment of all employees, regardless of classification or method of determining compensation. The employees include executives on straight salary plus bonus, office workers on monthly salary with or without overtime, salespeople on a commission basis, and factory and unionized personnel paid on an hourly basis.

The cycle is important for several reasons. First, the salaries, wages, employee benefits (e.g., Canada Pension, employment insurance, health and dental care), and other employer costs (e.g., workplace safety insurance) are a major expense in all companies. Second, labour is such an important consideration in the valuation of inventory in manufacturing and construction companies that the improper classification and allocation of labour can result in a material misstatement of net income. Finally, payroll is an area in which large amounts of company resources can be wasted through inefficiency or stolen through fraud.

The Hillsburg Hardware Limited trial balance in Chapter 5 includes typical general ledger accounts affected by the human resources and payroll cycle. They are

Human resources and payroll cycle—the transaction cycle that begins with the hiring of personnel, includes obtaining and accounting for services from the employees, and ends with payment to the employees for the services performed and to the government and other institutions for withheld and accrued employee benefits.

identified as human resource and payroll accounts by the letter P in the left column. In larger companies there may be 50 or more payroll expense accounts. As with the sales and collection cycle, the audit of the human resources and payroll includes obtaining an understanding of internal control, assessment of control risk, tests of controls, analytical procedures, and tests of details of balances.

There are several important differences between the human resources and payroll cycle and other cycles in a typical audit:

- There is only one class of transactions for payroll. Most cycles include at least two classes of transactions. For example, the sales and collection cycle includes both sales and cash receipts transactions and often sales returns and charge-off of uncollectables. Payroll has only one class because the receipt of services from employees and the payment for those services through payroll occur within a short period.
- Transactions are far more significant than related balance sheet accounts. Balances in payroll-related accounts such as accrued payroll and withheld taxes are usually small compared with the total amount of transactions for the year.
- Internal controls over payroll are effective for almost all companies, even small ones. The reasons for effective controls are harsh federal and provincial penalties for errors in withholding and paying payroll taxes, and employee morale problems if employees are not paid or are underpaid.

Because of these three characteristics, auditors typically emphasize tests of controls and analytical procedures in the audit of payroll.

The way in which accounting information flows through the various accounts in the human resources and payroll cycle is illustrated by T-accounts in Figure 15-1.

Figure 15-1 | Accounts in the Human Resources and Payroll Cycle

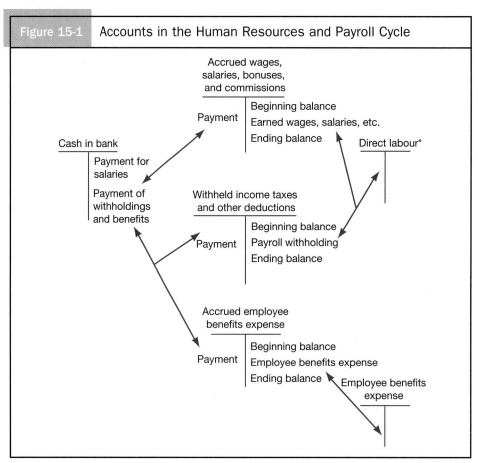

*Separate operating accounts for payroll also normally include officers' salaries and bonuses, office salaries, sales salaries and commissions, and indirect manufacturing labour. These accounts have the same relationship to accrued wages and withheld taxes and other deductions that is shown for direct labour. Some companies use a payroll service that performs all of the above functions.

Normally, the accrued wages and salaries account is used only at the end of an accounting period. Throughout the period, expenses are charged when the employees are actually paid rather than when the labour costs are incurred. The accruals for labour are recorded by adjusting entries at the end of the period for any earned but unpaid labour costs.

Risks of Fraud or Error in the Human Resources and Payroll Cycle

The payroll cycle is different from most cycles because we have many repeated transactions (such as an employee weekly salary). If there are errors in a wage rate, such errors can rapidly escalate into material amounts. As we did in the sales and cash chapters, we organize this cycle's major risks of fraud or error into three categories, as shown in Table 15-1.

A human resource and payroll cycle that has good controls will prevent or detect many of the potential consequences of the risks described in Table 15-1. The auditor of a private company converting to IFRS would need to look carefully at the quality of related party transactions, since IAS 24 Related Party Disclosures requires more disclosures (for example key management compensation) which has been in the past only required for public companies.

Table 15-1	Major Risks of Error or Fraud in the Human Resources and Payroll Cycle	
Risks of Error	**Risks of Misappropriation of Assets, Other Fraud or Illegal Acts**	**Risks of Inadequate Disclosure or Incorrect Presentation of Financial Information, Including Fraudulent Financial Reporting**
	Unauthorized wage rate increases, payment of overtime, overstated hours, or overstated commissions or bonuses.	
Undetected data entry errors (e.g., wage rates, hours worked, deduction codes, or others); employees paid twice, or other payment errors.		Overstated net income and inventory by recording excess labour costs in inventory.
	Set up and payment to fictitious employees.	
Late or incorrect provincial or federal payroll remittances.		Overstated net income by capitalizing excess labour costs as part of constructed fixed assets.
	Wages of terminated employees continue to be paid or are paid to unauthorized persons.	
Incorrect functional allocation of access rights, allowing employees to have unauthorized access to assets.		Understatement of pension obligations or pension costs (understating expenses or liabilities).
	Unauthorized access to confidential or private data leading to loss of cash (e-theft).	
Inappropriate response to phishing emails revealing access codes that lead to unauthorized access to assets and theft of assets.		Inadequate disclosure of related party transactions.

Next, we look at functions and internal controls in the human resources and payroll cycle, including those that mitigate the risks described in Table 15-1.

Functions in the Cycle, Related Documents and Records, and Internal Controls

The human resources and payroll cycle begins with the hiring of personnel and ends with payment to the employees for the services performed. Payment is made to the government and other institutions for employee withholdings (i.e., income tax, Canada [or Quebec] Pension Plan, employment insurance), and employee benefits (i.e., required contributions by the employer for the Canada [or Quebec] Pension Plan, employment insurance, workplace safety insurance, hospital insurance plans, provincial health and education taxes; and voluntary or negotiated employer contributions to company pension, medical, or dental plans). In between, the cycle involves obtaining services from the employees consistent with the objectives of the company and accounting for the services in a proper manner.

The first column of Table 14-2 (see page 453) lists the six business functions in a typical human resources and payroll cycle. The second column shows typical documents and records for each business function. These documents could be in paper form or electronic. The final column states the key purposes of the document or record for the human resources and payroll cycle.

PERSONNEL AND EMPLOYMENT The personnel (or human resources [HR]) department provides an independent source for interviewing and hiring of qualified personnel. Reference checks and a police check of new employees can identify past criminal activity and help prevent fraud. The HR department is also an independent source of records for the internal verification of wage information and for confirming segregation of duties by means of access rights.

Personnel records **Personnel records** (see Table 15-2) are used to keep track of semi-permanent information for employees. Here, documentation is kept of discretionary deductions (such as Canada Savings Bonds or registered pension plans), rates that should be used for calculating income taxes (by means of tax deduction codes), as well as the category of job the person is employed in and wage rates. Written or electronic documentation should be present for all changes, including changes to address, marital status, or wages.

Internal controls The most important control is clear, properly approved documentation of the employee's job responsibilities and wages by the appropriate level of authority. This could be a supervisor together with a controller, a manager together with human resources, or the Board of Directors. Note that in each case, at least two people should be involved in this approval process to prevent setup of fictitious employees. Refer to the partial organization chart of Hillsburg Hardware in Figure 10-2 on page 310. The hiring and wage rate of a new accounts payable supervisor would be approved by both the chief financial officer and human resources manager (not on the organization chart), for example.

Segregation of duties is extremely important, which helps prevent unauthorized changes to wage rates, deductions, or other payroll data. No individual with access to time recording, payroll records, or cheques should also be permitted access to personnel records. A second important control is the adequate investigation of the competence and trustworthiness of new employees, which helps prevent error (due to lack of competence) or fraud.

Master file change Master file data is the semi-permanent data in an employee's file. Any **master file change** needs to be adequately supported. For example, a change of marital status would be supported by a copy of a marriage certificate, and then the employee would be able to justify a reduction of income tax deductions by completing a change form that would be approved by a manager.

Personnel records—records that include such data as the date of employment, personnel investigations, rates of pay or changes to them, authorized deductions, performance evaluations, and termination of employment.

Master file change—the process used to change semi-permanent information in an employee record, such as deduction codes, addresses, or wage rates.

Table 15-2

Business Functions, Related Documents and Records, and their Purposes for the Human Resources and Payroll Cycle

Business function	Documents and Records	Purpose of Document or Record
Human resources and employment	Payroll and employment records	Track the employee's semi-permanent information, including wages, tax codes, and job responsibilities.
	Deduction authorization form	Documents employee approval of discretionary deductions and status of mandatory deductions, such as income tax deduction codes.
	Initial wage rate authorization form	Documents employee status and wage rate.
Master file change	Employee change form	Documents and approves changes in employee semi-permanent information, such as address, deduction code.
	Wage rate change form	Documents changes in wage rate and job responsibilities.
Access rights management	Access rights approval form	Describes the information systems functions (e.g., menu items) the person may have access to, including capabilities (e.g., read only or update).
	Access rights change form	Documents and approves changes to access rights based upon employee promotions, transfers, or terminations.
	Code of conduct statement	Signed by each employee, identifies responsibilities associated with information systems and organizational assets, including privacy, confidentiality, and ownership.
Timekeeping and payroll preparation	Time record	A document or electronic record tracking start time, end time, and total hours worked.
	Job time record	A record that allocates hours worked against a manufacturing or service job, allocating the work to a job order reference or client reference.
	Summary payroll report	List total wage costs by account number, department, job number, or other useful allocation.
	Payroll journal	List the details of the current pay, such as gross pay, hours worked, statutory withholdings, and net pay.
	Payroll master file	Electronic record of the current status of an employee (e.g., payments and deductions to date, name, address, employee number, social insurance number).
	Payroll transaction and history files	Electronic record of all payments and adjustments made to the employee master file.
Payment of payroll	Payroll cheque or direct bank deposit	Payment method of amounts due to employees.
	Employee remittance advice	Documentation of the details of employee payroll, such as gross pay, deductions, and net pay.
Preparation of employee withholdings and benefit remittance forms and their payment	T4 form	Provides totals of wage and benefit payments to and deductions from each employee for the calendar year.
	Employee withholdings and benefit remittance forms	Reporting and payment forms sent to federal and provincial authorities for the payment of withholdings and employee benefits and deductions.
	Other reporting forms	Other reporting forms may be required, such as group insurance forms, and workplace safety and health reports.

Internal controls All forms should be approved by at least two people. For example, a wage rate form that also documents a change in job responsibility should be approved by the immediate supervisor and perhaps the controller or human resources, to help prevent unauthorized changes in wage rates or deduction codes. At Hillsburg Hardware, wage rate changes for the accounts payable supervisor would be approved by the chief financial officer and the human resources manager. After data entry of the change into the information systems (by the payroll clerk at Hillsburg Hardware), a report of the changes should be automatically sent to and checked by a different person (i.e., not the person who did the data entry, such as the payroll supervisor at Hillsburg Hardware) to provide independent verification of the changes.

ACCESS RIGHTS MANAGEMENT This process includes identifying which information systems and which functions within a particular information system the employee is to have access to. When employees change jobs within the company (perhaps due to promotion), or leave the company, these access rights need to be updated. **Access rights management** is important because it is the organization's method of enforcing segregation of duties. Incorrect or weak access controls can provide unauthorized

Access rights management—the process used to identify and manage access to physical and logical assets (including information technology and user identification management)

access to data or programs, leading to the ability to issue payroll cheques or make unauthorized changes to wages or deductions. At Hillsburg Hardware, the accounts payable supervisor would be given access to payment processing functions only (the access rights form approved by the chief accountant and Chief Financial Officer).

Internal controls Management of access rights is an important function of the human resources and payroll cycle that helps prevent unauthorized access to data, programs, and electronic assets. It reflects the organization's attitudes toward segregation of duties. Clear policies and practices for employee setup and change of access rights include designation of the individuals who are authorized to approve access rights and independent comparison to check that they have been set up properly (to prevent error or unauthorized changes), with periodic review of master files (to detect unauthorized changes or terminated employees who are still being paid).

TIMEKEEPING AND PAYROLL PREPARATION This function is of major importance in the audit of payroll because it directly affects payroll expense for the period. **Timekeeping and payroll preparation** includes the preparation of time records by employee; the summarization and calculation of gross pay, deductions, and net pay; the preparation of payroll cheques; and the preparation of payroll records. Administrative employees are usually paid monthly, normally not requiring time records. Hourly employees, such as those working in a retail store at Hillsburg Hardware or working on a factory floor, would be paid hourly. Job time records are also used by service organizations, such as lawyers or accountants, who are required to submit time records indicating the client to be charged for their time.

Internal controls Adequate control over the time in the time records includes the use of a time clock and magnetic swipe card or other method of making certain that employees are paid for the number of hours they worked. There should also be controls to prevent anyone from checking in for several employees or submitting a fraudulent time record. Advanced information technology includes the use of fingerprint (biometric data) to record and track time. For example, **www.paypunch .com** illustrates the PayPunch time and attendance system. Employees clock in using an employee number and a hand or fingerprint. Instead of an employee number, for greater security, employees could use a PIN (personal identification number).

The summarization and calculation of the payroll can be controlled by well-defined policies for the payroll department, separation of duties to provide automatic cross-checks, reconciliation of payroll hours with independent production records, and independent internal verification of all important data. For example, payroll policies should require a competent, independent person to review actual hours worked, review for the proper approval of all overtime, and examine time records for deletions and alterations or for unusually long hours. These controls prevent unauthorized changes to the data and addition of unauthorized persons to the payroll (including continuing to pay terminated employees). Periodically, a printout of wage and withholding rates included in the computer files can be obtained and compared with authorized rates in the personnel files. Where the data volumes are large, such testing would be completed using audit software.

When manufacturing labour affects inventory valuation, a knowledgeable manager should approve wage allocations to make sure labour is distributed to the proper accounts. Independent comparison of the approved amounts to the actual data entered helps prevent error.

PAYMENT OF PAYROLL For **payment of payroll**, employees may be paid by cheque or direct bank deposit. In addition, employees must be informed of the details of their payments (gross pay, net pay, deductions) which would be on a separate remittance advice for bank payments or attached to their cheque.

Internal controls Controls over cheques or direct deposit authorization should include limiting the authorization to a responsible employee who does not have

Timekeeping and payroll preparation—processes used to record employee hours worked, allocate payroll costs to account, make payments to employees, and regulatory authorities.

Payment of payroll—payment of payroll amounts due to employees.

access to timekeeping or the preparation of the payroll, to prevent unauthorized changes. Payroll software should permit only one payment for each employee per pay period. Where physical cheques are used, the distribution of payroll should be by someone who is not involved in the other payroll functions to detect unauthorized payments or fictitious employees. Any unclaimed cheques should be immediately returned for redeposit. If a cheque-signing machine is used to replace a manual signature, the same controls are required; in addition, the cheque-signing machine must be carefully controlled.

To enable tracking, cheques, bank deposit transactions, and employee remittance advices should be sequentially numbered and accounted for.

Most companies use an **imprest payroll account** to prevent the payment of unauthorized payroll transactions. An imprest payroll account is a separate payroll account in which a small balance is maintained. A cheque for the exact amount of each net payroll is transferred from the general account to the imprest account immediately before the distribution of the payroll. The advantages of an imprest account are that it limits the client's exposure to payroll fraud (manual or electronic), allows the delegation of payroll cheque-signing duties, separates routine payroll expenditures from irregular expenditures, and facilitates cash management. It also simplifies the reconciliation of the payroll bank account if it is done at the low point in the payment cycle, for example, if the reconciliation is done a week after the last payroll and there is no payroll due in the current week.

Where employee payments are made directly into their bank account, reports produced by the bank or payroll service provider should be independently approved before the bank is given authority to transfer the funds.

> **Imprest payroll account**—a bank account to which the exact amount of payroll for the pay period is transferred by cheque from the employer's general cash account.

auditing in action 15-1

Wage Inflation or Deflation?

Throughout the audit risk assessment process, the auditor looks for management bias, perhaps management's misstating revenue or recording information in the incorrect period so that management can receive a larger bonus. The dollar effects of these deliberate errors can be large.

Throughout the financial trading community, traders and management are rewarded based upon organizational profits. For example, in 2006, Merrill Lynch paid out over $5 billion in bonuses, retaining $7.5 billion in earnings. However, these profits disappeared as mortgage-backed papers declined in value in the following years. Inadequate risk assessment and risk management resulted in huge bonuses being paid.

Another potential abuse is the back-dating of stock options. The incentive exists for stock options to be dated for a date when stock prices are low—then the recipient of the option can purchase the stock at a low price and resell to obtain an immediate profit. The options are to be disclosed, with tax consequences for the recipient and income effects upon the organization.

Research In Motion Ltd. of Waterloo, Ontario, one of over 200 companies investigated for back-dating of stock options in 2007, was the subject of a cease-trading order in 2007 for not releasing its financial statements on time. The delay occurred because restatements were required for the years 2005, 2006, and 2007 to correct information with respect to back-dating of stock options.

For tax purposes, options that are reported correctly in Canada are only taxed at the capital gains rate, whereas non-qualified options are taxed at the regular income tax rate. This means that in Canada, there is an incentive to record the tax options correctly.

Sources: 1. Canadian Press, "RIM files restated results," *Toronto Star*, May 18, 2007, **www.thestar.com**, Accessed: May 21, 2007. 2. Story, Louise, "On Wall Street, bonuses, not profits, were real," *The New York Times*, December 18, 2008, **www.nytimes.com**, Accessed: December 18, 2008. 3. Intuit, "Incentive Stock Options," **http://turbotax.intuit.com/tax-tools/tax-tips/Investments-and-Taxes/Incentive-Stock-Options/INF12049.html**; Accessed November 18, 2011.

C15-1 Why is it important for the auditor to audit the payroll cycle?

C15-2 Why is it likely that the auditor will focus on the audit of payroll transactions rather than payroll balances?

C15-3 How does the audit of access rights management in the payroll cycle affect the audit of other transaction cycles?

PREPARATION OF EMPLOYEE WITHHOLDINGS AND BENEFITS REMITTANCE FORMS AND THEIR PAYMENT The timely preparation and mailing of T4 slips and employee withholdings and benefits remittance forms is required by federal and provincial laws. Late payments result in heavy fines.

The nature and due date of the forms vary depending on the type of withholding or benefit and the size of the organization (e.g., weekly, monthly, or quarterly). These forms are prepared from information in the payroll master file or payroll history file. As dollar volume increases, more frequent remittances are required.

Internal controls The most important control in the preparation of these returns is a well-defined set of policies that carefully indicate when each form must be filed. Most automated payroll systems include the preparation of payroll tax returns using the information in the payroll transaction and master files. The independent verification of the output by a competent individual is an important control to prevent misstatements and potential liability for taxes and penalties.

② Internal Control Testing

Figure 15-2 shows the methodology for designing tests of controls for the human resources and payroll cycle. It is the same methodology used in Chapter 12 for the sales and collection cycle.

Internal control for payment of payroll is normally highly structured and well controlled in order to control cash disbursements and to minimize employee complaints and dissatisfaction. It is common to use information technology to prepare all journals

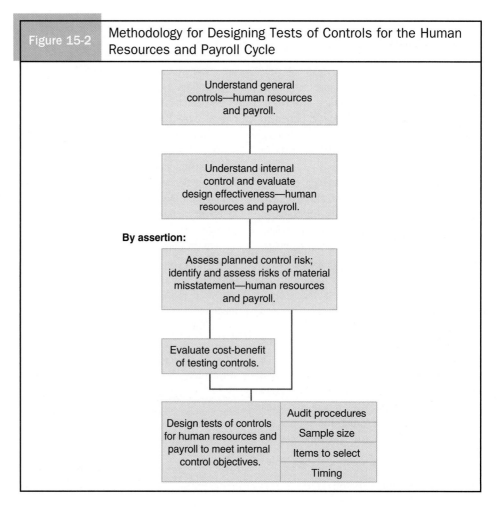

Figure 15-2 Methodology for Designing Tests of Controls for the Human Resources and Payroll Cycle

and payroll payments. In-house systems are used, or outside service-centre systems such as those of banks and financial institutions. Thus, general controls such as control over program changes and program updates and over access to data files must be evaluated, particularly over payroll calculations, since consistent errors could escalate into material amounts rapidly.

It is usually easy to establish good control over payments in the human resources and payroll cycle. For factory and office employees, there is usually a large number of relatively homogeneous, small-amount transactions. There are fewer executive payroll transactions, but they are consistent in timing, content, and amount. High-quality computer software packages are available, resulting in good controls over program changes. Auditors seldom expect to find exceptions in testing payroll transactions. Most monetary errors are corrected by internal verification controls or in response to employee complaints.

Where auditors tend to find problems is with management of access controls. Small- to medium-sized businesses may have inadequate controls over access to information systems, resulting in the need to rely solely on substantive tests. Larger organizations with more formal systems tend to have better controls over the initial set-up of employees but may have weaknesses in access-control change management.

Internal Controls and Tests of Controls

Tests of control procedures are the most important means of verifying account balances in the human resources and payroll cycle. The emphasis on tests of controls is due to the lack of independent third-party evidence, such as confirmation for verifying accrued wages, withholdings, accrued benefits payable, and other balance sheet accounts. In most audits, the amounts in the balance sheet accounts are small and can be easily verified if the auditor is confident that payroll transactions are correctly recorded and that withholding and benefit remittance forms are properly prepared.

There are three reasons for reducing tests in the human resources and payroll area: (1) employees are likely to complain to management if they are underpaid, (2) all payroll transactions are typically uniform and uncomplicated, and (3) payroll transactions are extensively audited by federal and provincial governments for income tax withholding and for pension, employment insurance, and health care payments.

Following the same approach used in Chapter 12 for tests of sales and cash receipts transactions, the internal controls and tests of controls for each objective and related monetary misstatements are summarized in Table 15-3. Note that:

- The internal controls will vary from company to company; so, the auditor must identify risks, document controls, and assess the design effectiveness of the controls.
- Controls the auditor intends to rely upon for reducing assessed control risk must be tested with tests of controls.
- The tests of controls will vary depending on the assessed control risk and the other considerations of the audit, such as the effect of payroll on inventory. Where an outside service organization is used to process payroll, the auditor must consider whether controls at the client are sufficient to ensure that the transaction-related audit objectives are satisfied. If not, the auditor may need to request evidence regarding controls at the service organization, including the existence of a service auditor's report on controls, discussed in the next section.

Three high-risk areas in human resources and payroll are first, payroll withholdings and remittances; second, the potential for misstatement of inventory of payroll including fraud; and third, the potential for non-existent (fictitious) employees. We look at these three topics in turn.

PAYROLL WITHHOLDINGS AND BENEFITS REMITTANCE FORMS AND PAYMENTS As discussed previously, this area is high risk since the amounts are often material and because the potential liability for failure to file forms in a timely manner can be severe.

Table 15-3	Summary of Transaction-Related Audit Objectives, Key Controls, and Tests of Controls for Payroll	

Transaction-Related Audit Objectives	Key Internal Controls	Common Tests of Controls
Recorded payroll payments are for work actually performed by existing employees (occurrence).	• Time records are approved by supervisors. • Time clock is used to record time. • Methods are in place to uniquely identify employees upon clocking in or out. • Adequately documented personnel files. • Separation of duties between personnel, timekeeping, and payroll disbursements supported by authorized access rights. • Setup and changes to payroll master files adequately documented and approved. • Independent authorization to issue cheques or initiate direct deposit payments.	• Examine time records for indication of approvals. • Review personnel policies. • Review organization chart, discuss with employees, and observe duties being performed. • Compare authorized duties with duties permitted on access rights forms. • Examine printouts of transactions rejected by the computer as having non-existent employee numbers, or determine whether invalid entries are accepted at point of entry.[†] • Examine personnel records for evidence of approval; compare wage rate to payroll master file or payroll journal. • Review the payroll journal, general ledger, and payroll earnings records for large or unusual amounts.[*†] • Compare cancelled cheques or direct deposit amounts with payroll journal for name, amount, and date. • Examine cancelled cheques for proper endorsement.
Existing payroll transactions are recorded (completeness).	• Payroll cheques are prenumbered and accounted for. • Independent preparation of bank reconciliation.	• Account for a sequence of payroll cheques or direct deposits, or conduct gap testing.[†] • Discuss payroll bank account reconciliation process with employees and observe reconciliation. • Reconcile the disbursements in the payroll journal with the disbursements on the payroll bank statement. • Prove the bank reconciliation.
Recorded payroll transactions are for the amount of time actually worked and at the proper pay rate; withholdings are properly calculated (accuracy).	• Independent verification of calculations and amounts. • Batch totals are compared with computer summary reports. • Authorization of wage rate, salary, or commission rate. • Authorization of withholdings, including amounts for insurance and Canada Savings Bonds.	• Examine indication of independent internal verification. • Examine file of batch totals for initials of approval; compare totals with summary reports.[†] • Examine personnel records for indication of independent approval. • Recompute hours worked from time records.[†] • Compare pay rates with union contract, approval by board of directors, or other source. • Recompute gross pay and net pay.[†] • Check withholdings by reference to appropriate tables[†] and authorization forms in personnel file. • Compare cancelled cheque or direct deposit with payroll journal for amount.
Payroll transactions are properly classified (classification).	• Adequate chart of accounts. • Internal independent verification of classification.	• Review chart of accounts. • Examine indication of internal verification; determine that software posts to correct accounts.[†] • Compare classification with chart of accounts or procedures manual. • Review time records for employee department and job records for job assignment, and trace through to labour distribution.
Payroll transactions are recorded on the correct dates (cutoff).	• Procedures requiring recording payroll transactions on a regular payment, immediately after payment. • Internal independent verification.	• Examine the procedures manual and observe when recording takes place. • Examine indication of internal verification. • Compare date of recorded cheques or direct deposits to the payroll journal dates and time records. • Compare date on cheque with date the cheque cleared the bank.
Payroll transactions are properly included in the payroll master file and transaction files; they are properly summarized (posting and summarization).	• Periodic independent comparison of payroll master file contents to personnel records. • Automatic posting of payroll transaction amounts to general ledger accounts.	• Examine initialled summary total reports indicating comparisons have been made. • Test clerical accuracy by footing the payroll journal and tracing postings to general ledger and the payroll master file.[†]

[*] This analytical procedure can also apply to other objectives, including completeness, valuation, and cutoff.

[†] This control would be tested on many audits by using the computer, possibly with generalized audit software.

Preparation of payroll withholdings and benefits remittance forms As a part of understanding the internal control structure, the auditor should review the preparation of at least one of each type of employee withholding and benefits remittance form that the client is responsible for filing.

A detailed reconciliation of the information on the remittance forms and the payroll records may be necessary when the auditor believes that there is a reasonable chance the remittance forms may be improperly prepared. Indications of high risk of errors in the forms include the past payment of penalties and interest for improper payments, new personnel in the payroll department who are responsible for the preparation of the remittance forms, the lack of independent verification of the information, and the existence of serious liquidity problems for the client.

Payment of the taxes withheld and other withholdings and benefits in a timely manner The withholdings of concern in these tests are such items as those for income taxes, Canada (or Quebec) Pension Plan, employment insurance, union dues, insurance, and Canada Savings Bonds. The auditor must first determine the client's requirements for submitting the payments. The requirements are determined by reference to such sources as tax laws, Canada Pension Plan rules, employment insurance rules, union contracts, and agreements with employees. Then, check whether the client has paid the proper amount on time by comparing the subsequent payment with the payroll records.

INVENTORY AND FRAUDULENT PAYROLL CONSIDERATIONS Risks of error or fraud are higher (1) when payroll significantly affects the valuation of inventory and (2) when the auditor is concerned about the possibility of material fraudulent payroll transactions.

Relationship between payroll and inventory valuation For audits where payroll is a significant portion of inventory (common for manufacturing and construction companies), the improper account classification of payroll can significantly affect asset valuation for accounts such as work in process, finished goods, or construction in process.

For example, the overhead charged to inventory at the balance sheet date can be overstated if the salaries of administrative personnel are charged to indirect manufacturing overhead. Similarly, the valuation of particular jobs is affected if the direct labour cost of individual employees is improperly charged to the wrong job or process. When some jobs are billed on a cost-plus basis, revenue and the valuation of particular jobs are both affected by charging labour to incorrect jobs.

When labour is a material factor in inventory valuation, there should be special emphasis on testing the internal controls over proper classification of payroll transactions. Trace job records or other evidence that an employee has worked on a particular job or process to the accounting records that affect inventory valuation. For example, if each employee must account for all of his or her time on a weekly basis by allocating individual job numbers, a useful test is to trace the recorded hours of several employees for a week to the related job-cost records to make sure each has been properly recorded. Trace from the job-cost records to employee summaries as a test for non-existent payroll charges being included in inventory.

TESTS FOR NON-EXISTENT PAYROLL Although auditors are not primarily responsible for the detection of fraud, they must extend audit procedures when internal controls over payroll are inadequate. There are several ways employees can significantly defraud a company in the payroll area. This discussion is limited to tests for the two most common types—non-existent employees and fraudulent hours.

The issuance of payroll payments to individuals who do not work for the company (non-existent employees) frequently results from continuing to pay an employee after his or her employment has been terminated. Usually, the person committing this type of defalcation is a payroll clerk, supervisor, fellow employee, or perhaps former employee. Certain procedures can be performed on cancelled cheques as a means of detecting defalcation. A procedure used on payroll audits is comparing the names on cancelled cheques with time cards and other records for authorized signatures and reasonableness of the endorsements. It is also common to scan endorsements on cancelled cheques for unusual or recurring second endorsements as an indication of a possible fraudulent cheque. The examination of cheques that are recorded as voided is also desirable to make sure they have not been fraudulently used. Where employees are paid automatically by bank deposits to the employees' accounts, the auditor can look for duplicated bank account numbers, post office boxes, or for common employee addresses using audit software.

A test for non-existent employees is tracing selected transactions recorded in the payroll journal to the human resources department to determine whether the employees were actually employed during the payroll period. The endorsement on the cancelled cheque written out to an employee is compared with the authorized signature on the employee's withholding authorization forms.

A procedure that tests for proper handling of terminated employees is selecting several files from the personnel records for employees who were terminated in the current year to determine whether each received his or her termination pay and severance. Continuing payments to terminated employees are tested by examining the payroll records in the subsequent period to verify that the employee is no longer being paid. This procedure is effective only if the personnel department is informed of terminations.

Fraudulent hours exist when an employee reports more time than was actually worked. Refer to Audit Challenge 15-1. Can you see how there are at least four people who can manipulate payroll information? Because of the lack of available evidence, it is usually difficult for an auditor to determine whether an employee records more time in his or her time record than was actually worked. One procedure is reconciling the total hours paid according to the payroll records with an independent record of the hours worked, such as those often maintained by production control.

concept check

C15-4 Why might auditors limit the number of transactions tested in the payroll cycle?

C15-5 Provide two examples of payroll tests that could be used to verify the accuracy of payroll costs included in inventory.

audit challenge 15-1
Improving Access Control Management

JEBRAH Manufacturing Limited (JML) is a medium-sized company with about 50 employees. It has a local area network, production systems software, timekeeping software, and accounting systems. These are all locally purchased and locally maintained software systems. There are no in-house information systems personnel.

The controller is responsible for setting up new users and changing user capabilities based upon scripts (standard instructions) provided by the network supplier. If she has any problems, she telephones the network supplier, who logs on to the system and makes the changes for her online.

All three accounting personnel and the owner of the company have access to all accounting systems. Manufacturing employees have access to timekeeping and production systems.

The controller prepares the bank reconciliation, but the owner signs payroll cheques and accounts payable cheques (with supporting documentation attached). The controller is responsible for recording all changes in wage rates in the accounting systems and writing off accounts receivable. The receptionist is responsible for printing reports, while there are two staff members who handle both accounts payable and accounts receivable transactions.

CRITICAL THINKING QUESTIONS

1. Describe the problems in segregation of duties for each application cycle: payroll, accounts receivable, and accounts payable. For each problem, state what could go wrong (the risk).
2. What are some of the practical changes that can be made at this company to improve internal controls? Justify your response.

3 Payroll Outsourcing and Third-Party Audits

The Nature of Outsourcing

Organizations face resource constraints, usually on time and expertise. In a small- to medium-sized business, the owner or senior manager may need to understand every aspect of the business, including payroll, investments, raw material pricing, and collection of accounts receivable. As management time becomes scarce, the owner can either hire new employees or use external assistance (contract assistance, consulting, or outsourcing). Outsourcing of some kind has existed for many years—think about factoring of accounts receivable, where the receivables are sold and someone else does the collection. Outsourcing has simply become more common. This is supported by internet communication of large volumes of information at low cost. A secondary driver for outsourcing is cost—reducing the cost of a function by outsourcing to an organization that specializes in that function helps the client organization.

Examples of functions that can be outsourced include call-centre functions, accounting functions, human resource functions, pension fund management, and recording and processing of transactions such as payroll.

We discuss outsourcing in this chapter because payroll is a commonly outsourced function, handled with a variety of technologies perhaps by the bank using batch processing on paper forms or online data entry, by another service bureau that specializes in payroll, or by an internet-based application service provider so that payroll transactions can be entered anywhere.

From the perspective of an assurance engagement described in CSAE 3416, Reporting on controls at a service organization, the outsourcing organization that provides services to a client is called the **service organization**. The client which uses the service organization is a **user entity**.

The remainder of this section focuses on the responsibilities of the **user auditor**, who is reporting on the financial statements of the user entity. In that role, the auditor needs to consider the types of controls available at both the user entity and the service organization and may rely upon third-party service organization reports as a source of information when conducting the audit. Responsibilities of the user auditor are described in CAS 402, Audit considerations relating to an entity using a service organization.

> **Service organization**—an outsourcing organization that provides services to the client.
>
> **User entity**—a client who uses a service organization.
>
> **User auditor**—the auditor reporting on the financial statements of the user entity.

---

audit challenge 15-2
Mini-outsourcing

PAYROLL is picky. The amounts have to be exact, many deductions have to be taken, and several remittances and forms must be submitted to regulatory agencies. Fines are heavy if you remit too little or if you remit late.

A small business owner could spend several hours per week doing payroll or checking the work of an employee who prepares the payroll, thus losing productive time.

NEBS Payweb.ca is an example of a payroll system that works for small and large businesses. Hours and wage rates are entered using the internet, from any location that has internet access. Then payroll payment is deposited directly to the employee bank account or to a debit card activated by the employer.

NEBS Payweb.ca also takes care of providing remittances (such as federal taxes), by withdrawing the funds from the company bank account and remitting to the regulatory agency

with the appropriate reports. Transaction reports can be viewed online or printed. You can view a presentation of the advantages of NEBS Payweb.ca at **www.payweb.ca/flash/**.

CRITICAL THINKING QUESTIONS

1. What are the risks associated with using NEBS Payweb.ca or other internet-based service providers for payroll processing?
2. How would you mitigate the risks that you identified in (1)?
3. NEBS Payweb.ca has thousands of clients. What would be the advantages and disadvantages of a service auditor's report for NEBS Payweb.ca?

Source: Bradbury, Danny, "Payroll work makes for a heavy load," *National Post*, February 11, 2008, p. FP4. 2. NEBS Payweb.ca, **www.payweb.ca**, Accessed: November 20, 2011.

ROLE OF RISK ASSESSMENT During the risk assessment phase of the financial statement audit, the financial statement auditor of the client will find out how the business of the client is managed. This includes finding out about service organizations (outsourcers) and what they do. If the client uses a service organization for the processing of payroll, the auditor may consider this to be significant, as payroll tends to be material. Payroll is normally a large part of the cost of goods sold, whether for service or manufacturing organizations.

The purpose of risk assessment includes determining the likelihood of material error in the account. The auditor may need to consider controls at both the user entity and at the service organization to assess control risk.

CONTROLS AT THE USER ENTITY Controls at the user entity will normally focus around input (submitting information to the service organization, such as wage rates and hours worked) and output (reviewing reports received, such as the payroll journal). If the client has controls to prevent or detect errors, then the auditor can spend less time considering the controls at the service organization.

For example, a form is used at the client to record new employees and their wage rates, approved by a manager. This form is provided as a data entry source to an online payroll service provider. All new employee data (or changes) are entered. Then the changed information is printed at the client location and checked independently (compared with the original wage-rate change form). Evidence of this checking is documented with an initial. This sequence of controls satisfies occurrence and accuracy (refer to Table 15-3).

For each pay, employees use a magnetic-stripe card to clock in and clock out. The data from the pay recording system are printed and approved by a manager before being transferred to the online payroll service provider. Then, the service provider creates the payroll records and transmits the payroll journal to the client. The controller reviews the payroll journal and compares the total hours worked with the payroll time records before entering a password that releases the pay for processing. He or she also prepares a requisition form, approved by executive management, for transfer of funds from the general bank account to the payroll service provider for payment of net pay and government tax remittances. These controls deal with accuracy and completeness and prevent unauthorized changes to wage rates or other payroll master file data.

Finally, the payroll journal is used to prepare a journal entry, posted by the controller to the general ledger (classification, cutoff, and posting and summarization).

The major control not performed by the client is the actual calculation of the payroll and its remittances. However, it is likely that material errors would be detected by the client review process listed above. Assuming that the activities at the client are conscientiously performed, the auditor would likely assess control risk as low, relying upon the client's controls and adding some substantive tests of the actual payroll calculations. There would be no need to test the controls at the service organization.

CONTROLS AT THE SERVICE ORGANIZATION Payroll could be complex, involving distributions to many cost centres. Perhaps there are 5,000 employees who are entering time from remote locations using multiple labour codes. Store managers enter passwords to approve wages but are not involved in calculating pay or in remittances. Head office simply takes the totals from the reports and posts them for monthly remittances. In this situation, reliance is placed heavily upon the service organization for calculation of pay and distribution of remittances. There could also be poor controls over checking for authorized employees, so the auditor might be concerned that someone at the service organization could enter an unauthorized employee and create a fictitious pay.

The auditor could go to the service organization and determine the controls directly or obtain a service auditor's report. CSAE 3416 describes the types of reports that an auditor can use to assist in that audit process.

CAS 402 applies where the service organization's services are part of the client's information systems and the transactions are material. It does not apply where the user specifically authorizes all transactions, such as the use of a chequing account at a bank.

OTHER CYCLES AND SERVICE AUDITOR REPORTS Any cycle or function can be outsourced. This includes the whole accounting function, internal audit, investment management, and human resources management. It becomes crucial for the auditor to work with the service organization (or a service auditor report) when the client has given up control over functions or transactions and the auditor determines that there is potential for material error when considering only the client controls.

Then the auditor will need either to contact the service organization directly to provide an unqualified report on the financial statements, or to obtain a service auditor report (described in CSAE 3416) that provides evidence that controls at the service organization are operating effectively.

concept check

C15-6 Provide two examples of outsourcing at an organization.

C15-7 When will the auditor need to consider controls at the outsourcing organization?

④ Analytical Review and Tests of Detail

Analytical Procedures

The use of analytical procedures is as important in the human resources and payroll cycle as it is in every other cycle. Table 15-4 illustrates analytical procedures for the balance sheet and income statement accounts in the human resources and payroll cycle. Most of the relationships included in Table 15-4 are highly predictable and are useful for uncovering areas in which additional audit work may be needed. The auditor should consider any changes in business policies or business practices when conducting the analytical procedures to help explain variations.

Tests of Details of Balances for Payroll Liability and Expense Accounts

Figure 15-3 summarizes the methodology for deciding the appropriate tests of details of balances for payroll liability accounts. The methodology is the same as that followed in Chapter 12 for accounts receivable. Normally, payroll-related liabilities are less material than accounts receivable, so there is less inherent risk.

The verification of the liability accounts associated with payroll, often termed **accrued payroll liability/expenses**, is straightforward if internal controls are operating effectively. When the auditor is satisfied that payroll transactions are being properly

> **Accrued payroll liability/ expenses**—the liability accounts associated with payroll including accounts for accrued salaries and wages, accrued commissions, accrued bonuses, and accrued employee benefits.

Table 15-4	Analytical Procedures for the Human Resources and Payroll Cycle	
Analytical Procedure	**Possible Misstatement Detected in**	
Compare payroll expense account balance with previous years (adjusted for pay rate increases and increases in volume).	Payroll expense accounts	
Compare direct labour as a percentage of sales with that of previous years.	Direct labour	
Compare commission expense as a percentage of sales with that of previous years.	Commission expense	
Compare payroll benefits expense as a percentage of salaries and wages with that of previous years (adjusted for changes in the benefits rates).	Payroll benefits expense and payroll benefits liability	
Compare accrued payroll benefits accounts with that of previous years.	Accrued payroll benefits and payroll benefits expense	

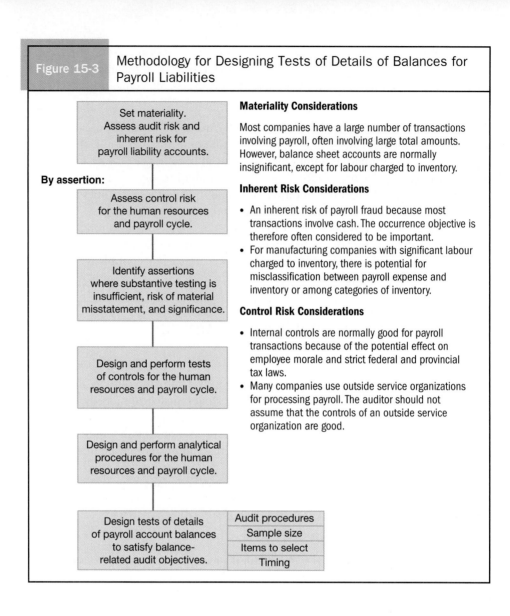

Figure 15-3 Methodology for Designing Tests of Details of Balances for Payroll Liabilities

Set materiality.
Assess audit risk and inherent risk for payroll liability accounts.

By assertion:

Assess control risk for the human resources and payroll cycle.

Identify assertions where substantive testing is insufficient, risk of material misstatement, and significance.

Design and perform tests of controls for the human resources and payroll cycle.

Design and perform analytical procedures for the human resources and payroll cycle.

Design tests of details of payroll account balances to satisfy balance-related audit objectives.

Audit procedures
Sample size
Items to select
Timing

Materiality Considerations

Most companies have a large number of transactions involving payroll, often involving large total amounts. However, balance sheet accounts are normally insignificant, except for labour charged to inventory.

Inherent Risk Considerations

- An inherent risk of payroll fraud because most transactions involve cash. The occurrence objective is therefore often considered to be important.
- For manufacturing companies with significant labour charged to inventory, there is potential for misclassification between payroll expense and inventory or among categories of inventory.

Control Risk Considerations

- Internal controls are normally good for payroll transactions because of the potential effect on employee morale and strict federal and provincial tax laws.
- Many companies use outside service organizations for processing payroll. The auditor should not assume that the controls of an outside service organization are good.

recorded in the payroll journal and the related employee withholding and benefits remittance forms are being accurately prepared and promptly paid, the tests of details of balances can be completed rapidly.

The objectives in testing payroll-related liabilities are to determine whether accruals in the trial balance are stated at correct amounts (accuracy) for all payroll accounts (completeness) and whether transactions in the human resources and payroll cycle are recorded in the proper period (cutoff). The primary concern in both objectives is to make sure there are no understated or omitted accruals. Table 15-5 illustrates examples of tests of details of balances for payroll liability and expense accounts.

Tests of details of the human resources and payroll accounts will be conducted if the amounts are significant or if the auditor considers that there is a risk of material misstatement. The auditor also considers the cost-effectiveness of testing. Most of the tests listed in Table 15-5 can be conducted efficiently, except for the recalculation of total commissions, payroll, and benefits, which can be complex since most benefits do not apply to all of a person's pay. For example, there are ceilings on pension and employment insurance benefits. This means that most auditors will conduct the tests listed for the liability accounts and for officers' compensation. The other tests will be conducted only if control risk is very high or the auditor suspects fraud or other material misstatements.

	Examples of Tests of Details of Balances for Payroll Liability and Expense Accounts
Table 15-5	

Account description	Test of detail and balance-related audit assertion
Liability Accounts	
Amounts withheld from employees' pay: Income taxes Canada (or Quebec) Pension Plan Employment Insurance Other: Union dues, bonds, insurance	Compare balance with payroll journal. (Completeness) Compare balance with subsequent period cash disbursements. (Allocation)
Accrued salaries and wages	Determine that policy for accruing wages is consistent with prior year. Evaluate reasonableness of the method. (Valuation) Recalculate the accrual. (Allocation, completeness, existence)
Accrued commissions	Determine nature of commission agreements or policies with employees. Evaluate consistency with prior year. (Allocation, valuation) Verify that the commission agreements or policies have been correctly applied to appropriate employees. (Allocation) Confirm amounts due with employees or compare balance with subsequent cash disbursements. (Allocation)
Accrued bonuses	Compare to amount authorized in the minutes of the board of director's meetings (or by owner of the company). (Allocation, Completeness)
Accrued statutory benefits, vacation pay, sick pay, and other benefits	Determine policy for accrual. Evaluate consistence with prior years. (Valuation) Recalculate the accruals. Examine remittance forms and recalculate amounts. (Allocation, completeness) Agree payments to subsequent payments. (Existence, allocation)
Expense Accounts	
Officers' compensation	Agree authorized salary to the minutes of the board of directors' meetings. (Existence, allocation) Compare authorized salary to amounts paid. (Allocation)
Commissions expense	See Accrued Commissions. In addition: Recalculate total commissions using stated policies or formulae, in total (for analytical review) or in detail (for particular employees or using generalized audit software). (Allocation, completeness)
Employee benefit expense	Reconcile annual payroll paid to total payroll stated on annual remittance forms. Multiple total payroll times benefit rate. (Allocation, completeness)
Total payroll	Reconcile total payroll paid to the annual T4 summary submitted to the Canada Revenue Agency. (Allocation, completeness)

Application of Audit Tests to Audit Objectives for Presentation and Disclosure

Figure 15-4 illustrates the categories of accounts in the human resources and payroll cycle and the types of audit tests used to audit these accounts. This figure also shows how the audit risk model discussed in Chapter 7 relates to the audit of the human resources and payroll cycle.

Table 15-5 shows that some of the audit tests conducted by the auditor pertain to assessing consistent presentation of information to prior years (such as methods of accrual and calculations of commissions). Similarly, tests of accuracy and cutoff help to determine that information is presented accurately and appropriately in the financial statements.

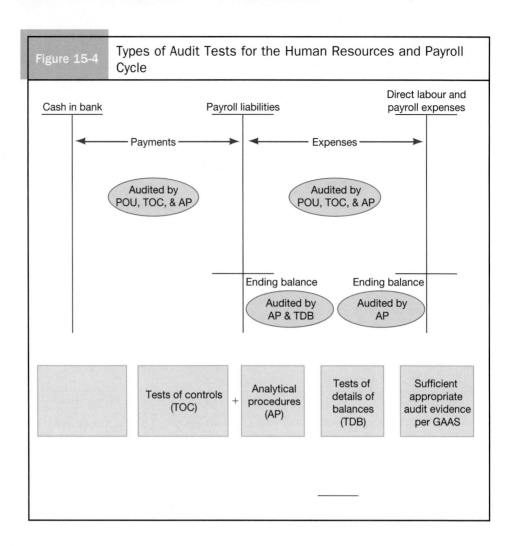

Figure 15-4 Types of Audit Tests for the Human Resources and Payroll Cycle

concept check

C15-8 Describe three assertions that are important when testing payroll-related liabilities, and provide an example of an audit test for each assertion.

C15-9 When would the auditor conduct tests of details of balances for payroll expense accounts?

The auditor would also need to consider the correctness, completeness, and adequacy of disclosure of management remuneration in the financial statements, as required by accounting standards. For example, disclosure of the salaries and other compensation of the top five officers is required by certain provincial securities commissions. IAS 24, Related party disclosures, requires that key management personnel be disclosed showing separately salary, share-based payments, and different categories of benefits.

The primary controls relating to adequate disclosure of financial information come from the control environment, discussed in Chapter 9. These relate to independent approval of account allocation, of journal entries, and of information disclosed in the financial statements. Such independent approval is of good quality when management is honest and trustworthy.

Summary

1. *Why is the human resources and payroll cycle important?* This cycle involves the employment and payment of all employees. Salaries, wages, and associated benefits are a major expense; labour is an important cost component for manufacturing and construction companies and, if improperly managed, could result in wasted resources.

What differentiates this cycle from other cycles? There is only one class of transaction. The total transaction value can be far more significant than balance sheet accounts. Internal control over payroll tends to be effective for most companies due to harsh federal and provincial penalties for errors in withholdings and taxes.

Describe the risks of fraud and error in the cycle and explain how the functions and records in the cycle help to prevent or detect fraud or error. Risks of error include incorrect or unauthorized wages, late payments of remittances, or overstatement of income by misallocating payroll to asset accounts. Clear access rights limited functions to authorized personnel help to prevent unauthorized changes, while an independent check of master file changes helps to prevent and detect error or unauthorized changes to master file data.

2. *List typical audit tests of controls by assertion.* Table 15-3 lists transaction-related audit objectives, key internal controls, and common tests of controls for payroll. For example, a test of occurrence is examining payroll records for evidence of approval.

3. *How does outsourcing affect the controls and audit of payroll?* If payroll is outsourced, then the outsourcing organization could conduct some controls that affect the reliability and auditability of the accounts or transactions. The auditor may need to assess or audit the controls at the service organization.

How do these principles apply to other application cycles? Other cycles are audited in a manner similar to that of payroll: the auditor considers controls at both the client and the service organization and may use a service auditor's report as part of the audit process.

4. *What misstatements could a payroll analytical review process detect?* Table 15-4 lists several analytical procedures that could detect potential errors in the following accounts: payroll expense, direct labour, commission expense, payroll benefits expenses, and liabilities.

Which liability and expense accounts in the payroll cycle are tested using tests of details? The auditor would test the following accounts: withholding benefits and taxes, accrued salaries and wages, accrued commissions, accrued vacation pay, accrued sick benefits, officers' compensation, commissions, employee benefits, and payroll costs.

How do audit tests of the human resources and payroll cycle affect presentation and disclosure of financial results? The auditor would conduct tests of the accuracy and completeness of disclosure of manager and officer remuneration, paying particular attention to adequacy and clarity of disclosure of related party transactions.

Review Questions

15-1 ❶ Explain the relationship between the human resources and payroll cycle and inventory valuation.

15-2 ❶ List three risks of error that could occur in the human resources and payroll cycle. For each risk of error, identify a control that would prevent or mitigate the error.

15-3 ❶ List three risks of misappropriation of assets or fraud that could occur in the human resources and payroll cycle. For each risk of misappropriation or fraud, identify a control that would prevent or mitigate the error.

15-4 ❶ List three risks of inadequate disclosure or fraudulent financial reporting in the human resources and payroll cycle. For each risk of inappropriate disclosure, identify a control that would prevent or detect it.

15-5 ❶ Explain why the percentage of total audit time in the cycle devoted to performing tests of controls may be less for the human resources and payroll cycle than for the sales and collection cycle.

15-6 ❶ Explain what is meant by an "imprest payroll account." What is its purpose as a control over payroll?

15-7 ❶ Distinguish among a payroll master file, a TD-1 form, and a T4 payroll summary return. Explain the purpose of each.

15-8 ❶ ❷ List the types of authorizations in the human resources and payroll cycle, and state the type of misstatement that is increased when each authorization is lacking.

15-9 ❶ ❷ What is the purpose of testing both employee access rights setup and employee access rights changes? What would be the impact upon the audit if either or both of these processes had control weaknesses?

15-10 ❶ ❷ The company you are auditing has a local area network with office automation software, accounting software, and point of sale equipment. Provide examples of five different categories of access rights, and state the control purpose of each access right category.

15-11 ❷ Evaluate the following comment by an auditor: "My job is to determine whether the payroll records are fairly stated in accordance with generally accepted accounting principles, not to find out whether the client is following proper hiring and termination procedures. When I conduct an audit of payroll, I keep out of the personnel department and stick to the time cards, journals, and payroll cheques. I don't care who the client hires and who it fires, as long as it properly pays the employees it has."

15-12 ❷ Distinguish between the following payroll audit procedures, and state the purpose of each: (1) Trace a random sample of sequentially numbered time records to the related payroll cheques in the payroll register, and compare the hours worked with the hours paid, and (2) trace a random sample of payroll cheques from the payroll register to the related time records, and compare the hours worked with the hours paid. Which of these two procedures is typically more important in the audit of payroll? Why?

15-13 ② List several audit procedures that the auditor can use to determine whether payroll transactions are recorded at the proper amount.

15-14 ③ DrinkOh Limited uses an application service provider to process its payroll. Its employees enter their hours using their smart phones. The payroll clerk collects the smart phone data and transmits it to the application service provider for payroll processing. Describe three controls that should be present over payroll processing at DrinkOh Limited. For each control, describe the risk of error or fraud that is mitigated or prevented by the control.

15-15 ④ In auditing payroll withholding and payroll benefits expense, explain why emphasis should normally be on evaluating the adequacy of the preparation procedures for employee withholding and benefits remittance forms rather than on the employee withholding and benefits liability. Explain the effect that inadequate preparation procedures will have on the remainder of the audit.

15-16 ④ List several analytical procedures for the human resources and payroll cycle, and explain the type of error that might be indicated when there is a significant difference in the comparison of the current year's and previous years' results for each of the tests.

15-17 ④ Explain why it is common to verify total officers' compensation even when the tests of controls results in payroll are excellent. What audit procedures can be used to verify officers' compensation?

Discussion Questions and Problems

15-18 ① ② Items 1 through 9 are selected questions typically found in questionnaires used by auditors to obtain an understanding of internal control in the human resources and payroll cycle. In using the questionnaire for a client, a "yes" response to a question indicates a possible internal control, whereas a "no" indicates a potential deficiency.

1. Does an appropriate official authorize initial rates of pay and any subsequent changes in rates?
2. Are written notices documenting reasons for termination required?
3. Are formal records such as time records used for keeping time?
4. Is approval by a department head or foreperson required for all time records before they are submitted for payment?
5. Does anyone verify pay rates, overtime hours, and computations of gross payroll before direct deposits are made?
6. Do adequate means exist for identifying jobs or products, such as work orders, job numbers, or some similar identification provided to employees to ensure proper coding of time records?
7. Are payroll direct deposits authorized by persons independent of timekeeping?
8. Are employees required to show identification when requesting changes to their address or other personal information in company files?
9. Are authorized master file change forms used to document and implement changes in functional access rights?

REQUIRED

a. For each of the questions, identify the nature of the potential financial misstatement(s) if the control is not in effect.
b. For each of the questions, state the transaction-related audit objective(s) being fulfilled if the control is in effect.
c. For each control, list a test of control to test its effectiveness.
d. For each of the potential misstatements in part (c), list a substantive audit procedure for determining whether a material misstatement exists.

15-19 ① ② Ling is responsible for planning the audit over inventory and payroll cycles for a new client. Her supervisor gave her an internal control questionnaire for payroll, on which the supervisor had written the client's answers to several questions about internal controls. After reviewing the internal control questionnaire, Ling felt that the questions asked were very thorough. Since the answers were all positive, indicating good internal controls, she recommended the internal control risk for payroll be assessed as low.

Ling proceeded to design substantive procedures for payroll transactions. She also tested the controls over the client's payroll processing and inventory count procedures at year end, just prior to the inventory count. Ling felt that she could not assess the control risks for the inventory count until she reviewed those procedures.

REQUIRED

State whether you agree with Ling's assessment of control risk and her plan of action. Justify your response.

(Extract from AU1 CGA - Canada Examinations developed by the Certified General Accountants Association of Canada © 2010 CGA-Canada. Reproduced with permission. All rights reserved.)

15-20 ❶ ❷ ❹ Following are some of the tests of controls and substantive tests of transactions procedures often performed in the human resources and payroll cycle. (Each procedure is to be done on a sample basis.)

1. Reconcile the monthly payroll total for direct manufacturing labour with the labour-cost distribution.
2. Examine time record reports for the approval of a foreperson.
3. Recompute hours on the time records, and compare the total with the total hours for which the employee has been paid.
4. Compare the employee name, date, cheque number, and amounts on cancelled cheques with the payroll journal.
5. Trace the hours from the employee time records to job records to make sure that the totals reconcile, and trace each job record to the job-cost report.
6. Account for a sequence of payroll cheques in the payroll journal.
7. Select employees who have been terminated from the personnel file, and determine whether their termination pay was in accordance with the union contract. As part of this procedure, examine two subsequent periods to determine whether the terminated employee is still being paid.

REQUIRED
a. Identify whether each of the procedures is primarily a test of control or a substantive test of transactions.
b. Identify the transaction-related audit objective(s) or balance-related audit objective(s) of each of the procedures.
c. For each procedure, identify the risk mitigated or the potential error quantified.

15-21 ❶ ❷ ❹ During the first-year audit of Omato Wholesale Stationery Ltd., you observe that commissions amount to almost 25 percent of total sales, which is somewhat higher than in previous years. Further investigation reveals that the industry typically has larger sales commissions than Omato and that there is significant variation in rates depending on the product sold.

At the time a sale is made, the salesperson records his or her commission rate and the total amount of the commissions on the office copy of the sales invoice. When sales are entered into the information system for the recording of sales, the debit to sales commission expense and credit to accrued sales commission are also recorded. As part of recording the sales and sales commission expense, the accounts receivable clerk verifies the prices, quantities, commission rates, and all calculations on the sales invoices. Both the customer master file and the salespersons' commission master files are updated when the sale and sales commission are recorded. On the fifteenth day after the end of the month, the salesperson is paid for the preceding month's sales commissions.

REQUIRED
a. What additional information do you require to complete the audit of sales commissions?
b. Develop an audit program, by assertion, to verify sales commission expense assuming that no audit tests have been conducted in any audit area to this point.
c. Develop an audit program, by assertion, to verify accrued sales commissions at the end of the year assuming that the tests you designed in part (a) resulted in no significant misstatements.

15-22 ❶ ❷ ❸ Janbec Limited is a distributor of health care products. It has about $450,000 in accounts receivable and about $600,000 in inventory. It has been a tough winter, with many people sick with the flu or falling on ice, breaking legs or dislocating shoulders so that they could not come in to work.

As a result, people have been helping out in various departments. For example, the accounts receivable clerk has been helping with payroll data entry and in receiving and shipping, making sure that forms and documents are filled in properly. The accounting manager has been helping the purchasing desk when placing needed orders for inventory replenishment, and the warehouse supervisor has also been helping out with purchasing, making sure that quantities are ordered that will fit on the shelves.

A new clerk in the accounts receivable department is all thumbs at the computer and is painfully slow at data entry. However, she is bright and cheerful and seems to be catching up on the filing backlog. Her excellent telephone manner seems to also have sped up some of the late payments from customers, resulting in an excellent collection ratio in accounts receivable.

Janbec uses an ASP (applications service provider) for its computing needs. Users log in via the internet, enter data, and request reports. The ASP is a local computer store a few blocks away, while the physical server is located downtown. Janbec prints all of the reports on premises after retrieving them from the ASP. If there are any problems with the software, they are dealt with by telephone.

REQUIRED
a. Explain control problems that could have arisen due to the employees "filling in" and how these potential problems could be mitigated by Janbec management.
b. How does the use of the ASP affect the audit engagement?
c. What risks are present for Janbec with respect to the ASP?

15-23 ❹ In comparing total employee benefits expense with that of the preceding year, Marilyn Brendin, public accountant, observed a significant increase, even though the total number of employees had increased only from 175 to 195. To investigate the difference, she selected a large sample of payroll disbursement transactions and carefully tested the withholdings for each employee in the sample by referring to Canada Pension Plan, employment insurance, and other benefits withholding tables. In her test, she found no exceptions; therefore, she concluded that employee benefits expense was fairly stated.

REQUIRED

a. Evaluate Brendin's approach to testing employee benefits expense.

b. Discuss a more suitable approach for determining whether employee benefits expense was properly stated in the current year.

Professional Judgment Problems

15-24 ❶❷❹ Cilly Stress, a fourth-year honours computer science student at a highly regarded university, was working as part-time cleaning staff at the Classy Manufacturing Company (CMC) when she was expelled from school for misuse of the university's computer resources.

Cilly was able to improve her employment status to full-time cleaning staff. She enjoyed working the night shift, where she found lots of time and opportunity to snoop around the company's office and computing centre. She learned from documentation in the recycling bins that CMC was in the process of updating its extensive policy and procedures documentation and placing it online.

Through continued efforts in searching waste bins and documents left on desktops and unlocked cabinets, as well as some careful observation of password entry by people who were working late, Cilly soon learned enough to log in to the company's information systems and ultimately to print out lists of user identification codes and passwords using a Trojan horse program. She was able to obtain all the passwords she needed to set herself up as a supplier, customer, and systems support technician.

As a customer, she was able to order enough goods so that the inventory procurement system would automatically trigger a need for purchase of products. Then, as a supplier, she was ready to deliver the goods at the specified price (by returning the goods that she had "purchased"). As a supervisor, she was able to write off the uncollected accounts receivable from her customer accounts while being paid as a supplier. On average, she was able to embezzle about $125,000 per month.

Cilly's fraud was detected by a suspicious delivery person, who wondered why he was delivering goods to an empty building lot.

REQUIRED

a. Describe weaknesses in human resources and access policies at CMC. For each weakness, indicate the impact and provide a recommendation for improvement.

b. Identify routine audit procedures that might have produced evidence that, with further investigation, could have revealed the fraud. Describe the evidence in the test results that would have triggered the investigation.

15-25 ❹ Archer Uniforms, Inc. is a distributor of professional uniforms to retail stores that sell work clothing to professionals such as doctors, nurses, and security guards. Traditionally, most of the sales are to retail stores throughout Canada and the United States. Most shipments are processed in bulk for direct delivery to retail stores or to the corporate warehouse distribution facilities for retail store chains. In early 2011, Archer Uniforms began offering the sale of uniforms directly to professionals through its company website. Professionals can access information about uniform styles, sizes, and prices. Purchases are charged to the customer's personal credit card. Management made this decision based on its conclusion that the online sales would tap a new market of professionals who do not have easy access to retail stores. Thus, the volume of shipments to retail stores is expected to remain consistent.

Given that Archer's IT staff lacked the experience necessary to create and support the online sales system, management engaged an IT consulting firm to design and maintain the online sales system.

REQUIRED

a. Before performing analytical procedures related to the human resources and payroll cycle accounts, develop expectations of how these recent events at Archer Uniforms, Inc. will affect payroll expense for the following departments during 2011 compared with prior years' payroll expense. Indicate the degree (extensive, moderate, little) to which you expect the payroll expense account balance to increase or decrease during 2011, with reasons supported by the facts of the case.

1. Warehouse and Shipping Department.
2. IT Department.
3. Accounts Receivable Department.
4. Accounts Payable Department.
5. Receiving Department.
6. Executive Management.
7. Marketing.

b. Provide additional audit procedures (by assertion) that might be required.

Case

15-26 ❶ You are assessing internal control in the audit of the human resources and payroll cycle for the Kowal Manufacturing Company, a company specializing in assembling computer systems from purchased parts. Kowal employs approximately two hundred hourly and thirty salaried employees in three locations. Each location has one foreman who is responsible for overseeing operations. The owner of the company lives in Victoria, B.C., and is not actively involved in the business. The two key executives are the vice president of sales and the controller, both of whom have been employed by the company for more than fifteen years.

Whenever there is a job opening at a location, the factory foreman interviews applicants and, on the basis of the interview, either hires or rejects them. When applicants are hired, they prepare a TD1 (employee's withholding exemption certificate) and give it to the foreman. The foreman writes the hourly rate of pay for the new employee in the corner of the TD1 form and then gives the form to the location's office manager as notice that the worker has been employed. The foreman verbally advises the office manager when there are wage rate adjustments.

Since each hourly employee works independently, Kowal has a highly flexible work schedule policy, as long as employees start after 7:00 a.m. and are finished by 6:00 p.m. Employees are issued magnetic stripe cards with a PIN (personal identification number) that they use to scan in and out. Every Friday at 6:00 p.m., the office manager retrieves the time records and prints the time records with hours worked. The foreman reviews the list and signs and dates it indicating his approval. Once the time records are approved, the office manager transmits the time records to head office in Mississauga, Ontario. Employees without a time record do not receive pay. In Mississauga, the accounting supervisor retrieves the file for transfer into the payroll system, which is used to calculate the pay amounts and create a payroll journal. The payroll journal for the three locations is printed and reviewed by the controller. The payroll package then generates a direct deposit file, which is sent to the bank by the accounting supervisor every Monday afternoon.

Except for the foremen and office managers, all salaried employees work at the Mississauga location. The vice president of sales or the controller hires all salaried employees, depending on their responsibilities, and determines their salaries and salary adjustments. The owner determines the salary of the vice president of sales and the controller. The accounting supervisor processes the payroll transactions for salaried employees using the same payroll software that is used for hourly employees. The monthly payroll journal is approved by the controller before the office manager transmits the salaried payroll direct deposit file to the bank.

The payroll software package has access controls that are set up by the controller. She is the only person who has access to the salary and wage rate module of the software. She updates the software for new wage rates and salaries and makes changes to existing ones. The accounting supervisor has access to all other payroll modules. The controller's assistant has been taught to reconcile bank accounts and does the monthly payroll bank reconciliation.

REQUIRED

a. List the risks of error or fraud that are present at Kowal Manufacturing. For each risk, state the type of misstatement that could occur.

b. State whether the fraud risk could lead to misappropriation of assets or fraudulent financial reporting. Explain how these frauds could take place.

c. For each risk of error or fraud, provide both preventive and detective controls to prevent or detect the fraud.
(Adapted from AICPA)

ACL Problem *ACL*

This problem requires the use of ACL software. For this problem, open an existing ACL Project, then choose the Sample Project data files. In the "Tables" folder, open the "Payroll Analysis" subfolder, then the "Payroll" file. The suggested command or other source of information needed to solve the problem requirement is included at the end of each question.

a. Determine the number of payroll transactions in the file (read the bottom of the Payroll file screen).

b. Determine the largest and smallest payroll transaction (gross pay) for the month of September (Quick Sort). How would the auditor use this information?

c. Determine gross pay for September (Total). Which general ledger account(s) would this total be reconciled to?

d. Determine and print gross pay by department (Summarize).

e. Recalculate net pay for each payroll transaction for September and compare it with the amount included in the file (Computed Fields or Filter). What would be your concern if there were any differences? What transaction-related and balance-related audit assertions are associated with this test?

f. Determine if there are any gaps or duplicates in the cheque numbers (Gaps and Duplicates). What would be your concern if there were gaps or duplicates?

Ongoing Small Business Case: Payroll at CondoCleaners.com

15-28 ❶ ❷ Jim is handling the payroll of his 15 full-time employees. As Jim allocates the work, he knows the hours that his employees have worked, and he records the data daily in a spreadsheet. At the end of the week, he uses the online calculator at Canada Revenue Agency's (CRA) website to calculate the gross pay and deductions. He then records this information in his spreadsheet. He uses a second spreadsheet to calculate the required remittances which he sends to the CRA every month. He then writes cheques and personally delivers them to his employees.

REQUIRED

What are the advantages and disadvantages of the methods that Jim uses to calculate payroll? What other low-cost alternatives are available to him?

16 Audit of the acquisition and payment cycle

How do you pay your bills? Do you have a credit card statement that is paid monthly? Do you have any payments that you pay by cheque or via electronic banking? Profit-oriented and other businesses have many different ways that they pay their bills. As auditors, we need to be concerned, first of all, that only appropriate bills are recorded in the financial statements and that none are omitted. Then, we also audit the payment process. Management accountants can design and monitor controls to help deter payment fraud, while auditors may focus on validity of payments.

LEARNING OBJECTIVES

1 Describe the major business functions, documents, and records in the acquisition and payment cycle. Describe the risks of error or fraud in the cycle. Explain how the functions and records in this cycle help to prevent or detect fraud or error.

2 Develop tests of controls for the acquisition and payment cycle. Describe the impact of information systems conversions on the audit process.

3 Design substantive tests (analytical review and tests of details) for accounts payable. Explain the relevance of understatement of accounts payable versus overstatement.

4 Consider the risks and audit processes for selected accounts. Explain the risks and audit processes for the audit of manufacturing equipment.

STANDARDS REFERENCED IN THIS CHAPTER

CICA Standard

CAS 550 – Related parties

Section 1000 – Financial statement concepts

Section 3061 – Property, Plant and Equipment

Section 3290 – Contingencies

IAS 1 – Presentation of financial statements

IAS 37 – Provisions, contingent liabilities and contingent assets

The High Cost of International Bribery

Siemens AG is an international engineering, construction, and telecommunications company with 2007 revenue of €72.5 billion. The company received unwelcome publicity commencing in November 2006 when the public became aware that Siemens seemed to have a "bribery expense account." Court proceedings later confirmed that more than €1.3 billion had been used to obtain contracts dating from 2001 through 2007 around the world, with figures as high as US$20 million for contracts to build power plants in Israel. What motivates this type of behaviour? Is it management bonuses, the drive for expansion, or simply the desire to be first? We will never know, for such data are unavailable from the more than 270 suspects focused on by the Munich, Germany, 2008, corruption trial that charged a former manager of a telecommunications division with 58 breach-of-trust charges.

Since Siemens' shares are traded on U.S. stock exchanges, the company was also fined by both the U.S. Department of Justice for bribery and falsification of corporate records and the Securities and Exchange Commission for violation of the Foreign Corrupt Practices Act. As of December 31, 2008, Siemens' costs with respect to the bribery were as follows:

1. €201 million. Fines in Munich, Germany, related to bribery (former telecommunications division).

2. €354 million. Fines in Munich, Germany, due to the failure of its supervisory committee (similar to a board of directors).

3. US$450 million. Levied by U.S. Department of Justice.

4. US$350 million. Levied by the U.S. Securities and Exchange Commission.

5. Estimated e850 million in accounting and legal fees.

This brings the total estimated cost to Siemens to about €2.5 billion. The company is also required to have a compliance monitor, reporting to the United States, who will report on the effectiveness of Siemen's organizational changes, its new internal controls, and new compliance director. The company's problems are not over, for in October 2008, Siemens' offices in Garfield Heights, United States, were raided and documents seized as part of an investigation into the awarding of contracts for the installation of lights, furnaces, and hot water heaters at 7,000 public housing units of the Cuyahoga Metropolitan Housing Authority.

IMPORTANCE TO AUDITORS

Auditors and accountants were called upon to quantify the scope of the bribes, document what had happened, and identify the weaknesses in internal controls that allowed the bribery to happen. It is unclear which levels of management were aware that the bribery was taking place.

continued >

New controls designed with the assistance of auditors will require that multiple levels of the organization be involved in controls to prevent, detect, and correct potential violations.

As discussed in Chapter 9, this will mean a top-down approach: board of director (Supervisory Board in Siemens case) and executive management approval; commitment and implementation by management, staff, and information systems; and regular monitoring, reporting, and revision.

WHAT DO YOU THINK?

1. Why do you think that employees would use bribery to obtain contracts?

2. Identify techniques that auditors can use to detect potential changes in business practices, such as bribery.

3. What actions should auditors take with respect to Siemens subsidiaries around the world?

Sources: 1. Annan, Grace, "German court hears first suspect in corruption scandal at Siemens," Global Insight Daily Analysis, May 26, 2008, Retrieved from Factiva Index database, **http://global.factiva.com.ezproxy.library. yorku.ca/ha/default.aspx**, Accessed: January 1, 2009. 2. Garrett, Amanda, "Siemens to pay $1.6 billion to settle bribery case," *The Plain Dealer*, December 31, 2008, Retrieved from Factiva Index database, **http://global.factiva. com.ezproxy.library.yorku.ca/ha/default.aspx**, Accessed: January 1, 2009. 3. Gow, David, "Record U.S. fine ends Siemens bribery scandal," *The Guardian*, December 16, 2008, **www.guardian.co.uk/business/2008/dec/16/ regulation-siemens-scandal-bribery**, Accessed: January 1, 2009. 4. Siemens Canada home page: **www.siemens.ca/ WEB/PORTAL/EN/Pages/Home.aspx,** Accessed: January 1, 2009.

AS our opening case illustrates, even large, well-run companies are susceptible to fraud risks. If those risks are not effectively managed, allowing bribery or other forms of corruption to occur, the costs to the company can be high. In addition to the costs listed above, Siemens' share values declined, and it is facing investigations in many countries around the world. Effective fraud management policies must cover risks related to payments.

In this chapter, the format for discussing internal control introduced in earlier chapters is repeated. Several important balance sheet accounts that are a part of the acquisition and payment cycle are included. These are manufacturing equipment, prepaid insurance, and provisions for liabilities (also called accrued liabilities). The chapter also discusses tests of details of income statement accounts included in the acquisition and payment cycle.

1 The Nature of the Acquisition and Payment Cycle

The acquisition of goods and services includes such items as the purchase of raw materials, equipment, supplies, utilities, repairs and maintenance, and research and development. The cycle does not include the acquisition and payment of employees' services or the internal transfers and allocations of costs within the organization. The former are a part of the human resources and payroll function, and the latter are audited as part of the verification of individual assets or liabilities. The acquisition and payment cycle also excludes the acquisition and repayment of capital (interest-bearing debt and owners' equity), which are considered separately in Chapter 18.

Acquisition and payment cycle— the transaction cycle that includes the acquisition of and payment for goods and services from suppliers outside the organization.

The **acquisition and payment cycle** includes two distinct classes of transactions— acquisitions of goods and services and cash disbursements for those acquisitions. Typical accounts used for acquisitions of goods and services are shown in Figure 16-1 and include inventory, manufacturing costs, selling expenses, and administrative expenses. Cash disbursements can be by cheque, electronic payments, or other methods (such as bank drafts). Purchase returns and allowances is also a class of transactions, but for many companies the amounts are immaterial.

The way the accounting information flows through the various accounts in the acquisition and payment cycle is illustrated by T-accounts in Figure 16-1 below. To keep the illustration manageable, only a control account is shown for the three major categories of expenses used by most companies (manufacturing expenses, selling expenses, and administrative expenses). For each control account, examples of the subsidiary expense accounts are also listed.

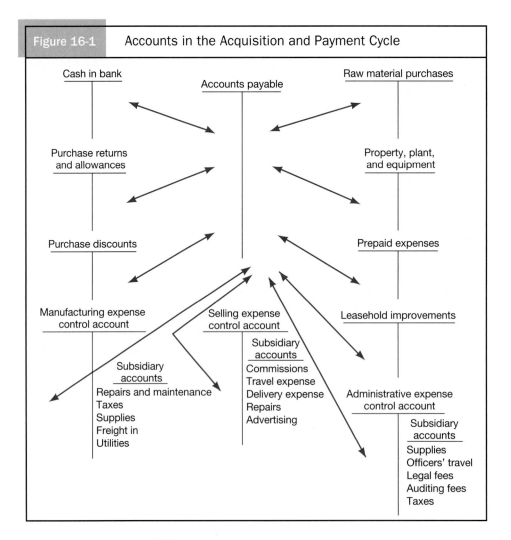

Figure 16-1 Accounts in the Acquisition and Payment Cycle

Table 16-1	Examples of Major Risks of Error or Fraud in the Acquisition and Payment Cycle		
Risks of Error	Risks of Misappropriation of Assets, Other Fraud or Illegal Acts	Risks of Inadequate Disclosure or Incorrect Presentation of Financial Information, including Fraudulent Financial Reporting	
	Deliberately recording accounts payable in the next period.		
Amounts posted to accounts payable are for goods in transit where shipping terms indicate that the risks and rewards of ownership have not yet passed to the entity.		Omitting disclosure of a related party transaction.	
	Use fictitious vendor allowances to reduce accounts payable.		
Provisions are understated because a provision has not been recorded.		Omitting disclosure of a contingent liability	
	Issue payments to fictitious vendors and steal the funds.		
Payments are posted to the wrong vendor account.		Incorrect disclosures relating to various components of plant, property, and equipment.	
	Theft of fixed assets, such as portable computing equipment.		
Incorrect rates used to amortize plant, property, and equipment.		Incorrect and confusing information disclosed about vendor allowances.	

The acquisition and payment cycle involves the decisions and processes necessary for obtaining the goods and services for operating a business. The cycle typically begins with the initiation of a purchase requisition by an authorized employee who needs the goods or services and ends with payment for the benefits received. Although the topics that follow deal with a small manufacturing company that makes tangible products for sale to third parties, the same principles apply to a service company, a government unit, or any other type of organization.

Risks of Fraud or Error in the Accounts Payable and Acquisition Cycle

Similar to other cycles, a client could make data entry errors, such as recording amounts in wrong periods or to wrong sub-ledger accounts (wrong vendors). Table 16-1 lists examples of major risks of error or fraud in this cycle. Cases of fraudulent financial reporting involving accounts payable are relatively common, although less frequent than frauds involving inventory or accounts receivable. Companies may engage in deliberate attempts to understate accounts payable and overstate income. This can be accomplished by not recording accounts payable until the subsequent period or by recording fictitious reductions to accounts payable.

Companies often have complex arrangements with suppliers, which results in reductions to accounts payable for advertising credits and other allowances. These arrangements may not be as well documented as acquisition transactions. Some companies have used fictitious reductions to accounts payable to overstate net income. Auditors should read agreements with suppliers when amounts are material and make sure the financial statements reflect the substance of the agreements.

The most common fraud in the acquisitions area is for the perpetrator to issue payments to fictitious vendors and deposit the cheques in a fictitious account. These frauds can be prevented by allowing payments to be made only to approved vendors and by having authorized personnel carefully scrutinize documentation supporting the acquisitions before payments are made. In other misappropriation cases, the accounts payable clerk or another employee steals a cheque to a legitimate vendor. The purchases information is then resubmitted for payment to the vendor. Such fraud can be prevented by cancelling supporting documents to prevent their being used to support multiple payments.

Fixed assets are a large balance sheet account for many companies and are often based on subjectively determined valuations. As a result, fixed assets may be a target for financial statement manipulation, especially for companies without material receivables or inventories. For example, companies may capitalize repairs or other operating expenses as fixed assets. Such frauds could be detected if the auditor examines evidence supporting fixed asset additions. Because of their value and saleability, fixed assets are also targets for theft. This is especially true for fixed assets that are readily portable, such as laptop computers. To reduce the potential for theft, fixed assets should be physically protected whenever possible, engraved or otherwise permanently labelled, and periodically inventoried.

Functions in the Cycle, Related Documents and Records, and Internal Controls

The first column of Table 16-2 identifies the five business functions in a typical acquisition and payment cycle, the documents and records that result from that business function, and the purposes of the documents and records. In the first three sections of this chapter, we focus on goods and services related to the cost of goods sold to the business. In the final section of this chapter, we consider asset acquisition and other selected accounts.

PROCESSING PURCHASE ORDERS The request for goods or services by the client's personnel is the starting point for the cycle. The exact form of the request and the required approval depend on the nature of the goods and services and company policy, but normally the request starts with an approved purchase order requisition that is used to create an approved purchase order for an authorized vendor. As purchase commitments are made, transaction details are recorded in the purchase order transaction file. Automated systems automatically number the purchase orders sequentially and assist in tracking purchase commitments, expected delivery dates, and items that have been back-ordered (i.e., when the vendor currently does not have stock but shipments are expected later).

Proper authorization for acquisitions and changes to the vendor master file (such as adding a new vendor) is an essential part of this function because it ensures that the goods and services acquired are for authorized company purposes, and it avoids the acquisition of excessive and unnecessary items. Most companies permit general authorization for the acquisition of regular operating needs, such as inventory at one level and acquisitions of capital assets or similar items at another. For example, acquisitions of capital assets in excess of a specified dollar limit may require board of directors' action; items acquired relatively infrequently, such as insurance policies and long-term service contracts, are approved by certain officers; supplies and services costing less than a designated amount are approved by supervisors and department heads; and some types of raw materials and supplies are re-ordered automatically whenever they fall to a predetermined level, often by direct communication with vendors' computers. Where automatic purchase orders are generated, care must be taken to ensure that re-order points are monitored so that only those

Table 16-2

Table 16-2 Business Functions, Related Documents and Records and their Purposes for the Acquisition and Payment Cycle

Business Function	Documents and Records	Purpose of Document or Record
Processing purchase orders	Purchase requisition	Provides a written internal record by an authorized employee to the purchasing department of a request to order materials or inventory or other goods and services (such as repairs or insurance) used by an entity.
	Purchase order	Records the description, quantity, and related information for goods and services that the company intends to purchase that constitutes a contract to buy with the vendor.
	Vendor master file	A computer file for maintaining a record for each vendor of individual acquisitions, cash disbursements, and acquisition returns and allowances, and vendor balances.
	Purchase transaction file	Contains purchase order details.
Receiving goods and services	Receiving report	Document prepared by the receiving department at the time tangible goods are received, indicating the description of the goods, the quantity received, the date received, and other relevant data.
Recognizing the liability	Vendor's invoice	Document that specifies the details of an acquisition transaction and amount of money owed to the vendor for an acquisition.
	Acquisitions journal	Lists vendor invoices received for physical goods and services. May also include returns and allowance transactions.
	Summary acquisitions report	Vendor invoices summarized by account type, division, or department.
	Debit memo	A document indicating a reduction in the amount owed to a vendor because of returned goods or an allowance granted.
	Vendor transaction file	Tracks details of acquisition transactions: invoices, debit memos, payments, and any other adjustments.
	Accounts payable trial balance	A listing by each vendor of the amount owed at a point in time; prepared directly from the accounts payable master file in either summary form (totals by vendor) or detail (showing the current month's transactions plus any unpaid transactions making up the opening balance).
	Vendor's statement	A statement prepared monthly by the vendor, which indicates the customer's beginning balance, acquisitions, payments, and ending balance.
Vendor master file changes	Vendor master file change form	An approved document that describes master file changes to be entered.
Processing and recording cash disbursements	Cheque or electronic payment record	Used to transfer funds to a supplier or service provider and provide a record of the payment.
	Payment transaction file	Records details of payments made by cheque or electronic payment.
	Cash disbursements journal	A listing of the details of payments made.

goods still required by the company are purchased. For good internal control, the purchasing department should not be responsible for authorizing the acquisition or receiving the goods.

RECEIVING GOODS AND SERVICES The receipt by the company of goods and services from the vendor is a critical point in the cycle because it is the point at which most companies first recognize the acquisition and related liability on their records. When goods are received, adequate control requires examination for description, quantity, timely arrival, and condition by a person independent of the accounts payable function. The receipt of goods and services in the normal course of business represents the date that clients normally recognize the liability for an acquisition. Where an organization has automated purchase order systems, the receipt needs to be entered into the computer system to signal that the goods have been received. This information would also be used to update perpetual inventory systems.

Most companies have the receiving department initiate a receiving report as evidence of the receipt and examination of goods. The receiving department uses it to update the quantity fields of the computer records, and then it is sent to the accounts payable department for matching to vendor invoices. To prevent theft and misuse, it is important that the goods be physically controlled from the time of their receipt until their use. The personnel in the receiving department should be independent of the warehouse personnel and the accounting department. Finally, the accounting records should transfer responsibility for the goods as they are transferred from receiving to storage and from storage to manufacturing or distribution to the customer.

RECOGNIZING THE LIABILITY The proper recognition of the liability for the receipt of goods and services requires prompt and accurate recording.

Supplier invoices (or debit memos) matched to both receiving reports and authorized purchase documents are recorded as an account payable and listed on the acquisitions journal. Individual transaction details are posted to the vendor transaction file with total amounts posted to the vendor master file. Acquisition journal totals are posted to the general ledger. The summary acquisitions report typically includes information analyzed by key components such as account classification, type of inventory, and division.

Unpaid transactions are used to prepare the accounts payable trial balance. The sum of the unpaid transactions should always agree with the sum of liabilities in the vendor master file and with the general ledger accounts payable total.

In some companies, the recording of the liability for acquisitions is made on the basis of the receipt of goods and services, and in other companies it is deferred until the vendor's invoice is received. In either case, the accounts payable department typically has responsibility for verifying the propriety of acquisitions. This is done by comparing the details on the purchase order, the receiving report, and the vendor's invoice to determine that the descriptions, prices, quantities, terms, and freight on the vendor's invoice are correct. Extensions and footings are recalculated and account distribution is also verified either manually or using automated systems.

The level of automation of the accounts payable system varies. Some organizations simply record the total amount of the vendor invoice into the accounts payable system. In that case, it is important that all of the above steps, including recalculation of the vendor invoice, are completed before the invoice is entered into the system. For highly integrated computer systems, the vendor invoice details entered manually or received electronically include each line of the invoice (i.e., the item number, description, quantity, price, and terms). The computer systems can then make the comparison with the purchase order details and recalculate the vendor invoice. Accurate and authorized entry of receiving order details by the organization's personnel is important so that the system can confirm that the quantity received is equal to the quantity ordered and the quantity billed by the vendor. An important control in the accounts payable and information processing departments is requiring that those personnel who record acquisitions do not have access to cash, marketable securities, and other assets.

PROCESSING AND RECORDING VENDOR MASTER FILE CHANGES New suppliers should undergo a credit check while other suppliers should be subject to periodic review for quality of service, product, delivery times, and other criteria approved by management. Then, after approval, new suppliers can be added to the supplier master file. The master file change forms should be independently approved (i.e., not by someone who approves payments, to prevent establishment of fictitious companies) and the data entry independently verified.

PROCESSING AND RECORDING CASH DISBURSEMENTS For most companies, payment is made by computer-prepared cheques (called cleared or cancelled cheques after they have cleared the bank) from information included in the acquisition transactions file at the time goods and services are received. Regular suppliers may be set up for direct deposit to their bank accounts using electronic data interchange (EDI) or other methods of electronic funds transfer (EFT). Printed cheques are typically prepared in a multi-copy format, with the original going to the payee, one copy being filed with the vendor's invoice and other supporting documents, and another copy being filed numerically. If laser-printed cheques are used, then normally only one copy is printed, as the documents are available electronically. Individual payments are recorded as cash disbursement transactions in the payment transaction file.

The most important controls in the cash disbursements function include the following:

- The signing of cheques (or authorization of payment release) by an individual with proper authority.
- Separation of responsibilities for approving the payments and performing the accounts payable function.
- Careful examination of the supporting documents by the cheque signer at the time the cheque is signed.
- Use of a password (preferably two different passwords by two people) before electronic payments are released.

The cheques should be prenumbered and printed on special paper that makes it difficult to alter the payee or amount. Care should be taken to provide physical control over blank, voided, and signed cheques. It is also important to have a method of cancelling the supporting documents to prevent their reuse as support for another cheque at a later time. A common method is to mark the documents as "entered" when recorded in the computer system and to write the cheque number or electronic payment number on the supporting documents when payments are made.

concept check

C16-1 Why is it important for an organization to use purchase orders?

C16-2 What is the purpose of matching receiving report and invoice details to purchase orders?

Tests of Controls

In a typical audit, the most time-consuming accounts to verify by tests of details of balances are accounts receivable, inventory, capital assets, accounts payable, and expense accounts. Of these five, all but accounts receivable are directly related to the acquisition and payment cycle. The audit time saved can be dramatic if the auditor can reduce tests of details by using tests of controls to verify the effectiveness of internal controls for acquisitions and cash disbursements.

Prior to considering tests in this cycle, the auditor will have assessed the quality of corporate governance, the risks of management override in the payment cycle, and the level of fraud risk associated with the cycle. Tests of controls for the acquisition and payment cycle are divided into two broad areas: tests of acquisitions and tests of payments. Acquisition tests concern four of the five functions discussed earlier in the chapter: processing purchase orders, vendor master file changes, receiving goods and services, and recognizing the liability. Tests of payments concern the fifth function, processing and recording cash disbursements.

The five transaction-related audit objectives developed in Chapter 5 are used as the frame of reference for designing tests of controls for acquisition and cash disbursement transactions. For each objective, the auditor must go through the same logical process that has been discussed in previous chapters. First, the auditor must understand the general controls applicable to the cycle and the cycle's internal controls to determine which controls exist and assess their design effectiveness. Then, an initial assessment of control risk and risk of material misstatement can be made for each objective. The auditor must decide which controls he or she plans to test to satisfy the initial assessment of control risk. After the auditor has developed the audit procedures for each objective, the procedures can be combined into an audit program that can be efficiently performed. Figure 16-2 summarizes that methodology. It is the same one used in Chapter 12 for sales and cash receipts.

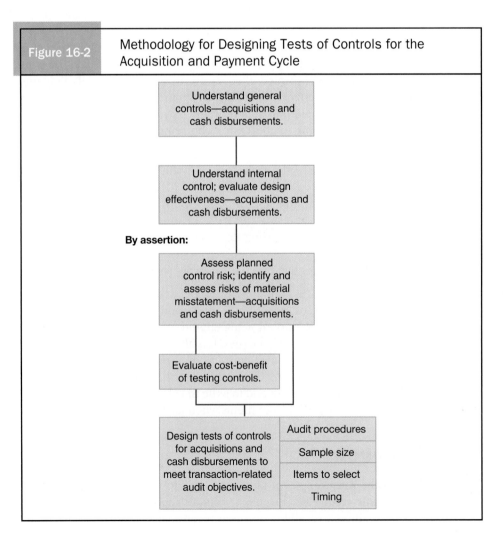

Figure 16-2 Methodology for Designing Tests of Controls for the Acquisition and Payment Cycle

Again, the emphasis in the methodology is on determining the appropriate audit procedures, sample size, items to select, and timing.

VERIFYING ACQUISITIONS Key internal controls and common tests of controls for each transaction-related audit objective are summarized in Table 16-3. An assumption underlying the internal controls and audit procedures is the existence of a separate acquisitions process for recording all acquisitions.

Four of the audit objectives for acquisitions deserve special attention. A discussion of each of these objectives follows.

Recorded acquisitions are for goods and services received, consistent with the best interests of the client (occurrence) If the auditor is satisfied that the controls are adequate for this objective, substantive tests for improper and non-existent transactions can be greatly reduced. In some instances, improper transactions can be readily identified, such as the acquisition of unauthorized personal items by employees or the actual embezzlement of cash by recording a duplicate purchase in the purchases journal. Others are more difficult to evaluate, such as the payment of officers' memberships in country clubs, expense-paid vacations to foreign countries for members of management and their families, and management-approved illegal payments to officials of foreign countries. If the controls over improper and non-existent transactions are inadequate, extensive examination of supporting documentation is necessary.

Existing acquisitions are recorded (completeness) Failure to record the acquisition of goods and services received directly affects the balance in accounts payable and may result in an overstatement of net income and owners' equity. Because of this, auditors are usually very concerned about the completeness objective.

Acquisitions are accurately recorded (accuracy) The controls over the acquisitions included in the perpetual records are normally tested as part of the tests of controls for acquisitions, and the controls over this objective play a key role in the audit. The inclusion of both quantity and unit costs in the inventory perpetual records permits a reduction in the tests of the physical count and the unit costs of inventory if the controls are operating effectively. As another example, if the auditor has found that controls over the accuracy of capital assets are good, it is acceptable to test fewer current period acquisitions.

Acquisitions are correctly classified (classification) Since performing documentation tests of current-period capital asset acquisitions and expense accounts for accuracy are relatively time-consuming audit procedures, if reliance on controls is possible, the saving in audit time can be significant.

Once the auditor has decided on audit procedures, the acquisitions and cash disbursements tests are typically performed concurrently. For example, for a transaction selected for examination from the acquisitions journal, the vendor's invoice and the receiving report are examined at the same time as the related cancelled cheque or direct deposit payment record.

ATTRIBUTE SAMPLING FOR TESTS OF CONTROLS Because of the importance of tests of controls for acquisitions and cash disbursements, the use of attribute sampling is common in this audit area. The approach is basically the same as for the tests of controls of sales discussed in Chapter 12. Many of the types of errors or fraud and other irregularities that may be found in this cycle represent a misstatement of earnings and are of significant concern to the auditor. For example, there may be inventory cutoff misstatements or an incorrect recording of an expense amount. Because of this, the tolerable exception rate selected by the auditor in tests of many of the attributes in this cycle is relatively low. Since the dollar amounts of individual transactions in the cycle cover a wide range, it is also common to segregate very large and unusual items and to test them on a 100-percent basis.

| Table 16-3 | Summary of Transaction-Related Audit Objectives, Key Controls, and Tests of Controls for Acquisitions | | |

Transaction-Related Audit Objective	Key Internal Control	Common Tests of Controls	
Recorded acquisitions are for goods and services received, consistent with the best interests of the client (occurrence).	Existence of purchase requisition, purchase order, receiving report, and vendor's invoice attached to the voucher.[†]	Inspect supporting documents for existence and match details (e.g., quantity, description, and amount).	Review the acquisitions journal, general ledger, and transaction files for large or unusual amounts.[*]
	Approval of acquisitions at the proper level.	Inspect invoice for indication of approval.	Inspect underlying documents for reasonableness and authenticity (vendors' invoices, receiving reports, purchase orders, and requisitions).
	Cancellation of documents to prevent their reuse.	Inspect invoice for indication of cancellation.	
			Trace inventory purchase details to inventory files.
	Independent verification of vendors' invoices, receiving reports, purchase orders, and purchase requisitions.[†]	Inspect invoice for indication of independent verification.[‡]	Physically inspect capital assets acquired.
		Inspect master file change forms for approval; trace details to vendor master file.	Inspect vendor master file for unusual credit terms, prices, or P.O. box addresses.[‡]
	New vendors and changes to vendor file approved.		
	Vendor master file independently examined periodically.	Discuss review and approval process with management.	
Existing acquisition transactions are recorded (completeness).	Purchase orders are prenumbered and accounted for.	Account for a sequence of purchase orders.[‡]	Trace from a file of vendors' invoices to the acquisitions journal.
	Receiving reports are prenumbered and accounted for.[†]	Account for a sequence of receiving reports.[‡]	Trace from a file of receiving reports to the acquisitions journal.[†]
Recorded acquisition transactions are accurate (accuracy).	Batch totals are compared with computer summary reports.	Examine file of batch totals for initials of data control clerk; compare totals to summary reports.[‡]	Compare recorded transactions in the acquisitions journal with the vendor's invoice, receiving report, and other supporting documentation.[†‡]
	Approval of acquisitions for prices and discounts.	Inspect for indication of approval.	Recompute the clerical accuracy on the vendors' invoices, including discounts and freight.[‡]
	Independent verification of calculations and amounts.	Inspect for indication of internal verification.[‡]	Test clerical accuracy by footing the journals and tracing postings to general ledger and accounts payable and inventory master files.[‡]
	Comparison of accounts payable master file or trial balance totals with general ledger balance.	Inspect initials on general ledger summary reports indicating comparison.	
Acquisition transactions are recorded on the correct dates (cutoff).	Procedures require recording transactions as soon as possible after the goods and services have been received.	Inspect procedures manual; observe whether unrecorded vendors' invoices exist.	Compare dates of receiving reports and vendors' invoices with dates in the acquisitions journal.[†]
	Transaction date must be system date (today's date) or a reasonable date.	Observe data entry process and dates used.	
Acquisition transactions are properly classified (classification).	Adequate chart of accounts.	Inspect procedures manual and chart of accounts.	Compare classification with chart of accounts by reference to vendors' invoices.
	Automatic updates of and posting to general ledger accounts.	Enter test transactions or observe entry; trace to correct file.	

[*] This analytical procedure can also apply to other objectives, including completeness, valuation, and cutoff.

[†] Receiving reports are used only for tangible goods and are therefore not available for services, such as utilities and repairs and maintenance. Frequently, vendors' invoices are the only documentation available.

[‡] This control would be tested on many audits by using the computer.

Audit of System Conversions

Organizations are not static. With time, as an organization grows or shrinks or changes its business objectives, the procedures within an organization also change. Often, when the auditor returns to conduct the audit, he or she identifies minor changes in procedures, causing minor changes in risk assessments, internal control testing, and tests of details.

At other times, the organization has undertaken a major change in its systems by implementing a new computer system or has made major changes to a system. For example, a client that previously processed its accounts payable and cash disbursements manually could use a standard accounting software package. A large client could change a batch-processing accounts payable and cash disbursements system to an online processing system, as described in Audit Challenge 16-1.

When an organization changes an entire system or set of systems, there are three issues that the auditor needs to address:

- A new system of internal controls will need to be documented and evaluated.
- The auditor will need to audit the actual data conversion process.
- The auditor will need to determine whether accounting policies have been changed.

NEW SYSTEM OF INTERNAL CONTROLS When new computer programs are put in place, the controls that are part of those programs will change. For example, if the system changes from batch to online, then controls to ensure data-entry accuracy will likely occur as information is entered rather than for a group of transactions. If a system changes from manual to automated, then new controls (such as automatic calculation of invoice extensions) will be present in the programs instead of being completed manually. Also, activities done by persons working with these systems may change.

The auditor needs to document the new procedures, evaluate them, and determine their effect on control risk. Should reliance on the programmed controls be tested, the auditor may have the option of using the same audit procedures as in prior years or may need to design new audit procedures, such as the creation of test

audit challenge 16-1
Conversion to New System Hides $5-Million Error

A large pharmaceutical distribution company had been using complex data processing methods for many years. It had custom-programmed accounting systems and used data communications to send and receive orders and other business documents. The accounts payable system was falling behind—it was based on batch processing and not integrated with the purchasing system.

Accordingly, the information systems personnel designed and tested many new programs for updating the accounts payable and purchasing systems. These systems were put in place at the company's year-end date, January 31. Systems were run in parallel (i.e., both the old and new systems were used) for the month of January, with the new system used exclusively effective February 1. The auditors relied on the equivalency of the two systems and on the fact that the company normally had excellent controls in accounts payable

and cash disbursements. However, due to excessive workload, goods received on January 31 were not recorded until February 1 and, therefore, were recorded only in the new system. Thus, accounts payable and purchases were understated by $5 million, resulting in an overstatement of income—a highly significant cutoff error.

This error was detected by the auditors in the following year's audit, resulting in a restatement of the prior financial statements. The client was very understanding but commented, "We knew the financial results last year were too good to be true!"

CRITICAL THINKING QUESTIONS

1. What analytical review procedures could have pointed to the cutoff error?
2. What audit procedures should the auditors have used to identify the error?

transactions to determine that programs are functioning as intended. If the client has run its systems in parallel (i.e., run both the old and the new systems for a certain period), then the auditor can evaluate the new system by examining the records kept during this parallel process.

AUDITING THE DATA CONVERSION PROCESS The mere occurrence of an information systems conversion raises the potential for material error, as illustrated by Audit Challenge 16-1. When computer systems are established for the first time, a major task is the creation of master files. For example, purchase orders cannot be processed or accounts payable vendor invoices entered if the vendor information such as name, address, and terms are not established in the vendor master file. Quantities ordered or received cannot be entered if the inventory item, description, and price do not exist in the inventory master file. The number of vendors could be in the hundreds, while the number of inventory items could number in the thousands.

Determining the audit procedures required involves a risk assessment process. Inherent risk may increase because these are new systems in place and employees may not be aware of the actions required. By determining the extent of employee training and the rigour of the implementation process, the auditor can assess whether inherent risk is affected. The rigour of the implementation process also affects control risk. If the implementation process is properly planned, conducted, and supervised, the auditor can rely on these controls. Conversely, if controls over the conversion process are poor or are not documented, the auditor must conduct tests of details. Table 16-4 combines the features of Tables 16-2 and 16-3 to describe audit objectives for the conversion of a batch system to an online system. Table 16-4 shows possible key controls, tests of controls, and also possible tests of details that would be required should controls be absent or not relied upon.

Note that three audit objectives are not included. Classification is not included, since accuracy and agreement between the two systems ensures that classification is satisfied. Rights and obligations as well as valuation apply to balances both before and after the conversion and would be audited separately, as of the year end.

A careful review of Table 16-4 shows that the tests can be simplified to the following three types:

Table 16-4	Audit Objectives, Key Controls, Tests of Controls, and Tests of Details for System Conversion of Accounts Payable			
Audit Objective	**Key Internal Control**	**Common Tests of Controls**	**Common Tests of Details**
Only authorized vendors are established with balances for goods and services actually received (occurrence/existence).	Agree vendor file details for each vendor from the new (online) system with those of the old (batch) system.	Inspect vendor file listings for evidence of agreement.	On a test basis, agree vendor file details for each vendor from the new (online) system to the old (batch) system.
All vendor balances as of the date of conversion are included (completeness and accuracy/allocation).	Agree aged accounts payable trial balance details from the old (batch) system with those of the new (online) system for each vendor and in total. Agree the total with that of general ledger.	Inspect aged accounts payable trial balance listings for evidence of comparison.	On a test basis, agree aged accounts payable trial balance details from the old (batch) system with those of the new (online) system for each vendor and in total. Agree total with that of general ledger.
Information is recorded in the appropriate system and is not omitted (cutoff/allocation).	Procedures exist to ensure appropriate cutoff of transactions (i.e., transactions are recorded only once in the proper system and are not omitted).	Conduct cutoff tests for receiving reports and vendor invoices.	Same as for tests of controls.

- Tests comparing details from the new system with those of the old system to verify that only accurate, authorized information has been established.
- Tests comparing details from the old system with those of the new system to ensure accuracy and that no transactions have been omitted.
- Cutoff testing to ensure that transactions are included in only the proper system and have not been omitted.

Thus, a **conversion audit** comprises the audit procedures required when an organization changes its system to a different information system. The emphasis is on the accurate and authorized establishment of new master files, the completeness and existence of the data within those files, and on the cut-off of transactions in the appropriate system.

DETERMINING WHETHER ACCOUNTING POLICIES HAVE CHANGED The new or changed automated system may have procedures that change accounting policies, such as asset capitalization or inventory costing. For example, assessing inventory accounting policy could be done concurrently with inventory costing. If inventory is counted only at year end (a periodic system), it would be costed on a FIFO (first-in, first-out) basis, whereas most computer systems use average costing or weighted average costing. Should the method of inventory costing change, the auditor would need to gather and include sufficient evidence that there is adequate disclosure in the financial statements for this change in accounting policy and determine whether the accounting policy change was handled retroactively.

③ Substantive Testing of Accounts Payable

Accounts payable are unpaid obligations (liabilities) for goods and services received in the ordinary course of business. It is sometimes difficult to distinguish between accounts payable and provisions for liabilities (also called accrued liabilities). The account payable is a liability if the total amount of the obligation is known and owed at the balance sheet date. The accounts payable account then includes obligations for the acquisition of raw materials, equipment, utilities, repairs, and many other types of goods and services that were received before the end of the year and will be paid in the next fiscal year. An obligation is an accrued liability under ASPE (or provision under IFRS) if a reliable estimate of the amount due can be made and there is an obligation to pay. The term "accrued liability" is still used under IFRS if the amount is known, such as for a trade payable. Examples of accruals include portions of realty taxes and portions of wages that belong to the current fiscal year but will be paid in the next fiscal year, while an example of a provision would be an estimated warranty expense. Table 16-5 lists terms pertaining to liabilities used by ASPE and IFRS. For further information on the term, refer to the *CICA Handbook* ASPE Section or IAS noted in the table.

> **concept check**
>
> C16-3 How do high-quality perpetual records affect the auditor's tests of controls of inventory acquisitions?
>
> C16-4 Provide examples of two controls that improve completeness over recording of acquisitions transactions.
>
> C16-5 When conducting a systems conversion audit, why does the auditor need to test the data details between the old and the new master files in both directions, that is, from old to new and from new to old?

Table 16-5	ASPE and IFRS Terms Used to Describe Liabilities and Contingent Assets		
ASPE Term	*CICA Handbook* ASPE Section Reference	IFRS Term	*CICA Handbook* IAS Reference
Liability	1000.28 to 1000.30	Liability	37.10
Accrued liability	N/A	Accrued liability or provision	37.10
		Obligating event	37.10
		Legal obligation	37.10
		Constructive obligation	37.10
Contingent loss	3290.05 and 3290.10	Contingent liability; Provision, when accrued	37.10
Contingent gain	3290.05	Contingent asset	37.10

The great majority of accounts payable can be recognized by the existence of vendors' invoices for the obligation. Accounts payable should be distinguished from interest-bearing obligations. If an obligation includes the payment of interest, it should be recorded properly as a note payable, contract payable, mortgage payable, or bond payable.

The methodology for designing tests of details for accounts payable is summarized in Figure 16-3. This methodology is the same as that used for accounts receivable in Chapter 13. It is common for accounts payable to be significant, with the potential for material error. Internal controls are often ineffective for accounts payable because many companies depend on the vendors to bill them and remind them of unpaid bills. This means that tests of details for accounts payable may need to be extensive.

INTERNAL CONTROLS The effects of the client's internal controls on accounts payable tests can be illustrated by two examples. In the first, assume that the client has highly effective internal controls over recording and paying for acquisitions. The receipt of goods is promptly documented by prenumbered receiving reports with receiving details entered into an online information system; receipt detail is automatically matched to purchase orders. When invoices are received, they are also immediately entered and matched online to the purchase order and receiving details. Cash disbursements are made promptly when due, and the disbursements are immediately recorded in the cash disbursements transactions file and the vendor master file. On a monthly basis, individual accounts payable balances in the vendor master file are

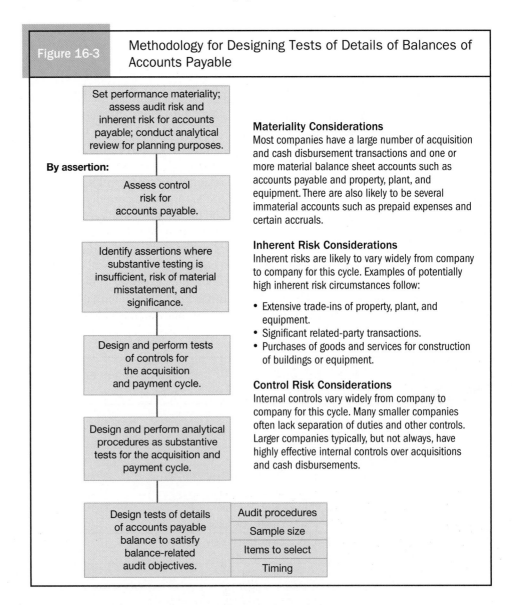

Figure 16-3 Methodology for Designing Tests of Details of Balances of Accounts Payable

Set performance materiality; assess audit risk and inherent risk for accounts payable; conduct analytical review for planning purposes.

By assertion:

Assess control risk for accounts payable.

Identify assertions where substantive testing is insufficient, risk of material misstatement, and significance.

Design and perform tests of controls for the acquisition and payment cycle.

Design and perform analytical procedures as substantive tests for the acquisition and payment cycle.

Design tests of details of accounts payable balance to satisfy balance-related audit objectives.
- Audit procedures
- Sample size
- Items to select
- Timing

Materiality Considerations
Most companies have a large number of acquisition and cash disbursement transactions and one or more material balance sheet accounts such as accounts payable and property, plant, and equipment. There are also likely to be several immaterial accounts such as prepaid expenses and certain accruals.

Inherent Risk Considerations
Inherent risks are likely to vary widely from company to company for this cycle. Examples of potentially high inherent risk circumstances follow:

- Extensive trade-ins of property, plant, and equipment.
- Significant related-party transactions.
- Purchases of goods and services for construction of buildings or equipment.

Control Risk Considerations
Internal controls vary widely from company to company for this cycle. Many smaller companies often lack separation of duties and other controls. Larger companies typically, but not always, have highly effective internal controls over acquisitions and cash disbursements.

reconciled with vendors' statements, unmatched receiving reports and purchase orders investigated, and the total of the accounts payable in the accounts payable subsystem (vendor master file) is compared with that in the general ledger by an independent person. Under these circumstances, the verification of accounts payable should require little audit effort once the auditor tests and concludes that internal controls are operating effectively.

In the second example, assume that receiving reports are not used, the client defers recording acquisitions until cash disbursements are made, and because of a weak cash position bills are frequently paid several months after their due date. When an auditor faces such a situation, there is a high likelihood of an understatement of accounts payable. Extensive tests of details of accounts payable are necessary to determine whether accounts payable are properly stated at the balance sheet date since payables will not be recorded until the following months when they are paid.

The most important controls over accounts payable have already been discussed as part of the control and recording of acquisitions and cash disbursements. In addition to these controls, it is important to have a monthly reconciliation of vendors' statements with recorded liabilities and of the outstanding unpaid invoice transaction file with the vendor master file and the general ledger. This should be done by an independent person or using computer software.

ANALYTICAL PROCEDURES The use of analytical procedures is as important in the acquisition and payment cycle as it is in every other cycle. Table 16-6 illustrates two analytical procedures for planning for the balance sheet and income statement accounts in the acquisition and payment cycle that are useful for uncovering areas in which additional investigation is desirable. It also shows two analytical procedures as substantive tests that can help quantify potential misstatements.

One of the most important analytical procedures for uncovering misstatements of accounts payable is comparing current-year expense totals with those of prior years. For example, by comparing current utilities expense with the prior years, the auditor may determine that the last utilities bill for the year was not recorded. Comparing expenses with prior years' is an effective analytical procedure for accounts payable because expenses from year to year are relatively stable if income is stable. Examples include rent, utilities, and other expenses billed on a regular basis.

BALANCE-RELATED AND PRESENTATION AND DISCLOSURE-RELATED AUDIT OBJECTIVES FOR TESTS OF DETAILS The overall objective in the audit of accounts payable is to determine whether accounts payable are fairly stated and properly disclosed. All but one of the balance-related (B-RAO) and presentation and disclosure-related audit objectives (P&D-RAO) discussed in Chapter 5 are applicable to accounts payable. Valuation is not applicable to liabilities.

Table 16-6	Analytical Procedures for the Acquisition and Payment Cycle
Analytical Procedure	Possible Misstatement
Analytical procedures for planning	
Compare acquisition-related expense account balances with prior years.	Misstatement of accounts payable and expenses.
Calculate ratios such as purchases divided by accounts payable, and accounts payable divided by current liabilities.	Unrecorded or non-existent accounts payable, or misstatements.
Analytical procedures as substantive tests	
Inspect list of accounts payable for unusual, non-vendor, and interest-bearing payables.	Classification misstatement for non-trade liabilities.
Compare individual accounts payable with previous years.	Unrecorded or non-existent accounts payable, or misstatements.

The difference in emphasis in auditing assets and liabilities results directly from the legal liability of public accountants. If, subsequent to the issuance of the audited financial statements, equity investors, creditors, and other users determine that owners' equity was materially overstated, a lawsuit against the public accounting firm is fairly likely. Since an overstatement of owners' equity can arise either from an overstatement of assets or from an understatement of liabilities, it is natural for public accountants to emphasize those two types of misstatements. This means that when auditing liabilities, the auditor looks primarily for understatements, which usually have the effect of understating liabilities and overstating income.

TESTS OF DETAILS OF ACCOUNTS PAYABLE Table 16-7 includes the balance-related audit objectives and common tests of details of balances procedures for accounts payable. The actual audit procedures will vary considerably depending on the nature of the entity, the materiality of accounts payable, the nature and effectiveness of internal controls, and inherent risk.

OUT-OF-PERIOD LIABILITY TESTS Because of the emphasis on understatements in liability accounts, out-of-period liability tests are important for accounts payable. The extent of tests to uncover unrecorded accounts payable, frequently referred to as "the

Table 16-7	Balance-Related and Presentation and Disclosure-Related Audit Objectives and Tests of Details of Balances for Accounts Payable
Audit Objective	**Common Tests of Details of Balances Procedures**
Accounts payable in the accounts payable trial balance, general ledger account, and financial statements exist (existence).	Trace from accounts payable list to vendors' invoices and statements. Confirm accounts payable, emphasizing large and unusual amounts.
Existing accounts payable are in the accounts payable list (completeness).	Perform out-of-period liability tests. The company has an obligation to pay the liabilities included in accounts payable (rights and obligations). Inspect vendors' statements, and confirm accounts payable.
Accounts payable in the accounts payable list agree with related master file, and the total is correctly added and agrees with that of the general ledger and financial statements (completeness and allocation).	Foot the accounts payable list.* Trace the total to the general ledger and the financial statements. Trace individual vendor's invoices to transaction file for names and amounts. Inquire of management for any additional accounts payable.
Accounts payable in the accounts payable trial balance and financial statements are properly classified (classification).	Inspect the aged accounts payable trial balance and master file for related parties, notes, or other interest-bearing liabilities, long-term payables, and debit balances. Discuss the nature and classification of accounts payable with management and compare audit findings with disclosures in the financial statements.
Transactions in the acquisition and payment cycle are recorded in the proper period (allocation).	Perform out-of-period liability tests. Perform detailed tests as a part of physical observation of inventory. Test for inventory in transit.
Accounts in the acquisition and payment cycle are clearly presented and disclosed (understandability).	Review financial statements to make sure material related-party, long-term, and interest-bearing liabilities are segregated and clearly disclosed. For IFRS clients, ensure that additional disclosure requirements are provided (IAS 1.125)

*This test of details would be conducted on many audits by using the computer.

search for unrecorded accounts payable," depends heavily on assessed control risk and the materiality of the potential balance in the account. The same audit procedures used to uncover unrecorded payables are applicable to the accuracy objective. The audit procedures that follow are typical tests.

Inspect underlying documentation for subsequent cash disbursements The purpose of this audit procedure is to uncover payments made in the subsequent accounting period that represent liabilities at the balance sheet date. The supporting documentation is inspected to determine whether a payment was for a current-period obligation. For example, if inventory was received prior to the balance sheet date but the invoice received in the following month, it will have the earlier date on the receiving report. Frequently, documentation for payments made in the subsequent period are examined for several weeks, especially when the client does not pay its bills on a timely basis. Any payment that is for a current-period obligation should be traced to the accounts payable trial balance to make sure it has been included as a liability.

Inspect underlying documentation for bills not paid several weeks after the year end This procedure is carried out in the same manner as the preceding one and serves the same purpose. The only difference is that it is done for unpaid obligations near the end of the examination rather than for obligations that have already been paid. For example, in an audit with a March 31 year end, if the auditor examines the supporting documentation for cheques paid until June 28, bills that are still unpaid at that date should be examined to determine whether they are obligations of the year ended March 31. For large audit engagements or for organizations with good internal controls, the auditor would limit these tests to a sample of transactions or reduce the period of investigation to a shorter period (perhaps two or three weeks).

Trace receiving reports issued before year end to related vendors' invoices All merchandise received before the year end of the accounting period, indicated by the issuance of a receiving report, should be included as accounts payable. By tracing receiving reports issued at and before year end to vendors' invoices and making sure they are included in accounts payable, the auditor is testing for unrecorded obligations.

Trace vendors' statements that show a balance due to the accounts payable trial balance If the client maintains a file of vendors' statements, any statement indicating a balance due can be traced to the accounts payable listing to make sure it is included as an account payable.

Send confirmations to client's vendors Although the use of confirmations for accounts payable is less common than for accounts receivable, it is common testing for vendors omitted from the accounts payable list, potential omitted transactions, and misstated account balances. Sending confirmations to active vendors for which a balance has not been included in the accounts payable list is a useful means of searching for omitted amounts. This type of confirmation is commonly referred to as "zero balance confirmation." See Figure 16-4 for an example.

CUTOFF TESTS Cutoff tests for accounts payable are intended to determine whether transactions recorded a few days before and after the balance sheet date are included in the correct period. The audit procedures discussed in the preceding section are directly related to cutoff for acquisitions, but they emphasize understatements. To test for overstatement cutoff amounts, the auditor should trace receiving reports issued after year end to related invoices to make sure they are not recorded as accounts payable (unless they are inventory in transit, which will be discussed shortly). Invoices for services would be examined to determine the date the service was performed.

Two aspects are expanded upon here: the examination of receiving reports and the determination of the amount of inventory in transit.

Relationship of cutoff to physical observation of inventory In determining that the accounts payable cutoff is correct, it is essential that the cutoff tests be coordinated

Figure 16-4   Accounts Payable Confirmation Request

Roger Mead Ltd.
1600 Westmount Ave. N.
Kenora, Ontario
P9N 1X7

January 15, 2012

Szabo Sales Co. Ltd.
2116 King Street
Kenora, Ontario
P9N 1G3

To Whom It May Concern:

Our auditors, Adams and Lelik, LLP, are conducting an audit of our financial statements. For this purpose, please furnish directly to them, at their address noted below, the following information as of December 31, 2011.

(1) Itemized statements of our accounts payable to you showing all unpaid items
(2) A complete list of any notes and acceptances payable to you (including any which have been discounted) showing the original date, dates due, original amount, unpaid balance, collateral, and endorsers
(3) An itemized list of your merchandise consigned to us

Your prompt attention to this request will be appreciated. A stamped, addressed envelope is enclosed for your reply.

Yours truly,

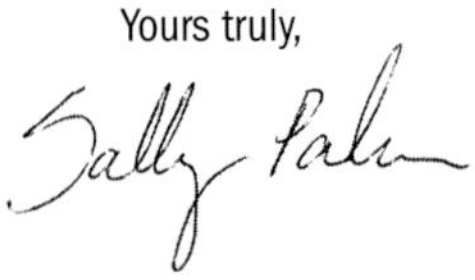

Sally Palm

Adams and Lelik, LLP
215 Tecumseh Crescent
Kenora, Ontario
P9N 2K5

Roger Mead Ltd.
per Sally Palm

---

with the physical observation of inventory. For example, assume that an inventory acquisition for $40,000 is received late in the afternoon of December 31, after the physical inventory is completed. If the acquisition is included in accounts payable and purchases but excluded from inventory, the result is an understatement of net earnings of $40,000. Conversely, if the acquisition is excluded from both inventory and accounts payable, there are understatements in the balance sheet, but the income statement is correct. The only way the auditor will know which type of misstatement has occurred is to coordinate cutoff tests with the observation of inventory.

The cutoff information for purchases should be obtained during the physical observation of the inventory. At this time, the auditor should review the procedures in the receiving department to determine that all inventory received was counted, and the auditor should record in his or her working papers the last inventory receiving report number. During the year-end fieldwork, the auditor should then test the accounting records for cutoff. The auditor should trace receiving report numbers to the accounts payable records to verify that they are correctly included or excluded.

Inventory in transit When inspecting accounts payable vendor invoices, the auditor needs to check for the method of shipping. With **FOB** (freight on board) **destination** shipping, title passes to the buyer when it is received for inventory. Therefore, inventory received prior to the balance sheet date should be included in inventory and accounts payable at year end. When an acquisition is on an **FOB origin** basis, title passes to the buyer when goods are shipped, so the inventory and related accounts payable must be recorded in the current period if shipment by the vendor occurred before the balance sheet date.

FOB destination—shipping contract in which title to the goods passes to the buyer when the goods are received.

FOB origin—shipping contract in which title to the goods passes to the buyer at the time that the goods are shipped.

RELIABILITY OF EVIDENCE In determining the appropriate evidence to accumulate for verifying accounts payable, it is essential that the auditor understand the relative reliability of the three primary types of evidence typically used: vendors' invoices, vendors' statements, and confirmations.

Evidence quality distinction between vendors' invoices and vendors' statements In verifying the amount due to a vendor, the auditor should make a major distinction between vendors' invoices and vendors' statements. In examining vendors' invoices and related supporting documents, such as receiving reports and purchase orders, the auditor gets highly reliable evidence about individual transactions. A vendor's statement is not as desirable as invoices for verifying individual transactions because a statement includes only the total amount of the transaction. The units acquired, price, freight, and other data are not included. However, a statement has the advantage of including the ending balance according to the vendor's records.

Which of these two documents is better for verifying the correct balance in accounts payable? The vendor's statement is superior for verifying accounts payable because it includes the ending balance. The auditor could compare existing vendors' invoices with the client's list and still not uncover missing ones, which is the primary concern in accounts payable.

Which of these two documents is better for testing acquisitions in tests of control? The vendor's invoice is superior for verifying transactions because the auditor is verifying individual transactions and the invoice shows the details of the acquisitions.

Evidence quality difference between vendors' statements and confirmations The most important distinction between a vendor's statement and a confirmation of accounts payable is the source of the information. A vendor's statement has been prepared by an independent third party, but it is in the hands of the client at the time the auditor examines it. This provides the client with an opportunity to alter a vendor's statement or to make particular statements unavailable to the auditor. A confirmation of accounts payable, which normally is a request for an itemized statement sent directly to the public accountant's office, provides the same information but can be regarded as more reliable. In addition, confirmations of accounts payable frequently include a request for information about notes and acceptances payable, as well as consigned inventory that is owned by the vendor but stored on the client's premises. An illustration of a typical accounts payable confirmation request is given in Figure 16-4.

The confirmation of accounts payable is less common than confirmation of accounts receivable. If the client has adequate internal controls and vendors' statements are available for examination, then confirmations are normally not sent. However, when the client's internal controls are weak, when statements are not available, or when the auditor questions the client's integrity, then it is desirable to send confirmation requests to vendors. Because of the emphasis on understatements of liability accounts, the accounts confirmed should include large accounts, active accounts, accounts with a zero balance, and a representative sample of all others.

When vendors' statements are examined or confirmations are received, there must be a reconciliation of the statement or confirmation with the accounts payable list. Frequently, differences are caused by inventory in transit, cheques mailed by the client but not received by the vendor at the statement date, and delays in processing the accounting records. The reconciliation is of the same general nature as that discussed in Chapter 13 for accounts receivable. The documents typically used to reconcile the balances on the accounts payable list with the confirmation or vendor's statement include receiving reports, vendors' invoices, and cancelled cheques.

Figure 16-5 illustrates the major accounts in the acquisition and payment cycle and the types of audit tests used to audit these accounts. This figure also shows how the audit risk model discussed in Chapter 7 relates to the audit of the acquisition and payment cycle.

concept check

C16-6 Why is an organization more likely to have poor internal controls over accounts payable than over accounts receivable?

C16-7 Provide two examples of analytical procedures that could indicate a possible misstatement in accounts payable.

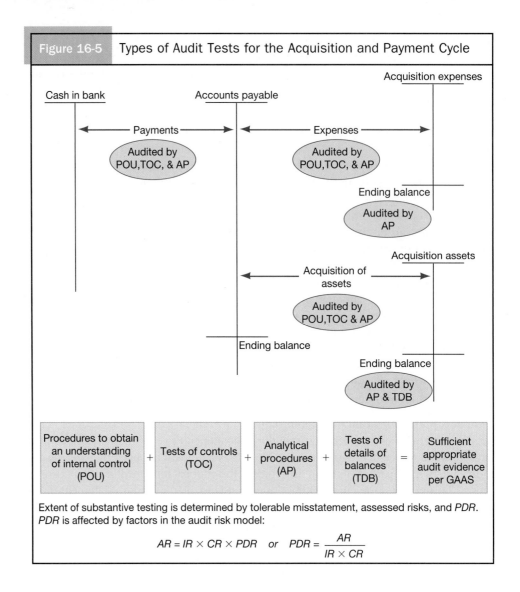

Figure 16-5 | Types of Audit Tests for the Acquisition and Payment Cycle

Extent of substantive testing is determined by tolerable misstatement, assessed risks, and *PDR*. *PDR* is affected by factors in the audit risk model:

$$AR = IR \times CR \times PDR \quad or \quad PDR = \frac{AR}{IR \times CR}$$

4 Completing the Tests in the Acquisition and Payment Cycle: Verification of Selected Accounts

Examining Other Accounts: Auditing Manufacturing Equipment

An important characteristic of the acquisition and payment cycle is the large number of accounts involved. These include accounts payable, professional fees, a variety of asset accounts, a variety of expense accounts, taxes payable, and others. Here, we will focus on the audit of manufacturing equipment as an example of auditing a capital asset account. The methodology for designing tests of details of balances for such a variety of accounts is the same as that shown in Figure 16-3 for accounts payable. Each account is a part of the acquisition and payment cycle. Therefore, the only change required in the figure is the replacement of accounts payable with the account being audited. For example, if the account being discussed is accrued property taxes, simply substitute accrued property taxes for accounts payable in the first, second, and last boxes in the figure. The types of audit tests used to audit the above accounts are the same as those shown in Figure 16-5, which also illustrates how the audit risk model discussed in Chapter 7 relates to the audit of these accounts.

Capital assets are assets that have expected lives of more than one year, are used in the business, and are not acquired for resale. The intention to use the assets as a part of the operation of the client's business and their expected life of more than one year are the significant characteristics that distinguish these assets from inventory, prepaid expenses, and investments.

Audit of Manufacturing Equipment

Organizations that do manufacturing may have highly material amounts of assets. For example, a small company with $200,000 in sales doing metal work may have $1.5 million or more in manufacturing equipment. Misallocations between the asset and repairs and maintenance (classification or allocation objectives) could be highly material. Errors in the class or in the depreciation rate could affect income (accuracy or allocation), while errors or deliberate manipulation of the estimates of remaining life of the asset could be used to smooth or alter income (accuracy, allocation). These risks are unique to assets that are amortized, with the nature of the accounting framework selected having a large impact, since IFRS is more complex than ASPE with respect to the accounting methods used to record asset values and depreciation.

The accounts commonly used for manufacturing equipment are illustrated in Figure 16-6. Since the source of debits in the asset account is the acquisitions journal, the accounting system has already been tested for recording the current period's additions to manufacturing equipment as part of the test of the acquisition and payment cycle.

The primary accounting record for manufacturing equipment and other capital asset accounts is generally a property or **capital asset master file** with supporting purchase, disposal, and amortization transactions. The contents of the data files must be understood for a meaningful study of the audit of manufacturing equipment. The files will be composed of a set of records, one for each piece of equipment and other types of property owned. In turn, each record will include descriptive information, date of acquisition, original cost, current-year amortization, and accumulated amortization for the property. The files will also contain information about property acquired and disposed of during the year. Proceeds, gains, and losses will be included for disposals. If IFRS is the financial reporting framework and the client is reporting assets at fair market value, then the capital asset master file will also need to track fair market value changes and the resulting effects on residual values and depreciation according to IAS 16. Note that the *CICA Handbook* Section 3061 for ASPE uses the term amortization rather than depreciation. We will be using these two terms interchangeably. Totals of the master file should agree to totals in the general ledger.

Capital asset master file—a computer file containing records for each piece of equipment and other types of property owned; the primary accounting record for manufacturing equipment and other capital asset accounts.

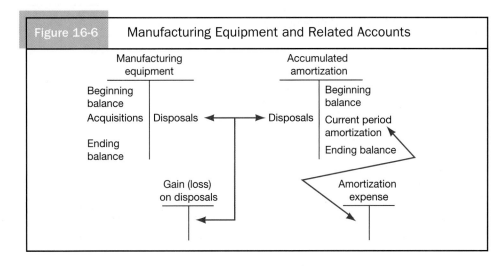

Figure 16-6 — Manufacturing Equipment and Related Accounts

DIFFERENCES WHEN AUDITING MANUFACTURING EQUIPMENT Manufacturing equipment is normally audited differently from current asset accounts for three reasons: (1) there are usually fewer current-period acquisitions of manufacturing equipment, (2) the amount of any given acquisition is often material, and (3) the equipment is likely to be kept and maintained in the accounting records for several years. Because of these differences, the emphasis in auditing manufacturing equipment is on the verification of current-period acquisitions and on changes to carrying values and useful life estimates rather than on the balance in the account carried forward from the preceding year. In addition, the expected life of assets over one year requires amortization and accumulated amortization accounts, which are verified as part of the audit of the assets. Additions should be traced to the capital cost allowance section of the tax working papers.

In response to these differences, the following audit procedures focus on current period changes.

ANALYTICAL PROCEDURES As in all audit areas, the nature of the analytical procedures depends on the nature of the client's operations. Table 16-8 provides examples of analytical procedure for planning for manufacturing equipment.

AUDIT OF CURRENT-YEAR ACQUISITIONS The proper recording of current-year additions is important because of the long-term effect the assets have on the financial statements. The failure to capitalize a capital asset, or the recording of an acquisition at the improper amount, affects the balance sheet until the firm disposes of the asset. The income statement is affected until the asset is fully amortized. Accuracy and classification are usually the major objectives for this part of the audit, although physical inspection would cover the existence objective.

Prior to the audit, the auditor requests from the client a schedule that provides relevant details by asset: the date of the acquisition, vendor, description, notation whether new or used, life of the asset for amortization purposes, amortization method, cost and revaluations (and salvage value, if any), and any relevant income tax information such as capital cost allowance rates and the investment tax credit if applicable. The information in this schedule is the focus of the audit. The audit steps conducted for current year acquisitions are:

- *Inspect supporting documentation for asset costs*: Vendors, invoices and receiving reports are examined to verify the nature of the asset, its cost, and the date acquired to determine that it has been recorded in compliance with the client's capitalization policies in the correct account. Costs should include foreign exchange, installation, and shipping. The sample would be at-risk transactions (large amounts, certain dates, or certain asset classes) as well as a sample of the remainder. The size of the sample for substantive testing depends upon the assessed inherent and control risks.

Table 16-8	Analytical Procedures for Planning for Manufacturing Equipment
Analytical Procedure	Possible Misstatement
Compare amortization expense divided by gross manufacturing equipment cost with previous years.	Misstatement in amortization expense and accumulated amortization.
Compare accumulated amortization divided by gross manufacturing equipment cost with previous years.	Misstatement in accumulated amortization.
Compare monthly or annual repairs and maintenance, supplies expense, small tools expense, and similar accounts with previous years.	Expensing amounts that should be capital items.
Compare gross manufacturing cost divided by some measure of production with previous years.	Idle equipment or equipment that has been disposed of but not written off.

- *Inspect grant documents:* Reading of grant documents provides information used to determine that the grant has been properly recorded, tax effects determined correctly, and its terms disclosed in the financial statements.
- *Inspect large repairs and maintenance documentation:* Similar to the first point above, verify details of the invoice to determine whether the transaction is in fact repairs and maintenance or should be capitalized or allocated to other accounts. While looking at asset acquisitions, the auditor would also determine whether any of the capitalized amounts inspected should be expensed. The auditor would consider both the client's policies as well as tax regulations during this assessment.
- *Search for trade-ins:* (see discussion under asset disposal)
- *Physically inspect the asset or repair:* Tour the physical location or ask for a photo of the asset to verify that it matches the supporting documentation.
- *Re-assess risks based upon findings:* If there are errors in classification to particular accounts or in accuracy of recording, the auditor may need to reassess risks or expand the extent of testing.

AUDIT OF CURRENT-YEAR DISPOSALS The next step is to audit current year disposals. Recording disposals relies more on internal controls than does the recording of acquisitions, since assets may be removed without receiving any funds (i.e., retired). Controls need to be in place to inform management and capital asset record-keeping of the authorized sale, trade-in, abandonment, or theft of recorded machinery and equipment. Once documented and notified, there should be independent verification of these changes to prevent unauthorized changes and ensure accuracy. The primary assertions for the following audit tests are occurrence and accuracy:

- *Inquiry of the nature of the disposals:* Inquire of management with respect to the quantity and nature of the disposals. For example, determine whether assets were replaced or simply retired, and how they were disposed of to identify the type of documentation that would be present for the disposal.
- *Inspect documentation of the disposal:* Inspect documentation to determine that the amounts were accurately recorded and allocated to the correct asset in the capital asset master files.
- *Recalculate gains and losses:* Recalculate the amounts and determine whether gains and losses were accurately recorded to the correct accounts (e.g., to miscellaneous income or expense).
- *Assess income tax effects:* Determine whether an asset class has been fully disposed of and whether recapture of capital cost allowance has occurred and is properly calculated.
- *Trace postings to the correct accounts:* As noted above, disposals should be removed from the asset master file (relieving both cost and accumulated amortization or depreciation) and gains and losses recorded to the correct income or expense account.
- *Physically inspect the plant location:* Tour the physical location (or obtain a photo) to determine that the asset is no longer on premises.
- *Inspect related accounts for potential unrecorded disposals:* Inspect postings to related accounts such as miscellaneous income or expense, goods and services or sales taxes, or details of insurance coverage for sold or removed assets.
- *While inspecting asset acquisition, search for trade-ins:* A common error on the part of the client is to record a new acquisition with a trade-in at the net amount (i.e., new cost less trade-in amount). By searching for trade-ins, the auditor can verify that the new asset has been recorded at full cost and that the disposed-of asset is properly removed from the accounts.

AUDIT OF OPENING AND CLOSING BALANCES Once assets and disposals have been verified, the auditor decides the extent of testing needed for opening and closing balances. Since the focus is on auditing additions and disposals, if the auditor audited the opening balance, and the client has a capital asset master file that agrees with the opening balance, the auditor would normally only check that the opening balance agrees to the ending balance of the prior year's audit for each fixed asset account. For the closing balance, two tests of accuracy (allocation) would need to be completed:

- *Reconcile opening to closing balance:* Opening balance plus additions minus disposals should agree to the ending balance.
- *Agree subsidiary totals to closing balance:* Add the capital asset master file and agree the total to the ending balance.

Additional tests of ending balances are the following:

- *Valuation objective:* Assets may need to be written down if their net realizable value has dropped due to changing technology or the presence of non-operating equipment. The auditor will need to be aware of the client's business environment, look at the cost of recent additions, and the replacement cost of comparable equipment. Non-operating equipment disclosures would need to be reviewed for completeness and understandability. Assets recorded at market value would require documentation, such as an independent appraisal to document the value used. The auditor would need to evaluate the competence and quality of the appraisal, and, if there is uncertainty regarding the quality of the appraisal, may need to have another independent appraisal conducted.
- *Completeness of disclosure:* Fixed assets are often used as collateral for loans or may be purchased using debt. The auditor would read the legal agreements that pertain to this debt to assess adequacy and thoroughness of disclosure in the financial statements.
- *Accuracy and understandability of disclosure:* Details of fixed assets need to be adequately and clearly shown in the financial statements, distinguishing between owned and leased assets, and identifying commitments for payments under leases and debt.

AUDIT OF AMORTIZATION EXPENSE Amortization expense is one of the few expense accounts that is not verified as a part of tests of controls since the recorded amounts are determined by internal **allocations** to particular expense accounts rather than by exchange transactions with outside parties. When amortization expense is material, more tests of details of amortization expense are required than for an account that has already been verified through tests of controls.

Allocation—the division of certain expenses, such as amortization and manufacturing overhead, among several expense accounts.

The most important objectives for amortization expense are valuation and accuracy. These involve determining whether the client is following a consistent amortization policy from period to period and whether the client's calculations are accurate.

When assessing amortization policy there are four considerations: the remaining useful life of assets, the method of amortization, the estimated salvage/residual value, and the policy of amortizing assets in the year of acquisition and disposition. The client's policies can be determined by having discussions with the client and comparing the responses with the information in the auditor's permanent files.

In deciding on the reasonableness of the useful lives assigned to assets, the auditor must consider a number of factors: any changes in value to the recorded assets, the actual physical life of the asset, the expected useful life (taking into account obsolescence and the company's normal policy of upgrading equipment), and established company policies on trading-in equipment. The effect of these on amortization must be carefully evaluated. The auditor needs to consider management bias toward higher or lower income and the overall risk of material misstatement when examining such accounting policies.

A useful method of testing amortization is to make a calculation of its overall reasonableness using analytical review as a substantive test. The calculation is made by multiplying the unamortized capital assets by the amortization rate for the year. In making these calculations, the auditor must make adjustments for current-year additions and disposals, assets with different lengths of life, and assets with different methods of amortization. The calculations can be made fairly easily if the public accounting firm includes in the permanent file a breakdown of the capital assets by method of amortization and length of life. If the overall calculations are reasonably close to the client's totals and if assessed control risk for amortization expense is low, tests of details for amortization can be minimized.

Checking the accuracy of amortization calculations is done by recomputing amortization expense for selected assets to determine whether the client is following a proper and consistent amortization policy. To be relevant, the detailed calculations should be tied into the total amortization calculations by footing the amortization expense in the capital asset master file and reconciling the total with the general ledger.

AUDIT OF ACCUMULATED AMORTIZATION Two objectives are usually emphasized in the audit of accumulated amortization (the ending balance):

- Accumulated amortization as stated in the asset master file agrees with the general ledger. This objective can be satisfied by test footing the accumulated amortization on the asset master file and tracing the total to the general ledger.
- Accumulated amortization in the master file is properly valued.

In some cases, the life of manufacturing equipment may be significantly reduced because of such changes as reductions in customer demands for products, unexpected physical deterioration, or a modification in operations. Because of these possibilities and if the decline in asset value is permanent, it may be appropriate to write the asset down to net realizable value, which could result in a change to the accumulated amortization.

Audit of Accrued Liabilities

Accrued liabilities (called provisions for liabilities in IFRS) are estimated unpaid obligations for services or benefits that have been received prior to the balance sheet date. Many accrued liabilities represent future obligations for unpaid services resulting from the passage of time but are not payable at the balance sheet date. For example, the benefits of property rental accrue throughout the year; therefore, at the balance sheet date, a certain portion of the total rent cost that has not been paid should be accrued. If the balance sheet date and the date of the termination of the rent agreement are the same, any unpaid rent is more appropriately called "rent payable" than an "accrued liability." Other examples are accrued wages, payroll taxes and bonuses, accrued pension costs and accrued professional fees. Some accruals, such as warranty expense, must be estimated and require evaluation of management's estimates and underlying assumptions.

The key risks for these accounts are existence (that they are all included), accuracy (that they are calculated correctly), and allocation (that they are allocated correctly among prior, current, and future fiscal periods). Accordingly, the auditor will use inquiry of management to determine which accruals exist, determine the policy for establishing the accrual, then re-calculate the accrual. The auditor will also inspect supporting documentation to verify the accrual, such as subsequent payroll journals for accrued wages, payroll taxes and bonuses, and an actuarial report for accrued pension costs.

Accrued liabilities—estimated unpaid obligations for services or benefits that have been received prior to the balance sheet date; include accrued commissions, accrued income taxes, accrued payroll, and accrued rent.

Review of Related-Party Transactions

CAS During the risk assessment process, CAS 550, Related parties, requires the auditor to consider risks of material misstatement or fraud that could be associated with related-party transactions. The auditor will also consider the controls and procedures that management has in place for the identification and disclosure of such transactions. In particular, if the client does not disclose related-party transactions to the auditor and the auditor discovers these, the auditor would need to carefully reassess why such transactions were not detected by the client's regular processes.

While the examination of underlying documents in the tests of controls is designed primarily to verify transactions with third parties, related transactions with affiliates and subdivisions within the client's organization are also included in the examination. The possibility of improper recording and disclosure of transactions between independent entities was discussed in Chapter 8 in the section dealing with related-party transactions.

CAS 550 adopts a risk-based approach and provides guidance to the auditor for assessing inherent and control risks and ultimately determining the extent of substantive testing for related-party transactions. The Application section of CAS 550 provides examples of audit procedures and of how related-party transactions could be measured.

When a client deals with related parties, the *CICA Handbook* requires that the nature of the relationship, the nature and extent of transactions, and amounts due to and from the related parties, including contractual obligations and contingencies, be properly disclosed for the financial statements to be in conformity with GAAS. Services and inventory acquired from related parties must be properly valued, and other exchange transactions must be carefully evaluated for propriety and reasonableness. Related-party transactions must be audited more extensively than those with third parties.

concept check

C16-8 What possible misstatements could occur with manufacturing equipment?

C16-9 Why does the auditor need to ask if any equipment purchases are from a related party?

Summary

1. *What are the major business functions, documents, and records in the acquisition and payment cycle?* Table 16-1 states that the business functions for acquisitions are processing purchase orders, receiving goods and services, recognizing liabilities, and vendor master file changes, while the business function for cash disbursements (payments) is the processing and recording of cash disbursements. The table also lists documents, records, and their purposes.

   Which accounts give rise to accrued liabilities? Typical accounts include payroll remittances (such as employment insurance and Canada Pension) and unpaid wages.

2. *How are tests of controls designed for the acquisition and payment cycle?* We follow the same methodology for the acquisition and payment cycle as for other cycles—after assessing risks at the organization level, we move to understanding controls at the cycle level so that risks can be assessed and tested by assertion. Then, tests of controls are designed for those assertions where the auditor chooses to place reliance upon the control.

   What is a system conversion? A system conversion occurs when an organization replaces or makes major changes to its existing systems (whether manual or automated).

   What issues does the auditor need to address during a conversion audit? The auditor needs to consider that there is likely a new system of internal controls that will need to be documented and evaluated. The auditor will also need to audit the actual data conversion process and determine whether there have been any changes in accounting policies.

3. *Why is accounts payable considered separately from acquisitions or payments?* Accounts payable is the ending balance

   sheet obligation, whereas acquisitions and payments are the transactions that occur throughout the year.

   How does the auditor design substantive tests for accounts payable? As for other cycles, the auditor considers risks, such as risks of understatement. Typical substantive tests include scrutinizing subsequent payments and reconciling supplier statements.

   Why is the auditor more concerned about understatement of accounts payable than overstatement? Should accounts payable be understated, income would be overstated. There is likely to be a greater legal liability to an auditor if a potential investor relies on overstated income than understated income.

4. *What process should be followed in the audit of manufacturing equipment, an asset?* The auditor needs to consider the risk of misstatement by audit objective in order to target testing. Analytical procedures (Table 16-8) can be helpful. Then, a sample of transactions would be selected for verification to supporting acquisitions documentation (e.g., invoices or purchase contracts) and tests of details conducted for relevant audit objectives.

   Why is the audit of prepaid expenses important? Prepaid expenses are important in the process of matching expenses with revenues. Misstatements in prepaid expenses would also result in misstatements in revenue.

   How are prepaid expenses audited? Risks and internal controls are assessed before designing audit tests that include determination of the period covered by the prepaid assets and calculation of the portion that is to be expensed.

What are some examples of typical accrued liabilities? Accruals include management bonuses, interest, payroll costs, property taxes, and insurance.

Why does the auditor need to consider related parties during the audit of the acquisition and payment cycle?

The nature of related parties and the details of the transactions need to be disclosed in notes to the financial statements in a clear and understandable way, so the auditor needs to audit such details as the exchange amount versus the carrying amount of such transactions.

MyAccountingLab

Make the grade with MyAccountingLab: The questions, exercises, and problems marked in orange can be found on MyAccountingLab. You can practise them as often as you want, and most feature step-by-step guided instructions to help you find the right answer.

Review Questions

16-1 ❶ What is the importance of cash discounts to the client, and how can the auditor verify whether they are being used in accordance with company policy?

16-2 ❶ Explain why most auditors consider the receipt of goods and services the most important point in the acquisition and payment cycle.

16-3 ❶❷ List one possible internal control for each of the five transaction-related audit objectives for cash disbursements. For each control, list a test of controls to test its effectiveness.

16-4 ❶❷ List one possible control for each of the five transaction-related audit objectives for acquisitions. For each control, list a test of controls to test its effectiveness.

16-5 ❶❸ Distinguish between a vendor's invoice and a vendor's statement. Which document should ideally be used as evidence in auditing acquisition transactions and which for directly verifying accounts payable balances? Why?

16-6 ❷ John has discovered that his client converted to an integrated set of software packages one month prior to the year end. During the last month of the fiscal year, the client ran systems in parallel. John decides that he can do the audit as usual because the old system is still in operation. Next year, he will have to audit only the new system because the old system will no longer be in use. Evaluate John's decision regarding the conduct of the audit.

16-7 ❷❸ What are the similarities and differences in the objectives of the following two procedures?
1. Select a random sample of receiving reports, and trace them to related vendors' invoices and acquisitions journal entries, comparing the vendor's name, type of material and quantity acquired, and total amount of the acquisition.
2. Select a random sample of acquisitions journal entries, and trace them to related vendors' invoices and receiving reports, comparing the vendor's name, type of material and quantity acquired, and total amount of the acquisition.

16-8 ❷❸ Explain the relationship between tests of the acquisition and payment cycle and tests of inventory. Give specific examples of how these two types of tests affect each other.

16-9 ❸ Explain the relationship between tests of the acquisition and payment cycle and tests of accounts payable. Give specific examples of how these two types of tests affect each other.

16-10 ❷❹ Explain the relationship between tests of controls for the acquisition and payment cycle and tests of details of balances for the verification of capital assets. Which aspects of capital assets are directly affected by the tests of controls, and which are not?

16-11 ❸ Explain why it is common for auditors to send confirmation requests to vendors with "zero balances" on the client's accounts payable listing but uncommon to follow the same approach in verifying accounts receivable.

16-12 ❸ In testing the cutoff of accounts payable at the balance sheet date, explain why it is important that auditors coordinate their tests with the physical observation of inventory. What can the auditor do during the physical inventory to enhance the likelihood of an accurate cutoff?

16-13 ❹ Explain why the emphasis in auditing capital assets is on the current-period acquisitions and disposals rather than on the balances in the account carried forward from the preceding year. Under what circumstances would the emphasis be on the balances carried forward?

16-14 ❹ What is the relationship between the audit of fixed assets accounts and the audit of repair and maintenance accounts? Explain how the auditor organizes the audit to take this relationship into consideration.

16-15 ❹ List and briefly state the purpose of all audit procedures that might reasonably be applied by an auditor to determine that all capital asset retirements have been recorded on the books.

16-16 ❹ In auditing amortization expense, what assertions should the auditor keep in mind? Explain how each can be verified.

16-17 ❹ List the factors that should affect the auditor's decision whether or not to analyze a particular account balance. Considering these factors, list four expense accounts that would be important to verify in audit engagements.

16-18 ❹ Why does the auditor examine transaction detail for subsidiaries, affiliates, officers, and directors?

Discussion Questions and Problems

16-19 ❶ ❷ Each year near the balance sheet date, when the president of Bargon Construction, Inc. takes a three-week vacation to Mexico, she signs several cheques to pay major bills during the period she is absent. Jack Morgan, head book-keeper for the company, uses this practice to his advantage. Morgan makes out a cheque to himself for the amount of a large vendor's invoice, and because there is no acquisitions journal, he records the amount in the cash disbursements journal as an acquisition from the supplier listed on the invoice. He holds the cheque until several weeks into the subsequent period to make sure that the auditors do not get an opportunity to examine the cancelled cheque. Shortly after the first of the year when the president returns, Morgan resub-mits the invoice for payment and again records the cheque in the cash disbursements journal. At that point, he marks the invoice "paid" and files it with all other paid invoices. Morgan has been following this practice successfully for several years and feels confident that he has developed a foolproof method.

REQUIRED

a. What is the auditor's responsibility for discovering this type of embezzlement?

b. What weaknesses exist in the client's internal control?

c. What evidence could the auditor use to uncover the fraud?

(Adapted from AICPA)

16-20 ❶ ❸ As part of the audit of different audit areas, it is important to be alert to the possibility of unrecorded liabilities. For each of the following audit areas or accounts, describe a liability that could be uncovered and the audit procedures that could uncover it.

a. Minutes of the board of directors' meetings.

b. Land and buildings.

c. Rent expense.

d. Interest expense.

e. Cash surrender value of life insurance.

f. Cash in the bank.

g. Officers' travel and entertainment expense.

(Adapted from AICPA)

16-21 ❷ ❸ Because of the small size of the company and the limited number of accounting personnel, Dry Goods Wholesale Company Ltd. initially records all acquisitions of goods and services at the time that cash disbursements are made. At the end of each quarter when financial statements for internal purposes are prepared, accounts payable are recorded by adjusting journal entries. The entries are reversed at the beginning of the subsequent period. Except for the lack of a purchasing system, the controls over acquisitions are excellent for a small company. (There are adequate prenumbered documents for all receipt of goods, proper approvals, and adequate internal verification wherever possible.)

Before the auditor arrives for the year-end audit, the bookkeeper prepares adjusting entries to record the accounts payable as of the balance sheet date. The aged trial balance is listed as of the year end, and a manual schedule is prepared adding the amounts that were entered in the following month. Thus, the accounts payable balance equals the aged trial balance plus the following month's journal entry for invoices received after the year end. All vendors' invoices supporting the journal entry are retained in a separate file for the auditor's use.

In the current year, the accounts payable balance has increased dramatically because of a severe cash shortage. (The cash shortage apparently arose from expansion of inventory and facilities rather than lack of sales.) Many accounts have remained unpaid for several months, and the client is getting pressure from several vendors to pay the bills. Since the company had a relatively profitable year, management is anxious to complete the audit as early as possible so that the audited statements can be used to obtain a larger bank loan.

REQUIRED

a. Explain how the lack of a complete aged accounts payable trial balance will affect the auditor's tests of controls for acquisitions and cash disbursements.

b. What should the auditor use as a sampling unit in performing tests of acquisitions?

c. Assume that no misstatements are discovered in the auditor's tests of controls for acquisitions and cash disbursements. How will that assumption affect the verification of accounts payable?

d. Discuss the reasonableness of the client's request for an early completion of the audit and the implications of the request from the auditor's point of view.

e. List the audit procedures that should be performed in the year-end audit of accounts payable to meet the cutoff objective.

f. State your opinion as to whether it is possible to conduct an adequate audit in these circumstances.

16-22 ❸ You were in the final stages of your examination of the financial statements of Ozine Corporation for the year ended December 31, 2011, when the corporation's president came to talk to you. He believed that there was no point to your examining the 2012 acquisitions data files and testing data in support of 2012 entries. He stated that (1) bills pertaining to 2011 that were received too late to be included in the December acquisitions data files were recorded by the corporation as of the year end by journal entry, (2) the internal auditor made tests after the year end, and (3) he would furnish you with a letter confirming that there were no unrecorded liabilities.

REQUIRED

a. Should a public accountant's test for unrecorded liabilities be affected by the fact that the client made a journal entry to record 2011 bills that were received late? Explain.

b. Should a public accountant's test for unrecorded liabilities be affected by the fact that a letter is obtained in which a responsible management official confirms that, to the best of his or her knowledge, all liabilities have been recorded? Explain.

c. Should a public accountant's test for unrecorded liabilities be eliminated or reduced because of the internal audit tests? Explain.

d. Assume that the corporation, which handled some government contracts, had no internal auditor but that an auditor from the Auditor General's office spent three weeks auditing the records and was just completing her work at this time. How would the public accountant's unrecorded liability test be affected by the work of the auditor from the Auditor General's office?

e. What sources in addition to the 2011 acquisitions data files should the public accountant consider to locate possible unrecorded liabilities?

16-23 ❹ Hardware Manufacturing Company Limited, a closely held corporation, has operated since 1994 but has not had its financial statements audited. The company now plans to issue additional share capital to be sold to outsiders and wishes to engage you to examine its 2011 transactions and render an opinion on the financial statements for the year ended December 31, 2011.

The company has expanded from one plant to three and has frequently acquired, modified, and disposed of all types of equipment. Capital assets have a net book value of 70 percent of total assets and consist of land and buildings, diversified machinery and equipment, and furniture and fixtures. Some property was acquired by donation from shareholders.

Amortization was recorded by several methods using various estimated lives.

REQUIRED

a. Should you confine your examination solely to 2011 transactions as requested by this prospective client whose financial statements have not previously been examined? Why or why not?

b. Prepare an audit program for the January 1, 2011, opening balances of the land, building, and equipment asset and accumulated amortization accounts of Hardware Manufacturing Company Limited, organized by audit objective.

(Adapted from AICPA)

Professional Judgment Problem

16-24 ❶ ❷ Donnen Designs Inc. is a small manufacturer of women's casual-wear jewellery, including bracelets, necklaces, earrings, and other moderately priced accessory items. Most of its products are made of silver, various low-cost stones, beads, and other decorative jewellery pieces. Donnen Designs is not involved in the manufacturing of high-end jewellery items such as those made of gold and semiprecious or precious stones.

Personnel responsible for purchasing raw material jewellery pieces for Donnen Designs would like to place orders directly with suppliers who offer their products for sale through websites. Most suppliers provide pictures of all jewellery components on their websites, along with pricing and other sales-term information. Customers that have valid business licenses are able to purchase the products at wholesale, rather than retail, prices. Customers can place orders online and pay for those goods immediately by using a valid credit card. Purchases made by credit card are shipped by the suppliers once the credit approval is received from the credit card agency, which usually occurs the same day. Customers can also place orders online with payment being made later by cheque. However, in that event, purchases are not shipped until the cheque is received and cashed by the supplier. Some of the suppliers have a 30-day full-payment refund policy, whereas other suppliers accept returns but only grant credit toward future purchases from that supplier.

REQUIRED

a. Identify advantages for Donnen Designs if management allows purchasing personnel to order goods online through supplier websites.

b. Identify potential risks associated with Donnen Designs' purchase of jewellery pieces through supplier websites.

c. Describe advantages of allowing purchasing agents to purchase products online using a Donnen Designs credit card.

d. Describe advantages of allowing purchasing agents to purchase products online with payment made only by cheque.

e. What internal controls could be implemented to ensure the following?

(1) Donnen allows purchasing agents to purchase jewellery items using Donnen credit cards, and purchasing agents do not use those credit cards to purchase non-jewellery items for their own purposes.

(2) Purchasing agents do not order jewellery items from the suppliers and ship those items to addresses other than Donnen addresses.

(3) Donnen does not end up with unused credits with jewellery suppliers as a result of returning unacceptable jewellery items to suppliers which only grant credit toward future purchases.

Case

16-25 ❷ ❸ The following procedures are used by EGO Company:

- EGO's purchasing manager approves all purchase above $250. The administrative staff use the petty cash system to purchase minor items that are needed for the office and the manufacturing plant.

- When a supplier invoice is received, the accounting department matches it to the corresponding purchase order and assigns the supplier invoice with purchasing order a sequential number (called a voucher number).

- Unmatched receiving reports are scanned and matched to the voucher. Once the receiving report is found that matches the purchase order and supplier invoice, the voucher (now comprising a supplier invoice, matching purchase order, and matching receiving report) is given to the accountant for entry into the acquisition journal.

- If there is no receiving report on file, the voucher with supplier invoice and attached purchase order remains in the unmatched supplier invoice file.

- The purchase order contains a description of the goods, the vendor name, the date of the purchase approval, whether the goods were purchased FOB destination or FOB origin, and the purchasing manager's initials showing her authorization for the purchase.

- When the company receives goods, the receiver prepares a receiving report and forwards it to the accounting department. The accounting department checks their unmatched supplier invoice file, and if there is no corresponding supplier invoice on hand, the receiving report is placed in an unmatched receiving reports file.

- The company's accounting system retains transaction files, an acquisition journal and supplier master file accounts for all authorized suppliers.

REQUIRED

You are conducting an external audit of the company's financial statements and are working at the client's office two weeks after the year end.

a. Design a test with *two* audit procedures, in addition to sample selection, using the unmatched supplier invoice file to test at least *one* control objectives. Specify which objective(s) you are testing, which documents and any other financial records you are using besides the unmatched supplier invoice file, and how your test would verify the objective(s). Do not use any analytical procedures.

b. Design a test with *two* audit procedures, in addition to sample selection, using the unmatched receiving report file to test *one* internal control objective. Specify which objective(s) you are testing, which documents and any other financial records you are using besides the unmatched receiving report file, and how your test would verify the objective(s). Do not use any analytical procedures.

(Extract from AU1 CGA - Canada Examinations developed by the Certified General Accountants Association of Canada © 2010 CGA-Canada. Reproduced with permission. All rights reserved.)

ACL Problem ACL

16-26 ❶ ❷ ❸ This problem requires the use of ACL software. For this problem, use the Metaphor_Trans_2002 file in ACL_Demo, which is a file of purchase transactions. The suggest command or other source of information needed to solve the problem requirement is included at the end of each question.

REQUIRED

a. Use Quick Sort for each column in the table and identify any concerns you have about the data. What are the internal control implications of the problems with the data? (Quick Sort)

b. Determine the total cost of all purchases, ignoring any concerns in part (a). What audit procedures would you conduct using the total figure? (Total)

c. Determine if there are any duplicates or missing numbers in the voucher file (Invoice column). State your audit concerns with any gaps or duplicates. Provide a possible explanation for any gaps or duplicates that you find. (Gaps and Duplicates)

d. Determine and print the total purchase for the period by product. (Summarize) Determine if the total cost is the same as in part (b). (Total) What product number has the greatest amount of purchases: (Quick Start) How would you further use this information during the conduct of the audit engagement?

e. Determine and print the percent of the total purchases by product. Save the classified file for use in requirement (f). (Classified) Based on that output, what percentage is product number 024133112 of the total amount?

f. Using the classified file from requirement (e), stratify and print the purchases by product. Exclude all items smaller than $1,000. Sort the items to determine the smallest and largest amounts. Use the smallest amount as the minimum in the Stratify window. Because the largest amount is significantly larger than all the other items, use the second highest amount as the maximum in the Stratify window. (Filter, Quick Sort, and Stratify) How would the auditor use this information during the audit?

Ongoing Small Business Case: E-Payments at CondoCleaners.com

16-27 **❹** In addition to payroll, the costs of running CondoCleaners.com are web services, telecommunications, cleaning supplies, and vehicle costs. Jim pays most of these costs using his personal credit card. He then separates the receipts, recording business expenses in a spreadsheet, marking any personal costs as "personal" on the credit card statement. He keeps the credit card statement and receipts in support of his expenses.

REQUIRED

Identify audit issues associated with the audit of expenses at CondoCleaners.com.

17 Audit of the inventory and distribution cycle

Look around your room. What is in it—bookshelves, a desk, carpeting, books, pens, pencils, paper supplies? All of these items are produced by companies, stored, and then sold to businesses that distribute or sell these products to consumers. The diversity of organizations involved in the manufacture, distribution, and sales of products is reflected in the many different types of accounting systems to track the costs and routing of inventory. Management accountants can help to develop and monitor controls and costs in such a supply chain, while auditors are interested in examining the effectiveness of such controls.

LEARNING OBJECTIVES

1 Describe the business functions, documents, and records of the inventory and distribution cycle. Describe the risks of error or fraud in the cycle. Explain how the functions and records in this cycle help to prevent fraud or error.

2 Select audit steps to audit the five different parts of the inventory and distribution cycle.

3 Explain the role of each of the following types of tests in the audit of inventory: (i) analytical review, (ii) physical observation of inventory, and (iii) pricing and compilation tests.

STANDARDS REFERENCED IN THIS CHAPTER

CICA Standard

CAS 501 – Audit evidence: specific considerations for selected items

Section 3031 – Inventories

IAS 2 – Inventories

Listeria Hysteria Caused by Meat Slicers

Ingestion of listeria bacteria (Listeria monocytogenes) can result in an illness called listeriosis. Listeriosis can result in mild flu-like symptoms, serious problems similar to food poisoning, or even death, as the lining of the brain can become inflamed. The bacteria are common in the environment but are readily destroyed with proper cooking procedures. They can build up in most raw meats and fish as well as in soft or semisoft cheeses made from unpasteurized milk. In August 2008, listeriosis cases suddenly increased across Canada, linked to over 20 deaths, a total of 38 confirmed cases of the disease, and many more suspected cases.

It appeared that the common element among those affected by the illness was ingestion of Maple Leaf deli meats such as ham, corned beef, roast beef, turkey, and salami. Independent tests conducted in mid-August 2008 on such Maple Leaf meats led to a massive recall of all Maple Leaf meat products and a shut down of a meat-processing facility in Toronto. The cost of the recall, clean-up, and additional marketing costs ultimately resulted in Maple Leaf Foods posting a loss for the quarter ended September 30, 2008, with sales reductions in the range of 30 to 50 percent. In early 2009, Maple Leaf Foods settled a resulting Canada-wide class action suit for $27 million.

IMPORTANCE TO AUDITORS

Auditors would be concerned about the value of inventory in the year that the listeria outbreak occurred. They would also check that clean-up costs and potential contingent liabilities (such as for lawsuits) were properly disclosed. Auditors would also be concerned about Maple Leaf's strategies for restoring food quality and consumer confidence to satisfy the going concern assumption for the business. In fact, in January 2012, Maple Leaf Foods was reported as "The best of 2011" for its work in product innovation and quality that restored consumer confidence and sales.

WHAT DO YOU THINK?

1. What types of questions would auditors ask about production quality control at a company such as Maple Leaf Foods?

Sources: 1. Lu, Vanessa, "Maple Leaf suspects slicers," *Toronto Star*, September 6, 2008, p. A4. 2. Flavelle, Dana, "Maple Leaf Foods profits sliced by listeria outbreak," *Toronto Star*, October 30, 2008, p. B1, B3. 3. Ministry of Health and Long-Term Care, "Diseases: Listeria," **www.health.gov.on.ca/english/public/pub/disease/listeria.html**, Accessed: April 9, 2009. 4. CBC News, "$27 M settlement reached in Maple Leaf listeriosis suits," February 5, 2009, **www.cbc.ca/news/story/2009/02/02/maple.html**, Accessed: March 24, 2012. 5. Laird, Kristin, "The Best of 2011," January 10, 2012, **www.marketingmag.ca/news/marketer-news/all-the-right-moves-43656**, January 10, 2012. Accessed: March 24, 2012.

continued >

continued

2. Identify other sources of information that the auditor would examine when considering the valuation of processed-meat inventories.

3. What is the role of corporate governance in the management of product quality control?

THE Maple Leaf Foods case illustrates difficulties or successes in areas that link to inventory management: production quality, distribution and recall processes, and effective marketing all play a role in moving good quality products to the consumer.

Table 17-1 illustrates major risks of fraud or error in the inventory or distribution cycle. For the reasons given below, the audit of inventories is often the most complex and time-consuming part of the audit:

- Inventory is generally a major item on the balance sheet, and it is often the largest item making up the accounts included in working capital, making it a high-risk audit area requiring substantial audit effort. If management is going to engage in fraud, it is often the inventory account that is likely to be involved.

- The inventory items are often in different locations, which makes physical control and counting difficult. Inventory is easily transportable, easy to steal, and may be hard to access.

- Such items as jewels, chemicals, and electronic parts present problems with observation and valuation and may need specialist assistance for both counting and valuation.

- Even when inventory looks good, it may be obsolete due to technological innovation in the marketplace.

- It is often returned by customers, causing accuracy, timing, and cut off issues with recording of the physical return and the corresponding credit in sales. Poor quality client return processes result in the need for increased audit tests.

- There are several acceptable inventory valuation methods under ASPE and IFRS, and the auditor must determine that the selected method has been applied consistently from year to year.

❶ The Nature of the Inventory and Distribution Cycle

Inventory takes many different forms, depending on the nature of the business. For retail or wholesale businesses, the most important inventory is merchandise on hand that is available for sale. For hospitals, it includes food, drugs, and medical supplies. A manufacturing company has raw materials, purchased parts, and supplies for use in production; goods in the process of being manufactured; and finished goods available for sale. For an organization to have the optimum quantity and quality of inventory, it needs to have a well-organized supply chain—a flow of materials, information, services, and funds. Figure 17-1 illustrates the accounts involved, supporting why the audit of accounts payable and purchasing (discussed in the previous chapter) needs to be linked with the audit of inventory.

| | | Risks of Inadequate Disclosure or Incorrect Presentation of |
Risks of Error	Risks of Misappropriation of Assets, Other Fraud or Illegal Acts	Financial Information, including Fraudulent Financial Reporting
	Intentional overstatement (or understatement) of inventory on consignment or on hand.	
Incorrect calculation used to determine inventory cost.		Intentional inclusion of inventory held on consignment as owned inventory.
	Intentional cut off errors (e.g., excluding returns from inventory or including shipments already sold).	
Valuation of obsolete value at full price.		Omission of disclosure that inventory is being used as collateral for debt.
	Employee theft of inventory.	
Incorrect valuation method used to determine cost of inventory.		Misallocation of inventory between raw material and finished goods.
	Unauthorized journal entries used to overstate inventory, so subsidiary records do not agree to the general ledger.	
Inventory counts done poorly, resulting in incorrect quantity on hand being recorded.		Accounting policy used for calculating inventory values is described in a confusing way.

Table 17-1 — Major Risks of Error or Fraud in the Inventory and Distribution Cycle

The physical flow of goods and the flow of costs in the **inventory and distribution cycle** for a manufacturing company are shown in Figure 17-1. The linkage of the inventory and distribution cycle to the acquisition and payment cycle and to the human resources and payroll cycle can be seen by examining the debits to the raw materials, direct labour, and manufacturing overhead T-accounts. The linkage to the sales and collection cycle occurs at the point where finished goods are relieved (credited) and a charge is made to cost of goods sold.

Inventory and distribution cycle— the transaction cycle that involves the physical flow of goods through the organization, as well as related costs.

Figure 17-1 Flow of Manufactured Inventory and Costs

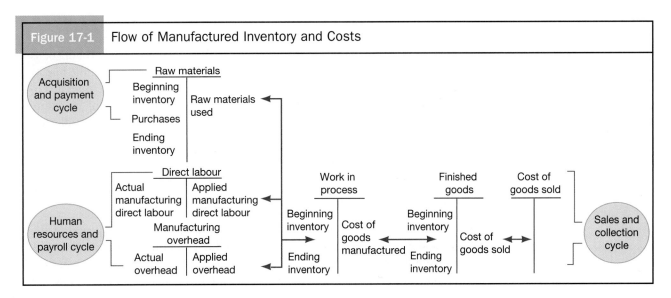

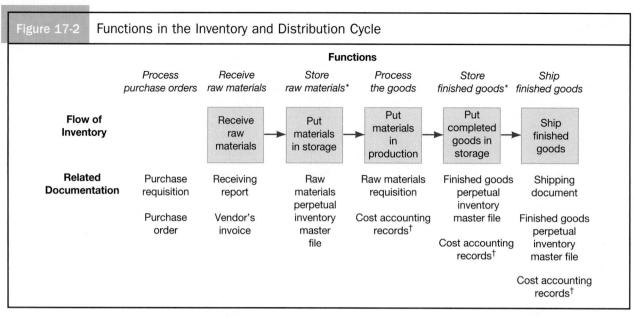

Figure 17-2 Functions in the Inventory and Distribution Cycle

Functions

	Process purchase orders	Receive raw materials	Store raw materials*	Process the goods	Store finished goods*	Ship finished goods
Flow of Inventory		Receive raw materials →	Put materials in storage →	Put materials in production →	Put completed goods in storage →	Ship finished goods
Related Documentation	Purchase requisition Purchase order	Receiving report Vendor's invoice	Raw materials perpetual inventory master file	Raw materials requisition Cost accounting records†	Finished goods perpetual inventory master file Cost accounting records†	Shipping document Finished goods perpetual inventory master file Cost accounting records†

* Inventory counts are taken and compared with perpetual inventory master files at any stage of the cycle. A count must ordinarily be taken at least once a year. If the perpetual system is operating well, this can be done on a cyclical basis throughout the year.
† Includes cost information for materials, direct labour, and overhead.

Business Functions in the Cycle and Internal Controls

The inventory and distribution cycle can be thought of as comprising two separate but closely related systems, one involving the actual physical flow of goods and the other the related costs. As inventories move through the company, there must be adequate controls over both their physical movement and their related costs. Figure 17-2 shows some of the business functions and reports of the cycle as a flow diagram, while Table 17-2 provides business functions analysis of the cycle. This analysis lists which cycle the business function is audited in, provides sample documents and records (as well as their purpose) and sample controls for the business function. Manufacturing organizations vary widely in the type of inventory that they have and how it is managed.

Distributing organizations, such as Hillsburg Hardware, would have many business functions similar to those described in Table 17-2. For example, Hillsburg needs to make sure that only authorized inventory is acquired that can be sold, that the inventory is priced correctly, and that costs of goods sold are recorded accurately when goods are sold.

② The Audit of Inventory

The overall objective in the audit of the inventory and distribution cycle is to determine that raw materials, work in process, finished goods inventory, and cost of goods sold are fairly stated on the financial statements. As Table 17-1 points out, the bias in recording inventory would be toward overstatement, accomplished by valuing inventory too high (the accuracy and valuation assertions), or toward including inventory that does not exist (occurrence). The auditor would keep in mind these risks of overstatement while auditing inventory. If other risks were identified during audit planning (for example, the potential for accuracy errors due to a complex information system), then the auditor would also consider those risks.

The audit of the inventory and distribution cycle can be divided into an examination of the five distinct business functions of the cycle shown in Table 17-2.

ACQUIRE AND RECORD RAW MATERIALS, LABOUR, AND OVERHEAD This part of the inventory and distribution cycle includes the first three functions in Figure 17-2: processing of purchase orders, receipt of raw materials, and storage of raw materials. The internal controls over these three functions are first studied, then tested, as part

Business Function (and cycle where tested)	Examples of Documents and Records (and purpose of document or record)	Sample Control Associated with the Document or Records (and assertion)
Acquire and record raw materials, overhead, (acquisition and payment cycle) and labour (human resources and payroll cycle).	Purchase requisition and purchase order (order materials or components).	Purchase requisitions and purchase orders should be approved (existence). Account for numerical sequence of purchase orders (completeness).
	Receiving report, vendor invoice, and cash disbursement (receive materials or components and pay for them).	Independent matching of details of receiving report to vendor invoice (existence, completeness, accuracy). Inspect goods received for quality and quantity (accuracy).
	Time records, payroll journal, payroll cost allocation report (use and allocate labour and other costs to inventory).	
Internal storage, production and transfer of inventory and costs (inventory and distribution).	Raw material, work in progress, and finished goods transaction files* (track activities associated with individual inventory items).	Independent verification of data entered or use of scanning devices to record transactions (accuracy). Automatic posting of transaction dollar totals to the general ledger (completeness, existence).
	Materials requisition (move materials internally).	Use of authorized materials requisition form for internal transfers (existence).
	Inventory master file* (provide status of inventory).	Totals of inventory master file should agree to the inventory general ledger account (allocation).
	Cost accounting records (describe inventory costs).	Changes to inventory costing methods should be independently verified (accuracy).
	Production forecasts and reports (plan production and describe production).	Production forecasts and actual production plans should be approved (existence).
Ship goods, record revenue and cost of goods sold (sales and collections).	Shipping documents and customer invoice (ship goods to and bill customers).	Credit check should be done on all new customers (existence).
Physically count inventory (inventory and distribution).	Count sheets or records (document inventory on hand).	Teams of two people should be used to count inventory (existence, accuracy).
	Inventory adjustment records (adjust records to agree with counted inventory).	Adjustments to inventory should be approved and independently verified (existence, accuracy).
	Obsolete or damaged goods report (provide support for adjusting inventory due to obsolescence or damage).	Obsolete or damaged goods adjustments should be approved by someone independent of custody of inventory (existence, valuation).
Price and compile inventory values (inventory and distribution).	Inventory price adjustments (correct or update inventory prices).	Inventory price adjustments should be verified for clerical accuracy (accuracy).
	Inventory sheets or reports (document inventory quantities and costs at a point in time).	Inventory count reports should be agreed to the general ledger inventory account (allocation).

* These documents and records are used for multiple business functions.

of performing tests of controls in the acquisition and payment cycle and the human resources and payroll cycle. At the completion of the acquisition and payment cycle, the auditor is likely to be satisfied that acquisitions of raw materials and manufacturing costs are correctly stated. Samples should be designed to ensure that these systems are adequately tested. Similarly, when labour is a significant part of inventory, the human resources and payroll cycle tests should verify the proper accounting for these costs.

INTERNAL STORAGE, PRODUCTION AND TRANSFER OF INVENTORY AND COSTS Internal transfers include the fourth and fifth functions in Figure 17-2: processing the goods and storing finished goods. The accounting records concerned with these functions of manufacture, processing, and storage are referred to as the **cost accounting records**.

Cost accounting records—the accounting records concerned with the manufacture and processing of the goods and storing finished goods.

Segregation of duties between production, inventory control, and accounting are important controls that the auditor would test by observation and inquiry.

SHIP GOODS AND RECORD REVENUE AND COST OF GOODS SOLD The recording of shipments and related costs, the last function in Figure 17-2, is part of the sales and collection cycle. The internal controls over this function are studied and tested as part of auditing the sales and collection cycle. The tests of controls should include procedures to verify the accuracy of the perpetual inventory master files.

PHYSICALLY OBSERVE INVENTORY Observing the client taking a physical inventory count is necessary to determine whether recorded inventory actually exists at the balance sheet date and is properly counted by the client.

PRICE AND COMPILE INVENTORY VALUES Costs used to value the physical inventory must be tested to determine whether the client has correctly followed an inventory method that is in accordance with generally accepted accounting principles and is consistent with the method of previous years. Audit procedures used to verify these inventory costs are referred to as **inventory price tests**. In addition, the auditor must verify whether the physical counts were correctly summarized, the inventory quantities and prices were correctly extended, and the extended inventory was correctly footed. These tests are called **inventory compilation tests**.

Depending upon the financial reporting framework used by the client, terminology used to work with inventory may be different. Table 17-3 lists the different terminology used. We will be using the terminology in the two columns synonymously.

Audit of Cost Accounting

The cost accounting systems and controls of different companies vary more than most other areas because of the wide variety of items of inventory and differences in the level of sophistication in tracking costs. For example, a company that manufactures an entire line of farm machines would have completely different kinds of cost records and internal controls than a steel fabricating shop that makes and installs custom-made metal cabinets.

COST ACCOUNTING CONTROLS **Cost accounting controls** are controls related to the physical inventory and its costs, from raw materials requisitioning through to completed manufacturing and storage. It is convenient to divide these controls into two broad categories: (1) physical controls over raw materials, work in process, and finished goods inventory; and (2) controls over the related costs.

Physical controls over assets prevent loss from misuse and theft. The use of physically segregated, limited-access storage areas for raw materials, work in process, and finished goods is one major control to protect assets. In some instances, the assignment of custody of inventory to specific responsible individuals may be necessary to protect the assets. Approved prenumbered documents for authorizing movement of inventory also protect the assets from improper use. Copies of these documents should be sent directly to accounting by the persons issuing them, bypassing people

Inventory price tests—audit procedures used to verify the costs used to value physical inventory.

Inventory compilation tests—audit procedures used to verify whether physical counts of inventory were correctly summarized, inventory quantities and prices were correctly extended, and extended inventory was correctly footed.

Cost accounting controls—controls over physical inventory and the related costs from the point at which raw materials are requisitioned to the point at which the manufactured product is completed and transferred to storage.

Table 17-3	Inventory Accounting Terminology
Term Used Prior to Implementation of ASPE and IFRS	**Term Used by ASPE Section 3031 and IFRS IAS 2**
Write off	Write down
Inventory allowance	Inventory provision
Lower of cost or market	Lower of cost or net realizable value
Cost of goods sold	Cost of sales
Construction in progress	Contract work in progress

with custodial responsibilities. An example of an effective document of this type is an approved materials requisition for obtaining raw materials from the storeroom.

Perpetual inventory data files maintained by persons who do not have custody of or access to assets are another important cost accounting control. Perpetual inventory data files provide a record of items on hand, which is used to initiate production or purchase of additional materials or goods; they provide a record of the use of raw materials and the sale of finished goods, which can be reviewed for obsolete or slow-moving items; and they provide a record that can be used to pinpoint responsibility for custody as part of the investigation of differences between physical counts and the amounts shown on the records.

TESTS OF COST ACCOUNTING The concepts in auditing cost accounting are from the same as those discussed in other transaction cycle. Figure 17-3 shows the methodology that the auditor should follow in determining which tests to perform. In auditing cost accounting, the auditor is concerned with four aspects: physical controls over inventory, documents and records for transferring inventory, perpetual inventory master files and transaction files, and unit cost records. If the auditor intends to rely upon these controls, they would be tested.

Physical controls over inventory The auditor's tests of the adequacy of the physical controls over raw materials, work in process, and finished goods are usually limited to observation and inquiry. For example, the auditor can examine the raw materials storage area to determine whether the inventory is protected from theft and misuse by the existence of a locked storeroom. The existence of an adequate storeroom with a competent custodian in charge also results in the orderly storage of inventory. If the auditor concludes that the physical controls are so inadequate that the inventory will be difficult to count, the auditor should expand his or her observation of physical inventory tests to ensure that an adequate count is carried out.

Documents and records for transferring inventory Relevant assertions are that the recorded transfers are valid (the inventory exists), the transfers that have actually taken place are recorded (completeness), and the quantity, description, and date of all recorded transfers are accurate (accuracy). First, it is necessary to understand the client's internal controls for recording transfers before relevant tests can be performed. Once the internal controls are understood, the tests can easily be performed

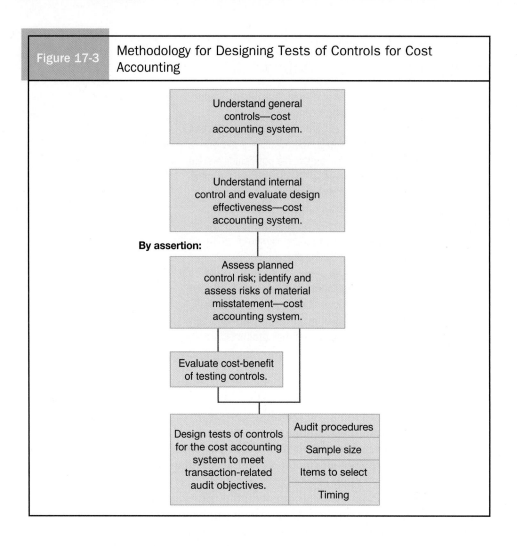

Figure 17-3 Methodology for Designing Tests of Controls for Cost Accounting

Understand general controls—cost accounting system.

Understand internal control and evaluate design effectiveness—cost accounting system.

By assertion:

Assess planned control risk; identify and assess risks of material misstatement—cost accounting system.

Evaluate cost-benefit of testing controls.

Design tests of controls for the cost accounting system to meet transaction-related audit objectives.	Audit procedures
	Sample size
	Items to select
	Timing

by inspecting documents and records. For example, a procedure to test the existence and accuracy of the transfer of goods from the raw materials storeroom to the manufacturing assembly line is accounting for a sequence of raw material requisitions, examining the requisitions for proper approval, and comparing the quantity, description, and date with the information on the raw material perpetual inventory transaction files.

Technology has improved the ability to track the movement of goods throughout production. For example, products are labelled with standardized bar codes (or RFID tags) that can be scanned by laser (or wireless scanners) to track the movement of inventory items.

Perpetual inventory master and transaction files The existence of adequate perpetual inventory master files has a major effect on the timing and extent of the auditor's physical examination of inventory. When there are accurate perpetual inventory master files, it is possible to test the physical inventory prior to the balance sheet date. An interim physical inventory audit can result in significant cost savings for both the client and the auditor and enables the client to receive the audited statements earlier. High-quality perpetual inventory master files also enable the auditor to reduce the extent of the tests of physical inventory when the assessed level of control risk related to physical observation of inventory is low.

Unit cost records Obtaining accurate cost data for raw materials, direct labour, and manufacturing overhead is an essential part of cost accounting. Adequate cost accounting records must be integrated with production and other accounting records in order to produce accurate costs of all products. The valuation of ending inventory depends on the proper design and use of these records.

Once the auditor understands internal control, the approach to internal verification involves the same concepts that were discussed in the verification of sales and acquisition transactions. Whenever possible, it is desirable to test the cost accounting records as part of the acquisition, payroll, and sales tests to avoid testing the records more than once. For example, when the auditor is testing acquisition transactions as part of the acquisition and payment cycle the auditor traces the units and unit costs of raw materials to the perpetual inventory data files and the total cost to the cost accounting records. Similarly, when payroll cost data are maintained for different jobs, the auditor traces data from the payroll summary directly to the job cost record as a part of testing the human resources and payroll cycle.

concept check

C17-3 The audit of inventory is broken down into five distinct parts (refer to Table 17-2). List and describe the three parts that are audited in the inventory cycle.

C17-4 Provide three examples of cost accounting controls. State the purpose of each control.

③ Conducting the Audit Tests

Analytical Procedures

Analytical procedures are as important in auditing inventory and distribution as in any other cycle. Table 17-4 includes several common analytical procedures and possible misstatements that may be indicated when fluctuations exist.

Tests of Details for Inventory

The methodology for deciding which tests of details of balances to do for inventory and distribution is essentially the same as that discussed for accounts receivable, accounts payable, and all other balance sheet accounts. It is shown in Figure 17-4. Note that test results of several other cycles besides inventory and distribution affect tests of details of balances for inventory.

Because of the complexity of auditing inventory, two aspects of tests of details of balances are discussed separately: (1) physical observation and (2) pricing and compilation.

Physical Observation of Inventory

Prior to the late 1930s, auditors generally avoided responsibility for determining either the physical existence of inventory or the accuracy of the count of inventory. Audit evidence for inventory quantities was usually restricted to obtaining a certificate from management as to the correctness of the stated amount. In 1938, the discovery of major fraud in the McKesson & Robbins Company in the United States caused a re-appraisal by the accounting profession of its responsibilities relating to inventory. In brief, the financial statements for McKesson & Robbins at December 31, 1937,

Table 17-4	Analytical Procedures for the Inventory and Distribution Cycle
Analytical Procedure	**Possible Misstatement**
Analytical Procedures for Planning Purposes	
Compare gross margin percentage with previous years.	Overstatement or understatement of inventory and cost of goods sold.
Compare inventory turnover (costs of goods sold divided by average inventory) with previous years.	Obsolete inventory, which affects inventory and cost of goods sold.
Analytical Procedures as Substantive Tests	
Compare unit costs of inventory with previous years.	Overstatement or understatement of inventory. Overstatement or understatement of unit costs.
Compare extended inventory value with previous years.	Misstatements in compilation, unit costs, or extensions that affect inventory and cost of goods sold.
Compare current-year manufacturing costs with previous years (variable costs should be adjusted for changes in volume).	Misstatements of unit costs of inventory, especially direct labour and manufacturing overhead, which affect inventory and cost of goods sold.

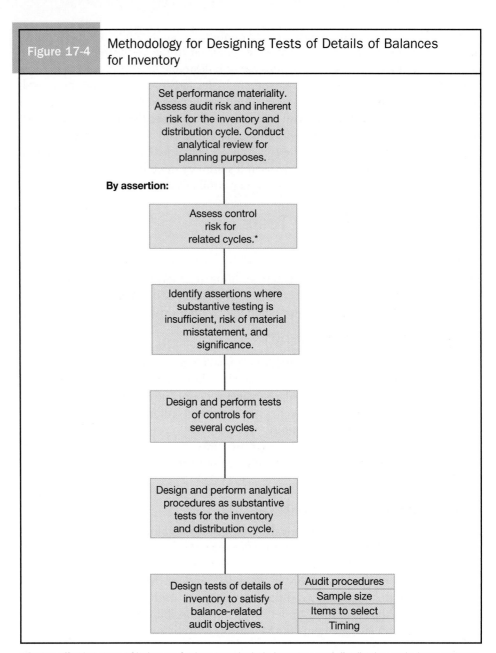

Figure 17-4 Methodology for Designing Tests of Details of Balances for Inventory

Set performance materiality. Assess audit risk and inherent risk for the inventory and distribution cycle. Conduct analytical review for planning purposes.

By assertion:

Assess control risk for related cycles.*

Identify assertions where substantive testing is insufficient, risk of material misstatement, and significance.

Design and perform tests of controls for several cycles.

Design and perform analytical procedures as substantive tests for the inventory and distribution cycle.

Design tests of details of inventory to satisfy balance-related audit objectives.	Audit procedures
	Sample size
	Items to select
	Timing

*Cycles affecting tests of balances for inventory include inventory and distribution cycle (cost accounting system), sales and collection cycle (sales only), acquisition and payment cycle (acquisitions only), and human resources and payroll (payroll costs in inventory).

which were "certified" by a major accounting firm, reported total consolidated assets of $87 million. Of this amount, approximately $19 million was subsequently determined to be fictitious ($10 million in inventory and $9 million in receivables). Due primarily to its adherence to the generally accepted auditing practices of that period, the auditing firm was not held directly at fault in the inventory area. However, it was noted that if certain procedures, such as observation of the physical inventory, had been carried out, the fraud would probably have been detected.

CAS Standards for the audit of inventory are provided by CAS 501, Audit evidence: specific considerations for selected items. When inventory is material, the auditor should attend the client's physical inventory count unless it is impractical to do so. The purpose of attendance is to observe that the inventory actually exists and its condition (to assist with the valuation objective). The CAS provides specific instructions for audit procedures that the auditor should perform (evaluation of the processes used during the count, including methods to record count results and tracking count results to their final recording into financial records).

If for some reason the auditor cannot attend the physical count, standards permit the auditor to apply other procedures. Absence at the inventory count must be justified. For example, an auditor who was appointed after a company's year end would not find it practical to count inventory; driving 100 km to attend an inventory count at a remote location may be neither practical nor convenient but would be required. Alternative procedures would need to be of high quality and considered in the context of management biases and assessed risks of material misstatement. For example, if appointed after the year end, the auditor could attend a current perpetual inventory count and roll backward with the records.

CONTROLS Regardless of the client's inventory record-keeping method, there must be a periodic physical count of the inventory items on hand, unless inventory is clearly immaterial. This can happen with just-in-time inventory practices, where the client is integrated heavily with supplier information systems and suppliers are required to provide inventory as needed for production. If a count is needed, it can be taken at or near the balance sheet date, at a preliminary date, or on a cycle basis throughout the year. The last two approaches are appropriate only if there are adequately controlled perpetual inventory master files and transaction files.

In connection with the client's physical count of inventory, adequate controls include proper instructions for the physical count, supervision by responsible personnel, independent internal verification of the counts, independent reconciliations of the physical counts with perpetual inventory master files, and adequate control over count tags, sheets, or computerized records.

An important aspect of the auditor's understanding of the client's physical inventory controls is complete familiarity with them before the inventory-taking begins. This is necessary to evaluate the effectiveness of the client's procedures, but it also enables the auditor to make constructive suggestions beforehand. If the inventory instructions do not provide adequate controls, the auditor must spend more time ensuring that the physical count is accurate.

Where procedures for managing inventory are highly automated, with a limited paper trail, the auditor will need to pay particular attention to controls, as tests of details may not be sufficient to provide adequate assurance with respect to the final inventory value.

AUDIT DECISIONS The auditor's decisions in the physical observation of inventory are of the same general nature as in any other audit area: selection of audit procedures, timing, determination of sample size, and selection of the items for testing. The selection of the audit procedures is discussed throughout this section; the other three decisions are discussed briefly at this time.

TIMING The auditor decides whether the physical count can be taken prior to year end primarily on the basis of the accuracy of the perpetual inventory files. When an interim physical count is performed, the auditor observes it then and also tests the accuracy of the perpetuals for transactions from the date of the count to year end. When the perpetuals are accurate, it may be unnecessary for the client to count the entire inventory every year. Instead, the auditor can compare the perpetuals with the actual inventory on a sample basis at a convenient time. When there are no perpetuals and the inventory is material, a complete physical inventory must be taken by the client near the end of the accounting period and tested by the auditor at the same time.

Sample size The emphasis during the tests is on observing the client's procedures rather than on selecting particular items for testing. A convenient way to think of sample size in physical observation is in terms of the total number of hours spent rather than the number of inventory items counted. The most important determinants of the amount of time needed to test the inventory are the adequacy of the internal controls over the physical counts, the accuracy of the perpetual inventory files, the total dollar amount and the type of inventory, the number of different significant inventory locations, and the nature and extent of misstatements discovered in previous years and other inherent risks.

Selection of items Care should be taken to observe the counting of the most significant items and a representative sample of typical inventory items. The auditor also inquires about items that are likely to be obsolete or damaged and discusses with management the reasons for excluding any material items.

PHYSICAL OBSERVATION TESTS Determining whether the physical count is being taken in accordance with the client's instructions affects multiple assertions (accuracy, completeness, and existence). The auditor should be present while the physical count is taking place. When the client's employees are not following the inventory instructions, the auditor must either contact the supervisor to correct the problem or modify the auditor's physical observation procedures. For example, if the procedures require one team to count the inventory and a second team to recount it as a test of accuracy, the auditor should inform management if he or she observes both teams counting together.

A proper understanding of the client's business and its industry enables the auditor to ask about and discuss such problems as inventory valuation, potential obsolescence, and existence of consignment inventory intermingled with owned inventory. A useful starting point for the auditor to become familiar with the client's inventory is a tour of the client's facilities, including receiving, storage, production, planning, and record-keeping areas. The tour should be led by a supervisor who can answer questions about production, especially about any changes in the past year.

Common tests of details audit procedures for physical inventory observation are shown in Table 17-5. The assumption throughout is that the client records inventory on prenumbered tags on the balance sheet date. Smaller businesses may use inventory sheets rather than inventory tags. Larger businesses with heavily automated systems will not use tags at all. Rather, individuals will use hand-held scanners to scan each inventory location and item code, then manually enter the amount counted. In such cases, information systems should list areas and items not counted to help ensure completeness of the count.

In addition to the detailed procedures included in Table 17-5, the auditor should walk through all areas where inventory is warehoused to make sure that all inventory has been counted and properly tagged. When inventory is in boxes or other containers, these should be opened on a sample basis during test counts. Compare high dollar value inventory with counts in the previous year and inventory master files as a test of reasonableness. These two procedures should be done after the client has completed the physical counts.

Audit of Pricing and Compilation

The purpose of pricing and compilation is to make certain the physical counts were properly priced and compiled. Pricing includes the tests of the client's unit prices to determine whether they are correct. Compilation includes the tests of the summarization of the physical counts, the extension of price times quantity, footing the inventory summary, and tracing the totals to the general ledger.

PRICING AND COMPILATION CONTROLS The existence of adequate internal control for unit costs that is integrated with production and other accounting helps ensure that reasonable costs are used for valuing ending inventory. When **standard cost records** are used, procedures must be designed to keep the standards updated for changes in production processes and costs. High variances may indicate that the standard costs are out of date or that production quantities are different than expected—both areas that the auditor should discuss with management. The review of unit costs for reasonableness by someone independent of the department responsible for developing the costs is a useful control over valuation.

An internal control designed to prevent the overstatement of inventory through the inclusion of obsolete inventory is a formal review and reporting of obsolete, slow-moving, damaged, and overstated inventory items by a competent employee. Any

Standard cost records—records that indicate variances between projected material, labour, and overhead costs, and the actual costs.

Balance-Related Audit Objective	Common Inventory Observation Procedures	Comments
Inventory as recorded on tags exists (existence and occurrence).	Select a random sample of tag numbers, and identify the tag with that number attached to the actual inventory. Observe whether movement of inventory takes place during the count.	The purpose is to uncover the inclusion of non-existent items as inventory.
The client has the right to inventory recorded on tags (rights and obligations).	Inquire as to consignment or customer inventory included on client's premises.	Be alert for inventory that is set aside or specially marked as indications of non-ownership.
Existing inventory is counted and tagged, and tags are accounted for to make sure none is missing (completeness).	Examine inventory to make sure it is tagged. Observe whether movement of inventory takes place during the count. Inquire as to inventory in other locations and how it is recorded and disclosed. Account for all used and unused tags to make sure none are lost or intentionally omitted. Record the tag numbers for those used and unused for subsequent follow-up.	Special concern should be directed to omission of large sections of inventory. This test should be done at the completion of the physical count.
Obsolete and unusable inventory items are excluded or noted (valuation).	Test for obsolete inventory by inquiry of factory employees and management, and be alert for items that are damaged, rust- or dust-covered, or located in inappropriate places.	This test should be done at the completion of the physical count.
Inventory is counted accurately (allocation and accuracy).	Recount client's counts to make sure the recorded counts are accurate on the tags (also check descriptions and unit of count, such as dozen or gross). Compare physical counts with perpetual inventory master file. Record client's counts for subsequent testing.	Recording client counts in the working papers on inventory count sheets is done for two reasons: to obtain documentation that an adequate physical examination was made and to test for the possibility that the client might change the recorded counts after the auditor leaves the premises.
Information is obtained to make sure sales and inventory purchases are recorded in the proper period (allocation).	Record in the working papers for subsequent follow-up the last shipping document number used at year end. Make sure the inventory for that item was excluded from the physical count. Review shipping area for inventory set aside for shipment but not counted and record the nature of such shipments. Record in the working papers for subsequent follow-up the last receiving report number used at year end. Make sure the inventory for that item was included in the physical count. Review receiving area for inventory that should be included in the physical count and verify that it has been included.	Obtaining proper cut-off information for sales and purchases is an essential part of inventory observation. The appropriate tests during the fieldwork were discussed for sales in Chapter 12 and for purchases in Chapter 16.
Inventory is classified correctly on the tags (classification).	Examine inventory descriptions on the tags and compare with the actual inventory for raw material, work in process, and finished goods. Evaluate whether the percent of completion recorded on the tags for work in process is reasonable.	These tests would be done as a part of the first procedure in the valuation objective.

write downs to the inventory values should be approved by a person independent of the physical inventory control. Compilation internal controls provide a means of ensuring that the physical counts are properly summarized, priced at the same amount as the unit perpetual records, correctly extended and totalled, and included in the general ledger at the proper amount. If the physical inventory is taken on prenumbered tags and carefully reviewed before the personnel are released from the physical examination of inventory, there should be little risk of misstatement in summarizing the tags. Internal control over accurate determination of prices, extensions, and footings are adequate controls over the programs that perform these calculations, with internal verification or review of entry of prices and of output reports by a competent, independent person.

PRICING AND COMPILATION PROCEDURES The frame of reference for applying these tests is a listing of inventory obtained from the client that includes each inventory item's description, quantity, unit price, and extended value. The inventory listing is in inventory item description order with raw material, work in process, and finished goods separated. The total equals the general ledger balance.

In performing pricing (valuation) tests, three things about the client's method of pricing are extremely important: the method must be in accordance with an acceptable financial accounting framework, the application of the method must be consistent from year to year, and cost versus market value (replacement cost or net realizable value) must be considered. Because the method of verifying the pricing of inventory depends on whether items are purchased or manufactured, these two categories are discussed separately.

Pricing purchased inventory The primary types of inventory included in this category are raw materials, purchased parts, and supplies. As a first step in verifying the valuation of purchased inventory, it is necessary to establish clearly the valuation method being used and how the calculations are being performed. The auditor also determines which costs should be included in the valuation of a particular item of inventory. For example, the auditor must find out whether freight, storage, discounts, and other costs are included and compare the findings with the preceding year's audit working papers to ensure that the methods are consistent.

In selecting specific inventory items for pricing, emphasis should be put on the larger dollar amounts and on products that are known to have wide fluctuations in price, but a representative sample of all types of inventory and departments should be included.

The auditor should list the inventory items he or she intends to verify for pricing and request that the client locate the appropriate vendors' invoices. It is important that a sufficient number of invoices be examined to account for the entire quantity of inventory for the particular item being tested, especially for the FIFO valuation method. If specific items or projects have different cost structures, the auditor should also be careful that the invoice relates to the specific item being tested (IAS 2.23), perhaps by checking serial numbers or locations. Examining a sufficient number of invoices is useful in uncovering situations in which clients value their inventory on the basis of the most recent invoice only and, in some cases, in discovering obsolete inventory. As an illustration, assume that the client's valuation of a particular inventory item is $12 per unit for 1,000 units, using FIFO. The auditor should examine the most recent invoices for acquisitions of that inventory item made in the year under audit until the valuation of all of the 1,000 units is accounted for. If the most recent acquisition of the inventory item was for 700 units at $12 per unit and the immediately preceding acquisition was for 600 units at $11.30 per unit, then the inventory item in question was overstated by $210 (300 × $0.70).

Pricing manufactured inventory The auditor must consider the cost of raw materials, direct labour, and manufacturing overhead in pricing work in process and finished goods. The need to verify each of these has the effect of making the audit of work-in-process and finished goods inventory more complex than the audit of purchased inventory.

In pricing raw materials in manufactured products, it is necessary to consider both the unit cost of the raw materials and the number of units required to manufacture a unit of output. The unit cost can be verified in the same manner as that used for other purchased inventory—by examining vendors' invoices or perpetual inventory master files. Then it is necessary to examine engineering specifications, inspect the finished product, or find a similar method to verify the number of units it takes to manufacture a particular product.

The hourly costs of direct labour and the number of hours it takes to manufacture a unit of output can be verified while testing direct labour. Hourly labour costs can be verified by comparison with authorized wage rates or union contracts. The number of hours needed to manufacture the product can be verified by reference to standard costs with associated variances, engineering specifications, or similar sources.

The proper manufacturing overhead in work in process and finished goods is dependent on the approach being used by the client. The auditor evaluates the method being used for consistency and reasonableness. Costs are recomputed to determine whether the overhead is correct. For example, if the rate is based on direct labour dollars, the auditor can divide the total manufacturing overhead by the total direct labour dollars to determine the actual overhead rate. This rate can then be compared with the overhead rate used by the client to determine unit costs.

Cost or market In pricing inventory, the auditor considers whether replacement cost or net realizable value is lower than historical cost. For purchased finished goods and raw materials, the most recent cost of an inventory item as indicated on a vendor's invoice of the subsequent period is a useful way to test for replacement cost. It is also necessary to consider the sales value of inventory items and the possible effect of rapid fluctuation of prices to determine net realizable value. Finally, in the evaluation process, it is necessary to consider the possibility of obsolescence with reference to recent sales, quality and age of inventory, and the client's technology environment. Audit Challenge 17-2 provides an example of how rapidly obsolesce can occur.

The auditor uses risk assessments to allocate audit tests by cycle and by assertion. Refer again to Figure 17-1 to see the relationship of inventory to other cycles.

concept check

C17-5 The inventory balance is highly material. Does the auditor have a choice with respect to observation of inventory? Why or why not?

C17-6 Why is the audit technique of observation important during the physical inventory count?

audit challenge 17-2
What's It Worth?

EVERYBODY loves toys, right? Wrong, when they have been painted with lead-based paint or contain raw materials with lead. Then the value plummets, media get involved, and toys are pulled off retailer shelves and recalled by manufacturers. This happened in fall 2008, worldwide, as many toys made in China were found to have lead-based paint or other lead-based components. Apparently, the largest recall on record was for themed RCMP products.

Toys found with lead included stuffed toys, kits to build jewellery, baby pacifiers, and costume jewellery. These toys were pulled from the retailers' shelves. If a retailer cannot get back its money for such toys, then it has lost the cost of the toys. Other costs might include returning products, as well as legal action, if large dollar amounts are involved.

The opposite, instant value of plastic 500-ml bottles, was created in January 1, 2009, when the bottles started attracting a 25-cent deposit. But what about the costs? Companies will now need a distribution system to collect and recycle the bottles.

CRITICAL THINKING QUESTIONS

1. Provide three different reasons why manufactured inventory could go down in value.
2. How would the auditor test to ensure that inventory has not gone down in value for the reasons that you described in part (1).

Sources: 1. Bruser, David, "Tests find toxic toys in stores across GTA," *Toronto Star*, October 4, 2008, p. A1, A16–A17.2. Flavelle, Dana, "Bottled water company to launch refund program," *Toronto Star*, October 2, 2008, p. B1, B4. 3. Torstar News Service, "RCMP toys recalled," *Metro*, November 19, 2008, p. 12.

Summary

1. *What are the components of the inventory and distribution cycle?* The inventory and distribution cycle normally has the following business functions: acquire and record raw materials, overhead, and labour; internal storage, production, and transfer of inventory costs; ship goods, record revenue and cost of goods sold; physically count inventory; and price and compile inventory values.
2. *Provide an overview of the process used to audit the inventory and distribution cycle.* In the context of the overall risk of the engagement and the cycle, the auditor documents general and application level controls, assesses control risks, and tests those controls, by assertion, where there is intended reliance. After assessing the results of the tests of controls, analytical procedures and tests of detail are conducted of the five business functions in the cycle.
3. *What role does each of the following types of tests play in the audit of inventory?* (i) Analytical review—This review assesses the likelihood of potential misstatements and targets tests of detail. (ii) Physical observation of inventory—This is a set of procedures that provides assurance for the following assertions: existence, completeness, accuracy, classification, cut-off, valuation, and rights and obligations; see Table 17-5. (iii) Pricing and compilation tests—These tests provide assurance with respect to the calculations used to develop costs of goods sold and the value of ending inventory.

MyAccountingLab

Make the grade with MyAccountingLab: The questions, exercises, and problems marked in orange can be found on MyAccountingLab. You can practise them as often as you want, and most feature step-by-step guided instructions to help you find the right answer.

Review Questions

17-1 **1** Give the reasons why inventory is often the most difficult and time-consuming part of many audit engagements.

17-2 **1** **2** Explain the relationship between the acquisition and payment cycle and the inventory and distribution cycle in the audit of a manufacturing company. List several audit procedures in the acquisition and payment cycle that support your explanation.

17-3 **2** **3** What is meant by "cost accounting records," and what is their importance in the conduct of an audit?

17-4 **2** **3** Many auditors assert that certain audit tests can be significantly reduced for clients with adequate perpetual records that include both unit and cost data. What are the most important tests of the perpetual records that the auditor must make before he or she can reduce the assessed level of control risk? Assuming the perpetuals are determined to be accurate, which tests can be reduced?

17-5 **3** Before the physical examination, the auditor obtains a copy of the client's inventory instructions and reviews them with the controller. In obtaining an understanding of inventory procedures for a small manufacturing company, these deficiencies are identified: shipping operations will not be completely halted during the physical examination, and there will be no independent verification of the original inventory count by a second counting team. Evaluate the importance of each of these deficiencies, and state its effect on the auditor's observation of inventory.

17-6 **3** At the completion of an inventory observation, the controller requested a copy of all recorded test counts from the auditor to facilitate the correction of all discrepancies between the client's and the auditor's counts. Should the auditor comply with the request? Why or why not?

17-7 **2** **3** What major audit procedures are involved in testing for the ownership of inventory during the observation of the physical counts and as part of subsequent valuation tests?

17-8 **3** In the verification of the amount of the inventory, the auditor should identify slow-moving and obsolete items. List the auditing procedures that could be employed to determine whether slow-moving or obsolete items have been included in inventory.

17-9 **3** During the taking of physical inventory, the controller intentionally withheld several inventory tags from the employees responsible for the physical count. After the auditor left the client's premises at the completion of the inventory observation, the controller recorded non-existent inventory on the tags and thereby significantly overstated earnings. How could the auditor have uncovered the misstatement, assuming there are no perpetual records?

17-10 **3** Explain why a proper cut off of purchases and sales is heavily dependent on the physical inventory observation. What information should be obtained during the physical count to make sure cut off is accurate?

17-11 **2** **3** Define what is meant by "compilation tests." List several examples of audit procedures to verify compilation.

17-12 **2** **3** Included in the December 31, 2011, inventory of Kupitz Supply Ltd. are 2,600 deluxe ring binders in the amount of $5,902. An examination of the most recent purchases of binders showed the following costs: January 26, 2012, 2,300 at $2.42 each; December 6, 2011, 1,900 at $2.28 each; and November 26,

2011, 2,400 at $2.07 each. What is the misstatement in valuation of the December 31, 2011, inventory for deluxe ring binders assuming FIFO inventory valuation? What would your answer be if the January 26, 2012, purchase were for 2,300 binders at $2.12 each?

17-13 ❸ Ruswell Manufacturing Ltd. applied manufacturing overhead to inventory at December 31, 2011, on the basis of $3.47 per direct labour hour. Explain how

you would evaluate the reasonableness of total direct labour hours and manufacturing overhead in the ending inventory of finished goods.

17-14 ❷ ❸ Assuming that the auditor properly documents receiving report numbers as part of the physical inventory observation procedures, explain how he or she should verify the proper cut off of purchases, including tests for the possibility of raw materials in transit, later in the audit.

Discussion Questions and Problems

17-15 ❶ In connection with her examination of the financial statements of Knutson Products Co. Ltd., an assembler of home appliances, for the year ended May 31, 2012, Raymonde Mathieu, public accountant, is reviewing with Knutson's controller the plans for a physical inventory at the company warehouse on May 31, 2012.

Finished appliances, unassembled parts, and supplies are stored in the warehouse, which is attached to Knutson's assembly plant. The plant will operate during the count. On May 30, the warehouse will deliver to the plant the estimated quantities of unassembled parts and supplies required for

May 31 production, but there may be emergency requisitions on May 31. During the count, the warehouse will continue to receive parts and supplies and to ship finished appliances. However, appliances completed on May 31 will be held in the plant until after the physical inventory.

REQUIRED
What procedures should the company establish to ensure that the inventory count includes all items that should be included and that nothing is counted twice?
(Adapted from AICPA)

17-16 ❶ ❷ ❸ Items 1 through 8 are selected questions typically found in questionnaires used by auditors to obtain an understanding of internal controls in the inventory and distribution cycle. In using the questionnaire for a particular client, a "yes" response to a question indicates a possible internal control, whereas a "no" indicates a potential weakness.

1. Does the receiving department prepare prenumbered receiving reports and account for the numbers periodically for all inventory received, showing the description and quantity of materials?
2. Is all inventory stored under the control of a custodian in areas where access is limited?
3. Are all shipments to customers authorized by prenumbered shipping documents?
4. Is a detailed perpetual inventory master file maintained for raw materials inventory?
5. Are physical inventory counts made by someone other than storekeepers and those responsible for maintaining the perpetual inventory master file?

6. Are standard cost records used for raw materials, direct labour, and manufacturing overhead?
7. Is there a stated policy with specific criteria for writing off obsolete or slow-moving goods?
8. Is the clerical accuracy of the final inventory compilation checked by a person independent of those responsible for preparing it?

REQUIRED
a. For each of the preceding questions, state the purpose of the internal control.
b. For each internal control, list a test of controls to test its effectiveness.
c. For each of the preceding questions, identify the nature of the potential financial misstatement(s) if the control is not in effect.
d. For each of the potential misstatements in part (c), list a substantive audit procedure to determine whether a material misstatement exists.

17-17 ❶ ❷ ❸ The following errors or omissions are included in the inventory and related records of Westbox Manufacturing Company Ltd.:

1. An inventory item was priced at $12 each instead of at the correct cost of $12 per dozen.
2. During the physical inventory-taking, the last shipments for the day were excluded from inventory and were not included as a sale until the subsequent year.
3. The clerk in charge of the perpetual inventory master file altered the quantity on an inventory tag to cover up

the shortage of inventory caused by his theft during the year.
4. After the auditor left the premises, several inventory tags were lost and were not included in the final inventory summary.
5. In recording raw materials purchases, the improper unit price was included in the perpetual inventory transaction file and master file. Therefore, the inventory valuation was misstated because the physical inventory was priced by referring to the perpetual records.

6. During the physical count, several obsolete inventory items were included.
7. Because of a significant increase in volume during the current year and excellent control over manufacturing overhead costs, the manufacturing overhead rate applied to inventory was far greater than actual cost.

REQUIRED
a. For each misstatement, state an internal control that should have prevented it from occurring.
b. For each misstatement, state a substantive audit procedure that could be used to uncover it.

17-18 ❷ The table below shows sales, cost of sales, and inventory data for Aladdin Products Supply Inc., a wholesale distributor of cleaning supplies. All amounts are in thousands.

	2012	2011	2010	2009
Sales	$23.2	$21.7	$19.6	$17.4
Cost of sales	17.1	16.8	15.2	13.5
Beginning inventory	2.3	2.1	1.9	1.5
Ending inventory	2.9	2.3	2.1	1.9

REQUIRED
a. Calculate the following ratios:
   (1) Gross margin as a percentage of sales.
   (2) Inventory turnover.
b. List several logical causes of the changes in the two ratios.
c. Assume that $500,000 is considered material for audit planning purposes for 2012. Could any of the fluctuations in the computed ratios indicate a possible material misstatement? Demonstrate this by performing a sensitivity analysis.
d. What should the auditor do to determine the actual cause of the changes?

17-19 ❷ ❸ You encountered the following situations during the December 31, 2011, physical inventory of Latner Shoe Distributing Corp.

a. Latner maintains a large portion of the shoe merchandise in 10 warehouses throughout eastern and central Canada. This ensures swift delivery service for its chain of stores. You are assigned alone to the Halifax warehouse to observe the physical inventory process. During the inventory count, several express trucks pulled in for loading. Although infrequent, express shipments must be attended to immediately. As a result, the employees who were counting the inventory stopped to assist in loading the express trucks. What should you do?
b. (1) In one storeroom of 10,000 items, you have test counted about 200 items of high value and a few items of low value. You found no misstatements. You also note that the employees are diligently following the inventory instructions. Do you think you have tested enough items? Explain.
   (2) What would you do if you counted 150 items and found a substantial number of counting errors?
c. In observing an inventory of liquid shoe polish, you note that a particular lot is five years old. From inspection of some bottles in an open box, you find that the material has solidified in most of the bottles. What action should you take?
d. During your observation of the inventory count in the main warehouse, you found that most of the prenumbered tags that had been incorrectly filled out are being destroyed and thrown away. What is the significance of this procedure, and what action should you take?

Professional Judgment Problem

17-20 ❶ Bill is a PA working on the financial statement audit of MEM-2 Inc., a company that manufactures computer memory devices for sale in Canada, England, and Europe. He reviewed the internal controls over purchasing, as well as background information on the client's industry, and made the following notes:
- The purchasing clerk receives materials requests from the inventory control clerk, initialled by the manufacturing manager indicating approval.
- The purchasing clerk looks up the part number and prepares the purchase order (P.O.) for the requested items, noting the authorized vendor number on the P.O.
- The purchasing manager verifies the vendor number and initials the P.O. to approve the purchase.
- The company occasionally purchases excess inventory from a related company in the United States.

- There are 22 authorized vendors in Canada, three in England, and four in China.
- Inventory may be overstated due to being obsolete, as technology for memory devices is changing rapidly.
- MEM-2 allows large retail stores to return unsold goods after a six-month holding period. The accounting manager will provide calculations for her estimate of goods that may be returned after year-end.
- Existing controls have been in place for one-and-a-half years. Control risk was high last year due to a change in accounting systems.
- Results of random sampling of purchase orders found no control deviations.

Bill assessed both control risk and inherent risk as low for purchasing and inventory based on his notes.

REQUIRED

a. State whether you agree with Bill's assessment of control risk, and explain your answer.
b. State whether you agree with Bill's assessment of inherent risk, and explain your answer.

Case

17-21 ❶ Technology Parts Inc. is a wholesaler of computer hardware components. The company purchases inventory items in bulk directly from parts manufacturers and sells the parts to computer and other technology equipment manufacturers that use them as components in their products. Technology Parts Inc. grants suppliers access to its inventory management system through its website. Suppliers have real-time access to information about the parts inventory, including information about quantities held, storage locations, and forecast of product demand. In addition, customers have access through the website to information containing product descriptions, price, delivery estimates, availability status, and quality and reliability ratings. Customers can also access information to assess the compatibility of selected parts with other components used in their production processes.

REQUIRED

a. Identify business objectives that Technology Parts' management may be able to achieve by providing this information online to key suppliers and customers.
b. How might the availability of the information to suppliers and customers increase Technology Parts' business risk?
c. What processes should Technology Parts' management implement to minimize business risks?
d. How might the availability of the information increase the risk of material misstatements in the financial statements?
e. How are the components of the audit risk model affected by the internet access?

ACL Problem *ACL*

17-22 ❶ ❷ This problem requires the use of ACL software. For this problem, start ACL, then click on "Open an existing project," and within the project, open "Sample Project.ACL." Click on the plus sign beside the "Tables" folder, which will reveal a series of files. We will be conducting an inventory review, so click on the plus sign beside "Inventory Review," then click on "Inventory" to open the inventory sample data file. The suggested command or other source of information needed to solve the problem requirement is included at the end of each question.

a. Obtain and print statistical information for both Inventory Value at Cost and Market Value. Determine how many inventory items have positive, negative, and zero values for both Inventory Value at Cost and Market Values (Statistics Command). How would you use this information during the audit?

b. Use Quick Sort Ascending and Descending for both Inventory Value at Cost and Market Value (Quick Sort). Use this information and the information from part (a) to identify any concerns you have in the audit of inventory.
c. Calculate the ratio of Inventory Value at Cost to Market Value and sort the result from low to high (Computed Fields and Quick Sort). Identify concerns about inventory valuation, if any.
d. What is the potential impact of your findings upon your field work? For example, if you found zero or negative amounts for inventory values, think about how these might arise at an organization. What might negative inventory values tell you about controls over inventory or over inventory data?

Ongoing Small Business Case: Supplies Inventory at CondoCleaners.com

17-23 ❸ Since CondoCleaners.com is a service organization, it does not have any inventory that is distributed or sold. However, Jim periodically buys large quantities of cleaning products for his business when they are on sale. As it turns out, just prior to the March year end, he purchased three months' worth of cleaning supplies at a local bulk store.

Although not a huge amount (about $5,000), this amount is material to his growing business.

REQUIRED

Explain how the audit of supplies inventory is similar to or different from the audit of inventory that is being held for resale.

18 Audit of the capital acquisition and repayment cycle

Owners' equity may be considered a residual account for corporations—this is where the result of current operations is posted. However, other large transactions, such as dividend payments, effects of revaluation of fixed assets, and the equity portion of financial instruments, also flow through this account. The auditor needs to carefully examine each of these potentially large transactions. Management accountants need to understand the impact of capitalization choices, while auditors need to assess realizable value as well as the cost of potentially complex financial instruments.

LEARNING OBJECTIVES

1 Describe the four key characteristics of the capital acquisition and repayment cycle and the risks of fraud or error in the cycle. Explain how the functions and records in the cycle help to prevent or detect fraud or error. State the methodology for designing tests of balances for notes payable. Itemize the purpose of conducting analytical procedures for notes payable.

2 Describe the difference in equity between public and closely held corporations. Provide examples of common internal controls over owners' equity transactions. List the main concerns when auditing capital stock.

STANDARDS REFERENCED IN THIS CHAPTER

IAS 32 – Financial Instruments: Presentation Audit Staff Continuity Supports Client Discontinuity

Audit Staff Continuity Supports Client Discontinuity

Flanagan Holdings was a growing consolidator of companies in the Canadian real estate industry. During the four years since its initial public offering, Flanagan had had significant staff turnover, including at senior executive levels. Geoff, the new CFO (chief financial officer) of Flanagan, was responsible for completing the unaudited interim financial statements for the quarter ended June 30, 2012. He had reviewed the company's working papers and loan agreements and had come to the conclusion that Flanagan was in breach of a bank loan with Big Blue Bank due to the devaluation of some of Flanagan's investment papers.

Geoff contacted the loan manager at his Big Blue branch (who was also new, having been assigned to his company's account for only six months), and they both agreed that it seemed that Flanagan had been in violation of the loan agreement since the inception of the loan two years ago. Feeling concerned, Geoff contacted the partner assigned to Flanagan's audit to find out what the financial statement disclosure issues were. The partner stated that if Flanagan were in breach of the loan agreement, the debt would be classified as a current liability and additional note disclosures explaining the breach would be required, unless the bank issued a waiver for the offending clause. However, the partner referred Geoff to Lana, the audit manager who had been working with Flanagan since its inception four years ago.

Lana reviewed the 2010 audit files—the year the lending agreement was executed. She remembered having analyzed the loan agreements carefully due to their magnitude. Lana found in the firm's permanent file her analysis of the loans and also a reference to a legal interpretation that the audit firm had obtained. The legal interpretation clarified the terms of the loan agreement and confirmed that Flanagan was not in violation of the loan. Lana provided a copy of the legal interpretation to Geoff and to Big Blue's loan manager.

IMPORTANCE TO AUDITORS

Flanagan's story illustrates the importance of maintaining well-documented and organized audit files in respect of client issues. The audit firm was able to support both the auditor's report and a client on an important issue. By understanding the impact to the financial statements and having legal support for a highly technical issue, the firm was able to provide continuity where both the client and the bank had employee turnover.

WHAT DO YOU THINK?

1. What are some other examples of ways specialists can assist auditors in the audit of the capital acquisition and repayment cycle?

2. Describe additional documentation that should have been present at both Flanagan and Big Blue.

continued >

LOAN agreements and methods of borrowing and investing funds are not stable—new types of instruments are regularly created. Some are stable, while others turn out to be problematic, such as the mortgage-backed papers that crashed in 2008 and 2009 and continue to have marketability problems. Specialists on the audit team help the firm assess risks and provide audit support for short-term and long-term financial instruments during the engagement. In this chapter, we focus on notes payable and certain owners' equity transactions to illustrate the audit of the capital acquisition cycle.

Source: Contributed by a qualified accountant in public practice.

① The Nature of the Capital Acquisition and Repayment Cycle

The final transaction cycle, capital acquisition and repayment, relates to the acquisition of capital resources such as interest-bearing debt and owners' equity as well as the repayment of capital. The **capital acquisition and repayment cycle** also includes the payment of interest and dividends and has a variety of accounts relating to debt payable, interest payments, and equity.

Four characteristics of the capital acquisition and repayment cycle significantly influence the audit of these accounts:

Capital acquisition and repayment cycle—the transaction cycle involving the acquisition of capital resources in the form of interest-bearing debt and owners' equity, and the repayment of the capital.

1. Relatively few transactions affect the account balances, but each transaction is often highly material in amount. For example, bonds are infrequently issued by most companies, but the amount of a bond issue is normally large. Due to the large size of most bond issues, it is common to verify each transaction taking place in the cycle for the entire year as part of verifying the balance sheet accounts. Audit working papers include the beginning balance of every account in the capital acquisition and repayment cycle and document every transaction that occurred during the year.

2. The exclusion of a single transaction could be material in itself. Considering the effect of understatements of liabilities and owners' equity, which was discussed in Chapter 16, omission (completeness assertion) is a major audit concern.

3. There is a legal relationship between the client entity and the holder of the stock, bond, or similar ownership document. In the audit of the transactions and amounts in the cycle, the auditor must ensure that the significant legal requirements affecting the financial statements have been properly fulfilled and adequately and clearly disclosed in the statements.

4. There is a direct relationship between the interest and dividend accounts and debt and equity. In the audit of interest-bearing debt, it is desirable to simultaneously verify the related interest expense and interest payable. This holds true for owners' equity, dividends declared, and dividends payable.

Careful audit of each transaction and of debt and equity documents should help detect errors or manipulations in these accounts. From these characteristics, we can summarize the risks of fraud and error for such accounts as follows:

- Errors in calculating interest payments, posting such amounts to the wrong period, or omitting them.
- Misclassifying debt as equity or vice versa, or misclassifications between current and long-term.
- Recording debt or equity transactions in the wrong period.
- Incorrect or inaccurate disclosure of terms or amounts.
- Deliberate misclassification of debt or equity as revenue or other fraudulent manipulations.

The methodology for determining tests of details of balances for capital acquisition accounts is the same as that followed for all other accounts. For example, the methodology for notes payable is shown in Figure 18-1.

Notes Payable

A **note payable** is a legal obligation to a creditor, which may be unsecured or secured by assets. Typically, a note is issued for a period somewhere between one month and one year, but there are also long-term notes of over a year. Notes are issued for many

Note payable—a legal obligation to a creditor, which may be unsecured or secured by assets.

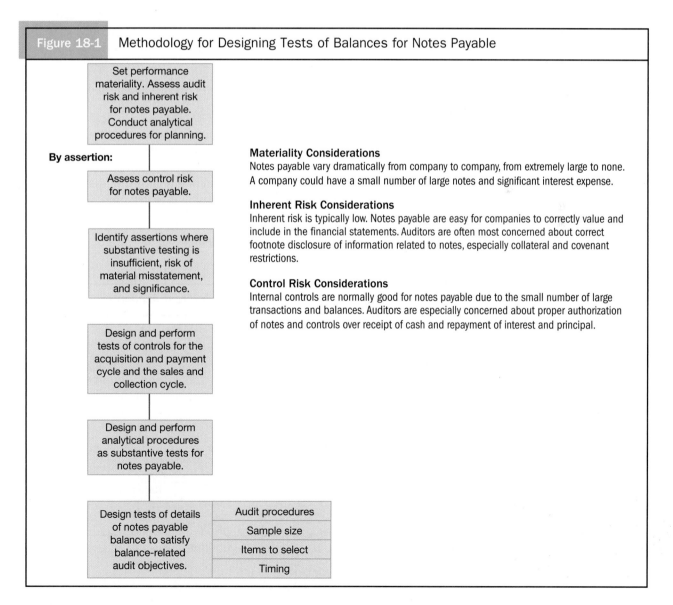

Figure 18-1 Methodology for Designing Tests of Balances for Notes Payable

Set performance materiality. Assess audit risk and inherent risk for notes payable. Conduct analytical procedures for planning.

By assertion:

Assess control risk for notes payable.

Identify assertions where substantive testing is insufficient, risk of material misstatement, and significance.

Design and perform tests of controls for the acquisition and payment cycle and the sales and collection cycle.

Design and perform analytical procedures as substantive tests for notes payable.

Design tests of details of notes payable balance to satisfy balance-related audit objectives.
- Audit procedures
- Sample size
- Items to select
- Timing

Materiality Considerations
Notes payable vary dramatically from company to company, from extremely large to none. A company could have a small number of large notes and significant interest expense.

Inherent Risk Considerations
Inherent risk is typically low. Notes payable are easy for companies to correctly value and include in the financial statements. Auditors are often most concerned about correct footnote disclosure of information related to notes, especially collateral and covenant restrictions.

Control Risk Considerations
Internal controls are normally good for notes payable due to the small number of large transactions and balances. Auditors are especially concerned about proper authorization of notes and controls over receipt of cash and repayment of interest and principal.

different purposes, and the pledged property includes a wide variety of assets such as securities, inventory, and capital assets. The principal and interest payments on the notes must be made in accordance with the terms of the loan agreement. For short-term loans, a principal and interest payment is usually required only when the loan becomes due; but for loans over 90 days, the note usually calls for monthly or quarterly interest payments.

OVERVIEW OF ACCOUNTS The accounts used for notes payable and related interest are shown in Figure 18-2.

OBJECTIVES The auditor considers risks of management bias when setting the objectives for auditing notes. For example, the auditor will consider the extent of related parties and the clarity of disclosure with respect to the notes. Assuming that disclosure is adequate and the auditor believes that management has fairly disclosed notes, the objectives of the auditor's examination of notes payable is to determine whether the following are true:

- The internal controls over notes payable are adequate.

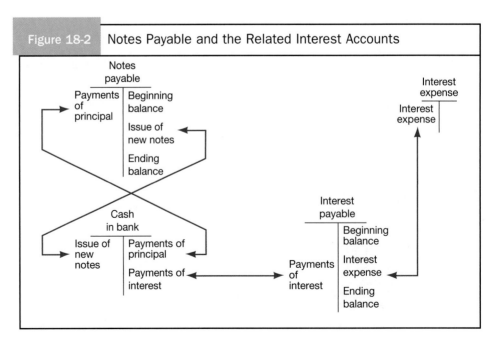

Figure 18-2 Notes Payable and the Related Interest Accounts

- Transactions for principal and interest involving notes are properly authorized and recorded as defined by the five transaction-related audit objectives.
- The liability for notes payable and the related interest expense and accrued liability are properly stated and fully and clearly disclosed as defined by the relevant balance-related and presentation and disclosure-related audit objectives. (Valuation is not applicable to liability accounts.)

INTERNAL CONTROLS There are four important controls over notes payable:

- *Proper authorization for the issue of new notes (existence):* Renewals or new notes should be approved by the Board of Directors (as evidenced in the minutes) or by senior management with two signatures, depending upon the size of the note. The amount of the loan, the interest rate, the repayment terms, and the particular assets pledged are all part of the approved agreement.
- *Adequate controls over the repayment of principal and interest (accuracy/allocation and completeness):* Due dates for interest and principal payments of notes should clearly be communicated to those responsible for cash disbursements, with payments appropriately approved.
- *Proper documents and records (existence and completeness):* These include the maintenance of subsidiary records and control over blank and paid notes by a responsible person. Paid notes should be cancelled and retained under the custody of an authorized official.
- *Periodic, independent verification (accuracy/allocation and completeness):* Authorized employees should perform independent recalculation of interest and reconciliation of the notes payable balance to the general ledger.

TESTS OF CONTROLS The audit tests are part of tests of controls for cash receipts for receipt of principal (Chapter 12) and cash disbursements for payment of interest and principal (Chapter 16). Additional tests of controls are often performed as part of tests of details of balances due to the materiality of individual transactions.

Tests of controls for notes payable and related interest should emphasize testing the four important internal controls discussed in the previous section.

ANALYTICAL PROCEDURES Analytical procedures are essential for notes payable because tests of details for interest expense and accrued interest can frequently be eliminated when results are favourable. Table 18-1 illustrates typical analytical procedures for notes payable and related interest accounts.

The auditor's independent estimate of interest expense, using average notes payable outstanding and average interest rates, tests the reasonableness of interest expense but also tests for omitted notes payable. If actual interest expense is materially larger than the auditor's estimate, one possible cause could be interest payments on unrecorded notes payable.

Table 18-1	Analytical Procedures for Notes Payable	

Analytical Procedure	Possible Misstatement
Analytical procedures for planning	
Compare total balance in notes payable, interest expense, and accrued interest with prior year's.	Misstatement of notes payable, interest expense, or accrued interest.
Analytical procedures as substantive tests	
Recalculate approximate interest expense on the basis of average interest rates and overall monthly notes payable.	Misstatement of interest expense or accrued interest, or omission of an outstanding note payable.
Compare individual notes outstanding with the prior year's.	Omission or misstatement of a note payable.

Figure 18-3   Schedule of Notes Payable and Accrued Interest

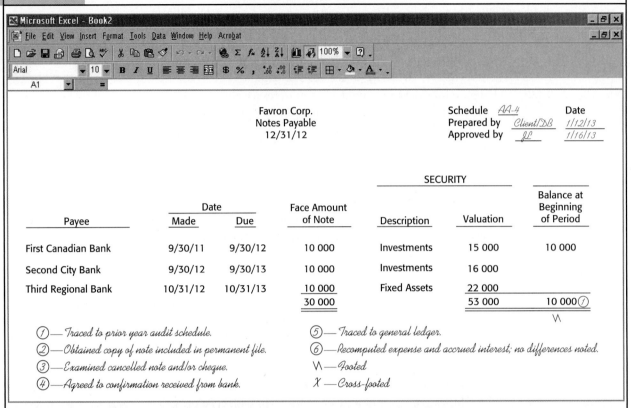

Favron Corp.
Notes Payable
12/31/12

	Schedule	*AA-4*	Date
Prepared by	*Client/DB*	*1/12/13*
Approved by	*JL*	*1/16/13*

Payee	Date Made	Date Due	Face Amount of Note	SECURITY Description	Valuation	Balance at Beginning of Period
First Canadian Bank	9/30/11	9/30/12	10 000	Investments	15 000	10 000
Second City Bank	9/30/12	9/30/13	10 000	Investments	16 000	
Third Regional Bank	10/31/12	10/31/13	10 000	Fixed Assets	22 000	
			30 000		53 000	10 000 ①
						⋀

① — Traced to prior year audit schedule.
② — Obtained copy of note included in permanent file.
③ — Examined cancelled note and/or cheque.
④ — Agreed to confirmation received from bank.
⑤ — Traced to general ledger.
⑥ — Recomputed expense and accrued interest; no differences noted.
⋀ — Footed
✗ — Cross-footed

	NOTES				INTEREST			
Additions	Payments	Balance at End of Period	Rate	Paid to	Accrued at Beginning of Period	Expense	Paid	Accrued at End of Period
	10 000 ③	-0- ④	9½% ④	Maturity	238	712 ⑥	950 ③	-0-
10 000 ②		10 000 ④	10% ④	Maturity		250 ⑥		250 ⑥
10 000 ②		10 000 ④	10% ④	Maturity		167 ⑥		167 ⑥
20 000	10 000	20 000 ⑤			238 ①	1129 ⑤	950	417 ⑤
⋀	⋀	⋀ ✗			⋀	⋀		⋀ ✗

TESTS OF DETAILS OF BALANCES The normal starting point for the audit of notes payable is a schedule of notes payable and accrued interest obtained from the client. A typical schedule is shown in Figure 18-3. The usual schedule includes detailed information for all transactions that took place during the entire year for principal and interest, the beginning and ending balances for notes and interest payable, and descriptive information about the notes, such as the due date, the interest rate, and the assets pledged as collateral. Such a schedule is also used to ensure adequate disclosure in the financial statements. Tests for presentation and disclosure are included in the last row of Table 18-2.

Table 18-2	Objectives and Tests of Details for Notes Payable and Interest	
Balance-Related Audit Objectives	**Common Tests of Details of Balances Procedures**	**Comments**
Notes payable in the schedule exist (existence).	Confirm notes payable. Examine duplicate copy of notes for authorization. Examine corporate minutes for loan approval.	
The company has an obligation to pay the notes payable (rights and obligations).	Examine notes to determine whether the company has obligations for payment.	
Existing notes payable are included in the notes payable schedule and in the general ledger (completeness).	Examine notes paid after year end to determine whether they were liabilities at the balance sheet date. Obtain a standard bank confirmation that includes specific reference to the existence of notes payable from all financial institutions with which the client does business. (Bank confirmations are discussed more fully in Chapter 14.) Review the bank reconciliation for new notes credited directly to the bank account by the bank. (Bank reconciliations are also discussed more fully in Chapter 14.) Obtain confirmations from creditors who have held notes from the client in the past and are not currently included in the notes payable schedule. This is the same concept as a "zero balance" confirmation in accounts payable. Analyze interest expense to uncover a payment to a creditor who is not included in the notes payable schedule. Examine paid notes for cancellation to make sure they are not still outstanding. Review the minutes of the board of directors for authorized but unrecorded notes.	This objective is important for uncovering both errors and fraud and other irregularities. The first three of these procedures are done on most audits. The next three are frequently done only when internal controls are weak. This procedure is automatically done if the schedule is similar to the one in Figure 18-3 because all interest payments are reconciled with the general ledger. They should be maintained in the client's files. Frequently, these are done on a 100-percent basis because of the small population size. Frequently, confirmations are done on a 100-percent basis because of the small population size. Interest expense is also normally analyzed on a 100-percent basis because of the small population size.
Balance-Related Audit Objectives	**Common Tests of Details of Balances Procedures**	**Comments**
	Foot the notes payable list for notes payable and accrued interest. Trace the totals to the general ledger. Trace the individual notes payable to the master file.	
Notes payable and accrued interest on the schedule are accurate and included in the correct period (accuracy and allocation).	Examine duplicate copies of notes for principal and interest rates. Confirm notes payable, interest rates, and last date for which interest has been paid with holders of notes. Recalculate accrued interest. Examine duplicate copies of notes to determine whether notes were dated on or before the balance sheet date.	In some cases, it may be necessary to calculate, using present-value techniques, the imputed interest rates, or the principal amount of the note. An example is when equipment is acquired for a note. Notes should be included as current-period liabilities when dated on or before the balance sheet date.
Notes payable in the schedule are properly classified, fully and clearly disclosed (classification, completeness, and understandability).	Examine due dates on duplicate copies of notes to determine whether all or part of the notes are a non-current liability. Review notes to determine whether any are related-party notes or accounts payable.	Note that these are presentation and disclosure audit objectives, rather than balance-related audit objectives.

The objectives and common audit procedures are summarized in Table 18-2. The amount of testing depends heavily on materiality of notes payable and the effectiveness of internal controls.

The most important balance-related audit objectives in notes payable are as follows:

- Existing notes payable are included (completeness).
- Notes payable in the schedule are accurately recorded (accuracy).
- Notes payable are fully and clearly presented and disclosed (completeness and understandability).

The first two objectives are important because a misstatement could be material if even one note is omitted or incorrect. Presentation and disclosure are important because generally accepted accounting principles require that the footnotes adequately describe the terms of notes payable outstanding and the assets pledged as collateral for the loans. If there are significant restrictions on the activities of the company required by the loans, such as compensating balance provisions or restrictions on the payment of dividends, these must also be disclosed in the footnotes.

 ## Owners' Equity

A major distinction must be made in the audit of owners' equity between publicly held and **closely held corporations** (also known as private corporations). Public companies are permitted by their articles of incorporation to issue shares to the public; closely held companies tend to be private companies with restricted share ownership. In most closely held corporations, there are few, if any, transactions during the year for capital stock accounts, and there are typically only a few shareholders. The only transactions entered in the owners' equity section are likely to be the change in owners' equity for the annual earnings or loss and the declaration of dividends, if any. The amount of time spent verifying owners' equity is frequently minimal for closely held corporations even though the auditor must test the existing corporate records.

For **publicly held corporations**, the verification of owners' equity is more complex due to the larger numbers of shareholders and frequent changes in the individuals holding the stock, and there may be more complex **equity instruments**. In this section, the appropriate tests for verifying the major accounts—capital stock, retained earnings, and the related dividends—in a publicly held corporation are discussed. The other accounts in owners' equity are verified in much the same way as these.

OBJECTIVES The objectives of the auditor's examination of owners' equity is to determine whether:

- The internal controls over capital stock and related dividends are adequate.
- Owners' equity transactions are recorded properly as defined by the transaction-related audit objectives.
- Owners' equity balances are properly presented and disclosed as defined by the balance-related and presentation and disclosure-related audit objectives for owners' equity accounts. (Rights and obligations and valuation are not applicable.) Audit Challenge 18-1 illustrates problems that can occur with credit.

INTERNAL CONTROLS Several important internal controls are of concern to the independent auditor in owners' equity:

- *Proper authorization of transactions:* Type, nature, timing, and terms (if any) should be approved by the Board of Directors as evidenced in the minutes of meetings.

Closely held corporation—a corporation whose stock is not publicly traded; typically, there are only a few shareholders and few, if any, capital stock account transactions during the year; also known as a private corporation.

Publicly held corporation—a corporation whose stock is publicly traded; typically, there are many shareholders and frequent changes in the ownership of the stock.

Equity instrument—an contract that has the characteristics of equity, i.e., there are residual interests in the assets of an entity, usually after deduction of a liability portion in the contract (IAS 32.11).

- *Proper record keeping and adequate segregation of duties between maintaining owners' equity records and handling cash and stock certificates:* In addition, there should be (1) well-defined policies for preparing share certificates and recording share transactions and (2) independent verification of both transaction details and amounts. One of the objectives of the controls is to maintain current share capital records, which will be used to pay dividends or repurchase shares (part of the Acquisitions and Payments cycle) and to record issues of shares.
- *The use of an independent registrar and share transfer agent:* The **independent registrar** issues shares in accordance with the provisions in the articles of incorporation and as authorized by the Board of Directors. The **share transfer agent** maintains shareholder records (including changes in ownership), adding independence to this process. The share transfer agent may also disburse dividends. A company may use one or two organizations for these processes.

AUDIT OF SHARE CAPITAL There are four main concerns in auditing capital stock:

- *Existing share capital transactions are recorded (completeness):* If a registrar or transfer agent is used, the auditor confirms balances and transactions with them. The auditor may also review minutes of Board of Directors' meetings, and examine client-held share records.
- *Recorded share capital transactions exist and are accurately recorded (occurrence and accuracy):* All capital stock transactions are verified (e.g., due to mergers, issuance, or repurchase) by looking for authorizations in the minutes of Board of Directors' meetings and agreement with share transfer agent records (using confirmations or physical inspection at their offices). Changes due to mergers and acquisitions will require inspection of relevant legal documents and may require auditor specialist assistance on the audit team.
- *Share capital is accurately recorded (accuracy):* Confirmation with the share transfer agent will provide balances and details. If the auditor inspects share records, then the auditor would verify mechanical accuracy of the records, check that certificates (if used) are properly cancelled, and determine that complex types of capital (such as convertible securities) have been properly figured into the calculations.
- *Capital stock is fully presented and clearly disclosed (completeness and understandability):* Based upon review of the prior audit working paper file, articles of incorporation and minutes of Directors' Meetings, the auditor evaluates the

Independent registrar—an outside person or organization engaged by a corporation to ensure that its stock is issued in accordance with capital stock provisions in the corporate charter and authorizations by the board of directors.

Share transfer agent—an outside person or organization engaged by a corporation to maintain the shareholder records and often to disburse cash dividends.

audit challenge 18-1
Credit Troubles

RECORDING long-term credit transactions sounds simple enough—record the debt, and expense the interest. Yet this is not always the case. Consider the ICAO (Institute of Chartered Accountants of Ontario). In July 2008, the ICAO announced that it was restating its financial statements due to an error of close to $1 million, which reduced members' equity. Costs associated with debt were capitalized rather than expensed when a complex swap took place with two different lenders.

The good thing is that the ICAO can readily obtain the credit that it needs. Consider another organization, such as Air Canada. The airline has been in and out of the news for many years, close to financial ruin. Air Canada's share price increased when it announced that it had signed a deal with CIBC (Canadian Imperial Bank of Commerce) for a loan of $100 million.

Other loans listed for Air Canada were with foreign organizations, such as one loan of US$195 million from General Electric Capital Corp. This might be a problem—with a changing U.S. dollar, the actual loan repayment and interest amounts will vary in terms of Canadian dollars unless the loan was hedged.

CRITICAL THINKING QUESTIONS

1. What are the risks associated with foreign currency loans? How would these risks be disclosed in the financial statements?
2. How does the financial stability of an organization affect its interest rates? How can the auditor use loan interest rate information during the conduct of the audit?

Sources: 1. Buckstein, Jeff, "ICAO 'embarrassed' by accounting glitch," *The Bottom Line*, 24(8), July, 2008, p. 1, 3, 2. The Canadian Press. "Air Canada lands credit," *Toronto Star*, January 1, 2009, p. B2.

completeness and quality of disclosure. Items to consider are type of capital, terms, amounts, dividend declaration dates, and similar matters.

AUDIT OF DIVIDENDS The emphasis in the audit of dividends is on the transactions rather than the ending balance. The exception is when there are dividends payable.

Dividends are usually audited or confirmed with outside agents on a 100-percent basis and cause few problems. The following are the most important objectives, including those concerning dividends payable:

- Recorded dividends occurred (occurrence).
- Existing dividends are recorded (completeness).
- Dividends are accurately recorded (accuracy).
- Dividends that exist are paid to shareholders (existence).
- Dividends payable are recorded (completeness).
- Dividends payable are accurately recorded (accuracy).

Existence of recorded dividends can be checked by examining the minutes of board of directors' meetings for the amount of the dividend per share and the dividend date. When the auditor examines the board of directors' minutes for dividends declared, the auditor should be alert to the possibility of unrecorded dividends declared, particularly shortly before the balance sheet date. A closely related audit procedure is reviewing the permanent audit working-paper file to determine if there are restrictions on the payment of dividends in bond indenture agreements or preferred share provisions.

The accuracy of a dividend declaration can be audited by recomputing the amount on the basis of the dividend per share and the number of shares outstanding. If the client uses a transfer agent to disburse dividends, the total can be traced to a cash disbursement entry to the agent and also confirmed.

When a client keeps its own dividend records and pays the dividend itself, the auditor can verify the total amount of the dividend by recalculation and reference to cash disbursed. In addition, it is necessary to verify whether the payment was made to the shareholders who owned the stock at the dividend record date. The auditor can test this by selecting a sample of recorded dividend payments and tracing the payee's name on the cancelled cheque to the dividend records to ensure the payee was entitled to the dividend. At the same time, the amount and the authenticity of the dividend cheque can be verified.

Tests of dividends payable should be done in conjunction with declared dividends. Any unpaid dividend should be included as a liability.

AUDIT OF RETAINED EARNINGS For most companies, the only transactions involving retained earnings are net earnings for the year and dividends declared. But there may also be corrections of prior-period earnings, prior-period adjustments charged or credited directly to retained earnings, and the setting up or elimination of appropriations of retained earnings.

The starting point for the audit of retained earnings is an analysis of retained earnings for the entire year. The audit schedule showing the analysis, which is usually part of the permanent file, includes a description of every transaction affecting the account. The audit of the credit to retained earnings for net income for the year (or the debit for a loss) is accomplished by tracing the entry in retained earnings to the net earnings figure on the income statement.

Once the auditor is satisfied that the recorded transactions are appropriately classified as retained earnings transactions, the next step is to decide whether they are accurately recorded. The audit evidence necessary to determine accuracy depends on the nature of the transactions. If there is a requirement for an appropriation of retained earnings for a bond sinking fund, the correct amount of the appropriation can be determined by examining the bond indenture agreement.

Another important consideration in the audit of retained earnings is evaluating whether there are any transactions that should have been included but were not. If a stock dividend was declared, for instance, the market value of the securities issued should be capitalized by a debit to retained earnings and a credit to capital stock. Similarly, if the financial statements include appropriations of retained earnings, the auditor should evaluate whether it is still necessary to have the appropriation as of the balance sheet date. As an example, an appropriation of retained earnings for a bond sinking fund should be eliminated by crediting retained earnings after the bond has been paid off.

Of primary concern in determining whether retained earnings are correctly disclosed on the balance sheet is the existence of any restrictions on the payment of dividends. Frequently, agreements with bankers, shareholders, and other creditors prohibit or limit the amount of dividends the client can pay. These restrictions must be disclosed in the footnotes to the financial statements.

concept check

C18-3 Provide examples of outsourcing as applied to management of share records.

C18-4 List examples of complex transactions that could affect retained earnings.

Summary

1. *What are the four key characteristics of the capital acquisition and repayment cycle?* (i) There are relatively few transactions, but these are often highly material. (ii) The exclusion of a single transaction could result in a material misstatement. (iii) A legal relationship exists between the client and the holder of the capital instrument. (iv) There is a direct relationship between interest or dividends paid and the corresponding debt or equity amount.

   What is the methodology for designing tests of balances for notes payable? After assessing risks and allocating materiality, tests of controls (if appropriate) are designed, tested, and evaluated. Then, analytical procedures are performed, followed by the design and execution of tests of details of balances.

   What is the purpose of conducting analytical procedures for notes payable? These calculations are designed to detect potential misstatements in interest expense, accrued interest, or notes payable, including the potential omission of a note.

2. *What is the difference in equity between publicly held and closely held corporations?* Publicly held companies tend to have a more complex share structure than closely held corporations, resulting in a greater variety of transactions. Also, as there are more shareholders, there tend to be more changes in ownership of share capital.

   Provide examples of common internal controls over owners' equity transactions. To ensure proper authorization, transactions such as declaration of dividends, purchase, redemption, and issuance of share capital should be approved by the board of directors. Adequate records should be kept of changes in share ownership to ensure payment of dividends to owners of shares. An independent registrar and share transfer agent may be used to help ensure adequate segregation of duties.

   What are the main concerns when auditing share capital? The auditor is concerned about the following assertions: completeness of all share capital transactions, accurate recording of share capital transactions, accurate recording of issued capital, and proper presentation and disclosure of share capital.

MyAccountingLab

Make the grade with MyAccountingLab: The questions, exercises, and problems marked in orange can be found on MyAccountingLab. You can practise them as often as you want, and most feature step-by-step guided instructions to help you find the right answer.

Review Questions

18-1 ❶ What characteristics do liabilities have in common? How do they differ?

18-2 ❶ Why are liability accounts that are included in the capital acquisition and repayment cycle audited differently from accounts payable?

18-3 ❶ It is common practice to audit the balance in notes payable in conjunction with the audit of interest expense and interest payable. Explain the advantages of this approach.

18-4 ❶ With which internal controls should the auditor be most concerned in the audit of notes payable? Explain the importance of each.

18-5 ❶ Which analytical procedures are most important in verifying notes payable? Which types of misstatements can the auditor uncover by the use of these tests?

18-6 ❶ Why is it more important to search for unrecorded notes payable than for unrecorded notes receivable?

List several audit procedures the auditor can use to uncover unrecorded notes payable.

18-7 ❶ What is the primary purpose of analyzing interest expense? Given this purpose, what primary considerations should the auditor keep in mind when doing the analysis?

18-8 ❶ Distinguish between the tests of controls and tests of details of balances for liability accounts in the capital acquisition and repayment cycle.

18-9 ❶ List four types of restrictions that long-term creditors often put on companies when granting them a loan. How can the auditor find out about each restriction?

18-10 ❷ What are the primary objectives in the audit of owners' equity accounts?

18-11 ❷ Evaluate the following statements: "The corporate charter and the bylaws of a company are legal documents; therefore, they should not be examined by the auditors. If the auditor wants information about these documents, a lawyer should be consulted."

18-12 ❷ What are the major internal controls over owners' equity?

18-13 ❷ Describe the duties of a share registrar and a transfer agent. How does the use of their services affect the client's internal controls?

18-14 ❷ What kinds of information can be confirmed with a transfer agent?

18-15 ❷ Evaluate the following statement: "The most important audit procedure to verify dividends for the year is a comparison of a random sample of cancelled dividend cheques with a dividend list that has been prepared by management as of the dividend record date."

18-16 ❷ Explain how the audit of dividends declared and paid is affected if a transfer agent disburses dividends for a client. What audit procedures are necessary to verify dividends paid when a transfer agent is used?

18-17 ❷ What should be the major emphasis in auditing the retained earnings account? Explain your answer.

18-18 ❷ Explain the relationship between the audit of owners' equity and the calculations of earnings per share. What are the main auditing considerations in verifying the earnings-per-share figure?

Discussion Questions and Problems

18-19 ❶ The following are frequently performed audit procedures for the verification of bonds payable issued in previous years:

1. Obtain a copy of the bond indenture agreement, and review its important provisions.
2. Determine that each of the bond indenture provisions has been met.
3. Analyze the general ledger account for bonds payable, interest expense, and unamortized bond discount or premium.
4. Reperform the client's calculations of interest expense, unamortized bond discount or premium, accrued interest, and bonds payable.

5. Obtain a confirmation from the bondholder.

REQUIRED
a. State the purpose of each of the five audit procedures listed.
b. List the provisions for which the auditor should be alert in examining the bond indenture agreement.
c. For each provision listed in part (b), explain how the auditor can determine whether its terms have been met.
d. Explain how the auditor should verify the unamortized bond discount or premium.
e. List the information that should be requested in the confirmation of bonds payable with the bondholder.

18-20 ❶ Evangeline Ltd. took out a 20-year mortgage for $2,600,000 on June 15, 2012, and pledged its only manufacturing building and the land on which the building stands as collateral. Each month a payment of $20,000 is paid to the mortgagor. You are in charge of the current-year audit for Evangeline, which has a balance sheet date of December 31, 2012. The client has been audited previously by your public accounting firm, but this is the first time Evangeline Ltd. has had a mortgage.

REQUIRED
a. Explain why it is desirable to prepare a working paper for the permanent file for the mortgage. What type of information should be included in the working paper?
b. Explain why the audits of mortgage payable, interest expense, and interest payable should all be done together.
c. List the audit procedures that should ordinarily be performed to verify the issue of the mortgage, the balance in the mortgage and interest payable accounts at December 31, 2012, and the balance in interest expense for the year 2012.

18-21 ❶ The Fox Company is a medium-sized industrial client that has been audited by your public accounting firm for several years. The only interest-bearing debt owed by Fox Company is $200,000 in long-term notes payable held by the bank. The notes were issued three years previously and will mature in six more years. Fox Company is highly profitable, has no pressing needs for additional financing, and has excellent internal controls over the recording of loan transactions and related interest costs.

a. Describe the auditing procedures that you think will be necessary for notes payable and related interest accounts in these circumstances.

b. How would your answer differ if Fox Company were unprofitable, had a need for additional financing, and had weak internal controls?

18-22 ❷ Bee Corporation's partial balance sheet includes the following information:

	2012	2011
Long-term investments		
Shares and negotiable securities	$400,000	$40,000
Shareholders' equity		
Common shares		
10,000,000 issued		
8,000,000 outstanding –		$16,000,000
December 31, 2011	$12,000,000	
6,000,000 outstanding –	$ 1,000,000	$ 6,000,000
December 31, 2012		
Contributed capital		

REQUIRED

a. Design two audit procedures to test existence related to the above investments for Bee's 2012 financial statements.

b. Design two audit procedures to test authorization related to the above investments for Bee's 2012 financial statements.

c. Assuming the company's share transactions are handled by a transfer agent, explain two important facts that the auditor would need to confirm or verify with the transfer agent for the 2012 audit.

(Extract from AU1 CGA-Canada Examinations developed by the Certified General Accountants Association of Canada © 2011 CGA-Canada. Reproduced with permission. All rights reserved.)

18-23 ❷ The following audit procedures are commonly performed by auditors in the verification of owners' equity:

1. Review the articles of incorporation and bylaws for provisions about owners' equity.
2. Review the minutes of the board of directors' meetings for the year for approvals related to owners' equity.
3. Analyze all owners' equity accounts for the year and document the nature of any recorded change in each account.
4. Account for all certificate numbers in the share capital listing for all shares outstanding.

5. Examine the share certificate listing for any shares that were cancelled.
6. Recompute earnings per share.
7. Review debt provisions and senior securities with respect to liquidation preferences, dividends in arrears, and restrictions on the payment of dividends or the issue of stock.

REQUIRED

a. State the purpose of each of these seven audit procedures, including the audit assertion(s).

b. List the type of misstatements the auditors could uncover by the use of each audit procedure.

18-24 ❷ The Bergonzi Corporation is a medium-sized wholesaler of grocery products with 4,000 shares of stock outstanding to approximately 25 shareholders. Because of the age of several retired shareholders and the success of the company, management has decided to pay dividends six times a year. The amount of the bimonthly dividend per share varies depending on the profits, but it is ordinarily between $5 and $7 per share. The chief accountant, who is also a shareholder, prepares the dividend cheques, records the cheques in the dividend journal, and reconciles the bank account. Important controls include manual cheque signing by the president and the use of an imprest dividend bank account.

The auditor verifies the dividends by maintaining a schedule of the total shares issued and outstanding in the permanent working papers. The total amount of shares outstanding is multiplied by the dividends per share authorized in the minutes to arrive at the current total dividend. This total is compared with the deposit that has been made to the imprest dividend account. Since the transfer of shares is infrequent, it is possible to verify dividends paid for the entire year in a comparatively short time.

REQUIRED

a. Evaluate the usefulness of the approach followed by the auditor in verifying dividends in this situation. Include both the strengths and the weaknesses of the approach.

b. List other audit procedures that should be performed in verifying dividends in this situation. Explain the purpose of each procedure.

Professional Judgment Problem

18-25 ❶ ❷ E-Antiques Inc. is an internet-based market for buyers and sellers of antique furniture and jewellery. The company allows sellers of antique items to list descriptions of those items on the E-Antiques website. Interested buyers review the website for antique items and then enter into negotiations directly with the seller for purchase. E-Antiques receives a commission for each transaction.

The company, founded in 2000, initially obtained capital through equity funding provided by the founders and through loan proceeds from financial institutions. In early 2012, E-Antiques became a publicly held company when it began selling shares on a national stock exchange. Although the company had never generated profits, the stock offering generated huge proceeds based on favourable expectations for the company, and the share price quickly increased to above $100 per share.

Management used the proceeds to pay off loans to financial institutions and to reacquire shares issued to the company founders. Proceeds were also used to fund purchases of hardware and software to support the online market. The balance of unused proceeds is currently held in the company's bank accounts.

REQUIRED

a. Before performing analytical procedures related to the capital acquisition and repayment cycle accounts, consider how the process of becoming publicly held would affect accounts at E-Antiques Inc. Describe whether each of the following balances would increase, decrease, or experience no change between 2011 and 2012 because of the public offering.
   (1) Cash.
   (2) Accounts receivable.
   (3) Property, plant, and equipment.
   (4) Accounts payable.
   (5) Long-term debt.
   (6) Common shares.
   (7) Retained earnings.
   (8) Dividends.
   (9) Revenues.

b. During 2012, the share price for E-Antiques plummeted to around $19 per share. No new shares were issued during 2012. Describe the impact of this drop in share price on the following accounts for the year ended December 31, 2012:
   (1) Common shares.
   (2) Retained earnings.

c. How does the decline in share price affect your assessment of client business risk and acceptable audit risk?

Case

18-26 ❶ The ending general ledger balance of $186,000 in notes payable for Sisam Manufacturing Inc. is made up of 20 notes to eight different payees. The notes vary in duration anywhere from 30 days to two years and in amount from $1,000 to $10,000. In some cases, the notes were issued for cash loans; in other cases, the notes were issued directly to vendors for the purchase of inventory or equipment. The use of relatively short-term financing is necessary because all existing properties are pledged for mortgages. Nevertheless, there is still a serious cash shortage.

Record-keeping procedures for notes payable are not good, considering the large number of loan transactions. There is neither a notes payable master file nor an independent verification of ending balances; however, the notes payable records are maintained by a secretary who does not have access to cash.

The audit has been done by the same public accounting firm for several years. In the current year, the following procedures were performed to verify notes payable:
1. Obtain a list of notes payable from the client, foot the notes payable balances on the list, and trace the total to the general ledger.

2. Examine duplicate copies of notes for all outstanding notes included on the listing. Compare the name of the lender, amount, and due date on the duplicate copy with the list.
3. Obtain a confirmation from lenders for all listed notes payable. The confirmation should include the due date of the loan, the amount, and interest payable at the balance sheet date.
4. Recompute accrued interest on the list for all notes. The information for determining the correct accrued interest is to be obtained from the duplicate copy of the note. Foot the accrued interest amounts, and trace the balance to the general ledger.

REQUIRED

a. What should be the emphasis in the audit of notes payable in this situation? Explain.
b. State the purpose of each of the four audit procedures listed.
c. Evaluate whether each of the four audit procedures was necessary. Evaluate the sample size for each procedure.
d. List other audit procedures that should be performed in the audit of notes payable in these circumstances.

Ongoing Small Business Case: Equity Accounts at CondoCleaners.com

18-27 ❶ When Jim established CondoCleaners.com the company was incorporated with two common shares with no par value. The shares have a book value of $2.00. The only other equity on the balance sheet is retained earnings.

REQUIRED

How does the audit of owners' equity for a closely held company such as CondoCleaners.com differ from that for a publicly held corporation? In what respect are there no significant differences?

4

Completing the audit, reporting, and offering other services

Chapter 1 introduced the many different types of accountants and the types of services they provide. The chapters in this part expand on this discussion. The provision of special skills during audit engagements, assurance services other than audits, and non-assurance services constitutes an important contribution by accountants to the business community, as long as the audit engagements are performed in conformity with the professional rules of conduct and while maintaining objectivity and independence.

The last part of Phase 7 of a financial statement audit is "Ongoing evaluation, quality control, and final evidence gathering," which is covered in Chapter 19. Even when the other phases of the audit are done well, if this final evidence gathering phase is done poorly, the quality of the audit will be low. If the planning phases and the other risk response phases are done well, the completion phase is typically relatively easy.

Chapter 20 addresses the final phase of the financial statement audit, reporting. We look at the standard audit report in detail, as well as alternatives to the standard audit report.

Chapter 21 focuses on small business, both non-profit and for-profit enterprises. Review and compilation engagements are the primary focus of this chapter. Chapter 21 also discusses the standards for assurance engagements, including compilation and review engagements, and provides a framework for the conduct of such engagements. Included is a discussion of interim financial information and future-oriented information, useful for businesses acquiring debt or share capital.

19 Completing the audit

As the audit progresses, the auditor continues to evaluate results to determine whether planned risks match actual risks. When all cycle, account, and assertion tests have been completed, the evidence as a whole needs to be examined, together with some additional tests that are non–cycle-specific. Then, the auditor can decide whether sufficient evidence has been collected to provide an audit opinion. Management accountants and internal auditors can use awareness of this phase to learn about the type of information that they would need to provide to the external auditors, while all auditors will benefit from understanding the type of evidence gathered in this final phase.

LEARNING OBJECTIVES

1 Design and perform audit tests related to presentation and disclosure audit objectives. Describe how the auditor searches for contingent liabilities, commitments, and contingent assets. State the purpose of obtaining a confirmation from the client's law firms. Explain why these "legal letters" must be in a specified format. Describe examples of procedures conducted during a review for subsequent events.

2 Provide examples of work completed as part of the final evidence-gathering process.

3 Describe the actions that the auditor takes to evaluate the adequacy of accumulated evidence. State how quality control procedures are incorporated into this final risk response phase of the audit.

4 Describe the communications the auditor is required to send after the completion of the audit.

STANDARDS REFERENCED IN THIS CHAPTER
CICA Standards

CAS 240 – The auditor's responsibilities relating to fraud in an audit of financial statements

CAS 250 – Consideration of laws and regulations in an audit of financial statements

CAS 260 – Communications with those charged with governance

CAS 450 – Evaluation of misstatements identified during the audit

CAS 501 – Audit evidence: specific considerations for selected items

CAS 520 – Analytical procedures

CAS 550 – Related parties

CAS 560 – Subsequent events

CAS 570 – Going concern

CAS 580 – Written representations

CAS 720 – The auditor's responsibility relating to other information in documents containing audited financial statements

Section 3290 – Contingencies

IAS 37 – Provisions, contingent liabilities and contingent assets

Good Review Requires More Than Looking at Working Papers

Larry Bedard, an audit senior at Messier, Nixon & Royce, assigned to staff assistant Clawson Lum the audit of accounts payable of Westside Industries Ltd., a large equipment manufacturer. Accounts payable is a major liability account for a manufacturing company, and testing accounts payable cut off is an important audit area. Testing primarily involves reviewing the liability recorded by the client by examining subsequent payments to suppliers and other creditors to assure that they were properly recorded in the correct period.

Larry observed that Clawson was spending a lot of time on the phone, apparently on personal matters. Shortly before the audit was completed, Clawson announced that he was leaving the firm. In spite of Clawson's distractions due to his personal affairs, he completed the audit work he was assigned within the budgeted time.

Because of Larry's concern about Clawson's work habits, he decided to review the working papers with extreme care. Every schedule he reviewed was properly prepared, with tick marks entered and explained by Clawson, indicating that he had made an extensive examination of underlying data and documents and had found the client's balance to be adequate as stated. Specifically, there were no payments subsequent to year end for inventory purchases received during the audit period that had not been accrued by Westside.

When Larry finished the audit, he turned the working papers over to Kelsey Mayburn, an audit manager on the engagement, for review. She had considerable knowledge about equipment manufacturers and about Westside Industries. Kelsey reviewed all the working papers, including the analytical procedures performed during the audit. After performing additional analytical procedures during her review, she contacted Larry to inform him that accounts payable did not seem reasonable to her. She asked him to do some additional checking. Larry went back and looked at all the documents that Clawson had indicated in the working papers that he had inspected. It was quickly apparent that Clawson either had not looked at the documents or did not know what he was doing when he inspected them. Almost $1 million of documents applicable to the December 31, 2012, audit period had not been included as liabilities. Kelsey's review likely saved Messier, Nixon & Royce significant embarrassment or worse consequences.

IMPORTANCE TO AUDITORS

This case illustrates the unfortunate fact that Clawson apparently violated the rules of conduct during his time at the Westside audit by preparing working papers that were incorrect. However, the positive side is that Kelsey discovered this through her experience in other audit engagements and by performing additional analytical review. This explains why audit firms will have a "cold review" on high-risk engagements (i.e., have someone who has not been involved in the engagement review the audit file) so that additional eyes can look for potential anomalies.

continued >

MANAGER and partner reviews are performed throughout the engagement and after the audit working paper file (including the audit steps discussed in this chapter) is completed. The review requires experience as well as an eye for detail to spot potential audit risks that are present or that have been poorly addressed, as in the Westside case presented above. The final risk response phase of the financial statement audit process includes final evidence gathering and the completion of checklists and review that wrap up the integration of the audit working paper file. It is also at that time that material is noted in the file for the following year's planning and for ensuring partner rotation.

❶ Phase 7 and Selected Final Audit Procedures

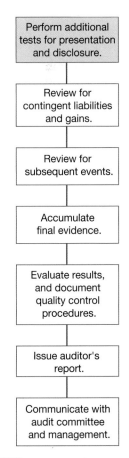

In this section, we discuss three specific types of audit procedures: performance of additional tests for presentation and disclosure, review for contingent liabilities (or assets), and review for subsequent events.

Perform Additional Tests for Presentation and Disclosure

Chapter 5 described the need to perform procedures to satisfy the three categories of audit objectives: transaction-related audit objectives, balance-related audit objectives, and presentation and disclosure-related audit objectives (P&D-RAO). This is done in the same way that auditors approach working with a particular cycle or account:

- Perform procedures to obtain an understanding of controls related to P&D-RAO as part of risk assessment procedures.
- Conduct tests of controls related to disclosures when the initial assessment of control risk is below maximum.
- Perform substantive procedures to obtain assurance that all audit objectives are achieved for information and amounts presented and disclosed in the financial statements.

Table 19-1 lists the P&D-RAO and examples of substantive procedures for each assertion. Since such procedures are usually integrated into cycle tests, in this phase the auditor determines whether adequate evidence was collected during that cycle test to determine whether additional evidence is required. The auditor would also evaluate whether the overall presentation of the financial statements and related notes

Table 19-1   Presentation and Disclosure Audit Objectives

Audit Objectives	Examples of Substantive Procedures
Occurrence and rights and obligations—Disclosed events and transactions have occurred and pertain to the entity.	Review debt contracts to determine that accounts receivable are pledged as collateral.
Completeness—All disclosures that should have been included in the financial statements have been included.	Use a disclosure checklist to determine if the financial statements include all disclosures required by accounting standards.
Classification and understandability—Financial information is appropriately presented and described, and disclosures are clearly expressed.	Review financial statements to determine if assets are properly classified between current and non-current categories. Read the notes for clarity.
Accuracy and valuation—Financial and other information are disclosed fairly and at appropriate amounts.	Reconcile amounts included in the long-term debt notes to information examined and supported in the auditor's long-term debt audit working papers.

Financial statement disclosure checklist—a questionnaire that reminds the auditor of disclosure problems commonly encountered in audits and that facilitates the final review of the entire audit by an independent partner.

Contingent liability—a potential future obligation to an outside party for an unknown amount resulting from activities that have already taken place.

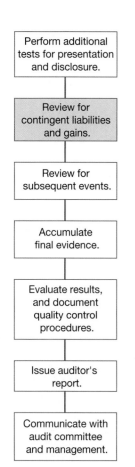

complies with the client's selected financial accounting framework standards on a basis consistent with prior years.

Unless the auditor is alert to disclosure problems throughout the audit, it is impossible to perform the final disclosure review adequately. For example, as part of the examination of accounts receivable, the auditor must be aware that accounts receivable, notes receivable, and other amounts due must be shown with clear distinctions between amounts due from affiliates (or other related parties) and those due from customers. Similarly, there must be a segregation of current from non-current receivables and a disclosure of the factoring or discounting of notes receivable if this has occurred.

As part of the final review for financial statement disclosure, many public accounting firms require the completion of a **financial statement disclosure checklist** for every engagement. This questionnaire is designed to remind the auditor of common disclosure problems encountered on audits and to facilitate the final review of the entire audit by an independent partner.

Due to the unique nature of the disclosures related to contingent liabilities and subsequent events, auditors often assess the risks as high that all required information may not be completely disclosed in the notes. Audit tests performed in earlier audit phases often do not provide sufficient appropriate evidence about contingent liabilities and subsequent events. Therefore, auditors design and perform procedures in every audit for contingent liabilities and subsequent events as part of their Phase 7 testing.

Review for Contingent Liabilities and Commitments

A **contingent liability** (or asset) is due to known events with uncertain outcomes. The terminology used under ASPE and IFRS differ, yet the general requirements under both financial accounting frameworks are similar: (1) if there is certainty regarding amount and timing, then the amount is to be accrued, while if (2) it is unlikely (or remote) that the amount needs to be paid or (3) it cannot be quantified, then it is to be disclosed. Table 19-2 describes the terminology used by both ASPE and IFRS as well as the financial accounting treatment.

Note that if the amount is accrued because it is likely and the amount is known, then under IFRS it is no longer considered to be a contingent liability, but rather is a provision for a liability. The decision as to the appropriate treatment requires considerable professional judgment. ASPE and IFRS agree that contingent gain (or contingent asset) should never be accrued, but rather, if its future confirmation is very likely, it should be disclosed in the notes.

Likelihood of Occurrence of Contingent Liability (ASPE Section 3290)	Likelihood of Occurrence of Event (IFRS IAS 37)	Term Used under IFRS (IAS 37)	Financial Statement Treatment
Table 19-2	**Likelihood of Occurrence of Contingencies and Financial Statement Treatment**		
Unlikely to occur	Likelihood is remote	Contingent liability	No disclosure is necessary.
Amount not determinable	Amount yet to be confirmed	Contingent liability	Note disclosure is necessary.
Likely to occur and the amount can be estimated	Probable that an outflow of resources is required	Provision	General ledger and financial statement accounts are adjusted (amount accrued).*
Likely to occur but the amount cannot be estimated	Outflow of resources is required, but cannot be reliably estimated	Contingent liability	Note disclosure is necessary.

* Note that the time value of money must be considered as part of the accrual process.

When the proper disclosure in the financial statements of material contingencies is through notes to the financial statements, the note should describe the nature of the contingency to the extent it is known, an estimate of the amount, or a statement that the amount cannot be estimated. The following is an illustration of a note related to pending litigation:

The Company is a defendant in a legal action instituted in the Alberta Court of the Queen's Bench by Mountain Supply Ltd. for alleged product defect. The amount claimed is $792,000 and the Company is vigorously contesting the claim. The Company's legal counsel is unable, at the present time, to give any opinion with respect to the merits of this action. Settlement, if any, that may be made with respect to these actions is expected to be accounted for as a charge against income for the period in which settlement is made.

Auditors are especially concerned about certain contingent liabilities:

- Pending litigation for patent infringement, product liability, or other actions.
- Income tax disputes.
- Product warranties.
- Notes receivable discounted.
- Guarantees of obligations of others.
- Unused balances in outstanding letters of credit.

Auditing standards make it clear that management, not the auditor, is responsible for identifying and deciding the appropriate accounting treatment for contingent liabilities. In many audits, it is impractical for auditors to uncover contingencies without management's cooperation.

The auditor's objectives in verifying contingent liabilities are (1) to evaluate the accounting treatment of known contingent liabilities to determine whether management has properly classified the contingency (classification P&D-RAO) and (2) to identify, to the extent practical, any contingencies not already identified by management (completeness P&D-RAO).

AUDIT PROCEDURES FOR FINDING CONTINGENCIES Many of these potential obligations are ordinarily verified as an integral part of various segments of the engagement rather than as a separate activity near the end of the audit. For example, guarantees of obligations of others may be tested as part of confirming bank balances and loans from banks. Similarly, income tax disputes can be checked as part of analyzing income tax expense, reviewing the general correspondence file, and examining Canada Revenue Agency reports and statements. Even if the contingencies are verified separately, it is common to perform the tests well before the last few days of completing the engagement to ensure their proper verification. The tests of contingent liabilities near the end of the engagement are more a review than an initial search.

The following are some audit procedures commonly used to search for contingent liabilities. The list is not all-inclusive, and each procedure is not necessarily performed on every audit.

- Inquire of management (orally and in writing) regarding the possibility of unrecorded contingencies. In these inquiries, the auditor must be specific in describing the different kinds of contingencies that may require disclosure. Naturally, inquiries of management are not useful in uncovering the intentional failure to disclose existing contingencies, but if management has overlooked a particular type of contingency or does not fully comprehend accounting disclosure requirements, the inquiry can be fruitful. At the completion of the audit, management is typically asked to make a written statement as part of the letter of representation that it is unaware of any undisclosed contingent liabilities.
- Review current and previous years' Canada Revenue Agency notices of assessment. The reports may indicate areas in which disagreement over unsettled years is likely to arise. If an audit by the Canada Revenue Agency has been in progress for a long time, there is an increased likelihood of an existing tax dispute.
- Review the minutes of directors' and shareholders' meetings for indications of lawsuits or other contingencies.
- Analyze legal expense for the period under audit, and review invoices and statements from the client's law firms for indications of contingent liabilities, especially lawsuits and pending tax assessments.
- Obtain a confirmation from all major law firms performing legal services for the client as to the status of pending litigation or other contingent liabilities. This procedure is discussed in more depth shortly.
- Review existing working papers for any information that may indicate a potential contingency. For example, bank confirmations may indicate notes receivable discounted or guarantees of loans.
- Obtain letters of credit in force as of the balance sheet date, and obtain a confirmation of the used and unused balances.
- Read contracts, agreements, and related correspondence and documents.

EVALUATION OF KNOWN CONTINGENT LIABILITIES If the auditor concludes that there are contingent liabilities, he or she must evaluate the significance of the potential liability and the nature of the disclosure that is necessary in the financial statements. The potential liability is sufficiently well known in some instances to be included in the statements as an actual liability. In other instances, disclosure may be unnecessary if the contingency is highly remote or immaterial.

Commitments—agreements that the entity will hold to a fixed set of conditions, such as the purchase or sale of merchandise at a stated price, at a future date, regardless of what happens to profits or to the economy as a whole.

COMMITMENTS Closely related to contingent liabilities are **commitments** (agreements that the entity will hold to a fixed set of conditions), such as to purchase raw materials or to lease facilities at a certain price, agreements to sell merchandise at a fixed price, bonus plans, profit-sharing and pension plans, royalty agreements, and similar items. For a commitment, the most important characteristic is the agreement to commit the firm to a set of fixed conditions in the future, regardless of what happens to profits or the economy as a whole. Commitments are ordinarily either described together in a separate note or combined in a note related to contingencies.

AUDIT PROCEDURES FOR FINDING COMMITMENTS The search for unknown commitments is usually performed as part of the audit of each audit area. For example, in verifying sales transactions, the auditor should be alert to sales commitments.

Obtain Confirmation from Client's Law Firms

A major procedure on which auditors rely for evaluating known litigation or other claims against the client and identifying additional ones is sending a letter of **inquiry of the client's law firms** (a confirmation letter in a specific format that requests information about pending litigation or other relevant information with respect to legal claims). There are two categories of lawsuits: an **outstanding** (or **asserted**) **claim** exists when a suit has been brought or when the client has been notified that a suit will be brought; a **possible** or **unasserted claim** exists when no suit has been filed but is possible. An example of the latter is a situation in which the lawyer is aware of a violation of a patent agreement that could be damaging to the client.

The auditor relies on the lawyer's expertise and knowledge of the client's legal affairs to provide a professional opinion about the expected outcome of existing lawsuits and the likely amount of the liability, including court costs. The lawyer is also likely to know of pending litigation and claims that management may have overlooked.

Many public accounting firms analyze legal expense for the entire year and have the client send a standard lawyer's letter to every law firm with which it has been involved in the current or preceding year, plus any law firm that it occasionally engages. In some cases, this involves a large number of law firms, including some dealing in aspects of law that are far removed from potential lawsuits.

The standard letter of confirmation to the client's law firm, which should be prepared on the client's letterhead and signed by one of the company's officials, should include the following:

- A list, prepared by management, of outstanding and possible claims with which the lawyer has had significant involvement.
- A description of the nature and the current status of each claim and possible claim.

Inquiry of the client's law firms—a confirmation letter in a specific format from the client's legal counsel informing the auditor of pending litigation or any other information involving legal counsel that is relevant to financial statement disclosure.

Outstanding claim—a lawsuit that has been brought against a client; also known as an "asserted claim."

Unasserted claim—a potential legal claim against a client where the condition for a claim exists but no claim has been filed; also known as "possible claim."

---

auditing in action 19-1

Will It Take Death or Disaster for the Client to Act?

As an auditor, assessing corporate governance includes assessing the organization's responsibility for the health and well-being of employees and other individuals. For example, the Basel Convention prohibits the exporting of electronic waste (e.g., computers, monitors, etc.), yet it seems that many organizations violate this convention.

In a more vivid example, employees of a Canadian waste management company complained about the speed and reckless manner in which a driver was operating a front-end loader in the plant. Subsequently, an employee who was acting as a "spotter" for a backward-driving task was killed by this same driver. The company was fined $300,000 for health and safety violations for failing to ensure that the front-end loader was driven by a competent person. On a separate occasion, the U.S. parent company refused to book correcting journal entries advised by its auditors. The auditors made a "deal" for the parent company to book these entries over a period of 10 years, which the company did not do. The auditors were fined US$7 million by the SEC for participating in this side deal.

It is important that auditors consider the behaviour of management with respect to known laws, regulations, and the health and safety of its employees, as this may be an indicator of management's attitude toward the integrity of the financial statements. Such behaviour could also lead to contingent liabilities such as fines as consequences of violations or to costs such as clean-up of environmentally polluted areas.

Sources: 1. Beasley, Mark S., Frank A. Buckless, Steven M. Glover, and Douglas F. Prawitt, *Auditing Cases, an Interactive Learning Approach*, Second Edition (Toronto: Prentice Hall, 2003). 2. Ontario Ministry of Labour, "Canadian Waste Services Inc. fined $300,000 for health and safety violation," 2004, **www.labour.gov.on.ca/english/news/pdf/2004/04-55.pdf**, Accessed: July 30, 2009. 3. Ross, Rachel, "Toxic exportation," *Toronto Star*, January 3, 2005, p. D1, D3.

- An indication of management's evaluation of the amount and likelihood of loss or gain for each listed claim and possible claim.
- A request that the lawyer reply to the client, with a signed copy going to the public accounting firm, advising whether management's descriptions and evaluations of the outstanding and possible claims are reasonable.

CAS Lawyers are not required to mention any omission of possible claims in their response to the inquiry letter and, thus, do not directly notify the auditor of them. Instead, lawyers discuss these possible claims with the client separately and inform management of its responsibility to inform the auditor. Whether management does so or not is its decision; CAS 501 par. 10 requires the auditor to obtain a letter of representation from management that it has disclosed all known outstanding and possible claims. In short, unless management discloses the existence of possible claims to the auditor, the auditor has no means of discovering whether or not any such claims exist.

Any differences between management's identification and assessment of outstanding and possible claims and the law firm's would be resolved, if possible, in a meeting of the law firm, the auditor, and management. Failure to resolve the differences would force the auditor to consider a reservation of opinion (discussed in the next chapter) on the auditor's report.

An example of a standard inquiry letter sent to a lawyer's office is shown in Figure 19-1. The letter should be sent toward the end of the audit so that the lawyer is communicating about contingencies up to approximately the date of the auditor's report.

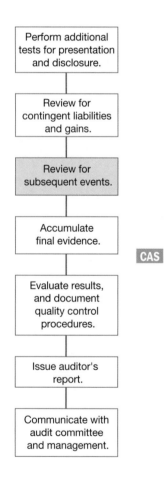

Perform additional tests for presentation and disclosure.

Review for contingent liabilities and gains.

Review for subsequent events.

Accumulate final evidence.

Evaluate results, and document quality control procedures.

Issue auditor's report.

Communicate with audit committee and management.

LIMITED OR NON-RESPONSES FROM LAW FIRMS Law firms in recent years have become reluctant to provide certain information to auditors because of their own exposure to legal liability for providing incorrect or confidential information. The nature of the refusal of law firms to provide auditors with complete information about contingent liabilities falls into two categories: the refusal to respond due to a lack of knowledge about matters involving contingent liabilities, and the refusal to disclose information that the lawyer regards as confidential. As an example of the latter, the lawyer might be aware of a violation of a patent agreement that could result in a significant loss to the client if the violation were public knowledge (possible claim). The inclusion of the information in a note could actually cause the lawsuit and therefore be damaging to the client. When the nature of the lawyer's legal practice does not involve contingent liabilities, the lawyer's refusal to respond causes no audit problems.

CAS A serious audit problem does arise, however, when a lawyer refuses to provide information that is within the lawyer's jurisdiction and may directly affect the fair presentation of financial statements. If a lawyer refuses to provide the auditor with information about material existing lawsuits (outstanding claims) or possible claims, the auditor's report would have to be modified to reflect the lack of available evidence. The "Joint Policy Statement concerning communications with law firms regarding claims and possible claims in connection with the preparation and audit of financial statements," an appendix to CAS 501 of the *CICA Handbook*, has the effect of encouraging lawyers to cooperate with auditors in obtaining information about contingencies, as the law firm's confidential relationship with its clients will not be violated. The Joint Policy Statement was approved by the Canadian Bar Association, the Council of the Bermuda Bar Association, and the Auditing Standards Committee (now the Auditing and Assurance Standards Board) of the CICA.

Review for Subsequent Events

Review for subsequent events—the auditing procedures performed by auditors to identify and evaluate subsequent events.

CAS The auditor must conduct a **review for subsequent events** (i.e., transactions and events occurring after the balance sheet date, see CAS 560) to determine whether anything occurred that might affect the fair presentation or disclosure of the statements being audited.

Figure 19-1   Typical Inquiry of Lawyer

Peppertree Produce Inc.
293 rue Crécy
Montréal, Québec

January 26, 2013

Rowan and Gunz
Barristers and Solicitors,
412 Côte des Neiges,
Montréal, Québec
H3C 1J7

To Whom It May Concern:

In connection with the preparation and audit of our financial statements for the fiscal period ended December 31, 2012, we have made the following evaluations of claims and possible claims with respect to which your firm's advice or representation has been sought:

Description	Evaluation
Calvert Growers vs. Peppertree Produce Inc., non-payment of debt in the amount of $16,000, trial date not set.	Peppertree Produce Inc. disputes this billing on the grounds that the produce was spoiled and expects to successfully defend this action.
Desjardins, Inc. vs. Peppertree Produce Inc., damages for breach of contract in the amount of $40,000, trial date not set.	It is probable that this action will be successfully defended.
Foodex Ltd. has a possible claim in connection with apples sold to them by Peppertree Produce Inc. The apples apparently had not been properly washed by the growers to remove insect spray, and a number of Foodex Ltd.'s customers became ill after eating said apples.	No claim has yet been made, and we are unable to estimate possible ultimate loss.

Would you please advise us, as of February 28, 2013, on the following points:
a. Are the claims and possible claims properly described?
b. Do you consider that our evaluations are reasonable?
c. Are you aware of any claims not listed above that are outstanding? If so, please include in your response letter the names of the parties and the amount claimed.

This inquiry is made in accordance with the Joint Policy Statement of January, 1978, approved by the Canadian Bar Association and the Auditing Standards Committee of the Canadian Institute of Chartered Accountants.

Please address your reply, marked "Privileged and Confidential," to this company, and send a signed copy of the reply directly to our auditors, Jeannerette & Cie, Comptables Agrées, 1133 rue Sherbrooke, Montréal, Québec, H3C 1M8.

Yours truly,

Charles D. Peppertree

Charles D. Peppertree, President

c.c. Jeannerette & Cie

The auditor's responsibility for reviewing for subsequent events is normally limited to the period beginning with the balance sheet date and ending with the date of the auditor's report. The date of the auditor's report corresponds with the approval of the financial statements by the Board of Directors or other executive management. The subsequent events review should be completed near the end of the engagement and may require returning to the client premises if approval of the financial statements is delayed. Figure 19-2 shows the period covered by a subsequent events review and the timing of that review.

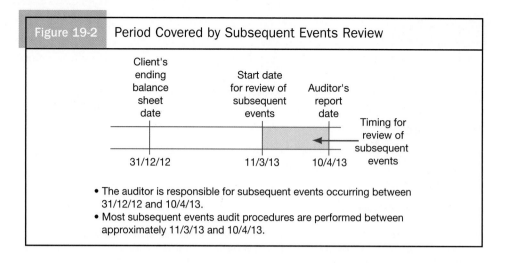

Figure 19-2 Period Covered by Subsequent Events Review

Client's ending balance sheet date

Start date for review of subsequent events

Auditor's report date

Timing for review of subsequent events

31/12/12   11/3/13   10/4/13

- The auditor is responsible for subsequent events occurring between 31/12/12 and 10/4/13.
- Most subsequent events audit procedures are performed between approximately 11/3/13 and 10/4/13.

Subsequent events—transactions and other pertinent events that occurred after the balance sheet date and that affect the fair presentation or disclosure of the statements being audited.

TYPES OF SUBSEQUENT EVENTS Two types of subsequent events require consideration by management and evaluation by the auditor: (1) those that have a direct effect on the financial statements and require adjustment and (2) those that have no direct effect on the financial statements but for which disclosure is required.

Those that have a direct effect on the financial statements and require adjustment These events or transactions provide additional information to management in determining the valuation of account balances as of the balance sheet date and to auditors in verifying the balances. For example, if the auditor is having difficulty determining the correct valuation of inventory because of obsolescence, the sale of raw material inventory as scrap in the subsequent period should be used as a means of determining the correct valuation of the inventory as of the balance sheet date.

Whenever subsequent events are used to evaluate the amounts included in the statements, care must be taken to distinguish between conditions that existed at the balance sheet date and those that came into being after the end of the year. The subsequent information should not be incorporated directly into the statements if the conditions causing the change in valuation did not take place until after year end. For example, the sale of scrap in the subsequent period would not be relevant in the valuation of inventory for obsolescence if the obsolescence took place after the end of the year. Also, an amount outstanding from a customer who declared bankruptcy after year end due to uninsured fire damage to its premises should not be removed from the accounts receivable balance until the year the damage took place.

Those that have no direct effect on the financial statements but for which disclosure is advisable Subsequent events of this type provide evidence of conditions that did not exist at the date of the balance sheet being reported on but are so significant that they require disclosure even though they do not require adjustment. Ordinarily, these events can be adequately disclosed by the use of notes, but occasionally one event may be so significant as to require supplementing the historical statements with statements that include the effect of the event as if it had occurred on the balance sheet date (i.e., pro forma statements).

Examples of events or transactions occurring in the subsequent period that may require disclosure rather than an adjustment in the financial statements include decline in the market value of investments, issuance of bonds or shares, and the purchase of a business or trademark.

AUDIT TESTS There are two categories of audit procedures for subsequent events review: (1) procedures normally integrated as part of the verification of year-end account balances and (2) those performed specifically for the purpose of discovering events or transactions that must be recognized as subsequent events.

The first category includes cut off and valuation tests that are done as part of the tests of details of balances. For example, subsequent-period sales and acquisition transactions are examined to determine whether the cut off is accurate. Similarly, many valuation tests involving subsequent events are also performed as part of the verification of account balances. As an example, it is common to test the collectability of accounts receivable by reviewing subsequent-period cash receipts. The second category of tests is performed specifically for the purpose of obtaining information that must be incorporated into the current year's account balances or notes. These tests include the following:

Inquire of management Inquiries vary from client to client but normally are about the existence of potential contingent liabilities or commitments, significant changes in the assets or capital structure of the company, the current status of items that were not completely resolved at the balance sheet date, and the existence of unusual adjustments made subsequent to the balance sheet date. Inquiries of management about subsequent events must be held with the proper client personnel to obtain meaningful answers. For example, discussing tax or union matters with the accounts receivable supervisor would not be appropriate. Most inquiries should be made of the controller, the vice-presidents, or the president, depending on the information desired.

Correspond with law firms Correspondence with law firms, which was previously discussed, takes place as part of the search for contingent liabilities. In obtaining confirmation letters from law firms, the auditor must remember his or her responsibility for testing for subsequent events up to the date of approval of the financial statements. A common approach is to request that the law firm date and mail the letter as of the expected approval date for the financial statements.

Review internal financial statements prepared subsequent to the balance sheet date The emphasis in the review should be on (1) changes in the business relative to results for the same period in the year under audit and (2) changes after year end. The auditor should pay particular attention to major changes in the business or environment in which the client is operating. The statements should be discussed with management to determine whether they are prepared on the same basis as the current-period statements, and there should be inquiries about significant changes in operating results.

Review records prepared subsequent to the balance sheet date Journals, data files, and ledgers should be reviewed to determine the existence and nature of any transaction related to the current year. If the journals are not kept up to date, the documents relating to the journals should be reviewed.

Examine minutes prepared subsequent to the balance sheet date The minutes of shareholders' and directors' meetings subsequent to the balance sheet date (including draft minutes) must be examined for important subsequent events affecting the current-period financial statements.

Obtain a letter of representation The letter of representation written by the client to the auditor formalizes statements the client has made about different matters throughout the audit, including discussions about subsequent events.

concept check

C19-1 Why are contingent liabilities difficult to identify?

C19-2 When reviewing legal expenses, which transactions should the auditor examine, and why?

C19-3 List three audit techniques that could be used to identify relevant subsequent events.

② Accumulate Final Evidence

The auditor has a few final accumulation responsibilities that apply to all cycles besides the search for contingent liabilities and the review for subsequent events. The four most important ones (final analytical review procedures [refer to CAS 520], evaluation of going concern assumption, client representation letter, and other information in annual reports), as well as review of management discussion and analysis, are discussed in this section. All are done late in the engagement.

FINAL ANALYTICAL PROCEDURES Analytical procedures were introduced in Chapter 8 and applied to specific cycles in several chapters. Analytical procedures are normally

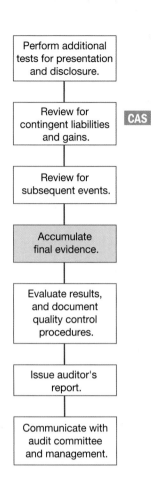

Perform additional
tests for presentation
and disclosure.

Review for
contingent liabilities
and gains.

Review for
subsequent events.

Accumulate
final evidence.

Evaluate results,
and document
quality control
procedures.

Issue auditor's
report.

Communicate with
audit committee
and management.

used as part of planning the audit, during the performance of detailed tests in each cycle as part of substantive procedures, and at the completion of the audit, where they are useful as a final review for material misstatements or financial problems not noted during other testing.

EVALUATION OF GOING-CONCERN ASSUMPTION The Commission to Study the Public's Expectation of Audits (Macdonald Commission) suggested in its Recommendation 10 that management should disclose in the financial statements if "there is significant danger that [the company] may not be able to continue as [a going concern] throughout the foreseeable future."[1] The implication of this and other recommendations is that the auditor should pay particular attention to the going-concern assumption during the audit, especially when performing the final review of the disclosures in the financial statements. CAS 570, Going concern, requires that the auditor evaluate management's assessment of the ability of the entity to continue as a going concern based upon evidence collected throughout the audit. This includes taking into account information obtained after the year end, as described in the subsequent events section of this chapter.

CAS 570 further requires that if the auditor concludes that there is substantial doubt of a going concern, that the auditor inquire of management and consider actions that management is taking, such as having specific plans for refinancing, that would enable the entity to continue in operations. If there is significant uncertainty, then the auditor's report should include an explanatory paragraph following the opinion paragraph to describe that conclusion, and the auditor may be required to further modify the auditor's report, as described in Chapter 20.

Auditing in Action 19-2 describes two businesses which dealt with going-concern issues in significantly different ways—resulting in ongoing business for one, and bankruptcy for the other.

auditing in action 19-2
Tumbling Revenue Troubles

Arpad Takacs had been the owner of Cam Tool & Die Ltd. for about 30 years. His sales dropped from $45 million in 2007 to $28 million in 2008 as a result of the difficulties in the automotive industry, the primary sector that Cam Tool served. The number of employees had gone from a high of 340 to only 90 just prior to closure.

Apparently, losses escalated rapidly after the barely profitable 2008 fiscal year, and the bank was distressed that Takacs had not kept it informed and had not considered other sources of capital. The 2008 financial results were delayed several months, and prospective business plans were not provided to the bank by the deadline it requested. Accordingly, the bank pushed the company into receivership.

Consider another company affected by the recession, Mattamy Homes, that laid off 50 employees in November 2008. The company's sales dropped from $1.5 billion in 2007

to below $1.4 billion in 2008, and Mattamy Homes was facing a real estate market where home sales were continuing to drop drastically. (For example, prices were down 35 percent for the first 11 months of 2008 in the Toronto area, which explains Mattamy's layoffs.)

Mattamy responded by closing one of its offices and pursuing partnerships with other builders to reduce its own investment costs. It continues to innovate and look for ways to reduce costs while maintaining quality, which has allowed the company to survive and do well in the cyclical real estate market. Auditors look at governance strategies to decide whether companies will survive.

Sources: 1. Hamilton, Tyler, "Tooling firm's demise 'big loss'," *Toronto Star*, April 15, 2009, p. B1, B6. 2. Wong, Tony, "Between bricks and a hard place," *Toronto Star*, January 17, 2009, p. B1, B6. 3, Mattamy Homes home page, **www.mattamyhomes.com**; Accessed: March 29, 2012.

---

[1] "50 ways to change our ways," *CAmagazine*, July 1988, p. 42. The July 1988 issue of *CAmagazine* includes several articles dealing with the report of the Commission to Study the Public's Expectations of Audits (Macdonald Commission).

CLIENT REPRESENTATION LETTER CAS 580, Written representations, requires that the auditor obtain a written management representation letter from management to confirm information that has been provided to the auditor during the audit engagement. The auditor may obtain written representations for any audit area. However, there are four specific situations where written client representations play an important role during most audit engagements:

1. CAS 250 requires written representation from management regarding awareness of non-compliance with laws and regulations.
2. CAS 550 indicates the auditor should have written representation with respect to related-party transactions and their disclosure.
3. CAS 560 states that the auditor would normally include, as part of a subsequent events review, written confirmation from management of any verbal representations and a statement that subsequent events have been adjusted or disclosed.
4. CAS 501 requires written representation from the client that outstanding and possible legal claims have been disclosed.

CAS 580 explains that a **written representation** is a written statement by management that documents management's representations or other audit evidence (normally oral information) that has been provided during the audit. The client representation letter is prepared on the client's letterhead, addressed to the public accounting firm, and signed by high-level corporate officials, usually the president and chief financial officer.

There are two purposes of the written representation (also called a management representation letter or client representation letter):

Written representation—a written statement by management that documents management's representations or other audit evidence (normally oral information) that has been provided during the audit.

- To impress upon management its responsibility for the assertions in the financial statements. For example, if the letter of representation includes a reference to pledged assets and contingent liabilities, honest management may be reminded of its unintentional failure to disclose the information adequately. To fulfill this objective, the written representation should be sufficiently detailed to act as a reminder to management.
- To document the responses from management to inquiries about various aspects of the audit. This provides written documentation of client representations in the event of disagreement or a lawsuit between the auditor and the client.

The letter should be dated subsequent to the date of completion of field work and prior to the date of the audit report. To prevent surprises, the auditor should discuss the type of representations with the client during the planning of the audit and as needed throughout the engagement. The representation letter implies that it has originated with the client, but it is common practice for the auditor to prepare the letter and request the client to type it on the company's letterhead and sign it if management is in agreement. Refusal by a client to prepare and sign the letter should probably cause the auditor to consider a qualified opinion or disclaimer of opinion of the auditor's report, as described further in the next chapter.

Many specific matters should be included, when applicable, in a client representation letter. A few of these follow:

- Management's acknowledgment of its responsibility for the fair presentation of the financial statements in conformity with Canadian generally accepted accounting principles or [an appropriate disclosed] basis of accounting.
- Availability of all financial records and related data.
- Completeness and availability of all minutes of meetings of shareholders, directors, and committees of directors.
- Information concerning related-party transactions and related amounts receivable or payable.
- Plans or intentions that may affect the carrying value or classification of assets or liabilities.

• Disclosure of compensating balances or other arrangements involving restrictions on cash balances and disclosure of lines of credit or similar arrangements.

A client written representation is a written statement from a non-independent source and therefore cannot be regarded as reliable evidence. Accordingly, where possible, the auditor should seek evidence to substantiate management's assertions. The letter does provide minimal evidence that management has been asked certain questions, but its primary purpose is psychological and to protect the auditor from potential claims by management that it was unaware of its responsibilities. There are occasions, though, when written representations may be the only source of audit evidence (for example, management intends to launch a new product line).

Other information in the annual report—information that is not a part of published financial statements but is published with them; must be read by auditors for inconsistencies with the financial statements and misleading information.

OTHER INFORMATION IN ANNUAL REPORTS CAS 720 details the auditor's responsibility for **other information in the annual report** of a company, which is published with the financial statements. The primary responsibility is to ensure that the financial statements and auditor's report are accurately reproduced in the annual report. If the company's annual report has not been issued, correcting any misstatement is relatively easy; the auditor can simply ask management to correct the misstatement in the report. On the other hand, if the financial statements and annual report have already been issued when the misstatement is discovered, the auditor must be satisfied that management will take "reasonable steps" to notify users about the misstatement. If the auditor is not so satisfied, notice should be given to the board of directors and consideration should be given to what further action should be taken.

Misstatement of fact—an inconsistency between the financial statements and additional information, such as the annual report.

CAS 720 also requires the auditor to review the additional information to determine if there is an inconsistency between the financial statements and the additional information, termed a **misstatement of fact**. For example, assume that the president's letter in the annual report refers to an increase in earnings per share from $2.60 to $2.93. The auditor is required to compare that information with that in the financial statements to make sure that it corresponds. If an error exists in the financial statements and the statements have not been issued yet, the auditor should have the error corrected or issue a reservation of opinion; if the statements have been issued, the auditor should treat the error as a subsequent discovery of a misstatement (CAS 560) and notify management. If it is the annual report that requires revision, the auditor should notify management.

If the auditor cannot gain satisfaction from management, including the audit committee and the board of directors, the auditor should consider what further action is warranted.

Management discussion and analysis (MD&A)—supplemental analysis and explanation by management that accompanies but does not form part of the financial statements.

MANAGEMENT DISCUSSION AND ANALYSIS In Canada and the United States, securities regulators, recognizing that there is a limit to the amount of information that can be communicated by the financial statements, including the notes, are requiring companies that borrow money from or sell stock to the public to provide a comment from management in the annual report; the comment is supplementary to the financial statements and provides information about management's expectations. Such a report by management supplementary to the financial statements has come to be known as **management discussion and analysis** (MD&A).

The general purpose of MD&A is to describe the performance of the company and the risks within which it operates. To assist boards of directors and senior management, the CICA established the Canadian Performance Reporting Board, which authorizes the CICA to publish guidance documents, issue papers, and research reports. An important guidance document is titled "Management's Discussion and Analysis: Guidance on Preparation and Disclosure." The guidance provides general disclosure principles, a disclosure framework, and a framework for overseeing the reliability and timeliness of disclosure. The intention is that the guidance be used by management, the board of directors, and the audit committee throughout the financial oversight process.

The auditor's role with respect to MD&A arises from the fact that MD&A is included in the annual report and thus falls under the auditor's review pursuant to CAS 720.

③ Evaluate Results and Document Quality Control Procedures

Ultimately, the auditor must decide whether sufficient appropriate audit evidence has been accumulated providing one integrated conclusion that the financial statements are stated in accordance with generally accepted accounting principles. Refer to the figure on the inside cover of this text. Phases 1 through 7 comprise the parts of the audit that must be reviewed in the evaluation of results. The emphasis is satisfactory mitigation of risks identified in the planning stage of the audit. The reviewer will also review the conclusions reached through tests of controls, analytical procedures, and tests of details of balances for each of the functional transaction cycles audited.

SUFFICIENCY OF EVIDENCE A major step in this process is reviewing the audit programs to make sure that all parts have been accurately completed and documented and that risks by audit objectives have been addressed. The reviewer evaluates whether the audit program is adequate considering the problem areas that were discovered as the audit progressed. For example, if misstatements were discovered as part of the tests of sales, the initial plans for the tests of details of accounts receivable balances may have been insufficient.

As an aid in drawing final conclusions about the adequacy of the audit evidence, auditors frequently use **completing the engagement checklists**. These are reminders of aspects of the audit that must not be overlooked. If the auditor concludes that he or she has not obtained sufficient evidence to draw a conclusion about the fairness of the client's representations, there are two choices: (1) additional evidence must be obtained, or (2) the audit report must be modified, as explained further in the next chapter.

Completing the engagement checklist—a reminder to the auditor of aspects of the audit that may have been overlooked.

EVIDENCE SUPPORTING AUDITOR'S OPINION An important part of evaluating whether the financial statements are fairly stated is summarizing the misstatements uncovered in the audit. Whenever the auditor uncovers misstatements that are individually material, entries should be proposed to the client to correct the statements. In addition to material misstatements, often there is discovered a large number of immaterial misstatements that are not adjusted at the time they are found. Most auditors use an **unadjusted misstatement worksheet** or summary of possible adjustments to track known and potential misstatements as shown in Figure 19-3.

Unadjusted misstatement worksheet—a summary of misstatements used to help the auditor assess whether the combined amount is material; also known as a summary of possible adjustments.

The auditor should consider carry-forward misstatements from the previous year in analyzing misstatements and the need for adjustment. For example, if closing inventory was understated by $15,000 in 2011 and overstated by $10,000 in 2012, the effect on income in 2012 would be $25,000. Although the individual misstatements may be immaterial, the combined effect might well be material and require adjustment.

If the auditor believes that there is sufficient evidence but that the financial statements are materially misstated, the auditor again has two choices: the statements must be revised to the auditor's satisfaction, or a modified audit opinion must be issued. To assist with this decision, the auditor will recalculate materiality if there are misstatements that affect the base that was used to calculate materiality (for example, net income).

WORKING PAPER REVIEW AND DOCUMENTATION OF SUPERVISION Regular planning meetings, consultation, and the use of specialists are part of the audit process for most large audit engagements. Records of these planning meetings and their results would be included in the working paper file. Ongoing **working paper review** consists primarily of documenting ongoing supervision that has taken place during the conduct

Working paper review—a review of the completed audit working papers by another member of the audit firm to ensure quality and counteract bias.

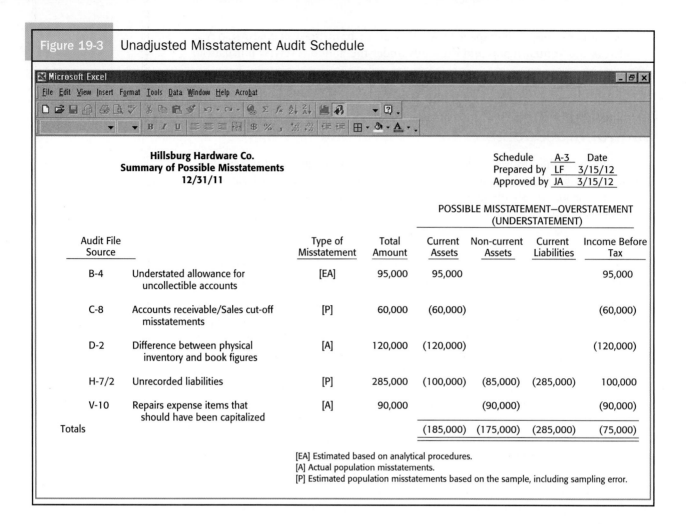

Figure 19-3   Unadjusted Misstatement Audit Schedule

Hillsburg Hardware Co.
Summary of Possible Misstatements
12/31/11

Schedule ___A-3___ Date
Prepared by ___LF___ 3/15/12
Approved by ___JA___ 3/15/12

Audit File Source		Type of Misstatement	Total Amount	POSSIBLE MISSTATEMENT—OVERSTATEMENT (UNDERSTATEMENT)			
				Current Assets	Non-current Assets	Current Liabilities	Income Before Tax
B-4	Understated allowance for uncollectible accounts	[EA]	95,000	95,000			95,000
C-8	Accounts receivable/Sales cut-off misstatements	[P]	60,000	(60,000)			(60,000)
D-2	Difference between physical inventory and book figures	[A]	120,000	(120,000)			(120,000)
H-7/2	Unrecorded liabilities	[P]	285,000	(100,000)	(85,000)	(285,000)	100,000
V-10	Repairs expense items that should have been capitalized	[A]	90,000		(90,000)		(90,000)
Totals				(185,000)	(175,000)	(285,000)	(75,000)

[EA] Estimated based on analytical procedures.
[A] Actual population misstatements.
[P] Estimated population misstatements based on the sample, including sampling error.

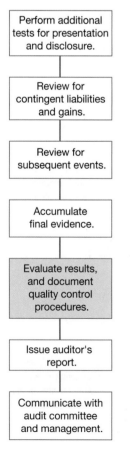

Perform additional tests for presentation and disclosure.

Review for contingent liabilities and gains.

Review for subsequent events.

Accumulate final evidence.

Evaluate results, and document quality control procedures.

Issue auditor's report.

Communicate with audit committee and management.

of the engagement by means of independent examination of the working papers by another member of the audit firm. There are three main reasons why it is essential that the working papers be thoroughly reviewed by another member of the audit firm at the completion of the audit:

• To evaluate the performance of inexperienced personnel.
• To make sure that the audit meets the public accounting firm's standard of performance.
• To counteract the bias that frequently enters into the auditor's judgment.

Except for a final independent review, which is discussed shortly, the review of the working papers should be conducted by someone who is knowledgeable about the client and the unique circumstances in the audit. Therefore, the initial review of the working papers prepared by any given auditor is normally done by the auditor's immediate supervisor. For example, the least experienced auditor's work is ordinarily reviewed by the audit senior; the senior's immediate supervisor, who is normally a supervisor or manager, reviews the senior's work and also reviews less thoroughly the papers of the inexperienced auditor.

When several staff are working together at an engagement, team review by means of interview is used. The senior meets with staff on a daily basis, discusses the nature of findings, and ensures that these are appropriately recorded in the electronic working papers before the actual client documents are returned to the client. Finally, the partner assigned to the audit must review all working papers, but the partner reviews those prepared by the supervisor or manager more thoroughly than the others. Except for the final independent review, most of the working paper review is done as each segment of the audit is completed.

INDEPENDENT REVIEW At the completion of larger audits, an **independent review** of the financial statements and the entire set of working papers is conducted by a completely independent reviewer who has not participated in the engagement. The audit team must be able to justify the evidence they have accumulated and the conclusions they have reached on the basis of the unique circumstances of the engagement. This type of review may also include a second independent review if the engagement is considered high risk by the audit firm.

Independent review—a review of the financial statements and the entire set of working papers by a completely independent reviewer to whom the audit team must justify the evidence accumulated and the conclusions reached.

ISSUE INDEPENDENT AUDITOR'S REPORT After completion of the audit and approval of the financial statements by the Board of Directors (or equivalent), the auditor issues the independent auditor's report (also known as the auditor's report). Auditor reporting is discussed in Chapter 20.

4 Auditor Communications and Subsequent Facts

Communicate with the Audit Committee and Management

CAS As part of the planning process, the auditor would have communicated the planned scope and timing of the audit with those charged with the governance of the entity. CAS 260 requires that the auditor examine the organizational structure of the entity to determine that reporting is being done to the appropriate person or group. In most large organizations, this will be the audit committee but will also include one or more individuals in executive management.

After the audit is completed, there are several potential communications from the auditor to client personnel. These would include significant findings from the audit, which could include misstatements, potential fraud, or difficulties encountered during the audit.

COMMUNICATE MISSTATEMENTS AND ILLEGAL ACTS CAS 260.12 requires that the auditor ensure that the appropriate level of management is informed of material weaknesses in the design, implementation, or operating effectiveness of internal control. CAS 450 requires that the auditor communicate all except clearly trivial misstatements and ask management to correct them. In addition, the auditor must ensure that the audit committee or similarly designated group (e.g., board of directors or board of trustees) is informed of all significant misstatements, whether or not they are adjusted. Misstatements include intentional (fraud or other irregularities) and unintentional (errors) misstatements. The audit committee can be informed by either the auditor or management, and this should be done on a timely basis.

Illegal acts are violations of laws or government regulations. CAS 250 requires the auditor to understand the regulatory environment in which the entity operates so that any observed illegal or possibly illegal acts, such as non-compliance with waste disposal regulations, can be communicated to the audit committee or equivalent group on a timely basis. The audit committee may also expect the auditor to communicate such matters as unusual actions that increase the risk of loss to the company; actions that could cause serious embarrassment to the entity, such as breaches of the company's code of conduct; significant transactions that appear to be inconsistent with the ordinary course of business; and other matters. The audit committee's wishes should be discussed and clarified with the audit committee prior to the auditor's start of the audit fieldwork.

COMMUNICATE REPORTABLE INTERNAL CONTROL CONDITIONS As discussed in Chapter 5, CAS 240 includes misstatements that indicate significant deficiencies in the design or operation of internal control in its definition of significant misstatements that must be reported to the audit committee. Although the auditor has no duty to report less significant internal control weaknesses identified during the audit to the client, he or she commonly does so as a client service. In addition, some auditors provide suggestions for improvements in internal control (called a "management letter,"

concept check

C19-6 What method does the auditor use to determine whether sufficient appropriate audit evidence has been collected?

C19-7 What is the purpose of independent review of the working papers?

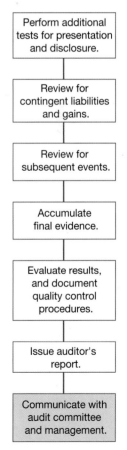

Perform additional tests for presentation and disclosure.

Review for contingent liabilities and gains.

Review for subsequent events.

Accumulate final evidence.

Evaluate results, and document quality control procedures.

Issue auditor's report.

Communicate with audit committee and management.

discussed below). In larger companies, communication of both reportable internal control conditions and other improvements are made to the audit committee, and in smaller companies, to the owners or senior management. The nature and form of this communication were discussed in Chapter 9.

OTHER COMMUNICATION WITH AUDIT COMMITTEE Like all communications with the audit committee (or alternative individuals responsible for the governance of the entity), the purpose of the following other communication is to keep the committee informed of auditing issues and findings that will assist it in performing its supervisory role for financial statements:

- The auditor's responsibilities under generally accepted auditing standards, including responsibility for understanding and evaluating internal control and the concept of reasonable rather than absolute assurance.
- Confirmation of the auditor's independence, including a breakdown (billed between audit and other services) of the fees, and a disclosure of any relationships between the auditor and the client (or its related entities or directors, officers, or employees).
- Planning of the current audit, including such matters as the general approach, areas of perceived high risk, materiality and risk levels selected, planned reliance on other auditors (including the internal audit department), and timing of the audit.
- The significant accounting principles and policies selected and applied to the financial statements, the existence of acceptable alternatives, and the acceptability of those selected by management.
- Management's judgments and estimates of sensitive accounting-related issues and the auditor's conclusions about the reasonableness of them.
- Disagreements with management about the scope of the audit, applicability of accounting principles under the selected financial reporting framework, and wording of the auditor's report, whether or not satisfactorily resolved.
- Difficulties encountered in performing the audit, such as lack of availability of client personnel, failure to obtain necessary information, and an unreasonable timetable in which to complete the audit.
- Any unresolved matters arising from review of the entire annual report and identification of misstatements in reproducing the financial statements or the auditor's report or of inconsistencies between the statements and other information in the annual report.
- The auditor's opinions about the subjects of any consultations with other accountants about accounting or auditing matters, if the auditor becomes aware of these consultations.
- Any major issues discussed with management in connection with the appointment of the auditor, including those related to the application of accounting principles, auditing standards, and fees.

Communication with the audit committee normally takes place more than once during each audit and can be oral, written, or both, although certain communications, such as the independence letter and possible material misstatements, must be in writing. For example, issues dealing with the auditor's responsibilities and significant accounting policies are usually discussed early in the audit, preferably during the planning phase. Disagreements with management and difficulties encountered in performing the audit would be communicated after the audit is completed or earlier if the problems hinder the auditor's ability to complete the audit. The most important matters are communicated in writing to minimize misunderstanding and to provide documentation in the event of subsequent disagreement.

MANAGEMENT LETTERS The purpose of a management letter (letter of recommendation) is to inform the client of the public accountant's recommendations for improving the client's business. The recommendations focus on suggestions for more efficient operations. The combination of the auditor's experience in various businesses and a thorough understanding gained in conducting the audit place the auditor in a unique position to provide management with assistance.

A management letter is different from the required communication of material weaknesses in internal control of CAS 260. The latter is required whenever there are significant internal control weaknesses. A management letter is optional and is intended to help the client operate its business more effectively. Auditors write management letters for two reasons: (1) to encourage a better relationship between the public accounting firm and management and (2) to suggest additional tax and management advisory services that the public accounting firm can provide.

There is no standard format or approach for writing management letters. Each letter should be developed to meet the style of the auditor and the needs of the client, consistent with the public accounting firm's concept of management letters. It should be noted that many auditors combine the management letter with the required communication on internal control-related matters.

concept check

C19-8 List two examples of information that must be communicated by the auditor to the audit committee.

C19-9 Why would an auditor submit a management letter to the client?

Summary

1. *Why does the auditor conduct final evidence gathering specific to presentation and disclosure audit objectives?* This is done (1) to collect any needed additional evidence pertaining to these assertions and (2) to evaluate the overall presentation of the financial statements and their notes for completeness, understandability, and consistency with prior years.

   How does the auditor search for contingent liabilities? Toward the end of the engagement, it is called a "review" for contingent liabilities, since each cycle has procedures that are intended to search for contingent liabilities (e.g., review of bank confirmations). At this stage, the auditor conducts final inquiries with management, reviews the working papers for comments about tax assessments, directors' and shareholders' meetings, and legal expenses, and ensures that legal documents such as contracts have been examined. Legal letters are reviewed for the responses received.

   What is the purpose of obtaining a confirmation from the client's law firms? These confirmations are used to evaluate known litigation or other claims against clients for potential contingent liabilities.

   Why must these "legal letters" be in a specified format? In order to protect their client's confidentiality, lawyers indicate whether they agree or disagree with the information that is provided by the client, in a format that has been approved by Bar Associations and the CICA.

   Describe examples of procedures conducted during a review for subsequent events. Testing is done in each transaction cycle (e.g., during cut off testing of documents). Other procedures include procedures listed with contingent liabilities above. In addition, the auditor reviews internal financial statements or budgets completed after the year end and reviews minutes and records prepared after the balance sheet date.

2. *Provide examples of work completed as part of the final evidence-gathering process.* The auditor will calculate final analytical procedures and again evaluate the going-concern assumption. The client will be asked to prepare and sign a representation letter. The auditor will review information that management plans to include in the annual report and the management discussion and analysis.

3. *What does the auditor do to evaluate the adequacy of accumulated evidence?* The partner and the engagement review team, in consultation with the audit team, will review the quality and sufficiency of evidence for all cycles, assertions, and end-of-engagement processes in the context of audit risk and the client risk profile.

   How are quality control procedures incorporated into this final risk response phase of the audit? In addition to the above review, an independent review or a standards department review helps to ensure that the audit is conducted to high standards.

4. *What communications is the auditor required to send after the completion of the audit?* The following communications are sent throughout the engagement (or on a timely basis after the engagement is completed): any reportable internal controls that could lead to material weaknesses, material misstatements, management letter, and independence letter. In addition, any other matters that need to be communicated, such as suspicion of fraud or illegal acts, would also be sent.

MyAccountingLab

Make the grade with MyAccountingLab: The questions, exercises, and problems marked in orange can be found on MyAccountingLab. You can practise them as often as you want, and most feature step-by-step guided instructions to help you find the right answer.

Review Questions

19-1 ❶ Identify and describe the four presentation and disclosure audit objectives.

19-2 ❶ Describe the purpose of a financial statement disclosure checklist and explain how it helps the auditor determine if there is sufficient appropriate evidence for each of the presentation and disclosure objectives.

19-3 ❶ Distinguish between a contingent liability and an actual liability, and give three examples of each.

19-4 ❶ In the audit of James Mobley Ltd., you are concerned about the possibility of contingent liabilities resulting from income tax disputes. Discuss the procedures you could use for an extensive investigation in this area.

19-5 ❶ Explain why the analysis of legal expense is an essential part of every audit engagement.

19-6 ❶ Describe the action that an auditor should take if a law firm refuses to provide information that is within its jurisdiction and may directly affect the fair presentation of the financial statements.

19-7 ❶ Distinguish between subsequent events requiring adjustment and those requiring disclosure. Give two examples of each type.

19-8 ❶ Explain why an auditor would be interested in a client's future commitments to purchase raw materials at a fixed price.

19-9 ❶ What major considerations should the auditor take into account in determining how extensive the review of subsequent events should be?

19-10 ❶ ❷ Compare and contrast the accumulation of audit evidence and the evaluation of the adequacy of the disclosures in the financial statements. Give two examples in which adequate disclosure could depend heavily on the accumulation of evidence and two others in which audit evidence does not normally affect the adequacy of the disclosure significantly.

19-11 ❷ Explain the meaning of the following: The auditor should actively evaluate whether there is substantial doubt about the client's ability to continue as a going concern.

19-12 ❷ Distinguish between a management representation letter and a management letter, and state the primary purpose of each. List some items that might be included in each letter.

19-13 ❷ What is meant by "reading other financial information" in annual reports? Give an example of the type of information that the auditor would be examining.

19-14 ❷ Explain why you think securities regulators in certain jurisdictions require public companies to provide MD&A in their annual reports.

19-15 ❸ Distinguish between regular working-paper review and independent review, and state the purpose of each. Give two examples of important potential findings in each of these two types of review.

19-16 ❹ Describe matters that the auditor must communicate to audit committees of public companies.

Discussion Questions and Problems

19-17 ❶ Kathy Choi, a public accountant, has completed the audit of notes payable and other liabilities for Valley River Electrical Services Ltd. and now plans to audit contingent liabilities and commitments.

REQUIRED

a. Distinguish between contingent liabilities and commitments, and explain why both are important in an audit.

b. Describe how Kathy's testing in Phases 1 to 6 of the audit of notes payable might help her obtain

evidence about the presentation and disclosure audit objectives.

c. Identify three useful audit procedures for uncovering contingent liabilities that Kathy would likely perform in the normal conduct of the audit, even if she had no responsibility for uncovering contingencies.

d. Identify three other procedures Kathy would likely perform specifically for the purpose of identifying undisclosed contingencies.

19-18 ❶ In an examination of Marco Corporation as of December 31, 2012, the following situations exist. No related entries have been made in the accounting records.

1. Marco Corporation has guaranteed the payment of interest on the 10-year, first-mortgage bonds of Chen Corp., an affiliate. Outstanding bonds of Chen Corp. amount to $150,000 with interest payable at 8 percent per annum, due June 1 and December 1 each year. The bonds were issued by Chen on December 31, 2010, and all interest payments have been met by that

company with the exception of the payment due December 1, 2012. Marco Corporation states that it will pay the defaulted interest to the bondholders on January 15, 2013.

2. During the year 2012, Marco Corporation was named as a defendant in a suit by Dalton Inc. for damages for breach of contract. A decision adverse to Marco Corporation was rendered, and Dalton Inc. was awarded $40,000 in damages. At the time of the audit, the case was under appeal to a higher court.

3. On December 23, 2012, Marco Corporation declared a common share dividend of 1,000 shares with a stated value of $100,000, payable February 2, 2013, to the common shareholders of record on December 30, 2012.

REQUIRED

a. Describe the audit procedures that you would use to learn about each of the above situations.

b. Describe the nature of the adjusting entries or disclosure, if any, that you would require for each of these situations. (Adapted from AICPA)

19-19 ❶ In analyzing legal expense for Boastman Bottle Company, Bart Little, a public accountant, observes that the company has paid legal fees to three different law firms during the current year. In accordance with his accounting firm's normal operating practice, Bart requests standard confirmation letters as of the balance sheet date from each of the three law firms.

On the last day of fieldwork, Bart notes that one of the confirmations has not yet been received. The confirmation from the second law firm contains a statement to the effect that the law firm deals exclusively in registering patents and refuses to comment on any lawsuits or other legal affairs of the client. The confirmation letter from the third law firm states that there is an outstanding unpaid bill due from the client and recognizes the existence of a potentially material lawsuit against the client but refuses to comment further to protect the legal rights of the client.

REQUIRED

a. Evaluate Bart's approach to requesting the confirmations and his follow-up on the responses.
b. What should Bart do about each of the confirmations?

19-20 ❷ Ruben Chavez, a public accountant, has prepared a management representation letter for the president and controller to sign. It contains references to the following items:

1. Inventory is fairly stated at the lower of cost or net realizable value and includes no obsolete items.
2. All actual and contingent liabilities are properly included in the statements.
3. All subsequent events of relevance to the financial statements have been disclosed.

REQUIRED

a. Why is it desirable to have a letter of representation from the client concerning the above matters when the audit evidence accumulated during the course of the engagement is meant to verify the same information?
b. To what extent is the letter of representation useful as audit evidence? Explain.
c. List several other types of information commonly included in a letter of representation.

19-21 ❷ Betty Ann Jarrett, a public accountant, was reading the annual report of Watgold Ltd. and noticed that the president's report contradicted several items in the audited financial statements included in the report.

REQUIRED

What are Betty Ann's responsibilities in this instance?

19-22 ❸ Melanie Adams is a public accountant in a medium-sized public accounting firm who takes an active part in the conduct of every audit she supervises. She follows the practice of reviewing all working papers of subordinates as soon as it is convenient, rather than waiting until the end of the audit.

When the audit is nearly finished, Melanie reviews the working papers again to make sure she has not missed anything significant. Since she makes most of the major decisions on the audit, there is rarely anything that requires further investigation. When she completes the review, she prepares a draft of the financial statements, gets them approved by management, and has them assembled in her firm's office. No other public accountant reviews the working papers because Melanie is responsible for signing the auditor's reports.

REQUIRED

a. Evaluate the practice of reviewing the working papers of subordinates on a continuing basis rather than when the audit is completed.
b. Is it acceptable for Melanie to prepare the financial statements rather than have the client assume that responsibility?
c. Evaluate the practice of not having a review of the working papers by another public accountant in the firm.

19-23 ④ In a letter to the audit committee of Cline Wholesale Company, Jerry Schwartz, a public accountant, informed it of weaknesses in the control of inventory. In a separate letter to senior management, he elaborated on how the weaknesses could result in a significant misstatement of inventory caused by the failure to recognize the existence of obsolete items. In addition, Jerry made specific recommendations in the management letter on how to improve internal control and save clerical time by installing a computer system for the company's perpetual records. Management accepted the recommendations and installed the system under Jerry's direction. For several months, the system worked beautifully, but unforeseen problems developed when a master file was erased. The cost of reproducing and processing the inventory records to correct the error was significant, and management decided to scrap the entire project. The company sued Jerry for failure to use adequate professional judgment in making the recommendations.

REQUIRED

a. What is Jerry's legal and professional responsibility in the issuance of management letters?

b. Discuss the major considerations that will determine whether he is liable in this situation.

c. Did Jerry abide by the Professional Rules of Conduct? Explain your reasoning.

Professional Judgment Problem

19-24 ① You are a public accountant in the public accounting firm of Lind and Hemming. One of your larger clients is Yukon Corp., a company incorporated under the Canada Business Corporations Act, which has a December 31 year end. Yukon's 2011 audit was completed in January 2012; the auditor's report was dated January 28, 2012.

It is now August 2012 and professional staff from your office are working at Yukon doing interim work on the December 31, 2012 audit. Yesterday, the senior in charge of the audit gave you a memo dated August 4, 2012, revealing that the staff have discovered that several large blocks of inventory were materially overpriced at December 31, 2011, and have since been written down to reflect their true value.

You have just finished reviewing again the 2011 working papers and have determined that the error was a sampling error; your firm does not appear to have been negligent.

REQUIRED

What action would you take and why? Support your answer.

Case

19-25 ① The controller of Kim Engineering Ltd. (KEL) sent a legal representation letter to KEL's law firm at the request of the company's auditors. The controller told the auditors that there are no lawsuits presently ongoing. The lawyers replied to the letter, agreeing that there were no outstanding or possible claims of which they have knowledge, or for which their advice has been sought.

However, the controller was not aware that the board of directors had sought legal advice from a second law firm regarding a harassment lawsuit. Due to the nature of the matter, the board of directors did not want anyone to know about the possible claim. There are no records outside of the president's office, but the auditor noticed it when reviewing the minutes of the board of directors' meetings. The auditor therefore requested that a letter be sent to the second law firm as well.

One of the members of the board is Yung, who started the company 20 years ago, but is now retired from any duties other than being a director. When the company first started, Yung performed almost all of the duties himself, but over the years, his duties have been assigned to other people. For example, only the controller or the president of the company can sign cheques on behalf of the company, and the controller's authority is limited to $15,000. Any cheque request must be supported by an authorized purchase requisition, and any request over $15,000 must be authorized by the president. The accounting manager does all of the bank reconciliations herself, but her assistant enters the journal entries according to the accounting manager's instructions.

REQUIRED

a. Indicate what the effect would be on the audit of the auditor receives no response from the second law firm.

b. If the second law firm replies and provides information to the auditor, indicate how the auditor should treat this information for financial statement purposes.

c. Provide an assessment of control risk (high, medium or low) and support your decision with four points.

(Extract from AU1 CGA-Canada Examinations developed by the Certified General Accountants Association of Canada © 2011 CGA-Canada. Reproduced with permission. All rights reserved.)

Ongoing Small Business Case: Subsequent Events at CondoCleaners.com

19-26 ① ② CondoCleaners.com is a typically well-run small business. There are no lawsuits, and Jim has never used a lawyer. He set up the company himself and maintains the share records, board of directors minutes and shareholder minutes as well. There were no unusual transactions either before or after the year end audit that require disclosure.

REQUIRED

Describe your responsibilities and audit procedures with respect to subsequent events at CondoCleaners.com, including those with respect to contingent liabilities.

20 Auditor reporting

Reports are essential to the audit and other attestation processes because they provide information about what is being attested to, what the public accountant did, and the conclusions reached based upon sufficient and appropriate evidence. Standard wording and rules about the types of reports guide their preparation. Accountants as users of these reports need to understand their meaning, while public accountants consider what type of report is available when.

LEARNING OBJECTIVES

1 State the requirements for a standard unqualified audit report. Describe the component parts and their significance. State the relevance of the audit report date and when dual dating might occur.

2 Describe how the standard audit report is changed to provide additional information to users. Select the appropriate format to match the nature of the information to be communicated, including disclosure of contingencies and doubts about the ability of the entity to continue as a going concern.

3 Describe the difference between an adverse opinion and a disclaimer of opinion. Explain how materiality is related to the wording changes used for these types of non-standard audit reports.

STANDARDS REFERENCED IN THIS CHAPTER

CICA Standards

CAS 560 – Subsequent events

CAS 600 – Special considerations: audits of group financial statements

CAS 620 – Using the work of an auditor's expert

CAS 700 – Forming an opinion and reporting on financial statements

CAS 705 – Modifications to the opinion in the independent auditor's report

CAS 706 – Emphasis of matter paragraphs and other matter(s) paragraphs in the independent auditor's report

CAS 710 – Comparative information: corresponding figures and comparative financial statements

Section 7110 – Auditor involvement with offering documents of public and private entities

Section 7115 – Auditor involvement with offering documents of public and private entities: current legislative and regulatory requirements

AuG – 48 – Legislative requirements to report on the consistent application of accounting principles in the applicable financial reporting framework

A Qualified Audit Report—Problems with Management Integrity

Halvorson & Co., public accountants, had been the auditors of Fine Furniture Inc. (FFI) for many years. Halvorson was a top-tier accounting firm with national offices across the country. It was proud of the quality of its staff and the type of service it provided to its clients. FFI was a medium-sized client that had been with the firm for over 20 years, a great accomplishment given the volatility of the furniture industry, and the local partners knew the owners well. Recently, Al Trent, one of the firm's senior qualified accountants, had joined Fine Furniture Inc. as the chief financial officer. Al was well liked and had been with Halvorson since he left university.

Bruce Marks, the partner in charge of the FFI audit, was livid as Steve Smith, a newly hired qualified accountant, left the partner's office with a dejected look on his face. Samantha, one of the audit seniors in the office, spoke to Bruce later in the day after he had calmed down. Bruce was steaming about a situation that had arisen the previous day. This year, Fine Furniture Inc. was going to receive a qualified independent auditor's report with respect to inventory. Bruce used phrases like "unable to determine the quantity of inventory on hand at year end" and "potential overstatement of expenses" as he explained what was going to happen to the audit report. Bruce was particularly angry because he was now faced with having to report Al Trent to the provincial institute of chartered accountants for unethical behaviour and having to discipline Steve Smith due to the events at FFI. He exclaimed that both of these highly qualified and competent men should have known better.

Steve had gone first to the east-end location of FFI to count inventory. The furniture inventory was well organized and labelled, and it had taken him only an hour to complete his test counts and gather necessary documentation. The inventory count had gone well. Al had shown him around and then offered to take Steve to lunch and for a round of golf. Steve knew Al only by reputation and had felt this was a good way to get to know the senior financial officer at the company while also getting in a round of golf.

About five hours later, Steve finally made it to the west-end location of FFI. Unfortunately, here, inventory was not that well organized. It was simply a storage location operated by part-time staff who looked particularly harried. The location was very busy, with shipments constantly leaving and arriving. It was almost as if the staff were not aware there was an inventory count that afternoon. Even though Steve was tired, he managed to jot down very specific details of inventory, including serial numbers. At that point he realized several of the items had the same serial numbers as those he had seen in the east-end location. It was like being hit with a tonne of bricks.

Without communicating his concerns to the FFI staff, Steve methodically went through the contents of the warehouse, staying late into the evening. Of the items he had counted at the east-end location, fully two-thirds were now here at the west end. Steve grimaced as he realized what Al had done while filling up his car with gasoline that afternoon. Al had purchased several

(continued)

food items at the gas bar and had asked the attendant to just "include it with the gas" as he paid for the bill with what looked like a company credit card. It must be routine if he did it even in Steve's presence—not material transactions, but clearly an indication of Al's ethics with respect to business practices.

Steve went home and wrote up what had happened that day, knowing that it was partially his own behaviour that had given FFI the opportunity to ship inventory from the east end to the west end. If he had not noted down serial numbers, the attempt to inflate inventory values would not have been detected.

IMPORTANCE TO AUDITORS

Users of financial statements rely on the auditor's report to provide assurance on the company's financial statements. Auditors assume that management is honest and that unethical behaviour (such as moving inventory from one location to another) will not be pursued. When such actions are detected, then the auditor must rethink the risks associated with the engagement.

WHAT DO YOU THINK?

1. What if Steve had not detected FFI's attempt to inflate inventory? Which users would have been affected and how?
2. Based upon the case facts above, what other accounts should the auditor further investigate before finalizing the audit report?

ISSUANCE of the auditor's report is part of the final phase in the risk-based audit process. Careful review of the working papers (including accumulated evidence) provides the auditor with the basis for the audit opinion. In most cases, the auditor is able to provide sufficient evidence to state that the financial statements present fairly the financial position of the company. In some cases, the evidence is unavailable, or the auditor disagrees with management about what has been presented in the financial statements. This chapter presents ways that the auditor provides a standard audit opinion or explains disagreements. We begin by describing the content of that standard auditor's report.

① The Standard Independent Auditor's Report

Standard Unqualified Independent Auditor's Report

The most common type of audit report is the **standard unqualified independent auditor's report**. It is also often referred to as the auditor's standard report. It is used when all auditing conditions have been met, no significant misstatements have been discovered and left uncorrected, and the auditor believes that the financial statements are fairly stated in accordance with the applicable financial reporting framework. The specific conditions required to issue this report are as follows:

1. An audit engagement has been undertaken to express an opinion on financial statements.
2. Generally accepted auditing standards (GAAS) have been followed by the auditor in all respects on the engagement.
3. Sufficient appropriate audit evidence has been accumulated, and the auditor has conducted the engagement in a manner that concludes that the examination standards have been met.
4. The financial statements, which include the balance sheet, the income statement, the statement of retained earnings, the cash flow statement, and the notes to the financial statements, are fairly presented in accordance with an appropriate applicable financial reporting framework.
5. There are no circumstances which, in the opinion of the auditor, would require modifying the wording of the report or adding an additional explanatory paragraph.

When these conditions are met, the standard unqualified auditor's report on the financial statements, as shown in Figure 20-1 (and also in Figure 20-5), is issued. Different auditors may vary the wording of the standard report slightly, but the meaning will be the same.

CAS **PARTS OF STANDARD UNQUALIFIED AUDITOR'S REPORT** Each standard unqualified auditor's report includes several distinct parts. These parts are labelled in bold letters in Figure 20-1.

1. *Report title.* CAS 700 par. 21 states that the auditor's report should have a title that clearly explains its purpose. CAS 700 emphasizes that the auditor is independent, so the title requires reference to the auditor's independence. This also distinguishes the report from other types of audit reports, such as those written by internal auditors.
2. *Addressee.* CAS 700 par. 22 and A16 require that the addressee be the parties who have hired the auditors, or as required by law in the local jurisdiction. Normally, the addressees are the shareholders, since it is usually they who appoint the auditor.
3. *Introductory statement.* The first part of the auditor's report does two things. First, it makes the simple statement that the public accounting firm has done an audit. (Later sections clarify what is meant by an audit.)
   Second, it lists the financial statements that were audited, including the statement of financial position (or balance sheet) date and the period for the (comprehensive) income statement, the statement of changes in equity (retained earnings), and the statement of cash flows and other explanatory information, which would include the notes to the financial statements. Private companies would have the audit report cover only one year (the current year under audit), while public companies such as Hillsburg Hardware Ltd. are required to have two years covered by the audit report.
4. *Management responsibility.* Management is responsible for developing fair financial statements using the financial reporting framework that they have selected (such as ASPE) or that is required for the company (most public companies require IFRS). Then, the paragraph explains that management is also responsible

Figure 20-1   Components of the Standard Auditor's Report

	Report section title
INDEPENDENT AUDITOR'S REPORT	**1. Report Title**
To the Shareholders of Hillsburg Hardware Ltd.	**2. Addressee**
We have audited the accompanying financial statements of Hillsburg Hardware Limited, which comprise the statements of financial position as at December 31, 2011 and December 31, 2010, and the statement of comprehensive income, statement of changes in equity, and statement of cash flows for the years then ended, and a summary of significant accounting policies and other explanatory information.	**3. Introductory statement**
Management's Responsibility for the Financial Statements	**4. Management responsibility**
Management is responsible for the preparation and fair presentation of these financial statements in accordance with International Financial Reporting Standards and for such internal control as management determines is necessary to enable the preparation of financial statements that are free from material misstatement, whether due to fraud or error.	
Auditor's Responsibility	**5. Auditor responsibility**
Our responsibility is to express an opinion on these financial statements based on our audits.	
We conducted our audits in accordance with Canadian generally accepted auditing standards. Those standards require that we comply with ethical requirements and plan and perform the audit to obtain reasonable assurance about whether the financial statements are free from material misstatement. An audit involves performing procedures to obtain audit evidence about the amounts and disclosures in the financial statements. The procedures selected depend on the auditor's judgment, including the assessment of the risks of material misstatement of the financial statements, whether due to fraud or error. In making those risk assessments, the auditor considers internal control relevant to the entity's preparation and fair presentation of the financial statements in order to design audit procedures that are appropriate in the circumstances, but not for the purpose of expressing an opinion on the effectiveness of the entity's internal control. An audit also includes evaluating the appropriateness of accounting policies used and the reasonableness of accounting estimates made by management, as well as evaluating the overall presentation of the financial statements.	
We believe that the audit evidence we have obtained is sufficient and appropriate to provide a basis for our audit opinion.	
Opinion	**6. Opinion paragraph**
In our opinion, the financial statements present fairly, in all material respects, the financial position of Hillsburg Hardware Limited as at December 31, 2011 and December 31, 2010, its financial performance and its cash flows for the years then ended in accordance with International Financial Reporting Standards.	
[signature of] Boritz, Kao, Kadous & Co., LLP	**7. Auditor's signature**
March 1, 2012	**8. Date of the auditor's report**
444 Transom Street Halifax, Nova Scotia B3M 3JP	**9. Auditor's address**

for the internal controls that prevent material misstatements either due to fraud or error. Review this paragraph carefully—you will see that it corresponds clearly to what we have discussed as the responsibility of management in previous chapters of this text.

5. *Auditor responsibility.* The auditor responsibility paragraph starts with a summary statement that explains the purpose of the audit—the expression of an opinion on the financial statements described in the first sentence. Then, further detail is provided, stating that the auditor followed generally accepted auditing standards during the performance of the audit. It tells the reader what those standards comprise: The audit is designed to obtain reasonable assurance whether the statements are free of material misstatement. The inclusion of the word "material" conveys the meaning that auditors search for significant misstatements, not minor errors that do not affect users' decisions. The use of the term "reasonable assurance" is intended to indicate that an audit cannot be expected to completely eliminate the possibility that a material error or fraud or other irregularity will exist in the financial

statements. In other words, an audit provides a high level of assurance, but not a guarantee.

The remainder briefly describes important aspects of what an audit does and does not include. It starts with the basis of the audit—that is, the auditor's use of professional judgment in the context of a risk assessment (considering risks of error or fraud) to select audit procedures for the conduct of the audit. It includes assessing internal controls over financial systems that affect the financial statements but does not provide an opinion over those controls (as internal controls can and do change over time).

While the management responsibility paragraph of the report states that management is responsible for the preparation and content of the financial statements, this paragraph explains how the auditor evaluates what management has done. It states that the auditor has the responsibility to evaluate the appropriateness of the accounting policies that are used and of the estimates made, as well as of the overall presentation of those financial statements. The auditor cannot simply accept management's representations about appropriateness. The final sentence refers to the quality of the evidence collected: sufficient and appropriate—that is, enough high-quality evidence has been obtained to allow the auditor to provide an opinion on the financial statements.

6. *Opinion paragraph.* The final paragraph in the standard auditor's report states the auditor's conclusions based on the results of the audit. This part of the auditor's report is so important that often the entire report is referred to as simply the auditor's opinion. The opinion paragraph is stated as an opinion, rather than as a statement of absolute fact or as a guarantee. The intent is to indicate that the conclusions are based on professional judgment. The phrase "in our opinion" indicates that there may be some information risk associated with the financial statements, even though the statements have been audited. Note that term "financial performance" rather than "results of operations" is used when describing the activity of the entity for the period under audit.

The opinion paragraph is directly related to the generally accepted auditing reporting standards described in Figure 20-4. The auditor is required to state an opinion about the financial statements taken as a whole, including a conclusion about whether the company followed an appropriate applicable financial reporting framework, such as ASPE or IFRS.

One of the most controversial parts of the auditor's report is the meaning of the term "presents fairly." The auditor means that the financial statements are fairly presented in accordance with the financial reporting framework described in the opinion paragraph. A layperson may mistake "presents fairly" to mean that the values in the financial statements represent the realizable values of the assets. It is important that lay people understand the auditor's message. The auditor cannot and does not check every transaction.

7. *(Signature) Name of public accounting firm.* The name identifies the public accounting firm or practitioner who has performed the audit. Typically, the firm's name is used since the entire firm has the legal and professional responsibility to make certain the quality of the audit meets professional standards as illustrated in Figure 20-1. CAS 700.A37 states that either the firm name or the personal name (or both) can be used.

CAS 8. *Date of the auditor's report.* CAS 700 par. 41(b) states that the audit report can be dated only after those with sufficient responsibility at the entity have taken responsibility for the financial statements. For most organizations this means that the board of directors must approve the financial statements. For smaller organizations it may be a primary shareholder, such as an owner/operator, who approves the financial statements.

This date is important to users because it indicates the last day of the auditor's responsibility for the review of significant events that occurred after the date of the financial statements. For example, if the balance sheet is dated December 31,

2011, and the audit report is dated March 1, 2012, the implication is that the auditor has searched for material, unrecorded transactions, and events that occurred up to March 1, 2012, that may have had an effect on the 2011 statements.

CAS

Dual Dating CAS 560, Subsequent Events, discusses, among other things, double dating of the auditor's report. Double dating is done when a material event occurs after the date of the auditor's report and before the date the report is issued. The preference is for the auditor to do additional field work based upon the revised, reapproved financial statements so that the audit report applies to the whole set of financial statements (CAS 560.11). However, if it is possible for the auditor to conduct work separately for the material event, the auditor may double date the report as follows:

> March 1, 2012
> except for Note 17 which is
> as of April 2, 2012

If the effect of the event were so material as to change the 2011 financial statements significantly, the auditor would probably extend the audit for the financial statements as a whole and date the report with the revised date as approved by the board. In the example provided, the new date of the auditor's report would be April 2, 2012.

9. *Auditor's address.* CAS 700.42 requires that the place of issue be identified. This could be in the letterhead on which the auditor's report is printed or at the foot of the report as is illustrated in Figure 20-1.

concept check

C20-1 What criteria does the auditor use to assess the client's financial statements?

C20-2 Provide four facets of the auditor's responsibility that are included in the Auditor Responsibility section of the independent auditor's report.

Variations to Unqualified Audit Reports

Most users of financial statements read the independent auditor's report. When the report consists of the standard paragraphs, they conclude that the five conditions described in the previous section have been met.

A deviation from the standard unqualified report will cause knowledgeable users of financial statements to recognize that the auditor intends to communicate additional or limiting information. The categorization of audit reports in Figure 20-2 is used throughout the remainder of this chapter. The departures from a standard unqualified report are considered increasingly severe as one follows down the figure. A disclaimer

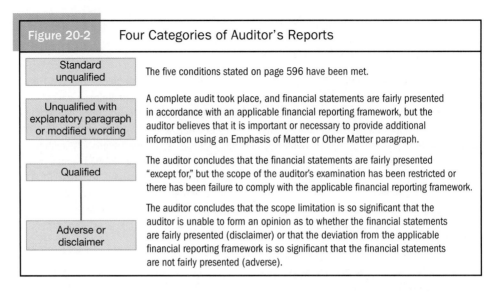

Figure 20-2 Four Categories of Auditor's Reports

Standard unqualified	The five conditions stated on page 596 have been met.
Unqualified with explanatory paragraph or modified wording	A complete audit took place, and financial statements are fairly presented in accordance with an applicable financial reporting framework, but the auditor believes that it is important or necessary to provide additional information using an Emphasis of Matter or Other Matter paragraph.
Qualified	The auditor concludes that the financial statements are fairly presented "except for," but the scope of the auditor's examination has been restricted or there has been failure to comply with the applicable financial reporting framework.
Adverse or disclaimer	The auditor concludes that the scope limitation is so significant that the auditor is unable to form an opinion as to whether the financial statements are fairly presented (disclaimer) or that the deviation from the applicable financial reporting framework is so significant that the financial statements are not fairly presented (adverse).

or adverse opinion is normally far more important to users than an unqualified report with the changes listed in Table 20-1.

Whenever the auditor believes that a variation in standard wording to the audit report is likely, the auditor is required to communicate this fact to those charged with governance as soon as possible (CAS 705.28). Before we look at the specific wording changes, we consider the difference between two key terms: *corresponding figures* and *comparative financial statements*.

Corresponding figures approach—the auditor reports only on the current year's financial statements.

Comparative financial statements approach—both periods under audit (current and prior) are reported on.

REPORTING ON COMPARATIVE FINANCIAL STATEMENTS The ASPE financial reporting framework normally requires the auditor to report only on the current year's financial statements, called the **corresponding figures approach**. Publicly listed organizations and those using IFRS must have audit reports that refer to both periods under audit, called the **comparative financial statements approach**. CAS 710 provides examples of what auditors do when there are transitions (for example different auditors in the two years, or if the audit opinion is different in the two years).

Table 20-1 Variations in Unqualified Audit Reports

Purpose of Variation	How It Is Accomplished	Example of When Used
Highlight or emphasize material that is **already in** the client financial statements or notes.	*Emphasis of Matter* paragraph (CAS 706.5[a])	Client has experienced a major data breach with lawsuits and fines pending of significant and uncertain amounts.
Provide information that is **not in** the client financial statements or notes.	*Other Matter* paragraph (CAS 706.5[b])	There are two sets of financial statements, for example one that is in compliance with an acceptable financial reporting framework such as IFRS and another that is in compliance with legislation (such as foreign tax legislation).
The financial statements are in compliance with a legislative framework that **is not fair** in accordance with a financial reporting framework.	State in the opinion paragraph that the financial statements *are prepared in accordance* with the legislation (CAS 700.36)	A country with high inflation requires financial statements fully prepared using current values with no use of historical cost.
Legislation requires **reporting on consistency** of accounting policies.	Add an Other Matter paragraph titled *Report on Other Legal and Regulatory Requirements* (AuG-48.5 and CAS 700.38)	Financial institutions are required to report on consistency of their accounting principles from one year to the next.

CAS **EMPHASIS OF MATTER PARAGRAPH** When the auditor is satisfied that the financial statements are fairly stated and has gathered sufficient evidence, there are times that the auditor would like to draw the user's attention to certain matters that are clearly disclosed in the financial statements but should have an impact on the user's decision making. For example, in Chapter 17 we talked about Maple Leaf Foods being connected to a liesteriosis outbreak. Another example could be a major data breach, such as occurred with Sony in 2011. In both cases, the companies would have disclosed some information about these events in their financial statements (perhaps due to pending lawsuits). An Emphasis of Matter paragraph is placed after the standard opinion paragraph and refers the reader to the note in the financial statements that discusses the matter.

CAS **OTHER MATTER PARAGRAPH** If the relevant information is **not** already in the financial statements, then the auditor provides the information in an Other Matter paragraph that is located in a relevant place in the financial statements. For example, the auditor would use such a paragraph to explain that the previous year's corresponding figures were not audited or were audited by other auditors. The Other Matters paragraph could be in various places—for example it could be right after the description of the auditor's responsibilities or it could be after the opinion paragraph.

CAS **UNQUALIFIED AUDITOR'S REPORT WHEN THE BASIS OF ACCOUNTING IS BASED ON REGULATIONS THAT DO NOT PROVIDE AN ACCEPTABLE FINANCIAL REPORTING FRAMEWORK** In certain situations, an unqualified auditor's report is issued when the disclosed basis of accounting is due to law or regulation rather than an acceptable financial reporting framework. If the structure of the resulting financial statements are not fair, in the auditor's view (for example, if the regulations provide for recording of assets or expenses at current value which does not provide fair presentation according to ASPE or IFRS), then the auditor might issue an unqualified audit report. However, rather than providing an audit opinion, the auditor would say that the financial statements had been "prepared" in accordance with the specified regulations.

CAS **CHANGES IN GAAS OR THE APPLICATION THEREOF** CAS 700.13 requires the auditor to evaluate a change in accounting principle or in the application of an accounting principle in the financial statements being reported on and to assess whether or not the new principle, or the application, is in accordance with the applicable financial reporting framework. In addition, the auditor must assess whether the method of accounting for the change, which may be retroactive or prospective, and the disclosure of the change, are also in accordance with that framework.

If the change, its application, and its disclosure are in accordance with the financial reporting framework, the auditor should express an unqualified opinion without reference to the change. However, some regulations, such as those pertaining to certain financial institutions, require those financial institutions to have the auditor assess their compliance with the consistency principle (see AuG-48). In that case, the auditor would place an Other Matter paragraph with the specific title *Report on Other Legal and Regulatory Requirements* after the opinion paragraph, and state whether the organization is in compliance (or not in compliance) with the regulations, and provide any additional reporting required under the regulations. Certain changes in the financial statements may not be changes in an accounting principle or in its application. Examples of such changes include the following:

1. Changes in an estimate, such as a decrease in the life of an asset for amortization purposes.
2. Error corrections not involving accounting principles, such as a previous year's mathematical error.
3. Variations in format and presentation of financial information.

4. Changes because of substantially different transactions or events, such as new endeavours in research and development or the sale of a subsidiary.

A change in estimate need not be disclosed in the notes nor in an Other Matter paragraph although disclosure may be desirable. A material error correction, on the other hand, must be fully disclosed.

DISCLOSURE OF UNUSUAL UNCERTAINTIES AFFECTING THE FINANCIAL STATEMENTS, INCLUDING USE OF GOING CONCERN ASSUMPTION Management customarily makes a number of estimates in the preparation of financial statements, including the useful lives of amortizable assets, the collectability of receivables, and the realizability of inventory and other assets. There is usually enough evidence to permit reasonable estimation of these items. Sometimes, the auditor encounters a situation in which the outcome of a matter cannot be reasonably estimated at the time the statements are being issued. These are contingencies, discussed further in the previous chapter. Examples include threats of the expropriation of assets, income tax or litigation contingencies (collectable or payable), and guarantees of the indebtedness of others.

The appropriate type of opinion to issue when either specific or general uncertainties exist depends on the materiality of the items in question and on the disclosure of the items by management in the notes. An unqualified opinion is appropriate if the uncertainty is not disclosed but is immaterial. If the amount involved is material but the accounting treatment, disclosure, and presentation of the contingency are in accordance with the applicable financial reporting framework, the auditor would refer to the uncertainty in the auditor's report by adding an Emphasis of Matter paragraph after the opinion paragraph.

The above examples or other less specific situations could bring into question the ability of the company to continue as a going concern. CAS 570, Going concern, explains that there are multiple alternatives:

- If adequate disclosure is made in the financial statements about material events or uncertainties that would cause doubt about the entity's ability to continue as a going concern, then the auditor uses an Emphasis of Matter paragraph to highlight the situation and reference the relevant note(s) in the financial statements.
- If there is not adequate disclosure in the financial statements of such material events or uncertainties, the auditor is required to express a qualified or adverse opinion (these types of opinions are discussed further in the next section).
- If the situation is so severe that the financial statements should not be prepared on a going-concern basis but have been prepared that way, then the auditor is required to express an adverse opinion.
- If the auditor is not being provided with sufficient evidence to provide a conclusion, then further assessment is required by the auditor (which would likely be considered a scope limitation and could result in a disclaimer of opinion).

③ Non-Standard Auditor's Reports

Conditions Requiring a Departure from an Unqualified Auditor's Report

In the study of auditor's reports that depart from an unqualified report, there are three closely related topics: (1) the conditions requiring a departure from an unqualified opinion, (2) the types of opinions other than unqualified, and (3) materiality.

The two conditions requiring a departure are that:

1. *The scope of the auditor's examination has been restricted.* When the auditor has not accumulated sufficient evidence to determine if financial statements are stated in accordance with an appropriate financial reporting framework, a scope

restriction exists. There are two major causes of scope restrictions: (1) those restrictions imposed by the client and (2) those caused by circumstances beyond either the client's or auditor's control. An example of a client restriction is management's refusal to permit the auditor to confirm material receivables or to physically examine material inventory. An example of a restriction caused by circumstances is when the engagement is not agreed upon until after the client's year end. It may not be possible to physically observe inventories, do certain cut-off tests, or perform other important procedures after the balance sheet date.

CAS 2. *The financial statements have not been prepared in accordance with the appropriate financial reporting framework.* CAS 705, Application and other explanatory material, describes examples of departures from accounting principles used by financial reporting frameworks that could result in material misstatement. These can generally be grouped into three categories:

1. An inappropriate accounting treatment, for example, failure to capitalize a capital lease.
2. An inappropriate valuation of an item in the financial statements, for example, failure to provide an adequate allowance for doubtful accounts.
3. A failure to disclose essential information in an informative manner, for example, failure to adequately disclose a going-concern problem or a material contingency.

Types of Non-Standard Auditor's Reports

Whenever either of the two conditions requiring a departure from an unqualified report exists and is material, a report other than an unqualified report must be issued. Four main types of auditor's reports are issued under these conditions: qualified opinion—scope limitation, qualified opinion—accounting principle violation, disclaimer of opinion, and adverse opinion.

QUALIFIED OPINION A **qualified opinion** can be used only as follows:

1. *For a scope limitation:* The auditor's fieldwork has been restricted, but the restriction is confined to a specific area such as opening inventory.
2. *For a departure from the accounting principles of the applicable financial reporting framework or other known material misstatement:* The financial statements are fairly presented except for failure to comply with one or more specific accounting principles or there is a known misstatement, and the effect can be quantified or isolated.

Instead of a qualified opinion, an **adverse opinion** or a disclaimer (discussed below) must be used if the auditor believes the condition being reported upon is extremely material or pervasive. For this reason, the qualified opinions (scope violation or accounting principle violation) are considered a less severe type of report for disclosing departures than an adverse opinion or a disclaimer.

Whenever an auditor issues one of the qualified opinions, he or she must use the term *except for* or, less frequently, *except that* or *except as* in the opinion paragraph. The implication is that the auditor is satisfied that the overall financial statements are correctly stated "except for" a particular part. Details of the exception are provided in a separate paragraph titled "Basis for Qualified Opinion" placed prior to the *Qualified Opinion* paragraph. Qualified opinions are fairly rare in practice. The provincial securities commissions will accept qualified statements from a public company only in rare circumstances. Lenders or creditors may not accept qualified statements from private companies. Consequently the conditions giving rise to the qualifications are often corrected.

DISCLAIMER OF OPINION A **disclaimer of opinion** is issued whenever the auditor has been unable to satisfy himself or herself that the overall financial statements are fairly presented. The necessity for denying ("disclaiming") happens because of a severe

Qualified opinion—a report issued when the auditor believes that financial statements are fairly stated but that either there was (a) a material, but not pervasive, limitation in the scope of the audit, or (b) there was a failure to follow the accounting principles of the applicable financial reporting framework that resulted in a material, but not pervasive, misstatement in the financial statements.

Adverse opinion—a report issued when the auditor believes the financial statements are materially misstated or misleading as a whole such that they do not present fairly the entity's financial position or the results of its operations and cash flows in conformity with the applicable financial reporting framework or there is a known material error.

Disclaimer of opinion—a report issued when the auditor has not been satisfied that the overall financial statements are fairly presented.

limitation on the scope of the audit examination, which would prevent the auditor from expressing an opinion on the financial statements as a whole.

The disclaimer is distinguished from an adverse opinion since it occurs due to a lack of knowledge by the auditor, but to express an adverse opinion the auditor must have knowledge that the financial statements are not fairly stated. Both disclaimers and adverse opinions are used only when the extent of the scope limitation or the effects of material misstatements are material and pervasive.

ADVERSE OPINION An adverse opinion is used only when the auditor concludes that the overall financial statements are materially misstated or misleading. This occurs because they do not present fairly the financial position or results of operations and changes in cash flows in conformity with the applicable financial reporting framework because of a departure from appropriate accounting principles or another known material error.

Materiality

Recall that **material misstatements** are misstatements in the financial statements, knowledge of which would affect or change the decision of a reasonable user of the statements.

In applying this definition, three levels are used for determining the type of opinion to issue. The relationship of level to type of opinion is presented in Table 20-2.

AMOUNTS ARE IMMATERIAL When a misstatement in the financial statements exists but is unlikely to affect the decisions of a reasonable user, it is considered to be immaterial. An unqualified opinion is therefore appropriate. For example, assume management recorded unexpired insurance as an asset in the previous year and decided to current year's insurance payments to reduce record-keeping costs, resulting in more than one year's insurance costs in the current year. Management failed to follow consistent accounting principles according to their financial reporting framework, but if the amounts are small, the misstatement would be immaterial, and a standard unqualified auditor's report would be appropriate.

Material misstatement—a misstatement in the financial statements, knowledge of which would affect a decision of a reasonable user of the statements.

Table 20-2	Relationship of Materiality to Type of Opinion and Significance in Terms of Reasonable User's Decision		
		Type of Audit Report	
			Auditing Related
		Accounting Related	**Financial Statements Not Prepared in Accordance with an Appropriate Financial Reporting Framework or Have Other Misstatements**
Materiality Level	**Significance in Terms of Reasonable User's Decisions**	**Scope Restricted by Client or Conditions**	
Immaterial	Decisions are unlikely to be affected.	Unqualified: Standard report	Unqualified: Standard report
Material but not pervasive	Decisions are likely to be affected only if the additional paragraph and qualified opinion (except for) information in question is important to the specific decisions being made. The overall financial statements are considered fairly stated. There is a material error, but it does not overshadow the financial statements as a whole.	Qualified (Accounting principle violation): Additional paragraph and qualified opinion (except for)	Qualified (scope limitation): Qualified scope, additional paragraph, and qualified opinion (except for)
Material and pervasive	Most or all decisions based on the financial statements are likely to be significantly affected. The overall fairness of the financial statements is in question.	Disclaimer of opinion	Adverse opinion

AMOUNTS ARE MATERIAL BUT NOT PERVASIVE The second level of materiality exists when a misstatement in the financial statements would affect a user's decision but the statements are still useful. For example, knowledge of a large misstatement in capital assets might affect a user's willingness to loan money to a company if the assets were the collateral. A misstatement of inventory does not mean that cash, accounts receivable, and other elements of the financial statements, or the financial statements as a whole, are materially incorrect.

To make materiality decisions when a condition requiring a departure from an unqualified report exists, the auditor must evaluate all effects on the financial statements. Assume the auditor is unable to satisfy himself or herself as to whether inventory is fairly stated (scope limitation) in deciding on the appropriate type of opinion. Because of the effect of a misstatement in inventory on other accounts and on totals in the statements, the auditor needs to consider the materiality of the combined effect on inventory, total current assets, total working capital, total assets, income taxes, income taxes payable, total current liabilities, cost of goods sold, net income before taxes, and net income after taxes.

When the auditor concludes that a misstatement is material but does not overshadow the financial statements as a whole (i.e., is not pervasive), a qualified opinion (using "except for") is appropriate.

AMOUNTS ARE MATERIAL AND PERVASIVE SUCH THAT OVERALL FAIRNESS OF STATEMENTS IS IN QUESTION The highest level of misstatement exists when users are likely to make incorrect decisions if they rely on the overall financial statements. Using the previous example of inventory, a large misstatement could be so material to the financial statements as a whole that the auditor's report should indicate the financial statements taken as a whole cannot be considered fairly stated. When the highest level of misstatement exists, the auditor must issue either a disclaimer of opinion or an adverse opinion.

When determining whether an exception is material and pervasive, the extent to which the exception affects different parts of the financial statements must be considered. This is referred to as pervasiveness. A misclassification between cash and accounts receivable affects only those two accounts and is therefore not pervasive. On the other hand, many accounts are affected by a failure to record a material sale. This type of error could be pervasive because it affects sales, accounts receivable, income tax expense, accrued income taxes, and retained earnings, which, in turn, affect current assets, total assets, current liabilities, total liabilities, owners' equity, gross margin, and operating income.

As misstatements become more pervasive, the likelihood of issuing an adverse opinion rather than a qualified opinion is increased. For example, if the auditor decides a misclassification between cash and accounts receivable is material, it should result in a qualified opinion; and if the failure to record a sale of the same dollar amount is pervasive, it should result in an adverse opinion.

MATERIALITY DECISIONS ARE TOUGH In theory, the effect of materiality on the type of opinion to issue is straightforward. In application, deciding upon actual materiality in a given situation can be a difficult judgment. There are no simple, well-defined guidelines that enable auditors to decide when something is immaterial, material, or material and pervasive.

MATERIALITY DECISIONS—ACCOUNTING PRINCIPLE VIOLATION OR OTHER MATERIAL MISSTATEMENT

Dollar amounts compared with a base The primary concern in measuring materiality when a client has failed to follow appropriate accounting principles is usually the total dollar misstatement in the accounts involved, compared to the performance materiality calculated during audit planning. A $10,000 misstatement might be material for a small company but not for a larger one. The auditor must combine all unadjusted errors and judge whether there may be individually immaterial errors that, when combined, significantly affect the statements. When comparing potential misstatements with a base, the auditor must carefully consider all accounts affected by a misstatement (pervasiveness). It is, for example, important to consider the effect of an understatement of ending inventory on cost of goods sold, income before taxes, income tax expense, and accrued income taxes payable.

Measurability The dollar error of some misstatements cannot be accurately measured. For example, a client's unwillingness to disclose an existing lawsuit or the acquisition of a new company subsequent to the balance sheet date is difficult, if not impossible, to measure in terms of dollar amounts. The materiality question the auditor must evaluate in such a situation is the effect on statement users of the failure to make the disclosure.

Nature of the item The decision of a user may also be affected by the kind of misstatement in the financial statements. The following may affect the user's decision and, therefore, the auditor's opinion, in a different way than most misstatements.

1. Transactions are illegal or fraudulent.
2. An item may materially affect some future period even though it is immaterial when only the current period is considered.
3. An item has a "psychological" effect (e.g., small profit versus small loss, or cash balance versus overdraft).
4. An item may be important in terms of possible consequences arising from contractual obligations (e.g., the effect of failure to comply with a debt restriction may result in a material loan being called).

MATERIALITY DECISIONS—SCOPE LIMITATIONS When there is a scope limitation in an audit, the audit report will be unqualified, qualified scope and opinion, or disclaimer, depending on the potential materiality and pervasiveness of the scope limitation. The auditor will consider the same three factors included in the previous discussion, but they will be considered differently. For example, if recorded accounts payable of $400,000 was not audited, the auditor must evaluate the potential misstatement in accounts payable and decide how materially the financial statements could be affected. There might be no dollar error, or the accounts payable might need to be double the amount at $800,000—if the amount was not audited, there is no way of knowing. The pervasiveness of these potential misstatements must also be considered.

Examples of Conditions Requiring a Departure

AUDITOR'S SCOPE HAS BEEN RESTRICTED Recall that there are two major categories of scope restrictions: (1) those caused by a client and (2) those caused by conditions beyond the control of either the client or the auditor.

For *client-imposed restrictions*, the auditor should be concerned about the possibility that management is trying to prevent discovery of misstated information. In such cases, it would be appropriate to issue a disclaimer of opinion whenever materiality and pervasiveness are uncertain. When restrictions are due to conditions beyond the client's control, a qualification of scope and opinion is more likely.

CAS 705, par. 11–13, emphasizes the severity of a scope restriction by providing an escalating set of actions that the auditor should take when a scope restriction is imposed by the client. First, the auditor should request that the scope restriction be removed. If that is not done, then the auditor is required to communicate with those charged with governance (such as the board of directors) to ensure that they are aware of the scope restriction and to describe the impact on the audit. If the scope limitation is both material and pervasive, the first choice is for the auditor to resign from the engagement—if the auditor cannot resign or this is considered impractical, only then would the auditor issue a disclaimer in the audit report.

Figure 20-3   Qualified Scope and Opinion Report Due to Scope Restriction

INDEPENDENT AUDITOR'S REPORT	Addressee, Introductory statement, Management responsibility
(Same addressee, introductory statement, and management responsibility paragraph as the standard report)	
(First two paragraphs of the auditor's responsibility section are unchanged.)	Auditor's responsibility
We believe that the audit evidence that we have obtained is sufficient and appropriate to provide a basis for our qualified audit opinion.	Last sentence—changed
Basis for Qualified Opinion	
We were unable to obtain audited financial statements supporting the Company's investment in a foreign affiliate stated at $475,000, or its equity in earnings of that affiliate of $365,000, which is included in net income, as described in Note X to the financial statements. Because of the nature of the Company's records, we were unable to satisfy ourselves as to the carrying value of the investment or the equity in its earnings by means of other auditing procedures.	Basis for Qualified Opinion paragraph—added
Qualified Opinion	
In our opinion, except for the effects of the matters described in the Basis for Qualified Opinion paragraph, the financial statements present fairly, in all material respects, the financial position of Laughlin Corporation as of December 31, 2012, and the results of its financial performance and its cash flows for the year then ended in accordance with International Financial Reporting Standards.	Opinion paragraph—qualified

Two restrictions occasionally imposed by clients on the auditor's scope relate to the observation of physical inventory and the confirmation of accounts receivable, but other restrictions may also occur. Reasons for client-imposed scope restrictions may be a desire to save audit fees and, in the case of confirming receivables, to prevent possible conflicts between the client and customer when amounts differ. Unfortunately, scope restrictions have also been used to hide fraud, so a scope restriction can be a huge warning sign with respect to potential fraud or financial statement manipulation.

The most common case in which conditions beyond the client's and auditor's control cause a scope restriction is an engagement agreed upon after the client's balance sheet date. Certain cut-off procedures, physical examination of inventory, and other important procedures may not be possible then. For example, the report in Figure 20-3 would be appropriate for an audit in which the amounts were material but not pervasive, and the auditor was unable to audit the financial statements of a company's foreign affiliate and could not gather evidence using alternative procedures. The introductory statement, management responsibility paragraph, and the bulk of the auditor responsibility section are omitted from the example because they contain standard wording. The final sentence of the auditor responsibility section is included, as it has changed: the word "qualified" has been added before the words "audit opinion." An explanatory basis paragraph has been added; the qualified opinion refers to that paragraph.

When the amounts are so material that a disclaimer of opinion is required, the introductory statement is modified to indicate that the auditors were engaged to audit (rather than conducted the audit). The management responsibility paragraph remains the same. The auditor's responsibility section is severely truncated, reflecting the fact that an audit could not be conducted, while an explanatory basis paragraph is included prior to the renamed and revised disclaimer of opinion paragraph as shown in Figure 20-4.

STATEMENTS ARE NOT IN CONFORMITY WITH IFRS (OR ANOTHER FINANCIAL REPORTING FRAMEWORK), OR OTHER KNOWN MISSTATEMENTS When the auditor knows that the financial statements may be misleading because material misstatements have been quantified or the statements were not prepared in conformity with the accounting principles of an applicable financial reporting framework, a qualified or an adverse opinion must be issued, depending on the materiality and pervasiveness of the item in question. The opinion must clearly state the nature and the amount of

INDEPENDENT AUDITOR'S REPORT	
(Same addressee)	Addressee
We were engaged to audit the accompanying financial statements of XiaPlus Company, which comprise the statement of financial position as at December 31, 2012, and the statement of comprehensive income, statement of changes in equity, and statement of cash flows for the year then ended, and a summary of significant accounting policies and other explanatory information.	Introductory statement—modified
(Management responsibility paragraph same as the standard report)	
Our responsibility is to express an opinion on these financial statements based on conducting an audit in accordance with Canadian generally accepted auditing standards. Because of the matter described in the Basis for Disclaimer of Opinion paragraph, however, we were not able to obtain sufficient appropriate evidence to provide a basis for an audit opinion.	Management responsibility—unchanged Auditor's responsibility—curtailed and modified
Basis for Disclaimer of Opinion	
Our examination indicated serious deficiencies in internal control of general fund transactions. As a consequence, we were unable to satisfy ourselves that all revenues and expenditures of the organization had been recorded nor were we able to satisfy ourselves that the recorded transactions were proper. As a result, we were unable to determine whether adjustments were required in respect of recorded and unrecorded assets, recorded and unrecorded liabilities, and the components making up the statements of comprehensive income, equity, and changes in cash flows.	Basis for Disclaimer of Opinion paragraph—added
Disclaimer of Opinion	Disclaimer of Opinion
Because of the significance of the matters described in the Basis for Disclaimer of Opinion paragraph, we have not been able to obtain sufficient appropriate audit evidence to provide a basis for an audit opinion. Accordingly, we do not express an opinion on the financial statements.	

the misstatement, if it is known. Figure 20-5 shows an example of a qualified opinion when a client did not capitalize leases as required by IFRS. The introductory statement, management's responsibility paragraph, and first two paragraphs of the auditor responsibility section in the example are omitted because they include standard wording.

When the amounts are so material and pervasive that an adverse opinion is required, the introductory statement, management's responsibility, and auditor's responsibility are fully described. The basis for the changed opinion could remain the same, but the opinion paragraph would be adverse as shown in Figure 20-6.

When the client fails to include information that is necessary for the fair presentation of financial statements in the body of the statements or in the narrative disclosures in the notes, it is the responsibility of the auditor to explain how these disclosures are misstated in a basis paragraph in the auditor's report and to issue a qualified or an adverse opinion, depending upon the auditor's assessment of the impact of the lack of disclosure. Figure 20-7 shows an example of an auditor's report in which the auditor considered the financial statement disclosure inadequate. As it is qualified due to the accounting principle violation, it follows a format similar to that of Figures 20-3 and 20-5.

CAS   **EXISTENCE OF MORE THAN ONE CONDITION REQUIRING A QUALIFICATION** Auditors may encounter situations involving more than one of the conditions requiring modification of the unqualified report. In these circumstances, the auditor should qualify or modify the opinion for each condition. CAS 705 requires a description of the basis for any modifications, the reasons why the auditor is including the information, and the material included in the Basis Paragraph. An example is presented in Figure 20-8.

CAS   **REPORTS INVOLVING RELIANCE ON ANOTHER AUDITOR OR A SPECIALIST** In Canada, although the main or primary auditor may rely on another auditor or a specialist in determining the appropriate opinion to issue on the financial statements, the primary auditor takes responsibility for that opinion, and only the name of the primary auditor appears on the auditor's report. During the audit engagement, it is the auditor's

Figure 20-5	Qualified Opinion Report Due to Use of Inappropriate Accounting Principles

	INDEPENDENT AUDITOR'S REPORT
Addressee, Introductory statement, Management responsibility	(Same addressee, introductory statement, and management responsibility paragraph as the standard report)
Auditor's responsibility	(First two paragraphs of the auditor's responsibility section are unchanged.)
Last sentence—changed	We believe that the audit evidence that we have obtained is sufficient and appropriate to provide a basis for our qualified audit opinion.
Basis for Qualified Opinion paragraph—added	Basis for Qualified Opinion
	The company has excluded from property and debt in the accompanying statement of financial position certain lease obligations that, in our opinion, should be capitalized in order to conform with International Financial Reporting Standards. If these lease obligations were capitalized, property would be increased by $4,600,000, long-term debt by $4,200,000, and equity by $400,000 as of December 31, 2012, and comprehensive income and earnings per share would be increased by $400,000 and $1.75, respectively, for the year then ended.
Opinion paragraph—qualified	Qualified Opinion
	In our opinion, except for the matter described in the Basis for Qualified Opinion paragraph, the financial statements present fairly, in all material respects, the financial position of Tonah Company as at December 31, 2012, and of its financial performance and its cash flows for the year then ended in accordance with International Financial Reporting Standards.

responsibility to ensure that the secondary auditor or any specialist hired is competent and conducts the field work to a high standard of quality while maintaining confidentiality. CAS 600 and CAS 620 deal with the (primary) auditor's reliance on another auditor and on a specialist, respectively. Inability to rely on the work of another auditor or a specialist is a scope limitation issue.

The auditor may rely on another auditor because the client's business is either too complex or widespread and the primary auditor either does not have the personnel or the proximity to all the client locations to do the audits with his or her own personnel. For example, the primary auditor, a public accounting firm located in Halifax, may rely on another public accounting firm located in Regina as the secondary auditor to audit the Halifax client's subsidiary located in Regina.

CAS

CAS 600 requires the primary auditor to assess the secondary auditor's professional qualifications, compliance with ethical requirements, quality control systems, and whether necessary access to documentation will be provided when determining whether or not to rely on the secondary auditor. As we explained in Chapter 4, the

Figure 20-6	Adverse Opinion Due to Use of Inappropriate Accounting Principles

	INDEPENDENT AUDITOR'S REPORT
Addressee, Introductory statement, Management responsibility	(Same addressee, introductory statement, and management responsibility paragraph as the standard report)
Auditor's responsibility	(First two paragraphs of the auditor's responsibility section are unchanged.)
Last sentence—changed	We believe that the audit evidence that we have obtained is sufficient and appropriate to provide a basis for our adverse audit opinion.
Basis for Adverse Opinion paragraph—added	Basis for Adverse Opinion
	(Same as contents of Basis for Qualified Opinion in Figure 20-5)
Opinion paragraph—adverse	Adverse Opinion
	In our opinion, because of the significance of the matter discussed in the Basis for Adverse Opinion paragraph, the financial statements do not present fairly the financial position of Tonah Company as at December 31, 2012, and of its financial performance and cash flows for the year then ended in accordance with International Financial Reporting Standards.

Figure 20-7   Qualified Opinion Due to Inadequate Disclosure

INDEPENDENT AUDITOR'S REPORT	Addressee, Introductory statement, Management responsibility
(Same addressee, introductory statement, and management responsibility paragraph as the standard report)	
(First two paragraphs of the auditor's responsibility section are unchanged.)	Auditor's responsibility
We believe that the audit evidence that we have obtained is sufficient and appropriate to provide a basis for our qualified audit opinion.	Last sentence—changed
Basis for Qualified Opinion	Basis for Qualified Opinion paragraph—added
On January 15, 2013, the company issued debentures in the amount of $3,600,000 for the purpose of financing plant expansion. The debenture agreement restricts the payment of future cash dividends to earnings after December 31, 2014. In our opinion, disclosure of this information is required to conform with International Financial Reporting Standards.	
Qualified Opinion	Opinion paragraph—qualified
In our opinion, except for matter described in the Basis for Qualified Opinion paragraph, the financial statements present fairly, in all material respects, the financial position of Tonah Company as at December 31, 2012, and of its financial performance and its cash flows for the year then ended in accordance with International Financial Reporting Standards.	

primary auditor who does rely on a secondary auditor is responsible for any deficiencies in the secondary auditor's work. The decision on whether or not to rely on that work is based on the primary auditor's judgment.

If the primary auditor decides that an unqualified opinion is appropriate, the name of the secondary auditor is not mentioned. If the quality of work of the secondary auditor is poor, then the primary auditor must somehow remedy the matter, perhaps by sending staff to the remote location. If this is not possible and the primary auditor decides that a qualified or disclaimer of opinion is appropriate and the qualification arises because of inability to rely on the work of the secondary auditor, the explanation of the qualification in the Basis for Disclaimer paragraph

INDEPENDENT AUDITOR'S REPORT	Addressee, Introductory statement, Management responsibility
(Same addressee, introductory statement, and management responsibility paragraph as the standard report)	
(First two paragraphs of the auditor's responsibility section are unchanged.)	Auditor's responsibility
We believe that the audit evidence that we have obtained is sufficient and appropriate to provide a basis for our qualified audit opinion.	Last sentence—changed
Basis for Qualified Opinion	Basis for Qualified Opinion paragraph—added
Management has advised us that the company may become liable with respect to guarantees given for indebtedness of a subsidiary located in another country. However, management has declined to provide us with further information and will not permit us to contact the subsidiary as management believes disclosure is not in the company's best interests. As a result, we have been unable to obtain sufficient audit evidence to form an opinion with respect to the possible liability. Further more, the matter has not been disclosed in the notes to the financial statements. In our opinion, such disclosure is required under International Financial Reporting Standards.	
Qualified Opinion	Opinion paragraph—qualified
In our opinion, except for the matter described in the Basis for Qualified Opinion paragraph, the financial statements present fairly, in all material respects, the financial position of Tonah Company as at December 31, 2012, and of its financial performance and its cash flows for the year then ended in accordance with International Financial Reporting Standards.	

could mention the name of the secondary auditor in explaining the reason for the qualification (scope limitation).

The auditor may have to rely on a specialist, such as an actuary, in completing the audit. Normally the auditor would not mention the specialist or reliance on the specialist, since if the quality of work of the specialist is poor, the auditor could hire another specialist. However, if the auditor believes that a qualified or disclaimer of opinion is appropriate and the qualification arises because of inability to rely on the work of the specialist, the explanation of the qualification in the Basis paragraph would mention the name of the specialist in explaining the reason for the qualification.

concept check

C20-5 What is the relationship among materiality, pervasiveness, and a qualified audit report?

C20-6 What type of audit report is issued when the only errors found during the audit are immaterial? Why?

C20-7 Why is a report that contains a disclaimer of opinion normally shorter than other reports?

Summary

1. *When can the public accountant issue a standard unqualified audit report?* It can be issued for an audit engagement where sufficient evidence has been collected using GAAS and where the financial statements are fairly presented in accordance with an applicable financial reporting framework.

   What parts are there in this report and why are they significant? Figure 20-1 shows the nine parts to the audit report: (1) the report title describes the document; (2) the addressee is identified; (3) the introductory statement provides a context for the report; (4) the management responsibility paragraph describes the responsibilities of management; (5) the auditor responsibility section describes the auditor's responsibilities, the criteria used to conduct the audit, and the nature of an audit engagement, and states that the auditor has gathered enough high-quality evidence to state an opinion on the financial statements; (6) provides an opinion on the financial statements; (7) identifies the audit firm, (8) identifies the date of the report; (9) identifies the place of issue.

   How is the date of the audit report decided? The audit report date is the date that management approves the financial statements, after the audit field work has been completed.

   When might dual dating of the audit report occur? If a significant event occurs after the audit report has been completed but not yet released, audit work could be completed with respect to that event only (disclosed in a note), and then the audit report would have two dates, with the second, later date pertaining only to the note with respect to the significant event.

2. *How can we categorize the auditor's report when there are variations in wording?* In addition to the standard unqualified report, there is (1) the unqualified report with an explanatory paragraph or modified wording, (2) a qualified (scope violation or inappropriate accounting principles), (3) adverse, or (4) disclaimer of opinion.

   Under what conditions would modified wording occur or an additional explanatory paragraph be added to an unqualified report? Such a report would be issued when a complete audit with satisfactory results has been completed, but the auditor believes it is necessary to provide additional information.

3. *What two types of situations would cause problems with issuing an opinion on financial statements?* When either the scope of the auditor's examination has been restricted or the financial statements have not been prepared in accordance with an acceptable financial reporting framework, the auditor may be unable to issue a standard unqualified report.

   How is materiality related to the wording changes used for these departures in audit opinion? A qualified report is likely to be used when the issue is material but does not overshadow the financial statements as a whole (pervasiveness). If problems are material and pervasive, then a disclaimer of opinion or an adverse opinion would result.

MyAccountingLab

Make the grade with MyAccountingLab: The questions, exercises, and problems marked in orange can be found on MyAccountingLab. You can practise them as often as you want, and most feature step-by-step guided instructions to help you find the right answer.

Review Questions

20-1 ① Explain why auditor's reports are important to users of financial statements.

20-2 ① What five circumstances are required for a standard unqualified report to be issued?

20-3 ① ③ List the nine parts of an unqualified auditor's report and explain the meaning of each part. How do the parts compare with those found in a qualified report?

20-4 ① What is the purpose of the introductory statement in the auditor's report? Identify the most important information included in the introductory statement.

20-5 ① What are the purposes of the management responsibility paragraph in the auditor's report? Identify the most important information included in the paragraph.

20-6 ① What are the purposes of the auditor responsibility section in the auditor's report? Identify the most important information included in the section.

20-7 ① What are the purposes of the opinion paragraph in the auditor's report? Identify the most important information included in the opinion paragraph.

20-8 ① On February 17, 2013, a public accountant completed the examination of the financial statements for Buckheizer Corporation for the year ended December 31, 2013. The audit is satisfactory in all respects. On February 26, the auditor completed the tax return and the pencil draft of the financial statements. Management approved these financial statements on March 1, 2013. The final auditor's report was completed, attached to the financial statements, and delivered to the client on March 7, 2013. What is the appropriate date on the auditor's report?

20-9 ② Explain what is meant by "contingencies." Give an example of a contingency, and discuss its appropriate disclosure in the financial statements.

20-10 ② Why would an auditor use an Emphasis of Matter or an Other Matters paragraph with an unqualified audit report?

20-11 ③ List the conditions requiring a departure from an unqualified opinion, and give one specific example of each of those conditions.

20-12 ③ Distinguish between a qualified opinion, an adverse opinion, and a disclaimer of opinion, and explain the circumstances under which each is appropriate.

20-13 ③ Define "materiality" as it is used in audit reporting. What conditions will affect the auditor's determination of materiality?

20-14 ③ Distinguish between the levels of materiality and pervasiveness an auditor considers when assessing how to deal with an inappropriate use of an accounting principle or known material error in the financial statements.

20-15 ① ③ How does an auditor's opinion differ between scope limitations caused by client restrictions and limitations resulting from conditions beyond the client's control? What is the effect of each on the auditor's work?

20-16 ③ Munroe Corp. had a bad year financially and the president, Jan de Boer, instructed the controller not to amortize the capital assets so that the company would show a small profit. The controller argued that ASPE required Munroe to amortize the capital assets on a regular basis and a qualified auditor's report would likely result. Jan told the controller to disclose the failure to record amortization in the notes to the financial statements. You are the auditor in charge on the Munroe audit. Write a memo to Jan in response to the controller's comments.

20-17 ③ At times, for a variety of reasons, an auditor must rely on another firm of auditors to perform part of an audit. What reference does the primary auditor make to the secondary auditor in the auditor's report? Justify your response.

Discussion Questions and Problems

20-18 ① ③ Roscoe, a public accountant, has completed the examination of the financial statements of Excelsior Corporation as of and for the year ended December 31, 2012. Roscoe also examined and reported on the Excelsior financial statements for the prior year. Roscoe drafted the following auditor's report for 2012:

We have audited the balance sheet and statements of income and retained earnings of Excelsior Corporation as of December 31, 2012.

MANAGEMENT'S RESPONSIBILITY

Management prepared the financial statements and is responsible for risk assessment and designing systems of internal control in response to those risks. It also selects and implements the accounting policies embedded in these financial statements.

AUDITOR RESPONSIBILITY

We were engaged to conduct an audit for the above-mentioned financial statements. We conducted our audit in accordance with Canadian generally accepted auditing standards. Those standards require that we plan and perform the audit to obtain reasonable assurance about whether the financial statements are free of misstatement.

We believe that our audit provides a reasonable basis for our opinion.

OPINION

In our opinion, the financial statements referred to above present fairly the financial position of Excelsior Corporation as of December 31, 2012, and the results of its operations for the year then ended in conformity with

International Financial Reporting Standards, applied on a basis consistent with those of the preceding year.

(Signed)

Roscoe, Public Accountant

OTHER INFORMATION:

- Excelsior is presenting comparative financial statements.
- Excelsior does not wish to present a cash flow statement for either year.
- During 2012, Excelsior changed its method of accounting for long-term construction contracts, properly reflected the effect of the change in the current year's financial statements, and restated the prior year's statements. Roscoe is satisfied with Excelsior's justification for making the change. The change is discussed in footnote 12.
- Roscoe was unable to perform normal accounts receivable confirmation procedures, but alternate procedures were used to satisfy Roscoe as to the existence of the receivables.

- Excelsior Corporation is the defendant in a lawsuit, the outcome of which is highly uncertain. If the case is settled in favour of the plaintiff, Excelsior will be required to pay a substantial amount of cash, which might require the sale of certain capital assets. The litigation and the possible effects have been properly disclosed in footnote 11.
- Excelsior issued debentures on January 31, 2012, in the amount of $10,000,000. The funds obtained from the issuance were used to finance the expansion of plant facilities. The debenture agreement restricts the payment of future cash dividends to earnings after December 31, 2013. Excelsior declined to disclose these essential data in the footnotes to the financial statements.

REQUIRED

a. Identify and explain any items included in "Other Information" that need not be part of the auditor's report.

b. Explain the deficiencies in Roscoe's auditor's report as drafted.

(Adapted from AICPA)

20-19 ❶ ❷ ❸ For the following independent situations, assume you are the audit partner on the engagement.

1. During your examination of Debold Batteries Ltd., you conclude there is a possibility that inventory is materially overstated. The client refuses to allow you to expand the scope of your examination sufficiently to verify whether the balance is actually misstated.

2. You are auditing Woodcolt Linen Services, Inc. for the first time. Woodcolt has been in business for several years but has never had an audit before. After the audit is completed, you conclude that the current year balance sheet is stated correctly in accordance with ASPE. The client did not authorize you to do test work for any of the previous years.

3. You were engaged to examine Cutter Steel Corp.'s financial statements after the close of the corporation's fiscal year. Because you were not engaged until after the balance sheet date, you were not able to physically observe inventory, which is very material. On the completion of your audit, you are satisfied that Cutter's financial statements are presented fairly, including inventory about which you were able to satisfy yourself by the use of alternative audit procedures.

4. Four weeks after the year-end date, a major customer of Prince Construction Ltd. declared bankruptcy. Because the customer had confirmed the balance due to Prince at the balance sheet date, management refuses to write off the account or otherwise disclose the information. The receivable represents approximately 10 percent of accounts receivable and 20 percent of net earnings before taxes.

5. You complete the audit of Johnson Department Store Ltd., and, in your opinion, the financial statements are fairly presented. On the last day of the examination, you discover that one of your supervisors assigned to the audit had a material investment in Johnson.

6. Auto Delivery Company Ltd. has a fleet of several delivery trucks. In the past, Auto Delivery had followed the policy of purchasing all equipment. In the current year, it decided to lease the trucks. This change in policy is fully disclosed in footnotes.

REQUIRED

For each situation, state the type of auditor's report that should be issued. If your decision depends on additional information, state the alternative reports you are considering and the additional information you need to make the decision.

20-20 ❶ ❷ ❸ For the following independent situations, assume you are the audit partner on the engagement.

1. Kieko Corporation has prepared financial statements but has decided to exclude the cash flow statement. Management explains to you that the users of its financial statements find that particular statement confusing and prefer not to have it included.

2. HardwareFromHome.com is an internet-based start-up company created to sell home hardware supplies online. Although the company had a promising start, a downturn in e-commerce retailing has negatively affected the company. The company's sales and cash position have deteriorated significantly, and you have reservations about the ability of the company to continue in operation for the next year.

3. Approximately 20 percent of the audit for Furtney Farms, Inc. was performed by a different public accounting firm, selected by you. You have reviewed its working papers and believe it did an excellent job on its portion of the audit. Nevertheless, you are unwilling to take complete responsibility for its work.

4. The controller of Fair City Hotels Co. Ltd. will not allow you to confirm the receivable balance from two of its major customers. The amount of the receivable is material in relation to Fair City's financial statements. You are unable to satisfy yourself as to the receivable balance by alternative procedures.

5. In the last three months of the current year, Oil Refining Corp. decided to change direction and go significantly into the oil-drilling business. Management recognizes that this business is exceptionally risky and could jeopardize the success of its existing refining business but that there are significant potential rewards. During the short period of operation in drilling, the company has had three dry wells and no successes. The facts are adequately disclosed in footnotes.

REQUIRED

a. For each situation, identify which of the conditions requiring modification of or a deviation from an unqualified standard report is applicable.

b. State the level of materiality as immaterial, material, or material and pervasive. If you cannot decide the level of materiality, state the additional information needed to make a decision.

c. Given your answers in parts (a) and (b), identify the appropriate auditor's report from the following choices:
   (1) Unqualified—standard wording.
   (2) Qualified opinion—inappropriate accounting policy or material misstatement.
   (3) Qualified opinion—scope limitation.
   (4) Disclaimer.
   (5) Adverse.

20-21 ❶ ❷ ❸ The following are independent situations for which you will recommend an appropriate auditor's report:

1. Subsequent to the date of the financial statements as part of the post-balance sheet date audit procedures, a public accountant learned of heavy damage to one of a client's two plants due to a recent fire; the loss will not be reimbursed by insurance. The newspapers described the event in detail. The financial statements and appended notes as prepared by the client do not disclose the loss caused by the fire.

2. A public accountant is engaged in the examination of the financial statements of a large manufacturing company with branch offices in many widely separate cities. The public accountant was not able to count the substantial undeposited cash receipts at the close of business on the last day of the fiscal year at all branch offices.

   As an alternative to this auditing procedure used to verify the accurate cut off of cash receipts, the public accountant observed that deposits in transit as shown on the year-end bank reconciliation appeared as credits on the bank statement on the first business day of the new year. The public accountant was satisfied as to the cut off of cash receipts by the use of the alternative procedure.

3. On January 2, 2013, the Retail Auto Parts Company Limited received a notice from its primary supplier that effective immediately all wholesale prices would be increased by 10 percent. On the basis of the notice, Retail Auto Parts revalued its December 31, 2012, inventory to reflect the higher costs. The inventory constituted a material proportion of total assets; however, the effect of the revaluation was material to current assets but not to total assets or net income. The increase in valuation is adequately disclosed in the footnotes.

4. E-lotions.com, Inc. is an online retailer of body lotions and other bath and body supplies. The company records revenues at the time customer orders are placed on the website, rather than when the goods are shipped, which is usually two days after the order is placed. The auditor determined that the amount of orders placed but not shipped as of the balance sheet date is not material.

5. During the course of the examination of the financial statements of a corporation for the purpose of expressing an opinion on the statements, a public accountant is refused permission to inspect the minute books. The corporate secretary instead offers to give the public accountant a certified copy of all resolutions and actions relating to accounting matters.

REQUIRED

a. For each situation, identify which of the conditions requiring a deviation from or modification of an unqualified standard report is applicable.

b. State the level of materiality as immaterial, material, or material and pervasive. If you cannot decide the level of materiality, state the additional information needed to make a decision.

c. Given your answers in parts (a) and (b), identify the appropriate auditor's report from the following alternatives:
   (1) Unqualified—standard wording.
   (2) Qualified opinion—inappropriate accounting policy or known material misstatement.
   (3) Qualified opinion—scope limitation.
   (4) Disclaimer.
   (5) Adverse.

(Adapted from AICPA)

20-22 **①②** You are in charge of the audit of Saskatoon Building Products Limited (SBP), a company listed on the Vancouver Stock Exchange. In the course of your audit, you discover that SBP's working capital ratio is below 2:1 and that, therefore, the company is in default on a substantial loan from Prairie Bank. Management announces to you its intention to sell a large block of provincial bonds, which were included in long-term investments, and some land that had been purchased for expansion, which was included in capital assets. Management proposes including the bonds and land as current assets pending disposition. Such inclusion would increase the current ratio to 2.2:1.

Prairie Bank and your client have not enjoyed cordial relations of late, and you have been advised by Avril Chui, the manager of the Saskatoon branch, that the bank is "looking forward to receiving the audited statements because we are concerned that SBP has been having problems."

REQUIRED
a. Draft the memo to your partner outlining the problem.
b. Draft the auditor's report.

Professional Judgment Problem

20-23 **③** Lesley, a PA, is auditing the financial statements of a jewellery store specializing in the sale of fine diamonds. Because of the difficulties in authenticating gemstones, Lesley reviews a report from a gemologist retained by the client who assisted in valuing the inventory. However, upon inquiry of various sources, Lesley is not satisfied that the gemologist is qualified to do the work. Accordingly, she selects a large sample of stones from those included on the client's inventory listing to ensure that they indeed exist and appear to be genuine. She does not notice anything unusual, and there-fore issues an unqualified opinion on the client's financial statements.

REQUIRED
Assess Lesley's actions.

(Extract from AU2 CGA-Canada Examinations developed by the Certified General Accountants Association of Canada © 2010 CGA-Canada. Reproduced with permission. All rights reserved.)

Case

20-24 **①** Materia Blues Inc. is a company that manufactures and distributes books internationally. The company has proposed that the following comments be included in the company's 2013 annual report to the shareholders:

"The integrity of the financial information reported by Materia Blues Inc. is the responsibility of the company's management. Fulfilling this responsibility requires the preparation of financial statements in accordance with International Financial Reporting Standards.

Materia Blues Inc. has established an excellent system of accounting and internal controls, used to gather and process financial data. Management believes that the role of the internal audit department is sufficient to ensure the high quality of the business practices and monitoring activities that are used to keep operations functioning smoothly at the company.

Our public accounting firm is engaged to provide an independent opinion on our financial statements. Together with our audit committee, they provide high-quality oversight over the financial accounting processes at Material Blues Inc. The audit committee has checked the audit report prepared by the auditors and believes that it is sound. The external auditors have had free and clear access to the audit committee and to management and employees of the company during the conduct of their audit engagement."

REQUIRED
Describe the incorrect assumptions that are implicit in the above comments. For each incorrect assumption, provide an example of more appropriate wording that might be included in the annual report to more accurately reflect healthy business practices.

Ongoing Small Business Case: Auditor's Report for CondoCleaners.com

20-25 **①②** CondoCleaners.com is now in its third year of operations. The prior two years' financial statements received a review engagement report. In the current year, Jim has decided that an audit will be completed for the annual financial statements. He has hired your local public accounting firm to do the audit, and you have been assigned as the senior in charge of the engagement.

REQUIRED
Assuming that the evidence that your firm needs to collect for the audit engagement is available, what type of audit opinion will CondoCleaners.com receive? Will there be a need for any additional information to be provided in the report? If so, what will that information be and how will it be organized?

21 Assurance services: Review and compilation engagements

In addition to financial statement audits, a public accountant performs a variety of services for clients with respect to financial information or business operations. This chapter begins by reviewing the nature of assurance engagements and their standards, then describes examples of specific engagements. Management accountants can use this information to determine alternative types of reporting, while potential auditors learn about the types of services they can offer.

LEARNING OBJECTIVES

1 Describe how assurance engagement general standards are different from and similar to audit standards. Provide examples of special reports that provide (i) high assurance and (ii) no assurance.

2 Explain the importance of review and compilation services. Relate evidence collection procedures to the assurance level provided for audits, reviews, and compilations.

3 Describe the type of report that the public accountant provides for interim financial information for public companies. Examine the alternatives for public accounting reporting on future-oriented information.

STANDARDS REFERENCED IN THIS CHAPTER

CICA Standards – High level of assurance (audit engagements)

CAS 700 – Forming an opinion and reporting on financial statements

CAS 805 – Special considerations audits of single financial statements and specific elements, accounts, or items of a financial statement

Section 5020 – Association (also applies to review and compilation engagements)

Section 5025 – Standards for assurance engagements (also applies to review level)

Section 5815 – Special reports: audit reports on compliance with agreements, statutes, and regulations

Section 5925 – An audit of internal control over financial reporting that is integrated with an audit of financial statements

Moderate level of assurance (review engagements)

Section 7050 – Auditor review of interim financial statements

Section 8100 – General review standards

Section 8200 – Public accountant's review of financial statements.

Section 8500 – Reviews of financial information other than financial statements

Section 8600 – Reviews of compliance with agreements and regulations

AuG-6 – Examination of a financial forecast or projection included in a prospectus or other public offering document

AuG-20 – Performance of a review of financial statements in accordance with sections 8100 and 8200

No assurance provided (compilation engagements)

Section 9100 – Reports on the results of applying specified auditing procedures to financial information other than financial statements

Section 9200 – Compilation engagements

AuG-16 – Compilation of a financial forecast or projection

Skepticism Applies to All Types of Engagements

Menard Construction Ltd. was a contractor specializing in apartment complexes in Alberta. The owner of the construction company, Tony Menard, reached an agreement with a promoter named Alice Mayberry to serve as contractor on three projects that Alice was currently marketing. One problem with the agreement was that Tony would not receive final payment for the construction work until all partnership units in the complexes were sold.

The first partnership offering was completely sold and Tony was paid. Unfortunately, the next two partnerships were not completely sold. To solve this problem, Tony loaned money to relatives and key employees who bought the necessary interests for the partnerships to close so that Tony would receive the final payment.

When Menard Construction Ltd. had a review engagement performed by Renée Fortin, a public accountant and sole practitioner, the accounting records showed loans receivable from a number of employees and individuals with the last name Menard. Fortin observed that the loans were made just before the second and third partnerships closed, and they were for amounts that were multiples of $15,000, the amount of a partnership unit. Renée asked Tony to explain what happened. Tony told her, "When I received the money from the first partnership escrow, I wanted to do something nice for relatives and employees who had been loyal to me over the years. This is just my way of sharing my good fortune with the ones I love. The equality of the amounts is just a coincidence."

IMPORTANCE TO ACCOUNTANTS[1]

Accountants need to consider the reasonableness of the information they receive. In this case, the timing was odd. Second, the identical amounts are an unusual coincidence. Third, if Tony really had wanted to do something special for these folks, why didn't he give them something, rather than loaning them money? When information does not match or seems unreasonable, it is important to ask for additional evidence. Fortin asked that the promoter, Alice, send her detailed information on the subscriptions to each partnership. Alice refused, stating that she was under legal obligation to keep all information confidential. When Renée pressed Tony, he also refused further cooperation, although he did say he would "represent" to her that the loans had nothing to do with closing the partnerships so he could get his money. At this point, Renée withdrew from the engagement. The appearance of Tony hiding something threw the rest of the financial information into question.

---

[1]As Renée Fortin is conducting a review engagement rather than an audit, Fortin would be referred to as the accountant rather than the auditor.

continued >

WHAT DO YOU THINK?

1. Why is Tony hiding the purchases made by his relatives? What adjustments or disclosures would need to be made to the financial statements?

2. What other financial information could be incorrect? Could review procedures compensate for these potential errors?

IT is difficult to resign from an engagement. As a professional accountant, to maintain your professional integrity and protect your business, you may have to resign from high-risk engagements at some time in your professional career. Think about difficult decisions that you have made in your life. How have they enhanced your ability to act with integrity?

In addition to being involved with audits of historical financial statements prepared in accordance with an appropriate financial reporting framework, public accountants commonly deal with situations involving other types of information, varying levels of assurance, and other types of reports. In this chapter, we talk about engagements that work with financial information as well as other types of engagements.

① Assurance Engagements

Chapter 1 described some of the services that a public accountant (PA) can provide. Users may misinterpret how a PA is involved with information, so it is very important that the PA properly communicate to users of information with whom he or she is associated both the nature and extent of the association (as described in *CICA Handbook* Section 5020). In studying the engagements and reports we highlight in this chapter, you should note similarities and differences between the reports and the auditor's report discussed in Chapter 20. Also note that it is highly recommended that an engagement letter be prepared and accepted by the client for all engagements.

There are three parties to an **assurance engagement**: (1) the practitioner, (2) the user(s), and (3) the person (or organization) who is accountable (usually management). Figure 21-1 (based on *CICA Handbook* Section 5025.07) illustrates this relationship. The user could be any stakeholder who will use the information on which the assurance is provided.

Section 5025 was designed to provide guidance for a broad range of services. For example, it considers both attest engagements and direct reporting engagements. **Attest engagements** are engagements where the auditor expresses a conclusion on a written assertion about a subject prepared by the accountable party, such as management. The assertion measures the subject matter using appropriate criteria. For example, a review engagement and a financial statement audit are both attest engagements, since management prepared the report (the financial statements), and specified criteria (such as ASPE) are used to measure the financial statements (the subject matter).

Assurance engagement—an engagement where there is an accountability relationship between two or more parties, and the practitioner is engaged to issue a written communication expressing a conclusion about subject matter for which the accountable party is responsible.

Attest engagement—an engagement where the auditor expresses a conclusion on a written assertion about a subject prepared by the accountable party, such as management; the assertion measures the subject matter using appropriate criteria.

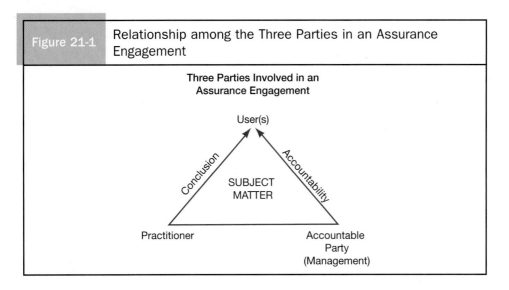

| Figure 21-1 | Relationship among the Three Parties in an Assurance Engagement |

Three Parties Involved in an Assurance Engagement

User(s)

Conclusion

Accountability

SUBJECT MATTER

Practitioner

Accountable Party (Management)

A **direct reporting engagement** is an engagement where the auditor directly expresses a conclusion on his or her evaluation of subject matter using criteria; management does not report in a direct reporting engagement. Perhaps the best example of a direct reporting engagement is the communication by the Auditor General to Parliament. In these reports the Auditor General of Canada describes what was found as a result of audits performed. The general standard in Section 5025.16 requires that the practitioner have sufficient information to decide whether the engagement can be completed in accordance with the assurance standards. The practitioner and all others involved with the assurance engagement should have adequate proficiency to perform the engagement and should collectively possess adequate knowledge of the subject matter. In addition, the engagement should be performed with due care and an objective state of mind. The practitioner should obtain some form of evidence that an accountability relationship exists (i.e., that management is responsible for the subject matter). The evidence will normally be an acknowledgment from management but may be in some other form.

Section 5025 requires the practitioner to identify or develop criteria that can be used to evaluate the subject matter. The importance of this requirement cannot be overemphasized. If the criteria are not suitable, the value of the assurance engagement is doubtful. The section suggests that the necessary characteristics of criteria are relevance, reliability, neutrality, understandability, and completeness. There are three performance standards outlined in the section:

- The work should be adequately planned, and there should be proper supervision.
- The practitioner should consider both significance (similar to materiality) and engagement risk (similar to audit risk) when planning and performing the engagement.
- Sufficient evidence should be gathered to support the conclusion the practitioner expresses in his or her report.

Detailed reporting standards (Section 5025.62) explain what should be included in an assurance report. The section also provides guidance on how to include additional information, or when the auditor will need to provide a reservation (for example, if not enough high quality evidence can be gathered).

These standards for assurance engagements apply to other engagements, such as the audit of internal controls over financial reporting that is integrated with the financial statement audit (covered in Section 5925, and required by Section 404 of the Sarbanes–Oxley Act). Figure 21-2 illustrates the form of communication that would be issued under Section 5925 if the report is provided as a stand-alone report, separate from the auditor's report on the financial statement. Note that the report in Figure 21-2 has the following features:

Direct reporting engagement— one where the auditor directly expresses a conclusion on his or her evaluation of subject matter using criteria; management does not report.

Figure 21-2

Example of an Assurance Report: Report on Internal Control over Financial Reporting

---

INDEPENDENT AUDITOR'S REPORT

To: The Shareholders of Gaa Corp.

We have audited the effectiveness of Gaa Corp.'s internal control over financial reporting as at December 31, 2012.

Management's Responsibility

The entity's management is responsible for maintaining effective internal control over financial reporting.

Auditor's Responsibility

Our responsibility is to express an opinion, based on our audit, on whether the entity's internal control over financial reporting was effectively maintained in accordance with criteria issued by the Committee of Sponsoring Organizations of the Treadway Commission (COSO).

We conducted our audit in accordance with the standard for audits of internal control over financial reporting set out in the CICA Handbook—Assurance. This standard requires that we plan and perform the audit to obtain reasonable assurance about whether effective internal control over financial reporting was maintained in all material respects. Our audit of internal control over financial reporting included obtaining an understanding of internal control over financial reporting, assessing the risk that a material weakness existed, testing and evaluating the design and operating effectiveness of internal control based on the assessed risk, and performing such other procedures as we considered necessary in the circumstances.

We believe that the audit evidence we have obtained is sufficient and appropriate to provide a basis for our opinion.

An entity's internal control over financial reporting is a process designed to provide reasonable assurance regarding the reliability of financial reporting and the preparation of financial statements for external purposes in accordance with an acceptable financial reporting framework. An entity's internal control over financial reporting includes those policies and procedures that (1) pertain to the maintenance of records that, in reasonable detail, accurately and fairly reflect the transactions and dispositions of the assets of the entity; (2) provide reasonable assurance that transactions are recorded as necessary to permit preparation of financial statements in accordance with an acceptable financial reporting framework, and that receipts and expenditures of the entity are being made only in accordance with authorizations of management and directors of the entity; and (3) provide reasonable assurance regarding prevention or timely detection of unauthorized acquisition, use, or disposition of the entity's assets that could have a material effect on the financial statements.

Because of its inherent limitations, internal control over financial reporting may not prevent or detect misstatements. Also, projections of any evaluation of effectiveness to future periods are subject to the risk that controls may become inadequate because of changes in conditions, or that the degree of compliance with the policies or procedures may deteriorate.

Opinion

In our opinion, the entity maintained, in all material respects, effective internal control over financial reporting as at December 31, 2012, in accordance with criteria issued by the Committee of Sponsoring Organizations of the Treadway Commission (COSO).

We have also audited, in accordance with Canadian generally accepted auditing standards, the statement of financial position and the statements of comprehensive income, equity, and cash flows of Gaa Corp. and issued our report dated February 7, 2013, which is the same as the date of the report on the effectiveness of internal control over financial reporting.

Brunkof + Makepeace

Edmonton, Alberta

February 7, 2013

Chartered Accountants

- An introductory paragraph describing the purpose of the engagement (the subject matter), the responsibilities of management (the accountable party) and the auditor, and the criteria used (the criteria for the engagement are COSO standards, from the Committee of Sponsoring Organizations of the Treadway Commission; see **www.coso.org**).

Figure 21-3   Example of a Report under Section 9100

ACCOUNTANTS' REPORT IN CONNECTION WITH GROSS SALES

To Garner Limited:

As requested by Okanagan Stores Limited, we report that the gross sales of the company's store at King Street, Kelowna, B.C., for the year ended June 30, 2012, are recorded in the amount of $790,000 in the general ledger sales account of the company and form part of the company's gross sales in its financial statements for the year then ended, on which we reported on August 3, 2012.

Our examination of the company's financial statements for the year ended June 30, 2012, was not directed to the determination of gross sales or other financial information of individual stores. We have not performed an audit of and accordingly do not express an opinion on the amount of gross sales referred to in the preceding paragraph.

It is understood that this report is to be used solely for computing percentage rental and is not to be referred to or distributed to any person who is not a member of management of Garner Limited or Okanagan Stores Limited.

Kelowna, B.C.

August 8, 2012

Carter ◦ Wilhelm

Certified General Accountants

- A scope paragraph that summarizes standards used to conduct the field work.
- A definition paragraph that defines the nature of internal control over financial reporting and the general purposes of such controls.
- An opinion paragraph that provides a conclusion.
- An inherent limitations paragraph.
- A final paragraph that provides a cross reference to the audit opinion with respect to the financial statements (see also Chapter 20).

These paragraphs are examples of additional information that the practitioner includes to make the auditor's report more informative.

You should compare Figure 21-2 to Figure 20-1 in order to understand the differences and similarities between a standard auditor's report and a report issued in connection with an assurance engagement (report on internal control over financial reporting).

REPORTS ON THE RESULTS OF APPLYING SPECIFIED AUDITING PROCEDURES TO FINANCIAL INFORMATION OTHER THAN FINANCIAL STATEMENTS (SECTION 9100) At the opposite end of the assurance spectrum, we have an engagement that includes audit procedures but provides no assurance, covered by Section 9100. This section is concerned with an accountant's application of prespecified procedures to financial information. The engagement is not an assurance engagement and an expression of an opinion is not expected. Since the client specifies what procedures are to be applied and the form of report that is to be issued, distribution of the report is normally restricted. The accountant reaches an agreement with the client with respect to these issues before beginning the engagement. In this situation, the accountant should comply both with the general assurance standard and the first examination standard.

Figure 21-3 is an illustration of such a report. It was prepared in the situation where the financial statements were audited, but gross sales were not audited on a store-by-store basis.

concept check

C21-1 How are attest and assurance engagements related?

C21-2 Describe the three performance standards that apply to all assurance engagements.

② Review and Compilation Services

Many public accountants are involved with non-public clients that do not have audits. A company may believe an audit is unnecessary due to the active involvement of the owners in the business, lack of significant debt, or absence of regulations requiring the

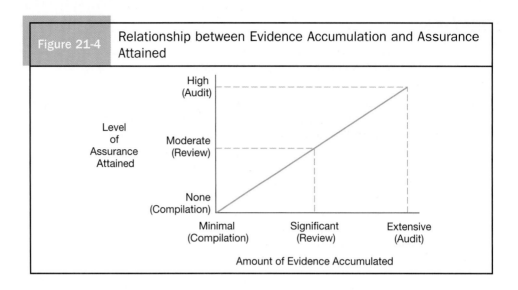

Figure 21-4 Relationship between Evidence Accumulation and Assurance Attained

Level of Assurance Attained

- High (Audit)
- Moderate (Review)
- None (Compilation)

Amount of Evidence Accumulated

- Minimal (Compilation)
- Significant (Review)
- Extensive (Audit)

company to have one. Common examples are smaller companies and professional organizations such as partnerships of physicians and lawyers.

These organizations often engage a public accountant to provide tax services and to assist in the preparation of accurate financial information without an audit. Providing these services is a significant part of the practice of many smaller public accounting firms. When a public accountant provides any services involving financial statements, specific requirements exist. The requirements for review engagements are covered in *CICA Handbook* Sections 8100, 8200, 8500, and 8600. Requirements for compilation engagements appear in Section 9200.

The assurance provided by reviews and compilations is considerably below that of audits, and the practitioners' reports are intended to convey that difference. Similarly, the extent of evidence accumulation differs among the three types of engagements (i.e., audit, review, and compilation). Figure 21-4 illustrates the difference in both the evidence accumulation and the level of assurance provided. The amount of assurance and extent of evidence accumulation, shown in Figure 21-4, are not well defined by the profession. This is because both evidence accumulation and assurance are subjective. Only a practitioner in the circumstances of an engagement can judge how much evidence is sufficient and what level of assurance has actually been attained. Table 21-1 compares audits, reviews, and compilations on a number of dimensions.

TERMS OF ENGAGEMENT While the *CICA Handbook* sections covering review and compilation engagements do not require an engagement letter (although it is advisable to have one), they do require that the public accountant and the client reach an understanding and agreement regarding the services to be provided. An engagement letter would include items such as:

- A description of the services to be provided.
- A discussion of the client's responsibility for providing complete and accurate information.

Table 21-1 Comparison of Audit, Review, and Compilation Engagements

Type of Engagement	Amount of Evidence	Level of Assurance	Form of Conclusion	Communication Title
Audit	Extensive	High	Positive	Independent Auditors' Report
Review	Moderate	Moderate	Negative	Review Engagement Report
Compilation	Minor	None	None	Notice to Reader

Small Business Risks

A review engagement focuses on plausibility, or reasonableness, of financial information. This includes assessing the likelihood of fraud, and of the entity's compliance with laws and regulations.

Small business systems may be basic. For example, what would an organization do to comply with privacy legislation? It would need to have clear procedures when dealing with client information, and use a very powerful tool—the shredder! Combined with owner vigilance over employees and access to information, the shredder is important in destroying paper records that may contain private data.

Even small businesses may use electronic means to transmit and receive funds via inter-mediate organizations such as PayPal, an electronic payment service. The business would need to monitor the service to ensure that it is not hacked and to make sure that they receive their funds on time—one convenient method is to have a separate bank account or credit card with a relatively low limit to mitigate the likelihood of loss. A small business that has had its electronic payment systems "hijacked" could literally close its doors if large amounts of funds are taken.

Sources: 1. Kandra, Anne, "The problem with PayPal," *PC World*, January 3, 2005. 2. Perkins, Tara, "Information theft: security firms boom," *Toronto Star*, January 20, 2007, p. D1, D4. 3. Corbin, Kenneth, "New developments in PayPal Class Action Lawsuit over payment holds," **www.ecommercebytes.com**, November 11, 2011, Accessed: April 11, 2012.

- A statement that an audit is not to be performed and that, consequently, no opinion will be expressed. In the case of a compilation engagement, the fact that no assurance results should be stated.
- A note on any restrictions on the distribution of the statements.
- A statement that each page of the statements should be clearly marked "unaudited."
- The probable content of the communication, to be attached by the accountant.
- The fact that the engagement cannot be relied on to detect error or fraud and other irregularities.
- Possibly a comment to the effect that the statements do not satisfy any statutory requirements.

REVIEW   A **review engagement** is described by the *CICA Handbook* (Section 8100.05) by describing the procedures used to conduct it. The accountant would use inquiry, analytical procedures, and discussion during the engagement. Rather than providing reasonable assurance, the accountant's objective is to provide an opinion on "plausibility" of the information using appropriate criteria. Plausible can be defined as being worthy of belief.

General review standards   Section 8100, General review standards, discusses the acceptance of an engagement and the standards applicable to review engagements. These include knowledge of the client's business, review procedures, documentation, and reporting. Review engagements should be accepted by a public accountant only if the accountant believes that he or she has the necessary competence in the subject matter to be reported on and is independent of the client.

Procedures suggested for reviews   Reviews imply a level of assurance somewhere between that of an audit and the absence of assurance provided by a compilation. A review does not include obtaining an understanding of internal controls or tests of controls, independent confirmation, or physical inspection. The emphasis in reviews is on four broad areas:

- Obtain knowledge of the client's business. The information should be about the nature of the client's organization and business transactions; its accounting records and employees; the basis, form, and content of the financial statements; and accounting matters peculiar to the client's business and industry.

Review engagement—one that consists primarily of inquiry, analytical procedures, and discussion with the limited objectives of assessing whether the information being reported on is plausible within the framework of appropriate criteria.

- Make inquiries of client personnel. The objective of these inquiries is to determine whether the financial statements are fairly presented, assuming that management does not intend to deceive the accountant. The CICA Assurance and Related Services Guideline AuG-20, Performance of a review of financial statements in accordance with sections 8100 and 8200, provides a thorough list of questions that can be asked.
- Perform analytical procedures. These are meant to identify relationships and individual items that appear to be unusual. Analytical procedures performed during a review engagement would normally be less extensive than those performed during an audit. The appropriate analytical procedures are the same as the ones already studied in Chapter 8 and in those chapters dealing with substantive procedures. Explanations for relationships and items that appear to be unusual would be obtained by inquiry of appropriate client personnel.
- Have discussions with management concerning information received and the information being reported on.

Generally accepted review standards The standards for review engagements are similar to generally accepted auditing standards, except that they deal with reviews and not audits. Based on Section 8100.15, these standards comprise the following:

- A general standard indicating that the engagement and its resulting report should be completed by individuals with sufficient training and competence, who are independent and conduct the work with due care.
- Review standards that cover similar areas as GAAS. These are as follows:

  (i) The engagement should be properly planned and executed, with any assistants adequately supervised.
  (ii) Adequate knowledge of the business is gathered as the basis for the completion of the engagement.
  (iii) Techniques used should be used to measure the plausibility of the subject matter against specified criteria (e.g., ASPE). Techniques would normally be limited to inquiry, analytical procedures, and discussion. Only if there were uncertainty with respect to the plausibility of the subject matter would the accountant conduct additional procedures.

- Reporting standards describe the required contents of the report, as illustrated in Figure 21-5.

Figure 21-5   Example of a Report under Section 8200

REVIEW ENGAGEMENT REPORT

To R. Fortin:

I have reviewed the balance sheet of Leger Inc. as at December 31, 2012, and the statements of income, retained earnings, and cash flows for the year then ended. My review was made in accordance with Canadian generally accepted standards established for review engagements and accordingly consisted primarily of inquiry, analytical procedures, and discussion related to information supplied to me by the company.

A review does not constitute an audit, and, consequently, I do not express an audit opinion on these financial statements.

Based on my review, nothing has come to my attention that causes me to believe that these financial statements are not, in all material respects, in accordance with Canadian generally accepted accounting principles.

Montréal, Québec
February 18, 2013

a. Vachon

Certified General Accountant

Review Inquiry Relevant to Not-for-Profit Organizations

Not-for-profit organizations (NPOs) do not have shareholders, but they do have a board of directors. These directors are elected by members, rather than shareholders, so the accountant needs to find out how membership is determined. If the accountant is a member (such as of a golf club), his or her independence might be questioned. One possibility is to ask for a bylaw stating that the accountant cannot vote for board members. This is particularly relevant, since the accountant must report a number of issues to the audit committee (a subcommittee of the board).

Important issues for NPOs include the following:

- *Awareness of fraud risks:* Is leadership organized, rather than chaotic, and aware of the risks of fraud? Are random supervision and volunteer/staff rotation used to encourage early detection? Does the environment make it easy to report suspicious behaviour?

- *Completeness of revenues:* Are numbered receipts issued? How is fundraising handled? What is the mix between government grants and fundraising?

- *Valuation of donated assets or services:* How are donated services or donated assets valued? Are charitable donation receipts given for these items and services? Are valued amounts defensible for tax purposes? Is volunteer time recorded at nil?

- *Existence of donated assets:* Are these items added to a capital assets ledger, even if they were donated and have been recorded at a nil value?

- *Compliance with regulations:* Are funds disbursed in accordance with their intended purpose? Is an accounting system in place that properly tracks and distributes restricted funds? How does the NPO ensure that directors do not receive any funds or benefits?

The requirement that the accountant have sufficient knowledge of the client's enterprise and type of business is made so that the accountant can assess whether the information to be reported on is plausible in the circumstances. The accountant would not be able to make the required inquiry and assessment of the information obtained without such knowledge. For instance, the accountant would not be able to assess the plausibility of manufactured inventory unless he or she had knowledge of the company's product and manufacturing processes.

The review standards should be appropriate to the particular engagement; for example, it is likely that procedures would differ between a review of financial statements and financial information. The review procedures do not preclude audit procedures if the accountant believes that more extensive procedures are required to assess plausibility. However, once the accountant decides to use more extensive procedures, such as audit procedures, the particular procedure must be carried out to completion. The accountant should not carry out an audit procedure to partial completion simply because the engagement is a review.

Materiality would be measured in the same manner as with an audit.

Negative assurance should be expressed only when the standards applicable to a review engagement described above have been met.

As illustrated in Figure 21-5, the report first indicates the type of engagement, then identifies the information presented (a set of financial statements as of a specific date) and the criteria used (ASPE). The report states that a review does not constitute an audit after clearly indicating the procedures used (primarily inquiry, analytical procedures, and discussion) were performed in accordance with generally accepted standards for review engagements. The purpose of stating that a review does not constitute an audit is to ensure that financial statement users are aware that a review provides a lower level of assurance than an audit. As illustrated in the last sentence of the

Figure 21-6 Example of a Report under Section 8500

REVIEW ENGAGEMENT REPORT

To Kamloops Limited:

At the request of Pacific Limited, I have reviewed the plant and equipment of Pacific Limited as at March 31, 2012 (calculated in accordance with the provisions of section 10 of the mortgage agreement with Kamloops Limited dated May 5, 2009, and the interpretations set out in note 1). My review was made in accordance with Canadian generally accepted standards for review engagements and accordingly consisted primarily of inquiry, analytical procedures, and discussion related to information supplied to me by the company.

A review does not constitute an audit, and, consequently, I do not express an audit opinion on this plant and equipment.

Based on my review, nothing has come to my attention that causes me to believe that this plant and equipment are not presented fairly in accordance with the provisions of section 10 of the mortgage agreement with Kamloops Limited dated May 5, 2009, and the interpretations set out in note 1.

Vancouver, B.C.

June 7, 2012

L. Dayl

Chartered Accountant

---

report, the accountant should also state, except when a reservation is required, that nothing has come to his or her attention as a result of his or her review that causes him or her to believe that the information is not, in all material respects, in accordance with an appropriate disclosed basis of accounting. The appropriate disclosed basis of accounting would be ASPE, ASNPO, or IFRS, except in special circumstances or, in the case of non-financial information, other appropriate criteria. This is called "negative assurance." In addition, each page of information reported on would be marked "unaudited."

Reservations may be required in the accountant's report when the review cannot be completed, when there is a departure from the appropriate criteria, or when the accountant concludes that the client's interpretation of an agreement or regulation is not reasonable. The reservation would be disclosed in a reservation paragraph in the review engagement report, which would appear immediately preceding the negative assurance paragraph. The reason for the reservation and the effect of the reservation on the information reported on should also be disclosed.

The discovery of a misstatement after the release of the report by the accountant should be treated in the same way as the discovery of a misstatement by an auditor after the release of audited financial statements.

CAS **Reviews of financial information other than financial statements** Section 8500 describes the sorts of financial information that might be included under this grouping. This section is parallel to CAS 805. When the information is prepared in accordance with an agreement or a regulation and that agreement requires interpretations, the report should refer to such interpretations. Figure 21-6 shows the form a communication might take when the auditor is reporting on financial information other than financial statements.

Reviews of compliance with agreements and regulations Section 8600 is parallel to Section 5815. The accountant should read the relevant provisions of the agreement or regulation, inquire about how the client monitors its compliance with the provisions, and consider whether the provisions have been consistently applied. In the review engagement report, the PA should identify the provisions of the agreement or regulation that establish the criteria on which his or her assessment of compliance is based. As well, any significant interpretations of the criteria made by the accountant

Figure 21-7   Example of a Report Under Section 8600

REVIEW ENGAGEMENT REPORT

To J. O'Sullivan:

I have reviewed Separate Limited's compliance as at December 31, 2012, with covenants to be complied with described in sections 8 to 10 inclusive of the agreement dated November 3, 2010, with Waterloo Inc. My review was made in accordance with Canadian generally accepted standards for review engagements and accordingly consisted primarily of inquiry, analytical procedures, and discussion related to information supplied to me by the company.

A review does not constitute an audit, and, consequently, I do not express an audit opinion on this matter.

Based on my review, nothing has come to my attention that causes me to believe that the company is not in compliance with covenants to be complied with as described in sections 8 to 10 inclusive of this agreement.

Calgary, Alberta

January 18, 2013

G. On

Certified General Accountant

---

when the criteria were non-specific and any significant changes in interpretations from the previous year should be identified. Figure 21-7 presents an example of a report that the accountant might issue.

COMPILATION Compilation services are bookkeeping services that lead to the completion of financial statements. It is common for smaller public accounting firms to provide bookkeeping services, monthly or quarterly financial statements, and tax services for smaller clients.

In **compilation engagements**, discussed in Section 9200, the public accountant provides assistance in compiling financial statements but is not required to provide any assurance about the statements; the engagement is not an assurance engagement. The statements may be complete (i.e., include balance sheet, income statement, statement of retained earnings, and statement of cash flows); they may be part of a complete set of financial statements; or they may be for the whole enterprise or for a part of the enterprise. The accountant assembles the information supplied by the client and ensures that it is arithmetically correct; the accountant is concerned with neither the accuracy or completeness of the information nor whether the financial statements comply with an acceptable financial reporting framework. Although the accountant should not be associated with false or misleading financial statements, determining whether the statements are false or misleading can be difficult because of the limited involvement.

Section 9200.12 sets out the criteria for accepting a compilation engagement: the accountant must have no reason to believe that the statements are false or misleading, and the client clearly understands the nature and scope of the engagement, including its limitations.

Professional standards The compilation services should be performed and the report prepared by individuals who have adequate technical training and proficiency in accounting, and who completed their work with due care. Like other types of engagements, planning and proper conduct of the work is required. Any assistants should be properly supervised.

If something comes to the attention of the public accountant that could indicate that the financial statements may be false or misleading, additional information must be obtained and the statements amended, or the accountant should resign from the engagement.

Form of report The communication from the public accountant in a compilation engagement is entitled "Notice to Reader." Each page of the statements should include either the "Notice to Reader" heading itself or the statement "Unaudited— See Notice to Reader." An example of a "Notice to Reader" appears in Figure 21-8.

> **Compilation engagement—** non-audit engagement in which the public accountant provides assistance in compiling financial statements but is not expected to provide assurance about the statements.

Figure 21-8	Example of Report under Section 9200

NOTICE TO READER

On the basis of information provided by management, I have compiled the balance sheet of New B Ltd. as at March 31, 2012, and the statements of income, retained earnings, and cash flows for the year then ended.

I have not performed an audit or a review engagement in respect of these financial statements and, accordingly, I express no assurance thereon.

Readers are cautioned that these statements may not be appropriate for their purposes.

Halifax, N.S.

June 12, 2012

R. Fundy

Chartered Accountant

The example illustrates key aspects of the report: it is clearly labelled, with the work and the financial statements (including period covered) described. The report states that the accountant has not audited or otherwise checked the information that was provided by management. Because the statements might not be in accordance with an acceptable financial reporting framework, the report also includes a warning with respect to the use of the financial statements.

Departures from an acceptable financial reporting framework should not be referred to in the report as this may suggest that the public accountant has a responsibility to detect and report all such departures.

Compilation standards also apply to the financial information included in a client's tax return. Thus, accountants should include a "Notice to Reader" with financial information included with personal tax returns prepared on behalf of clients.

Interim Financial Information and Future-Oriented Information

Interim Financial Information

Interim financial information may be audited, reviewed, or compiled by a public accountant. The decision depends on how much assurance is desired from the accountant's involvement and how timely the information must be. Estimates normally have to be made in order to prepare the information on a timely basis. Therefore, the information may not be as reliable as annual financial information. Since the objective of producing interim financial information is to provide up-to-date information to users of the statements, such information is usually not audited. Section 7050, Auditor review of interim financial statements, provides thorough guidance for review of financial statements for a financial reporting period that is shorter than the fiscal year. Sections 8100, 8200, 8500, and 8600 can also be consulted when interim financial information is reviewed. If the information is compiled, Section 9200 is relevant.

Future-Oriented Financial Information

Future-oriented financial information (FOFI) is prospective information about results of operations or other financial information that is based on assumptions about future economic conditions and courses of action. It may be presented either as a forecast or a projection. AuG-6 describes the nature of FOFI and provides guidance for providing assurance on FOFI. This Guideline is directed at prospective information included in offering documents.

Future-oriented financial information (FOFI)—information about prospective results of operations, financial position, and/or changes in financial position based on assumptions about future economic conditions and courses of action; may be presented either as a forecast or projection.

Assurance and Related Services Guideline AuG-16, Compilation of a financial forecast or projection, indicates the standards that the public accountant should follow when compiling a forecast or projection for a client who does not require the public accountant to provide any assurance.

Chapter 1 pointed out that Assurance and Related Services Guidelines do not have the force of Recommendations. Their intent is to provide guidance in the absence of Recommendations.

FORECASTS AND PROJECTIONS Future-oriented financial information deals with the future, not with the past. There are two general types of future-oriented financial information: forecasts and projections. A **forecast** is prospective financial information prepared using assumptions reflecting management's judgment as to the most probable courses of action for the entity. The information is presented to the best of management's knowledge and belief. A **projection** is prepared using one or more assumptions (hypotheses) that do not necessarily reflect the most likely course of action in management's judgment.

USE OF PROSPECTIVE FINANCIAL STATEMENTS **Prospective financial statements** refer to predicted or expected financial statements in some future period (income statement) or at some future date (balance sheet). They can be for either general use or special use. General use refers to use by any third party. An example of general use would be inclusion of a financial forecast in a prospectus for the sale of shares of a large public company. Special use refers to use by third parties with whom the responsible party is negotiating directly. An example of special purpose future-oriented financial information would be the inclusion of a financial projection in a takeover bid circular aimed at current shareholders of the company or in an entity's application for a bank loan.

ACCEPTANCE OF THE ENGAGEMENT The following discussion pertains to Assurance and Related Service Guideline AuG-6. As with other types of engagements performed by the public accountant, it is important to ensure that the nature and terms of involvement with future-oriented financial information are understood and agreed to by management, preferably in writing. Management should also acknowledge its responsibilities related to the financial information. AuG-6 identifies a number of matters that should be agreed to by management and the public accountant and included in an engagement letter:

- The anticipated form of the financial forecast.
- The period of time to be covered.
- The fact that management will prepare and present the forecast in accordance with an applicable financial reporting framework and in accordance with any applicable securities requirements.
- The fact that management is responsible for the forecast: its presentation, the process of preparation, and the assumptions used.
- The fact that management is responsible for obtaining or developing appropriate support for the assumptions sufficient to enable the public accountant to report without reservation.
- The need for the public accountant to have access to outside specialists and third-party reports obtained by management (e.g., a feasibility study).
- The anticipated form and content of the public accountant's report.
- The fact that the public accountant has no responsibility to update his or her report for events and circumstances occurring after the date of that report.

Before accepting such an engagement, the public accountant should ensure that management will act with integrity during the engagement, providing relevant information, and that sufficient evidence will be available to conduct the engagement.

Professional standards As with other types of reports, FOFI services should be performed by someone with adequate technical training and proficiency; the examination

Forecast—prospective financial information prepared using assumptions as to the most probable courses of action for the entity.

Projection—prospective financial information prepared using assumptions reflecting management's judgment as to the most probable course of action for the entity; prepared using one or more assumptions (hypotheses) that do not necessarily reflect the most likely course of action in management's judgment.

Prospective financial statements—financial statements that deal with expected/projected future data rather than with historical data.

should be carefully supervised and properly performed; and the report should be prepared with due care. Enough evidence should be obtained about the assumptions and the underlying data to provide a reasonable basis for the report. Supporting documentation and evidence should be retained in a working paper file.

EXAMINATION OF PROSPECTIVE FINANCIAL STATEMENTS An examination of future-oriented financial information involves evaluating the preparation of the future-oriented financial information and the underlying assumptions and assessing the plausibility of hypotheses. In addition, the public accountant would evaluate the presentation of the financial information for appropriate presentation and disclosure (including understandability) and ensure that accounting policies are consistent with those used in the historical financial statements. The public accountant would obtain a written letter of representation from management acknowledging its responsibility for preparing the forecast or projection and indicating that forecast figures are management's best estimate of the forecast results. Finally, the accountant would issue an examination report.

These evaluations are based primarily on accumulating evidence about the completeness and reasonableness of the underlying assumptions as disclosed in the prospective financial information. This requires the accountant to become familiar with the client's business and industry, to identify the significant matters on which the client's future results are expected to depend ("key factors"), and to determine that appropriate assumptions have been included with respect to these.

REPORTING The accountant's report on an examination of financial statements is illustrated in Figure 21-9. Like other examples in this chapter, the report is clearly identified, and the information that was examined is described. Then, the role of management and the accountants is stated. For FOFI, the auditor states an opinion about the underlying assumptions rather than the data presented in the financial statements themselves. Finally, the last paragraph in the report includes a warning that the results may not be achieved and that the accountant cannot provide any kind of opinion about such future events.

The date of the report would be the date of the completion of the fieldwork by the public accountant.

concept check

C21-5 What is the purpose of interim financial information?

C21-6 The difference between a forecast and a projection relates to the nature of the underlying assumptions. Describe that difference.

Figure 21-9	Example of a Report on a Financial Forecast

AUDITOR'S REPORT ON FINANCIAL FORECAST

To the Directors of Nomad Corp.:

The accompanying financial forecast of Nomad Corp. consisting of a balance sheet as at June 30, 2013, and the statements of income, retained earnings, and changes in financial position for the period then ending have been prepared by management using assumptions with an effective date of June 30, 2012. We have examined the support provided by management for the assumptions, and the preparation and presentation of this forecast. Our examination was made in accordance with Auditing Guideline AuG-6 as set out in the *CICA Handbook*–Assurance. We have no responsibility to update this report for events and circumstances occurring after the date of our report.

In our opinion, as of the date of this report, the assumptions developed by management are suitably supported and consistent with the plans of the Company and provide a reasonable basis for the forecast; this forecast reflects such assumptions; and the financial forecast complies with the presentation and disclosure standards as set out in the *CICA Handbook*–Accounting.

Since this forecast is based on assumptions regarding future events, actual results will vary from the information presented and the variations may be material. Accordingly, we express no opinion as to whether this forecast will be achieved.

Toronto, Ontario

August 15, 2012

McWhite & Kedwell

Chartered Accountants

Summary

1. *How is the assurance engagement general standard different from the audit standard?* The assurance standard requires that the public accountant believe it is possible to complete the engagement. The equivalent statement (i.e., having a reasonable basis to conduct an audit) is not present in the audit standard.

   How is it similar? Both general standards require adequate proficiency to perform the engagement, having knowledge of the business or subject matter, and that the engagement be completed with due care and an objective state of mind.

   Provide an example of a special report that provides the following:
   (i) High assurance—an auditor's report concerning the effectiveness of the system of internal control over financial reporting.
   (ii) No assurance—an accountant's report on gross sales that were not audited.

2. *Why are review and compilation services important?* Many businesses and other organizations do not require the assurance level that is provided by an audit. Even some banks require only moderate assurance (i.e., a review engagement) for bank loans. A key service that may not require assurance is the preparation of information included with a tax return.

   How are the evidence collection procedures related to the assurance level provided for audits, reviews, and compilations? Audits require the greatest amount of evidence collection, with the requirement that objective evidence be collected, where possible. This results in the audit providing the greatest assurance level of the three engagements. Reviews require less evidence, and the procedures are normally limited to inquiry, analysis, and discussion, while compilations provide no assurance—the accountant does not gather any evidence.

3. *What type of report does the public accountant provide for interim financial information?* Interim financial information can be audited, reviewed, or compiled. The type of report depends on the type of engagement.

   How does the public accountant report on future-oriented information? The public accountant evaluates the assumptions used by management and checks that the information has been compiled correctly (compilation engagement).

MyAccountingLab

Make the grade with MyAccountingLab: The questions, exercises, and problems marked in orange can be found on MyAccountingLab. You can practise them as often as you want, and most feature step-by-step guided instructions to help you find the right answer.

Review Questions

21-1 ❶ Distinguish between an "attest engagement" and a "direct reporting engagement."

21-2 ❶ Explain why criteria are so important with respect to assurance engagements.

21-3 ❶ Identify the three parties to an accountability relationship, and explain the roles of each.

21-4 ❶ Give three examples of the special reports that a public accountant may be asked to issue. Explain why these reports would be requested.

21-5 ❶ Why do public accountants prepare reports on the results of applying specified auditing procedures to financial information other than financial statements?

21-6 ❷ How do the general standards applicable to review engagements differ from generally accepted auditing standards?

21-7 ❷ Contrast the level of assurance provided by negative assurance discussed in Sections 8100, 8200, 8500, and 8600 of the *CICA Handbook* with the level of assurance provided by the opinion given in the auditor's report.

21-8 ❷ What is the intention of Section 9200, Compilation engagements, in the *CICA Handbook*?

21-9 ❷ Discuss the standards for compilation engagements, and explain why they differ from those for review engagements and audits.

21-10 ❷ The financial statements prepared for a compilation engagement may not be complete according to an acceptable financial reporting framework. Why is this exception permitted? Provide examples of information that might be excluded.

21-11 ❷ Explain how the review engagement for an NPO differs from the review engagement for a profit-oriented entity.

21-12 ❸ On what does the auditor comment in his or her report on financial forecasts? On what does the auditor disclaim an opinion and why?

Discussion Questions and Problems

21-13 ❶ ❷ Joseph, a public accountant, has been keeping the books for his father's business, JoPar Tech Ltd., in the evenings, while working with other clients during the day. Yesterday, Joseph's father proudly announced that he had negotiated a loan with the Federal Business Development Bank at favourable rates so that he could purchase $120,000 in new machinery and equipment. Upon reviewing the loan agreement, Joseph discovered that one of the requirements of the loan agreement is that JoPar Tech Ltd. submit financial statements that have been reviewed by a public accountant within 90 days of the fiscal year end.

REQUIRED

a. Can Joseph complete a review engagement report for JoPar Tech Ltd.? Why or why not?

b. What type of engagement can Joseph complete with respect to the financial statements of JoPar Tech Ltd.?

c. What would you advise Joseph to do? Why?

21-14 ❶ ❷ You are doing a review engagement and the related tax work for Regency Tools, Inc., a tool and die company with $2,000,000 in sales. Inventory is recorded at $125,000. Prior-year unaudited statements, prepared by the company without assistance from a public accounting firm, disclose that the inventory is based on "historical cost estimated by management." You obtain the following facts:

1. The company has been growing steadily for the past five years.
2. The unit cost of typical material used by Regency Tools has increased dramatically for several years.
3. The inventory cost has been approximately $125,000 for five years.
4. Management intends to use a value of $125,000 again for the current year-end financial statements.

When you discuss with management the need to get a physical count and an accurate inventory, the response is negative. Management is concerned about the effects on income taxes of a more realistic inventory. The company has never been audited and has always estimated the historical cost of inventory. You are convinced, based upon inquiry and ratio analysis, that a conservative evaluation would be $500,000 at historical cost.

REQUIRED

a. What are the generally accepted accounting requirements for valuation and disclosure of inventory for unaudited financial statements with a review report?

b. Identify the potential legal and professional problems that you face in this situation.

c. What procedures would you normally follow for a review engagement when the inventory is a material amount? Be as specific as possible.

d. How should you resolve the problem in this situation? Identify alternatives, and evaluate the costs and benefits of each.

21-15 ❶ ❷ O'Sullivan, a public accountant, has completed the audit of Sarawak Lumber Supply Co. Ltd. and has issued a standard unqualified report. In addition to a report on the overall financial statements, the company needs a special audit report on three specific accounts: sales, net fixed assets, and inventory valued at FIFO. The report is to be issued to Sarawak's lessor, who bases annual rentals on these three accounts. O'Sullivan was not aware of the need for the special report until after the overall audit was completed.

REQUIRED

a. Explain why O'Sullivan is unlikely to be able to issue the special audit report without additional audit tests.

b. What additional tests are likely to be needed before the special report can be issued?

c. Assume that O'Sullivan is able to satisfy all the requirements needed to issue the special report. Write the report, making any necessary assumptions.

21-16 ❷ The following items represent a series of unrelated procedures that an accountant may consider performing in an engagement to review or compile the financial statements of a non-public entity. Procedures may apply to only one, both, or neither type of engagement.

1. The accountant should establish an understanding with the entity regarding the nature and limitations of the services to be performed.
2. The accountant should make inquiries concerning actions taken at the board of directors' meetings.
3. The accountant should obtain a level of knowledge of the accounting principles and practices of the entity's industry.
4. The accountant should obtain an understanding of the entity's internal control.
5. The accountant should perform analytical procedures designed to identify relationships that appear to be unusual.

6. The accountant should send a letter of inquiry to the entity's lawyer to corroborate the information furnished by management concerning litigation.
7. The accountant should obtain a management representation letter from the entity.
8. The accountant should make inquiries about events subsequent to the date of the financial statements that would have a material effect on the financial statements.
9. The accountant should perform a physical examination of inventory.

REQUIRED

a. Indicate which procedures are required to be performed on a review engagement.

b. Indicate which procedures are required to be performed on a compilation engagement.

21-17 ❷ Chow, a PA, is assisting his client, Western Resources Inc., a closely held company, that is seeking to secure a new line of credit from a local bank. Chow has performed a review of the company's financial statements for several years and always issued a review engagement report without modification or reservation. However, the bank is not satisfied with the reviewed financial statements and is particularly concerned about the value of the client's accounts receivable, which will be pledged as collateral for the new line of credit.

The CEO of Western Resources has asked Chow to perform his normal review of the financial statements this year, as well as confirm a large sample (to be jointly selected by the CEO and Chow) of the company's accounts receivable at year end directly with debtors. He then wants Chow to write a special report to the bank describing his findings with respect to the confirmation of receivables. Chow agrees to perform both of these services for the client for a fixed fee of $15,000, which is about 50 percent more than the usual fee for performing a review.

REQUIRED

Discuss reporting issues with respect to the new engagement.
(Extract from AU2 CGA-Canada Examinations developed by the Certified General Accountants Association of Canada © 2009 CGA-Canada. Reproduced with permission. All rights reserved.)

Professional Judgment Problem

21-18 ❷ Ballantine Church has been located on a central downtown street in Toronto for over 120 years. Originally, the church was in the middle of farmland, but is now surrounded by high-rise apartments and condominiums. The church has an active parish community that engages in fundraising in the neighbourhood, assisting the homeless, and providing drop-in housing during the winter. Francine, the parish priest, and the church board have decided it is time to have a review engagement completed for the church finances. In the past, this work has been done by church members on a part-time basis.

The church organizes its finances based on five funds: operating, endowment, youth, homeless, and music scholarship. Any transfers from the endowment fund to the operating fund must be approved by the board. The church has about $1.2 million in cash and marketable securities in the bank. The church is valued at zero on the balance sheet.

The church also owns a large house. Francine lives in a section of the house and the rest of the property is used for storage, as office space for three permanent church staff, and as meeting space.

REQUIRED

a. What should you do before you accept the review engagement?

b. Outline the process for conducting the review engagement and describe any analytical review procedures that you would conduct specific to the church. What types of questions would you ask that are specific to the church to address plausibility of financial information?

Case

21-19 ❶ Quality Review is the franchisor of a national accounting review course for candidates taking CA, CGA, and CMA examinations. Quality Review is responsible for providing all materials, including DVDs, doing all national and local advertising, and giving assistance in effectively organizing and operating local franchises. The fee to the participant is $1,500 for the full course if all parts of the examination are taken. Quality Review gets 50 percent of the total fee.

The materials for the review course are purchased by Quality Review from Ronnie Johnson, a highly qualified writer of review materials. Quality Review receives one copy of those materials from Ronnie and reproduces them for candidates. Quality Review must pay Ronnie a $60 royalty for each full set of materials used and 12 percent of the participant fee for partial candidates. The contract between Ronnie and Quality Review requires an audited report to be provided by Quality Review on royalties due to Ronnie. Recorded gross fees for the 2009 review course are $1,500,000.

Even before the audit was started, there was a dispute between Quality Review and Ronnie. Quality Review does not intend to pay royalties on certain materials. Ronnie disagrees with that conclusion, but the contract does not specify anything about it. The table on the right lists the disputed sales on which Quality Review refuses to pay royalties:

1. Materials sent to instructors for promotion	$31,000
2. Uncollected fees due to bad debts	6,000
3. Candidates who paid no fee because they performed administrative duties during the course	16,000
4. Refunds to customers who were dissatisfied with the course	22,000
Total	$75,000

REQUIRED

a. Assume that you are engaged to do the ordinary audit of Quality Review and the special audit of royalties for Ronnie. What additional audit testing beyond the normal tests of royalties is required because of the special audit?

b. Assume that the financial statements of Quality Review are found to be fairly stated except for the unresolved dispute between Ronnie and Quality Review. Write the appropriate audit report.

c. Write the report for total royalties to Ronnie, assuming that the information as stated in the case is correct and the dispute is not resolved.

Ongoing Small Business Case: Potential Expansion at CondoCleaners.com

21-20 ❸ It is now March 2013 and Jim, the owner of CondoCleaners.com, has requested you work with him in preparing three-year forecast information for the upcoming year end and two subsequent years. Jim intends to use the forecasts, together with the audited financial statements, to seek additional financing to expand the business. Jim is very busy and is counting on you to assist in any way possible. He wants the most supportive opinion possible from your firm to add to the credibility of the forecast. He informs you that he is willing to do anything necessary to help you prepare the forecast.

First, Jim wants projections of sales and revenues and earnings from the existing business, which he believes could continue to be financed from existing capital.

Second, Jim intends to buy a company in a closely related business that is currently operating unsuccessfully (a cleaning franchise that is being poorly managed). He believes that his skills will make the combined company highly successful. He has made an offer on the new business, subject to obtaining proper financing.

REQUIRED

a. Explain circumstances under which it would and would not be acceptable to undertake the engagement.

b. Why is it important that Jim understand the nature of your reporting requirements before the engagement proceeds?

c. What information will Jim have to provide you before you can complete the forecasted statements? Be as specific as possible.

d. Discuss, in as specific terms as possible, the nature of the report you will issue with the forecasts, assuming that you are able to properly complete them.

Index

The suffix -*f* indicates a figure, -*t* indicates a table, and –*n* indicates a note.

manual controls, 293
manufactured inventory, 537f
manufacturing equipment audit, 522–523, 523f
  analytical procedures for planning, 524, 524t
  differences, 524
Maremont, Mark, 381n
master file change, 480–481
  forms, 397f
material misstatements, 184, 604
  accounting principle violation, 605–606
  assessing risk of, 284
  comparing, 199
  difficult, 605
  estimating, 199
  identifying at-risk assertions, 415
  immaterial, 604
  incentives for, 260
  levels of, 193
  material and pervasive, 605
  material but not pervasive, 605
  opportunities for, 260
  potential for, 279
  scope limitations, 606–607
  tone at the top and, 260
materiality, 181, 192, 604
  allocation of, 198
  balance sheet allocation, 198–199
  bases for evaluating, 195
  calculation of performance, 198t
  characteristics of, 192–193
  comparison of maximum possible misstatement
      for, 200t
  concepts of, 192
  establishing performance step in applying, 197
  estimating and comparing steps in evaluating, 199–200
  factors affecting judgment of, 194–195
  general cash account and, 455
  guidelines, 196f
  illustrative guidelines, 195–197
  performance, 193
  planning in segments step in applying, 197–198
  preliminary judgment, 196t
  qualitative factors in applying, 195
  relationship to opinion type and
      significance, 604t
  relationship to risk and evidence, 203–204
  relative not absolute concept of, 194
  review engagements, 625
  setting step in applying, 193–194, 413
  steps in applying, 193–198, 194f, 196f
maximum possible misstatements, 193
  comparing, 200
McClellan, Amy, 7n
McConnell, Donald K., 423n
McDonald, M., 40n
McKesson & Robbins Company, 543–544
McMillan, Robert, 541n
MD&A. See management discussion and analysis (MD&A)
Mejri, Sofiane, 78n
Miles, William, 369n
Millen, David R., 476n
MIS. See management information systems (MIS)
misstatement of fact, 585
  auditor's responsibilities for reporting, 587
  bounds, 439t
  calculating bounds, 440t
  found, 438t
  percent, 439t
mitigating control, 289
monetary unit sampling (MUS), 345, 346, 352, 408

  calculating misstatement bounds, 441t
  decision rule for, 442
  offsetting amounts and, 440
  problems with, 436
  sampling steps, 347t
  tainting and, 435
money laundering, 76, 77
monitoring, 272
Morgan, Brian, 80n
Morris, Floyd, 56n
Murthy, Raja, 450n
MUS. See monetary unit sampling (MUS)
Mzhen, Vadim A., 381n

N

narrative, 284
  characteristics, 284
National Post, 489n
negative confirmation, 426f
negligence, tort of, 74, 81
  auditors defences, 83
  level of care, 82
New Canadian Auditing Standards, 89
New York Times, The, 254n, 450n, 483n
Nielsen Media Research Canada, 9
no (or reduced) damages, 83–84
non-assurance services, 9, 13
  compared to assurance services, 9
  relationship to assurance services, 9f
non-negligent performance, 86
nonsampling risk (error), 338
  causes of, 338
nonstandard auditor's reports, 602–603
  types, 603–604
nonprobalistic sample selection, 339–340
  methods, 340
Norris, Floyd, 450n
not-for-profit organizations (NPOs), 11
  review engagements and, 625
notes payable, 557–558, 557f
  analytical procedures, 559–561, 559f, 559t
  audit objectives, 558–559, 559t
  designing tests of balances, 557f
  internal controls, 559
  objectives and tests of details, 561t
  related interest accounts, 558, 558f
  schedule, 560f
  tests of balances for, 557
  tests of control, 559
  tests of details of balances, 561–562, 561f, 562t
Notices to Readers (NTRs), 13
NPOs. See not-for-profit organizations (NPOs)
NTRs. See Notices to Readers (NTRs)

O

OAG. See Office of the Auditor General (OAG)
OAP tools. See online analytical processing
      (OAP) tools
observation, 223
obtain reasonable assurance, 181
occurrence rate, 344, 345
Office of the Auditor General (OAG), 3
Office of the Superintendent of Financial Institutions, 39
Olive, David, 222n
online analytical processing (OAP) tools, 343
online processing, 365
online resources, 29
Ontario Internal Audit Division, 4
Ontario Ministry of Finance, 4

University of Waterloo Centre for Information Integrity and Information Systems Assurance, 88
unusual fluctuations, 234
upper misstatement bound (UMB), 442
user auditor, 489
    outsourcing, 489
user entity, 489
    controls at, 490
user identification codes (user IDs), 366

V

value-added services, 158
variables sampling, 345
VeriSign verification, 427
viral networking, 476
vouching, 228

W

Wall Street Journal, The, 254n
weakness investigation tests, 377–378
web portal, 508

WebTrust certification, 427
WebTrust service, 12
Wong, Tony, 582n
working paper review, 585–586
    contents, 169f
    electronic, 170t
    reasons for, 586
    well-designed, 172f
written representation, 583
    inclusion in, 584–585
    purposes, 584

Y

York University, 27

Z

Zappos.com, 190n
Zeffer, Kim, 275n
Zelikman, Rita, 158n
Zuckerberg, Mark, 275n